W9-CLQ-345

THE JEWISH ANNOTATED NEW TESTAMENT

New Revised
Standard Version

THE JEWISH ANNOTATED NEW TESTAMENT

New Revised Standard Version Bible Translation

Amy-Jill Levine and Marc Zvi Brettler

Editors

Oxford University Press, Inc., publishes works that further Oxford University's objective of excellence in research, scholarship, and education.

Oxford New York
Auckland Cape Town Dar es Salaam Hong Kong Karachi Kuala Lumpur
Madrid Melbourne Mexico City Nairobi New Delhi Shanghai Taipei Toronto

With offices in
Argentina Austria Brazil Chile Czech Republic France Greece Guatemala
Hungary Italy Japan Poland Portugal Singapore South Korea Switzerland
Thailand Turkey Ukraine Vietnam

Published by Oxford University Press, Inc.
198 Madison Avenue, New York, New York 10016

http://www.oup.com

Design and typesetting by 2Krogh AS, Denmark.

20 19 18 17 16 15 14 13
Printed in the USA

EDITORS AND CONTRIBUTORS

Alan J. Avery-Peck – *The Second Letter of Paul to the Corinthians*
Herbert Basser – *The Letter of James*
Daniel Boyarin – Logos, *A Jewish Word: John's Prologue as Midrash*
Marc Zvi Brettler, Editor – *The New Testament between the Hebrew Bible (Tanakh) and Rabbinic Literature*
Jonathan Brumberg-Kraus – *The Third Letter of John*
Shaye J. D. Cohen – *The Letter of Paul to the Galatians; Judaism and Jewishness; Josephus*
Michael Cook – *The Letter of Paul to the Philippians*
Pamela Eisenbaum – *The Letter to the Hebrews*
Michael Fagenblat – *The Concept of Neighbor in Jewish and Christian Ethics*
Charlotte Elisheva Fonrobert – *Judaizers, Jewish Christians, and Others*
David Frankfurter – *The Revelation to John*
David M. Freidenreich – *Food and Table Fellowship*
Julie Galambush – *The Second Letter of John*
Aaron M. Gale – *The Gospel According to Matthew*
Joshua D. Garroway – Ioudaios
Barbara Geller – *The Letter of Paul to Philemon*
Gary Gilbert – *The Acts of the Apostles*
Martin Goodman – *Jewish History, 331 BCE–135 CE*
Leonard Greenspoon – *The Septuagint*
Michael R. Greenwald – *The Second Letter of Peter; The Canon of the New Testament*
Adam Gregerman – *The Second Letter of Paul to the Thessalonians*
Maxine Grossman – *The Letter of Paul to the Ephesians; The Dead Sea Scrolls*
Susannah Heschel – *Jesus in Modern Jewish Thought*
Martha Himmelfarb – *Afterlife and Resurrection*
Tal Ilan – *The Second Letter of Paul to Timothy*
Andrew S. Jacobs – *The Letter of Jude*
Jonathan Klawans – *The Law*
Naomi Koltun-Fromm – *The First Letter of Paul to Timothy*
Jennifer L. Koosed – *The Letter of Paul to Titus*
Ross S. Kraemer – *Jewish Family Life in the First Century CE*
Shira Lander – *The First Letter of Paul to the Corinthians*
Daniel R. Langton – *Paul in Jewish Thought*
Rebecca Lesses – *Divine Beings*
David B. Levenson – *Messianic Movements*
Amy-Jill Levine, Editor – *The Gospel According to Luke; Bearing False Witness: Common Errors Made about Early Judaism*
Lee I. Levine – *The Synagogue*
Martin Lockshin – *Jesus in Medieval Jewish Tradition*
Michele Murray – *The First Letter of John*
Mark D. Nanos – *The Letter of Paul to the Romans; Paul and Judaism*
Adele Reinhartz – *The Gospel According to John*
David Fox Sandmel – *The First Letter of Paul to the Thessalonians*
David Satran – *Philo of Alexandria*
Daniel R. Schwartz – *Jewish Movements of the New Testament Period*
Naomi Seidman – *Translation of the Bible*
Claudia Setzer – *The First Letter of Peter; Jewish Responses to Believers in Jesus*
David Stern – *Midrash and Parables in the New Testament*
Geza Vermes – *Jewish Miracle Workers in the Late Second Temple Period*
Burton L. Visotzky – *Jesus in Rabbinic Tradition*
Lawrence M. Wills – *The Gospel According to Mark*
Peter Zaas – *The Letter of Paul to the Colossians*

CONTENTS

The Editors' Preface xi
Acknowledgments xv
To the Reader xvii
Alphabetical Listing of the Books of the New Testament xix
Abbreviations xxi

The New Testament

Matthew .... *Introduction and Annotations by Aaron M. Gale* 1
Mark .... *Introduction and Annotations by Lawrence M. Wills* 55
Luke .... *Introduction and Annotations by Amy-Jill Levine* 96
John .... *Introduction and Annotations by Adele Reinhartz* 152
Acts of the Apostles .... *Introduction and Annotations by Gary Gilbert* 197
Romans .... *Introduction and Annotations by Mark D. Nanos* 253
1 Corinthians .... *Introduction and Annotations by Shira Lander* 287
2 Corinthians .... *Introduction and Annotations by Alan J. Avery-Peck* 315
Galatians .... *Introduction and Annotations by Shaye J. D. Cohen* 332
Ephesians .... *Introduction and Annotations by Maxine Grossman* 345
Philippians .... *Introduction and Annotations by Michael Cook* 354
Colossians .... *Introduction and Annotations by Peter Zaas* 362
1 Thessalonians .... *Introduction and Annotations by David Fox Sandmel* 372
2 Thessalonians .... *Introduction and Annotations by Adam Gregerman* 378
1 Timothy .... *Introduction and Annotations by Naomi Koltun-Fromm* 383
2 Timothy .... *Introduction and Annotations by Tal Ilan* 391
Titus .... *Introduction and Annotations by Jennifer L. Koosed* 397
Philemon .... *Introduction and Annotations by Barbara Geller* 402
Hebrews .... *Introduction and Annotations by Pamela Eisenbaum* 406
James .... *Introduction and Annotations by Herbert Basser* 427
1 Peter .... *Introduction and Annotations by Claudia Setzer* 436
2 Peter .... *Introduction and Annotations by Michael R. Greenwald* 443
1 John .... *Introduction and Annotations by Michele Murray* 448
2 John .... *Introduction and Annotations by Julie Galambush* 456
3 John .... *Introduction and Annotations by Jonathan Brumberg-Kraus* 458
Jude .... *Introduction and Annotations by Andrew S. Jacobs* 460
Revelation .... *Introduction and Annotations by David Frankfurter* 463

Maps, Charts, Sidebar Essays, and Diagrams

The Virgin Birth 4
Righteousness 7
The Geography of the Gospel of Matthew 8
The Beatitudes 10
Peter in Matthew's Gospel 31
Paying Taxes 40
Pharisees and Judas 41
Eschatological Elements in Matthew 44
The Geography of the Gospel of Mark 60
Impurity and Healing 63
Pharisees and Tax Collectors 64
Parables and Kingdom 68
Scripture Fulfillments 89
Jesus' Synagogue Sermon 107
The Geography of the Gospel of Luke 108
Pharisees in Luke 110
Parable of the Good Samaritan 123
Parable of the Prodigal Son 133
Parable of the Pharisee and the Tax Collector 138
The Geography of the Gospel of John 162
The Native Lands of Pentecost Pilgrims 201
Jews and the Death of Jesus 204
Gamaliel 209
Stephen's Speech 211
Sites of Early Christian Missionary Activities 215
First Missionary Journey of Paul 224
Second Missionary Journey of Paul 228
Third Missionary Journey of Paul 235
Paul and the Jews 243
Paul's Journey to Rome 250
Faith 255
Diatribe 257
Law 258
Circumcision and "Works of Law" 259
Circumcision of the Heart 260
God is One for All Humanity 260
The Source of Authority in Interpretation 274
Grafting the Olive Branch 276
Restoration of Israel 278
Food that is "Profane" 283
Paul and the Trinity 293
Freedom from the Law 296
Sexual Mores 298
Headcovering 305
Eucharist and Passover 306
Cursing Jesus 307
Spiritual Gifts 307
Paul and the Rabbis on Moses' Radiant Face 320
Places Mentioned in Galatians 1–2 334
Christ Hymn 357
"Beware of the Dogs" 359
Colossians and Ephesians: Parallels 365
Diatribe against the Jews 374
Slavery in the Roman Empire 404
Perfection through Suffering 408
The High Priest in Jewish Tradition 412
Melchizedek 415
Heroes of the Faith 421
Implanted Word 429
Suffering under Persecution 438
Use of Israel's Scripture 439
Oral and Written Prophecy 466
Christ as Manifestation of God 467
The Letters to the Seven Congregations 468
So-Called Jews and Their Synagogues of Satan 469
Revelation 2–3: The Seven Churches 470
John, A New Ezekiel 473
The Numerology of Revelation 475
The Heavenly Temple Cult 478
Chaos Monsters 483
Names Inscribed on the Body 485
Woman and the Symbolism of Pollution 489
A Holy City without a Holy Temple 496

Essays

INTRODUCTORY ESSAYS

Bearing False Witness: Common Errors Made about Early Judaism 501
Amy-Jill Levine
The New Testament between the Hebrew Bible (Tanakh) and Rabbinic Literature . . . 504
Marc Zvi Brettler

HISTORY AND SOCIETY

Jewish History, 331 BCE–135 CE
Martin Goodman 507
Judaism and Jewishness
Shaye J. D. Cohen 513
The Law
Jonathan Klawans 515
The Synagogue
Lee I. Levine 519
Food and Table Fellowship
David M. Freidenreich 521
Ioudaios
Joshua D. Garroway 524
Jewish Movements of the New Testament Period
Daniel R. Schwartz 526
Messianic Movements
David B. Levenson 530
Jewish Miracle Workers in the Late Second Temple Period
Geza Vermes 536
Jewish Family Life in the First Century CE
Ross S. Kraemer 537
The Concept of Neighbor in Jewish and Christian Ethics
Michael Fagenblat 540
Divine Beings
Rebecca Lesses 544
Logos, a Jewish Word: John's Prologue as Midrash
Daniel Boyarin 546
Afterlife and Resurrection
Martha Himmelfarb 549
Paul and Judaism
Mark D. Nanos 551
Judaizers, Jewish Christians, and Others
Charlotte Elisheva Fonrobert 554

LITERATURE

The Canon of the New Testament
Michael R. Greenwald 557
Translation of the Bible
Naomi Seidman.......... 560
The Septuagint
Leonard Greenspoon 562
Midrash and Parables in the New Testament
David Stern 565
The Dead Sea Scrolls
Maxine Grossman.......... 569
Philo of Alexandria
David Satran.......... 572
Josephus
Shaye J. D. Cohen 575

JEWISH RESPONSES TO THE NEW TESTAMENT

Jewish Responses to Believers in Jesus
Claudia Setzer.......... 577
Jesus in Rabbinic Tradition
Burton L. Visotzky 580
Jesus in Medieval Jewish Tradition
Martin Lockshin 581
Jesus in Modern Jewish Thought
Susannah Heschel.......... 582
Paul in Jewish Thought
Daniel R. Langton.......... 585

Tables, Glossary, Index

TIMELINE.......... 588
CHRONOLOGICAL TABLE OF RULERS.......... 590
SOME TANNAITIC RABBIS.......... 592
SOME AMORAIC RABBIS 593
CALENDAR.......... 594
WEIGHTS AND MEASURES 595
PARALLEL TEXTS.......... 596
CHAPTER/VERSE DIFFERENCES 598
CANONS OF THE HEBREW BIBLE/OLD TESTAMENT WITH ADDITIONS 600
TRANSLATIONS OF ANCIENT TEXTS 601
DIVISIONS AND TRACTATES OF THE MISHNAH, TALMUD, AND TOSEFTA.......... 603

GLOSSARY 604

INDEX.......... 619

THE EDITORS' PREFACE

". . . for my family, my kin of the flesh: Israelites they are, and to them are due the sonship, the glory, the covenants, the giving of Torah, the worship, the promises; of them were the patriarchs, and from them is the messiah in the flesh—who is over all, and whom God blessed, forever . . . for the gifts and the calling of God are irrevocable.

Saul (Paul) of Tarsus, Letter to the community in Rome, 9.3–5; 11.29"

It is almost two millennia since the earliest texts incorporated into the New Testament were composed. For the most part, these centuries have seen a painful relationship between Jews and Christians. Although Jewish perceptions of Christians and Christian perceptions of Jews have improved markedly in recent decades, Jews and Christians still misunderstand many of each other's texts and traditions. The landmark publication of this book is a witness to that improvement; ideally, it will serve to increase our knowledge of both our common histories and the reasons why we came to separate.

The word "Jewish" in the title *The Jewish Annotated New Testament* serves several roles. First, this volume highlights in its annotations and essays aspects of first- and second-century Judaism that enrich the understanding of the New Testament: customs, literature, and interpretations of biblical texts. We believe that it is important for both Jews and non-Jews to understand how close, in many aspects, significant parts of the New Testament are to the Jewish practices and beliefs reflected in the works of the Dead Sea Scrolls, Philo and Josephus, the Pseudepigrapha and Deuterocanonical literature, the Targumim (Aramaic translations of the Bible), and slightly later rabbinic literature, and that the New Testament has, in many passages, Jewish origins. Jesus was a Jew, as was Paul; likely the authors known as Matthew and John were Jews, as were the authors of the Epistle of James and the book of Revelation. When they were writing, the "parting of the ways" had not yet occurred. Other authors, such as the individual who composed the Gospel of Luke and the Acts of the Apostles, while probably not Jewish themselves, were profoundly influenced by first- and second-century Jewish thought and by the Jewish translation of Tanakh into Greek, the Septuagint. Thus, understanding the diverse Jewish populations of the early Roman Empire—their habits, their conventions, their religious practices—is as crucial to understanding the New Testament writings as is general familiarity with the Roman world. In turn, familiarity with the New Testament helps Jews to recover some of our own history.

Second, we highlight connections between the New Testament material and later Jewish (especially rabbinic) literature, so readers can track similar as well as distinct ideas across time. For example, in most rabbinic literature, the entire book of Psalms is attributed to David, even though fewer than half of the psalms have a Davidic superscription and several are explicitly attributed to other people, such as Korach. How and when did the rabbis' understanding of all of Psalms as Davidic (*b. B. Bat.* 14b) develop? Here, Acts 4.25 introduces Psalm 2—a psalm with no explicit Davidic superscription—by saying "it is you who said by the Holy Spirit through our ancestor David, your servant." The verse offers important evidence that the idea of the Davidic authorship of Psalms already existed in the first or early second century CE, and was not a rabbinic innovation. Similarly, seeing certain ascetic tendencies, interests in resurrection and heaven and hell, views of fallen angels and Satanic evil in some New Testament texts can make readers aware that such ideas existed in early Judaism as well.

Third, the volume addresses problems that Jewish readers in particular may find in reading the New Testament, especially passages that have been used to perpetuate anti-Judaism and the stereotypes that non-Jewish readers sometimes bring to the texts. Therefore, in addition to emphasizing the Jewish background—or better, the Jewish contexts—of the New Testament, we pay special attention to passages that negatively stereotype Jews or groups of Jews, such as the Pharisees or the "Jews" in John's Gospel. Jews have for too long been accused of being "Christ killers" (see 1 Thess 2.14b–16), or regarded as Judases, or seen as the venal descendants of the Temple's "money changers" (Mt 21.12; Mk 11.15; Jn 2.14–15, cf. Lk 16.14). The authors in this volume do not engage in apologetics by claiming that these statements are harmless. In some cases, they contextualize them by showing how they are part of the exaggerated language of debate of the first century, while elsewhere they note that the statements may not have always been understood accurately by later Christian tradition. An excellent example of the latter is reflected in the annotations to Matthew 27.25: "Then the people as a whole answered, 'His blood be on us and on our children!'" (a verse unique to Matthew's Gospel). The annotation observes that the verse may be referring to the destruction of the Second Temple in 70 CE, and the "children" may be specifically the generation after Jesus who experienced that destruction, and not Jews in perpetuity. Similarly, the notes to Revelation propose that the polemic against the "synagogue of Satan, who say that they are Jews and are not" (Rev 3.9) is not against Jews at all, but is against Gentile followers of Jesus who promote Jewish practices. These annotations cannot undo the harm that such verses have done for two millennia, but they may help both Jews and Christians see that certain pernicious interpretations of the New Testament are not based on the actual texts, as they have been assumed to be. At the very least, the annotations and essays should provide guidance to Christian teachers and preachers, so that when they proclaim the "good news" (the meaning of the Greek term *euangelion* or "gospel") of Jesus, they will not stain that good news by anti-Jewish stereotypes.

At times, the reader must wrestle with these New Testament texts (and we would argue the same point for the materials in the shared Scriptures—the Tanakh of the Synagogue and the Old Testament of the Church) since they sometimes express ideas that might make us uncomfortable, or worse. The point in studying such texts is not to justify them, but to understand them in their historical contexts and to recognize that the heirs of those texts have different interpretations of them. For example, some New Testament texts appear to promote a supersessionist agenda. Supersessionism (also sometimes called "replacement theology") is the claim, expressed in its starkest form, that by rejecting Jesus and then killing him, the Jews have lost their role as a people in covenant with God, and that the promises made to Abraham now apply only to the followers of Jesus. In other words, this view regards Jews and Judaism as having been superseded by or replaced with Christians and Christianity. This theology is most evident in Hebrews 8.13, which states: "In speaking of 'a new covenant' [Jer 31.31–34] he has made the first one obsolete. And what is obsolete and growing old will soon disappear." Study leads to deeper knowledge and therefore understanding of how those of differing beliefs or traditions develop.

Indeed, for many Jews, including the editors of this volume, study of the New Testament also has made us better, more informed Jews. Familiarity with the New Testament allows readers to see the various options open to Jews in the first century (to follow Jesus, or John the Baptist; to join the community at the Dead Sea or to affiliate with Pharisaic teaching; to align with Rome or with the rebels, and so on), and so have a better sense of why most Jews did not follow Jesus or the movement that developed in his name. At times, we find that many of the passages in the New Testament provide an excellent encapsulation of basic, ongoing Jewish values: of love of God and love of neighbor (Lk 10.25–28, quoting Deut 6.5; Lev 19.18; Josh 22.5; on love of God see *Avot de R. Natan* 48 [67a]; on the primacy of Lev 19.18, see R. Akiva in *y. Ned.* 9.4, who notes that "it is a great principle of the Torah"); of *tzedakah* (righteousness expressed as charity) (Mk 10.21; Mt 25.34–40; see Jer 22.3; Prov 21.3; on its primacy in rabbinic texts, see *b. B. Bat.* 9a; *b. Sukk.* 49b); of longing for the kingdom or reign of God (Mt 16.24–26) and the repair of the world (Rev 21.1—4); compare the *Aleinu* prayer: "To repair the world through the kingdom of heaven." It is very possible for the non-Christian to respect a great deal of the (very Jewish) message of much of the New Testament, without worshiping the messenger.

Many Jews are unfamiliar with, or even afraid of reading, the New Testament. Its content and genres are foreign, and they need notes to guide their reading. Other Jews may think that the New Testament writings are irrelevant to their lives, or that any annotated New Testament is aimed at persuasion, if not conversion. This volume, edited and written by Jewish scholars, should not raise that suspicion. Our intention is not to convert, whether to convert Jews to Christianity, or to convert Christians away from their own churches. Rather, this book is designed to allow all readers to understand what the texts of the New Testament meant within their own social, historical, and religious context; some of the essays then describe the impact that the New Testament has had on Jewish-Christian relations. Moreover, we strongly believe that Jews should understand the Christian Bible—what is called from the Christian perspective the Old Testament and New Testament—because it is Scripture for most English-speaking people: it is difficult for Jews to understand their neighbors, and the broader society of which Jewish citizens are a part, without familiarity with the New Testament. Just as we as Jews wish our neighbors to understand our texts, beliefs, and practices, we should understand the basics of Christianity.

Additional reasons commend Jewish familiarity with these texts. The New Testament is the origin of much of the great literature, art, and music of Western culture. To appreciate fully Bach's masterpieces, it helps to know the texts on which they are based; familiarity with the infancy narratives in the Gospels of Matthew and Luke helps readers to appreciate the magnificent portraits of the Madonna and her child; New Testament literacy provides the necessary background to understand how cultures over time have come to represent Jesus and Judas, Mary Magdalene and Peter. The New Testament is not only a book of religious significance; it is a book of cultural importance as well.

The term "Jewish" in the title has a final, important function: it reflects the sensitivities of the contributors. It is not the case that only Jews have the competence to provide these annotations, many of which assume knowledge of Hebrew, Tanakh, Second Temple, and rabbinic texts. The indebtedness of all the contributors to scholarship of authors from all religious backgrounds is evident throughout. At the same time, the increase in the number of Jews having expertise in this material, allowing us to find sufficient contributors, is testimony to the openness of the study of religious texts, and it also highlights the increasing cooperation of Jewish and Christian scholars in understanding both the differences and similarities between early Christianity and Judaism of that period.

As professional scholars, the authors of the annotations and essays approach the text with the respect that all religious texts deserve. A precise understanding of the Greek in which the New Testament is written, and deep knowledge of the Greek and Roman literary conventions that it employs, are crucial for understanding the New Testament—just as understanding of ancient Near Eastern culture and languages is crucial for understanding the scriptures Jews and Christians share. The annotations not only display a sensitivity to what may be perceived to be Jewish interests, they also provide data about history, nuance of language, and connection to earlier biblical texts that any annotated Bible provides. The annotations do not, and cannot, provide the final word on the meaning of the texts either in antiquity or today: new discoveries and new theoretical models will continue to advance our knowledge. Moreover, in some cases the contributors to this volume disagree with each other, and in other cases the editors disagreed with the contributors. This is the nature of biblical studies. We believe that the discussions included in this volume fit the category of disputes for the sake of divine service. As *m. Avot* 5.20a states

> "Any controversy waged in the service of God shall in the end be of lasting worth, but any that is not shall in the end lead to no permanent result. Which controversy was an example of being waged in the service of God? Such was the controversy of Hillel and Shammai. And which was not for God? Such was the controversy of Korah and all his company."

Such study can also have a much loftier result. The late Krister Stendahl, a Lutheran New Testament scholar, Emeritus Bishop of Stockholm, and former professor and Dean of the Harvard Divinity School, coined the term "holy envy" to express the idea that a religious tradition different from the one we practice may express beautiful and meaningful notions. No religion contains all wisdom expressed perfectly and there is much in the New Testament that we find both beautiful and meaningful. For example, Paul's description of love in 1 Corinthian 13.4–7 is deeply compelling:

> Love is patient; love is kind; love is not envious or boastful or arrogant or rude. It does not insist on its own way; it is not irritable or resentful; it does not rejoice in wrongdoing, but rejoices in the truth. It bears all things, believes all things, hopes all things, endures all things.

Just as we have learned much working on this milestone project together, the first time that Jewish scholars have annotated and written essays on the complete New Testament, we hope and anticipate that all who read the annotations and essays will gain a deeper appreciation of this central religious work. We hope that non-Jewish readers will learn to appreciate that significant sections of the New Testament derive from the heart of Judaism, and that they will be able to understand these texts without importing false notions of the tradition of Jesus and his earliest followers. We further hope that this volume will make the New Testament more welcoming to Jewish readers (many of whom are unfamiliar with its contents), that these new readers may become better acquainted with the traditions of their neighbors, and that perhaps they may even experience "holy envy" in the reading.

AMY-JILL LEVINE
MARC ZVI BRETTLER
28 Sivan 5771 / 30 June 2011

ACKNOWLEDGMENTS

No project such as this can possibly be brought to completion without the combined efforts of numerous people. We particularly thank our supportive families and friends for their patience while this volume took shape. We are grateful to all of the contributors, who shared their scholarship and who made the effort to make their knowledge accessible to all readers. We also wish to thank Oxford University Press, whose willingness to undertake this project will advance both interest and awareness of biblical interpretation and Jewish-Christian relations in the wider culture. Among those who labored on this volume, we thank: Elisabeth Nelson, of Oxford University Press; Mary Sutherland, copyeditor, who worked long and hard to achieve consistency of spelling and usage in the great variety of submissions and who prepared the text for composition; Claudia Dukeshire, who oversaw the typesetting and proofreading; 2Krogh, who designed and typeset the text; and Peachtree Editorial and Proofreading Service, who proofread the typeset pages. The project could not have been completed without the wisdom, insight, experience and superb guidance of Donald Kraus, Executive Editor for Bibles for Oxford University Press. Joshua ben Perachyah said: "Provide for yourself a teacher and get yourself a friend" (*m. Avot* 1.6); in Don, we have found both.

A.-J.L.

M.Z.B.

TO THE READER

[The following prefatory essay, "To the Reader," is part of the New Revised Standard Version Bible translation (NRSV), and is reprinted here in accordance with the requirements of the National Council of the Churches of Christ in the U.S.A., which holds copyright to the NRSV.]

This preface is addressed to you by the Committee of translators, who wish to explain, as briefly as possible, the origin and character of our work. The publication of our revision is yet another step in the long, continual process of making the Bible available in the form of the English language that is most widely current in our day. To summarize in a single sentence: the New Revised Standard Version of the Bible is an authorized revision of the Revised Standard Version, published in 1952, which was a revision of the American Standard Version, published in 1901, which, in turn, embodied earlier revisions of the King James Version, published in 1611.

The need for issuing a revision of the Revised Standard Version of the Bible arises from three circumstances: (*a*) the acquisition of still older Biblical manuscripts, (*b*) further investigation of linguistic features of the text, and (*c*) changes in preferred English usage. Consequently, in 1974 the Policies Committee of the Revised Standard Version, which is a standing committee of the National Council of the Churches of Christ in the U.S.A., authorized the preparation of a revision of the entire RSV Bible.

For the New Testament the Committee has based its work on the most recent edition of *The Greek New Testament*, prepared by an interconfessional and international committee and published by the United Bible Societies (1966; 3rd ed. corrected, 1983; information concerning changes to be introduced into the critical apparatus of the forthcoming 4th edition was available to the Committee). As in that edition, double brackets are used to enclose a few passages that are generally regarded to be later additions to the text, but which we have retained because of their evident antiquity and their importance in the textual tradition. Only in very rare instances have we replaced the text or the punctuation of the Bible Societies' edition by an alternative that seemed to us to be superior. Here and there in the footnotes the phrase, "Other ancient authorities read," identifies alternative readings preserved by Greek manuscripts and early versions. Alternative renderings of the text are indicated by the word "Or."

As for the style of English adopted for the present revision, among the mandates given to the Committee in 1980 by the Division of Education and Ministry of the National Council of Churches of Christ (which now holds the copyright of the RSV Bible) was the directive to continue in the tradition of the King James Bible, but to introduce such changes as are warranted on the basis of accuracy, clarity, euphony, and current English usage. Within the constraints set by the original texts and by the mandates of the Division, the Committee has followed the maxim, "As literal as possible, as free as necessary." As a consequence, the New Revised Standard Version (NRSV) remains essentially a literal translation. Paraphrastic renderings have been adopted only sparingly, and then chiefly to compensate for a deficiency in the English language—the lack of a common gender third person singular pronoun.

During the almost half a century since the publication of the RSV, many in the churches have become sensitive to the danger of linguistic sexism arising from the inherent bias of the English language towards the masculine gender, a bias that in the case of the Bible has often restricted or obscured the meaning of the original text. The mandates from the Division specified that, in references to men and women, masculine-oriented language should be eliminated as far as this can be done without altering passages that reflect the historical situation of ancient patriarchal culture. As can be appreciated, more than once the Committee found that the several mandates stood in tension and even in conflict. The various concerns had to be balanced case by case in order to provide a faithful and acceptable rendering without using contrived English. In the vast majority of cases, however, inclusiveness has been attained by simple rephrasing or by introducing plural forms when this does not distort the meaning of the passage. Of course, in narrative and in parable no attempt was made to generalize the sex of individual persons.

It will be seen that in prayers addressed to God the archaic second person singular pronouns (*thee*, *thou*, *thine*) and verb forms (*art*, *hast*, *hadst*) are no longer used. Although some readers may regret this change, it should be pointed out that in the original languages neither the Old Testament nor the New makes any linguistic distinction between addressing a human being and addressing the Deity. Furthermore, in the tradition of the King James Version one will not expect to find the use of capital letters for pronouns that refer to the Deity—such capitalization is an unnecessary innovation that has only recently been introduced into a few English translations of the Bible. Finally, we have left to the discretion of the licensed publishers such matters as section headings, cross-references, and clues to the pronunciation of proper names.

This new version seeks to preserve all that is best in the English Bible as it has been known and used through the years. It is intended for use in public reading and congregational worship, as well as in private study, instruction, and meditation. We have resisted the temptation to introduce terms and phrases that merely reflect current moods, and have tried to put the message of the Scriptures in simple, enduring words and expressions that are worthy to stand in the great tradition of the King James Bible and its predecessors.

For the Committee,
BRUCE M. METZGER

ALPHABETICAL LISTING OF THE BOOKS OF THE NEW TESTAMENT

Acts of the Apostles 197
Colossians 362
1 Corinthians 287
2 Corinthians 315
Ephesians 345
Galatians 332
Hebrews 406
James 427
John 152
1 John 448
2 John 456
3 John 458
Jude 460
Luke 96
Mark 55
Matthew 1
1 Peter 436
2 Peter 443
Philemon 402
Philippians 354
Revelation 463
Romans 253
1 Thessalonians 372
2 Thessalonians 378
1 Timothy 383
2 Timothy 391
Titus 397

LIST OF ABBREVIATIONS

Books of the Bible: Abbreviation First

HEBREW BIBLE

TORAH

Gen	Genesis
Ex	Exodus
Lev	Leviticus
Num	Numbers
Deut	Deuteronomy

NEVI'IM

Josh	Joshua
Judg	Judges
1 Sam	1 Samuel
2 Sam	2 Samuel
1 Kings	1 Kings
2 Kings	2 Kings
Isa	Isaiah
Jer	Jeremiah
Ezek	Ezekiel
Hos	Hosea
Joel	Joel
Am	Amos
Ob	Obadiah
Jon	Jonah
Mic	Micah
Nah	Nahum
Hab	Habakkuk
Zeph	Zephaniah
Hag	Haggai
Zech	Zechariah
Mal	Malachi

KETHUVIM

Ps	Psalms
Prov	Proverbs
Job	Job
Song	Song of Solomon
Ruth	Ruth
Lam	Lamentations
Eccl	Ecclesiastes
Esth	Esther
Dan	Daniel
Ezra	Ezra
Neh	Nehemiah
1 Chr	1 Chronicles
2 Chr	2 Chronicles

THE APOCRYPHAL / DEUTEROCANONICAL BOOKS

Tob	Tobit
Jdt	Judith
Add Esth	Esther (Greek)
Wis	The Wisdom of Solomon
Sir	Sirach
Bar	Baruch
Let Jer	The Letter of Jeremiah
Song of Thr	Azariah and the Three Jews
Sus	Susanna
Bel	Bel and the Dragon
1 Macc	1 Maccabees
2 Macc	2 Maccabees
1 Esd	1 Esdras
Pr Man	The Prayer of Manasseh
Ps 151	Psalm 151
3 Macc	3 Maccabees
2 Esd	2 Esdras
4 Macc	4 Maccabees

NEW TESTAMENT

Mt	Matthew
Mk	Mark
Lk	Luke
Jn	John
Acts	Acts of the Apostles
Rom	Romans
1 Cor	1 Corinthians
2 Cor	2 Corinthians
Gal	Galatians
Eph	Ephesians
Phil	Philippians
Col	Colossians
1 Thess	1 Thessalonians
2 Thess	2 Thessalonians
1 Tim	1 Timothy
2 Tim	2 Timothy
Titus	Titus
Philem	Philemon
Heb	Hebrews
Jas	James
1 Pet	1 Peter
2 Pet	2 Peter
1 Jn	1 John
2 Jn	2 John
3 Jn	3 John
Jude	Jude
Rev	Revelation

In the translators' notes to the books of the Bible, the following abbreviations are used:

Ant. — Josephus, *Antiquities of the Jews*
Aram — Aramaic
Ch, chs — Chapter, chapters
Cn — Correction; made where the text has suffered in transmission and the versions provide no satisfactory restoration but where the Standard Bible Committee agrees with the judgment of competent scholars as to the most probable reconstruction of the original text.
Gk — Septuagint, Greek version of the Old Testament [also used in the New Testament, where it means simply Greek]
Heb — Hebrew of the consonantal Masoretic Text of the Old Testament
Josephus — Flavius Josephus (Jewish historian, about CE 37 to about 95)
Macc. — The book(s) of the Maccabees
Ms(s) — Manuscript(s)
MT — The Hebrew of the pointed Masoretic Text of the Old Testament
OL — Old Latin
Q Ms(s) — Manuscript(s) found at Qumran by the Dead Sea
Sam — Samaritan Hebrew text of the Old Testament
Syr — Syriac Version of the Old Testament
Syr H — Syriac Version of Origen's Hexapla
Tg — Targum
Vg — Vulgate, Latin Version of the Old Testament

The following general abbreviations and abbreviations of additional ancient works are used in the introductions, annotations to the biblical books, sidebar essays, and in the general essays at the end of the volume:

1Q26 — *Wisdom apocryphon* (4Q Sapiential Work A)
1Q27 — *Mysteries*
1QapGen — *Genesis Apocryphon*
1QH — *Hodayot*[a] or *Thanksgiving Hymns*[a] (1QH[a]) from Qumran Cave 1
1QIsa[a] — *Isaiah*[a]
1QIsa[b] — *Isaiah*[b]
1QM — *Milhamah* or *War Scroll* from Qumran Cave 1
1QpHab — *Pesher Habakkuk* from Qumran Cave 1
1QpNahum — *Pesher Nahum*
1QS — *Serek Hayahad* or *Rule of the Community* from Qumran Cave 1
1QSa — *Rule of the Congregation* (1Q28a)
1QSb — *Rule of the Blessings* (1Q28b)
4Q163 — *Pesher Isaiah*
4Q186 — *Horoscope*
4Q246 — *Apocryphon of Daniel* (4QapocrDan ar)
4Q265 — *Serek Damascus* (4QSD)
4Q285 — *Sefer Hamilhamah*
4Q372 — *Apocryphon of Joseph*
4Q415-418 — *Sapiential Work A* (Instruction)
4Q423 — *Sapiential Work A* (Instruction) Same
4Q460 — *Pseudepigraphic work (Narr. Work and Prayer)*
4Q491 — *War Scroll*
4Q496 — *War Scroll* (one of the copies)
4Q504 — *Words of the Luminaries*[a] (4QDibHam[a])

4Q510	*Shirot*[a] or *Songs of the Sage*[a] (4QShir[a])
4Q511	*Shir (Songs of the Sage)*
4Q521	*Messianic Apocalypse* (4QMessAp)
4Q525	*Beatitudes* (4QBeat)
4QCatena[a]	*Catena*[a] also *Midrash on Eschatology*[b] (4Q177)
4QFlor	*Florilegium*, also *Midrash on Eschatology*[a] (4Q174)
4QMMT	*Miqsat Maase ha-Torah* ("matters of the Torah") (4Q394)
4QpIsa[a]	4Q161 (Pesher Isaiah[a]) (4Q161)
4QpNahum	4Q169 (Pesher Nahum) (4Q169)
4QPrNab ar	*Prayer of Nabonidus* (4Q242)
4QSam[a]	4Q51 (Samuel) (4Q51)
4QShirShabb[a]	*Songs of the Sabbath Sacrifice*[a] (4Q400)
4QTest	*Testimonia* (4Q175)
11QMelch	*Melchizedek* scroll from Qumran Cave 11 (11Q13)
11QPs[a]	*Psalms Scroll*[a] from Qumran Cave 11 (11Q5)
11QShirShabb	*Sabbath Songs*
11QSTemple	*Temple Scroll*[a] (11Q19); *Temple Scroll*[b] (11Q20);Qumran Cave 11

Note: The abbreviation "Q," unless specified as "Quelle" ("Source") for the posited document of non-Markan material common to Matthew and Luke, refers to Qumran, and manuscripts from Qumran are identified by the cave number, which precedes the Q, and the official manuscript number, which follows it; thus, 1Q34 = Manuscript 34 from Cave 1 at Qumran; 4Q174 = Manuscript 174 from Cave 4; etc.

Acts Pet.	*Acts of Peter*
Acts Pil.	*Acts of Pilate*
Ant.	Josephus, *Antiquities of the Jews*
Apoc. Abr.	*Apocalypse of Abraham*
Apoc. El.	*Apocalypse of Elijah*
Apoc. Mos.	*Apocalypse of Moses*
Apoc. Sedr.	*Apocalypse of Sedrach*
Apoc. Zeph.	*Apocalypse of Zephaniah*
Arak.	Talmudic Tractate *Arakhin* ("vows of valuation")
Aram	Aramaic (language)
Aram. Apoc.	*Aramaic Apocalypse*
Aratus, *Phaen.*	Aratus, *Phaenomena*
Aristophanes, *Thesm.*	Aristophanes, *Thesmophoriazusae*
Aristotle, *Eth. nic.*	Aristotle, *Nicomachean Ethics*
Aristotle, *Pol.*	Aristotle, *Politics*
Ascen. Isa.	*Ascension of Isaiah*
Augustine, *Doctr. chr.*	Augustine, On *Christian Doctrine*
Augustine, *Op. mon.*	Augustine, *The Work of Monks*
Avot de R. Natan	*Avot of Rabbi Nathan*
b.	Tractates of the Babylonian Talmud (Bavli)
2 Bar.	*2 Baruch* (another name for the *Apocalypse of Baruch*)
3 Bar.	*3 Baruch*
B. Bat.	Talmudic Tractate *Bava Bathra* ("last gate")
B. Kamma	Talmudic Tractate *Bava Kamma* ("first gate")
B. Metz.	Talmudic Tractate *Bava Metzia* ("second gate")
BCE	Before the Common Era
Bek.	Talmudic Tractate *Bekhorot* ("firstlings")
Ber.	Talmudic Tractate *Berakot* ("blessings")
Bik.	Talmudic Tractate *Bikkurim* ("first-fruits")

BS	*Beit She'arim. Vol II: The Greek Inscriptions*. Ed. Moshe Schwabe and Baruch Lifshitz. Jerusalem: Inst. Of Arch., 1974
ca.	*circa*, about, approximately
CD	Cairo Genizah copy of the *Damascus Document*
CE	Common Era
cf.	*confer*, compare
ch, chs	chapter, chapters
Cicero, *Cael.*	Cicero, *Pro Caelio*
Cicero, *Cat.*	Cicero, *In Catalinam*
Cicero, *Clu.*	Cicero, *Pro Cluentio*
Cicero, *De or.*	Cicero, *De oratore*
Cicero, *Flac.*	Cicero, *Pro Flacco*
Cicero, *Off.*	Cicero, *De officiis*
Cicero, *Philipp.*	Cicero, *Orationes philippicae*
Cicero, *Somn. Scip.*	Cicero, *Dream of Scipio*
Cicero, *Verr.*	Cicero, *In Verrem*
CIJ	*Corpus Inscriptionum Judaicarum*, Ed. Jean Baptiste Frey
1 Clem.	*1 Clement* (First Epistle of Clement)
Clement, *Paed.*	Clement of Alexandria, *Paedogogus*
Clement, *Strom.*	Clement of Alexandria, *Stromata*
Cod. Just.	*Codex Justinian* (5th century)
CPJ	*Corpus papyrorum judaicorum*. Ed. V. Tcherikover
d.	died
Did.	*Didache*
Dio Chrys., *Or.*	Dio Chrysostom, *Orationes*
Diod. Sic.	Diodorus of Sicily *(Library of History)*
Dionysius, *Ant. rom.*	Dionysius, *Roman Antiquities*
DSS	Dead Sea Scrolls
e.g.	*exempli gratia*, for example
Ed.	Talmudic Tractate *Eduyot* ("testimonies")
1 En.	*1 Enoch*
2 En.	*2 Enoch*
3 En.	*3 Enoch*
Ep. Arist.	*Letter of Aristeas*
Ep. Barn.	*Letter of Barnabas*
Epictetus, *Diatr.*	Epictetus, *Diatribai (Discourses)*
Eruv.	Talmudic Tractate *Eruvin* ("Sabbath limits")
esp.	especially
etc.	*et cetera*, and so forth
Euripides, *Bacch.*	Euripides, *Bacchae (Bacchanals)*
Eusebius, *Hist. eccl.*	Eusebius, *Ecclesiastical History*
ff.	and following
fl.	*floruit*, flourished
Gaius, *Inst.*	Gaius, *Institutiones*
Git.	Talmudic Tractate *Gittin* ("bills of divorce")
Gk	Greek (language)
Gk. Apoc. Ezra	*Greek Apocalypse of Ezra*
Gos. Nic.	*Gospel of Nicodemus*
Gos. Pet.	*Gospel of Peter*
Gos. Thom.	*Gospel of Thomas*
Hag.	Talmudic Tractate *Ḥagigah* ("festal offering")
HB	Hebrew Bible

Heb	Hebrew (language)
Herm. *Vis.*	*Shepherd of Hermas, Vision*
Homer, *Od.*	Homer, *Odyssey*
Hor.	Talmudic Tractate *Horayot* ("instructions")
Horace, *Sat.*	Horace, *Satires*
Hul.	Talmudic Tractate *Hullin* ("animals killed for food")
i.e.	*id est,* that is
ibid.	*ibidem,* in the same place
Ignatius, *Eph.*	Ignatius, *Letter to the Ephesians*
Ignatius, *Magn.*	Ignatius, *Letter to the Magnesians*
Ignatius, *Philad.*	Ignatius, *Letter to the Philadelphians*
Ignatius, *Pol.*	Ignatius, *Letter to Polycarp, Bishop of Smyrna*
Irenaeus, *Adv. Haer.*	Irenaeus, *Against Heresies*
J. Chrys., *Hom. 2 Thess.*	John Chrysostom, *Homiliae in epistulam ii ad Thessalonicenses*
JIGRE	*Jewish Inscriptions of Graeco-Roman Egypt.* Ed. Horbury and Noy
Jos. Asen.	*Joseph and Aseneth*
Josephus, *Ag. Ap.*	Josephus, *Against Apion*
Josephus, *J.W.*	Josephus, *Jewish War*
Josephus, *Life*	Josephus, *The Life*
Jub.	*Jubilees*
Justin , *Dial.*	Justin Martyr, *Dialogue with Trypho*
Justin, *Apol.*	Justin Martyr, 1 or 2 *Apology*
Ker.	Talmudic Tractate *Kerithot* ("extirpation")
Ketub.	Talmudic Tractate *Ketubbot* ("marriage deeds")
Kil.	Talmudic Tractate *Kilaim* ("diverse kinds")
KJV	King James Version (1611)
L.A.B.	*Pseudo-Philo (Liber Antiquitatum Biblicarum)*
L.A.E.	*Life of Adam and Eve*
Lat	Latin (language)
lit.	literally
LXX	Septuagint
m.	Tractates of the Mishnah
Ma'as.	Talmudic Tractate *Ma'aserot* ("tithes")
Ma'as. S.	Talmudic Tractate *Ma'aser Sheni* ("second tithe")
Makk.	Talmudic Tractate *Makkot* ("stripes")
Maks.	Talmudic Tractate *Makshirin* ("predisposers")
Mart. Isa.	*Martyrdom of Isaiah*
Mart. Pol.	*Martyrdom of Polycarp*
Me'il.	Talmudic Tractate *Me'ilah* ("sacrilege")
Meg.	Talmudic Tractate *Megillah* ("scroll" [of Esther])
Meg. Ta'an.	*Megillat Ta'anit* (list of holy days)
Mek.	*Mekhilta* (commentary on Exodus)
Men.	Talmudic Tractate *Menahot* ("meal offerings")
Midd.	Talmudic Tractate *Middot* ("measurements")
Midr.	*Midrash* (an interpretation of a text)
Midr. Min.	*Midrash Minayin*
Midr. Mishle	*Midrash Mishle* (Proverbs)
Midr. Tann.	*Midrash Tannaim*
Mo'ed Qat.	Talmudic Tractate *Mo'ed Qatan* ("mid-festival days")
Ms, Mss	manuscript, manuscripts
MT	Masoretic Text
n., nn.	annotation, annotations

Naz.	Talmudic Tractate *Nazir* ("Nazirites")
Ned.	Talmudic Tractate *Nedarim* ("vows")
Nidd.	Talmudic Tractate *Niddah* ("the menstruant")
NJPS	New Jewish Publication Society (Tanakh translation)
NRSV	New Revised Standard Version
NT	New Testament
Odes Sol.	*Odes of Solomon*
Origen, *Cels.*	Origen, *Against Celsus*
Origen, *Hom. Ps.*	Origen, *Homiliae in Psalmos*
Ovid, *Ars*	Ovid, *Ars amatoria*
Ovid, *Metam.*	Ovid, *Metamorphoses*
p., pp.	page, pages
P.	papyrus
Pausanias , *Descr.*	Pausanias, *Description of Greece*
Pesah.	Talmudic Tractate *Pesaḥim* ("Passover")
Pesiq. Rab.	*Pesikta Rabbati*
Pesiq. Rav Kah.	*Pesikta de-Rav Kahana*
Philo, *Abr.*	Philo, *On the Life of Abraham*
Philo, *Cher.*	Philo, *On the Cherubim*
Philo, *Confusion*	Philo, *On the Confusion of Tongues*
Philo, *Cont. Life*	Philo, *On the Contemplative Life*
Philo, *Decalogue*	Philo, *On the Decalogue*
Philo, *Dreams*	Philo, *On Dreams* 1, 2
Philo, *Drunkenness*	Philo, *On Drunkenness*
Philo, *Flaccus*	Philo, *Against Flaccus*
Philo, *Giants*	Philo, *On Giants*
Philo, *Good Person*	Philo, *That Every Good Person Is Free*
Philo, *Heir*	Philo, *Who Is the Heir of Divine Things?*
Philo, *Hypoth.*	Philo, *Hypothetica*
Philo, *Joseph*	Philo, *On the Life of Joseph*
Philo, *Leg. all.*	Philo, *Allegorical Interpretation*
Philo, *Leg. Gai.*	Philo, *On the Embassy to Gaius*
Philo, *Life of Moses*	Philo, *On the Life of Moses* 1, 2
Philo, *Migr.*	Philo, *On the Migration of Abraham*
Philo, *Names*	Philo, *On the Change of Names*
Philo, *On the Creation*	Philo, *On the Creation of the World*
Philo, *Planting*	Philo, *On Planting*
Philo, *Posterity*	Philo, *Posterity and Exile of Cain*
Philo, *Prelim. Studies*	Philo, *On Mating with the Preliminary Studies*
Philo, *Providence*	*On Providence* 1, 2
Philo, *QG*	Philo, *Questions and Answers on Genesis*
Philo, *Rewards*	Philo, *On Rewards and Punishments*
Philo, *Sacr.*	Philo, *On the Sacrifices of Cain and Abel*
Philo, *Spec. Laws*	Philo, *On the Special Laws*
Philo, *Virtues*	Philo, *On the Virtues*
Philo, *Worse*	Philo, *That the Worse Attacks the Better*
Pirqe R. El.	*Pirqe Rabbi Eliezer*
pl.	plural
Plato, *Apol.*	Plato, *Apology of Socrates*
Plato, *Leg.*	Plato, *Laws*
Plato, *Resp.*	Plato, *Republic*
Plato, *Tim.*	Plato, *Timaeus*

Pliny, *Nat.*	Pliny the Elder, *Natural History*
Plutarch, *Alc.*	Plutarch, *Alcibiades*
Plutarch, *Cic.*	Plutarch, *Life of Cicero*
Plutarch, *Is. Os.*	Plutarch, *De Iside et Osiride*
Plutarch, *Mor.*	Plutarch, *Moralia*
Plutarch, *Pyth. orac.*	Plutarch, *On the Pythian Responses*
Plutarch, *Quaest. conv.*	Plutarch, *Quaestionum convivialum libri IX*
Plutarch, *Quaest. rom.*	Plutarch, *Quaestiones romanae et graecae*
Plutarch, *Superst.*	Plutarch, *De superstition*
Polycarp, *Phil.*	Polycarp, *To the Philippians*
Pr. Azar.	*Prayer of Azariah*
Pr. Jos.	*Prayer of Joseph*
Pseudo-Phocylides, *Sent.*	Pseudo-Phocylides, *Sentences*
Pss. Sol.	*Psalms of Solomon*
Qidd.	Talmudic Tractate *Qiddushin* ("betrothals")
R.	Rabbi
Rab.	*Rabbah* (comments on scripture)
RSV	Revised Standard Version
Sanh.	Talmudic Tractate *Sanhedrin* ("the Sanhedrin")
Seb.	Talmudic Tractate *Shebiit* ("seventh year")
Sebu.	Talmudic Tractate *Shebuot* ("oaths")
Seder Olam Rab.	*Seder Olam Rabbah*
Sem.	*Semahot* ("mourning," rabbinic tractate of regulations for death and dying)
Seneca, *Ep.*	Seneca, *Epistulae morales*
Seqal.	Talmudic Tractate *Sheqalim* ("shekel tax")
Shabb.	Talmudic Tractate *Shabbat* ("Sabbath")
Shir. Rab.	*Shir ha-Shirim Rabbah (Midrash Hazita)*
Sib. Or.	*Sibylline Oracles*
sing.	singular
Sot.	Talmudic Tractate *Sotah* ("adulteress")
Strabo, *Geogr.*	Strabo, *Geography*
Suetonius, *Aug.*	Suetonius, *Augustus Caesar*
Suetonius, *Claud.*	Suetonius, *Divus Claudius*
Suetonius, *Vesp.*	Suetonius, *Life of Vespasian*
Sukk.	Talmudic Tractate *Sukkah* ("Tabernacles/Booths")
t.	*Tractates of the Tosefta*
T.	*Testament*
T. 12 Patr.	*Testaments of the Twelve Patriarchs*
T. Abr.	*Testament of Abraham*
T. Ash.	*Testament of Asher*
T. Benj.	*Testament of Benjamin*
T. Dan	*Testament of Dan*
T. Gad	*Testament of Gad*
T. Iss.	*Testament of Issachar*
T. Job	*Testament of Job*
T. Jud.	*Testament of Judah*
T. Levi	*Testament of Levi*
T. Levi^{ar}	*Aramaic Testament of Levi*
T. Moses	*Testament of Moses*
T. Naph.	*Testament of Naphtali*
T. Reuben	*Testament of Reuben*
T. Sim.	*Testament of Simeon*

T. Sol.	*Testament of Solomon*
T. Zeb.	*Testament of Zebulun*
Ta'an.	Talmudic Tractate *Ta'anit* ("fasts")
Tacitus, *Ann.*	Tacitus, *Annales*
Tacitus, *Germ.*	Tacitus, *Germania*
Tacitus, *Hist.*	Tacitus, *Historiae*
Tanh.	*Tanhuma* (a rabbi whose interpretations are in the *Midr. Tanh.)*
Tanh. Vay.	*Tanhuma Vayetzei*
Tehar.	Talmudic Tractate *Teharot* ("cleannesses")
Ter.	Talmudic Tractate *Terumot* ("heave offerings")
Tertullian, *Apol.*	Tertullian, *Apology*
Tertullian, *Exh. cast.*	Tertullian, *Exhortation to Chastity*
Tertullian, *Marc.*	Tertullian, *Against Marcion*
Tertullian, *Prax.*	Tertullian, *Against Praxeas*
Tertullian, *Pud.*	Tertullian, *Modesty*
Tertullian, *Scorp.*	Tertullian, *Antidote for the Scorpion's Sting*
Tertullian, *Spect.*	Tertullian, *The Shows*
Tg.	*Targum* (Aramaic translations of the Bible)
Tg. Cant.	*Targum to Canticles*
Tg. Neb.	*Targum of the Prophets/Targum Jonathan*
Tg. Neof.	*Targum Neofiti*
Tg. Onq.	*Targum Onqelos*
Tg. Ps.-J.	*Targum Pseudo-Jonathan*
Thucydides, *Hist.*	Thucydides, *History*
v., vv.	verse, verses
Vit. Phil.	Diogenes Laertius, *Lives of the Philosophers*
vs.	versus
Xenophon, *Mem.*	Xenophon, *Memorabilia*
y.	Tractates of the *Yerushalmi*, Jerusalem (Palestinian) Talmud
Yad.	Talmudic Tractate *Yadaim* ("hands")
Yebam.	Talmudic Tractate *Yebamot* ("sisters-in-law")
Zeb.	Talmudic Tractate *Zebahim* ("animal offerings")
||	parallel
§	section

Note: In chapter/verse references, or following a verse number, the letter "a" means the first section of the verse, "b" means the second section, and so on.

THE GOSPEL ACCORDING TO MATTHEW

TITLE AND AUTHORSHIP

According to the fourth-century church historian Eusebius, a bishop named Papias (writing ca. 125) noted that the disciple Matthew (Mt 9.9; see also Mk 3.18; Lk 6.15; Acts 1.13) recorded sayings of Jesus in the Hebrew language. The text of the first Gospel, however, neither claims Matthean authorship nor reads like a translation from the Hebrew. The Gospel appears rather to be a Greek text written with strong knowledge of and attachment to Jewish Scripture, tradition, and belief.

While some scholars argue that Matthew's Gospel served as a source for both Mark and Luke and possibly John, most agree that Matthew is dependent on both Mark's Gospel (90 percent of Mark's material is contained within Matthew's text) and a hypothetical text called Q, from the German *Quelle*, meaning "source." This presumed document or source consisted primarily of teaching materials, such as the Beatitudes (Mt 5.3–12; cf. Lk 6.20–23) and the Lord's Prayer (Mt 6.9–13; cf. Lk 11.2–4), and can be reconstructed from the verses shared by Matthew and Luke but absent from Mark. That Matthew's text depends on earlier traditions and texts does not preclude Matthean authorship but nonetheless calls it into question.

DATE AND SETTING

The Gospel of Matthew suggests that the Jerusalem Temple has been destroyed (see 12.6; 22.7), and thus must date after 70 CE. The earliest reference to the Gospel may be from Ignatius, bishop of Antioch, ca. 110 CE. His *Letter to the Philadelphians* seems to reference some Matthean traditions. Hence, a date for the Gospel of 80–90 CE seems reasonable. Antioch (in Syria) is a plausible setting for several reasons: Matthew is the only Gospel to mention awareness in Syria of Jesus' ministry (4.24); later texts mention the prominence of Jesus' followers there (see Acts 11.19–27; 13.1; 14.22–23; Gal 2.11); Peter has connections both to the city and to Matthew's Gospel (see 16.17–19); and, as noted earlier, there is a possible connection of the Gospel to Ignatius. A Galilean setting is also possible, given the Gospel writer's interest in the region (see 4.12; 21.11; 26.32; 28.10).

PLACEMENT IN NEW TESTAMENT

Matthew's Gospel appears as the first Gospel in the New Testament for several reasons: it was popular throughout the early Christian world (it is the most cited Gospel); it contains instructions for the church (e.g., 18.15–20); and its opening genealogy provides a smooth transition between the Scriptures of Israel and the story of Jesus. Whether the Gospel was written for a particular Christian (or specifically, a Jewish Christian) community or served as a text for all Jesus' followers remains debated.

STRUCTURE AND MAJOR THEMES

Matthew is divided into five major discourses, separated by the formula "when Jesus had finished" (7.28; 11.1; 13.53; 19.1; 26.1), suggesting a recapitulation of the Pentateuch. The themes of the discourses, however, (the Sermon on the Mount, evangelism, parables, church organization, and eschatology) do not match the contents of the Pentateuchal books. (The book of Psalms is similarly divided into five parts, which do not match the Torah books.) Matthew's Gospel relies upon Israel's Scriptures more than any other early Christian text, with approximately fifty quotations and allusions to the Septuagint (LXX, the Greek translation of the Tanakh). Matthew frequently uses the formula ". . . to fulfill what was spoken . . . by the prophet" (e.g., 1.22–23; 2.15; 4.14; 8.17; 12.14–17; 13.35; 21.4–5; 27.9–10) and depicts Jesus as the fulfillment of Torah and prophets (see 5.17; 7.12; 17.3,12).

The text also displays substantial interest in Jewish observance, from Jesus' insistence "Do not think that I have come to abolish the law or the prophets; I have come not to abolish but to fulfill" (5.17), to the elimination of Mark's claim (7.19) that Jesus had declared all foods clean, to the observance of Sabbath laws (12.1–14). Jesus shows how to understand the Jewish laws and how to apply them to the circumstances of an early church community comprised of both Jewish and Gentile members.

Also anchoring Jesus in Jewish tradition are Matthew's comparisons between Jesus and Moses. This connection may begin in ch 1, with Mary's miraculous pregnancy, Joseph's resolve to divorce her, and the divine instructions to marry her, which bear some connection to midrashic accounts of Moses' conception (see e.g., *Ant.* 2.205–17; *L.A.B.* 9.1–10; *Tg. Ps.-J.; Ex. Rab.* 1.13; *Sefer ha-Zikronot*). Connections are clear in ch 2: Jesus, like Moses, is rescued in infancy and travels to Egypt; like Moses, after leaving Egypt Jesus crosses water (the baptism), enters the wilderness (the temptation), and climbs a mountain before beginning his instruction (the "Sermon on the Mount" [5.1]). At the end of the Gospel, Jesus gives instructions to his followers from a mountain, as Moses did (28.16; cf. Deut 32.48).

Matthew's Jesus is not only depicted as the "new Moses" who interprets Torah for the people of Israel, but he is also Moses' superior. For example, in Matthew's temptation story (4.1–11), Jesus, like Moses, fasts for forty days and nights (4.2; cf. Deut 9.9), is challenged to command stones (4.3; cf. Num 20.8), and is shown "the kingdom" (4.8; cf. Deut 34.1). There, Jesus is shown "all the kingdoms" of the world, but Moses is shown only Canaan. Furthermore, whereas Moses dies outside the Promised Land, Jesus returns (28.16–20); whereas Moses leads the people to their earthly home; Jesus leads followers to the kingdom of heaven. Moses receives the Torah from God and gives it to Israel; Jesus is the fulfillment of Torah as well as its authoritative interpreter.

Jesus is also, for Matthew, the "son of David," the long-awaited future ideal Davidic king, called messiah in Jewish postbiblical literature (1.1; see the genealogy). The Gospel frequently uses phrases such as "son of David" as well as references to Jesus' kingship (1.1; 2.2; 9.27; 12.23; 15.22; 20.30; 22.42; 27.11). Judas, only in Matthew, hangs himself (27.5) as did Ahithophel, David's betrayer (2 Sam 17.23). But even the title "son of David" is surpassed, since Matthew presents Jesus also as the divine Son of God who will save his people (1.21; 2.15; 3.17; 4.3,6; 8.29; 14.33; 16.16; 26.63). The concept of Jesus as the *shekhinah*, the physical manifestation of the divine presence, frames Matthew's entire Gospel (see 1.18; 18.20; 28.20); as the Son of God and the incarnation of the divine on earth, Jesus thus replaces the Temple as the locus of divine presence.

MATTHEW AND JUDAISM

Along with adducing biblical imagery, Matthew also reveals links to rabbinic scriptural interpretation. The rabbis utilize different forms of argumentation (or exegetical rules) to interpret the Torah, including the *qal vahomer* ("light and heavy") and the *binyan 'av* ("construction of a father"), both of which appear in the Matthew's Gospel. See *b. B. Metz.* 87b; *m. Qidd.* 4.14; *b. Pesah.* 66a; *b. Sanh.* 17a; *y. Seb.* 9.1.38d; *Gen. Rab.* 92.7. The *qal vahomer* involves arguing from a minor to a major premise: if God takes care of the birds, how much more will he look after his followers (6.26; see also 10.29–31). The *binyan 'av* entails using one Torah passage to reach a conclusion regarding another. When questioned by the Pharisees regarding divorce (19.3–6), Jesus cites Gen 1.27; 2.23 to issue an authoritative decision regarding another, Deut 24.1–4. Similarly, when some Pharisees express concern that Jesus' disciples are plucking grain on the Sabbath (12.1–9; *b. Shabb.* 73b; the rabbis would have prohibited the plucking of grain since it would have been equated with "reaping"), Jesus responds by arguing that other Jews violated Sabbath laws when they were in need. Matthew makes the need clear in 12.1 by adding to Mark 2.23 that the disciples were hungry. Matthew's Jesus is thus depicted as utilizing Jewish exegetical methods to create new authoritative rulings.

Despite these close connections to Jewish texts, Torah interpretation, and images, other passages—the parables of the vineyard (21.33–45) and the wedding feast (22.1–14), the invectives against the Pharisees (23.3–36), and the self-curse of "all the people" that Jesus' "blood be on us and on our children!" (27.25)—suggest a strained if not broken relationship between Matthew's intended readers and the synagogue.

That final citation—the infamous "blood cry"—was used by some Christians through the centuries to claim that all Jews in all times and places were collectively responsible for the death of Jesus. More likely, the phrase reflects Matthew's interpretation of the tragic events of 70 CE, when Rome destroyed Jerusalem and burned the Temple: the "children" of the Jerusalem crowd were the ones to witness that destruction.

Following this tragic event, in which thousands of Jews were killed or exiled, the survival of Judaism was in doubt. New leaders were needed to preserve the Jewish traditions as well as to interpret the Torah for a changing world. The conflict inherent in Matthew's Gospel may reflect this competition for survival, thereby explaining the harsh attitude exhibited toward the Pharisees, who were the forerunners of the rabbis. Matthew's Gospel thus may provide a look into the tensions that existed between Jewish Christians and traditional Jews following 70 CE.

Aaron M. Gale

1 An account of the genealogy[a] of Jesus the Messiah,[b] the son of David, the son of Abraham.

[2] Abraham was the father of Isaac, and Isaac the father of Jacob, and Jacob the father of Judah and his brothers, [3] and Judah the father of Perez and Zerah by Tamar, and Perez the father of Hezron, and Hezron the father of Aram, [4] and Aram the father of Aminadab, and Aminadab the father of Nahshon, and Nahshon the father of Salmon, [5] and Salmon the father of Boaz by Rahab, and Boaz the father of Obed by Ruth, and Obed the father of Jesse, [6] and Jesse the father of King David.

And David was the father of Solomon by the wife of Uriah, [7] and Solomon the father of Rehoboam, and Rehoboam the father of Abijah, and Abijah the father of Asaph,[c] [8] and Asaph[c] the father of Jehoshaphat, and Jehoshaphat the father of Joram, and Joram the father of Uzziah, [9] and Uzziah the father of Jotham, and Jotham the father of Ahaz, and Ahaz the father of Hezekiah, [10] and Hezekiah the father of Manasseh, and Manasseh the father of Amos,[d] and Amos[d] the father of Josiah, [11] and Josiah the father of Jechoniah and his brothers, at the time of the deportation to Babylon.

[12] And after the deportation to Babylon: Jechoniah was the father of Salathiel, and Salathiel the father of Zerubbabel, [13] and Zerubbabel the father of Abiud, and Abiud the father of Eliakim, and Eliakim the father of Azor, [14] and Azor the father of Zadok, and Zadok the father of Achim, and Achim the father of Eliud, [15] and Eliud the father of Eleazar, and Eleazar the father of Matthan, and Matthan the father of Jacob, [16] and Jacob the father of Joseph the husband of Mary, of whom Jesus was born, who is called the Messiah.[e]

[17] So all the generations from Abraham to David are fourteen generations; and from

[a] Or *birth*
[b] Or *Jesus Christ*
[c] Other ancient authorities read *Asa*
[d] Other ancient authorities read *Amon*
[e] Or *the Christ*

1.1–17: The genealogy. The genealogy is unusual in citing women, non-Jews, and morally questionable characters among the ancestors. **1:** *Genealogy*, Gk "geneseōs," perhaps an allusion to the book of Genesis. *Messiah*, from the Hebrew "anointed one"; Gk "Christos" (see Dan 9:25,26 LXX; 11QMelch 2.9–13). This term is never used in Tanakh (the Hebrew Bible) of the future ideal Davidic king, though it is used that way in the Dead Sea Scrolls and rabbinic literature. *David*, traditional Jewish belief held that the messiah would descend from King David (Isa 11.1; Jer 23.5; *b. Sukk.* 52a; *b. Sanh.* 97a), perhaps based on the idea of an everlasting line of Davidic kings in 2 Sam 7.12–16. **2:** *Abraham*, see 3.9, was regarded both as the first Jew and as the first proselyte. Luke (3.23–38) traces Jesus' genealogy to Adam; from David to Jesus, the two NT genealogies of Matthew and Luke are inconsistent. **3:** *Tamar*, ancient sources variously consider her a Gentile, a proselyte to Judaism, and an Israelite (Gen 38; Ruth 4.18; 1 Chr 2.4; *L.A.B.* 9.5). She conceives twins with her father-in-law Judah (Gen 38.18; *T. Jud.* 12.8). **5:** *Rahab*, the Canaanite prostitute faithful to Joshua's spies; she and her family are spared from Jericho's destruction (Josh 6.25; *Ruth Rab.* on 1.1). *B. Meg.* 14b lists her as the wife of Joshua. *Ruth*, a Moabite woman regarded as a proselyte (Ruth 1.16–18; *Midr. Gen. Rab.* 59.9; *b. Sukk.* 49b). **6:** *Wife of Uriah*, Bathsheba, who committed adultery with David (2 Sam 11.2–12.24; 1 Kings 15.5; *b. Shabb.* 56a; *b. Qidd.* 43a). **7:** *Abijah . . . Asaph*, Abijah's son was Asa, not Asaph (1 Chr 3.10). **10:** *Amos*, the name evokes the biblical prophet; the son of *Manasseh* was Amon (1 Chr 3.14). **11:** *Deportation to Babylon*, in 597, a decade before the destruction of the First Temple and exile in 586 BCE. Matthew omits the kings Ahaziah, Joash, and Amaziah to have the list add up to fourteen (v. 7). For *y. Ber.* 2.4, the destruction of the Second Temple (70 CE) is the beginning of the period awaiting the messiah. **12:** *Zerubbabel*, Davidic descendant (Hag 2.23; Zech 4.6–10), who governed Jerusalem following the Babylonian exile. Only the names Jechoniah, Salathiel, and Zerubbabel, in the third group, are mentioned in the Tanakh. **16:** *Jacob the father of Joseph*, see Gen 35.24; Matthew evokes Israel's ancestors. *Joseph . . . of whom Jesus was born*, although not Jesus' biological father, Joseph is his legal parent. **17:** *Fourteen*, the sum of the numerical values ("gematriah") of the Hebrew letters "dalet" (=4), "vav" (=6), "dalet" (=4), spelling "David." Seven, the number of days in the week, may symbolize completeness. The genealogy omits five kings (Ahaziah, Joash, Amaziah, Jehoiakin, and Zedekiah) to make the numbers add up to fourteen. *From the deportation*, Matthew lists only thirteen generations for the last set.

THE VIRGIN BIRTH

Matthew's rendering of the LXX's *parthenos* from Isa 7.14 ("A virgin will conceive and bear a son" [Mt 1.23]) remains a site of popular piety and scholarly debate. The Hebrew word translated by *parthenos* in the LXX is *'almah*, which is used in the Tanakh in Isa 7.14 and six other times (Gen 24.43; Ex 2.8; Ps 68.26; Prov 30.19; and Song 1.3; 6.8) in the sense of "a young woman" but does not necessarily suggest "virgin." The Greek *parthenos* does not, for the LXX, necessarily connote "virgin," although that is the predominant translation. It appears in Gen 34.3 in reference to Dinah, who had just had intercourse with Shechem. The Hebrew term *betulah*, used more than fifty times, including several times in Isaiah, usually (but not always) carries the technical sense of "virgin." Thus for the Hebrew text of Isa 7.14, and perhaps even the Greek text, the prophet is saying, "The young woman is pregnant. . . ." There is no reason to presume her pregnancy was miraculous.

Most biblical scholars date Isa 7.14 to the eighth century BCE, during the reign of King Ahaz of Judah (see Isa 7.1). Isaiah tells Ahaz about the birth of child who will be named "Immanuel," "God with us." The name is a sign for the king, just as Isaiah's children have special names that indicate messages to the community (see Isa 7.3). The context of the passage indicates that a birth will occur soon. Some Jewish responses to Christian claims proposed that Isaiah was speaking of the birth of King Ahaz's son, Hezekiah (see Justin, *Dial.* 43; contrast Rashi, who sees the reference to be to Isaiah's own son; cf. Isa 8.1–3).

Traditional Christian readings favor a reference to a miraculous conception. However, some interpreters argue that Matthew was not speaking of a literal conception that took place apart from sexual intercourse. Others propose that Matthew borrowed from pagan traditions, in which a male god engages in intercourse with a human woman (cf. Gen 6.1–4); or that the tradition of miraculous conception arose in order to explain what would otherwise be seen as an illegitimate conception; still others see behind Matthew's account a midrash similar to Jewish ones concerning the miraculous birth of Moses. He was supposed to have been born, as he was conceived, without pain (hence his mother was not subject to the punishment of Eve, Gen 3.16); when he was born the house was filled with light; and he was said to have been born already circumcised (*b. Sot.* 12a).

David to the deportation to Babylon, fourteen generations; and from the deportation to Babylon to the Messiah,[a] fourteen generations.

[18] Now the birth of Jesus the Messiah[b] took place in this way. When his mother Mary had been engaged to Joseph, but before they lived together, she was found to be with child from the Holy Spirit. [19] Her husband Joseph, being a righteous man and unwilling to expose her to public disgrace, planned to dismiss her quietly. [20] But just when he had resolved to do this, an angel of the Lord appeared to him in a dream and said, "Joseph, son of David, do not be afraid to take Mary as your wife, for the child conceived in her is from the Holy Spirit. [21] She will bear a son, and you are to name him Jesus, for he will save his people from their sins." [22] All this took place to fulfill what had been spoken by the Lord through the prophet:

[a] Or *the Christ*
[b] Or *Jesus Christ*

1.18–25: The nativity (birth narrative) (Luke 1.26–2.40). **18:** *Before they lived together, m. Ketub.* 1.2; 5.2, note the bethrothal period prior to the marriage. *B. Yebam.* 62b suggests betrothal took place around the age of twelve (see also *m. Ned.* 10.5; *Gen. Rab.* 95), although the rabbinic ideal may not reflect first-century practice. The betrothal was formalized with a marriage contract (Heb "ketubah") (Tob 7.14; *m. Ketub.* 5.2; *m. Ned.* 10.5). *Holy Spirit*, God's creative and enduring presence (Gen 1.2; 2.7; 8.1; Ex 13.21–22; Josh 2.16; Ps 51.11; *b. Hag.* 12a,b). **19:** *Righteousness*, a Matthean theme (3.15; 5.6,10,20; 6.33; 9.13; 10.41; 21.32; 25.37,46; compare Lk 1.6). Righteousness was linked to justice, ethics, and Torah observance (Gen 6.9; Lev 18.5; Deut 6.25; Ps 85.11). *Dismiss*, divorce; see *m. Ned.* 11.12. **20:** *Angel*, angels often mediate prophecies in apocalyptic literature of this period. *Dream*, evoking the Joseph of Genesis and Amram, the father of Moses (*Ant.* 2.210–17). **21:** *Jesus*, Heb "Yehoshua," Joshua, "God saves." Jesus' mission is to save his people from their sins (9.1–8; 20.28; 26.28). Jews traditionally saw salvation as a part of the covenant (Ps 130.8; 2 Chr 7.14; *m. Sanh.* 10.1), and understood continuing divine presence to be part of the ideal future (see e.g., Ezek 48.35). **23:** *Virgin*, Matthew quotes the

[23] "Look, the virgin shall conceive and
bear a son, and they shall name him
Emmanuel,"

which means, "God is with us." [24] When Joseph awoke from sleep, he did as the angel of the Lord commanded him; he took her as his wife, [25] but had no marital relations with her until she had borne a son;[a] and he named him Jesus.

2 In the time of King Herod, after Jesus was born in Bethlehem of Judea, wise men[b] from the East came to Jerusalem, [2] asking, "Where is the child who has been born king of the Jews? For we observed his star at its rising,[c] and have come to pay him homage." [3] When King Herod heard this, he was frightened, and all Jerusalem with him; [4] and calling together all the chief priests and scribes of the people, he inquired of them where the Messiah[d] was to be born. [5] They told him, "In Bethlehem of Judea; for so it has been written by the prophet:

[6] 'And you, Bethlehem, in the land of
Judah,
are by no means least among the rulers
of Judah;
for from you shall come a ruler
who is to shepherd[e] my people
Israel.'"

[7] Then Herod secretly called for the wise men[b] and learned from them the exact time when the star had appeared. [8] Then he sent them to Bethlehem, saying, "Go and search diligently for the child; and when you have found him, bring me word so that I may also go and pay him homage." [9] When they had heard the king, they set out; and there, ahead of them, went the star that they had seen at its rising,[c] until it stopped over the place where the child was. [10] When they saw that the star had stopped,[f] they were overwhelmed with joy. [11] On entering the house, they saw the child with Mary his mother; and they knelt down and paid him homage. Then, opening their treasure chests, they offered him gifts of gold, frankincense, and myrrh. [12] And having been warned in a dream not to return to Herod, they left for their own country by another road.

[13] Now after they had left, an angel of the Lord appeared to Joseph in a dream and said, "Get up, take the child and his mother, and flee to Egypt, and remain there until I tell you; for Herod is about to search for the child, to destroy him." [14] Then Joseph[g] got up, took the child and his mother by night, and went to Egypt, [15] and remained there until the death of Herod. This was to fulfill what had been spoken by the Lord through

[a] Other ancient authorities read *her firstborn son*
[b] Or *astrologers*; Gk *magi*
[c] Or *in the East*
[d] Or *the Christ*
[e] Or *rule*
[f] Gk *saw the star*
[g] Gk *he*

Greek translation of Isa 7.14, which reads "parthenos." See "The Virgin Birth," p. 4. *Emmanuel*, lit., "God with us," frames the Gospel (18.20; 28.20). **25:** *No marital relations*, the phrase does not preclude their having relations after Jesus' birth. The view of Mary's perpetual virginity develops in the second century.

2.1–12: King Herod and the magi. 1: *King*, Matthew emphasizes the title to contrast Herod's rule with that of Jesus, the son of David. *Herod* ruled 37–4 BCE. *Bethlehem*, five miles south of Jerusalem. The *wise men*, Gk "Magi"; early Jewish readers may have regarded these Persian astrologers not as wise but as foolish or evil. Philo calls Balaam a "magos" (*Life of Moses* 1.264); see also Dan 2.2 LXX. Like the genealogy's Tamar, Rahab, and Ruth, they foreshadow the Gentile mission (28.19). **2:** *King of the Jews*, see 27.11,29,37. *Star*, perhaps here suggesting an angel (Num 24.17, related to Balaam's prophecy; CD 7.18–26; *T. Levi* 18.3); no ancient sources confirm this astronomical phenomenon. **3:** *All Jerusalem*, Matthew has a negative view of Jerusalem (21.10; 23.37). **4:** *He inquired*, Herod, although viewed as a Jew, does not know the tradition. *Messiah*, see 1.1n. **5–6:** Matthew paraphrases Mic 5.2 (HB 5.1). See v. 2; a star rising (see also v. 9). **8:** *Search diligently*, Herod seeks to deceive the Magi. **11:** *Gold, frankincense, and myrrh*, perhaps alluding to Isa 60.6 (see also Ps 72.10,15), underlying the tradition that the Magi are kings.

2.13–23: Flight to Egypt. As a new Moses, Jesus is rescued in infancy and travels to safety. **13:** *Dream*, see 1.20n. *Egypt*, a traditional place of refuge (1 Kings 11.40; 2 Kings 25.26; Jer 26.21; 43.1–7). **15:** *Out of Egypt*, Hos 11.1, originally referring to the people Israel. The literary context of Hosea's quote does not support Matthew's use of the verse, but such decontextualizing is typical of biblical interpretation in postbiblical

the prophet, "Out of Egypt I have called my son."

[16] When Herod saw that he had been tricked by the wise men,[a] he was infuriated, and he sent and killed all the children in and around Bethlehem who were two years old or under, according to the time that he had learned from the wise men.[a] [17] Then was fulfilled what had been spoken through the prophet Jeremiah:

[18] "A voice was heard in Ramah,
wailing and loud lamentation,
Rachel weeping for her children;
she refused to be consoled, because
they are no more."

[19] When Herod died, an angel of the Lord suddenly appeared in a dream to Joseph in Egypt and said, [20] "Get up, take the child and his mother, and go to the land of Israel, for those who were seeking the child's life are dead." [21] Then Joseph[b] got up, took the child and his mother, and went to the land of Israel. [22] But when he heard that Archelaus was ruling over Judea in place of his father Herod, he was afraid to go there. And after being warned in a dream, he went away to the district of Galilee. [23] There he made his home in a town called Nazareth, so that what had been spoken through the prophets might be fulfilled, "He will be called a Nazorean."

3 In those days John the Baptist appeared in the wilderness of Judea, proclaiming, [2] "Repent, for the kingdom of heaven has come near."[c] [3] This is the one of whom the prophet Isaiah spoke when he said,

"The voice of one crying out in the
wilderness:
'Prepare the way of the Lord,
make his paths straight.'"

[4] Now John wore clothing of camel's hair with a leather belt around his waist, and his food was locusts and wild honey. [5] Then the people of Jerusalem and all Judea were going out to him, and all the region along the Jordan, [6] and they were baptized by him in the river Jordan, confessing their sins.

[7] But when he saw many Pharisees and Sadducees coming for baptism, he said to them, "You brood of vipers! Who warned you to flee from the wrath to come? [8] Bear fruit worthy of repentance. [9] Do not presume to say to yourselves, 'We have Abraham as

a Or *astrologers*; Gk *magi*
b Gk *he*
c Or *is at hand*

and rabbinic periods. **16:** *Killed all the children*, the "Slaughter of the Innocents" evokes Ex 1.16. **18:** Jer 31.15, this chapter from Jeremiah, a favorite of Jesus' early followers, predicts a "new covenant" (31.31). *Ramah*, approximately six miles north of Jerusalem. **19:** Herod died ca. 4 BCE. Jesus' birth is usually placed between 6 and 4 BCE. **20:** *Are dead*, reworking Ex 4.19. **22:** *Archelaus*, deposed in 6 CE and replaced by direct Roman rule. *Galilee*, ruled by Archelaus's brother Herod Antipas (14.1). **23:** *Nazareth*, a small town about an hour's walk from Sepphoris. *Spoken through the prophets*, Matthew's citation is not in the Tanakh, but see Jdg 13.5,7; Isa 11.1; 60.21. .

3.1–12: John the Baptist (Mk 1.2–8; Lk 3.1–20; Jn 1.19–28). **1:** *John the Baptist*, a popular figure admired by some Jews (*Ant.* 18.116–19). *Baptist*, from the Greek meaning "dip" or "immerse." *Wilderness of Judea*, west of the Dead Sea. **2:** *Repent*, a prophetic call (e.g., Ezek 18.30). *Kingdom of heaven*, rather than, as in the other Gospels, "kingdom of God"; the circumlocution preserves the holiness of God's name. John anticipates the messianic age (see Zech 14.9). See *Pesiq. Rab.* 2, associating the "kingdom of heaven" with Zech 14.9. **3:** Isa 40.3, written originally to encourage Jews in Babylonian exile to return to Judea. 1QS 8.12–14 also locates the *voice* in the *wilderness*. The Masoretic cantillation marks, which also serve as punctuation, understand the words "in the wilderness" as belonging with what follows rather than with what precedes. **4:** *Hair . . . belt*, recalling Elijah (2 Kings 1.8; see Mt 11.14; 17.11–13), who is also depicted in the Tanakh as a new Moses. **6:** *River Jordan*, for water purification rites see Isa 4.4; 44.3; Jer 4.14; Ezek 36.25–27; Zech 13.1; *m. Yoma* 8.9; Josephus, *J.W.* 4.205. *Confessing their sins*, see *t. Yoma* 2.1; *y. Yoma* 8.9; *Lev. Rab.* 3.3. On the power of the Jordan, see 2 Kings 5.1–19, concerning Elijah's disciple Elisha. **7:** *Pharisees and Sadducees*, Jewish movements (Josephus *J.W.* 2.164–65; *Ant.* 13.278–79; 17.42; 18.16–17). See "Jewish Movements of the NT Period," p. 526. Lk 3.7 has John address his invective to the crowds. *Brood of vipers*, newborn vipers were believed to eat through their mother's stomach, killing her. *Wrath to come*, eschatological judgment. **8:** *Fruit*, good deeds; baptism itself is not sufficient. **9:** *Abraham*, see Gen. 17.7; Prov 17.2; *b.*

RIGHTEOUSNESS

Matthew's Gospel emphasizes the concepts of obedience and righteousness (see 1.19; 3.15; 5.10–11; 6.1, 33; 9.13; 10.41; 13.43; 21.31–32; 22.14; 23.35; 25.46). Righteousness (Gk *dikaiosynē*; Heb *tzedakah*, as in the term *tzaddik*, a righteous person) means, for Matthew, obedience to the divine will, often through Jesus' interpretation of the Jewish *mitzvot* ("commandments," as seen in the Sermon on the Mount, 5.10–11). Joseph is a "righteous" man in his resolve to divorce Mary quietly (1.19) and so not create a scandal. Jesus himself models this higher righteousness in insisting that John baptize him (3.15) and so submitting himself to John. Adherence to Jesus' teachings (being "righteous") and living a moral life ensured admission into the kingdom of heaven. As the parable of the sheep and the goats (25.31–46) makes clear, proper action in terms of care for others is mandatory.

our ancestor'; for I tell you, God is able from these stones to raise up children to Abraham. [10] Even now the ax is lying at the root of the trees; every tree therefore that does not bear good fruit is cut down and thrown into the fire.

[11] "I baptize you with[a] water for repentance, but one who is more powerful than I is coming after me; I am not worthy to carry his sandals. He will baptize you with[a] the Holy Spirit and fire. [12] His winnowing fork is in his hand, and he will clear his threshing floor and will gather his wheat into the granary; but the chaff he will burn with unquenchable fire."

[13] Then Jesus came from Galilee to John at the Jordan, to be baptized by him. [14] John would have prevented him, saying, "I need to be baptized by you, and do you come to me?" [15] But Jesus answered him, "Let it be so now; for it is proper for us in this way to fulfill all righteousness." Then he consented. [16] And when Jesus had been baptized, just as he came up from the water, suddenly the heavens were opened to him and he saw the Spirit of God descending like a dove and alighting on him. [17] And a voice from heaven said, "This is my Son, the Beloved,[b] with whom I am well pleased."

4 Then Jesus was led up by the Spirit into the wilderness to be tempted by the devil. [2] He fasted forty days and forty nights, and afterwards he was famished. [3] The tempter came and said to him, "If you are the Son of God, command these stones to become loaves of bread." [4] But he answered, "It is written,

'One does not live by bread alone,
but by every word that comes from the
mouth of God.'"

[5] Then the devil took him to the holy city and placed him on the pinnacle of the temple, [6] saying to him, "If you are the Son of God, throw yourself down; for it is written,

[a] Or *in*
[b] Or *my beloved Son*

Yebam. 64a; *Gen. Rab.* 60.2. *As our ancestor*, perhaps referring to the "merits of the fathers" (Heb "zekut avot"), see *Gen. Rab.* 60.2. *Stones . . . children*, a pun in Hebrew ("avanim . . . banim," "stones . . . sons"). **11:** *Fire* was used for purification (Num 31.23; *b. Sanh.* 39a).

3.13–17: Jesus' baptism (Mk 1.9–11; Lk 3.21–22; Jn 1.29–34). **14:** John recognizes Jesus' superiority. **15:** *Fulfill all righteousness*, a messianic accomplishment (Jer 23.5–6; 33.15–16; *T. Jud.* 24.1), see 3.19n. **16:** *Heavens were opened*, Isa 63.19; Ezek 1.1. *Spirit of God*, Isa 11.2; 42.1; 61.1; *b. Hag.* 15a. **17:** *Voice from heaven*, Jewish tradition speaks of the "bat qol," Heb. lit. "daughter of [the] voice," a heavenly voice (Dan 4.28; *b. Ber.* 3a; *b. Sot.* 48.2; *Tg. Cant.* on 2.12). *This is my Son*, cf. Deut 14.1; 2 Sam 7.14; Isa 42.1; Jer 31.9; Ps 2.7; on son and beloved together, see the binding of Isaac (Gen 22.2) and Hos 11.1.

4.1–11: Jesus' temptation (Mk 1.12–13; Lk 4.1–13). **1:** *Led up by the Spirit*, suggests God destined the temptation (see e.g., Isa 63.14; Ps 107.7; also 1 Sam 16.13; 1 Kings 18.12; 2 Kings 2.16; Ezek 3.14). *Tempted*, *m. Avot* 5.5 and its parallels state that Abraham endured ten trials. *Devil*, Gk "diabolos," equivalent to Heb "satan," "accuser" (see Num 22.2; Zech 3.1; Job 6.1; Ps 109.6; 1 Chr 21.1; *b. Shabb.* 89b). **2:** *He fasted*, Moses fasted while on Sinai (Deut 9.9; see also Ex 24.18). *Forty days and forty nights*, evoking Noah, Moses, the wilderness period, Elijah, etc. (Gen 7.12; Ex 24.18; 34.28; Num 13.25; Deut 8.2; 1 Kings 19.8; Ezek 4.6; Jon 3.4). **3:** *Command these stones*, see Num 20.8. **4:** Deut 8.3 (Jesus' responses are all from Deuteronomy, which is the most-quoted book of the Torah in the NT, the DSS,

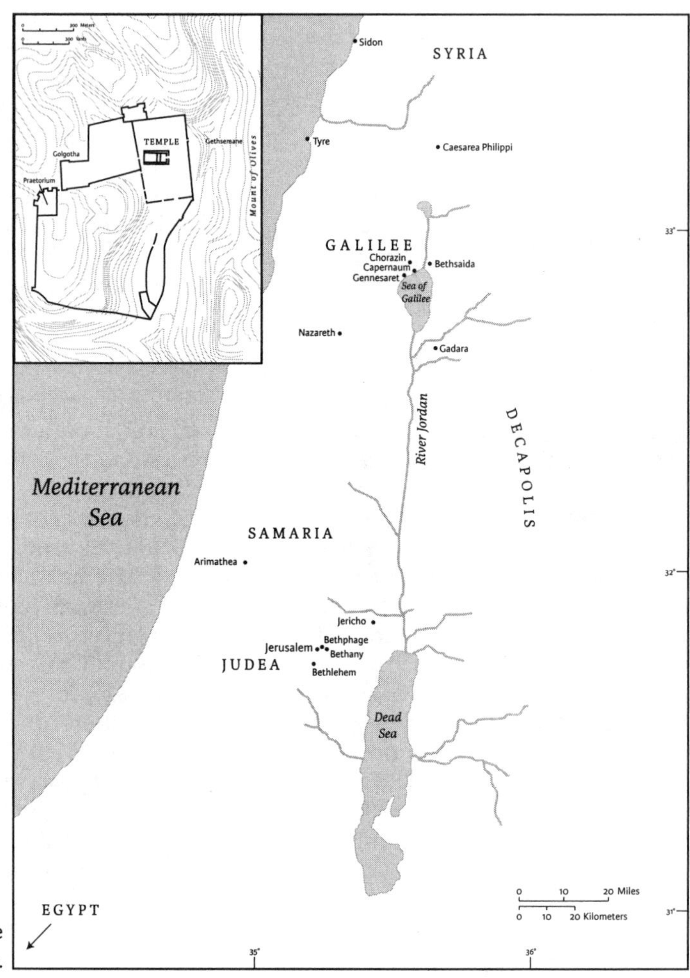

The geography of the Gospel of Matthew.

'He will command his angels concerning you,'
and 'On their hands they will bear you up,
so that you will not dash your foot against a stone.'"

[7] Jesus said to him, "Again it is written, 'Do not put the Lord your God to the test.'"

[8] Again, the devil took him to a very high mountain and showed him all the kingdoms of the world and their splendor; [9] and he said to him, "All these I will give you, if you will fall down and worship me." [10] Jesus said to him, "Away with you, Satan! for it is written,
'Worship the Lord your God,
and serve only him.'"

[11] Then the devil left him, and suddenly angels came and waited on him.

[12] Now when Jesus[a] heard that John had been arrested, he withdrew to Galilee. [13] He

[a] Gk *he*

and rabbinic literature). **6:** Ps 91.11–12. **7:** Deut 6.16; see also Isa 7.12; Sir 3.26; *b. Shabb.* 32a. **8:** *All the kingdoms*, the offer presumes that the world is in Satanic control; see 20.28. **10:** Deut 6.13. **11:** *Angels came*, God, directly or by means of divine servants, attends the faithful (4.6–7,11n.; 13.41–42; 16.27; 18.10n.; 24.30–31; cf. 1 Kings 19.5–8; Ps 78.25; Heb 1.14; 12–17; *Apoc. Sedr.* 5; *Gk. Apoc. Ezra* 2).

4.12–17: Jesus' ministry begins (Mk 1.14–15; Lk 4.14–15; Jn 1.35–51). **12:** *Arrested*, by Herod Antipas (see 14.3). *Withdrew to Galilee*, far north of the Dead Sea, Jesus' home and a future center of rabbinic Judaism (*t. Maks.* 1.3;

left Nazareth and made his home in Capernaum by the sea, in the territory of Zebulun and Naphtali, [14] so that what had been spoken through the prophet Isaiah might be fulfilled:

[15] "Land of Zebulun, land of Naphtali,
on the road by the sea, across the
Jordan, Galilee of the Gentiles—
[16] the people who sat in darkness
have seen a great light,
and for those who sat in the region and
shadow of death
light has dawned."

[17] From that time Jesus began to proclaim, "Repent, for the kingdom of heaven has come near." [a]

[18] As he walked by the Sea of Galilee, he saw two brothers, Simon, who is called Peter, and Andrew his brother, casting a net into the sea—for they were fishermen. [19] And he said to them, "Follow me, and I will make you fish for people." [20] Immediately they left their nets and followed him. [21] As he went from there, he saw two other brothers, James son of Zebedee and his brother John, in the boat with their father Zebedee, mending their nets, and he called them. [22] Immediately they left the boat and their father, and followed him.

[23] Jesus[b] went throughout Galilee, teaching in their synagogues and proclaiming the good news[c] of the kingdom and curing every disease and every sickness among the people. [24] So his fame spread throughout all Syria, and they brought to him all the sick, those who were afflicted with various diseases and pains, demoniacs, epileptics, and paralytics, and he cured them. [25] And great crowds followed him from Galilee, the Decapolis, Jerusalem, Judea, and from beyond the Jordan.

5 When Jesus[d] saw the crowds, he went up the mountain; and after he sat down, his disciples came to him. [2] Then he began to speak, and taught them, saying:

[3] "Blessed are the poor in spirit, for theirs is the kingdom of heaven.

[4] "Blessed are those who mourn, for they will be comforted.

[5] "Blessed are the meek, for they will inherit the earth.

[6] "Blessed are those who hunger and thirst for righteousness, for they will be filled.

[7] "Blessed are the merciful, for they will receive mercy.

a Or *is at hand*
b Gk *He*
c Gk *gospel*
d Gk *he*

b. Eruv. 29a; *b. Sot.* 45a; *b. Qidd.* 20a; *b. Arak.* 30b). **13:** *Capernaum,* town on the northwestern shore of the Sea of Galilee. **15–16:** Isa 9.1. *Galilee of the Gentiles,* "Gentiles" refers to non-Jews. Galilee was mostly Jewish at the time of Jesus (Josephus, *Ant.* 13.337; 18.37; *Life* 12.14; 65; 112–14; 128; 134; 190–192; 418; *m. Shabb.* 16.7; 22.3; *b. Shabb.* 146a). **17:** *Repent,* Jesus' message echoes that of John the Baptist (see 3.2).

4.18–25: The first disciples (Mk 1.16–20; Lk 5.1–11). **18:** *Simon,* Gk derivative of Heb "Shim'on," "[God] has heard." *Peter,* Gk for "rock" (see 16.18). It was common at the time to have both a Hebrew and a Greek (or Latin) name (see Acts 12.25). *Andrew,* a Greek form of "man." John 1.44 indicates that Peter and Andrew are from Bethsaida. **23:** *Synagogues,* Jewish assemblies, not necessarily buildings (9.35; 10.17; 12.9; 13.54) See "The Synagogue," p. 519. *Good news,* Gk "euangelion," the term translated "gospel." **24:** *Syria* had large Jewish population (Josephus, *J.W.* 2.461–68). *Demoniacs,* people possessed by demons (*Ant.* 8.42–49). **25:** *Decapolis,* ten cities, nine of which were located east of the Jordan: Philadelphia, Gerasa, Gadara, Pella, Dion, Raphana, Damascus, Canatha, Hippos, and Scythopolis (Pliny, *Nat.* 5.74; *b. Git.* 7b calls this area "land of the Gentiles").

5.1–7.29: The Sermon on the Mount (Lk 6.17–7.1). Cf. Luke's "Sermon on the Plain."

5.1–12: The Beatitudes. "Beatitude" from Lat "beatus," translation of Gk "makarios," "blessed, fortunate" (see "The Beatitudes," p. 10). Similar blessings appear in Jewish literature (Gen 30.3; Job 5.17; Dan 12.12; Sir 14.1–2; 4Q525 2.2.1–6). **1–2:** Like Moses, Jesus escapes death, enters Egypt, enters the water, goes into the wilderness, and ascends a mountain (Ex 19.3). **3:** *Blessed,* Gk "makarioi," compare Heb "'ashrei" (e.g., Ps 1.1). *Poor in spirit,* humble (see Isa 61.1; 66.2; Zeph 2.3; 1QM 14.7; *b. Eruv.* 13b). **4:** *Those who mourn,* the suffering righteous, a Matthean (5.10–12; 7.15–22; 10.23; 13.53–58; 16.24–25; 19.28; 21.12–13; 24.9–10) and generally Jewish theme (Isa 61.1–3; 66.10; Tob 13.14). **5:** Ps 37.7. *Meek . . . inherit the earth,* based on Ps 37.11. *Meek,* people who do not take advantage of their position (Isa 49.13; Ps 22.27; Prov 16.19; *b. Shabb.* 30b; *b. Ned.* 38a; *Pesiq. Rab.* 36; *Ant.* 19.330;

THE BEATITUDES

The expression "blessed are" (Gk *makarioi*) appears sixty-eight times in the LXX, usually for the Hebrew *ashrei* ("happy are . . . "; see, e.g., Ps 84.4, "Happy are those who live in your house, ever singing your praise. *Selah*") known from the Jewish liturgy, where it introduces Ps 145. In terms of content as well, the Beatitudes draw upon scriptural precedent. For example, "Blessed are the poor in spirit" and "Blessed are those who mourn" may be dependent on Isa 61.1–3, which also speaks of the poor and those who mourn. "Blessed are the meek, for they shall inherit the earth" is a near-quotation of Ps 37.11 (LXX 36.11; see also LXX Isa 61.7). The Hebrew of the psalm speaks of inheriting the "land" (*'aretz*), which should be taken as a reference to the land of Israel. The LXX and hence the New Testament reads *gē*, which could be translated as either "land" or "earth"; the reading of "earth" serves to de-Judaize Jesus by disconnecting him from any specific concern for the land of Israel. The concern for those who "hunger and thirst" evokes Ps 107.5–6,9 (see also Ps 22.26); LXX Prov 14.21 (LXX; see also LXX Prov 17.5) underlies the concern for the merciful. "Pure in heart" or "clean of heart" recalls Ps 24.3–6 (see also Ps 73.1), another reference to the land; it also echoes Ps 51.10 (Heb 51.12; LXX 50.12), *kardian katharan* in the Greek text of the Psalm and *katharoi tē kardia* in Matthew.

[8] "Blessed are the pure in heart, for they will see God.

[9] "Blessed are the peacemakers, for they will be called children of God.

[10] "Blessed are those who are persecuted for righteousness' sake, for theirs is the kingdom of heaven.

[11] "Blessed are you when people revile you and persecute you and utter all kinds of evil against you falsely[a] on my account. [12] Rejoice and be glad, for your reward is great in heaven, for in the same way they persecuted the prophets who were before you.

[13] "You are the salt of the earth; but if salt has lost its taste, how can its saltiness be restored? It is no longer good for anything, but is thrown out and trampled under foot.

[14] "You are the light of the world. A city built on a hill cannot be hid. [15] No one after lighting a lamp puts it under the bushel basket, but on the lampstand, and it gives light to all in the house. [16] In the same way, let your light shine before others, so that they may see your good works and give glory to your Father in heaven.

[17] "Do not think that I have come to abolish the law or the prophets; I have come not to abolish but to fulfill. [18] For truly I tell

[a] Other ancient authorities lack *falsely*

Philo, *Life of Moses* 2.279). **6:** See 1.19n. (cf. Isa 51.1–5; *1 En.* 58.2–3). **7:** *Merciful*, a highly regarded human attribute and one of the two primary aspects of God (along with justice; see Ps 145.9; *b. Shabb.* 151b; *Gen. Rab.* 33). **8:** See Ps 24.3–4; *Lev. Rab.* 23.13. *Heart* represents the center of thought and conviction (Deut 28.47; Prov 27.11; Isa 35.4). **9:** *Peacemakers*, see *b. Ber.* 64a; *Pesiq. Rav Kah.* 18:6–9. **10–11:** *Persecuted for righteousness' sake*, Jesus' followers faced hostility from both Jews and pagans (cf. 1 Thess 2.2,14–15; 1 Pet 3.14; 4.14; 5.8; see also Ps 37.11). **12:** See 23.30–37; Acts 7.52.

5.13–16: Salt and light (Mk 9.49–50; Lk 14.34–35). **13:** *Salt*, following ancient Mesopotamian notions, symbolizing purity and wisdom (Ex 30.35; 2 Kings 2.19–22; Ezek 16.4; *m. Sot.* 9.15). **14:** *Light of the world*, Phil 2.15; Jn 8.12 applies the epithet to Jesus. See also Isa 42.6; 49.6; 51.4–5; Dan 12.3; Prov 6.23; Jn 1.4–5; Sir 31.17; *Midr. Tanh.* 2; 1QS 2.3; 3.3,19–21; 1QM 13.5–6,14–15). **16:** *Good works*, Matthew insists that faith be accompanied by action (see 25.32–46).

5.17–20: Views concerning the Torah. 17: *Law*, Gk "nomos," in LXX for Heb "torah." Here the reference (accompanied by "the prophets," Gk "prophētēs,") is to the writings, the Torah and Nevi'im of the Tanakh (as opposed to the prophets themselves in v. 12). *Not to abolish*, Matthew upholds Torah. Some of Jesus' followers believed that he abrogated Torah (cf. Rom 8.4; 13.8; Gal 5.4; Acts 6.14; Heb 8). The Rabbis believed that the Torah should not be altered at all; it was the heretics who dismissed much or all of the Torah laws (*b. Shabb.* 31a; 116a–b; *Ex. Rab.* 47.1). **18:** Mk 13.31. *Not one letter*, Gk "iota," for Heb "yod," the smallest letter (see translators' note *a* on the next page). *Not one stroke of a letter*, rabbinic teachings do not allow a letter of Torah to be altered (*b. Sanh.* 90a; *y. Sanh.* 2.6; *Ex. Rab.* 6.1; *Lev. Rab.* 19.2). The "stroke" is the smallest part of a letter that differentiates it from another letter. **19:**

you, until heaven and earth pass away, not one letter,[a] not one stroke of a letter, will pass from the law until all is accomplished. [19] Therefore, whoever breaks[b] one of the least of these commandments, and teaches others to do the same, will be called least in the kingdom of heaven; but whoever does them and teaches them will be called great in the kingdom of heaven. [20] For I tell you, unless your righteousness exceeds that of the scribes and Pharisees, you will never enter the kingdom of heaven.

[21] "You have heard that it was said to those of ancient times, 'You shall not murder'; and 'whoever murders shall be liable to judgment.' [22] But I say to you that if you are angry with a brother or sister,[c] you will be liable to judgment; and if you insult[d] a brother or sister,[e] you will be liable to the council; and if you say, 'You fool,' you will be liable to the hell[f] of fire. [23] So when you are offering your gift at the altar, if you remember that your brother or sister[g] has something against you, [24] leave your gift there before the altar and go; first be reconciled to your brother or sister,[g] and then come and offer your gift. [25] Come to terms quickly with your accuser while you are on the way to court[h] with him, or your accuser may hand you over to the judge, and the judge to the guard, and you will be thrown into prison. [26] Truly I tell you, you will never get out until you have paid the last penny.

[27] "You have heard that it was said, 'You shall not commit adultery.' [28] But I say to you that everyone who looks at a woman with lust has already committed adultery with her in his heart. [29] If your right eye causes you to sin, tear it out and throw it away; it is better for you to lose one of your members than for your whole body to be thrown into hell.[f] [30] And if your right hand causes you to sin, cut it off and throw it away; it is better for you to lose one of your members than for your whole body to go into hell.[f]

[31] "It was also said, 'Whoever divorces his wife, let him give her a certificate of divorce.' [32] But I say to you that anyone who divorces

a Gk *one iota*
b Or *annuls*
c Gk *a brother*; other ancient authorities add *without cause*
d Gk *say Raca to* (an obscure term of abuse)
e Gk *a brother*
f Gk *Gehenna*
g Gk *your brother*
h Gk lacks *to court*

Least of these commandments, all Torah commandments to be followed, but some are weightier than others (Deut 22.6–7; cf. Jas 2.10; *m. Avot* 2.1; 4.2; *m. Qidd.* 1.10; *b. Ned.* 39b; *b. Shabb.* 70b; *Avot de R. Natan* 35). **20:** *Exceeds that of the scribes and Pharisees*, setting the bar high, as Pharisees were known as righteous.

5.21–48: Antitheses. The common term "antitheses" (lit., "oppositions") for these six teachings is inaccurate; some teachings proclaim not antithesis, but intensification (comparable to "making a fence around the Torah"; see *m. Avot* 1.1). **21:** *You shall not murder*, Ex 20.13; Deut 5.17. *Whoever murders...*, perhaps paraphrasing Gen 9.6; Ex 21.12. *Judgment*, a sentence for murder could only be ordered by a Jewish court (Deut 16.18; 21.1–9. See *m. Sanh.* 1.4; 7.1; *b. Sanh.* 35a; 72a–b). **22:** *Insult*, name-calling could be a legal offense (*m. B. Kamma* 8.1; *m. Ketub.* 3.7; see also *b. B. Metz.* 58b). *Council* (Gk "sanhedrin") refers to the Jewish high council in Jerusalem, or a local court (see 26.57; *m. Makk.* 1.10; *m. Sanh.* 1.6; *t. Sanh.* 1.7). *Hell* (Gk "Gehenna"), based on Heb "Gehinnom," a valley south of Jerusalem associated with child sacrifice (2 Kings 23.10; Jer 7.31; 2 Chr 28.3; 33.6). Gehinnom later became associated with purgatory and/or hell, where the wicked, according to some traditions, are tortured after death (cf. 25.41; see also *b. Eruv.* 19a; *b. Pesah.* 54a; *m. Ed.* 2.9–10; *b. Rosh Ha-Shanah* 17a; *t. Sanh.* 13.3; cf. *1 En.* 90.24; *2 Bar.* 59.10; 85.13; *Sib. Or.* 1.103; 2.292; 4.186; Rev 19.20; 20.14–15). **23–24:** *At the altar*, Matthew presumes Jesus' audience continued to participate in Temple sacrifice; perhaps also an allusion to Gen 4 (Cain and Abel). **24:** *Be reconciled*, Jews were required to seek peace with their neighbors before reconciliation with God was possible (Prov 6.1–5; 16.7; *m. Avot* 3.10; *m. Yoma* 8.9; *Gen. Rab.* 93.1). **25–26:** (Lk 12.57–59), see Prov. 6.1–5. **27:** *Adultery*, Ex 20.14; Lev 20.10; Deut 5.18. **28:** *Lust*, Jewish sources show a deep disdain for this offense (e.g., Job 31.1,9; Sir 9.8; 23.35; 41.21; *b. Ber.* 16a; *Lev. Rab.* 23.12 [on the adulterous eye]; 11QTemple 59.14). **29–30:** (Mk 9.43–48); Mt 18.8–9. *Cut it off*, Jewish sources linked the loss of limbs to martyrdom (e.g., 2 Macc 7.7–11; 4 Macc 10.20). The language here is hyperbolic. **31:** *Certificate of divorce* (Heb "get"), see 19.9; Deut 24.1–4. **32:**

his wife, except on the ground of unchastity, causes her to commit adultery; and whoever marries a divorced woman commits adultery.

[33] "Again, you have heard that it was said to those of ancient times, 'You shall not swear falsely, but carry out the vows you have made to the Lord.' [34] But I say to you, Do not swear at all, either by heaven, for it is the throne of God, [35] or by the earth, for it is his footstool, or by Jerusalem, for it is the city of the great King. [36] And do not swear by your head, for you cannot make one hair white or black. [37] Let your word be 'Yes, Yes' or 'No, No'; anything more than this comes from the evil one.[a]

[38] "You have heard that it was said, 'An eye for an eye and a tooth for a tooth.' [39] But I say to you, Do not resist an evildoer. But if anyone strikes you on the right cheek, turn the other also; [40] and if anyone wants to sue you and take your coat, give your cloak as well; [41] and if anyone forces you to go one mile, go also the second mile. [42] Give to everyone who begs from you, and do not refuse anyone who wants to borrow from you.

[43] "You have heard that it was said, 'You shall love your neighbor and hate your enemy.' [44] But I say to you, Love your enemies and pray for those who persecute you, [45] so that you may be children of your Father in heaven; for he makes his sun rise on the evil and on the good, and sends rain on the righteous and on the unrighteous. [46] For if you love those who love you, what reward do you have? Do not even the tax collectors do the same? [47] And if you greet only your brothers and sisters,[b] what more are you doing than others? Do not even the Gentiles do the same? [48] Be perfect, therefore, as your heavenly Father is perfect.

6 "Beware of practicing your piety before others in order to be seen by them; for then you have no reward from your Father in heaven.

[a] Or *evil*

[b] Gk *your brothers*

Unchastity (Gk "porneia"; see 19.3–9; cf. Mk 10.2–12; Lk 16.18; 1 Cor 7.11–13), encompasses more than adultery, e.g., marriages viewed by Leviticus (18.6–18) as incestuous. Jesus' sexual ethics are stricter than found in most other branches of early Judaism, but see 11QTemple 57.17–19; CD 4.12–5.14; *m. Ned.* 11.12; *b. Sanh.* 22a. **33:** *Swear falsely*, paraphrase of Ex 20.7; Lev 19.12; Num 30.3–15; Deut 5.11; 21.21–23. **34:** *Do not swear at all*, see Eccl 5.4 and Jas 5.12. Some rabbis forbid certain oaths (*m. Sebu.* 4.13; *m. Ned.* 1.3; *m. Sanh.* 3.2), but Jesus goes farther. *Throne of God*, see 23.22; Heb 12.2; Rev 7.15; 22.1,2. **35:** Isa 66.1. **37:** See *b. B. Metz.* 49a; *Ruth Rab.* 7.6. **38:** *An eye for an eye*, Ex 21.23–25; Lev 24.19–20; Deut 19.21; 11QTemple 61.10–12; *Jub.* 4.31–32; *L.A.B.* 44.10; Cf. Lk 6.27–36). *M. Bava Kamma* 8 states that such injuries should be compensated financially. **39–40:** Cf. 1 Thess 5.15. Jesus will be slapped and have his cloak removed (26.67; 27.35). *Right cheek*, presumes a back-handed slap. *Turn the other*, respond with neither violence nor abjection (see also Lam 3.30). *Give your cloak*, most people owned only two garments; to strip naked would uncover the judiciary injustice. **41:** *Second mile*, Roman soldiers could conscript locals to carry their gear for one mile; going the second is nonviolent resistance. Giving to charity was mandated in the Torah; interest was forbidden on loans as well (see Ex 22.25; Lev 25.36–37; Deut 15.7–11). **43:** *Love your neighbor*, Lev 19.18. *Hate your enemy*, no biblical text records this saying but cf. 1QS 9.21. **44:** *Love your enemies*, Jews were not to mistreat enemies. See Prov 24.17; 25.21; Josephus, *Ag. Ap.* 2.211. **45:** (Lk 6.35; 10.6; Jn 8.39). *Children of your Father*, see Jn 1.12; Rom 8.14–15; Gal 3.26–27; 4.5; Eph 1.5. Jewish sources also portray God in parental terms (2 Sam 7.14; Ps 82.6; 1 Chr 22.9–10; *b. Qidd.* 36a; *Ex. Rab.* 46.4). **46:** *Tax collectors*, agents of Rome; for Matthew, those needing evangelization (9.10–11; 11.19; 18.17; 21.31–32). **48:** Cf. Lk 6.36; Rom 12.2; Col 3.13; 1 Jn 4.19. *Be perfect* (Gk "teleios"), the word in this sense appears in the NT only in Matthew's Gospel (19.21) and the Letter of James (1.4; 3.2); it implies maturity or wisdom (19.21; cf. Lev 19.2; Deut 18.13 [and Targumic commentaries]; 1QS 1.8–9,13; 2.1–2; 8.9–10; *Midr. Tehillim* 119:3; Lk 6.36 demands disciples be merciful). In Jewish tradition, Heb "tamim" ("complete, sound"; see Gen 6.9, where Noah is "blameless") could indicate "completeness" with God, though not necessarily in a moral sense (e. g. Deut 18.13; 32.4).

6.1–8: Piety. 1: *Piety* (Gk "dikaiosynē"), lit., "righteousness" (in LXX for Heb "tzedakah"); see 1.19n.; 3.15; 5.6, 10,20; 6.33; 9.13; 21.32; 25.37,46; cf. 1 Sam 16.7; Rom 2.28–9; *b. Meg.* 20a. *To be seen by them*, on practicing righteousness in private, see *b. Sukk.* 49b. *Y. Ber.* 4.6 and *y. Meg.* 3.1 mention prayer recited in streets and markets. *Reward*, see *m. Avot* 1.3 ("Be not like servants who minister unto their master for the sake of

[2] "So whenever you give alms, do not sound a trumpet before you, as the hypocrites do in the synagogues and in the streets, so that they may be praised by others. Truly I tell you, they have received their reward. [3] But when you give alms, do not let your left hand know what your right hand is doing, [4] so that your alms may be done in secret; and your Father who sees in secret will reward you.[a]

[5] "And whenever you pray, do not be like the hypocrites; for they love to stand and pray in the synagogues and at the street corners, so that they may be seen by others. Truly I tell you, they have received their reward. [6] But whenever you pray, go into your room and shut the door and pray to your Father who is in secret; and your Father who sees in secret will reward you.[a]

[7] "When you are praying, do not heap up empty phrases as the Gentiles do; for they think that they will be heard because of their many words. [8] Do not be like them, for your Father knows what you need before you ask him.

[9] "Pray then in this way:
Our Father in heaven,
hallowed be your name.
[10] Your kingdom come.
Your will be done,
on earth as it is in heaven.
[11] Give us this day our daily bread.[b]
[12] And forgive us our debts,
as we also have forgiven our debtors.
[13] And do not bring us to the time of trial,[c]
but rescue us from the evil one.[d]
[14] For if you forgive others their trespasses, your heavenly Father will also forgive you; [15] but if you do not forgive others, neither will your Father forgive your trespasses.

[a] Other ancient authorities add *openly*
[b] Or *our bread for tomorrow*
[c] Or *us into temptation*
[d] Or *from evil.* Other ancient authorities add, in some form, *For the kingdom and the power and the glory are yours forever. Amen.*

receiving a reward . . ."). *Father in heaven,* see 5.45n. **2:** *Alms,* Deut 14.28–29; 15.11; 19.24; Tob 4.7; 12.8; cf. *b. Git.* 11b; an increasingly valued practice in Hellenistic and rabbinic Judaism. *Trumpet,* Jews did not, contrary to popular Christian preaching, have trumpets announce donations. *Hypocrite,* originally a Gk term for "actor," came to mean one who seeks public praise or is deceitful; Matthew uses it to refer to Jesus' enemies, usually Pharisees (6.2,5,16; 7.5; 15.7; 22.18; 23 passim; see Hab 2.5; Prov 21.24; *Pss. Sol.* 4.1–6,20; 2 Macc 6.25; Josephus, *J.W.* 2.587; *m. Avot* 1.3; *b. Sanh.* 103a). The polemic likely reflects religious rivalries in Matthew's own time. *Synagogues,* see 4.23n. **4:** *Alms may be done in secret,* the twelfth-century Jewish philosopher Maimonides advocated secret almsgiving as the second-highest of his eight levels of "tzedakah," or charity. See also *b. Sukk.* 49b. **5–6:** cf. Lk 18.10–14. *Whenever you pray,* traditional Jewish prayers are said three times daily: morning, late afternoon, and early evening (Dan 6.10; cf. Acts 3.1; 10.2–3,30; *Did.* 8.3; *m. Ber.* 4.1; *t. Ber.* 3.6; *b. Ber.* 26b;). Jesus is not forbidding public prayer but condemning those who seek attention by their manner of praying (cf. 23.5–7; Isa 26.20; *t. Ber.* 3.1). The exhortation to private prayer in v. 6, however, seems to indicate a preference for nonpublic piety, and not for such venues as congregational common prayer. **7:** *Empty phrases, b. Ber.* 55a condemns verbosity in prayer. **8:** *Your Father knows,* Philo, *Life of Moses* 2.217.

6.9–15: The "Lord's Prayer" (Lk 11.2–4). **9:** *Father in heaven,* see 5.45n. *Hallowed be your name,* see Ps 105.3, "Exult in His holy name," and the Aramaic "Kaddish" prayer (from Heb "qadosh," "holy," e.g., Isa 6.3, source of the prayer), which became popular during the Talmudic era (*b. Yebam.* 79a; *b. Sot.* 49a; *Sifre Deut.* 32.3; *Midr. Ps.* 25.13), begins "May his great name grow exalted and glorified" (see Lev 22.32; Isa 23.23; Ezek 36.23; Ps 113.2; cf. Deut 32.3; Jn 17; *Did.* 8.2; 9.2–4; 1QM 11.15). **10:** *Your will be done,* the rabbis emphasize obedience to divine will (*m. Avot* 1.11; *t. Ber.* 3.7; *b. Ber.* 29b; *b. Meg.* 29b; *b. Yoma* 53b; 86b). *As it is in heaven,* angels have no independent power according to biblical texts (see e.g., Job 1–2). **11:** *Daily bread,* likely reflecting an Aramaic original meaning "bread for tomorrow" or the eschatological banquet. **12:** *Debts,* sins were considered "debts" (Deut 15.1–2; see also *m. Avot* 3.17; *Gen. Rab.* 85.2; 92.9; *Ex. Rab.* 25.6; 31.1; *Pesiq. Rab.* 11.23; 51.8). Cf. Lk 11.4, which uses "sin." See 18.23–35n. **13:** *Time of trial,* or testing, cf. 2 Thess 3.3; Jas 1.13. *Evil one,* Satan. *B. Ber.* 60b offers examples of similar prayers. **14:** *Father will also forgive you,* God forgives those who forgive others (5.21–48; 18.35; see also Sir 28.1–8; *Midr. Tanh.* to Deut 13.18).

[16] "And whenever you fast, do not look dismal, like the hypocrites, for they disfigure their faces so as to show others that they are fasting. Truly I tell you, they have received their reward. [17] But when you fast, put oil on your head and wash your face, [18] so that your fasting may be seen not by others but by your Father who is in secret; and your Father who sees in secret will reward you.[a]

[19] "Do not store up for yourselves treasures on earth, where moth and rust[b] consume and where thieves break in and steal; [20] but store up for yourselves treasures in heaven, where neither moth nor rust[b] consumes and where thieves do not break in and steal. [21] For where your treasure is, there your heart will be also.

[22] "The eye is the lamp of the body. So, if your eye is healthy, your whole body will be full of light; [23] but if your eye is unhealthy, your whole body will be full of darkness. If then the light in you is darkness, how great is the darkness!

[24] "No one can serve two masters; for a slave will either hate the one and love the other, or be devoted to the one and despise the other. You cannot serve God and wealth.[c]

[25] "Therefore I tell you, do not worry about your life, what you will eat or what you will drink,[d] or about your body, what you will wear. Is not life more than food, and the body more than clothing? [26] Look at the birds of the air; they neither sow nor reap nor gather into barns, and yet your heavenly Father feeds them. Are you not of more value than they? [27] And can any of you by worrying add a single hour to your span of life?[e] [28] And why do you worry about clothing? Consider the lilies of the field, how they grow; they neither toil nor spin, [29] yet I tell you, even Solomon in all his glory was not clothed like one of these. [30] But if God so clothes the grass of the field, which is alive today and tomorrow is thrown into the oven, will he not much more clothe you—you of little faith? [31] Therefore do not worry, saying, 'What will we eat?' or 'What will we drink?' or 'What will we wear?' [32] For it is the Gentiles who strive for all these things; and indeed your heavenly Father knows that you need all these things. [33] But strive first for the kingdom of God[f] and his[g] righteousness, and all these things will be given to you as well.

[34] "So do not worry about tomorrow, for tomorrow will bring worries of its own. Today's trouble is enough for today.

[a] Other ancient authorities add *openly*
[b] Gk *eating*
[c] Gk *mammon*
[d] Other ancient authorities lack *or what you will drink*
[e] Or *add one cubit to your height*
[f] Other ancient authorities lack *of God*
[g] Or *its*

6.16–18: Fasting. A method of Jewish religious devotion associated with mourning, repentance, and self discipline; Jesus fasted (4.1; see also Lev 16.34; Num 29.7–11; 2 Sam 12.22–23; 1 Kings 21.27–29; Isa 58.3–7; Jer 14.11–12; Joel 1.14; 2.15; Jon 3.5; Zech 8.19; Dan 9.3; Jdt 8.5; 1 Macc 3.47; *t. Ta'an.* 2.4; Josephus, *J.W.* 3.47).

6.19–34: Wealth and the kingdom of heaven (Mk 4.21–23; Lk 12.33–34; 11.33–34; 16.13; 12.22–31). **19–20:** *Treasures on earth*, Jewish law does not prohibit possessions (Deut 28.1–14; Prov 3.9–10; 13.18; Tob 4.8–9; *Sib. Or.* 3.783; *m. Avot* 4.9; *m. Qidd.* 4.14), but decries obsession with material wealth (Prov 11.4; Sir 31.8–11; *1 En.* 63.10; 94.8; 96.4; 97.8; 1QS 10.18–19; 11.2; CD 4.17; 8.7; Josephus, *J.W.* 2.50; *y. Peah* 1.1). *Treasures in heaven* (see Lk 12.19–21), spiritual wealth and eschatological reward accumulated through right practice (cf. *2 Bar.* 24.1; *T. Job* 33; *b. B. Bat.* *11a*). **21:** See 5.8n. **22:** *Full of light*, see 5.6; Lk 16.8. Jewish sources connect light and spiritual goodness (Isa 25.; 60.20; Hab 3.3–4; Ps 56.13; 104.2; Prov 15.30; Dan 2.22; Tob 10.5; 11.14). **24:** *Wealth*, lit., "mammon," Gk "mamonas," transliteration of Aram "mamona," a word which had come to mean "riches" but which originally was derived from "'aman," "trust, reliance," meaning "that in which [other than God] one places one's trust"; see Lk 16.9,11,13. **25:** Lk 10.41; 12.11; Phil 4.6. The promise recalls Deut 28.1–14. **26:** *Birds . . . are you not of more value? B. Qidd.* 82b makes a similar argument. For the "qal vahomer" ("light and heavy") rabbinic form of argument in general, see *m. Qidd.* 4.14; *b. Pesah.* 66a; *b. Sanh.* 17a; *y. Seb.* 9.1.38d; *Gen. Rab.* 92.7). See also 10.24; 12.10–12; 20.26–28. **29:** *Solomon*, David's son (1.6–7). **30:** *Little faith*, a frequent charge against the disciples (8.26; 14.31; 16.8; 17.20). **33:** See 1.19n.; Mk 10.29–30; Lk 18.29–30. **34:** *Today's trouble is enough*, see *b. Ber.* 9b; Ex. Rab. 3.7.

7 "Do not judge, so that you may not be judged. [2] For with the judgment you make you will be judged, and the measure you give will be the measure you get. [3] Why do you see the speck in your neighbor's[a] eye, but do not notice the log in your own eye? [4] Or how can you say to your neighbor,[b] 'Let me take the speck out of your eye,' while the log is in your own eye? [5] You hypocrite, first take the log out of your own eye, and then you will see clearly to take the speck out of your neighbor's[a] eye.

[6] "Do not give what is holy to dogs; and do not throw your pearls before swine, or they will trample them under foot and turn and maul you.

[7] "Ask, and it will be given you; search, and you will find; knock, and the door will be opened for you. [8] For everyone who asks receives, and everyone who searches finds, and for everyone who knocks, the door will be opened. [9] Is there anyone among you who, if your child asks for bread, will give a stone? [10] Or if the child asks for a fish, will give a snake? [11] If you then, who are evil, know how to give good gifts to your children, how much more will your Father in heaven give good things to those who ask him!

[12] "In everything do to others as you would have them do to you; for this is the law and the prophets.

[13] "Enter through the narrow gate; for the gate is wide and the road is easy[c] that leads to destruction, and there are many who take it. [14] For the gate is narrow and the road is hard that leads to life, and there are few who find it.

[15] "Beware of false prophets, who come to you in sheep's clothing but inwardly are ravenous wolves. [16] You will know them by their fruits. Are grapes gathered from thorns, or figs from thistles? [17] In the same way, every good tree bears good fruit, but the bad tree bears bad fruit. [18] A good tree cannot bear bad fruit, nor can a bad tree bear good fruit. [19] Every tree that does not bear good fruit is cut down and thrown into the fire. [20] Thus you will know them by their fruits.

[21] "Not everyone who says to me, 'Lord, Lord,' will enter the kingdom of heaven, but only the one who does the will of my Father in heaven. [22] On that day many will say to me, 'Lord, Lord, did we not prophesy in your name, and cast out demons in your name, and do many deeds of power in your name?' [23] Then I will declare to them, 'I never knew you; go away from me, you evildoers.'

a Gk *brother's*
b Gk *brother*
c Other ancient authorities read *for the road is wide and easy*

7.1–6: Judging others (Mk 4.24–25; Lk 6.37–42; cf. Rom 14.10). **1–2:** See Ps 18.25–26. *Do not judge*, rabbinic sources discuss the importance of fair judgment (*m. Avot* 2.4–5; 4.8; *m. Sot.* 1.7; *b. Ta'an.* 8a; *b. Shabb.* 127b). **3:** *Speck*, see *b. B. Bat.* 15b; *b. Arak.* 16b. **6:** *Dogs*, a generic, not ethnic, insult.

7.7–15: Ethical guides. 7: *Knock, and the door will be opened*, see 21.22; Jn 15.7; 16.23–24. Vigilant prayer is the pathway to God's rewards (2 Kings 1.10,12–15; Ps 37.4; Prov 8.17; Isa 55.6; *b. Bek.* 44b; cf. *b. Meg.* 6b). **9:** Lk 11.11 (cf. *Lev. Rab.* 34.14). **11:** *How much more*, see 6.26n. *Father in heaven*, see 5.45n. **12:** *Do to others*, see "The Concept of Neighbor," p. 540; Lev 19.18; cf. Tob 4.15; *b. Shabb.* 31a, the story of Hillel. *Law and the prophets*, see 5.17n.; 22.34–40. Matthew sees the "golden rule" as the guide for interpreting all other laws; the rule does not substitute for the rest of Torah. **13–14:** (Lk 13.23–24). The imagery of two paths appears in Jewish sources (cf. Deut 30.15; Ps 1.1; *2 Bar.* 85.13; *m. Avot* 2.9; *T. Ash.* 1.3, 5). **15:** (Mk 13.22). *Beware of false prophets*, imposters claiming to be the true messengers (Deut 13.1–5 [Heb 2–6]; 18.15–22; Jer 5.6,31; 6.13–14; 8.11; 23.2; Ezek 22.27–28; Zech 13.2; Mic 3.5–8; Jn 10.12; Acts 20.29; *Did.* 16.3–4; Josephus, *J.W.* 6.285–288).

7.16–29: Ethical Warnings (Lk 6.43–45). **16:** *Fruits*, their actions (see Prov 11.30; 1 Sam 24.13). The phrase is repeated (vv. 16,20) for emphasis (see also 3.10; 7.22; 12.33–37; 24.5,24). **19:** *Every tree*, see Deut 20.20; Lk 13.6–9; Jas 3.12; *Gos. Thom.* 45. *Thrown into the fire*, eschatological warning. **21:** See Ps 6.8. *The will of my Father*, 6.10n. Jesus demands proper action more than religious confession. **22:** *On that day*, see 19.22,29,36,38; 26.29; the day of judgment (Isa 2.11,17,20; Hos 1.5; Joel 1.15; 3.18). See *b. Sanh.* 108a; *y. Rosh Ha-Shanah* 1.3. *Many will say to me*, Jesus as eschatological judge (cf. 10.32–33; 11.17; 13.24–30,36–40,47–50; 16.27; 19.28; 24.29–31; 25.31–46; 26.64; 28.18; Jn 3.35; Acts 10.42; 17.31; Rom 2.16; 2 Cor. 5.10; Phil 2.9–11; 1 Pet 5.4; Rev 19.11). *Did we not do . . . many deeds of power*, righteous action rather the deeds of power grants salvation (Jer 14.14; Lk 10.20; 1 Cor 12–14). **23:** Cf. Ps

24 "Everyone then who hears these words of mine and acts on them will be like a wise man who built his house on rock. 25 The rain fell, the floods came, and the winds blew and beat on that house, but it did not fall, because it had been founded on rock. 26 And everyone who hears these words of mine and does not act on them will be like a foolish man who built his house on sand. 27 The rain fell, and the floods came, and the winds blew and beat against that house, and it fell—and great was its fall!"

28 Now when Jesus had finished saying these things, the crowds were astounded at his teaching, 29 for he taught them as one having authority, and not as their scribes.

8 When Jesus[a] had come down from the mountain, great crowds followed him; 2 and there was a leper[b] who came to him and knelt before him, saying, "Lord, if you choose, you can make me clean." 3 He stretched out his hand and touched him, saying, "I do choose. Be made clean!" Immediately his leprosy[b] was cleansed. 4 Then Jesus said to him, "See that you say nothing to anyone; but go, show yourself to the priest, and offer the gift that Moses commanded, as a testimony to them."

5 When he entered Capernaum, a centurion came to him, appealing to him 6 and saying, "Lord, my servant is lying at home paralyzed, in terrible distress." 7 And he said to him, "I will come and cure him." 8 The centurion answered, "Lord, I am not worthy to have you come under my roof; but only speak the word, and my servant will be healed. 9 For I also am a man under authority, with soldiers under me; and I say to one, 'Go,' and he goes, and to another, 'Come,' and he comes, and to my slave, 'Do this,' and the slave does it." 10 When Jesus heard him, he was amazed and said to those who followed him, "Truly I tell you, in no one[c] in Israel have I found such faith. 11 I tell you, many will come from east and west and will eat with Abraham and Isaac and Jacob in the kingdom of heaven, 12 while the heirs of the kingdom will be thrown into the outer darkness, where there will be weeping and gnashing of teeth." 13 And to the centurion Jesus said, "Go; let it be done for you according to your faith." And the servant was healed in that hour.

a Gk *he*
b The terms *leper* and *leprosy* can refer to several diseases
c Other ancient authorities read *Truly I tell you, not even*

6.8. **24–27:** (Lk 6.47–49). Cf. *m. Avot* 1.17. **28–29:** *When Jesus had finished,* a common ending to Jesus' discourses (11.1; 13.53; 19.1; 26.1; cf. Ex 34.33; Deut 31.1; *2 Bar.* 87.1). *Their scribes,* see 13.52n. Scribes were religious experts (8.18; 9.3; 13.52; 15.1; 20.18; 21.15; 23.2) who typically appealed to precedent whereas Jesus teaches on his own authority.

8.1–17: Jesus' authority as healer. 1–4: Healing of the man with leprosy (Mk 1.40–45; Lk 5.12–16). **1:** *Down from the mountain,* Jesus, like Moses, descends (Ex 34.29; see also 5.1–2n.). Moses received divine commandments; Jesus interprets them. **2:** *A leper,* biblical leprosy, a type of scaly skin disease (not Hansen's disease, what we now call leprosy), created serious ritual impurity (Lev 5.2–6; 13–14; Num 12; *b. Sanh.* 47a; *b. Hor.* 10a; *b. Ned.* 64b; *Ant.* 2.264; *Gen. Rab.* 71.6). Curing leprosy indicates a prophetic role (2 Kings 5.8), missionary work (10.8) and eschatological sign (11.5). **3:** *Touched him,* rabbinic sources mention healing by touch (e.g., *b. Ber.* 5b). No law forbids touching people with leprosy. **4:** *Say nothing,* messianic secret; see Introduction to the Gospel of Mark, pp. 55–57. *Show yourself to the priest,* to be pronounced clean. *Gift that Moses commanded,* Lev 14.2–9. *Testimony to them,* the priests.

8.5–13: Healing the centurion's servant (Lk 7.1–10; Jn 4.46–54). **5:** *Capernaum,* 4.13n. *Centurion,* Roman (Gentile) army officer. Since Rome in the 20s through the 30s stationed no troops in Galilee, the centurion may be a pensioned officer. **7:** *I will come and cure him,* the sentence could be read as a question indicating Jesus' hesitance to perform a healing for Rome's representative. **8:** *I am not worthy,* the centurion occupied a higher social position than Jesus, yet recognizes Jesus' superiority. **10:** *Faith,* anticipates the Gentile mission (see also 15.28; 18.6; 21.21; 24.13–14; 28.19). **11:** Lk 13.28–30. *From east and west,* evoking the eschatological hope of the restoration of the ten lost tribes. *Kingdom of heaven,* see 3.2n. **12:** *Outer darkness,* eschatological punishment. *Gnashing of teeth,* indicates anger or frustration (13.42; 22.13; 24.51; 25.30; cf. Ps 112.10; Acts 7.54). **13:** *According to your faith,* see 15.28.

[14] When Jesus entered Peter's house, he saw his mother-in-law lying in bed with a fever; [15] he touched her hand, and the fever left her, and she got up and began to serve him. [16] That evening they brought to him many who were possessed with demons; and he cast out the spirits with a word, and cured all who were sick. [17] This was to fulfill what had been spoken through the prophet Isaiah, "He took our infirmities and bore our diseases."

[18] Now when Jesus saw great crowds around him, he gave orders to go over to the other side. [19] A scribe then approached and said, "Teacher, I will follow you wherever you go." [20] And Jesus said to him, "Foxes have holes, and birds of the air have nests; but the Son of Man has nowhere to lay his head." [21] Another of his disciples said to him, "Lord, first let me go and bury my father." [22] But Jesus said to him, "Follow me, and let the dead bury their own dead."

[23] And when he got into the boat, his disciples followed him. [24] A windstorm arose on the sea, so great that the boat was being swamped by the waves; but he was asleep. [25] And they went and woke him up, saying, "Lord, save us! We are perishing!" [26] And he said to them, "Why are you afraid, you of little faith?" Then he got up and rebuked the winds and the sea; and there was a dead calm. [27] They were amazed, saying, "What sort of man is this, that even the winds and the sea obey him?"

[28] When he came to the other side, to the country of the Gadarenes,[a] two demoniacs coming out of the tombs met him. They were so fierce that no one could pass that way. [29] Suddenly they shouted, "What have you to do with us, Son of God? Have you come here to torment us before the time?" [30] Now a large herd of swine was feeding at some distance from them. [31] The demons begged him, "If you cast us out, send us into the herd of swine." [32] And he said to them, "Go!" So they came out and entered the swine; and suddenly, the whole herd rushed down the steep bank into the sea and perished in the water. [33] The swineherds ran off, and on going into the town, they told the whole story about what had happened to the demoniacs. [34] Then the whole town came out to meet Jesus; and when they saw him, they begged him to leave their neighborhood.

9 [1] And after getting into a boat he crossed the sea and came to his own town.

[2] And just then some people were carrying a paralyzed man lying on a bed. When

[a] Other ancient authorities read *Gergesenes*; others, *Gerasenes*

8.14–17: Healing the sick and possessed (Mk 1.29–34; Lk 4.38–41). **14:** Cf. Jn 4.52; Acts 28.8. **15:** *Touched her hand*, a typical healing gesture. Jesus violates no ritual law or social rule. *To serve*, Gk "diakonein," whence the English "deacon," can connote ministerial service. **16:** 8.28–34. *Demons . . . spirits*, see Lev 16.8,10,26; Isa 13.21; 34.14; Tob 6.7–8,16–17; 8.2–3; 1QM 13.11–12; *b. Ber.* 6a; *b. Git.* 70a.; *Ant.* 8.45–49; *Jub.* 10.10–13. **17:** Isa 53.4. The "suffering servant" motif is linked elsewhere to redemption from sin (see 5.4n.; 1 Pet 2.18–25).

8.18–34: Stilling the storm and casting out demons. 19: *Scribe*, see 7.28–29n. **20:** *Son of Man*, rabbinic sources, following Dan 7.13–14, use the phrase in an eschatological sense linked to the messiah (*b. Sanh.* 98a; *y. Ta'an.* 2.1; cf. 10.23n.). **21–22:** Lk 9.57–62. *Bury my father*, cf. 1 Kings 19.19–21. Jews observed a seven-day period of mourning (Heb "shiva," "seven"; Jdt 16.24; Sir 22.12; *Apoc. Mos.* 43.3; *b. Sanh.* 47b). *Let the dead bury their own dead*, Jewish sources note the importance of accompanying a corpse to burial (*b. Ber.* 18a, citing Prov 17.5). **23–27:** (Mk 4.35–41; Lk 8.22–25). **24:** *Windstorm*, Gk "seismos," usually translated as "earthquake," suggesting an apocalyptic theme (cf. 24.7; 27.51; 28.2). *He was asleep*, relaxing in a crisis indicated faith (Lev 26.6; Jon 1.5; Ps 3.5–6; 4.8; Prov 3.24–26; Job 11.18–19; Acts 12.6). **26:** *Rebuked the winds*, Matthew portrays Jesus, like God, as lord over nature, thus surpassing Jonah. **28–34:** (Mk 5.1–20; Lk 8.26–39). **28:** *Gadarenes*, the people of Gadara, a town six miles southeast of the Sea of Galilee (cf. Mk 5.1, citing Gerasa; see Josephus, *Life* 9.42). Matthew changed the location to fit the story's details. **29:** *Before the time*, judgment day (see *1 En.* 16.1; *Jub.* 10.7–10). **31:** *Swine*, pigs are not kosher (Lev 11.7; Deut 14.8; Isa 65.4; 66.3,17; 1 Macc 1.47; 2 Macc 6.18–23); Gadara is Gentile territory. **32:** *Go*, rabbinic tradition cites an instance where R. Shimon bar Yoḥai performed an exorcism with this command (*b. Me'il.* 17b). *Whole herd . . . perished*, the story illustrates Jesus' authority over evil spirits; pigs can swim. **34:** *Begged him to leave*, For the Gadarenes, economic interests trump miraculous healing.

9.1–8: Jesus heals a paralytic (Mk 2.1–12; Lk 5.17–26). **1:** *His own town*, Capernaum (cf. 4.13; 8.5). **2:** *Sins are forgiven*, some sources connect sickness to sinfulness (Ex 20.5; Lev 26.14–17; Ps 103.3; 2 Chr 21.12–15; 4Q510; 1QS

Jesus saw their faith, he said to the paralytic, "Take heart, son; your sins are forgiven." [3] Then some of the scribes said to themselves, "This man is blaspheming." [4] But Jesus, perceiving their thoughts, said, "Why do you think evil in your hearts? [5] For which is easier, to say, 'Your sins are forgiven,' or to say, 'Stand up and walk'? [6] But so that you may know that the Son of Man has authority on earth to forgive sins"—he then said to the paralytic—"Stand up, take your bed and go to your home." [7] And he stood up and went to his home. [8] When the crowds saw it, they were filled with awe, and they glorified God, who had given such authority to human beings.

[9] As Jesus was walking along, he saw a man called Matthew sitting at the tax booth; and he said to him, "Follow me." And he got up and followed him.

[10] And as he sat at dinner[a] in the house, many tax collectors and sinners came and were sitting[b] with him and his disciples. [11] When the Pharisees saw this, they said to his disciples, "Why does your teacher eat with tax collectors and sinners?" [12] But when he heard this, he said, "Those who are well have no need of a physician, but those who are sick. [13] Go and learn what this means, 'I desire mercy, not sacrifice.' For I have come to call not the righteous but sinners."

[14] Then the disciples of John came to him, saying, "Why do we and the Pharisees fast often,[c] but your disciples do not fast?" [15] And Jesus said to them, "The wedding guests cannot mourn as long as the bridegroom is with them, can they? The days will come when the bridegroom is taken away from them, and then they will fast. [16] No one sews a piece of unshrunk cloth on an old cloak, for the patch pulls away from the cloak, and a worse tear is made. [17] Neither is new wine put into old wineskins; otherwise, the skins burst, and the wine is spilled, and the skins are destroyed; but new wine is put into fresh wineskins, and so both are preserved."

[18] While he was saying these things to them, suddenly a leader of the synagogue[d] came in and knelt before him, saying, "My daughter has just died; but come and lay your hand on her, and she will live." [19] And Jesus got up and followed him, with his disciples. [20] Then suddenly a woman who had been suffering from hemorrhages for twelve years came up behind

[a] Gk *reclined*
[b] Gk *were reclining*
[c] Other ancient authorities lack *often*
[d] Gk lacks *of the synagogue*

3.20–24; 4QPrNab; *m. Avot.* 2.7; *t. Ber.* 6.3). **3:** *Blaspheming,* profaning God's name; there is no indication that Jesus has blasphemed, according to the standards in Jewish sources. The authority to forgive sins belongs to God (Ex 34.7; Num 14.37; 2 Sam 12.13; Isa 6.7; 43.25; 44.22; Dan 9.9), but others can speak on God's behalf. **6:** *Son of Man,* see 8.20n. **8:** *Glorified God,* see 6.9n. The people do not regard Jesus' action as blasphemous. *Given such authority to human beings,* see *b. Ber.* 58a.

9.9–13: Sinners and tax collectors (Mk. 2.14; Lk 5.27–28). **9:** *Matthew,* Heb "mattityahu," "gift of the Lord" (cf. Mt 10.3; Mk 3.18; Lk 6.15; Acts 1.13). **10:** *Tax collectors,* see 5.46n., cf. Mk 2.15–16; Lk 3.12–13; 15.1; *m. B. Kamma* 10.1; *b. Sanh.* 25b; *b. Bek.* 31a; *y. Hag.* 2.2; Philo, *Spec. Laws* 3.30. *Sinners,* those who violate familial or community welfare (cf. 15.2; see also Tob 4.17; *Pss. Sol.* 2.34; 13.1; 14.6–7; *Sib. Or.* 3.304; *Sifre Deut.* 48.4.1; *b. Ber.* 61a). **11:** *Eat with,* see *m. Avot* 1.3 on avoiding evil doers. **13:** *I desire mercy . . .,* Hos 6.6. The rhetorical form, for both Hosea and Jesus, is that mercy takes precedence over sacrifice, not that sacrifice is eliminated (see 5.23–24).

9.14–17: Fasting (Mk 2.18–22; Lk 5.33–39). **14:** *Disciples of John,* that John (the Baptist) kept disciples suggests that he did not view Jesus as the messiah. *Pharisees fast,* see 6.16–18n.; Lev 16.34; Num 29.7–11; 2 Sam 12.22–23; 1 Kings 21.27–29; Zech 8.19; on dates of fasts, see *b. Rosh Ha-Shanah* 18b. **15:** *Bridegroom,* an early Christian metaphor for Jesus, the church's bridegroom (Jn 3.29; 2 Cor 11.2; Eph 5.21–33; Rev 19.7; 21.2,9; 22.17); Jesus likely used the term as a self-designation. For bridegrooms' exemptions from certain practices during the time of the wedding, see *t. Ber.* 2.10; *b. Sukk.* 25b. **17:** *Both are preserved,* both biblical law and Jesus/the church's interpretation of it.

9.18–26: Jesus heals two women (Mk. 5.21–43; Lk 8.40–56). **18:** *Leader of the synagogue,* the Gk reads "archon," "leader"; "synagogue" comes from Mk 5.22; Lk 8.41. **20:** *Hemorrhages,* probably vaginal or uterine. *Fringe* (cf. Heb pl. "tzitzit"), Jewish men (and possibly women) wore fringes to remind them of the commandments

him and touched the fringe of his cloak, [21] for she said to herself, "If I only touch his cloak, I will be made well." [22] Jesus turned, and seeing her he said, "Take heart, daughter; your faith has made you well." And instantly the woman was made well. [23] When Jesus came to the leader's house and saw the flute players and the crowd making a commotion, [24] he said, "Go away; for the girl is not dead but sleeping." And they laughed at him. [25] But when the crowd had been put outside, he went in and took her by the hand, and the girl got up. [26] And the report of this spread throughout that district.

[27] As Jesus went on from there, two blind men followed him, crying loudly, "Have mercy on us, Son of David!" [28] When he entered the house, the blind men came to him; and Jesus said to them, "Do you believe that I am able to do this?" They said to him, "Yes, Lord." [29] Then he touched their eyes and said, "According to your faith let it be done to you." [30] And their eyes were opened. Then Jesus sternly ordered them, "See that no one knows of this." [31] But they went away and spread the news about him throughout that district.

[32] After they had gone away, a demoniac who was mute was brought to him. [33] And when the demon had been cast out, the one who had been mute spoke; and the crowds were amazed and said, "Never has anything like this been seen in Israel." [34] But the Pharisees said, "By the ruler of the demons he casts out the demons." [a]

[35] Then Jesus went about all the cities and villages, teaching in their synagogues, and proclaiming the good news of the kingdom, and curing every disease and every sickness. [36] When he saw the crowds, he had compassion for them, because they were harassed and helpless, like sheep without a shepherd. [37] Then he said to his disciples, "The harvest is plentiful, but the laborers are few; [38] therefore ask the Lord of the harvest to send out laborers into his harvest."

10 Then Jesus[b] summoned his twelve disciples and gave them authority over unclean spirits, to cast them out, and to cure every disease and every sickness. [2] These are the names of the twelve apostles: first, Simon, also known as Peter, and his brother Andrew; James son of Zebedee, and his brother John; [3] Philip and Bartholomew; Thomas and Matthew the tax collector; James son of Alphaeus, and Thaddaeus;[c] [4] Simon the Cananaean, and Judas Iscariot, the one who betrayed him.

[5] These twelve Jesus sent out with the following instructions: "Go nowhere among the Gentiles, and enter no town of the Samaritans, [6] but go rather to the lost sheep

a Other ancient authorities lack this verse
b Gk *he*
c Other ancient authorities read *Lebbaeus*, or *Lebbaeus called Thaddaeus*

(Num 15.38; Deut 22.12; *b. Men.* 14a; 43b); see 14.36; 23.5; *Tg. Onq.* to Num. 15.38 and Deut 22.12 uses an Aramaic cognate to the Greek term "kraspedon" ("fringe"). **22:** *Made you well*, Gk "sōzō," which can mean "save" (cf. 1.21; 10.22; 16.25; 19.25; 24.13). **23:** *Flute players*, see *m. Ketub.* 4.4. **24:** *Sleeping*, see Dan 12.21; 1 Thess 5.10. **25:** Cf. 1 Kings 17.22–23; 2 Kings 4.17–37.

9.27–34: Two blind men and the demoniac (Mk 10.46–52; 3.22; Lk 18.35–43; 11.14–15). **27:** *Two blind men*, cf. 20.29–34. Blindness often symbolizes spiritual lack. *Son of David*, cf. 12.23; 15.22; 17.15; 20.30; 21.9; cf. *T. Sol.* 20.1. The title can suggest King Solomon (1.6), known for his healing powers. **29:** *According to your faith*, 8.10n.; 15.28. **30:** *See that no one knows*, see 8.4n. **34:** Pharisees do not deny Jesus' power but attribute it to demons (12.24; 15.22–24). A rabbinic source attributes it to sorcery (*b. Sanh.* 43a).

9.35–38: Anticipating the mission (Mk 1.39; 6.34; Lk 8.1; 10.2). See 4.23–25. **35:** *Good news*, see 4.23n. **36:** Num 27.17; 1 Kings 22.17; Ezek 34.5; Zech 10.2. **37:** *Laborers are few*, compare *m. Avot* 2.15.

10.1–42: Missionary instructions. 1–4: Twelve disciples (Mk 6.7; 3.13–19; Lk 6.12–16; 9.1). **1:** *Twelve*, number of the tribes of Israel (see 19.28; Gen 35.22–26; Num 1). **2:** *Apostles*, from Gk "apostolos," "one who is sent" (cf. Heb "shaliaḥ," "messenger"). *Peter*, see 16.18. **3:** *Matthew*, see 9.9. **4:** *Cananaean*, likely from an Aramaic term ("Canai"; see *Avot de R. Natan* 6) indicating Zealot affiliation. *Judas*, 26.14–16,20–25,47–56; 27.3–10. *Iscariot*, perhaps from "Kerioth," a town in southern Judea (see Josh 15.25).

10.5–15: Specific instructions. 5: *Nowhere among the Gentiles*, Jesus restricts the mission to Jews; 28.19 expands it to Gentiles. *Samaritans*, Jews and Samaritans had mutual animosity (cf. Lk 9.51–56; 10.29–37; Jn 4.9;

of the house of Israel. [7] As you go, proclaim the good news, 'The kingdom of heaven has come near.'[a] [8] Cure the sick, raise the dead, cleanse the lepers,[b] cast out demons. You received without payment; give without payment. [9] Take no gold, or silver, or copper in your belts, [10] no bag for your journey, or two tunics, or sandals, or a staff; for laborers deserve their food. [11] Whatever town or village you enter, find out who in it is worthy, and stay there until you leave. [12] As you enter the house, greet it. [13] If the house is worthy, let your peace come upon it; but if it is not worthy, let your peace return to you. [14] If anyone will not welcome you or listen to your words, shake off the dust from your feet as you leave that house or town. [15] Truly I tell you, it will be more tolerable for the land of Sodom and Gomorrah on the day of judgment than for that town.

[16] "See, I am sending you out like sheep into the midst of wolves; so be wise as serpents and innocent as doves. [17] Beware of them, for they will hand you over to councils and flog you in their synagogues; [18] and you will be dragged before governors and kings because of me, as a testimony to them and the Gentiles. [19] When they hand you over, do not worry about how you are to speak or what you are to say; for what you are to say will be given to you at that time; [20] for it is not you who speak, but the Spirit of your Father speaking through you. [21] Brother will betray brother to death, and a father his child, and children will rise against parents and have them put to death; [22] and you will be hated by all because of my name. But the one who endures to the end will be saved. [23] When they persecute you in one town, flee to the next; for truly I tell you, you will not have gone through all the towns of Israel before the Son of Man comes.

[24] "A disciple is not above the teacher, nor a slave above the master; [25] it is enough for the disciple to be like the teacher, and the slave like the master. If they have called the master of the house Beelzebul, how much more will they malign those of his household!

[26] "So have no fear of them; for nothing is covered up that will not be uncovered, and nothing secret that will not become known. [27] What I say to you in the dark, tell in the light; and what you hear whispered, proclaim from the housetops. [28] Do not fear those who kill the body but cannot kill the soul; rather fear him who can destroy both soul and body in hell.[c] [29] Are not two sparrows sold for a penny? Yet not one of them will fall to the ground apart

a Or *is at hand*

b The terms *leper* and *leprosy* can refer to several diseases

c Gk *Gehenna*

Josephus, *J.W.* 1.63; *Ant.* 11; 13.255; *T. Levi* 5–7). **6:** *Lost sheep of the house of Israel,* see 15.24; either all Israel depicted as lost or the people as opposed to the religious and political leaders. **7:** *Kingdom of heaven has come near,* see 3.2n. **8:** *Raise the dead,* see *Lev. Rab.* 10.4 on similar rabbinic abilities. **9:** *Take no gold, or silver, or copper,* God provides for those who study and/or teach the Torah (*m. Avot* 1.3; *b. Bek.* 29a; *Tanh. Ex.* 29). **10:** *Laborers deserve their food,* missionaries should receive hospitality (1 Cor 9.14; see *b. Shabb.* 127a on the importance of hospitality). **15:** *Sodom and Gomorrah,* destroyed for lack of charity and hospitality according to Ezek 16.49 (see also Gen 13.13; 18.20; 19.24–28; Deut 29.23; Isa 13.19; Jer 50.40; Zeph 2.9; *b. Sanh.* 109a).

10.16–25: The disciples' fate (Mk 13.9–13,22; Lk 12.11–12; 21.12–19; Jn 16.2; 15.18–20). **16:** *Wise as serpents,* see *Song Rab.* 2.30. **17:** *Flog,* see *m. Makk.* 3.12. **18:** *Them,* the persecutors are Jews, given "their synagogues" (see 1 Thess 1.6; 2.1–2,14–16; 3.4; 2 Cor 11.24). **20:** *Spirit . . . through you,* the Spirit of God was seen as making it possible for ordinary people to speak out, as in Num 11.25. **21:** *Brother will betray brother,* see *m. Sot.* 9.15 on familial breakdown prior to the messianic age. **23:** *Son of Man comes,* final judgment (see 8.20n.; 10.23; 19.28; 25.30–31; cf. Dan 7.13). **25:** *Slave like the master, b. Ber.* 58b; *Gen. Rab.* 49.2. *Beelzebul,* from Hebrew, "lord of lofty abode," a Canaanite god, whose name was changed pejoratively to Beelzebub, "Lord of the flies" in 2 Kings 1.2–3,6,16, and later associated with the demonic in early Jewish and Christian tradition (*T. Sol.* 3.6; 6.1–2; Origen, *Cels.* 8.25).

10.26–42: Final instructions (Mk 8.34–35; Lk 12.1–12,49–53). **26:** *So have no fear of them,* likely reflecting the dedication of Jeremiah (1.8). **28:** *Fear him,* see Heb 10.31. *Hell,* lit., "Gehenna"; see 5.22n. **29–31:** *Sparrows,* if God cares for seemingly insignificant animals, how much more so will God care for human beings (a "qal vahomer" argument, 6.26n.; 10.30–32; *b. B. Metz.* 85a; cf. *y. Seb.* 9.1; *Gen. Rab.* 33.18; see also Lk 12.6).

from your Father. [30] And even the hairs of your head are all counted. [31] So do not be afraid; you are of more value than many sparrows.

[32] "Everyone therefore who acknowledges me before others, I also will acknowledge before my Father in heaven; [33] but whoever denies me before others, I also will deny before my Father in heaven.

[34] "Do not think that I have come to bring peace to the earth; I have not come to bring peace, but a sword.

[35] For I have come to set a man against his father,
and a daughter against her mother,
and a daughter-in-law against her mother-in-law;
[36] and one's foes will be members of one's own household.

[37] Whoever loves father or mother more than me is not worthy of me; and whoever loves son or daughter more than me is not worthy of me; [38] and whoever does not take up the cross and follow me is not worthy of me. [39] Those who find their life will lose it, and those who lose their life for my sake will find it.

[40] "Whoever welcomes you welcomes me, and whoever welcomes me welcomes the one who sent me. [41] Whoever welcomes a prophet in the name of a prophet will receive a prophet's reward; and whoever welcomes a righteous person in the name of a righteous person will receive the reward of the righteous; [42] and whoever gives even a cup of cold water to one of these little ones in the name of a disciple—truly I tell you, none of these will lose their reward."

11 Now when Jesus had finished instructing his twelve disciples, he went on from there to teach and proclaim his message in their cities.

[2] When John heard in prison what the Messiah[a] was doing, he sent word by his[b] disciples [3] and said to him, "Are you the one who is to come, or are we to wait for another?" [4] Jesus answered them, "Go and tell John what you hear and see: [5] the blind receive their sight, the lame walk, the lepers[c] are cleansed, the deaf hear, the dead are raised, and the poor have good news brought to them. [6] And blessed is anyone who takes no offense at me."

[7] As they went away, Jesus began to speak to the crowds about John: "What did you go out into the wilderness to look at? A reed shaken by the wind? [8] What then did you go out to see? Someone[d] dressed in soft robes? Look, those who wear soft robes are in royal palaces. [9] What then did you go out to see? A prophet?[e] Yes, I tell you, and more than a prophet. [10] This is the one about whom it is written,

'See, I am sending my messenger ahead of you,
who will prepare your way before you.'

[11] Truly I tell you, among those born of women no one has arisen greater than John the Baptist; yet the least in the kingdom of heaven is greater than he. [12] From the days of John the Baptist until now the kingdom of heaven has suffered violence,[f] and the violent take it by force. [13] For all the prophets and the law prophesied until John came;

[a] Or *the Christ*
[b] Other ancient authorities read *two of his*
[c] The terms *leper* and *leprosy* can refer to several diseases
[d] Or *Why then did you go out? To see someone*
[e] Other ancient authorities read *Why then did you go out? To see a prophet?*
[f] Or *has been coming violently*

33: *Whoever denies me,* a warning to be faithful despite persecution. **34–36:** Mic 7.6; cf. Ezek 38.21. **37–39:** 16.24–25. **38:** *Take up the cross,* risk suffering (*Gen. Rab.* 56). **41:** *Righteous,* see 1.19n. **42:** *Little ones,* possibly missionaries (see 25.45).

11.1–19: John questions Jesus. 1: *Finished instructing,* Jesus does not send the disciples on an independent mission (contrast Mk 3.13; Lk 7.18–35). **2–3:** *Prison,* Josephus locates John's imprisonment at Macherus, five miles east of the Dead Sea (*Ant.* 18.116–119). *Messiah,* see 3.13–17. *By his disciples,* 9.14n.; 14.12. **4–5:** *What you hear and see,* Jesus fulfills some messianic expectations, although beliefs varied (Isa 35.4–6,9–10; see also Isa 26.19; 29.18–19; cf. *2 Bar.* 29.6; 4Q521; 11QMelch 18). Matthew omits "freeing the captive" (Isa 61.1). Jesus may avoid answering directly since a report to John in prison saying "I am the Messiah" would be heard by Herod's guards, and could lead to Jesus' arrest as well. **10:** Mal 3.1. **11:** *Born of women,* mortals; see Job 14.1; 15.14; 25.4; *b. Shabb.*

[14] and if you are willing to accept it, he is Elijah who is to come. [15] Let anyone with ears[a] listen!

[16] "But to what will I compare this generation? It is like children sitting in the marketplaces and calling to one another,

[17] 'We played the flute for you, and you did not dance;
we wailed, and you did not mourn.'

[18] For John came neither eating nor drinking, and they say, 'He has a demon'; [19] the Son of Man came eating and drinking, and they say, 'Look, a glutton and a drunkard, a friend of tax collectors and sinners!' Yet wisdom is vindicated by her deeds."[b]

[20] Then he began to reproach the cities in which most of his deeds of power had been done, because they did not repent. [21] "Woe to you, Chorazin! Woe to you, Bethsaida! For if the deeds of power done in you had been done in Tyre and Sidon, they would have repented long ago in sackcloth and ashes. [22] But I tell you, on the day of judgment it will be more tolerable for Tyre and Sidon than for you. [23] And you, Capernaum,

will you be exalted to heaven?
No, you will be brought down to Hades.

For if the deeds of power done in you had been done in Sodom, it would have remained until this day. [24] But I tell you that on the day of judgment it will be more tolerable for the land of Sodom than for you."

[25] At that time Jesus said, "I thank[c] you, Father, Lord of heaven and earth, because you have hidden these things from the wise and the intelligent and have revealed them to infants; [26] yes, Father, for such was your gracious will.[d] [27] All things have been handed over to me by my Father; and no one knows the Son except the Father, and no one knows the Father except the Son and anyone to whom the Son chooses to reveal him.

[28] "Come to me, all you that are weary and are carrying heavy burdens, and I will give you rest. [29] Take my yoke upon you, and learn from me; for I am gentle and humble in heart, and you will find rest for your souls. [30] For my yoke is easy, and my burden is light."

12 At that time Jesus went through the grainfields on the sabbath; his disciples were hungry, and they began to pluck heads of grain and to eat. [2] When the Pharisees saw it, they said to him, "Look, your disciples are doing what is not lawful to do on the sabbath." [3] He said to them, "Have you not read what

a Other ancient authorities add *to hear*
b Other ancient authorities read *children*
c Or *praise*
d Or *for so it was well-pleasing in your sight*

88b. *Least in the kingdom*, those among Jesus' followers. **13:** *Prophets and the law*, regarded as anticipating the Messiah (Acts 3.24; *b. Ber.* 34b; *b. Shabb.* 63a; *b. Sanh.* 99a). Some early Christians understood that John the Baptist's arrival negated Torah (Tertullian, *Pud.* 8). **14–15:** See Jn 1.21. *Elijah*, messianic forerunner (Mal 4.4–5 [Heb 3.23]; see also Sir 48.10; *b. Sukk.* 5a; *b. Meg.* 16b; *b. Sanh.* 98a). **18:** *Neither eating nor drinking*, engaging in ascetic practices. **19:** *Son of Man*, see 8.20n. *Glutton and a drunkard*, allusion to the rebellious son (Deut 21.20). *Tax collectors and sinners*, see 5.46n.; 9.10n. *Wisdom* (Gk "Sophia"; Heb "hohkmah"), the feminine manifestation of the divine (Prov. 1–9; Wis 7.21–8.1).

11.20–24: Jesus condemns three cities (Lk 10.13–15). **21:** *Woe to you*, a prophetic formula (Isa 5.11–17; 23.1–12; 29.15–21). *Chorazin . . . Bethsaida*, Jewish cities on the northern tip of the Sea of Galilee, near Capernaum (cf. Mk 6.45; 8.22; Lk 9.10–17; Jn 1.44). *Tyre and Sidon*, Mediterranean cities rebuked for extravagant wealth (Isa 23; Ezek 28; cf. Jer 25.22; 27.3; 47.4; Joel 3.4–7; Zech 9.1–4). **23:** *Capernaum*, 4.13n. *Hades*, the realm of the dead, synonymous with Gehenna (see 5.22n.). *Sodom*, see 10.15n.

11.25–30: Jesus' authority (Lk 10.21–22). **25:** See 10.42; 18.10. *Infants*, Jewish tradition speaks of teaching children (or the "simple") (Ps 8.2; 19.7; Prov 1.4; Sir. 3.19; 1QH 7.21–22). **27:** Jesus claims unique knowledge of the divine. **29:** *Yoke*, connected to the study of Torah (Sir 51.23,26; *m. Avot* 3.5; *m. Ber.* 2.2), discipline, and obedience (Gen. 27.40; Jer 5.5; cf. *1 En.* 103.11; *Pss. Sol.* 7.30; 17.30; *Sib. Or.* 3.391–92; 448, 508, 537, 567).

12.1–14: Sabbath instructions (Mk 2.23–3.6; Lk 6.1–11). **1:** *Hungry*, added by Matthew. *Pluck heads of grain*, the thirty-nine types of work forbidden on the Sabbath according to rabbinic law (Ex 34.21) include reaping, but not explicitly plucking; *m. Pesah.* 4.8; *m. Shabb.* 7.2; *b. Shabb.* 73b). **2:** *Not lawful*, the disciples do not violate Torah (which prohibits "work" [Ex 20.10; Deut 5.14]) since the Sabbath should be a time of joy (Isa 58.13). Health supersedes Sabbath prohibitions (*m. Yoma* 8.6; *b. Men.* 96a; *t. Shabb.* 15.16). **3–4:** *What David did*, 1 Sam 21.1–6; Jesus

David did when he and his companions were hungry? [4] He entered the house of God and ate the bread of the Presence, which it was not lawful for him or his companions to eat, but only for the priests. [5] Or have you not read in the law that on the sabbath the priests in the temple break the sabbath and yet are guiltless? [6] I tell you, something greater than the temple is here. [7] But if you had known what this means, 'I desire mercy and not sacrifice,' you would not have condemned the guiltless. [8] For the Son of Man is lord of the sabbath."

[9] He left that place and entered their synagogue; [10] a man was there with a withered hand, and they asked him, "Is it lawful to cure on the sabbath?" so that they might accuse him. [11] He said to them, "Suppose one of you has only one sheep and it falls into a pit on the sabbath; will you not lay hold of it and lift it out? [12] How much more valuable is a human being than a sheep! So it is lawful to do good on the sabbath." [13] Then he said to the man, "Stretch out your hand." He stretched it out, and it was restored, as sound as the other. [14] But the Pharisees went out and conspired against him, how to destroy him.

[15] When Jesus became aware of this, he departed. Many crowds [a] followed him, and he cured all of them, [16] and he ordered them not to make him known. [17] This was to fulfill what had been spoken through the prophet Isaiah:

[18] "Here is my servant, whom I have chosen,
my beloved, with whom my soul is well pleased.
I will put my Spirit upon him,
and he will proclaim justice to the Gentiles.
[19] He will not wrangle or cry aloud,
nor will anyone hear his voice in the streets.
[20] He will not break a bruised reed
or quench a smoldering wick
until he brings justice to victory.
[21] And in his name the Gentiles will hope."

[22] Then they brought to him a demoniac who was blind and mute; and he cured him, so that the one who had been mute could speak and see. [23] All the crowds were amazed and said, "Can this be the Son of David?" [24] But when the Pharisees heard it, they said, "It is only by Beelzebul, the ruler of the demons, that this fellow casts out the demons." [25] He knew what they were thinking and said to them, "Every kingdom divided against itself is laid waste, and no city or house divided against itself will stand. [26] If Satan casts out Satan, he is divided against himself; how then will his kingdom stand? [27] If I cast out demons by Beelzebul, by whom do your own exorcists[b] cast them out? Therefore they will be your judges. [28] But if it is by the Spirit of God that I cast out demons, then the kingdom of God has come to you. [29] Or how can one enter a strong man's house and plunder his property, without first tying up the strong man? Then indeed the house can be plundered. [30] Whoever is not with me is against me, and whoever does not gather with me scatters. [31] Therefore I tell you, people will be forgiven

[a] Other ancient authorities lack *crowds*
[b] Gk *sons*

argues from biblical precedent. See also Lev 24.5–9. **5:** Num 28.9–10. **6:** *Greater than the Temple*, Jesus' presence grants his disciples authority to define Sabbath practices. **7:** *Mercy and not sacrifice*, see 9.13n. **8:** *Son of Man*, see 8.20n. According to the Torah, the Sabbath was God's gift to the people (Ex 16.29; see also *Mek.* 31.12–17). In Matthew, Jesus is the authoritative interpreter of the Sabbath laws. **10–12:** See 9.26n. Rabbinic law permitted alleviating an animal's distress on the Sabbath (*t. Shabb.* 15.1; *b. Shabb.* 128b), although some Jews disagreed (CD 11.13). **13:** *It was restored*, the passive construction both suggests divine healing and indicates that Jesus did no "work."

12.15–21: Healing the multitudes (Mk 3.7–12; Lk 6.17–19). **16:** *Not to make him known*, messianic secret: see 8.4n. **18–21:** Isa 42.1–4, but not an exact quotation of either Hebrew or Greek texts. **18:** *My servant*, here meaning the Messiah (cf. *2 Bar.* 70.9). The "servant" usually referred to Israel (Isa 42.18–29; 44.1,21; 49.3,5–7; *Pss. Sol.* 12.6; 17.21). **21:** *Gentiles*, 8.10; 15.28; 18.6; 21.21; 24.13–14; 28.20. Here Matthew is closer to LXX Isaiah.

12.22–37: Jesus' powers (Mk 3.20–30; Lk 11.14–23; 12.10; 6.43–45). **22–24:** See 9.34n. *Son of David*, 1.1n. *Beelzebul*, 10.25n. **26:** *Satan casts out Satan*, a demon would not expel fellow demons (cf. *T. Sol.* 5.5; 15.8). **27:** Cf. 7.22–23; Mk 9.38; Acts 19.13–19. *Your own exorcists*, see *Ant.* 8.46–49. **28:** *Kingdom of God*, see 3.2n. **30:** *Is against me*, a dualistic view of humanity. **31:** See 9.3n. *Blasphemy against the Spirit*, certain sins against God are not for-

for every sin and blasphemy, but blasphemy against the Spirit will not be forgiven. [32] Whoever speaks a word against the Son of Man will be forgiven, but whoever speaks against the Holy Spirit will not be forgiven, either in this age or in the age to come.

[33] "Either make the tree good, and its fruit good; or make the tree bad, and its fruit bad; for the tree is known by its fruit. [34] You brood of vipers! How can you speak good things, when you are evil? For out of the abundance of the heart the mouth speaks. [35] The good person brings good things out of a good treasure, and the evil person brings evil things out of an evil treasure. [36] I tell you, on the day of judgment you will have to give an account for every careless word you utter; [37] for by your words you will be justified, and by your words you will be condemned."

[38] Then some of the scribes and Pharisees said to him, "Teacher, we wish to see a sign from you." [39] But he answered them, "An evil and adulterous generation asks for a sign, but no sign will be given to it except the sign of the prophet Jonah. [40] For just as Jonah was three days and three nights in the belly of the sea monster, so for three days and three nights the Son of Man will be in the heart of the earth. [41] The people of Nineveh will rise up at the judgment with this generation and condemn it, because they repented at the proclamation of Jonah, and see, something greater than Jonah is here! [42] The queen of the South will rise up at the judgment with this generation and condemn it, because she came from the ends of the earth to listen to the wisdom of Solomon, and see, something greater than Solomon is here!

[43] "When the unclean spirit has gone out of a person, it wanders through waterless regions looking for a resting place, but it finds none. [44] Then it says, 'I will return to my house from which I came.' When it comes, it finds it empty, swept, and put in order. [45] Then it goes and brings along seven other spirits more evil than itself, and they enter and live there; and the last state of that person is worse than the first. So will it be also with this evil generation."

[46] While he was still speaking to the crowds, his mother and his brothers were standing outside, wanting to speak to him. [47] Someone told him, "Look, your mother and your brothers are standing outside, wanting to speak to you." [a] [48] But to the one who had told him this, Jesus [b] replied, "Who is my mother, and who are my brothers?" [49] And pointing to his disciples, he said, "Here are my mother and my brothers! [50] For whoever does the will of my Father in heaven is my brother and sister and mother."

13 That same day Jesus went out of the house and sat beside the sea. [2] Such great crowds gathered around him that he got into a boat and sat there, while the whole crowd

[a] Other ancient authorities lack verse 47
[b] Gk *he*

given (cf. Ex 20.7; Num 15.30–31; *Jub.* 15.34; 1QS 7.15–17, 22–23; CD 10.3; *Sifre Deut.* 328). **32:** See 8.20n.; 10.23n. *Son of Man*, see 8.20n. *Age to come*, Heb "Olam ha-ba," the messianic age (*m. Sanh.* 10.1; *b. Sanh.* 90a; *b. Shabb.* 127a; *b. Men.* 44a; *b. Pesah.* 50a; *b. Qidd.* 39b, etc.). **34:** *Brood of vipers*, see 3.7n.; 23.33. **36:** *Day of judgment*, see 7.22n. **37:** *Justified*, put in a right relationship with God.

12.38–42: Demand for a sign (16.1–4; Mk 8.11–13; Lk 11.29–32; Jn 6.30). **38:** *A sign from you*, the Pharisees ask Jesus to prove he is the Messiah. **39:** Jon 1.17. *Evil and adulterous*, sinful (Deut 1.35; 32.5; Hos 1.2; 2.2; 4.15,18; 9.1; *Jub.* 23.14; 1QSb 3.7). In Matthew, those who lack faith in Jesus (12.39; 16.4; cf. Mk 8.38). **40:** *Jonah*, see Jon 2.1. *In the heart of the earth*, often linked to the legend of Jesus' harrowing of hell (Acts 2.27,31; 1 Pet 3.19; 4.6) to redeem faithful people who died before his crucifixion. Early Christian sarcophagi frequently depicted Jonah as a symbol of resurrection. **41:** Jon 3.5; see *y. Sanh.* 11.5. **42:** *Queen of the South*, Queen of Sheba (1 Kings 10.1–13; 2 Chr 9.1–12).

12.43–45: The return of the unclean spirit (Lk 11.24–26). The description accounts for failed exorcisms or medical relapses. **45:** *Evil generation*, see 12.39n.

12.46–50: Jesus' true family (Mk 3.31–35; Lk 8.19–21). See 13.55; Jude 1.1. The true family includes only those who have faith. **46:** *Mother and his brothers*, see 1.25n. **50:** *Will of my Father*, see 6.10n. Jewish sources cite a similar belief as it relates to faith in God (Deut 33.9; Prov 4.3; 1QS 1–9; *y. Qidd.* 1.7).

13.1–53: Parables of the kingdom. 1–2: Introduction to the parables (Mk 4.1). **3:** *Parables*, Gk "parabolē, meaning "comparison" (Heb "mashal"). Parables appear in various forms throughout Jewish literature (2 Sam

stood on the beach. [3] And he told them many things in parables, saying: "Listen! A sower went out to sow. [4] And as he sowed, some seeds fell on the path, and the birds came and ate them up. [5] Other seeds fell on rocky ground, where they did not have much soil, and they sprang up quickly, since they had no depth of soil. [6] But when the sun rose, they were scorched; and since they had no root, they withered away. [7] Other seeds fell among thorns, and the thorns grew up and choked them. [8] Other seeds fell on good soil and brought forth grain, some a hundredfold, some sixty, some thirty. [9] Let anyone with ears[a] listen!"

[10] Then the disciples came and asked him, "Why do you speak to them in parables?" [11] He answered, "To you it has been given to know the secrets[b] of the kingdom of heaven, but to them it has not been given. [12] For to those who have, more will be given, and they will have an abundance; but from those who have nothing, even what they have will be taken away. [13] The reason I speak to them in parables is that 'seeing they do not perceive, and hearing they do not listen, nor do they understand.' [14] With them indeed is fulfilled the prophecy of Isaiah that says:

'You will indeed listen, but never
understand,
and you will indeed look, but never
perceive.
[15] For this people's heart has grown dull,
and their ears are hard of hearing,
and they have shut their eyes;
so that they might not look with
their eyes,
and listen with their ears,
and understand with their heart and
turn—
and I would heal them.'

[16] But blessed are your eyes, for they see, and your ears, for they hear. [17] Truly I tell you, many prophets and righteous people longed to see what you see, but did not see it, and to hear what you hear, but did not hear it.

[18] "Hear then the parable of the sower. [19] When anyone hears the word of the kingdom and does not understand it, the evil one comes and snatches away what is sown in the heart; this is what was sown on the path. [20] As for what was sown on rocky ground, this is the one who hears the word and immediately receives it with joy; [21] yet such a person has no root, but endures only for a while, and when trouble or persecution arises on account of the word, that person immediately falls away.[c] [22] As for what was sown among thorns, this is the one who hears the word, but the cares of the world and the lure of wealth choke the word, and it yields nothing. [23] But as for what was sown on good soil, this is the one who hears the word and understands it, who indeed bears fruit and yields, in one case a hundredfold, in another sixty, and in another thirty."

[24] He put before them another parable: "The kingdom of heaven may be compared to someone who sowed good seed in his field;

[a] Other ancient authorities add *to hear*
[b] Or *mysteries*
[c] Gk *stumbles*

12.1–7; Isa 5.1–7; *1 En.* 1.2–3; 37–71; Sir 1.24; 3.29; 20.20; 39.2; 47.17; *T. Job* 18.7–8; *m. Sot.* 9.15; *t. Sot.* 5.9; *b. Ber.* 61b; see "Midrash and Parables in the NT," p. 565).

13.3–9: Parable of the sower (Mk 4.2–9; Lk 8.4–8). Cf. *Gos. Thom.* 9. **3:** *Sower*, refers to Jesus (13.37). "Sowing" related to doing the work of God (Jer 31.27–28; Ezek 36.9; Hos 2.21–23; *4 Ezra* 9.31; *2 Bar.* 32.1). **4:** *Seeds*, later identified as "the word of the kingdom" (13.19; cf. *b. Ta'an.* 4a).

13.10–23: Jesus explains his teaching (Mk 4.10–12; Lk 8.9–10,18; 19.26; Jn 12.40). **11:** *Secrets*, indicating a divine plan previously unrevealed (Dan 2.18,19,27; 1QpHab 7.8; 1QS 3.23; 1QM 3.9). **13:** *Nor do they understand*, the message is open to a select few (like the disciples; see 13.16–17) having faith in Jesus. **14–15:** Isa 6.9–10; Lk 8.10; Jn 12.37–41; Acts 28.26–27; admonition aimed at those who fail to grasp Jesus' teachings. Even though Isa 6 refers to the audience contemporary with the prophet, it is understood here as being fulfilled more than seven hundred years later. **16–17:** Lk 10.23–4. **18–23:** Mk 4.13–20; Lk 8.11–15. Jewish parables often included explanations (e.g., Isa 5; *4 Ezra* 4.13–18,20–21). **19:** *Evil one*, see 8.16n.; 6.13; 13.19,38; Jn 17.15; *Jub.* 11.11–12; *Apoc. Abr.* 13.

13.24–30: Parable of the wheat and the weeds (Mk 4.13–20; Lk 8.11–15). Cf. *Gos. Thom.* 57. **25:** *Enemy*, identified as the devil (13.39). **30:** *Both of them grow together*, unfaithful people in the church will be rooted out in the

[25] but while everybody was asleep, an enemy came and sowed weeds among the wheat, and then went away. [26] So when the plants came up and bore grain, then the weeds appeared as well. [27] And the slaves of the householder came and said to him, 'Master, did you not sow good seed in your field? Where, then, did these weeds come from?' [28] He answered, 'An enemy has done this.' The slaves said to him, 'Then do you want us to go and gather them?' [29] But he replied, 'No; for in gathering the weeds you would uproot the wheat along with them. [30] Let both of them grow together until the harvest; and at harvest time I will tell the reapers, Collect the weeds first and bind them in bundles to be burned, but gather the wheat into my barn.'"

[31] He put before them another parable: "The kingdom of heaven is like a mustard seed that someone took and sowed in his field; [32] it is the smallest of all the seeds, but when it has grown it is the greatest of shrubs and becomes a tree, so that the birds of the air come and make nests in its branches."

[33] He told them another parable: "The kingdom of heaven is like yeast that a woman took and mixed in with[a] three measures of flour until all of it was leavened."

[34] Jesus told the crowds all these things in parables; without a parable he told them nothing. [35] This was to fulfill what had been spoken through the prophet:[b]

"I will open my mouth to speak in
parables;
I will proclaim what has been hidden
from the foundation of the
world."[c]

[36] Then he left the crowds and went into the house. And his disciples approached him, saying, "Explain to us the parable of the weeds of the field." [37] He answered, "The one who sows the good seed is the Son of Man; [38] the field is the world, and the good seed are the children of the kingdom; the weeds are the children of the evil one, [39] and the enemy who sowed them is the devil; the harvest is the end of the age, and the reapers are angels. [40] Just as the weeds are collected and burned up with fire, so will it be at the end of the age. [41] The Son of Man will send his angels, and they will collect out of his kingdom all causes of sin and all evildoers, [42] and they will throw them into the furnace of fire, where there will be weeping and gnashing of teeth. [43] Then the righteous will shine like the sun in the kingdom of their Father. Let anyone with ears[d] listen!

[44] "The kingdom of heaven is like treasure hidden in a field, which someone found and hid; then in his joy he goes and sells all that he has and buys that field.

[45] "Again, the kingdom of heaven is like a merchant in search of fine pearls; [46] on finding one pearl of great value, he went and sold all that he had and bought it.

[47] "Again, the kingdom of heaven is like a net that was thrown into the sea and caught fish of every kind; [48] when it was full, they drew it ashore, sat down, and put the good into baskets but threw out the bad. [49] So it will be at the end of the age. The angels will come out and separate the evil from the righteous [50] and throw them into the furnace

a Gk *hid in*
b Other ancient authorities read *the prophet Isaiah*
c Other ancient authorities lack *of the world*
d Other ancient authorities add *to hear*

eschaton; even those expelled should be re-evangelized (see 18.17n.). *Harvest,* metaphor for final judgment (Jer 51.33; Hos 6.11; Joel 3.13).

13.31–52: Parables of mustard seed and yeast (Mk 4.30–34; Lk 13.18–21). Cf. *Gos. Thom.* 8,20,76,96,109. **31–32:** *Mustard seed,* symbolizing smallness (17.20; *m. Nidd.* 5.2; *m. Tehar.* 8.8; *b. Ber.* 31a; cf. Lk 17.6), although the plant can grow as high as five feet. *Becomes a tree,* an ironic comment; the parable is a parody (Ezek 17.23; 31.5; Dan 4.7–9,17–19). **33:** *Yeast,* which permeates and expands. *Three measures,* approximately sixty pounds; like the previous parable, an account of ironic and unexpected exaggeration. **35:** Ps 78.2 (following the LXX). **37:** *Son of Man,* see 8.20n. **42:** See 8.12n.; 22.13. *Furnace,* represents judgment (Dan 3.6; *1 En.* 54.6; *4 Ezra* 7.36). **43:** Dan 12.3. **44:** Cf. Prov 2.4; Sir. 20.30; *2 Bar.* 6.7–9. According to rabbinic sources, once a person acquired property all contents belonged to him/her (see *m. B. Bat.* 4.8–9). **45:** *Pearls,* Jewish sources relate pearls to piety and Torah study (*Pesiq. Rab.* 23.6; *Avot de R. Natan* 18A; cf. *Acts Pet.* 20). **48:** Fishermen in the Sea of Galilee would have had to separate kosher and nonkosher fish from their nets.

of fire, where there will be weeping and gnashing of teeth.

[51] "Have you understood all this?" They answered, "Yes." [52] And he said to them, "Therefore every scribe who has been trained for the kingdom of heaven is like the master of a household who brings out of his treasure what is new and what is old." [53] When Jesus had finished these parables, he left that place.

[54] He came to his hometown and began to teach the people[a] in their synagogue, so that they were astounded and said, "Where did this man get this wisdom and these deeds of power? [55] Is not this the carpenter's son? Is not his mother called Mary? And are not his brothers James and Joseph and Simon and Judas? [56] And are not all his sisters with us? Where then did this man get all this?" [57] And they took offense at him. But Jesus said to them, "Prophets are not without honor except in their own country and in their own house." [58] And he did not do many deeds of power there, because of their unbelief.

14 At that time Herod the ruler[b] heard reports about Jesus; [2] and he said to his servants, "This is John the Baptist; he has been raised from the dead, and for this reason these powers are at work in him." [3] For Herod had arrested John, bound him, and put him in prison on account of Herodias, his brother Philip's wife,[c] [4] because John had been telling him, "It is not lawful for you to have her." [5] Though Herod[d] wanted to put him to death, he feared the crowd, because they regarded him as a prophet. [6] But when Herod's birthday came, the daughter of Herodias danced before the company, and she pleased Herod [7] so much that he promised on oath to grant her whatever she might ask. [8] Prompted by her mother, she said, "Give me the head of John the Baptist here on a platter." [9] The king was grieved, yet out of regard for his oaths and for the guests, he commanded it to be given; [10] he sent and had John beheaded in the prison. [11] The head was brought on a platter and given to the girl, who brought it to her mother. [12] His disciples came and took the body and buried it; then they went and told Jesus.

[13] Now when Jesus heard this, he withdrew from there in a boat to a deserted place by himself. But when the crowds heard it, they followed him on foot from the towns. [14] When he went ashore, he saw a great crowd; and he had compassion for them and cured their sick. [15] When it was evening, the disciples came to him and said, "This is a deserted place, and the hour is now late; send the crowds away so that they may go into the villages and buy food for themselves." [16] Jesus said to them, "They need not go away; you give them something

a Gk *them*
b Gk *tetrarch*
c Other ancient authorities read *his brother's wife*
d Gk *he*

52: *Scribe . . . trained for the kingdom of heaven*, elsewhere, scribes are condemned (ch 23), suggesting this positive reference relates to Matthew's own scribes (cf. 5.17–20; 8.18; 9.3; 13.52; 15.1; 20.18; 21.15; 23). *What is new and what is old*, see 9.17n.

13.53–58: Rejection in Nazareth (Mk 6.1–6; Lk 4.16–30; Jn 4.44). See 12.46–50n. **54:** *Hometown*, Nazareth, see 2.23n. **55:** *Carpenter* (Gk "tektōn"), a builder, not just a woodworker. **57:** *Took offense*, Hebrew prophets were also rejected (Jer 11.21–23; 12.6; Am 7.10–17). *Prophets are not without honor*, in the Tanakh, Jeremiah was also rejected by his own people (Jer 1.1; 11.21). **58:** *Did not do many deeds*, Matthew makes the lack of miracles a matter of volition, not capability (contrast Mk 6.5).

14.1–12: John the Baptist is beheaded (Mk 6.14–29; Lk 9.7–11). Cf. *Ant.* 18.109–19. **1:** *Herod* Antipas, son of Herod the Great (see 2.1n.), ruled Galilee from 4 BCE–39 CE. **2:** *John the Baptist*, see 3.1–12. *Raised from the dead*, an ironic comment, given that Matthew depicts Jesus, not John, as eventually raised. **3:** *Herodias*, niece of Herod the Great, sister of Agrippa I (Acts 12.1), and wife not of Antipas's brother Philip but of another half-brother, Herod Boethus. **4:** *Not lawful*, marrying a brother's wife constituted incest (Lev 18.16; 20.21; Deut 25.5–10; *Ant.* 18.136; cf. 5.31–32). **5:** *Feared the crowd*, Josephus confirms John's popularity. **6:** *Daughter of Herodias*, Josephus names her Salome (*Ant.* 18.136–37). **7:** *Whatever she might ask*, a rash promise; see Esth 5.3. **10:** *Had John beheaded*, see 17.12–13. **12:** *His disciples came*, an ironic foreshadowing of Jesus' death, where the twelve disciples desert him (see 27.57).

14.13–21: Feeding more than five thousand (Mk 6.30–44; Lk 9.12–17; Jn 6.1–15 [the only miracle reported in all four canonical Gospels]). **19:** *Blessed and broke the loaves*, see 26.20–29; the description recollects the feeding

to eat." [17] They replied, "We have nothing here but five loaves and two fish." [18] And he said, "Bring them here to me." [19] Then he ordered the crowds to sit down on the grass. Taking the five loaves and the two fish, he looked up to heaven, and blessed and broke the loaves, and gave them to the disciples, and the disciples gave them to the crowds. [20] And all ate and were filled; and they took up what was left over of the broken pieces, twelve baskets full. [21] And those who ate were about five thousand men, besides women and children.

[22] Immediately he made the disciples get into the boat and go on ahead to the other side, while he dismissed the crowds. [23] And after he had dismissed the crowds, he went up the mountain by himself to pray. When evening came, he was there alone, [24] but by this time the boat, battered by the waves, was far from the land,[a] for the wind was against them. [25] And early in the morning he came walking toward them on the sea. [26] But when the disciples saw him walking on the sea, they were terrified, saying, "It is a ghost!" And they cried out in fear. [27] But immediately Jesus spoke to them and said, "Take heart, it is I; do not be afraid."

[28] Peter answered him, "Lord, if it is you, command me to come to you on the water." [29] He said, "Come." So Peter got out of the boat, started walking on the water, and came toward Jesus. [30] But when he noticed the strong wind,[b] he became frightened, and beginning to sink, he cried out, "Lord, save me!" [31] Jesus immediately reached out his hand and caught him, saying to him, "You of little faith, why did you doubt?" [32] When they got into the boat, the wind ceased. [33] And those in the boat worshiped him, saying, "Truly you are the Son of God."

[34] When they had crossed over, they came to land at Gennesaret. [35] After the people of that place recognized him, they sent word throughout the region and brought all who were sick to him, [36] and begged him that they might touch even the fringe of his cloak; and all who touched it were healed.

15 Then Pharisees and scribes came to Jesus from Jerusalem and said, [2] "Why do your disciples break the tradition of the elders? For they do not wash their hands before they eat." [3] He answered them, "And why do you break the commandment of God for the sake of your tradition? [4] For God said,[c] 'Honor your father and your mother,' and, 'Whoever speaks evil of father or mother must surely die.' [5] But you say that whoever tells father or mother, 'Whatever support you might have had from me is given to God,'[d] then that person need not honor the father.[e] [6] So, for the sake of your tradition, you make void the word[f] of God. [7] You hypocrites! Isaiah prophesied rightly about you when he said:

a Other ancient authorities read *was out on the sea*
b Other ancient authorities read *the wind*
c Other ancient authorities read *commanded, saying*
d Or *is an offering*
e Other ancient authorities add *or the mother*
f Other ancient authorities read *law*; others, *commandment*

of Israel in the wilderness (Ex 16) and anticipates the Last Supper. *2 Bar.* 29.8 connects Ex 16 with the messianic age. **20:** *All ate and were filled,* recollects the feeding of Israel in the wilderness (Ex 16.15–18; Num 11.31–32; cf Jn 6.31–33; Rev 2.17) and the miracle of Elisha (2 Kings 4.42–44).

14.22–36: Jesus walks on water (Mk 6.45–52; Jn 6.16–21). **25:** *Walking toward them on the sea,* like God, Jesus has power over the seas (Gen 1.9–10,21; Ex 14.21–22; Isa 43.16; 51.9–10; Hab 3.15; Ps 77.19; Job 9.8; 26.11–12). See 16.33n. **26:** *Ghost,* Gk "phantasma," "apparition"; the term does not mean that the disciples thought Jesus was dead, only that there was some sort of visible manifestation. **27:** Ex 3.14; Deut 31.6. A rabbinic story depicts the recitation of scripture during a storm (*b. B. Bat.* 73a). **28–30:** Perhaps a foreshadowing of Peter's later lack of faith. **31:** *Little faith,* a frequent rebuke of the disciples, 6.30; 8.26; 14.31; 16.8; 17.20. *Doubt,* see 28.17. **33:** *Son of God,* here indicating Jesus' divine nature (cf. 2.15; 3.17; 4.3,6; 8.29); the phrase may have been a messianic reference (4Q246; *4 Ezra* 7.28–29; 13.32); no Jewish texts identify the Messiah as the son of God. **34:** Mk 6.53. *Gennesaret,* on the northwestern shore of the Sea of Galilee (Josephus, *J.W.* 3.516–21). **36:** *Fringe,* see 9.20n.

15.1–20: Tradition of the elders (Mk 7.1–23). **2:** *Do not wash,* see Ex 30.17–21, concerning priests; rabbinic thought extends several Temple purity practices to the household (see *m. Yad.* 1.1–2.4; *b. Ber.* 53b; *b. Git.* 15b; *b. Pesah.* 115a–b; *b. Sukk.* 26b; 27a). **4:** *Honor your father and your mother,* Ex 20.12; Deut 5.16. *Whoever speaks evil,* Ex 21.17; Lev 20.9. **5:** *Given to God,* the "Korban" offering dedicates property to the Temple (see *m. Ned.* 3.2; 5.6).

[8] 'This people honors me with their lips,
but their hearts are far from me;
[9] in vain do they worship me,
teaching human precepts as doctrines.'"

[10] Then he called the crowd to him and said to them, "Listen and understand: [11] it is not what goes into the mouth that defiles a person, but it is what comes out of the mouth that defiles." [12] Then the disciples approached and said to him, "Do you know that the Pharisees took offense when they heard what you said?" [13] He answered, "Every plant that my heavenly Father has not planted will be uprooted. [14] Let them alone; they are blind guides of the blind.[a] And if one blind person guides another, both will fall into a pit." [15] But Peter said to him, "Explain this parable to us." [16] Then he said, "Are you also still without understanding? [17] Do you not see that whatever goes into the mouth enters the stomach, and goes out into the sewer? [18] But what comes out of the mouth proceeds from the heart, and this is what defiles. [19] For out of the heart come evil intentions, murder, adultery, fornication, theft, false witness, slander. [20] These are what defile a person, but to eat with unwashed hands does not defile."

[21] Jesus left that place and went away to the district of Tyre and Sidon. [22] Just then a Canaanite woman from that region came out and started shouting, "Have mercy on me, Lord, Son of David; my daughter is tormented by a demon." [23] But he did not answer her at all. And his disciples came and urged him, saying, "Send her away, for she keeps shouting after us." [24] He answered, "I was sent only to the lost sheep of the house of Israel." [25] But she came and knelt before him, saying, "Lord, help me." [26] He answered, "It is not fair to take the children's food and throw it to the dogs." [27] She said, "Yes, Lord, yet even the dogs eat the crumbs that fall from their masters' table." [28] Then Jesus answered her, "Woman, great is your faith! Let it be done for you as you wish." And her daughter was healed instantly.

[29] After Jesus had left that place, he passed along the Sea of Galilee, and he went up the mountain, where he sat down. [30] Great crowds came to him, bringing with them the lame, the maimed, the blind, the mute, and many others. They put them at his feet, and he cured them, [31] so that the crowd was amazed when they saw the mute speaking, the maimed whole, the lame walking, and the blind seeing. And they praised the God of Israel.

[32] Then Jesus called his disciples to him and said, "I have compassion for the crowd, because they have been with me now for three days and have nothing to eat; and I do not want to send them away hungry, for they might faint on the way." [33] The disciples said

[a] Other ancient authorities lack *of the blind*

8–9: Isa 29.13 (following the LXX). **11:** Cf. *Gos. Thom.* 14. *Defiles*, spiritual purity is more important than physical purity of the body (5.19–20; cf. Ps 24.3–4; 51; 2 Chr 30.18–20; *Pesiq. Rav Kah.* 4.7; *Pesiq. Rab.* 14.14). **13:** Isa 60.21; Jer 12.12. **14:** *Blind guides* (Lk 6.39; cf. *Gos. Thom.* 34), Matthew warns against following Pharisaic rather than church teachers. *Fall into a pit*, suffer misfortune (Isa 24.18; Jer 48.44 ; Ps 7.15; Prov 26.27). **15–16:** See 13.13n. *Still without understanding*, the disciples by now should not require explanations (13.16). **18:** See 15.11n. **20:** *To eat with unwashed hands does not defile*, Matthew omits Mark's claim (7.19) that Jesus declared all foods clean; for Matthew, dietary laws remain in place, but some "traditions of the elders" are not followed.

15.21–28: The Canaanite woman (Mk 7.24–30). Cf. 1 Kings 17.8–24. **21:** *Tyre and Sidon*, see 11.21n. **22:** *Canaanite*, Israel's traditional enemies; the region was associated with Baal worship (Gen 9.25; Judg 2.11–12; 3.7; 8.33; Hos 2.13). *Came out*, Jesus and the woman meet at the border; it is not clear that Jesus enters the Gentile district. *Son of David*, Jesus' Jewish messianic title (1.1; 9.27; 12.23; 15.22; 17.15; 20.30; 21.9; cf. *T. Sol.* 20.1). The woman foreshadows the conversion of the Gentiles (see also 8.10n.; 18.6; 21.21; 24.13–14; 28.19). **23:** *He did not answer*, his silence is explained in v. 24. *Send her away*, Gk "apoluson" can alternatively mean "loose her," i.e., perform the exorcism. **24:** *Lost sheep*, see 10.6n. **26:** *Dogs*, see 7.6n. **27:** *The dogs eat the crumbs*, the woman acknowledges her marginal position but still insists on her rights. **28:** *Faith*, see 8.10; 9.2,20–22,27; 11.6,25; 12.46–50; 15.28; 18.6; 21.21.

15.29–31: Jesus heals (Mk 7.31–37). **31:** *God of Israel*, see 1 Kings 1.48; Ps 41.13; 68.35; 69.6; 1 Chr 16.36; 1QM 13.2; 14.4; *t. Hag.* 2.1. Here the phrase might indicate a Gentile crowd.

15.32–39: Feeding more than four thousand (Lk 9.12–17; Jn 6.1–17). See 14.15–21; 8.1–10. Given the previous two accounts, the story may suggest a feeding of Gentiles. **39:** *Magadan*, an unknown city.

to him, "Where are we to get enough bread in the desert to feed so great a crowd?" 34 Jesus asked them, "How many loaves have you?" They said, "Seven, and a few small fish." 35 Then ordering the crowd to sit down on the ground, 36 he took the seven loaves and the fish; and after giving thanks he broke them and gave them to the disciples, and the disciples gave them to the crowds. 37 And all of them ate and were filled; and they took up the broken pieces left over, seven baskets full. 38 Those who had eaten were four thousand men, besides women and children. 39 After sending away the crowds, he got into the boat and went to the region of Magadan.[a]

16 The Pharisees and Sadducees came, and to test Jesus[b] they asked him to show them a sign from heaven. 2 He answered them, "When it is evening, you say, 'It will be fair weather, for the sky is red.' 3 And in the morning, 'It will be stormy today, for the sky is red and threatening.' You know how to interpret the appearance of the sky, but you cannot interpret the signs of the times.[c] 4 An evil and adulterous generation asks for a sign, but no sign will be given to it except the sign of Jonah." Then he left them and went away.

5 When the disciples reached the other side, they had forgotten to bring any bread. 6 Jesus said to them, "Watch out, and beware of the yeast of the Pharisees and Sadducees." 7 They said to one another, "It is because we have brought no bread." 8 And becoming aware of it, Jesus said, "You of little faith, why are you talking about having no bread? 9 Do you still not perceive? Do you not remember the five loaves for the five thousand, and how many baskets you gathered? 10 Or the seven loaves for the four thousand, and how many baskets you gathered? 11 How could you fail to perceive that I was not speaking about bread? Beware of the yeast of the Pharisees and Sadducees!" 12 Then they understood that he had not told them to beware of the yeast of bread, but of the teaching of the Pharisees and Sadducees.

13 Now when Jesus came into the district of Caesarea Philippi, he asked his disciples, "Who do people say that the Son of Man is?" 14 And they said, "Some say John the Baptist, but others Elijah, and still others Jeremiah or one of the prophets." 15 He said to them, "But who do you say that I am?" 16 Simon Peter answered, "You are the Messiah,[d] the Son of the living God." 17 And Jesus answered him, "Blessed are you, Simon son of Jonah! For flesh and blood has not revealed this to you, but my Father in heaven. 18 And I tell you, you are Peter,[e] and on this rock[f] I will build

[a] Other ancient authorities read *Magdala* or *Magdalan*
[b] Gk *him*
[c] Other ancient authorities lack 2*When it is ... of the times*
[d] Or *the Christ*
[e] Gk *Petros*
[f] Gk *petra*

16.1–4: Demand for a sign (Mk 8.11–13; Lk 11.29–32; 12.54–56). **1:** *Sadducees*, aristocrats and priestly officials linked to the Temple. Political rivals of Pharisees (Josephus, *J.W.* 2.164–66; *Ant.* 13.171–73,297–98; 18.11,16–17), their being paired with them here suggests rejection by all Jewish leaders. *Sign from heaven*, divine validation of Jesus' claims (Lk 15.18; Rom 1.18; cf. Jer 10.2; Dan 4.26; *1 En.* 6.2; 13.8; *m. Avot* 1.3; *t. B. Kamma.* 7.5). **4:** *Evil and adulterous generation*, see 12.39n. *Sign of Jonah*, see 12.40n.

16.5–12: Yeast of the Pharisees and Sadducees (Mk 8.14–21; Lk 12.1). **5:** *Forgotten to bring any bread*, ironic, given two miraculous multiplications of loaves. **6:** *Yeast*, see 13.33n.; here a negative reference to Pharisaic teaching (16.11–12). **8:** *Little faith*, see 6.30n. **9:** *Five loaves*, see 14.30–31. **10:** *Seven loaves*, see 15.32–38.

16.13–23: The keys of the kingdom (Mk 8.27–33; Lk 9.18–22). Cf. *Gos. Thom.* 13. **13:** *Caesarea Philippi*, a predominantly Gentile city about twenty-five miles north of the Sea of Galilee. *Son of Man*, see 8.20n. **14:** *John the Baptist*, see 14.2. *Elijah*, see 11.14–15n.; Mal 4.5–6 (Heb 3.23–24); Sir 48.10. **16:** *Messiah*, see 1.1n. *Living God*, see 15.33n. On the Messiah in Judaism, see 3.14n.; 8.20n.; 11.14–15n.; 17.12–13n.; 26.53–54. **17:** *Flesh and blood*, faith in Jesus is based in revelation, not argument. **18:** *Peter*, a play on Gk "petra," "rock"; the underlying Aram, "Kepha," relates to the name Cephas (Jn 1.42; 1 Cor 1.12, and elsewhere). *This rock*, Christian traditions disagree on whether the "rock" is Peter (leading to claims for the papacy), or his faith. *Church*, Gk "ekklēsia" (cf. 18.18), comparable to Heb "qahal," "congregation" (Deut 4.10; 9.10; 18.16; 31.30; 2 Sam 7; 1 Chr 17; 1QM 4.10). Matthew is the only canonical Gospel to use this term. *Gates of Hades*, see 11.21n. **19:** *Keys*, linked to knowledge and authority (Isa 22.22; Lk 11.52; Rev. 3.7; *2 Bar.* 10.18; *3 Bar.* 11.2; *3 En.*

PETER IN MATTHEW'S GOSPEL

Unlike Mark, one of its sources, Matthew's Gospel presents a positive portrayal of the disciples (see, e.g., 13.16 in contrast to Mk 4.13). Only Matthew's Gospel confirms Peter as the "rock of the church" to whom is given the "keys of the kingdom" (16.18–19). Peter is the leader of the disciples (16.19), is present at the Transfiguration (17.1–9), and, despite his fear, follows Jesus after his arrest (26.58). He is also the only disciple to attempt to walk on water with Jesus (14.28–30). Roman Catholic tradition identifies Peter as the first bishop of Rome, thereby making him the first pope (although the title was not officially used until almost two hundred years later).

my church, and the gates of Hades will not prevail against it. [19] I will give you the keys of the kingdom of heaven, and whatever you bind on earth will be bound in heaven, and whatever you loose on earth will be loosed in heaven." [20] Then he sternly ordered the disciples not to tell anyone that he was[a] the Messiah.[b]

[21] From that time on, Jesus began to show his disciples that he must go to Jerusalem and undergo great suffering at the hands of the elders and chief priests and scribes, and be killed, and on the third day be raised. [22] And Peter took him aside and began to rebuke him, saying, "God forbid it, Lord! This must never happen to you." [23] But he turned and said to Peter, "Get behind me, Satan! You are a stumbling block to me; for you are setting your mind not on divine things but on human things."

[24] Then Jesus told his disciples, "If any want to become my followers, let them deny themselves and take up their cross and follow me. [25] For those who want to save their life will lose it, and those who lose their life for my sake will find it. [26] For what will it profit them if they gain the whole world but forfeit their life? Or what will they give in return for their life?

[27] "For the Son of Man is to come with his angels in the glory of his Father, and then he will repay everyone for what has been done. [28] Truly I tell you, there are some standing here who will not taste death before they see the Son of Man coming in his kingdom."

17 Six days later, Jesus took with him Peter and James and his brother John and led them up a high mountain, by themselves. [2] And he was transfigured before them, and his face shone like the sun, and his clothes became dazzling white. [3] Suddenly there appeared to them Moses and Elijah, talking

[a] Other ancient authorities add *Jesus*
[b] Or *the Christ*

18.18; *Sifre Deut.* 32.25; *b. Shabb.* 31a–b). *Bound . . . loose,* indicating "forbid and permit" (in a legal sense), according to rabbinic teachings (*m. Pesah.* 4.5; *b. Ter.* 5.4; cf. 18.18); see 9.17n. **20:** *Not to tell anyone,* messianic secret; see 8.4n. **21:** *Great suffering,* precedes the time of redemption (Isa 52–53; Hos 6.2; Zech 13.7–9; Dan 7). *Elders . . . chief priests . . . scribes,* Matthew attributes Jesus' suffering to Jewish, not Roman, authorities. *On the third day* (Hos 6.2; Jon 1.17; 2.10; *b. Sanh.* 97a). The rabbis indicated that God would resurrect humanity on the third day following the desolation of the world. **22:** *God forbid,* Peter does not expect the messiah to die (see 1.1n.; 3.14n.; *Pss. Sol.* 17.21–25,32; 1QM; cf. Dan 9.24–27; Zech 9.9). **23:** *Satan,* Peter is cast in the role of tempting Jesus (4.10). *Stumbling block,* Gk "skandalon."

16.24–28: Jesus calls the disciples again (Mk 8.34–9.1; Lk 9.23–27; Jn 12.25). See 4.18–22; 10.38. **24:** Lk 14.27. *Take up their cross,* see 10.38n. **25:** *Will find it,* eternal life. The statement is in the form of a paradox (Gk "paradoxa," "against common opinion"): holding tightly to something in fact risks losing it; letting it go in the right cause preserves it. **27:** *Son of Man,* see 8.20n. Ps 62.13; Prov 24.12; Rom 2.6; 1 Jn 2.28; Rev 2.23; 22.12. **28:** *Will not taste death,* the messianic era is imminent (Mk 9.1; Lk 9.27 see also Jn 8.51–52; 1 Thess 4.15; see 28.20n.).

17.1–8: The Transfiguration (Mk 9.2–8; Lk 9.28–34). **1:** *Peter . . . James . . . John,* like Moses, Jesus takes three named disciples for a revelatory experience (cf. Ex 24.1). *High mountain,* associated with Moses and Elijah (see 5.1–2n.; Ex 19.20; 24.9–18; 1 Kings 19.8–18). **2:** *Transfigured,* Gk "metamorphoō," "change in form or appearance" (cf. Rom 12.2; 2 Cor 3.18). *His face shone,* allusion to Moses (Ex 34.35); *like the sun,* (*L.A.B.* 12.1; 19.16; *b. B. Bat.* 75a; cf. Dan 10.6; 2 Cor 3.18; Rev 10.1; *2 En.* 19.1; *3 En.* 18.25; 22.4–9; 26.2–7; 35.2; *4 Ezra* 9.7). **3:** *Moses and Elijah,* suggesting that Jesus is the fulfillment of the Law and the Prophets (cf. 5.17; 7.12; 17.12; Deut 18.15,18; *Apoc. Zeph.* 9.5).

with him. [4] Then Peter said to Jesus, "Lord, it is good for us to be here; if you wish, I[a] will make three dwellings[b] here, one for you, one for Moses, and one for Elijah." [5] While he was still speaking, suddenly a bright cloud overshadowed them, and from the cloud a voice said, "This is my Son, the Beloved;[c] with him I am well pleased; listen to him!" [6] When the disciples heard this, they fell to the ground and were overcome by fear. [7] But Jesus came and touched them, saying, "Get up and do not be afraid." [8] And when they looked up, they saw no one except Jesus himself alone.

[9] As they were coming down the mountain, Jesus ordered them, "Tell no one about the vision until after the Son of Man has been raised from the dead." [10] And the disciples asked him, "Why, then, do the scribes say that Elijah must come first?" [11] He replied, "Elijah is indeed coming and will restore all things; [12] but I tell you that Elijah has already come, and they did not recognize him, but they did to him whatever they pleased. So also the Son of Man is about to suffer at their hands." [13] Then the disciples understood that he was speaking to them about John the Baptist.

[14] When they came to the crowd, a man came to him, knelt before him, [15] and said, "Lord, have mercy on my son, for he is an epileptic and he suffers terribly; he often falls into the fire and often into the water. [16] And I brought him to your disciples, but they could not cure him." [17] Jesus answered, "You faithless and perverse generation, how much longer must I be with you? How much longer must I put up with you? Bring him here to me." [18] And Jesus rebuked the demon,[d] and it[e] came out of him, and the boy was cured instantly. [19] Then the disciples came to Jesus privately and said, "Why could we not cast it out?" [20] He said to them, "Because of your little faith. For truly I tell you, if you have faith the size of a[f] mustard seed, you will say to this mountain, 'Move from here to there,' and it will move; and nothing will be impossible for you."[g]

[22] As they were gathering[h] in Galilee, Jesus said to them, "The Son of Man is going to be betrayed into human hands, [23] and they will kill him, and on the third day he will be raised." And they were greatly distressed.

[24] When they reached Capernaum, the collectors of the temple tax[i] came to Peter and said, "Does your teacher not pay the temple tax?"[i] [25] He said, "Yes, he does." And when

[a] Other ancient authorities read *we*
[b] Or *tents*
[c] Or *my beloved Son*
[d] Gk *it* or *him*
[e] Gk *the demon*
[f] Gk *faith as a grain of*
[g] Other ancient authorities add verse 21, *But this kind does not come out except by prayer and fasting*
[h] Other ancient authorities read *living*
[i] Gk *didrachma*

5: Ps 2.7. *Bright cloud,* indicating God's presence (Ex 40.35–38; cf. Rev 14.14; *Ant.* 4.326). *Listen to him,* see 3.17; cf. Deut 18.15 of the prophet like Moses; 2 Pet 1.17–18.

17.9–13: Elijah the prophet (Mk 9.9–13). **9:** *Tell no one,* messianic secret; see 8.4n. Cf. 9.30; 16.20. **10:** *Scribes,* see 8.28–29n.; 13.52n. *Elijah must come first,* as messianic forerunner (Mal 4.4–6 [Heb 3.22–24]; see 11.4–5n.). **12–13:** *Elijah has already come,* referencing John the Baptist (3.3; Lk 1.17; cf. Jn 1.21; Isa 40.3). Rabbinic literature varies regarding Elijah's precise messianic role (*m. Ed.* 8.7; *b. Sanh.* 98a; *b. B. Metz.* 85b; *b. Eruv.* 43b; *Mek.* 16.33; *Ex. Rab.* 18.12; *Deut. Rab.* 6.7; *Pesiq. Rab.* 35.4).

17.14–21: Jesus heals an epileptic boy (Mk 9.14–29; 11.22–23; Lk 9.37–43; 17.6). **16:** *Could not cure him,* the disciples' faith has not sufficiently matured (16.20). **17–19:** *Faithless and perverse,* see 12.39n.; 16.4. Epilepsy, like many other diseases leading to uncontrolled behavior, was understood to be caused by demonic possession (see 8.16,28–34). **20–21:** *Mustard seed,* 13.31–32n.; 14.30–31n.; cf. 6.30; 8.26; 1 Cor 13.2.

17.22–23: Second Passion prediction (Mk 9.30–32; Lk 9.43–45). Cf. 16.21; 20.17–19; 26.2.

17.24–27: Temple tax. Cf. 22.15–22. **24:** *Capernaum,* see 4.13n. *Temple tax,* Jewish males annually paid the half-shekel tax for the Jerusalem Temple (Ex 30.11–16; Neh 10.33; cf. *t. Ketub.* 13.3). Some rabbinic texts state that all males over the age of twenty (i.e., non-minors) paid the tax (*m. Seqal.* 1.1–3); others indicate debate (*m. Seqal.* 1.4; *b. Men.* 65a). *Does your teacher not pay,* Jesus' teachings may have aroused suspicion (12.6). The question would also be pertinent to Jews within Matthew's community. **26:** *Children are free,* Jesus, the Son, and his followers, are technically exempt. **27:** *We do not give offense,* a lesson for Matthew's day when Rome

he came home, Jesus spoke of it first, asking, "What do you think, Simon? From whom do kings of the earth take toll or tribute? From their children or from others?" [26] When Peter [a] said, "From others," Jesus said to him, "Then the children are free. [27] However, so that we do not give offense to them, go to the sea and cast a hook; take the first fish that comes up; and when you open its mouth, you will find a coin;[b] take that and give it to them for you and me."

18 At that time the disciples came to Jesus and asked, "Who is the greatest in the kingdom of heaven?" [2] He called a child, whom he put among them, [3] and said, "Truly I tell you, unless you change and become like children, you will never enter the kingdom of heaven. [4] Whoever becomes humble like this child is the greatest in the kingdom of heaven. [5] Whoever welcomes one such child in my name welcomes me.

[6] "If any of you put a stumbling block before one of these little ones who believe in me, it would be better for you if a great millstone were fastened around your neck and you were drowned in the depth of the sea. [7] Woe to the world because of stumbling blocks! Occasions for stumbling are bound to come, but woe to the one by whom the stumbling block comes!

[8] "If your hand or your foot causes you to stumble, cut it off and throw it away; it is better for you to enter life maimed or lame than to have two hands or two feet and to be thrown into the eternal fire. [9] And if your eye causes you to stumble, tear it out and throw it away; it is better for you to enter life with one eye than to have two eyes and to be thrown into the hell[c] of fire.

[10] "Take care that you do not despise one of these little ones; for, I tell you, in heaven their angels continually see the face of my Father in heaven.[d] [12] What do you think? If a shepherd has a hundred sheep, and one of them has gone astray, does he not leave the ninety-nine on the mountains and go in search of the one that went astray? [13] And if he finds it, truly I tell you, he rejoices over it more than over the ninety-nine that never went astray. [14] So it is not the will of your [e] Father in heaven that one of these little ones should be lost.

[15] "If another member of the church[f] sins against you,[g] go and point out the fault when the two of you are alone. If the member listens to you, you have regained that one.[h] [16] But if you are not listened to, take one or two others along with you, so that every word may be confirmed by the evidence of two or three witnesses. [17] If the member refuses to listen to them, tell it to the church; and if the offender refuses to listen even to the church, let such a one be to you as a Gentile and a

a Gk *he*
b Gk *stater*; the stater was worth two didrachmas
c Gk *Gehenna*
d Other ancient authorities add verse 11, *For the Son of Man came to save the lost*
e Other ancient authorities read *my*
f Gk *If your brother*
g Other ancient authorities lack *against you*
h Gk *the brother*

required Jews to pay the "Fiscus Judaicus" for supporting the temple of Jupiter Capitolina. *Fish*, rabbinic literature speaks of fish containing riches (*b. Shabb.* 15a). *Coin*, a Tyrian "stater," worth four drachmas, enough to pay for two men.

18.1–5: Becoming like children (Mk 9.33–37; Lk 9.46–50). See 19.13–14; 20.20–28; *Gos. Thom.* 12. **1:** *Who is the greatest*, the question is inappropriate in that it seeks status. **3:** Mk 10.13–16; Lk 18.15–17. *Become like children*, children represent those without power and who are dependent on others.

18.6–9: Stumbling blocks. 6: *Stumbling block*, see 16.23n. **8:** *Cut it off*, see 5.29–30n.

18.10–14: The lost sheep (Lk 15.3–7). Cf. *Gos. Thom.* 107. **10:** *Angels*, see 4.6–7,11n.; 13.41–42; 16.27; 18.10; 24.30–31. Angels guard human beings (Gen 48.16; Job 33.23; cf. Tob 12.10; *1 En.* 40.6,9; 104.1; *T. Levi* 3.5; 5.6; Acts 12.15; Heb 1.4). **12–13:** *One of them has gone astray*, every community member is important (Ezek 34; 1 Tim 2.4–5; 2 Pet 3.9; cf. *Mek.* 19.21; *Ex. Rab.* 2.2).

18.15–20: Church discipline. 15: Lk 17.1–4. Rabbinic sources indicated that a person should never shame another publicly or he/she could be excluded from the world to come (*b. Sanh.* 107a). **16:** *Two or three witnesses*, Jewish law required witnesses for a charge to be leveled (Deut 17.6–7; 19.15; cf. *t. Sanh.* 8.3; Rev 11). **17:** *Gentile and*

tax collector. [18] Truly I tell you, whatever you bind on earth will be bound in heaven, and whatever you loose on earth will be loosed in heaven. [19] Again, truly I tell you, if two of you agree on earth about anything you ask, it will be done for you by my Father in heaven. [20] For where two or three are gathered in my name, I am there among them."

[21] Then Peter came and said to him, "Lord, if another member of the church[a] sins against me, how often should I forgive? As many as seven times?" [22] Jesus said to him, "Not seven times, but, I tell you, seventy-seven[b] times.

[23] "For this reason the kingdom of heaven may be compared to a king who wished to settle accounts with his slaves. [24] When he began the reckoning, one who owed him ten thousand talents[c] was brought to him; [25] and, as he could not pay, his lord ordered him to be sold, together with his wife and children and all his possessions, and payment to be made. [26] So the slave fell on his knees before him, saying, 'Have patience with me, and I will pay you everything.' [27] And out of pity for him, the lord of that slave released him and forgave him the debt. [28] But that same slave, as he went out, came upon one of his fellow slaves who owed him a hundred denarii;[d] and seizing him by the throat, he said, 'Pay what you owe.' [29] Then his fellow slave fell down and pleaded with him, 'Have patience with me, and I will pay you.' [30] But he refused; then he went and threw him into prison until he would pay the debt. [31] When his fellow slaves saw what had happened, they were greatly distressed, and they went and reported to their lord all that had taken place. [32] Then his lord summoned him and said to him, 'You wicked slave! I forgave you all that debt because you pleaded with me. [33] Should you not have had mercy on your fellow slave, as I had mercy on you?' [34] And in anger his lord handed him over to be tortured until he would pay his entire debt. [35] So my heavenly Father will also do to every one of you, if you do not forgive your brother or sister[e] from your heart."

19

When Jesus had finished saying these things, he left Galilee and went to the region of Judea beyond the Jordan. [2] Large crowds followed him, and he cured them there.

[3] Some Pharisees came to him, and to test him they asked, "Is it lawful for a man to di-

a Gk *if my brother*
b Or *seventy times seven*
c A talent was worth more than fifteen years' wages of a laborer
d The denarius was the usual day's wage for a laborer
e Gk *brother*

a tax collector, people requiring evangelization. **18:** *Bind . . . loose*, see 16.19n. **20:** *Two or three are gathered*, rabbinic teachings stated that the Divine (Heb "shekhinah") is present when people study Torah (*m. Avot* 3.2,6).

18.21–22: Forgiveness. 21: *Church*, see 16.18n. *Seven times*, rabbinic sources indicate that one is only required to seek forgiveness three times (e.g., *b. Yoma* 86b–87a). **22:** *Seventy-seven times*, the same phrasing as Gen 4.24 (LXX).

18.23–35: Parable of the unforgiving servant. See Lk 7.41–43. This parable is found only in Matthew's Gospel. The "debt" in question probably has nothing to do with material wealth. Although Matthew references wealth several times throughout the Gospel, in the parable the talents refer to spiritual goods rather than physical ones. Hence, Matthew is linking debt to sin. This connection is already present in Aramaic-speaking Judaism, where the term "ḥob" could connote both "debt" and "sin." Other Matthean passages also address the theme of "debt." Most notably, the "Lord's Prayer" in 6.12 reads "forgive us our debts"; in Luke's version (11.4), the word "sin" appears in place of "debt." In the Torah and the rabbinic writings, debt is also linked to sinfulness (see *m. Avot* 3.17; *Gen. Rab.* 85.2; 92.9; etc.). **23:** *King*, traditionally interpreted as God; the allegorical connection also appears in rabbinic sources (*b. Ber.* 33b; *b. Hag.* 16a; *t. Ber.* 6.18; *t. B. Kamma* 7.2; *t. Sanh.* 8.9; *t. Sukk.* 2.6). **24:** *Ten thousand talents*, millions of dollars in today's currency (see Esth 3.9), probably representing sin (see 6.12n.). **25:** *Ordered him to be sold*, biblical and Roman law allowed debt-slavery (Ex 22.2; 1 Sam 22.2; Isa 50.1; Am 2.6). **35:** *My heavenly Father will also do*, harsh eschatological judgment.

19.1–12: Divorce and marriage (Mk 10.2–12). **1–2:** *Beyond the Jordan*, east of the Jordan. Jesus probably avoided Samaria (10.5). **3–9:** Lk 16.18. **3:** *Test him*, see 12.2–4; 16.1–4; 22.15–22,34–40. *For any cause*, Jewish teachers permitted divorce (following Deut 24.1–4) but debated reasons to permit it (5.31–32nn.; *m. Git.* 9.10; *m. Ketub.*

Man will be handed over to the chief priests and scribes, and they will condemn him to death; [19] then they will hand him over to the Gentiles to be mocked and flogged and crucified; and on the third day he will be raised."

[20] Then the mother of the sons of Zebedee came to him with her sons, and kneeling before him, she asked a favor of him. [21] And he said to her, "What do you want?" She said to him, "Declare that these two sons of mine will sit, one at your right hand and one at your left, in your kingdom." [22] But Jesus answered, "You do not know what you are asking. Are you able to drink the cup that I am about to drink?"[a] They said to him, "We are able." [23] He said to them, "You will indeed drink my cup, but to sit at my right hand and at my left, this is not mine to grant, but it is for those for whom it has been prepared by my Father."

[24] When the ten heard it, they were angry with the two brothers. [25] But Jesus called them to him and said, "You know that the rulers of the Gentiles lord it over them, and their great ones are tyrants over them. [26] It will not be so among you; but whoever wishes to be great among you must be your servant, [27] and whoever wishes to be first among you must be your slave; [28] just as the Son of Man came not to be served but to serve, and to give his life a ransom for many."

[29] As they were leaving Jericho, a large crowd followed him. [30] There were two blind men sitting by the roadside. When they heard that Jesus was passing by, they shouted, "Lord,[b] have mercy on us, Son of David!" [31] The crowd sternly ordered them to be quiet; but they shouted even more loudly, "Have mercy on us, Lord, Son of David!" [32] Jesus stood still and called them, saying, "What do you want me to do for you?" [33] They said to him, "Lord, let our eyes be opened." [34] Moved with compassion, Jesus touched their eyes. Immediately they regained their sight and followed him.

21

When they had come near Jerusalem and had reached Bethphage, at the Mount of Olives, Jesus sent two disciples, [2] saying to them, "Go into the village ahead of you, and immediately you will find a donkey tied, and a colt with her; untie them and bring them to me. [3] If anyone says anything to you, just say this, 'The Lord needs them.' And he will send them immediately.[c]" [4] This took place to fulfill what had been spoken through the prophet, saying,

[5] "Tell the daughter of Zion,
Look, your king is coming to you,
humble, and mounted on a donkey,
and on a colt, the foal of a donkey."

[6] The disciples went and did as Jesus had directed them; [7] they brought the donkey and the colt, and put their cloaks on them, and he sat on them. [8] A very large crowd[d] spread their cloaks on the road, and others

[a] Other ancient authorities add *or to be baptized with the baptism that I am baptized with?*
[b] Other ancient authorities lack *Lord*
[c] Or *'The Lord needs them and will send them back immediately.'*
[d] Or *Most of the crowd*

20.20–28: The mother of James and John (Mk 10.35–45; Lk 22.24–27). Mark and Luke have the brothers pose the question. Cf. 15.21–28; 1 Kings 1.15–21. **20:** *Sons of Zebedee*, James and John (4.21). **21:** *Right hand . . . at your left*, positions of honor. Ironically the two on Jesus' right and left hands are crucified thieves (27.38). **23:** *Cup*, suffering and death (26.27–28; Jn 18.11; cf. Isa 5.13; 51.17; Jer 25.15; Ezek 23.31; Hab 2.16; Ps 75.8). Disciples must share Jesus' suffering (cf. 5.10–12; 7.15–22; 10.23; 13.53–58; 16.24–25; 19.28; 21.12–13; 24.9–10; Rom 8.17; Rev 1.9; 20.4). **25:** *Rulers of the Gentiles*, pagan Rome and its client kings. **27:** *Must be your slave*, true rulers serve those in their charge. **28:** *Ransom* (Mark 10.45). See Ex 6.6; 15.33; Isa 43.1; 44.22, Ps 77.16 (76 LXX), in the sense of divine liberation from slavery and exile. To "save his people" (1.21; cf. Jn 13.13–15; 1 Tim 2.5–6; 1 Pet 1.18–19), Jesus pays the penalty ("ransom") of their debt/sins

20.29–34: Jesus heals the two blind men (Mk 10.46–52; Lk 18.35–43). Cf. 9.27–31. **29:** *Jericho*, a city (with an oasis) 15 mi (24 km) east of Jerusalem and 8 mi (13 km) north of the Dead Sea. **30:** *Son of David*, see 1.1n.; 9.27n. **31:** *Ordered them to be quiet*, perhaps in order to hear any teaching that Jesus might give.

21.1–11: Triumphal entry (Mk 11.1–11; Lk 19.28–40; Jn 12.12–19). **1:** *Bethphage*, the specific location cannot be identified. *Mount of Olives*, east of Jerusalem, was linked to messianic and eschatological fulfillment (Ezek 11.23; Zech 14.4). **2:** *Donkey . . . and a colt*, Zech 9.9; *b. Sanh.* 98a. **4–5:** *The prophet*, Matthew combines Isa 62.11 and Zech 9.9. **8:** *Cut branches*, see Lev 23.39–40; 2 Kings 9.13; 2 Macc 10.5–8; only Jn 12.13 mentions palms.

cut branches from the trees and spread them on the road. [9] The crowds that went ahead of him and that followed were shouting,

"Hosanna to the Son of David!
Blessed is the one who comes in the name of the Lord!
Hosanna in the highest heaven!"

[10] When he entered Jerusalem, the whole city was in turmoil, asking, "Who is this?" [11] The crowds were saying, "This is the prophet Jesus from Nazareth in Galilee."

[12] Then Jesus entered the temple[a] and drove out all who were selling and buying in the temple, and he overturned the tables of the money changers and the seats of those who sold doves. [13] He said to them, "It is written,

'My house shall be called a house of prayer';
but you are making it a den of robbers."

[14] The blind and the lame came to him in the temple, and he cured them. [15] But when the chief priests and the scribes saw the amazing things that he did, and heard[b] the children crying out in the temple, "Hosanna to the Son of David," they became angry [16] and said to him, "Do you hear what these are saying?" Jesus said to them, "Yes; have you never read,

'Out of the mouths of infants and nursing babies
you have prepared praise for yourself'?"

[17] He left them, went out of the city to Bethany, and spent the night there.

[18] In the morning, when he returned to the city, he was hungry. [19] And seeing a fig tree by the side of the road, he went to it and found nothing at all on it but leaves. Then he said to it, "May no fruit ever come from you again!" And the fig tree withered at once. [20] When the disciples saw it, they were amazed, saying, "How did the fig tree wither at once?" [21] Jesus answered them, "Truly I tell you, if you have faith and do not doubt, not only will you do what has been done to the fig tree, but even if you say to this mountain, 'Be lifted up and thrown into the sea,' it will be done. [22] Whatever you ask for in prayer with faith, you will receive."

[23] When he entered the temple, the chief priests and the elders of the people came to him as he was teaching, and said, "By what authority are you doing these things, and who gave you this authority?" [24] Jesus said to them, "I will also ask you one question; if you tell me the answer, then I will also tell you by what

[a] Other ancient authorities add *of God*
[b] Gk lacks *heard*

Palms were normally connected to the fall Jewish harvest festival of Sukkot. The cloaks and branches mentioned in Matthew were therefore meant for a different purpose: to connect Jesus to the kingship of Israel, as the practice in 2 Kings 9.13 indicates. **9:** *Hosanna,* Hebrew "save now" (Ps 118.26). A form of this term ("Help!") is earlier used in connection with King David (2 Sam 14.4), making it clear that Jesus is the Davidic king. *Son of David,* see 9.27n. *Blessed is the one who comes,* from the "hallel" ("praise") psalms (Ps 115–18) recited during Passover according to rabbinic tradition (*b. Arak.* 10a; *t. Sukk.* 3.2). **10:** *Whole city was in turmoil,* see 2.3; cf. Ruth 1.19. **11:** *Prophet Jesus,* the crowds do not address him as messiah. *From Nazareth in Galilee,* Matthew favors Galilee over Jerusalem.

21.12–17: Temple incident (Mk 11.15–19; Lk 19.45–48; Jn 2.13–22). **12:** *Selling and buying,* to purchase animals for sacrificial offering (*m. Seqal.* 1.3; *m. Ker.* 1.7). *Money changers* converted foreign currency into Tyrian shekels, high-quality silver coinage accepted by the Temple. *Doves,* Lev 5.7. **13:** *House of prayer,* Isa 56.7; 1 Macc 7.37; cf. 6.5; Ps 141.2; 2 Macc 10.26. *Den of robbers,* Jer 7.11 (see 12.6), a place where criminals feel safe. **14:** *Blind and the lame,* present in the Temple, contrast 2 Sam 5.8 LXX. **15:** *Hosanna,* see 21.9n. **16:** Ps 8.1–2 (Heb vv. 2–3); 11.25n.; 17.23n. **17:** *Bethany,* east of Jerusalem (26.6).

21.18–22: The fig tree (Mk 11.12–14; Lk 13.6–9). **19:** *Fig tree,* here symbolizing judgment (see Isa 34.4; Jer 8.13; 24.1–10; Hos 2.12; Joel 1.7). *Withered,* Temple leaders and the people of Jerusalem are condemned because they lack faith in Jesus (24.2).

21.23–27: Jesus' authority is questioned (Mk 11.27–33; Lk 20.1–8). **23:** Temple authorities challenge Jesus (cf. 9.34; 12.22–24; 19.3–9; 22.15–22,34–46). *Chief priests,* Gk "archiereus," in sing. "high priest," in pl. "chief priests," including previous high priests and family members. In Lk 3.2 there is mention of "the high priesthood of Annas and Caiaphas": Annas had been deposed by the Romans in 15 CE and was succeeded by sons and a

authority I do these things. [25] Did the baptism of John come from heaven, or was it of human origin?" And they argued with one another, "If we say, 'From heaven,' he will say to us, 'Why then did you not believe him?' [26] But if we say, 'Of human origin,' we are afraid of the crowd; for all regard John as a prophet." [27] So they answered Jesus, "We do not know." And he said to them, "Neither will I tell you by what authority I am doing these things.

[28] "What do you think? A man had two sons; he went to the first and said, 'Son, go and work in the vineyard today.' [29] He answered, 'I will not'; but later he changed his mind and went. [30] The father[a] went to the second and said the same; and he answered, 'I go, sir'; but he did not go. [31] Which of the two did the will of his father?" They said, "The first." Jesus said to them, "Truly I tell you, the tax collectors and the prostitutes are going into the kingdom of God ahead of you. [32] For John came to you in the way of righteousness and you did not believe him, but the tax collectors and the prostitutes believed him; and even after you saw it, you did not change your minds and believe him.

[33] "Listen to another parable. There was a landowner who planted a vineyard, put a fence around it, dug a wine press in it, and built a watchtower. Then he leased it to tenants and went to another country. [34] When the harvest time had come, he sent his slaves to the tenants to collect his produce. [35] But the tenants seized his slaves and beat one, killed another, and stoned another. [36] Again he sent other slaves, more than the first; and they treated them in the same way. [37] Finally he sent his son to them, saying, 'They will respect my son.' [38] But when the tenants saw the son, they said to themselves, 'This is the heir; come, let us kill him and get his inheritance.' [39] So they seized him, threw him out of the vineyard, and killed him. [40] Now when the owner of the vineyard comes, what will he do to those tenants?" [41] They said to him, "He will put those wretches to a miserable death, and lease the vineyard to other tenants who will give him the produce at the harvest time."

[42] Jesus said to them, "Have you never read in the scriptures:

'The stone that the builders rejected
has become the cornerstone;[b]
this was the Lord's doing,
and it is amazing in our eyes'?

[43] Therefore I tell you, the kingdom of God will be taken away from you and given to a people that produces the fruits of the kingdom.[c] [44] The one who falls on this stone will be broken to pieces; and it will crush anyone on whom it falls."[d]

[45] When the chief priests and the Pharisees heard his parables, they realized that he was speaking about them. [46] They wanted to arrest him, but they feared the crowds, because they regarded him as a prophet.

22 Once more Jesus spoke to them in parables, saying: [2] "The kingdom of heaven may be compared to a king who gave

[a] Gk *He*
[b] Or *keystone*
[c] Gk *the fruits of it*
[d] Other ancient authorities lack verse 44

son-in-law, Caiaphas, who was high priest 18–36 CE. **25:** *Baptism of John*, see 3.1–12. **26:** *Regard John as a prophet*, see 17.12–13n.

21.28–32: Parable of the two sons. See 20.1–16. **29:** *Changed his mind*, the first son represents those who repent. **30:** *But he did not go*, the second son, a liar and a hypocrite, represents those who preach but do not practice (see 23.2–3).

21.33–46: Parable of the vineyard (Mk 12.1–12; Lk 20.9–19). *Gos. Thom.* 65. **33:** *Vineyard*, a reworking of the earlier parable in Isa 5.1–2, 7; see 20.1–16n. *Tenants*, chief priests and Pharisees (see 21.45). **34:** *Slaves*, prophets of Israel (22.3). **37:** *His son*, Jesus (21.41,43; see 7.16–20n.). **39:** *Out of the vineyard*, Jesus was crucified outside Jerusalem's walls (27.32–34; Mk 15.20; Lk 23.26–33; Jn 19.17; cf. Heb 13.12–13); executions occurred outside the walls of Jerusalem. **41:** 8.11; Acts 13.46. The leaders condemn themselves. **42:** Ps 118.22–23, also from the Hallel prayer (see 21.9n.); cf. Acts 4.11; 1 Pet 2.7. **43:** *People that produces the fruits*, followers of Jesus, both Jews and Gentiles. **46:** *Prophet*, see 21.11. There is nothing surprising about this contention—although later rabbinic sources claimed that prophecy had ceased centuries earlier, Josephus and others suggest a widespread belief that prophecy continued through the late Second Temple period.

PAYING TAXES

Matthew's Gospel indicates that tax collectors were associated with sinfulness (9.10), and Luke alludes to the likelihood that office holders routinely took more money than they were entitled to (Lk 3.12–13). Rabbinic sources view tax collecting with disdain (*m. Sanh.* 3.3; *b. Sanh.* 25b). Throughout the larger Roman empire, tax collectors were also viewed negatively (Cicero, *Off.* 1.42.150). Despite this fact, Jesus' instructions concerning tax collecting are surprisingly tame, to the point that he can be seen as endorsing paying the required tributes to Rome (22.15–22). However, the famous "render . . . unto Caesar" comment (Mt 22.21 [KJV]) is enigmatic, not to say ambiguous or ambivalent: if one believes Caesar is due taxes, then pay; if one believes everything belongs to God, then do not pay. Thus Jesus avoids the anger of both Rome and Rome's opponents, even as he forces his interlocutors to answer their question about taxes themselves.

a wedding banquet for his son. [3] He sent his slaves to call those who had been invited to the wedding banquet, but they would not come. [4] Again he sent other slaves, saying, 'Tell those who have been invited: Look, I have prepared my dinner, my oxen and my fat calves have been slaughtered, and everything is ready; come to the wedding banquet.' [5] But they made light of it and went away, one to his farm, another to his business, [6] while the rest seized his slaves, mistreated them, and killed them. [7] The king was enraged. He sent his troops, destroyed those murderers, and burned their city. [8] Then he said to his slaves, 'The wedding is ready, but those invited were not worthy. [9] Go therefore into the main streets, and invite everyone you find to the wedding banquet.' [10] Those slaves went out into the streets and gathered all whom they found, both good and bad; so the wedding hall was filled with guests.

[11] "But when the king came in to see the guests, he noticed a man there who was not wearing a wedding robe, [12] and he said to him, 'Friend, how did you get in here without a wedding robe?' And he was speechless. [13] Then the king said to the attendants, 'Bind him hand and foot, and throw him into the outer darkness, where there will be weeping and gnashing of teeth.' [14] For many are called, but few are chosen."

[15] Then the Pharisees went and plotted to entrap him in what he said. [16] So they sent their disciples to him, along with the Herodians, saying, "Teacher, we know that you are sincere, and teach the way of God in accordance with truth, and show deference to no one; for you do not regard people with partiality. [17] Tell us, then, what you think. Is it lawful to pay taxes to the emperor, or not?" [18] But Jesus, aware of their malice, said, "Why are you putting me to the test, you hypocrites? [19] Show me the coin used for the tax." And they brought him a denarius. [20] Then he said to them, "Whose head is this, and whose title?" [21] They answered, "The emperor's." Then he said to them, "Give therefore to the emperor the things that are the emperor's, and to God the things that are God's." [22] When they heard this, they were amazed; and they left him and went away.

22.1–14: Parable of the wedding banquet (Lk 14.15–24). Cf. 21.33–41; *Gos. Thom.* 64. **2:** *Wedding banquet,* kingdom of heaven (25.1–13; Prov 9; *b. Ber.* 64a; *b. Shabb.* 153a). **3:** *Slaves,* see 21.34n. **5:** *Made light of it,* a gross insult to the host. **6:** *Killed them,* the tenants move from insult to rebellion. **7:** *Burned their city,* a reference to Jerusalem's destruction; Israel's prophets predicted the destruction of the First Temple, (Isa 5.24–25; Jer 4.5–8). **10:** *Whom they found,* for Matthew, Jew and Gentile (see, e.g., 13.47). **11–12:** *Wedding robe,* a garment representing righteous deeds or a righteous state. Clothing often symbolized righteousness (Rom 13.12; Gal 3.27; Rev 3.4–5,18; 6.11; 7.13–14; 19.8; 22.14). **13:** *Outer darkness,* 8.12; 25.30. **14:** *Few are chosen,* some reject Jesus' message; others apostasize.

22.15–22: Taxes to Caesar (Mk 12.13–17; Lk 20.20–26). *Gos. Thom.* 100; cf. 17.24–27. **16:** *Herodians,* Political group supporting the royal family, Rome's client rulers. **17:** *Pay taxes to the emperor,* Rome levied an annual census tax of one denarius (Lk 2.1–2; Josephus, *J.W.* 1.154; 2.118; Tacitus, *Ann.* 2.42). See "Paying Taxes" above. **18:** *Putting me to the test,* see 4.7; 16.1; 19.3; 22:35. *Hypocrites,* see 6.2,5,16; 15.7; 23 passim; 24.51. **19:** *Denarius,* a day's wage; see 20.2n.;

PHARISEES AND JUDAS

Jesus' enemies are more persistent in Matthew's Gospel than in Mark's, as the expanded role of Judas indicates (27.3–5). Judas's acceptance of the thirty pieces of silver in exchange for his betrayal of Jesus (a Matthean addition) contributes to the stereotype of the venal and disloyal Jew. Jesus' other opponents, such as the Pharisees, appear more devious than in Mark's Gospel. Matthew alone contains the famous "woe to you scribes and Pharisees" in ch 23. The Pharisees (sometimes accompanied by other adversaries) constantly question and harass Jesus, especially regarding observance of Torah (9.10–13; 12.1–8,24–28; 15.1–9; 16.1–4; 19.3–9; 22.15–22, 34–40). Even the word "rabbi" has a negative connotation in Matthew: Judas refers to Jesus by that title while betraying him (26.49). Matthew's Pharisees may represent rival Jewish scribes competing for community loyalty following the Roman war, and thus Matthew's Gospel may provide a look into the tensions existing between Jesus' followers and other Jews in the late first century. (See "Jewish Movements of the NT Period," p. 526.) Adherents of a particular group or set of beliefs often polemicize most strongly against those who share similar, but not identical, beliefs; this may be responsible for some of the strong anti-Pharisaic rhetoric in Matthew.

[23] The same day some Sadducees came to him, saying there is no resurrection;[a] and they asked him a question, saying, [24] "Teacher, Moses said, 'If a man dies childless, his brother shall marry the widow, and raise up children for his brother.' [25] Now there were seven brothers among us; the first married, and died childless, leaving the widow to his brother. [26] The second did the same, so also the third, down to the seventh. [27] Last of all, the woman herself died. [28] In the resurrection, then, whose wife of the seven will she be? For all of them had married her."

[29] Jesus answered them, "You are wrong, because you know neither the scriptures nor the power of God. [30] For in the resurrection they neither marry nor are given in marriage, but are like angels[b] in heaven. [31] And as for the resurrection of the dead, have you not read what was said to you by God, [32] 'I am the God of Abraham, the God of Isaac, and the God of Jacob'? He is God not of the dead, but of the living." [33] And when the crowd heard it, they were astounded at his teaching.

[34] When the Pharisees heard that he had silenced the Sadducees, they gathered together, [35] and one of them, a lawyer, asked him a question to test him. [36] "Teacher, which commandment in the law is the greatest?" [37] He said to him, " 'You shall love the Lord your God with all your heart, and with all your soul, and with all your mind.' [38] This is the greatest and first commandment. [39] And a second is like it: 'You shall love your neighbor

[a] Other ancient authorities read *who say that there is no resurrection*

[b] Other ancient authorities add *of God*

18.28; 20.10; 22.19. **21:** Jesus asks the interlocutors to determine for themselves what belongs to God. His early followers generally paid taxes (see 17.27n.; Rom 14.13–23; 1 Cor 9.19–23; 1 Pet 2.17; contrast Rev, particularly ch 13).

22.23–33: Questions about resurrection (Mk 12.18–27; Lk 20.27–40). **24:** *Saying there is no resurrection,* Sadducees denied the concept of bodily resurrection (Acts 4.1–2; 23.6–10). See 3.7n. **25:** *His brother shall marry the widow,* see 1.3n.; Gen. 38.8; Deut 25.5–10; *Ant.* 4.254–56; *m. Yebam.* 2.2. **28:** *Whose wife of the seven will she be,* the Sadducees reason that heavenly existence is equivalent to earthly life (cf. *2 Bar.* 51.10–11; *1 En.* 39.5; 69.11; Josephus, *J.W.* 3.374 [the righteous dead in the world to come "dwell in chaste bodies"] *b. Ber.* 17a). **32:** *God of Abraham . . . Jacob,* Ex 3.6. Torah emphasizes the eternal nature of God's relationship with Israel (cf. *2 En.* 22.3–14; 62.15–16; 2 Macc 7.9, 36).

22.34–40: The greatest commandment (Mk 12.28–34; Lk 10.25–29). **35:** *Lawyer,* Gk "nomikos"; the word occurs only here in Matthew, and in Lk 7.30; 10.25; 11.45,46,52; 14.3; Titus 3.13. Except for Titus, where "Zenas the lawyer" seems to be a member of the community, lawyers appear only in the gospels, as here, to provoke Jesus with a question. There is not enough textual evidence either in the NT or elsewhere to determine whether this title indicates a special class of Jewish authorities different from the scribes (on the latter, see 7.28–29n.; 13.52n.). *Test,* see 4.7; 16.1; 19.3; 22.18. **36:** *Which commandment,* the traditional number of commandments in later rabbinic literature is 613; some attempted to epitomize the Law (see, e.g., *b. Makk.* 23b; *b. Yebam.* 47b, citing Mic 6.8

as yourself.' [40] On these two commandments hang all the law and the prophets."

[41] Now while the Pharisees were gathered together, Jesus asked them this question: [42] "What do you think of the Messiah?[a] Whose son is he?" They said to him, "The son of David." [43] He said to them, "How is it then that David by the Spirit[b] calls him Lord, saying,

[44] 'The Lord said to my Lord,
"Sit at my right hand,
until I put your enemies under your feet" '?

[45] If David thus calls him Lord, how can he be his son?" [46] No one was able to give him an answer, nor from that day did anyone dare to ask him any more questions.

23 Then Jesus said to the crowds and to his disciples, [2] "The scribes and the Pharisees sit on Moses' seat; [3] therefore, do whatever they teach you and follow it; but do not do as they do, for they do not practice what they teach. [4] They tie up heavy burdens, hard to bear,[c] and lay them on the shoulders of others; but they themselves are unwilling to lift a finger to move them. [5] They do all their deeds to be seen by others; for they make their phylacteries broad and their fringes long. [6] They love to have the place of honor at banquets and the best seats in the synagogues, [7] and to be greeted with respect in the marketplaces, and to have people call them rabbi. [8] But you are not to be called rabbi, for you have one teacher, and you are all students.[d] [9] And call no one your father on earth, for you have one Father—the one in heaven. [10] Nor are you to be called instructors, for you have one instructor, the Messiah.[e] [11] The greatest among you will be your servant. [12] All who exalt themselves will be humbled, and all who humble themselves will be exalted.

[13] "But woe to you, scribes and Pharisees, hypocrites! For you lock people out of the kingdom of heaven. For you do not go in yourselves, and when others are going in, you stop them.[f] [15] Woe to you, scribes and Pharisees, hypocrites! For you cross sea and land to make a single convert, and you make the new convert twice as much a child of hell[g] as yourselves.

[16] "Woe to you, blind guides, who say, 'Whoever swears by the sanctuary is bound by nothing, but whoever swears by the gold of the sanctuary is bound by the oath.' [17] You blind fools! For which is greater, the gold or the sanctuary that has made the gold sacred? [18] And you say, 'Whoever swears by the altar

[a] Or *Christ*
[b] Gk *in spirit*
[c] Other ancient authorities lack *hard to bear*
[d] Gk *brothers*
[e] Or *the Christ*
[f] Other authorities add here (or after verse 12) verse 14, *Woe to you, scribes and Pharisees, hypocrites! For you devour widows' houses and for the sake of appearance you make long prayers; therefore you will receive the greater condemnation*
[g] Gk *Gehenna*

and other verses). **37:** *You shall love the Lord,* Deut 6.5. Deut 6.4–5 is the "Shema," the basic affirmation of Jewish belief. **39:** *Love your neighbor,* Lev 19.18; *m. Avot* 1.2; cf. Rom 13.9; Gal 5.14; Jas 2.8. **40:** *Hang all the law,* see 7.12n.

22.41–46: Jesus questions the Pharisees (Mk 12.35–37; Lk 20.41–44). **42:** *Son of David,* see 1.1n.; 9.27n. **44:** Ps 110.1; cf. Acts 2.34–35; 1 Cor 15.25; Heb 1.13; 10.12–13. *The Lord said to my Lord,* in Ps 110, the first usage refers to God, the second to David. **45:** Jesus implicitly claims he is superior to David, since in his interpretation of the psalm David (presumed author of Ps 110) calls the messiah "Lord."

23.1–36: Seven woes against scribes and Pharisees (Mk 12.38–40; Lk 11.37–52). **2:** *Sit on Moses' seat,* Jesus acknowledges the Pharisees' Torah knowledge (cf. *Pesiq. Rav Kah.* 1.7). **4:** *Heavy burdens,* Jesus accuses Pharisees of imposing harsh teachings (contrast 11.28–29). Jews traditionally look upon Torah as a blessing, not a burden. **5:** *Phylacteries* (Gk "phylaktēria," "safeguard"; Heb "tefillin," from "tefillah," "prayer"), boxes containing scriptural passages (Ex 13.1–10; 13.11–16; Deut 6.4–9; 11.13–21), which are worn on the forehead and arm during prayer (Ex 13.9,16; Deut 6.8; 11.15; *b. Ber.* 6a; *b. Men.* 34b; 35b; 37a). *Fringes,* see 9.20n. **7:** *Rabbi,* Heb, lit., "my great one," meaning "teacher" or "master," a negative term in Matthew (e.g., 26.49; contrast Jn 20.16). **11:** *Greatest among you,* (Mk 9.33–37; 10.41–45; Lk 9.46–50). See 18.4; 20.26. **12:** 18.4; Lk 14.11; 18.14. **13:** *Woe to you,* see 11.21n. *Scribes and Pharisees,* the pairing suggests scribes of the Pharisees (cf. *m. Sot.* 3.4; *b. Sot.* 22; contrast Mt 13.52; 23.2). *Hypocrites,* see 6.2n. *Lock people out,* for Matthew, to follow Pharisees is to be damned. **15:** *To make a single convert* (Gk "proselytos"), there was some active Jewish proselytizing at the time of the Roman Empire, although the practice was not formally condoned (see *Ant.* 20.17,34–36). Here the concern is Pharisees attempting to convince other

is bound by nothing, but whoever swears by the gift that is on the altar is bound by the oath.' [19] How blind you are! For which is greater, the gift or the altar that makes the gift sacred? [20] So whoever swears by the altar, swears by it and by everything on it; [21] and whoever swears by the sanctuary, swears by it and by the one who dwells in it; [22] and whoever swears by heaven, swears by the throne of God and by the one who is seated upon it.

[23] "Woe to you, scribes and Pharisees, hypocrites! For you tithe mint, dill, and cummin, and have neglected the weightier matters of the law: justice and mercy and faith. It is these you ought to have practiced without neglecting the others. [24] You blind guides! You strain out a gnat but swallow a camel!

[25] "Woe to you, scribes and Pharisees, hypocrites! For you clean the outside of the cup and of the plate, but inside they are full of greed and self-indulgence. [26] You blind Pharisee! First clean the inside of the cup,[a] so that the outside also may become clean.

[27] "Woe to you, scribes and Pharisees, hypocrites! For you are like whitewashed tombs, which on the outside look beautiful, but inside they are full of the bones of the dead and of all kinds of filth. [28] So you also on the outside look righteous to others, but inside you are full of hypocrisy and lawlessness.

[29] "Woe to you, scribes and Pharisees, hypocrites! For you build the tombs of the prophets and decorate the graves of the righteous, [30] and you say, 'If we had lived in the days of our ancestors, we would not have taken part with them in shedding the blood of the prophets.' [31] Thus you testify against yourselves that you are descendants of those who murdered the prophets. [32] Fill up, then, the measure of your ancestors. [33] You snakes, you brood of vipers! How can you escape being sentenced to hell?[b] [34] Therefore I send you prophets, sages, and scribes, some of whom you will kill and crucify, and some you will flog in your synagogues and pursue from town to town, [35] so that upon you may come all the righteous blood shed on earth, from the blood of righteous Abel to the blood of Zechariah son of Barachiah, whom you murdered between the sanctuary and the altar. [36] Truly I tell you, all this will come upon this generation.

[37] "Jerusalem, Jerusalem, the city that kills the prophets and stones those who are sent to it! How often have I desired to gather your children together as a hen gathers her brood under her wings, and you were not willing! [38] See, your house is left to you, desolate.[c] [39] For I tell you, you will not see me again until you say, 'Blessed is the one who comes in the name of the Lord.'"

24 As Jesus came out of the temple and was going away, his disciples came to point out to him the buildings of the temple.

[a] Other ancient authorities add *and of the plate*
[b] Gk *Gehenna*
[c] Other ancient authorities lack *desolate*

Jews to follow their teaching (Acts 2.11; 6.5; 13.43; *b. Sanh.* 99b; *b. Shabb.* 31a; *Gen. Rab.* 47.10; 98.5; *Num. Rab.* 8.4). **16:** *Blind guides,* see 15.14n. *Swears,* see 5.33–37; 23.24. **17:** Ex 30.29. **21:** Ex 29.37. **23:** *Tithe,* Lev 27.30; Deut 14.22–23; Mic 6.8. *Mint, dill, and cumin,* dill and cumin were well-known aromatic plants (Isa 28.25,27; *m. Ma'as* 4.5; *m. Demai* 2.1), but mint is never mentioned in Jewish sources as a tithing herb. Jesus was likely criticizing the Pharisees' attention to detail, at the expense of more important matters. *Weightier matters of the law,* see 7.12; 22.34–40. **24:** *Strain out a gnat,* see Lev 11.4,41–45; compare 19.24. **25–26:** *Clean the outside,* Lk 11.33–34. Jesus charges the Pharisees with having impure hearts (6.22; 15.16–20), while outwardly appearing pious (23.2; cf. *b. Ber.* 28a; *b. Yoma* 72b). **27:** *Whitewashed tombs,* marked so that people could avoid corpse impurity; see Num 19.11–22; Lk 11.44. **33:** *Brood of vipers,* see 3.17n.; 12.34; Lk 3.7. **34:** Lk 11.49–51. *Prophets, sages, and scribes,* the heroes of the Tanakh and their successors (2 Chr 36.15–16). *You will kill,* see 16.24n.; 20.19n. *Flog in your synagogues,* see 5.10–11n. **35:** *Blood of righteous Abel,* Gen 4.8. *Zechariah son of Barachiah,* Zech 1.1 is conflated with 2 Chr 24.20–22. Jewish sources link shedding of blood to judgment (*Sib. Or.* 3.12; *T. Zeb.* 3.2; *b. Shabb.* 33a; *b. Yoma* 9b). **36:** *Upon this generation,* Matthew condemns those who rejected Jesus (11.16; 12.41–42,45; 17.17; 24.24).

23.37–39: Jesus laments over Jerusalem (Lk 13.34–35). **37:** *Hen gathers her brood,* see Ps 17.8; 91.4. **38:** *Your house is left to you, desolate,* the divine presence would leave the Temple upon its destruction (Jer 12.7; cf. Tob 14.4; *Pss. Sol.* 7.1; Josephus, *Ag. Ap.* 1.132,154). **39:** *Blessed is the one . . . ,* Ps 118.26 (again, from Hallel; see 21.9n.); Rom 11.25–27.

ESCHATOLOGICAL ELEMENTS IN MATTHEW

In Matthew 24, the disciples ask Jesus when the Temple will be destroyed. The resulting discourse discusses in detail the signs that will precede Jesus' return, as well as how to prepare for the final judgment.

Most prominent among these signs are earthquakes, which, starting in the Bible, were often linked to God's power and coming judgment (see Isa 5.25; 24.17–18; Ezek 37.13; 38.19; Zech 14.5; 1QH 3.12–13; *b. Ber.* 59a). All four gospels contain accounts of the events immediately following Jesus' death on the cross, but in Matthew's Gospel alone "The earth shook, and the rocks were split. The tombs also were opened, and many bodies of the saints who had fallen asleep were raised. After his resurrection they came out of the tombs and entered the holy city and appeared to many" (27.51b–53).

It is possible that behind the earthquake at the cross is the rabbinic view, attested to only later, that the death of a righteous person could usher in tragic repercussions (*b. Sanh.* 113b; *b. Ned.* 32a; one less righteous person weakens the world). The "saints" (Gk *hagioi*, "holy ones") are most likely righteous Jews who died. Since many Jews, as well as many of Jesus' followers, believed that the messianic age would inaugurate a general resurrection of the dead (see Dan 12.2; 1 Cor 15.20,23; 1 Thess 4.13–17), Matthew's scene announces that the general resurrection has begun.

[2] Then he asked them, "You see all these, do you not? Truly I tell you, not one stone will be left here upon another; all will be thrown down."

[3] When he was sitting on the Mount of Olives, the disciples came to him privately, saying, "Tell us, when will this be, and what will be the sign of your coming and of the end of the age?" [4] Jesus answered them, "Beware that no one leads you astray. [5] For many will come in my name, saying, 'I am the Messiah!'[a] and they will lead many astray. [6] And you will hear of wars and rumors of wars; see that you are not alarmed; for this must take place, but the end is not yet. [7] For nation will rise against nation, and kingdom against kingdom, and there will be famines[b] and earthquakes in various places: [8] all this is but the beginning of the birth pangs.

[9] "Then they will hand you over to be tortured and will put you to death, and you will be hated by all nations because of my name. [10] Then many will fall away,[c] and they will betray one another and hate one another. [11] And many false prophets will arise and lead many astray. [12] And because of the increase of lawlessness, the love of many will grow cold. [13] But the one who endures to the end will be saved. [14] And this good news[d] of the kingdom will be proclaimed throughout the world, as a testimony to all the nations; and then the end will come.

[15] "So when you see the desolating sacrilege standing in the holy place, as was spoken of by the prophet Daniel (let the reader understand), [16] then those in Judea must flee to the mountains; [17] the one on the

[a] Or *the Christ*
[b] Other ancient authorities add *and pestilences*
[c] Or *stumble*
[d] Or *gospel*

24.1–14: The Temple's destruction (Mk 13.1–13; Lk 21.5–19). **1–2:** *All will be thrown down*, evoking earlier prophetic threats against the Temple (e.g., Jer 26.4–6; Mic 3.12; see also Mt 26.67; 27.40; Acts 6.14; 2 Macc 2.22; Josephus, *J.W.* 6.267; 1QpHab 9.6–7; *b. Sukk.* 51b). Temple renovations begun by Herod the Great ca. 19 BCE were not completed in Jesus' time. **3:** *Mount of Olives*, see 21.1n.; the Temple could be seen from there. *Sign*, like the Pharisees, the disciples seek a sign; Jesus offers a prediction. *Your coming*, Gk "parousia," a term associated with military and imperial parades. Later, as here, it came to mean the return of the messiah to begin the new age (e.g., 1 Thess 2.19). **5:** *I am the Messiah*, see 7.15n. on false prophets. Josephus lists several first-century messianic claimants (Josephus, *J.W.* 6.259–63; 288). See "Messianic Movements," p. 530. **6:** *Rumors of wars*, Isa 19.1–4; Jer 51.46; Zech 14.1–37; Dan 7.21; 9.26; 11; cf. *Pss. Sol.* 15.7–15; *2 Bar.* 27.3–5; *4 Ezra* 13.31–32; *Sib. Or.* 3.635–51; Rev 6.4,12–17. **8:** *Birth pangs*, Isa 26.17; Dan 2.28; *4 Ezra* 13.31–32; see also Joel 2.10–11; Am 4.6–13; Zech 14.5; *2 Bar.* 27.6; 70.8; Rev 6.8; 18.8; *m. Ber.* 9.2; *b. Ber.* 55a. **9:** *Hand you over*, 10.16–25n.; 16.24n.; Jn 15.18–21. **10–12:** *Will betray one another*, see 18.6n. **14:** *All the nations*, both Jews and Gentiles (see 8.10n.; 9.17; 15.28; 18.6; 21.21; 28.19). Matthew defers the eschaton until the world is evangelized (see 28.19–20nn.). See also Dan 12.12.

housetop must not go down to take what is in the house; [18] the one in the field must not turn back to get a coat. [19] Woe to those who are pregnant and to those who are nursing infants in those days! [20] Pray that your flight may not be in winter or on a sabbath. [21] For at that time there will be great suffering, such as has not been from the beginning of the world until now, no, and never will be. [22] And if those days had not been cut short, no one would be saved; but for the sake of the elect those days will be cut short. [23] Then if anyone says to you, 'Look! Here is the Messiah!'[a] or 'There he is!'—do not believe it. [24] For false messiahs[b] and false prophets will appear and produce great signs and omens, to lead astray, if possible, even the elect. [25] Take note, I have told you beforehand. [26] So, if they say to you, 'Look! He is in the wilderness,' do not go out. If they say, 'Look! He is in the inner rooms,' do not believe it. [27] For as the lightning comes from the east and flashes as far as the west, so will be the coming of the Son of Man. [28] Wherever the corpse is, there the vultures will gather.

[29] "Immediately after the suffering of those days

the sun will be darkened,
 and the moon will not give its light;
the stars will fall from heaven,
 and the powers of heaven will be
  shaken.

[30] Then the sign of the Son of Man will appear in heaven, and then all the tribes of the earth will mourn, and they will see 'the Son of Man coming on the clouds of heaven' with power and great glory. [31] And he will send out his angels with a loud trumpet call, and they will gather his elect from the four winds, from one end of heaven to the other.

[32] "From the fig tree learn its lesson: as soon as its branch becomes tender and puts forth its leaves, you know that summer is near. [33] So also, when you see all these things, you know that he[c] is near, at the very gates. [34] Truly I tell you, this generation will not pass away until all these things have taken place. [35] Heaven and earth will pass away, but my words will not pass away.

[36] "But about that day and hour no one knows, neither the angels of heaven, nor the Son,[d] but only the Father. [37] For as the days of Noah were, so will be the coming of the Son of Man. [38] For as in those days before the flood they were eating and drinking, marrying and giving in marriage, until the day Noah entered the ark, [39] and they knew nothing until the flood came and swept them all away, so too will be the coming of the Son of Man. [40] Then two will be in the field; one will be taken and one will be left. [41] Two women will be grinding meal together; one will be taken and one will be left. [42] Keep awake therefore, for you do not know on what day[e] your Lord is coming. [43] But understand this: if the owner of the house had known in what part of the night the thief was coming, he would have stayed awake and would not have let his house be broken into. [44] Therefore you also must be ready, for the Son of Man is coming at an unexpected hour.

a Or *the Christ*
b Or *christs*
c Or *it*
d Other ancient authorities lack *nor the Son*
e Other ancient authorities read *at what hour*

24.15–35: The coming of the Son of Man (Mk 13.14–32; Lk 21.20–33). **15:** *Desolating sacrilege*, Dan 9.27; 11.31; 12.11. This refers to the action of Antiochus IV (called "Epiphanes") in setting up a statue of Zeus in the Temple at Jerusalem in 168 or 167 BCE (1 Macc 1.54). **16:** *Flee*, Matthew may be referring to the revolt of 66–70 CE when Jews fled Jerusalem (Eusebius, *Hist. eccl.* 3.5.3); see also Zech 14.5. **20:** *On a sabbath*, breaking Sabbath laws is permissible to preserve life (see 12.1n.; 1 Macc 2.41; *b. Shabb.* 128b; *b. Yoma* 85a–b). **21–22:** Joel 2.2; Dan 12.1. *Elect*, for Matthew, faithful church members (Ex 19.16; Deut 30.3–4; Isa 11.11,16; 18.3; 27.13; Ezek 39.27). *Days will be cut short*, Sir 36.8; *2 Bar.* 20.1–2; 54.1; 83.1; *4 Ezra* 4.26. **23–24:** See 24.5n. **28:** *Vultures*, Gk "aetoi," lit., "eagles"; perhaps referring to Roman troops. **29:** Isa 19.10; Ezek 32.7; Joel 2.10–11; Am 8.9; Zeph 1.15. **30:** *Sign*, i.e., the coming of the Son of Man, who is his own sign. *Son of Man coming on the clouds*, see 8.20n.; 10.23n.; 26.64; Dan 7.13–14; 1 Thess 4.16. **31:** *Trumpet*, see Isa 27.13; Zech 9.14. **34:** 10.23; 16.28n.; 23.36n. *His elect*, 24.22n.

24.36–44: Watchfulness (Mk 13.33–37; Lk 21.34–36; 17.26–35). **36:** 11.27. The Son appears subordinate to the Father (cf. Jn 14.28; 1 Cor 15.28). Only God knows when the time will arrive (Zech 14.7; *2 Bar.* 21.8). **37:** *Days of Noah*, time of sinfulness (Gen 6.11–12). *Coming of the Son of Man*, suddenly and without warning (Gen 7.6–24;

[45] "Who then is the faithful and wise slave, whom his master has put in charge of his household, to give the other slaves[a] their allowance of food at the proper time? [46] Blessed is that slave whom his master will find at work when he arrives. [47] Truly I tell you, he will put that one in charge of all his possessions. [48] But if that wicked slave says to himself, 'My master is delayed,' [49] and he begins to beat his fellow slaves, and eats and drinks with drunkards, [50] the master of that slave will come on a day when he does not expect him and at an hour that he does not know. [51] He will cut him in pieces[b] and put him with the hypocrites, where there will be weeping and gnashing of teeth.

25 "Then the kingdom of heaven will be like this. Ten bridesmaids[c] took their lamps and went to meet the bridegroom.[d] [2] Five of them were foolish, and five were wise. [3] When the foolish took their lamps, they took no oil with them; [4] but the wise took flasks of oil with their lamps. [5] As the bridegroom was delayed, all of them became drowsy and slept. [6] But at midnight there was a shout, 'Look! Here is the bridegroom! Come out to meet him.' [7] Then all those bridesmaids[c] got up and trimmed their lamps. [8] The foolish said to the wise, 'Give us some of your oil, for our lamps are going out.' [9] But the wise replied, 'No! there will not be enough for you and for us; you had better go to the dealers and buy some for yourselves.' [10] And while they went to buy it, the bridegroom came, and those who were ready went with him into the wedding banquet; and the door was shut. [11] Later the other bridesmaids[c] came also, saying, 'Lord, lord, open to us.' [12] But he replied, 'Truly I tell you, I do not know you.' [13] Keep awake therefore, for you know neither the day nor the hour.[e]

[14] "For it is as if a man, going on a journey, summoned his slaves and entrusted his property to them; [15] to one he gave five talents,[f] to another two, to another one, to each according to his ability. Then he went away. [16] The one who had received the five talents went off at once and traded with them, and made five more talents. [17] In the same way, the one who had the two talents made two more talents. [18] But the one who had received the one talent went off and dug a hole in the ground and hid his master's money. [19] After a long time the master of those slaves came and settled accounts with them. [20] Then the one who had received the five talents came forward, bringing five more talents, saying, 'Master, you handed over to me five talents; see, I have made five more talents.' [21] His master said to him, 'Well done, good and trustworthy slave; you have been trustworthy in a few things, I will put you in charge of many things; enter into the joy of your master.' [22] And the one with the two talents also came forward, saying, 'Master, you handed over to me two talents; see, I have made two more talents.' [23] His master said to him, 'Well done, good and trustworthy slave; you have been trustworthy in a few things, I will put you in charge of many things; enter into the joy of your master.' [24] Then the one who had received the one talent also came forward, saying, 'Master, I knew that you were a harsh man, reaping where you did not sow, and gathering where you did not scatter seed; [25] so I was afraid, and I went and hid your

[a] Gk *to give them*
[b] Or *cut him off*
[c] Gk *virgins*
[d] Other ancient authorities add *and the bride*
[e] Other ancient authorities add *in which the Son of Man is coming*
[f] A talent was worth more than fifteen years' wages of a laborer

Dan 7.13–14; *Mek.* 16.32). **40–41:** *In the field . . . grinding meal,* a gendered pair. **42:** *Keep awake,* 25.13 (see Mk 13.35,37; 14.34; 1 Thess 5.6). **43:** *Thief,* see 1 Thess 5.2; Rev 3.3; 16.15.

24.45–51: Parable of the faithful servant (Lk 12.42–46). **45:** *Faithful and wise slave,* Matthean community leaders, responsible for keeping other followers faithful until Jesus' (the "master's") return. *Food,* spiritual nourishment (2 Tim 2.15). **51:** 8.12n.; 13.42,50; 21.41; 22.13; 25.30,41,46.

25.1–13: Parable of the bridesmaids (Lk 12.35–36). Cf. 22.1–14; Rev 19.7–10; *b. Shabb.* 152b–153a. **1:** *Bridesmaids,* Gk "parthenoi," "virgins." They accompany the bridegroom to the house of the bride and then escort both to the house where the wedding and the feast will take place. *Bridegroom,* 9.15n. **3–4:** *Oil,* metaphor for righteousness or good deeds (Ps 119.105; Prov 6.23; 13.9; Job 18.5; *2 Bar.* 59.2; *4 Ezra* 14.20–21). **13:** *Keep awake,* 24.42.

talent in the ground. Here you have what is yours.' [26] But his master replied, 'You wicked and lazy slave! You knew, did you, that I reap where I did not sow, and gather where I did not scatter? [27] Then you ought to have invested my money with the bankers, and on my return I would have received what was my own with interest. [28] So take the talent from him, and give it to the one with the ten talents. [29] For to all those who have, more will be given, and they will have an abundance; but from those who have nothing, even what they have will be taken away. [30] As for this worthless slave, throw him into the outer darkness, where there will be weeping and gnashing of teeth.'

[31] "When the Son of Man comes in his glory, and all the angels with him, then he will sit on the throne of his glory. [32] All the nations will be gathered before him, and he will separate people one from another as a shepherd separates the sheep from the goats, [33] and he will put the sheep at his right hand and the goats at the left. [34] Then the king will say to those at his right hand, 'Come, you that are blessed by my Father, inherit the kingdom prepared for you from the foundation of the world; [35] for I was hungry and you gave me food, I was thirsty and you gave me something to drink, I was a stranger and you welcomed me, [36] I was naked and you gave me clothing, I was sick and you took care of me, I was in prison and you visited me.' [37] Then the righteous will answer him, 'Lord, when was it that we saw you hungry and gave you food, or thirsty and gave you something to drink? [38] And when was it that we saw you a stranger and welcomed you, or naked and gave you clothing? [39] And when was it that we saw you sick or in prison and visited you?' [40] And the king will answer them, 'Truly I tell you, just as you did it to one of the least of these who are members of my family,[a] you did it to me.' [41] Then he will say to those at his left hand, 'You that are accursed, depart from me into the eternal fire prepared for the devil and his angels; [42] for I was hungry and you gave me no food, I was thirsty and you gave me nothing to drink, [43] I was a stranger and you did not welcome me, naked and you did not give me clothing, sick and in prison and you did not visit me.' [44] Then they also will answer, 'Lord, when was it that we saw you hungry or thirsty or a stranger or naked or sick or in prison, and did not take care of you?' [45] Then he will answer them, 'Truly I tell you, just as you did not do it to one of the least of these, you did not do it to me.' [46] And these will go away into eternal punishment, but the righteous into eternal life."

26 When Jesus had finished saying all these things, he said to his disciples, [2] "You know that after two days the Passover is coming, and the Son of Man will be handed over to be crucified."

[a] Gk *these my brothers*

25.14–30: Parable of the talents (Lk 19.11–27). Cf. 18.23–35; 25.1–13. **15:** *Talents*, equal to several years' wages. **19:** *The master . . . came*, Jesus' second coming. *Settled accounts*, final judgment in which all are held accountable for their actions (18.23). **25:** *Hid your talent*, people buried money to keep it safe from thieves (cf. Horace, *Sat.* 1.1.41–42). Here the phrase refers to those who fail to act righteously. **29–30:** Lk 8.18; 13.28. *For to all those who have, more will be given*, see *Gos. Thom.* 41; cf. *b. Ber.* 40a; 55a. *Outer darkness*, 8.12; 22.13.

25.31–46: The final judgment. 31: *Son of Man*, see Dan 7.13–14; see 8.20n. **32:** *All the nations*, see 24.13n. The judgment of both Jews and Gentiles (see 5.21–22; 7.2; 12.36,41–42; 16.27; cf. Isa 66.18; Ezek 34.17; Mic 4.3; Rom 2.13–16). *Separate people*, Jewish writings attested to an exalted human being who will judge the nations (*2 Bar.* 72.2–6; 11QMelch 2.13), although in rabbinic sources God is the judge (*b. Rosh Ha-Shanah.* 8a; 16a–b). *Sheep from the goats*, representing righteous and wicked, respectively (see Ezek 34.12). **33:** *Right hand*, the side of righteousness and justice (20.21–23; 1 Kings 22.19; Ps 110.1; cf. 1 Kings 2.19; Ps 45.9; Rom 8.34). **34:** 5.3; Lk 12.32; Rev 13.8; 17.8. **35–36:** Isa 58.7; Jas 2.15–16; Heb 13.2; 2 Tim 1.16. **40:** 10.42. **41:** *Eternal fire*, see 7.19n. **46:** See Dan 12.2; Jn 5.29; *2 Bar.* 51.6. *Righteous*, salvation is based on works of compassion (1.19n.; 3.14n.; 5.6; 6.1; 10.11; 21.32; 22.14; cf. Jn 5.29).

26.1–28.20: Passion and resurrection. The name "Passion" for the narrative of Jesus' arrest, trial, and crucifixion comes from the Lat "passio," "suffered." (Mk 14.1–15.47; Lk 22.1–23.56; Jn 13.1–19.42).

26.1–2: Fourth Passion prediction. See 16.21–23; 17.22–23; 20.17–19. **2:** *Passover*, pilgrimage festival celebrating the Israelites' exodus from Egypt and bringing tens of thousands of pilgrims to Jerusalem.

[3] Then the chief priests and the elders of the people gathered in the palace of the high priest, who was called Caiaphas, [4] and they conspired to arrest Jesus by stealth and kill him. [5] But they said, "Not during the festival, or there may be a riot among the people."

[6] Now while Jesus was at Bethany in the house of Simon the leper, [a] [7] a woman came to him with an alabaster jar of very costly ointment, and she poured it on his head as he sat at the table. [8] But when the disciples saw it, they were angry and said, "Why this waste? [9] For this ointment could have been sold for a large sum, and the money given to the poor." [10] But Jesus, aware of this, said to them, "Why do you trouble the woman? She has performed a good service for me. [11] For you always have the poor with you, but you will not always have me. [12] By pouring this ointment on my body she has prepared me for burial. [13] Truly I tell you, wherever this good news [b] is proclaimed in the whole world, what she has done will be told in remembrance of her."

[14] Then one of the twelve, who was called Judas Iscariot, went to the chief priests [15] and said, "What will you give me if I betray him to you?" They paid him thirty pieces of silver. [16] And from that moment he began to look for an opportunity to betray him.

[17] On the first day of Unleavened Bread the disciples came to Jesus, saying, "Where do you want us to make the preparations for you to eat the Passover?" [18] He said, "Go into the city to a certain man, and say to him, 'The Teacher says, My time is near; I will keep the Passover at your house with my disciples.'" [19] So the disciples did as Jesus had directed them, and they prepared the Passover meal.

[20] When it was evening, he took his place with the twelve; [c] [21] and while they were eating, he said, "Truly I tell you, one of you will betray me." [22] And they became greatly distressed and began to say to him one after another, "Surely not I, Lord?" [23] He answered, "The one who has dipped his hand into the bowl with me will betray me. [24] The Son of Man goes as it is written of him, but woe to that one by whom the Son of Man is betrayed! It would have been better for that one not to have been born." [25] Judas, who

[a] The terms *leper* and *leprosy* can refer to several diseases

[b] Or *gospel*

[c] Other ancient authorities add *disciples*

26.3–5: Jewish leaders conspire (Mk 14.1–2; Lk 22.1–2; Jn 11.47–53). **3:** *High priest,* nominal head of the people absent a king (Josephus, *J.W.* 2.232–44; 6.300–309; *Ant.* 20.199–203). *Caiaphas,* high priest from 18–36 CE (*Ant.* 18.35). **4:** *They conspired,* priests and elders are Jesus' primary opponents in the Passion narrative. **5:** *Riot,* see 27.24.

26.6–13: Anointing woman. 6: *Bethany,* see 21.17n. *Simon,* nothing is known of him beyond this story. **7:** *Poured it on his head,* kings were anointed with oil (e.g., 1 Sam 10.1; 16.13; 2 Kings 9.6). **8–9:** *Money given to the poor,* rabbinic tradition mandates selling luxury items to provide for the poor (*b. Ta'an.* 20b). Passover was a time for giving charity (*m. Pesah.* 9.10; 11.1). **11:** *You always have the poor,* cf. Deut 15.4. **12:** *Prepared me for burial,* in the late Second Temple period, Jews anointed corpses in preparation for burial (Jn 19.39–40; *T. Abr.* 20.11; *Ant.* 17.199; *m. Sanh.* 23.5).

26.14–16: Judas agrees to betray Jesus (Mk 14.10–11; Lk 22.3–6). **14:** *Judas Iscariot,* see 10.4n. To this point, Judas has been a faithful disciple. **15:** *What will you give me,* Matthew offers greed as a motive. Lk (22.3–6) and Jn (13.2,27) link Judas to Satan. *Thirty pieces of silver,* Ex 21.32; Zech 11.12–13. The silver coin most likely in circulation at this time that could correspond to a shekel was the Athenian tetradrachm (four drachmas), the rough equivalent of four denarii. A denarius was a day's wage for a laborer, so the fee mentioned here is 120 days' wages.

26.17–29: The Last Supper (Mk 14.12–31; Lk 22.7–34; Jn 13.21–30). **17:** *Unleavened Bread,* Heb "matzah," see 26.19n. *Eat the Passover,* the ritually sacrificed lamb (Ex 12.3,6; *m. Pesah.* 7.9; 10.3,9; *Ant.* 3.249; CD 11.18–21). **19:** *Passover meal,* Heb "seder," lit., "order," where Jews recount the Israelites' exodus from Egypt and, with their families, eat special foods (matzah, paschal lamb, bitter herbs) (Ex 12.18–27; Lev 23.4–8; Num 9.1–14; 28.17; Deut 16.1–8; cf. *m. Pesah.*). The seder ritual as we know it, however, is largely a rabbinic, postbiblical rite. **24:** *Son of Man,* see 8.20n. **25:** *Rabbi,* see 23.7n. **26–28:** *This is my body . . . this is my blood,* the origin of the Christian Eucharist, "communion," or "Lord's Supper," a reenactment or remembrance of the Last Supper (see also Ex 24.6–8; Isa 53.11–12; 1 Cor 11.23–25; Heb 9.20). *My blood of the covenant,* taken by some Christians to refer to Jesus' "new"

betrayed him, said, "Surely not I, Rabbi?" He replied, "You have said so."

26 While they were eating, Jesus took a loaf of bread, and after blessing it he broke it, gave it to the disciples, and said, "Take, eat; this is my body." 27 Then he took a cup, and after giving thanks he gave it to them, saying, "Drink from it, all of you; 28 for this is my blood of the[a] covenant, which is poured out for many for the forgiveness of sins. 29 I tell you, I will never again drink of this fruit of the vine until that day when I drink it new with you in my Father's kingdom."

30 When they had sung the hymn, they went out to the Mount of Olives.

31 Then Jesus said to them, "You will all become deserters[b] because of me this night; for it is written,

'I will strike the shepherd,
  and the sheep of the flock will be
    scattered.'

32 But after I am raised up, I will go ahead of you to Galilee." 33 Peter said to him, "Though all become deserters because of you, I will never desert you." 34 Jesus said to him, "Truly I tell you, this very night, before the cock crows, you will deny me three times." 35 Peter said to him, "Even though I must die with you, I will not deny you." And so said all the disciples.

36 Then Jesus went with them to a place called Gethsemane; and he said to his disciples, "Sit here while I go over there and pray." 37 He took with him Peter and the two sons of Zebedee, and began to be grieved and agitated. 38 Then he said to them, "I am deeply grieved, even to death; remain here, and stay awake with me." 39 And going a little farther, he threw himself on the ground and prayed, "My Father, if it is possible, let this cup pass from me; yet not what I want but what you want." 40 Then he came to the disciples and found them sleeping; and he said to Peter, "So, could you not stay awake with me one hour? 41 Stay awake and pray that you may not come into the time of trial;[c] the spirit indeed is willing, but the flesh is weak." 42 Again he went away for the second time and prayed, "My Father, if this cannot pass unless I drink it, your will be done." 43 Again he came and found them sleeping, for their eyes were heavy. 44 So leaving them again, he went away and prayed for the third time, saying the same words. 45 Then he came to the disciples and said to them, "Are you still sleeping and taking your rest? See, the hour is at hand, and the Son of Man is betrayed into the hands of sinners. 46 Get up, let us be going. See, my betrayer is at hand."

47 While he was still speaking, Judas, one of the twelve, arrived; with him was a large crowd with swords and clubs, from the chief priests and the elders of the people. 48 Now the betrayer had given them a sign, saying, "The one I will kiss is the man; arrest him." 49 At once he came up to Jesus and said, "Greetings, Rabbi!" and kissed him. 50 Jesus said to him, "Friend, do what you are here to do." Then they came and laid hands on Jesus and arrested him. 51 Suddenly, one of those with Jesus put his hand on his sword, drew it, and struck the slave of the high priest, cutting off his ear. 52 Then Jesus said to him, "Put your sword back into its place; for all who take the sword will perish by the sword. 53 Do you think that I cannot appeal to my Father, and he will at once send me more than twelve

a Other ancient authorities add *new*
b Or *into temptation*

covenant (Jer 31.31; cf. Ex 24.8; Zech 9.11; see translators' note *a*). *For the forgiveness of sins*, Jesus' blood, like that of sin offerings, has the power to forgive sins (12.6; see also 1.21; 9.2,3,8n.; 12.6; 20.28; 21.12–13).

26.30–35: Predicting Peter's denial. 30: *Sung the hymn*, see 21.9n. *Mount of Olives*, see 21.1n.; 24.3n. **31:** Zech 13.7; Jn 16.32. *Become deserters*, Gk "skandalisthēsesthe," lit., "be made to stumble" (from "skandalon," stumbling-block; see 18.6n.). **32:** *Galilee*, 4.12n.; 21.11; 28.7,10; Luke and John set resurrection appearances in Judea.

26.36–56: Gethsemane (Mk 14.32–52; Lk 22.39–54; Jn 18.1–12). **36:** *Gethsemane*, Heb "oil press" ("gat shemen"), near the Mount of Olives. **37:** *Sons of Zebedee*, see 20.20n. **38:** *Deeply grieved*, an inner struggle, similar to those found in the Psalms (cf. Ps 31; 42.5–6). *Stay awake*, 24.42. **39:** *Let this cup pass*, see 20.22n.; 26.27–28; cf. Ezek 23.31–34. **41:** *Time of trial*, see 6.13n. Cf. Rom 6.19. **42:** *My Father . . . your will be done*, see 6.9–13. **48:** *Kiss*, greeting used by Jesus' followers (Rom 16.16; 1 Cor 16.20; 2 Cor 13.12; 1 Thess 5.26; 1 Pet 5.14), but also a sign of betrayal (2 Sam 20.9). **49:** *Rabbi*, 23.7n.; 26.5. **50:** *Friend*, see 20.13n. **52:** *Perish by the sword*, see Gen 9.6; Jer 15.2; Rev 13.10.

legions of angels? [54] But how then would the scriptures be fulfilled, which say it must happen in this way?" [55] At that hour Jesus said to the crowds, "Have you come out with swords and clubs to arrest me as though I were a bandit? Day after day I sat in the temple teaching, and you did not arrest me. [56] But all this has taken place, so that the scriptures of the prophets may be fulfilled." Then all the disciples deserted him and fled.

[57] Those who had arrested Jesus took him to Caiaphas the high priest, in whose house the scribes and the elders had gathered. [58] But Peter was following him at a distance, as far as the courtyard of the high priest; and going inside, he sat with the guards in order to see how this would end. [59] Now the chief priests and the whole council were looking for false testimony against Jesus so that they might put him to death, [60] but they found none, though many false witnesses came forward. At last two came forward [61] and said, "This fellow said, 'I am able to destroy the temple of God and to build it in three days.'" [62] The high priest stood up and said, "Have you no answer? What is it that they testify against you?" [63] But Jesus was silent. Then the high priest said to him, "I put you under oath before the living God, tell us if you are the Messiah,[a] the Son of God." [64] Jesus said to him, "You have said so. But I tell you,

From now on you will see the Son of Man
seated at the right hand of Power
and coming on the clouds of heaven."

[65] Then the high priest tore his clothes and said, "He has blasphemed! Why do we still need witnesses? You have now heard his blasphemy. [66] What is your verdict?" They answered, "He deserves death." [67] Then they spat in his face and struck him; and some slapped him, [68] saying, "Prophesy to us, you Messiah![a] Who is it that struck you?"

[69] Now Peter was sitting outside in the courtyard. A servant-girl came to him and said, "You also were with Jesus the Galilean." [70] But he denied it before all of them, saying, "I do not know what you are talking about." [71] When he went out to the porch, another servant-girl saw him, and she said to the bystanders, "This man was with Jesus of Nazareth."[b] [72] Again he denied it with an oath, "I do not know the man." [73] After a little while the bystanders came up and said to Peter, "Certainly you are also one of them, for your accent betrays you." [74] Then he began to curse, and he swore an oath, "I do not know the man!" At that moment the cock crowed. [75] Then Peter remembered what Jesus had said: "Before the cock crows, you will deny me three times." And he went out and wept bitterly.

27 When morning came, all the chief priests and the elders of the people conferred together against Jesus in order to bring about his death. [2] They bound him, led him away, and handed him over to Pilate the governor.

[3] When Judas, his betrayer, saw that Jesus[c] was condemned, he repented and brought

[a] Or *Christ*
[b] Gk *the Nazorean*
[c] Gk *he*

53: *Legions*, Roman military cohorts. **54:** *Scriptures*, Matthew cites none; no pre-Christian sources predict the arrest, suffering, and crucifixion of the messiah. **55:** Jn 18.19–21. **56:** *Scriptures of the prophets*, see 26.54n.

26.57–68: Sanhedrin trial (Mk 14.53–72; Lk 22.54–71; Jn 18.13–14). **57:** *Caiaphas*, see 26.3n. The historicity of this Sanhedrin trial, which is not attested in John's Gospel, is highly questionable. It would have been illegal since hearings were forbidden on festivals (*m. Sanh.* 4.1; *t. Yom Tov* 4.4). **59:** *Whole council*, the Sanhedrin (unlikely to be convened the first night of Passover). **60:** *False witnesses*, at least two witnesses were needed to pronounce a death sentence (18.16n.; cf. Deut 17.6–7; 19.15; *t. Sanh.* 8.3; Rev 11). **61:** 24.2; 27.40; Jn 2.19; *Gos. Thom.* 71. **63:** *Silent*, perhaps alluding to Isa 53.7. *Son of God*, see 14.33n. **64:** *You have said so*, Matthew demurs from Mark's "I am" (Mk 14.62). *Son of Man . . . heaven*, Dan 7.13–14. **65:** *Tore his clothes*, indicating mourning. *He has blasphemed*, technically, Jesus does not blaspheme. *M. Sanh.* 7.4–5 defines blasphemy as uttering the divine name (see also Lev 24.10–16). The verdict, as presented here, is as trumped up as the trial (see 9.3n.; 11.31). **66:** *He deserves death*, Jewish leaders may not have had the authority of capital punishment (Jn 18.31; Josephus, *J.W.* 6.126; *y. Sanh.* 18a, 24b).

26.69–74: Peter's denial. *He swore an oath*, Peter violates Jesus' teachings (5.33–37).

27.1–10: Judas's suicide. 1–2: (Mk 15.1; Lk 23.1). *Pilate*, Roman governor in Judea from 18–36 CE, known for cruelty (Tacitus, *Ann.* 15.44; Josephus, *J.W.* 2.166–77; *Ant.* 18.35,55–64,85–89,177). **3:** *He repented*, a point unique to

back the thirty pieces of silver to the chief priests and the elders. [4] He said, "I have sinned by betraying innocent[a] blood." But they said, "What is that to us? See to it yourself." [5] Throwing down the pieces of silver in the temple, he departed; and he went and hanged himself. [6] But the chief priests, taking the pieces of silver, said, "It is not lawful to put them into the treasury, since they are blood money." [7] After conferring together, they used them to buy the potter's field as a place to bury foreigners. [8] For this reason that field has been called the Field of Blood to this day. [9] Then was fulfilled what had been spoken through the prophet Jeremiah,[b] "And they took[c] the thirty pieces of silver, the price of the one on whom a price had been set,[d] on whom some of the people of Israel had set a price, [10] and they gave[e] them for the potter's field, as the Lord commanded me."

[11] Now Jesus stood before the governor; and the governor asked him, "Are you the King of the Jews?" Jesus said, "You say so." [12] But when he was accused by the chief priests and elders, he did not answer. [13] Then Pilate said to him, "Do you not hear how many accusations they make against you?" [14] But he gave him no answer, not even to a single charge, so that the governor was greatly amazed.

[15] Now at the festival the governor was accustomed to release a prisoner for the crowd, anyone whom they wanted. [16] At that time they had a notorious prisoner, called Jesus[f] Barabbas. [17] So after they had gathered, Pilate said to them, "Whom do you want me to release for you, Jesus[f] Barabbas or Jesus who is called the Messiah?"[g] [18] For he realized that it was out of jealousy that they had handed him over. [19] While he was sitting on the judgment seat, his wife sent word to him, "Have nothing to do with that innocent man, for today I have suffered a great deal because of a dream about him." [20] Now the chief priests and the elders persuaded the crowds to ask for Barabbas and to have Jesus killed. [21] The governor again said to them, "Which of the two do you want me to release for you?" And they said, "Barabbas." [22] Pilate said to them, "Then what should I do with Jesus who is called the Messiah?"[g] All of them said, "Let him be crucified!" [23] Then he asked, "Why, what evil has he done?" But they shouted all the more, "Let him be crucified!"

[24] So when Pilate saw that he could do nothing, but rather that a riot was beginning, he took some water and washed his hands before the crowd, saying, "I am innocent of this

[a] Other ancient authorities read *righteous*
[b] Other ancient authorities read *Zechariah* or *Isaiah*
[c] Or *I took*
[d] Or *the price of the precious One*
[e] Other ancient authorities read *I gave*
[f] Other ancient authorities lack *Jesus*
[g] Or *the Christ*

Matthew. *Thirty pieces of silver,* see 26.15n. **4:** *Innocent blood,* cf. Deut 27.25; Jer 19.4. Judas (27.4), Jewish leaders (26.59), Pilate (27.23–25), Pilate's wife (27.19), crowds (27.18), and the centurion (27.54) proclaim Jesus' righteousness and innocence. **5:** *Hanged himself,* Matthew is the only gospel that includes this account (contrast Acts 1.16–20), paralleling the death of David's betrayer, Ahithophel (2 Sam 17.23). **6:** *Blood money,* money related to death cannot be used for holy purposes. **9–10:** A combination of Zech 11.12–13; Jer 18.1–19; 32.6–15.

27.11–26: Jesus before Pilate (Mk 15.2–5; 23.1–7,13–25; Jn 18.29–19.16). **11:** *King of the Jews,* Pilate would view a Jewish "king" as a threat to the Empire. **14:** *Gave him no answer,* see 26.63n.; 1 Tim 6.13. **15:** *Release a prisoner,* Rome sometimes released prisoners but not those "plainly worthy of death" (*Ant.* 20.215; cf. *m. Pesah.* 8.6). **16:** Mk 15.7; Lk 23.25. Rome would not release a *notorious prisoner. Jesus Barabbas,* Aram, lit., "son of [the/a] father." Some early manuscripts lack "Jesus." The name "Barabbas" appears in rabbinic literature (*b. Ber.* 18b). The names make a theological point: the innocent "Jesus 'son of the father'" pays the ransom for his guilty counterpart. **19–20:** *His wife,* mentioned only by Matthew (cf. *Acts Pil.* 2.1). Her *dream* recollects Joseph (Mt 1–2). **22:** *Crucified,* Roman method of execution for insurrectionaries, sometimes in large groups; it was usually preceded by scourging or whipping (Josephus, *J.W.* 5.11.449–51). The victim was nailed (through the wrists) or bound to the transverse piece; part of the punishment was the public exposure (victims were often naked) and the lingering nature of the death, by asphyxiation, as the victim's exhaustion made it progressively more difficult, and then impossible, to raise the body in order to breathe. **24:** *Washed his hands,* linked to purification or redemption (Deut 21.1–9; Ps 26.6; 73.13). Pilate, failing to

man's blood;[a] see to it yourselves." [25] Then the people as a whole answered, "His blood be on us and on our children!" [26] So he released Barabbas for them; and after flogging Jesus, he handed him over to be crucified.

[27] Then the soldiers of the governor took Jesus into the governor's headquarters,[b] and they gathered the whole cohort around him. [28] They stripped him and put a scarlet robe on him, [29] and after twisting some thorns into a crown, they put it on his head. They put a reed in his right hand and knelt before him and mocked him, saying, "Hail, King of the Jews!" [30] They spat on him, and took the reed and struck him on the head. [31] After mocking him, they stripped him of the robe and put his own clothes on him. Then they led him away to crucify him.

[32] As they went out, they came upon a man from Cyrene named Simon; they compelled this man to carry his cross. [33] And when they came to a place called Golgotha (which means Place of a Skull), [34] they offered him wine to drink, mixed with gall; but when he tasted it, he would not drink it. [35] And when they had crucified him, they divided his clothes among themselves by casting lots;[c] [36] then they sat down there and kept watch over him. [37] Over his head they put the charge against him, which read, "This is Jesus, the King of the Jews."

[38] Then two bandits were crucified with him, one on his right and one on his left. [39] Those who passed by derided[d] him, shaking their heads [40] and saying, "You who would destroy the temple and build it in three days, save yourself! If you are the Son of God, come down from the cross." [41] In the same way the chief priests also, along with the scribes and elders, were mocking him, saying, [42] "He saved others; he cannot save himself.[e] He is the King of Israel; let him come down from the cross now, and we will believe in him. [43] He trusts in God; let God deliver him now, if he wants to; for he said, 'I am God's Son.'" [44] The bandits who were crucified with him also taunted him in the same way.

[45] From noon on, darkness came over the whole land[f] until three in the afternoon. [46] And about three o'clock Jesus cried with a loud voice, "Eli, Eli, lema sabachthani?" that is, "My God, my God, why have you forsaken me?" [47] When some of the bystanders heard it, they said, "This man is calling for Elijah." [48] At once one of them ran and got a sponge, filled it with sour wine, put it on a stick, and gave it to him to drink. [49] But the others said, "Wait, let

[a] Other ancient authorities read *this righteous blood*, or *this righteous man's blood*
[b] Gk *the praetorium*
[c] Other ancient authorities add *in order that what had been spoken through the prophet might be fulfilled, "They divided my clothes among themselves, and for my clothing they cast lots."*
[d] Or *blasphemed*
[e] Or *is he unable to save himself?*
[f] Or *earth*

uphold justice, is complicit in Jesus' execution. **25:** *His blood be on us and on our children*, this unique Matthean addition resulted in Jews throughout the generations being blamed for Jesus' death (cf. Jer 26.15; see also 21.37–39n.). Matthew's first readers likely related the verse to the Jerusalem population, devastated in 70 CE.

27.27–54: The crucifixion (Mk 15.16–41; Lk 23.26–49; Jn 19.17–37). **27–31: Mocking.** Mk 15.16–20; Lk 23.26–32; Jn 19.1–2; *Gos. Pet.* 2.5–3.9. Matthew's theme of prophetic fulfillment continues (20.19; cf. Isa 50.6; Jer 48.17; cf. Ps 22.7). *Cohort*, around 600 men. *Scarlet robe*, a Roman soldier's tunic (contrast with the other Gospels' "purple," a royal color; see Mk 15.17; Jn 19.2). **32:** *Cyrene*, in modern-day Libya; there was in the first century a large Jewish community there. **33:** *Golgotha*, Gk transliteration of the Aram, "skull." **34:** *Offered him wine*, to dull the pain (Prov 31.6; *b. Sanh.* 43a; cf. Mk 15.23). *He would not drink it*, see 26.29. **35:** *Divided his clothes*, Ps 22.18. **38:** *Two bandits*, see 20.21n. **39:** *Derided him* (Gk, lit., "blasphemed him"), 9.3n.; Ps 22.7–8; 109.25. **40:** *Destroy the temple*, see 1.11n., 23.38n., 24.1–2n. *If you are the Son of God*, recalls the devil's challenge (4.3,5; see also 26.61). **46:** *Eli, Eli, lema sabachthani*, Ps 22.1. The first two words are in Hebrew, followed by Aramaic, the vernacular of the period; the psalm, which informs much of the description of the crucifixion, ends on a triumphal note. **47:** *Elijah* (Heb "Eli-yahu"), the prophet expected to announce the messiah/messianic age (11.14–15n.). According to rabbinic tradition, Elijah aided the righteous in their time of need (*b. Avodah Zara* 17b; *Ta'an.* 21a). **51–53:** Ex 26.31–35; Heb 9.8; 10.19. **48:** *Sour wine*, Ps 69.21. **51:** *Curtain of the temple*, could symbolize the Temple destruction, Jesus'

us see whether Elijah will come to save him."[a] [50] Then Jesus cried again with a loud voice and breathed his last.[b] [51] At that moment the curtain of the temple was torn in two, from top to bottom. The earth shook, and the rocks were split. [52] The tombs also were opened, and many bodies of the saints who had fallen asleep were raised. [53] After his resurrection they came out of the tombs and entered the holy city and appeared to many. [54] Now when the centurion and those with him, who were keeping watch over Jesus, saw the earthquake and what took place, they were terrified and said, "Truly this man was God's Son!"[c]

[55] Many women were also there, looking on from a distance; they had followed Jesus from Galilee and had provided for him. [56] Among them were Mary Magdalene, and Mary the mother of James and Joseph, and the mother of the sons of Zebedee.

[57] When it was evening, there came a rich man from Arimathea, named Joseph, who was also a disciple of Jesus. [58] He went to Pilate and asked for the body of Jesus; then Pilate ordered it to be given to him. [59] So Joseph took the body and wrapped it in a clean linen cloth [60] and laid it in his own new tomb, which he had hewn in the rock. He then rolled a great stone to the door of the tomb and went away. [61] Mary Magdalene and the other Mary were there, sitting opposite the tomb.

[62] The next day, that is, after the day of Preparation, the chief priests and the Pharisees gathered before Pilate [63] and said, "Sir, we remember what that impostor said while he was still alive, 'After three days I will rise again.' [64] Therefore command the tomb to be made secure until the third day; otherwise his disciples may go and steal him away, and tell the people, 'He has been raised from the dead,' and the last deception would be worse than the first." [65] Pilate said to them, "You have a guard[d] of soldiers; go, make it as secure as you can."[e] [66] So they went with the guard and made the tomb secure by sealing the stone.

28 After the sabbath, as the first day of the week was dawning, Mary Magdalene and the other Mary went to see the tomb. [2] And suddenly there was a

[a] Other ancient authorities add *And another took a spear and pierced his side, and out came water and blood*

[b] Or *gave up his spirit*

[c] Or *a son of God*

[d] Or *Take a guard*

[e] Gk *you know how*

function as the "forgiver of sins" and the "divine presence," thereby replacing the Temple (12.6; 21.12–13n.; 23.38n.; see also 1.23; 18.20; 28.20; cf. *Acts Pil.* 11.1), or divine mourning. *Earth shook*, Gk "seismos," lit., "earthquake" (see 8.24n.; 24.7; 28.2; cf. Judg 5.4; Isa 24.19–22; 29.6; Ps 18.6–8; Rev 6.12; 8.5; 11.13,19). No non-Christian sources record these events. **52:** *Saints*, Gk "hagioi," lit., "holy ones." *Were raised*, many Jews expected a general resurrection as part of the messianic age (see Jn 11.24). **54:** *Centurion*, see 8.8,10n.

27.55–56: Women witnesses. 55: *Provided for him*, women served as patrons (see Lk 8.1–3). Matthew mentions female followers by name for the first time (see 27.61). **56:** *Mary Magdalene*, on Magdala, see 15.39n. *Mary the mother of James and Joseph*, otherwise unknown. *Mother of the sons of Zebedee*, see 20.20n.

27.57–61: Jesus' entombment (Mk 15.42–47; Lk 23.50–56; Jn 19.38–42). **57–58:** *When it was evening*, burials were not permitted on the Sabbath (*m. Shabb.* 23.5; see also Jn 19.31). Jewish law requires that the deceased be buried quickly (Deut 21.22–23; cf. Tob 1.17–18; 2.3–7; *m. Ber.* 3.1; *b. Ber.* 14b). No mention is made of what happens to the other crucified men. *Arimathea*, a Judean town of uncertain location. *Rich*, see Isa 53.9. Later Christian traditions have Joseph conducting missionary work in Britain. **61:** The wife of Zebedee does not go to the tomb.

27.62–66: Pharisees ironically remember the prediction. 62: *Day of Preparation*, Gk "paraskeuē," "making ready," an ambiguous term. It appears in the NT here and in Mk 15.42; Lk 23.54, where it means the day preceding the Sabbath (Passover has already begun); in Jn 19.14,31,42, where it means the day preceding Passover, although 19.42 implies that Passover fell on a Sabbath. **63:** *After three days . . .*, Hos 6.2; cf. *Gos. Pet.* 8.28–32. **64:** *Command the tomb to be made secure*, Dan 6.17; *Apoc. Mos.* 42.1.

28.1–10: The empty tomb (Mk 16.1–8; Lk 24.1–11; Jn 20.1–18). **1:** *First day of the week*, Sunday, the third day after Jesus' death. Some Jews believed the soul departed from the body after three days (*y. Mo'ed Qat.* 8.5; *b. Yebam.* 16.3; *b. Sanh.* 90b–91a; *b. Shabb.* 151b; *Gen. Rab.* 100; *Sem.* 8.1). *Went to see the tomb*, women as well as men were allowed to visit and attend to tombs, for both male and female deceased persons. **2:** Cf. *Acts Pil.* 13.

great earthquake; for an angel of the Lord, descending from heaven, came and rolled back the stone and sat on it. [3] His appearance was like lightning, and his clothing white as snow. [4] For fear of him the guards shook and became like dead men. [5] But the angel said to the women, "Do not be afraid; I know that you are looking for Jesus who was crucified. [6] He is not here; for he has been raised, as he said. Come, see the place where he[a] lay. [7] Then go quickly and tell his disciples, 'He has been raised from the dead,[b] and indeed he is going ahead of you to Galilee; there you will see him.' This is my message for you." [8] So they left the tomb quickly with fear and great joy, and ran to tell his disciples. [9] Suddenly Jesus met them and said, "Greetings!" And they came to him, took hold of his feet, and worshiped him. [10] Then Jesus said to them, "Do not be afraid; go and tell my brothers to go to Galilee; there they will see me."

[11] While they were going, some of the guard went into the city and told the chief priests everything that had happened. [12] After the priests[c] had assembled with the elders, they devised a plan to give a large sum of money to the soldiers, [13] telling them, "You must say, 'His disciples came by night and stole him away while we were asleep.' [14] If this comes to the governor's ears, we will satisfy him and keep you out of trouble." [15] So they took the money and did as they were directed. And this story is still told among the Jews to this day.

[16] Now the eleven disciples went to Galilee, to the mountain to which Jesus had directed them. [17] When they saw him, they worshiped him; but some doubted. [18] And Jesus came and said to them, "All authority in heaven and on earth has been given to me. [19] Go therefore and make disciples of all nations, baptizing them in the name of the Father and of the Son and of the Holy Spirit, [20] and teaching them to obey everything that I have commanded you. And remember, I am with you always, to the end of the age."[d]

[a] Other ancient authorities read *the Lord*
[b] Other ancient authorities lack *from the dead*
[c] Gk *they*
[d] Other ancient authorities add *Amen*

Great earthquake, see 8.24n.; 27.51–53n. **3:** *Clothing white as snow*, Dan 7.9; 10.6; cf. Rev 1.14; 2.18; 1QS 3.20; 1QM 13.9–10. **4:** *Became like dead men*, the guards are more frightened than the women. **6:** *He is not here*, many Jews believed in bodily resurrection, which would occur at the dawn of the messianic age (Dan 12.2; Josephus, *J.W.* 2.158,163; 3.374; *Ant.* 10.277–80; 16.397–98; 18.14; *Pss. Sol.* 3.12–13; 5.12–13; *1 En.* 22.13; *b. Sanh.* 90b; *Gen. Rab.* on Gen. 95). **7:** *Tell his disciples*, the women are commissioned as evangelists. **7:** *To Galilee*, 4.12; 25.32n. **9:** *Jesus met them*, two women are the first resurrection witnesses (cf. Jn 20.14–18). *Worshiped him*, Gk "proskyneō," "make obeisance, do reverence," lit., "kiss towards" (in LXX for Heb "shahah," "bow down" in worship, e.g. Ps 5.7 [Heb, LXX 5.8]), i.e., as divine. Cf. v. 17.

28.11–15: The guards' report. 13: *His disciples came by night and stole him away*, the story remained in circulation (Justin, *Dial.* 102.8). Matthew's account is unlikely: Roman guards would not claim that *we were asleep*. **15:** *To this day*, a biblical formula used here to refer to the time of Matthew's authorship (11.26; 27.8; cf. Gen 35.20; Deut 11.4).

28.16–20: The Great Commission. The name comes from the command or commission in v. 19, directing the mission "to all nations." See also references to Jeremiah at v. 20n. Cf. *Acts Pil.* 14.1. **16:** Like Moses, Jesus' final instructions are given from a mountain (cf. Deut 32.48). **17:** *Some doubted*, doubt and belief are not mutually exclusive (28.13). **18:** *All authority in heaven and on earth*, the risen Christ's domain has become the entire world (cf. 11.27; Dan 7.14,18,27; Eph 1.20–23; Phil 2.9–11). **19:** *Make disciples of all nations*, the change in Jesus' status prompts the expansion of the mission (10.6; 15.24) to include both Jews and Gentiles (8.10; 9.17; 15.28; 18.6; 21.21; 24.13–14; 28.20). *All nations* (Gk "panta ta ethne"), also can be translated as "all the Gentiles." The mission to Israel is never abrogated. *Father and of the Son and of the Holy Spirit*, the Trinity did not become an integral part of Christian theological doctrine until at least the second century (*Did.* 7.1–3; Ignatius, *Magn.* 3.2; cf. Eph 4.6; 1 Cor 8.6); a similar formula is found only in 2 Cor 13.13. This occurrence may reflect liturgical usage in Matthew's community, as other accounts of baptism (e.g., Acts 2.38) do not use this formula. **20:** *I am with you always*, the Gospel's frame (1.23; 18.20; 28.20). By depicting Jesus as always present and mandating the evangelization of the world, the Great Commission decreases tension over the delay of the second coming. Cf. Ex 3.14, concerning YHWH, and Jer 1.19, "I am with you," following 1.17, "tell them everything that I command you" as the prophetic commission.

THE GOSPEL ACCORDING TO MARK

This Gospel was titled "According to Mark" in the earliest manuscripts, but the names of the Gospels were likely added later to establish their authority. Still, it is possible that the author is the same as the John Mark of Acts 12.12; 15.37, and the Mark mentioned in Col 4.10; 2 Tim 4.11; Philem 24; and 1 Pet 5.13. Papias, a Christian bishop in Asia Minor in the early second century (Eusebius, *Hist. eccl.* 3.39.15–16), believed that Mark had accompanied Peter to Rome and recorded what Peter had said, but he considered Mark less dependable as a Gospel author than Matthew, since Matthew was presumed (based on Mt 9.9) to be one of Jesus' original followers. This traditional view of the relative authority of the first two Gospels continued throughout Christian history until the nineteenth and twentieth centuries, when the lack of literary artifice of the Gospel came to be viewed as a virtue: scholars theorized that Mark was the earliest of the Gospels and therefore preserved more faithfully the words and deeds of Jesus. This view of Mark as prior to Matthew, however, also made it easier to downplay the Jewish practices of Jesus, which are more prominently discussed in Matthew.

AUTHORSHIP AND DATE

Jesus was crucified in about 30 CE, but the Gospel of Mark was likely written between 64 and 72 CE, during the events of the horrific Jewish War, when Jerusalem and the entire region were re-pacified by the Romans, and the Jewish Temple was destroyed. The reference to the Temple's destruction in 13.2 and to wars in 13.7, as well as the depiction of refugees in 13.14–17, could apply to the events of that period, although the descriptions are vague and so not necessarily derived from the uprising and the Roman response.

Mark probably utilized a number of sources for the Gospel: a passion tradition (that is, the account of the days leading up to the crucifixion of Jesus), stories of healing and conflict, parables, and other teachings. The shortest of the Gospels, Mark was likely one of the sources for Matthew and Luke; the Gospel of John may reflect an indirect knowledge of Mark, but it is also possibly independent. Mark reflects a rich use of scripture (the Bible was that used by Jews, in Greek translation, and given the traditional abbreviation LXX [Septuagint] in the annotations that follow), but a few texts—Daniel, Isaiah, Deuteronomy, Zechariah, and some of the Psalms—are quoted often and may have been known from collections of favorite passages ("testimonia") or from oral tradition. These texts were also among the most popular with various Jewish groups of the time, as shown for instance by their presence (sometimes in multiple copies) among the Dead Sea Scrolls and in later rabbinic citations.

As to the location of its writing, cogent arguments have been made for Rome, where early tradition (see Papias, above) placed Mark as the assistant to Peter, but also for southern Galilee, northern Galilee, or Antioch in southern Syria (see map, p. 60). It is also possible that Mark spent much of his life in Jerusalem, even if he did not write from there. Of these possibilities, a composition in the region of Antioch in Syria is perhaps the most likely.

STYLE AND CONTENT

While Mark quotes Jewish Scriptures often and generally places Jesus' and John the Baptist's preaching within the range of Jewish religious concepts (on possible exceptions see annotations), like some groups within Judaism, Mark expresses ambivalence or even antagonism to Jewish religion centered upon the Temple in Jerusalem (see annotations to 11.12–25). Mark follows in a Jewish tradition, heightened in apocalyptic texts, in which election and forgiveness pass from "this generation" to the new community (9.19n.). Mark also follows in the tradition of Amos, Isaiah 1, Micah 6, and some other prophets in presenting a stronger critique of economic inequality than do the other Gospels.

Although Mark presents an earthly Jesus and not the heavenly mediator emphasized in Paul's letters, Mark and Paul share several important themes: the centrality of faith, the emphasis on Jesus' death rather than his resurrection, reservations about Peter's importance and role, and an emphasis on the present community's needs over apocalyptic hopes. They both contain passages that assert that all foods are clean (Mk 7.19; Rom 14.20). Yet the "Gentile focus" of Mark is not as certain as it was once held to be. In this Gospel Jesus goes to Gentile areas (i.e., the region of Tyre) where he engages individual Gentiles such as the Syrophoenician woman (7.24–30), "cleanses" all foods, and says that the good news must be announced to all nations. However all of these things, even the apocalyptic cleansing of formerly impure items, are found in Jewish tradition, and some have roots in Jewish Scriptures (cleansing of a man with leprosy, 2 Kings 5.1–14; cleansing of formerly impure items, Zech 14.20–21). Further, the evidence that is often adduced that Mark was a Gentile or advocated a mission without the law is ambiguous. Mark's apparent inaccuracy on Jewish practices and his statement that Jesus "cleansed all foods" (7.3–4,19) does not appear in the parallel story in Matthew, and v. 19 does not relate precisely to the question being debated. The passages may have been inserted into the text after Mark's writing (see "Impurity and Healing," p. 63). In addition, Mark's counting of days from sunrise instead of sundown (14.1,12) is unusual, but not unknown in ancient Judaism (see annotation at 14.1–2). Just as it is not clear where Mark was written, it is also not clear whether Mark was Jewish or Gentile, whether the first audience of the Gospel was predominantly Jewish or Gentile, or whether Mark advocated the abrogation of the laws of Torah to facilitate a mission to the Gentiles without the law as Paul had done. What we do know is that at some point the Gospel became associated with Rome and with Pauline views of a Gentile mission and the abrogation of Jewish law.

STRUCTURE AND GENRE

The story of Jesus' days in Jerusalem—the trial, crucifixion, and burial—are referred to as the passion narrative, and although Mark is sometimes characterized as a passion narrative with a long introduction, the Gospel as a whole is much more comprehensive in its structure than would be the case if the first ten chapters served merely as a prologue to the Passion.

1.1–15	Introduction
1.16–8.21	Enacting the kingdom of God
8.22–10.52	Passion predictions and radical social teachings
11.1–16.8	Passion narrative and death

Scholars continue to debate the literary category of Mark. The "gospel genre" is not found among the Dead Sea Scrolls, rabbinic literature, or other Jewish sources. Although the contemporary Jewish philosopher Philo composed a long biography of Moses (*Life of Moses*), rabbinic literature interwove biographical episodes of important figures into the larger discourses on law and scripture. Various terms were used by Christians in the second century to describe the texts about Jesus—reminiscences, histories, gospels—but none of these terms goes back to the first century as a reference to a particular kind of book ("good news" or "gospel" in Mk 1.1 refers to the message or preaching, not the book of Mark as a whole). Some have argued in modern times that the Gospels were a new and distinctive type of writing invented by the followers of Jesus, but many scholars now argue that the Gospels, including that of Mark, are similar to ancient genres. The Gospels created longer and more connected narratives of their subject than were found in the stories of the rabbis, more in keeping with Greek (*bios*) and Roman biography. However, the usual ethos of an ancient biography was to present a continuing model of virtues. As a result, other scholars classify Mark (if not the other Gospels) not as a biography but as a kind of apocalyptic history based on biblical history.

The contents of the book and its style have also suggested similarities to other genres as well. Central to Mark are the prophetic stances of John the Baptist and Jesus, and parallels to the biblical prophets are prominent (see annotations). Other aspects of Mark's narrative have been compared to ancient novels and the epics of Homer. The heart of Mark's narrative, however, is the depiction of the tragic end of a divinely favored figure—a messiah, Son of God, Son of Man—who is also very human. This depiction is influenced by Jewish traditions of the suffering servant (Isa 52–53), psalms of lament (e.g., Ps 22), and the persecuted righteous person (Wis 2–5). In keeping with these texts, Mark tells a story in which Jesus suffers a downward spiral of being abandoned by those around him. Jesus has a conflictual relationship with Pharisees, Herodians, and scribes, but it is often wrongly assumed that he is consistently embraced by others. Jesus is eventually rejected by all of "his people"—however that may be understood. He was rejected by Jews and Gentiles: family (3.19b–21), townspeople (6.1–6), Gentiles who witness his healing power (5.17), Peter (8.32; 14.71), disciples (14.50), chief priests and Sanhedrin, and the "crowd" influenced by them (ch. 14; 15.8,11,15), those who "passed by" (15.29), the two men crucified with him (15.32), and finally, even God (15.34).

SOME KEY THEMES: IRONY AND THE "MESSIANIC SECRET"

Mark, in keeping with many of the authors of the Jewish Scriptures, was a master of irony. Dramatic irony is the potentially profound reading experience that occurs when the audience knows things that the characters themselves do not perceive. Irony suggests that there is a real truth behind appearances: the reader who understands the irony understands God's ultimate purpose. It is often assumed, for example, that the Gospel of Mark presented a very human Jesus (called "low Christology") because it was early and the idea of a fully divine Christ had not yet been articulated. But "high Christologies" of a divine or pre-existent Christ also existed at a very early stage (Phil 2.6–11), and Mark may have deliberately sought to minimize divine or heavenly claims for Jesus (16.5n.). At times Jesus is even said to be lacking in power (6.5) or faith (14.36; 15.34), but the audience already knows the ending of the story: Jesus is the true Messiah and will be resurrected and vindicated by God. Thus there is an ironic distance between the expectation of a triumphant Jesus and the depiction of a struggling messiah. It is probably for this reason that a triumphant conclusion to the story is not included (16.8)—a final irony.

One of the most important examples of irony in Mark is the messianic secret: at a number of points Jesus commands people not to tell anyone about what they have witnessed. Indeed, in some Jewish texts of this period it is stated that the identity of the messiah, or the time of his coming, is hidden until the very end (2 Esd [4 *Ezra*] 7.28; *1 En.* 62.7; *b. Pesah.* 54b; *b. Sanh.* 97a). But in 1901, the German scholar William Wrede attributed the reason for these commands of secrecy not to Jesus but to Mark's own attempt to make sense of why more people did not embrace Jesus as messiah during his lifetime. Despite the power of the messianic secret theme (taken up also by Matthew and Luke, but almost totally lacking in John), it is still not clear what it would have communicated to the first audience. The messianic secret could be a narrative technique, the use of irony to increase awe of Jesus (that is, the audience knows the true meaning of the secret). It may suggest to the audience that a "low profile" is the best response to persecution. It may also reflect Mark's tendency to contrast expectations of Jesus' triumph with the difficulties Jesus actually encounters, including the crucifixion. Mark thus carries the messianic secret through to the end by minimizing the apocalyptic expectations of vindication (ch 13) and the triumphal appearance of a risen Christ (ch 16). The Gospel communicates the idea that Jesus' messianic identity ironically includes suffering and death, and it cannot be fully understood until after his resurrection; thus the Gospel's audience fully understands Jesus' significance, even though the disciples are depicted as not completely understanding it during his lifetime. Mark depicts a more human and vulnerable Jesus than is encountered in the Gospel of John, for example.

The deceptive simplicity of Mark came to be fully appreciated in the late twentieth century, as literary scholars and theologians alike took note of its arresting narrative realism: whether the stories themselves actually happened, they are told realistically and with evocative details of everyday life. Mark, more than the other Gospels, never loses sight of the real lives of ordinary people—the economic and the social, the earthly over the cosmic, the present over the future.

Lawrence M. Wills

1 The beginning of the good news[a] of Jesus Christ, the Son of God.[b]
[2] As it is written in the prophet Isaiah,[c]
"See, I am sending my messenger ahead
of you,[d]
who will prepare your way;
[3] the voice of one crying out in the
wilderness:
'Prepare the way of the Lord,
make his paths straight,'"

[a] Or *gospel*
[b] Other ancient authorities lack *the Son of God*
[c] Other ancient authorities read *in the prophets*
[d] Gk *before your face*

1.1–15: Introduction. Mark's overture strikes a number of gospel themes: repentance and forgiveness (v. 4), the Spirit (vv. 8,10), Jesus the Son (v. 11), the kingdom of God (v. 15), but unlike Matthew and Luke, it does not include an account of Jesus' birth.

1.1–11: John's baptism (Mt 3.1–17; Lk 3.1–22; Jn 1.6–34). **1:** *Good news* (Gk "euangelion") or gospel was not used in the first century to refer to a book; in Israel it was the good news of God's coming deliverance (Isa 52.7 (Heb "mebaser," "bringing [good] tidings"; Gk [LXX] "euangelizomenos," "announcing good news") and in the Roman world the good news of the peace brought by the emperor. Both sets of resonances would have reverberated with the readers of Mark, but with new meanings. Jesus' identity as messiah ("anointed one"; Gk "christos," Heb "mashiaḥ"—the Gk term is the source of the title "Christ") is announced in the first clause, even

[4] John the baptizer appeared[a] in the wilderness, proclaiming a baptism of repentance for the forgiveness of sins. [5] And people from the whole Judean countryside and all the people of Jerusalem were going out to him, and were baptized by him in the river Jordan, confessing their sins. [6] Now John was clothed with camel's hair, with a leather belt around his waist, and he ate locusts and wild honey. [7] He proclaimed, "The one who is more powerful than I is coming after me; I am not worthy to stoop down and untie the thong of his sandals. [8] I have baptized you with[b] water; but he will baptize you with[b] the Holy Spirit."

[9] In those days Jesus came from Nazareth of Galilee and was baptized by John in the Jordan. [10] And just as he was coming up out of the water, he saw the heavens torn apart and the Spirit descending like a dove on him. [11] And a voice came from heaven, "You are my Son, the Beloved;[c] with you I am well pleased."

[12] And the Spirit immediately drove him out into the wilderness. [13] He was in the wilderness

[a] Other ancient authorities read *John was baptizing*
[b] Or *in*
[c] Or *my beloved Son*

though the significance of "messiah" will have new meanings as well. Messiah, the one anointed by God, was applied to the king of Israel, the high priest, the prophet, and even the king of Persia when he enacted God's plan (Isa 45.1), but never in the Hebrew Bible to the ideal future Davidic king (although the promise that the Davidic line will endure in Ps 89.19–37 implies an eternal "anointing"). *Son of God* is present here in some ancient manuscripts; see translators' note *b* on the previous page and 1.9–11n. It too could be understood as a royal title (see Ps 2.7; 89.26–27). **2–3:** *Isaiah* was one of the biblical books most quoted by Jews and followers of Jesus, but this quotation actually begins with Mal 3.1; Matthew and Luke correct this misattribution by removing "See . . . your way" (see Mt 3.3; Lk 3.4–6). Mark may have known these texts from "testimonia," collections of verses on a common theme, in this case, God's *way*. "Way" is common in Greek, Jewish, and Christian ethical discourse, especially the choosing of the good and difficult path as opposed to the immoral and easy path. The ways of God are emphasized in biblical passages such as Deut 5.33 and Jer 7.23. From this, the word "way" can be likened to Jewish notions of "halakhah," how one walks, and "derekh eretz," the way of the land (cf. *Jub.* 12.21; *4 Ezra* 7.12–13). At *1 En.* 71.17 we also find the "upright way" of the Son of Man. "Way" will have a central place in Mark 8–10, and according to Acts 9.2 the first followers of Jesus called themselves not Christians but "belong[ing] to the Way." The Way is one name for the community as a religious movement, and it also suggests a new exodus—one as a release from oppression, equating Rome and Egypt—a common rallying cry for other Jewish prophetic leaders of this period. **4–5:** *John,* the Baptist began a movement similar to but still separate from that of Jesus, in preaching repentance and forgiveness. Jesus and John are a coordinated pair in the Gospels, much like Moses and Aaron, David and Jonathan, Elijah and Elisha, Ezra and Nehemiah, and Peter and Paul in Acts; this aspect of paired figures even extends to their deaths (6.29; 15.45–46). Water purifications occur in the Tanakh (e.g., Lev 13.6; 15.5–10), but at the turn of the Common Era there arose a strong interest in water purification rites among a number of Jewish groups. Judith 12.7–9, written about 100 BCE, already mentions bathing as purification, and "mikvaot" have been discovered in a variety of locations, although whether these concerns would have registered in the first century outside Judea is unclear. Likewise, the Pharisees, probably centered more in Jerusalem, advocated ritual washing of hands before meals (7.2). *Baptism of repentance,* a ritual bathing that was understood to effect the *forgiveness of sin.* **6:** John the Baptist is likened to Elijah (9.13; 2 Kings 1.8). **8:** *Baptize you with the Holy Spirit,* perhaps an anticipation of the practices in the early Christian community (Acts 2.1–4; 8.14–17). **9–11:** The rabbis referred to words from heaven as "bat qol," "the daughter of the voice"; here they combine Ps 2.7 and Isa 42.1–2. The former is a psalm of royal adoption; when anointed, the Davidic king becomes a son of God. Jesus is never called "Son of God" by the disciples, but he is by God, by unclean spirits (5.7), by Jewish authorities (14.61, in a question) and by a Roman soldier (15.39). In some Christian circles Son of God was elevated to include preexistence (as in the prologue to John's Gospel, 1.1–14) and equality with God (Jn 5.18), but this only became a general view in Christian doctrine later. In Mark, Son of God was more likely understood as the raising of a human being to a special status with God, influenced both by the model of the Davidic king and the Roman emperor (Livy 1.16). This view of Jesus' status, had it been adopted by the community as a whole, would have been that God "adopted" Jesus as God's son, as the king was adopted by God at the ceremony of installation (as in 2.7 cited above). *Torn apart,* see 15.38n. *Dove,* perhaps symbolizing gentleness (Ps 74.19).

forty days, tempted by Satan; and he was with the wild beasts; and the angels waited on him.

[14] Now after John was arrested, Jesus came to Galilee, proclaiming the good news[a] of God,[b] [15] and saying, "The time is fulfilled, and the kingdom of God has come near;[c] repent, and believe in the good news."[a]

[16] As Jesus passed along the Sea of Galilee, he saw Simon and his brother Andrew casting a net into the sea—for they were fishermen. [17] And Jesus said to them, "Follow me and I will make you fish for people." [18] And immediately they left their nets and followed him. [19] As he went a little farther, he saw James son of Zebedee and his brother John, who were in their boat mending the nets. [20] Immediately he called them; and they

[a] Or *gospel*
[b] Other ancient authorities read *of the kingdom*
[c] Or *is at hand*

1.12–13: Jesus' testing (Mt 4.1–11; Lk 4.1–13). Mark's story here lacks the drama of Matthew's and Luke's; Mark has understated it. *Satan*, the "adversary" or "accuser," was not mentioned in the Hebrew Bible until after the exile, when, under Persian influence, this figure becomes prominent (Job 1.6; Zech 3.1–2; *Gen. Rab.* 57.4). In *Jub.* 17.18 Satan is called by a different name, Mastema. *Wilderness* and *forty days* suggest both the wilderness wanderings during the Exodus (Ex 15.22ff.) and also the fasts of Moses and Elijah (Deut 9.18; 1 Kings 19.8).

1.14–15: Announcement of the kingdom of God (Mt 4.12–17; Lk 4.14–15). Jesus' message is similar to John the Baptist's, emphasizing the kingdom of God and the urgency of the times. **14:** *Galilee* is the region north of Judea and Samaria, west of the Sea of Galilee, where most of the action of the Gospel will occur until Jesus comes to Jerusalem. It was part of the land given to the twelve tribes (roughly that assigned to Issachar, Zebulun, Naphtali, and Asher). More rural and less Hellenized in the first century CE than Judea, archaeological evidence indicates that beginning at the end of the first century BCE—right before Jesus' childhood begins in Nazareth of Galilee—and into the first century CE Galilee was changing rapidly. Jewish identity markers are more in evidence in pottery, as is the stronger profile of non-Jews, specifically Phoenicians. **15:** *Kingdom of God*, the concept that God is the true king is present in the Hebrew Bible (see, e.g., Ps 5.2; 10.16; 103.19; 145.11,13) and also in Second Temple literature (Wis 10.10), mostly as a future promise or an ideal state not yet accomplished here and now. *Repent*, Gk "metanoia," "change of mind" where "mind" has the sense of the whole inner being; usually the translation in LXX of Heb "n-ḥ-m," "suffer regret, repent"; in Jer 31.19 "niḥam" is paired with "shuv," "turn, turn back." Here repentance is not in regard to individual sins but in the sense of "returning" to God. *Believe in the good news*, "faith" as a noun and "believe" as a verb (from the same root in Greek) are strongly emphasized in the NT (e.g., Mt 8; 10; 24.23; Mk 13.11; Jn 11.40; 1 Cor 11.18; many other occurrences). In ancient Israel "faith" and "believe" ("'aman" root; cf. "amen," 3.28n.) often connoted faithfulness or trustworthiness regarding both humans (e.g., Isa 38.3) and God (e.g, Ps 71.22); cf. also the "amanah" or faith-covenant in Neh 9.38 (10.1). In the Greek period faith/believe also took on a new emphasis: conviction, confession, even conversion (Jdt 14.10; Wis 1.2; 16.26; Sir 1.14; 2.6). The Pharisees also gave the "'aman" concept a major boost by using it to characterize the first level of initiates into their group: those who tithed carefully were called "ne'emanim" or faithful ones. Faith and believe are key terms in almost all texts of the Jesus movement, describing a personal commitment to Jesus or the kingdom. Mark often discusses faith and Torah, although he never contrasts faith and law as Paul does (but see 2.1–12). If Mark were indebted to Paul, it is strange that this Gospel never opposes faith and law, but it is possible that Mark recognized such a view as Pauline and not attributable to Jesus.

1.16–8.21: First major section: Bringing about the kingdom of God.

1.16–20: Call of the first disciples (Mt 4.18–22; Lk 5.1–11; Jn 1.35–42). **17:** *Fish for people*, fishing is used both positively and negatively in biblical texts (Jer 16.16; Am 4.2), and in the Cairo Damascus Document there is reference to the net of Belial (CD 4.15–16), but some rabbinic texts are more similar to Mark's image of fish as new disciples (*Avot de R. Natan A* 40). **19:** *James son of Zebedee* is not the same as James the brother of Jesus, associated with those early followers of Jesus who continued to observe the Torah. In Greek and Roman philosophical circles and in rabbinic Judaism students are described as seeking out teachers rather than being suddenly called by them (as indeed is the case in John 1.35–40; cf. *b. Eruv.* 30a; *b. Ketub.* 66b). However, a precedent for Jesus' method here can be seen in Elijah's call of Elisha (1 Kings 19.19–21). Both Jesus and Elijah take the active role in calling; the disciples and Elisha both respond immediately, leaving their parents in order to follow.

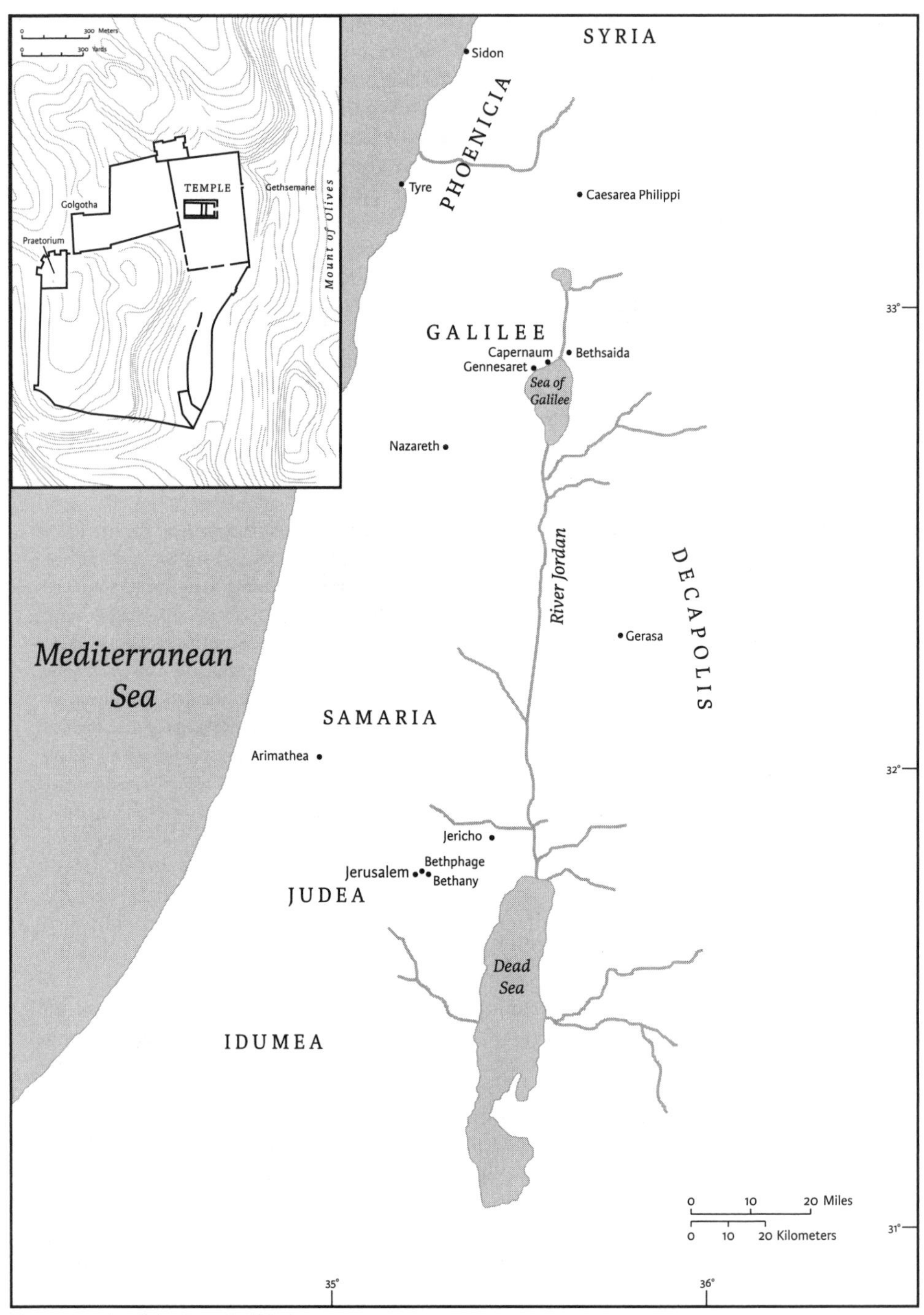

The geography of the Gospel of Mark.

left their father Zebedee in the boat with the hired men, and followed him.

[21] They went to Capernaum; and when the sabbath came, he entered the synagogue and taught. [22] They were astounded at his teaching, for he taught them as one having authority, and not as the scribes. [23] Just then there was in their synagogue a man with an unclean spirit, [24] and he cried out, "What have you to do with us, Jesus of Nazareth? Have you come to destroy us? I know who you are, the Holy One of God." [25] But Jesus rebuked him, saying, "Be silent, and come out of him!" [26] And the unclean spirit, convulsing him and crying with a loud voice, came out of him. [27] They were all amazed, and they kept on asking one another, "What is this? A new teaching—with authority! He[a] commands even the unclean spirits, and they obey him." [28] At once his fame began to spread throughout the surrounding region of Galilee.

[29] As soon as they[b] left the synagogue, they entered the house of Simon and Andrew, with James and John. [30] Now Simon's mother-in-law was in bed with a fever, and they told him about her at once. [31] He came and took her by the hand and lifted her up. Then the fever left her, and she began to serve them.

[32] That evening, at sunset, they brought to him all who were sick or possessed with demons. [33] And the whole city was gathered around the door. [34] And he cured many who were sick with various diseases, and cast out many demons; and he would not permit the demons to speak, because they knew him.

[a] Or *A new teaching! With authority he*
[b] Other ancient authorities read *he*

1.21–45: A series of healings without opposition. Diseased people in the ancient world were often thought to be possessed by demonic forces (*b. Ketub.* 61b). In Mark the healings enact the eschatological promises of Isa 35.5–6 and establish Jesus' power over Satan's minions at the end of time, evidence that the kingdom of God has drawn near. The unclean spirits were sometimes understood to have been descended from fallen angels (*1 En.* 15.8,34; *Jub.* 7.21; 10.1; 11QPs[a] 19.15; 1QM 13.5). In *1 En.* 9–10 the giants of Gen 6 were called "mamzerin," illegitimate mixed offspring of heavenly beings and human women, and evil spirits derived from these could be considered "bastard spirits." Although there has been a tendency in the modern period to distinguish Jesus' healings from those of contemporary Jews and others, this is a theological not a historical judgment. The miracles in the Gospels contain the same procedures, healing formulae (e.g., "be muzzled," "rebuked" v. 25, often retaining the original Aramaic, e.g., 7.34 "ephphatha"), and demonological lore as the magic of the ancient world.

1:21–28: Exorcising and teaching with authority (Mt 7.28–29; Lk 4.31–37). **21:** In the first century, synagogues were probably just coming into existence as local Jewish town meetings or civic associations, in some cases providing lodging as well, but they were also beginning to be centers of study and worship. Because Mark states here that people were gathered in the *synagogue* specifically on the *sabbath,* Mark assumes some worship function (see also 6.2). **22:** Jesus' teaching consists in marshalling the kingdom of God against the kingdom of Satan, and in this he proves he has more authority than the *scribes.* **23–24:** *Unclean spirit,* one from the demonic realm, perhaps seen as the encroachment of death into the person's life. *Holy One of God,* applied to Elisha (2 Kings 4.9); as counter to the *unclean spirit,* such a prophet would restore the correct boundary between the demonic realm of death and the world of life created by God. **25:** *Rebuked,* a common word in Jewish exorcisms (Gk "epitimaō," Heb "ga'ar"). See Zech 3.2; Ps 6.9; 68.31; 78.6; 80.16; see also 1QM 14.9–11 where the Heb is used of God defeating foes in battle or overcoming Satan. *Be silent,* lit., "be muzzled," also refers to the control of unclean spirits. **27:** *Authority* (Gk "exousia," meaning the freedom to express one's powers; in LXX for Heb "memshalah," "rule, dominion," e.g., Ps 136.8, referring to the "rule" of the sun over the day), shown partly in commanding *unclean spirits* and partly in teaching on his own, not referring to other teachers.

1.29–34: Summary statement of many healings (Mt 8.14–17; Lk 4.38–41). Summaries of people thronging to Jesus suggest that the growth of the kingdom at the end of time should be ironically contrasted with Jesus' commands to silence (2.1–2; 3.7–8; 6.53–56). *Simon's* [Peter's] *mother-in-law,* there is no other mention of her in the NT, so it is not clear whether she is living in Simon's house because she is a widow, because Simon's wife has died and she is the female relative who can keep house for him, or for some other reason.

[35] In the morning, while it was still very dark, he got up and went out to a deserted place, and there he prayed. [36] And Simon and his companions hunted for him. [37] When they found him, they said to him, "Everyone is searching for you." [38] He answered, "Let us go on to the neighboring towns, so that I may proclaim the message there also; for that is what I came out to do." [39] And he went throughout Galilee, proclaiming the message in their synagogues and casting out demons.

[40] A leper[a] came to him begging him, and kneeling[b] he said to him, "If you choose, you can make me clean." [41] Moved with pity,[c] Jesus[d] stretched out his hand and touched him, and said to him, "I do choose. Be made clean!" [42] Immediately the leprosy[a] left him, and he was made clean. [43] After sternly warning him he sent him away at once, [44] saying to him, "See that you say nothing to anyone; but go, show yourself to the priest, and offer for your cleansing what Moses commanded, as a testimony to them." [45] But he went out and began to proclaim it freely, and to spread the word, so that Jesus[d] could no longer go into a town openly, but stayed out in the country; and people came to him from every quarter.

2 When he returned to Capernaum after some days, it was reported that he was at home. [2] So many gathered around that there was no longer room for them, not even in front of the door; and he was speaking the word to them. [3] Then some people[e] came, bringing to him a paralyzed man, carried by four of them. [4] And when they could not bring him to Jesus because of the crowd, they removed the roof above him; and after having dug through it, they let down the mat on which the paralytic lay. [5] When Jesus saw their faith, he said to the paralytic, "Son, your sins are forgiven." [6] Now some of the

[a] The terms *leper* and *leprosy* can refer to several diseases
[b] Other ancient authorities lack *kneeling*
[c] Other ancient authorities read *anger*
[d] Gk *he*
[e] Gk *they*

1.35–39: Jesus gives a hint as to his mission (Mt 4.23–25; Lk 4.42–44). The disciples will continually misunderstand his exact identity and mission, and indeed Jesus is often indirect. Mark's audience, however, would know the stories well and were told in 1.1 what Jesus' significance was. *Deserted place . . . he prayed*, Jesus regularly prayed alone (e.g., 1.1; 14.35; cf. Mt 4.1–11).

1.40–45: Healing one suffering from a skin disease (Mt 8.2–4; Lk 5.12–16). The English term *leprosy* (see translators' note *a*) refers to Hansen's disease, a serious, disfiguring, contagious illness, but Heb "tsara'at" (Gk "lepros," "scaly, rough," from which Eng "leprosy" is derived) is more likely psoriasis, eczema, or fungus infections (see Lev 13–14 for laws regarding skin disease and the required actions to regain purity after it is healed), minor skin diseases which were at that time considered a serious impurity of the skin. By *touching* the unclean man, Jesus does not reject the purity laws; rather, as the text clearly implies, he restores the man to a clean state, leaving the purity codes intact: four times Mark emphasizes that Jesus makes the man *clean* of his disease, not that he critiques the law in any way. The cleansing of this leper does not abrogate the purity laws any more than does the cleansing of Naaman in 2 Kings 5.10. Indeed, Jesus commands the man to present the *offering* prescribed by law.

2.1–3.6: Collection of controversy stories. Although Jesus' first "day" of miracles was greeted positively, here he meets opposition in five conflicts with authorities. The theme is a new understanding of the law: those who have in some way seemed to violate Jewish law are brought into a larger vision of the law. In each case there is ambiguity: does Jesus oppose "Jewish law" or merely some interpretations of Jewish law, much as rabbis often disagreed with each other?

2.1–12: Faith and the forgiveness of sin (Mt 9.1–8; Lk 5.17–26). This dramatic scene of healing and forgiveness has been of central importance to Christian audiences for centuries, despite the improbable premise of Jesus teaching in a crowded room while bits of the roof are falling down from above. There is a limit to realism in accounts that are told primarily to serve as moral examples, which affects the interpretation of other illustrative stories as well (6.33; 12.43–44). **5:** There is no mention of the repentance of sinners here (contrast 1.4,15; 6.12); *faith* (in Jesus' healing power) is the defining marker of the community (1.15n.). *Forgiven*, Christian tradition has seen in this story an opposition between a Judaism with restricted forgiveness and a Christian community that

IMPURITY AND HEALING

A central issue in Mark is the relation of the followers of Jesus to the purity rules of Judaism, rules that helped to define Jewish identity. The rules distinguished several categories: the Temple was sacred (Heb *qodesh*, Gk *hagios*), while in relation to that, most people, places, and things were "common"—neutral or mundane (Heb *ḥol*, Gk *bebēlos, koinos*). On the other end of the spectrum, certain things were "unclean" or polluting (Heb *tame'*, Gk *akathartos*), such as a corpse, and in relation to that most people or things were "clean" (Heb *tahor*, Gk *katharos*). The two sets of opposites can be superimposed in this way:

holy	common
clean	unclean

This system, spelled out in Lev 10.10–11, was simplified in Mark's usage by combining the categories on one spectrum:

holy	common	unclean

Many apocalyptic texts, such as the War Scroll from Qumran, assume a parallel between the conflicts in this world and conflicts on a cosmic level. Mark, more than many other early Christian texts, characterizes the spirit world in terms of a distinction between the *holy* spirit and *unclean* spirits. (Cf. Zech 13.1–2, both in the Heb and Gk texts; *1 En.* 10.17–11.2; 38.2; 1QS 4.20–21; 9.3). In rabbinic Judaism it was believed that a purification could occur near the altar (*m. Zeb.* 9.1); in the apocalyptic texts it was assumed that this cleansing could fall on the saved community away from the Temple as well. (Cf. also Paul's discussion, 1 Cor 7.14.) In Mark, Jesus may not be erasing the Jewish distinctions of impurity as much as *defeating* impure spirits through the end-time actions of the Holy Spirit. It is part of the transformations at the end of time; purity codes are not set aside, but people are cleansed of their impurities.

scribes were sitting there, questioning in their hearts, [7] "Why does this fellow speak in this way? It is blasphemy! Who can forgive sins but God alone?" [8] At once Jesus perceived in his spirit that they were discussing these questions among themselves; and he said to them, "Why do you raise such questions in your hearts? [9] Which is easier, to say to the paralytic, 'Your sins are forgiven,' or to say, 'Stand up and take your mat and walk'? [10] But so that you may know that the Son of Man has authority on earth to forgive sins"—he said to the paralytic— [11] "I say to you, stand up, take your mat and go to your home."

offers forgiveness before it is requested. Neither of these is accurate. Judaism, like other religions, has a variety of understandings of the route back to acceptance for sinners and the forgiveness of sins. The earliest texts of the followers of Jesus, in addition to the offer of forgiveness, also affirm exclusion, segregation from sinners, shunning, cursing of sinners, and even the death of sinners (Mt 18.17; Acts 5.1–11; 1 Cor 5.1–5,9–11; 2 Cor 6.14–7.1). **6–7:** In a largely illiterate society, *scribes* played the role of interpreters of the law. They are portrayed, as here and in what immediately follows, in negative terms as rule-bound and unable to grasp the significance of Jesus' ministry. Since it is God who forgives, the statement is *blasphemy* from their point of view, but followers of Jesus claimed the power of forgiveness for their movement (cf. Mt 16.19; 18.18; Jn 20.22–23). In an earlier Jewish text, "Prayer of Nabonidus," a Jewish exorcist is said to have pardoned the sins of the Babylonian king Nabonidus and thus cured him. **10:** The title for Jesus used most often in Mark is *Son of Man* or "son of humanity" ("ho huios tou anthrōpou"). Although this title was originally simply an evocative way to say "human being" (Ezek 2.1), it underwent a significant transformation, as reflected in Dan 7.13, referring to the angel of judgment (probably Michael) as "one like a son of man" (KJV), that is, one who looked like a human being. When this image was taken up in apocalyptic Jewish texts, "Son of Man" became a term for God's heavenly judge at the end of time. Jesus may have spoken of the Son of Man as a figure other than himself, the coming judge, but in Mark this figure is identified with Jesus. A similar development occurs in *1 En.* 37–71, when the future Son of Man is identified with Enoch. A similar notion of the Son of Man as God's judge at the end of time is also found in the Sayings Source Q and in John, but Mark introduced an important nuance (which was then retained by Matthew and Luke): the Son of Man also suffers and is killed. The suffering servant (Isa 52.13–53.12) and the suffering righteous person (Wis 2–5) already existed in Jewish thought, but Mark connected them to the messiah and Son of Man, and thus transformed the latter into an evocative image of the human Jesus. This new meaning is central to the three Passion predictions (8.27–33n.).

PHARISEES AND TAX COLLECTORS

On the Pharisees, see "Jewish Movements of the NT Period," p. 526, but note here and in a number of passages in Matthew, Mark, and Luke, the Pharisees are contrasted specifically with tax collectors. This aspect is crucial for understanding the Gospels' view of both Pharisees and tax collectors: they are both presented as symbolic as well as real. As a lay movement outside of the Temple administration, the goal of the Pharisees was to renew and extend the observance of Jewish practice in society. But while Mark and Matthew could allow for the existence of good scribes (Mk 12.28–34; Mt 13.52), they do not recognize the possibility of a good Pharisee (contrast Acts 15.5). The conflict between the Jesus of the Gospels and the Pharisees, as representatives of Judaism in daily life, has therefore set up an opposition that has been perpetuated in Christian attitudes toward Judaism to this day.

The tax collectors, on the other hand, enjoy a special role, even a favored status in Matthew, Mark, and Luke. Yet if Jesus himself engaged them, it is odd that they should be totally absent in Paul, John, and in most early Christian texts. Not collectors of Roman direct taxes or of the Jewish Temple tax, tax collectors in the New Testament belonged to that group of functionaries responsible for local duties and tolls: in some cases they controlled local monopolies, such as the sale of salt. Since they kept as their own income whatever was in excess of the amount they had agreed to supply to the Roman administration, they were easily portrayed (justly or not) as extortionists. Contrary to some scholarly speculation, they were not likely slaves or poor, but low-level entrepreneurial figures. In both rabbinic and Christian texts, tax collectors are depicted as morally questionable, unsavory types who are the least likely to engage in heartfelt repentance and lead a good life (Lk 3.12–13; 7.34; Mt 5.46; 21.31; *m. Hag.* 3.6; *m. Ned.* 3.4; *m. B. Kamma* 10.1–2).

But aside from our understanding of the Pharisees and tax collectors separately, they must be understood together. The role of the tax collectors—*in both the Gospels and in rabbinic sources*—is generally as a foil to the Pharisees. In early rabbinic traditions, the Pharisees and their likely allies, the *ḥaverim* or "comrades" are particularly condemning of tax collectors, since they were viewed as lax about observance of the law and unscrupulous in terms of business practices. The tax collectors are thus likely favored in the gospels precisely because they were maligned by the Pharisees.

[12] And he stood up, and immediately took the mat and went out before all of them; so that they were all amazed and glorified God, saying, "We have never seen anything like this!"

[13] Jesus[a] went out again beside the sea; the whole crowd gathered around him, and he taught them. [14] As he was walking along, he saw Levi son of Alphaeus sitting at the tax booth, and he said to him, "Follow me." And he got up and followed him.

[15] And as he sat at dinner[b] in Levi's[c] house, many tax collectors and sinners were also sitting[d] with Jesus and his disciples—for there were many who followed him. [16] When the scribes of[e] the Pharisees saw that he was eating with sinners and tax collectors, they said to his disciples, "Why does he eat[f] with tax collectors and sinners?" [17] When Jesus heard this, he said to them, "Those who are well have no need of a physician, but those who are sick; I have come to call not the righteous but sinners."

[18] Now John's disciples and the Pharisees were fasting; and people[a] came and said to him, "Why do John's disciples and the disciples of the Pharisees fast, but your disciples

a Gk *He*
b Gk *reclined*
c Gk *his*
d Gk *reclining*
e Other ancient authorities read *and*
f Other ancient authorities add *and drink*

2.13–17: Jesus associates with tax collectors and sinners (Mt 9.9–13; Lk 5.27–32). *Sinners,* 2.5n.

2.18–22: Fasting (Mt 9.14–17; Lk 5.33–39). The followers of Jesus and John the Baptist never fully merged (Mt 11.18–19). The modern Mandaeans, a small group most of whom live on the border of Iran and Iraq, trace their origins to John the Baptist. *Fasting* was not a general practice for Jews except at Yom Kippur, during mourning (including mourning the destruction of the Temple, Zech 7.3, a practice that the same prophet rescinds in 8.19), and as a preparation for urgent supplications to God (Joel 1.14; Esth 4.16; Ezra 8.21). Some Jews took up

do not fast?" [19] Jesus said to them, "The wedding guests cannot fast while the bridegroom is with them, can they? As long as they have the bridegroom with them, they cannot fast. [20] The days will come when the bridegroom is taken away from them, and then they will fast on that day.

[21] "No one sews a piece of unshrunk cloth on an old cloak; otherwise, the patch pulls away from it, the new from the old, and a worse tear is made. [22] And no one puts new wine into old wineskins; otherwise, the wine will burst the skins, and the wine is lost, and so are the skins; but one puts new wine into fresh wineskins."[b]

[23] One sabbath he was going through the grainfields; and as they made their way his disciples began to pluck heads of grain. [24] The Pharisees said to him, "Look, why are they doing what is not lawful on the sabbath?" [25] And he said to them, "Have you never read what David did when he and his companions were hungry and in need of food? [26] He entered the house of God, when Abiathar was high priest, and ate the bread of the Presence, which it is not lawful for any but the priests to eat, and he gave some to his companions." [27] Then he said to them, "The sabbath was made for humankind, and not humankind for the sabbath; [28] so the Son of Man is lord even of the sabbath."

3 Again he entered the synagogue, and a man was there who had a withered hand. [2] They watched him to see whether he would cure him on the sabbath, so that they might accuse him. [3] And he said to the man who had the withered hand, "Come forward." [4] Then he said to them, "Is it lawful to do good or to do harm on the sabbath, to save life or to kill?" But they were silent. [5] He looked around at them with anger; he was grieved at their hardness of heart and said to the man, "Stretch out your hand." He stretched it out, and his hand was restored. [6] The Pharisees went out and immediately conspired with the Herodians against him, how to destroy him.

[a] Gk *they*
[b] Other ancient authorities lack *but one puts new wine into fresh wineskins*

a discipline of fasting, such as the Pharisees and John the Baptist, as did some followers of Jesus (Mt 6.16–18; *Did.* 8.1), but here and in Lk 7.33–34 fasting while the *bridegroom*, the eschatological Son of Man, is present, is evidently not affirmed.

2.23–28: Plucking grain on the Sabbath (Mt 12.1–8; Lk 6.1–5). This typical controversy story involves a legal challenge, presented as petty and mean-spirited, and a pithy rejoinder that transcends the legal challenge to address the underlying human need (v. 27). Before that response, however, the text includes a scriptural and legal argument: if David could supersede law to meet human needs, so could Jesus and his disciples (vv. 25–26; cf. 7.6–13; 10.3–8; 12.26–27). However, Mark does not accurately follow the biblical text, 1 Sam 21.1–6, making the question—*Have you never read?*—perhaps accidentally ironic. *David* acts alone in 1 Samuel, does not act from hunger, and does not enter the *house of God* to eat *the bread of Presence*. Further, the priest is Ahimelech, not *Abiathar*. Pharisees would also not likely be out in the fields on the Sabbath to observe behavior, so the story, like other conflict stories in the Gospels, is likely created to define the identities of Jesus' followers and their opponents. **27–28:** Here Jesus advocates a humanitarian Sabbath exception such as those often discussed in Jewish law. Since *Son of Man* could simply mean a person and not Jesus or the judge at the end of time (2.10n.), it is possible that this saying originally meant that a person is *lord even of the Sabbath* in the sense that he or she is to enjoy the Sabbath and is not constricted by the Sabbath (*b. Yoma* 85b). Later, however, this saying was interpreted to mean that Jesus had authority to revoke the rules of Sabbath rest.

3.1–6: Healing on the Sabbath (Mt 12.9–14; Lk 6.6–11). Jesus responds with another humanitarian Sabbath exception, found also in rabbinic tradition: "Any danger to life overrides the prohibitions of the Sabbath" (*m. Yoma* 8.6). In the Cairo Damascus Document, however, many such exceptions were not allowed (CD 11.32–33). **4:** Although Jesus characterizes the healing in this way—*good* or *harm*, *save life* or *kill*—the man's condition is not life-threatening, and therefore the incident is understood to have wider significance. **5:** *Was restored*, the passive may indicate that Jesus in fact did not do anything that could be considered "work." **6:** In the Gospels Jesus is often opposed by the Pharisees, but it is the chief priests, scribes, and elders who wish to have him executed (8.31; 14.1–2). Only here does Mark say that the Pharisees tried to *destroy* Jesus. *Herodians*, members of the court of Herod Antipas, the ruler of Galilee installed by Rome, and those who supported them.

[7] Jesus departed with his disciples to the sea, and a great multitude from Galilee followed him; [8] hearing all that he was doing, they came to him in great numbers from Judea, Jerusalem, Idumea, beyond the Jordan, and the region around Tyre and Sidon. [9] He told his disciples to have a boat ready for him because of the crowd, so that they would not crush him; [10] for he had cured many, so that all who had diseases pressed upon him to touch him. [11] Whenever the unclean spirits saw him, they fell down before him and shouted, "You are the Son of God!" [12] But he sternly ordered them not to make him known.

[13] He went up the mountain and called to him those whom he wanted, and they came to him. [14] And he appointed twelve, whom he also named apostles,[a] to be with him, and to be sent out to proclaim the message, [15] and to have authority to cast out demons. [16] So he appointed the twelve:[b] Simon (to whom he gave the name Peter); [17] James son of Zebedee and John the brother of James (to whom he gave the name Boanerges, that is, Sons of Thunder); [18] and Andrew, and Philip, and Bartholomew, and Matthew, and Thomas, and James son of Alphaeus, and Thaddaeus, and Simon the Cananaean, [19] and Judas Iscariot, who betrayed him.

Then he went home; [20] and the crowd came together again, so that they could not even eat. [21] When his family heard it, they went out to restrain him, for people were saying, "He has gone out of his mind." [22] And the scribes who came down from Jerusalem said, "He has Beelzebul, and by the ruler of the demons he casts out demons." [23] And he called them to him, and spoke to them in parables, "How can Satan cast out Satan? [24] If a kingdom is divided against itself, that kingdom cannot stand. [25] And if a house is divided against itself, that house will not be able to stand. [26] And if Satan has risen up against himself and is divided, he cannot stand, but his end has come. [27] But no one can enter a strong man's house and plunder his property without first tying up the strong man; then indeed the house can be plundered.

[28] "Truly I tell you, people will be forgiven for their sins and whatever blasphemies they utter; [29] but whoever blasphemes against the Holy Spirit can never have forgiveness, but is

[a] Other ancient authorities lack *whom he also named apostles*

[b] Other ancient authorities lack *So he appointed the twelve*

3.7–12: Summary of Jesus' successes (Mt 12.15–21; Lk 6.17–19; 4.41). Texts like Isa 2.1–4 predict the ingathering of Israel and the streaming of Gentiles to Jerusalem; here that process is focused on Jesus and not Jerusalem, and seems primarily (if not exclusively) to mean Jews from the immediate Diaspora; Gentiles are not explicitly indicated. **11:** *Unclean spirits,* see "Impurity and Healing," p. 63. *Son of God,* 1.9–11n. **12:** See Introduction on the messianic secret.

3.13–19a: Appointing the twelve (Mt 10.1–4; Lk 6.12–16). **14:** The *twelve* suggests the twelve tribes of Israel, a symbolic number (since the twelve tribes were no longer in existence) essentially standing for the people of God. The twelve are disciples (Gk "mathetes," originally "learners, students" who gathered around a teacher); they are here named *apostles* (Gk "apostolos," "one sent out" as a representative or to carry out a mission). The only female disciple specified in the NT is Tabitha in Acts 9.36, though Jesus had female followers such as Mary Magdalene (16.1). In addition, Paul claimed the status of apostle (Gal 1–2). The only specific occurrence of a word similar to "disciple" in the Hebrew Bible is in Isaiah (8.16; 50.4; 54.13; Heb "lammud," "one who is taught"). Elisha was in a similar relation to Elijah, and there were schools of prophets (e.g., 2 Kings 2.3, "sons of the prophets").

3.19b–35: Beelzebul and Satan (Mt 12.22–32,46–50; Lk 8.19–21; 11.14–23; 12.10). **21:** *His family . . . restrain him,* Jesus' near relatives are sometimes portrayed in the Gospels as misunderstanding him, or opposing his ministry (Mt 12.46–50; Lk 8.19–21). **22:** *Beelzebul,* a name for Satan, derived ultimately from the Canaanite high god Baal, meaning perhaps "Baal, the prince" (2 Kings 1.2,3 spells the name "Baal-zebub," "lord of flies," an insulting parody). This passage shows how charges of magic develop: the perceived miracles of one group are assigned to demonic forces by another. **23–27:** The *parables* refute the accusation of demonic power in casting out demons by drawing an analogy with a human *kingdom* working at cross-purposes with itself, which would be self-defeating. Jesus then draws another analogy, comparing himself to one who has bound *a strong man* so that his property *can be plundered* as Jesus is plundering the demonic world by defeating Satan. **28–30:** As

guilty of an eternal sin"— [30] for they had said, "He has an unclean spirit."

[31] Then his mother and his brothers came; and standing outside, they sent to him and called him. [32] A crowd was sitting around him; and they said to him, "Your mother and your brothers and sisters[a] are outside, asking for you." [33] And he replied, "Who are my mother and my brothers?" [34] And looking at those who sat around him, he said, "Here are my mother and my brothers! [35] Whoever does the will of God is my brother and sister and mother."

4 Again he began to teach beside the sea. Such a very large crowd gathered around him that he got into a boat on the sea and sat there, while the whole crowd was beside the sea on the land. [2] He began to teach them many things in parables, and in his teaching he said to them: [3] "Listen! A sower went out to sow. [4] And as he sowed, some seed fell on the path, and the birds came and ate it up. [5] Other seed fell on rocky ground, where it did not have much soil, and it sprang up quickly, since it had no depth of soil. [6] And when the sun rose, it was scorched; and since it had no root, it withered away. [7] Other seed fell among thorns, and the thorns grew up and choked it, and it yielded no grain. [8] Other seed fell into good soil and brought forth grain, growing up and increasing and yielding thirty and sixty and a hundredfold." [9] And he said, "Let anyone with ears to hear listen!"

[10] When he was alone, those who were around him along with the twelve asked him about the parables. [11] And he said to them, "To you has been given the secret[b] of the kingdom of God, but for those outside, everything comes in parables; [12] in order that

'they may indeed look, but not perceive,
and may indeed listen, but not understand;
so that they may not turn again and be forgiven.'"

[13] And he said to them, "Do you not understand this parable? Then how will you understand all the parables? [14] The sower sows the word. [15] These are the ones on the path where the word is sown: when they hear, Satan immediately comes and takes away the word that is sown in them. [16] And these are the ones sown on rocky ground: when they hear the word, they immediately receive it with joy. [17] But they have no root, and endure only for a while; then, when trouble or persecution arises on account of the word, immediately they fall away.[c] [18] And others are those sown among the thorns: these are the ones who hear the word, [19] but the cares of the world, and the lure of wealth, and the desire for other things come in and choke the word, and it yields nothing. [20] And these are the ones sown on the good soil: they hear the word and accept it and bear fruit, thirty and sixty and a hundredfold."

[21] He said to them, "Is a lamp brought in to be put under the bushel basket, or under the

[a] Other ancient authorities lack *and sisters*
[b] Or *mystery*
[c] Or *stumble*

in some Jewish apocalypses (*1 En.* 38.2), the Holy Spirit was the divine power that brought the new community into existence. In rabbinic texts unforgivable sins were also sins against God and the sanctity of the community (*m. Avot* 3.12: "R. Eleazar of Modiim said: If a man profanes the hallowed things and despises the set feasts and puts his fellow to shame publicly and makes void the covenant of Abraham our father, and discloses meanings in the law which are not according to the *Halakah*, even though a knowledge of the law and good works are his, he has no share in the world to come.") **28:** *Truly,* Heb "amen," see 1.14–15n. Jesus uses the word "amen" not in the typical Jewish way as an affirmation of what someone else has just prayed, but as a solemn affirmation of what he is about to say (cf. Jer 28.6, where the prophet's use of "Amen" at the beginning of his speech relates [probably ironically] to the previous speech of the prophet Hananiah). **31–35:** New religious movements often create "fictive families" of social networks outside of traditional families, with members called "brothers and sisters," "saints," and so on.

4.1–34: Parables and the kingdom of God (Mt 13; Lk 8.4–18; 13.18–19). The central teaching section of Mark is this parables chapter, perhaps based on an earlier collection (see "Parables and Kingdom," p. 68). **11–12:** *Those outside* do not *understand*, as those who heard Isaiah's prophecies (Isa 6.9–10) did not grasp their import, but it is not clear if the lack of understanding is from a willful refusal or from a clouding of their

PARABLES AND KINGDOM

Because of their prominent place in the first three Gospels, parables are, as scholars have argued, among the most likely teachings to go back to the historical Jesus. Ironically, however, their elusive quality has not yielded a consensus as to what they meant for Jesus or his first followers. Gk *parabolē* (lit., "throw alongside," that is, talk about one thing in terms of another) and Heb *mashal* (from a verb meaning "compare") referred to any figurative comparison, from clear proverbs to obscure riddles. The rabbis also told many parables of God's relation to Israel (e.g., *Gen. Rab.* 3.1; *Lam. Rab.* 1.1)

The first parable in Mk 4 (vv. 2–9) seems clear to the modern audience, but Jesus' followers have difficulty understanding. For Mark, the secret of the kingdom of God, communicated through the parables, is explained to the insiders, but those outside only hear the impenetrable shell (vv. 11–12,33–34). Thus Mark suggests that the parables, without an explanation, are impenetrable, although most of them succeed at least on a suggestive level. Mark's presentation also rigidly and irrevocably separates insiders from outsiders, and the latter are lost. Jesus speaks in parables *in order that* the outsiders may not understand and seek forgiveness. (This hard line may have been softened in Mt 13.13.) Mark is here quite emphatic that the community is a separate entity with insiders' understanding and restricted salvation. The parables also express "the secret [lit., 'mystery'] of the kingdom of God" (v. 11). It is left ambiguous whether the kingdom is present now or lies in the future. In the parable of the sower, the extended comparison is stretched: the "seed" stands for the "word" that the believer hears, and yet the plants that spring from the seed are the believers themselves.

bed, and not on the lampstand? [22] For there is nothing hidden, except to be disclosed; nor is anything secret, except to come to light. [23] Let anyone with ears to hear listen!" [24] And he said to them, "Pay attention to what you hear; the measure you give will be the measure you get, and still more will be given you. [25] For to those who have, more will be given; and from those who have nothing, even what they have will be taken away."

[26] He also said, "The kingdom of God is as if someone would scatter seed on the ground, [27] and would sleep and rise night and day, and the seed would sprout and grow, he does not know how. [28] The earth produces of itself, first the stalk, then the head, then the full grain in the head. [29] But when the grain is ripe, at once he goes in with his sickle, because the harvest has come."

[30] He also said, "With what can we compare the kingdom of God, or what parable will we use for it? [31] It is like a mustard seed, which, when sown upon the ground, is the smallest of all the seeds on earth; [32] yet when it is sown it grows up and becomes the greatest of all shrubs, and puts forth large branches, so that the birds of the air can make nests in its shade."

[33] With many such parables he spoke the word to them, as they were able to hear it; [34] he did not speak to them except in parables, but he explained everything in private to his disciples.

[35] On that day, when evening had come, he said to them, "Let us go across to the other side." [36] And leaving the crowd behind, they took him with them in the boat,

minds caused by God. **26–29:** This parable is similar to the previous parable of the sower, but without the long introduction allegorized by Mark. **27:** *He does not know how,* many of the parables involve miraculous appearance and inexplicable growth as a metaphor for the kingdom. Exaggeration for effect, or hyperbole, is a common rhetorical device. **31–32:** Great trees, typically cedars, were symbols of powerful empires (Ezek 17.22–23; Dan 4.20–22), but *mustard* plants are invasive shrubs that grow to be a few feet high. Like many other parables, this one is satirical and humorous, and highly suggestive: the kingdom is like a scrubby, invasive bush! The parable suggests that *the kingdom* arises from a very small beginning and nevertheless grows miraculously.

4.35–41: Stilling of the storm (Mt 8.23–27; Lk 8.22–25). Like Jonah, Jesus is sleeping in the midst of a storm, but unlike Jonah Jesus calms the storm (see Jon 1.4–6). **35:** *Go across to the other side.* Here Jesus leaves a predominantly Jewish section of Galilee for the first time to go by sea to the eastern, predominantly Gentile

just as he was. Other boats were with him. [37] A great windstorm arose, and the waves beat into the boat, so that the boat was already being swamped. [38] But he was in the stern, asleep on the cushion; and they woke him up and said to him, "Teacher, do you not care that we are perishing?" [39] He woke up and rebuked the wind, and said to the sea, "Peace! Be still!" Then the wind ceased, and there was a dead calm. [40] He said to them, "Why are you afraid? Have you still no faith?" [41] And they were filled with great awe and said to one another, "Who then is this, that even the wind and the sea obey him?"

5 They came to the other side of the sea, to the country of the Gerasenes.[a] [2] And when he had stepped out of the boat, immediately a man out of the tombs with an unclean spirit met him. [3] He lived among the tombs; and no one could restrain him any more, even with a chain; [4] for he had often been restrained with shackles and chains, but the chains he wrenched apart, and the shackles he broke in pieces; and no one had the strength to subdue him. [5] Night and day among the tombs and on the mountains he was always howling and bruising himself with stones. [6] When he saw Jesus from a distance, he ran and bowed down before him; [7] and he shouted at the top of his voice, "What have you to do with me, Jesus, Son of the Most High God? I adjure you by God, do not torment me." [8] For he had said to him, "Come out of the man, you unclean spirit!" [9] Then Jesus[b] asked him, "What is your name?" He replied, "My name is Legion; for we are many." [10] He begged him earnestly not to send them out of the country. [11] Now there on the hillside a great herd of swine was feeding; [12] and the unclean spirits[c] begged him, "Send us into the swine; let us enter them." [13] So he gave them permission. And the unclean spirits came out and entered the swine; and the herd, numbering about two

[a] Other ancient authorities read *Gergesenes*; others, *Gadarenes*
[b] Gk *he*
[c] Gk *they*

coast. **38–40:** Mark here and elsewhere depicts the disciples as uncomprehending, weak-willed, or cowardly (4.13,38,40; 5.31; 6.52; 7.18; 8.17). It is possible that Mark is indicating that they do not deserve the authority they held in the early communities of Jesus' followers, but the audience may also be able to identify with their level of weakness, and gain encouragement for renewed efforts to be faithful followers. In the wilderness wanderings of Exodus there is a recurrent motif of the murmurings of the people. Further, the boat here is likely intended as a metaphor for the tiny, buffeted community; this was certainly the way the boat was interpreted in later Christian art. **39:** Jesus *rebuked the wind* and *sea,* which takes up an ancient Near Eastern and Israelite evocation of the god who conquers the sea (e.g., Ps 65.7; 89.9; 107.29).

5.1–20: Gerasene demoniac and the legion of unclean spirits (Mt 8.28–34; Lk 8.26–39). This first exorcism in Gentile territory parallels Jesus' first exorcism in Jewish Galilee (1.21–28). Here Jesus encounters the man outside; in the first exorcism the man with an unclean spirit was inside the synagogue. This man is much more violent and self-destructive. The demons possessing the first man were simply expelled; here they are allowed to enter a herd of swine. But in both exorcisms the demons recognize Jesus, and he expels them with commands, not performing any actions. The onlookers also quickly report the events. **1:** *Gerasenes,* Gerasa is forty miles from the Sea of Galilee, which is inconsistent with v. 13. Some have taken this as evidence that Mark was not from northern Galilee, but this is not conclusive evidence. Further, Gerasa may evoke Heb "gerash," which means expel, and was used in some of the biblical accounts of God driving the nations out of the land (Ex 23.28), as here the swine, unclean animals, are driven out (see also 16.7n.). **2:** *Unclean spirit,* see "Impurity and Healing," p. 63. **7:** The spirit recognizes Jesus as *Son of the Most High God* (Gk "hypsistos," in LXX for "'elyon," "Most High" [e.g., Ps 9.2]) and tries to negotiate. **9:** *What is your name,* in exorcisms knowledge of the names of angels and demons was essential to enlist or control them. *Legion,* a Latin loan-word, denotes a unit of 6,000 soldiers in the Roman army. Many Jewish and Christian texts, especially apocalyptic texts, express a belief that God would destroy the Romans and establish a kingdom of God—albeit conceived in different ways. This story remains evocative of several far-reaching possibilities without clarifying them: Do the swine represent the expulsion ("gerash") of unclean animals or the Roman armies? Are the Gerasenes angry over a symbolic battle or the loss of their herds? What is the significance of a Gentile asking to follow Jesus? Why is

thousand, rushed down the steep bank into the sea, and were drowned in the sea.

[14] The swineherds ran off and told it in the city and in the country. Then people came to see what it was that had happened. [15] They came to Jesus and saw the demoniac sitting there, clothed and in his right mind, the very man who had had the legion; and they were afraid. [16] Those who had seen what had happened to the demoniac and to the swine reported it. [17] Then they began to beg Jesus[a] to leave their neighborhood. [18] As he was getting into the boat, the man who had been possessed by demons begged him that he might be with him. [19] But Jesus[b] refused, and said to him, "Go home to your friends, and tell them how much the Lord has done for you, and what mercy he has shown you." [20] And he went away and began to proclaim in the Decapolis how much Jesus had done for him; and everyone was amazed.

[21] When Jesus had crossed again in the boat[c] to the other side, a great crowd gathered around him; and he was by the sea. [22] Then one of the leaders of the synagogue named Jairus came and, when he saw him, fell at his feet [23] and begged him repeatedly, "My little daughter is at the point of death. Come and lay your hands on her, so that she may be made well, and live." [24] So he went with him.

And a large crowd followed him and pressed in on him. [25] Now there was a woman who had been suffering from hemorrhages for twelve years. [26] She had endured much under many physicians, and had spent all that she had; and she was no better, but rather grew worse. [27] She had heard about Jesus, and came up behind him in the crowd and touched his cloak, [28] for she said, "If I but touch his clothes, I will be made well." [29] Immediately her hemorrhage stopped; and she felt in her body that she was healed of her disease. [30] Immediately aware that power had gone forth from him, Jesus turned about in the crowd and said, "Who touched my clothes?" [31] And his disciples said to him, "You see the crowd pressing in on you; how can you say, 'Who touched me?'" [32] He looked all around to see who had done it. [33] But the woman, knowing what had happened to her, came in fear and trembling, fell down before him, and told him the whole truth. [34] He said to her, "Daughter, your faith has made you well; go in peace, and be healed of your disease."

[35] While he was still speaking, some people came from the leader's house to say, "Your daughter is dead. Why trouble the teacher any further?" [36] But overhearing[d] what they said, Jesus said to the leader of the synagogue, "Do not fear, only believe." [37] He allowed no one to follow him except Peter, James, and John, the brother of James. [38] When they came to the house of the leader of the synagogue, he saw a commotion, people weeping and wailing loudly. [39] When he had entered, he said to them, "Why do you make a commotion and weep? The child is not dead but sleeping."

[a] Gk *him*
[b] Gk *he*
[c] Other ancient authorities lack *in the boat*
[d] Or *ignoring*; other ancient authorities read *hearing*

there no messianic secret here? **20:** The *Decapolis* was a federation of ten predominantly Gentile cities to the east of the Sea of Galilee.

5.21–43: Healing of Jairus's daughter and a woman with a hemorrhage (Mt 9.18–26; Lk 8.40–56). No sooner has Jesus crossed the sea to the more Gentile side than he retraces his route back to the western, more Jewish side. Mark never comments on what the regions may mean to Jesus' mission to Jews and Gentiles (but cf. 13.10; Mt 10.5–6). **22:** *Leaders of the synagogue*, in the first century probably not a religious officer but rather a prominent person in the community. Jewish law distinguished between a woman in menses ("niddah") and a woman with a continuous flow of blood beyond her monthly period ("zavah"; Lev 15.19–30). The result in either case is that the woman is in an impure state. **24–34:** Leviticus 15 addresses normal and abnormal genital discharges. All cause ritual impurity, with different responses commanded. Whether such ritual impurity—an issue not mentioned in the text—would have mattered in a local village, where access to the temple compound is not an issue, is not clear. Mark's story is concerned with a woman with a flow of blood for twelve years, which would have resulted in continuous impurity. It is often assumed that this healing miracle contrasts menstrual impurity codes and Jesus' liberation of women from them, but it is more likely that the contrast is between sickness on one hand and miraculous healing based on faith on the other, as the text twice states (vv. 28–29,34; cf. 1.40–45

[40] And they laughed at him. Then he put them all outside, and took the child's father and mother and those who were with him, and went in where the child was. [41] He took her by the hand and said to her, "Talitha cum," which means, "Little girl, get up!" [42] And immediately the girl got up and began to walk about (she was twelve years of age). At this they were overcome with amazement. [43] He strictly ordered them that no one should know this, and told them to give her something to eat.

6 He left that place and came to his hometown, and his disciples followed him. [2] On the sabbath he began to teach in the synagogue, and many who heard him were astounded. They said, "Where did this man get all this? What is this wisdom that has been given to him? What deeds of power are being done by his hands! [3] Is not this the carpenter, the son of Mary[a] and brother of James and Joses and Judas and Simon, and are not his sisters here with us?" And they took offense[b] at him. [4] Then Jesus said to them, "Prophets are not without honor, except in their hometown, and among their own kin, and in their own house." [5] And he could do no deed of power there, except that he laid his hands on a few sick people and cured them. [6] And he was amazed at their unbelief.

Then he went about among the villages teaching. [7] He called the twelve and began to send them out two by two, and gave them authority over the unclean spirits. [8] He ordered them to take nothing for their journey except a staff; no bread, no bag, no money in their belts; [9] but to wear sandals and not to put on two tunics. [10] He said to them, "Wherever you enter a house, stay there until you leave the place. [11] If any place will not welcome you and they refuse to hear you, as you leave, shake off the dust that is on your feet as a testimony against them." [12] So they went out and proclaimed that all should repent. [13] They cast out many demons, and anointed with oil many who were sick and cured them.

[14] King Herod heard of it, for Jesus'[c] name had become known. Some were[d] saying,

[a] Other ancient authorities read *son of the carpenter and of Mary*
[b] Or *stumbled*
[c] Gk *his*
[d] Other ancient authorities read *He was*

and "Impurity and Healing," p. 63). The elect community at the end of time is liberated from impurity, not impurity codes (Zech 13.1–2; 14.20–21). **41:** *Talitha cum,* the original Aramaic of Jesus' words of healing is retained; this is presumably a vestige of the stage of oral tradition before the narratives that make up the Gospel were translated into Greek. **42:** *Twelve years of age,* the girl's age is the same as the period of the woman's suffering from hemorrhage, suggesting a reference to the renewal of Israel as a whole ("twelve" can stand for the twelve tribes, thereby indicating the whole Israelite people).

6.1–13: Second rejection in Jesus' hometown and the mission of the twelve (Mt 13.53–58; 10.1–14; Lk 4.16–30; 9.1–6). **3:** *Brother, sisters,* Christian tradition has sometimes explained these family members as children of Joseph and a wife other than Mary, or as cousins. The Hebrew, Aramaic, and Greek words for brother and sister can mean relative, even a marriageable person from one's extended family, or "kissing cousin" (Tob 7.9). In ancient Israel, these would have been the members of the "mishpachah" or clan, but such traditional extended kinship categories may not have been so precise by this period. The context suggests close family members, and the virginal conception of Jesus is not mentioned in Mark (Mt 1.18–25; Lk 1.34–35). The point, as in 3.19b–30, is that Jesus' own family and hometown rejected him. Such rejection is part of both the paradigm of the prophet and of the hero cross-culturally (see Introduction). **4:** *Prophets are not without honor,* the origin of the later Hebrew expression "There is no prophet in his own city" ("Ein nabi be'iro") is unknown, but it may ultimately derive from this verse. **5–6a:** The lack of faith limits Jesus' power. **6b–13:** Jesus' own rejection is followed by the mission of the twelve. There is a parallel between the power and authority of the disciples and that of Jesus himself; as *m. Ber.* 5.5 says, "A person's representative is as the person himself." **7:** *Two by two,* perhaps to ensure that there would be two witnesses in accordance with Deut 17.6; this would be relevant for the *testimony* in v. 11. **13:** *Anointed with oil,* a common medicinal practice in the ancient world (Isa 1.6; Josephus, *J. W.* 1.657).

6.14–29: Beheading of John the Baptist (Mt 14.1–12; Lk 9.7–9). The Jewish historian Josephus indicates that John the Baptist was a well-known and respected figure (*Ant.* 18.116–19; Mk 11.30–32). Mark presents John as a prophet who condemns *Herod* Antipas for violating Jewish law (Lev 18.16) by marrying his *brother's wife* (in a

"John the baptizer has been raised from the dead; and for this reason these powers are at work in him." [15] But others said, "It is Elijah." And others said, "It is a prophet, like one of the prophets of old." [16] But when Herod heard of it, he said, "John, whom I beheaded, has been raised."

[17] For Herod himself had sent men who arrested John, bound him, and put him in prison on account of Herodias, his brother Philip's wife, because Herod[a] had married her. [18] For John had been telling Herod, "It is not lawful for you to have your brother's wife." [19] And Herodias had a grudge against him, and wanted to kill him. But she could not, [20] for Herod feared John, knowing that he was a righteous and holy man, and he protected him. When he heard him, he was greatly perplexed;[b] and yet he liked to listen to him. [21] But an opportunity came when Herod on his birthday gave a banquet for his courtiers and officers and for the leaders of Galilee. [22] When his daughter Herodias[c] came in and danced, she pleased Herod and his guests; and the king said to the girl, "Ask me for whatever you wish, and I will give it." [23] And he solemnly swore to her, "Whatever you ask me, I will give you, even half of my kingdom." [24] She went out and said to her mother, "What should I ask for?" She replied, "The head of John the baptizer." [25] Immediately she rushed back to the king and requested, "I want you to give me at once the head of John the Baptist on a platter." [26] The king was deeply grieved; yet out of regard for his oaths and for the guests, he did not want to refuse her. [27] Immediately the king sent a soldier of the guard with orders to bring John's[d] head. He went and beheaded him in the prison, [28] brought his head on a platter, and gave it to the girl. Then the girl gave it to her mother. [29] When his disciples heard about it, they came and took his body, and laid it in a tomb.

[30] The apostles gathered around Jesus, and told him all that they had done and taught. [31] He said to them, "Come away to a deserted place all by yourselves and rest a while." For many were coming and going, and they had no leisure even to eat. [32] And they went away in the boat to a deserted place by themselves. [33] Now many saw them going and recognized them, and they hurried there on foot from all the towns and arrived ahead of them. [34] As he went ashore, he saw a great crowd; and he had compassion for them, because they were like sheep without a shepherd; and he began to teach them many things. [35] When it grew late, his disciples came to him and said, "This is a deserted place, and the hour is now very late; [36] send them away so that they may go into the surrounding country and villages and buy something for themselves to eat." [37] But he answered them, "You give them something to eat." They said to him, "Are we to go and buy two hundred denarii[e] worth of bread, and give it to them to eat?" [38] And he said to them, "How many loaves have you? Go and see." When they had found out, they said, "Five, and two fish." [39] Then he ordered them to get all the people to sit down in groups on

a Gk *he*
b Other ancient authorities read *he did many things*
c Other ancient authorities read *the daughter of Herodias herself*
d Gk *his*
e The denarius was the usual day's wage for a laborer

situation where the levirate law [Deut 25.5–6] did not apply, because Herod's brother did not die childless). **14:** The *powers* of Israelite heroes were great (see Introduction). **15:** *Elijah,* Mk 8.28. *John . . . has been raised,* Herod apparently sees Jesus as the resurrected John the Baptist, since their preaching was similar and they both attracted crowds. Resurrection of the righteous in Israel was a common belief, though not universal (Ezek 37; Mk 12.18).

6.30–44: Feeding of the five thousand (Mt 14.13–21; Lk 9.10–17; Jn 6.1–13). There are two miraculous feedings in Mark, the first in predominantly Jewish territory, the second (8.1–10) in a predominantly Gentile area. Matthew includes both, while Luke and John have only one. A number of motifs evoke the Exodus and Elisha's miracles (Ex 16–18; 2 Kings 4.42–44). **33:** Improbably, the people see them leaving by boat, recruit others from *all the towns,* and run ahead on foot, and yet are able to arrive at the deserted place ahead of them (2.1–12n.). This emphasizes the miraculous nature of the kingdom and the ingathering of peoples at the end of time. **34:** *Sheep without a shepherd,* 1 Kings 22.17. It is typical of hero legends that the hero is called out of his preferred isolation (v. 31) by *compassion* for the people (e.g., Moses; Ex 3–4), who will ultimately abandon him. *Shepherd,*

the green grass. [40] So they sat down in groups of hundreds and of fifties. [41] Taking the five loaves and the two fish, he looked up to heaven, and blessed and broke the loaves, and gave them to his disciples to set before the people; and he divided the two fish among them all. [42] And all ate and were filled; [43] and they took up twelve baskets full of broken pieces and of the fish. [44] Those who had eaten the loaves numbered five thousand men.

[45] Immediately he made his disciples get into the boat and go on ahead to the other side, to Bethsaida, while he dismissed the crowd. [46] After saying farewell to them, he went up on the mountain to pray.

[47] When evening came, the boat was out on the sea, and he was alone on the land. [48] When he saw that they were straining at the oars against an adverse wind, he came towards them early in the morning, walking on the sea. He intended to pass them by. [49] But when they saw him walking on the sea, they thought it was a ghost and cried out; [50] for they all saw him and were terrified. But immediately he spoke to them and said, "Take heart, it is I; do not be afraid." [51] Then he got into the boat with them and the wind ceased. And they were utterly astounded, [52] for they did not understand about the loaves, but their hearts were hardened.

[53] When they had crossed over, they came to land at Gennesaret and moored the boat. [54] When they got out of the boat, people at once recognized him, [55] and rushed about that whole region and began to bring the sick on mats to wherever they heard he was. [56] And wherever he went, into villages or cities or farms, they laid the sick in the marketplaces, and begged him that they might touch even the fringe of his cloak; and all who touched it were healed.

7 Now when the Pharisees and some of the scribes who had come from Jerusalem gathered around him, [2] they noticed that some of his disciples were eating with defiled hands, that is, without washing them. [3] (For the Pharisees, and all the Jews, do not eat unless they thoroughly wash their hands,[a] thus observing the tradition of the elders; [4] and they do not eat anything from the market

[a] Meaning of Gk uncertain

Num 27.17; Isa 40.11. **41:** *Taking . . . blessed . . . broke . . . gave* are reminiscent of the blessing at a Jewish Sabbath meal (based on Deut 8.7–10 and developed into the "blessing for nourishment" ["birchat ha-mason"] used at mealtime), but they are especially close to words used in the Lord's Supper (Mk 14.22–25n.), thus providing a foreshadowing, while also suggesting the banquet prophesied at Isa 25.6, taken up also at Qumran (1QM 2.11–22; cf. *1 En.* 10.18–19). **43:** *Twelve baskets* suggests the twelve tribes gathered at the end of time, and by extension, the twelve disciples.

6.45–52: Walking on the water (Mt 14.22–33; Jn 6.15–21). Each of the feeding miracles in Mark is joined with a water miracle, evoking the Exodus miracles (e.g., God parting the waters [Ex 14.19–31], God feeding the people in the wilderness [Ex 16.13–21]). **48–51:** *Intended to pass them by,* perhaps meaning that the stilling of the waves did not require Jesus to enter the boat, but the disciples mistaking him for a ghost and their fear did. **52:** The disciples' misunderstanding is a serious condition, akin to that of Pharaoh who oppressed the Israelites (Ex 7–11). *Hearts . . . hardened,* as with Pharaoh (e.g., Ex 7.14) but also the people (Ps 95.8), hardness of heart can mean a willful inability to understand.

6.53–56: A Markan summary (Mt 14.34–36). See 1.29–34n. **56:** *Fringe of his cloak,* the blue threads ("tzitzit") commanded by God to be worn by Israelite males at the corners of their cloaks (Num 15.37–40). Jesus here is shown observing a requirement of Torah.

7.1–23. Washing of hands and the commandment of God (Mt 15.1–20). The issue of following Torah rules for kosher food and ritual purity was, along with circumcision for Gentile male converts, one of the contentious areas that followers of Jesus had to resolve (see Acts 15.19–20). **2:** *Defiled,* see "Impurity and Healing," p. 63. **3–4:** That Mark must explain these practices indicates that the audience (though not the setting) is largely Gentile; this explanation is lacking in Mt 15.2 (Luke and John lack this story). The Pharisees were known for observing *traditions of the elders* not found in scripture, including hand washing (an observance that acknowledged the likelihood of contact with things that were ritually unclean in the course of daily life, but that did not require total immersion), but it is probably incorrect that *all the Jews* observed these laws at this time. Sadducees—and most Jews?—did not follow the Pharisees in this matter. This raises the possibility that even if Jesus'

unless they wash it;[a] and there are also many other traditions that they observe, the washing of cups, pots, and bronze kettles.[b]) [5] So the Pharisees and the scribes asked him, "Why do your disciples not live[c] according to the tradition of the elders, but eat with defiled hands?" [6] He said to them, "Isaiah prophesied rightly about you hypocrites, as it is written,

'This people honors me with their lips,
but their hearts are far from me;
[7] in vain do they worship me,
teaching human precepts as doctrines.'

[8] You abandon the commandment of God and hold to human tradition."

[9] Then he said to them, "You have a fine way of rejecting the commandment of God in order to keep your tradition! [10] For Moses said, 'Honor your father and your mother'; and, 'Whoever speaks evil of father or mother must surely die.' [11] But you say that if anyone tells father or mother, 'Whatever support you might have had from me is Corban' (that is, an offering to God[d])— [12] then you no longer permit doing anything for a father or mother, [13] thus making void the word of God through your tradition that you have handed on. And you do many things like this."

[14] Then he called the crowd again and said to them, "Listen to me, all of you, and understand: [15] there is nothing outside a person that by going in can defile, but the things that come out are what defile."[e]

[17] When he had left the crowd and entered the house, his disciples asked him about the parable. [18] He said to them, "Then do you also fail to understand? Do you not see that whatever goes into a person from outside cannot defile, [19] since it enters, not the heart but the stomach, and goes out into the sewer?" (Thus he declared all foods clean.) [20] And he said, "It is what comes out of a person that defiles. [21] For it is from within, from the human heart, that evil intentions come: fornication, theft, murder, [22] adultery, avarice, wickedness, deceit, licentiousness, envy, slander, pride, folly.

a Other ancient authorities read *and when they come from the marketplace, they do not eat unless they purify themselves*
b Other ancient authorities add *and beds*
c Gk *walk*
d Gk lacks *to God*
e Other ancient authorities add verse 16, *"Let anyone with ears to hear listen"*

followers disagreed with the Pharisees on hand washing, they were in agreement with many, if not most Jews. **6–8:** Isa 29.13. Mark recognized the *commandment of God,* but disputes arise here over which are still binding (v. 19), and also which practices are merely human tradition. *Hypocrite,* a term from Greek drama, means one who plays a part, applied to a person who has only the appearance of righteousness (12.15; Mt 23; *Did.* 8.1). As in 2.25–26, there are multiple responses to the challenge; one response was the exaggerated, humorous, and even scatological (v. 15), implicitly comparing eliminated body waste to nonkosher food, a comparison that is undercut in vv. 20–22. Another response is the scriptural and legal arguments (vv. 6–13). **11:** The controversy here involves both the determination of which part of Torah, honoring parents or keeping vows, supersedes the other, and also whether a vow can be repudiated. In the Mishnah (*m. Ned.* 9.1) there is a discussion of "opening the way" to repentance (i.e., of allowing one who has vowed something to be released from the vow if it leads to a conflict with something more important). *Corban,* Heb ("korban") for a gift to God. When something had been declared devoted to God, it was generally not permitted for the giver to take back the gift. Rabbinic tradition, as noted above, also allowed release from "korban" when it deprived parents of their due. **14–23:** The witty rejoinder is now treated as a special revelation: *Listen . . . understand* (v. 14), *parable* (v. 17); cf. 4.3n. **18–23:** Like other parables, this one requires an interpretation. **19:** *Declared all foods clean,* literally and more accurately, "cleansed all foods." The first issue, washing practices, is expanded here to refer to all kosher laws. Matthew omits this addition and Luke does not include this episode. There are several distinct possibilities here. The declaration may reflect Mark's rejection of Jewish food laws (cf. Rom 14.20), or an older Jewish apocalyptic tradition of the transformations of impurity at the end (Zech 14.20; "Impurity and Healing," p. 63). Further, since this line and the descriptions of Jewish practices in vv. 3–4 above are not found in Matthew, they may have been added when the Gospel was brought into an understanding of Jesus' teaching that was compatible with Paul. Concerning Jesus' own teaching on this point, it is unlikely that the controversy over Torah among the early followers of Jesus would have been as intense if there had been a tradition going back to him that nullified Torah in this way. In either case, v. 19 likely goes beyond Jesus' own practice, even if he had said v. 15.

[23] All these evil things come from within, and they defile a person."

[24] From there he set out and went away to the region of Tyre.[a] He entered a house and did not want anyone to know he was there. Yet he could not escape notice, [25] but a woman whose little daughter had an unclean spirit immediately heard about him, and she came and bowed down at his feet. [26] Now the woman was a Gentile, of Syrophoenician origin. She begged him to cast the demon out of her daughter. [27] He said to her, "Let the children be fed first, for it is not fair to take the children's food and throw it to the dogs." [28] But she answered him, "Sir,[b] even the dogs under the table eat the children's crumbs." [29] Then he said to her, "For saying that, you may go—the demon has left your daughter." [30] So she went home, found the child lying on the bed, and the demon gone.

[31] Then he returned from the region of Tyre, and went by way of Sidon towards the Sea of Galilee, in the region of the Decapolis. [32] They brought to him a deaf man who had an impediment in his speech; and they begged him to lay his hand on him. [33] He took him aside in private, away from the crowd, and put his fingers into his ears, and he spat and touched his tongue. [34] Then looking up to heaven, he sighed and said to him, "Ephphatha," that is, "Be opened." [35] And immediately his ears were opened, his tongue was released, and he spoke plainly. [36] Then Jesus[c] ordered them to tell no one; but the more he ordered them, the more zealously they proclaimed it. [37] They were astounded beyond measure, saying, "He has done everything well; he even makes the deaf to hear and the mute to speak."

8 In those days when there was again a great crowd without anything to eat, he called his disciples and said to them, [2] "I have compassion for the crowd, because they have been with me now for three days and have nothing to eat. [3] If I send them away hungry to their homes, they will faint on the way—and some of them have come from a great distance." [4] His disciples replied, "How can one feed these people with bread here in the desert?" [5] He asked them, "How many loaves do you have?" They said, "Seven." [6] Then he ordered the crowd to sit down on the ground; and he took the seven loaves, and after giving thanks he broke them and gave them to his disciples to distribute; and they distributed them to the crowd. [7] They had also a few small fish; and after blessing them, he ordered that these too should be distributed.

[a] Other ancient authorities add *and Sidon*
[b] Or *Lord*; other ancient authorities prefix *Yes*
[c] Gk *he*

7.24–30: Syrophoenician woman (Mt 15.21–28). **26:** *Gentile*, lit., "Hellenis," i.e., "Greek," here used as a general term for non-Jew. *Syrophoenician* refers to Phoenicians from Syria as opposed to North Africa. Those nations who inhabited the land before Israel's arrival—Canaanites, Moabites, and so on—were viewed as inherently wicked and dangerous, but there were surprising exceptions, such as Ruth the Moabite, Achior the Ammonite, or the craftsmen of Tyre and Sidon, Phoenician (Canaanite) cities (1 Kings 5.1–12). Elijah and Elisha had also healed Gentiles (1 Kings 17.8–16; 2 Kings 5.1–14), and at Isa 56.1–8 foreigners (and eunuchs) are accepted. The Syrophoenician woman is another such surprising example; she may represent Gentile converts among the early followers of Jesus in general. **27–29:** *Dogs*, a highly insulting name, dogs were regarded as shameless and unclean (the term is still used in a derogatory way in Rev 22.15). Jesus' first meeting with Gentiles was not successful (5.17), but after this episode his attitude becomes more open (8.1–10).

7.31–37: Healing a deaf man (Mt 15.29–31). In rabbinic sources a deaf person, "ḥeresh," is often considered similar to being a minor, "qatan," or mentally ill, "shoteh"; that is, such a person is not considered responsible for observing the law (*b. Yebam.* 99b). **33–34:** *Spat . . . touched . . . sighed*, on the physical aspects of healings in this period see Introduction. *Ephphatha*, Aramaic, another indication (see 5.41n.) of the original Aramaic-language versions of Gospel narratives. **36:** The ironic contrast between the messianic secret and the thronging of followers is emphasized. **37:** Isa 35.5–6.

8.1–10: Feeding of four thousand (Mt 15.32–39). A second feeding miracle, this time in a predominantly Gentile area (see 6.30–44n.). There were two instances of feeding in the wilderness during the Exodus (Ex 16; Num 12). **5:** *Seven* may be a symbolic number for completeness, as it is in the days of creation (Gen 1) or the fullness of praise ("seven times a day," Ps 119.164).

[8] They ate and were filled; and they took up the broken pieces left over, seven baskets full. [9] Now there were about four thousand people. And he sent them away. [10] And immediately he got into the boat with his disciples and went to the district of Dalmanutha.[a]

[11] The Pharisees came and began to argue with him, asking him for a sign from heaven, to test him. [12] And he sighed deeply in his spirit and said, "Why does this generation ask for a sign? Truly I tell you, no sign will be given to this generation." [13] And he left them, and getting into the boat again, he went across to the other side.

[14] Now the disciples[b] had forgotten to bring any bread; and they had only one loaf with them in the boat. [15] And he cautioned them, saying, "Watch out—beware of the yeast of the Pharisees and the yeast of Herod."[c] [16] They said to one another, "It is because we have no bread." [17] And becoming aware of it, Jesus said to them, "Why are you talking about having no bread? Do you still not perceive or understand? Are your hearts hardened? [18] Do you have eyes, and fail to see? Do you have ears, and fail to hear? And do you not remember? [19] When I broke the five loaves for the five thousand, how many baskets full of broken pieces did you collect?" They said to him, "Twelve." [20] "And the seven for the four thousand, how many baskets full of broken pieces did you collect?" And they said to him, "Seven." [21] Then he said to them, "Do you not yet understand?"

[22] They came to Bethsaida. Some people[d] brought a blind man to him and begged him to touch him. [23] He took the blind man by the hand and led him out of the village; and when he had put saliva on his eyes and laid his hands on him, he asked him, "Can you see anything?" [24] And the man[e] looked up and said, "I can see people, but they look like trees, walking." [25] Then Jesus[e] laid his hands

a Other ancient authorities read *Mageda* or *Magdala*
b Gk *they*
c Other ancient authorities read *the Herodians*
d Gk *They*
e Gk *he*

8.11–13: Pharisees demand a sign (Mt 12.38–39; 16.1–4; Lk 11.16,29). **11:** *Sign,* Gk "sēmeion," Heb "'ot," is the action of the prophet that verifies that he has been sent from God, commonly used for the end-time prophets that Josephus describes (*Ant.* 20.167–70). Mark characterizes Jesus' miracles in different terms by calling them "acts of power," "dunameis," rather than signs; see 13.22, and contrast Jn 2.11; 4.54. In the Hebrew Bible signs are sometimes ignored (e.g., Ex 4.8,9); God provides them as indications of promise (Judg 6, where Gideon is given three signs; Isa 7.11–14, where the king demurs and is given a sign anyway).

8.14–21: Leaven (yeast) of the Pharisees and Herod (Mt 16.5–12; Lk 12.1). **15:** *Pharisees . . . Herod,* see Introduction. *Yeast* or leaven (Heb "ḥamets"), dough made of wheat, barley, spelt, rye, or oats, mixed with water and allowed to stand until soured. It is not eaten on Passover (Ex 12.39), and anyone who does consume it then is considered to be cut off (Ex 12.19). It is not allowed as part of the meal offering (Lev 2.11). **18:** *Eyes . . . see . . . ears . . . hear,* proverbial for failure to heed the word of God (Isa 6.9–10; Jer 5.21) but also characteristic of idols (Ps 115.3–8).

8.22–10.52: Second major section: Passion predictions and social teachings. This section begins and ends with miracles of people who are blind but then are able to see. At the center are three nearly identical predictions of the suffering and death of Jesus, associated with the concept of "way" (8.27–33; 9.30–37; 10.32–34), and social teachings. The literary practice employed here—circling back to the beginning of a passage by echoing it at the end—is called "inclusio," and in the absence of chapter breaks and other such visual indicators was a means of showing where a unit in an ancient narrative was completed. By using this device, Mark emphasizes true understanding into the meaning of Jesus' role—and lack thereof.

8.22–26: Healing of a blind man (Jn 9.1–7). **22:** *Bethsaida* was located at the upper end of the Sea of Galilee, in the territory of (Herod) Philip, one of Herod the Great's sons, who ruled from 4 BCE to 34 CE. Philip rebuilt the city and renamed it "Bethsaida Julias" after Julia, one of Caesar's daughters. Both Matthew and Luke omit this episode, perhaps because it depicts Jesus' inability to heal immediately. This depiction of a two-stage healing may anticipate the two-stage reception of Jesus' messianic identity: the disciples have lack of clear vision (they understand Jesus is the "messiah," but they don't know what the term means) and they only grasp the full reality later, after Jesus' death (and after the close of Mark's Gospel; see 16.8n.).

on his eyes again; and he looked intently and his sight was restored, and he saw everything clearly. [26] Then he sent him away to his home, saying, "Do not even go into the village."[a]

[27] Jesus went on with his disciples to the villages of Caesarea Philippi; and on the way he asked his disciples, "Who do people say that I am?" [28] And they answered him, "John the Baptist; and others, Elijah; and still others, one of the prophets." [29] He asked them, "But who do you say that I am?" Peter answered him, "You are the Messiah."[b] [30] And he sternly ordered them not to tell anyone about him.

[31] Then he began to teach them that the Son of Man must undergo great suffering, and be rejected by the elders, the chief priests, and the scribes, and be killed, and after three days rise again. [32] He said all this quite openly. And Peter took him aside and began to rebuke him. [33] But turning and looking at his disciples, he rebuked Peter and said, "Get behind me, Satan! For you are setting your mind not on divine things but on human things."

[34] He called the crowd with his disciples, and said to them, "If any want to become my followers, let them deny themselves and take up their cross and follow me. [35] For those who want to save their life will lose it, and those who lose their life for my sake, and for the sake of the gospel,[c] will save it. [36] For what will it profit them to gain the whole world and forfeit their life? [37] Indeed, what can they give in return for their life? [38] Those who are ashamed of me and of my words[d] in this

[a] Other ancient authorities add *or tell anyone in the village*
[b] Or *the Christ*
[c] Other ancient authorities read *lose their life for the sake of the gospel*
[d] Other ancient authorities read *and of mine*

8.27–33: Peter's confession and Jesus' first Passion prediction (Mt 16.13–23; Lk 9.18–22). Mark subordinates the expectation of a future Son of Man coming in power to the Son of Man suffering and being crucified. Although up to now Jesus has been opposed by Pharisees, on only one occasion (3.6) was there a suggestion that they wanted to kill him. From this point on it is the *elders, chief priests, and the scribes* who will reject Jesus and turn him over to the Roman governor to be *killed.* The Pharisees drop out of the Passion narrative. **27:** *Caesarea Philippi,* originally Panion after the god Pan, to whom there was an important cult site, was re-founded under Herod's son Philip, who renamed it in honor of the emperor and himself. A major temple, probably dedicated to the emperor, has been discovered nearby. Perhaps because it was situated near a spring, a source of the Jordan River, and below a sacred mountain (Mount Hermon), it became a sacred site. The ancient Israelite shrine of Dan was near here, and this was the site of the revelations to Enoch (*1 En.* 13.7) . Not only Peter's confession but also the Transfiguration (9.2–10) are located at this center, important to Jews and non-Jews alike. The mountain of the Transfiguration is not named, but the geographical indications in the text indicate that the mountain was likely to have been Mount Hermon: after the Transfiguration and the healing in 9.14–29, Jesus and his disciples went into Galilee and ended up at Capernaum (9.35), on the northwestern shore of the Sea of Galilee and not far from the border with Philip's tetrarchy. **27–28:** The disciples say that Jesus has been associated with prophetic figures, but now Peter articulates a different identity, that of the messiah (see 1.1n.). **30–32:** The messianic secret is most explicit here; *quite openly* clearly applies only to Jesus' discourse with his disciples. Peter's fuller confession is found at Mt 16.16–22. **31:** *Must undergo* expresses the determinism of God's plan, similar to apocalyptic texts like Daniel, *4 Ezra*, and *1 Enoch*. However, from the audience's perspective, this "future" is already in the past and confirmed by history. **32–33:** Peter cannot imagine a messiah who suffers and dies. Cf. Zech 3.2 where in the presence of Joshua the high priest—Jesus in Greek!—God rebukes Satan with similar language. Jewish tradition often turned to the question of the suffering of good people (Prov 3.12, "the LORD reproves the one he loves," and *b. Sanh.* 101a–b), but here the discrepancy in understanding appears to concern the role of the messiah and Son of Man. Later Christian tradition understood the suffering of the messiah by referring to Isa 52.13–53.12.

8.34–9.1: On discipleship (Mt 16.24–28; Lk 9.23–27; cf. Mt 10.32–33; Lk 12.4–9). **8.34–38:** Mark emphasizes the high stakes, necessity of decision, and the potential for persecution; the greater the eternal danger, the greater the salvation, and the greater the necessity of being part of the elect community. The turbulent events and interparty strife of the period leading up to the Jewish War and afterwards would make this language even more compelling. **35:** *Save . . . lose . . . lose . . . save,* self-preservation cannot be the highest value. **38:** *This adul-*

adulterous and sinful generation, of them the Son of Man will also be ashamed when he comes in the glory of his Father with the holy angels." **9** [1] And he said to them, "Truly I tell you, there are some standing here who will not taste death until they see that the kingdom of God has come with[a] power."

[2] Six days later, Jesus took with him Peter and James and John, and led them up a high mountain apart, by themselves. And he was transfigured before them, [3] and his clothes became dazzling white, such as no one[b] on earth could bleach them. [4] And there appeared to them Elijah with Moses, who were talking with Jesus. [5] Then Peter said to Jesus, "Rabbi, it is good for us to be here; let us make three dwellings,[c] one for you, one for Moses, and one for Elijah." [6] He did not know what to say, for they were terrified. [7] Then a cloud overshadowed them, and from the cloud there came a voice, "This is my Son, the Beloved;[d] listen to him!" [8] Suddenly when they looked around, they saw no one with them any more, but only Jesus.

[9] As they were coming down the mountain, he ordered them to tell no one about what they had seen, until after the Son of Man had risen from the dead. [10] So they kept the matter to themselves, questioning what this rising from the dead could mean. [11] Then they asked him, "Why do the scribes say that Elijah must come first?" [12] He said to them, "Elijah is indeed coming first to restore all things. How then is it written about the Son of Man, that he is to go through many sufferings and be treated with contempt? [13] But I tell you that Elijah has come, and they did to him whatever they pleased, as it is written about him."

[14] When they came to the disciples, they saw a great crowd around them, and some scribes arguing with them. [15] When the whole crowd saw him, they were immediately overcome with awe, and they ran forward to greet him. [16] He asked them, "What are you arguing about with them?" [17] Someone from the crowd answered him, "Teacher, I brought you my son; he has a spirit that makes him unable to speak; [18] and whenever it seizes

[a] Or *in*
[b] Gk *no fuller*
[c] Or *tents*
[d] Or *my beloved Son*

terous and sinful generation, like those who murmured against Moses (Deut 32.20). Adultery, as in the Hebrew Bible, is a stand-in for sin generally, especially the sin of idolatry (e.g., Jer 3.1–5). The *Son of Man* is the figure who will carry out the divine judgment. **9.1:** *Some standing here,* depending on how readers understood this promise, it can mean the crucifixion (the *power* of the *kingdom of God* as the expression of sacrificial love) or the beginning of the eschatological age (perhaps seen as the destruction of the Temple in 70 CE). See 13.30–33 for a different expression of the promise followed by an absolute expression of ignorance about its timing.

9.2–13: Transfiguration of Jesus and prophecies about Elijah (Mt 17.1–13; Lk 9.28–36). Mark's Gospel lacks a depiction of the resurrected Christ (16.8n.), and some scholars argue that the Transfiguration was originally a resurrection appearance (like those in Mt 28, Lk 24, and Jn 20), but one that was placed back into the narrative of the life of Jesus before the crucifixion—a representation of the glorified, resurrected Jesus within the human life of Jesus. Although it lacks the commissioning motif typical of the other Gospels' resurrection appearances (see e.g., Mt 28.18–20), that element would be omitted had the scene been moved. Further, this passage is similar to the "departures" of Moses (Deut 34.6) and Elijah (2 Kings 2.11), and to Roman depictions of the ascension of the emperor to heaven (Livy 1.16). **2:** The *mountain* is likely Mount Hermon (see 8.27n.). **4:** *Moses, Elijah,* these figures represent the covenant of Torah and the prophetic denunciations of corruption and idolatry, respectively. Moses, who spoke with God face to face, died, but his burial place was unknown (Deut 34.6); Elijah was taken up in the whirlwind to heaven by the chariots and horses of fire (2 Kings 2.1–12). Both therefore can represent those who stand in God's presence and communicate God's word. **5:** The *dwellings* may suggest Sukkot. There were prophets who believed God would intervene at one of the pilgrimage festivals, usually Passover or Sukkot (Zech 14.16). **7:** The *cloud* could evoke either the biblical motif of God as storm god (Dan 7.13), or perhaps more specifically the cloud of the tent of meeting (Ex 40.34–38). *My Son, the Beloved,* Mk 1.9–11n.

9.14–29: Healing of a possessed boy (Mt 17.14–21; Lk 9.37–43). **14:** The argument with the *scribes* is not explained. **17–19:** The failure of the *disciples* is attributed to lack of faith, as contrasted with the father and with Jesus' promise (v. 23). An account in the Hebrew Bible (2 Kings 4.11–37) relates a failure of Elisha's servant, Gehazi,

him, it dashes him down; and he foams and grinds his teeth and becomes rigid; and I asked your disciples to cast it out, but they could not do so." [19] He answered them, "You faithless generation, how much longer must I be among you? How much longer must I put up with you? Bring him to me." [20] And they brought the boy[a] to him. When the spirit saw him, immediately it convulsed the boy,[a] and he fell on the ground and rolled about, foaming at the mouth. [21] Jesus[b] asked the father, "How long has this been happening to him?" And he said, "From childhood. [22] It has often cast him into the fire and into the water, to destroy him; but if you are able to do anything, have pity on us and help us." [23] Jesus said to him, "If you are able!—All things can be done for the one who believes." [24] Immediately the father of the child cried out,[c] "I believe; help my unbelief!" [25] When Jesus saw that a crowd came running together, he rebuked the unclean spirit, saying to it, "You spirit that keeps this boy from speaking and hearing, I command you, come out of him, and never enter him again!" [26] After crying out and convulsing him terribly, it came out, and the boy was like a corpse, so that most of them said, "He is dead." [27] But Jesus took him by the hand and lifted him up, and he was able to stand. [28] When he had entered the house, his disciples asked him privately, "Why could we not cast it out?" [29] He said to them, "This kind can come out only through prayer."[d]

[30] They went on from there and passed through Galilee. He did not want anyone to know it; [31] for he was teaching his disciples, saying to them, "The Son of Man is to be betrayed into human hands, and they will kill him, and three days after being killed, he will rise again." [32] But they did not understand what he was saying and were afraid to ask him.

[33] Then they came to Capernaum; and when he was in the house he asked them, "What were you arguing about on the way?" [34] But they were silent, for on the way they had argued with one another who was the greatest. [35] He sat down, called the twelve, and said to them, "Whoever wants to be first must be last of all and servant of all." [36] Then he took a little child and put it among them; and taking it in his arms, he said to them, [37] "Whoever welcomes one such child in my name welcomes me, and whoever welcomes me welcomes not me but the one who sent me."

[38] John said to him, "Teacher, we saw someone[e] casting out demons in your name, and we tried to stop him, because he was not following us." [39] But Jesus said, "Do not stop him; for no one who does a deed of power in my name will be able soon afterward to speak evil of me. [40] Whoever is not against us is for us. [41] For truly I tell you, whoever gives you a cup of water to drink because you bear the name of Christ will by no means lose the reward.

a Gk *him*
b Gk *He*
c Other ancient authorities add *with tears*
d Other ancient authorities add *and fasting*
e Other ancient authorities add *who does not follow us*

to carry out a healing that Elisha later accomplishes. **18:** 6.7,13. **19:** Jesus despairs over this *generation* (8.38n.), lumping together both followers and others (cf. Deut 1:34–40; Isa 44.22; Ezek 10–11; 43–44; Zech 13.1–2; 14.20–21; 1QS 9.4, *Gen. Rab.* 30.1). **22–24:** Central is the role of faith; see 2.1–12n. The father's cry is an expression of faith in the person present—Jesus—possibly leading to faith in the God of Israel. *All things can be done*, a promise, of seemingly boundless reach, that implicitly presumes oneness of will with God.

9.30–32: Second Passion prediction (Mt 17.22–23; Lk 9.43–45). This shorter prediction contains the elements of the first (see 8.27–33n.). **31:** *Betrayed*, Isa 53.8.

9.33–10.31: Social teachings. The followers of Jesus, like those in most movements of religious renewal, understood themselves as holding to a superior ethical standard. This unit begins (9.33–35) and ends (10.31) with exhortations or statements that the first shall be last and the last first. See annotation on "inclusio," 8.22–10.52.

9.33–50: Receiving disciples (Mt 18.1–9; Lk 9.46–50). **34–37:** *Servant*, an exhortation to prepare for a lower-status position, followed up by the example. The *child* did not represent innocence but a secondary status, a

[42] "If any of you put a stumbling block before one of these little ones who believe in me,[a] it would be better for you if a great millstone were hung around your neck and you were thrown into the sea. [43] If your hand causes you to stumble, cut it off; it is better for you to enter life maimed than to have two hands and to go to hell,[b] to the unquenchable fire.[c] [45] And if your foot causes you to stumble, cut it off; it is better for you to enter life lame than to have two feet and to be thrown into hell.[b,c] [47] And if your eye causes you to stumble, tear it out; it is better for you to enter the kingdom of God with one eye than to have two eyes and to be thrown into hell,[b] [48] where their worm never dies, and the fire is never quenched.

[49] "For everyone will be salted with fire.[d] [50] Salt is good; but if salt has lost its saltiness, how can you season it?[e] Have salt in yourselves, and be at peace with one another."

10 He left that place and went to the region of Judea and[f] beyond the Jordan. And crowds again gathered around him; and, as was his custom, he again taught them.

[2] Some Pharisees came, and to test him they asked, "Is it lawful for a man to divorce his wife?" [3] He answered them, "What did Moses command you?" [4] They said, "Moses allowed a man to write a certificate of dismissal and to divorce her." [5] But Jesus said to them, "Because of your hardness of heart he wrote this commandment for you. [6] But from the beginning of creation, 'God made them male and female.' [7] 'For this reason a man shall leave his father and mother and be joined to his wife,[g] [8] and the two shall become one flesh.' So they are no longer two, but one flesh. [9] Therefore what God has joined together, let no one separate."

[10] Then in the house the disciples asked him again about this matter. [11] He said to them, "Whoever divorces his wife and marries another commits adultery against her; [12] and if she divorces her husband and marries another, she commits adultery."

[a] Other ancient authorities lack *in me*
[b] Gk *Gehenna*
[c] Verses 44 and 46 (which are identical with verse 48) are lacking in the best ancient authorities
[d] Other ancient authorities either add or substitute *and every sacrifice will be salted with salt*
[e] Or *how can you restore its saltiness?*
[f] Other ancient authorities lack *and*
[g] Other ancient authorities lack *and be joined to his wife*

lesser human. Symbolically, accepting a child *in my name*, as a true human representative, is analogous to receiving Jesus as sent from God (10.13–16). **42:** *Put a stumbling block* in this context means to discourage people, no matter how low their status in the outer world, from staying within the movement. **43:** *Hell* or "Gehenna" (see translators' note *b*), originally a valley south of Jerusalem. The site of rites condemned in Jer 7.31, it became the term for hell (Mt 5.22; Lk 12.5). The image, like that of being drowned (v. 42), is one of the destruction of the person (drowning, burning, being devoured by worms all destroy the body). **43–47:** *Hand . . . foot . . . eye*, in general, the means of carrying out sinful deeds (stealing, coveting, etc.); if sexual sins are meant specifically, there may be allusions to Heb "foot" as euphemism for genitals (Isa 7.20) and of "eye" as transgressing sexual boundaries (Lev 20.17–21). **49:** *Salted with fire*, perhaps preserved (from worse fate) by punishment that is short of destruction.

10.1–16: Marriage, divorce, and children (Mt 19.1–15; Lk 18.15–17). **1:** Jesus' travels bring him into Judea, the region of Jerusalem. **2–9:** As in 2.25–26, it appears that after a challenge from the Pharisees (v. 2), the original clever retort (v. 9) was supplemented by a scriptural and legal argument (vv. 3–8). Here a rigor greater than that in Torah is held up for emulation: the *commandment* allowing divorce was given because of *hardness of heart*. Mark insists that the prohibition of divorce (Deut 24.1–4) goes back to creation (Gen 1.27; 2.24), a legal move not unlike Paul's critique of the law (Gal 3.17). The prohibition of divorce appears in many early texts of the followers of Jesus (Mt 5.32; 1 Cor 7.10–11) and may derive from Jesus himself. Some interpreters argue that it was introduced to protect women from being abandoned without support, but there is nothing in any of these texts to suggest this. Further, the Qumran sect also prohibited divorce with the same scriptural argument as here: marriage was ordained at creation (CD 4.19–5.2). Among his followers the prohibition of divorce might have addressed the situation of those who were separating for celibacy (Mt 19.10–12; Lk 18.29–30; 1 Cor 7.5). The same may be true for the affirmation of children in vv. 13–16 (contrast Wis 4.1–9). **11–12:** Biblical law allowed only men

[13] People were bringing little children to him in order that he might touch them; and the disciples spoke sternly to them. [14] But when Jesus saw this, he was indignant and said to them, "Let the little children come to me; do not stop them; for it is to such as these that the kingdom of God belongs. [15] Truly I tell you, whoever does not receive the kingdom of God as a little child will never enter it." [16] And he took them up in his arms, laid his hands on them, and blessed them.

[17] As he was setting out on a journey, a man ran up and knelt before him, and asked him, "Good Teacher, what must I do to inherit eternal life?" [18] Jesus said to him, "Why do you call me good? No one is good but God alone. [19] You know the commandments: 'You shall not murder; You shall not commit adultery; You shall not steal; You shall not bear false witness; You shall not defraud; Honor your father and mother.'" [20] He said to him, "Teacher, I have kept all these since my youth." [21] Jesus, looking at him, loved him and said, "You lack one thing; go, sell what you own, and give the money[a] to the poor, and you will have treasure in heaven; then come, follow me." [22] When he heard this, he was shocked and went away grieving, for he had many possessions.

[23] Then Jesus looked around and said to his disciples, "How hard it will be for those who have wealth to enter the kingdom of God!" [24] And the disciples were perplexed at these words. But Jesus said to them again, "Children, how hard it is[b] to enter the kingdom of God! [25] It is easier for a camel to go through the eye of a needle than for someone who is rich to enter the kingdom of God." [26] They were greatly astounded and said to one another,[c] "Then who can be saved?" [27] Jesus looked at them and said, "For mortals it is impossible, but not for God; for God all things are possible."

[28] Peter began to say to him, "Look, we have left everything and followed you." [29] Jesus said, "Truly I tell you, there is no one who has left house or brothers or sisters or mother or father or children or fields, for my sake and for the sake of the good news,[d] [30] who will not receive a hundredfold now in this age—houses, brothers and sisters, mothers and children, and fields, with persecutions—and in the age to come eternal life. [31] But many who are first will be last, and the last will be first."

[32] They were on the road, going up to Jerusalem, and Jesus was walking ahead of them; they were amazed, and those who followed were afraid. He took the twelve aside again and began to tell them what was to happen to him, [33] saying, "See, we are going up to Jerusalem, and the Son of Man will be handed over to the chief priests and the scribes, and they will condemn him to death; then they will hand

a Gk lacks *the money*
b Other ancient authorities add *for those who trust in riches*
c Other ancient authorities read *to him*
d Or *gospel*

to initiate divorce (Deut 24.1–4), but in this period Jewish women, in accordance with Roman law, also initiated divorces, as Mark and Paul assumed. **13–16:** Perhaps the *disciples* spoke *sternly* to those bringing children because they were still concerned with distinctions of status; see 9.34. *Receive the kingdom of God as a little child,* without regard to one's position in it; perhaps also without insisting that it come to one by merit, but simply as given, just as children "receive" their upbringing.

10.17–31: Riches and entering the kingdom of God (Mt 19.16–30; Lk 18.18–30). **17:** *Eternal life,* life with God (the only eternal being); here treated as synonymous with entering the kingdom of God (v. 24). **18:** *Why do you call me good?* Jesus' reply is going to be based on the Torah that the young man has known all his life; he does not need a new teaching from Jesus, but rather the old teaching from the *God* who is *good.* **19–20:** The *commandments* here are from the second half of the Ten Commandments (Ex 20.1–17), those concerning relations among people, but the man's performance of deeds for others has fallen short of the care of the poor (cf. Deut 24.17–22; Am 2.6 and many other passages in the Hebrew Bible; 2 Cor 8,9; Jas 2.1–7; Acts 2.43–47; 4.32–5.11). **21:** *Loved him,* perhaps meaning "wished for his good." **25:** Contrary to a commonly cited medieval legend, there is no narrow "Eye of the Needle" gate in Jerusalem. A Talmudic parallel (*b. Ber.* 55b) uses a needle's eye and an elephant to make the same point.

him over to the Gentiles; [34] they will mock him, and spit upon him, and flog him, and kill him; and after three days he will rise again."

[35] James and John, the sons of Zebedee, came forward to him and said to him, "Teacher, we want you to do for us whatever we ask of you." [36] And he said to them, "What is it you want me to do for you?" [37] And they said to him, "Grant us to sit, one at your right hand and one at your left, in your glory." [38] But Jesus said to them, "You do not know what you are asking. Are you able to drink the cup that I drink, or be baptized with the baptism that I am baptized with?" [39] They replied, "We are able." Then Jesus said to them, "The cup that I drink you will drink; and with the baptism with which I am baptized, you will be baptized; [40] but to sit at my right hand or at my left is not mine to grant, but it is for those for whom it has been prepared."

[41] When the ten heard this, they began to be angry with James and John. [42] So Jesus called them and said to them, "You know that among the Gentiles those whom they recognize as their rulers lord it over them, and their great ones are tyrants over them. [43] But it is not so among you; but whoever wishes to become great among you must be your servant, [44] and whoever wishes to be first among you must be slave of all. [45] For the Son of Man came not to be served but to serve, and to give his life a ransom for many."

[46] They came to Jericho. As he and his disciples and a large crowd were leaving Jericho, Bartimaeus son of Timaeus, a blind beggar, was sitting by the roadside. [47] When he heard that it was Jesus of Nazareth, he began to shout out and say, "Jesus, Son of David, have mercy on me!" [48] Many sternly ordered him to be quiet, but he cried out even more loudly, "Son of David, have mercy on me!" [49] Jesus stood still and said, "Call him here." And they called the blind man, saying to him, "Take heart; get up, he is calling you." [50] So throwing off his cloak, he sprang up and came to Jesus. [51] Then Jesus said to him, "What do you want me to do for you?" The blind man said to him, "My teacher,[a] let me see again." [52] Jesus said to him, "Go; your faith has made you well." Immediately he regained his sight and followed him on the way.

11 When they were approaching Jerusalem, at Bethphage and Bethany, near the Mount of Olives, he sent two of his disciples [2] and said to them, "Go into the village ahead

[a] Aramaic *Rabbouni*

10.32–45: Third Passion prediction (Mt 20.17–28; Lk 18.31–34; 22.24–27). **38:** *Cup*, a metaphor for consequences that must be accepted (Ps 75.8; cf. Isa 51.17,22), usually merited suffering resulting from one's wrongdoing; Jesus' use of the metaphor indicates that he is accepting the cup in place of others; see 14.36. *Baptism*, John had predicted (1.8) that Jesus would baptize "with the Holy Spirit"; Jesus here accepts the consequences of that baptism. **42–45:** Mark provides a concise description of the Roman aristocratic political system. As the previous two chapters indicate, the followers of Jesus are to create an alternative community. **42:** *Great ones*, 9.33–37. **45:** The climax of this middle section: even James and John expect the Son of Man to come in glory, but he will serve and die as a ransom, Gk "lytron," Heb "'asham." Though there has been lengthy discussion among Christian thinkers about how such ransom is deemed to work, and what it accomplishes, there is no settled agreement about the meaning of this phrase, *give his life a ransom for many*. Theories have included the idea that the payment was made to satisfy a penalty for human wrongdoing, to avert divine retribution (see above on "cup," v. 38n.), or as a sacrifice (like the Temple sacrifices) to cleanse the followers of Jesus from their sins. The phrase *for many* may indicate an expiatory sacrifice (see 14.24n.; Isa 53.12), but only in the eleventh century did this notion come to dominate western Christian theology.

10.46–52: Blind Bartimaeus (Mt 20.29–34; Lk 18.35–43). **46:** *Bartimaeus* means *son of Timaeus*. **47:** *Son of David, have mercy on me* was likely a standardized form of words in a petitionary prayer. Some Jewish healers healed in the name of Solomon, the original son of David (*Ant.* 8.42–49). In *Pss. Sol.* 17.21, the coming king will be the son of David: "See, O Lord, and raise up for them their king, the son of David / at the time which you choose, O God, to rule over Israel your servant." In both Matthew (1.6–7) and Luke (1.27; 3.31) Joseph is given a genealogy that includes David, but Mark does not have any such information.

11.1–16.8: Last major section. Passion and death.

11.1–11: Entry into Jerusalem (Mt 21.1–9; Lk 19.28–38; Jn 12.12–19). **1:** *Mount of Olives* or Olivet is the site of the final battle against the nations according to Zech 14.4. A contemporary prophet-leader, the so-called Egyptian

of you, and immediately as you enter it, you will find tied there a colt that has never been ridden; untie it and bring it. [3] If anyone says to you, 'Why are you doing this?' just say this, 'The Lord needs it and will send it back here immediately.'" [4] They went away and found a colt tied near a door, outside in the street. As they were untying it, [5] some of the bystanders said to them, "What are you doing, untying the colt?" [6] They told them what Jesus had said; and they allowed them to take it. [7] Then they brought the colt to Jesus and threw their cloaks on it; and he sat on it. [8] Many people spread their cloaks on the road, and others spread leafy branches that they had cut in the fields. [9] Then those who went ahead and those who followed were shouting,

"Hosanna!
 Blessed is the one who comes in the name of the Lord!
 [10] Blessed is the coming kingdom of our ancestor David!
 Hosanna in the highest heaven!"

[11] Then he entered Jerusalem and went into the temple; and when he had looked around at everything, as it was already late, he went out to Bethany with the twelve.

[12] On the following day, when they came from Bethany, he was hungry. [13] Seeing in the distance a fig tree in leaf, he went to see whether perhaps he would find anything on it. When he came to it, he found nothing but leaves, for it was not the season for figs. [14] He said to it, "May no one ever eat fruit from you again." And his disciples heard it.

[15] Then they came to Jerusalem. And he entered the temple and began to drive out those who were selling and those who were buying in the temple, and he overturned the tables of the money changers and the seats of those who sold doves; [16] and he would not allow anyone to carry anything through the temple. [17] He was teaching and saying, "Is it not written,

prophet, had also announced that God would appear on the Mount of Olives (*Ant.* 20.168–72). **2:** The apocalyptic vision of Zech 9.9 prophesies the need for a colt, but the coronation of a king in Israel also included the colt (Gen 49.11), as well as including the garments of v. 8 (2 Kings 9.13). **8:** *Leafy branches*, see 1 Macc 13.51. **9:** *Hosanna*, "save, we pray!" in Aramaic, not Hebrew. The quotation is from Ps 118.25–26, sung at the pilgrimage festivals of Passover, Shavuot (Weeks), and Sukkot (Booths). **10:** Not a quotation, but an addition to make the connection with the *coming* Davidic *kingdom*.

11.12–25: Cursing of the fig tree and the prophetic judgment against the temple (Mt 21.12–13,18–22; Lk 19.45–48). **15–18:** The Gospel of John places the temple action very early (2.13–22), but Mark, followed by Matthew and Luke, depicts it as preceding the trial and crucifixion. The scholarly consensus is that Mark has the correct placement: the Temple scene was likely the act of Jesus that provoked his execution by the Roman authorities. The *temple* compound was the largest in the ancient world in terms of area. In the outer court (only later called the court of the Gentiles) money changers and animal merchants conducted the business necessary for pilgrims to provide sacrifices. **14:** The reason for this curse is not given in the text. Destruction or withering of a fig tree is one image of God's judgment (Isa 34.4; Jer 5.17). **15–17:** Why Jesus objects is not clear. Christian tradition has held that Jesus condemns Temple sacrifices and worship in principle and is announcing the transition from Jewish law to faith in Christ. The text nowhere suggests this. Scholars are split in focusing on (1) a violation of the sanctity of the Temple (cf. *m. Ber.* 9.5, not relating to money but with general behavior in the Temple precincts); (2) *for all the nations* as meaning an end to the exclusion of Gentiles; or (3) the purported economic injustice of the Roman-appointed Temple establishment in requiring money to be changed at a discount favorable to the Temple. But the text does not explicitly mention any of these possible motivations. The fall of the first Temple as a result of sin is mourned in some of the prophets, e.g., Isa 64:11. Mark combines Isa 56.7 and Jer 7.11, while John 2.16–17 quotes Ps 69.9 and alludes to Zech 14.21. The original account may therefore not have included a quotation, since the two versions of it give different ones; the passage may have been presented as a prophetic act. Mark's quotations are often interpreted as an affirmation of the inclusion of Gentiles, but the Isaiah quotation concerns the acceptance of both eunuchs and foreigners; the former are included and the latter observe God's laws without necessarily becoming Jews. The allusion to Jer 7.11, *den of robbers*, may suggest that Mark is opposed to abuses by Temple authorities or the selling of sacrificial animals in the outer court of the Temple, as v. 16 indicates. The context of Jer 7.1–15 is a condemnation of abuses by the people and the false sense of security that they may take in the Temple; it is not clear what particular abuses Mark may have in mind.

'My house shall be called a house of prayer
for all the nations'?
But you have made it a den of robbers."
[18] And when the chief priests and the scribes heard it, they kept looking for a way to kill him; for they were afraid of him, because the whole crowd was spellbound by his teaching. [19] And when evening came, Jesus and his disciples[a] went out of the city.

[20] In the morning as they passed by, they saw the fig tree withered away to its roots. [21] Then Peter remembered and said to him, "Rabbi, look! The fig tree that you cursed has withered." [22] Jesus answered them, "Have[b] faith in God. [23] Truly I tell you, if you say to this mountain, 'Be taken up and thrown into the sea,' and if you do not doubt in your heart, but believe that what you say will come to pass, it will be done for you. [24] So I tell you, whatever you ask for in prayer, believe that you have received[c] it, and it will be yours.

[25] "Whenever you stand praying, forgive, if you have anything against anyone; so that your Father in heaven may also forgive you your trespasses."[d]

[27] Again they came to Jerusalem. As he was walking in the temple, the chief priests, the scribes, and the elders came to him [28] and said, "By what authority are you doing these things? Who gave you this authority to do them?" [29] Jesus said to them, "I will ask you one question; answer me, and I will tell you by what authority I do these things. [30] Did the baptism of John come from heaven, or was it of human origin? Answer me." [31] They argued with one another, "If we say, 'From heaven,' he will say, 'Why then did you not believe him?' [32] But shall we say, 'Of human origin'?"—they were afraid of the crowd, for all regarded John as truly a prophet. [33] So they answered Jesus, "We do not know." And Jesus said to them, "Neither will I tell you by what authority I am doing these things."

12 Then he began to speak to them in parables. "A man planted a vineyard, put a fence around it, dug a pit for the wine press, and built a watchtower; then he leased it to tenants and went to another country. [2] When the season came, he sent a slave to the tenants to collect from them his share of the produce of the vineyard. [3] But they seized him, and beat him, and sent him away empty-handed. [4] And again he sent another slave to them; this one they beat over the head and insulted. [5] Then he sent another, and that one they killed. And so it was with many others; some they beat, and others they killed. [6] He had still one other, a beloved son. Finally he sent him to them, saying, 'They will respect my son.' [7] But those tenants said to one another, 'This is the heir; come, let us kill him, and the inheritance will be ours.' [8] So they seized him, killed him, and threw him out of the vineyard. [9] What then will the owner of the vineyard do? He will come and destroy the tenants and give the vineyard to others. [10] Have you not read this scripture:

a Gk *they*: other ancient authorities read *he*
b Other ancient authorities read *"If you have*
c Other ancient authorities read *are receiving*
d Other ancient authorities add verse 26, *"But if you do not forgive, neither will your Father in heaven forgive your trespasses."*

20–25: In Mark's treatment, the significance of the fig tree is raised dramatically, since it is now associated with a prayer that the Temple mount, the place of orderly worship and acknowledgment of God's rule, would be *taken up and thrown into the sea*, the place of primal chaos which God subdues in creation (Isa 27.1; Ps 89.9; Job 26.12). Continuing the use of fig symbolism from the prophets (Mic 7.1; Hos 9.10; cf. Lk 13.6–9), here Mark may prophesy the coming destruction of the Temple or of Israel's leaders. **25:** *Forgive. . . your Father in heaven may also forgive*, Mark does not include the Lord's Prayer (Mt 6.9–13; Lk 11.2–4), but this language echoes one of its sections. *Father*, see 14.36n.

11.27–33: Question on authority (Mt 21.23–27; Lk 20.1–8). **29–30:** The leaders try to force Jesus to make a dangerous statement, but he turns their challenge back against them by placing them in a similar dilemma.

12.1–12: Parable of the vineyard (Mt 21.33–46; Lk 20.9–19). The thrust of this parable is more judgment/less kingdom than the other parables, and requires an allegorical reading: the vineyard is Israel (Isa 5.1–7), the tenants are Israel's leaders, the servants are God's prophets, and the heir is Jesus. In Isaiah the vineyard is condemned for not producing edible grapes (idolatry and injustice are compared to wild grapes), and its destruction is predicted. Christian tradition sees this parable as a blueprint for the replacement of Judaism by the

'The stone that the builders rejected
has become the cornerstone;[a]
[11] this was the Lord's doing,
and it is amazing in our eyes'?"

[12] When they realized that he had told this parable against them, they wanted to arrest him, but they feared the crowd. So they left him and went away.

[13] Then they sent to him some Pharisees and some Herodians to trap him in what he said. [14] And they came and said to him, "Teacher, we know that you are sincere, and show deference to no one; for you do not regard people with partiality, but teach the way of God in accordance with truth. Is it lawful to pay taxes to the emperor, or not? [15] Should we pay them, or should we not?" But knowing their hypocrisy, he said to them, "Why are you putting me to the test? Bring me a denarius and let me see it." [16] And they brought one. Then he said to them, "Whose head is this, and whose title?" They answered, "The emperor's." [17] Jesus said to them, "Give to the emperor the things that are the emperor's, and to God the things that are God's." And they were utterly amazed at him.

[18] Some Sadducees, who say there is no resurrection, came to him and asked him a question, saying, [19] "Teacher, Moses wrote for us that if a man's brother dies, leaving a wife but no child, the man[b] shall marry the widow and raise up children for his brother. [20] There were seven brothers; the first married and, when he died, left no children; [21] and the second married the widow[c] and died, leaving no children; and the third likewise; [22] none of the seven left children. Last of all the woman herself died. [23] In the resurrection[d] whose wife will she be? For the seven had married her."

[24] Jesus said to them, "Is not this the reason you are wrong, that you know neither the scriptures nor the power of God? [25] For when they rise from the dead, they neither marry nor are given in marriage, but are like angels in heaven. [26] And as for the dead being raised, have you not read in the book of Moses, in the story about the bush, how God said to him, 'I am the God of Abraham, the God of Isaac, and the God of Jacob'? [27] He is God not of the dead, but of the living; you are quite wrong."

[28] One of the scribes came near and heard them disputing with one another, and seeing

[a] Or *keystone*
[b] Gk *his brother*
[c] Gk *her*
[d] Other ancient authorities add *when they rise*

church, but it can also be understood as Jesus' condemnation of Jewish officials in collusion with Rome. **10:** Ps 118.22–23. *Cornerstone*, Gk "kephalen gonias," Heb "rosh pinna," "head of the corner." A "keystone" (see translators' note *a*) is the top stone in an arch that holds the whole arch in place; a *cornerstone* is the stone on which everything else is based.

12.13–17: Taxes for Caesar (Mt 22.15–22; Lk 20.20–26). As in 11.27–33, the opponents try to elicit a politically dangerous pronouncement. In 6–7 CE a prophetic leader named Judas (also mentioned in Acts 5.37) organized a movement to worship God alone and refuse to pay the tax to Caesar (Josephus, *J.W.* 2.117–18). *Putting me to the test*, putting me on trial. The answer allows for a limited realm in which Roman rule is legitimate, but keeps Jewish practice inviolate from that realm.

12.18–27: Dispute with the Sadducees (Mt 22.23–33; Lk 20.27–40). Resurrection of the dead was not a belief in early Israel; life was believed to continue after death in the form of children and lineage (e.g., Ps 25.13). "Sheol," a place of shadowy existence (Ps 6.5), is a realm of death similar to the Greek Hades; in 1 Sam 28.7, Saul uses a "woman of spirits," a medium, to bring Samuel up from the realm of the dead ("the ground") to prophesy for him (Sheol is not mentioned in this passage, but the shadowy existence is clear). Resurrection appears first in the "Isaiah Apocalypse" (Isa 26.19) and in Dan 12.2–3 (cf. 2 Macc 7; 4 Macc; Wis 2–5; 1 Cor 15). The *Sadducees* were an aristocratic party who observed the written laws of the Torah only and not the traditions of the elders as the Pharisees did, and also differed in denying resurrection; the Pharisees, like Jesus' followers, believed in resurrection (Acts 23.6–10), and rabbinic tradition followed Pharisaic belief (*b. Sanh.* 90b–92b). **19–23:** The absurdity of the test case is meant to disprove the idea of resurrection. **25:** *Like angels*, describes beliefs similar to those found in contemporary Jewish apocalyptic texts (2 *Bar.* 51.5). **26–27:** *Story about the bush*, Ex 3.1–6. The argument surprisingly does not hinge on predictions of Jesus' resurrection, but rather on the present tense: "I am," not "I was." *God* as *living* is a common description in the Hebrew Bible (e.g., Ps 18.46; 42.2).

that he answered them well, he asked him, "Which commandment is the first of all?" [29] Jesus answered, "The first is, 'Hear, O Israel: the Lord our God, the Lord is one; [30] you shall love the Lord your God with all your heart, and with all your soul, and with all your mind, and with all your strength.' [31] The second is this, 'You shall love your neighbor as yourself.' There is no other commandment greater than these." [32] Then the scribe said to him, "You are right, Teacher; you have truly said that 'he is one, and besides him there is no other'; [33] and 'to love him with all the heart, and with all the understanding, and with all the strength,' and 'to love one's neighbor as oneself,'—this is much more important than all whole burnt offerings and sacrifices." [34] When Jesus saw that he answered wisely, he said to him, "You are not far from the kingdom of God." After that no one dared to ask him any question.

[35] While Jesus was teaching in the temple, he said, "How can the scribes say that the Messiah[a] is the son of David? [36] David himself, by the Holy Spirit, declared,

'The Lord said to my Lord,
"Sit at my right hand,
until I put your enemies under your feet."'

[37] David himself calls him Lord; so how can he be his son?" And the large crowd was listening to him with delight.

[38] As he taught, he said, "Beware of the scribes, who like to walk around in long robes, and to be greeted with respect in the marketplaces, [39] and to have the best seats in the synagogues and places of honor at banquets! [40] They devour widows' houses and for the sake of appearance say long prayers. They will receive the greater condemnation."

[41] He sat down opposite the treasury, and watched the crowd putting money into the treasury. Many rich people put in large sums. [42] A poor widow came and put in two small copper coins, which are worth a penny. [43] Then he called his disciples and said to them, "Truly I tell you, this poor widow has put in more than all those who are contributing to the treasury. [44] For all of them have contributed out of their abundance; but she out of her poverty has put in everything she had, all she had to live on."

13 As he came out of the temple, one of his disciples said to him, "Look, Teacher, what large stones and what large

[a] Or *the Christ*

12.28–34: The greatest commandment (Mt 22.34–40; Lk10.25–28). **29:** Jesus quotes Deut 6.4–5 and Lev 19.18 (combining the two quotations may not have been original to Jesus: in Luke 10.25–28, Jesus elicits the quotation from a lawyer); when Hillel was faced with a similar question he summed up the law with a dictum that is not in the Torah: "Do not do to anyone else what is hateful to you" (*b. Shabb.* 31a; cf. Tob 4.15; Mt 7.12). *Hear,* Heb "shema"; the latter became the name of the prayer recited by Jews twice a day, composed of Deut 6.4–9; 11.13–21; Num 15.37–41. **32–34:** Despite the context of the episodes before and after, the *scribe* answers Jesus positively and warmly, and Jesus responds in kind. Matthew and Luke omit these lines. Nowhere else does Mark depict scribes positively, but cf. Mt 13.52. **33:** Hos 6.6; Mic 6.6–8. **34:** *Not far from the kingdom* is presented as a warm response from Jesus, but it may be limited.

12.35–37: The messiah and David's son? (Mt 22.41–46; Lk 20.41–44). Interjected here is a short scriptural argument to the effect that the messiah is not just the son of David (i.e., a king of the Davidic line) but something greater. (See 10.47n.) Mark may have been opposing those who, during the Jewish War, longed for the military intervention of the son of David (13.6). Elsewhere Mark affirms Jesus' connection with David (2.25–26; 10.47), but the idea of "messiah" presented in Mark does not correspond to the expectations of Jesus' contemporaries. **36:** Most Jews assumed that it was David's voice who speaks in the Psalms: "The LORD (God) says to my lord (the messiah, not David) . . . ." The argument assumes that David, the purported speaker of Ps 110 (v. 1), called the messiah "my lord," indicating that the messiah was David's superior.

12.38–44: Rich scribes and a poor widow (Mt 23.6; Lk 20.46–47; 21.1–4). Matthew 23 develops this critique. Mark's version does not mention Pharisees, and is more explicitly economic: the class pretensions of the scribes lead directly to a comparison with a poor widow (omitted in Matthew). **43–44:** Some scholars suggest that Mark is critical of the woman's over-generosity, but the text does not suggest that. The Temple is a place where both rich and poor can contribute.

buildings!" [2] Then Jesus asked him, "Do you see these great buildings? Not one stone will be left here upon another; all will be thrown down."

[3] When he was sitting on the Mount of Olives opposite the temple, Peter, James, John, and Andrew asked him privately, [4] "Tell us, when will this be, and what will be the sign that all these things are about to be accomplished?" [5] Then Jesus began to say to them, "Beware that no one leads you astray. [6] Many will come in my name and say, 'I am he!'[a] and they will lead many astray. [7] When you hear of wars and rumors of wars, do not be alarmed; this must take place, but the end is still to come. [8] For nation will rise against nation, and kingdom against kingdom; there will be earthquakes in various places; there will be famines. This is but the beginning of the birth pangs.

[9] "As for yourselves, beware; for they will hand you over to councils; and you will be beaten in synagogues; and you will stand before governors and kings because of me, as a testimony to them. [10] And the good news[b] must first be proclaimed to all nations. [11] When they bring you to trial and hand you over, do not worry beforehand about what you are to say; but say whatever is given you at that time, for it is not you who speak, but the Holy Spirit. [12] Brother will betray brother to death, and a father his child, and children will rise against parents and have them put to death; [13] and you will be hated by all because of my name. But the one who endures to the end will be saved.

[14] "But when you see the desolating sacrilege set up where it ought not to be (let the reader understand), then those in Judea must flee to the mountains; [15] the one on the housetop must not go down or enter the house to take anything away; [16] the one in the field must not turn back to get a coat. [17] Woe to those who are pregnant and to those who are nursing infants in those days! [18] Pray that it may not be in winter. [19] For in those days there will be suffering, such as has not been from the beginning of the creation that God created until now, no, and never will be. [20] And if the Lord had not cut short those days, no one would be saved; but for the sake of the elect, whom he chose, he has cut short those days. [21] And if anyone says to you at that time, 'Look! Here is the Messiah!'[c] or 'Look! There he is!'—do not believe it. [22] False messiahs[d] and false prophets will appear and produce signs and omens, to lead astray, if possible, the elect. [23] But be alert; I have already told you everything.

[24] "But in those days, after that suffering,
the sun will be darkened,

a Gk *I am*
b Gk *gospel*
c Or *the Christ*
d Or *christs*

13.1–37: Prediction of the destruction of the Temple and the events of the end (Mt 24.1–36; Lk 21.5–36). Although this section of Mark is often referred to as the Markan Apocalypse, the chapter resembles prophetic texts as well (Isa 13.11; 51.6). The main themes are that apocalyptic messengers are deceitful and that discerning people will keep watch, waiting for the real end (vv. 32–33). *Beware* implies resisting the false messianic prophets, but it also implies readiness for the true events about to unfold (vv. 26–27). **3:** *Mount of Olives,* 11.1n. *Privately,* see "Parables and Kingdom," p. 68. **6:** *In my name* suggests that other followers of Jesus would have varying understandings of the events of the end-time. **7–8:** In contrast to texts such as Dan 8–12, the events of the end are disordered and cannot be treated as orderly predictions (cf. Isa 19.2; 4 *Ezra* 13.31–32). Some of the phrases here echo prophetic passages about the invasions of Jerusalem (e.g., Ezek 7.21–27). **9:** Although Mark may condemn specific *councils* and *synagogues,* they still have authority over some Jewish followers of Jesus (cf. 2 Cor 11.24–25). There is not a clean break from Judaism in the early years after Jesus' life. **10:** This verse was perhaps inserted by Mark. Jesus himself probably did not emphasize a mission to the Gentiles, certainly not a mission without the law. **14:** *Desolating sacrilege,* from Dan 11.31; 12.11 ("shiqquts meshomem"), the image of Zeus placed in the Temple by the Seleucids at the outbreak of the Maccabean Revolt in 167 BCE. In Mark it may refer to Caligula's image of himself that he intended to erect in the Temple; his assassination in 40 CE removed the threat. **19–32:** Apocalyptic motifs are incorporated here (Dan 12; *1 En.* 8.2; 83.1), and accompanied by warnings to be alert. **19:** Mark alters the apocalyptic prediction in Dan 12.1 (LXX from "until that day")—looking into the future—to "until now" (cf. Mk 10.30). **22:** *Signs and omens,* see 8.11n. *Elect* refers to those predetermined

and the moon will not give its light,
[25] and the stars will be falling from heaven,
and the powers in the heavens will be shaken.

[26] Then they will see 'the Son of Man coming in clouds' with great power and glory. [27] Then he will send out the angels, and gather his elect from the four winds, from the ends of the earth to the ends of heaven.

[28] "From the fig tree learn its lesson: as soon as its branch becomes tender and puts forth its leaves, you know that summer is near. [29] So also, when you see these things taking place, you know that he[a] is near, at the very gates. [30] Truly I tell you, this generation will not pass away until all these things have taken place. [31] Heaven and earth will pass away, but my words will not pass away.

[32] "But about that day or hour no one knows, neither the angels in heaven, nor the Son, but only the Father. [33] Beware, keep alert;[b] for you do not know when the time will come. [34] It is like a man going on a journey, when he leaves home and puts his slaves in charge, each with his work, and commands the doorkeeper to be on the watch. [35] Therefore, keep awake—for you do not know when the master of the house will come, in the evening, or at midnight, or at cockcrow, or at dawn, [36] or else he may find you asleep when he comes suddenly. [37] And what I say to you I say to all: Keep awake."

14 It was two days before the Passover and the festival of Unleavened Bread. The chief priests and the scribes were looking for a way to arrest Jesus[c] by stealth and kill him; [2] for they said, "Not during the festival, or there may be a riot among the people."

[3] While he was at Bethany in the house of Simon the leper,[d] as he sat at the table, a woman came with an alabaster jar of very costly ointment of nard, and she broke open the jar and poured the ointment on his head. [4] But some were there who said to one another in anger, "Why was the ointment wasted in this way? [5] For this ointment could have been sold for more than three hundred denarii,[e] and the money given to the poor." And they scolded her. [6] But Jesus said, "Let her alone; why do you trouble her? She has performed a good service for me. [7] For you always have the poor with you, and you can show kindness to them whenever you wish; but you will not always have me. [8] She has done what she could; she has anointed my body beforehand for its burial. [9] Truly I tell

[a] Or *it*
[b] Other ancient authorities add *and pray*
[c] Gk *him*
[d] The terms *leper* and *leprosy* can refer to several diseases
[e] The denarius was the usual day's wage for a laborer

to be saved. **24–26:** Ps 68.4; see 1.9–11n. **26:** Dan 7.13; see 2.10n. **27:** See 3.7–12n. **30:** *Generation,* see 8.38n. **31:** Isa 51.6; 54.10. **32–35:** *No one knows* is not necessarily a rejection of apocalyptic reasoning, but rather a further reason to *keep awake*; cf. *4 Ezra* 4.52.

14.1–2: Conspiracy to kill Jesus (Mt 26.1–5; Lk 22.1–2; Jn 11.47–53). The three pilgrimage festivals—Passover, Shavuot (Weeks or Pentecost), and Sukkot (Booths)—brought crowds to Jerusalem and therefore heightened tension; the Romans consequently paid careful attention at the times of these events. *Passover* was especially explosive because of its association with the Exodus; each year at the festival the Roman governor moved troops to Jerusalem to discourage an uprising. **1:** *Passover... Unleavened Bread,* Mark's phrasing suggests that he saw these as two separate events, but in fact, although they arose from different starting points—Passover as the celebration of release from bondage in Egypt, Unleavened Bread as the celebration of ripening ears of grain in the spring—they were combined into one festival with the sacrifice of the paschal lamb and eating of unleavened bread during the seven days following. Mark here and in v. 12 appears to count the days sunrise to sunrise, rather than the more typically Jewish method of sundown to sundown. This has been taken as evidence that Mark was not Jewish (see Introduction), but counting a day as sunrise to sunrise is found in some Jewish texts (*m. Pesah.* 5.1; *Ant.* 6.248,336).

14.3–11. Anointment and prediction of betrayal (Mt 26.6–16; Lk 22.3–6; Jn 12.1–8). Jesus is anointed; the action could be either that of anointing a king or of preparing a body for burial. Mark's principle of irony would suggest both. **3:** *Alabaster jar,* a small, probably globular container of carved, translucent gypsum; its long neck would be broken so the contents could be poured out. *Ointment of nard,* ointment scented with the flower of spikenard, which grows in the Himalayan region. **9:** The anointing will be retold *in remembrance of her,* but her

SCRIPTURE FULFILLMENTS

From this point Mark highlights a number of events in such a way as to fulfill scriptures (mainly Psalms and Isaiah).

MARK		
14.1	to kill by stealth	Ps 10.7–8
14.10–11	betray him	Isa 53.6,12
14.18	the one eating with me	Ps 41.9
14.24	blood poured out for many	Isa 53.12
14.57	false testimony	Ps 27.12; 35.11
14.61; 15.5	silence before accusers	Ps 38.13–14; Isa 53.7
14.65	spit on, slap him	Isa 50.6
15.5,39	amazement of nations and kings	Isa 52.15
15.6–15	criminal saved, righteous killed	Isa 53.6,12
15.24	divided his clothes	Ps 22.18
15.29	derided him and shook their heads	Ps 22.7; 109.25
15.30–31	save yourself!	Ps 22.8
15.32	taunted him	Ps 22.6
15.34	why have you forsaken me?	Ps 22.1
15.36	gave him sour wine to drink	Ps 69.21

This observation has called into question whether these details actually occurred or were composed in order to establish that Jesus died "according to the scriptures" (1 Cor 15.3–4). Readers should decide for themselves whether actual incidents were being interpreted through a scriptural lens or were suggested to the writer from the use of favorite biblical texts.

you, wherever the good news[a] is proclaimed in the whole world, what she has done will be told in remembrance of her."

[10] Then Judas Iscariot, who was one of the twelve, went to the chief priests in order to betray him to them. [11] When they heard it, they were greatly pleased, and promised to give him money. So he began to look for an opportunity to betray him.

[12] On the first day of Unleavened Bread, when the Passover lamb is sacrificed, his disciples said to him, "Where do you want us to go and make the preparations for you to eat the Passover?" [13] So he sent two of his disciples, saying to them, "Go into the city, and a man carrying a jar of water will meet you; follow him, [14] and wherever he enters, say to the owner of the house, 'The Teacher asks, Where is my guest room where I may eat the Passover with my disciples?' [15] He will

[a] Or *gospel*

name is not given. Perhaps the omission of her name is ironic: the unnamed "everywoman" understands him, while the named disciples, the authority figures of old (from the audience's point of view), do not. She could also be like the unnamed centurion (15.39) who understands while the disciples again do not. In addition, she is contrasted to the three named women who attempt to anoint the body, but fail (16.1–8), just as the unnamed centurion is contrasted to the three named disciples who fail in Gethsemane (14.33). Women characters were also emphasized in the Jewish novellas of this period (Esther, Judith, Susanna, *Jos. Asen.*); they became central protagonists for the exploration of the religious concerns of the audience, as they would also in the centuries to follow in the Greek novels. **10–11:** Only in Jn 12.4–6 are we told that Judas was the one who urged that the money be given to the poor.

14.12–25: The Last Supper (Mt 26.17–29; Lk 22.7–20). See 1 Cor 11.23–26. In Mark the Last Supper is the Passover meal (though not a Seder, which probably developed later, after destruction of the Temple in 70 CE), while at Jn 19.31 Jesus is crucified on the day of preparation for Passover. Deut 16.1–8 established that the Pass-

show you a large room upstairs, furnished and ready. Make preparations for us there." [16] So the disciples set out and went to the city, and found everything as he had told them; and they prepared the Passover meal.

[17] When it was evening, he came with the twelve. [18] And when they had taken their places and were eating, Jesus said, "Truly I tell you, one of you will betray me, one who is eating with me." [19] They began to be distressed and to say to him one after another, "Surely, not I?" [20] He said to them, "It is one of the twelve, one who is dipping bread[a] into the bowl[b] with me. [21] For the Son of Man goes as it is written of him, but woe to that one by whom the Son of Man is betrayed! It would have been better for that one not to have been born."

[22] While they were eating, he took a loaf of bread, and after blessing it he broke it, gave it to them, and said, "Take; this is my body." [23] Then he took a cup, and after giving thanks he gave it to them, and all of them drank from it. [24] He said to them, "This is my blood of the[c] covenant, which is poured out for many. [25] Truly I tell you, I will never again drink of the fruit of the vine until that day when I drink it new in the kingdom of God."

[26] When they had sung the hymn, they went out to the Mount of Olives. [27] And Jesus said to them, "You will all become deserters; for it is written,

'I will strike the shepherd,
and the sheep will be scattered.'

[28] But after I am raised up, I will go before you to Galilee." [29] Peter said to him, "Even though all become deserters, I will not." [30] Jesus said to him, "Truly I tell you, this day, this very night, before the cock crows twice, you will deny me three times." [31] But he said vehemently, "Even though I must die with you, I will not deny you." And all of them said the same.

[32] They went to a place called Gethsemane; and he said to his disciples, "Sit here while I pray." [33] He took with him Peter and James and John, and began to be distressed and agitated. [34] And he said to them, "I am deeply grieved, even to death; remain here, and keep awake." [35] And going a little farther, he threw himself on the ground and prayed that, if it were possible, the hour

[a] Gk lacks *bread*
[b] Other ancient authorities read *same bowl*
[c] Other ancient authorities add *new*

over could only be eaten in Jerusalem. **22–25:** Churches recite the words of the Last Supper as the Eucharist (Gk for "giving thanks"); it is also referred to in various Christian traditions as "Holy Communion" or "The Lord's Supper." It is treated here as a real meal, as also in 1 Cor 11.20–32. A different early Eucharist is found in the early Christian document *Did.* 9.1–10.15, which is more typical of Jewish meal prayers (*m. Ber.* 7.1–5) and theology, but the one here became dominant in the Christian tradition. Christians over the centuries have disagreed about whether Christ is literally or symbolically present in the bread and wine, whether the wine is to be consumed by priests alone while the congregation consumes bread only, whether alcoholic wine is used, or wafer or a loaf of bread is used. Various denominations have also differed about the meaning of this practice: whether, for instance, it participates in Jesus' sacrifice of his life on the cross, or is a memorial of that event. The language of consuming Jesus' *body* and *blood* is perhaps deliberately shocking, since consumption of animal blood is forbidden for Jews (Lev 17.10–11). **22:** *Bread,* in keeping with Passover, this should be unleavened bread (Heb "matzah"). **24:** The *covenant* is ratified by Jesus' blood just as Moses ratified the Sinai covenant with blood (Ex 24.1–8; Zech 9.11). Mark's language suggests a covenant renewal rather than a new covenant. Matthew explicitly adds "for the forgiveness of sins" (cf. 1 Cor 15.3; Heb 9.11–22; 1 Pet 1.18–19). **25:** On the messiah's future banquet, cf. Isa 25.6, taken up also at Qumran (1QM 2.11–22; cf. *1 En.* 10.18–19).

14.26–31: Peter's denial prophesied (Mt 26.30–35; Lk 22.39). **26:** The Passover *hymns* were Ps 114; 115 (*m. Pesah.* 10.6); 118, the Hallel psalms. *Mount of Olives,* see 11.1n. **27:** Zech 13.7. Mark assumes that God is the agent of Jesus' suffering; see 14.36n. **28:** *Go before,* see 16.7n.

14.32–42: Prayer in Gethsemane (Mt 26.36–46; Lk 22.40–46). **32:** *Gethsemane* means "oil press"; it is located on the Mount of Olives (Lk 22.39). **33:** *Peter, James, John,* see 9.2–13. **36:** *Abba,* Aramaic for father (not Heb for "daddy," as some scholars have argued). Followers of Jesus, perhaps by his lead, emphasized their relationship to God as father (11.25; Mt 6.9; Lk 11.2; Rom 8.15–17; Gal 4.6–7). The image was infrequent, but not unknown, in the Hebrew Bible (Isa 63.16; 64.8; Jer 3.4,19; Ps 68.5; 89.26; 103.13). *Remove this cup,* see Isa

might pass from him. [36] He said, "Abba,[a] Father, for you all things are possible; remove this cup from me; yet, not what I want, but what you want." [37] He came and found them sleeping; and he said to Peter, "Simon, are you asleep? Could you not keep awake one hour? [38] Keep awake and pray that you may not come into the time of trial;[b] the spirit indeed is willing, but the flesh is weak." [39] And again he went away and prayed, saying the same words. [40] And once more he came and found them sleeping, for their eyes were very heavy; and they did not know what to say to him. [41] He came a third time and said to them, "Are you still sleeping and taking your rest? Enough! The hour has come; the Son of Man is betrayed into the hands of sinners. [42] Get up, let us be going. See, my betrayer is at hand."

[43] Immediately, while he was still speaking, Judas, one of the twelve, arrived; and with him there was a crowd with swords and clubs, from the chief priests, the scribes, and the elders. [44] Now the betrayer had given them a sign, saying, "The one I will kiss is the man; arrest him and lead him away under guard." [45] So when he came, he went up to him at once and said, "Rabbi!" and kissed him. [46] Then they laid hands on him and arrested him. [47] But one of those who stood near drew his sword and struck the slave of the high priest, cutting off his ear. [48] Then Jesus said to them, "Have you come out with swords and clubs to arrest me as though I were a bandit? [49] Day after day I was with you in the temple teaching, and you did not arrest me. But let the scriptures be fulfilled." [50] All of them deserted him and fled.

[51] A certain young man was following him, wearing nothing but a linen cloth. They caught hold of him, [52] but he left the linen cloth and ran off naked.

[53] They took Jesus to the high priest; and all the chief priests, the elders, and the scribes were assembled. [54] Peter had followed him at a distance, right into the courtyard of the high priest; and he was sitting with the guards, warming himself at the fire. [55] Now the chief priests and the whole council were looking for testimony against Jesus to put him to death; but they found none. [56] For many gave false testimony against him, and their testimony did not agree. [57] Some stood up and gave false testimony against him, saying, [58] "We heard him say, 'I will destroy this temple that is made with hands, and in three days I will build another, not made with hands.'" [59] But even on this point their testimony did not agree. [60] Then the high priest stood up before them and asked Jesus, "Have you no answer? What is it that they testify against you?" [61] But he was silent and did not answer.

[a] Aramaic for *Father*
[b] Or *into temptation*

51.12,17, where God removes the cup of wrath from the people; see also 10.38n. *Not what I want* implies that Jesus resists God's plan, much as Peter had resisted in 8.32; both Matthew and Luke omit this line. **37–41:** In 13.37 the disciples were told to *keep awake,* yet here three times they are found sleeping. The three naps also anticipate Peter's three denials.

14.43–65: Jesus arrested and tried before the Sanhedrin (Mt 26.47–68; Lk 22.47–71; Jn 18.2–11). **44–45:** The *kiss* is an expected greeting (Lk 7.45; Gen 45.15), though ironic here. It was perhaps necessary as an identification of Jesus in the dark. **47–52:** These provocative symbolic acts have not been convincingly explained. The attack on the high priest's slave implies that Jesus' followers were armed, thereby indicating that they anticipated an armed rebellion. *Young man . . . wearing nothing but a cloth,* perhaps a comment on the exposure of the followers as unfaithful. **53:** *Chief priests, the elders, and the scribes* constitute the Sanhedrin, or Jerusalem city council. It had authority over Jewish life in Judea, but Romans reserved control over some areas, especially capital punishment. For this reason, and because this trial is placed on Passover when such activities would be strictly forbidden by Jewish law (*m. Pesah.* 4.1,5–6 makes clear that one may work at most up until noon on the day on which Passover begins at sundown), the scene is of questionable historicity. **55–59:** Biblical law forbade suborning perjury (Ex 20.16) and convicting based on conflicting evidence (Deut 19.15), so the proceedings are presented as violations of Jewish criminal procedure. Yet although the *testimony* is depicted as *false,* Mark previously stated that Jesus had predicted the destruction of the Temple (11.15; 13.2). **61–64:** Jesus is *silent* like the suffering servant at Isa 53.7. *Blessed One,* the chief

Again the high priest asked him, "Are you the Messiah,[a] the Son of the Blessed One?" [62] Jesus said, "I am; and

'you will see the Son of Man
seated at the right hand of the Power,'
and 'coming with the clouds of heaven.'"

[63] Then the high priest tore his clothes and said, "Why do we still need witnesses? [64] You have heard his blasphemy! What is your decision?" All of them condemned him as deserving death. [65] Some began to spit on him, to blindfold him, and to strike him, saying to him, "Prophesy!" The guards also took him over and beat him.

[66] While Peter was below in the courtyard, one of the servant-girls of the high priest came by. [67] When she saw Peter warming himself, she stared at him and said, "You also were with Jesus, the man from Nazareth." [68] But he denied it, saying, "I do not know or understand what you are talking about." And he went out into the forecourt.[b] Then the cock crowed.[c] [69] And the servant-girl, on seeing him, began again to say to the bystanders, "This man is one of them." [70] But again he denied it. Then after a little while the bystanders again said to Peter, "Certainly you are one of them; for you are a Galilean." [71] But he began to curse, and he swore an oath, "I do not know this man you are talking about." [72] At that moment the cock crowed for the second time. Then Peter remembered that Jesus had said to him, "Before the cock crows twice, you will deny me three times." And he broke down and wept.

15 As soon as it was morning, the chief priests held a consultation with the elders and scribes and the whole council. They bound Jesus, led him away, and handed him over to Pilate. [2] Pilate asked him, "Are you the King of the Jews?" He answered him, "You say so." [3] Then the chief priests accused him of many things. [4] Pilate asked him again, "Have you no answer? See how many charges they bring against you." [5] But Jesus made no further reply, so that Pilate was amazed.

[6] Now at the festival he used to release a prisoner for them, anyone for whom they asked. [7] Now a man called Barabbas was in prison with the rebels who had committed murder during the insurrection. [8] So the crowd came and began to ask Pilate to do for them according to his custom. [9] Then he answered them, "Do you want me to release for you the King of the Jews?" [10] For he realized that it was out of jealousy that the chief priests had handed him over. [11] But the chief priests stirred up the crowd to have him release Barabbas for them instead. [12] Pilate spoke to them again, "Then what do you wish me to do[d] with the man you call[e] the King of the Jews?" [13] They shouted back, "Crucify him!" [14] Pilate asked them, "Why, what evil has he done?" But they

[a] Or *the Christ*
[b] Or *gateway*
[c] Other ancient authorities lack *Then the cock crowed*
[d] Other ancient authorities read *what should I do*
[e] Other ancient authorities lack *the man you call*

priest uses a circumlocution for God, similar to the rabbinic "Holy One, Blessed be He" ("Ha-Qadosh barukh hu"). The titles *Messiah* and *Son of the Blessed One* are not *blasphemy,* since a Jewish king could be both, but they are politically dangerous. However, according to Mark the high priest takes Jesus' quotations of Ps 110.1 and Dan 7.13, and his identification of himself with the judging Son of Man, as blasphemy from the Sanhedrin's point of view; see 2.6–7n.

14.66–72: Peter's denial (Mt 26.69–75; Lk 22.56–62; Jn 18.17,25–27). By beginning the scene with Peter in v. 54 and completing it here, Mark ironically conveys that Peter's "self-acquittal" is occurring simultaneously with Jesus' conviction. Just as the witnesses against Jesus offered false testimony, so does Peter concerning himself. This incident culminates in a solemn denial of Jesus that is like the pronouncement of guilt by the high priest.

15.1–15: Jesus condemned by Pilate (Mt 27.1–2,11–26; Lk 23.1–5,18–25; Jn 18.28–40; 19.4–16). **1:** *Handed him over to Pilate,* only the Romans could impose a sentence of death (see Jn 18.31); in addition, the charges apparently are not completely clear (v. 3). **2:** *King of the Jews,* a claim that the Romans would understand as dangerous; they could tolerate no kings except those, like the Herods, whom they had appointed. **6–15:** *Barabbas* is Aramaic for "son of the father," and is likely an invented double for Jesus. There is no evidence that the Romans released prisoners, much less insurrectionaries, at Passover. Further, if the point is to release him for the festival, the timing is off: the paschal lamb was eaten the night before. **14–15:** Mark places the blame on the Jews,

shouted all the more, "Crucify him!" [15] So Pilate, wishing to satisfy the crowd, released Barabbas for them; and after flogging Jesus, he handed him over to be crucified.

[16] Then the soldiers led him into the courtyard of the palace (that is, the governor's headquarters[a]); and they called together the whole cohort. [17] And they clothed him in a purple cloak; and after twisting some thorns into a crown, they put it on him. [18] And they began saluting him, "Hail, King of the Jews!" [19] They struck his head with a reed, spat upon him, and knelt down in homage to him. [20] After mocking him, they stripped him of the purple cloak and put his own clothes on him. Then they led him out to crucify him.

[21] They compelled a passer-by, who was coming in from the country, to carry his cross; it was Simon of Cyrene, the father of Alexander and Rufus. [22] Then they brought Jesus[b] to the place called Golgotha (which means the place of a skull). [23] And they offered him wine mixed with myrrh; but he did not take it. [24] And they crucified him, and divided his clothes among them, casting lots to decide what each should take.

[25] It was nine o'clock in the morning when they crucified him. [26] The inscription of the charge against him read, "The King of the Jews." [27] And with him they crucified two bandits, one on his right and one on his left.[c] [29] Those who passed by derided[d] him, shaking their heads and saying, "Aha! You who would destroy the temple and build it in three days, [30] save yourself, and come down from the cross!" [31] In the same way the chief priests, along with the scribes, were also mocking him among themselves and saying, "He saved others; he cannot save himself. [32] Let the Messiah,[e] the King of Israel, come down from the cross now, so that we may see and believe." Those who were crucified with him also taunted him.

[33] When it was noon, darkness came over the whole land[f] until three in the afternoon. [34] At three o'clock Jesus cried out with a loud voice, "Eloi, Eloi, lema sabachthani?" which means, "My God, my God, why have you forsaken me?"[g] [35] When some of the bystanders heard it, they said, "Listen, he is calling for Elijah." [36] And someone ran, filled a sponge with sour wine, put it on a stick, and gave it to him to drink, saying, "Wait, let us see whether Elijah will come to take him down." [37] Then Jesus gave a loud cry and breathed his last. [38] And the curtain of the temple was torn in two, from top to bottom. [39] Now when the centurion, who stood facing him, saw that in this way he[h] breathed his last, he said, "Truly this man was God's Son!"[i]

a Gk *the praetorium*
b Gk *him*
c Other ancient authorities add verse 28, *And the scripture was fulfilled that says, "And he was counted among the lawless."*
d Or *blasphemed*
e Or *the Christ*
f Or *earth*
g Other ancient authorities read *made me a reproach*
h Other ancient authorities add *cried out and*
i Or *a son of God*

an increasing tendency in subsequent accounts. After the dissemination of the Gospels, Pilate was even considered a convert to Christianity, and he is honored as a martyr in the Coptic Orthodox Church; his feast day is June 25. The transfer of guilt from the Romans—who crucified Jesus—to the Jews was then complete. *Flogging* was a way of weakening the victim before crucifixion. **16–20:** Jesus is mocked by the Romans as a king, a parody of "Hail, Caesar!" The shaming is emphasized more than physical pain. The *purple cloak* evokes royal robes, and the *crown of thorns* a gold circlet, or perhaps a laurel wreath.

15. 20–47: The crucifixion and burial (Mt 27.27–61; Lk 23.18–56; Jn 19.1–3,17–42). **22:** *Golgotha*, the sites of Jesus' last days are significant: Mount of Olives (11.1n.) and Place of the Skull. **23:** *Wine mixed with myrrh*, see "Scripture Fulfillments," p. 89. **24:** The crucifixion is stated in only one sentence. The extreme physical agony would have been known by all, but the Gospels emphasize the shame of the punishment much more than the physical suffering. Crucifixion was the most extreme form of execution, reserved for slaves and insurrectionaries. **33:** In apocalypses (e.g., *2 Bar.* 32), the conditions at the end of time will replay those of creation; cf. Gen 1.2–3. **34:** Jesus' "cry of dereliction" from Ps 22.1 in mixed Hebrew/Aramaic is ironically misunderstood by the people. As in 15.11–15, Jesus is abandoned by his own people, a theme of the psalms of lament, such as Ps 22. **36:** *Sour wine*, a mild anesthetic. **38:** *Was torn*, Mk 1.10; Isa 64.1. The tearing of the *curtain* could symbolize the presence of God's power at the moment of Jesus' death, the access to God, or a critique of the Temple and

[40] There were also women looking on from a distance; among them were Mary Magdalene, and Mary the mother of James the younger and of Joses, and Salome. [41] These used to follow him and provided for him when he was in Galilee; and there were many other women who had come up with him to Jerusalem.

[42] When evening had come, and since it was the day of Preparation, that is, the day before the sabbath, [43] Joseph of Arimathea, a respected member of the council, who was also himself waiting expectantly for the kingdom of God, went boldly to Pilate and asked for the body of Jesus. [44] Then Pilate wondered if he were already dead; and summoning the centurion, he asked him whether he had been dead for some time. [45] When he learned from the centurion that he was dead, he granted the body to Joseph. [46] Then Joseph[a] bought a linen cloth, and taking down the body,[b] wrapped it in the linen cloth, and laid it in a tomb that had been hewn out of the rock. He then rolled a stone against the door of the tomb. [47] Mary Magdalene and Mary the mother of Joses saw where the body[b] was laid.

16 When the sabbath was over, Mary Magdalene, and Mary the mother of James, and Salome bought spices, so that they might go and anoint him. [2] And very early on the first day of the week, when the sun had risen, they went to the tomb. [3] They had been saying to one another, "Who will roll away the stone for us from the entrance to the tomb?" [4] When they looked up, they saw that the stone, which was very large, had already been rolled back. [5] As they entered the tomb, they saw a young man, dressed in a white robe, sitting on the right side; and they were alarmed. [6] But he said to them, "Do not be alarmed; you are looking for Jesus of Nazareth, who was crucified. He has been raised; he is not here. Look, there is the place they laid him. [7] But go, tell his disciples and Peter that he is going ahead of you to Galilee; there you will see him, just as he told you." [8] So they went out and fled from the tomb, for terror and amazement had seized them; and they said nothing to anyone, for they were afraid.[c]

a Gk *he*

b Gk *it*

c Some of the most ancient authorities bring the book to a close at the end of verse 8. One authority concludes the book with the shorter ending; others include the shorter ending and then continue with verses 9-20. In most authorities verses 9-20 follow immediately after verse 8, though in some of these authorities the passage is marked as being doubtful.

anticipation of its destruction. (Although a curtain is made for the wilderness tabernacle [Ex 36] to separate the inner area where the ark is kept, there is no curtain mentioned in the construction of the Temple, either Solomon's or the Second Temple.) **39:** At the climactic point in the Gospel, the centurion declares what the followers of Jesus cannot (cf. Jn 11.49–52). **40–41:** The *women* are mentioned again in v. 47, witnessing the burial, and in 16.1–8, seeing the empty tomb. **42:** *Day of Preparation, . . . the day before the Sabbath* (2 Macc 8.26); this implies that the crucifixion was on a Friday. The Gospel of John (19.14) states that the crucifixion occurred on the day of Preparation for the Passover, not for the Sabbath. **43:** Others expected the kingdom of God, so *Joseph* is not necessarily a follower of Jesus; cf. 12.34. By moving to take down Jesus' dead body, Joseph fulfills Deut 21.22–23 (cf. Tob 1–2).

16.1–8: The empty tomb (Mt 28.1–8; Lk 24.1–11; Jn 20.1–10). **1:** Jewish customs of anointing for burial can also be found at *m. Shabb.* 23.5, where the limitations on preparation of the body on the Sabbath are also noted. Thus the women wait until *the Sabbath [is] over* to prepare Jesus' body for proper burial. Two different tombs of Jesus have been marked in Jerusalem over the centuries, but neither has any historical claim. **5–6:** *Young man,* Mark once again understates the divine significance: the figure is *dressed* as a vindicated martyr (Dan 11.35, "be made white"). Similarly, Jesus' clothing in the Transfiguration (9.3,6) is white. **7:** Mark predicts Jesus' appearance in *Galilee* (cf. 14.28), which is followed by Matthew's account; Luke puts the appearances in Jerusalem, Emmaus, and Bethany, all in Judea; John 21 places an appearance by the Sea of Tiberias (the Sea of Galilee) in Galilee, while John 20 and the longer ending of Mark (see below), like Luke, place the resurrection appearances in Jerusalem. **8:** The ending does not provide the anticipated appearance, which would have been well known

THE SHORTER ENDING OF MARK

⟦And all that had been commanded them they told briefly to those around Peter. And afterward Jesus himself sent out through them, from east to west, the sacred and imperishable proclamation of eternal salvation.[a]⟧

THE LONGER ENDING OF MARK

[9] ⟦Now after he rose early on the first day of the week, he appeared first to Mary Magdalene, from whom he had cast out seven demons. [10] She went out and told those who had been with him, while they were mourning and weeping. [11] But when they heard that he was alive and had been seen by her, they would not believe it.

[12] After this he appeared in another form to two of them, as they were walking into the country. [13] And they went back and told the rest, but they did not believe them.

[14] Later he appeared to the eleven themselves as they were sitting at the table; and he upbraided them for their lack of faith and stubbornness, because they had not believed those who saw him after he had risen.[b] [15] And he said to them, "Go into all the world and proclaim the good news[c] to the whole creation. [16] The one who believes and is baptized will be saved; but the one who does not believe will be condemned. [17] And these signs will accompany those who believe: by using my name they will cast out demons; they will speak in new tongues; [18] they will pick up snakes in their hands,[d] and if they drink any deadly thing, it will not hurt them; they will lay their hands on the sick, and they will recover."

[19] So then the Lord Jesus, after he had spoken to them, was taken up into heaven and sat down at the right hand of God. [20] And they went out and proclaimed the good news everywhere, while the Lord worked with them and confirmed the message by the signs that accompanied it.[a]⟧

[a] Other ancient authorities add *Amen*

[b] Other ancient authorities add, in whole or in part, *And they excused themselves, saying, "This age of lawlessness and unbelief is under Satan, who does not allow the truth and power of God to prevail over the unclean things of the spirits. Therefore reveal your righteousness now"—thus they spoke to Christ. And Christ replied to them, "The term of years of Satan's power has been fulfilled, but other terrible things draw near. And for those who have sinned I was handed over to death, that they may return to the truth and sin no more, that they may inherit the spiritual and imperishable glory of righteousness that is in heaven."*

[c] Or *gospel*

[d] Other ancient authorities lack *in their hands*

to the audience (cf. 1 Cor 15.3–5). The Gospel ends with one last example of irony: followers are now, at the resurrection, told to proclaim what they have heard, but out of fear they remain silent.

Two alternative endings to Mark. These two endings were not likely found in the copies of Mark that Matthew and Luke utilized. The shorter ending is not attested in any manuscript earlier than fourth century CE. **16.9–20: Traditional longer ending.** This was not likely the original ending of Mark; it is possibly an early version of the ending of the Gospel story, added to Mark to supply a conclusion, but most scholars assume that it was a pastiche of phrases from the other Gospels composed in the second century CE. For centuries it was accepted as the authentic conclusion of Mark's Gospel. It provides the scriptural basis for modern practices still occasionally found among Christian groups regarding snake-handling and drinking poison while "in the spirit."

THE GOSPEL ACCORDING TO LUKE

NAME, AUTHORSHIP, AND SOURCES

The Gospel according to Luke, also known as the Third Gospel, and the book of Acts are traditionally ascribed to Luke, a physician who accompanied Paul on his missions (Col 4.14; 2 Tim 4.11; Philem 1.24). Neither the Gospel nor Acts, however, claims Lukan authorship, and sufficient distinctions between the portrait of Paul provided in his authentic epistles and his depiction in Acts call into question the author's personal familiarity with the apostle.

Whoever composed the Gospel was not an eyewitness (1.2); the author, henceforth "Luke," not only utilized earlier sources but also sought to correct them (1.1–4). These sources likely included Mark's Gospel (although not Mk 6.45–8.26; 9.41–10.12); a written text today called Q (from the German word for "source," *Quelle*), reconstructed from materials common to the Gospels of Luke and Matthew and comprising mostly sayings material such as the beatitudes (Mt 5.3–11||Lk 6.20–23) and the "Lord's Prayer" (Mt 6.9–13||Lk 11.2–4); independent material called L for Luke's special source (e.g., Lk 1–2); and the author's own commentary. Luke also shares some common material with John, such as stories about Jesus' friends Mary and Martha (Lk 10.38–42||Jn 11–12) and the notice that Satan possessed Judas Iscariot (Lk 22.3||Jn 13.2).

STYLE, CONTENTS, AND STRUCTURE

Luke's style ranges from the elegant Greek of the prologue (1.1–4 comprise a single Greek sentence) to an evocation of the Septuagint in the first two chapters. By casting the nativity stories of John the Baptist and Jesus in the cadences of Israel's Scriptures, the Gospel suggests continuity between ancient Israel and the Christian story.

The narrative follows that of the other canonical Gospels, but it is distinguished by the "travel" account (9.51–18.14) inserted into the Markan scheme (contrast Mk 9.41–10.12). Here Luke includes some of the most familiar of Jesus' teachings, including the parable of the good Samaritan (10.29–37) and the parable of the prodigal son (15.11–32). Distinct as well are Luke's nativity stories, with their focus on John the Baptist and the virgin Mary, and resurrection and ascension accounts.

INTERPRETATION AND READING GUIDE

The Gospel has been traditionally seen as interested in society's "marginal": women, children, the sick, the poor, tax collectors and sinners, and Gentiles. This configuration begs the question, "marginal to what?" Luke's Gospel instead reveals that (Jewish) women had freedom of travel (1.39; 8.2–3; 23.27,55–56) and access to their own funds (7.37; 8.3; 15.8; 21.2); undertook patronage roles (8.1–3); owned homes (10.38; see also Acts 12.12); and appeared in synagogues (13.10–17) and the Temple (2.22,36–37,41–50). Children, of utmost value in Jewish culture, appear in the care of parents and caregivers who so love them that they seek Jesus' healing and blessing. The sick, who should not be confused with the ritually impure, are often presented as embedded in caring social networks. Most people in antiquity were poor, and the Jewish system, starting with the Tanakh, mandated communal responsibility for their care. To regard Jesus, appropriately, as caring for women, children, the sick and the poor, embeds him within Judaism rather than separates him from it.

The Lukan Jesus does have a particular interest in associating with "tax collectors and sinners." Rather than seen as suspect because of laxity in halakhic observance, they are people who have removed themselves from community welfare. Tax collectors, for example, work for the Roman government. Finally, Gentiles—including Rome's representatives—are hardly marginal. Luke instead depicts them as welcome within the Jewish community (see 7.1–11).

The Gospel's presentation of Jews and Judaism is complex. On the one hand, especially in the first two chapters, it solidly locates Jesus within a vibrant Jewish environment of faithful Jews engaged in faithful Jewish practice. The Gospel opens with the priest Zechariah, the father of John the Baptist, receiving divine revelation in the Jerusalem Temple; Joseph and Mary visit the Temple to dedicate their son and to celebrate the Passover. Luke even describes the circumcisions of both John and Jesus. On the other hand, Luke depicts the synagogue as a place of violence (4.28–29), details Israel's continual failures while highlighting the fidelity of Gentiles and Samaritans (e.g., 7.9; 17.16–18), and engages in scathing caricatures of Pharisees (see "Pharisees in Luke," p. 110) and chief priests. The harsh rhetoric resembles that of the biblical prophets and the Qumran writings (Dead Sea Scrolls); the distinction is, however, that Jesus' criticisms against his fellow Jews are now embedded in a text directed primarily to Gentiles. Nor does Luke know, or presume readers know, Jewish customs: Jewish practices are defined (e.g., 22.1) and sometimes erroneously presented (e.g., 2.22). Thus the consensus view is that the author is a Gentile writing to a primarily Gentile audience, sometime in the late first or early second century. Indeed, some scholars suggest that the first two chapters are additions, created in the early second century and designed not to foreground the practice of Judaism, but to counter the arguments of Marcion, a Christian teacher who promoted the idea that the God of the Old Testament was not the one revealed by Jesus (the stereotype of the "Old Testament God of wrath" vs. the "New Testament God of love" is a recrudescence of the Marcionite heresy).

Luke's view of Jews and Judaism is also complicated by the relationship of the Gospel to Luke's second volume. Acts of the Apostles depicts the beginnings of the church as firmly within Judaism, with Jesus' followers in the Temple and as being well regarded by their Jewish neighbors. Yet Acts accuses "the entire house of Israel" (2.36) with crucifying Jesus and having "killed the Author of life" (3.14–15); the text ends not in Jerusalem but in Rome, with Paul announcing that the Jews will "never understand" (28.26), but that the Gentiles "will listen" (28.28). One plausible reading of the two volumes is that Luke depicts Jesus as the fulfillment of God's plan and the church as the true heirs of Moses and the Prophets, while presenting non-Christian Jews as hypocritical, intolerant, and violent. Readers should attend to the tension between Luke's depiction of Jesus the Jew and of Jesus' early followers as observant Jews, and Luke's presentation of those Jews who did not become Christian as having fallen short of God's intentions and thus, ultimately, having become foes of Jesus himself and of his followers.

Amy-Jill Levine

1 Since many have undertaken to set down an orderly account of the events that have been fulfilled among us, [2] just as they were handed on to us by those who from the beginning were eyewitnesses and servants of the word, [3] I too decided, after investigating everything carefully from the very first,[a] to write an orderly account for you, most excellent Theophilus, [4] so that you may know the truth concerning the things about which you have been instructed.

[5] In the days of King Herod of Judea, there was a priest named Zechariah, who belonged to the priestly order of Abijah. His wife was a descendant of Aaron, and her name was Elizabeth. [6] Both of them were righteous before God, living blamelessly according to all the commandments and regulations of the Lord. [7] But they had no children, because Elizabeth was barren, and both were getting on in years.

[8] Once when he was serving as priest before God and his section was on duty, [9] he was chosen by lot, according to the custom of

[a] Or *for a long time*

1.1–4: Prologue. Comprising one Greek sentence, the opening follows classical and Hellenistic conventions (see Josephus, *J.W.* 1.17; *Ag. Ap.* 1.1–18). **1:** *Fulfilled*, suggests prophetic fulfillment. **3:** *Most excellent Theophilus*, the address (also Acts 1.1) suggests a patron. Whether Theophilus (a common name meaning "friend of God") is an actual or ideal reader cannot be determined. **4:** *Instructed*, Gk "katēchēthēs," whence "catechism"; the ideal reader likely has some knowledge of both Jewish Scripture and the story of Jesus.

1.5–10: Zechariah and Elizabeth. **5:** *Days of King Herod*, ruled ca. 37–4 BCE; Mt. 2.1,15 places Jesus' birth during Herod's latter years. *Priestly order of Abijah*, the eighth of twenty-four divisions of Levites (1 Chr 24.10); each division served in the Jerusalem Temple twice annually. *Aaron*, Moses' brother and progenitor of the priestly line. **6:** *Righteous . . . living blamelessly . . . commandments and regulations*, Luke emphasizes their halakhic fidelity. **7:** *Elizabeth was barren . . . getting on in years*, the elderly, faithful, childless couple anticipates an angelic annunciation and the conception of a special son (Gen 11.30; see also 16.1; 25.21; 29.31; Judg 13.2–3;

the priesthood, to enter the sanctuary of the Lord and offer incense. [10] Now at the time of the incense offering, the whole assembly of the people was praying outside. [11] Then there appeared to him an angel of the Lord, standing at the right side of the altar of incense. [12] When Zechariah saw him, he was terrified; and fear overwhelmed him. [13] But the angel said to him, "Do not be afraid, Zechariah, for your prayer has been heard. Your wife Elizabeth will bear you a son, and you will name him John. [14] You will have joy and gladness, and many will rejoice at his birth, [15] for he will be great in the sight of the Lord. He must never drink wine or strong drink; even before his birth he will be filled with the Holy Spirit. [16] He will turn many of the people of Israel to the Lord their God. [17] With the spirit and power of Elijah he will go before him, to turn the hearts of parents to their children, and the disobedient to the wisdom of the righteous, to make ready a people prepared for the Lord." [18] Zechariah said to the angel, "How will I know that this is so? For I am an old man, and my wife is getting on in years." [19] The angel replied, "I am Gabriel. I stand in the presence of God, and I have been sent to speak to you and to bring you this good news. [20] But now, because you did not believe my words, which will be fulfilled in their time, you will become mute, unable to speak, until the day these things occur."

[21] Meanwhile the people were waiting for Zechariah, and wondered at his delay in the sanctuary. [22] When he did come out, he could not speak to them, and they realized that he had seen a vision in the sanctuary. He kept motioning to them and remained unable to speak. [23] When his time of service was ended, he went to his home.

[24] After those days his wife Elizabeth conceived, and for five months she remained in seclusion. She said, [25] "This is what the Lord has done for me when he looked favorably on me and took away the disgrace I have endured among my people."

1 Sam 1.2; cf. 2 Kings 4.14). **9:** *Chosen by lot*, see Acts 1.26; *m. Tamid* 5.2–6.3. *Offer incense*, there being so many priests, this was likely Zechariah's only time. **10:** *Time of the incense offering*, Ex 30.7–8 (see also Ps 141.2); Josephus (*Ant.* 13.10.3) states that the Maccabean king, John Hyrcanus, received a divine revelation during the incense offering. *Whole assembly* (lit., "All the number of the people"), Luke here portrays the Jews in Jerusalem as faithful and pious.

1.11–23: Annunciation of John's conception. 11: *Angel*, heavenly messengers (see 1.7n.) gain distinct personalities in postbiblical Jewish texts. **13:** *Afraid*, common response to an angelophany. *Prayer has been heard*, suggesting that Zechariah had prayed for a child. *You will name him*, in Gen 16.11, an angel commands Hagar to name her son "Ishmael"; see 1.31. *John* (Heb "Yoḥanan"), "favor/grace of YHWH/YHWH is gracious," a name attested in Jer 40.8 and increasingly in later Jewish texts. **15:** *Wine or strong drink*, indicting a Nazirite, a person dedicated to God (Num 6.1–4; Judg 13.4–6). The annunciation in the Temple draws a particular connection between John and Samuel. *Holy Spirit*, a major Lukan theme, indicating the presence of the divine (e.g., Ps 51.11 [51.13 LXX]; Wis 9.17); the concept came into later Jewish thought primarily in the depiction of the "Shekhinah" (derived from Heb "dwell" [e.g., Ex 29.45], a cognate of the Hebrew "mishkan," or "tabernacle"), the feminine presence of God that dwells with Israel (e.g., *b. Sanh.* 39a, 103b; *b. Yoma* 56b). **16:** *People of Israel*, Jews; the eschatological promises come first to Israel. **17:** *Elijah* the prophet (1 Kings 17–19,21) was expected to announce the messianic age (see Mal 3.23 [4.5–6]; Mt 11.14); his traditional appearance at the Passover seder anticipates that final liberation; his appearance at the ritual circumcision ("brit milah") proves that he is not alone among the faithful in Israel (1 Kings 19.14). *Turn the hearts of parents*, Elijah's role in Mal 3.24 [4.6]; Sir 48.10. *Prepared for the Lord*, "Lord" (Gk "kyrios") can mean "sir" (Heb "'adon"), but it is also the standard translation of the Hebrew YHWH; Christians accord this title to Jesus. **19:** *Gabriel*, with Michael, one of two angels named in the Tanakh (Dan 8.16; 9.21; see also *1 En.* 9, 20, 40; *Jub.* 2.18; 54.6; 1QH 6.13; 1QM 9.14–16; 15.14). *Presence of God*, the heavenly throneroom. *Good news*, the noun form of this term is "euangellion," "gospel"; in Roman society "euangellion" was, e.g., proclamation of tax relief or the emperor's birthday; for the LXX (Ps. 40.9 [Heb v. 10]; 68.11 [Heb v. 12]; 96.2; Isa 40.9 and elsewhere), the verbal form [Heb "basar," noun "besorah"] can refer to divine salvation. **20:** *Become mute*, see Ezek 3.26; 24.27; 33.22. **22:** *Vision in the sanctuary*, see Acts 22.17–21.

1.24–25: John's conception. 25: *Disgrace*, see Gen. 30.23, where Rachel's reproach may be from Leah. In the Tanakh, God opens and closes wombs (Gen 16.2; 25.21; 1 Sam 1.1–18).

[26] In the sixth month the angel Gabriel was sent by God to a town in Galilee called Nazareth, [27] to a virgin engaged to a man whose name was Joseph, of the house of David. The virgin's name was Mary. [28] And he came to her and said, "Greetings, favored one! The Lord is with you."[a] [29] But she was much perplexed by his words and pondered what sort of greeting this might be. [30] The angel said to her, "Do not be afraid, Mary, for you have found favor with God. [31] And now, you will conceive in your womb and bear a son, and you will name him Jesus. [32] He will be great, and will be called the Son of the Most High, and the Lord God will give to him the throne of his ancestor David. [33] He will reign over the house of Jacob forever, and of his kingdom there will be no end." [34] Mary said to the angel, "How can this be, since I am a virgin?"[b] [35] The angel said to her, "The Holy Spirit will come upon you, and the power of the Most High will overshadow you; therefore the child to be born[c] will be holy; he will be called Son of God. [36] And now, your relative Elizabeth in her old age has also conceived a son; and this is the sixth month for her who was said to be barren. [37] For nothing will be impossible with God." [38] Then Mary said, "Here am I, the servant of the Lord; let it be with me according to your word." Then the angel departed from her.

[39] In those days Mary set out and went with haste to a Judean town in the hill country, [40] where she entered the house of Zechariah and greeted Elizabeth. [41] When Elizabeth heard Mary's greeting, the child leaped in her womb. And Elizabeth was filled with the Holy Spirit [42] and exclaimed with a loud cry, "Blessed are you among women, and blessed is the fruit of your womb. [43] And why has this happened to me, that the mother of my Lord comes to me? [44] For as soon as I heard the sound of your greeting, the child in my womb leaped for joy. [45] And blessed is she who believed that there would be[d] a fulfillment of what was spoken to her by the Lord."

[a] Other ancient authorities add *Blessed are you among women*

[b] Gk *I do not know a man*

[c] Other ancient authorities add *of you*

[d] Or *believed, for there will be*

1.26–38: The annunciation. 26: *Sixth month,* after John's conception. *Gabriel,* see 1.19. *Galilee,* northern Israel. *Nazareth,* a small village (cf. Jn 1.46) in southern Galilee, outside of the NT unattested in first-century literature. Although Matthew and Luke locate Jesus' birth in Bethlehem (Mt 2.6 specifies in Judea), Jesus was known as being from Nazareth (see, e.g., Jn 1.46). **27:** *Virgin* (Gk "parthenos"); Luke emphasizes the term (also v. 34). *Engaged,* the wedding contract ("ketubah") had been signed. *M. Avot* 5.21 sets the ideal age for a man to marry at eighteen; Josephus, following Roman norms, married at about thirty. *House of David,* one dominant Jewish messianic expectation was that the messiah would be David's descendant (see 2 Sam 7.12). *Mary* (Gk "Mariam"), from Heb "Miryam"; the name, recollecting both Moses' sister Miriam and Herod's Hasmonean wife Mariamme, was common among first-century Jewish women. **28:** *Greetings,* a traditional Greek salutation, which can also be translated "Hail" as in "Hail Mary" (Lat "Ave Maria"). *The Lord is with you,* see Judg 6.12; 2 Sam 7.3; 2 Chr 15.2. **29:** *Perplexed* (Gk "diatarassō"), the related term ("tarassō") in 1.12, referring to Zechariah's vision, is translated "terrified." **31:** *You will name him,* 1.13n. *Jesus,* Gk "Iesous," from Heb "Yehoshua," "the Lord saves" (see Mt 1.21), a common name in the Tanakh and subsequently. **32:** *Son of the Most High,* indicating royal authority (2 Sam 7.13–16) and rectitude (Sir 4.10; see also Dan 7.25); "Most High" translates the Heb "El Elyon" or "YHWH Elyon" (e.g., Gen 14.18–22; Ps 78.35). *Throne of his ancestor David,* v. 27n.; on the promises to David, see also Ps 89; Jer 23.5–8; *Pss. Sol.* 17.4,6,21; etc. **33:** *House of Jacob,* synonym for Israel (Ex 19.3; Isa 46.3; 48.1, Jer 2.4; Ps 114.1; and elsewhere). *Kingdom there will be no end,* See 2 Sam 7.13,16, which use the Hebrew "'ad 'olam," "forever," of the Davidic dynasty. **35:** *Holy Spirit . . . overshadow,* see 1.15n., Ex 40.35. *Son of God,* in 3.38, Adam is a "son of God"; cf. 2 Sam 7.14. Luke develops Jesus' divine nature throughout the narrative. The virginal conception is clearer in Mt 1.23. No Jewish texts regard Isa 7.14 as predicting the messiah's birth or take *Son of God* as indicating anything other than divine adoption (2 Sam 7.14; Ps 2.7; 4QFlor 10–13). **36:** *Your relative Elizabeth,* indicating Mary's priestly ancestry. **37:** *Nothing will be impossible,* see Gen 18.14 concerning the birth of Isaac; Jer 32.17; Zech 8.6. **38:** *Servant,* Gk "doulē," "slave."

1.39–45: The visitation. 39: *Judean,* in southern Israel, where Jerusalem is located. **41:** *Filled with the Holy Spirit,* 1.15n. **43:** *Lord* (Gk "Kyrios"), here a divine title.

[46] And Mary[a] said,
"My soul magnifies the Lord,
[47] and my spirit rejoices in God my Savior,
[48] for he has looked with favor on the lowliness of his servant.
Surely, from now on all generations will call me blessed;
[49] for the Mighty One has done great things for me,
and holy is his name.
[50] His mercy is for those who fear him
from generation to generation.
[51] He has shown strength with his arm;
he has scattered the proud in the thoughts of their hearts.
[52] He has brought down the powerful from their thrones,
and lifted up the lowly;
[53] he has filled the hungry with good things,
and sent the rich away empty.
[54] He has helped his servant Israel,
in remembrance of his mercy,
[55] according to the promise he made to our ancestors,
to Abraham and to his descendants forever."

[56] And Mary remained with her about three months and then returned to her home.

[57] Now the time came for Elizabeth to give birth, and she bore a son. [58] Her neighbors and relatives heard that the Lord had shown his great mercy to her, and they rejoiced with her.

[59] On the eighth day they came to circumcise the child, and they were going to name him Zechariah after his father. [60] But his mother said, "No; he is to be called John." [61] They said to her, "None of your relatives has this name." [62] Then they began motioning to his father to find out what name he wanted to give him. [63] He asked for a writing tablet and wrote, "His name is John." And all of them were amazed. [64] Immediately his mouth was opened and his tongue freed, and he began to speak, praising God. [65] Fear came over all their neighbors, and all these things were talked about throughout the entire hill country of Judea. [66] All who heard them pondered them and said, "What then will this child become?" For, indeed, the hand of the Lord was with him.

[67] Then his father Zechariah was filled with the Holy Spirit and spoke this prophecy:
[68] "Blessed be the Lord God of Israel,
for he has looked favorably on his people and redeemed them.
[69] He has raised up a mighty savior[b] for us
in the house of his servant David,
[70] as he spoke through the mouth of his holy prophets from of old,

[a] Other ancient authorities read *Elizabeth*
[b] Gk *a horn of salvation*

1.46–56: Mary's Magnificat. The first of four canticles in Lk 1–2. The song is modeled on Hannah's prayer (1 Sam 2.1–10; for similar songs by women see Ex 15.19–20 [Miriam]; Judg 5.1–31 [Deborah]; Jdt 16.1–17 [Judith]). **46:** *Magnifies*, Lat "Magnificat." **48:** See 1 Sam 1.11[LXX]; Mary's *lowliness* is the same Gk word ("tapeinōsis," "low estate") as Hannah's "misery." **49:** *Holy is his name*, see 11.1n. **50:** *Generation to generation* (Heb "dor [le]'dor"), see Ex 17.16; Isa 34.10; Ps 79.13; *T. Levi* 18.8, and elsewhere. **54:** *His servant Israel*, Isa 44.1; Ps 136.22; 1 Chr 16.13. **55:** *Promise he made*, Gen. 12.3; 15.5; 17.7; 18.18; 22.17; Mic 7.20, and elsewhere. Combining covenants with David and *Abraham*, to this point, Luke emphasizes the promises to Israel first, and then, via Israel, to the nations.

1.57–66: John's birth and naming. 59: *Circumcise*, the sign of the covenant (Heb "brit") between God and Israel, in accord with Gen 17.11–12; 21.4; Lev 12.3; see also Lk 2.21; *m. Shabb.* 18.3. *Zechariah after his father* (see Tob 1.1; Josephus, *J.W.* 5.13.2; *Ant.* 14.1.3), a tradition maintained in Sephardic (Mediterranean) but not Ashkenazic (Eastern European) Jewish culture; in the latter, children are named after deceased relatives. Naming sons at circumcision is not attested in Jewish sources until the post-Talmudic period (eighth century). Earlier Jewish texts attest naming after grandfathers, but not after fathers (unless the father is deceased). **60:** *John*, see 1.13n. **66:** *Hand of the Lord*, Ex 9.3; 16.3; Josh 4.24; 22.31; Isa 41.20; 66.14; and elsewhere, often in contexts of judgment.

1.67–79: The second canticle, called the "Benedictus" (Lat "blessed"; see v. 68). **67:** *Holy Spirit*, see 1.15n.; Joel 2.28–31 (Acts 2.17–18) on the connection between the *Spirit* and prophecy. **68:** *Blessed be the Lord*, familiar blessing in the Tanakh (1 Sam 25.32; 1 Kings 1.48; 8.15; etc.). *Redeemed*, Zechariah speaks as if redemption has already occurred (see 2.38; 24.21n.). **69:** *Mighty savior*, lit., "horn [Heb "qeren"] of salvation," see 2 Sam 22.3; Ps 18.2; see also Ps 89.17–24; 132.17; 148.14; Sir 51.12. **70:** *Holy prophets*, the Tanakh depicts prophets as God's

[71] that we would be saved from our enemies and from the hand of all who hate us.
[72] Thus he has shown the mercy promised to our ancestors,
and has remembered his holy covenant,
[73] the oath that he swore to our ancestor Abraham,
to grant us [74] that we, being rescued from the hands of our enemies,
might serve him without fear, [75] in holiness and righteousness
before him all our days.
[76] And you, child, will be called the prophet of the Most High;
for you will go before the Lord to prepare his ways,
[77] to give knowledge of salvation to his people
by the forgiveness of their sins.
[78] By the tender mercy of our God,
the dawn from on high will break upon[a] us,
[79] to give light to those who sit in darkness and in the shadow of death,
to guide our feet into the way of peace."

[80] The child grew and became strong in spirit, and he was in the wilderness until the day he appeared publicly to Israel.

2 In those days a decree went out from Emperor Augustus that all the world should be registered. [2] This was the first registration and was taken while Quirinius was governor of Syria. [3] All went to their own towns to be registered. [4] Joseph also went from the town of Nazareth in Galilee to Judea, to the city of David called Bethlehem, because he was descended from the house and family of David. [5] He went to be registered with Mary, to whom he was engaged and who was expecting a child. [6] While they were there, the time came for her to deliver her child. [7] And she gave birth to her firstborn son and wrapped him in bands of cloth, and laid him in a manger, because there was no place for them in the inn.

[8] In that region there were shepherds living in the fields, keeping watch over their flock by night. [9] Then an angel of the Lord stood before them, and the glory of the Lord shone around them, and they were terrified. [10] But

[a] Other ancient authorities read *has broken upon*

servants (Ezek 38.1) but not usually as holy; contrast Wis 11.1; Eph 3.5; *2 Bar.* 85.1. **72–73:** *Remembered his holy covenant*, e.g., Ex 2.24; Lev 26.42; Ps 105.8, as well as the "ḥesed avot" ["steadfast love of the fathers"] of Mic 7.20; Ps 106.45; etc. *Oath*, see Gen 26.3. *Holy covenant*, Dan 11.30; 1 Macc 1.15,63. **76:** *Most High*, 1.32n. *Prepare his ways*, 3.4n. **77:** *Forgiveness of their sins*, see 3.3n. **78:** *Tender mercy*, evoking Heb "raḥamim," see, e.g., Isa 54.7; 63.7; Jer 42.12; Ps 25.6; 103.4. **79:** *Sit in darkness*, see Isa 42.7; Mic 7.8; Ps 107.10; 143.3; Lam 3.6. *Shadow of death* (Mt 4.16), Ps 23.4. *Peace*, a major concern for the Tanakh. **80:** *Grew and became strong*, compare 2.52. *Wilderness*, see 3.4; site of Israel's encounter with God at Sinai; here, by the Jordan River; see also Judg 13.25.

2.1–7: Jesus' birth (Mt 1.18–25). **1:** *Augustus*, who ruled 27 BCE–14 CE, was called "god," "son of god," "savior," and "father." *Registered*, this census is not externally attested. Rome registered its citizens primarily to determine taxes; in Jewish thought, counting people directly is contrary to divine will (see Ex 30.12; 2 Sam 24). Acts 5.37 dates the revolt of Judas the Galilean to the "time of the census" and thus contrasts Joseph and Mary's obedience to Judas's revolution. **2:** *Quirinius*, appointed "legatus" (military governor) to suppress the revolt by the Homonadensians in Cilicia; the actual governor was Varus. Josephus (*Ant.* 17.354; 18.1–2; cf. *J.W.* 2.117; 7.253) reports a census under Quirinius in 6 CE, not during Herod's reign. **3–4:** *Their own towns*, the census explains how Jesus can be born in *Bethlehem*, the *city of David* (1 Sam 17; 20; Mic 5.2 predicts a ruler from Bethlehem; see Mt 2.5–6). Bethlehem is approximately five miles from Jerusalem, eighty-five miles from Nazareth. **7:** *Firstborn* (Gk "prototokos"; Heb "ḅor") can indicate that which is dedicated to God (Ex 13.2,12,15; Num 3.12–13; Deut 21.17); Israel is God's "firstborn son" (Ex 4.22). *Manger*, feeding trough; the symbolism anticipates the Last Supper (22.19). *Inn*, Luke gives no indication residents rejected the family; there may have been no room for the privacy needed for the birth.

2.8–20: Annunciation to shepherds (cf. Mt 2.1–12). **8:** *Shepherds*, contrary to some Christian teaching, Jews of the time did not view shepherds as outcast or unclean, as numerous positive images of shepherds in Israel's Scriptures, the association of Moses and David with shepherding, and the connection of sheep with the sacrificial system indicate (see also Philo, *Spec. Laws* 1.133,136). **9:** *Glory of the Lord*, compare Heb "kavod" [of YHWH]

the angel said to them, "Do not be afraid; for see—I am bringing you good news of great joy for all the people: [11] to you is born this day in the city of David a Savior, who is the Messiah,[a] the Lord. [12] This will be a sign for you: you will find a child wrapped in bands of cloth and lying in a manger." [13] And suddenly there was with the angel a multitude of the heavenly host,[b] praising God and saying,

[14] "Glory to God in the highest heaven,
and on earth peace among those whom he favors!"[c]

[15] When the angels had left them and gone into heaven, the shepherds said to one another, "Let us go now to Bethlehem and see this thing that has taken place, which the Lord has made known to us." [16] So they went with haste and found Mary and Joseph, and the child lying in the manger. [17] When they saw this, they made known what had been told them about this child; [18] and all who heard it were amazed at what the shepherds told them. [19] But Mary treasured all these words and pondered them in her heart. [20] The shepherds returned, glorifying and praising God for all they had heard and seen, as it had been told them.

[21] After eight days had passed, it was time to circumcise the child; and he was called Jesus, the name given by the angel before he was conceived in the womb.

[22] When the time came for their purification according to the law of Moses, they brought him up to Jerusalem to present him to the Lord [23] (as it is written in the law of the Lord, "Every firstborn male shall be designated as holy to the Lord"), [24] and they offered a sacrifice according to what is stated in the law of the Lord, "a pair of turtledoves or two young pigeons."

[25] Now there was a man in Jerusalem whose name was Simeon;[d] this man was righteous and devout, looking forward to the consolation of Israel, and the Holy Spirit rested on him. [26] It had been revealed to him by the Holy Spirit that he would not see death before he had seen the Lord's Messiah.[e] [27] Guided by the Spirit, Simeon[f] came into the temple; and when the parents brought in the child Jesus, to do for him what was customary under the law, [28] Simeon[g] took him in his arms and praised God, saying,

[29] "Master, now you are dismissing your servant[h] in peace,
according to your word;
[30] for my eyes have seen your salvation,
[31] which you have prepared in the presence of all peoples,
[32] a light for revelation to the Gentiles
and for glory to your people Israel."

[a] Or *the Christ*
[b] Gk *army*
[c] Other ancient authorities read *peace, goodwill among people*
[d] Gk *Symeon*
[e] Or *the Lord's Christ*
[f] Gk *In the Spirit, he*
[g] Gk *he*
[h] Gk *slave*

(Ex 16.7,10; 24.16–17; Isa 40.5; Ps 104.31; etc.). **10:** *Good news,* 1.19n. *All the people* (Heb "kol ha'am"), would be heard by a Jewish audience as concerning the "people Israel." **11:** *City of David,* 1.3n. *Messiah* (Gk "Christos") *the Lord,* 1.17n. *Pss. Sol.* 17.32 mentions a *Lord, the anointed* in reference to a Davidic king; see also the "LORD'S anointed" in Lam 4.20; 1 Sam 24.7 (in reference to King Saul). **12:** *Wrapped in bands,* KJV: "swaddling cloths"; see Wis 7.4–5. *Manger,* 1.7n. **13:** *Heavenly host,* Deut 4.19; 33.2; 1 Kings 22.19; Jer 8.2; Ps 33.6; etc., the angels who serve God. **19:** See 2.51.

2.21–24: Jesus' circumcision and presentation. 21: *Eight days had passed,* lit., "had been fulfilled"; the circumcision took place on the eighth day after birth; see 1.59n. *Called Jesus,* 1.31n. **22:** *Their purification,* no purification rites were required for fathers or newborns. For the mother's purification (forty days after the birth of a son), see Lev 12 and "The Law," p. 515. *Jerusalem,* a Lukan focus. *Present him,* possible allusion to the "pidyon ha-ben," "redemption of the firstborn" (Ex 13.2,12,15; Num 18.15–16; Neh 10.35–36); no law prescribes this presentation; presenting children at the Temple is not a recognized custom. **23:** Paraphrasing Ex 13.2.

2.25–38: Simeon and Anna. 25: *Jerusalem,* see 1.21. *Simeon,* not otherwise attested. *Consolation* (Gk "paraklēsis"), here synonymous with redemption, 1.68n.; 24.21n.; see also Isa 40 [LXX]; *2 Bar.* 44.7. *Holy Spirit,* 1.15n. **27:** *What was customary,* see 2.21–22n. **29:** *Now you are dismissing,* Lat "Nunc dimittis." The canticle is often referred to by this name. **30–31:** *Your salvation,* see 3.6. **32:** *Revelation to the Gentiles,* see Isa 49.6; Judaism gen-

[33] And the child's father and mother were amazed at what was being said about him. [34] Then Simeon[a] blessed them and said to his mother Mary, "This child is destined for the falling and the rising of many in Israel, and to be a sign that will be opposed [35] so that the inner thoughts of many will be revealed—and a sword will pierce your own soul too."

[36] There was also a prophet, Anna[b] the daughter of Phanuel, of the tribe of Asher. She was of a great age, having lived with her husband seven years after her marriage, [37] then as a widow to the age of eighty-four. She never left the temple but worshiped there with fasting and prayer night and day. [38] At that moment she came, and began to praise God and to speak about the child[c] to all who were looking for the redemption of Jerusalem.

[39] When they had finished everything required by the law of the Lord, they returned to Galilee, to their own town of Nazareth. [40] The child grew and became strong, filled with wisdom; and the favor of God was upon him.

[41] Now every year his parents went to Jerusalem for the festival of the Passover. [42] And when he was twelve years old, they went up as usual for the festival. [43] When the festival was ended and they started to return, the boy Jesus stayed behind in Jerusalem, but his parents did not know it. [44] Assuming that he was in the group of travelers, they went a day's journey. Then they started to look for him among their relatives and friends. [45] When they did not find him, they returned to Jerusalem to search for him. [46] After three days they found him in the temple, sitting among the teachers, listening to them and asking them questions. [47] And all who heard him were amazed at his understanding and his answers. [48] When his parents[d] saw him they were astonished; and his mother said to him, "Child, why have you treated us like this? Look, your father and I have been searching for you in great anxiety." [49] He said to them, "Why were you searching for me? Did you not know that I must be in my Father's house?"[e] [50] But they did not understand what he said to them. [51] Then he went down with them and came to Nazareth, and was obedient to them. His mother treasured all these things in her heart.

a Gk *Symeon*
b Gk *Hanna*
c Gk *him*
d Gk *they*
e Or *be about my Father's interests?*

erally taught that salvation was for all people, not only for Jews. *Glory to your people Israel*, see Isa 46.13. **33:** *Father*, Joseph (also 2.48; 3.23). **34:** *Blessed them*, perhaps hinting at a priestly blessing (see Num 6.23; 1 Sam 2.20). *Falling and the rising*, Jesus' preaching, and the preaching about him, create division among Jews; Luke frequently depicts Jews who do not accept Jesus as violently opposed to him and his followers (see 4.28–29). **35:** *Sword will pierce your own soul*, views of Mary's righteousness, suffering, and intercession will develop in Christian thought. **36:** *Prophet, Anna*, comparable to women prophets in Judaism (Miriam [Exod 15.20], Deborah [Judg 4.4], Huldah [2 Kings 22.14], and possibly Isaiah's wife [Isa 8.3]). **37:** *As a widow*, Luke favors celibacy. **38:** *Redemption of Jerusalem*, 1.68n.; 24.21n.

2.39–40: Jesus' childhood. 39: *Required by the law*, Luke emphasizes the family's connection to Torah.

2.41–52: Jesus in the Temple. 41: *Every year*, Luke continues the themes of Jerusalem, Temple, and Torah. *Passover*, one of three pilgrimage festivals (with Sukkot/Booths and Shavuot/Weeks), see Ex 23.14–17; Deut 16.1–8,16; also Lk 22.7–13. **42:** *Twelve years old*, the story is not, contrary to popular teaching, Jesus' bar mitzvah; for thirteen as the age of adult responsibility, see *m. Nidd.* 5.6; *m. Avot* 5.21; *Gen. Rab.* 63.10; for twelve, regarding vows and fasting, *Sifre Num.* 22; *b. Ber.* 24a. **47:** Stories of heroes' prodigious wisdom are conventional (e.g., Cyrus [Herodotus I, 114f.], Alexander the Great [Plutarch, *Life of Alexander* 5], Moses [*Ant.* 2.230; Philo, *Life of Moses* 1.21]; Josephus, *Life* 9, records: "when I was a child, about fourteen years of age, I was commended by all for the love I had of learning; on which account the high priests and principal men of the city frequently came to me together, to know my opinion about the accurate understanding of points of the law"). **48:** *Father*, see 2.33n., anticipating the irony of Jesus' response in 2.49. **49:** *Father's house*, the phrase is common in the Tanakh but not in reference to the Temple. **51:** See 2.19. **52:** 1 Sam 2.26; Lk 1.80; 2.40; similar terms describe Moses (*Ant.* 2.231; Philo, *Life of Moses* 1.19); see also Prov 3.4.

[52] And Jesus increased in wisdom and in years,[a] and in divine and human favor.

3

In the fifteenth year of the reign of Emperor Tiberius, when Pontius Pilate was governor of Judea, and Herod was ruler[b] of Galilee, and his brother Philip ruler[b] of the region of Ituraea and Trachonitis, and Lysanias ruler[b] of Abilene, [2] during the high priesthood of Annas and Caiaphas, the word of God came to John son of Zechariah in the wilderness. [3] He went into all the region around the Jordan, proclaiming a baptism of repentance for the forgiveness of sins, [4] as it is written in the book of the words of the prophet Isaiah,

"The voice of one crying out in the
wilderness:
'Prepare the way of the Lord,
make his paths straight.
[5] Every valley shall be filled,
and every mountain and hill shall be
made low,
and the crooked shall be made straight,
and the rough ways made smooth;
[6] and all flesh shall see the salvation of
God.'"

[7] John said to the crowds that came out to be baptized by him, "You brood of vipers! Who warned you to flee from the wrath to come? [8] Bear fruits worthy of repentance. Do not begin to say to yourselves, 'We have Abraham as our ancestor'; for I tell you, God is able from these stones to raise up children to Abraham. [9] Even now the ax is lying at the root of the trees; every tree therefore that does not bear good fruit is cut down and thrown into the fire."

[10] And the crowds asked him, "What then should we do?" [11] In reply he said to them, "Whoever has two coats must share with anyone who has none; and whoever has food must do likewise." [12] Even tax collectors came to be baptized, and they asked him, "Teacher, what should we do?" [13] He said to them, "Collect no more than the amount prescribed for you." [14] Soldiers also asked him, "And we, what should we do?" He said to them, "Do not extort money from anyone by threats or false accusation, and be satisfied with your wages."

[a] Or *in stature*
[b] Gk *tetrarch*

3.1–6: John the Baptist (Mt 3.1–6; Mk 1.2–6). See also *Ant.* 18.5.2. Some scholars believe the original version of Luke's Gospel began here (see Introduction and compare Mk 1). **1:** *Tiberius* ruled 14–37 CE. *Pontius Pilate,* Roman *governor* of *Judea,* Samaria, and Idumea (26–36 CE). *Herod* Antipas (see 23.6–7) ruled *Galilee* and Perea (4 BCE–29 CE). *Philip,* ruled 4 BCE–34 CE; see 3.19–20. *Lysanias,* Roman tetrarch of Abilene (west of Damascus), ca. 25–30 CE. **2:** *Annas,* high priest 6–15 CE when deposed by Rome. He was succeeded by his sons, then his son-in-law *Caiaphas* (18–36 CE). On dating by reigning powers, see e.g. Isa 6.1; Jer 1.1–3; Ezek 1.1–3. *Zechariah,* 1.5–23,59–80. *Wilderness,* 1.80n. **3:** *Baptism,* from a Gk term meaning "dip," ritual immersion in water. Unlike "miqveh" immersion for ritual purity, John's baptism was apparently a singular event. For washing as symbolizing God's cleansing, see e.g., Ezek 36.25; Ps 51.2; for the renunciation of evil see Isa 1.16. Josephus (*Ant.* 18.117) states that John's baptism did not wash away sins; rather, it served as public testimony of repentance. For 1QS 5.7–15, immersion functions as a rite of initiation; there is no evidence of John's connection to the Qumran community. "Jewish proselyte baptism" (i.e., immersion as part of the ritual of conversion to Judaism) appears to be a post-70s practice (*b. Yebam.* 46a). For immersion prior to offering sacrifice, see *m. Pesah.* 8.8. **4–6:** Isa 40.3–5 (see also 1QS 8.12–16). For Isaiah, *salvation* was Israel's return from Babylonian exile to its homeland ("A voice cries out: 'In the wilderness, prepare . . .'"); however, cantillation marks (for chanting the text in the synagogue) place "in the wilderness" with "prepare the way." See also Mal 3.1.

3.7–18: John's teaching. 7: *Crowds,* Mt 3.7–10 addresses John's invective to Pharisees and Sadducees. *Brood of vipers,* Matthew's designation for Pharisees, scribes, and Sadducees (Mt 3.7; 12.34; 23.33). *Wrath to come,* God's final judgment. **8:** *Abraham as . . . ancestor* (see Jn 8.33–39), Jewish tradition speaks of "zukhut 'avot," the "merits of the fathers" (see e.g., *b. Shabb.* 55a). See also 1.72n. *Stones . . . children,* an Aramaic ("avnayya . . . benayya") and Hebrew ("avanim . . . banim") pun. **11:** *Share,* care for the disadvantaged is a major Jewish value (see, e.g., Isa 1.10–20; 58.6–7; Ezek 18.5–9; Tob 1.16–17; 4.16; *Gen. Rab.* 30; *b. Ber.* 5a; etc.). **12:** *Tax collectors,* most likely Jews in Rome's employ, regarded as traitors and known for corrupt practices. **14:** *Soldiers,* including Jews in service to Herod Antipas (see *Ant.* 18.5.1). The teaching conforms to Josephus's description of John (*Ant.* 18.117), "A good man who commanded the Jews to exercise virtue, both as to righteousness towards one another and

[15] As the people were filled with expectation, and all were questioning in their hearts concerning John, whether he might be the Messiah,[a] [16] John answered all of them by saying, "I baptize you with water; but one who is more powerful than I is coming; I am not worthy to untie the thong of his sandals. He will baptize you with[b] the Holy Spirit and fire. [17] His winnowing fork is in his hand, to clear his threshing floor and to gather the wheat into his granary; but the chaff he will burn with unquenchable fire."

[18] So, with many other exhortations, he proclaimed the good news to the people. [19] But Herod the ruler,[c] who had been rebuked by him because of Herodias, his brother's wife, and because of all the evil things that Herod had done, [20] added to them all by shutting up John in prison.

[21] Now when all the people were baptized, and when Jesus also had been baptized and was praying, the heaven was opened, [22] and the Holy Spirit descended upon him in bodily form like a dove. And a voice came from heaven, "You are my Son, the Beloved;[d] with you I am well pleased."[e]

[23] Jesus was about thirty years old when he began his work. He was the son (as was thought) of Joseph son of Heli, [24] son of Matthat, son of Levi, son of Melchi, son of Jannai, son of Joseph, [25] son of Mattathias, son of Amos, son of Nahum, son of Esli, son of Naggai, [26] son of Maath, son of Mattathias, son of Semein, son of Josech, son of Joda, [27] son of Joanan, son of Rhesa, son of Zerubbabel, son of Shealtiel,[f] son of Neri, [28] son of Melchi, son of Addi, son of Cosam, son of Elmadam, son of Er, [29] son of Joshua, son of Eliezer, son of Jorim, son of Matthat, son of Levi, [30] son of Simeon, son of Judah, son of Joseph, son of Jonam, son of Eliakim, [31] son of Melea, son of Menna, son of Mattatha, son of Nathan, son of David, [32] son of Jesse, son of Obed, son of Boaz, son of Sala,[g] son of Nahshon, [33] son of Amminadab, son of Admin, son of Arni,[h] son of Hezron, son of Perez, son of Judah, [34] son of Jacob, son of Isaac, son of Abraham, son of Terah, son of Nahor, [35] son of Serug, son of Reu, son of Peleg, son of Eber, son of Shelah, [36] son of Cainan, son of Arphaxad, son of Shem, son of Noah, son of Lamech, [37] son of Methuselah, son of Enoch, son of Jared, son of Mahalaleel, son of Cainan, [38] son of Enos, son of Seth, son of Adam, son of God.

a Or *the Christ*
b Or *in*
c Gk *tetrarch*
d Or *my beloved Son*
e Other ancient authorities read *You are my Son, today I have begotten you*
f Gk *Salathiel*
g Other ancient authorities read *Salmon*
h Other ancient authorities read *Amminadab, son of Aram*; others vary widely

piety towards God." **15:** Some regarded *John* as the *Messiah*. **16–18:** (Mt 3.11–12; Mk 1.7–8). *Holy Spirit*, see 1.15n., Acts 2.1–4. **18:** Good news, 1.19n.

3.19–20: John's imprisonment (Mt 14.3–4; Mk 6.17–18). Herod Antipas divorced the daughter of the Nabatean king in order to marry Herodias, his niece, who had divorced his brother, Herod Philip. Josephus (*Ant.* 18.5.1) provides details. Jewish law prohibited marrying one's brother's wife (Lev 18.16; 20.21). *Rebuked*, on "rebuking" (Heb "tokheiḥah"), see Lev 19.17; *b. Tamid* 28a; *Gen. Rab.* 54.3; *Sifra* 89a–89b.

3.21–22: Jesus' baptism (Mt 3.13–17; Mk 1.9–11). **21:** *Praying*, indication of Jewish piety (5.16; 6.12; 9.18,28; 11.1; 22.32,41–46). *Heaven was opened*, Isa 64.1; Ezek 1.1; *2 Bar.* 22.1, indicating direct divine revelation. **22:** *Holy Spirit*, see 1.15n. *Voice came from heaven*, Heb "bat qol" ("daughter of the voice"), a rare means of divine communication (e.g., *b. B. Metz.* 59b; see also Lk 9.35). *Son*, suggesting Isa 42.1; Ps 2.7. For Jewish messianic interpretation of Ps 2, see *Pss. Sol.* 17.23–24; 4QFlor.

3.23–38: Jesus' genealogy (Mt 1.1–17). Luke traces Jesus' lineage to Adam (Gen 5.1), also a "son of God" (v. 38; see Philo, *Virtues* 204–5). Matthew's genealogy goes through Solomon (1.6) rather than Nathan (2 Sam 5.14; Lk 3.31), and names Joseph's father Jacob (Mt 1.15–16), not Heli (Lk 3.23). The seventy-seven names (compare Matthew's three divisions of 14) suggest completion. For *Adam* to *David*, see Gen 5.3–32; 11.10–26; Ruth 4.18–22; 1 Chr 1.1–4,24–28; 2.1–15. **23:** *Thirty*, conventional age of service: Gen 41.46; Num 4.3,23; 2 Sam 5.4; Dionysius, *Ant. rom.* 4.6. **38:** *Son of Adam, son of God*, without parallel in Jewish tradition.

4 Jesus, full of the Holy Spirit, returned from the Jordan and was led by the Spirit in the wilderness, [2] where for forty days he was tempted by the devil. He ate nothing at all during those days, and when they were over, he was famished. [3] The devil said to him, "If you are the Son of God, command this stone to become a loaf of bread." [4] Jesus answered him, "It is written, 'One does not live by bread alone.'"

[5] Then the devil[a] led him up and showed him in an instant all the kingdoms of the world. [6] And the devil[a] said to him, "To you I will give their glory and all this authority; for it has been given over to me, and I give it to anyone I please. [7] If you, then, will worship me, it will all be yours." [8] Jesus answered him, "It is written,

'Worship the Lord your God,
and serve only him.'"

[9] Then the devil[a] took him to Jerusalem, and placed him on the pinnacle of the temple, saying to him, "If you are the Son of God, throw yourself down from here, [10] for it is written,

'He will command his angels concerning you,
to protect you,'

[11] and

'On their hands they will bear you up,
so that you will not dash your foot against a stone.'"

[12] Jesus answered him, "It is said, 'Do not put the Lord your God to the test.'" [13] When the devil had finished every test, he departed from him until an opportune time.

[14] Then Jesus, filled with the power of the Spirit, returned to Galilee, and a report about him spread through all the surrounding country. [15] He began to teach in their synagogues and was praised by everyone.

[16] When he came to Nazareth, where he had been brought up, he went to the synagogue on the sabbath day, as was his custom. He stood up to read, [17] and the scroll of the prophet Isaiah was given to him. He unrolled the scroll and found the place where it was written:

[18] "The Spirit of the Lord is upon me,
because he has anointed me
to bring good news to the poor.
He has sent me to proclaim release to the captives
and recovery of sight to the blind,
to let the oppressed go free,
[19] to proclaim the year of the Lord's favor."

[a] Gk *he*

4.1–13: The temptation (Mt 4.1–11; Mk 1.12–13). **1:** *Holy Spirit*, 1.15n. **2:** *Forty days* in the *wilderness* (v. 1) recalls Israel's testing (Deut 8.2; Ps 106). *Tempted*, or "tested" (see 11.16). *Ate nothing*, see Deut 9.9; 1 Kings 19.8; Jesus enacts the roles of Moses and Elijah. **3:** *Devil*, Satan; in Jewish thought (cf. Zech 3.1–2 and Job 1–2 ["the Satan," i.e., the "Accuser"]; 1 Chr 21.1) is a member of the heavenly court; his role is to test the righteous. **4:** Deut 8.3. Jesus counters Satan's citation of Psalms by quoting Deuteronomy (the citations are closer to the LXX than the MT). **5:** Compare Deut 34.1–4. **6:** *Given over to me*, suggests Satan presently rules the world. **8:** Deut 6.13; 10.20. *Lord your God* here can subtly refer to Jesus (1.17n.). **9:** *Jerusalem*, see 2.22n. Matthew places this temptation second and ends with the temptation to universal rule. **10–11:** Ps 91.11–12. **12:** Deut 6.16. *Lord your God*, see v. 8n. **13:** *Opportune time*, see 22.3,28.

4.14–15: Teaching in Galilee (Mt 4.12–17; Mk 1.14–15). **14:** *Spirit*, 1.15n. **15:** *Synagogues*, locations of Jewish worship, teaching, and community gathering; see 4.44; see also "The Synagogue," p. 519. *Praised by everyone*, initial Jewish reception is unequivocally positive.

4.16–30: Rejection in Nazareth. See Mt 13.53–58; Mk 6.1–6; a scene unique to Luke (perhaps a rewriting of Mk 6.1–6; cf. Mt 13.53–58). See "Jesus' Synagogue Sermon," p. 107. **16:** *As was his custom*, referring to v. 15. *To read*, most people in antiquity were illiterate. **17:** *Scroll of the prophet Isaiah*, whether Nazareth had a separate synagogue building or was prosperous enough to own an Isaiah scroll remains debated. Jesus would be reading the "haftarah", a passage from the Prophets ("Nevi'im") complementing the weekly Torah portion. The earliest rabbinic reference to this practice is *t. Meg.* 4 (3).1; however, both Lk 4 and Acts 13.15 suggest it as might Philo. The text Jesus reads does not appear among the "haftarot." **18–19:** Isa 61.1–2; see also Isa 58.6 and the Jubilee tradition of Lev 25 (see *b. Sanh.* 102a). For messianic interpretations of Isa 61, see 1QH 18.14; 11QMelch 1.18. *Spirit . . . is upon me*, 3.22. *Release to the captives*, ironic, given John's imprisonment (3.19–20). Luke omits Isaiah's

JESUS' SYNAGOGUE SERMON (LK 4.16–30)

Replacing Mark's account (Mk 6.2–6) of Jesus' rejection in Nazareth, this depiction of Jesus' preaching in the local synagogue is generally recognized as the Gospel's signature story: Jesus announces that Isaiah's predictions about the one "anointed" (4.18: the Greek *echrisen* is related to the term "Christ") are fulfilled in his ministry; the Gentile mission is suggested; and the Jews in the synagogue violently reject him.

Rather than manifest the "recovery of sight to the blind" or the letting "the oppressed go free" (4.18), Jesus first goes on the offensive against the people in the synagogue and next cites two precedents to his ministry: the prophets Elijah and Elisha performed miracles not for Jews but for Gentiles. Luke then describes how the congregation was "filled with rage," "drove Jesus out of the town," and sought to "hurl him off the cliff" (4.28–29). Christian sermons occasionally explain the fury of the congregation by claiming that the Jews, as not only ethnocentric but also xenophobic, wanted to reserve the messianic benefits for themselves; therefore, they seek to kill Jesus because he has a positive message for the Gentiles.

Such conclusions misread Jewish history. Jews in general had positive relations with Gentiles, as witnessed by the Court of the Gentiles in the Jerusalem Temple, Gentiles as patrons of synagogues (7.1–10), and Gentiles as god-fearers (Acts 10). They also expected the redemption of righteous Gentiles, who would come streaming to Zion, as Zech 8.23 states, "In those days ten men from nations of every language shall take hold of a Jew, grasping his garment and saying, 'Let us go with you, for we have heard that God is with you.'" The rejection of Jesus is not prompted by xenophobia; it is prompted by Jesus' refusal to provide his hometown with messianic blessings.

[20] And he rolled up the scroll, gave it back to the attendant, and sat down. The eyes of all in the synagogue were fixed on him. [21] Then he began to say to them, "Today this scripture has been fulfilled in your hearing." [22] All spoke well of him and were amazed at the gracious words that came from his mouth. They said, "Is not this Joseph's son?" [23] He said to them, "Doubtless you will quote to me this proverb, 'Doctor, cure yourself!' And you will say, 'Do here also in your hometown the things that we have heard you did at Capernaum.'" [24] And he said, "Truly I tell you, no prophet is accepted in the prophet's hometown. [25] But the truth is, there were many widows in Israel in the time of Elijah, when the heaven was shut up three years and six months, and there was a severe famine over all the land; [26] yet Elijah was sent to none of them except to a widow at Zarephath in Sidon. [27] There were also many lepers[a] in Israel in the time of the prophet Elisha, and none of them was cleansed except Naaman the Syrian." [28] When they heard this, all in the synagogue were filled with rage. [29] They got up, drove him out of the town, and led him to the brow of the hill on which their town was built, so that they might hurl him off the cliff. [30] But he passed through the midst of them and went on his way.

[31] He went down to Capernaum, a city in Galilee, and was teaching them on the sabbath. [32] They were astounded at his teaching, because he spoke with authority. [33] In the synagogue there was a man who had the spirit of an unclean demon, and he cried out with a loud voice, [34] "Let us alone! What

[a] The terms *leper* and *leprosy* can refer to several diseases

reference to "the day of vengeance" (61.2). **22:** *Joseph's son*, see 2.33,48; 3.23. **23:** *Doctor, cure yourself*, a similar proverb appears in *Gen. Rab.* 23.4. *You did at Capernaum*, Luke does not describe these events; see 4.31–41. *Capernaum* (from "Kefar-Nahum," Nahum's village), a fishing center on the Sea of Galilee. **24:** *Truly* (Gk/Heb "amen," lit., "so be it"; the only Hebrew word Luke uses), a term usually found at the end of prayers, but Jesus' usage is not unique (e.g., Jer 28.6). **25–26:** See 1 Kings 17.8–16. **27:** 2 Kings 5.1–4. **28:** *Filled with rage*, not because of beneficence shown to Gentiles but to Jesus' withholding his powers from them. **29:** *Cliff*, Nazareth is not built on a cliff.

4.31–37: Capernaum healing (Mt 4.13; 7.28–29; Mk 1.21–28). The first of five Sabbath healings (4.31,38; 6.6; 13.10; 14.1). No offense is taken at these healings; Jesus violates no Sabbath commandment. **31:** *Capernaum*, see v. 23n. **32:** *With authority* (also v. 36), perhaps indicating that he speaks on his authority rather than cites earlier

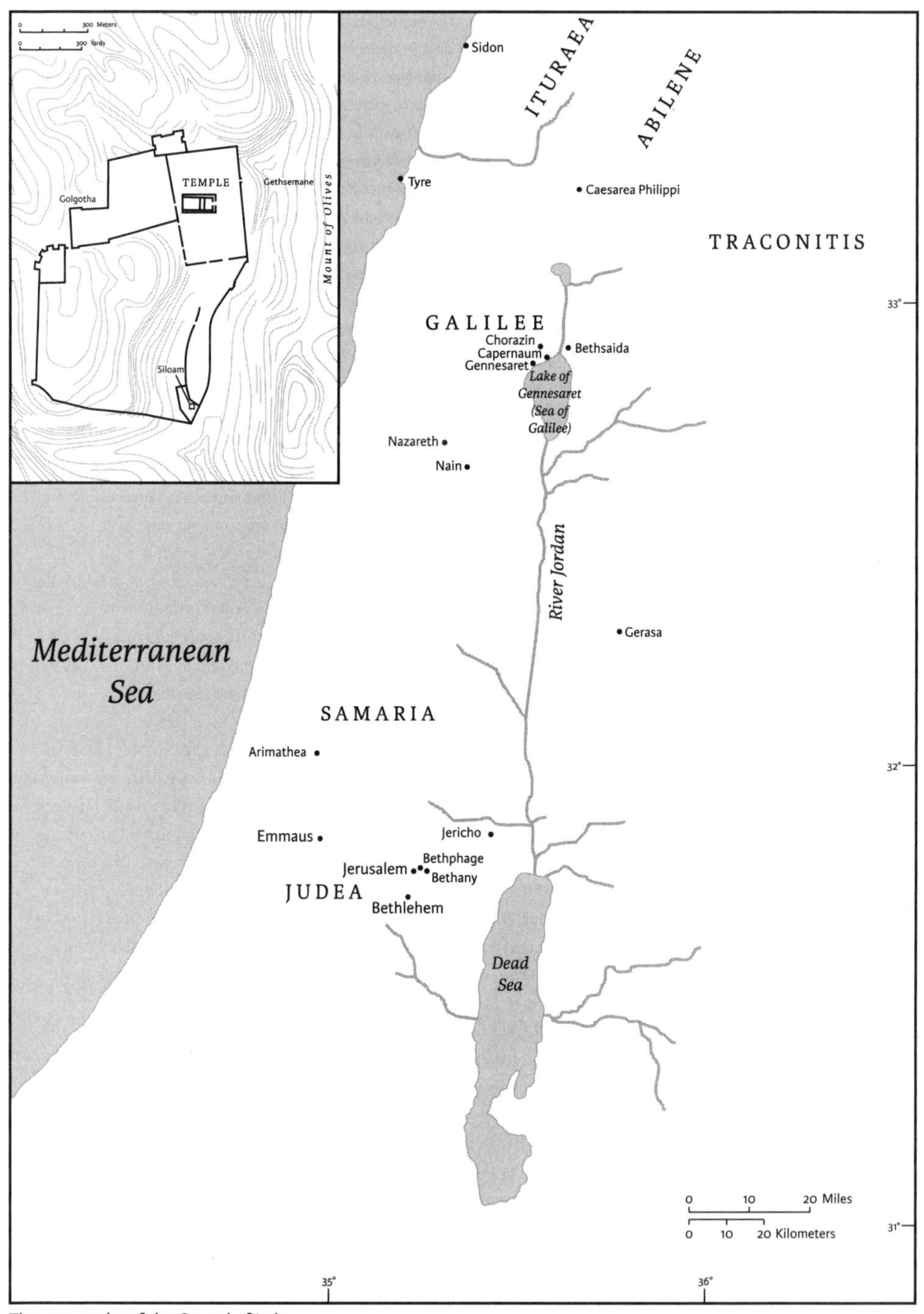

The geography of the Gospel of Luke.

have you to do with us, Jesus of Nazareth? Have you come to destroy us? I know who you are, the Holy One of God." [35] But Jesus rebuked him, saying, "Be silent, and come out of him!" When the demon had thrown him down before them, he came out of him without having done him any harm. [36] They were all amazed and kept saying to one another, "What kind of utterance is this? For with authority and power he commands the unclean spirits, and out they come!" [37] And a report about him began to reach every place in the region.

[38] After leaving the synagogue he entered Simon's house. Now Simon's mother-in-law was suffering from a high fever, and they asked him about her. [39] Then he stood over her and rebuked the fever, and it left her. Immediately she got up and began to serve them.

[40] As the sun was setting, all those who had any who were sick with various kinds of diseases brought them to him; and he laid his hands on each of them and cured them. [41] Demons also came out of many, shouting, "You are the Son of God!" But he rebuked them and would not allow them to speak, because they knew that he was the Messiah.[a]

[42] At daybreak he departed and went into a deserted place. And the crowds were looking for him; and when they reached him, they wanted to prevent him from leaving them. [43] But he said to them, "I must proclaim the good news of the kingdom of God to the other cities also; for I was sent for this purpose." [44] So he continued proclaiming the message in the synagogues of Judea.[b]

5 Once while Jesus[c] was standing beside the lake of Gennesaret, and the crowd was pressing in on him to hear the word of God, [2] he saw two boats there at the shore of the lake; the fishermen had gone out of them and were washing their nets. [3] He got into one of the boats, the one belonging to Simon, and asked him to put out a little way from the shore. Then he sat down and taught the crowds from the boat. [4] When he had finished speaking, he said to Simon, "Put out into the deep water and let down your nets for a catch." [5] Simon answered, "Master, we have worked all night long but have caught nothing. Yet if you say so, I will let down the nets." [6] When they had done this, they caught so many fish that their nets were beginning to break. [7] So they signaled their partners in the other boat to come and help them. And they came and filled both boats, so that they began to sink. [8] But when Simon Peter saw it, he fell down at Jesus' knees, saying, "Go away from me, Lord, for I am a sinful man!" [9] For he and all who were with him were amazed at the catch of fish that they had taken; [10] and so also were James and John, sons of Zebedee, who were partners with Simon. Then Jesus said to Simon, "Do not be afraid; from now

[a] Or *the Christ*
[b] Other ancient authorities read *Galilee*
[c] Gk *he*

tradition (see e.g., *m. Avot* 1.1); see Mt 7.29. **36:** *Commands the unclean spirits*, Tob 3.17; Josephus (*J.W.* 7.185; *Ant.* 8.45–49); 1QapGen 20.16–29; Acts 19.13, and other sources attest Jewish exorcists. The expression "unclean spirit" appears in the Tanakh only at Zech 13.2.

4.38–39: Simon Peter's mother-in-law (Mt 8.14–15; Mk 1.29–31). This is the second Sabbath healing (see 4.31–37n.). **38:** *Simon*, see 5.1–11; 6.13–14. *Mother-in-law*, the Gospels do not mention the wife (but see 1 Cor 9.5). **39:** *Rebuked*, suggesting that a demon caused the fever (see 4.35). **39:** *Serve* (Gk "diakonei"), origin of the term "deacon" (see also 8.3; 10.40; 22.26–27).

4.40–41: Evening healings (Mt 8.16–17; Mk 1.32–34). **40:** *Sun was setting*, concluding the Sabbath.

4.42–44: Missionary mandate (Mt 4.23; Mk 1.35–39). **42:** *Crowds*, Jesus retains popular support among the Jewish people. **43:** *Kingdom of God*, the major content of Jesus' preaching; cf. Zech 14.9; Ps 93–99; the "Kiddush"; "May He give reign to His kingship in your lifetimes . . ." ("vayamlikh malkhutei beḥayeikhon uveyomeikhon . . ."), *b. Ber.* 14b. **44:** *Synagogues*, 4.15n. *Judea*, Jesus' teaching expands beyond Galilee.

5.1–11: Great catch of fish (Mt 13.1–3a; 4.18–22; Mk 1.16–20; 4.1–2; Jn 21.4–7). **1:** *Lake of Gennesaret*, Sea of Galilee, called "Kinneret" (NRSV: Chinnereth) in the Tanakh (Num 34.11; Deut 3.17; Josh 13.27). *Word of God*, the Torah as interpreted by Jesus and/or a prophetic revelation from him. **5:** *Master* (Gk "epistatēs"), Luke's equivalent for "Rabbi" (see Lk 9.33 || Mk 9.5). **8:** *Lord*, 1.17n. *Sinful*, Luke does not detail Peter's transgressions.

PHARISEES IN LUKE (LK 5.17–39)

Scholars correctly describe the Gospel's presentation of Pharisees as puzzling, inconsistent, and complex. Positively, Luke mentions no Pharisees in the passion narrative, but does mention Pharisees as members of the Christian community (Acts 15.5). However, in the Gospel, the first words attributed to Pharisees—"Who is this who is speaking blasphemies" (5.21)—show them at best misunderstanding Jesus, if not in opposition to him. They next appear grumbling at Jesus' disciples, where they accuse Jesus of inappropriate table fellowship (5.30; a point repeated in 15.2) and question the disciples for their failure to fast (5.33). By 6.1–5 "some" Pharisees are accosting the disciples for violating Sabbath injunctions, and in 6.6–11, Pharisees seek to accuse Jesus directly of Sabbath violation.

Luke 7.29–30 depicts the Pharisees as rejecting John's baptism, which for the Gospel means rejecting the plan of God. The story continues in 7.36–50, which, together with 11.37–54; 14.1–24, depict Pharisees hosting Jesus at table. In each case, Jesus verbally attacks his hosts, for example, by the accusation that they "neglect justice and the love of God" (11.42). Teaching his disciples, but within the hearing of several thousand listeners, Jesus advises, "Beware of the yeast of the Pharisees, that is, their hypocrisy" (12.1). In 16.14–15, Luke has added that Pharisees are self-righteous (a point potentially reinforced by 18.9–14) and "lovers of money." Josephus would beg to differ: he states, "Pharisees simplify their standard of living, making no concession to luxury" (*Ant.* 13.171–73).

Given these and other excoriations, potentially neutral or even friendly actions of Pharisees take on more ominous hues. When "some Pharisees" warn Jesus that Herod seeks to kill him (13.31), they can be seen as attempting to thwart Jesus from his mission. When a Pharisee inquires about the timing of the kingdom of God (17.20–21), he could be seen as misunderstanding Jesus' program. In their last appearance (19.37–40), "some" Pharisees exhort Jesus to rebuke his disciples for hailing Jesus as a king. Rather than see them as fearing that the acclamation would prompt Roman reprisal, they can equally be seen as seeking to reject the disciples' claims.

on you will be catching people." [11] When they had brought their boats to shore, they left everything and followed him.

[12] Once, when he was in one of the cities, there was a man covered with leprosy.[a] When he saw Jesus, he bowed with his face to the ground and begged him, "Lord, if you choose, you can make me clean." [13] Then Jesus[b] stretched out his hand, touched him, and said, "I do choose. Be made clean." Immediately the leprosy[a] left him. [14] And he ordered him to tell no one. "Go," he said, "and show yourself to the priest, and, as Moses commanded, make an offering for your cleansing, for a testimony to them." [15] But now more than ever the word about Jesus[c] spread abroad; many crowds would gather to hear him and to be cured of their diseases. [16] But he would withdraw to deserted places and pray.

[17] One day, while he was teaching, Pharisees and teachers of the law were sitting near by (they had come from every village of Galilee and Judea and from Jerusalem); and the power of the Lord was with him to

[a] The terms *leper* and *leprosy* can refer to several diseases
[b] Gk *he*
[c] Gk *him*

Confession of sin is not a typical response to a miracle, but here appropriate, cf. 5.32. **11:** *Left everything*, including families (see 5.28; 8.21; 9.61; 18.29 and compare 1 Kings 19.20).

5.12–16: Healing the man with leprosy (Mt 8.1–4; Mk 1.40–45). See also Lev 13–14; Num 12.9–15; 2 Kings 5.1–14; Lk 4.27; 17.11–19; *Ant.* 3.264. **12:** *Leprosy*, generic skin ailment, not Hansen's disease. The man is not depicted as outcast. *Make me clean*, cured, thus ritually pure. **13:** *Touched*, contrary to many homiletic appropriations, no Jewish law forbids touching a person with leprosy (Josephus, *Ag. Ap.* 1.281, suggests that one who touches a person suffering from leprosy would be "esteemed unclean"). **14:** *Tell no one*, the "messianic secret," as this motif is commonly known, is more prevalent in Luke's source, Mark. Its rationale remains debated; suggestions include to emphasize teaching over miracles and to avoid Antipas's attention (see 8.56; also 7.22; 22.70; 23.3). *Show yourself to the priest*, the priest needs to pronounce him as having been cleansed (Lev 13). *Moses commanded*, Lev 14.1–57. **16:** *Pray*, see 3.21n.

heal.[a] [18] Just then some men came, carrying a paralyzed man on a bed. They were trying to bring him in and lay him before Jesus;[b] [19] but finding no way to bring him in because of the crowd, they went up on the roof and let him down with his bed through the tiles into the middle of the crowd[c] in front of Jesus. [20] When he saw their faith, he said, "Friend,[d] your sins are forgiven you." [21] Then the scribes and the Pharisees began to question, "Who is this who is speaking blasphemies? Who can forgive sins but God alone?" [22] When Jesus perceived their questionings, he answered them, "Why do you raise such questions in your hearts? [23] Which is easier, to say, 'Your sins are forgiven you,' or to say, 'Stand up and walk'? [24] But so that you may know that the Son of Man has authority on earth to forgive sins"—he said to the one who was paralyzed—"I say to you, stand up and take your bed and go to your home." [25] Immediately he stood up before them, took what he had been lying on, and went to his home, glorifying God. [26] Amazement seized all of them, and they glorified God and were filled with awe, saying, "We have seen strange things today."

[27] After this he went out and saw a tax collector named Levi, sitting at the tax booth; and he said to him, "Follow me." [28] And he got up, left everything, and followed him.

[29] Then Levi gave a great banquet for him in his house; and there was a large crowd of tax collectors and others sitting at the table[e] with them. [30] The Pharisees and their scribes were complaining to his disciples, saying, "Why do you eat and drink with tax collectors and sinners?" [31] Jesus answered, "Those who are well have no need of a physician, but those who are sick; [32] I have come to call not the righteous but sinners to repentance."

[33] Then they said to him, "John's disciples, like the disciples of the Pharisees, frequently fast and pray, but your disciples eat and drink." [34] Jesus said to them, "You cannot make wedding guests fast while the bridegroom is with them, can you? [35] The days will come when the bridegroom will be taken away from them, and then they will fast in those days." [36] He also told them a parable: "No one tears a piece from a new garment and sews it on an old garment; otherwise the new will be torn, and the piece from the new will not match the old. [37] And no one puts new wine into old wineskins; otherwise the new wine will burst the skins and will be spilled, and the skins will be destroyed. [38] But new wine must be put into

a Other ancient authorities read *was present to heal them*
b Gk *him*
c Gk *into the midst*
d Gk *Man*
e Gk *reclining*

5.17–26: Healing the paralyzed man (Mt 9.1–8; Mk 2.1–12). **17:** *Pharisees*, see, "Jewish Movements of the NT Period," p. 526. *Teachers of the law* (see Acts 5.34; 1 Tim 1.7), a Christian rather than Jewish term. **19:** *Tiles*, Mark describes a mud-plaster roof; Luke gives the home an upgrade. **20:** *Sins are forgiven*, the comment implies a connection between infirmity and sin (see Ex 34.7; Jn 9.2). Jews also recognized illness as caused by demons (see 4.39n.), as tests of the righteous (especially Job), and as part of life. **21:** *Scribes*, Heb "soferim." *Blasphemies*, a capital offense (see Lev 24.14–16), although Jesus does not here blaspheme by using the divine name. Were Jesus guilty of blasphemy, his opponents would do more than question *in [their] hearts* (v. 22). In 4QPrNab, a Jewish exorcist forgives the sins of an ailing man. **24:** *Son of Man*, Jesus' self-designation, variously indicating a mortal (Ezek 2.1; Ps 8.4) or an apocalyptic redeemer (Dan 7.13–14; *1 En.* 71). **25:** *Glorifying God*, also 18.43. Luke does not directly equate Jesus with "God" here, but later readers could make the connection (see 4.8n.).

5.27–28: Levi's call (Mt 9.9–13; Mk 2.13–17). **27:** *Tax collector*, 3.12n. **28:** *Left everything*, 5.11n.

5.29–39: Table fellowship (Mt 9.14–17; Mk 2.18–22). See "Food and Table Fellowship," p. 521. **29:** *Banquet*, settings for instruction (7.36; 10.38; 11.37; 14.1,7,12,15) and suggesting symposiums. **33:** *Fast*, for spiritual discipline (not a reference to fast days such as Yom Kippur); Tacitus (*Hist.* 5.4) suggests fasting can be seen as a distinctly Jewish activity. **34–35:** *Bridegroom*, a frequent (self-)designation for Jesus (cf. Jn 3.29); see Isa 62.5; the term connotes creation of new families, celebration, and potentially precedence over other obligations (Deut 24.5). **35:** *Those days*, after Jesus departs. **36:** *Parable*, see "Midrash and Parables in the NT," p. 565. **39:** *The old is*

fresh wineskins. [39] And no one after drinking old wine desires new wine, but says, 'The old is good.'"[a]

6 One sabbath[b] while Jesus[c] was going through the grainfields, his disciples plucked some heads of grain, rubbed them in their hands, and ate them. [2] But some of the Pharisees said, "Why are you doing what is not lawful[d] on the sabbath?" [3] Jesus answered, "Have you not read what David did when he and his companions were hungry? [4] He entered the house of God and took and ate the bread of the Presence, which it is not lawful for any but the priests to eat, and gave some to his companions?" [5] Then he said to them, "The Son of Man is lord of the sabbath."

[6] On another sabbath he entered the synagogue and taught, and there was a man there whose right hand was withered. [7] The scribes and the Pharisees watched him to see whether he would cure on the sabbath, so that they might find an accusation against him. [8] Even though he knew what they were thinking, he said to the man who had the withered hand, "Come and stand here." He got up and stood there. [9] Then Jesus said to them, "I ask you, is it lawful to do good or to do harm on the sabbath, to save life or to destroy it?" [10] After looking around at all of them, he said to him, "Stretch out your hand." He did so, and his hand was restored. [11] But they were filled with fury and discussed with one another what they might do to Jesus.

[12] Now during those days he went out to the mountain to pray; and he spent the night in prayer to God. [13] And when day came, he called his disciples and chose twelve of them, whom he also named apostles: [14] Simon, whom he named Peter, and his brother Andrew, and James, and John, and Philip, and Bartholomew, [15] and Matthew, and Thomas, and James son of Alphaeus, and Simon, who was called the Zealot, [16] and Judas son of James, and Judas Iscariot, who became a traitor.

[17] He came down with them and stood on a level place, with a great crowd of his disciples and a great multitude of people from all Judea, Jerusalem, and the coast of

a Other ancient authorities read *better*; others lack verse 39

b Other ancient authorities read *On the second first sabbath*

c Gk *he*

d Other ancient authorities add *to do*

good (see Sir 9.10; *m. Avot* 4.20); although enigmatic (parables often are), the saying likely indicates that the old (non-messianic Judaism) and the new (Jesus' teachings) are incompatible.

6.1–11: Sabbath practices (Mt 12.1–14; Mk 2.23–3.6). **1:** Early (especially non-Jewish) followers of Jesus debated *Sabbath* practice (see Col 2.16); whereas the Tanakh enjoins "work" on the Sabbath (e.g., Ex 20.10; 31.14–15; Lev 23.3), it does not define what constitutes work. **2:** *Not lawful*, Ex 34.21; for stricter rabbinic rules, see *m. Shabb.* 7.2. Plucking grain in another's field is legal (Deut 23.24–25). **3:** *What David did*, 1 Sam 21.1–6. **4.** *Bread of the Presence*, see Lev 24.5–9. **5:** *Son of Man*, 5.24n. If this expression is taken in a non-messianic way, v. 5 is comparable to Rabbi Simeon B. Menasya's comment on Ex 31.14 ("You shall keep the Sabbath, because it is holy for you"): "The words 'unto you' imply that the Sabbath is given to you, and that you are not given to the Sabbath" (*Mek., Ki Tissa* [to Ex 31]). **6:** *Synagogue*, 4.15n. **7:** *Cure on the Sabbath*, see 4.21–27n. **9:** *Save life*, "Pikuach nefesh" ("saving a life") always overrides other Sabbath laws, see 6.5n.; 1 Macc 2.40–41; *b. Yoma* 84b. **10:** *Hand was restored*, Jesus does not touch the man, and therefore prevents suspicion of "working." **11:** *Fury*, Gk "anoia" connotes "madness" or "lack of understanding." *What they might do*, Pharisees have no political or juridical authority.

6.12–16: The twelve apostles (Mt 10.1–4; Mk 3.13–19a). See also Acts 1.13. **12:** *Pray*, see 3.21n. **13:** *Twelve* (8.1; Acts 6.2; etc.) symbolizes reconstitution of the twelve tribes of Israel. *Apostles* (Gk "apostolos," "those sent"), compare Heb "shaliaḥ" who, whether a man or a woman, was the agent or emissary of the sender; the concept of "shaliaḥ shel 'adam kemoto" ["a person's agent is as the person himself"] and thus fully representative of the sender (see *m. Ber.* 5.5; *b. Qidd.* 42b–43a). **14:** *Peter*, nickname meaning "rock." The names of the Twelve vary among Gospels, but Peter is always named first and Judas Iscariot last. *John*, Gk "Ioannēs," Heb "Yoḥanan." *James*, Gk "Iacobos," Heb "Ya'aqov" (Jacob). *Bartholomew*, Heb/Aram "Bar Tolmai," "Son of Tolmai." **15:** *Zealot*, in the revolt against Rome (66–70), a political revolutionary; here the term suggests Phineas (Num 25.11) and Elijah (1 Kings 18.40; 19.10); see also 2 Cor 7.7,11,12. **16:** *Iscariot*, perhaps "a man [from the Judean village] of Kerioth" (Josh 15.25); if so, Judas was the only Judean among the Twelve; perhaps from the Aram "sheqarya," "false one, liar."

Tyre and Sidon. [18] They had come to hear him and to be healed of their diseases; and those who were troubled with unclean spirits were cured. [19] And all in the crowd were trying to touch him, for power came out from him and healed all of them.

[20] Then he looked up at his disciples and said:

"Blessed are you who are poor,
  for yours is the kingdom of God.
[21] "Blessed are you who are hungry now,
  for you will be filled.
"Blessed are you who weep now,
  for you will laugh.

[22] "Blessed are you when people hate you, and when they exclude you, revile you, and defame you[a] on account of the Son of Man. [23] Rejoice in that day and leap for joy, for surely your reward is great in heaven; for that is what their ancestors did to the prophets.

[24] "But woe to you who are rich,
  for you have received your consolation.
[25] "Woe to you who are full now,
  for you will be hungry.
"Woe to you who are laughing now,
  for you will mourn and weep.

[26] "Woe to you when all speak well of you, for that is what their ancestors did to the false prophets.

[27] "But I say to you that listen, Love your enemies, do good to those who hate you, [28] bless those who curse you, pray for those who abuse you. [29] If anyone strikes you on the cheek, offer the other also; and from anyone who takes away your coat do not withhold even your shirt. [30] Give to everyone who begs from you; and if anyone takes away your goods, do not ask for them again. [31] Do to others as you would have them do to you.

[32] "If you love those who love you, what credit is that to you? For even sinners love those who love them. [33] If you do good to those who do good to you, what credit is that to you? For even sinners do the same. [34] If you lend to those from whom you hope to receive, what credit is that to you? Even sinners lend to sinners, to receive as much again. [35] But love your enemies, do good, and lend, expecting nothing in return.[b] Your reward will be great, and you will be children of the Most High; for he is kind to the ungrateful and the wicked. [36] Be merciful, just as your Father is merciful.

[a] Gk *cast out your name as evil*
[b] Other ancient authorities read *despairing of no one*

6.17–49: Sermon on the plain (Mt 5–7). **17:** *Level place,* contrasts Matthew's "Sermon on the Mount."

6.20–23: Beatitudes (Mt 5.3–12). For the form, see Ps 1.1; 34.8; etc.; *blessed* (Gk "makarioi") corresponds to Heb "'ashrei," "fortunate"; see Ps 1.1. **20:** *You poor,* compare Matthew's "poor in spirit." Jewish tradition regards the poor, the hungry, etc. not as cursed or impure but as deserving recipients of divine and earthly care (e.g., Deut 15.11; Isa 49.10; Jer 31.25; Ezek 34.29). **22:** *Exclude you,* see Isa 66.5. *Son of Man,* 5.24n.; here, Jesus. **23:** *Their ancestors,* e.g., Neh 9.26; 2 Chr 13.15–16.

6.24–26: Woes. 24: Luke descries the *rich* who refuse to give alms (6.30n.) and encourages extreme generosity (11.41; 12.13–21,33–34; 16.13,19–31; 18.18–30; see *1 En.* 94.8); the condemnation of wealth is stronger in this Gospel than in, e.g., 1 Tim 6.10 and Heb 13.5 (where the issue is "love of money"; see also, e.g., Hab 2.5). See 6.30n.

6.27–36: Avoiding violence (Mt 5.38–48; 7.12). **27:** *Love your enemies,* Jewish teaching commands helping enemies (see e.g., Ex 23.4–5; Prov 24.17; 25.21); rabbinic commentary speaks of aiding (not "loving") enemies in order to "subdue the evil inclination" (*b. B. Metz.* 32b). See "Parable of the Good Samaritan" p. 123. **28:** *Pray for those who abuse,* see 23.34. **29:** *Takes away your coat,* Mt 5.40 suggest a lawsuit; Luke suggests robbery. **30:** *Give to everyone,* Luke sanctions voluntary poverty (see also 6.24n.; 12.33; 18.22); rabbinic sources do not, as personal impoverishment would create greater hardships for the community. Jewish sources mandate the giving of alms ("tzedakah"); see e.g., Deut 15.11. Rav Assi (third century) called almsgiving "equal in value to all other commandments" (*b. B. Bat.* 9a). **31:** *Do to others,* compare Hillel's "What is hateful to you, do not do to anyone else" (*b. Shabb.* 31a; Tob 4.15). **32–34:** *What credit,* Luke reflects the reciprocal system of benefaction. **35:** *Expecting nothing in return,* Ex 22.25; Lev 25.36–37. *Children of the Most High,* see 1.32,35; 8.28. **36:** *Be merciful,* compare Mt 5.48, where the injunction is perfection; for imitating divine compassion (Ex 34.6), see *b. Shabb.* 133b; *Mek.* 15.2; *Sifre Deut.* 11.22; 49 ("As God is called compassionate and gracious, so you too must be compassionate and gracious, giving gifts freely").

[37] "Do not judge, and you will not be judged; do not condemn, and you will not be condemned. Forgive, and you will be forgiven; [38] give, and it will be given to you. A good measure, pressed down, shaken together, running over, will be put into your lap; for the measure you give will be the measure you get back."

[39] He also told them a parable: "Can a blind person guide a blind person? Will not both fall into a pit? [40] A disciple is not above the teacher, but everyone who is fully qualified will be like the teacher. [41] Why do you see the speck in your neighbor's[a] eye, but do not notice the log in your own eye? [42] Or how can you say to your neighbor,[b] 'Friend,[b] let me take out the speck in your eye,' when you yourself do not see the log in your own eye? You hypocrite, first take the log out of your own eye, and then you will see clearly to take the speck out of your neighbor's[a] eye.

[43] "No good tree bears bad fruit, nor again does a bad tree bear good fruit; [44] for each tree is known by its own fruit. Figs are not gathered from thorns, nor are grapes picked from a bramble bush. [45] The good person out of the good treasure of the heart produces good, and the evil person out of evil treasure produces evil; for it is out of the abundance of the heart that the mouth speaks.

[46] "Why do you call me 'Lord, Lord,' and do not do what I tell you? [47] I will show you what someone is like who comes to me, hears my words, and acts on them. [48] That one is like a man building a house, who dug deeply and laid the foundation on rock; when a flood arose, the river burst against that house but could not shake it, because it had been well built.[c] [49] But the one who hears and does not act is like a man who built a house on the ground without a foundation. When the river burst against it, immediately it fell, and great was the ruin of that house."

7 After Jesus[d] had finished all his sayings in the hearing of the people, he entered Capernaum. [2] A centurion there had a slave whom he valued highly, and who was ill and close to death. [3] When he heard about Jesus, he sent some Jewish elders to him, asking him to come and heal his slave. [4] When they came to Jesus, they appealed to him earnestly, saying, "He is worthy of having you do this for him, [5] for he loves our people, and it is he who built our synagogue for us." [6] And Jesus went with them, but when he was not far from the house, the centurion sent friends to say to him, "Lord, do not trouble yourself, for I am not worthy to have you come under my roof; [7] therefore I did not presume to come to you. But only speak the word, and let my servant be healed. [8] For I also am a man set under authority, with soldiers under me; and I say to one, 'Go,' and

a Gk *brother's*
b Gk *brother*
c Other ancient authorities read *founded upon the rock*
d Gk *he*

6.37–42: Judging (Mt 7.1–5; 12.36–37; 15.14; Mk 4.24–25). **37:** *Do not judge*, see *b. Rosh Ha-Shanah* 16b; *b. Meg.* 28a. **41–42:** *Log in your own eye*, *b. Arak.* 16b; *b. Hor.* 3b. *Hypocrite*, see Ps 26.4; Sir 1.29; 32.15.

6.43–45: Bearing good fruit (Mt 7.15–20; 12.33–35). See also Jas 3.11–12. **45:** *Heart*, the moral center (see Gen 8.21; Deut 6.5–6; etc.). On the relation of heart (Heb "lev") to lips (Heb "peh") see Ps 19.15.

6.46–49: Wise and foolish builders (Mt 7.21–27). See also Jas 1.22–25. **46:** *Lord, Lord*, confession without attendant works is meaningless. For the invocation, see Ex 34.6 and compare the recitation of the thirteen "midot ha-raḥamim" ("attributes of [divine] mercy") in the *Seliḥot* (penitential prayers). **47–49**, See R. Eleazar b. Azariah's similar story concerning trees with weak vs. strong roots (*m. Avot* 3.22).

7.1–10: The centurion's slave (Mt 8.5–13; see also Jn 4.46–54). **1:** *Capernaum*, 4.23n. **2:** *Centurion*, officer in charge of a company of soldiers; either attached to the customs service under Antipas's jurisdiction, or pensioned. No Roman troops occupied Galilee under Antipas. For centurions in Luke-Acts see also 23.47; Acts 10.1; 22.25–26; 24.43; 27.43. **2:** *Valued highly* (Gk "entimos," from "timē," "honor"), suggesting honorable service (Phil 2.29; 1 Pet 2.4,6), and used in contemporary papyri for soldiers who performed honorably. **5:** *Built our synagogue*, one of several historically attested Gentile patrons of synagogues (e.g., Tation [*CIJ* 2.738]; Julia Severa [*CIJ* 2.766]). The comment belies Peter's statement (Acts 10.28) that it is unlawful for Jews to associate with Gentiles. Tacitus (*Hist.* 3.24) comments on soldiers adapting the religions of areas where they were stationed. **9:** *Not even in Israel*, Luke hails this Gentile's piety. **10:** *They found the slave*, for rabbinic

he goes, and to another, 'Come,' and he comes, and to my slave, 'Do this,' and the slave does it." [9] When Jesus heard this he was amazed at him, and turning to the crowd that followed him, he said, "I tell you, not even in Israel have I found such faith." [10] When those who had been sent returned to the house, they found the slave in good health.

[11] Soon afterwards[a] he went to a town called Nain, and his disciples and a large crowd went with him. [12] As he approached the gate of the town, a man who had died was being carried out. He was his mother's only son, and she was a widow; and with her was a large crowd from the town. [13] When the Lord saw her, he had compassion for her and said to her, "Do not weep." [14] Then he came forward and touched the bier, and the bearers stood still. And he said, "Young man, I say to you, rise!" [15] The dead man sat up and began to speak, and Jesus[b] gave him to his mother. [16] Fear seized all of them; and they glorified God, saying, "A great prophet has risen among us!" and "God has looked favorably on his people!" [17] This word about him spread throughout Judea and all the surrounding country.

[18] The disciples of John reported all these things to him. So John summoned two of his disciples [19] and sent them to the Lord to ask, "Are you the one who is to come, or are we to wait for another?" [20] When the men had come to him, they said, "John the Baptist has sent us to you to ask, 'Are you the one who is to come, or are we to wait for another?'" [21] Jesus[c] had just then cured many people of diseases, plagues, and evil spirits, and had given sight to many who were blind. [22] And he answered them, "Go and tell John what you have seen and heard: the blind receive their sight, the lame walk, the lepers[d] are cleansed, the deaf hear, the dead are raised, the poor have good news brought to them. [23] And blessed is anyone who takes no offense at me."

[24] When John's messengers had gone, Jesus[b] began to speak to the crowds about John:[e] "What did you go out into the wilderness to look at? A reed shaken by the wind? [25] What then did you go out to see? Someone[f] dressed in soft robes? Look, those who put on fine clothing and live in luxury are in royal palaces. [26] What then did you go out to see? A prophet? Yes, I tell you, and more than a prophet. [27] This is the one about whom it is written,

> 'See, I am sending my messenger ahead of you,
> who will prepare your way before you.'

[28] I tell you, among those born of women no one is greater than John; yet the least in the kingdom of God is greater than he." [29] (And all the people who heard this, including the tax collectors, acknowledged the justice of God,[g] because they had been baptized with John's baptism. [30] But by refusing to be baptized by him, the Pharisees and the lawyers rejected God's purpose for themselves.)

[31] "To what then will I compare the people of this generation, and what are they like? [32] They are like children sitting in the marketplace and calling to one another,

a Other ancient authorities read *Next day*
b Gk *he*
c Gk *He*
d The terms *leper* and *leprosy* can refer to several diseases
e Gk *him*
f Or *Why then did you go out? To see someone*
g Or *praised God*

healings at a distance, see, e.g., *b. Ber.* 34b on Rabbi Ḥanina ben Dosa's healing children; see "Jewish Miracle Workers," p. 536.

7.11–17: The widow's son. 11: *Nain,* about 23 miles (37 km) southwest of Capernaum. **12:** *Gate of the town,* cemeteries were usually located outside residential areas. *Widow,* a Lukan concern (see 2.37; 4.26; 18.3; 20.28,47; 21.2–3; Acts 6.1; 9.39–41). Her economic condition is not mentioned. **13:** *Compassion,* see 15.20. **16:** *Great prophet,* Jesus' healing evokes those attributed to Elijah (1 Kings 17.17–24; see Lk 4.25–26) and Elisha (2 Kings 4.32–37).

7.18–35: Jesus and John the Baptist (Mt 11.2–19). **18:** *John,* Luke does not mention that John was imprisoned (cf. Mt 11.2–9). **19:** *One who is to come,* the messiah. **21:** Jewish sources do not traditionally speak of the messiah as a miracle worker. **22:** Echoing Lk 4.18–19 and evoking Isa 29.18; 42.18; 26.19; see also Isa 35.5–6; 61.1; no reference to freeing captives is made (see 4.18). Jesus does not answer the Baptist's disciples directly (see 5.14n.; 22.70; 23.3). **27:** Mal 3.1, connecting John to Elijah's role (see Mal 3.23). **29:** *Tax collectors,* see 3.12n. **30:** *Pharisees and the lawyers,* conventional opponents of Jesus (11.39,42–43,53; 12.1; etc.; on their rejection of John, see 20.5). **31:** *Generation,* see 9.41.

'We played the flute for you, and you did not dance;
we wailed, and you did not weep.'

[33] For John the Baptist has come eating no bread and drinking no wine, and you say, 'He has a demon'; [34] the Son of Man has come eating and drinking, and you say, 'Look, a glutton and a drunkard, a friend of tax collectors and sinners!' [35] Nevertheless, wisdom is vindicated by all her children."

[36] One of the Pharisees asked Jesus[a] to eat with him, and he went into the Pharisee's house and took his place at the table. [37] And a woman in the city, who was a sinner, having learned that he was eating in the Pharisee's house, brought an alabaster jar of ointment. [38] She stood behind him at his feet, weeping, and began to bathe his feet with her tears and to dry them with her hair. Then she continued kissing his feet and anointing them with the ointment. [39] Now when the Pharisee who had invited him saw it, he said to himself, "If this man were a prophet, he would have known who and what kind of woman this is who is touching him—that she is a sinner." [40] Jesus spoke up and said to him, "Simon, I have something to say to you." "Teacher," he replied, "speak." [41] "A certain creditor had two debtors; one owed five hundred denarii,[b] and the other fifty. [42] When they could not pay, he canceled the debts for both of them. Now which of them will love him more?" [43] Simon answered, "I suppose the one for whom he canceled the greater debt." And Jesus[c] said to him, "You have judged rightly." [44] Then turning toward the woman, he said to Simon, "Do you see this woman? I entered your house; you gave me no water for my feet, but she has bathed my feet with her tears and dried them with her hair. [45] You gave me no kiss, but from the time I came in she has not stopped kissing my feet. [46] You did not anoint my head with oil, but she has anointed my feet with ointment. [47] Therefore, I tell you, her sins, which were many, have been forgiven; hence she has shown great love. But the one to whom little is forgiven, loves little." [48] Then he said to her, "Your sins are forgiven." [49] But those who were at the table with him began to say among themselves, "Who is this who even forgives sins?" [50] And he said to the woman, "Your faith has saved you; go in peace."

8 Soon afterwards he went on through cities and villages, proclaiming and bringing the good news of the kingdom of God. The twelve were with him, [2] as well as some women who had been cured of evil spirits and infirmities: Mary, called Magdalene, from whom seven demons had gone out, [3] and Joanna, the wife of Herod's steward Chuza, and Susanna, and many others, who provided for them[d] out of their resources.

[a] Gk *him*
[b] The denarius was the usual day's wage for a laborer
[c] Gk *he*
[d] Other ancient authorities read *him*

33: *Eating no bread,* Jews recognized fasting as a spiritual discipline but did not generally promote asceticism. *Has a demon,* explaining unconventional behavior. **34:** *Son of Man,* 5.24n. *Glutton and a drunkard,* evoking the rebellious son, punished with death (Deut 21.18–21). **35:** *Wisdom* (Gk "Sophia"; Heb "Ḥokhmah"), here personified; cf. Prov 1–9; Wis passim. *Vindicated* (Gk "dikaiō"), lit., "justified," demonstrated to be in the right.

7.36–50: The Pharisee and the woman who loved much. 36: *To eat with him,* the first of three dinners with Pharisees (see 11.37; 14.1). **37:** *Sinner,* no specific sin is mentioned or need be inferred. **38:** *Behind him at his feet,* Jesus reclined on a dining couch. *Dry them with her hair,* an intimate and hardly common practice. Loosened hair indicated grief, gratefulness, propitiation of a god, or pleading, and need not be taken as erotic. *Anointing,* see Mt 26.6–13; Mk 14.3–9; Jn 12.1–8. Later tradition associated this unnamed woman with Mary Magdalene (see 8.2). **44:** *Gave me no water,* a breach of etiquette. **49:** *Forgives sins,* see 5.20n. **50:** *Faith has saved you,* see 8.48; 17.19; 18.42. This *faith,* although not defined, suggests faith in Jesus as Lord and so the forgiveness he grants.

8.1–3: Jesus' patrons. 1: *Good news,* 1.19n. *Kingdom of God,* 4.43n. **2:** *Some women,* see 23.49. *Cured,* only Luke describes Jesus' women followers as beneficiaries of healing. *Magdalene,* see 7.38n. Magdala (Tarichaea) was a fishing village on the western shore of the Sea of Galilee. **3:** *Wife of Herod's steward,* suggesting elite class. *Provided for them,* women served as patrons to various individuals and groups, including synagogues and Pharisees (see 7.5n.). Luke does not here explicitly call them "disciples" (contrast Acts 9.36).

8.4–15: Parable of the sower (Mt 13.1–23; Mk 4.1–20). **9:** *What this parable meant,* this parable requires an allegorical key (see 15.7; 18.1). **10:** Paraphrasing Isa 6.9–10 (see also Jer 5.21; Ezek 12.2). Here, the purpose of

[4] When a great crowd gathered and people from town after town came to him, he said in a parable: [5] "A sower went out to sow his seed; and as he sowed, some fell on the path and was trampled on, and the birds of the air ate it up. [6] Some fell on the rock; and as it grew up, it withered for lack of moisture. [7] Some fell among thorns, and the thorns grew with it and choked it. [8] Some fell into good soil, and when it grew, it produced a hundredfold." As he said this, he called out, "Let anyone with ears to hear listen!"

[9] Then his disciples asked him what this parable meant. [10] He said, "To you it has been given to know the secrets[a] of the kingdom of God; but to others I speak[b] in parables, so that

'looking they may not perceive,
and listening they may not understand.'

[11] "Now the parable is this: The seed is the word of God. [12] The ones on the path are those who have heard; then the devil comes and takes away the word from their hearts, so that they may not believe and be saved. [13] The ones on the rock are those who, when they hear the word, receive it with joy. But these have no root; they believe only for a while and in a time of testing fall away. [14] As for what fell among the thorns, these are the ones who hear; but as they go on their way, they are choked by the cares and riches and pleasures of life, and their fruit does not mature. [15] But as for that in the good soil, these are the ones who, when they hear the word, hold it fast in an honest and good heart, and bear fruit with patient endurance.

[16] "No one after lighting a lamp hides it under a jar, or puts it under a bed, but puts it on a lampstand, so that those who enter may see the light. [17] For nothing is hidden that will not be disclosed, nor is anything secret that will not become known and come to light. [18] Then pay attention to how you listen; for to those who have, more will be given; and from those who do not have, even what they seem to have will be taken away."

[19] Then his mother and his brothers came to him, but they could not reach him because of the crowd. [20] And he was told, "Your mother and your brothers are standing outside, wanting to see you." [21] But he said to them, "My mother and my brothers are those who hear the word of God and do it."

[22] One day he got into a boat with his disciples, and he said to them, "Let us go across to the other side of the lake." So they put out, [23] and while they were sailing he fell asleep. A windstorm swept down on the lake, and the boat was filling with water, and they were in danger. [24] They went to him and woke him up, shouting, "Master, Master, we are perishing!" And he woke up and rebuked the wind and the raging waves; they ceased, and there was a calm. [25] He said to them, "Where is your faith?" They were afraid and amazed, and said to one another, "Who then is this, that he commands even the winds and the water, and they obey him?"

[26] Then they arrived at the country of the Gerasenes,[c] which is opposite Galilee. [27] As he stepped out on land, a man of the city who had demons met him. For a long time he had worn[d] no clothes, and he did not live in a

[a] Or *mysteries*
[b] Gk lacks *I speak*
[c] Other ancient authorities read *Gadarenes*; others, *Gergesenes*
[d] Other ancient authorities read *a man of the city who had had demons for a long time met him. He wore*

parables is to conceal truth; Luke omits Mark's point (4.12) that parables prevent conversion and forgiveness. *Secrets*, veiled notices of God's plan (see Dan 2.18–19,44–47 LXX; 1 Cor 2.1–7). **15:** *Heart*, see 6.45n.

8.16–18: Independent sayings (Mt 5.15; 10.26; 13.12; Mk 4.21–25). **18:** *Will be taken away*, see 19.26; those who do not follow Jesus will suffer eschatological loss.

8.19–21: Jesus' family (Mt 12.46–50; Mk 3.31–35). **19:** *Brothers*, Mk 6.3 lists four brothers and mentions sisters. **21:** Mk 3.20–21,33 increases the distance between Jesus and his natal family. *My mother and my brothers*, Jesus subordinates biological and marital relations to loyalty to God (5.11n.; 10.61), although the Greek can be taken as indicating the mother and brothers as model disciples.

8.22–25: Stilling the storm (Mt 8.23–27; Mk 4.35–41). **23:** *Fell asleep*, one of several connections between Jesus and Jonah (see Jon 1.5). **24:** *Rebuked the wind*, controlling nature indicates divine power (Ps 107.28–30).

8.26–39: Gerasene demoniac (Mt 8.28–34; Mk 5.1–20). **26:** *Gerasenes*, Gerasa, *opposite Galilee*, in the Transjordan, had a largely non-Jewish population. Mt 8.28 situates this event in Gadara, southeast of the Sea of

house but in the tombs. [28] When he saw Jesus, he fell down before him and shouted at the top of his voice, "What have you to do with me, Jesus, Son of the Most High God? I beg you, do not torment me"— [29] for Jesus[a] had commanded the unclean spirit to come out of the man. (For many times it had seized him; he was kept under guard and bound with chains and shackles, but he would break the bonds and be driven by the demon into the wilds.) [30] Jesus then asked him, "What is your name?" He said, "Legion"; for many demons had entered him. [31] They begged him not to order them to go back into the abyss.

[32] Now there on the hillside a large herd of swine was feeding; and the demons[b] begged Jesus[c] to let them enter these. So he gave them permission. [33] Then the demons came out of the man and entered the swine, and the herd rushed down the steep bank into the lake and was drowned.

[34] When the swineherds saw what had happened, they ran off and told it in the city and in the country. [35] Then people came out to see what had happened, and when they came to Jesus, they found the man from whom the demons had gone sitting at the feet of Jesus, clothed and in his right mind. And they were afraid. [36] Those who had seen it told them how the one who had been possessed by demons had been healed. [37] Then all the people of the surrounding country of the Gerasenes[d] asked Jesus[c] to leave them; for they were seized with great fear. So he got into the boat and returned. [38] The man from whom the demons had gone begged that he might be with him; but Jesus[a] sent him away, saying, [39] "Return to your home, and declare how much God has done for you." So he went away, proclaiming throughout the city how much Jesus had done for him.

[40] Now when Jesus returned, the crowd welcomed him, for they were all waiting for him. [41] Just then there came a man named Jairus, a leader of the synagogue. He fell at Jesus' feet and begged him to come to his house, [42] for he had an only daughter, about twelve years old, who was dying.

As he went, the crowds pressed in on him. [43] Now there was a woman who had been suffering from hemorrhages for twelve years; and though she had spent all she had on physicians,[e] no one could cure her. [44] She came up behind him and touched the fringe of his clothes, and immediately her hemorrhage stopped. [45] Then Jesus asked, "Who touched me?" When all denied it, Peter[f] said, "Master, the crowds surround you and press in on you." [46] But Jesus said, "Someone touched me; for I noticed that power had gone out from me." [47] When the woman saw that she could not remain hidden, she came trembling; and falling down before him, she declared in the presence of all the people why she had touched him, and how she had been immediately healed. [48] He said to her, "Daughter, your faith has made you well; go in peace."

a Gk *he*
b Gk *they*
c Gk *him*
d Other ancient authorities read *Gadarenes*; others, *Gergesenes*
e Other ancient authorities lack *and though she had spent all she had on physicians*
f Other ancient authorities add *and those who were with him*

Galilee. **28:** *Son of the Most High*, 1.32n.; the demoniac's identification contrasts with the apostles' confusion (8.25). **30:** *What is your name*, knowledge of one's name provides advantage (see Gen 32.29). *Legion*, Roman army unit of approximately five thousand troops, suggesting Rome's demonic power. **31:** *Abyss*, where God confines demons (Rev 9.1–11; 11.7; 17.8; 20.1–3); demonology, like angelology, developed during the Hellenistic period. **32:** *Swine*, indicating a non-Jewish area; archaeological investigation of lower Galilee shows no pig bones (see Lev 11.7; Deut 14.8). **39:** *Jesus had done*, in contrast to Jesus' command to proclaim what "God" had done (but see 4.8; 5.25).

8.40–56: Jairus's daughter and hemorrhaging woman (Mt 9.18–26; Mk 5.21–43). **41:** *Leader of the synagogue*, one who oversaw congregational activities. **42:** *Only daughter*, Jewish parents consistently display concern for their children (e.g., 2.48; 9.38; 11.7,11–13; 14.5; 18.15). **43:** *Hemorrhages*, probably vaginal or uterine (see Lev 15.25–30); no recounting of her story mentions matters of purity. **44:** *Fringe*, Heb "tzitzit," see Num 15.38. Her hands would not convey impurity. **48:** *Daughter*, one of several linkages with Jairus's daughter. *Made you well*,

[49] While he was still speaking, someone came from the leader's house to say, "Your daughter is dead; do not trouble the teacher any longer." [50] When Jesus heard this, he replied, "Do not fear. Only believe, and she will be saved." [51] When he came to the house, he did not allow anyone to enter with him, except Peter, John, and James, and the child's father and mother. [52] They were all weeping and wailing for her; but he said, "Do not weep; for she is not dead but sleeping." [53] And they laughed at him, knowing that she was dead. [54] But he took her by the hand and called out, "Child, get up!" [55] Her spirit returned, and she got up at once. Then he directed them to give her something to eat. [56] Her parents were astounded; but he ordered them to tell no one what had happened.

9 Then Jesus[a] called the twelve together and gave them power and authority over all demons and to cure diseases, [2] and he sent them out to proclaim the kingdom of God and to heal. [3] He said to them, "Take nothing for your journey, no staff, nor bag, nor bread, nor money—not even an extra tunic. [4] Whatever house you enter, stay there, and leave from there. [5] Wherever they do not welcome you, as you are leaving that town shake the dust off your feet as a testimony against them." [6] They departed and went through the villages, bringing the good news and curing diseases everywhere.

[7] Now Herod the ruler[b] heard about all that had taken place, and he was perplexed, because it was said by some that John had been raised from the dead, [8] by some that Elijah had appeared, and by others that one of the ancient prophets had arisen. [9] Herod said, "John I beheaded; but who is this about whom I hear such things?" And he tried to see him.

[10] On their return the apostles told Jesus[c] all they had done. He took them with him and withdrew privately to a city called Bethsaida. [11] When the crowds found out about it, they followed him; and he welcomed them, and spoke to them about the kingdom of God, and healed those who needed to be cured.

[12] The day was drawing to a close, and the twelve came to him and said, "Send the crowd away, so that they may go into the surrounding villages and countryside, to lodge and get provisions; for we are here in a deserted place." [13] But he said to them, "You give them something to eat." They said, "We have no more than five loaves and two fish—unless we are to go and buy food for all these people." [14] For there were about five thousand men. And he said to his disciples, "Make them sit down in groups of about fifty each." [15] They did so and made them all sit down. [16] And taking the five loaves and the two fish, he looked up to heaven, and blessed and broke them, and gave them to the disciples to set before the crowd. [17] And all ate and were filled. What was left over was gathered up, twelve baskets of broken pieces.

[a] Gk *he*
[b] Gk *tetrarch*
[c] Gk *him*

lit., "saved you"; see 7.50. **51:** *Peter, John, and James,* the inner circle (9.28). **54:** *By the hand,* Jesus violates no ritual taboos. **56:** *Tell no one,* 5.14n.

9.1–6: Commissioning of the apostles (Mt 10.1–14; Mk 6.6b–13). **3:** *Take nothing,* apostles are dependent on God and those to whom they minister. **5:** *Shake the dust off,* indicating they are not responsible for the fate of the inhospitable. **6:** *Good news,* see 1.19n.

9.7–9: Herod's speculations (Mt 14.1–2; Mk 6.14–16). *Herod* Antipas, 3.1n. **8:** *Elijah,* 1.17n.; see also 9.18–19. *Prophets,* perhaps a reference to Deut 18.15, understanding "raise" as raise from the dead. **9:** *John I beheaded,* see Mk 6.17–29 (Luke does not directly describe John's death). *Tried to see him,* see 23.7–12.

9.10–11: Successful mission (Mt 14.12–14; Mk 6.30–34). **10:** *Bethsaida,* north of the Sea of Galilee.

9.12–17: Feeding of the five thousand (Mt 14.15–21; Mk 6.35–44; Jn 6.5–14). See 2 Kings 4.43–44. **14:** *Five thousand men,* Mt 14.21 adds that the five thousand did not include the women and children also present. **16:** *Blessed,* traditional Jewish blessing before eating (see Deut 8.10; *b. Ber.* 48b; *Num. Rab.* 20.21; the traditional blessing over bread ["birchat ha-motsi"] is based on Ps 104.14). The scene here anticipates 22.17–20. **17:** *Twelve baskets,* perhaps suggesting Israel's twelve tribes. Luke recounts a miracle, comparable to the giving of manna (Ex 16; 2 Kings 4.43–44; cf. Jn 6.31; *b. Yoma* 75a on the sufficiency of manna), and not a sharing of resources.

[18] Once when Jesus[a] was praying alone, with only the disciples near him, he asked them, "Who do the crowds say that I am?" [19] They answered, "John the Baptist; but others, Elijah; and still others, that one of the ancient prophets has arisen." [20] He said to them, "But who do you say that I am?" Peter answered, "The Messiah[b] of God."

[21] He sternly ordered and commanded them not to tell anyone, [22] saying, "The Son of Man must undergo great suffering, and be rejected by the elders, chief priests, and scribes, and be killed, and on the third day be raised."

[23] Then he said to them all, "If any want to become my followers, let them deny themselves and take up their cross daily and follow me. [24] For those who want to save their life will lose it, and those who lose their life for my sake will save it. [25] What does it profit them if they gain the whole world, but lose or forfeit themselves? [26] Those who are ashamed of me and of my words, of them the Son of Man will be ashamed when he comes in his glory and the glory of the Father and of the holy angels. [27] But truly I tell you, there are some standing here who will not taste death before they see the kingdom of God."

[28] Now about eight days after these sayings Jesus[a] took with him Peter and John and James, and went up on the mountain to pray. [29] And while he was praying, the appearance of his face changed, and his clothes became dazzling white. [30] Suddenly they saw two men, Moses and Elijah, talking to him. [31] They appeared in glory and were speaking of his departure, which he was about to accomplish at Jerusalem. [32] Now Peter and his companions were weighed down with sleep; but since they had stayed awake,[c] they saw his glory and the two men who stood with him. [33] Just as they were leaving him, Peter said to Jesus, "Master, it is good for us to be here; let us make three dwellings,[d] one for you, one for Moses, and one for Elijah"—not knowing what he said. [34] While he was saying this, a cloud came and overshadowed them; and they

a Gk *he*
b Or *The Christ*
c Or *but when they were fully awake*
d Or *tents*

9.18–20: Peter's confession (acknowledgment) of Jesus' messiahship (Mt 16.13–19; Mk 8.27–29). **19:** *John . . . Elijah . . . ancient prophets*, some of many messianic figures; see "Messianic Movements," p. 530. **20:** *Messiah of God*, Gk "ho Christos tou Theou," "God's anointed."

9.21–22: First Passion prediction (Mt 16.20–21; Mk 8.30–31). **21:** *Not to tell anyone*, Given the earlier mission (9.2–6) and miracles, a problematic point. **22:** *Son of Man*, see 5.24n. *Elders, chief priests, and scribes*, Jewish leadership. *Be killed*, the passive subtly exonerates Pilate. Contemporaneous Jewish thought displays limited evidence of either a suffering messiah or "Son of Man."

9.23–27: Discipleship (Mt 16.24–28; Mk 8.34–9.1). **23:** *Deny themselves*, see 7.33n. *Take up their cross*, the Greek is singular (lit., "anyone . . . his"), making the challenge personal. *Daily*, discipleship is a permanent state; Luke spiritualizes Mark's focus on action leading to death to suggest continual self-denial (cf. 5.11; 8.21; 10.61). **26:** *Son of Man*, 5.24n. *Comes in his glory*, the "second coming" and final judgment. Jewish tradition does not separate the messiah and messianic age and thus has no "second coming." **27:** *Not taste death*, enigmatic saying perhaps refers to those who witness Jesus' resurrection or the successful mission; see 21.31.

9.28–36: The Transfiguration (Mt 17.1–9; Mk 9.2–10). **28:** *About eight days*, Jewish thought associates eight days with circumcision (Gen 17.12; 21.4; Lev 12.3), perhaps here subtly anticipating Jesus' resurrection on the "first day" after the old week. *Peter and John and James*, 8.51n. *To pray*, 3.21n. **29:** *Face*, see Ex 34.29–34. *Dazzling*, suggests mystical experience (Ex 34.29–35; also Dan 12.3). **30:** *Moses and Elijah*, unlikely representing "Torah" and "Nevi'im" (Prophets); perhaps representing the heavenly elect, righteous caught up to heaven, fidelity, or prophets rejected by (some of) the people. **31:** *Glory*, 2.9n. *Departure* (Gk "exodus," "road out"), referring to Jesus' death, resurrection, and ascension. **32:** *Sleep*, anticipating 22.45. **33:** *Dwellings*, "tents" or "tabernacles." *Not knowing*, Peter wants Moses and Elijah to remain. **34:** *Cloud*, indicating the divine presence (e.g., Ex 13.21–22). **35:** *Voice*, see 3.22n. *Chosen*, cf. Isa 42.1; Jewish tradition affirms the people Israel as God's chosen (Gen 18.19; Deut 7.6; Isa 43.20; Ps 33.12; 89.19; 105.6; 1 Chr 16.13, and elsewhere). For God's choosing particular people, see e.g., Neh 9.7 (Abraham).

were terrified as they entered the cloud. [35] Then from the cloud came a voice that said, "This is my Son, my Chosen;[a] listen to him!" [36] When the voice had spoken, Jesus was found alone. And they kept silent and in those days told no one any of the things they had seen.

[37] On the next day, when they had come down from the mountain, a great crowd met him. [38] Just then a man from the crowd shouted, "Teacher, I beg you to look at my son; he is my only child. [39] Suddenly a spirit seizes him, and all at once he[b] shrieks. It convulses him until he foams at the mouth; it mauls him and will scarcely leave him. [40] I begged your disciples to cast it out, but they could not." [41] Jesus answered, "You faithless and perverse generation, how much longer must I be with you and bear with you? Bring your son here." [42] While he was coming, the demon dashed him to the ground in convulsions. But Jesus rebuked the unclean spirit, healed the boy, and gave him back to his father. [43] And all were astounded at the greatness of God.

While everyone was amazed at all that he was doing, he said to his disciples, [44] "Let these words sink into your ears: The Son of Man is going to be betrayed into human hands." [45] But they did not understand this saying; its meaning was concealed from them, so that they could not perceive it. And they were afraid to ask him about this saying.

[46] An argument arose among them as to which one of them was the greatest. [47] But Jesus, aware of their inner thoughts, took a little child and put it by his side, [48] and said to them, "Whoever welcomes this child in my name welcomes me, and whoever welcomes me welcomes the one who sent me; for the least among all of you is the greatest."

[49] John answered, "Master, we saw someone casting out demons in your name, and we tried to stop him, because he does not follow with us." [50] But Jesus said to him, "Do not stop him; for whoever is not against you is for you."

[51] When the days drew near for him to be taken up, he set his face to go to Jerusalem. [52] And he sent messengers ahead of him. On their way they entered a village of the Samaritans to make ready for him; [53] but they did not receive him, because his face was set toward Jerusalem. [54] When his disciples James and John saw it, they said, "Lord, do you want us to command fire to come down from heaven and consume them?"[c] [55] But he turned and rebuked them. [56] Then[d] they went on to another village.

[57] As they were going along the road, someone said to him, "I will follow you

[a] Other ancient authorities read *my Beloved*
[b] Or *it*
[c] Other ancient authorities add *as Elijah did*
[d] Other ancient authorities read *rebuked them, and said, "You do not know what spirit you are of, [56] for the Son of Man has not come to destroy the lives of human beings but to save them." Then*

9.37–43a: Healing the afflicted boy (Mt 17.14–21; Mk 9.14–29). **38:** *Only child,* cf. 8.42n. **41:** *Faithless and perverse generation,* evoking Moses' speech in Deut 32.5; see also 7.31. **42:** *Rebuked,* see 4.35,39,41; 8.24.

9.43b–45: Second Passion prediction (Mt 17.22–23; Mk 9.30–32). **44:** See 9.22; 17.25; 18.31–34. *Son of Man,* see 5.14n. **45:** *Was concealed,* see 24.16. Faith in Jesus requires divine support.

9.46–48: True greatness (Mt 18.1–5; Mk 9.33–37). **47:** *Little child,* see 8.42n. A *child* is dependent on others and lacks patronage rights.

9.49–50: The unknown exorcist (Mk 9.38–41). **50:** *Whoever is not against you,* contrast 11.23; see also Num 11.26–29 (Elded and Medad).

9.51–19.27: Jesus' journey to Jerusalem (Mt 19.1–20.34; Mk 10.1–52), a section substantially unique to Luke. **51: The necessity of going to Jerusalem** (Mt 19.1–2; Mk 10.1). *Taken up* suggests both crucifixion and ascension. *He set his face,* a Semitic idiom (Isa 50.7).

9.52–56: Samaritans' rejection. 52–53: See Mt 10.5. *Samaritans,* inhabitants of Samaria, the capital of the former Northern Kingdom of Israel conquered by Assyria in 722 BCE. *Samaritans* became a distinct ethnic group, in tension with Jews (Jn 4.9; *Ant.* 20.118). **54:** *Command fire,* like Elijah in 2 Kings 1.9–16; contrast Lk 9.3–5. See "Parable of the Good Samaritan," p. 123.

wherever you go." [58] And Jesus said to him, "Foxes have holes, and birds of the air have nests; but the Son of Man has nowhere to lay his head." [59] To another he said, "Follow me." But he said, "Lord, first let me go and bury my father." [60] But Jesus[a] said to him, "Let the dead bury their own dead; but as for you, go and proclaim the kingdom of God." [61] Another said, "I will follow you, Lord; but let me first say farewell to those at my home." [62] Jesus said to him, "No one who puts a hand to the plow and looks back is fit for the kingdom of God."

10 After this the Lord appointed seventy[b] others and sent them on ahead of him in pairs to every town and place where he himself intended to go. [2] He said to them, "The harvest is plentiful, but the laborers are few; therefore ask the Lord of the harvest to send out laborers into his harvest. [3] Go on your way. See, I am sending you out like lambs into the midst of wolves. [4] Carry no purse, no bag, no sandals; and greet no one on the road. [5] Whatever house you enter, first say, 'Peace to this house!' [6] And if anyone is there who shares in peace, your peace will rest on that person; but if not, it will return to you. [7] Remain in the same house, eating and drinking whatever they provide, for the laborer deserves to be paid. Do not move about from house to house. [8] Whenever you enter a town and its people welcome you, eat what is set before you; [9] cure the sick who are there, and say to them, 'The kingdom of God has come near to you.'[c] [10] But whenever you enter a town and they do not welcome you, go out into its streets and say, [11] 'Even the dust of your town that clings to our feet, we wipe off in protest against you. Yet know this: the kingdom of God has come near.'[d] [12] I tell you, on that day it will be more tolerable for Sodom than for that town.

[13] "Woe to you, Chorazin! Woe to you, Bethsaida! For if the deeds of power done in you had been done in Tyre and Sidon, they would have repented long ago, sitting in sackcloth and ashes. [14] But at the judgment it will be more tolerable for Tyre and Sidon than for you. [15] And you, Capernaum,

will you be exalted to heaven?
No, you will be brought down to Hades.

[16] "Whoever listens to you listens to me, and whoever rejects you rejects me, and whoever rejects me rejects the one who sent me."

[17] The seventy[b] returned with joy, saying, "Lord, in your name even the demons submit to us!" [18] He said to them, "I watched Satan fall from heaven like a flash of lightning. [19] See, I have given you authority to tread on snakes and scorpions, and over all the power of the enemy; and nothing will hurt you. [20] Nevertheless, do not rejoice at this, that the spirits submit to you, but rejoice that your names are written in heaven."

[a] Gk *he*
[b] Other ancient authorities read *seventy-two*
[c] Or *is at hand for you*
[d] Or *is at hand*

9.57–62: Demands of discipleship (Mt 8.18–22). **58:** *Son of Man*, see 5.14n. **59:** *Bury my father*, necessary filial piety (see Tob 4.3; 6.15; *b. Ber.* 18a); v. 60 suggests the father was not yet dead. **61:** *Let me first say farewell*, see 1 Kings 19.20. Separation from the natal family is a hallmark of Jesus' teaching (see 4.11; 9.61; 14.26).

10.1–12: Mission of the seventy (Mt 9.37–38; 10.7–16). **1:** *Seventy*, see Gen 10.2–31 (LXX lists seventy-two names); *Jub.* 44.34; in the wilderness, Moses was aided by *seventy* elders (Ex 24.1,9; Num 11.16,24–25). *Sent them on ahead*, perhaps echoing Deut 1.22–25. **4:** *Carry no purse, See* 9.3n. *Greet no one*, see 2 Kings 4.29. **5:** *Peace*, a standard greeting; see 24.36; 1 Sam 25.6; Tob 12.17. **7:** *Laborer deserves to be paid*, see Deut 24.15; classical rabbis were not paid for teaching. **8:** *Eat what is set before you*, anticipating Acts 10. Since no Gentile mission is yet enjoined, the context suggests kosher food. **11:** *Dust*, 9.5n. **12:** *Sodom*, see Gen 19.24–28; for the comparative fate, Ezek 16.45–58; Lam 4.6.

10.13–16: Woes to unrepentant cities (Mt 11.20–24). **13:** *Chorazin*, 2 miles (3 km) north of Capernaum. *Bethsaida*, see 9.10n. *Tyre and Sidon*, Gentile cities, originally Philistine, north of Galilee; see Isa 23; Ezek 26–28. *Sackcloth and ashes*, Isa 58.5; Esth 4.1,3; Dan 9.3. **15:** *Capernaum*, see 4.22n. *Hades*, hell, comparable to Heb "Sheol" (Isa 14; Tob 3.10; 4.19; Wis 1.14 and elsewhere). By the first century CE, the concept of "hell" as a permanent place of damnation had begun to develop. **16:** Cf. Mt 10.40.

10.17–20: The seventy return (Mt 11.25–27). **17:** *Seventy*, see 10.1n. **18:** *Watched Satan fall*, a visionary experience (see Jn 12.31; Rev 12.7–12; cf. Isa 14.12). The Hebrew "Day Star" comes into Latin as "Lucifer" (lit., "light

PARABLE OF THE GOOD SAMARITAN (LK 10.25–37)

The account opens with a "lawyer" (*nomikos*) "testing" Jesus and thus depicting the lawyer not as a neutral questioner, but as another of Jesus' opponents. The term "test [or trial]," also translated "tempt," appears in 11.4: "Do not bring us to the test." Further, by testing Jesus, the lawyer takes Satan's role (4.12). His question is also misguided. "Eternal life" is not a commodity gained by a limited action; it is a gift freely given.

Jesus responds with a question of his own: "What is written in the law?" The lawyer responds by combining verses of the Torah known to all Jews of his time. Deuteronomy 6.5, on love of God, is still is recited in Judaism's daily liturgy. Leviticus 19.18, on love of neighbor, is, according to R. Akiva, Torah's greatest teaching (*Sifra Kedoshim* [ch 4] on Lev 19.18). Deuteronomy 6 and Lev 19 had already been combined in Jewish thought (*T. Iss.* 5.2; *T. Dan* 5.3), and the same combination appears in different contexts in Mt 22.37 and Mk 12.29–31.

For Judaism, everyone must be treated as a neighbor. It is necessary to read Lev 19.18 in the context of the statement further in the same chapter. For Lev 19.33–34, the neighbor whom one is to love is the *ger*, the "stranger" whom "you shall love . . . as yourself." The LXX translates *ger* as *prosēlytos*, "one who has come," i.e., "stranger," but also "proselyte"; viewing the "stranger" as a "proselyte" is a tradition also found in rabbinic literature. In Lev 25.47 the *ger* is also the *toshav*, the "sojourner," the resident alien (the LXX reads respectively *proselytos*, stranger, proselyte, and *paroikos*, which can mean "neighbor" but also "alien"). More striking, in Hebrew the words "neighbor" (*re'a*, "one who dwells nearby, fellow-citizen," as in Lev 19.18) and "enemy/evil [one]" (*ra'*, as in 1 Sam 30.22, *'ish-ra'*, "evil person") share the same consonants (*resh* and *ayin*); they differ only in the vowels, which are not included in the text. When Jesus asks the lawyer, "What do you *read* there?" he is asking, "Are you able to see, in Torah's words, the command to love both neighbor (narrowly defined) and those you would see as enemies?" (See "The Concept of Neighbor," p. 540.)

Regarding the robbers, some commentators depict them as Jewish Robin Hoods displaced from their land by over-taxation and urbanization, and who protest their socio-economic disenfranchisement by taking from the rich and giving to the poor. The text does not suggest this, and the word for "robber," *lēstēs* (compare rabbinic Hebrew *listim*), connotes violent criminal.

Nor, contrary to one popular view, do the priest and the Levite bypass the injured man because of ritual purity concerns. Numbers 19.10b–13 prescribes ritual ablutions after contacting a corpse, but this law does not prohibit saving a life or burying a corpse. Tobit (1.16–20) and Josephus (*Ag. Ap.* 2.30.211) demonstrate the strong Jewish concern for the respectful treatment of the dead. While Lev 21 forbids priests, *but not Levites*, from touching corpses, *m. Naz.* 7.1, insists even "A high priest or a Nazirite [a person under utmost purity] . . . may contract uncleanness because of a neglected corpse" (see also *b. Naz.* 43b; *y. Naz.* 56a). Levites are not forbidden from contact with corpses, and the priest is not going up to Jerusalem, where his impurity would have prevented him from participating in the Temple service, but "down from" (Gk *katabainō*; 10.31) the city. To import questions of purity into the parable is to misread it.

Priest and Levite indicate not an interest in purity but a point about community. Jews generally then, and now, fit into one of three groups: priests (*kohanim*) descended from Aaron; Levites (*levi'im*) descended from other children of Levi, and Israelites, descended from children of Jacob other than Levi. The citation of the first two anticipates the mention of the third. The parable shocks by making the third person not the expected Israelite but the unexpected Samaritan, the enemy of the Jews. It thus evokes 2 Chr 28.8–15, wherein enemy Samaritans care for Jewish victims, even as it reframes the lawyer's question. The issue is not "who is my neighbor?" but "can we recognize that the enemy might be our neighbor and can we accept this disruption of our stereotypes?

[21] At that same hour Jesus[a] rejoiced in the Holy Spirit[b] and said, "I thank[c] you, Father, Lord of heaven and earth, because you have

[a] Gk *he*
[b] Other authorities read *in the spirit*
[c] Or *praise*

bringer"). **19:** *Snakes and scorpions*, see Ps 90.13 LXX. *Enemy*, Satan. **20:** *Written in heaven*, an ancient Mesopotamian idea found in Ex 32.32; Ps 69.28; Dan 12.1; *1 En.* 47.3; 104.1; *Jub.* 19.9; Rev 3.5; etc., and reflected in the traditional Rosh Ha-Shanah greeting: "May you be inscribed for a good year."

10.21–24: Knowledge of God (Mt 11.25–27). **21:** *In the Holy Spirit*, in communion with God. See 1.15n. *Father*,

hidden these things from the wise and the intelligent and have revealed them to infants; yes, Father, for such was your gracious will.[a] [22] All things have been handed over to me by my Father; and no one knows who the Son is except the Father, or who the Father is except the Son and anyone to whom the Son chooses to reveal him."

[23] Then turning to the disciples, Jesus[b] said to them privately, "Blessed are the eyes that see what you see! [24] For I tell you that many prophets and kings desired to see what you see, but did not see it, and to hear what you hear, but did not hear it."

[25] Just then a lawyer stood up to test Jesus.[c] "Teacher," he said, "what must I do to inherit eternal life?" [26] He said to him, "What is written in the law? What do you read there?" [27] He answered, "You shall love the Lord your God with all your heart, and with all your soul, and with all your strength, and with all your mind; and your neighbor as yourself." [28] And he said to him, "You have given the right answer; do this, and you will live."

[29] But wanting to justify himself, he asked Jesus, "And who is my neighbor?" [30] Jesus replied, "A man was going down from Jerusalem to Jericho, and fell into the hands of robbers, who stripped him, beat him, and went away, leaving him half dead. [31] Now by chance a priest was going down that road; and when he saw him, he passed by on the other side. [32] So likewise a Levite, when he came to the place and saw him, passed by on the other side. [33] But a Samaritan while traveling came near him; and when he saw him, he was moved with pity. [34] He went to him and bandaged his wounds, having poured oil and wine on them. Then he put him on his own animal, brought him to an inn, and took care of him. [35] The next day he took out two denarii,[d] gave them to the innkeeper, and said, 'Take care of him; and when I come back, I will repay you whatever more you spend.' [36] Which of these three, do you think, was a neighbor to the man who fell into the hands of the robbers?" [37] He said, "The one who showed him mercy." Jesus said to him, "Go and do likewise."

[38] Now as they went on their way, he entered a certain village, where a woman named Martha welcomed him into her home. [39] She had a sister named Mary, who sat at the Lord's feet and listened to what he was saying. [40] But Martha was distracted by her many tasks; so she came to him and asked, "Lord, do you not care that my sister has left me to do all the work by myself? Tell her then to help me." [41] But the Lord answered her, "Martha, Martha, you are worried and distracted by many things; [42] there is need of

a Or *for so it was well-pleasing in your sight*
b Gk *he*
c Gk *him*
d The denarius was the usual day's wage for a laborer

Lord . . . , (Tob 7.17; Jdt 9.12). **22:** *Son . . . Father,* see Jn 3.35; 10.15; 17.21. Knowledge of God is only fully known by and through Jesus. **23–24:** See Mt 13.16–17.

10.25–28: Lawyer's challenge (Mt 22.34–40; Mk 12.28–34; cf. Lk 18.9–14). **25:** *Lawyer,* expert in Torah and a negative foil for Luke (see 7.30; 11.45–46,52; 14.3). *Test,* in the role of Satan, see 4.2; cf. 11.16. *Inherit eternal life,* eternal life was part of Israel's covenant (see *m. Sanh.* 10.1). **26:** *Law,* Torah (2.22–24,27,39; 5.17; 16.16–17; 24.44). **27:** Deut 6.5 (cf. Josh 22.5); Lev 19.18 (R. Akiva, *Sifre* on Lev 19.18, calls this the "greatest principle in the Law"). On combining the two commandments, *T. Dan* 5.3; *T. Iss.* 5.2.

10.29–37: Parable of the good samaritan. See "Parable of the Good Samaritan," p. 123. **29:** *Justify himself,* present himself in the right. **30:** *Jerusalem to Jericho,* 17–18 miles, with a steep drop-off. *Robbers,* thieves, not freedom fighters (see 19.46; 22.52; Jn 10.8; 18.40; 2 Cor 11.26). **31:** *Priest* (Heb "kohen"), such as Zechariah (see 1.5). *Going down,* not up to Jerusalem, where purity may have been an issue. **32:** *Levite,* Temple functionary. **33:** *Samaritan,* 9.52n. *Pity,* translated "compassion" in 7.33; 15.20. **34:** *Oil,* see Isa 1.6. *Wine,* an antiseptic. **35:** *Two denarii,* providing the cost of lodging. The full imagery evokes 2 Chr 28.8–15. **36:** *Was a neighbor,* Jesus changes the original question. **37:** *The one,* the lawyer cannot voice "Samaritan."

10.38–42: Martha and Mary (see Jn 11–12). **38:** *Her home,* Martha is a householder; Jesus criticizes her as he does other householders (see 5.29n.). **39:** *Sat at the Lord's feet,* 1.17n.; women received instruction in synagogues (see 13.11), homes, patronage capacities (8.3n.), and personal conversations. **40:** *Many tasks:* Gk "pollēn diakonian," lit., "much serving" (see 4.39). **42:** *Better part,* listening to Jesus precedes service.

only one thing.[a] Mary has chosen the better part, which will not be taken away from her."

11 He was praying in a certain place, and after he had finished, one of his disciples said to him, "Lord, teach us to pray, as John taught his disciples." 2 He said to them, "When you pray, say:

Father,[b] hallowed be your name.
Your kingdom come.[c]
3 Give us each day our daily bread.[d]
4 And forgive us our sins,
for we ourselves forgive everyone
indebted to us.
And do not bring us to the time of trial."[e]

5 And he said to them, "Suppose one of you has a friend, and you go to him at midnight and say to him, 'Friend, lend me three loaves of bread; 6 for a friend of mine has arrived, and I have nothing to set before him.' 7 And he answers from within, 'Do not bother me; the door has already been locked, and my children are with me in bed; I cannot get up and give you anything.' 8 I tell you, even though he will not get up and give him anything because he is his friend, at least because of his persistence he will get up and give him whatever he needs.

9 "So I say to you, Ask, and it will be given you; search, and you will find; knock, and the door will be opened for you. 10 For everyone who asks receives, and everyone who searches finds, and for everyone who knocks, the door will be opened. 11 Is there anyone among you who, if your child asks for[f] a fish, will give a snake instead of a fish? 12 Or if the child asks for an egg, will give a scorpion? 13 If you then, who are evil, know how to give good gifts to your children, how much more will the heavenly Father give the Holy Spirit[g] to those who ask him!"

14 Now he was casting out a demon that was mute; when the demon had gone out, the one who had been mute spoke, and the crowds were amazed. 15 But some of them said, "He casts out demons by Beelzebul, the ruler of the demons." 16 Others, to test him, kept demanding from him a sign from heaven. 17 But he knew what they were thinking and said to them, "Every kingdom divided against itself becomes a desert, and house falls on house.

a Other ancient authorities read *few things are necessary, or only one*
b Other ancient authorities read *Our Father in heaven*
c A few ancient authorities read *Your Holy Spirit come upon us and cleanse us.* Other ancient authorities add *Your will be done, on earth as in heaven*
d Or *our bread for tomorrow*
e Or *us into temptation.* Other ancient authorities add *but rescue us from the evil one* (or *from evil*)
f Other ancient authorities add *bread, will give a stone; or if your child asks for*
g Other ancient authorities read *the Father give the Holy Spirit from heaven*

11.1–4: The Lord's Prayer (Mt 6.9–13). **1:** *Praying,* 3.21n. **2:** *Father,* Jewish address for God, especially in postbiblical prayers (Sir 23.1; 51.10; Tob 13.4). *Hallowed be your name,* the sanctity of God's name is a biblical theme: Lev 20.3; 22.2; Ezek 36.20; Ps 30.4; 1 Chr 16.10,35; see also the "Kiddush" (an early Aramaic prayer): "Magnified and sanctified be your great name." *Your kingdom come,* expressing hope for the messianic age. **3:** *Daily bread,* the obscure Greek term "epiousion," although translated "daily," may express an underlying future aspect, suggesting "bread for tomorrow," i.e., the messianic banquet (13.29; 14.15; see Isa 25.6–8; 1QSa 2.11–22; *1 En.* 25.4–6; *m. Avot* 3.17; *Num. Rab.* 13.2) and perhaps a reference to manna (Ex 16.15; Neh 9.15; Ps 78.24; Wis 16.20), which came to symbolize the world-to-come ("olam ha-ba"). **4:** *Sins . . . indebted,* Aram "ḥov" can be translated "sin" or "debt"; in rabbinic, but not biblical literature, sins were considered debts against God. *We ourselves forgive,* see *m. Yoma* 8.9; *b. Shabb.* 151b; *b. Rosh Ha-Shanah* 17a; *b. Meg.* 28a; *Midr. Tanh., Hukkat* 19.1–22.1. *Time of trial,* test or temptation, see Gen 22.1, Abraham, Job, and for Israel, Ex 16.4; Deut 8.2.

11.5–8: Importuning friend. 8: *Persistence,* in prayer (see also 18.1–8).

11.9–13: Assurance of God's attention (Mt 7.7–11). **11:** *Anyone* (Gk "pater"), "father"; see 8.42n. **13:** *Holy Spirit,* see 1.15n.

11.14–23: Beelzebul controversy (Mt 12.22–30; Mk 3.22–27). **15:** *Beelzebul,* Satan (see v. 18); Beelzebul, "exalted Baal," originally a title of the Canaanite Baal (2 Kings 1.2; Baal-zebub is a parody of the name, meaning "lord of the flies"). *B. Sanh.* 43a, 107b attributes Jesus' wonder-workings to demonic powers. **16:** *Sign,* see Mt 16.1 and Mk 8.11. Jewish tradition recognized mighty works; the question was whether they were miracle or magic,

[18] If Satan also is divided against himself, how will his kingdom stand?—for you say that I cast out the demons by Beelzebul. [19] Now if I cast out the demons by Beelzebul, by whom do your exorcists[a] cast them out? Therefore they will be your judges. [20] But if it is by the finger of God that I cast out the demons, then the kingdom of God has come to you. [21] When a strong man, fully armed, guards his castle, his property is safe. [22] But when one stronger than he attacks him and overpowers him, he takes away his armor in which he trusted and divides his plunder. [23] Whoever is not with me is against me, and whoever does not gather with me scatters.

[24] "When the unclean spirit has gone out of a person, it wanders through waterless regions looking for a resting place, but not finding any, it says, 'I will return to my house from which I came.' [25] When it comes, it finds it swept and put in order. [26] Then it goes and brings seven other spirits more evil than itself, and they enter and live there; and the last state of that person is worse than the first."

[27] While he was saying this, a woman in the crowd raised her voice and said to him, "Blessed is the womb that bore you and the breasts that nursed you!" [28] But he said, "Blessed rather are those who hear the word of God and obey it!"

[29] When the crowds were increasing, he began to say, "This generation is an evil generation; it asks for a sign, but no sign will be given to it except the sign of Jonah. [30] For just as Jonah became a sign to the people of Nineveh, so the Son of Man will be to this generation. [31] The queen of the South will rise at the judgment with the people of this generation and condemn them, because she came from the ends of the earth to listen to the wisdom of Solomon, and see, something greater than Solomon is here! [32] The people of Nineveh will rise up at the judgment with this generation and condemn it, because they repented at the proclamation of Jonah, and see, something greater than Jonah is here!

[33] "No one after lighting a lamp puts it in a cellar,[b] but on the lampstand so that those who enter may see the light. [34] Your eye is the lamp of your body. If your eye is healthy, your whole body is full of light; but if it is not healthy, your body is full of darkness. [35] Therefore consider whether the light in you is not darkness. [36] If then your whole body is full of light, with no part of it in darkness, it will be as full of light as when a lamp gives you light with its rays."

[37] While he was speaking, a Pharisee invited him to dine with him; so he went in and took his place at the table. [38] The Pharisee was amazed to see that he did not first wash before dinner. [39] Then the Lord said to him, "Now you Pharisees clean the outside of the cup and of the dish, but inside you are full of greed and wickedness. [40] You fools! Did not the one who made the outside make the inside also? [41] So give for alms those things that are within; and see, everything will be clean for you.

[42] "But woe to you Pharisees! For you tithe mint and rue and herbs of all kinds, and neglect justice and the love of God; it is these you ought to have practiced, without neglecting the others. [43] Woe to you Pharisees! For you love to have the seat of honor in the

a Gk *sons*

b Other ancient authorities add *or under the bushel basket*

facilitated by God or Satan. **18:** *Satan,* 4.2n. **19:** *Your exorcists,* Jewish miracle workers (see *Ant.* 8.45 on Solomon's power to exorcise). **20:** *Finger of God,* Ex 8.19; Deut 9.10. **21–22:** *One stronger,* here Jesus' self-reference. **23:** Cf. 9.50; one either follows Jesus or is his enemy.

11.24–26: (Mt 12.43–45), accounting for the relapse of the exorcised individuals.

11.27–28: True family. 27: *Woman in the crowd,* there is nothing unusual about her presence or her voice; see "Jewish Family Life," p. 537. *Blessed,* blessings of both individuals (e.g., Judg 5.24 for Jael) and groups are common in the Tanakh. **28:** *Blessed rather,* see 8.21.

11.29–32: Sign of Jonah (Mt 12.38–42; Mk 8.11–12). **29:** *Sign,* see 11.16. *Sign of Jonah,* Jonah's successful preaching to the (Gentile) Ninevites but also his rescue from the fish (analogous to resurrection). **30:** *Son of Man,* see 5.24n. **31:** *Queen of the South,* of Sheba (1 Kings 10.1–10; 2 Chr 9.1–9), a Gentile. *Will rise,* at the resurrection; see Dan 12.2–3.

11.33–36: Internal light. 33: *Lamp,* see 8.16; Mt 5.15; Mk 4.21. **34–36:** *Eye,* see Mt 6.22–23.

11.37–48: Invectives against Pharisees and lawyers. 37: *Pharisee invited him to dine,* see 7.36n. **38:** *Did not first wash* (see Mk 7.1–5; Mt 15.1–9), "Nitilat yadayim," washing hands before eating, a ritual of sanctification (see *m.*

synagogues and to be greeted with respect in the marketplaces. [44] Woe to you! For you are like unmarked graves, and people walk over them without realizing it."

[45] One of the lawyers answered him, "Teacher, when you say these things, you insult us too." [46] And he said, "Woe also to you lawyers! For you load people with burdens hard to bear, and you yourselves do not lift a finger to ease them. [47] Woe to you! For you build the tombs of the prophets whom your ancestors killed. [48] So you are witnesses and approve of the deeds of your ancestors; for they killed them, and you build their tombs. [49] Therefore also the Wisdom of God said, 'I will send them prophets and apostles, some of whom they will kill and persecute,' [50] so that this generation may be charged with the blood of all the prophets shed since the foundation of the world, [51] from the blood of Abel to the blood of Zechariah, who perished between the altar and the sanctuary. Yes, I tell you, it will be charged against this generation. [52] Woe to you lawyers! For you have taken away the key of knowledge; you did not enter yourselves, and you hindered those who were entering."

[53] When he went outside, the scribes and the Pharisees began to be very hostile toward him and to cross-examine him about many things, [54] lying in wait for him, to catch him in something he might say.

12 Meanwhile, when the crowd gathered by the thousands, so that they trampled on one another, he began to speak first to his disciples, "Beware of the yeast of the Pharisees, that is, their hypocrisy. [2] Nothing is covered up that will not be uncovered, and nothing secret that will not become known. [3] Therefore whatever you have said in the dark will be heard in the light, and what you have whispered behind closed doors will be proclaimed from the housetops.

[4] "I tell you, my friends, do not fear those who kill the body, and after that can do nothing more. [5] But I will warn you whom to fear: fear him who, after he has killed, has authority[a] to cast into hell.[b] Yes, I tell you, fear him! [6] Are not five sparrows sold for two pennies? Yet not one of them is forgotten in God's sight. [7] But even the hairs of your head are all counted. Do not be afraid; you are of more value than many sparrows.

[8] "And I tell you, everyone who acknowledges me before others, the Son of Man also will acknowledge before the angels of God; [9] but whoever denies me before others will be denied before the angels of God. [10] And everyone who speaks a word against the Son of Man will be forgiven; but whoever blasphemes against the Holy Spirit will not be forgiven. [11] When they bring you before the synagogues, the rulers, and the authorities, do not worry about how[c] you are to defend

[a] Or *power*
[b] Gk *Gehenna*
[c] Other ancient authorities add *or what*

Yad. 2.4). **39:** *Lord,* 1.17n. **41:** *Alms* (Heb "tzedaqah"), 6.30n. **42:** *Woe to you Pharisees,* see Mt 23.13–33. *Tithe,* Deut 14.22. **44:** *Unmarked graves,* graves were whitewashed (Mt 23.27) to prevent corpse impurity (see "The Law," p. 515), not to conceal. **46:** *Burdens hard to bear,* see Mt 23.4. **47:** *You build the tombs,* logically, this should indicate repudiation of rather than complicity in the murders. *Your ancestors killed,* Jesus casts the lawyers and Pharisees as killers of prophets and distinguishes himself from them (7.30n.).

11.49–52: Murderous people. 49: *Wisdom of God,* see 7.35n. The quotation cannot be located, but see Jer 7.25–26. **50:** *Charged with the blood,* see Mt 27.25. **51:** *Abel,* Gen 4.8; Jewish tradition does not regard Abel as a "prophet." *Zechariah,* probably referring to 2 Chr 24.20–22 (and so naming murder victims from Genesis through Chronicles, which according to *b. B. Bat.* 14b concludes the canon) although Josephus (*J.W.* 4.335–44) mentions a Zechariah killed in the Temple during the first revolt against Rome. **52:** *Did not enter,* see Mt 23.13.

11.53–54: Growing opposition. See 6.11; 19.47–48; 20.19–20; 22.2.

12.1–12: Instructions to disciples (Mt 16.5–6; Mk 8.14–15). **1:** *Yeast* could symbolize corruption (1 Cor 5.6–8), but see 13.21. *Derekh Eretz Zuta* on Lev 26.6 (citing R. Yehoshua ben Levi) states, "Great is peace, for it is as the leaven to dough. If the Holy One had not given peace to the world, sword and beast would devour up the whole world." **5:** *Hell,* Gk/Heb "Gehenna"; see 2 Kings 23.10; see also 10.15n. **6:** *Penny* ("assarion"), one-sixteenth of a denarius (see 12.59n.). **8:** *Son of Man,* 5.24n.; 9.26; Mk 8.38. **10:** *Blasphemes against the Holy Spirit* (Mt 12.31–32; Mk 3.28–30), attributing the Spirit's works to Satan; see 1.15n. and Isa 63.10–11. **11:** *Bring you before the syna-*

yourselves or what you are to say; [12] for the Holy Spirit will teach you at that very hour what you ought to say."

[13] Someone in the crowd said to him, "Teacher, tell my brother to divide the family inheritance with me." [14] But he said to him, "Friend, who set me to be a judge or arbitrator over you?" [15] And he said to them, "Take care! Be on your guard against all kinds of greed; for one's life does not consist in the abundance of possessions." [16] Then he told them a parable: "The land of a rich man produced abundantly. [17] And he thought to himself, 'What should I do, for I have no place to store my crops?' [18] Then he said, 'I will do this: I will pull down my barns and build larger ones, and there I will store all my grain and my goods. [19] And I will say to my soul, Soul, you have ample goods laid up for many years; relax, eat, drink, be merry.' [20] But God said to him, 'You fool! This very night your life is being demanded of you. And the things you have prepared, whose will they be?' [21] So it is with those who store up treasures for themselves but are not rich toward God."

[22] He said to his disciples, "Therefore I tell you, do not worry about your life, what you will eat, or about your body, what you will wear. [23] For life is more than food, and the body more than clothing. [24] Consider the ravens: they neither sow nor reap, they have neither storehouse nor barn, and yet God feeds them. Of how much more value are you than the birds! [25] And can any of you by worrying add a single hour to your span of life?[a] [26] If then you are not able to do so small a thing as that, why do you worry about the rest? [27] Consider the lilies, how they grow: they neither toil nor spin;[b] yet I tell you, even Solomon in all his glory was not clothed like one of these. [28] But if God so clothes the grass of the field, which is alive today and tomorrow is thrown into the oven, how much more will he clothe you—you of little faith! [29] And do not keep striving for what you are to eat and what you are to drink, and do not keep worrying. [30] For it is the nations of the world that strive after all these things, and your Father knows that you need them. [31] Instead, strive for his[c] kingdom, and these things will be given to you as well.

[32] "Do not be afraid, little flock, for it is your Father's good pleasure to give you the kingdom. [33] Sell your possessions, and give alms. Make purses for yourselves that do not wear out, an unfailing treasure in heaven, where no thief comes near and no moth destroys. [34] For where your treasure is, there your heart will be also.

[35] "Be dressed for action and have your lamps lit; [36] be like those who are waiting for their master to return from the wedding banquet, so that they may open the door for him as soon as he comes and knocks. [37] Blessed are those slaves whom the master finds alert when he comes; truly I tell you, he will fasten his belt and have them sit down to eat, and he will come and serve them. [38] If he comes during the middle of the night, or near dawn, and finds them so, blessed are those slaves.

[a] Or *add a cubit to your stature*
[b] Other ancient authorities read *Consider the lilies; they neither spin nor weave*
[c] Other ancient authorities read *God's*

gogues, for discipline (see 21.12; Mt 10.17; 23.34; Mk 13.9; Acts 22.19; 26.11). **12:** *Holy Spirit will teach you* (Mt 10.19–20; Mk 13.11), no rehearsed speeches are needed.

12.13–21: Warnings against wealth. 13: *Divide the family inheritance*, Deut 21.17 mandates that the oldest sons receive a double portion, but postbiblical practice allowed parents freedom in bequests. **14:** Cf. Ex 2.14. **16:** *Rich man*, parables with this phrase are critical of wealth not used to support the poor (16.1–19). **19:** *Eat, drink, and be merry*, a proper response to God's good gifts: Eccl 8.15; Tob 7.10; *1 En.* 97.8–9. **20:** Cf. 12.33–34; Jer 17.11. *Is being demanded*, lit., "they demand"; the antecedent may be God, angels, or the man's possessions. **21:** *Store up treasures*, see 12.33; Tob 4.9–11; Mt 6.19–20; *t. Pe'ah* 4.18.

12.22–32: Lessons from nature (Mt 6.25–34). **24:** *Ravens*, scavengers (Lev 11.15; Deut 14.14; cf. Job 38.41). **27:** *Solomon in all his glory*, see 1 Kings 10. **32:** *Flock*, those shepherded by the messiah (Ezek 34.23). *Father*, see 10.21n. For illustrations from nature, see Prov 30.24–28 and elsewhere.

12.33–34: Treasure in heaven (Mt 6.19–21). Cf. Mk 10.21; Lk 18.22; Acts 2.45; 4.32–35. **33:** *Sell your possessions*, see 6.30n. *Unfailing treasure in heaven*, 12.21n.

12.35–48: Watchfulness and prudence (Mt 24.42–51). **35:** *Dressed for action*, lit., "your loins girded." **36:** *Master*, Gk "kyrios," 1.17n. *Wedding banquet*, a messianic image (see 5.34–35). **37:** *Serve them*, see 17.7–8; 22.27; Jn

[39] "But know this: if the owner of the house had known at what hour the thief was coming, he[a] would not have let his house be broken into. [40] You also must be ready, for the Son of Man is coming at an unexpected hour."

[41] Peter said, "Lord, are you telling this parable for us or for everyone?" [42] And the Lord said, "Who then is the faithful and prudent manager whom his master will put in charge of his slaves, to give them their allowance of food at the proper time? [43] Blessed is that slave whom his master will find at work when he arrives. [44] Truly I tell you, he will put that one in charge of all his possessions. [45] But if that slave says to himself, 'My master is delayed in coming,' and if he begins to beat the other slaves, men and women, and to eat and drink and get drunk, [46] the master of that slave will come on a day when he does not expect him and at an hour that he does not know, and will cut him in pieces,[b] and put him with the unfaithful. [47] That slave who knew what his master wanted, but did not prepare himself or do what was wanted, will receive a severe beating. [48] But the one who did not know and did what deserved a beating will receive a light beating. From everyone to whom much has been given, much will be required; and from the one to whom much has been entrusted, even more will be demanded.

[49] "I came to bring fire to the earth, and how I wish it were already kindled! [50] I have a baptism with which to be baptized, and what stress I am under until it is completed! [51] Do you think that I have come to bring peace to the earth? No, I tell you, but rather division! [52] From now on five in one household will be divided, three against two and two against three; [53] they will be divided:

father against son
  and son against father,
mother against daughter
  and daughter against mother,
mother-in-law against her daughter-in-law
  and daughter-in-law against mother-in-law."

[54] He also said to the crowds, "When you see a cloud rising in the west, you immediately say, 'It is going to rain'; and so it happens. [55] And when you see the south wind blowing, you say, 'There will be scorching heat'; and it happens. [56] You hypocrites! You know how to interpret the appearance of earth and sky, but why do you not know how to interpret the present time?

[57] "And why do you not judge for yourselves what is right? [58] Thus, when you go with your accuser before a magistrate, on the way make an effort to settle the case,[c] or you may be dragged before the judge, and the judge hand you over to the officer, and the officer throw you in prison. [59] I tell you, you will never get out until you have paid the very last penny."

13 At that very time there were some present who told him about the Galileans whose blood Pilate had mingled with their sacrifices. [2] He asked them, "Do you think that because these Galileans suffered in this way they were worse sinners than all other Galileans? [3] No, I tell you; but unless you repent, you will all perish as they did. [4] Or those eighteen who were killed when the tower of Siloam fell on them—do you think that they were worse offenders than all the

a Other ancient authorities add *would have watched and*
b Or *cut him off*
c Gk *settle with him*

13.3–16. **39:** *Thief*, 1 Thess 5.2; 2 Pet 3.10; Rev 16.15. **40:** *Son of Man*, 5.24n. *Unexpected hour*, see Mk 13.35. **46:** *Cut him in pieces*, eschatological punishment. **48:** See 8.18; 19.26.

12.49–53: Familial division (Mt 10.34–36). **49:** *Fire*, symbolizing judgment (Mt 3.11; 7.19; Mk 9.48; Lk 3.16). **50:** *Baptism*, here, Jesus' death. **51:** *Division*, 8.21; 9.61; 18.29. **53:** See Mic 7.6.

12.54–56: Interpreting signs (Mt 16.2–3). **56:** *Hypocrites*, see 13.15.

12.57–59: Avoiding litigation (Mt 5.25–26). **59:** *Penny*, Gk "lepton," the smallest Greek coin. Two "lepta" make a "quadrans" (Mt 5.26; Mk 12.42), eight an assarion (12.6n.).

13.1–5: Understanding evil occurrences. 1: *Galileans whose blood Pilate had mingled*, the event is unknown; on Pilate's ruthless treatment of those he governed see, e.g., Philo, *Leg. Gai.* 37–38; Josephus, *J.W.* 2.9.2–4; *Ant.* 18.2.2; 18.3.1–2; 18.4.1–2. *With their sacrifices*, Galileans fully participated in Temple worship. Tragic death does not indicate a sinful life. **4:** *Tower of Siloam*, another unknown accident. Siloam, southwest Jerusalem (Isa 8.6; Neh 3.15; Jn 9.7).

others living in Jerusalem? [5] No, I tell you; but unless you repent, you will all perish just as they did."

[6] Then he told this parable: "A man had a fig tree planted in his vineyard; and he came looking for fruit on it and found none. [7] So he said to the gardener, 'See here! For three years I have come looking for fruit on this fig tree, and still I find none. Cut it down! Why should it be wasting the soil?' [8] He replied, 'Sir, let it alone for one more year, until I dig around it and put manure on it. [9] If it bears fruit next year, well and good; but if not, you can cut it down.'"

[10] Now he was teaching in one of the synagogues on the sabbath. [11] And just then there appeared a woman with a spirit that had crippled her for eighteen years. She was bent over and was quite unable to stand up straight. [12] When Jesus saw her, he called her over and said, "Woman, you are set free from your ailment." [13] When he laid his hands on her, immediately she stood up straight and began praising God. [14] But the leader of the synagogue, indignant because Jesus had cured on the sabbath, kept saying to the crowd, "There are six days on which work ought to be done; come on those days and be cured, and not on the sabbath day." [15] But the Lord answered him and said, "You hypocrites! Does not each of you on the sabbath untie his ox or his donkey from the manger, and lead it away to give it water? [16] And ought not this woman, a daughter of Abraham whom Satan bound for eighteen long years, be set free from this bondage on the sabbath day?" [17] When he said this, all his opponents were put to shame; and the entire crowd was rejoicing at all the wonderful things that he was doing.

[18] He said therefore, "What is the kingdom of God like? And to what should I compare it? [19] It is like a mustard seed that someone took and sowed in the garden; it grew and became a tree, and the birds of the air made nests in its branches."

[20] And again he said, "To what should I compare the kingdom of God? [21] It is like yeast that a woman took and mixed in with[a] three measures of flour until all of it was leavened."

[22] Jesus[b] went through one town and village after another, teaching as he made his way to Jerusalem. [23] Someone asked him, "Lord, will only a few be saved?" He said to them, [24] "Strive to enter through the narrow door; for many, I tell you, will try to enter and will not be able. [25] When once the owner of the house has got up and shut the door, and you begin to stand outside and to knock at the door, saying, 'Lord, open to us,' then in reply he will say to you, 'I do not know where you come from.' [26] Then you will begin to say, 'We ate and drank with you, and you taught in our streets.' [27] But he will say, 'I do not know where you come from; go away from me, all you evildoers!' [28] There will be weeping and gnashing of teeth when you see Abraham and Isaac and Jacob and all the prophets in the kingdom of God, and you yourselves

[a] Gk *hid in*
[b] Gk *He*

13.6–9: The unfruitful fig tree (Mt 21.18–19; Mk 11.12–14). **7:** *Cut it down*, see 3.9. **8:** *One more year*, limited time left for the people to repent.

13.10–17: Sabbath healing (see 4.31–37n.). **14:** *Leader of the synagogue*, see 8.41n. *Sabbath*, see Ex 20.9–10; Lev 23.3; Deut 5.13–14; see 6.1–11n. **15:** *Untie his ox*, a rabbinic "qal vahomer" (from lesser to greater) argument. **16:** *Daughter of Abraham*, Jewish woman (4 Macc 15.28; 17.6; 18.20; cf. Lk 19.9). **17:** *Entire crowd was rejoicing*, the people celebrate the healing; they correctly find no violation of halakhah.

13.18–19: Parable of the mustard seed (Mt 13.31–32; Mk 4.30–32). **19:** *Became a tree*, an exaggeration. *Made nests in its branches*, see Ps 104.12; Dan 4.12,21.

13.20–21: Parable of the yeast (Mt 13.33). **21:** *Yeast*, see 12.1n. *Mixed* (Gk "enegkrypsen"), lit., "hid." *Three measures*, 50–60 pounds. Another parable of hyperbole, contrast, growth, and transformation of domestic images (mustard seed, yeast).

13.22–30: Who will be saved (Mt 7.13–14,22–23; 8.11–12; 19.30; Mk 10.31). **23:** *A few be saved*, a concern of much apocalyptic literature (see especially 4 *Ezra*), but not rabbinic literature, which takes a generous view of salvation (e.g., *m. Sanh.* 10.1). **24:** *Will not be able*, restricted access to salvation. **28:** *Weeping and gnashing of teeth*, Mt 8.12; 13.42,50; 22.13; 24.51; 25.30. *Abraham and Isaac and Jacob*, unity with the ancestors in the world-to-come. **29:** *People*

thrown out. [29] Then people will come from east and west, from north and south, and will eat in the kingdom of God. [30] Indeed, some are last who will be first, and some are first who will be last."

[31] At that very hour some Pharisees came and said to him, "Get away from here, for Herod wants to kill you." [32] He said to them, "Go and tell that fox for me,[a] 'Listen, I am casting out demons and performing cures today and tomorrow, and on the third day I finish my work. [33] Yet today, tomorrow, and the next day I must be on my way, because it is impossible for a prophet to be killed outside of Jerusalem.' [34] Jerusalem, Jerusalem, the city that kills the prophets and stones those who are sent to it! How often have I desired to gather your children together as a hen gathers her brood under her wings, and you were not willing! [35] See, your house is left to you. And I tell you, you will not see me until the time comes when[b] you say, 'Blessed is the one who comes in the name of the Lord.'"

14 On one occasion when Jesus[c] was going to the house of a leader of the Pharisees to eat a meal on the sabbath, they were watching him closely. [2] Just then, in front of him, there was a man who had dropsy. [3] And Jesus asked the lawyers and Pharisees, "Is it lawful to cure people on the sabbath, or not?" [4] But they were silent. So Jesus[c] took him and healed him, and sent him away. [5] Then he said to them, "If one of you has a child[d] or an ox that has fallen into a well, will you not immediately pull it out on a sabbath day?" [6] And they could not reply to this.

[7] When he noticed how the guests chose the places of honor, he told them a parable. [8] "When you are invited by someone to a wedding banquet, do not sit down at the place of honor, in case someone more distinguished than you has been invited by your host; [9] and the host who invited both of you may come and say to you, 'Give this person your place,' and then in disgrace you would start to take the lowest place. [10] But when you are invited, go and sit down at the lowest place, so that when your host comes, he may say to you, 'Friend, move up higher'; then you will be honored in the presence of all who sit at the table with you. [11] For all who exalt themselves will be humbled, and those who humble themselves will be exalted."

[12] He said also to the one who had invited him, "When you give a luncheon or a dinner, do not invite your friends or your brothers or your relatives or rich neighbors, in case they may invite you in return, and you would be repaid. [13] But when you give a banquet, invite the poor, the crippled, the lame, and the blind. [14] And you will be blessed, because they cannot repay you, for you will be repaid at the resurrection of the righteous."

a Gk lacks *for me*
b Other ancient authorities lack *the time comes when*
c Gk *he*
d Other ancient authorities read *a donkey*

will come, perhaps originally referring to the ingathering of the exiles, a sign of the messianic age (see Isa 60.4; Zech 10.6–10; Ps 107.3); for Luke, a hint of the Gentile mission. *Eat in the kingdom*, the messianic banquet (11.3n.).

13.31–33: Herod's threat. 31: See "Pharisees in Luke," p. 110. *Here*, Galilee and Perea (see 3.1n.). **32:** *Go and tell*, Jesus presumes Pharisees have access to Herod. *Fox*, an insult. **33:** *Prophet*, Jesus accepts this designation.

13.34–35: Lament over Jerusalem (Mt 23.37–39; see also Lk 18.41–42). **34:** *City that kills the prophets*, see 6.23; 11.47–50. The lament anticipates Stephen's death (Acts 7). *Gather*, perhaps referring to the ingathering of the exiles (see v. 29n.). **35:** *House*, Temple, see Jer 22.5. *Blessed is the one who comes*, Ps 118.26, from the Hallel Psalms (113–18), recited on festivals, including Passover; see Lk 19.37–38.

14.1–6: Sabbath healing. 1: *Eat a meal*, see 7.36n. **2:** *Dropsy*, edema. **3:** *Lawful to cure people on the sabbath*, 13.14n. **5:** *Child*, the variant "donkey" (see translators' note *d*) connects the example to 13.15. *Will you not . . . pull it out*, another "qal vahomer" argument (13.15n.; contrast CD ms. A 11.13–17; 4Q265, which prohibit lifting an animal from a ditch on the Sabbath).

14.7–14: Instructions on humility. 8: See Prov 25.6–7. **11:** See 13.30; 18.14; Ezek 21.16; Mt 23.12. **12:** *Rich neighbors*, Luke presumes elite readers (see 1.3). **13:** *The poor*, those unlikely to be able to reciprocate. **14:** *You will be repaid*, heavenly reward based on earthly action. *Resurrection of the righteous*, Dan 12.2–3; *m. Sanh.* 10.1; *b. Rosh Ha-Shanah* 16b–17a.

[15] One of the dinner guests, on hearing this, said to him, "Blessed is anyone who will eat bread in the kingdom of God!" [16] Then Jesus[a] said to him, "Someone gave a great dinner and invited many. [17] At the time for the dinner he sent his slave to say to those who had been invited, 'Come; for everything is ready now.' [18] But they all alike began to make excuses. The first said to him, 'I have bought a piece of land, and I must go out and see it; please accept my regrets.' [19] Another said, 'I have bought five yoke of oxen, and I am going to try them out; please accept my regrets.' [20] Another said, 'I have just been married, and therefore I cannot come.' [21] So the slave returned and reported this to his master. Then the owner of the house became angry and said to his slave, 'Go out at once into the streets and lanes of the town and bring in the poor, the crippled, the blind, and the lame.' [22] And the slave said, 'Sir, what you ordered has been done, and there is still room.' [23] Then the master said to the slave, 'Go out into the roads and lanes, and compel people to come in, so that my house may be filled. [24] For I tell you,[b] none of those who were invited will taste my dinner.'"

[25] Now large crowds were traveling with him; and he turned and said to them, [26] "Whoever comes to me and does not hate father and mother, wife and children, brothers and sisters, yes, and even life itself, cannot be my disciple. [27] Whoever does not carry the cross and follow me cannot be my disciple. [28] For which of you, intending to build a tower, does not first sit down and estimate the cost, to see whether he has enough to complete it? [29] Otherwise, when he has laid a foundation and is not able to finish, all who see it will begin to ridicule him, [30] saying, 'This fellow began to build and was not able to finish.' [31] Or what king, going out to wage war against another king, will not sit down first and consider whether he is able with ten thousand to oppose the one who comes against him with twenty thousand? [32] If he cannot, then, while the other is still far away, he sends a delegation and asks for the terms of peace. [33] So therefore, none of you can become my disciple if you do not give up all your possessions.

[34] "Salt is good; but if salt has lost its taste, how can its saltiness be restored?[c] [35] It is fit neither for the soil nor for the manure pile; they throw it away. Let anyone with ears to hear listen!"

15 Now all the tax collectors and sinners were coming near to listen to him. [2] And the Pharisees and the scribes were grumbling and saying, "This fellow welcomes sinners and eats with them."

[3] So he told them this parable: [4] "Which one of you, having a hundred sheep and losing one of them, does not leave the ninety-nine in the wilderness and go after the one that is lost until he finds it? [5] When he has found it, he lays it on his shoulders and rejoices. [6] And when he comes home, he calls together his friends and neighbors, saying to them, 'Rejoice with me, for I have found my sheep that was lost.' [7] Just so, I tell you, there will be more joy in heaven over one sinner who repents than over ninety-nine righteous persons who need no repentance.

[a] Gk *he*
[b] The Greek word for *you* here is plural
[c] Or *how can it be used for seasoning?*

14.15–24: Parable of the great dinner (Mt 22.1–14). **15:** *Bread in the kingdom of God,* messianic banquet (11.3n.). **18–20:** Cf. Deut 20.5–8, although the excuses here shame the host. **21:** *Poor . . . lame,* see 14.13. **24:** *My dinner,* 11.3n.

14.25–35: Costs of discipleship (Mt 10.37–38). **26:** See Mt 10.37; Jn 12.25. *Hate,* hyperbolic (see Prov 13.24), but consistent with Luke's interest in severing familial and economic ties (12.51n.). **27:** *Carry the cross,* risk death (see Mk 8.34). **28:** *Intending to build a tower,* suggesting an elite audience. **33:** *Give up all your possessions,* see 6.30n. **34–35:** *Salt has lost its taste,* Mt 5.13; Mk 9.49–50.

15.1–2: Sinners and Pharisees. 1: *Tax collectors,* see 3.12n. *Sinners,* those who fracture community welfare. **2:** *Eats with them,* suggesting approval.

15.3–7: Parable of the lost sheep (Mt 18.12–14). **4:** *Having a hundred sheep,* indicating a person of some wealth. *Go after the one,* for God as shepherd see Ps 23; 78.52; 80.1; 100.3; for the people as lost sheep, see Jer 50.6; Ezek 34.15–16; Ps 119.176. *Ex. Rab.* 2.2 depicts Moses as the good shepherd who seeks after a lost sheep, and so receives a divine commission to shepherd God's people, Israel. **7:** *One sinner who repents,* Luke allegorizes the parable, which focuses on the effort of the search and the joy of finding (see 8.9n.; 18.1).

PARABLE OF THE PRODIGAL SON (LK 15.11–32)

The juxtaposed parables of the lost sheep and lost coin that immediately precede this parable suggest that it is about something more or other than repenting (despite the assertion in 15.10), for neither sheep nor coins repent. The focus of the first two is on the *search* for the lost and the *joy* of the finding.

Jews would likely identify with the younger son (recalling Abel, Isaac, Jacob, and Ephraim). However, this younger son makes a rude, presumptuous request (see Sir 33.20–24) and then shames himself by dissolute practices. Listeners are thus shocked into the possibility of identifying with the elder son.

Although many interpreters see the younger son as repenting, the text does not make this point. The prodigal's motive for returning to his father may be economic need rather than theological recognition. Other interpreters see the father as symbolizing God, the son's comment in 15.18 suggests rather a distinction. Incorrect is the common view that the father's generous response to the prodigal—whether the father is seen loving parent or representative of God—would be surprising to Jesus' Jewish audience. Jewish tradition sees fathers as loving their children (see 8.42n.), and God as always reaching out to bring the sinner home.

A third common reading is the identification of the older brother as the recalcitrant Pharisee, who refuses to welcome sinners. However, if the father is seen as God and the elder as the Pharisee, then the parable necessarily sees the Pharisees as heirs to God's promises (15.31).

[8] "Or what woman having ten silver coins,[a] if she loses one of them, does not light a lamp, sweep the house, and search carefully until she finds it? [9] When she has found it, she calls together her friends and neighbors, saying, 'Rejoice with me, for I have found the coin that I had lost.' [10] Just so, I tell you, there is joy in the presence of the angels of God over one sinner who repents."

[11] Then Jesus[b] said, "There was a man who had two sons. [12] The younger of them said to his father, 'Father, give me the share of the property that will belong to me.' So he divided his property between them. [13] A few days later the younger son gathered all he had and traveled to a distant country, and there he squandered his property in dissolute living. [14] When he had spent everything, a severe famine took place throughout that country, and he began to be in need. [15] So he went and hired himself out to one of the citizens of that country, who sent him to his fields to feed the pigs. [16] He would gladly have filled himself with[c] the pods that the pigs were eating; and no one gave him anything. [17] But when he came to himself he said, 'How many of my father's hired hands have bread enough and to spare, but here I am dying of hunger! [18] I will get up and go to my father, and I will say to him, "Father, I have sinned against heaven and before you; [19] I am no longer worthy to be called your son; treat me like one of your hired hands."' [20] So he set off and went to his father. But while he was still far off, his father saw him and was filled with compassion; he ran and put his arms around him and kissed him. [21] Then the son said to him, 'Father, I have sinned against heaven and before you; I am no longer worthy to be called your son.'[d] [22] But the father said to his slaves, 'Quickly, bring out a robe—the best one—and put it on him; put a ring on his finger and sandals on his feet. [23] And get the fatted calf and kill it, and let us eat and

a Gk *drachmas*, each worth about a day's wage for a laborer

b Gk *he*

c Other ancient authorities read *filled his stomach with*

d Other ancient authorities add *Treat me like one of your hired servants*

15.8–10: Parable of the lost coin. 8: If the shepherd in 15.3–7 is understood as God, so should this woman be. Female images of God are occasionally found in the Tanakh, e.g. Isa 49.15–16. *Silver coins*, drachmas. **9:** *Friends and neighbors*, feminine nouns, indicating female associates. **10:** *One sinner who repents*, 15.7n.

15.11–32: Parable of the lost. See "Parable of the Prodigal Son" above. **12:** *Divided his property*, see 12.13n.; Sir 33.19–23. **15:** *Pigs*, see 8.32n. **17:** *Came to himself*, Luke does not mention "repentance" (15.7,10). **18:** *I have sinned*, see Ex 10.16. **20:** *Compassion*, see 10.32n. **23:** *Fatted calf*, see 1 Sam 28.24; Am 6.4.

celebrate; [24] for this son of mine was dead and is alive again; he was lost and is found!' And they began to celebrate.

[25] "Now his elder son was in the field; and when he came and approached the house, he heard music and dancing. [26] He called one of the slaves and asked what was going on. [27] He replied, 'Your brother has come, and your father has killed the fatted calf, because he has got him back safe and sound.' [28] Then he became angry and refused to go in. His father came out and began to plead with him. [29] But he answered his father, 'Listen! For all these years I have been working like a slave for you, and I have never disobeyed your command; yet you have never given me even a young goat so that I might celebrate with my friends. [30] But when this son of yours came back, who has devoured your property with prostitutes, you killed the fatted calf for him!' [31] Then the father[a] said to him, 'Son, you are always with me, and all that is mine is yours. [32] But we had to celebrate and rejoice, because this brother of yours was dead and has come to life; he was lost and has been found.'"

16 Then Jesus[a] said to the disciples, "There was a rich man who had a manager, and charges were brought to him that this man was squandering his property. [2] So he summoned him and said to him, 'What is this that I hear about you? Give me an accounting of your management, because you cannot be my manager any longer.' [3] Then the manager said to himself, 'What will I do, now that my master is taking the position away from me? I am not strong enough to dig, and I am ashamed to beg. [4] I have decided what to do so that, when I am dismissed as manager, people may welcome me into their homes.' [5] So, summoning his master's debtors one by one, he asked the first, 'How much do you owe my master?' [6] He answered, 'A hundred jugs of olive oil.' He said to him, 'Take your bill, sit down quickly, and make it fifty.' [7] Then he asked another, 'And how much do you owe?' He replied, 'A hundred containers of wheat.' He said to him, 'Take your bill and make it eighty.' [8] And his master commended the dishonest manager because he had acted shrewdly; for the children of this age are more shrewd in dealing with their own generation than are the children of light. [9] And I tell you, make friends for yourselves by means of dishonest wealth[b] so that when it is gone, they may welcome you into the eternal homes.[c]

[10] "Whoever is faithful in a very little is faithful also in much; and whoever is dishonest in a very little is dishonest also in much. [11] If then you have not been faithful with the dishonest wealth,[b] who will entrust to you the true riches? [12] And if you have not been faithful with what belongs to another, who will give you what is your own? [13] No slave can serve two masters; for a slave will either hate the one and love the other, or be devoted to the one and despise the other. You cannot serve God and wealth."[b]

[14] The Pharisees, who were lovers of money, heard all this, and they ridiculed him. [15] So he said to them, "You are those who justify yourselves in the sight of others; but God knows

[a] Gk *he*
[b] Gk *mammon*
[c] Gk *tents*

25: *He heard music,* unlike the lost sheep and coin, the lost son is not sought. **29:** *Working like a slave,* some Christian interpreters compare the older son to Pharisees, whom they negatively stereotype as serving God joylessly and mechanically; v. 32 disrupts this reading. **30:** *This son of yours,* sibling enmity (see Gen 4.2–8; 25.27–34; 27.1–36; 37.1–4). **31:** *All that is mine is yours,* see v. 12. **32:** *Brother of yours,* the father seeks to reconcile the sons.

16.1–9: Parable of the dishonest manager. 1: *Rich man,* see 12.16n. *Squandering,* see 15.13. **6:** *Make it fifty,* some commentators, but not the parable, suggest the manager was removing the interest charge (Ex 22.25; Lev 25.36–37; Deut 23.19; Ps 15.5). **8:** *His master* (Gk "kyrios," "lord," with no possessive), scholars disagree as to whether this "master" is the rich man, or the "lord" (i.e., here, Jesus; 1.17n.). *Children of light,* Jn 12.36; Eph 5.8; 1 Thess 5.5; 1QM. **9:** *Wealth,* lit., "mammon," Gk transliteration of a Semitic word for money. The parable defies any fully satisfactory explanation.

16.10–13: Fiduciary fidelity. 11,13: *Wealth,* see v. 9n. **13:** See Mt 6.24.

your hearts; for what is prized by human beings is an abomination in the sight of God.

[16] "The law and the prophets were in effect until John came; since then the good news of the kingdom of God is proclaimed, and everyone tries to enter it by force.[a] [17] But it is easier for heaven and earth to pass away, than for one stroke of a letter in the law to be dropped.

[18] "Anyone who divorces his wife and marries another commits adultery, and whoever marries a woman divorced from her husband commits adultery.

[19] "There was a rich man who was dressed in purple and fine linen and who feasted sumptuously every day. [20] And at his gate lay a poor man named Lazarus, covered with sores, [21] who longed to satisfy his hunger with what fell from the rich man's table; even the dogs would come and lick his sores. [22] The poor man died and was carried away by the angels to be with Abraham.[b] The rich man also died and was buried. [23] In Hades, where he was being tormented, he looked up and saw Abraham far away with Lazarus by his side.[c] [24] He called out, 'Father Abraham, have mercy on me, and send Lazarus to dip the tip of his finger in water and cool my tongue; for I am in agony in these flames.' [25] But Abraham said, 'Child, remember that during your lifetime you received your good things, and Lazarus in like manner evil things; but now he is comforted here, and you are in agony. [26] Besides all this, between you and us a great chasm has been fixed, so that those who might want to pass from here to you cannot do so, and no one can cross from there to us.' [27] He said, 'Then, father, I beg you to send him to my father's house— [28] for I have five brothers—that he may warn them, so that they will not also come into this place of torment.' [29] Abraham replied, 'They have Moses and the prophets; they should listen to them.' [30] He said, 'No, father Abraham; but if someone goes to them from the dead, they will repent.' [31] He said to him, 'If they do not listen to Moses and the prophets, neither will they be convinced even if someone rises from the dead.'"

17 Jesus[d] said to his disciples, "Occasions for stumbling are bound to come, but woe to anyone by whom they come! [2] It would be better for you if a millstone were hung around your neck and you were thrown

[a] Or *everyone is strongly urged to enter it*
[b] Gk *to Abraham's bosom*
[c] Gk *in his bosom*
[d] Gk *He*

16.14–15: Criticism of Pharisees. See "Pharisees in Luke," p. 110. **14:** *Lovers of money*, a conventional Greco-Roman insult. For Luke, love of money is a major sin. See 1 Tim 6.10; Heb 13.5; *1 En.* 92–105.

16.16–17: Torah's permanence (Mt 11.12–13; 5.18; cf. Lk 21.33). **16:** *Law and the prophets*, the first two parts of the Tanakh ("Torah" and "Nevi'im"). See 16.29; 24.27,44; Sir (Prologue, 0.1); 2 Macc 15.9. *Good news*, 1.19n. **17:** *To be dropped*, Torah remains, although for the church it is interpreted through Jesus.

16.18: Forbidding remarriage after divorce (Mt 19.9; Mk 10.11–12). *Marries another*, the injunction may be against divorce designed to facilitate remarriage. See 3.19–20n. Jews generally agreed that divorce was permissible (given Deut 24.1–4) but debated the legitimate grounds; Bet Hillel (the School of Hillel) permitted divorce for extremely flimsy reasons; Bet Shammai (the School of Shammai) permitted it only in cases of unchastity (*m. Git.* 9.10). See "Jewish Family Life," p. 537. Because Jewish women had marriage contracts ("ketubot"), divorce was financially prohibitive; it was also not desirable (Mal 2.16; *b. Sanh.* 22a: "Even [God] shares tears when anyone divorces his wife").

16.19–31: Parable of the rich man and Lazarus. 19: *Rich man*, commonly called "dives" (Latin for "rich man"); see 6.24; 12.16n. *Purple*, expensive dyed cloth (Prov 31.22; Lam 4.5; Dan 5.7,16,29; see also Mk 15.17,20; Jn 19.2, 5; Acts 16.14). **20:** *Lazarus*, the only named character in a parable. There may be some connection between the parable and Jn 11.1–44; 12.1,9. **21:** *Longed to satisfy his hunger*, see 14.13. **22:** *To be with Abraham*, paradise (see 13.28–29); salvation in the Gospel of Luke is not contingent upon Jesus' sacrificial death. Lazarus's moral character is ignored. **23:** *Hades*, 10.15n. **24:** *Send Lazarus*, the rich man regards Lazarus as a servant. **25:** *He is comforted*, see 13.30. **29:** *Moses and the prophets*, see v. 16n. Israel's Scriptures provide needed guidance. **31:** *Rises from the dead*, evoking Jesus' resurrection; see also Jn 11.45–46.

17.1–4: Sin and forgiveness (Mt 18.6–7; Mk 9.42). **1:** *Stumbling* (Gk "skandala"; cf. English "scandalize"); offense or cause of sin (see, e.g., Lev 19.14). **2:** *Millstone*, ca. 12–18 in (30–40 cm) in diameter and 2–4 in (5–10 cm) thick, for

into the sea than for you to cause one of these little ones to stumble. [3] Be on your guard! If another disciple[a] sins, you must rebuke the offender, and if there is repentance, you must forgive. [4] And if the same person sins against you seven times a day, and turns back to you seven times and says, 'I repent,' you must forgive."

[5] The apostles said to the Lord, "Increase our faith!" [6] The Lord replied, "If you had faith the size of a[b] mustard seed, you could say to this mulberry tree, 'Be uprooted and planted in the sea,' and it would obey you.

[7] "Who among you would say to your slave who has just come in from plowing or tending sheep in the field, 'Come here at once and take your place at the table'? [8] Would you not rather say to him, 'Prepare supper for me, put on your apron and serve me while I eat and drink; later you may eat and drink'? [9] Do you thank the slave for doing what was commanded? [10] So you also, when you have done all that you were ordered to do, say, 'We are worthless slaves; we have done only what we ought to have done!'"

[11] On the way to Jerusalem Jesus[c] was going through the region between Samaria and Galilee. [12] As he entered a village, ten lepers[d] approached him. Keeping their distance, [13] they called out, saying, "Jesus, Master, have mercy on us!" [14] When he saw them, he said to them, "Go and show yourselves to the priests." And as they went, they were made clean. [15] Then one of them, when he saw that he was healed, turned back, praising God with a loud voice. [16] He prostrated himself at Jesus'[e] feet and thanked him. And he was a Samaritan. [17] Then Jesus asked, "Were not ten made clean? But the other nine, where are they? [18] Was none of them found to return and give praise to God except this foreigner?" [19] Then he said to him, "Get up and go on your way; your faith has made you well."

[20] Once Jesus[c] was asked by the Pharisees when the kingdom of God was coming, and he answered, "The kingdom of God is not coming with things that can be observed; [21] nor will they say, 'Look, here it is!' or 'There it is!' For, in fact, the kingdom of God is among[f] you."

[22] Then he said to the disciples, "The days are coming when you will long to see one of the days of the Son of Man, and you will not see it. [23] They will say to you, 'Look there!' or 'Look here!' Do not go, do not set off in pursuit. [24] For as the lightning flashes and lights up the sky from one side to the other,

[a] Gk *your brother*
[b] Gk *faith as a grain of*
[c] Gk *he*
[d] The terms *leper* and *leprosy* can refer to several diseases
[e] Gk *his*
[f] Or *within*

grinding grain. *Little ones*, disciples. **3:** *Rebuke the offender*, compare rabbinic injunctions to "tokheiḥah," "rebuke" (e.g., Lev 19.17; *Gen. Rab.* 54.3; *Sifra* 89a–89b). **3–4:** *Must forgive*, see Mt 18.15,21–22.

17.5–6: Saying concerning faith (Mt 17.19–21; Mk 9.28–29). **5:** *Faith* (Gk "pistis"; Heb "'emunah"). **6:** *Mustard seed*, see 13.19.

17.7–10: Service without desire for reward. 7: *Would say to your slave*, see 14.11n. 10: *What we ought to have done*, obedience as a duty, but see 12.35–38. Compare *m. Avot* 1.3: "Be not like slaves that serve the master for the sake of a reward . . . ."

17.11–19: Ten men with leprosy. See 5.12–16. **12:** *Keeping their distance*, suggesting Lev 13.45–46. **14:** *Priests*, Lev 13.2–3; 14.2–32. **16:** *Samaritan*, see 9.52n. The Samaritan would have gone to the priest on Mount Gerizim in Samaria; the *other nine* (v. 17), presumably Jews, would go to Jerusalem. **18:** *Foreigner* (Gk "allogenēs"), see 7.9n. **19:** *Made you well*, lit., "saved you" (see 7.50; 8.48; 18.42).

17.20–21: Kingdom of God. 20: *When the kingdom . . . was coming*, pressing question also for Jesus' followers (19.11; 21.7; Acts 1.6). **21:** *Among you*, the Greek could also be translated "within you." The kingdom, redefined away from traditional Jewish views of general resurrection, ingathering of the exiles, universal peace, is present in Jesus' activities (see 11.20).

17.22–37: The day of the Son of Man (Mt 24.17–18,23,26–28,37–41; Mk 13.14–16,19–23). **22:** *Days are coming*, see 2 Kings 20.17; Isa 36.9; Jer 51.47. *Son of Man*, 5.24n. **25:** *Endure much suffering*, 9.22. **26–27:** *Noah*, see Gen 6–7. **28–29:** *Lot*, Gen 18.16–19.28. **32:** *Lot's wife*, Gen 19.26. **33:** 9.24. **34:** *Two in one bed*, Mt 24.40 offers "two

so will the Son of Man be in his day.[a] [25] But first he must endure much suffering and be rejected by this generation. [26] Just as it was in the days of Noah, so too it will be in the days of the Son of Man. [27] They were eating and drinking, and marrying and being given in marriage, until the day Noah entered the ark, and the flood came and destroyed all of them. [28] Likewise, just as it was in the days of Lot: they were eating and drinking, buying and selling, planting and building, [29] but on the day that Lot left Sodom, it rained fire and sulfur from heaven and destroyed all of them [30]—it will be like that on the day that the Son of Man is revealed. [31] On that day, anyone on the housetop who has belongings in the house must not come down to take them away; and likewise anyone in the field must not turn back. [32] Remember Lot's wife. [33] Those who try to make their life secure will lose it, but those who lose their life will keep it. [34] I tell you, on that night there will be two in one bed; one will be taken and the other left. [35] There will be two women grinding meal together; one will be taken and the other left."[b] [37] Then they asked him, "Where, Lord?" He said to them, "Where the corpse is, there the vultures will gather."

18 Then Jesus[c] told them a parable about their need to pray always and not to lose heart. [2] He said, "In a certain city there was a judge who neither feared God nor had respect for people. [3] In that city there was a widow who kept coming to him and saying, 'Grant me justice against my opponent.' [4] For a while he refused; but later he said to himself, 'Though I have no fear of God and no respect for anyone, [5] yet because this widow keeps bothering me, I will grant her justice, so that she may not wear me out by continually coming.'"[d] [6] And the Lord said, "Listen to what the unjust judge says. [7] And will not God grant justice to his chosen ones who cry to him day and night? Will he delay long in helping them? [8] I tell you, he will quickly grant justice to them. And yet, when the Son of Man comes, will he find faith on earth?"

[9] He also told this parable to some who trusted in themselves that they were righteous and regarded others with contempt: [10] "Two men went up to the temple to pray, one a Pharisee and the other a tax collector. [11] The Pharisee, standing by himself, was praying thus, 'God, I thank you that I am not like other people: thieves, rogues, adulterers, or even like this tax collector. [12] I fast twice a week; I give a tenth of all my income.' [13] But the tax collector, standing far off, would not even look up to heaven, but was beating his breast and saying, 'God, be merciful to me, a sinner!' [14] I tell you, this man went down to his home justified rather than the other; for all who exalt themselves will be humbled, but all who humble themselves will be exalted."

[a] Other ancient authorities lack *in his day*
[b] Other ancient authorities add verse 36, *"Two will be in the field; one will be taken and the other left."*
[c] Gk *he*
[d] Or *so that she may not finally come and slap me in the face*

[men] in the field," in parallel to the *two women grinding* of v. 35 (Mt 24.41). **[36]:** A scribal addition of Mt 24.20. **37:** Mt 24.28. On the unburied *corpse*, see "Parable of the Good Samaritan," p. 123. *Vultures*, Gk "aetoi," can be translated "eagles," a symbol of Rome.

18.1–8: Parable of the unjust judge and persistent widow. 1: *Need to pray*, an allegorical interpretation (8.9n.; 15.7). For Luke's interest in prayer, see 6.28; 11.1–2; 18.1–14; 22.40,46. **2:** *Neither feared . . . nor had respect*, negative traits rather than praise for objectivity (see Sir 35.14–26). **3:** *Grant me justice*, lit., "avenge me"; the widow need be neither poor nor righteous (Deut 27.19 is usually cited as background; the parable may overturn the stereotype). **5:** *Wear me out*, boxing term suggesting "punch in the eye" (see translators' note *d*). **7:** *Chosen ones*, here, followers of Jesus (Mt 24.22,24,31; Mk 13.20,22; 27; Rom 8.33; Col 3.12; Titus 1.1; 1 Pet 2.9; Rev 17.14); the argument is a "qal vahomer" (13.15n.; if the unjust judge responds, so with the just judge). **8:** *Comes*, to judge (see 17.22–37; Dan 7.13–14).

18.9–14: Parable of the Pharisee and tax collector. See "Parable of the Pharisee and the Tax Collector," p. 138. **9:** *Righteous*, see 1.16–17; 5.32; 15.7; 23.50. **10:** *Tax collector*, see 1.23n. **12:** *Fast twice a week . . . give a tenth of all*, supererogatory practice. For Jewish fasting practices, see *Pss. Sol.* 3.9; *Did.* 8; Tacitus, *Hist.* 5.4; Suetonius, *Aug.* 76.3; *Meg. Ta'an.* **13:** *Beating his breast*, indicating contrition (as Jews do on Yom Kippur when reciting the "'al ḥet," the litany of sins). **14:** *Justified*, restored to a right relationship with God. *Rather than*, the Greek could be translated "alongside," indicating both were justified. *All who exalt*, see 13.30; 14.11; Mt 23.12.

PARABLE OF THE PHARISEE AND THE TAX COLLECTOR (LK 18.9–14)

Some Christian readers dismiss the Pharisee as hypocritical, sanctimonious, and legalistic, and in turn identify with the tax collector, the appropriately repentant and humble sinner. However, this reading traps interpreters: to conclude (following 18.11), "God, I thank you that I am not like *this Pharisee*" places the readers in the very position they condemn. Moreover, this interpretation overlooks the Pharisee's numerous supererogatory qualities: tithing, fasting, giving thanks without asking for something in return.

Other readers presume that the tax collector stands "far off" (18.13) because other worshipers ostracize him, believing him to be ritually impure. The parable says nothing about either ostracism or impurity; to the contrary, to enter the Temple a person must be ritually pure. Even were he ostracized, the cause would not be impurity but employment: he works for Rome, the occupation government.

Still other readers perceive the Temple to have become an elitist, xenophobic, misogynist, fully corrupt "domination system." Again, the parable thwarts this stereotype, since it is in the Temple that repentance and reconciliation occur.

Finally, might we see the Pharisee as helping the tax collector. Just as the sin of one person impacts the community (hence, e.g., "forgive us our sins" [11.4] rather than "forgive me my sins"), so the merits of the righteous can benefit the community (see Gen 18.24–33; hence one view of the cross: the sacrifice of one can save the many). Perhaps the Jews who first heard this parable understood the Pharisee's merit positively to have impacted the tax collector. This would be the parable's shock: not only that the agent of Rome is justified but that the Pharisee's own good works helped in that justification.

[15] People were bringing even infants to him that he might touch them; and when the disciples saw it, they sternly ordered them not to do it. [16] But Jesus called for them and said, "Let the little children come to me, and do not stop them; for it is to such as these that the kingdom of God belongs. [17] Truly I tell you, whoever does not receive the kingdom of God as a little child will never enter it."

[18] A certain ruler asked him, "Good Teacher, what must I do to inherit eternal life?" [19] Jesus said to him, "Why do you call me good? No one is good but God alone. [20] You know the commandments: 'You shall not commit adultery; You shall not murder; You shall not steal; You shall not bear false witness; Honor your father and mother.'" [21] He replied, "I have kept all these since my youth." [22] When Jesus heard this, he said to him, "There is still one thing lacking. Sell all that you own and distribute the money[a] to the poor, and you will have treasure in heaven; then come, follow me." [23] But when he heard this, he became sad; for he was very rich. [24] Jesus looked at him and said, "How hard it is for those who have wealth to enter the kingdom of God! [25] Indeed, it is easier for a camel to go through the eye of a needle than for someone who is rich to enter the kingdom of God."

[26] Those who heard it said, "Then who can be saved?" [27] He replied, "What is impossible for mortals is possible for God."

[28] Then Peter said, "Look, we have left our homes and followed you." [29] And he said to them, "Truly I tell you, there is no one who has left house or wife or brothers or parents or children, for the sake of the kingdom of God, [30] who will not get back very much more in this age, and in the age to come eternal life."

[a] Gk lacks *the money*

18.15–17: Little children (Mt 19.13–15; Mk 10.13–16). **15:** *Bringing even infants*, see 9.42n. *Touch*, for a blessing. **17:** *As a little child*, with dependence, not pride.

18.18–30: The rich ruler (Mt 19.16–30; Mk 10.17–31). **18:** *Good teacher*, a respectful address. *Inherit eternal life*, see 10.25n. **19:** Jesus distinguishes himself from God; see 1.17n.; 4.8; 5.25; 8.39. **20:** *Commandments*, Ex 20.12–16; Deut 5.16–20, following the Septuagint's order. **22:** *Sell all that you own*, see 6.30n.; 14.33. *Treasure in heaven*, see 12.33–34. **23:** *Very rich*, see 12.16n. **24:** *Those who have wealth*, see 16.14n. **25:** *Eye of a needle*, contrary to popular legend, Jerusalem had no "needle gate" through which camels passed with difficulty. **27:** *Possible for God*, see 1.37; Gen 18.14; Jer 32.17; Job 42.2. **28:** *Left our homes*, 5.1–11. **29:** *Wife*, an addition to Matt 19.29; Luke continues

[31] Then he took the twelve aside and said to them, "See, we are going up to Jerusalem, and everything that is written about the Son of Man by the prophets will be accomplished. [32] For he will be handed over to the Gentiles; and he will be mocked and insulted and spat upon. [33] After they have flogged him, they will kill him, and on the third day he will rise again." [34] But they understood nothing about all these things; in fact, what he said was hidden from them, and they did not grasp what was said.

[35] As he approached Jericho, a blind man was sitting by the roadside begging. [36] When he heard a crowd going by, he asked what was happening. [37] They told him, "Jesus of Nazareth[a] is passing by." [38] Then he shouted, "Jesus, Son of David, have mercy on me!" [39] Those who were in front sternly ordered him to be quiet; but he shouted even more loudly, "Son of David, have mercy on me!" [40] Jesus stood still and ordered the man to be brought to him; and when he came near, he asked him, [41] "What do you want me to do for you?" He said, "Lord, let me see again." [42] Jesus said to him, "Receive your sight; your faith has saved you." [43] Immediately he regained his sight and followed him, glorifying God; and all the people, when they saw it, praised God.

19 He entered Jericho and was passing through it. [2] A man was there named Zacchaeus; he was a chief tax collector and was rich. [3] He was trying to see who Jesus was, but on account of the crowd he could not, because he was short in stature. [4] So he ran ahead and climbed a sycamore tree to see him, because he was going to pass that way. [5] When Jesus came to the place, he looked up and said to him, "Zacchaeus, hurry and come down; for I must stay at your house today." [6] So he hurried down and was happy to welcome him. [7] All who saw it began to grumble and said, "He has gone to be the guest of one who is a sinner." [8] Zacchaeus stood there and said to the Lord, "Look, half of my possessions, Lord, I will give to the poor; and if I have defrauded anyone of anything, I will pay back four times as much." [9] Then Jesus said to him, "Today salvation has come to this house, because he too is a son of Abraham. [10] For the Son of Man came to seek out and to save the lost."

[11] As they were listening to this, he went on to tell a parable, because he was near Jerusalem, and because they supposed that the kingdom of God was to appear immediately. [12] So he said, "A nobleman went to a distant country to get royal power for himself and then return. [13] He summoned ten of his slaves, and gave them ten pounds,[b] and said to them, 'Do business with these

[a] Gk *the Nazorean*

[b] The mina, rendered here by *pound,* was about three months' wages for a laborer

the theme of familial disruption (see 12.51n.). **30:** *Age to come,* the "olam ha-ba," see 11.2; *m. Avot* 4.17: "Better is one hour of repentance and good works in this world than the whole life in the world to come, and better is one hour of bliss in the world to come than the whole life of this world."

18.31–34: Third Passion prediction (Mt 20.17–19; Mk 10.32–34). See 9.22,44–45; 17.25. **31:** *Son of Man,* 5.24n. The passages usually cited as *written about . . . by the prophets* (e.g., Isa 53; Zech 13.7; Ps 22) do not use the phrase "Son of Man." Most of these passages receive messianic interpretation only in Christian sources. **34:** *Was hidden from them,* see 24.16.

18.35–43: Healing a blind man (Mt 20.29–34; Mk 10.46–52). **35:** *Jericho,* see 10.30n.; 19.1. **38:** *Son of David,* 1.27n.; 3.31; see also Mt 22.42; Mk 12.35. **42:** *Faith has saved you,* see 7.50n.; 8.48; 17.19. **43:** *All the people* (Gk "pas ho laos"; see 2.10; Mt 27.25); Jesus retains the support of the Jewish population.

19.1–10: Zacchaeus. 1: *Jericho,* a customs center (see 10.30n.; 19.1). **2:** *Zacchaeus,* from the Hebrew for "righteous" or "upright," as in R. Yoḥanan ben Zakkai. *Chief tax collector,* 3.12n. *Rich,* see 6.24n.; 18.18–23. **7:** *Sinner,* 5.1n.,30; 15.1–2. **8:** *I will give . . . will pay back,* lit., "give . . . do pay back" (present tense): Zaccheus is less repenting than he is attesting his righteousness. *Four times,* see Ex 22.1. **9:** *Son of Abraham,* see 13.16n. **10:** *Son of Man,* 5.24.

19.11–27: Parable of the pounds (Mt 25.14–30; Mk 13.34). **11:** *Kingdom of God was to appear,* the messianic age would dawn. See 17.21n. **12:** *To get royal power,* reminiscent of Archelaus's visit to Rome in 4 BCE to seek his father Herod's kingdom (*Ant.* 17.9.4; 17.10). **13:** *Pounds* (Gk "minas"), gold coins worth 100 drachmas (see 15.8n.),

until I come back.' [14] But the citizens of his country hated him and sent a delegation after him, saying, 'We do not want this man to rule over us.' [15] When he returned, having received royal power, he ordered these slaves, to whom he had given the money, to be summoned so that he might find out what they had gained by trading. [16] The first came forward and said, 'Lord, your pound has made ten more pounds.' [17] He said to him, 'Well done, good slave! Because you have been trustworthy in a very small thing, take charge of ten cities.' [18] Then the second came, saying, 'Lord, your pound has made five pounds.' [19] He said to him, 'And you, rule over five cities.' [20] Then the other came, saying, 'Lord, here is your pound. I wrapped it up in a piece of cloth, [21] for I was afraid of you, because you are a harsh man; you take what you did not deposit, and reap what you did not sow.' [22] He said to him, 'I will judge you by your own words, you wicked slave! You knew, did you, that I was a harsh man, taking what I did not deposit and reaping what I did not sow? [23] Why then did you not put my money into the bank? Then when I returned, I could have collected it with interest.' [24] He said to the bystanders, 'Take the pound from him and give it to the one who has ten pounds.' [25] (And they said to him, 'Lord, he has ten pounds!') [26] 'I tell you, to all those who have, more will be given; but from those who have nothing, even what they have will be taken away. [27] But as for these enemies of mine who did not want me to be king over them—bring them here and slaughter them in my presence.'"

[28] After he had said this, he went on ahead, going up to Jerusalem.

[29] When he had come near Bethphage and Bethany, at the place called the Mount of Olives, he sent two of the disciples, [30] saying, "Go into the village ahead of you, and as you enter it you will find tied there a colt that has never been ridden. Untie it and bring it here. [31] If anyone asks you, 'Why are you untying it?' just say this, 'The Lord needs it.'" [32] So those who were sent departed and found it as he had told them. [33] As they were untying the colt, its owners asked them, "Why are you untying the colt?" [34] They said, "The Lord needs it." [35] Then they brought it to Jesus; and after throwing their cloaks on the colt, they set Jesus on it. [36] As he rode along, people kept spreading their cloaks on the road. [37] As he was now approaching the path down from the Mount of Olives, the whole multitude of the disciples began to praise God joyfully with a loud voice for all the deeds of power that they had seen, [38] saying,

"Blessed is the king
  who comes in the name of the Lord!
Peace in heaven,
  and glory in the highest heaven!"

[39] Some of the Pharisees in the crowd said to him, "Teacher, order your disciples to stop." [40] He answered, "I tell you, if these were silent, the stones would shout out."

[41] As he came near and saw the city, he wept over it, [42] saying, "If you, even you, had only recognized on this day the things that make for peace! But now they are hidden from your eyes. [43] Indeed, the days will come upon you, when your enemies will set up

a very large amount. **14:** *Sent a delegation*, the response of the Judeans to Archelaus; in 6 CE Rome replaced Archelaus with direct rule in Judea. **23:** *Bank* (Gk "trapeza"; lit., "table"), to invest. **26:** See 8.18. **27:** *Slaughter them*, scholars debate whether the reference is to earthly political abuse and so a warning about governments, or to the final judgment.

19.28–40: Triumphal procession (Mt 21.1–9; Mk 11.1–10; Jn 12.12–18). **29:** *Bethphage*, otherwise unknown; *Bethany*, east of Jerusalem (see 10.38n.). *Mount of Olives*, hill opposite Jerusalem, on the eastern side of Kidron Valley; traditional place for the Messiah's appearance (see Zech 14.4). **30:** *You will find*, Jesus has local supporters. *Colt*, see Zech 9.9. **32:** *Found it as he had told them*, see 22.13. **36:** *Spreading their cloaks*, to greet a king (see 2 Kings 9.13). **37:** *Disciples*, distinct from the crowd (contrast other versions of this event). **38:** Combination of Ps 118.26, part of the Hallel prayer (see 13.35n.) and Zech 9.9 (see also Lk 2.14; 13.35). *King*, the charge against Jesus (23.2–3,37–38). **39:** *Pharisees*, their last appearance in this Gospel, apparently trying to prevent Roman reprisal (see 13.31n.). **40:** *Stones would shout*, see Hab 2.11; perhaps related to the concept of nature rejoicing, Ps 93–99.

19.41–44: Second lament over Jerusalem. See 13.33–34; cf. 23.27–31. **42:** *Things that make for peace*, the verse likely reflects knowledge of Jerusalem's destruction in 70 CE (see 19.44; 21.6,20–24). The name "Jerusalem" sug-

ramparts around you and surround you, and hem you in on every side. [44] They will crush you to the ground, you and your children within you, and they will not leave within you one stone upon another; because you did not recognize the time of your visitation from God."[a]

[45] Then he entered the temple and began to drive out those who were selling things there; [46] and he said, "It is written,

'My house shall be a house of prayer';
but you have made it a den of robbers."

[47] Every day he was teaching in the temple. The chief priests, the scribes, and the leaders of the people kept looking for a way to kill him; [48] but they did not find anything they could do, for all the people were spellbound by what they heard.

20 One day, as he was teaching the people in the temple and telling the good news, the chief priests and the scribes came with the elders [2] and said to him, "Tell us, by what authority are you doing these things? Who is it who gave you this authority?" [3] He answered them, "I will also ask you a question, and you tell me: [4] Did the baptism of John come from heaven, or was it of human origin?" [5] They discussed it with one another, saying, "If we say, 'From heaven,' he will say, 'Why did you not believe him?' [6] But if we say, 'Of human origin,' all the people will stone us; for they are convinced that John was a prophet." [7] So they answered that they did not know where it came from. [8] Then Jesus said to them, "Neither will I tell you by what authority I am doing these things."

[9] He began to tell the people this parable: "A man planted a vineyard, and leased it to tenants, and went to another country for a long time. [10] When the season came, he sent a slave to the tenants in order that they might give him his share of the produce of the vineyard; but the tenants beat him and sent him away empty-handed. [11] Next he sent another slave; that one also they beat and insulted and sent away empty-handed. [12] And he sent still a third; this one also they wounded and threw out. [13] Then the owner of the vineyard said, 'What shall I do? I will send my beloved son; perhaps they will respect him.' [14] But when the tenants saw him, they discussed it among themselves and said, 'This is the heir; let us kill him so that the inheritance may be ours.' [15] So they threw him out of the vineyard and killed him. What then will the owner of the vineyard do to them? [16] He will come and destroy those tenants and give the vineyard to others." When they heard this, they said, "Heaven forbid!" [17] But he looked at them and said, "What then does this text mean:

'The stone that the builders rejected
has become the cornerstone'?[b]

[18] Everyone who falls on that stone will be broken to pieces; and it will crush anyone on whom it falls." [19] When the scribes and chief priests realized that he had told this parable

[a] Gk lacks *from God*
[b] Or *keystone*

gests a city of *peace* (Heb "shalom"). **43–44:** *You did not recognize*, Luke suggests the city's destruction is caused by its failure to follow Jesus. Earlier prophets predicted the Babylonian destruction of Jerusalem in 586 BCE (see Isa 29.3; Jer 6.6; Ezek 4.2). *Hem you in*, Roman troops surrounded the city to starve the population. *One stone upon another*, only the Kotel (Western Wall) of the Temple retaining mound remains standing.

19.45–46: Temple disruption (Mt 21.12–13; Mk 11.15–17; Jn 2.13–17). **45:** *Selling*, for sacrificial offerings (see 2.24); because Luke does not specify the reason for the vendors, the text can suggest venal activity. **46:** *House of prayer*, Isa 56.7. *Den of robbers*, Jer 7.11, a place where thieves go with their ill-gotten gains. The point is not priestly corruption or vendors overcharging, but ritual without accompanying repentance and good deeds.

19.47–48: Teaching in the Temple (Mk 11.18–19). **47:** *Chief priests, the scribes, and the leaders*, Jesus' adversaries in Jerusalem (see 20.19).

20.1–8: Questioning Jesus' authority (Mt 21.23–27; Mk 11.27–33; Jn 2.18–22). **1:** *Good news*, 1.19n. **4:** *Baptism of John*, 3.3–21.

20.9–19: Parable of the wicked tenants (Mt 21.33–46; Mk 12.1–12). **9:** *Vineyard*, symbol for Israel (Isa 5.1–7). **13:** *Beloved* (see 3.22) identifies the son with Jesus. **16:** *Destroy those tenants*, see 19.27n. *Others*, here, Jesus' followers. **17:** Ps 118.22; see Isa 28.16; Acts 4.11; Eph 2.20; 1 Pet 2.6. The Hallel Psalms (113–118) sung on pilgrimage festivals were adapted by Jesus' followers. **18:** See Isa 8.14–15. **19:** See 19.47.

against them, they wanted to lay hands on him at that very hour, but they feared the people.

[20] So they watched him and sent spies who pretended to be honest, in order to trap him by what he said, so as to hand him over to the jurisdiction and authority of the governor. [21] So they asked him, "Teacher, we know that you are right in what you say and teach, and you show deference to no one, but teach the way of God in accordance with truth. [22] Is it lawful for us to pay taxes to the emperor, or not?" [23] But he perceived their craftiness and said to them, [24] "Show me a denarius. Whose head and whose title does it bear?" They said, "The emperor's." [25] He said to them, "Then give to the emperor the things that are the emperor's, and to God the things that are God's." [26] And they were not able in the presence of the people to trap him by what he said; and being amazed by his answer, they became silent.

[27] Some Sadducees, those who say there is no resurrection, came to him [28] and asked him a question, "Teacher, Moses wrote for us that if a man's brother dies, leaving a wife but no children, the man[a] shall marry the widow and raise up children for his brother. [29] Now there were seven brothers; the first married, and died childless; [30] then the second [31] and the third married her, and so in the same way all seven died childless. [32] Finally the woman also died. [33] In the resurrection, therefore, whose wife will the woman be? For the seven had married her."

[34] Jesus said to them, "Those who belong to this age marry and are given in marriage; [35] but those who are considered worthy of a place in that age and in the resurrection from the dead neither marry nor are given in marriage. [36] Indeed they cannot die anymore, because they are like angels and are children of God, being children of the resurrection. [37] And the fact that the dead are raised Moses himself showed, in the story about the bush, where he speaks of the Lord as the God of Abraham, the God of Isaac, and the God of Jacob. [38] Now he is God not of the dead, but of the living; for to him all of them are alive." [39] Then some of the scribes answered, "Teacher, you have spoken well." [40] For they no longer dared to ask him another question.

[41] Then he said to them, "How can they say that the Messiah[b] is David's son? [42] For David himself says in the book of Psalms,

'The Lord said to my Lord,
"Sit at my right hand,
[43] until I make your enemies your
footstool." '

[44] David thus calls him Lord; so how can he be his son?"

[45] In the hearing of all the people he said to the[c] disciples, [46] "Beware of the scribes, who like to walk around in long robes, and love to be greeted with respect in the

[a] Gk *his brother*
[b] Or *the Christ*
[c] Other ancient authorities read *his*

20.20–26: Paying taxes to the emperor (Mt 22.15–22; Mk 12.13–17). **22:** *Lawful*, according to Jewish law. **24:** *Denarius*, coin depicting a portrait of the emperor (12.59n.). **25:** *Things that are God's*, Jesus' interlocutors would need to determine whether anything belongs to the emperor, or whether everything (including coinage) belongs to God. Christian tradition reads the saying as advocating payment (see Rom 13.6–7). Jesus' opponents charge him with forbidding paying taxes, a plausible interpretation of his response (23.2).

20.27–40: Question concerning resurrection (Mt 22.23–33; Mk 12.18–27). **27:** *Sadducees*, the elite, Jerusalem-based party; see "Jewish Movements of the NT Period," p. 526. *There is no resurrection*, either they rejected the idea of physical resurrection (see Acts 4.1–2; 23.6–10; *Ant.* 18.1.4) or denied that it could be found in Torah (see *m. Sanh.* 10.1). **28:** *Raise up children*, levirate marriage, designed to protect widows and preserve the dead husband's name and estate (Deut 25.5–10; see also Gen 38.8). **34–35:** *Marry and are given in marriage*, see 17.27. **36:** *Like angels*, having no need to procreate. **37:** *Story about the bush*, Ex 3.6.

20.41–44: A question about David's son (Mt 22.41–46; Mk 12.35–37a). **42–43:** Citation of Ps 110.1 (early Christian writings, but not Jewish ones, frequently cite this text in reference to the Messiah; see Acts 2.34–35; 1 Cor 15.25; Heb 1.4). **44:** *How can he be his son*, the psalm depicts God ("the Lord") speaking to David or another king ("my Lord"); the superscription ascribes it to David.

20.45–47: Warnings concerning the scribes (see Mt 23.6–7; Mk 12.37b–40). **46:** In 11.43, Jesus places the same charge against Pharisees.

marketplaces, and to have the best seats in the synagogues and places of honor at banquets. [47] They devour widows' houses and for the sake of appearance say long prayers. They will receive the greater condemnation."

21 He looked up and saw rich people putting their gifts into the treasury; [2] he also saw a poor widow put in two small copper coins. [3] He said, "Truly I tell you, this poor widow has put in more than all of them; [4] for all of them have contributed out of their abundance, but she out of her poverty has put in all she had to live on."

[5] When some were speaking about the temple, how it was adorned with beautiful stones and gifts dedicated to God, he said, [6] "As for these things that you see, the days will come when not one stone will be left upon another; all will be thrown down."

[7] They asked him, "Teacher, when will this be, and what will be the sign that this is about to take place?" [8] And he said, "Beware that you are not led astray; for many will come in my name and say, 'I am he!'[a] and, 'The time is near!'[b] Do not go after them.

[9] "When you hear of wars and insurrections, do not be terrified; for these things must take place first, but the end will not follow immediately." [10] Then he said to them, "Nation will rise against nation, and kingdom against kingdom; [11] there will be great earthquakes, and in various places famines and plagues; and there will be dreadful portents and great signs from heaven.

[12] "But before all this occurs, they will arrest you and persecute you; they will hand you over to synagogues and prisons, and you will be brought before kings and governors because of my name. [13] This will give you an opportunity to testify. [14] So make up your minds not to prepare your defense in advance; [15] for I will give you words[c] and a wisdom that none of your opponents will be able to withstand or contradict. [16] You will be betrayed even by parents and brothers, by relatives and friends; and they will put some of you to death. [17] You will be hated by all because of my name. [18] But not a hair of your head will perish. [19] By your endurance you will gain your souls.

[20] "When you see Jerusalem surrounded by armies, then know that its desolation has come near.[d] [21] Then those in Judea must flee to the mountains, and those inside the city must leave it, and those out in the country must not enter it; [22] for these are days of vengeance, as a fulfillment of all that is written. [23] Woe to those who are pregnant and to those who are nursing infants in those days! For there will be great distress on the earth and wrath against this people; [24] they will fall by the edge of the sword and be taken away as captives among all nations; and Jerusalem will be trampled on by the Gentiles, until the times of the Gentiles are fulfilled.

[a] Gk *I am*
[b] Or *at hand*
[c] Gk *a mouth*
[d] Or *is at hand*

21.1–4: The widow's offering (Mk 12.41–44). **1:** *Treasury*, a receptacle for free-will offerings (see *m. Seqal.* 2.1; 6.1; in Jn 8.20 the term refers to a room in the Temple). **2:** *Copper coin* (Gk "lepton"), see 12.59n. **4:** *All she had*, Jesus praises the women's charity (see 6.30n.; *Lev. Rab.* 107a); he does not, contrary to some speculation, condemn the Temple for exploitation. Had Jesus wished to protect the woman, he could have advised her to keep her coins.

21.5–6: Predicting the Temple's destruction (Mt 24.1–2; Mk 13.1–2). **5:** *Beautiful stones*, see Josephus, *Ant.* 15.392; *J.W.* 5.210f., 222. **6:** See 19.43–44n.

21.7–11: End-time signs (Mt 24.3–8; Mk 13.3–8). **7:** *When will this be*, see 17.20–21n.; Acts 1.6. **10:** *Nation will rise against nation*, conventional language (Isa 19.2; 2 Chr 15.6). **11:** *Earthquakes . . . famines . . . plagues*, conventional apocalyptic language.

21.12–19: Prediction of the disciples' persecution (Mt 24.9–14; Mk 13.9–13). **12:** *Synagogues*, 12.11n. **14–15:** 12.11–12. **16:** *Parents and brothers*, 12.51n. **18:** *Hair of your head*, indicating immunity; see 12.7; Acts 27.34; 1 Sam 14.45; 2 Sam 14.11; 1 Kings 1.52. **19:** *Gain your souls*, have eternal life.

21.20–24: The desolation of Jerusalem (Mt 24.15–22; Mk 13.14–20). **20:** *Surrounded by armies*, see 19.43–44n. **22:** *Days of vengeance*, see Isa 63.4; Hos 9.7. **23:** *Pregnant . . . nursing*, see 12.51n. **24:** *Times of the Gentiles*, perhaps referring to the Gentile mission (see Rom 11.25); the period has no distinguishing markers or temporal limits.

[25] "There will be signs in the sun, the moon, and the stars, and on the earth distress among nations confused by the roaring of the sea and the waves. [26] People will faint from fear and foreboding of what is coming upon the world, for the powers of the heavens will be shaken. [27] Then they will see 'the Son of Man coming in a cloud' with power and great glory. [28] Now when these things begin to take place, stand up and raise your heads, because your redemption is drawing near."

[29] Then he told them a parable: "Look at the fig tree and all the trees; [30] as soon as they sprout leaves you can see for yourselves and know that summer is already near. [31] So also, when you see these things taking place, you know that the kingdom of God is near. [32] Truly I tell you, this generation will not pass away until all things have taken place. [33] Heaven and earth will pass away, but my words will not pass away.

[34] "Be on guard so that your hearts are not weighed down with dissipation and drunkenness and the worries of this life, and that day does not catch you unexpectedly, [35] like a trap. For it will come upon all who live on the face of the whole earth. [36] Be alert at all times, praying that you may have the strength to escape all these things that will take place, and to stand before the Son of Man."

[37] Every day he was teaching in the temple, and at night he would go out and spend the night on the Mount of Olives, as it was called. [38] And all the people would get up early in the morning to listen to him in the temple.

22 Now the festival of Unleavened Bread, which is called the Passover, was near. [2] The chief priests and the scribes were looking for a way to put Jesus[a] to death, for they were afraid of the people.

[3] Then Satan entered into Judas called Iscariot, who was one of the twelve; [4] he went away and conferred with the chief priests and officers of the temple police about how he might betray him to them. [5] They were greatly pleased and agreed to give him money. [6] So he consented and began to look for an opportunity to betray him to them when no crowd was present.

[7] Then came the day of Unleavened Bread, on which the Passover lamb had to be sacrificed. [8] So Jesus[b] sent Peter and John, saying, "Go and prepare the Passover meal for us that we may eat it." [9] They asked him, "Where do you want us to make preparations for it?" [10] "Listen," he said to them, "when you have entered the city, a man carrying a jar of water will meet you; follow him into the house he enters [11] and say to the owner of the house, 'The teacher asks you, "Where is the guest room, where I may eat the Passover with my disciples?"' [12] He will show you a large room upstairs, already furnished. Make preparations for us there." [13] So they went and found everything as he had told them; and they prepared the Passover meal.

a Gk *him*
b Gk *he*

21.25–28: The coming of the Son of Man (Mt 24.29–31; Mk 13.24–27). **25–27:** Apocalyptic elements drawn from Joel 3.3–4; Isa 24.19 (LXX); Ps 65.8; 46.4; 89.10; Wis 5.22. **25:** Isa 13.10; Joel 2.10; Zeph 1.15. **26:** *Powers of the heavens*, either celestial bodies or supernatural beings (see Rom 8.38; Eph 6.12; Col 1.16; Heb 6.4; 1 Pet 3.22). **27:** *Son of Man*, see 5.24n. *Cloud*, see Dan 7.13; Acts 1.9.

21.29–33: Lesson of the fig tree (Mt 24.32–36; Mk 13.28–32). **32:** See 9.27n. **33:** Cf. 16.17.

21.34–36: Admonition to alertness (cf. Mt 24.43–51; 25.13; Mk 13.33–37; see also Luke 12.35–48). **34:** *Drunkenness*, see Tob 4.15; Sir 31.30; Rom 13.13; Gal 5.21; 1 Pet 4.3. **36:** *Son of Man*, see 5.24n.; 21.25–28.

21.37–38: Jesus' Jerusalem activities. 37: *Mount of Olives*, 19.29n.

22.1–6: Judas Iscariot. 1: *Festival of Unleavened Bread* (Mt 26.2–5; Mk 14.1–2; Jn 11.47–53), Ex 12.17; 23.15; 34.18; Lev 23.6; Num 28.17; Deut 16.16; 2 Chr 8.13; etc. *Called the Passover*, explanation for Gentile readers. **3–6:** Mt 26.14–16; Mk 14.10–11. *Satan*, 4.2n.; his reappearance is the "opportune time" of 4.13; see also Jn 13.2. *Judas*, 6.16n. *Chief priests*, 19.47n.

22.7–13: Passover preparations (Mt 26.17–19; Mk 14.12–16; Jn 13.1). **7:** *Day of Unleavened Bread*, see 22.1n. *Passover lamb*, Ex 12.8,21. For *Passover*, see 2.41n. **10:** *A man carrying a jar of water*, contrary to popular readings, there is no clear indication this was women's work. See 19.30n. **13:** *Prepared*, including obtaining a lamb sacrificed in the Temple, unleavened bread, and bitter herbs (details in *m. Pesah.*). *Passover meal*, according to the Synoptic Gospels, the Last Supper is a Passover meal; in John's Gospel, it is not.

[14] When the hour came, he took his place at the table, and the apostles with him. [15] He said to them, "I have eagerly desired to eat this Passover with you before I suffer; [16] for I tell you, I will not eat it[a] until it is fulfilled in the kingdom of God." [17] Then he took a cup, and after giving thanks he said, "Take this and divide it among yourselves; [18] for I tell you that from now on I will not drink of the fruit of the vine until the kingdom of God comes." [19] Then he took a loaf of bread, and when he had given thanks, he broke it and gave it to them, saying, "This is my body, which is given for you. Do this in remembrance of me." [20] And he did the same with the cup after supper, saying, "This cup that is poured out for you is the new covenant in my blood.[b] [21] But see, the one who betrays me is with me, and his hand is on the table. [22] For the Son of Man is going as it has been determined, but woe to that one by whom he is betrayed!" [23] Then they began to ask one another which one of them it could be who would do this.

[24] A dispute also arose among them as to which one of them was to be regarded as the greatest. [25] But he said to them, "The kings of the Gentiles lord it over them; and those in authority over them are called benefactors. [26] But not so with you; rather the greatest among you must become like the youngest, and the leader like one who serves. [27] For who is greater, the one who is at the table or the one who serves? Is it not the one at the table? But I am among you as one who serves.

[28] "You are those who have stood by me in my trials; [29] and I confer on you, just as my Father has conferred on me, a kingdom, [30] so that you may eat and drink at my table in my kingdom, and you will sit on thrones judging the twelve tribes of Israel.

[31] "Simon, Simon, listen! Satan has demanded[c] to sift all of you like wheat, [32] but I have prayed for you that your own faith may not fail; and you, when once you have turned back, strengthen your brothers." [33] And he said to him, "Lord, I am ready to go with you to prison and to death!" [34] Jesus[d] said, "I tell you, Peter, the cock will not crow this day, until you have denied three times that you know me."

[35] He said to them, "When I sent you out without a purse, bag, or sandals, did you lack anything?" They said, "No, not a thing." [36] He said to them, "But now, the one who has a purse must take it, and likewise a bag. And the one who has no sword must sell his cloak and buy one. [37] For I tell you, this scripture must be fulfilled in me, 'And he was counted among the lawless'; and indeed what is written about me is being fulfilled." [38] They said, "Lord, look, here are two swords." He replied, "It is enough."

[a] Other ancient authorities read *never eat it again*
[b] Other ancient authorities lack, in whole or in part, verses 19b-20 (*which is given . . . in my blood*)
[c] Or *has obtained permission*
[d] Gk *He*

22.14–20: The Last Supper (Mt 26.26–29; Mk 14.22–25; cf. Jn 6.51–58). **14:** *The hour,* of the meal, after sundown. **17:** *Giving thanks,* blessing before drinking. Only Luke presents the cup prior to the bread as well as after. **18:** *Kingdom of God comes,* focusing on the future rather than present kingdom (contrast 17.21). **19:** *Loaf,* Gk "artos," "bread," could refer to unleavened bread. *Given thanks,* 9.14n. *This is my body,* see 1 Cor 11.23–26. Jews found the idea of eating human flesh abhorrent. **20:** *New covenant,* see Jer 31.31; 1 Cor 11.25; 2 Cor 3.6; Heb 8.8,13; 9.15; 12.24. On the connection of covenant and blood, see Ex 24.8.

22.21–23: Predicting the betrayal (Mt 26.21–25; Mk 14.18–21; Jn 13.21–30). **21:** *His hand is on the table,* possible allusion to Ps 41.9. **22:** *Son of Man,* 5.24n. *Woe to that one,* despite Jesus' foreordained and willing death, Judas is still held responsible.

22.24–30: Servant leadership (Mt 20.24–28; Mk 10.41–45; cf. John 13.3–16). **25:** *Benefactors* (Gk "euergetai," lit., "good works doers"), a title typically bestowed on kings. **27:** See 12.37n. **30:** *At my table,* 11.3n. *Sit on thrones,* Mt 19.28.

22.31–34: Predicting Peter's denial (Mt 26.30–35; Mk 14.26–31; Jn 13.36–38). **32:** *I have prayed,* 3.21n. **34:** See vv. 54–62.

22.35–38: Preparation for Jesus' arrest. 35: See 9.3; 10.4. **37:** Isa 53.12. **38:** *Two swords,* Jesus' followers are armed (see 22.49–50; Jesus rejects violent reprisal).

[39] He came out and went, as was his custom, to the Mount of Olives; and the disciples followed him. [40] When he reached the place, he said to them, "Pray that you may not come into the time of trial."[a] [41] Then he withdrew from them about a stone's throw, knelt down, and prayed, [42] "Father, if you are willing, remove this cup from me; yet, not my will but yours be done." [43] Then an angel from heaven appeared to him and gave him strength. [44] In his anguish he prayed more earnestly, and his sweat became like great drops of blood falling down on the ground.[b] [45] When he got up from prayer, he came to the disciples and found them sleeping because of grief, [46] and he said to them, "Why are you sleeping? Get up and pray that you may not come into the time of trial."[a]

[47] While he was still speaking, suddenly a crowd came, and the one called Judas, one of the twelve, was leading them. He approached Jesus to kiss him; [48] but Jesus said to him, "Judas, is it with a kiss that you are betraying the Son of Man?" [49] When those who were around him saw what was coming, they asked, "Lord, should we strike with the sword?" [50] Then one of them struck the slave of the high priest and cut off his right ear. [51] But Jesus said, "No more of this!" And he touched his ear and healed him. [52] Then Jesus said to the chief priests, the officers of the temple police, and the elders who had come for him, "Have you come out with swords and clubs as if I were a bandit? [53] When I was with you day after day in the temple, you did not lay hands on me. But this is your hour, and the power of darkness!"

[54] Then they seized him and led him away, bringing him into the high priest's house. But Peter was following at a distance. [55] When they had kindled a fire in the middle of the courtyard and sat down together, Peter sat among them. [56] Then a servant-girl, seeing him in the firelight, stared at him and said, "This man also was with him." [57] But he denied it, saying, "Woman, I do not know him." [58] A little later someone else, on seeing him, said, "You also are one of them." But Peter said, "Man, I am not!" [59] Then about an hour later still another kept insisting, "Surely this man also was with him; for he is a Galilean." [60] But Peter said, "Man, I do not know what you are talking about!" At that moment, while he was still speaking, the cock crowed. [61] The Lord turned and looked at Peter. Then Peter remembered the word of the Lord, how he had said to him, "Before the cock crows today, you will deny me three times." [62] And he went out and wept bitterly.

[63] Now the men who were holding Jesus began to mock him and beat him; [64] they also blindfolded him and kept asking him, "Prophesy! Who is it that struck you?" [65] They kept heaping many other insults on him.

[66] When day came, the assembly of the elders of the people, both chief priests and scribes, gathered together, and they brought him to their council. [67] They said, "If you are

[a] Or *into temptation*

[b] Other ancient authorities lack verses 43 and 44

22.39–46: Anguish on the Mount of Olives (Mt 26.36–46; Mk 14.32–42; Jn 18.1–2; Luke avoids Aramaisms, like "Gethsemane"). **39:** *His custom*, 21.37. *Mount of Olives*, 19.29n. **40, 46:** *Time of trial*, See 11.4. **41:** *Prayed*, 3.21n. 42: *Cup*, symbolizing destiny (Ps 11.6; 16.5) and divine wrath (Isa 51.17; Ps 75.8). **43–44:** Major early manuscripts lack these verses. **45:** *Because of grief*, Luke tempers the disciples' failure to remain awake.

22.47–53: Jesus' arrest (Mt 26.47–56; Mk 14.43–52; Jn 18.2–12). **47:** *Kiss*, see 2 Sam 20.9; the greeting of early followers of Jesus (Rom 16.16; 1 Cor 16.20; 2 Cor 13.12; 1 Thess 5.26; 1 Pet 5.14). **48:** *Son of Man*, 5.24n. **49:** *Sword*, see 22.36–38. **52:** *Chief priests*, mentioned only in Luke's account of the arrest (see 19.47n.). *Bandit* (Gk "lēstēs"), not a simple robber but one who uses violence (10.30,36; 19.46). **53:** *Power of darkness*, 1.79; 11.35–36; 23.33; Gal 1.13; Luke depicts the chief priests' authority as cosmically evil (see also Ps 82.5; 107.10,14, and elsewhere).

22.54–62: Peter's denials (Mt 26.69–75; Mk 14.66–72; Jn 18.12–27). **59:** *Galilean*, likely identifiable by his accent. **61:** *The Lord . . . looked*, unique to Luke's Gospel.

22.63–65: The mockery of Jesus (Mt 26.67–68; 27.27–31a; Mk 14.65; 15.16–20a; cf. Jn 18.22–24).

22.66–71: Sanhedrin condemnation (Mt 27.1; 26.59–65; Mk 14.55–63; 15.1; Jn 18.13–14,19–23). **66:** *Council* (Gk "synedrion," Sanhedrin; related to Heb "bet din," "house of judgment"), the judicial authority. *Mishnah Sanh.* records a "Great Sanhedrin" of seventy-one that met in the Temple; it was ruled by the high priest but consisted

the Messiah,[a] tell us." He replied, "If I tell you, you will not believe; [68] and if I question you, you will not answer. [69] But from now on the Son of Man will be seated at the right hand of the power of God." [70] All of them asked, "Are you, then, the Son of God?" He said to them, "You say that I am." [71] Then they said, "What further testimony do we need? We have heard it ourselves from his own lips!"

23 Then the assembly rose as a body and brought Jesus[b] before Pilate. [2] They began to accuse him, saying, "We found this man perverting our nation, forbidding us to pay taxes to the emperor, and saying that he himself is the Messiah, a king."[c] [3] Then Pilate asked him, "Are you the king of the Jews?" He answered, "You say so." [4] Then Pilate said to the chief priests and the crowds, "I find no basis for an accusation against this man." [5] But they were insistent and said, "He stirs up the people by teaching throughout all Judea, from Galilee where he began even to this place."

[6] When Pilate heard this, he asked whether the man was a Galilean. [7] And when he learned that he was under Herod's jurisdiction, he sent him off to Herod, who was himself in Jerusalem at that time. [8] When Herod saw Jesus, he was very glad, for he had been wanting to see him for a long time, because he had heard about him and was hoping to see him perform some sign. [9] He questioned him at some length, but Jesus[d] gave him no answer. [10] The chief priests and the scribes stood by, vehemently accusing him. [11] Even Herod with his soldiers treated him with contempt and mocked him; then he put an elegant robe on him, and sent him back to Pilate. [12] That same day Herod and Pilate became friends with each other; before this they had been enemies.

[13] Pilate then called together the chief priests, the leaders, and the people, [14] and said to them, "You brought me this man as one who was perverting the people; and here I have examined him in your presence and have not found this man guilty of any of your charges against him. [15] Neither has Herod, for he sent him back to us. Indeed, he has done nothing to deserve death. [16] I will therefore have him flogged and release him."[e]

[18] Then they all shouted out together, "Away with this fellow! Release Barabbas for us!" [19] (This was a man who had been put in prison for an insurrection that had taken place in the city, and for murder.) [20] Pilate, wanting to release Jesus, addressed them

[a] Or *the Christ*
[b] Gk *him*
[c] Or *is an anointed king*
[d] Gk *he*
[e] Here, or after verse 19, other ancient authorities add verse 17, *Now he was obliged to release someone for them at the festival*

of sages (rabbis). This report's historicity is questionable, given the Mishnah's tendency to promote the authority of the sages. John's Gospel, lacking a Sanhedrin hearing, depicts only a hearing before Annas. **67:** *If you are the Messiah,* a charge against Jesus in 23.2. **69:** *Son of Man,* see 5.24n. *Seated at the right hand,* see also Col 3.1; Heb 8.1. **70:** *You say,* Jesus does not provide a direct answer (contrast Mk 14.62). **71:** No charge is directly applied to Jesus; he has not technically blasphemed nor engaged in sedition.

23.1–5: Jesus before Pilate (Mt 27.1–14; Mk 15.1–5; Jn 18.28–38). **1:** *Pilate,* see 3.1n. *Perverting our nation,* perhaps an allusion to Deut 13.1–11, suggesting Jesus is a false prophet. *Forbidding us to pay taxes,* see 20.25. *A king,* see 19.38. **3:** *You say so* does not answer the question. **4:** *I find no basis,* 23.14,22,41; Jn 19.4,6; Acts 13.28. The Gospels portray Pilate as seeking to free Jesus but succumbing to pressure by the Jewish rulers and population.

23.6–12: Jesus before Herod. An episode unique to Luke's Gospel. Son of Herod the Great (see 3.1n.), Herod [Antipas] arrested (3.19–20) and beheaded (9.9) John the Baptist. **7:** *Sent him off to Herod,* Perhaps alluding to Ps 2.2. **8:** See 9.9; Acts 4.27–28. **9:** *Gave him no answer,* see Mt 27.12; Mk 15.5. **10:** *Chief priests and scribes,* 19.47n. **11:** *Mocked him,* see Jn 19.2–3.

23.13–16 [17]: Pilate declares Jesus innocent. **13:** *Chief priests* (19.47n.) together with *the people* condemn Jesus. **14:** *Not found this man guilty,* vv. 4,22,41. **15:** *Herod,* vv. 6–12. **[17]:** Scribal addition from Mk 15.6.

23.18–25: The people condemn Jesus (Mt 27.15–26; Mk 15.6–15; Jn 18.39–40; 19.16). See Acts 3.13–14. **18:** *Barabbas* (see Mt 27.15–23; Mk 15.6–14; Jn 18.39–40), Aramaic, "Son of the Father." Luke omits Mark's reference to the (unlikely) custom of releasing a prisoner and so makes the crowds' demand for Barabbas more perverse. **19:** *Insurrection,* Barabbas is guilty of sedition, the charge leveled against Jesus (23.38).

again; [21]but they kept shouting, "Crucify, crucify him!" [22]A third time he said to them, "Why, what evil has he done? I have found in him no ground for the sentence of death; I will therefore have him flogged and then release him." [23]But they kept urgently demanding with loud shouts that he should be crucified; and their voices prevailed. [24]So Pilate gave his verdict that their demand should be granted. [25]He released the man they asked for, the one who had been put in prison for insurrection and murder, and he handed Jesus over as they wished.

[26]As they led him away, they seized a man, Simon of Cyrene, who was coming from the country, and they laid the cross on him, and made him carry it behind Jesus. [27]A great number of the people followed him, and among them were women who were beating their breasts and wailing for him. [28]But Jesus turned to them and said, "Daughters of Jerusalem, do not weep for me, but weep for yourselves and for your children. [29]For the days are surely coming when they will say, 'Blessed are the barren, and the wombs that never bore, and the breasts that never nursed.' [30]Then they will begin to say to the mountains, 'Fall on us'; and to the hills, 'Cover us.' [31]For if they do this when the wood is green, what will happen when it is dry?"

[32]Two others also, who were criminals, were led away to be put to death with him. [33]When they came to the place that is called The Skull, they crucified Jesus[a] there with the criminals, one on his right and one on his left. [34]Then Jesus said, "Father, forgive them; for they do not know what they are doing."[b] And they cast lots to divide his clothing. [35]And the people stood by, watching; but the leaders scoffed at him, saying, "He saved others; let him save himself if he is the Messiah[c] of God, his chosen one!" [36]The soldiers also mocked him, coming up and offering him sour wine, [37]and saying, "If you are the King of the Jews, save yourself!" [38]There was also an inscription over him,[d] "This is the King of the Jews."

[39]One of the criminals who were hanged there kept deriding[e] him and saying, "Are you not the Messiah?[c] Save yourself and us!" [40]But the other rebuked him, saying, "Do you not fear God, since you are under the same sentence of condemnation? [41]And we indeed have been condemned justly, for we are getting what we deserve for our deeds, but this man has done nothing wrong." [42]Then he said, "Jesus, remember me when you come into[f] your kingdom." [43]He replied, "Truly I tell you, today you will be with me in Paradise."

[44]It was now about noon, and darkness came over the whole land[g] until three in the afternoon, [45]while the sun's light failed;[h]

a Gk *him*
b Other ancient authorities lack the sentence *Then Jesus . . . what they are doing*
c Or *the Christ*
d Other ancient authorities add *written in Greek and Latin and Hebrew* (that is, *Aramaic*)
e Or *blaspheming*
f Other ancient authorities read *in*
g Or *earth*
h Or *the sun was eclipsed.* Other ancient authorities read *the sun was darkened*

20–25: *Wanting to release Jesus,* Luke places the blame for Jesus' death on the Jewish people (cf. Acts 2.23; 3.13–15; 4.10; 5.30; 7.52; 13.27–29).

23.26–31: Journey to the cross (Mt 27.31b–32; Mk 15.20b–21; Jn 19.17a). **26:** *Cyrene,* in Libya. *The cross,* the horizontal beam. **27:** *Beating their breasts,* likely indicating mourning rather than repentance (cf. 18.3; 23.48). **28–31:** See 21.23–24; 19.41–44. **29:** *Blessed are the barren,* see 21.23. **30:** Suggestive of Hos 10.8. **31:** The analogy is not clear: either the saying means that if the innocent Jesus suffers, how much more will the guilty Jerusalem suffer, or if evil occurs with Jesus present, how much more will occur in his absence (see 1 Pet 4.17–18).

23.32: Two criminals. 32: *Criminals,* Luke does not specify their crimes.

23.33–49: The crucifixion. (Mt 27.33–43; Mk 15.22–32a; Jn 19.17b–27). **33:** *Skull* (Gk "kranion"), Matthew and Mark give the Aramaic "Golgotha." **34:** See textual note *b;* cf. Acts 7.60. *Cast lots,* alluding to Ps 22.18. **36:** *Sour wine,* alluding to Ps 69.21. **39–43:** (Mt 27.44; Mk 15.32b). **41:** *Has done nothing wrong,* a point affirmed by Pilate and Herod Antipas (vv. 4,14,22). **42:** *Remember,* a psalmic cry for aid (Ps 74.2,18,22). **43:** *Paradise,* originally referring to the Garden of Eden (Gen 2.8–10 LXX); here the home of the righteous dead prior to the resurrection; cf.

and the curtain of the temple was torn in two. [46] Then Jesus, crying with a loud voice, said, "Father, into your hands I commend my spirit." Having said this, he breathed his last. [47] When the centurion saw what had taken place, he praised God and said, "Certainly this man was innocent."[a] [48] And when all the crowds who had gathered there for this spectacle saw what had taken place, they returned home, beating their breasts. [49] But all his acquaintances, including the women who had followed him from Galilee, stood at a distance, watching these things.

[50] Now there was a good and righteous man named Joseph, who, though a member of the council, [51] had not agreed to their plan and action. He came from the Jewish town of Arimathea, and he was waiting expectantly for the kingdom of God. [52] This man went to Pilate and asked for the body of Jesus. [53] Then he took it down, wrapped it in a linen cloth, and laid it in a rock-hewn tomb where no one had ever been laid. [54] It was the day of Preparation, and the sabbath was beginning.[b] [55] The women who had come with him from Galilee followed, and they saw the tomb and how his body was laid. [56] Then they returned, and prepared spices and ointments.

On the sabbath they rested according to the commandment.

24 But on the first day of the week, at early dawn, they came to the tomb, taking the spices that they had prepared. [2] They found the stone rolled away from the tomb, [3] but when they went in, they did not find the body.[c] [4] While they were perplexed about this, suddenly two men in dazzling clothes stood beside them. [5] The women[d] were terrified and bowed their faces to the ground, but the men[e] said to them, "Why do you look for the living among the dead? He is not here, but has risen.[f] [6] Remember how he told you, while he was still in Galilee, [7] that the Son of Man must be handed over to sinners, and be crucified, and on the third day rise again." [8] Then they remembered his words, [9] and returning from the tomb, they told all this to the eleven and to all the rest. [10] Now it was Mary Magdalene, Joanna, Mary the mother of James, and the other women with them who told this to the apostles. [11] But these words seemed to them an idle tale, and they did not believe them. [12] But Peter got up and ran to the tomb; stooping and looking in, he saw the linen cloths by themselves; then he went home, amazed at what had happened.[g]

a Or *righteous*
b Gk *was dawning*
c Other ancient authorities add *of the Lord Jesus*
d Gk *They*
e Gk *but they*
f Other ancient authorities lack *He is not here, but has risen*
g Other ancient authorities lack verse 12

16.22. **44–48:** (Mt 27.45–54; Mk 15.33–39; Jn 19.28–30). **45:** *Sun's light failed,* the translation is uncertain; see Am 8.9; Joel 2.31. *Curtain of the temple,* Ex 26.31–35. *Torn in two,* indicating mourning (Gen 37.29,34; 44.13; Num 14.6; Josh 7.6; 11.35; etc.) and perhaps prefiguring the Temple's destruction. The point is not, contrary to some readings, new access to God, since God had always been accessible outside of the Jerusalem Temple. **47:** *Innocent,* Gk "dikaios," lit., "righteous." **48:** *Beating their breasts,* see v. 27n. **49:** (Mt 27.55–56; Mk 15.40–41; Jn 19.25–27). *Including the women,* see 23.55; cf. 8.1–3; 24.10.

23.50–56: Jesus' entombment (Mt 27.57–60; Mk 15.42–46; Jn 19.38–42). **50:** *Council,* 22.66n. **51:** *Arimathea* (likely from Heb "Ramataim," cf. *Ramoth, Ramah*), near Jerusalem. **53:** *Laid it in a rock-hewn tomb,* Luke does not record who cared for the bodies of the other two crucified men. **54:** *Day of Preparation,* Friday, before sunset. *Sabbath was beginning,* at sundown. **55–56:** Mt 27.61; Mk 15.47–16.1; *m. Shabb.* 23.5. **55:** Cf. 24.10. **56:** *Spices and ointments* were applied to the corpse; see Mk 16.1; Jn 19.40. Preparation of the corpse should precede burial. The women presume that Jesus will not be resurrected. *They rested,* see Ex 20.10.

24.1–12: Women at the tomb (Mt 28.1–8; Mk 16.1–8; Jn 20.1–13). **1:** *Taking the spices,* see 23.55–56n. **4:** *Dazzling clothes* suggest angels (see v. 23), as does sudden appearance and supernatural knowledge (vv. 5–7). **6:** *He told you,* 9.22; 13.32–33. **10:** See 8.1–3; Jn 19.25; 20.2. **11:** *They did not believe,* many commentators claim, incorrectly, that the men did not believe because Jews do not accept women's testimony; to the contrary, the eleven do not believe because they do not expect Jesus to rise (see Jn 20.25).

[13] Now on that same day two of them were going to a village called Emmaus, about seven miles[a] from Jerusalem, [14] and talking with each other about all these things that had happened. [15] While they were talking and discussing, Jesus himself came near and went with them, [16] but their eyes were kept from recognizing him. [17] And he said to them, "What are you discussing with each other while you walk along?" They stood still, looking sad.[b] [18] Then one of them, whose name was Cleopas, answered him, "Are you the only stranger in Jerusalem who does not know the things that have taken place there in these days?" [19] He asked them, "What things?" They replied, "The things about Jesus of Nazareth,[c] who was a prophet mighty in deed and word before God and all the people, [20] and how our chief priests and leaders handed him over to be condemned to death and crucified him. [21] But we had hoped that he was the one to redeem Israel.[d] Yes, and besides all this, it is now the third day since these things took place. [22] Moreover, some women of our group astounded us. They were at the tomb early this morning, [23] and when they did not find his body there, they came back and told us that they had indeed seen a vision of angels who said that he was alive. [24] Some of those who were with us went to the tomb and found it just as the women had said; but they did not see him." [25] Then he said to them, "Oh, how foolish you are, and how slow of heart to believe all that the prophets have declared! [26] Was it not necessary that the Messiah[e] should suffer these things and then enter into his glory?" [27] Then beginning with Moses and all the prophets, he interpreted to them the things about himself in all the scriptures.

[28] As they came near the village to which they were going, he walked ahead as if he were going on. [29] But they urged him strongly, saying, "Stay with us, because it is almost evening and the day is now nearly over." So he went in to stay with them. [30] When he was at the table with them, he took bread, blessed and broke it, and gave it to them. [31] Then their eyes were opened, and they recognized him; and he vanished from their sight. [32] They said to each other, "Were not our hearts burning within us[f] while he was talking to us on the road, while he was opening the scriptures to us?" [33] That same hour they got up and returned to Jerusalem; and they found the eleven and their companions gathered together. [34] They were saying, "The Lord has risen indeed, and he has appeared to Simon!" [35] Then they told what had happened on the road, and how he had been made known to them in the breaking of the bread.

[36] While they were talking about this, Jesus himself stood among them and said to them, "Peace be with you."[g] [37] They were

[a] Gk *sixty stadia;* other ancient authorities read *a hundred sixty stadia*
[b] Other ancient authorities read *walk along, looking sad?"*
[c] Other ancient authorities read *Jesus the Nazorean*
[d] Or *to set Israel free*
[e] Or *the Christ*
[f] Other ancient authorities lack *within us*
[g] Other ancient authorities lack *and said to them, "Peace be with you."*

24.13–35: Emmaus incident. 13: *Two of them,* Cleopas (v. 18) and an unidentified follower, who may be a woman. *Seven miles,* lit., "sixty stadia"; a "stadion" was approximately 600 feet (180 m). The location of Emmaus is uncertain. **16:** *Their eyes were kept from recognizing,* 9.35n.; 18.34. **20:** *Chief priests and leaders,* Cleopas does not blame all Jews, although he ignores Roman involvement. **21:** *Redeem* (Gk "lutroō," "ransom"; see Mt 20.28; Mk 10.45; 1 Tim 2.6), bring about the messianic age. There is no reason to presume only a political import (see 1.68). **22:** *Women,* see 24.11n. **25:** *Prophets have declared,* Jesus' followers searched the scriptures for allusions to him. **26:** *The messiah should suffer,* not part of general Jewish messianic views. **27:** *Moses and all the prophets,* see 16.16n.; 24.44; Acts 28.23; Moses was regarded as having written the Torah. **30:** *Took bread, blessed and broke,* see 9.16; 22.19. **31:** *Their eyes were opened,* revelation is connected with the breaking of bread in a fellowship meal (see v. 35; Acts 2.42; 20.7; 1 Cor 10.16). The "recognition" scene ("anagnorisis") was conventional in Greek and Roman literature. **34:** *Appeared to Simon,* see 1 Cor 15.5.

24.36–43: Jesus' appearance to his disciples (Jn 20.19–23). **36:** *Peace be with you,* see 10.5n. **37:** *Ghost,* a mistaken identification (see vv. 39–40 on Jesus' corporeality); Luke stresses the reality of Jesus' resurrection. **42:** *Broiled fish* (cf. Jn 21.9–13). **43:** *He . . . ate,* ghosts, like angels, do not eat.

startled and terrified, and thought that they were seeing a ghost. [38] He said to them, "Why are you frightened, and why do doubts arise in your hearts? [39] Look at my hands and my feet; see that it is I myself. Touch me and see; for a ghost does not have flesh and bones as you see that I have." [40] And when he had said this, he showed them his hands and his feet.[a] [41] While in their joy they were disbelieving and still wondering, he said to them, "Have you anything here to eat?" [42] They gave him a piece of broiled fish, [43] and he took it and ate in their presence.

[44] Then he said to them, "These are my words that I spoke to you while I was still with you—that everything written about me in the law of Moses, the prophets, and the psalms must be fulfilled." [45] Then he opened their minds to understand the scriptures, [46] and he said to them, "Thus it is written, that the Messiah[b] is to suffer and to rise from the dead on the third day, [47] and that repentance and forgiveness of sins is to be proclaimed in his name to all nations, beginning from Jerusalem. [48] You are witnesses[c] of these things. [49] And see, I am sending upon you what my Father promised; so stay here in the city until you have been clothed with power from on high."

[50] Then he led them out as far as Bethany, and, lifting up his hands, he blessed them. [51] While he was blessing them, he withdrew from them and was carried up into heaven.[d] [52] And they worshiped him, and[e] returned to Jerusalem with great joy; [53] and they were continually in the temple blessing God.[f]

[a] Other ancient authorities lack verse 40
[b] Or *the Christ*
[c] Or *nations. Beginning from Jerusalem [48]you are witnesses*
[d] Other ancient authorities lack *and was carried up into heaven*
[e] Other ancient authorities lack *worshiped him, and*
[f] Other ancient authorities add *Amen*

24.44–53: Final teachings and ascension (see Mk 16.15,19). **44:** Vv. 26–27; Acts 28.23. *Written about me,* Luke continues to stress that Israel's Scriptures predicted Jesus' life, death, and resurrection (see vv. 25–26). The *Psalms* formed the opening and the longest part of the Ketuvim ("Writings"; see 16.16n.). **45:** *Opened their minds,* without divine revelation, readers would not see the predictions about Jesus in the Scriptures (24.32). **46:** *It is written,* no text explicitly states that "the messiah" should suffer, and Luke cites no specific text. Isaiah 53 and Hos 6.2 are sometimes claimed as proof texts (see also 1 Cor 15.3–4). **47:** *Repentance and forgiveness of sins* (see Acts 5.31; 10.43; 13.38; 26.18), Jews believed God is always ready to forgive the repentant. *To all nations,* anticipates the Gentile mission (see Acts 1.8). **49:** *What my Father promised,* the Holy Spirit (see Acts 2.1–21). **50:** *Bethany,* see 19.29n. *Lifting up his hands,* see Lev 9.22. **51:** *Was carried up into heaven,* Acts 1.9–11. The verse explains why Jesus no longer appears. **53:** *Continually in the temple,* Jesus' followers continue as faithful Jews (see Acts 2.46).

THE GOSPEL ACCORDING TO JOHN

The Gospel according to John, also known as the Fourth Gospel due to its placement in the New Testament, is one of paradoxes and contradictions both in its content and in the reactions it evokes in its readers. It tells the story of the Son of God who becomes flesh and dwells in the world, and dies an ignominious death that nevertheless marks his exaltation, ascension to God, and the divine triumph over the forces of evil. It presents a sublime vision of a future salvation that is also in some inexplicable way already a present reality. Many readers love this Gospel because of its sublime language and imagery, and its ability to lift its readers out of the historical moments of Jesus' life to the lofty heights of the cosmos. Others dislike it because of its insistence on the exclusive truth of its message, and the absence of space for any other way of viewing the world.

The paradox that this Gospel presents extends to its relationship to Judaism. It makes abundant use of the Hebrew Bible, through direct quotations and allusions, as well as, more subtly, through its appropriation of some of its characters, motifs and stories that are then interpreted through the lens of faith in Jesus as Christ and Son of God. This Gospel also has numerous parallels to other Jewish sources, from the second temple and rabbinic periods, as well as references to Jewish practices. At the same time, the Gospel is highly disturbing in its representation of "the Jews." "The Jews" are the archenemies of Jesus and his followers; they are blind to the truth and relentless in pursuit of Jesus to the point of masterminding his demise. Their behavior toward Jesus and their failure to believe demonstrate that they have relinquished their covenantal relationship with the God of Israel, and show them to be instead the children of the devil. For this reason, John's Gospel has been called the most Jewish and the most anti-Jewish of the Gospels.

DATE AND HISTORICAL CONTEXT

John's Gospel is generally considered the latest of the four canonical gospels to be written. This view was held as early as the second century CE. The church father Clement of Alexandria (ca. 150–211/216), was quoted by the fourth century Christian historian Eusebius of Caesarea (*Hist. eccl.* 6.14.7), to the effect that John's Gospel was written to supplement the other Gospels. Today, the question of John's relationship to the Synoptics (Matthew, Mark, and Luke) remains controversial. To be sure, there are a number of significant parallels between John and the Synoptics, such as the feeding of the multitudes (6.1–14; cf. Mt 14.13–21; Mk 16.32–44; Lk 9.10–17) and Jesus' walking on water (6.16–21; cf. Mt 14.22; Mk 6.45–51). On the basis of these parallels, some scholars have argued that John is familiar with one or more of these Gospels. Yet most of the stories, such as the wedding at Cana (2.1–13), Jesus' encounter with the Samaritan woman (4.1–42), and the raising of Lazarus (11.1–44), are unique to the Fourth Gospel. The Gospel also has a distinctive perspective on Jesus, such as belief in his identity as the preexistent Word and the Word's role in the creation (1.1–5). It seems reasonable to suggest that while all the Gospels had access to some common traditions, insufficient evidence exists to determine whether the Fourth Gospel had access to a complete text of one or more of the Synoptics. For this reason, it is not possible to date John on the basis of a literary dependence upon one or more other canonical Gospels.

Dating the Gospel based on its theology is equally problematic. A late first-century or early second-century dating has been suggested on the basis of the Gospel's high Christology, which focuses primarily on Jesus' role as the Son of God rather than on his human aspect. Earlier examples of exalted views of Jesus, such as Paul's letter to the Philippians (2.6–11), make this a less useful criterion for determining the Gospel's date.

Nor are the historical circumstances in which the Gospel has been written of much assistance. No external evidence exists for the historical first audience of the Gospel, but on the basis of internal evidence it has been argued that the Gospel was written within and for a particular group of Christ-believers, often referred to in scholarly literature as the Johannine community. The particular circumstances that led to the final version of the Gospel are often reconstructed from three references to expulsion from the synagogue on account of confessing Jesus to be the messiah (9.22; 12.42; 16.2). Because expulsion on these grounds would be anachronistic to the time of Jesus, it is often argued that these passages refer to an exclusion of Jewish believers in Christ from the synagogue, either in John's community or more broadly. Exclusion from the synagogue, it is argued, would have been tantamount to complete and forcible removal from the Jewish community, with numerous social and economic consequences. Proponents of this interpretation argue that the traumatic experience of expulsion was written into the community's story of Jesus and suggest that experience can be reconstructed by reading the Gospel on two levels: as a story of Jesus set in the first third of the first century CE that simultaneously recounts a story of the Johannine community set in the last decade or two of the first century. External corroboration for this hypothesis has been sought in the liturgical curse on the heretics, "Birchat ha-minim," euphemistically called a Blessing on the Heretics, that was added to the Eighteen Benedictions that constitute the central prayers of the Jewish liturgy. The theory is that at some point in the late first century, Jewish authorities added this curse to the daily liturgy as a way of flushing undesirables, including Jewish Christ-confessors, out of the worship service and thereby from the community as a whole. If this theory is correct, it would provide a basis for dating the Gospel to the late first century, after 85 CE.

This construction is flawed on both literary and historical grounds. From a literary-critical point of view, there is no evidence that the Gospel in fact encodes the history and experience of the community in its story of Jesus. With the exception of the expulsion passages, no other parts of the Gospel lend themselves easily to this two-level reading. The well-documented theological diversity within first-century Judaism, as evidenced by the widely differing views of the Pharisees and Sadducees on fundamental matters such as the authority of oral tradition and the belief in bodily resurrection and the distinctive views expressed in the Dead Sea Scrolls, makes it unlikely that Jews would have been excluded from the synagogue for believing Jesus to be the Messiah. Indeed, in the period of 132–135 similar claims were apparently made for Simeon Bar Kosiba to be a messiah, by the prominent Rabbi Akiva, whose status and stature within early rabbinic Judaism did not suffer as a result. Finally, the manuscript evidence for Birchat ha-minim as a whole does not support the view that the curse would have been in existence at this time in a form that could have served to exclude Jewish Christ-confessors from the synagogue. For these reasons, it is difficult to use historical circumstances as a basis for dating the Gospel.

The most persuasive evidence for the date of the Gospel is textual. The earliest material evidence for the Gospel is a small Egyptian codex fragment of John 18.31–33,37–38, known as the Rylands Library Papyrus 52. This fragment is dated to 135–160. Because circulation of the Gospel from Asia Minor, where it was likely written, to Egypt would have taken a few decades, the existence of this fragment suggests a late first- or early second-century dating for the final version of the Gospel. For these reasons, John's Gospel is generally thought to have been completed ca. 85–95 CE.

HISTORY OF COMPOSITION

This dating applies to the final version of the Gospel found in the most complete manuscripts of the New Testament, such as Sinaiticus, Alexandrinus, and Vaticanus. This final version, however, was the product of a lengthy and complicated history of composition. It is likely that pre-Johannine sources or early versions of the Gospel circulated for some decades before the date of final composition. Evidence for a lengthy process of composition includes narrative inconsistencies and awkward narrative transitions. For example, whereas ch 5, which recounts the healing of a lame man, is set in Jerusalem, ch 6, v. 1 abruptly situates Jesus on the "other side of the Sea of Galilee." Also puzzling is the comment in 14.31, in which Jesus says, "Rise, let us be on our way," and then continues to speak, with no change in setting, for three more chapters.

Some scholars posit that a written "signs source" served as the basis for the Gospel's narrative. The Gospel recounts a series of "signs" (Gk "semeia") or wondrous deeds, often, though not always, accompanied by lengthy discourses. These signs are not mere miracles but rather witnesses to Jesus' identity as God's only son; the accounts of these signs are intended to foster or deepen the faith of the Gospel's audience.

The version of John's Gospel now found in the New Testament contains one passage that did not originally belong: the story of the woman caught in adultery (7.53–8.13) is absent from some of the earliest manuscripts, and in some manuscripts it appears after Luke 21.38 (where it fits better narratively). Questions have also been raised regarding John 21. On the grounds of both content and style, some scholars believe that this final chapter is a later addition, written by someone other than the author(s) of the rest of the Gospel. In antiquity, later traditions were often added at a book's end.

AUTHORSHIP AND PROVENANCE

The Gospel identifies the beloved disciple (or "the disciple whom Jesus loved") as the eyewitness author (19.35; 21.24). This anonymous figure first appears in the scene of Jesus' last meal with his disciples (13.23). He is presented as the disciple who is closest to Jesus, and at the cross, Jesus appoints him to take care of his mother (19.25–27). Since the second century, Christian tradition has identified the beloved disciple with John son of Zebedee, one of the twelve disciples mentioned in the Synoptics. This tradition is unlikely to be correct, however, both because

John the son of Zebedee, a Galilean fisherman, does not match the Jerusalem-based depiction of the beloved disciple, and because the Gospel does not identify the beloved disciple as John. Therefore, the Gospel's author is better understood to be anonymous and probably not an original follower of Jesus or an eyewitness. The final version of the Gospel has traditionally been assigned to Ephesus in Asia Minor (Izmir, in modern-day Turkey), though it is possible that an early version originated orally or in written form with a group from Judea.

AUDIENCE AND PURPOSE

John 20.30–31 states the purpose for the Gospel: "Now Jesus did many other signs in the presence of his disciples, which are not written in this book. But these are written so that you may come to believe that Jesus is the Messiah, the Son of God, and that through believing you may have life in his name." This translation implies that the purpose is to bring readers to faith in Jesus as the Messiah (Christ) and Son of God. However, the verb translated "that you may come to believe" reflects one manuscript tradition; other manuscripts contain a different form of the verb that is better translated "that you may continue to believe." This second form suggests that the Gospel was intended to strengthen the faith of those already within the community. The latter interpretation suits the overall tone and content of the Gospel, which does not emphasize openness to nonbelievers, but focuses on a set of specific views of Jesus (Christology), the end times (eschatology), and salvation (soteriology).

The view that the Gospel was written for a specific community is closely related to the historical context of the Gospel. The predominantly negative role played by "the Jews" in the narrative suggests that the text was written in a context of overt conflict between Jews and the members of the Johannine community. Even if the expulsion theory is tenuous, the Gospel's hostility toward the Jews is certainly real. It is possible that the Gospel reflects a stage in the process by which Johannine believers came to see themselves as separate from and, to some extent, over and against Jews and Judaism. Views on the size and ethnic character of the intended audience vary widely: they range from seeing the audience as comprised of all followers of Jesus to the view that the first audience was a small and select community of Israelites who were the direct descendants of those who had remained in Judea after the destruction of the First Temple (see "John's Prologue as Midrash" p. 546). If the first view is correct, the conflict portrayed within the Gospel may well reflect a widespread separation between Jews and Christ-confessors (the term "Christian" may not yet have been in effect for those who believed in Jesus as the Messiah). If the second view is correct, the Gospel reflects an inner-Jewish controversy but not a widespread or even local parting of the ways.

There are significant clues within the Gospel itself, however, to suggest that the intended audience included not only those of Jewish origin but those of Samaritan and Gentile origin as well. John 4 describes Jesus' encounter with a Samaritan woman, as a result of which many other Samaritans came to believe in Jesus. John 12 describes the strong interest of some "Greeks," perhaps Jews from the Diaspora but more likely Gentiles, in Jesus, after which Jesus declares that his death will draw all people to himself. If the intended audience, and therefore the Johannine community, included Jews, Gentiles, and Samaritans, then it could be plausibly argued that they needed to create their own identity that overcame the social, historical and theological boundaries existing between their groups of origin. An important part of doing this work would have been to create an identity quite distinct from those other groups, especially from Jews and Judaism, from which this new group has appropriated much of its symbolism, scripture, and theology. The Gospel stresses Jesus' superiority to Moses (1.18; 3.14–15). John 2.13–22 implies that Jesus replaces the Jerusalem Temple as the place where God dwells, a claim that is made explicitly in 4.21 and illustrated in 6.1–4, in which Jews flock to Jesus in the Galilee region instead of to Jerusalem for the Passover pilgrimage festival.

JEWS AND JUDAISM

John's knowledge of first-century Judaism

The Gospel of John reflects deep and broad knowledge of Jerusalem, Jewish practice, and methods of biblical interpretation. Some references to early first-century Jerusalem topography and landmarks, such as the pool at Beth-zatha near the Sheep Gate in Jerusalem (5.2) are supported archaeologically, suggesting direct knowledge of the city and surroundings. The Gospel refers to the Sabbath and Passover as well as to the Feast of Tabernacles (5.1) and Hanukkah (10.22). It explains ritual hand-washing before meals (2.6), a comment that supports the hypothesis, mentioned earlier, that at least some of the Gospel's intended audience is not of Jewish origin. Most strikingly, the Gospel alludes to a broad range of Jewish ideas. For example, in Jn 6, often called the Bread of Life discourse (6.25–71), it employs argument similar to later rabbinic midrashic traditions. In 5.17, Jesus responds to the Jews' accusations that he breaks the Sabbath by asserting: "My Father is still working, and I also am working." This response recalls the discussion by the Hellenistic Jewish philosopher, Philo of Alexandria (ca. 20 BCE–50 CE) on the question of whether God works on the Sabbath (*Cher.* 86–890; *Leg. all.* 1.5–6). The same issue is discussed in rabbinic literature, e.g., *Ex. Rab.* 11.10; 30.9; though this text in its present form postdates the Gospel of John by several centuries, it may reflect traditions that were already present in the first century. The Gospel's prologue applies concepts associated with Lady Wisdom in Prov 8.22–31 and Sir 24 to "the Word" (incarnated in Jesus); the Word is portrayed as preexistent and instrumental in the creation of the world. And like Lady Wisdom, the Word is instructed to take on flesh and dwell in the world (1.14; cf. Sir 24.8).

John and Jewish sources

Despite the striking parallels between John and Hellenistic Jewish sources such as the Apocrypha and pseudepigrapha, and the works of Philo, there is no evidence of John's direct knowledge and use of these sources. Rather, the similarities reflect ideas that were "in the air" in Asia Minor, where the final version of the Gospel may have been written. The parallels to rabbinic literature also do not reveal any dependence or direct knowledge of rabbinic texts, all of which are dated to a period at least two centuries after the completion of the Gospel. For this reason, John's similarities to some rabbinic traditions and his use of similar exegetical methods do not demonstrate dependence but rather help to establish the existence in the first century of beliefs, practices, or methods that may otherwise be known only from much later Jewish texts. John is therefore a source for the antiquity of some rabbinic traditions, not the other way around.

The most important, and the only documentable, textual sources used by John's Gospel are the Jewish scriptures, most likely in a Greek translation. The Gospel includes numerous quotations and allusions to the Pentateuch (Torah) and prophetic literature, as well as the writings (see annotations for examples). Important biblical figures, such as Abraham, Moses, and Jacob, are mentioned. More subtly, certain biblical narratives form the basis of several of the major discourses. The figure of Lady Wisdom, and her association with God and with creation is a major feature of the prologue (Jn 1.1–18; Prov 8; Sir 24; Wis 10; cf. Philo, *On the Creation*). The Abraham cycle (Gen 12–36) underlies Jn 8.31–59, especially the contrast between Ishmael and Isaac (Gen 16 and 21; cf. Jn 8.34–35), Abraham's hospitality to three angelic visitors (Gen 18; cf. Jn 8.39–44), and the tradition that Abraham was given a vision of the future times and heavenly worlds (Gen 15.17–20; cf. *T. Abr.*; Jn 8:53–58). The story of the Exodus from Egypt is evoked throughout Jn 6.

At the same time, it must be stressed that the Gospel also alludes to non-Jewish practices and ideas. The notion of the Logos as a creative power in the world is a feature not only of Jewish wisdom literature but also of Greek philosophy, e.g., in the work of Heraclitus, Aristotle, and the Stoics. John 6 refers not only to the book of Exodus but also to Greco-Roman mystery cults and perhaps even Roman accusations against Christianity as engaging in cannibalism and other immoral practices. John 4 also has strong allusions to Samaritan messianic beliefs.

John and anti-Judaism

Although the Gospel draws extensively on Jewish tradition, its explicit references to Jews and Judaism are often hostile. The Greek term *hoi Ioudaioi* or variations appears more than seventy times. The literal translation is "the Judeans," that is, the inhabitants of Judea, or, as became commonplace, "the Jews." (See "Ioudaios," p. 524.) The appropriate translation of this term is one of the most contentious issues in Johannine studies. Some suggest that the term should be translated as "the Jews" when used neutrally or positively, as in references to the festivals of the Jews (e.g., 2.13; 5.1; 6.4), but not when it is used negatively to refer to Jesus' enemies. In these latter cases, *hoi Ioudaioi* does not designate the Jews or even the Judeans as a whole. The crowds who eat the "bread of life" (Jn 6), or who hear Jesus teach in the Temple during the Feast of Tabernacles (Jn 7) are Jews, yet they are not arrayed against Jesus. In addition, Jesus says in his conversation with the Samaritan woman at the well that "salvation is from the Jews" (4.22). These examples show that the specific referent of *hoi Ioudaioi* within the narrative varies according to its literary context.

Yet this does not quite resolve the issue. More important than the referent of each usage is the overall rhetorical effect of the relentless repetition of the words *hoi Ioudaioi*. The Gospel's use of the term serves two important functions: it blurs the boundaries among various Jewish groups, and it employs the term to designate the forces that are hostile to Jesus. Notably, *hoi Ioudaioi* is never used to describe the disciples and other followers, who are certainly

Jewish with regard to their religious and ethnic origins, though not residents of Judea for the most part. Similarly, Jesus is not referred to as a "Jew" except once, by the Samaritan woman, who wonders that Jesus, a Jew, asks a drink of a Samaritan woman (4.9). Instead, the Gospel uses "Israelite" and "Israel" as positive terms. Jesus refers to Nathanael approvingly, as an "Israelite in whom there is no deceit" (1.47). Nathanael in turn declares Jesus to be the King of Israel (1.49) and the enthusiastic crowds who greet Jesus as he enters Jerusalem before his final Passover do the same (12.13). The effect is to distance the reader from any group designated as *hoi Ioudaioi*, regardless of the specific referent. On the basis of these arguments, the generic translation of *hoi Ioudaioi* as "the Jews" is the most suitable.

The Jews are from the outset portrayed as the people who reject Jesus (1.11), persecute him (5.16), seek his death (8.40), expel believers from the synagogue (9.22), plot Jesus' death (9.49–52), and persecute his followers (16.2). Furthermore, both the Gospel narrator and the Johannine Jesus employ dualistic language that contrasts spirit and flesh, light and darkness, life and death, salvation and eternal damnation, God and Satan, belief and nonbelief. Those who believe Jesus to be the Messiah and Son of God are firmly associated with the positive element in each pair, whereas those who reject him—epitomized by "the Jews"—are associated with the negative elements. The most extreme example appears in Jn 8, in which Jesus declares to his Jewish audience: "You are from your father the devil, and you choose to do your father's desires" (8.44). This accusation has contributed to anti-Judaism and anti-Semitism from ancient times to the present day.

In using the term "the Jews" to indicate, and to condemn, those who do not believe in Jesus, the Gospel of John encourages its readers to dissociate themselves from any who would identify with that designation. For that reason it may also be considered "anti-Jewish," insofar as it declares that Jews who do not believe in Jesus as the Christ and Son of God thereby relinquish their covenantal relationship with God (8.47). It must be emphasized that the Gospel is not anti-Semitic in a racial sense, as it is not one's origins that are decisive but one's beliefs. Nevertheless, it has been used to promote anti-Semitism. Most damaging has been Jn 8.44, in which Jesus declares that the Jews have the devil as their father. The association of the Jews with Satan or the devil is pervasive in anti-Semitic discourse and imagery, from woodcuts (such as the image of *[T]he Jew calling the Devil from a Vessel of Blood*, a 1560 woodcut found in the *Histoires Prodigieuses* by the important French humanist, Pierre Boaistuau, ca. 1517–66) to plays such Shakespeare's *The Merchant of Venice*, in which the Jewish merchant Shylock is referred to as "a kind of devil," "the devil himself," and "the very devil incarnate" (act 2, scene 2), and on present-day white supremacist websites, to name but a few examples.

While John's difficult rhetoric should not be facilely dismissed, it can be understood as part of the author's process of self-definition, of distinguishing the followers of Jesus from the synagogue and so from Jews and Judaism. This distancing may have been particularly important if the ethnic composition of the Johannine community included Jews, Samaritans, and Gentiles. This approach does not excuse the Gospel's rhetoric, but it may make it possible for readers to understand the narrative's place in the process by which Christianity became a separate religion, to appreciate the beauty of its language, and to recognize the spiritual power that it continues to have in the lives of many of its Christian readers.

STRUCTURE AND LITERARY FEATURES

The Gospel of John falls into two main sections, traditionally called the Book of Signs (chs 1–12) and the Book of Glory (chs 13–21). For details on the subsections under each main section, see the headings in the annotations.

The Johannine narrative

As a "life" of Jesus, the Gospel of John tells what we might term a "historical tale," in that it situates Jesus' story in its historical context of Galilee and Judea, during the decades leading up to the first Jewish Revolt against Rome. The Gospel also tells a cosmological story of the preexistent Word of God who enters the world, conquers Satan, and returns to the Father. This cosmological tale exists within and behind the account of Jesus' words and deeds. The historical tale, which describes his interactions with his followers and his opponents, is evident primarily through the plot, which traces Jesus' life from the moment of his identification by John the Baptist (1.19–36) through to his crucifixion (ch 19) and his resurrection appearances to the disciples (chs 20–21). The cosmological tale is told both by the narrator and by Jesus, in their comments and reflections upon Jesus' life and death.

The Gospel of John employs a number of literary devices, which direct the reader's attention to its main themes and help to bridge the historical and cosmological tales. These include repetition (e.g., "The hour is coming, and is now here"; 4.21,23; 5.25,28; 16.2,25,32), double entendre (e.g., "be lifted up" in 3.14–15 as meaning both crucifixion and exaltation), misunderstanding (cf. Nicodemus's question on how it is possible to be "born a second time," 3.3–5), and irony (e.g., 7.34–35, in which the crowd thinks that Jesus might "go to" the Diaspora when the reader knows he is speaking of his death and return to the Father).

Narrative patterning

The Gospel of John narrates fewer events than do the Synoptics, but the stories are more developed and stylized, perhaps in order to make them easier to follow. The narrative structures of these stories are easily discernible and tend to follow similar patterns. One example consists of "signs" stories, the accounts of Jesus' miracles. These tend to have the following structure or a variation thereof: (1) the identification of a problem, (2) the expectation that Jesus will remedy the problem, (3) the apparent frustration of this expectation, (4) the miracle itself, and (5) the aftermath. For example, in ch 2, the wedding at Cana, Jesus' mother points out to Jesus that the wine has run out, clearly expecting him to do something about this; he apparently rebukes her (2.4), saying that his hour has not yet come. He then performs the miracle, the steward marvels, and the narrator explains that "Jesus did this, the first of his signs, in Cana of Galilee, and revealed his glory; and his disciples believed in him" (2.11). The purpose of this pattern seems to be to convey to the audience that Jesus' miracles are not intended to demonstrate his superhuman abilities but to testify to his identity as the Son of God. This aspect of the Johannine signs calls to mind Ex 10.2, in which the LORD tells Moses that the signs that he has done among the Egyptians were in order that the people might know that "I am the LORD."

A second example of close narrative patterning can be found in the stories that narrate the call of the disciples. In almost every case, it is someone who already believes that testifies to others and brings them to encounter Jesus, after which they believe as well. For example, John the Baptist tells two of his disciples to follow Jesus. One of them, Andrew, tells his brother Simon Peter, who then comes to Jesus and becomes a disciple himself (1.42). Jesus finds Philip, who tells Nathanael, who comes to encounter Jesus and becomes a disciple (1.49). The Samaritan woman meets Jesus by the well and testifies to her Samaritan community; they invite Jesus to stay with them, after which they become believers (4.41–42). The purpose of this pattern becomes clear at the end of the Gospel, when Thomas refuses to believe the disciples' testimony that Jesus has risen from the dead unless he can see for himself. Jesus returns and invites him to see and touch him, but he offers a gentle rebuke: "Have you believed because you have seen me? Blessed are those who have not seen and yet have come to believe" (20.29). Here the Johannine Jesus is clearly addressing later readers who will not have the capacity to see Jesus directly but will believe in any case. The Gospel's concluding statement (20.30–31) indicates that for later generations, it is the Gospel of John itself that will be a basis for faith, the means through which believers can encounter Jesus.

Adele Reinhartz

1 In the beginning was the Word, and the Word was with God, and the Word was God. [2] He was in the beginning with God. [3] All things came into being through him, and without him not one thing came into being. What has come into being [4] in him

1.1–18: Prologue. In contrast to Matthew and Luke, John does not include an infancy narrative describing Jesus' conception and birth; neither Joseph nor Mary figures in the account of Jesus' human origins. Rather, Jesus' arrival in the world is described in cosmological terms, and his role as God's son emphasized. **1–3:** *In the beginning*, echoing the opening of Genesis. *The Word* signifies God's power of creation and redemption; as a means of expression, reason (or truth), and grace it is identified with Jesus (vv. 9,14,17). It suggests Wisdom terminology (Ps 33.6; Prov 8.7–30; Wis 9.1,9; 18.15; Sir 24.9; 43.26). For the Alexandrian Jewish philosopher Philo, God's Logos was the very first fruit of creation; *Leg. all.* 3.175. In the Wisdom of Ben Sirach, Wisdom is strongly associated and even identified with the divine commandment, that is, the Torah (Sir 24.22–23), This identification persists well into the rabbinic period, as attested by its presence in *Gen. Rab.* 1.10, probably redacted no earlier than the fifth century. See also the use of "memra" ("word") in the Aramaic Targumim to Genesis (see "John's Prologue as Midrash," p. 546). *With God*, as in Prov 8.22–31, "I [Wisdom] was there . . . I was beside him [the LORD]." **4:** *Life*, whose source is God (Gen 1.20–25); *light*, the first created thing (Gen 1.3); a frequent image for God or God's presence or favor (Isa 2.5; Ps 27.1; 36.9). Cf.

was life,[a] and the life was the light of all people. [5] The light shines in the darkness, and the darkness did not overcome it.

[6] There was a man sent from God, whose name was John. [7] He came as a witness to testify to the light, so that all might believe through him. [8] He himself was not the light, but he came to testify to the light. [9] The true light, which enlightens everyone, was coming into the world.[b]

[10] He was in the world, and the world came into being through him; yet the world did not know him. [11] He came to what was his own,[c] and his own people did not accept him. [12] But to all who received him, who believed in his name, he gave power to become children of God, [13] who were born, not of blood or of the will of the flesh or of the will of man, but of God.

[14] And the Word became flesh and lived among us, and we have seen his glory, the glory as of a father's only son,[d] full of grace and truth. [15] (John testified to him and cried out, "This was he of whom I said, 'He who comes after me ranks ahead of me because he was before me.'") [16] From his fullness we have all received, grace upon grace. [17] The law indeed was given through Moses; grace and truth came through Jesus Christ. [18] No one has ever seen God. It is God the only Son,[e] who is close to the Father's heart,[f] who has made him known.

[a] Or [3]*through him. And without him not one thing came into being that has come into being.* [4]*In him was life*

[b] Or *He was the true light that enlightens everyone coming into the world*

[c] Or *to his own home*

[d] Or *the Father's only Son*

[e] Other ancient authorities read *It is an only Son, God,* or *It is the only Son*

[f] Gk *bosom*

also Wis 7.26. **5:** Creation (Gen 1.2). The *light/darkness* contrast, a prominent theme in the Gospel of John, is evident also in the Dead Sea Scrolls, e.g., 1QS 3.13–4.26, but direct influence of the DSS on the Gospel is unlikely. **6–8:** These verses preview 1.19–34. *John* the Baptist is also mentioned by Josephus, *Ant.* 18.116–119. **10–12:** These verses summarize the basic plot of the Gospel, on both the historical and cosmological levels: Jesus' own people, the Jews, failed to accept him and indeed they led him to his death; those who did accept him become God's children and receive eternal life. *The world* (Gk "kosmos") is used in two senses, meaning both creation and humankind, or, more specifically, that portion of humankind that rejected Jesus (cf. 12.31; 16.11). **11:** *His own people* are the Jews (4.22; cf. Ex 19.5). **12–13:** Contrast between a biologically based covenant, such as that of the Jews, and a faith-based covenant, such as that the Gospel proposes (cf. 8.33–40). *Believed in his name*, gave him due honor. *Children of God*, contrast Deut 14.1, where the "children" are enjoined from following other religious practices than those given to them. **14:** *Word became flesh*, a paradoxical formulation since "flesh" is all that is perishable and "logos" is a divine quality that is eternal; cf. Isa 40.6–8, "All people [lit., 'flesh'] are grass . . . The grass withers . . . but the word of our God will stand forever." This point marks the "incarnation," the moment at which the Word becomes a human being. The idea that a divine being, "God's son," can simultaneously be human is seen as a major dividing line between Judaism and Christianity by many Jews and Christians today. It should be noted, however, that Jews in the Second Temple period believed in the existence of supernatural beings, such as angels, who could at times take human form (e.g., Raphael in the book of Tobit). This is not to say that Christ-confessors believed Jesus was human in form only (this was argued by the Docetists, a group labeled as heretical by the developing Christian church), but simply that the boundaries between human and divine were understood in a more porous and less absolute way at this time. *Lived among us*, the Gk means "tabernacled," an allusion to the Tabernacle that the Israelites constructed in the wilderness and the precursor of the Jerusalem Temple (e.g., Ex 25.9). There may also be a connection to the Heb "shekhinah", which in some texts, such as *Tg. Onq.* at Deut 12.5, was used as a technical term for God's presence among God's people. *Glory*, Gk "doxa" is the usual LXX equivalent of Heb "kavod," the visible manifestation of God's presence (e.g., Ex 16.10). **17–18:** Contrast between Jesus and Moses, and the superiority of the Gospel to the Torah (Ex 34.18). *Grace and truth*, both God's loving presence (Heb "ḥesed," "steadfast love," e.g., Ps 85.10) and God's firm faithfulness (Heb "'emet," "truth" that does not give way).

1.19–34: The testimony of John the Baptist. 19: *The Jews*, here refers to the Jerusalem authorities most closely associated with ritual purification. **20:** John the Baptist was revered by the Mandaeans, a little-known

[19] This is the testimony given by John when the Jews sent priests and Levites from Jerusalem to ask him, "Who are you?" [20] He confessed and did not deny it, but confessed, "I am not the Messiah."[a] [21] And they asked him, "What then? Are you Elijah?" He said, "I am not." "Are you the prophet?" He answered, "No." [22] Then they said to him, "Who are you? Let us have an answer for those who sent us. What do you say about yourself?" [23] He said,

"I am the voice of one crying out in the wilderness,
'Make straight the way of the Lord,'"

as the prophet Isaiah said.

[24] Now they had been sent from the Pharisees. [25] They asked him, "Why then are you baptizing if you are neither the Messiah,[a] nor Elijah, nor the prophet?" [26] John answered them, "I baptize with water. Among you stands one whom you do not know, [27] the one who is coming after me; I am not worthy to untie the thong of his sandal." [28] This took place in Bethany across the Jordan where John was baptizing.

[29] The next day he saw Jesus coming toward him and declared, "Here is the Lamb of God who takes away the sin of the world! [30] This is he of whom I said, 'After me comes a man who ranks ahead of me because he was before me.' [31] I myself did not know him; but I came baptizing with water for this reason, that he might be revealed to Israel." [32] And John testified, "I saw the Spirit descending from heaven like a dove, and it remained on him. [33] I myself did not know him, but the one who sent me to baptize with water said to me, 'He on whom you see the Spirit descend and remain is the one who baptizes with the Holy Spirit.' [34] And I myself have seen and have testified that this is the Son of God."[b]

[a] Or *the Christ*
[b] Other ancient authorities read *is God's chosen one*

monotheistic group, adherents of which still exist today, mostly in Iraq. **21:** *Elijah* (2 Kings 2.11) and *the prophet* were believed to be the forerunners of the messiah (Mal 4.5 [3.23 in MT]). Elijah's ascent to heaven in a fiery chariot (1 Kings 2.11) led to speculation that he was still alive and would return before the messianic age. Elijah's role as a forerunner of the messiah is indicated in a number of rabbinic stories, e.g., *b. Sanh.* 98a; "the prophet" may be a reference to the expectation that the messiah would be a "prophet like Moses" (Deut 18.15–18; see also 1 Macc 4.46; 14.41). The expectation of a prophet-messiah is also present in the DSS (e.g., 1QS 9.11). The inclusion of this interrogation may be part of a polemic against those who viewed John the Baptist as a messianic figure. **23:** The quotation from Isa 40.3 reflects the Septuagint (LXX) version, in which "in the wilderness" modifies "voice," rather than the Hebrew (MT) version, in which the phrase modifies "way of the Lord." **24:** *Pharisees* were a group with spiritual authority. Rabbinic tradition, e.g., *m. Avot* 1.1, later portrays the Pharisees as the forerunners of the rabbis who developed Jewish law and practice after the destruction of the Temple. It is not apparent, however, that the author of this Gospel is aware of this tradition, as it uses the terms Pharisees and Jews interchangeably (1.19; 7.32,45; 11.45–57; 18.3,12). **25:** Cleansing with water was an important means of ritual purification in biblical law (e.g., Ex 19.10; Lev 14.8). Although the language of purity and impurity is occasionally used in the discussion of moral issues, there are no sources that unambiguously point to the use of immersion in the "cleansing" from sin. **28:** *Bethany*, this Bethany is a town in the Transjordan, of which no trace now remains, and not the Judean town mentioned in Jn 11.18. While the name is open to a symbolic interpretation (lit., "house of response"), place names in John are generally factual even if they take on a degree of symbolic significance, e.g., Galilee as the place where Jesus is accepted, and Judea as the place where he is rejected (cf. Jn 4.1–2). **29:** *Lamb*, a possible allusion to the sacrificial Passover lamb (Ex 12). **31:** *Israel* refers to the people Israel, a positive designation in John meaning the "children of God" who know God through his son (see 1.18). **32:** In contrast to the Synoptic Gospels, John does not describe Jesus' actual baptism. The simile connecting *Spirit* and *dove* is present in all of the canonical Gospels. The positive symbolism attached to the dove is present in the Hebrew Bible (e.g., Gen 8; Ps 68.13; Song 2.14; Isa 60.8) though not the direct association of dove and the Spirit of God. **34:** *Son of God*, Jesus is seen as God's Son who resembles his father, does his will, and serves as his agent (e.g., 6.38). Although some have seen John's use of this title against the background of non-Jewish Greek and Roman usage, it is likely that it has its origins in the Hebrew Bible and postbiblical literature, in which "son of God" can refer to Israel and the righteous more generally (e.g., Ex 4.22–23; Hos 11.1; Wis 2.13; 18.13; Sir 4.10; *Pss. Sol.* 13.9; *Jub.* 1.224–25).

[35] The next day John again was standing with two of his disciples, [36] and as he watched Jesus walk by, he exclaimed, "Look, here is the Lamb of God!" [37] The two disciples heard him say this, and they followed Jesus. [38] When Jesus turned and saw them following, he said to them, "What are you looking for?" They said to him, "Rabbi" (which translated means Teacher), "where are you staying?" [39] He said to them, "Come and see." They came and saw where he was staying, and they remained with him that day. It was about four o'clock in the afternoon. [40] One of the two who heard John speak and followed him was Andrew, Simon Peter's brother. [41] He first found his brother Simon and said to him, "We have found the Messiah" (which is translated Anointed[a]). [42] He brought Simon[b] to Jesus, who looked at him and said, "You are Simon son of John. You are to be called Cephas" (which is translated Peter[c]).

[43] The next day Jesus decided to go to Galilee. He found Philip and said to him, "Follow me." [44] Now Philip was from Bethsaida, the city of Andrew and Peter. [45] Philip found Nathanael and said to him, "We have found him about whom Moses in the law and also the prophets wrote, Jesus son of Joseph from Nazareth." [46] Nathanael said to him, "Can anything good come out of Nazareth?" Philip said to him, "Come and see." [47] When Jesus saw Nathanael coming toward him, he said of him, "Here is truly an Israelite in whom there is no deceit!" [48] Nathanael asked him, "Where did you get to know me?" Jesus answered, "I saw you under the fig tree before Philip called you." [49] Nathanael replied, "Rabbi, you are the Son of God! You are the King of Israel!" [50] Jesus answered, "Do you believe because I told you that I saw you under the fig tree? You will see greater things than these." [51] And he said

[a] Or *Christ*
[b] Gk *him*
[c] From the word for *rock* in Aramaic (*kepha*) and Greek (*petra*), respectively

1.35–51: Call of the disciples. 37: One disciple is Andrew (v. 40); the anonymous other is sometimes identified as the beloved disciple. **38:** *Rabbi,* originally meaning "my master," became at an uncertain date the term for one qualified to pronounce on matters of Jewish law and practice. The Hebrew root of *rabbi* is "rav," meaning "great" in biblical Hebrew, often a title denoting reverence. In Second Temple Judaism it did not refer to a religious functionary or clergyperson but primarily to a person whose authority was accepted by the speaker. *Teacher* is therefore not a literal translation but captures the general sense of the term. In Hebrew sources it does not appear before the Mishnah, though the Gospels of Matthew (e.g., 26.25), Mark (e.g., 9.5), and John use the term to refer to Jesus; Mt 3.7–8 refers more generically to "rabbis" and may be the earliest evidence of its usage to denote a classification of learned individuals. **41:** *Messiah* is the Greek transliteration of the Aramaic, "meshiḥa" ("the anointed one"); the Gk translation is "Christos" (Christ). This term recurs in 4.25 and 4.29 but nowhere else in the NT. **42:** *Cephas* means "rock" in Aramaic; this disciple is also called Peter (Gk "Petros," also "rock"); cf. Mt 16.18. **43:** The narrative implies that Jesus was still in Bethany (cf. 1.28) **44:** *Bethsaida,* close to the Sea of Galilee. Although the Gospel implies that Bethsaida is in Galilee, it was in fact in Gaulanitis, across the border from Herod's Galilee, in the territory controlled by Philip. **45:** Philip's words to Nathanael imply that he, and others, were waiting or searching for a messiah who would fulfill the Torah and prophecies in the scriptures. The reference may be to the "prophet like Moses" described in Deut 18.15–18, the son of man ("one like a human being," Dan 7.13; 8.17), and/or Elijah (Mal 4.5). For *Jesus* as the *son of Joseph,* see also Jn 6.42 and Mt 1.23. This may reflect a historical detail as it is possible that Jesus was known as Joseph's son within the Jewish community in which he lived. Despite the prominence of the "Son of God" title, and Jesus' frequent references to himself as the Son, the Gospel does not refer or allude to the idea that Jesus' mother was a virgin. **46:** *Nazareth,* approximately 15 mi (26 km) west of the Sea of Galilee. **47:** *Israelite,* the Israelite Nathanael recognizes Jesus as *the King of Israel* (v. 49). *No deceit,* an allusion to Jacob, also known as Israel (Gen 32.28–29) who deceitfully supplanted his twin brother, Esau, in receiving his father Isaac's blessing (Gen 27.35) **48:** *Fig tree,* associated with abundance, as well as with the eschaton; "gathering figs" was an expression that in later sources means "studying," apparently because the tree of knowledge in Gen 3 was believed to be a fig tree (*b. Ber.* 40a). **49:** *Son of God . . . King of Israel,* treated as synonymous expressions; Ps 2.6–7 uses adoption language in relating the king to God. **51:** *Very truly,* lit., "amen, amen" (Heb "amen," "it is so," "it is true"). A formula used for emphasis (cf. 3.3,5,11; 5.19,24ff.; 6.26,32,47,53; 8.34,51,58; 10.1,7; 12.24; 13.16,20ff.,38; 14.12; 16.20,23; 21.18). *Son of Man,*

to him, "Very truly, I tell you,[a] you will see heaven opened and the angels of God ascending and descending upon the Son of Man."

2 On the third day there was a wedding in Cana of Galilee, and the mother of Jesus was there. [2] Jesus and his disciples had also been invited to the wedding. [3] When the wine gave out, the mother of Jesus said to him, "They have no wine." [4] And Jesus said to her, "Woman, what concern is that to you and to me? My hour has not yet come." [5] His mother said to the servants, "Do whatever he tells you." [6] Now standing there were six stone water jars for the Jewish rites of purification, each holding twenty or thirty gallons. [7] Jesus said to them, "Fill the jars with water." And they filled them up to the brim. [8] He said to them, "Now draw some out, and take it to the chief steward." So they took it. [9] When the steward tasted the water that had become wine, and did not know where it came from (though the servants who had drawn the water knew), the steward called the bridegroom [10] and said to him, "Everyone serves the good wine first, and then the inferior wine after the guests have become drunk. But you have kept the good wine until now." [11] Jesus did this, the first of his signs, in Cana of Galilee, and revealed his glory; and his disciples believed in him.

[12] After this he went down to Capernaum with his mother, his brothers, and his disciples; and they remained there a few days.

[13] The Passover of the Jews was near, and Jesus went up to Jerusalem. [14] In the temple he found people selling cattle, sheep, and doves, and the money changers seated at their tables. [15] Making a whip of cords, he drove all of them out of the temple, both the sheep and the cattle. He also poured out the coins of the money changers and overturned their tables. [16] He told those who were selling the doves, "Take these things out of here! Stop making my Father's house a marketplace!" [17] His disciples remembered that it was written, "Zeal for your house will consume me." [18] The Jews then said to him, "What sign can you show us for doing this?" [19] Jesus answered them, "Destroy this temple,

[a] Both instances of the Greek word for *you* in this verse are plural

"Bar Enosh" in Aramaic (cf. Dan 7.13), a cosmic messianic figure associated strongly with apocalyptic eschatology (views of the end of times as including a violent battle). *Angels . . . ascending and descending,* an allusion to Jacob's dream (Gen 28.12), implying that Jesus is the ladder connecting heaven and earth.

2.1–12: Jesus' first sign: wedding at Cana. 1: *Third day* may foreshadow the resurrection, just as the wedding may allude to the messianic banquet, the feast that will celebrate the inauguration of God's rule. *Cana,* village in the Galilee, about 9 mi (15 km) north of Nazareth. *Mother of Jesus,* Jesus' mother is never mentioned by name in this Gospel. **3:** Jesus' mother expects him to remedy the situation. **4:** *Woman,* an unusual address to one's mother, but used in this Gospel to introduce a revelation to a woman (cf. 4.21; 19.26; 20.13,15). *Hour,* the hour of Jesus' death and glorification. **6:** *Rites of purification,* ritual hand-washing that precedes the meal. This practice is later described in *b. Ber.* 53b; *b. Shabb.* 62b; its presence in John indicates that the ritual was already common in the first century. Since the jars needed to be filled (again), presumably the washing had already taken place. The size of the jars may indicate that there were many guests. **9:** *Bridegroom,* a double entendre referring to the bridegroom of the wedding and alluding to Jesus as the eschatological bridegroom (cf. 4.29). **11:** *First of his signs,* possible evidence for a "signs source" underlying the narrative (cf. 2.23; 3.2; 4.48,54; 6.14; 10.41; 12.18; 20.30). *Glory,* see 1.14n. **12:** *Capernaum,* a town on the northwestern shore of the Sea of Galilee. *Brothers,* see 7.3; 20.17; 21.23; Mk 6.3.

2.13–25: Jesus' sign of authority over the Temple (see Mt 21.17; Mk 11.15–19; Lk 9.45–48). In the other Gospels, this incident occurs at the end of Jesus' ministry; in John it is, in effect, his inaugural public appearance. **13:** *Passover,* the week-long spring festival celebrating the Exodus from Egypt and the barley harvest (Ex 12.1–18). Passover is closely associated with liberation from oppression and divine salvation, past and future. *Of the Jews,* a redundancy that may indicate the lack of acquaintance with Judaism on the part of at least some members of John's audience. **14:** Animals (unblemished and therefore acceptable for sacrifice) were sold at the Temple, and foreign currencies had to be exchanged for the official half-shekel for the Temple tax (Ex 30.11–16). **17:** Ps 69.9; see Zech 14.21; Mal 3.1. **18:** *The Jews,* here, Temple authorities. *What sign . . . ,* may be a challenge to Jesus' authority. **19:** *Destroy this temple . . . ,* alludes to the tradition of Temple critique (4.21; see Jer 7.1–15; Ezek 10.18–19; Acts

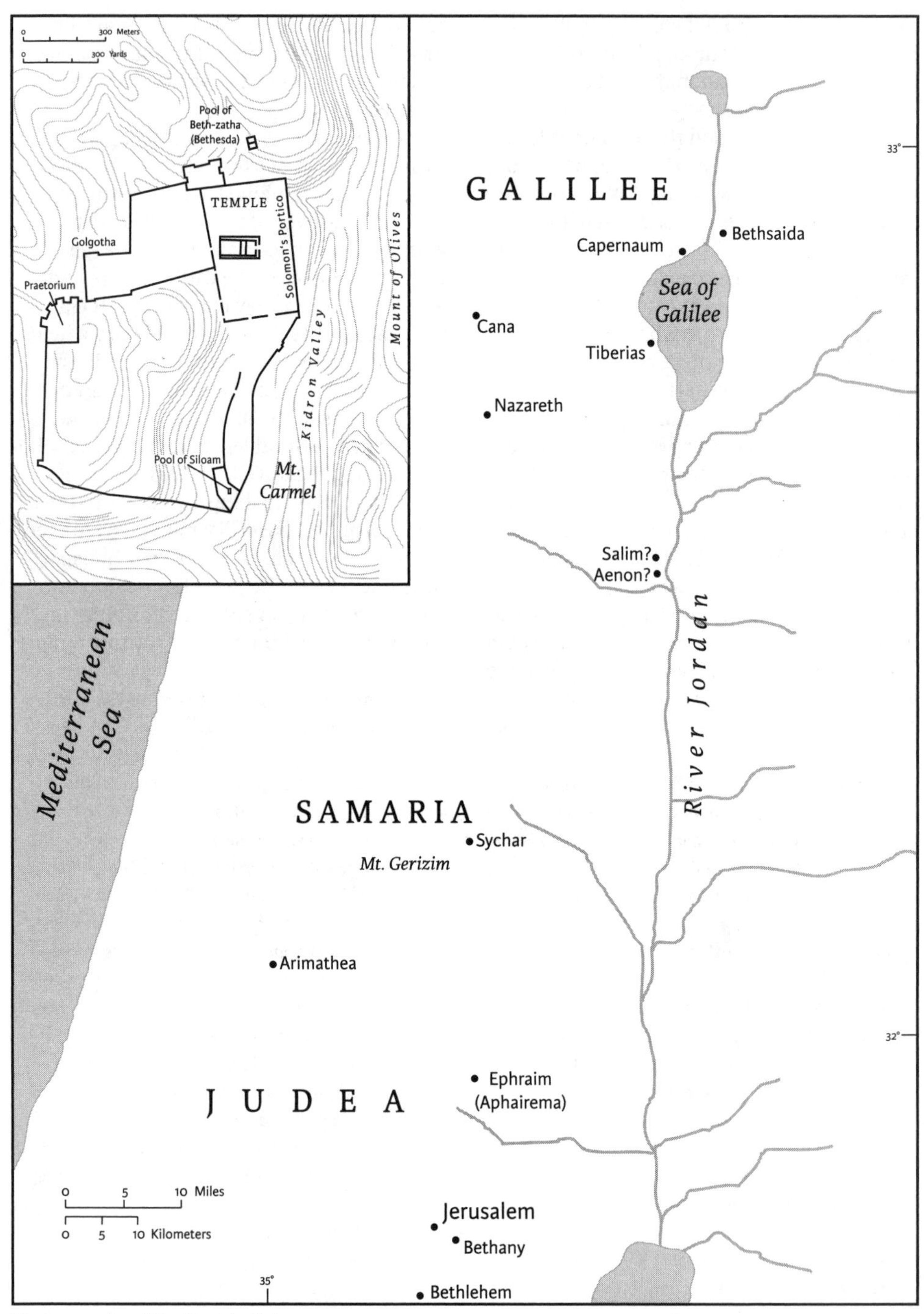

The geography of the Gospel of John.

and in three days I will raise it up." [20] The Jews then said, "This temple has been under construction for forty-six years, and will you raise it up in three days?" [21] But he was speaking of the temple of his body. [22] After he was raised from the dead, his disciples remembered that he had said this; and they believed the scripture and the word that Jesus had spoken.

[23] When he was in Jerusalem during the Passover festival, many believed in his name because they saw the signs that he was doing. [24] But Jesus on his part would not entrust himself to them, because he knew all people [25] and needed no one to testify about anyone; for he himself knew what was in everyone.

3 Now there was a Pharisee named Nicodemus, a leader of the Jews. [2] He came to Jesus[a] by night and said to him, "Rabbi, we know that you are a teacher who has come from God; for no one can do these signs that you do apart from the presence of God." [3] Jesus answered him, "Very truly, I tell you, no one can see the kingdom of God without being born from above."[b] [4] Nicodemus said to him, "How can anyone be born after having grown old? Can one enter a second time into the mother's womb and be born?" [5] Jesus answered, "Very truly, I tell you, no one can enter the kingdom of God without being born of water and Spirit. [6] What is born of the flesh is flesh, and what is born of the Spirit is spirit.[c] [7] Do not be astonished that I said to you, 'You[d] must be born from above.'[e] [8] The wind[c] blows where it chooses, and you hear the sound of it, but you do not know where it comes from or where it goes. So it is with everyone who is born of the Spirit." [9] Nicodemus said to him, "How can these things be?" [10] Jesus answered him, "Are you a teacher of Israel, and yet you do not understand these things?

[11] "Very truly, I tell you, we speak of what we know and testify to what we have seen; yet you[f] do not receive our testimony. [12] If I have told you about earthly things and you do not believe, how can you believe if I tell

a Gk *him*
b Or *born anew*
c The same Greek word means both *wind* and *spirit*
d The Greek word for *you* here is plural
e Or *anew*
f The Greek word for *you* here and in verse 12 is plural

7.48) and continues the theme of Jesus' authority over the Temple. **20:** *Forty-six years,* according to Josephus, (*Ant.* 15.11.1) construction began in the eighteenth year of the rule of Herod the Great (20/19 BCE) and concluded under Herod Agrippa II in 64 CE. **22:** *The word,* Jesus' own prophecies are treated as of equal authority to scripture. **23:** *His name,* the expression of his true being and power. **24:** *Entrust himself,* rely upon others to vouch for his authority. **25:** *Needed no one to testify,* forensic (courtroom) language evokes the theme of God as judge. *He himself knew,* Jesus' foreknowledge appears first with Nathanael (1.48; cf. 4.17–18; 6.70).

3.1–21: Nicodemus. 1: *Nicodemus's* leadership role is not specified. The Pharisees are normally counted among Jesus' opponents (but see also 12.42). "Nicodemus" is a Greek name that was apparently used among Jews as "Naqdimon" (*b. Ta'an.* 20a). The Sanhedrin, the governing body, was responsible primarily for the internal and autonomous affairs of the Jewish people. Membership included Sadducees and Pharisees. **2:** *By night,* secretly. Night and darkness are associated with those—such as the Jewish authorities—who are spiritually blind (cf. 9.39–41). **3:** *Very truly,* see 1.51n. *Kingdom of God,* used by John only in 3.3,5, but prominent in the other Gospels, referring to the divine domain that will arise at some future point in this world (Mk 9.1) or in some other place in which the righteous will dwell (Lk 13.29), or an altered state of existence in the here and now (Lk 17.21). The Hebrew term, "malkut shamayim" (Dan 4.3; 1 Chr 29.10–12) implies the divine reign in this world. *Born from above,* "born anew"; the origin of the term "born-again Christian." **4:** Puns and double entendres are a frequent literary device in John, as they are also in the Hebrew Bible (e.g., Dan 5.25–28), classical Greek literature (e.g., Ovid, *Metam.*); and rabbinic literature (e.g., *Lam. Rab.* 1.1) **5:** *Water and spirit,* suggesting that baptism is the act of rebirth that allows one to enter or see (v. 3) the kingdom. The combination may suggest both the baptismal act and the gift of the Spirit (Acts 1.5). **6:** Spiritual birth contrasted with biological birth; cf. 8.12–59 that dismisses genealogy as the basis for being a child of God. **8:** *Wind,* Gk "pneuma," like Heb "ruaḥ," can mean wind, breath, or spirit. Each is unpredictable and cannot be seen or grasped but is essential for life and can express great power. **11:** Jesus views Nicodemus as a representative of his opponents. **13:** Allusions to

you about heavenly things? [13] No one has ascended into heaven except the one who descended from heaven, the Son of Man.[a] [14] And just as Moses lifted up the serpent in the wilderness, so must the Son of Man be lifted up, [15] that whoever believes in him may have eternal life.[b]

[16] "For God so loved the world that he gave his only Son, so that everyone who believes in him may not perish but may have eternal life.

[17] "Indeed, God did not send the Son into the world to condemn the world, but in order that the world might be saved through him. [18] Those who believe in him are not condemned; but those who do not believe are condemned already, because they have not believed in the name of the only Son of God. [19] And this is the judgment, that the light has come into the world, and people loved darkness rather than light because their deeds were evil. [20] For all who do evil hate the light and do not come to the light, so that their deeds may not be exposed. [21] But those who do what is true come to the light, so that it may be clearly seen that their deeds have been done in God."[b]

[22] After this Jesus and his disciples went into the Judean countryside, and he spent some time there with them and baptized. [23] John also was baptizing at Aenon near Salim because water was abundant there; and people kept coming and were being baptized [24]—John, of course, had not yet been thrown into prison.

[25] Now a discussion about purification arose between John's disciples and a Jew.[c] [26] They came to John and said to him, "Rabbi, the one who was with you across the Jordan, to whom you testified, here he is baptizing, and all are going to him." [27] John answered, "No one can receive anything except what has been given from heaven. [28] You yourselves are my witnesses that I said, 'I am not the Messiah,[d] but I have been sent ahead of him.' [29] He who has the bride is the bridegroom. The friend of the bridegroom, who stands and hears him, rejoices greatly at the bridegroom's voice. For this reason my joy

a Other ancient authorities add *who is in heaven*
b Some interpreters hold that the quotation concludes with verse 15
c Other ancient authorities read *the Jews*
d Or *the Christ*

1.51 and Gen 28 (Jacob's ladder). The statement seems to ignore Enoch (Gen 5.22,24) and Elijah (2 Kings 2.11), both of whom were taken up to heaven instead of undergoing death; *ascended* may imply some agency on the part of the *Son of Man*. **14:** Jesus is here described as superior to Moses, who held up the bronze serpent to save Israel from a plague of snakes (Num 21.4–9; cf. 2 Kings 18.4, in which King Hezekiah demolishes the bronze serpent). **16–21:** Because the Greek manuscripts do not include punctuation, it is not always easy to identify the speaker in these long discourses. These verses are often attributed to the narrator rather than Jesus. **16:** Jesus is God's son; Jesus' death testifies to God's love for the world, and is necessary for salvation. *Perish . . . eternal life*, the contrast implies that eternal life is not intrinsic to persons but is given to them, or withheld from them, according to their relationship to the Son or to God. **19–20:** Here *evil* is not a moral category but a theological one, referring to the failure to believe.

3.22–36: Baptizing. 22–23: *Aenon* comes from the Aramaic plural of "spring"; *Salim* comes from the Semitic root for "peace." The exact sites are uncertain, as tradition has located this event in Transjordan, in the northern Jordan Valley, and in Samaria. In contrast to the Synoptic Gospels, in which Jesus' main ministry takes place after John's imprisonment, this passage suggests that the missions of John and Jesus overlapped in time. The Synoptics do not mention that Jesus baptized. **24:** An allusion to John's imprisonment, which the Gospel does not recount (cf. Mk 6.14–29). **25:** *Purification*, implying that baptism is related to Jewish practices of dealing with ritual purity (see e.g., Lev 14.8), rather than the "Christian" baptism as such. **27–30:** *Receive . . . except what has been given*, a statement about authority, not a predetermination. John is the *friend* to the *bridegroom* Jesus. *Bridegroom* is a prophetic image of one who rejoices (Isa 62.5; Jer 16.9); in the other Gospels the bridegroom is the symbol of one who is to arrive, after which festivities can begin (Mt 25.1ff.) or the one in whose presence rejoicing takes place (Mt 9.15; Mk 2.9; Lk 5.34). It also (Rev 18.23) became the symbol of the messiah united with God's people at the wedding banquet celebrating the new age. This symbol, like the wedding at Cana, may be an allusion to the Jewish idea of the eschatological banquet, as a metaphor for the joy and abundance that will be experienced in the messianic age (Isa 25.6–8; Exek 34.17–30; see also 4Q521 2, II 5–13). The notion of a

has been fulfilled. [30] He must increase, but I must decrease."[a]

[31] The one who comes from above is above all; the one who is of the earth belongs to the earth and speaks about earthly things. The one who comes from heaven is above all. [32] He testifies to what he has seen and heard, yet no one accepts his testimony. [33] Whoever has accepted his testimony has certified[b] this, that God is true. [34] He whom God has sent speaks the words of God, for he gives the Spirit without measure. [35] The Father loves the Son and has placed all things in his hands. [36] Whoever believes in the Son has eternal life; whoever disobeys the Son will not see life, but must endure God's wrath.

4 Now when Jesus[c] learned that the Pharisees had heard, "Jesus is making and baptizing more disciples than John" [2]—although it was not Jesus himself but his disciples who baptized— [3] he left Judea and started back to Galilee. [4] But he had to go through Samaria. [5] So he came to a Samaritan city called Sychar, near the plot of ground that Jacob had given to his son Joseph. [6] Jacob's well was there, and Jesus, tired out by his journey, was sitting by the well. It was about noon.

[7] A Samaritan woman came to draw water, and Jesus said to her, "Give me a drink." [8] (His disciples had gone to the city to buy food.) [9] The Samaritan woman said to him, "How is it that you, a Jew, ask a drink of me, a woman of Samaria?" (Jews do not share things in common with Samaritans.)[d] [10] Jesus answered her, "If you knew the gift of God, and who it is that is saying to you, 'Give me a drink,' you would have asked him, and he would have given you living water." [11] The woman said to him, "Sir, you have no bucket, and the well is deep. Where do you get that living water? [12] Are you greater than our ancestor Jacob, who gave us the well, and with his sons and his flocks drank from it?" [13] Jesus said to her, "Everyone who drinks of this water will be thirsty again, [14] but those who drink of the water that I will give them will never be thirsty. The water that I will give will become in them a spring of water gushing up to eternal life." [15] The woman said to him, "Sir, give

a Some interpreters hold that the quotation continues through verse 36
b Gk *set a seal to*
c Other ancient authorities read *the Lord*
d Other ancient authorities lack this sentence

messianic banquet also occurs later, in rabbinic literature, e.g., *b. Sanh.* 96–99. John's acknowledgement that Jesus' movement must expand and his (John's) decrease may be a historical reminiscence of the development of these two groups and/or an element in the Gospel's polemic against the baptising group. **32–33:** *No one accepts . . . whoever has accepted,* a contradictory formulation, but intended presumably to convey that those who do not accept the testimony are doubting not just the one who testifies but also that God is *true* (trustworthy or faithful). **34–35:** *Spirit . . . all things in his hands,* the Son's authority from God includes the granting of God's spirit (see 3.5ff.). **36:** See 3.16n.

4.1–42: The Samaritan woman. 4: *Samaria,* between Judea and Galilee. Samaritans are descendants of two distinct groups: the remnant of the ten tribes associated with the Northern Kingdom of Israel who were not deported when the Northern Kingdom fell in 722 BCE, and foreign colonists from Babylonia and Media brought by the Assyrian conquerors of Samaria (cf. 2 Kings 17.24–41). Tension between the Samaritans and the Jews who returned from the Babylonian exile was created in part by the Samaritans' opposition to the rebuilding of the Temple (Ezra 4.6–24). Avoiding Samaria would have required going through the non-Jewish territory east of the Jordan River. **5:** *Sychar,* near Shechem; see Gen 33.19; 48.22; Josh 23.32. **6–8:** *Well,* a place where women gathered (see e.g., Gen 24, where Abraham's servant meets Rebekah at the spring of water); the overtones of an encounter between a man and a woman at a well are those of courtship. The fact that the woman is there at *noon* serves to contrast the woman favorably with Nicodemus, who first met Jesus at night (3.2). Jesus' thirst is mentioned again only in 19.28, at the crucifixion, also at noon. **9:** This passage suggests that in the view of the Gospel writer, Jews and Samaritans would not eat together. Whether this is due to the issue of purity or to other matters is not possible to determine. **10:** *Living water,* flowing water, as in a spring or river (Num 19.17) and refreshing (Jer 2.14; 17.13). **11:** Perhaps in a parallel with Nicodemus (3.4), the woman takes Jesus literally and therefore misunderstands him. **13:** *Everyone who drinks . . . ,* see Sir 24.21, in which Wisdom personified promises that those who taste wisdom will thirst for more. Continuous thirst

me this water, so that I may never be thirsty or have to keep coming here to draw water."

[16] Jesus said to her, "Go, call your husband, and come back." [17] The woman answered him, "I have no husband." Jesus said to her, "You are right in saying, 'I have no husband'; [18] for you have had five husbands, and the one you have now is not your husband. What you have said is true!" [19] The woman said to him, "Sir, I see that you are a prophet. [20] Our ancestors worshiped on this mountain, but you[a] say that the place where people must worship is in Jerusalem." [21] Jesus said to her, "Woman, believe me, the hour is coming when you will worship the Father neither on this mountain nor in Jerusalem. [22] You worship what you do not know; we worship what we know, for salvation is from the Jews. [23] But the hour is coming, and is now here, when the true worshipers will worship the Father in spirit and truth, for the Father seeks such as these to worship him. [24] God is spirit, and those who worship him must worship in spirit and truth." [25] The woman said to him, "I know that Messiah is coming" (who is called Christ). "When he comes, he will proclaim all things to us." [26] Jesus said to her, "I am he,[b] the one who is speaking to you."

[27] Just then his disciples came. They were astonished that he was speaking with a woman, but no one said, "What do you want?" or, "Why are you speaking with her?" [28] Then the woman left her water jar and went back to the city. She said to the people, [29] "Come and see a man who told me everything I have ever done! He cannot be the Messiah,[c] can he?" [30] They left the city and were on their way to him.

[31] Meanwhile the disciples were urging him, "Rabbi, eat something." [32] But he said to them, "I have food to eat that you do not know about." [33] So the disciples said to one another, "Surely no one has brought him something to eat?" [34] Jesus said to them, "My food is to do the will of him who sent me and to complete his work. [35] Do you not say, 'Four months more, then comes the harvest'? But I tell you, look around you, and see how the fields are ripe for harvesting. [36] The reaper is already receiving[d] wages and is gathering fruit for eternal life, so that sower and reaper may rejoice together. [37] For here the saying holds true, 'One sows and another reaps.' [38] I sent you to reap that for which you did not labor. Others have labored, and you have entered into their labor."

[39] Many Samaritans from that city believed in him because of the woman's testimony, "He told me everything I have ever done." [40] So when the Samaritans came to him, they asked him to stay with them; and he stayed there two days. [41] And many more believed

a The Greek word for *you* here and in verses 21 and 22 is plural

b Gk *I am*

c Or *the Christ*

d Or [35] . . . *the fields are already ripe for harvesting.* [36] *The reaper is receiving*

is contrasted with the fulfillment Jesus claims to provide. **19–20:** *Prophet*, not one who predicts the future but one who has God-given insight into a current situation. **21:** Jesus looks toward a time when worship will not be localized in either Jerusalem or Mount Gerizim, the Samaritans' holy place (see 2 Macc 6.2). **22:** The Gospel's only unequivocally positive statement about Jews. It may refer to the view that the people of Israel were God's special people with a special mission (see Deut 4.37; 7.6–7; 10.15; 1 Kings 3.8; Isa 44.1–2; 45.4; 65.9,15,22; Am 3.2). *From* may imply "arising among" or "originating in." **27:** The disciples' comment implies that they were not accustomed to seeing Jesus speak with a woman, even though Jesus does so in their presence on other occasions (e.g., ch 11). One might have expected them to be surprised that he is speaking with a Samaritan woman specifically (cf. 4.9), but this does not seem to be a particular concern. Some Second Temple and rabbinic texts warn against speaking with a woman (Sir 9.1–9; *m. Avot* 1.5), but it is obvious that men, including teachers, did so (for rabbinic texts, see, e.g., *b. Kelim* 1.8,9 and the Beruriah traditions). **29:** Here the Samaritan woman is depicted as a preacher, one who brings others to meet Jesus, just as Andrew and Philip do in 1.41,45. **35:** Apparently a proverbial saying; see v. 37. Harvest imagery is associated with the eschatological era in numerous biblical texts such as Gen 24.12; Ps 144.13. **36:** *Wages*, the harvest of believers; cf. Mt 9.37–38. **37–38:** *Sows . . . reaps*, ordinarily those who sow and those who reap are the same, but here the reapers (perhaps those who are spreading the gospel) are, like the Israelites in Deut 6.10–11, benefiting from the labors of those who have gone before, or whom they have displaced. **39–42:** Like Andrew and Philip

because of his word. [42] They said to the woman, "It is no longer because of what you said that we believe, for we have heard for ourselves, and we know that this is truly the Savior of the world."

[43] When the two days were over, he went from that place to Galilee [44] (for Jesus himself had testified that a prophet has no honor in the prophet's own country). [45] When he came to Galilee, the Galileans welcomed him, since they had seen all that he had done in Jerusalem at the festival; for they too had gone to the festival.

[46] Then he came again to Cana in Galilee where he had changed the water into wine. Now there was a royal official whose son lay ill in Capernaum. [47] When he heard that Jesus had come from Judea to Galilee, he went and begged him to come down and heal his son, for he was at the point of death. [48] Then Jesus said to him, "Unless you[a] see signs and wonders you will not believe." [49] The official said to him, "Sir, come down before my little boy dies." [50] Jesus said to him, "Go; your son will live." The man believed the word that Jesus spoke to him and started on his way. [51] As he was going down, his slaves met him and told him that his child was alive. [52] So he asked them the hour when he began to recover, and they said to him, "Yesterday at one in the afternoon the fever left him." [53] The father realized that this was the hour when Jesus had said to him, "Your son will live." So he himself believed, along with his whole household. [54] Now this was the second sign that Jesus did after coming from Judea to Galilee.

5 After this there was a festival of the Jews, and Jesus went up to Jerusalem.

[2] Now in Jerusalem by the Sheep Gate there is a pool, called in Hebrew[b] Beth-zatha,[c] which has five porticoes. [3] In these lay many invalids—blind, lame, and paralyzed.[d] [5] One man was there who had been ill for thirty-eight years. [6] When Jesus saw him lying there and knew that he had been there a long time, he said to him, "Do you want to be made well?" [7] The sick man answered him, "Sir, I have no one to put me into the pool when the water is stirred up; and while I am making my way, someone else steps down ahead of me."

[a] Both instances of the Greek word for *you* in this verse are plural

[b] That is, *Aramaic*

[c] Other ancient authorities read *Bethesda*, others *Bethsaida*

[d] Other ancient authorities add, wholly or in part, *waiting for the stirring of the water; [4]for an angel of the Lord went down at certain seasons into the pool, and stirred up the water; whoever stepped in first after the stirring of the water was made well from whatever disease that person had.*

in 1.41–45, the woman now acts as an apostle to her townspeople. **42:** *Savior* (Gk "soter," in LXX for Heb "yesha," basis for Yehoshua [Jesus]; see Mt 1.21), the word could mean "deliverer" (from enemies) and was a common title for rulers. The Samaritan term is "Taheb."

4.43–54: Second sign: healing of the official's son (Mt 8.5–13; Lk 7.1–10). **44:** See Mk 6.4; Lk 4.24. This proverb has close parallels in the Synoptic tradition (Mk 6.1–6; Mt 13.53–58; Lk 4.22–24) and *Gos. Thom.*, logion 31 (logion = a saying of Jesus). It is unlikely that John took it from any of these sources; rather, this proverb had circulated in different forms. In the Johannine context, it contrasts the generally warm reception that the Johannine Jesus receives in Galilee with the suspicion that his activities arouse in Judea. While this may be a historical reminiscence, it also serves a symbolic purpose, drawing attention to the opposition to Jesus largely among the Jewish authorities based in Judea, especially the Temple precinct. It is possible to read this as an ironic saying, in that for both groups, Galileans and Judeans alike, a faith based only on observing the signs is considered inadequate (cf. 2.23–25). **45:** *Galileans*, a geographical designation, but since they were at the festival in Jerusalem, it follows that they are Jews. **46:** *Cana*, see 2.1–11. *A royal official*, likely under the aegis of Herod Antipas, tetrarch of Galilee 4 BCE–39 CE. **48:** *You* is plural. *Signs and wonders*, if "signs" only produce awe and not faith, they have failed in their role. **50:** Biblical parallels to the healing of a son include 1 Kings 17.23 (Elijah) and 2 Kings 8.9 (Elisha).

5.1–47: Third sign: healing of the lame man. 1: *Festival of the Jews*, perhaps one of the three pilgrimage festivals, Passover, Weeks (Shavuot), or Tabernacles (Sukkot). **2:** *Sheep Gate* is a gate to the Temple precinct (cf. Neh 3.1). Remains of a second-century healing sanctuary and pool with five porticoes have been discovered

[8] Jesus said to him, "Stand up, take your mat and walk." [9] At once the man was made well, and he took up his mat and began to walk.

Now that day was a sabbath. [10] So the Jews said to the man who had been cured, "It is the sabbath; it is not lawful for you to carry your mat." [11] But he answered them, "The man who made me well said to me, 'Take up your mat and walk.'" [12] They asked him, "Who is the man who said to you, 'Take it up and walk'?" [13] Now the man who had been healed did not know who it was, for Jesus had disappeared in[a] the crowd that was there. [14] Later Jesus found him in the temple and said to him, "See, you have been made well! Do not sin any more, so that nothing worse happens to you." [15] The man went away and told the Jews that it was Jesus who had made him well. [16] Therefore the Jews started persecuting Jesus, because he was doing such things on the sabbath. [17] But Jesus answered them, "My Father is still working, and I also am working." [18] For this reason the Jews were seeking all the more to kill him, because he was not only breaking the sabbath, but was also calling God his own Father, thereby making himself equal to God.

[19] Jesus said to them, "Very truly, I tell you, the Son can do nothing on his own, but only what he sees the Father doing; for whatever the Father[b] does, the Son does likewise. [20] The Father loves the Son and shows him all that he himself is doing; and he will show him greater works than these, so that you will be astonished. [21] Indeed, just as the Father raises the dead and gives them life, so also the Son gives life to whomever he wishes. [22] The Father judges no one but has given all judgment to the Son, [23] so that all may honor the Son just as they honor the Father. Anyone who does not honor the Son does not honor the Father who sent him. [24] Very truly, I tell you, anyone who hears my word and believes him who sent me has eternal life, and does not come under judgment, but has passed from death to life.

[25] "Very truly, I tell you, the hour is coming, and is now here, when the dead will hear the voice of the Son of God, and those who hear will live. [26] For just as the Father has life in himself, so he has granted the Son also to have life in himself; [27] and he has given him authority to execute judgment, because he is the Son of Man. [28] Do not be astonished at this; for the hour is coming when all who are in their graves will hear his voice [29] and will come out—those who have done good, to the resurrection of life, and those who have done evil, to the resurrection of condemnation.

[30] "I can do nothing on my own. As I hear, I judge; and my judgment is just, because I seek to do not my own will but the will of him who sent me.

[a] Or *had left because of*
[b] Gk *that one*

near the church of St. Anne in Jerusalem. **8:** *Stand up*, in Mk 2.11, this is offered as proof of Jesus' authority to forgive sins. **9:** The healing story becomes an account of conflict over Sabbath observance, in which carrying any object outside the domain of one's household was prohibited (Jer 17.21–22). According to later rabbinic law, the healing of an acute, life-threatening illness or condition was permitted, even mandated, on the Sabbath, but the healing of a chronic illness was not, on the grounds that treatment could just as easily take place before or after the Sabbath (see *b. Yoma* 84b). The Johannine passage suggests that this law was in place, at least in the eyes of some, in the first century. **14:** Jesus implies that illness is punishment for sin; see 9.2–3 (on disease as punishment for specific sins, see Ex 4.11; Lev 26.16; Num 12.9–10; Deut 32.39; 2 Chr 7.13; 21.14–15). **16–17:** *Persecuting*, although no specific persecution is mentioned, use of the word (as in Mt 5.10 and Acts 9.4) calls to mind the persecution of the early Christian community. *Sabbath*, according to Gen 2.2–3, God rested on the seventh day of creation. Hellenistic Jewish speculation (Philo, *Cher.* 86–90; *Leg. All.* 1.5–6) conceded that God did not rest on subsequent Sabbaths, given that vegetation grew, children were born, and other natural processes continued. Jesus declares his filial relationship to and imitation of God as a creative force (cf. 1.1–4); there is no explicit statement in the Gospel that abrogates Jewish Sabbath observance (cf. Mk 2.28, "the Son of Man is lord even of the sabbath"). **18:** For Jesus' Jewish audience, this statement violated monotheism; see 10.30–33; Phil 2.6. **19:** This statement implies that Jesus' actions are like what *the Father does*, not in the sense of slavish imitation but rather acting within a specific context according to the will of God. **21:** An anticipatory statement (or perhaps anachronism) regarding the resurrection of Christians, but perhaps a reference to Jewish belief in resurrection; the idea that resurrection is God's act is an established one (Ezek 37.5).

[31] "If I testify about myself, my testimony is not true. [32] There is another who testifies on my behalf, and I know that his testimony to me is true. [33] You sent messengers to John, and he testified to the truth. [34] Not that I accept such human testimony, but I say these things so that you may be saved. [35] He was a burning and shining lamp, and you were willing to rejoice for a while in his light. [36] But I have a testimony greater than John's. The works that the Father has given me to complete, the very works that I am doing, testify on my behalf that the Father has sent me. [37] And the Father who sent me has himself testified on my behalf. You have never heard his voice or seen his form, [38] and you do not have his word abiding in you, because you do not believe him whom he has sent.

[39] "You search the scriptures because you think that in them you have eternal life; and it is they that testify on my behalf. [40] Yet you refuse to come to me to have life. [41] I do not accept glory from human beings. [42] But I know that you do not have the love of God in[a] you. [43] I have come in my Father's name, and you do not accept me; if another comes in his own name, you will accept him. [44] How can you believe when you accept glory from one another and do not seek the glory that comes from the one who alone is God? [45] Do not think that I will accuse you before the Father; your accuser is Moses, on whom you have set your hope. [46] If you believed Moses, you would believe me, for he wrote about me. [47] But if you do not believe what he wrote, how will you believe what I say?"

6 After this Jesus went to the other side of the Sea of Galilee, also called the Sea of Tiberias.[b] [2] A large crowd kept following him, because they saw the signs that he was doing for the sick. [3] Jesus went up the mountain and sat down there with his disciples. [4] Now the Passover, the festival of the Jews, was near. [5] When he looked up and saw a large crowd coming toward him, Jesus said to Philip, "Where are we to buy bread for these people to eat?" [6] He said this to test him, for he himself knew what he was going to do. [7] Philip answered him, "Six months' wages[c] would not buy enough bread for each of them to get a little." [8] One of his disciples, Andrew, Simon Peter's brother, said to him, [9] "There is a boy here who has five barley loaves and two fish. But what are they among so many people?" [10] Jesus said, "Make the people sit down." Now there was a great deal of grass in the place; so they[d] sat down, about five thousand in all. [11] Then Jesus took the loaves, and when he had given thanks, he distributed them

[a] Or *among*
[b] Gk *of Galilee of Tiberias*
[c] Gk *Two hundred denarii*; the denarius was the usual day's wage for a laborer
[d] Gk *the men*

24: A characteristic of this Gospel's presentation of ideas is that God's goals, as expressed in Jesus' ministry, have already been accomplished (a position known as "realized eschatology," meaning that the conditions of the "last days" [Gk "eschata"] are already present ["realized"]). **25–30:** Jesus' voice reaches the realm of the dead who will be called to final judgment (see 11.1–44; cf. Dan 12.1–3; 1 Thess 4.13–18). **31–47:** Deut 17.6 specifies that in capital cases, two or three witnesses are required. Continuing the juridical motif, Jesus acts as his own lawyer and calls John the Baptist (v. 33), his works and God's works (v. 36), God (v. 37), and the scriptures (vv. 39–47) as witnesses. Thereby he accuses his Jewish opponents of misunderstanding their scriptures and alienating God. **41:** *Accept glory*, rely on God for authority.

6.1–71: Fourth sign: feeding of the multitudes and bread of life discourse. 6.1–15: The five thousand; see Mt 14.13–21; Mk 16.32–44; Lk 9.10–17. **1:** *The other side*, the eastern shore of the Sea of Galilee. **3:** *Up the mountain*, as in the discourse in Mt 5–7. Speaking from the side of a hill was a way to reach more hearers; a mountain was also a place in which to seek God's word (as did Moses, Ex 19.3; Elijah, 1 Kings 19.11). **4:** In contrast to his usual practice, Jesus does not go on pilgrimage to Jerusalem but stays in the Galilee, where others flock to him instead of to the Temple (cf. 4.4,21–23). This is a fulfillment of his prophecy to the Samaritan woman in 4.21 and may reflect a postdestruction (70 CE) perspective in which worship in the Temple is no longer possible, and perhaps, from John's point of view, no longer necessary. **6:** *Test*, presumably their faith in Jesus' ability. **9:** *Barley*, grain harvested at Passover. **11:** Jesus thanks God, following Jewish practice ("birchat ha-mason," "blessing [or benediction] for nourishment," from Deut 8.10; *b. Ber.* 35a). Gk "eucharistein,"—"giving thanks"—may allude to the Eucharist, the Lord's Supper (bread and wine that represent Jesus' body and blood; Mk 14.22–25; 1 Cor

to those who were seated; so also the fish, as much as they wanted. [12] When they were satisfied, he told his disciples, "Gather up the fragments left over, so that nothing may be lost." [13] So they gathered them up, and from the fragments of the five barley loaves, left by those who had eaten, they filled twelve baskets. [14] When the people saw the sign that he had done, they began to say, "This is indeed the prophet who is to come into the world."

[15] When Jesus realized that they were about to come and take him by force to make him king, he withdrew again to the mountain by himself.

[16] When evening came, his disciples went down to the sea, [17] got into a boat, and started across the sea to Capernaum. It was now dark, and Jesus had not yet come to them. [18] The sea became rough because a strong wind was blowing. [19] When they had rowed about three or four miles,[a] they saw Jesus walking on the sea and coming near the boat, and they were terrified. [20] But he said to them, "It is I;[b] do not be afraid." [21] Then they wanted to take him into the boat, and immediately the boat reached the land toward which they were going.

[22] The next day the crowd that had stayed on the other side of the sea saw that there had been only one boat there. They also saw that Jesus had not got into the boat with his disciples, but that his disciples had gone away alone. [23] Then some boats from Tiberias came near the place where they had eaten the bread after the Lord had given thanks.[c] [24] So when the crowd saw that neither Jesus nor his disciples were there, they themselves got into the boats and went to Capernaum looking for Jesus.

[25] When they found him on the other side of the sea, they said to him, "Rabbi, when did you come here?" [26] Jesus answered them, "Very truly, I tell you, you are looking for me, not because you saw signs, but because you ate your fill of the loaves. [27] Do not work for the food that perishes, but for the food that endures for eternal life, which the Son of Man will give you. For it is on him that God the Father has set his seal." [28] Then they said to him, "What must we do to perform the works of God?" [29] Jesus answered them, "This is the work of God, that you believe in him whom he has sent." [30] So they said to him, "What sign are you going to give us then, so that we may see it and believe you? What work are you performing? [31] Our ancestors ate the manna in the wilderness; as it is written, 'He gave them bread from heaven to eat.'" [32] Then Jesus said to them, "Very truly, I tell you, it was not Moses who gave you the bread from heaven, but it is my Father who gives you the true bread from heaven. [33] For the bread of God is that which[d] comes down from heaven and gives life to the world." [34] They said to him, "Sir, give us this bread always."

[35] Jesus said to them, "I am the bread of life. Whoever comes to me will never be hungry, and whoever believes in me will never be thirsty. [36] But I said to you that you have seen me and yet do not believe. [37] Everything that

[a] Gk *about twenty-five or thirty stadia*
[b] Gk *I am*
[c] Other ancient authorities lack *after the Lord had given thanks*
[d] Or *he who*

11.23–26). **12–13:** *Gather up the fragments*, see Mk 6.43. The Hebrews during the Exodus and wilderness wanderings were fed by manna that they gathered, including gathering enough for two days to avoid work on the Sabbath (Ex 16.14–26). *Twelve baskets*, perhaps a correspondence with the number of tribes of Israel, or the number of Jesus' apostles, thereby signifying God's people. **15:** The risk in being made king by popular acclaim, rather than as a Roman vassal, was that the Romans would regard such an act as treasonous and would execute the would-be ruler. **16–21:** *Walking* on water demonstrates power over the natural world (cf. Mt 14.22; Mk 6.45–51). Similarly, Elisha makes an ax head float (2 Kings 6.4–7). God is the one who calms waves (Ps 89.9).

6.22–71: The bread of life discourse. The imagery of the eucharistic body and blood is extended in this section. **23:** *The Lord had given thanks*, this phrase may not be original (see translators' note *c*). Calling Jesus *Lord* here is anachronistic. **27:** *Perishes . . . endures*, manna perished after one night; in contrast to God's provision of manna at the time of Moses, *eternal life* can only result from *the bread of life* (v. 35), Jesus himself. *Seal*, a symbol of authority (see Rev 5.2). **28–29:** *Works of God . . . believe in him whom [God] has sent*: the contrast is between "working" for food (v. 27) and participating in God's life (v. 33). **31:** *Manna* (Ex 16.4,15; Num 11.8; Ps 78.24 [quoted]; 105.40). Like Nicodemus and the Samaritan woman, the crowds misunderstand Jesus' meaning (cf.

the Father gives me will come to me, and anyone who comes to me I will never drive away; [38] for I have come down from heaven, not to do my own will, but the will of him who sent me. [39] And this is the will of him who sent me, that I should lose nothing of all that he has given me, but raise it up on the last day. [40] This is indeed the will of my Father, that all who see the Son and believe in him may have eternal life; and I will raise them up on the last day."

[41] Then the Jews began to complain about him because he said, "I am the bread that came down from heaven." [42] They were saying, "Is not this Jesus, the son of Joseph, whose father and mother we know? How can he now say, 'I have come down from heaven'?" [43] Jesus answered them, "Do not complain among yourselves. [44] No one can come to me unless drawn by the Father who sent me; and I will raise that person up on the last day. [45] It is written in the prophets, 'And they shall all be taught by God.' Everyone who has heard and learned from the Father comes to me. [46] Not that anyone has seen the Father except the one who is from God; he has seen the Father. [47] Very truly, I tell you, whoever believes has eternal life. [48] I am the bread of life. [49] Your ancestors ate the manna in the wilderness, and they died. [50] This is the bread that comes down from heaven, so that one may eat of it and not die. [51] I am the living bread that came down from heaven. Whoever eats of this bread will live forever; and the bread that I will give for the life of the world is my flesh."

[52] The Jews then disputed among themselves, saying, "How can this man give us his flesh to eat?" [53] So Jesus said to them, "Very truly, I tell you, unless you eat the flesh of the Son of Man and drink his blood, you have no life in you. [54] Those who eat my flesh and drink my blood have eternal life, and I will raise them up on the last day; [55] for my flesh is true food and my blood is true drink. [56] Those who eat my flesh and drink my blood abide in me, and I in them. [57] Just as the living Father sent me, and I live because of the Father, so whoever eats me will live because of me. [58] This is the bread that came down from heaven, not like that which your ancestors ate, and they died. But the one who eats this bread will live forever." [59] He said these things while he was teaching in the synagogue at Capernaum.

[60] When many of his disciples heard it, they said, "This teaching is difficult; who can accept it?" [61] But Jesus, being aware that his disciples were complaining about it, said to them, "Does this offend you? [62] Then what if you were to see the Son of Man ascending to where he was before? [63] It is the spirit that gives life; the flesh is useless. The words that I have spoken to you are spirit and life. [64] But among you there are some who do not believe." For Jesus knew from the first who were the ones that did not believe, and who was the one that would betray him. [65] And he said, "For this reason I have told you that no one can come to me unless it is granted by the Father."

[66] Because of this many of his disciples turned back and no longer went about with him. [67] So Jesus asked the twelve, "Do you also wish to go away?" [68] Simon Peter answered him, "Lord, to whom can we go? You have the words of eternal life. [69] We have come to believe and know that you are the

3.5; 4.15). **35:** *I am* expresses divinity and implies Jesus' unity with God (Ex 3.14; Jn 1.1–3; 6.20; 8.58). **38:** Jesus is not identical with God but rather is God's agent. **39–40:** *Raise it up . . . raise them up . . . last day*, Gk "anasteso . . . te eschate hemera," lit., "resurrect . . . the day at the end of the age." **41:** *Jews began to complain*, Jesus' claim to be from heaven is offensive, given their knowledge of his parentage. **45:** *Prophets*, Isa 54.13; cf. Jer 31.34. **51–58:** In contrast to the Synoptic Gospels, John's Gospel does not provide an account of the memorial meal during the Last Supper. Jesus alludes to his death and resurrection, in that he became flesh (1.14) and offered himself to God, thus sacrificing his life for the life of the world. **53:** *Flesh . . . blood*, the literal meaning is not only repellent but offensive because Jews do not ingest the blood of an animal along with its flesh (Gen 9.4; Lev 7.26–27; 17.15). The passage may allude to the practice of theophagy associated with Greco-Roman mystery cults such as the cults of Demeter and Dionysus. If so, this may be one indication that the Gospel's intended audience included non-Jews. **59:** *Synagogue at Capernaum*, as in Mk 1.21; Lk 4.31; the sudden mention of this place may indicate that various traditions have been combined into one discourse. **60:** Many followers were offended by this teaching, perhaps because of its cannibalistic overtones. Ingesting blood was forbidden (see v. 53n.). **63:** *Flesh . . . useless*, an indication that the meaning of terms in this Gospel is fluid (see also "world," 3.16; 16.33; 17.14–16).

Holy One of God."[a] [70] Jesus answered them, "Did I not choose you, the twelve? Yet one of you is a devil." [71] He was speaking of Judas son of Simon Iscariot,[b] for he, though one of the twelve, was going to betray him.

7 After this Jesus went about in Galilee. He did not wish[c] to go about in Judea because the Jews were looking for an opportunity to kill him. [2] Now the Jewish festival of Booths[d] was near. [3] So his brothers said to him, "Leave here and go to Judea so that your disciples also may see the works you are doing; [4] for no one who wants[e] to be widely known acts in secret. If you do these things, show yourself to the world." [5] (For not even his brothers believed in him.) [6] Jesus said to them, "My time has not yet come, but your time is always here. [7] The world cannot hate you, but it hates me because I testify against it that its works are evil. [8] Go to the festival yourselves. I am not[f] going to this festival, for my time has not yet fully come." [9] After saying this, he remained in Galilee.

[10] But after his brothers had gone to the festival, then he also went, not publicly but as it were[g] in secret. [11] The Jews were looking for him at the festival and saying, "Where is he?" [12] And there was considerable complaining about him among the crowds. While some were saying, "He is a good man," others were saying, "No, he is deceiving the crowd." [13] Yet no one would speak openly about him for fear of the Jews.

[14] About the middle of the festival Jesus went up into the temple and began to teach. [15] The Jews were astonished at it, saying, "How does this man have such learning,[h] when he has never been taught?" [16] Then Jesus answered them, "My teaching is not mine but his who sent me. [17] Anyone who resolves to do the will of God will know whether the teaching is from God or whether I am speaking on my own. [18] Those who speak on their own seek their own glory; but the one who seeks the glory of him who sent him is true, and there is nothing false in him.

[19] "Did not Moses give you the law? Yet none of you keeps the law. Why are you looking for an opportunity to kill me?" [20] The crowd answered, "You have a demon! Who is trying to kill you?" [21] Jesus answered them, "I performed one work, and all of you are astonished. [22] Moses gave you circumcision (it is, of course, not from Moses, but from the patriarchs), and you circumcise a man on the sabbath. [23] If a man receives circumcision on the sabbath in order that the law of Moses

[a] Other ancient authorities read *the Christ, the Son of the living God*
[b] Other ancient authorities read *Judas Iscariot son of Simon;* others, *Judas son of Simon from Karyot* (Kerioth)
[c] Other ancient authorities read *was not at liberty*
[d] Or *Tabernacles*
[e] Other ancient authorities read *wants it*
[f] Other ancient authorities add *yet*
[g] Other ancient authorities lack *as it were*
[h] Or *this man know his letters*

69: *Holy One of God,* this title is not present elsewhere in the Fourth Gospel. See Judg 13.7; 16.17 in reference to Samson as a Nazirite, and Ps 106.16 in reference to Aaron. **70:** Judas is aligned with the cosmic forces hostile to Jesus. This verse foreshadows Judas's role as the betrayer, which in 13.2 is associated with the devil entering into him **71:** *Judas,* the name of Judah the Maccabee, who led a revolt against the Seleucid (Greek) rulers of Judah in 167–164 BCE; *Iscariot,* that is, a man (Heb "'ish") from the town of Kerioth.

7.1–52: Festival of Tabernacles. 1: *Judea* was the location of the Temple in Jerusalem, where the leadership would have been hostile to Jesus if they saw him as a possible insurrectionary who would bring down Roman power to crush even their limited autonomy. **2:** Tabernacles, or *Booths* (Heb "Sukkot"), a weeklong fall pilgrimage festival celebrating the harvest and commemorating Israel's sojourn in the desert after the Exodus. It was required that all males attend this festival (Lev 23.42; Deut 16.16, which specifies Passover, Weeks, and Booths as required). Jesus' refusal (v. 8), followed by his covert attendance (v. 10), shows that he meant to obey the requirement. **3:** *His brothers,* likely biological relations, rather than disciples (for "brothers" as disciples, see 20.17). **6–7:** Jesus' brothers, like "the Jews," represent the hostile world. **8:** Jesus tries to hide his intentions. Despite this statement, he secretly goes to Jerusalem (v. 9). **11:** *The Jews,* here the Jewish crowds in Jerusalem. **13:** *The Jews,* here Jewish authorities. **14–18:** Jesus teaches openly in the Temple (see 8.20n.), which he mentions when interrogated by Annas (18.20). **15:** *The Jews,* here the crowd that was listening to Jesus. **18:** An implicit criticism of Jewish authorities as self-glorifying (cf. Mt 23.5–7). **22–24:** Jesus refers to the healing of the lame

may not be broken, are you angry with me because I healed a man's whole body on the sabbath? [24] Do not judge by appearances, but judge with right judgment."

[25] Now some of the people of Jerusalem were saying, "Is not this the man whom they are trying to kill? [26] And here he is, speaking openly, but they say nothing to him! Can it be that the authorities really know that this is the Messiah?[a] [27] Yet we know where this man is from; but when the Messiah[a] comes, no one will know where he is from." [28] Then Jesus cried out as he was teaching in the temple, "You know me, and you know where I am from. I have not come on my own. But the one who sent me is true, and you do not know him. [29] I know him, because I am from him, and he sent me." [30] Then they tried to arrest him, but no one laid hands on him, because his hour had not yet come. [31] Yet many in the crowd believed in him and were saying, "When the Messiah[a] comes, will he do more signs than this man has done?"[b]

[32] The Pharisees heard the crowd muttering such things about him, and the chief priests and Pharisees sent temple police to arrest him. [33] Jesus then said, "I will be with you a little while longer, and then I am going to him who sent me. [34] You will search for me, but you will not find me; and where I am, you cannot come." [35] The Jews said to one another, "Where does this man intend to go that we will not find him? Does he intend to go to the Dispersion among the Greeks and teach the Greeks? [36] What does he mean by saying, 'You will search for me and you will not find me' and 'Where I am, you cannot come'?"

[37] On the last day of the festival, the great day, while Jesus was standing there, he cried out, "Let anyone who is thirsty come to me, [38] and let the one who believes in me drink. As[c] the scripture has said, 'Out of the believer's heart[d] shall flow rivers of living water.'" [39] Now he said this about the Spirit, which believers in him were to receive; for as yet there was no Spirit,[e] because Jesus was not yet glorified.

[a] Or *the Christ*
[b] Other ancient authorities read *is doing*
[c] Or *come to me and drink.* [38]*The one who believes in me, as*
[d] Gk *out of his belly*
[e] Other ancient authorities read *for as yet the Spirit* (others, *Holy Spirit*) *had not been given*

man (ch 5). *Moses*, the Torah (Gen 17.10; Lev 12.3), including *the patriarchs*, traditions predating the time of Moses. **25:** The *people of Jerusalem* know the sentiment against Jesus (contrast the crowd of v. 20). A distinction is drawn between the people and the authorities; significantly, Gk "hoi Ioudaioi" ("the Jews") is not used of either group in vv. 25–26. **27:** *No one will know . . .*, a possible allusion to the tradition of the "hidden messiah," one of several different strands of messianic expectation in the first century (cf. *1 En.* 46.1–3). **27–28:** Although the crowd claims to know where Jesus came from—perhaps an allusion to Nazareth (see 1.45; 6.42)—Jesus asserts that they do not know where he really comes from. He does therefore fulfill the expectations of the "hidden messiah" tradition. **30:** *They*, perhaps the people of Jerusalem (v. 25), but their attempt to arrest him suggests that "they" refers specifically to the authorities. **31:** The crowd continues to be divided in their assessment of Jesus, with some believing that he fulfills the criteria of the messiah, such as doing signs. **32:** *Pharisees* and *chief priests*, implies that "the Jews" as a whole are hostile to Jesus: the Pharisees, who held to a more expansive interpretation of Torah, including oral tradition, were often at odds with the priesthood, most of whom were Sadducees who differed from the Pharisees in that they relied on the Written Torah and did not believe in a bodily resurrection after death. *Temple police*, the guards who kept order in the Temple. **34–35:** Another misunderstanding. The Jews think that Jesus refers to a trip to the Dispersion (the Diaspora), yet readers know that Jesus is alluding to his death. *The Greeks*, Gentiles. **37–39:** According to rabbinic sources, it was customary at Sukkot to bring water in a golden pitcher from the pool of Siloam to the Temple to remind the people of the water from the rock in the desert (Num 20.2–13) and as a symbol of hope for messianic deliverance (Isa 12.3). On each day of the festival there was a procession including prayers for deliverance (Heb "hoshana," pl. "hoshanot," meaning "deliver" or "save"); on *the last day* was "Hoshana Rabbah," the "great" hosanna, the culmination of these prayers (*b. Sukk.* 53a). The Johannine material suggests that these practices may have been known to the author in the first century. **38:** *As the scripture has said*, allusions to Isa 44.3; 58.11; Prov 18.4. **39:** *The Spirit*, NRSV capitalizes this word to identify this as the Holy Spirit predicted in 14.26ff. and given in 20.22.

[40] When they heard these words, some in the crowd said, "This is really the prophet." [41] Others said, "This is the Messiah."[a] But some asked, "Surely the Messiah[a] does not come from Galilee, does he? [42] Has not the scripture said that the Messiah[a] is descended from David and comes from Bethlehem, the village where David lived?" [43] So there was a division in the crowd because of him. [44] Some of them wanted to arrest him, but no one laid hands on him.

[45] Then the temple police went back to the chief priests and Pharisees, who asked them, "Why did you not arrest him?" [46] The police answered, "Never has anyone spoken like this!" [47] Then the Pharisees replied, "Surely you have not been deceived too, have you? [48] Has any one of the authorities or of the Pharisees believed in him? [49] But this crowd, which does not know the law—they are accursed." [50] Nicodemus, who had gone to Jesus[b] before, and who was one of them, asked, [51] "Our law does not judge people without first giving them a hearing to find out what they are doing, does it?" [52] They replied, "Surely you are not also from Galilee, are you? Search and you will see that no prophet is to arise from Galilee."

8 ⟦[53] Then each of them went home, [1] while Jesus went to the Mount of Olives. [2] Early in the morning he came again to the temple. All the people came to him and he sat down and began to teach them. [3] The scribes and the Pharisees brought a woman who had been caught in adultery; and making her stand before all of them, [4] they said to him, "Teacher, this woman was caught in the very act of committing adultery. [5] Now in the law Moses commanded us to stone such women. Now what do you say?" [6] They said this to test him, so that they might have some charge to bring against him. Jesus bent down and wrote with his finger on the ground. [7] When they kept on questioning him, he straightened up and said to them, "Let anyone among you who is without sin be the first to throw a stone at her." [8] And once again he bent down and wrote on the ground.[c] [9] When they heard it, they went away, one by one, beginning with the elders; and Jesus was left alone with the woman standing before him. [10] Jesus straightened up and said to her, "Woman, where are they? Has no one condemned you?" [11] She said, "No one, sir."[d] And Jesus said, "Neither do I condemn you. Go your way, and from now on do not sin again."⟧[e]

a Or *the Christ*
b Gk *him*
c Other ancient authorities add *the sins of each of them*
d Or *Lord*
e The most ancient authorities lack 7.53—8.11; other authorities add the passage here or after 7.36 or after 21.25 or after Luke 21.38, with variations of text; some mark the passage as doubtful.

It thus may allude to the spirit that will infuse the community after Jesus' death (cf. 15.26). *Glorified*, a reference to Jesus' death and resurrection (13.31). **40–42:** These verses reflect one set of speculations, according to which the messiah was to be born in Bethlehem of Judea, not in Galilee (cf. Mic 5.2; Mt 2.1; Lk 2.1–7), and descended from King David (on the basis of the promise in 2 Sam 7.16 that David's throne would stand forever). *Bethlehem*, David's home town (1 Sam 17.12). **49:** *Crowd . . . does not know the law*, that is, ordinary Jews are not experts in legal matters. **50:** *Nicodemus* (see 3.1n.). **51:** *A hearing*, Deut 19.15–21 mandates taking testimony from accusers and witnesses to assess the truth of an accusation. Nicodemus's defense of Jesus may point to his growing belief in Jesus as the Messiah.

7.53–8.11: The adulterous woman. This episode is an interpolation and therefore not part of the original Gospel. It appears in Mss of other Gospels, particularly after Lk 21.38, where it fits the narrative much better. Here the conclusion of the incident, in v. 11, does not lead into the following v. 12; in addition, *scribes and Pharisees* is not a phrase in John's Gospel (John uses the term "Pharisees," but not "scribes"), but is frequent in Luke. **1:** *Mount of Olives*, a ridge overlooking the Jerusalem Temple. **3:** The sole reference to *the scribes* in John's Gospel; in the Synoptics they are closely associated with the chief priests (e.g., Mt 2.4; Mk 8.31; Lk 20.19) and the Pharisees (Mt 23.2; Mk 2.16; Lk 6.7). **5:** Lev 20.10; Deut 22.23–24. Roman law did not permit execution for adultery. Jesus' opponents may have been trying to test his faithfulness to the law. **6:** What Jesus wrote in the sand is not known, though it may be an allusion to Jer 17.13, which declares that those who depart from God shall be written in the earth ("underworld" in NRSV). Perhaps it is simply the fact that he is writing—thereby

[12] Again Jesus spoke to them, saying, "I am the light of the world. Whoever follows me will never walk in darkness but will have the light of life." [13] Then the Pharisees said to him, "You are testifying on your own behalf; your testimony is not valid." [14] Jesus answered, "Even if I testify on my own behalf, my testimony is valid because I know where I have come from and where I am going, but you do not know where I come from or where I am going. [15] You judge by human standards;[a] I judge no one. [16] Yet even if I do judge, my judgment is valid; for it is not I alone who judge, but I and the Father[b] who sent me. [17] In your law it is written that the testimony of two witnesses is valid. [18] I testify on my own behalf, and the Father who sent me testifies on my behalf." [19] Then they said to him, "Where is your Father?" Jesus answered, "You know neither me nor my Father. If you knew me, you would know my Father also." [20] He spoke these words while he was teaching in the treasury of the temple, but no one arrested him, because his hour had not yet come.

[21] Again he said to them, "I am going away, and you will search for me, but you will die in your sin. Where I am going, you cannot come." [22] Then the Jews said, "Is he going to kill himself? Is that what he means by saying, 'Where I am going, you cannot come'?" [23] He said to them, "You are from below, I am from above; you are of this world, I am not of this world. [24] I told you that you would die in your sins, for you will die in your sins unless you believe that I am he."[c] [25] They said to him, "Who are you?" Jesus said to them, "Why do I speak to you at all?[d] [26] I have much to say about you and much to condemn; but the one who sent me is true, and I declare to the world what I have heard from him." [27] They did not understand that he was speaking to them about the Father. [28] So Jesus said, "When you have lifted up the Son of Man, then you will realize that I am he,[c] and that I do nothing on my own, but I speak these things as the Father instructed me. [29] And the one who sent me is with me; he has not left me alone, for I always do what is pleasing to him." [30] As he was saying these things, many believed in him.

[a] Gk *according to the flesh*
[b] Other ancient authorities read *he*
[c] Gk *I am*
[d] Or *What I have told you from the beginning*

evoking the Written Torah?—that is important.

8.12–59: Confrontation with the Jews. **12:** *Again,* apparently following 7.52. *Light of the world,* recalls 1.5,8,9. **13:** *Testimony is not valid,* see 5.31–47n. **15:** *Human standards,* i.e., by appearances, not as God (and Jesus as associated with God) would judge. **17:** *Your law,* here Jesus dissociates himself from the Jewish law (cf. also 10.34). This, along with the near absence of the connection of the term "Jew" with Jesus, is part of the rhetorical strategy whereby the Gospel encourages its readership to distance themselves from "the Jews." Deut 19.15 requires the testimony of *two witnesses* for capital cases. **18:** The two witnesses are Jesus and God (v. 16). *The Father* (God) and Jesus (the human being) are separate; the later development in Christian thought of the doctrine of the Trinity (three persons in one God) is not the issue here. **19:** More misunderstanding; the Jews inquire as to Jesus' paternity, whereas Jesus claims God as his father. **20:** *Treasury,* not a strongroom but apparently (see Mk 12.41) the publicly available receptacles into which offerings could be placed. Both men and women had access to these, and therefore this is a reference to a public place in the Temple precincts to which anyone could have access. Jesus later refers (18.20) to the fact that he has taught publicly. **21:** *Going away,* i.e., to death and then to eternal life with the Father. **22:** *Kill himself . . . ,* as in ch 7, the Jews misunderstand: Jesus is not committing suicide but willingly moving toward his own death (cf. 3.16). **23:** Jesus and the Jews occupy opposite ends of the spiritual pole. **24:** Continuation of the trial motif; Jesus judges the Jews and condemns them for their refusal to believe. **25:** *Why do I speak to you at all?,* another rendering, making more sense in the context, is given in translators' note *d,* "[I am] what I have told you from the beginning." **28:** *I am he,* a divine claim, alluding to the theophany of Ex 3.14. *Lifted up,* i.e., in the crucifixion (see 12.32); for this Gospel, crucifixion is transformed from a shameful form of death to Jesus' exaltation and glorification, which in turn are seen as essential to the completion of God's work and Jesus' resurrection. **30–59:** The rest of the chapter initially appears to be addressed to former believers; as the discussion proceeds, the sense that the audi-

[31] Then Jesus said to the Jews who had believed in him, "If you continue in my word, you are truly my disciples; [32] and you will know the truth, and the truth will make you free." [33] They answered him, "We are descendants of Abraham and have never been slaves to anyone. What do you mean by saying, 'You will be made free'?"

[34] Jesus answered them, "Very truly, I tell you, everyone who commits sin is a slave to sin. [35] The slave does not have a permanent place in the household; the son has a place there forever. [36] So if the Son makes you free, you will be free indeed. [37] I know that you are descendants of Abraham; yet you look for an opportunity to kill me, because there is no place in you for my word. [38] I declare what I have seen in the Father's presence; as for you, you should do what you have heard from the Father."[a]

[39] They answered him, "Abraham is our father." Jesus said to them, "If you were Abraham's children, you would be doing[b] what Abraham did, [40] but now you are trying to kill me, a man who has told you the truth that I heard from God. This is not what Abraham did. [41] You are indeed doing what your father does." They said to him, "We are not illegitimate children; we have one father, God himself." [42] Jesus said to them, "If God were your Father, you would love me, for I came from God and now I am here. I did not come on my own, but he sent me. [43] Why do you not understand what I say? It is because you cannot accept my word. [44] You are from your father the devil, and you choose to do your father's desires. He was a murderer from the beginning and does not stand in the truth, because there is no truth in him. When he lies, he speaks according to his own nature, for he is a liar and the father of lies. [45] But because I tell the truth, you do not believe me. [46] Which of you convicts me of sin? If I tell the truth, why do you not believe me? [47] Whoever is from God hears the words of God. The reason you do not hear them is that you are not from God."

[48] The Jews answered him, "Are we not right in saying that you are a Samaritan and have a demon?" [49] Jesus answered, "I do not have a demon; but I honor my Father, and you dishonor me. [50] Yet I do not seek my own glory; there is one who seeks it and he is the judge. [51] Very truly, I tell you, whoever keeps my word will never see death." [52] The Jews said to him, "Now we know that you have a demon. Abraham died, and so did the proph-

[a] Other ancient authorities read *you do what you have heard from your father*

[b] Other ancient authorities read *If you are Abraham's children, then do*

ence within the narrative constitutes a specific Jewish subset recedes, and the impression is created that the Johannine Jesus is speaking to, and about, all Jews who are not believers. **32:** *The truth will make you free,* Heb "emet," "truth," implies reliability or steadfastness, something to depend on, which can provide a firm basis for one's life. For John, this can only be knowledge of and faith in Jesus' identity as the Messiah and Son of God. Jesus' statement could be taken in combination with his later claim, "I am the way, the truth, and the life" (14.6) to mean "The one who knows me knows the truth and is thereby free." This statement, and the passage as a whole, plays on the contrast between Isaac and Ishmael that is present also in Gal 4: Isaac as the son of the free woman Sarah, and Ishmael as the son of the slave woman Hagar. Faith in Jesus is a sign of one's own freedom and therefore one's identity as the son of Isaac and heir to the covenant between God and Abraham. **33–59:** The Jews claim their covenantal relationship with the one God, and declare that Jesus contravenes monotheism by asserting divine sonship. Jesus denies their covenantal relationship on the grounds that they reject God's son. **33:** Two claims are made: the Jews are children of Abraham (cf. Gen 12; Deut 14.1), and that they have never been enslaved. The Israelites were enslaved in Egypt (Ex 13.3); the reference here is likely to idolatry, which is sometimes referred to as enslavement to foreign gods (Jer 2.10–14). **34–36:** The distinction between *the slave* and *the son* is one of property and inheritance. As in ch 2, Jesus claims to be the true "son" who has inherited the Temple and all that it symbolizes, in contrast to the Jews, who serve in the Temple but do not inherit it. **39:** Jesus argues that paternity is shown by behavior. *Abraham's children* implies offspring sharing the characteristics of their ancestor, not merely physical "descendants" as in v. 37. **41–47:** In trying to kill Jesus, the Jews show that they are not God's children but the devil's. **41:** *We are not illegitimate,* perhaps an implied contrast to Jesus' supposed illegitimacy (Origen, *Cels* 1.28). **44:** This verse is the source of the association of the Jews with Satan. **48–52:** The Jews express their growing inability to believe Jesus' words, especially

ets; yet you say, 'Whoever keeps my word will never taste death.' [53] Are you greater than our father Abraham, who died? The prophets also died. Who do you claim to be?" [54] Jesus answered, "If I glorify myself, my glory is nothing. It is my Father who glorifies me, he of whom you say, 'He is our God,' [55] though you do not know him. But I know him; if I would say that I do not know him, I would be a liar like you. But I do know him and I keep his word. [56] Your ancestor Abraham rejoiced that he would see my day; he saw it and was glad." [57] Then the Jews said to him, "You are not yet fifty years old, and have you seen Abraham?"[a] [58] Jesus said to them, "Very truly, I tell you, before Abraham was, I am." [59] So they picked up stones to throw at him, but Jesus hid himself and went out of the temple.

9 As he walked along, he saw a man blind from birth. [2] His disciples asked him, "Rabbi, who sinned, this man or his parents, that he was born blind?" [3] Jesus answered, "Neither this man nor his parents sinned; he was born blind so that God's works might be revealed in him. [4] We[b] must work the works of him who sent me[c] while it is day; night is coming when no one can work. [5] As long as I am in the world, I am the light of the world." [6] When he had said this, he spat on the ground and made mud with the saliva and spread the mud on the man's eyes, [7] saying to him, "Go, wash in the pool of Siloam" (which means Sent). Then he went and washed and came back able to see. [8] The neighbors and those who had seen him before as a beggar began to ask, "Is this not the man who used to sit and beg?" [9] Some were saying, "It is he." Others were saying, "No, but it is someone like him." He kept saying, "I am the man." [10] But they kept asking him, "Then how were your eyes opened?" [11] He answered, "The man called Jesus made mud, spread it on my eyes, and said to me, 'Go to Siloam and wash.' Then I went and washed and received my sight." [12] They said to him, "Where is he?" He said, "I do not know."

[13] They brought to the Pharisees the man who had formerly been blind. [14] Now it was a sabbath day when Jesus made the mud and opened his eyes. [15] Then the Pharisees also began to ask him how he had received his sight. He said to them, "He put mud on my eyes. Then I washed, and now I see." [16] Some of the Pharisees said, "This man is not from God, for he does not observe the sabbath." But others said, "How can a man who is a sinner perform such signs?" And they were divided. [17] So they said again to the blind man, "What do you say about him? It was your eyes he opened." He said, "He is a prophet."

[18] The Jews did not believe that he had been blind and had received his sight until they called the parents of the man who had received his sight [19] and asked them, "Is this your son, who you say was born blind? How then does he now see?" [20] His parents answered, "We know that this is our son, and

[a] Other ancient authorities read *has Abraham seen you?*
[b] Other ancient authorities read *I*
[c] Other ancient authorities read *us*

the claim that belief overcomes death. **48:** *Samaritan*, here apparently a general term for one outside Judaism (see 4.4ff.). **51:** *Death* here may mean not so much the physical death that ends human life but the ultimate death that is the opposite of "eternal life." **56–58:** *Abraham . . . see my day*, this may be a reference to the traditions described in *T. Abr.*, in which God gives Abraham a tour of the heavens and provides him with knowledge of the final judgment, before his own death. *I am*, an allusion to God's revelation to Moses at the burning bush (Ex 3.14), also perhaps a claim to preexistence (1.1–3).

9.1–41: Fifth sign: healing of the blind man. 2–3: Illness and disability were sometimes attributed to sin; cf. 5.14. **4:** A reference to Jesus' death. **5:** See 1.4–5; 8.12. This verse indicates that Jesus is viewing the man's blindness and later the restoration of his sight as symbolic of the spiritual journey from darkness to light, from unbelief to belief. **6:** *Saliva* was seen to have medicinal value (cf. Pliny, *Nat.* 28.4). **7:** *Pool of Siloam*, Isa 8.6; Neh 3.15. *Siloam* is Gk spelling of Heb "shiloaḥ," possibly from "sh-l-ḥ," "send." It is the end point of the tunnel built by King Hezekiah to provide Jerusalem with water. **14:** Only now does the Gospel mention that it was the *Sabbath* as in ch 5. **16:** The interrogators are here referred to as Pharisees, but in v. 18 as Jews. **17:** The *man* like the Samaritan woman (4.19) declares Jesus to be a prophet based on firsthand experience. **18–34:** The Jewish authorities conduct a legal investigation. Whether interrogations or trials were undertaken on the Sabbath in

that he was born blind; [21] but we do not know how it is that now he sees, nor do we know who opened his eyes. Ask him; he is of age. He will speak for himself." [22] His parents said this because they were afraid of the Jews; for the Jews had already agreed that anyone who confessed Jesus[a] to be the Messiah[b] would be put out of the synagogue. [23] Therefore his parents said, "He is of age; ask him."

[24] So for the second time they called the man who had been blind, and they said to him, "Give glory to God! We know that this man is a sinner." [25] He answered, "I do not know whether he is a sinner. One thing I do know, that though I was blind, now I see." [26] They said to him, "What did he do to you? How did he open your eyes?" [27] He answered them, "I have told you already, and you would not listen. Why do you want to hear it again? Do you also want to become his disciples?" [28] Then they reviled him, saying, "You are his disciple, but we are disciples of Moses. [29] We know that God has spoken to Moses, but as for this man, we do not know where he comes from." [30] The man answered, "Here is an astonishing thing! You do not know where he comes from, and yet he opened my eyes. [31] We know that God does not listen to sinners, but he does listen to one who worships him and obeys his will. [32] Never since the world began has it been heard that anyone opened the eyes of a person born blind. [33] If this man were not from God, he could do nothing." [34] They answered him, "You were born entirely in sins, and are you trying to teach us?" And they drove him out.

[35] Jesus heard that they had driven him out, and when he found him, he said, "Do you believe in the Son of Man?"[c] [36] He answered, "And who is he, sir?[d] Tell me, so that I may believe in him." [37] Jesus said to him, "You have seen him, and the one speaking with you is he." [38] He said, "Lord,[d] I believe." And he worshiped him. [39] Jesus said, "I came into this world for judgment so that those who do not see may see, and those who do see may become blind." [40] Some of the Pharisees near him heard this and said to him, "Surely we are not blind, are we?" [41] Jesus said to them, "If you were blind, you would not have sin. But now that you say, 'We see,' your sin remains.

10 "Very truly, I tell you, anyone who does not enter the sheepfold by the gate but climbs in by another way is a thief and a bandit. [2] The one who enters by the gate is the shepherd of the sheep. [3] The

a Gk *him*
b Or *the Christ*
c Other ancient authorities read *the Son of God*
d *Sir* and *Lord* translate the same Greek word

the first century is uncertain, but unlikely; later rabbis explicitly forbid courts to be in session on the Sabbath (*y. Sanh.* 4.6). **21:** Traditionally, a male comes *of age* at thirteen ("bar mitzvah") though in this instance the parents are merely pointing out that their son is an adult and therefore capable of explaining his own situation. **22:** It is difficult to know what is meant here. Exclusion of Christ-confessors from the synagogue would be anachronistic for the time of Jesus, and for that reason the verse has often been understood as a reference to the historical experience of the Johannine community at the end of the first century CE. It is understood not as a one-time event but as a type of excommunication that would involve not only the exclusion from participation in worship services but also social ostracism. Yet this interpretation is problematic on many grounds (see Introduction), and whether it has any historical referent at all cannot be demonstrated. **24:** *Give glory to God*, i.e., do not credit Jesus with the healing. **28:** This passage sets up a contrast between the disciples of Jesus and the *disciples of Moses*. There is no evidence, however, that Jews referred to themselves as *disciples of Moses*. **31:** That Jesus could heal the man is evidence that he is not a sinner. **32:** In the book of Tobit, however, the protagonist is healed of blindness by his son Tobias (Tob 11.11). **34:** *Born entirely in sins* likely refers back to v. 2 and the common belief that congenital blindness is somehow related to the sin of the man or his parents, a view that Jesus rejects (vv. 3–4). **38:** Bowing in worship is a biblical response to a theophany; cf. Gen 17.3. **39–41:** Comments on the literal and figurative meanings of blindness and sight echo 9.5. *Become blind*, see Isa 6.9–10.

10.1–42: Good shepherd discourse. 1–6: A *figure of speech* (v. 6 comparing Jesus to a good shepherd). **1,8:** The *thieves* and *bandits* may be a reference to the Jewish leadership though this is not certain **2:** The passage alludes to biblical *shepherds* such as Moses (Ex 3.1); David (e.g., 2 Sam 5.2), and God (Ps 23). **3:** The language (*hear his voice, calls his own sheep by name, leads them out*) recalls 5.5 and anticipates 11.43. This may be an al-

gatekeeper opens the gate for him, and the sheep hear his voice. He calls his own sheep by name and leads them out. [4] When he has brought out all his own, he goes ahead of them, and the sheep follow him because they know his voice. [5] They will not follow a stranger, but they will run from him because they do not know the voice of strangers." [6] Jesus used this figure of speech with them, but they did not understand what he was saying to them.

[7] So again Jesus said to them, "Very truly, I tell you, I am the gate for the sheep. [8] All who came before me are thieves and bandits; but the sheep did not listen to them. [9] I am the gate. Whoever enters by me will be saved, and will come in and go out and find pasture. [10] The thief comes only to steal and kill and destroy. I came that they may have life, and have it abundantly.

[11] "I am the good shepherd. The good shepherd lays down his life for the sheep. [12] The hired hand, who is not the shepherd and does not own the sheep, sees the wolf coming and leaves the sheep and runs away—and the wolf snatches them and scatters them. [13] The hired hand runs away because a hired hand does not care for the sheep. [14] I am the good shepherd. I know my own and my own know me, [15] just as the Father knows me and I know the Father. And I lay down my life for the sheep. [16] I have other sheep that do not belong to this fold. I must bring them also, and they will listen to my voice. So there will be one flock, one shepherd. [17] For this reason the Father loves me, because I lay down my life in order to take it up again. [18] No one takes[a] it from me, but I lay it down of my own accord. I have power to lay it down, and I have power to take it up again. I have received this command from my Father."

[19] Again the Jews were divided because of these words. [20] Many of them were saying, "He has a demon and is out of his mind. Why listen to him?" [21] Others were saying, "These are not the words of one who has a demon. Can a demon open the eyes of the blind?"

[22] At that time the festival of the Dedication took place in Jerusalem. It was winter, [23] and Jesus was walking in the temple, in the portico of Solomon. [24] So the Jews gathered around him and said to him, "How long will you keep us in suspense? If you are the Messiah,[b] tell us plainly." [25] Jesus answered, "I have told you, and you do not believe. The works that I do in my Father's name testify to me; [26] but you do not believe, because you do not belong to my sheep. [27] My sheep hear my voice. I know them, and they follow me. [28] I give them eternal life, and they will never perish. No one will snatch them out of my hand. [29] What my Father has given me is greater than all else, and no one can snatch it out of the Father's hand.[c] [30] The Father and I are one."

[31] The Jews took up stones again to stone him. [32] Jesus replied, "I have shown you many good works from the Father. For which of these are you going to stone me?" [33] The Jews answered, "It is not for a good work that we are going to stone you, but for blasphemy,

[a] Other ancient authorities read *has taken*
[b] Or *the Christ*
[c] Other ancient authorities read *My Father who has given them to me is greater than all, and no one can snatch them out of the Father's hand*

lusion to the "harrowing of hell," the idea that Jesus spent the days between his crucifixion and resurrection in Hades bringing the dead to faith (1 Pet 3.19, as interpreted in the Apostles' Creed, *Gos. Nic.*). **7:** *I am the gate,* the figure changes from the one who calls to his sheep to the one who is the means by which they are brought in. **10:** *Life . . . abundantly,* i.e., eternal life. **12:** The *hired hand* may refer to the Jewish leadership (see Ezek 34.1–10). *Wolf,* evil; a more specific referent cannot be determined **16:** *Other sheep* may refer to Gentile followers. **22:** *Festival of the Dedication,* Hanukkah (beginning on 25 Chislev, a date that falls in December), commemorating the rededication of the Temple (164 BCE), after it had been desecrated by the Seleucid king Antiochus IV (1 Macc 4.52–59). It is unclear clear how this feast was observed in the first century. **30:** Jesus reiterates his unity with God, which the Jews see as blasphemy (v. 33). **31:** *Took up stones,* in biblical and rabbinic law, stoning is the prescribe penalty for blasphemy (Lev 29.16; *m. Sanh.* 7.4). It is difficult to know, however, what exactly constituted blasphemy in the late first century. The context suggests, however, that Jesus' utterances, here, and elsewhere (e.g., 5.17) are seen by the Johannine Jews as a violation of monotheism, that

because you, though only a human being, are making yourself God." [34] Jesus answered, "Is it not written in your law,[a] 'I said, you are gods'? [35] If those to whom the word of God came were called 'gods'—and the scripture cannot be annulled— [36] can you say that the one whom the Father has sanctified and sent into the world is blaspheming because I said, 'I am God's Son'? [37] If I am not doing the works of my Father, then do not believe me. [38] But if I do them, even though you do not believe me, believe the works, so that you may know and understand[b] that the Father is in me and I am in the Father." [39] Then they tried to arrest him again, but he escaped from their hands.

[40] He went away again across the Jordan to the place where John had been baptizing earlier, and he remained there. [41] Many came to him, and they were saying, "John performed no sign, but everything that John said about this man was true." [42] And many believed in him there.

11 Now a certain man was ill, Lazarus of Bethany, the village of Mary and her sister Martha. [2] Mary was the one who anointed the Lord with perfume and wiped his feet with her hair; her brother Lazarus was ill. [3] So the sisters sent a message to Jesus,[c] "Lord, he whom you love is ill." [4] But when Jesus heard it, he said, "This illness does not lead to death; rather it is for God's glory, so that the Son of God may be glorified through it." [5] Accordingly, though Jesus loved Martha and her sister and Lazarus, [6] after having heard that Lazarus[d] was ill, he stayed two days longer in the place where he was.

[7] Then after this he said to the disciples, "Let us go to Judea again." [8] The disciples said to him, "Rabbi, the Jews were just now trying to stone you, and are you going there again?" [9] Jesus answered, "Are there not twelve hours of daylight? Those who walk during the day do not stumble, because they see the light of this world. [10] But those who walk at night stumble, because the light is not in them." [11] After saying this, he told them, "Our friend Lazarus has fallen asleep, but I am going there to awaken him." [12] The disciples said to him, "Lord, if he has fallen asleep, he will be all right." [13] Jesus, however, had been speaking about his death, but they thought that he was referring merely to sleep. [14] Then Jesus told them plainly, "Lazarus is dead. [15] For your sake I am glad I was not there, so that you may believe. But let us go to him." [16] Thomas, who was called the Twin,[e] said to his fellow disciples, "Let us also go, that we may die with him."

[17] When Jesus arrived, he found that Lazarus[d] had already been in the tomb four days. [18] Now Bethany was near Jerusalem, some two miles[f] away, [19] and many of the Jews had come to Martha and Mary to console them about their brother. [20] When Martha heard that Jesus was coming, she went and met him, while Mary stayed at home. [21] Martha said to Jesus, "Lord, if you had been here, my

[a] Other ancient authorities read *in the law*
[b] Other ancient authorities lack *and understand*; others read *and believe*
[c] Gk *him*
[d] Gk *he*
[e] Gk *Didymus*
[f] Gk *fifteen stadia*

is, of the fundamental belief in the one, unique God of Israel. **33:** *Good work*, perhaps a reference to healings. **34:** *Your law*, see 8.17n. *'I said, you are gods,'* see Ps 82.6. This is Jesus' answer to the charge that he is making himself God (v. 33): it is God who has consecrated him as God's son. This is consistent with the biblical and Second Temple idea that certain people such as Jeremiah (Jer 1.5), the priests (2 Chr 26.18) or Moses (Sir 45.4) are chosen to do God's work. **41–42:** John the Baptist's testimony cited as corroborating Jesus' claims (see 1.19–28; 3.27–30).

11.1–57: Sixth sign: raising of Lazarus and its aftermath. 1: *Lazarus*, Gk "Eleazar" (see also Lk 16.20–25). *Bethany*, a village near Jerusalem. *Mary and Martha*, see Lk 10.38–42. **2:** This reference anticipates 12.1–3. **3:** *Lord*, as elsewhere depending on context could be translated "Sir." **4:** As in 9.3, Lazarus's illness is an opportunity to demonstrate Jesus' relationship to God. **5:** Deliberately ignoring the expectation, Jesus remains where he is, apparently to make sure that Lazarus is dead and buried. According to some rabbinic sources (e.g., *Gen. Rab.* 50.10) and some non-Jewish belief systems (e.g., Zoroastrianism), the spirit hovers near the body for three days. This view may have been known to the Gospel writer or the traditions that he used, as he has Jesus approach the tomb only on the fourth day (v. 17). **8:** The disciples fear for Jesus' life. **11:** *Asleep . . . awaken*, metaphors for death and resurrection (cf. Dan 12.2). **19:** In contrast to the parents of the man born blind (9.22), Mary and Martha are unafraid to

brother would not have died. [22] But even now I know that God will give you whatever you ask of him." [23] Jesus said to her, "Your brother will rise again." [24] Martha said to him, "I know that he will rise again in the resurrection on the last day." [25] Jesus said to her, "I am the resurrection and the life.[a] Those who believe in me, even though they die, will live, [26] and everyone who lives and believes in me will never die. Do you believe this?" [27] She said to him, "Yes, Lord, I believe that you are the Messiah,[b] the Son of God, the one coming into the world."

[28] When she had said this, she went back and called her sister Mary, and told her privately, "The Teacher is here and is calling for you." [29] And when she heard it, she got up quickly and went to him. [30] Now Jesus had not yet come to the village, but was still at the place where Martha had met him. [31] The Jews who were with her in the house, consoling her, saw Mary get up quickly and go out. They followed her because they thought that she was going to the tomb to weep there. [32] When Mary came where Jesus was and saw him, she knelt at his feet and said to him, "Lord, if you had been here, my brother would not have died." [33] When Jesus saw her weeping, and the Jews who came with her also weeping, he was greatly disturbed in spirit and deeply moved. [34] He said, "Where have you laid him?" They said to him, "Lord, come and see." [35] Jesus began to weep. [36] So the Jews said, "See how he loved him!" [37] But some of them said, "Could not he who opened the eyes of the blind man have kept this man from dying?"

[38] Then Jesus, again greatly disturbed, came to the tomb. It was a cave, and a stone was lying against it. [39] Jesus said, "Take away the stone." Martha, the sister of the dead man, said to him, "Lord, already there is a stench because he has been dead four days." [40] Jesus said to her, "Did I not tell you that if you believed, you would see the glory of God?" [41] So they took away the stone. And Jesus looked upward and said, "Father, I thank you for having heard me. [42] I knew that you always hear me, but I have said this for the sake of the crowd standing here, so that they may believe that you sent me." [43] When he had said this, he cried with a loud voice, "Lazarus, come out!" [44] The dead man came out, his hands and feet bound with strips of cloth, and his face wrapped in a cloth. Jesus said to them, "Unbind him, and let him go."

[45] Many of the Jews therefore, who had come with Mary and had seen what Jesus did, believed in him. [46] But some of them went to the Pharisees and told them what he had done. [47] So the chief priests and the Pharisees called a meeting of the council, and said, "What are we to do? This man is performing many signs. [48] If we let him go on like this, everyone will believe in him, and the Romans will come and destroy both our holy place[c] and our nation." [49] But one of them, Caiaphas, who was high priest that year, said to them, "You know nothing at all!

[a] Other ancient authorities lack *and the life*
[b] Or *the Christ*
[c] Or *our temple*; Greek *our place*

be known as Jesus' followers. The presence of many Jews with them implies that they are engaged in a somewhat ritualized mourning observance, but it is unclear whether the formal practice of "sitting shiva" (observing a week of home-based mourning during which time others come to console the mourners) was already in existence at the time. **24:** Pharisees believed in bodily resurrection (*Ant.* 18.1.4; see Dan 12.1–3; 2 Macc 7.9), whereas Sadducees did not (Mk 12.18). **25–27:** Jesus reveals his identity as *the resurrection and the life*, God's gift of new existence (cf. 20.30–31). **33–35:** Here (repeated in v. 38) and 13.21 are the only passages in which the Gospel ascribes emotion to Jesus. **39:** The references to the stench in the tomb emphasize that Lazarus is really and truly dead, and therefore stresses in anticipation the marvel of his return to life **40:** *Glory*, bringing Lazarus back to life is a manifestation of God's glory, a term associated with divine splendor (11.4). **41:** Jesus prays to show that the resurrection of Lazarus manifests God's power, not Jesus'. **43:** Jesus calls Lazarus by name (cf. 5.25; 10.4). Lazarus's revival foreshadows Jesus' own (chs 20–21). **44:** In the first century, Jews were buried in linen shrouds and their bodies laid in a sealed tomb so that the flesh would decompose. After a period of eleven months, the tomb would be unsealed, and the bones would be placed in an ossuary (bone box) and stored on a shelf in the tomb. **47:** *The council*, perhaps the Sanhedrin. **48:** The fear on the part of the authorities is that the Romans will see Jesus' activities as tantamount to being a claim as king, and they will therefore crush not only Jesus' followers but the religion of the Jewish peo-

[50] You do not understand that it is better for you to have one man die for the people than to have the whole nation destroyed." [51] He did not say this on his own, but being high priest that year he prophesied that Jesus was about to die for the nation, [52] and not for the nation only, but to gather into one the dispersed children of God. [53] So from that day on they planned to put him to death.

[54] Jesus therefore no longer walked about openly among the Jews, but went from there to a town called Ephraim in the region near the wilderness; and he remained there with the disciples.

[55] Now the Passover of the Jews was near, and many went up from the country to Jerusalem before the Passover to purify themselves. [56] They were looking for Jesus and were asking one another as they stood in the temple, "What do you think? Surely he will not come to the festival, will he?" [57] Now the chief priests and the Pharisees had given orders that anyone who knew where Jesus[a] was should let them know, so that they might arrest him.

12 Six days before the Passover Jesus came to Bethany, the home of Lazarus, whom he had raised from the dead. [2] There they gave a dinner for him. Martha served, and Lazarus was one of those at the table with him. [3] Mary took a pound of costly perfume made of pure nard, anointed Jesus' feet, and wiped them[b] with her hair. The house was filled with the fragrance of the perfume. [4] But Judas Iscariot, one of his disciples (the one who was about to betray him), said, [5] "Why was this perfume not sold for three hundred denarii[c] and the money given to the poor?" [6] (He said this not because he cared about the poor, but because he was a thief; he kept the common purse and used to steal what was put into it.) [7] Jesus said, "Leave her alone. She bought it[d] so that she might keep it for the day of my burial. [8] You always have the poor with you, but you do not always have me."

[9] When the great crowd of the Jews learned that he was there, they came not only because of Jesus but also to see Lazarus, whom he had raised from the dead. [10] So the chief priests planned to put Lazarus to death as well, [11] since it was on account of him that many of the Jews were deserting and were believing in Jesus.

[12] The next day the great crowd that had come to the festival heard that Jesus was coming to Jerusalem. [13] So they took branches of palm trees and went out to meet him, shouting,

"Hosanna!
Blessed is the one who comes in the name
of the Lord—
the King of Israel!"

[14] Jesus found a young donkey and sat on it; as it is written:

[15] "Do not be afraid, daughter of Zion.
Look, your king is coming,
sitting on a donkey's colt!"

[16] His disciples did not understand these things at first; but when Jesus was glorified, then they remembered that these things had been written of him and had been done

[a] Gk *he*
[b] Gk *his feet*
[c] Three hundred denarii would be nearly a year's wages for a laborer
[d] Gk lacks *She bought it*

ple, including their Temple. **49:** *Caiaphas*, high priest between 18–36 CE (*Ant.* 18.90–95). **50–52:** The evangelist emphasizes that Caiaphas's statement is, ironically, truer than he knows. *Dispersed children*, either the Jews of the Diaspora, those who live outside Judea, or the non-Jewish members of the Christian community. **54:** *Ephraim*, twelve miles north-northeast of Jerusalem. **55:** The third Passover in this Gospel. *Before the Passover to purify themselves*, i.e., those who had to travel allowed extra time for a purification rite in case they had encountered anything in their journey that might have made them ritually unclean.

12.1–11: Anointing at Bethany (Mk 14.3–11). **1:** *Bethany*, 11.18. **2:** In Lk 10.38–42, Martha serves and Mary sits at Jesus' feet. **3:** A Roman *pound*, 327.45 grams (11 or 12 ounces). *Nard*, oil of a plant, the spikenard, the rhizomes of which can be crushed to extract an aromatic oil used as perfume; cf. Mk 14.3. **5:** A denarius was approximately one day's wages for a laborer. **7:** Jesus interprets Mary's act as foreshadowing his death. **8:** Deut 15.11. **10–11:** The Jewish leaders are motivated not only by political concerns (see 11.50) but also by the number of Jews that were *deserting* them. This formulation suggests that one could no longer be both a "Jew" and a follower of Jesus.

12.12–19: Triumphal entry (Mt 21.1–9; Mk 11.1–10; Lk 19.28–38). **13:** *Hosanna*, Heb meaning "please save," "save now," most directly associated with the Feast of Tabernacles (Booths) (see 7.37–39n.). Ps 118.26; *King of*

to him. [17] So the crowd that had been with him when he called Lazarus out of the tomb and raised him from the dead continued to testify.[a] [18] It was also because they heard that he had performed this sign that the crowd went to meet him. [19] The Pharisees then said to one another, "You see, you can do nothing. Look, the world has gone after him!"

[20] Now among those who went up to worship at the festival were some Greeks. [21] They came to Philip, who was from Bethsaida in Galilee, and said to him, "Sir, we wish to see Jesus." [22] Philip went and told Andrew; then Andrew and Philip went and told Jesus. [23] Jesus answered them, "The hour has come for the Son of Man to be glorified. [24] Very truly, I tell you, unless a grain of wheat falls into the earth and dies, it remains just a single grain; but if it dies, it bears much fruit. [25] Those who love their life lose it, and those who hate their life in this world will keep it for eternal life. [26] Whoever serves me must follow me, and where I am, there will my servant be also. Whoever serves me, the Father will honor.

[27] "Now my soul is troubled. And what should I say—'Father, save me from this hour'? No, it is for this reason that I have come to this hour. [28] Father, glorify your name." Then a voice came from heaven, "I have glorified it, and I will glorify it again." [29] The crowd standing there heard it and said that it was thunder. Others said, "An angel has spoken to him." [30] Jesus answered, "This voice has come for your sake, not for mine. [31] Now is the judgment of this world; now the ruler of this world will be driven out. [32] And I, when I am lifted up from the earth, will draw all people[b] to myself." [33] He said this to indicate the kind of death he was to die. [34] The crowd answered him, "We have heard from the law that the Messiah[c] remains forever. How can you say that the Son of Man must be lifted up? Who is this Son of Man?" [35] Jesus said to them, "The light is with you for a little longer. Walk while you have the light, so that the darkness may not overtake you. If you walk in the darkness, you do not know where you are going. [36] While you have the light, believe in the light, so that you may become children of light."

After Jesus had said this, he departed and hid from them. [37] Although he had performed so many signs in their presence, they did not believe in him. [38] This was to fulfill the word spoken by the prophet Isaiah:

"Lord, who has believed our message,
and to whom has the arm of the Lord
been revealed?"

[39] And so they could not believe, because Isaiah also said,

[40] "He has blinded their eyes
and hardened their heart,
so that they might not look with their eyes,
and understand with their heart and
turn—
and I would heal them."

[41] Isaiah said this because[d] he saw his glory and spoke about him. [42] Nevertheless many, even of the authorities, believed in him. But

[a] Other ancient authorities read *with him began to testify that he had called . . . from the dead*
[b] Other ancient authorities read *all things*
[c] Or *the Christ*
[d] Other ancient witnesses read *when*

Israel is absent from the psalm. **15:** Zeph 3.16; Zech 9.9. **16:** The disciples do not fully understand this event until after Jesus' resurrection (2.22). **19:** The Jewish leaders' concern over Jesus' popularity continues to mount.

12.20–50: End of Jesus' public ministry. 20: *Greeks*, likely Gentiles rather than Greek-speaking Jews (cf. 7.34–35). **21–22:** Would-be followers initially encounter Jesus indirectly, through someone who is already a disciple. They may approach Philip because his name is Greek ("horse-lover"). **23:** *The hour has come*, perhaps a foreshadowing that the Gospel will be preached to "Greeks" (i.e., Gentiles). **24–25:** Jesus apparently refuses to meet with the Greeks. On grain imagery, see 1 Cor 15.36. **28:** *A voice . . . from heaven*, a rabbinic term was Heb "bat qol," "daughter of the voice" or "echo," (cf. 11.41). **29:** Cf. the Israelites' response at Mount Sinai (Ex 19.18–19). Heb "qol," at Sinai (esp. Ex 19.19), may be voice or thunder as well. **31:** The trial motif concludes. *Ruler of this world*, the devil (14.30; 16.11). **34:** *Law* refers to Torah in this context. The reference may be to Ps 89.36 saying that David's seed remains forever; the psalm is interpreted messianically in Acts 13.22 and Rev 1.5; 3.24. **38:** Isa 53.1. **40:** Isa 6.10. The quotations are used to explain why the Jews as a whole did not recognize Jesus as the messiah, though individual Jews did do so. In the original the second quotation is in the imperative ("Make . . . blind," "Harden . . . heart"). **42:** See 9.22. Pharisees do not in fact run synagogues.

because of the Pharisees they did not confess it, for fear that they would be put out of the synagogue; [43] for they loved human glory more than the glory that comes from God.

[44] Then Jesus cried aloud: "Whoever believes in me believes not in me but in him who sent me. [45] And whoever sees me sees him who sent me. [46] I have come as light into the world, so that everyone who believes in me should not remain in the darkness. [47] I do not judge anyone who hears my words and does not keep them, for I came not to judge the world, but to save the world. [48] The one who rejects me and does not receive my word has a judge; on the last day the word that I have spoken will serve as judge, [49] for I have not spoken on my own, but the Father who sent me has himself given me a commandment about what to say and what to speak. [50] And I know that his commandment is eternal life. What I speak, therefore, I speak just as the Father has told me."

13 Now before the festival of the Passover, Jesus knew that his hour had come to depart from this world and go to the Father. Having loved his own who were in the world, he loved them to the end. [2] The devil had already put it into the heart of Judas son of Simon Iscariot to betray him. And during supper [3] Jesus, knowing that the Father had given all things into his hands, and that he had come from God and was going to God, [4] got up from the table,[a] took off his outer robe, and tied a towel around himself. [5] Then he poured water into a basin and began to wash the disciples' feet and to wipe them with the towel that was tied around him. [6] He came to Simon Peter, who said to him, "Lord, are you going to wash my feet?" [7] Jesus answered, "You do not know now what I am doing, but later you will understand." [8] Peter said to him, "You will never wash my feet." Jesus answered, "Unless I wash you, you have no share with me." [9] Simon Peter said to him, "Lord, not my feet only but also my hands and my head!" [10] Jesus said to him, "One who has bathed does not need to wash, except for the feet,[b] but is entirely clean. And you[c] are clean, though not all of you." [11] For he knew who was to betray him; for this reason he said, "Not all of you are clean."

[12] After he had washed their feet, had put on his robe, and had returned to the table, he said to them, "Do you know what I have done to you? [13] You call me Teacher and Lord—and you are right, for that is what I am. [14] So if I, your Lord and Teacher, have washed your feet, you also ought to wash one another's feet. [15] For I have set you an example, that you also should do as I have done to you. [16] Very truly, I tell you, servants[d] are not greater than their master, nor are messengers greater than the one who sent them. [17] If you know these things, you are blessed if you do them. [18] I am not speaking of all of you; I know whom I have chosen. But it is to fulfill the scripture, 'The one who ate my bread[e] has lifted his heel against me.' [19] I tell you this now, before it occurs, so that when it does occur, you may believe that I am he.[f] [20] Very truly, I tell you, whoever receives one whom I send receives me; and whoever receives me receives him who sent me."

[21] After saying this Jesus was troubled in spirit, and declared, "Very truly, I tell you,

[a] Gk *from supper*
[b] Other ancient authorities lack *except for the feet*
[c] The Greek word for *you* here is plural
[d] Gk *slaves*
[e] Other ancient authorities read *ate bread with me*
[f] Gk *I am*

44–50: Jesus here claims that his authority, his offer of eternal life and salvation, and the judgment that he announces, are not from himself but from God.

13.1–38: Final dinner. 1: *Passover* begins here on Friday night, in contrast to in the Synoptics, where it begins on Thursday (see Mt 26.17; Mk 14.12–16; Lk 22.15). This "supper" is not a Passover meal—it lacks the pascal lamb, and there is no institution of the Eucharist (contrast Mt 26.26–29; Mk 14.22–25; Lk 22.13–20). **2:** *The devil . . . Judas*, Jesus makes one more appeal to Judas (v. 27), after which Judas leaves to begin his betrayal. **5–10:** The foot washing is unique to John, and it indicates that members of the community should be willing to perform acts of service for one another. The foot washing was not an act of hygiene but a ritual act of purification. **13:** *Teacher . . . Lord*, both one who offers instruction and insight and one who acts with authority. **14:** The foot washing was an exemplary act of humility. **16:** See Mt 10.24; Lk 6.40. **18:** Ps 41.9. **20:** *Receives . . . whom I send*,

one of you will betray me." [22] The disciples looked at one another, uncertain of whom he was speaking. [23] One of his disciples—the one whom Jesus loved—was reclining next to him; [24] Simon Peter therefore motioned to him to ask Jesus of whom he was speaking. [25] So while reclining next to Jesus, he asked him, "Lord, who is it?" [26] Jesus answered, "It is the one to whom I give this piece of bread when I have dipped it in the dish."[a] So when he had dipped the piece of bread, he gave it to Judas son of Simon Iscariot.[b] [27] After he received the piece of bread,[c] Satan entered into him. Jesus said to him, "Do quickly what you are going to do." [28] Now no one at the table knew why he said this to him. [29] Some thought that, because Judas had the common purse, Jesus was telling him, "Buy what we need for the festival"; or, that he should give something to the poor. [30] So, after receiving the piece of bread, he immediately went out. And it was night.

[31] When he had gone out, Jesus said, "Now the Son of Man has been glorified, and God has been glorified in him. [32] If God has been glorified in him,[d] God will also glorify him in himself and will glorify him at once. [33] Little children, I am with you only a little longer. You will look for me; and as I said to the Jews so now I say to you, 'Where I am going, you cannot come.' [34] I give you a new commandment, that you love one another. Just as I have loved you, you also should love one another. [35] By this everyone will know that you are my disciples, if you have love for one another."

[36] Simon Peter said to him, "Lord, where are you going?" Jesus answered, "Where I am going, you cannot follow me now; but you will follow afterward." [37] Peter said to him, "Lord, why can I not follow you now? I will lay down my life for you." [38] Jesus answered, "Will you lay down your life for me? Very truly, I tell you, before the cock crows, you will have denied me three times.

14 "Do not let your hearts be troubled. Believe[e] in God, believe also in me. [2] In my Father's house there are many dwelling places. If it were not so, would I have told you that I go to prepare a place for you?[f] [3] And if I go and prepare a place for you, I will come again and will take you to myself, so that where I am, there you may be also. [4] And you know the way to the place where I am going."[g] [5] Thomas said to him, "Lord, we do not know where you are going. How can we know the way?" [6] Jesus said to him, "I am the way, and the truth, and

a Gk *dipped it*
b Other ancient authorities read *Judas Iscariot son of Simon*; others, *Judas son of Simon from Karyot* (Kerioth)
c Gk *After the piece of bread*
d Other ancient authorities lack *If God has been glorified in him*
e Or *You believe*
f Or *If it were not so, I would have told you; for I go to prepare a place for you*
g Other ancient authorities read *Where I am going you know, and the way you know*

an apostle (Gk "one who is sent") is a full representative of the sender. **22:** The identity of Jesus' betrayer is not known to the other disciples. Cf. Mt 26.21; Mk 14.17. **23:** The first appearance of the anonymous "beloved disciple," but apparently Jesus' closest disciple and the eyewitness who "wrote" the Gospel; cf. 19.25–27; 20.2; 21.1–14,20–24. From this point on, the Gospel subordinates Peter to the beloved disciple in their relationship to Jesus and leadership of the disciples. **30:** *Night*, see 3.19. **31:** *Now . . . glorified*, the events are now underway. **34:** *New commandment*, the *commandment* (Gk "entolē," in LXX for "mitzvah," "commandment, order") is not "new" in the sense of not having been given before; Lev 19.18,34 enjoins love of one's fellow and of the stranger (see "The Concept of Neighbor," p. 540). "Hillel would say, Be of the followers of Aaron, loving peace, pursuing peace, loving your fellow human beings and bringing them to Torah" (*m. Avot* 1.12). Instead, it is part of the new life to which the disciples are invited (14.15; 15.12–17). **36–38:** Mt 26.33–35; Mk. 14.29–30; Lk 22.33–34. **38:** See 18.15–27.

14.1–16.33: Farewell discourses. 2: *My father's house* implies that eternal life pertains to another realm. There may be an allusion here to the Jewish "Hekhalot" ("palaces") tradition, involving stories in which a seer visits the heavenly realm and explores its different rooms (based on the chariot vision in Ezek 1, and in such works as *1 En.* 17, 18). More immediately, the verse also alludes to the Temple, which Jesus called his Father's house in 2.16 and to the son/slave contrast in 8.35. **6:** *The way*, a summary of Johannine Christology. Christ-believers called themselves "the Way" (Acts 9.2). *Truth . . . life*, knowledge of truth is more like a personal relationship, instead of

the life. No one comes to the Father except through me. [7] If you know me, you will know[a] my Father also. From now on you do know him and have seen him."

[8] Philip said to him, "Lord, show us the Father, and we will be satisfied." [9] Jesus said to him, "Have I been with you all this time, Philip, and you still do not know me? Whoever has seen me has seen the Father. How can you say, 'Show us the Father'? [10] Do you not believe that I am in the Father and the Father is in me? The words that I say to you I do not speak on my own; but the Father who dwells in me does his works. [11] Believe me that I am in the Father and the Father is in me; but if you do not, then believe me because of the works themselves. [12] Very truly, I tell you, the one who believes in me will also do the works that I do and, in fact, will do greater works than these, because I am going to the Father. [13] I will do whatever you ask in my name, so that the Father may be glorified in the Son. [14] If in my name you ask me[b] for anything, I will do it.

[15] "If you love me, you will keep[c] my commandments. [16] And I will ask the Father, and he will give you another Advocate,[d] to be with you forever. [17] This is the Spirit of truth, whom the world cannot receive, because it neither sees him nor knows him. You know him, because he abides with you, and he will be in[e] you.

[18] "I will not leave you orphaned; I am coming to you. [19] In a little while the world will no longer see me, but you will see me; because I live, you also will live. [20] On that day you will know that I am in my Father, and you in me, and I in you. [21] They who have my commandments and keep them are those who love me; and those who love me will be loved by my Father, and I will love them and reveal myself to them." [22] Judas (not Iscariot) said to him, "Lord, how is it that you will reveal yourself to us, and not to the world?" [23] Jesus answered him, "Those who love me will keep my word, and my Father will love them, and we will come to them and make our home with them. [24] Whoever does not love me does not keep my words; and the word that you hear is not mine, but is from the Father who sent me.

[25] "I have said these things to you while I am still with you. [26] But the Advocate,[d] the Holy Spirit, whom the Father will send in my name, will teach you everything, and remind you of all that I have said to you. [27] Peace I leave with you; my peace I give to you. I do not give to you as the world gives. Do not let your hearts be troubled, and do not let them be afraid. [28] You heard me say to you, 'I am going away, and I am coming to you.' If you loved me, you would rejoice that I am going to the Father, because the Father is greater than I. [29] And now I have told you this before it occurs, so that when it does occur, you may believe. [30] I will no longer talk much with you, for the ruler of this world is coming. He has no power over me; [31] but I do as the Father has commanded me, so that the world may know that I love the Father. Rise, let us be on our way.

15 "I am the true vine, and my Father is the vinegrower. [2] He removes every branch in me that bears no fruit. Every

[a] Other ancient authorities read *If you had known me, you would have known*
[b] Other ancient authorities lack *me*
[c] Other ancient authorities read *me, keep*
[d] Or *Helper*
[e] Or *among*

an intellectual experience. *No one . . . except through me*, the basis for exclusive claims in later Christian history. **7–11:** To "see" Jesus is not a visual experience but one of personal knowledge; therefore to know Jesus and to understand his life is to understand and know the life of God. **12–14:** *Works* means not just "signs" but Jesus' willingness to offer his life (15.13). *In my name*, in accordance with my true character. **15:** Jesus, like Moses, has given commandments, which are now central to the covenantal relationship between the believer and God. (See "The Concept of Neighbor," p. 540.) **16–17:** The community will receive an *Advocate* (Gk "parakletos," "one who stands beside," a supporter or comforter), who is the *Spirit of truth*. This passage influenced later Christian thought about the nature and role of the Holy Spirit. **20:** John's Gospel suggests that Jesus is equivalent to God (10.30) and that Jesus is God's son and agent (6.38). **22:** *Judas*, apparently two disciples had this name; see Lk 6.16; Acts 1.13. **30:** *The ruler of this world*, Satan (cf. 12.31; 16.11). For John's Gospel, the Jews, who plotted Jesus' death, are Satan's agents (cf. 8.44). **31:** The discourse seems to be at an end, yet Jesus continues to speak for three more chapters.

branch that bears fruit he prunes[a] to make it bear more fruit. [3] You have already been cleansed[a] by the word that I have spoken to you. [4] Abide in me as I abide in you. Just as the branch cannot bear fruit by itself unless it abides in the vine, neither can you unless you abide in me. [5] I am the vine, you are the branches. Those who abide in me and I in them bear much fruit, because apart from me you can do nothing. [6] Whoever does not abide in me is thrown away like a branch and withers; such branches are gathered, thrown into the fire, and burned. [7] If you abide in me, and my words abide in you, ask for whatever you wish, and it will be done for you. [8] My Father is glorified by this, that you bear much fruit and become[b] my disciples. [9] As the Father has loved me, so I have loved you; abide in my love. [10] If you keep my commandments, you will abide in my love, just as I have kept my Father's commandments and abide in his love. [11] I have said these things to you so that my joy may be in you, and that your joy may be complete.

[12] "This is my commandment, that you love one another as I have loved you. [13] No one has greater love than this, to lay down one's life for one's friends. [14] You are my friends if you do what I command you. [15] I do not call you servants[c] any longer, because the servant[d] does not know what the master is doing; but I have called you friends, because I have made known to you everything that I have heard from my Father. [16] You did not choose me but I chose you. And I appointed you to go and bear fruit, fruit that will last, so that the Father will give you whatever you ask him in my name. [17] I am giving you these commands so that you may love one another.

[18] "If the world hates you, be aware that it hated me before it hated you. [19] If you belonged to the world,[e] the world would love you as its own. Because you do not belong to the world, but I have chosen you out of the world—therefore the world hates you. [20] Remember the word that I said to you, 'Servants[f] are not greater than their master.' If they persecuted me, they will persecute you; if they kept my word, they will keep yours also. [21] But they will do all these things to you on account of my name, because they do not know him who sent me. [22] If I had not come and spoken to them, they would not have sin; but now they have no excuse for their sin. [23] Whoever hates me hates my Father also. [24] If I had not done among them the works that no one else did, they would not have sin. But now they have seen and hated both me and my Father. [25] It was to fulfill the word that is written in their law, 'They hated me without a cause.'

[26] "When the Advocate[g] comes, whom I will send to you from the Father, the Spirit of truth who comes from the Father, he will testify on my behalf. [27] You also are to testify because you have been with me from the beginning.

a The same Greek root refers to pruning and cleansing
b Or *be*
c Gk *slaves*
d Gk *slave*
e Gk *were of the world*
f Gk *Slaves*
g Or *Helper*

Jesus and his followers do not go out until 18.1, perhaps indicating that two or more sources have been combined into one final speech. **15.1–6:** *Vine*, a common image for God's people; see Isa 5.1–10. **3:** *Cleansed*, or "pruned" (see translators' note *a*). The image is of the necessary cutting back on a vine so that it will produce fruit. **5:** *Vine . . . branches*, the branches are part of the vine; the comparison is not "stem" and "branches." **6:** The wood of the vine cannot be put to any other use if it does not produce fruit. See also Mt 3.10. **12:** The notion of dying for one's friends is also expressed in Aristotle's extensive comments on friendship in the *Nicomachean Ethics* 9.1169a, which may underlie the Gospel's entire discussion on friendship and love in the farewell discourses chs 14–16). **16:** *I chose you*, probably not an expression of predestination, but of Jesus' calling his followers (e.g., 1.43). **18–25:** Prophecy of persecution perhaps intended to help the Johannine community through a time of difficulty. *The world* is both the opposition to the work of Jesus and the community of his followers, and the area where that work takes place (17.15–18). **22–24:** Those who knew Jesus and saw his works cannot claim ignorance as an excuse for their opposition to him. **24:** Allusion to 9.39–41, implying that the Jews are agents of persecution. **25:** *Law*, used by extension of the entire Bible, since the quotation is not from the Torah but from Ps 35.19; 69.4. The opponents of Jesus do not understand *their* own *law*. **26:** *Advocate*, see 14.15ff. **27:** *Testify*, presumably in public.

16 "I have said these things to you to keep you from stumbling. [2] They will put you out of the synagogues. Indeed, an hour is coming when those who kill you will think that by doing so they are offering worship to God. [3] And they will do this because they have not known the Father or me. [4] But I have said these things to you so that when their hour comes you may remember that I told you about them.

"I did not say these things to you from the beginning, because I was with you. [5] But now I am going to him who sent me; yet none of you asks me, 'Where are you going?' [6] But because I have said these things to you, sorrow has filled your hearts. [7] Nevertheless I tell you the truth: it is to your advantage that I go away, for if I do not go away, the Advocate[a] will not come to you; but if I go, I will send him to you. [8] And when he comes, he will prove the world wrong about[b] sin and righteousness and judgment: [9] about sin, because they do not believe in me; [10] about righteousness, because I am going to the Father and you will see me no longer; [11] about judgment, because the ruler of this world has been condemned.

[12] "I still have many things to say to you, but you cannot bear them now. [13] When the Spirit of truth comes, he will guide you into all the truth; for he will not speak on his own, but will speak whatever he hears, and he will declare to you the things that are to come. [14] He will glorify me, because he will take what is mine and declare it to you. [15] All that the Father has is mine. For this reason I said that he will take what is mine and declare it to you.

[16] "A little while, and you will no longer see me, and again a little while, and you will see me." [17] Then some of his disciples said to one another, "What does he mean by saying to us, 'A little while, and you will no longer see me, and again a little while, and you will see me'; and 'Because I am going to the Father'?" [18] They said, "What does he mean by this 'a little while'? We do not know what he is talking about." [19] Jesus knew that they wanted to ask him, so he said to them, "Are you discussing among yourselves what I meant when I said, 'A little while, and you will no longer see me, and again a little while, and you will see me'? [20] Very truly, I tell you, you will weep and mourn, but the world will rejoice; you will have pain, but your pain will turn into joy. [21] When a woman is in labor, she has pain, because her hour has come. But when her child is born, she no longer remembers the anguish because of the joy of having brought a human being into the world. [22] So you have pain now; but I will see you again, and your hearts will rejoice, and no one will take your joy from you. [23] On that day you will ask nothing of me.[c] Very truly, I tell you, if you ask anything of the Father in my name, he will give it to you.[d] [24] Until now you have not asked for anything in my name. Ask and you will receive, so that your joy may be complete.

[25] "I have said these things to you in figures of speech. The hour is coming when I will no longer speak to you in figures, but will tell you plainly of the Father. [26] On that day you will ask in my name. I do not say to you that I will ask the Father on your behalf; [27] for the Father himself loves you, because you have loved me and have believed that I came from

a Or *Helper*
b Or *convict the world of*
c Or *will ask me no question*
d Other ancient authorities read *Father, he will give it to you in my name*

16.1–4a: Synagogue expulsion (9.22; 12.42). **2:** *Those who kill you*, a general reference, but in context a suggestion that Jews will kill Jesus' followers. **4:** *Their hour* could mean either the hour of the opponents' ascendancy (Lk 22.53) or the hour of seeming defeat that is actually triumph (17.1). **4b–14:** The Paraclete (see 14.15ff.). **8–11:** *Sin* is here the failure to believe or trust in Jesus and therefore to separate oneself from God; *righteousness* is Jesus' reunion with the Father, which the opponents do not acknowledge; *judgment* is the recognition that the power of opposition and evil that organizes this *world* has already been deposed. **12–14:** These statements about the *Spirit* and the *Father* were important in the later development of Christian doctrine about God as Trinity. **16:** *A little while*, perhaps an indication that the end is near; cf. Hag 2.6. **20–22:** Apocalyptic imagery prophesying the end times. *Woman . . . labor*, see Isa 21.3; 42.14. **25–28:** Jesus speaks plainly of his death and return to the Father, and the state of being he occupied before coming into the world (cf. 1.1–18).

God.[a] [28] I came from the Father and have come into the world; again, I am leaving the world and am going to the Father."

[29] His disciples said, "Yes, now you are speaking plainly, not in any figure of speech! [30] Now we know that you know all things, and do not need to have anyone question you; by this we believe that you came from God." [31] Jesus answered them, "Do you now believe? [32] The hour is coming, indeed it has come, when you will be scattered, each one to his home, and you will leave me alone. Yet I am not alone because the Father is with me. [33] I have said this to you, so that in me you may have peace. In the world you face persecution. But take courage; I have conquered the world!"

17 After Jesus had spoken these words, he looked up to heaven and said, "Father, the hour has come; glorify your Son so that the Son may glorify you, [2] since you have given him authority over all people,[b] to give eternal life to all whom you have given him. [3] And this is eternal life, that they may know you, the only true God, and Jesus Christ whom you have sent. [4] I glorified you on earth by finishing the work that you gave me to do. [5] So now, Father, glorify me in your own presence with the glory that I had in your presence before the world existed.

[6] "I have made your name known to those whom you gave me from the world. They were yours, and you gave them to me, and they have kept your word. [7] Now they know that everything you have given me is from you; [8] for the words that you gave to me I have given to them, and they have received them and know in truth that I came from you; and they have believed that you sent me. [9] I am asking on their behalf; I am not asking on behalf of the world, but on behalf of those whom you gave me, because they are yours. [10] All mine are yours, and yours are mine; and I have been glorified in them. [11] And now I am no longer in the world, but they are in the world, and I am coming to you. Holy Father, protect them in your name that you have given me, so that they may be one, as we are one. [12] While I was with them, I protected them in your name that[c] you have given me. I guarded them, and not one of them was lost except the one destined to be lost,[d] so that the scripture might be fulfilled. [13] But now I am coming to you, and I speak these things in the world so that they may have my joy made complete in themselves.[e] [14] I have given them your word, and the world has hated them because they do not belong to the world, just as I do not belong to the world. [15] I am not asking you to take them out of the world, but I ask you to protect them from the evil one.[f] [16] They do not belong to the world, just as I do not belong to the world. [17] Sanctify them in the truth; your word is truth. [18] As you have sent me into the world, so I have sent them into the world. [19] And for their sakes I sanctify myself, so that they also may be sanctified in truth.

[20] "I ask not only on behalf of these, but also on behalf of those who will believe in me through their word, [21] that they may all be one. As you, Father, are in me and I am in you, may they also be in us,[g] so that the world may believe that you have sent me. [22] The glory that you have given me I have given them, so that they may be one, as we are one, [23] I in them and you in me, that they may become completely one, so that the world may know that you have sent me and have loved them even as you have loved me. [24] Father, I desire that those also, whom you have given me, may be with me where I am, to see my glory, which you have given me because you loved me before the foundation of the world.

[a] Other ancient authorities read *the Father*
[b] Gk *flesh*
[c] Other ancient authorities read *protected in your name those whom*
[d] Gk *except the son of destruction*
[e] Or *among themselves*
[f] Or *from evil*
[g] Other ancient authorities read *be one in us*

17.1–26: Jesus' prayer. Jesus addresses God on behalf of his followers (Mt 6.9–13; Lk 11.2–4). In Mt and Lk, Jesus teaches his followers how and what to pray; here he prays for himself and on their behalf. **3:** *Eternal life,* defined as faith in Christ. **4:** Glorification refers to the revelation of God's power and expresses Jesus' desire to return to the Father. **5:** *Before the world existed,* see 1.1–3; 8.58. **12:** *Destined to be lost,* Judas Iscariot. **15:** *Evil one,* Satan. **17:** *Truth,* see 8.32; 14.6. **24:** *Foundation of the world,* Jesus' preexistence (1.1–18).

[25] "Righteous Father, the world does not know you, but I know you; and these know that you have sent me. [26] I made your name known to them, and I will make it known, so that the love with which you have loved me may be in them, and I in them."

18 After Jesus had spoken these words, he went out with his disciples across the Kidron valley to a place where there was a garden, which he and his disciples entered. [2] Now Judas, who betrayed him, also knew the place, because Jesus often met there with his disciples. [3] So Judas brought a detachment of soldiers together with police from the chief priests and the Pharisees, and they came there with lanterns and torches and weapons. [4] Then Jesus, knowing all that was to happen to him, came forward and asked them, "Whom are you looking for?" [5] They answered, "Jesus of Nazareth."[a] Jesus replied, "I am he."[b] Judas, who betrayed him, was standing with them. [6] When Jesus[c] said to them, "I am he,"[b] they stepped back and fell to the ground. [7] Again he asked them, "Whom are you looking for?" And they said, "Jesus of Nazareth."[a] [8] Jesus answered, "I told you that I am he.[b] So if you are looking for me, let these men go." [9] This was to fulfill the word that he had spoken, "I did not lose a single one of those whom you gave me." [10] Then Simon Peter, who had a sword, drew it, struck the high priest's slave, and cut off his right ear. The slave's name was Malchus. [11] Jesus said to Peter, "Put your sword back into its sheath. Am I not to drink the cup that the Father has given me?"

[12] So the soldiers, their officer, and the Jewish police arrested Jesus and bound him. [13] First they took him to Annas, who was the father-in-law of Caiaphas, the high priest that year. [14] Caiaphas was the one who had advised the Jews that it was better to have one person die for the people.

[15] Simon Peter and another disciple followed Jesus. Since that disciple was known to the high priest, he went with Jesus into the courtyard of the high priest, [16] but Peter was standing outside at the gate. So the other disciple, who was known to the high priest, went out, spoke to the woman who guarded the gate, and brought Peter in. [17] The woman said to Peter, "You are not also one of this man's disciples, are you?" He said, "I am not." [18] Now the slaves and the police had made a charcoal fire because it was cold, and they were standing around it and warming themselves. Peter also was standing with them and warming himself.

[19] Then the high priest questioned Jesus about his disciples and about his teaching. [20] Jesus answered, "I have spoken openly to the world; I have always taught in synagogues and in the temple, where all the Jews come together. I have said nothing in secret. [21] Why do you ask me? Ask those who heard what I said to them; they know what I said." [22] When he had said this, one of the police standing nearby struck Jesus on the face, saying, "Is that how you answer the high priest?" [23] Jesus answered, "If I have spoken wrongly, testify to the wrong. But if I have spoken rightly, why do you strike me?" [24] Then Annas sent him bound to Caiaphas the high priest.

a Gk *the Nazorean*
b Gk *I am*
c Gk *he*

18.1–19.42: Passion narrative (Mt 26.30–27.61; Mk 14.26–15.47; Lk 22.39–23.56).

18.1–40: Arrest and trial. 1: *Kidron valley*, east of Jerusalem. A *garden*, called Gethsemane in Mt 26.36; Mk 14.32. **3:** Jesus' arrest was carried out by Roman and Jewish police. *Pharisees* would not have had their own police; perhaps the Pharisees came along with the Temple police. **5:** Double entendre. Jesus identifies himself with the "I am" formula (Ex 3.14; cf. Jn 6.35; 8.58). **6:** *Fell to the ground*, perhaps suggesting a theophany. **9:** Cf. 6.39; 10.28; 17.12. Jesus' words, thoughout the Gospel, are viewed as prophecies, with the same authority as the scriptures. **10:** Mt 26.51–52; Mk 14.47; Lk 22.50. Only John names perpetrator (*Peter*) and victim (*Malchus*). **11:** *Drink the cup*, see e.g., Isa 51.17; Ps 16.5; Lam 4.21. **13:** *Annas*, high priest 6–15 CE. **14:** Cf. 11.49–52. **15–27:** Peter's interrogation by the high priest's slaves and police is interwoven with Jesus' interrogation before Annas. **15:** *Known to the high priest*, suggesting a Temple connection, but one that is not specified. Peter's unwillingness to admit that he is Jesus' follower fulfills Jesus' prophecy in 13.38. **20:** See 7.14,37; 8.20n.,59. Such passages demonstrate Jesus' assertion that he has spoken openly in the Temple and synagogue. **24:**

[25] Now Simon Peter was standing and warming himself. They asked him, "You are not also one of his disciples, are you?" He denied it and said, "I am not." [26] One of the slaves of the high priest, a relative of the man whose ear Peter had cut off, asked, "Did I not see you in the garden with him?" [27] Again Peter denied it, and at that moment the cock crowed.

[28] Then they took Jesus from Caiaphas to Pilate's headquarters.[a] It was early in the morning. They themselves did not enter the headquarters,[a] so as to avoid ritual defilement and to be able to eat the Passover. [29] So Pilate went out to them and said, "What accusation do you bring against this man?" [30] They answered, "If this man were not a criminal, we would not have handed him over to you." [31] Pilate said to them, "Take him yourselves and judge him according to your law." The Jews replied, "We are not permitted to put anyone to death." [32] (This was to fulfill what Jesus had said when he indicated the kind of death he was to die.)

[33] Then Pilate entered the headquarters[a] again, summoned Jesus, and asked him, "Are you the King of the Jews?" [34] Jesus answered, "Do you ask this on your own, or did others tell you about me?" [35] Pilate replied, "I am not a Jew, am I? Your own nation and the chief priests have handed you over to me. What have you done?" [36] Jesus answered, "My kingdom is not from this world. If my kingdom were from this world, my followers would be fighting to keep me from being handed over to the Jews. But as it is, my kingdom is not from here." [37] Pilate asked him, "So you are a king?" Jesus answered, "You say that I am a king. For this I was born, and for this I came into the world, to testify to the truth. Everyone who belongs to the truth listens to my voice." [38] Pilate asked him, "What is truth?"

After he had said this, he went out to the Jews again and told them, "I find no case against him. [39] But you have a custom that I release someone for you at the Passover. Do you want me to release for you the King of the Jews?" [40] They shouted in reply, "Not this man, but Barabbas!" Now Barabbas was a bandit.

19 Then Pilate took Jesus and had him flogged. [2] And the soldiers wove a crown of thorns and put it on his head, and they dressed him in a purple robe. [3] They kept coming up to him, saying, "Hail, King of the Jews!" and striking him on the face. [4] Pilate went out again and said to them, "Look, I am bringing him out to you to let you know that I find no case against him." [5] So Jesus came out, wearing the crown of thorns and the purple robe. Pilate said to them, "Here is the man!" [6] When the chief priests and the police saw him, they shouted, "Crucify him! Crucify him!" Pilate said to them, "Take him yourselves and crucify him; I find no case against him." [7] The Jews answered him, "We have a law, and according to that law he ought to die because he has claimed to be the Son of God."

[a] Gk *the praetorium*

In contrast to Matthew, John depicts no trial before Caiaphas, which, if any of the Gospel trial accounts is historical, is not possible to determine (cf. Mt 26.57–68). **28:** *Avoid ritual defilement*, an ironic statement. "Defilement" could mean touching leaven during Passover or anything associated with a corpse. **31:** Jews were not allowed to impose the death penalty; thus Jesus is crucified, a Roman penalty. **33:** *King of the Jews*, anyone claiming kingship without Roman permission would have been regarded as a potential or actual insurrectionist. The ruler(s) of the Jewish territories owed their primary loyalty to Rome. **36:** *My kingdom is not from this world*, in context, this is an argument against seeing Jesus as a political threat. **38:** More irony: Pilate cannot see the *truth* in front of him. **39:** This tradition has no external historical support (cf. Mt 27.15; Mk 15.6; Lk 23.17). **40:** *Barabbas* could be translated "son of a [or the] father." *Bandit*, probably meaning a revolutionary rather than a thief.

19.1–16: Condemnation. 1: *Flogged*, Lk 23.22. This was a common penalty (2 Cor 11.23–25), but here was perhaps meant to weaken Jesus' resistance. **2:** *Crown . . . purple*, symbols of kingship used in mockery. **5:** *Here is the man*, famous in its Latin version, "Ecce Homo." **6–7:** In John it is the Temple party, and not the people as a whole, who call for crucifixion (contrast Mt 27.25); this indicates that John saw the opposition to Jesus primarily in the leadership. **7:** *Law*, probably a reference to the prohibition of blasphemy (Lev 24.16), the penalty for which

[8] Now when Pilate heard this, he was more afraid than ever. [9] He entered his headquarters[a] again and asked Jesus, "Where are you from?" But Jesus gave him no answer. [10] Pilate therefore said to him, "Do you refuse to speak to me? Do you not know that I have power to release you, and power to crucify you?" [11] Jesus answered him, "You would have no power over me unless it had been given you from above; therefore the one who handed me over to you is guilty of a greater sin." [12] From then on Pilate tried to release him, but the Jews cried out, "If you release this man, you are no friend of the emperor. Everyone who claims to be a king sets himself against the emperor."

[13] When Pilate heard these words, he brought Jesus outside and sat[b] on the judge's bench at a place called The Stone Pavement, or in Hebrew[c] Gabbatha. [14] Now it was the day of Preparation for the Passover; and it was about noon. He said to the Jews, "Here is your King!" [15] They cried out, "Away with him! Away with him! Crucify him!" Pilate asked them, "Shall I crucify your King?" The chief priests answered, "We have no king but the emperor." [16] Then he handed him over to them to be crucified.

So they took Jesus; [17] and carrying the cross by himself, he went out to what is called The Place of the Skull, which in Hebrew[c] is called Golgotha. [18] There they crucified him, and with him two others, one on either side, with Jesus between them. [19] Pilate also had an inscription written and put on the cross. It read, "Jesus of Nazareth,[d] the King of the Jews." [20] Many of the Jews read this inscription, because the place where Jesus was crucified was near the city; and it was written in Hebrew,[c] in Latin, and in Greek. [21] Then the chief priests of the Jews said to Pilate, "Do not write, 'The King of the Jews,' but, 'This man said, I am King of the Jews.'" [22] Pilate answered, "What I have written I have written." [23] When the soldiers had crucified Jesus, they took his clothes and divided them into four parts, one for each soldier. They also took his tunic; now the tunic was seamless, woven in one piece from the top. [24] So they said to one another, "Let us not tear it, but cast lots for it to see who will get it." This was to fulfill what the scripture says,

"They divided my clothes among
themselves,
and for my clothing they cast lots."

[25] And that is what the soldiers did.

Meanwhile, standing near the cross of Jesus were his mother, and his mother's sister, Mary the wife of Clopas, and Mary Magdalene. [26] When Jesus saw his mother and the disciple whom he loved standing beside her, he said to his mother, "Woman, here is your son." [27] Then he said to the disciple, "Here is your mother." And from that hour the disciple took her into his own home.

[28] After this, when Jesus knew that all was now finished, he said (in order to fulfill the scripture), "I am thirsty." [29] A jar full of sour wine was standing there. So they put a

[a] Gk *the praetorium*
[b] Or *seated him*
[c] That is, *Aramaic*
[d] Gk *the Nazorean*

was death by stoning. **8:** *Afraid*, perhaps of making the wrong judgment. **12:** The Jews threaten to blackmail Pilate if he releases Jesus. **13:** *Gabbatha*, an outdoor platform, perhaps meaning "elevated place." It is at this point that Pilate actually renders judgment (previously he has, in effect, been conducting an inquiry). **14:** *Day of Preparation*, when the Passover lambs are slaughtered in the Temple. **15–16:** When the Jewish leaders affirm the kingship of Caesar, Pilate agrees to have Jesus crucified. The execution will be carried out by Romans.

19.17–37: The crucifixion. 17: *Cross*, the crossbeam rather than the entire cross. There is no mention that someone else (Simon of Cyrene, Mk 15.21) carries the cross instead of Jesus. *Golgotha*, likely just outside the city walls to the northwest. **19–20:** *Inscription . . . in Hebrew, in Latin, and in Greek*, it is uncertain whether such inscriptions were usual; this seems mostly to indicate that Jesus' claims were addressed to all who would pass by. **23:** *Tunic*, undergarment. **24:** Ps 22.18. In Mk 15.34, Jesus quotes the first verse of this psalm, "My God, my God, why have you forsaken me?" **25:** *His mother*, unnamed in the Gospel (cf. 2.1). *Mary the wife of Clopas*, perhaps the mother of James and Joses (Mk 15.40). In the Synoptics the women must stand at a distance (Mk 15.40). **28:** Ps. 69.21. **29:** The only time in the Gospel that Jesus explicitly consumes food or drink. *Hyssop* was used to mark

sponge full of the wine on a branch of hyssop and held it to his mouth. [30] When Jesus had received the wine, he said, "It is finished." Then he bowed his head and gave up his spirit.

[31] Since it was the day of Preparation, the Jews did not want the bodies left on the cross during the sabbath, especially because that sabbath was a day of great solemnity. So they asked Pilate to have the legs of the crucified men broken and the bodies removed. [32] Then the soldiers came and broke the legs of the first and of the other who had been crucified with him. [33] But when they came to Jesus and saw that he was already dead, they did not break his legs. [34] Instead, one of the soldiers pierced his side with a spear, and at once blood and water came out. [35] (He who saw this has testified so that you also may believe. His testimony is true, and he knows[a] that he tells the truth.) [36] These things occurred so that the scripture might be fulfilled, "None of his bones shall be broken." [37] And again another passage of scripture says, "They will look on the one whom they have pierced."

[38] After these things, Joseph of Arimathea, who was a disciple of Jesus, though a secret one because of his fear of the Jews, asked Pilate to let him take away the body of Jesus. Pilate gave him permission; so he came and removed his body. [39] Nicodemus, who had at first come to Jesus by night, also came, bringing a mixture of myrrh and aloes, weighing about a hundred pounds. [40] They took the body of Jesus and wrapped it with the spices in linen cloths, according to the burial custom of the Jews. [41] Now there was a garden in the place where he was crucified, and in the garden there was a new tomb in which no one had ever been laid. [42] And so, because it was the Jewish day of Preparation, and the tomb was nearby, they laid Jesus there.

20 Early on the first day of the week, while it was still dark, Mary Magdalene came to the tomb and saw that the stone had been removed from the tomb. [2] So she ran and went to Simon Peter and the other disciple, the one whom Jesus loved, and said to them, "They have taken the Lord out of the tomb, and we do not know where they have laid him." [3] Then Peter and the other disciple set out and went toward the tomb. [4] The two were running together, but the other disciple outran Peter and reached the tomb first. [5] He bent down to look in and saw the linen wrappings lying there, but he did not go in. [6] Then Simon Peter came, following him, and went into the tomb. He saw the linen wrappings lying there, [7] and the cloth that had been on Jesus' head, not lying with the linen wrappings but rolled up in a place by itself. [8] Then the other disciple, who reached the tomb first, also went in, and he saw and believed; [9] for as yet they did not

[a] Or *there is one who knows*

the doorposts with the blood of lambs at the time of the Passover before the Exodus from Egypt (Ex 12.22). Its mention here may be intended to recall the theme of Jesus as the Passover sacrifice. **31:** *Day of Preparation*, see 19.14n. The legs of crucifixion victims were often broken to hasten death. In keeping with the sacrificial theme, the fact that Jesus' legs were not broken may have symbolized his suitability as a Passover sacrifice given his unblemished nature, both physical and spiritual (cf. Ex 12.46; Heb 9.14). **34:** *Blood and water*, signifying both birth and the rituals of baptism and the eucharistic meal. **36:** Ex 12.46; Ps 34.20. Jesus is the Passover lamb, as lambs were slaughtered for the Passover sacrifice (see also 1.29). **37:** Zech 12.10.

19.38–42: Burial. 38: *Joseph of Arimathea*, cf. Mt 27.57–60; Mk 15.43; Lk 23.50–53. **39:** *Nicodemus*, see 3.1–17; 7.50–52. *Myrrh*, resinous gum mixed with *aloes*, used for embalming; this may recall Jesus' anointing (12.3). A hundred Roman pounds = 75 lbs. **40:** The explanation implies a non-Jewish audience. **41–42:** The *garden* is not literally *in the place where he was crucified*, but *nearby*. There was not much time to complete the burial preparations before sunset, when Passover would begin.

20.1–31: Resurrection appearances. (Mt 28; Mk 16; Lk 24). **1–18: The empty tomb. 1:** *First day*, Sunday. Mary had to wait until the Sabbath was over. *Mary Magdalene* is named in Mt and Mk; Lk does not name the women at the tomb, but here, Mary Magdalene is alone. **3–8:** A foot race between the contenders for Jesus' closest disciple. This passage may intimate the Johannine effort to elevate itself over churches who viewed Peter as the principal disciple. **8:** The "beloved disciple" may have believed the prophecy of Jesus' resurrection, or simply the testimony of Mary Magdalene. **9:** There is no specific quotation referring to this from the Tanakh.

understand the scripture, that he must rise from the dead. [10] Then the disciples returned to their homes.

[11] But Mary stood weeping outside the tomb. As she wept, she bent over to look[a] into the tomb; [12] and she saw two angels in white, sitting where the body of Jesus had been lying, one at the head and the other at the feet. [13] They said to her, "Woman, why are you weeping?" She said to them, "They have taken away my Lord, and I do not know where they have laid him." [14] When she had said this, she turned around and saw Jesus standing there, but she did not know that it was Jesus. [15] Jesus said to her, "Woman, why are you weeping? Whom are you looking for?" Supposing him to be the gardener, she said to him, "Sir, if you have carried him away, tell me where you have laid him, and I will take him away." [16] Jesus said to her, "Mary!" She turned and said to him in Hebrew,[b] "Rabbouni!" (which means Teacher). [17] Jesus said to her, "Do not hold on to me, because I have not yet ascended to the Father. But go to my brothers and say to them, 'I am ascending to my Father and your Father, to my God and your God.'" [18] Mary Magdalene went and announced to the disciples, "I have seen the Lord"; and she told them that he had said these things to her.

[19] When it was evening on that day, the first day of the week, and the doors of the house where the disciples had met were locked for fear of the Jews, Jesus came and stood among them and said, "Peace be with you." [20] After he said this, he showed them his hands and his side. Then the disciples rejoiced when they saw the Lord. [21] Jesus said to them again, "Peace be with you. As the Father has sent me, so I send you." [22] When he had said this, he breathed on them and said to them, "Receive the Holy Spirit. [23] If you forgive the sins of any, they are forgiven them; if you retain the sins of any, they are retained."

[24] But Thomas (who was called the Twin[c]), one of the twelve, was not with them when Jesus came. [25] So the other disciples told him, "We have seen the Lord." But he said to them, "Unless I see the mark of the nails in his hands, and put my finger in the mark of the nails and my hand in his side, I will not believe."

[26] A week later his disciples were again in the house, and Thomas was with them. Although the doors were shut, Jesus came and stood among them and said, "Peace be with you." [27] Then he said to Thomas, "Put your finger here and see my hands. Reach out your hand and put it in my side. Do not doubt but believe." [28] Thomas answered him, "My Lord and my God!" [29] Jesus said to him, "Have you

[a] Gk lacks *to look*
[b] That is, *Aramaic*
[c] Gk *Didymus*

11: The language echoes Song 2.9. **14–16:** Mary, possibly through tears, does not recognize Jesus by sight nor by his voice, but she does know him when he speaks her name; perhaps a reference to the shepherd calling the sheep by name (10.3). **15:** *Woman,* signaling that Jesus is about to impart a revelation. *Whom are you looking for,* echoes 1.38. **17:** It is not clear whether Jesus is asking Mary to let go of him or warning her not to touch him. See Song 3.4. *Ascending,* see 14.3; 16.10. Jesus leaves both to return to the Father and to prepare to receive his followers.

20.19–29: Appearances to the disciples. An important theme in this passage is Jesus' postcrucifixion corporeality. On the one hand, he can walk through walls in order to appear in the room with the disciples, suggesting that his body does not have the substance that it had before his death, or that the process of resurrection is not yet complete. On the other hand, he invites Thomas to touch his wounds, implying that he does indeed have a physical body with the same properties as mortal humans do. **19:** *Fear of the Jews* is a recurrent theme (7.13; 19.38) and echoes Jesus' prediction that those who believe in him will be persecuted just as he was (16.2–3). *Peace be with you,* traditional greeting (cf. Tob 12.47). **22:** *He breathed on them,* giving them new life (cf. 3.5; Gen 2.7). *Spirit,* perhaps alluding to the Paraclete or Advocate (14.16,26; 15.26; 16.7; compare the account in Acts 2). **23:** *Forgive . . . retain,* the authority to decide who can become or remain a member of the community; in Matthew, Jesus grants this power before the crucifixion (Mt 16.19; 18.18). **24:** *Thomas,* also known as the *Twin* and Doubting Thomas. Thomas's other statements perhaps express resignation (11.16) or puzzlement (14.5). **28:** *Lord . . . God,* a full recognition of Jesus' being, as given at the beginning (1.1–14).

believed because you have seen me? Blessed are those who have not seen and yet have come to believe."

[30] Now Jesus did many other signs in the presence of his disciples, which are not written in this book. [31] But these are written so that you may come to believe[a] that Jesus is the Messiah,[b] the Son of God, and that through believing you may have life in his name.

21 After these things Jesus showed himself again to the disciples by the Sea of Tiberias; and he showed himself in this way. [2] Gathered there together were Simon Peter, Thomas called the Twin,[c] Nathanael of Cana in Galilee, the sons of Zebedee, and two others of his disciples. [3] Simon Peter said to them, "I am going fishing." They said to him, "We will go with you." They went out and got into the boat, but that night they caught nothing.

[4] Just after daybreak, Jesus stood on the beach; but the disciples did not know that it was Jesus. [5] Jesus said to them, "Children, you have no fish, have you?" They answered him, "No." [6] He said to them, "Cast the net to the right side of the boat, and you will find some." So they cast it, and now they were not able to haul it in because there were so many fish. [7] That disciple whom Jesus loved said to Peter, "It is the Lord!" When Simon Peter heard that it was the Lord, he put on some clothes, for he was naked, and jumped into the sea. [8] But the other disciples came in the boat, dragging the net full of fish, for they were not far from the land, only about a hundred yards[d] off.

[9] When they had gone ashore, they saw a charcoal fire there, with fish on it, and bread. [10] Jesus said to them, "Bring some of the fish that you have just caught." [11] So Simon Peter went aboard and hauled the net ashore, full of large fish, a hundred fifty-three of them; and though there were so many, the net was not torn. [12] Jesus said to them, "Come and have breakfast." Now none of the disciples dared to ask him, "Who are you?" because they knew it was the Lord. [13] Jesus came and took the bread and gave it to them, and did the same with the fish. [14] This was now the third time that Jesus appeared to the disciples after he was raised from the dead.

[15] When they had finished breakfast, Jesus said to Simon Peter, "Simon son of John, do you love me more than these?" He said to him, "Yes, Lord; you know that I love you." Jesus said to him, "Feed my lambs." [16] A second time he said to him, "Simon son of John, do you love me?" He said to him, "Yes, Lord; you know that I love you." Jesus said to him, "Tend my sheep." [17] He said to him the third time, "Simon son of John, do you love me?" Peter felt hurt because he said to him the third time, "Do you love me?" And he said to him, "Lord, you know everything; you know that I love you." Jesus said to him, "Feed my sheep. [18] Very truly, I tell you, when you were younger, you used to fasten your own belt and to go wherever you wished. But when you grow old, you will stretch out your hands, and someone else will fasten a belt around you and take you where you do not wish to go." [19] (He said this to indicate the kind of death by which he would glorify God.) After this he said to him, "Follow me."

[20] Peter turned and saw the disciple whom Jesus loved following them; he was the one who had reclined next to Jesus at the supper and had said, "Lord, who is it that is going to betray you?" [21] When Peter saw him, he said to Jesus, "Lord, what about him?" [22] Jesus said

[a] Other ancient authorities read *may continue to believe*
[b] Or *the Christ*
[c] Gk *Didymus*
[d] Gk *two hundred cubits*

20.30–31: Conclusion and statement of purpose. **30:** *Other signs*, implying that a selection has been made. *This book*, the Gospel of John. **31:** *Come to believe*, or, continue to believe.

21:1–25: Epilogue. On the basis of its content and literary style, this chapter has sometimes been viewed as an addition, written by someone other than the author of chs 1–20. Unlike 7.53–8.11, however, the manuscript evidence does not show that it circulated separately from the rest of the Gospel or that the Gospel originally ended with ch 20. **2:** Not a full listing of Jesus' disciples; the sons of Zebedee are mentioned here for the first time (cf. Mk 1.19–20). **3:** *Fishing*, recalling the prior occupation of the disciples but also symbolizing their new

to him, "If it is my will that he remain until I come, what is that to you? Follow me!" [23] So the rumor spread in the community[a] that this disciple would not die. Yet Jesus did not say to him that he would not die, but, "If it is my will that he remain until I come, what is that to you?"[b]

[24] This is the disciple who is testifying to these things and has written them, and we know that his testimony is true. [25] But there are also many other things that Jesus did; if every one of them were written down, I suppose that the world itself could not contain the books that would be written.

[a] Gk *among the brothers*
[b] Other ancient authorities lack *what is that to you*

role of gathering disciples. **7:** It is odd that Peter dresses but then jumps into the sea. **9:** The passage recalls the multiplication of loaves and fishes in ch 6. **11:** Numerous theories have been proposed to account for the number 153, e.g., Jerome states that Greek zoologists had recorded 153 different types of fish, in which case the number symbolizes the universality of the Gospel's message and mission; Augustine notes that 153 is the sum of all numbers from 1–17. **15–17:** The referent of *these* is not certain. Jesus commissions Peter as the leader of his lambs (cf. 10.1–5). The triple question undoes the triple denial (18.17,25–27). These verses include extraordinary variation in Greek terminology that is not generally evidence in English translation, including two verbs for "to love," "to know," and "to feed or tend." It is not clear that this variation has significance in terms of meaning. **18:** This verse contrasts the agility of the young with the infirmity of the old, who cannot even fasten their own belts. **19:** This comparison refers to Peter's martyrdom, which will glorify God, to which he will be led by others. This may be a reference to the death of Peter. **23:** The beloved disciple has apparently died. This verse corrects the rumor that Jesus had promised him eternal life. **24–25:** A second ending to the Gospel, identifying the beloved disciple as the author, or, alternatively, its authoritative witness. *World . . . could not contain the books*, an example of hyperbole that is a common literary convention in first-century Jewish and Greco-Roman literature (cf. Eccl 12.12).

THE ACTS OF THE APOSTLES

TITLE OF BOOK AND MEANING

The Acts of the Apostles (Acts) appears fifth in the canonical order of the books of the New Testament, but most scholars now see it as the second part of a two-volume work (1.1) written by the author of the third Gospel, traditionally identified as Luke. The two works (Luke-Acts) have a common literary style, narrative parallels, and thematic similarities. While the title "Acts of the Apostles" refers in general to all the apostles, the work focuses on Peter and Paul.

AUTHORSHIP

The attribution of Acts to Luke, often considered a physician and companion of Paul (Col 4.14; 2 Tim 4.11; Philem 24), first appears in the second century (Irenaeus, *Adv. Haer.* 3.1.1; 3.14.1; Tertullian, *Marc.* 4.2.2; Clement, *Paed.* 2.1.15; *Strom.* 5.12.82). The author had considerable familiarity with the Septuagint, Jewish customs and institutions such as Sabbath restrictions on travel (1.12), Greek literary traditions (Paul quotes from Greek poets in 17.28), and Roman political structures (e.g., legal proceedings in ch 24).

DATE

The Gospel of Luke probably alludes to the destruction of the Jerusalem Temple (cf. 19.41–44; 21.20–24), which places its composition after 70 CE. While a precise date is impossible to establish, Acts was most likely composed early in the second century CE.

LITERARY HISTORY

Modern scholarship has long debated the historical reliability of Acts. The author describes the writing as an orderly narrative based on careful investigation (cf. Lk 1.3). Several characters, such as the Roman proconsul Gallio (18.12) and Judean procurators Felix and Festus (ch 24), were historical figures. Other details, such as the sailing routes and nautical practices (e.g., 27.9–44), references to Roman law (ch 24), and, beginning in ch 16, the frequent use of first-person plural ("we"), may suggest that the author was present at the events narrated or had access to firsthand accounts. It is also possible, however, that these details were included to add verisimilitude to the story. Many of the deeds and words of Peter, Paul, and the other apostles cannot be confirmed, and in several instances the information presented in Acts contradicts what we know from other sources, including the letters of Paul. For instance, the result of the Jerusalem council's decision on the admission of Gentiles to the community, including abstention from eating "whatever has been strangled" (15.20), in keeping with the Torah's prohibitions of eating carrion (e.g., Lev 17.15), is not borne out in Paul's letter to the Galatians (2.10), which mentions only service to "the poor" as the requirement. Whatever historical information may be present in Acts, the selection of events, their ordering, the content of the speeches, and many of the details were determined by the theological and literary interests of the author.

STRUCTURE AND CONTENTS

Acts presents an account of the expansion of the church from its origins among the small group of Jesus' followers in Jerusalem to a movement spread throughout the Roman Empire. The narrative trajectory is summarized in the initial instructions that the resurrected Jesus imparts to his disciples: they should be his "witnesses in Jerusalem, in all Judea and Samaria, and to the ends of the earth" (1.8). The action unfolds in two main units. The first, chs 1–12, focuses largely on activities that take place in Jerusalem, Judea, and Samaria. Peter, the central figure, delivers speeches, performs healings, and, as the climax of this section, baptizes the first Gentile convert, the Roman centurion Cornelius. (Philip had previously baptized an Ethiopian eunuch, 8.26–40, but he is characterized as already worshiping God in Jerusalem.) Beginning in ch 13, the focus shifts to Paul, his missionary activity in Asia Minor (present-day Turkey) and Greece, his arrest by Jewish authorities, questioning before Roman and Jewish authorities, and his journey to Rome, where he is to plead his case before the emperor. Although the author surely knew that Paul was dead, likely killed during Nero's persecution of Jesus' followers in 64 CE, the book concludes with Paul preaching openly in Rome.

INTERPRETATION

Scholars have long attempted to identify the genre of Acts, whether as history, biography, or novel. Considerable attention also has also been paid to ascertain its purpose: a defense of Christians in the eyes of Romans, a defense of Romans in the eyes of Christians, a defense of Paul's memory, particularly against charges of antinomianism, an explanation or reassurance to Christians who grew anxious about the delay of Jesus' return, and/or an attempt to harmonize diverging opinions among early Christians. While the author may have wanted to help Christians understand the Roman government as legitimate or to reassure Romans that Christians were not a threat to their authority (as in the treatment of Paul in the latter part of the book), it is also likely that the author was highly critical of certain Roman political claims, such as Rome as ruler of the world.

GUIDE TO READING

Acts shares with other early Christian writings many ideas that later become central to Christian tradition, although it presents them without the more developed argumentation such as is found Paul's letters. Acts highlights the power of the Holy Spirit to guide and protect Christians (e.g., 19.21), the resurrection as the core proof of Jesus' identity (e.g., 2.22–32), and the offer of salvation to all persons (10.34–35). Other themes, such as martyrdom (chs 6–7) and the sharing of possessions (2.45), find widespread acceptance in later Christian thought.

Acts paints an idealized church expanding in an orderly, harmonious fashion, from Jerusalem to Rome and from Jew to Gentile, and comprising persons who live according to a common set of values, such as the sharing of possessions and observing an agreed-upon set of ethical norms, as members of God's people.

The book devotes considerable importance to the inclusion of Gentiles among the people of God. According to Acts, the importance of any distinction between Jew and Gentile has ceased. As Peter says, "God shows no partiality" (10.34). While the opening to Gentiles comes as a divine act (ch 10), subsequent moves in this direction stem from the rejection by Jews of the Christian preaching (13.46; 18.5–6; 28.23).

While Acts conceives all persons comprising the people of God, it creates new categories for those who believe in Jesus as resurrected Messiah and those who do not. Those who reject Jesus are excluded from God's community and do not share in the blessings of salvation. Only those who believe can expect salvation (4.12). Acts replaces an ethnic distinction with a theological distinction that comes to define, according to Acts, the new people of God.

Aspects of Roman government and culture constitute another important element in the narrative. The Roman government is represented by its magistrates, soldiers, and legal practices, and Paul identifies himself as a Roman citizen (22.25–29), a claim not verified from Paul's letters. Generally, Roman figures treat Christians with respect. Several Romans show sympathy with Christian figures (e.g., Lysias, 23.26–30) and a few, such as the centurion Cornelius, convert to Christianity (10.44–48). Beyond any historical reminiscence, the author may have used this largely positive portrayal of Roman power to convince Christian readers to see their religious community as a legitimate and welcomed part of the Roman world. Acts also employs language and images (Jesus as "Lord of all" [10.36]) used to justify Roman imperial power and applies such language to Jesus and the early church. Acts presents Jesus, rather than the emperor, as the true savior of the world.

Jewish elements, including prominent historical figures such as Rabbi Gamaliel, Agrippa I, Agrippa II, and institutions, such as synagogues and the Temple, occupy a prominent place throughout Acts. Acts identifies the Pharisees as those who believe in resurrection in contrast to the Sadducees who do not (23.6–10). Acts provides important information on Jewish institutions and customs of that time. The Jerusalem Temple is the site of worship and sacrifice (2.46; 3.1; 5.21; 21.26) and involves rituals of purification (21.26). Acts mentions other Jewish customs, including the taking of vows (18.18), the festivals of Passover (20.6; cf. Lk 22.1) and Shavuot (2.1), circumcision (16.3), and frequently portrays synagogues as important communal institutions, describing Jews participating in synagogue activities, such as reading and discussion of scripture on the Sabbath. It also depicts Gentiles, often referred to as God-fearers (Gk *sebomenos/phoboumenos ton theon*), engaged in Jewish religious activities, such as the Ethiopian eunuch worshiping at the Temple and reading Isaiah (8.27–28; 10.2) or the Gentiles who frequently are found in the Diaspora synagogues.

Acts includes quotations from several books of the Bible, most commonly Psalms and Isaiah, but also verses from Exodus, Jeremiah, Joel, Amos, and Habakkuk. In every instance Acts presents the Greek translation, commonly used by Greek-speaking Jews, known as the Septuagint (LXX). Characters are also described as reading from the "law" (i.e., the Pentateuch) and prophets (13.15; 28.23). Acts makes clear that Scripture, properly understood, foretells who Jesus is and how people will come to respond to him (13.41,47; 15.16–18; 28.26–27). Jews respond to these teachings in different ways, some accepting what the apostles preach (2.41; 13.42) and others rejecting it (7.54; 17.2). The book culminates with Paul's fiery denunciation of Jewish unbelief, punctuated by a quote from Isaiah that predicts Jewish intransigence and justifies the opening of God's promises to Gentiles (28.25–28).

Luke-Acts depicts the believers in Jesus as possessing the proper understanding of scripture, obedient to God, and serving as the true recipients of the divine promises and blessings. Jesus' followers point to the fulfillment of prophecies (e.g., 2.14–28) as they exhort Jews to accept Jesus as the Messiah. Some Jews, however, generally prove unwilling to convert or are incapable of comprehending God's actions. In contrast the ease with which many Gentiles, including God-fearers, come to this recognition casts further condemnation upon Jews for their unbelief.

Gary Gilbert

1 In the first book, Theophilus, I wrote about all that Jesus did and taught from the beginning [2] until the day when he was taken up to heaven, after giving instructions through the Holy Spirit to the apostles whom he had chosen. [3] After his suffering he presented himself alive to them by many convincing proofs, appearing to them during forty days and speaking about the kingdom of God. [4] While staying[a] with them, he ordered them not to leave Jerusalem, but to wait there for the promise of the Father. "This," he said, "is what you have heard from me; [5] for John baptized with water, but you will be baptized with[b] the Holy Spirit not many days from now."

[6] So when they had come together, they asked him, "Lord, is this the time when you will restore the kingdom to Israel?" [7] He replied, "It is not for you to know the times or periods that the Father has set by his own authority. [8] But you will receive power when the Holy Spirit has come upon you; and you will be my witnesses in Jerusalem, in all Judea and Samaria, and to the ends of the earth." [9] When he had said this, as they were watching, he was lifted up, and a cloud took him out of their sight. [10] While he was going and they

[a] Or *eating*
[b] Or *by*

1.1–14: Introduction. 1: Like the Gospel of Luke, Acts opens with a formal, conventional address (cf. Lk 1.3). *Theophilus* may have been Luke's benefactor, although the name, meaning "lover of God," may symbolize all readers who display such character. **2–3:** The verses connect to the Gospel by several key themes: Holy Spirit, resurrection, kingdom of God, Jerusalem, and God's promises. *Taken up to heaven*, entering the realm of the divine (1 Kings 2.9–15). *Holy Spirit*, the power of God working in a human life (cf. Ps 51.11 [Heb v. 13]). *Apostles*, "ones sent out," ambassadors or representatives. *Forty days* contradicts Lk 24.50–53, which describes the ascension as taking place on the same day as the resurrection. On the number forty representing divinely ordained periods, see Gen 7.4; Ex 16.35; 24.18; Deut 2.7. **4:** *Father*, not the usual way of referring to God in the Tanakh, but not unknown see Jer 3.19; Ps 89.26; Sir 23.1; *m. Rosh Ha-Shanah.* 3.8. **5:** *John* the Baptist, see Lk 3.1–20; baptism with the Holy Spirit occurs in 2.1–4. **6:** A traditional Jewish expectation that the messiah would restore Israel's independence (cf. Lk 24.21; *Pss. Sol.* 17; the 14th and 15th benedictions in the daily Jewish prayer called the "Amidah"/Eighteen Benedictions). **7–8:** Jesus intimates that the apostles have a faulty understanding; God's act of redemption is not found in a political change, but in the bestowing of the Spirit. *Witnesses*, Gk "martyres," from which comes the English word "martyr." "Witness" is an important theme in Acts, by which those who have seen or participated in the experience of the community are thereby empowered to testify to it; see 1.22; 2.32; 3.15; 5.32; 10.39,41; 13.31; 22.15. *Jerusalem . . . ends of the earth*, the outline of the narrative's geographic progression: Jerusalem (chs 1–7); Judea and Samaria (chs 8–11), ends of the earth (chs 13–28): Acts concludes with Paul in Rome, the capital of the empire. *Ends of the earth* may also connote the ethnic progression of God's promise from Jews to Gentiles (cf. Lk 24.47). **9–12: The ascension.** Within the NT, only Luke-Acts reports this event. **9:** *Cloud*, common symbol for divine presence (Ex 24.15; Dan 7.13). **10:** *Two men in white*, similar figures appear in

were gazing up toward heaven, suddenly two men in white robes stood by them. [11] They said, "Men of Galilee, why do you stand looking up toward heaven? This Jesus, who has been taken up from you into heaven, will come in the same way as you saw him go into heaven."

[12] Then they returned to Jerusalem from the mount called Olivet, which is near Jerusalem, a sabbath day's journey away. [13] When they had entered the city, they went to the room upstairs where they were staying, Peter, and John, and James, and Andrew, Philip and Thomas, Bartholomew and Matthew, James son of Alphaeus, and Simon the Zealot, and Judas son of[a] James. [14] All these were constantly devoting themselves to prayer, together with certain women, including Mary the mother of Jesus, as well as his brothers.

[15] In those days Peter stood up among the believers[b] (together the crowd numbered about one hundred twenty persons) and said, [16] "Friends,[c] the scripture had to be fulfilled, which the Holy Spirit through David foretold concerning Judas, who became a guide for those who arrested Jesus— [17] for he was numbered among us and was allotted his share in this ministry." [18] (Now this man acquired a field with the reward of his wickedness; and falling headlong,[d] he burst open in the middle and all his bowels gushed out. [19] This became known to all the residents of Jerusalem, so that the field was called in their language Hakeldama, that is, Field of Blood.) [20] "For it is written in the book of Psalms,

'Let his homestead become desolate,
and let there be no one to live in it';

and

'Let another take his position of overseer.'

[21] So one of the men who have accompanied us during all the time that the Lord Jesus went in and out among us, [22] beginning from the baptism of John until the day when he was taken up from us—one of these must become a witness with us to his resurrection." [23] So they proposed two, Joseph called Barsabbas, who was also known as Justus, and Matthias. [24] Then they prayed and said, "Lord, you know everyone's heart. Show us which one of these two you have chosen [25] to take the place[e] in this ministry and apostleship from which Judas turned aside to go to his own place." [26] And they cast lots for them, and the lot fell on Matthias; and he was added to the eleven apostles.

[a] Or *the brother of*
[b] Gk *brothers*
[c] Gk *Men, brothers*
[d] Or *swelling up*
[e] Other ancient authorities read *the share*

Jesus' tomb (Lk 24.4; Jn 20.12). **11:** *Come in the same way,* Zech 14.4 identifies the Mount of Olives as the site where the LORD (God, in Heb YHWH) will appear. **12:** *Olivet,* Mount of Olives, to the east of Jerusalem. See 1.11n. *Sabbath's day journey,* restrictions on travel during the Sabbath appear in the Dead Sea Scrolls (1,000 cubits, CD 10.21; 2,000 cubits when pasturing animals, CD 11.5) and rabbinic tradition (2,000 cubits, *m. Eruv.* 4.3; 5.7; *Mek. Vayassa* 6; *b. Eruv.* 51a); 2,000 cubits is approximately 1 kilometer (.6 mi). **13:** The same names, in a different order and minus Judas Iscariot, appear in Lk 6.14–16. *Zealot,* not necessarily a member of a group aiming at violent revolution; perhaps an epithet indicating ardent or enthusiastic commitment. **14:** *His* (Jesus') *brothers,* Mk 6.3 names four brothers; one, James, becomes a church leader (12.17; 15.13; 21.18; Gal 2.9; 1 Cor 15.7; *Ant.* 20.200).

1.15–12.25: Peter and the expansion of the church.

1.15–26: Appointment of Matthias and Judas's death. **16:** *Scripture . . . fulfilled,* God's plan, knowable through the correct reading of scripture, included both Judas's actions and the appointment of Matthias. The reference is not to a particular text but to scripture generally. *Guide,* Lk 22.3–4,47–48 identifies Judas as leading the chief priests and others to arrest Jesus. **18–20: Judas's death.** Mt 27.3–10 reports that Judas regretted his involvement in Jesus' condemnation and died by hanging himself. **18:** Judas's death occurs as an act of divine judgment (cf. death of Herod Agrippa in 12.23). **19:** *Hakeldama . . . Field of Blood,* the location is given first in a transliteration of Aram "heikhal dama," then Gk. **20:** Ps 69.25 and 109.8. **21–26: Selection of Matthias.** **22:** *Witness,* see 1.8n. *Resurrection,* according to Acts, the central message of Christianity (2.31; 4.2,33; 17.18,32; 23.6; 24.21; 26.23). **23:** *Matthias,* nothing more is reported about him. **26:** *Lots,* common practice for making decisions, revealing divine intent (e.g., Lev 16.8; Num 26.55–56; Jon 1.7; Esth 3.7; 9.24; 1 Chr 25.8–9; 1QS 5.3; Philo, *Heir* 179; *m. Yoma* 2.2; *b. Shabb.* 149b; *b. Yoma* 39b–40a; *b. Sanh.* 43b). **26:** *Eleven,* the need to expand the number to twelve may have been influenced by the thought of the community's leadership corresponding to the twelve tribes.

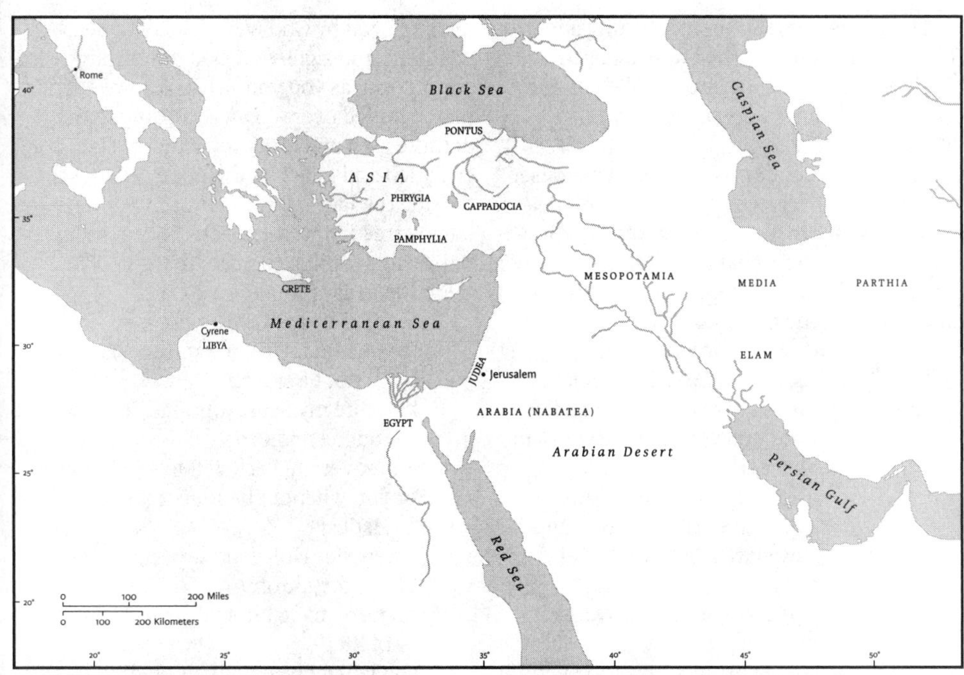

2.9–11: The native lands of Pentecost pilgrims.

---

2 When the day of Pentecost had come, they were all together in one place. [2] And suddenly from heaven there came a sound like the rush of a violent wind, and it filled the entire house where they were sitting. [3] Divided tongues, as of fire, appeared among them, and a tongue rested on each of them. [4] All of them were filled with the Holy Spirit and began to speak in other languages, as the Spirit gave them ability.

[5] Now there were devout Jews from every nation under heaven living in Jerusalem. [6] And at this sound the crowd gathered and was bewildered, because each one heard them speaking in the native language of each. [7] Amazed and astonished, they asked, "Are not all these who are speaking Galileans? [8] And how is it that we hear, each of us, in our own native language? [9] Parthians, Medes, Elamites, and residents of Mesopotamia, Judea and Cappadocia, Pontus and Asia, [10] Phrygia and Pamphylia, Egypt and the parts of Libya belonging to Cyrene, and visitors from Rome, both Jews and proselytes, [11] Cretans and Arabs—in our

2.1–41: Holy Spirit and Peter's preaching. The events take place during Shavuot ("Weeks," Lev 23.15–21), a harvest festival (*m. Bik.* 3; *b. Shabb.* 86b) and in later Jewish tradition the time when Moses received the Torah (*b. Pesah.* 68b).

2.1–13: Sending of the Spirit. The act parallels Jesus' reception of the Spirit, Lk 3.21–22. **1:** *Pentecost*, Gk "fiftieth," the day seven full weeks (fifty days) after Pesach (Passover), the name of the festival used by Greek-speaking Jews, 2 Macc 12.32; Josephus, *J. W.* 6.299. **3:** *Tongues as of fire*, the specific image (Isa 5.24; *1 En.* 14.8–25; 71.5) and fire in general (Ex 3.2; 14.24; 19.18; Isa 5.24) symbolize divine presence. **4:** *Filled with Holy Spirit* fulfills 1.5. *Other languages*, here, as opposed to the discussion of tongues in 1 Cor 14.6–19, the speaking is in languages that are understood by native speakers in attendance. **5:** *Devout Jews from every nation*, Shavuot, one of the three pilgrimage festivals (along with Pesach [Passover] and Sukkot [Booths]) that attracted many Jews to Jerusalem. The reference suggests that these Jews reside there. **7:** *Galileans*, rabbinic commentary sometimes treated Galileans as ignorant (*m. Eruv.* 2.4; *y. Shabb.* 15d; *b. Eruv.* 53a–b). **9–11:** List of Nations. The list adds geographic detail to *every nation under heaven* (v. 5) and foreshadows the spread of Christianity throughout the world. The order is roughly from east to west. **10:** *Proselytes*, converts

own languages we hear them speaking about God's deeds of power." [12] All were amazed and perplexed, saying to one another, "What does this mean?" [13] But others sneered and said, "They are filled with new wine."

[14] But Peter, standing with the eleven, raised his voice and addressed them, "Men of Judea and all who live in Jerusalem, let this be known to you, and listen to what I say. [15] Indeed, these are not drunk, as you suppose, for it is only nine o'clock in the morning. [16] No, this is what was spoken through the prophet Joel:

[17] 'In the last days it will be, God declares,
that I will pour out my Spirit upon all flesh,
and your sons and your daughters shall prophesy,
and your young men shall see visions,
and your old men shall dream dreams.
[18] Even upon my slaves, both men and women,
in those days I will pour out my Spirit;
and they shall prophesy.
[19] And I will show portents in the heaven above
and signs on the earth below,
blood, and fire, and smoky mist.
[20] The sun shall be turned to darkness
and the moon to blood,
before the coming of the Lord's great and glorious day.
[21] Then everyone who calls on the name of the Lord shall be saved.'

[22] "You that are Israelites,[a] listen to what I have to say: Jesus of Nazareth,[b] a man attested to you by God with deeds of power, wonders, and signs that God did through him among you, as you yourselves know— [23] this man, handed over to you according to the definite plan and foreknowledge of God, you crucified and killed by the hands of those outside the law. [24] But God raised him up, having freed him from death,[c] because it was impossible for him to be held in its power. [25] For David says concerning him,

'I saw the Lord always before me,
for he is at my right hand so that I will not be shaken;
[26] therefore my heart was glad, and my tongue rejoiced;
moreover my flesh will live in hope.
[27] For you will not abandon my soul to Hades,
or let your Holy One experience corruption.
[28] You have made known to me the ways of life;
you will make me full of gladness with your presence.'

[29] "Fellow Israelites,[d] I may say to you confidently of our ancestor David that he both died and was buried, and his tomb is with us to this day. [30] Since he was a prophet, he knew that God had sworn with an oath to

[a] Gk *Men, Israelites*
[b] Gk *the Nazorean*
[c] Gk *the pains of death*
[d] Gk *Men, brothers*

to Judaism. **13:** *New wine* has not yet had time to begin turning to vinegar, so its alcoholic content is at its height.

2.14–36: Peter's speech. 14–21: Teaching on Pentecost. 17–21: Joel 2.28–32 (MT 3.1–5). Rabbinic literature understands Joel as referring to the world to come (*Num. Rab.* 15.25; *Deut. Rab.* 6.14; *Tanh. Miqqetz* 10). Luke adds *in the last days*, presenting the plan as realized in the giving of the Spirit. *Slaves* indicates the inclusion of all orders of society in the world to come. **22–36: Jesus the Messiah. 22:** *Israelites*, perhaps of wider reference, since those being addressed include pilgrims from outside Judea. *Deeds of power, wonders, and signs*, common expressions for proof of divine activity (Deut 4.34; 6.22; 26.8; Isa 8.18; Jer 32.20; Ps 78.43; Dan 4.1–3 [MT 3.31–33]). **23:** Jesus' death was the result of both divine plan and Jewish action (3.13; 4.10; 5.30; 7.52; 13.27). Divine involvement does not absolve human responsibility. *Outside the law*, may refer Romans (who are not subject to Torah) or Jews (who transgressed against God; cf. Lk 22.37). **24:** *God raised him up*, the Jews who killed Jesus acted in opposition to God (2.36; 3.15; 4.10; 5.30,38–39; 10.39–40; 13.29–30). **25–28:** Ps 16.8–11. **25:** Traditional Jewish understanding regards *David* as the author of Psalms. **27:** *Hades*, Heb "Sheol," ultimate destination after death (Isa 38.10,18; Ps 6.5; 89.48; 116.3; Job 7.9). Jewish writings in Greek adopted the Greek term (Wis 2.1; 16.13; 2 Macc 6.23; *Pss. Sol.* 16.2). Later Jewish writings come to imagine Sheol/Hades as a place of judgment and punishment (*1 En.* 63.10; *t. Yoma* 4.11). **29:** The tomb of David was known (Josephus, *J.W.* 1.61; *Ant.* 7.393; 13.249). David's death, for Peter, excludes him as the person the psalm mentions. Rather, the psalm speaks of the resurrection of the messiah (v.

him that he would put one of his descendants on his throne. [31] Foreseeing this, David[a] spoke of the resurrection of the Messiah,[b] saying,

'He was not abandoned to Hades,
nor did his flesh experience corruption.'

[32] This Jesus God raised up, and of that all of us are witnesses. [33] Being therefore exalted at[c] the right hand of God, and having received from the Father the promise of the Holy Spirit, he has poured out this that you both see and hear. [34] For David did not ascend into the heavens, but he himself says,

'The Lord said to my Lord,
"Sit at my right hand,
[35] until I make your enemies your footstool."'

[36] Therefore let the entire house of Israel know with certainty that God has made him both Lord and Messiah,[d] this Jesus whom you crucified."

[37] Now when they heard this, they were cut to the heart and said to Peter and to the other apostles, "Brothers,[e] what should we do?" [38] Peter said to them, "Repent, and be baptized every one of you in the name of Jesus Christ so that your sins may be forgiven; and you will receive the gift of the Holy Spirit. [39] For the promise is for you, for your children, and for all who are far away, everyone whom the Lord our God calls to him." [40] And he testified with many other arguments and exhorted them, saying, "Save yourselves from this corrupt generation." [41] So those who welcomed his message were baptized, and that day about three thousand persons were added. [42] They devoted themselves to the apostles' teaching and fellowship, to the breaking of bread and the prayers.

[43] Awe came upon everyone, because many wonders and signs were being done by the apostles. [44] All who believed were together and had all things in common; [45] they would sell their possessions and goods and distribute the proceeds[f] to all, as any had need. [46] Day by day, as they spent much time together in the temple, they broke bread at home[g] and ate their food with glad and generous[h] hearts, [47] praising God and having the goodwill of all the people. And day by day the Lord added to their number those who were being saved.

[a] Gk *he*
[b] Or *the Christ*
[c] Or *by*
[d] Or *Christ*
[e] Gk *Men, brothers*
[f] Gk *them*
[g] Or *from house to house*
[h] Or *sincere*

31). Jesus' resurrection, as witnessed, proves he is the messiah (v. 32). **30:** *Prophet, Ant.* 6.166; 7.334; 8.109; 11QPs[a] 27.11; *y. Sot.* 9.24b. *One of his descendants,* 2 Sam 7.12–13. Jesus is a descendant of David (Lk 3.31; 18.38–39). **32:** *Witnesses,* see 1.8n. **34–35:** Ps 110.1; Christian tradition often understands the psalm as speaking about Jesus, not David (Mk 12.36; 1 Cor 15.25; Heb 1.13). **36:** Luke again (v. 24) distinguishes between God's act in making Jesus Messiah and Jews who crucify him. **36:** *Made . . . Lord and Messiah,* the view that God "adopted" Jesus as messiah, as shown in the resurrection. This may be an indication of one early explanation of Jesus' messiahship.

2.37–41: Teaching on repentance. Repentance often appears as a central teaching (3.19; 5.31; 8.22; 11.18; 17.30; 20.21; 26.20). **38:** *Repent,* turn from what one has been and done; the reference is general, not to a specific act. *Be baptized,* some Jews associated baptism or ritual immersion with repentance (Isa 1.16; Ps 51.7 [Heb v. 9]; Lk 3.3; *Sib. Or.* 4.162–70; 1QS 3.6–9). Baptism in Jesus' name, however, distinguishes the new community (2.41; 10.48; 19.5). *Sins may be forgiven,* unspecified; the *sins* most likely include killing Jesus (v. 23). **40:** *Save,* a key concept in Acts, connoting rescue from sin and falsehood (as here) and entry into the reign of God (4.12; 11.14; 13.47; 15.1; 16.30–31). *Corrupt generation,* Deut 32.20; Ps 78.8. **41:** Such summaries appear regularly (4.32–35; 5.12–16; 6.11; 9.31), and emphasize the astounding success in attracting believers. *Three thousand,* many in Jerusalem become believers (2.47; 4.4; 5.14; 6.1; 21.20).

2.42–47: Early community life. The ideal life is one of prayer and communal fellowship. **42:** *Teaching and fellowship, . . . breaking of bread . . . prayers,* three characteristics (instruction, community, worship) followed by a fourth (care for others) in v. 44. **44:** *Had all things in common,* communal ownership (4.36–5.11; 6.1–6), existed among the Jewish community at Qumran (1QS 1.11), and was highly valued in philosophical teachings (Aristotle, *Eth. nic.* 9.8, Cicero, *Off.* 1.16.51). The actual practice may have been different; see 5.1–2. **46:** *Temple,* the apostles often congregate in the Temple for prayer and teaching (3.1–10; 5.21,42; 21.26–30; 22.17). **47:** Summary statement depicting church growth (see 4.32–35; 5.12–16; 6.7; 9.31; 16.5; 19.20).

JEWS AND THE DEATH OF JESUS

Luke-Acts presents Jews as those primarily responsible for the death of Jesus. In Luke, the Roman governor Pilate had declared Jesus innocent (Lk 22.4; 23.22) and was prepared to release him (Lk 23.20,22), but he acquiesced to the demands of the Jewish leaders and multitudes (23.18–25). The theme continues in Acts. At several points Peter accuses Jews as having killed Jesus (2.23,36; 3.15; 4.10; 5.30; 10.39), a charge repeated by Stephen (7.52) and Paul (13.27–29). At the same time, both Luke's Gospel and Acts note that Jesus' death happened according to divine plan (2.23; 3.18; 4.28; 13.28; cf. Lk 24.26) and that the Jews acted in ignorance (3.17; 13.27; cf. Lk 23.34). Neither claim, however, exonerates the Jews or lessens their culpability. Their ignorance, rather than justifying their action, becomes inexcusable because they should have been able to discern God's plan as set forth in the words of the prophets (13.27).

3 One day Peter and John were going up to the temple at the hour of prayer, at three o'clock in the afternoon. [2] And a man lame from birth was being carried in. People would lay him daily at the gate of the temple called the Beautiful Gate so that he could ask for alms from those entering the temple. [3] When he saw Peter and John about to go into the temple, he asked them for alms. [4] Peter looked intently at him, as did John, and said, "Look at us." [5] And he fixed his attention on them, expecting to receive something from them. [6] But Peter said, "I have no silver or gold, but what I have I give you; in the name of Jesus Christ of Nazareth,[a] stand up and walk." [7] And he took him by the right hand and raised him up; and immediately his feet and ankles were made strong. [8] Jumping up, he stood and began to walk, and he entered the temple with them, walking and leaping and praising God. [9] All the people saw him walking and praising God, [10] and they recognized him as the one who used to sit and ask for alms at the Beautiful Gate of the temple; and they were filled with wonder and amazement at what had happened to him.

[11] While he clung to Peter and John, all the people ran together to them in the portico called Solomon's Portico, utterly astonished. [12] When Peter saw it, he addressed the people, "You Israelites,[b] why do you wonder at this, or why do you stare at us, as though by our own power or piety we had made him walk? [13] The God of Abraham, the God of Isaac, and the God of Jacob, the God of our ancestors has glorified his servant[c] Jesus, whom you handed over and rejected in the presence of Pilate, though he had decided to release him. [14] But you rejected the Holy and Righteous One and asked to have a murderer given to you, [15] and you killed the Author of life, whom God raised from the dead. To this we

[a] Gk *the Nazorean*
[b] Gk *Men, Israelites*
[c] Or *child*

3.1–10: Peter heals a crippled man. An example of *wonders and signs* (2.43). **1:** *Three o'clock*, when the evening daily offerings (Ex 29.39; Lev 6.20) were performed (*Ant.* 14.65) and when prayer took place (Jdt 9.1). **2:** *Beautiful Gate*, otherwise unattested, possibly a reference to the impressive bronze Nicanor Gate (Josephus, *J.W.* 5.201; *m. Midd.* 1.4; 2.3). **4:** *Intently*, typical practice during healing (13.9; 14.9). **6:** *Name of Jesus Christ*, the power of Jesus, not the apostles, creates the miracle (3.16; 4.10,12,17,18,30; 16.18; 19.13).

3.11–26: Peter's speech in Solomon's Portico. As with the giving of the spirit (2.15), the crowd's misperception prompts Peter's teaching. **11:** *Solomon's Portico*, this was in the eastern part of the Temple Mount (*Ant.* 20.221; 15.401). **13:** *God of Abraham . . . Isaac . . . Jacob*, Ex 3.6,15,16; 4.5; first benediction in "Amidah"/Eighteen Benedictions. *Glorified his servant*, Jesus is identified as God's servant (3.26; 4.27,30), possibly alluding to the servant figure in Isaiah who suffers but is vindicated and exalted by God (Isa 52.13; 53.1–12). *Handed over and rejected*, Jews are responsible for Jesus' execution (see 2.23). *Pilate*, Roman prefect of Judea 26–36 CE. The desire of Jews to kill Jesus is juxtaposed to the desire of Pilate to release him (Lk 23.4,14–16,20–25; but see Acts 4.27). **14:** *Righteous One*, attribute of Isaianic servant (Isa 53.11), and possibly meant as messianic title (*1 En.* 38.2; 53.6). *Murderer*, Barabbas (Lk 23.18–19). **15:** *Author*, Gk "archēgos," can mean "first entrant, pioneer," as well as "founder" or "source." Contrast between Jews who killed Jesus and God who raised him. *Witnesses*, see 1.8n.

are witnesses. [16] And by faith in his name, his name itself has made this man strong, whom you see and know; and the faith that is through Jesus[a] has given him this perfect health in the presence of all of you.

[17] "And now, friends,[b] I know that you acted in ignorance, as did also your rulers. [18] In this way God fulfilled what he had foretold through all the prophets, that his Messiah[c] would suffer. [19] Repent therefore, and turn to God so that your sins may be wiped out, [20] so that times of refreshing may come from the presence of the Lord, and that he may send the Messiah[d] appointed for you, that is, Jesus, [21] who must remain in heaven until the time of universal restoration that God announced long ago through his holy prophets. [22] Moses said, 'The Lord your God will raise up for you from your own people[b] a prophet like me. You must listen to whatever he tells you. [23] And it will be that everyone who does not listen to that prophet will be utterly rooted out of the people.' [24] And all the prophets, as many as have spoken, from Samuel and those after him, also predicted these days. [25] You are the descendants of the prophets and of the covenant that God gave to your ancestors, saying to Abraham, 'And in your descendants all the families of the earth shall be blessed.' [26] When God raised up his servant,[e] he sent him first to you, to bless you by turning each of you from your wicked ways."

4 While Peter and John[f] were speaking to the people, the priests, the captain of the temple, and the Sadducees came to them, [2] much annoyed because they were teaching the people and proclaiming that in Jesus there is the resurrection of the dead. [3] So they arrested them and put them in custody until the next day, for it was already evening. [4] But many of those who heard the word believed; and they numbered about five thousand.

[5] The next day their rulers, elders, and scribes assembled in Jerusalem, [6] with Annas

a Gk *him*
b Gk *brothers*
c Or *his Christ*
d Or *the Christ*
e Or *child*
f Gk *While they*

16: *Faith in his name,* trust in his true being ("name" as communicating the true nature of a person). **17:** *Ignorance,* although ignorance can explain why Jews killed Jesus (7.60; 13.27), it can no longer justify failure to recognize Jesus' messianic identity (17.30). **18:** *His Messiah would suffer,* such a prophecy does not appear in the biblical prophets; Luke may have in mind an interpretation of Isa 53 or Zech 12.10; 13.7. The statement makes clear that Jesus' death was part of a divine plan (Lk 24.25–27,46; Acts 17.2–3; 26.22–23). **19:** *Repent,* shown by accepting Jesus as Messiah. **20:** *Times of refreshing,* opportunities for renewal. **21:** *Universal restoration,* expansion of the Jewish eschatological concept of restoration/turn (Mal 4.6 [MT 3.24]) to include all persons. **22–23:** Deut 18.15,18–19. Jesus is the anticipated prophet; he is regarded here in a way similar to Moses, who is recognized by some Jews as an eschatological figure (1QS 9.11). **23:** *Rooted out of the people,* punishment for failure to heed the prophet is infrequent in Deut (see 18.19); Luke possibly draws on Lev 23.29. Peter insists here and in 4.12 that rejecting Jesus results in exclusion from the people of God. **24:** *Samuel,* included among the prophets (as in the Jewish canon, where Sam [1 and 2] is the first book of the "former prophets"). **25:** *Descendants of the . . . covenant,* Jews are not the only partners, since the covenant includes "all the families of the earth" (Gen 12.3; 18.18; 22.18; 26.4). **26:** *First to you,* Jews will be followed by Gentiles in God's plan for salvation. *Wicked ways,* from which Jews must repent (v. 19).

4.1–31: Conflict with Jewish authorities. The first of several scenes that display conflict between the apostles and Jewish authorities. **1–3: Arrest of Peter and John. 1:** *Priests, the captain of the temple and the Sadducees,* the *priests* appear as the leading authorities in Jerusalem and central figures opposed to the apostles (5.21; 9.1,14,21; 22.5,30; 23.2–5; 24.1; 25.2). *Captain of the temple,* a position with authority over Temple personnel and ritual (5.24,26). *The Sadducees,* often contrasted to Pharisees and said to have rejected ideas not explicitly found in the Tanakh, such as resurrection (23.6–8; Josephus, *J.W.* 2.164–166; *Ant.* 13.173; 18.16–17). Many were responsible for overseeing Temple rituals. **4: Summary.** *Five thousand,* the rejection by the Jewish authorities is contrasted with the acceptance by thousands of Jews. Acts emphasizes rapid growth of the community; the number may be exaggerated. **5–7: Questioning of Peter. 5:** *Rulers, elders, and scribes,* members of the council, the Sanhedrin. *Annas . . . , Caiaphas, John, and Alexander,* Annas/Ananus was high priest in 6–15 CE (Josephus, *J.W.* 18.26–35) and retained

the high priest, Caiaphas, John,[a] and Alexander, and all who were of the high-priestly family. [7] When they had made the prisoners[b] stand in their midst, they inquired, "By what power or by what name did you do this?" [8] Then Peter, filled with the Holy Spirit, said to them, "Rulers of the people and elders, [9] if we are questioned today because of a good deed done to someone who was sick and are asked how this man has been healed, [10] let it be known to all of you, and to all the people of Israel, that this man is standing before you in good health by the name of Jesus Christ of Nazareth,[c] whom you crucified, whom God raised from the dead. [11] This Jesus[d] is

'the stone that was rejected by you, the builders;

it has become the cornerstone.'[e]

[12] There is salvation in no one else, for there is no other name under heaven given among mortals by which we must be saved."

[13] Now when they saw the boldness of Peter and John and realized that they were uneducated and ordinary men, they were amazed and recognized them as companions of Jesus. [14] When they saw the man who had been cured standing beside them, they had nothing to say in opposition. [15] So they ordered them to leave the council while they discussed the matter with one another. [16] They said, "What will we do with them? For it is obvious to all who live in Jerusalem that a notable sign has been done through them; we cannot deny it. [17] But to keep it from spreading further among the people, let us warn them to speak no more to anyone in this name." [18] So they called them and ordered them not to speak or teach at all in the name of Jesus. [19] But Peter and John answered them, "Whether it is right in God's sight to listen to you rather than to God, you must judge; [20] for we cannot keep from speaking about what we have seen and heard." [21] After threatening them again, they let them go, finding no way to punish them because of the people, for all of them praised God for what had happened. [22] For the man on whom this sign of healing had been performed was more than forty years old.

[23] After they were released, they went to their friends[f] and reported what the chief priests and the elders had said to them. [24] When they heard it, they raised their voices together to God and said, "Sovereign Lord, who made the heaven and the earth, the sea, and everything in them, [25] it is you who said by the Holy Spirit through our ancestor David, your servant:[g]

[a] Other ancient authorities read *Jonathan*
[b] Gk *them*
[c] Gk *the Nazorean*
[d] Gk *This*
[e] Or *keystone*
[f] Gk *their own*
[g] Or *child*

the title (Lk 3.1–2; Jn 18.12–24; Josephus, *J.W.* 2.240,256). Caiaphas was Annas's son-in-law and high priest in 18–36/37; he served as high priest during the execution of Jesus (Mt 26.3; Jn 18.13–28). John may be Jonathan, one of Annas's sons and Caiaphas's successor (*Ant.* 18.95,122–24; 20.162–64). Alexander is otherwise unknown. **7:** *Power . . . name,* a query about the sources—perhaps demonic, in their view—of the deeds of the apostles. **8–12: Peter's defense.** Peter's speech summarizes several Lukan themes. **8:** *Holy Spirit,* see 1.2–3n. **10:** *Name of Jesus Christ,* see 3.6. The contrast between the Jews who crucified Jesus and God who raised him, see 2.24. **11:** Ps 118.22; early Christian tradition applies the image to Jesus (Lk 20.17; Mt 21.42; 1 Pet 2.7). The psalm is the last one recited at Passover (Ps 113–118, the "Egyptian Hallel"); v. 19 was recited in acclamation for those coming to Jerusalem, and is shouted by the crowd when Jesus enters riding on a colt, Lk 19.38. **12:** *Salvation . . . saved,* Jesus is the sole agent of salvation; see 2.40n. (cf. 3.23). **13–22: Deliberations of the council. 13:** *Boldness,* the apostles often speak fearlessly to authorities (2.29; 4.29,31; 9.27,28; 13.46; 14.3; 18.26; 19.8; 26.26; 28.31), a useful quality for rhetoricians. **15:** *Council,* Sanhedrin, the supreme judicial body in Jerusalem. **19:** *Listen to you rather than to God,* a similar idea is attributed to the Pharisee Gamaliel (5.29). *Listen,* with the added understanding of obey, as in the "Shema" ("Hear, O Israel") prayer. Jewish and Greek philosophical traditions often rank obedience to God as more important than obedience to human authority (Plato, *Apol.* 29d; 2 Macc 7.2; 4 Macc 5.16–21; *Ant.* 17.158–59; 18.268). **21:** *Because of the people,* the apostles receive widespread support (2.41,47). **23–31: Reaction of the community. 24:** God is frequently invoked as creator of all (Isa 37.16; Ps 146.6; Neh 9.6). **25–26:** Ps 2.1–2. **27:** The quotation leads Luke to implicate Pilate in Jesus' death; elsewhere responsibility falls to Jews (see 2.23).

'Why did the Gentiles rage,
and the peoples imagine vain things?
[26] The kings of the earth took their stand,
and the rulers have gathered together
against the Lord and against his
Messiah.'[a]

[27] For in this city, in fact, both Herod and Pontius Pilate, with the Gentiles and the peoples of Israel, gathered together against your holy servant[b] Jesus, whom you anointed, [28] to do whatever your hand and your plan had predestined to take place. [29] And now, Lord, look at their threats, and grant to your servants[c] to speak your word with all boldness, [30] while you stretch out your hand to heal, and signs and wonders are performed through the name of your holy servant[b] Jesus." [31] When they had prayed, the place in which they were gathered together was shaken; and they were all filled with the Holy Spirit and spoke the word of God with boldness.

[32] Now the whole group of those who believed were of one heart and soul, and no one claimed private ownership of any possessions, but everything they owned was held in common. [33] With great power the apostles gave their testimony to the resurrection of the Lord Jesus, and great grace was upon them all. [34] There was not a needy person among them, for as many as owned lands or houses sold them and brought the proceeds of what was sold. [35] They laid it at the apostles' feet, and it was distributed to each as any had need. [36] There was a Levite, a native of Cyprus, Joseph, to whom the apostles gave the name Barnabas (which means "son of encouragement"). [37] He sold a field that belonged to him, then brought the money, and laid it at the apostles' feet.

5 But a man named Ananias, with the consent of his wife Sapphira, sold a piece of property; [2] with his wife's knowledge, he kept back some of the proceeds, and brought only a part and laid it at the apostles' feet. [3] "Ananias," Peter asked, "why has Satan filled your heart to lie to the Holy Spirit and to keep back part of the proceeds of the land? [4] While it remained unsold, did it not remain your own? And after it was sold, were not the proceeds at your disposal? How is it that you have contrived this deed in your heart? You did not lie to us[d] but to God!" [5] Now when Ananias heard these words, he fell down and died. And great fear seized all who heard of it. [6] The young men came and wrapped up his body,[e] then carried him out and buried him.

[7] After an interval of about three hours his wife came in, not knowing what had happened. [8] Peter said to her, "Tell me whether you and your husband sold the land for such and such a price." And she said, "Yes, that was the price." [9] Then Peter said to her, "How is it that you have agreed together to put the

a Or *his Christ*
b Or *child*
c Gk *slaves*
d Gk *to men*
e Meaning of Gk uncertain

27–28: Luke sees no contradiction to understanding Jesus' death as having taken place according to divine plan and human action; see 2.23. **29:** *Boldness*, see vv. 13,31. **30:** *Signs and wonders . . . through the name*, see 3.6. **31:** *Filled with the Holy Spirit*, 2.2; 4.8; 9.17; 13.9,52.

4.32–5.11: Communal possessions. 32–37: Luke paints a harmonious image of the church: unity of believers, sharing of wealth, absence of material deprivation. See 2.42–44. **32:** *Heart and soul*, often paired to represent the completeness of one's obedience to God (Deut 6.5; 10.12; 11.13; 26.16). *Held in common*, see 2.44. **33:** *Testimony to the resurrection*, what the apostles were appointed to do (see 1.8n.). **36:** *Levite*, member of the priestly tribe. *Barnabas*, he worked closely together with Paul (9.27; 11.22–30; 12.25; 13.1–15.8; 1 Cor 9.6; Gal 2.1,9), although the two later separated (15.36–41; Gal 2.13). Here he stands as the proper model of behavior in contrast to Ananias and Sapphira who follow. **5.1–11: Ananias and Sapphira.** A narrative concerning withholding what is devoted to God's purpose, resulting in the death of the offender, is in Josh 7. **3–4:** Once *Ananias* sold the property, it was expected that he would donate the entire sum (4.34). *Satan*, the leader of demonic forces who tempted Jesus (Lk 4.1–12) and led Judas to betray Jesus (Lk 22.3,31). While Ananias may have been influenced by Satan, he remains responsible. *Holy Spirit*, because Ananias's transgression is against the Holy Spirit, he merits immediate and severe punishment (v. 5; cf. Lk 12.10). **6.** *Buried him*, speedy burial, including the use of a shroud, is expected. See Tob 2.8; Josephus, *Ag. Ap.* 2.221; *b. Sanh.* 47a.

Spirit of the Lord to the test? Look, the feet of those who have buried your husband are at the door, and they will carry you out." [10] Immediately she fell down at his feet and died. When the young men came in they found her dead, so they carried her out and buried her beside her husband. [11] And great fear seized the whole church and all who heard of these things.

[12] Now many signs and wonders were done among the people through the apostles. And they were all together in Solomon's Portico. [13] None of the rest dared to join them, but the people held them in high esteem. [14] Yet more than ever believers were added to the Lord, great numbers of both men and women, [15] so that they even carried out the sick into the streets, and laid them on cots and mats, in order that Peter's shadow might fall on some of them as he came by. [16] A great number of people would also gather from the towns around Jerusalem, bringing the sick and those tormented by unclean spirits, and they were all cured.

[17] Then the high priest took action; he and all who were with him (that is, the sect of the Sadducees), being filled with jealousy, [18] arrested the apostles and put them in the public prison. [19] But during the night an angel of the Lord opened the prison doors, brought them out, and said, [20] "Go, stand in the temple and tell the people the whole message about this life." [21] When they heard this, they entered the temple at daybreak and went on with their teaching.

When the high priest and those with him arrived, they called together the council and the whole body of the elders of Israel, and sent to the prison to have them brought. [22] But when the temple police went there, they did not find them in the prison; so they returned and reported, [23] "We found the prison securely locked and the guards standing at the doors, but when we opened them, we found no one inside." [24] Now when the captain of the temple and the chief priests heard these words, they were perplexed about them, wondering what might be going on. [25] Then someone arrived and announced, "Look, the men whom you put in prison are standing in the temple and teaching the people!" [26] Then the captain went with the temple police and brought them, but without violence, for they were afraid of being stoned by the people.

[27] When they had brought them, they had them stand before the council. The high priest questioned them, [28] saying, "We gave you strict orders not to teach in this name,[a] yet here you have filled Jerusalem with your teaching and you are determined to bring this man's blood on us." [29] But Peter and the apostles answered, "We must obey God rather than any human authority.[b] [30] The God of our ancestors raised up Jesus, whom you had killed by hanging him on a tree. [31] God exalted him at his right hand as Leader and Savior that he might give repentance to Israel and forgiveness of sins. [32] And we are witnesses to these things, and so is the Holy Spirit whom God has given to those who obey him."

a Other ancient authorities read *Did we not give you strict orders not to teach in this name?*

b Gk *than men*

11: *Fear,* awe, a positive response or attitude toward God (2.43; 9.31; 10.2,35; 13.16,26; 19.17). *Church,* the term frequently designates a specific community (8.1; 11.22,26; 13.1; 14.23,27; 15.3,4; 16.5; 18.22; 20.17) or more generally all those who believe in Jesus (9.31; 20.28).

5.12–16: Miraculous deeds. Miraculous healing often results in attracting believers (9.35; 19.11–20). **12:** *Solomon's Portico,* see 3.11n. **15:** Similar miracles are also ascribed to Paul (19.12).

5.17–42: Apostles appear before the council. The miraculous deeds and the enthusiastic response prompt opposition by Jewish authorities (3.1–4.22). **17:** *High priest . . . Sadducees,* see 4.1n. *Jealousy,* 13.45; 17.5. **18:** *Public prison,* the local or municipal prison. **19:** Miraculous escape from prison occurs elsewhere, 12.6–11; 16.25–26. **21,25:** *Temple,* the frequent location of teaching, see 4.1; 5.20,42. **26:** *Stoned,* the opening chapters portray significant popular support for apostles (2.41,47; 4.4,21; 5.13–14). **28–29:** See 4.17–20. *Bring this man's blood on us,* blame us for this man's death (cf. notorious "blood cry" of Mt 27.25). **30:** *God of our ancestors,* one basis for the claim that the community of Jesus followers fulfills and continues the promises God made to the patriarchs. *God . . . raised up Jesus, whom you had killed,* see 2.24; 3.15. *Hanging him on a tree,* Deut 21.22–23; cf. Gal 3.13; 1QpNahum. **31–32:** Obedience to God requires acknowledging God's exaltation of Jesus; that acknowledg-

GAMALIEL

Gamaliel (Gamliel in Hebrew) was a well-respected, first-century sage. According to one rabbinic tradition, "When Rabban Gamliel the Elder died, the glory of the law ceased and purity and abstinence died" (*m. Sot.* 9.15). Acts' portrait of Gamaliel is often regarded as a positive representation of a Jew. While Gamaliel does prevent his colleagues from killing the apostles, and he is identified as Paul's teacher (22.3, an assertion not confirmed in Paul's own writings), the real power belongs to divine providence. That a major Jewish leader plays a supporting role in the origin of Christianity further tarnishes those Jews who continue in their opposition.

[33] When they heard this, they were enraged and wanted to kill them. [34] But a Pharisee in the council named Gamaliel, a teacher of the law, respected by all the people, stood up and ordered the men to be put outside for a short time. [35] Then he said to them, "Fellow Israelites,[a] consider carefully what you propose to do to these men. [36] For some time ago Theudas rose up, claiming to be somebody, and a number of men, about four hundred, joined him; but he was killed, and all who followed him were dispersed and disappeared. [37] After him Judas the Galilean rose up at the time of the census and got people to follow him; he also perished, and all who followed him were scattered. [38] So in the present case, I tell you, keep away from these men and let them alone; because if this plan or this undertaking is of human origin, it will fail; [39] but if it is of God, you will not be able to overthrow them—in that case you may even be found fighting against God!"

They were convinced by him, [40] and when they had called in the apostles, they had them flogged. Then they ordered them not to speak in the name of Jesus, and let them go. [41] As they left the council, they rejoiced that they were considered worthy to suffer dishonor for the sake of the name. [42] And every day in the temple and at home[b] they did not cease to teach and proclaim Jesus as the Messiah.[c]

6 Now during those days, when the disciples were increasing in number, the Hellenists complained against the Hebrews because their widows were being neglected in the daily distribution of food. [2] And the twelve called together the whole community of the disciples and said, "It is not right that we should neglect the word of God in order to wait on tables.[d] [3] Therefore, friends,[e] select from among yourselves seven men of good

[a] Gk *Men, Israelites*
[b] Or *from house to house*
[c] Or *the Christ*
[d] Or *keep accounts*
[e] Gk *brothers*

ment shows repentance that brings about forgiveness. **33–39: Speech of Gamaliel. 34:** *Pharisee,* Acts depicts Pharisees as believers in divine providence (5.39), resurrection (23.7–8), and strict adherence to Torah (15.5), prominent qualities Josephus confirms (*J.W.* 1.110–14; 2.162–66; *Ant.* 13.171–173; 18.12–15). *Gamaliel,* according to rabbinic tradition, a learned and highly esteemed leader of the rabbinic community before the destruction of the Temple (*m. Sot.* 9.15). **36–37:** *Theudas,* eschatological prophet who in the mid-40s CE gathered a group of followers near the Jordan and was executed under orders of the Roman procurator (*Ant.* 20.97–98). *Judas the Galilean,* in 6 CE, before *Theudas,* Judas led a revolt against the Roman census in Judea (Josephus, *J.W.* 2.117–19,433; *Ant.* 18.2–10,23–25). See "Messianic Movements," p. 530. **38–39:** Gamaliel's teaching echoes Peter's earlier statement (v. 29). See similar opinion of R. Yoḥanan the Sandal-maker, *m. Avot* 4.11. By placing the instruction in the mouth of a respected Jewish leader, Acts portrays subsequent Jewish opposition to Christianity as an act against God and contrary to Judaism. **41:** *Suffer dishonor,* suffering on behalf of Jesus is understood as honorable rather than shameful (9.16; Phil 1.29; 2 Tim 1.8). **42:** Teaching in the *temple,* v. 25.

6.1–7: Hellenists and Hebrews. Problems threatening to divide the community are amicably resolved. **1:** *Hellenists . . . Hebrews,* the text implies the division is based largely on language, between those speaking Aramaic and those speaking Greek. *Widows,* neglect of widows, seen as representing the poor or marginal in general, is contrary to communal assistance (4.32–37), and receives particular condemnation (Deut 24.17–21; Isa 10.1–3; Zech 7.10). **2:** *Wait,* not table service per se, but providing service to the community, especially its poor (which

standing, full of the Spirit and of wisdom, whom we may appoint to this task, [4] while we, for our part, will devote ourselves to prayer and to serving the word." [5] What they said pleased the whole community, and they chose Stephen, a man full of faith and the Holy Spirit, together with Philip, Prochorus, Nicanor, Timon, Parmenas, and Nicolaus, a proselyte of Antioch. [6] They had these men stand before the apostles, who prayed and laid their hands on them.

[7] The word of God continued to spread; the number of the disciples increased greatly in Jerusalem, and a great many of the priests became obedient to the faith.

[8] Stephen, full of grace and power, did great wonders and signs among the people. [9] Then some of those who belonged to the synagogue of the Freedmen (as it was called), Cyrenians, Alexandrians, and others of those from Cilicia and Asia, stood up and argued with Stephen. [10] But they could not withstand the wisdom and the Spirit[a] with which he spoke. [11] Then they secretly instigated some men to say, "We have heard him speak blasphemous words against Moses and God." [12] They stirred up the people as well as the elders and the scribes; then they suddenly confronted him, seized him, and brought him before the council. [13] They set up false witnesses who said, "This man never stops saying things against this holy place and the law; [14] for we have heard him say that this Jesus of Nazareth[b] will destroy this place and will change the customs that Moses handed on to us." [15] And all who sat in the council looked intently at him, and they saw that his face was like the face of an angel.

7 Then the high priest asked him, "Are these things so?" [2] And Stephen replied:

"Brothers[c] and fathers, listen to me. The God of glory appeared to our ancestor Abraham when he was in Mesopotamia, before he lived in Haran, [3] and said to him, 'Leave your country and your relatives and go to the land that I will show you.' [4] Then he left the country of the Chaldeans and settled in Haran. After his father died, God had him move from there to this country in which you are now living. [5] He did not give him any of it as a

[a] Or *spirit*
[b] Gk *the Nazorean*
[c] Gk *Men, brothers*

may be financial help, as in translators' note *d*, previous page); see 11.29; 12.25. This is not a reference to the Lord's Supper or Eucharist. **3–4:** The division of labor does not hold: none of the seven serves food, and both Stephen and Philip pray and preach. **5:** *Pleased the whole community,* the community once divided is now united. Only Stephen (6.8–8.1) and Philip (8.5–40; 21.8) appear again. **6:** *Laid their hands,* sign of appointment for divine service (Num 27.18; Deut 34.9; 1 Tim 4.14; 5.22; 2 Tim 1.6). **7:** *Priests,* formerly characterized as opponents of the apostles (5.17), join the believers (2.41; 4.4; 5.14).

6.8–8.1a: Stephen's arrest, speech, and martyrdom. Luke models the story of Stephen's trial and death on that of Jesus (see annotations and Lk chs 22–23; parallels Mk chs 15–16, Mt chs 26–27).

6.8–15: Stephen's arrest. 8: *Wonders and signs,* actions performed by the apostles (2.43; 4.30; 5.12). **9:** *Synagogue of the Freedmen. . . , Cyrenians, Alexandrians,* most of the opposition to Stephen comes from diaspora Jews, perhaps in contrast to the Jerusalem Jews who are supportive of the apostles, perhaps because as Hellenistic Jews they encounter Stephen, whose Greek name indicates that he also might be Hellenistic. The term "synagogue" might mean "persons assembled," "congregation," or "building where persons assemble." The names designate characteristics of the members, including former slaves (Philo, *Leg. all.* 155; Tacitus, *Ann.* 2.85) and persons from established Jewish communities in North Africa (Cyrene and Alexandria) and Asia Minor (Cilicia and Asia). **11:** *Blasphemous words* would carry the sentence of death (Lev 24.16). *Against Moses and God,* an ironic statement; Stephen's speech and the rest of Acts claim that Jews, who reject Jesus, are the ones who are against God and "Moses," i.e., the Torah (7.53; 11.18). **13:** *False witnesses,* also used against Jesus (Mt 26.59–61; Mk 14.55–58, though not mentioned in Lk). **14:** *Will destroy this place,* according to the Gospels, Jesus speaks about the destruction of the Temple (Mt 26.61; Lk 21.6; Jn 2.19), and he is accused of seeking its destruction (Mk 14.58). *Change the customs,* Acts often states that this accusation is false (15.21; 16.3; 21.26). **15:** *Face of an angel,* a divinely illuminated face indicates that Stephen speaks with wisdom and divine authority (Ex 34.29; 1 Sam 29.9; 2 Sam 14.17; 19.27).

7.1–53: Stephen's speech. 2–8: Abraham. Gen 12–21. **2:** *Glory,* Gk "doxa," in LXX for Heb "kavod," the divine attribute of honor or worthiness. *Mesopotamia . . . Haran,* locations outside Israel; Stephen points to God's freedom

STEPHEN'S SPEECH

After some Jews accuse Stephen of blasphemy (though his offense was apparently to characterize the Temple as "made with hands," that is, a merely human construction), they bring him before the council where they present false witnesses who charge him with saying things against the Temple and law (6.8–15; see Mk 14.56 for a parallel in Jesus' trial). Stephen launches into a speech, the longest in Acts, that rehearses Israel's history, beginning with Abraham. The speech develops two themes that become a major part of the larger Lukan narrative, particularly in its representation of Jews. First, it highlights Jewish disobedience. The speech, rather than offering any response to the high priest's question, rehearses major events in Israel's sacred narrative. After mentioning Abraham, Joseph, and other early ancestors, the focus shifts to Moses and the continual disobedience of Israel. The speech presents Moses' story in terms of Israel's primal disobedience to God and God's messengers, and it identifies the present generation as persisting in the same spirit. By contrast, Nehemiah 9 also combines historical review with rebuke of the people's rebellious nature, yet God is merciful and faithful to the covenant (see also Ps 78). Second, the critical references to building the Temple elevate the value of God's universal presence over a possible implicit belief that God is particularly present in the Temple. Stephen's consequent martyrdom continues the parallel with Jesus in his quotation from Ps 31.6 and his plea for forgiveness for his persecutors (Lk 23.34,46).

heritage, not even a foot's length, but promised to give it to him as his possession and to his descendants after him, even though he had no child. [6] And God spoke in these terms, that his descendants would be resident aliens in a country belonging to others, who would enslave them and mistreat them during four hundred years. [7] 'But I will judge the nation that they serve,' said God, 'and after that they shall come out and worship me in this place.' [8] Then he gave him the covenant of circumcision. And so Abraham[a] became the father of Isaac and circumcised him on the eighth day; and Isaac became the father of Jacob, and Jacob of the twelve patriarchs.

[9] "The patriarchs, jealous of Joseph, sold him into Egypt; but God was with him, [10] and rescued him from all his afflictions, and enabled him to win favor and to show wisdom when he stood before Pharaoh, king of Egypt, who appointed him ruler over Egypt and over all his household. [11] Now there came a famine throughout Egypt and Canaan, and great suffering, and our ancestors could find no food. [12] But when Jacob heard that there was grain in Egypt, he sent our ancestors there on their first visit. [13] On the second visit Joseph made himself known to his brothers, and Joseph's family became known to Pharaoh. [14] Then Joseph sent and invited his father Jacob and all his relatives to come to him, seventy-five in all; [15] so Jacob went down to Egypt. He himself died there as well as our ancestors, [16] and their bodies[b] were brought back to Shechem and laid in the tomb that Abraham had bought for a sum of silver from the sons of Hamor in Shechem.

[17] "But as the time drew near for the fulfillment of the promise that God had made to Abraham, our people in Egypt increased and multiplied [18] until another king who had not known Joseph ruled over Egypt. [19] He dealt craftily with our race and forced our ancestors to abandon their infants so that they would die. [20] At this time Moses was born,

[a] Gk *he*
[b] Gk *they*

of action in self-revelation apart from those in the land of promise. **3:** Gen 12.1. **5:** Gen 13.15; 17.8; 48.4. *Heritage . . . possession,* the promise is absolute: ownership, not inheritance. **6–7:** *A country . . . four hundred years,* refers to Egypt: Gen 15.13–14; the punishment of the Egyptians and the plunder of the Israelites are not mentioned. **8:** Gen 17.10–13; 21.4. **9–16: Joseph. 9:** Gen 37. **10–16:** Gen 39–50. **14:** *Seventy-five,* Gen 46.27; the number given in the LXX and two Dead Sea Scrolls; the traditional Hebrew version has seventy. **16:** The burial of Joseph in *Shechem,* in land purchased by Jacob not Abraham (Josh 24.32), may have influenced the suggestion that the ancestors were buried there, despite the tradition that Abraham, Isaac, and Jacob were buried at Hebron (Gen 49.30; 50.13). **17–43: Moses and the Exodus. 17–19:** Ex 1 identifies only male infants as victims of Pharaoh's command. **20–22:** Ex 2.1–10.

and he was beautiful before God. For three months he was brought up in his father's house; [21] and when he was abandoned, Pharaoh's daughter adopted him and brought him up as her own son. [22] So Moses was instructed in all the wisdom of the Egyptians and was powerful in his words and deeds.

[23] "When he was forty years old, it came into his heart to visit his relatives, the Israelites.[a] [24] When he saw one of them being wronged, he defended the oppressed man and avenged him by striking down the Egyptian. [25] He supposed that his kinsfolk would understand that God through him was rescuing them, but they did not understand. [26] The next day he came to some of them as they were quarreling and tried to reconcile them, saying, 'Men, you are brothers; why do you wrong each other?' [27] But the man who was wronging his neighbor pushed Moses[b] aside, saying, 'Who made you a ruler and a judge over us? [28] Do you want to kill me as you killed the Egyptian yesterday?' [29] When he heard this, Moses fled and became a resident alien in the land of Midian. There he became the father of two sons.

[30] "Now when forty years had passed, an angel appeared to him in the wilderness of Mount Sinai, in the flame of a burning bush. [31] When Moses saw it, he was amazed at the sight; and as he approached to look, there came the voice of the Lord: [32] 'I am the God of your ancestors, the God of Abraham, Isaac, and Jacob.' Moses began to tremble and did not dare to look. [33] Then the Lord said to him, 'Take off the sandals from your feet, for the place where you are standing is holy ground. [34] I have surely seen the mistreatment of my people who are in Egypt and have heard their groaning, and I have come down to rescue them. Come now, I will send you to Egypt.'

[35] "It was this Moses whom they rejected when they said, 'Who made you a ruler and a judge?' and whom God now sent as both ruler and liberator through the angel who appeared to him in the bush. [36] He led them out, having performed wonders and signs in Egypt, at the Red Sea, and in the wilderness for forty years. [37] This is the Moses who said to the Israelites, 'God will raise up a prophet for you from your own people[c] as he raised me up.' [38] He is the one who was in the congregation in the wilderness with the angel who spoke to him at Mount Sinai, and with our ancestors; and he received living oracles to give to us. [39] Our ancestors were unwilling to obey him; instead, they pushed him aside, and in their hearts they turned back to Egypt, [40] saying to Aaron, 'Make gods for us who will lead the way for us; as for this Moses who led us out from the land of Egypt, we do not know what has happened to him.' [41] At that time they made a calf, offered a sacrifice to the idol, and reveled in the works of their hands. [42] But God turned away from them and handed them over to worship the host of heaven, as it is written in the book of the prophets:

'Did you offer to me slain victims and
sacrifices
forty years in the wilderness, O house
of Israel?

[a] Gk *his brothers, the sons of Israel*
[b] Gk *him*
[c] Gk *your brothers*

20: *Beautiful,* Philo (*Life of Moses* 1.18) and Josephus (*Ant.* 2.224) comment on Moses' attractive physical appearance. **22:** *Wisdom of the Egyptians,* ancient Jewish writers portray Moses as a master of Egyptian culture (Artapanus; Philo, *Life of Moses* 1.21–4). **23–29:** Ex 2.11–22. **23:** *Forty years old, Sifre Deut.* 357 (a postbiblical tradition). **25:** Stephen emphasizes the fact that Moses' own people did not understand him. On misunderstanding or rejecting a divinely chosen servant or God see vv. 35,39,51,53. **30–34:** Ex 3.1–10. **30:** *Forty years had passed, Sifre Deut.* 357. **35–43:** Luke juxtaposes the image of Moses as simultaneously appointed by God (vv. 36–38) and rejected by his people (vv. 39–43). **36:** *Wonders and signs,* Acts 2.22,43; 4.30; 5.12; 6.8. **37:** Acts 3.22; cf. Deut 18.15. **38–39:** The brief mention of the giving of the Torah is followed immediately by the report of Israel's disobedience. **38:** *Angel,* belief in the presence of angels at Sinai was common among Jews (Deut 33.2 [LXX]; *Jub.* 1.29; *Ant.* 15.136; *Pesiq. Rab.* 21.7–10) and Christians (Gal 3.19; Heb 2.2). *Living oracles,* the teaching given to Moses. **40:** Ex 32.1,23. **41:** Ex 32.4–6. *Works of their hands,* idolatry; see similar language applied to the Temple, v. 48. **42–43:** *God turned away,* Ex 32.9–10; unmentioned is God's repentance (Ex 32.14). *Host of heaven,* astral deities. Am 5.25–27; the accusation is that Jews practiced idolatry (i.e., disobedience against God) from early times. *Moloch . . . Rephan,* Moloch was

[43] No; you took along the tent of Moloch,
and the star of your god Rephan,
the images that you made to worship;
so I will remove you beyond Babylon.'

[44] "Our ancestors had the tent of testimony in the wilderness, as God[a] directed when he spoke to Moses, ordering him to make it according to the pattern he had seen. [45] Our ancestors in turn brought it in with Joshua when they dispossessed the nations that God drove out before our ancestors. And it was there until the time of David, [46] who found favor with God and asked that he might find a dwelling place for the house of Jacob.[b] [47] But it was Solomon who built a house for him. [48] Yet the Most High does not dwell in houses made with human hands;[c] as the prophet says,

[49] 'Heaven is my throne,
and the earth is my footstool.
What kind of house will you build for me,
says the Lord,
or what is the place of my rest?
[50] Did not my hand make all these things?'

[51] "You stiff-necked people, uncircumcised in heart and ears, you are forever opposing the Holy Spirit, just as your ancestors used to do. [52] Which of the prophets did your ancestors not persecute? They killed those who foretold the coming of the Righteous One, and now you have become his betrayers and murderers. [53] You are the ones that received the law as ordained by angels, and yet you have not kept it."

[54] When they heard these things, they became enraged and ground their teeth at Stephen.[d] [55] But filled with the Holy Spirit, he gazed into heaven and saw the glory of God and Jesus standing at the right hand of God. [56] "Look," he said, "I see the heavens opened and the Son of Man standing at the right hand of God!" [57] But they covered their ears, and with a loud shout all rushed together against him. [58] Then they dragged him out of the city and began to stone him; and the witnesses laid their coats at the feet of a young man named Saul. [59] While they were stoning Stephen, he prayed, "Lord Jesus, receive my spirit." [60] Then he knelt down and cried out in a loud voice, "Lord, do not hold this sin against them."

8 When he had said this, he died.[e] [1] And Saul approved of their killing him.

That day a severe persecution began against the church in Jerusalem, and all

[a] Gk *he*
[b] Other ancient authorities read *for the God of Jacob*
[c] Gk *with hands*
[d] Gk *him*
[e] Gk *fell asleep*

one of the supposed gods in Canaan; Rephan is not otherwise known. **44–50: Places of worship. 44:** Ex 25.8–9; 33.7. **45:** Josh 3.14–17. **46:** *Found favor,* 2 Sam 15.25. *Find a dwelling place,* 2 Sam 7.2. **47:** 2 Sam 7.13; 1 Kings 6. **48–50:** Stephen argues that building the Temple was contrary to God's wishes. Most Jewish tradition maintained that although God is universal, the Temple is no less a legitimate location where to worship (2 Macc 14.35; *Ant.* 8.107). **48:** *Most High,* common term for God (Deut 32.8; Ps 91.1,9). *Does not dwell in houses made with human hands,* while the general sentiment accords with Jewish tradition (1 Kings 8.27), *made with human hands* implies that the building of the Temple was an idolatrous act (Isa 2.8; 37.19; Mic 5.13 [MT 5.12]; Ps 115.4; 135.15). **49–50:** Isa 66.1–2. **51–53: Final condemnation. 51:** *Stiff-necked,* Ex 32.9; 33.3,5. *Uncircumcised in heart and ears,* Lev 26.41; Jer 6.10. *Your ancestors,* Stephen had spoken of *our ancestors* (vv. 2,11,12,15,19,38,39,44,45), but now separates himself from his Jewish audience and associates them with their rebellious and murderous ancestors (also v. 52). **52:** *Prophets . . . persecute,* a common motif in the "Lives of the Prophets," an ancient Jewish work. *Murderers,* Stephen suggests that those who do not accept Jesus have make themselves guilty of his murder. **53:** Stephen answers the original question (6.13–7.1) by turning the tables on his accusers. He is not guilty of saying things against the Torah (6.13); rather they are the ones who continually violate it. *Ordained by angels,* see v. 38.

7.54–8.1a: The stoning of Stephen. The story is modeled on the death of Jesus. Christian tradition understands Stephen as the first martyr. **54:** *Ground their teeth,* image used of God's enemies (Lk 13.28; Ps 35.16; 112.10; Job 16.9). **55:** *Right hand,* position of power, as of a judge (cf. Ps 110.1). **56:** *Son of Man,* see Lk 22.69. Outside the gospels, the term (often denoting Jesus as judge) appears only here and in Rev 1.13; 14.14. **58:** Stoning was the main method of execution in the Tanakh (e.g., Lev 20.2); here, however, it seems to be a spontaneous mob action, like a lynching; as noted in John 18.31. *Saul,* the first appearance of Paul. **58–59:** Stephen's final words echo those of Jesus (Lk 23.34,46). **60:** *Do not hold,* Stephen intercedes on behalf of his killers, possibly modeled on the image of the servant in Isa 53.12.

except the apostles were scattered throughout the countryside of Judea and Samaria. [2] Devout men buried Stephen and made loud lamentation over him. [3] But Saul was ravaging the church by entering house after house; dragging off both men and women, he committed them to prison.

[4] Now those who were scattered went from place to place, proclaiming the word. [5] Philip went down to the city[a] of Samaria and proclaimed the Messiah[b] to them. [6] The crowds with one accord listened eagerly to what was said by Philip, hearing and seeing the signs that he did, [7] for unclean spirits, crying with loud shrieks, came out of many who were possessed; and many others who were paralyzed or lame were cured. [8] So there was great joy in that city.

[9] Now a certain man named Simon had previously practiced magic in the city and amazed the people of Samaria, saying that he was someone great. [10] All of them, from the least to the greatest, listened to him eagerly, saying, "This man is the power of God that is called Great." [11] And they listened eagerly to him because for a long time he had amazed them with his magic. [12] But when they believed Philip, who was proclaiming the good news about the kingdom of God and the name of Jesus Christ, they were baptized, both men and women. [13] Even Simon himself believed. After being baptized, he stayed constantly with Philip and was amazed when he saw the signs and great miracles that took place.

[14] Now when the apostles at Jerusalem heard that Samaria had accepted the word of God, they sent Peter and John to them. [15] The two went down and prayed for them that they might receive the Holy Spirit [16] (for as yet the Spirit had not come[c] upon any of them; they had only been baptized in the name of the Lord Jesus). [17] Then Peter and John[d] laid their hands on them, and they received the Holy Spirit. [18] Now when Simon saw that the Spirit was given through the laying on of the apostles' hands, he offered them money, [19] saying, "Give me also this power so that anyone on whom I lay my hands may receive the Holy Spirit." [20] But Peter said to him, "May your silver perish with you, because you thought you could obtain God's gift with money! [21] You have no part or share in this, for your heart is not right before God. [22] Repent therefore of this wickedness of yours, and pray to the Lord that, if possible, the

[a] Other ancient authorities read *a city*
[b] Or *the Christ*
[c] Gk *fallen*
[d] Gk *they*

8.1b–3: Church developments. The death of Stephen marks a turning point in the narrative. For the first time the church experiences widespread opposition, and because the persecution drives followers out of Judea, it gains a presence outside of Jerusalem. Both themes dominate the rest of the work. **1:** *Judea and Samaria,* see 1.8. The stories of Philip and Peter in chs 8–10 dramatize the expansion. **3:** Paul reports his persecution of the church (1 Cor 15.9; Gal 1.13,23).

8.4–25: Preaching in Samaria. Fulfilling Jesus' instructions in 1.8. Samaritans, living particularly around Mount Gerizim, were descended from the remnants of the population of the Northern Kingdom of Israel and those brought into the region by the Assyrian conquerors in 722 BCE; therefore they had close historical and religious ties to Jews, though there were religious differences. Samaritans appear in the Gospel of Luke as faithful to Jesus' teaching (Lk 10.33; 17.16; cf. 9.53). **4:** *Scattered,* like the Jewish people in the Diaspora. **5:** *Philip,* one of the seven, 6.5. *City of Samaria,* no exact location is given; Luke may have had in mind Sebaste, formerly Samaria, once the capital of the Kingdom of Israel, but renamed by Herod in honor of the emperor Augustus (Josephus, *J.W.* 1.403; *Ant.* 15.217,292–98). **6–7:** Exorcisms and healings; cf. 3.7; 5.12; 9.34; 14.18; 16.18. **9–25: Simon.** Luke distinguishes the magic of *Simon,* "the great power" (v. 10) with the miraculous great powers (here translated as miracles) of Philip (v. 13). Acts champions Christians as the legitimate conveyers of divine power in contrast to those who practice base magic (13.6–11; 16.16–24; 19.13–20,23–40). **9:** *Practiced magic,* hence the name often given as Simon "Magus," originally indicating a member of the Persian priestly class, but commonly carrying a pejorative connotation. **12:** *Kingdom of God,* in Acts, the term refers to the general content of Christian preaching; see 19.8; 20.25; 28.23,31. **14:** Jesus' instructions concerning *Samaria* (1.8) are fulfilled. The apostles continue to oversee the expansion of the church (15.1–21). **15–16:** Holy Spirit is independent of any ritual act, even laying on of hands (10.44). **18–19:** Simon's offer is the origin of the term "simony" for any

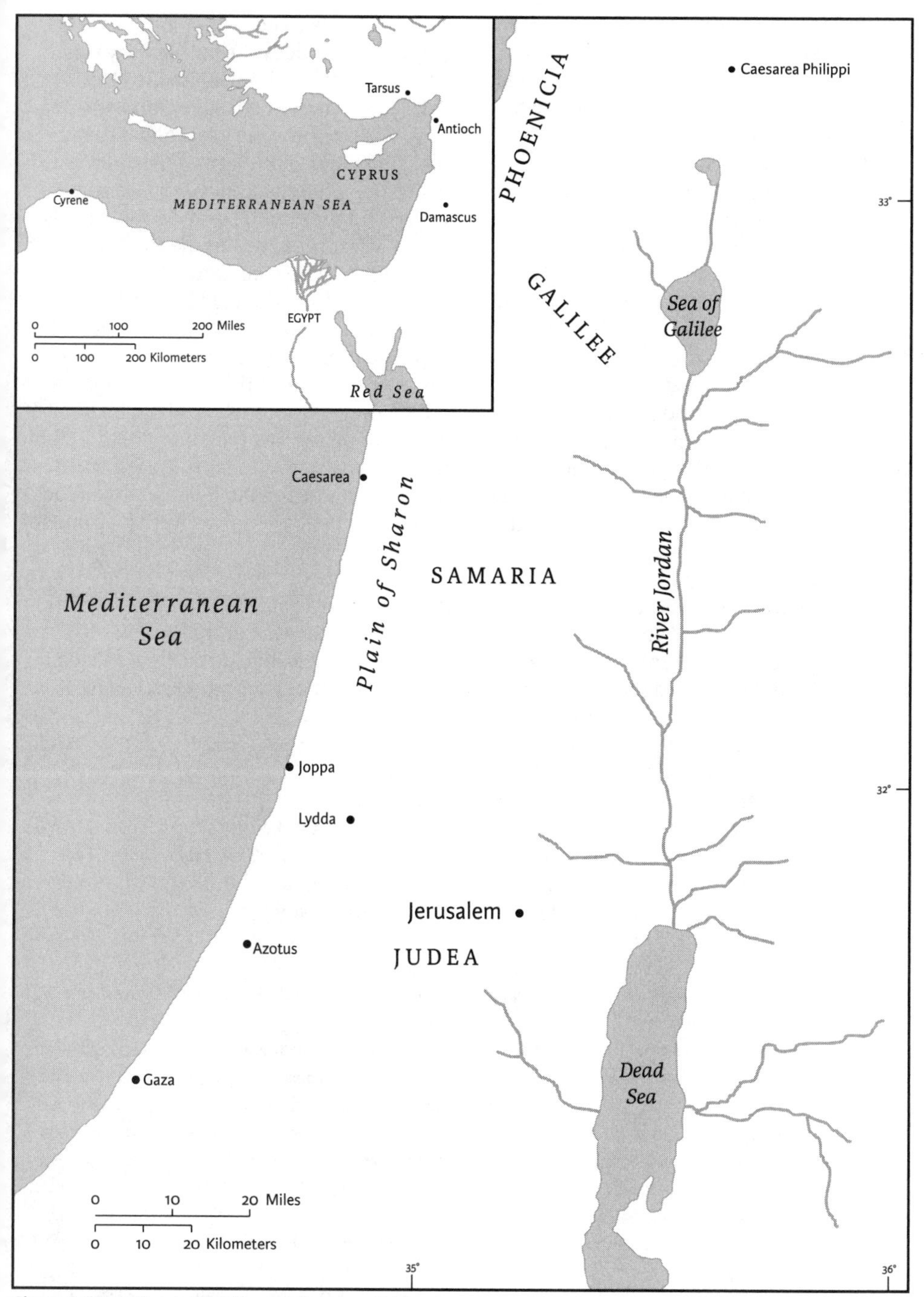

Chs 8–11: Sites of early Christian missionary activities.

intent of your heart may be forgiven you. [23] For I see that you are in the gall of bitterness and the chains of wickedness." [24] Simon answered, "Pray for me to the Lord, that nothing of what you[a] have said may happen to me."

[25] Now after Peter and John[b] had testified and spoken the word of the Lord, they returned to Jerusalem, proclaiming the good news to many villages of the Samaritans.

[26] Then an angel of the Lord said to Philip, "Get up and go toward the south[c] to the road that goes down from Jerusalem to Gaza." (This is a wilderness road.) [27] So he got up and went. Now there was an Ethiopian eunuch, a court official of the Candace, queen of the Ethiopians, in charge of her entire treasury. He had come to Jerusalem to worship [28] and was returning home; seated in his chariot, he was reading the prophet Isaiah. [29] Then the Spirit said to Philip, "Go over to this chariot and join it." [30] So Philip ran up to it and heard him reading the prophet Isaiah. He asked, "Do you understand what you are reading?" [31] He replied, "How can I, unless someone guides me?" And he invited Philip to get in and sit beside him. [32] Now the passage of the scripture that he was reading was this:

"Like a sheep he was led to the slaughter,
and like a lamb silent before its shearer,
so he does not open his mouth.
[33] In his humiliation justice was denied him.
Who can describe his generation?
For his life is taken away from the earth."

[34] The eunuch asked Philip, "About whom, may I ask you, does the prophet say this, about himself or about someone else?" [35] Then Philip began to speak, and starting with this scripture, he proclaimed to him the good news about Jesus. [36] As they were going along the road, they came to some water; and the eunuch said, "Look, here is water! What is to prevent me from being baptized?"[d] [38] He commanded the chariot to stop, and both of them, Philip and the eunuch, went down into the water, and Philip[e] baptized him. [39] When they came up out of the water, the Spirit of the Lord snatched Philip away; the eunuch saw him no more, and went on his way rejoicing. [40] But Philip found himself at Azotus, and as he was passing through the region, he proclaimed the good news to all the towns until he came to Caesarea.

9 Meanwhile Saul, still breathing threats and murder against the disciples of the Lord, went to the high priest [2] and asked him for letters to the synagogues at Damascus,

a The Greek word for *you* and the verb *pray* are plural
b Gk *after they*
c Or *go at noon*
d Other ancient authorities add all or most of verse 37, *And Philip said, "If you believe with all your heart, you may." And he replied, "I believe that Jesus Christ is the Son of God."*
e Gk *he*

attempt to buy a church office. **23:** *Gall of bitterness,* the allusion to Deut 29.18 (Heb 29.17) implies that Simon is guilty of serving other gods.

8.26–40: The Ethiopian official. 26: *Angel of the Lord,* God, through agents such as angels and the Spirit, directs the expansion of the church (10.19–20; 13.4; 16.6,7). **27:** *Ethiopian eunuch,* Ethiopia is probably meant to evoke a far distant land (Am 9.7; Homer, *Od.* 1.23). *Candace,* a royal title for *queen of the Ethiopians* rather than a personal name. *Jerusalem to worship,* no indication of what form of worship is intended. Eunuchs were excluded from participation in Temple rituals (Lev 21.20) and entrance, as proselytes, into the community of Israel (Deut 23.1; *Ant.* 4.292). His presence in Jerusalem possibly is meant as fulfillment of Ps 68.31 (Heb 68.32) that speaks of Ethiopia reaching out to God, and Isa 56.3–5 that anticipates the future inclusion of eunuchs among God's people (cf. Wis 3.14). Gentiles interested in Judaism appear often in Acts (10.2; 13.16; 16.14; 18.7). **28:** *Isaiah,* often quoted in Luke-Acts (Lk 3.4; 4.17; Acts 28.25) or alluded to (2.3; 3.13–14; 7.58; 8.26). **29:** *The Spirit,* see 8.39; 10.19; 11.12; 13.2,4; 15.28; 16.6,7; 21.4,11; 28.25. **30:** *Heard him,* reading was typically aloud. **32–33:** Isa 53.7–8. **35:** Lk 24.27. For Luke, although Jews and Christians possess the same sacred text, only Christians can interpret it correctly. See similar understanding attributed to the Teacher of Righteousness in the Qumran community, e.g., 1QpHab. **40:** *Azotus,* between Gaza and Joppa; *Caesarea,* Caesarea Maritima, the major harbor city rebuilt by Herod I, seat of Roman administration in the province of Judea.

9.1–31: Conversion of Saul/Paul. Account repeated, with minor variations, in 22.1–21; 26.9–18. Paul describes himself (Gal 1.13–14; Phil 3.6) as having persecuted the church. **2:** *Way,* title for Christian community

so that if he found any who belonged to the Way, men or women, he might bring them bound to Jerusalem. [3] Now as he was going along and approaching Damascus, suddenly a light from heaven flashed around him. [4] He fell to the ground and heard a voice saying to him, "Saul, Saul, why do you persecute me?" [5] He asked, "Who are you, Lord?" The reply came, "I am Jesus, whom you are persecuting. [6] But get up and enter the city, and you will be told what you are to do." [7] The men who were traveling with him stood speechless because they heard the voice but saw no one. [8] Saul got up from the ground, and though his eyes were open, he could see nothing; so they led him by the hand and brought him into Damascus. [9] For three days he was without sight, and neither ate nor drank.

[10] Now there was a disciple in Damascus named Ananias. The Lord said to him in a vision, "Ananias." He answered, "Here I am, Lord." [11] The Lord said to him, "Get up and go to the street called Straight, and at the house of Judas look for a man of Tarsus named Saul. At this moment he is praying, [12] and he has seen in a vision[a] a man named Ananias come in and lay his hands on him so that he might regain his sight." [13] But Ananias answered, "Lord, I have heard from many about this man, how much evil he has done to your saints in Jerusalem; [14] and here he has authority from the chief priests to bind all who invoke your name." [15] But the Lord said to him, "Go, for he is an instrument whom I have chosen to bring my name before Gentiles and kings and before the people of Israel; [16] I myself will show him how much he must suffer for the sake of my name." [17] So Ananias went and entered the house. He laid his hands on Saul[b] and said, "Brother Saul, the Lord Jesus, who appeared to you on your way here, has sent me so that you may regain your sight and be filled with the Holy Spirit." [18] And immediately something like scales fell from his eyes, and his sight was restored. Then he got up and was baptized, [19] and after taking some food, he regained his strength.

For several days he was with the disciples in Damascus, [20] and immediately he began to proclaim Jesus in the synagogues, saying, "He is the Son of God." [21] All who heard him were amazed and said, "Is not this the man who made havoc in Jerusalem among those who invoked this name? And has he not come here for the purpose of bringing them bound before the chief priests?" [22] Saul became increasingly more powerful and confounded the Jews who lived in Damascus by proving that Jesus[c] was the Messiah.[d]

[23] After some time had passed, the Jews plotted to kill him, [24] but their plot became known to Saul. They were watching the gates day and night so that they might kill him; [25] but his disciples took him by night and let him down through an opening in the wall,[e] lowering him in a basket.

[a] Other ancient authorities lack *in a vision*
[b] Gk *him*
[c] Gk *that this*
[d] Or *the Christ*
[e] Gk *through the wall*

(19.9,23; 22.4; 24.14); it may suggest that Christians follow the divine appointed path (cf. Deut 5.33; 10.12; 30.16; Isa 42.24; Zech 3.7; CD 20.18; 1QS 9.17–18). **3–7:** Common elements of divine appearances include flashing light (4 Macc 4.10), falling to the ground (Ezek 1.28; Dan 10.9), double naming (Gen 22.11; 46.2; Ex 3.4; 1 Sam 3.4,10), and commission (Gen 12.1; 22.2). **5:** *Lord,* a title of respect as well as of divinity. **8–9:** Connection between physical and spiritual sight (Lk 24.16,31). *Neither ate nor drank,* extended fasting is associated with intense piety and spiritual transformation (Lk 4.2; Jdt 8.6; *Jos. Asen.* 10.1). **10:** *Disciple in Damascus,* Acts does not report how Christianity spread to the Syrian city. *Vision,* divine instruction often takes place in visions (10.3,17,19; 16.9). *Here I am,* conventional response to God (Gen 22.1; 31.11; 46.2; Ex 3.4). **11:** *Tarsus,* city of Cilicia in southeast Asia Minor. **12:** *Lay . . . hands,* technique used in healing (Lk 4.40; 13.11–13). **13:** *Saints,* lit., "holy ones," a standard term. It is rare in Acts (9.32; 26.10), but frequent in Paul (e.g., Rom 1.7; 15.25; 1 Cor 16.1; 2 Cor 8.4; 13.13; Phil 1.1) to designate members of the Christian community. **15:** *Gentiles . . . kings . . . Israel,* Paul accomplishes this mission. Jesus offers a similar command to his disciples (cf. Mt 10.18; 28:19; Mk 13.9–10). **16:** *Suffer,* the mission will be difficult; Paul recites his ordeals in 2 Cor 11.24–29. **18:** *Scales,* Tob 3.17; 11.13. **22:** *Jesus was the Messiah,* the claim that Jesus is Messiah often provokes opposition among Jews (17.3–5; 18.5–6,28). **23–25:** Paul's version of the escape (2 Cor 11.32–33) identifies the source of hostility as an official of the Nabatean king, not Jews.

[26] When he had come to Jerusalem, he attempted to join the disciples; and they were all afraid of him, for they did not believe that he was a disciple. [27] But Barnabas took him, brought him to the apostles, and described for them how on the road he had seen the Lord, who had spoken to him, and how in Damascus he had spoken boldly in the name of Jesus. [28] So he went in and out among them in Jerusalem, speaking boldly in the name of the Lord. [29] He spoke and argued with the Hellenists; but they were attempting to kill him. [30] When the believers[a] learned of it, they brought him down to Caesarea and sent him off to Tarsus.

[31] Meanwhile the church throughout Judea, Galilee, and Samaria had peace and was built up. Living in the fear of the Lord and in the comfort of the Holy Spirit, it increased in numbers.

[32] Now as Peter went here and there among all the believers,[b] he came down also to the saints living in Lydda. [33] There he found a man named Aeneas, who had been bedridden for eight years, for he was paralyzed. [34] Peter said to him, "Aeneas, Jesus Christ heals you; get up and make your bed!" And immediately he got up. [35] And all the residents of Lydda and Sharon saw him and turned to the Lord.

[36] Now in Joppa there was a disciple whose name was Tabitha, which in Greek is Dorcas.[c] She was devoted to good works and acts of charity. [37] At that time she became ill and died. When they had washed her, they laid her in a room upstairs. [38] Since Lydda was near Joppa, the disciples, who heard that Peter was there, sent two men to him with the request, "Please come to us without delay." [39] So Peter got up and went with them; and when he arrived, they took him to the room upstairs. All the widows stood beside him, weeping and showing tunics and other clothing that Dorcas had made while she was with them. [40] Peter put all of them outside, and then he knelt down and prayed. He turned to the body and said, "Tabitha, get up." Then she opened her eyes, and seeing Peter, she sat up. [41] He gave her his hand and helped her up. Then calling the saints and widows, he showed her to be alive. [42] This became known throughout Joppa, and many believed in the Lord. [43] Meanwhile he stayed in Joppa for some time with a certain Simon, a tanner.

10 In Caesarea there was a man named Cornelius, a centurion of the Italian Cohort, as it was called. [2] He was a devout man who feared God with all his household; he gave alms generously to the people and prayed constantly to God. [3] One afternoon at about three o'clock he had a vision in which he clear-

a Gk *brothers*
b Gk *all of them*
c The name Tabitha in Aramaic and the name Dorcas in Greek mean *a gazelle*

26: *Come to Jerusalem,* Paul reports that he initially traveled to Arabia and did not go to Jerusalem for three years (Gal 1.17–18). **27:** *Barnabas,* see 4.36n. He joins Paul as a fellow missionary (12.25; 13.2–50; 14.12–20; 15.2–39; cf. 1 Cor 9.6; Gal 2.1–13). *Apostles,* Paul reports that on his initial visit to Jerusalem he met only with Cephas (Peter) and James (Gal 1.18–19). *Spoken boldly,* see 4.13. **29:** *Hellenists,* Greek speaking Jews, as in 6.1. **30:** *Tarsus,* Paul's hometown, see v. 11. **31:** A concluding summary reporting the expansion of the church in size and location (2.41,47; 5.12–16; 19.20).

9.32–43: Peter's travels. The story returns to Peter who performs two miraculous healings. Elsewhere in Acts, healing rarely prompts conversion (13.11–12), and more often stirs interest (5.16) and misunderstanding (14.11–12; 28.6). **32:** *Saints,* see 9.13n. *Lydda,* on the road from Jerusalem to Joppa; present-day Lod. **36–42:** Peter's act of resuscitation is modeled on those of Elijah (1 Kings 17.17–24), Elisha (2 Kings 4.18–37), and Jesus (Lk 7.11–17; 8.41–42,49–56). **36:** *Joppa,* present-day Yaffa/Yafo. *Tabitha,* only woman in the NT explicitly called a disciple. Like Paul and John Mark (12.12,25), she has both a Hebrew or Aramaic name and a Greek (or Latin) one (see translators' note *c*). **39:** *Widows,* for widows involved in prayer and mourning, see Lk 2.37; 1 Tim 5.5.

10.1–11.18: Conversion of Cornelius. The conversion of the Roman centurion marks the decisive step in extending the church to Gentiles. **10.1–33: Peter and Cornelius.** Visions, angelic messengers, and heavenly voices underscore the point that God has directed the conversion of Gentiles. **1:** *Caesarea,* see 8.40. *Centurion of the Italian Cohort,* an officer in the Roman army, who, along with other centurions, would have led a group of several hundred soldiers. **2:** *Devout,* adheres to Jewish ideas and practices. See also Lk 7.1–10; Acts 13.16,26; 16.14; 17.4,12; 18.7. **3:** *Three o'clock,* see 3.1. *Vision,* see 9.10. *Angel,* see 5.19; 8.26; 12.7; 27.23.

ly saw an angel of God coming in and saying to him, "Cornelius." [4] He stared at him in terror and said, "What is it, Lord?" He answered, "Your prayers and your alms have ascended as a memorial before God. [5] Now send men to Joppa for a certain Simon who is called Peter; [6] he is lodging with Simon, a tanner, whose house is by the seaside." [7] When the angel who spoke to him had left, he called two of his slaves and a devout soldier from the ranks of those who served him, [8] and after telling them everything, he sent them to Joppa.

[9] About noon the next day, as they were on their journey and approaching the city, Peter went up on the roof to pray. [10] He became hungry and wanted something to eat; and while it was being prepared, he fell into a trance. [11] He saw the heaven opened and something like a large sheet coming down, being lowered to the ground by its four corners. [12] In it were all kinds of four-footed creatures and reptiles and birds of the air. [13] Then he heard a voice saying, "Get up, Peter; kill and eat." [14] But Peter said, "By no means, Lord; for I have never eaten anything that is profane or unclean." [15] The voice said to him again, a second time, "What God has made clean, you must not call profane." [16] This happened three times, and the thing was suddenly taken up to heaven.

[17] Now while Peter was greatly puzzled about what to make of the vision that he had seen, suddenly the men sent by Cornelius appeared. They were asking for Simon's house and were standing by the gate. [18] They called out to ask whether Simon, who was called Peter, was staying there. [19] While Peter was still thinking about the vision, the Spirit said to him, "Look, three[a] men are searching for you. [20] Now get up, go down, and go with them without hesitation; for I have sent them." [21] So Peter went down to the men and said, "I am the one you are looking for; what is the reason for your coming?" [22] They answered, "Cornelius, a centurion, an upright and God-fearing man, who is well spoken of by the whole Jewish nation, was directed by a holy angel to send for you to come to his house and to hear what you have to say." [23] So Peter[b] invited them in and gave them lodging.

The next day he got up and went with them, and some of the believers[c] from Joppa accompanied him. [24] The following day they came to Caesarea. Cornelius was expecting them and had called together his relatives and close friends. [25] On Peter's arrival Cornelius met him, and falling at his feet, worshiped him. [26] But Peter made him get up, saying, "Stand up; I am only a mortal." [27] And as he talked with him, he went in and found that many had assembled; [28] and he said to them, "You yourselves know that it is unlawful for a Jew to associate with or to visit a Gentile; but God has shown me that I should not call anyone profane or unclean. [29] So when I was sent for, I came without objection. Now may I ask why you sent for me?"

[30] Cornelius replied, "Four days ago at this very hour, at three o'clock, I was praying in my house when suddenly a man in dazzling clothes stood before me. [31] He said, 'Cornelius, your prayer has been heard and your alms have been remembered before God. [32] Send therefore to Joppa and ask for Simon, who is called Peter; he is staying in the home

[a] One ancient authority reads *two*; others lack the word
[b] Gk *he*
[c] Gk *brothers*

4: *Lord,* see 9.5n. *Ascended as a memorial,* language frequently used of sacrifice (Lev 2.2; 5.12; 6.15; Sir 38.11). **9:** *Noon,* not a typical time for prayer; meals might be served then (*b. Shabb.* 10a). **13–15:** *Voice,* the divine presence is heard, not seen, but the communication is important; see 9.4,11. **14:** *Profane or unclean,* Peter affirms his adherence to Jewish dietary practices (Lev 11 and Deut 14). **19:** *Spirit,* on communication by the Spirit, see 1.16; 2.4; 6.10; 13.2; 16.6; 21.11; 28.5. **22:** *Well spoken of,* similar description of Gamaliel (5.34). **28:** *Unlawful for a Jew to associate with or to visit a Gentile,* fear of committing idolatry and desire to avoid prohibited foods required care in how Jews associated with Gentiles. Peter's statement, however, is rarely reflected in Jewish writings (cf. *Jub.* 22.16), but represents a common perspective among Gentiles (e.g., Philo, *Spec. Laws* 2.167; Tacitus, *Hist.* 5.1–13). Actual practice among Jews would not have supported this view, as for instance the existence of a "Court of the Gentiles" at the Temple would indicate. *Not call anyone profane,* Peter applies his vision of animals to human associations. **30:** *Dazzling clothes,* attribute of angelic being (Lk 24.4; Rev 19.8).

of Simon, a tanner, by the sea.' [33] Therefore I sent for you immediately, and you have been kind enough to come. So now all of us are here in the presence of God to listen to all that the Lord has commanded you to say."

[34] Then Peter began to speak to them: "I truly understand that God shows no partiality, [35] but in every nation anyone who fears him and does what is right is acceptable to him. [36] You know the message he sent to the people of Israel, preaching peace by Jesus Christ—he is Lord of all. [37] That message spread throughout Judea, beginning in Galilee after the baptism that John announced: [38] how God anointed Jesus of Nazareth with the Holy Spirit and with power; how he went about doing good and healing all who were oppressed by the devil, for God was with him. [39] We are witnesses to all that he did both in Judea and in Jerusalem. They put him to death by hanging him on a tree; [40] but God raised him on the third day and allowed him to appear, [41] not to all the people but to us who were chosen by God as witnesses, and who ate and drank with him after he rose from the dead. [42] He commanded us to preach to the people and to testify that he is the one ordained by God as judge of the living and the dead. [43] All the prophets testify about him that everyone who believes in him receives forgiveness of sins through his name."

[44] While Peter was still speaking, the Holy Spirit fell upon all who heard the word. [45] The circumcised believers who had come with Peter were astounded that the gift of the Holy Spirit had been poured out even on the Gentiles, [46] for they heard them speaking in tongues and extolling God. Then Peter said, [47] "Can anyone withhold the water for baptizing these people who have received the Holy Spirit just as we have?" [48] So he ordered them to be baptized in the name of Jesus Christ. Then they invited him to stay for several days.

11 Now the apostles and the believers[a] who were in Judea heard that the Gentiles had also accepted the word of God. [2] So when Peter went up to Jerusalem, the circumcised believers[b] criticized him, [3] saying, "Why did you go to uncircumcised men and eat with them?" [4] Then Peter began to explain it to them, step by step, saying, [5] "I was in the city of Joppa praying, and in a trance I saw a vision. There was something like a large sheet coming down from heaven, being lowered by its four corners; and it came close to me. [6] As I looked at it closely I saw four-footed animals, beasts of prey, reptiles, and birds of the air. [7] I also heard a voice saying to me,

a Gk *brothers*
b Gk lacks *believers*

34–43: Peter's speech. The speech summarizes major themes in Acts: Jesus is the prophesied anointed one and Lord (2.36; 4.33; 8.16; 15.11; 16.31; 19.5; 28.31); his death has been vindicated by God (2.24,32; 3.15; 4.10; 5.30; 13.30); the apostles are chosen witnesses to proclaim Jesus (1.8; 2.32; 3.15; 13.31; 23.11; 26.16); all experience forgiveness of sins through believing in Jesus (2.38; 5.31; 13.38; 26.18). **34:** *No partiality,* God's quality of judging impartially, regardless of status or wealth (Deut 10.17–18; Sir 35.12–13), now extends to ethnic distinctions between Jews and Gentiles (cf. Rom 2.11). **35:** *Fears him,* Ps 15.1–2; Cornelius models this description, vv. 2,22. Fearing God and doing right echo the Jewish teaching that two most important actions are loving God (Deut 6) and one's neighbor (Lev 19) (e.g., *T. Dan* 5.3; Philo, *Spec. Laws* 2.63). To be God's people is no longer constituted by the ethnic division between Jew and Gentile but by a religious distinction, those who do/do not fear God and do what is right. **36:** *Preaching peace,* the message of reconciliation (2 Cor 5.18–19). *Lord of all,* title of pagan gods (Plutarch, *Is. Os.* 355E), Roman emperors (Epictetus, *Diatr.* 4.1.12), and God (Josh 3.11; Zech 6.5; Ps 97.5; Wis 6.7; 8.3). **39:** *They,* most likely meant as Jews/Jewish leaders who were responsible for the crucifixion (2.23; 3.15; 5.30). *Tree,* the cross (see 5.30; 13.29). **44–48:** The scene repeats the events of Pentecost: Spirit poured out (2.17–18), speaking in tongues (2.4–11), astonished reaction (2.12), but now offered to Gentiles (v. 45). **44:** *Holy Spirit,* confirming sign of divine favor and transformation, see 1.8; 2.4; 4.31. **11.1–18: Peter's report to the "circumcised believers."** Peter reviews the events that led to the baptism of Cornelius, and the apostles acknowledge that the divine gifts have been extended to Gentiles. Luke often repeats stories, such as Jesus' ascent into heaven (Lk 24.51; Acts 1.9) or Paul's reports of his vision of Jesus (9.1–9; 22.4–11; 26.12–18), most likely used as an indication of an important transitional moment. **3:** The objection to Peter's eating with Gentiles, rather than converting them, reinforces an image of Jewish xenophobia. **5–9:** Peter repeats the ac-

'Get up, Peter; kill and eat.' [8] But I replied, 'By no means, Lord; for nothing profane or unclean has ever entered my mouth.' [9] But a second time the voice answered from heaven, 'What God has made clean, you must not call profane.' [10] This happened three times; then everything was pulled up again to heaven. [11] At that very moment three men, sent to me from Caesarea, arrived at the house where we were. [12] The Spirit told me to go with them and not to make a distinction between them and us.[a] These six brothers also accompanied me, and we entered the man's house. [13] He told us how he had seen the angel standing in his house and saying, 'Send to Joppa and bring Simon, who is called Peter; [14] he will give you a message by which you and your entire household will be saved.' [15] And as I began to speak, the Holy Spirit fell upon them just as it had upon us at the beginning. [16] And I remembered the word of the Lord, how he had said, 'John baptized with water, but you will be baptized with the Holy Spirit.' [17] If then God gave them the same gift that he gave us when we believed in the Lord Jesus Christ, who was I that I could hinder God?" [18] When they heard this, they were silenced. And they praised God, saying, "Then God has given even to the Gentiles the repentance that leads to life."

[19] Now those who were scattered because of the persecution that took place over Stephen traveled as far as Phoenicia, Cyprus, and Antioch, and they spoke the word to no one except Jews. [20] But among them were some men of Cyprus and Cyrene who, on coming to Antioch, spoke to the Hellenists[b] also, proclaiming the Lord Jesus. [21] The hand of the Lord was with them, and a great number became believers and turned to the Lord. [22] News of this came to the ears of the church in Jerusalem, and they sent Barnabas to Antioch. [23] When he came and saw the grace of God, he rejoiced, and he exhorted them all to remain faithful to the Lord with steadfast devotion; [24] for he was a good man, full of the Holy Spirit and of faith. And a great many people were brought to the Lord. [25] Then Barnabas went to Tarsus to look for Saul, [26] and when he had found him, he brought him to Antioch. So it was that for an entire year they met with[c] the church and taught a great many people, and it was in Antioch that the disciples were first called "Christians."

[27] At that time prophets came down from Jerusalem to Antioch. [28] One of them named Agabus stood up and predicted by the Spirit that there would be a severe famine over all the world; and this took place during the reign of Claudius. [29] The disciples determined that according to their ability, each would send relief to the believers[d] living in Judea; [30] this they did, sending it to the elders by Barnabas and Saul.

a Or *not to hesitate*
b Other ancient authorities read *Greeks*
c Or *were guests of*
d Gk *brothers*

count of his vision, see 10.11–15. **14:** *Household,* the conversion of the head of the household can bring about the conversion of the entire household (16.15,34; 18.8). *Will be saved,* see 4.12. **15:** *Holy Spirit,* see 10.44n. **16:** See 1.5n. **18:** *Repentance,* shown by belief in Jesus.

11.19–30: The church in Antioch. 19: *Scattered,* see 8.1. *Phoenicia,* on the Mediterranean coast north of Mount Carmel. *Antioch,* seat of Roman administration in Syria and site of an early largely Gentile church (Gal 2.11–14). **20:** *Cyrene,* important city in North Africa. *Hellenists,* here apparently Greek-speaking Gentiles, rather than Greek-speaking Jews (6.1; 9.29). **22:** Sending representatives from the Jerusalem church (cf. 8.14) sanctions the expansion. **25:** *Tarsus,* see 9.30. **26:** *Christians,* the origin of the name is uncertain, but perhaps a Latin word "partisans of Christ." The creation of a new name, especially in the account of the first Gentile church, indicates that the church is no longer fully identifiable with Jews. **27:** *Prophets,* recognized role among Jews (Josephus, *J.W.* 1.78–80; 2.112–13,258–63; 6.283–87,300–309; 7.437–50; *Ant.* 14.22–24,172–76; 15.373–79; 17.345–48; 20.97–99,167–72,188) and early Christians (1 Cor 12.28–29; 14.29–37; Eph 4.11). **28:** *Agabus,* see 21.10. *Famine,* while local famines, including in Judea, are known from this time (*Ant.* 20.51–53,101), this report both reflects Lukan hyperbole and portrays Rome as the failed ruler. *Claudius,* Roman emperor 41–54 CE. **30:** *Elders,* Gk "presbyteroi"; church leaders (14.23; 15.2,4,22,23; 16.4; 20.17; 21.18; 1 Tim 4.14; 5.17,19; Titus 1.5; Jas 5.14; Rev 4.4). This title was used in many Jewish communities, including Qumran (1QS 6.8, Heb "zekeinim").

12 About that time King Herod laid violent hands upon some who belonged to the church. [2] He had James, the brother of John, killed with the sword. [3] After he saw that it pleased the Jews, he proceeded to arrest Peter also. (This was during the festival of Unleavened Bread.) [4] When he had seized him, he put him in prison and handed him over to four squads of soldiers to guard him, intending to bring him out to the people after the Passover. [5] While Peter was kept in prison, the church prayed fervently to God for him.

[6] The very night before Herod was going to bring him out, Peter, bound with two chains, was sleeping between two soldiers, while guards in front of the door were keeping watch over the prison. [7] Suddenly an angel of the Lord appeared and a light shone in the cell. He tapped Peter on the side and woke him, saying, "Get up quickly." And the chains fell off his wrists. [8] The angel said to him, "Fasten your belt and put on your sandals." He did so. Then he said to him, "Wrap your cloak around you and follow me." [9] Peter[a] went out and followed him; he did not realize that what was happening with the angel's help was real; he thought he was seeing a vision. [10] After they had passed the first and the second guard, they came before the iron gate leading into the city. It opened for them of its own accord, and they went outside and walked along a lane, when suddenly the angel left him. [11] Then Peter came to himself and said, "Now I am sure that the Lord has sent his angel and rescued me from the hands of Herod and from all that the Jewish people were expecting."

[12] As soon as he realized this, he went to the house of Mary, the mother of John whose other name was Mark, where many had gathered and were praying. [13] When he knocked at the outer gate, a maid named Rhoda came to answer. [14] On recognizing Peter's voice, she was so overjoyed that, instead of opening the gate, she ran in and announced that Peter was standing at the gate. [15] They said to her, "You are out of your mind!" But she insisted that it was so. They said, "It is his angel." [16] Meanwhile Peter continued knocking; and when they opened the gate, they saw him and were amazed. [17] He motioned to them with his hand to be silent, and described for them how the Lord had brought him out of the prison. And he added, "Tell this to James and to the believers."[b] Then he left and went to another place.

[18] When morning came, there was no small commotion among the soldiers over what had become of Peter. [19] When Herod had searched for him and could not find him, he examined the guards and ordered them to be put to death. Then he went down from Judea to Caesarea and stayed there.

[20] Now Herod[c] was angry with the people of Tyre and Sidon. So they came to him in a body; and after winning over Blastus, the

[a] Gk *He*
[b] Gk *brothers*
[c] Gk *he*

12.1–19: Persecution of apostles. 1: *King Herod,* Agrippa I, grandson of Herod I, who ruled the Herodian kingdom, mainly Judea (under Roman authority) 41–44 CE. Only Acts refers to Agrippa by the name "Herod," possibly to build continuity with Herod Antipas, who was involved in the deaths of John the Baptist (Lk 3.18–20; 9.7–9) and Jesus (Lk 13.31; 23.6–12; Acts 4.27), and with his grandfather, Herod the Great (37–4 BCE) (Lk 1.5; 3.1). In Jewish tradition, Agrippa is remembered as a fair, generous, and religious observant Jewish ruler (*Ant.* 19.330). **2.** *James, the brother of John,* James the son of Zebedee. Both he and his brother were early disciples of Jesus (Lk 5.10; 6.14). **3:** *Pleased the Jews,* Jews as a whole, not just individuals such as the high priest or groups such as Sadducees, frequently appear in Acts as persecutors of Christians (13.45; 14.2,19; 17.5; 18.12; 20.3; 21.27; 22.30; 23.12; 24.9; 25.2,7; 26.2,21). *Unleavened bread,* Passover, the festival during which Jesus was arrested and executed (Lk 22.1,7). **4:** *Squad,* Gk "stratiōtos," a small group of soldiers probably consisting of about ten men; the number (forty or so, altogether) emphasizes the impossibility of escape (as do the chains, v. 6). **6–11: Miraculous release from prison.** See 5.17–21; 16.23–29. **7:** *Angel,* see, for angelic help, 5.19; 27.23; Ex 23.20; 1 Kings 19.5; Dan 3.19–28; 6.22; 2 Macc 11.6. **12:** *John . . . Mark,* 12.25; 15.37. **13:** *Outer gate,* suggesting a large house. **17:** *James,* the brother of Jesus, leader of Jerusalem church (15.13–21; 21.18).

12.20–25: Death of Herod. Agrippa I died in 44 CE. According to Josephus (*Ant.* 19.343–52), Agrippa, while presiding over public spectacles in Caesarea, was acclaimed as a god. He accepted the flattery but almost im-

king's chamberlain, they asked for a reconciliation, because their country depended on the king's country for food. [21] On an appointed day Herod put on his royal robes, took his seat on the platform, and delivered a public address to them. [22] The people kept shouting, "The voice of a god, and not of a mortal!" [23] And immediately, because he had not given the glory to God, an angel of the Lord struck him down, and he was eaten by worms and died.

[24] But the word of God continued to advance and gain adherents. [25] Then after completing their mission Barnabas and Saul returned to[a] Jerusalem and brought with them John, whose other name was Mark.

13 Now in the church at Antioch there were prophets and teachers: Barnabas, Simeon who was called Niger, Lucius of Cyrene, Manaen a member of the court of Herod the ruler,[b] and Saul. [2] While they were worshiping the Lord and fasting, the Holy Spirit said, "Set apart for me Barnabas and Saul for the work to which I have called them." [3] Then after fasting and praying they laid their hands on them and sent them off.

[4] So, being sent out by the Holy Spirit, they went down to Seleucia; and from there they sailed to Cyprus. [5] When they arrived at Salamis, they proclaimed the word of God in the synagogues of the Jews. And they had John also to assist them. [6] When they had gone through the whole island as far as Paphos, they met a certain magician, a Jewish false prophet, named Bar-Jesus. [7] He was with the proconsul, Sergius Paulus, an intelligent man, who summoned Barnabas and Saul and wanted to hear the word of God. [8] But the magician Elymas (for that is the translation of his name) opposed them and tried to turn the proconsul away from the faith. [9] But Saul, also known as Paul, filled with the Holy Spirit, looked intently at him [10] and said, "You son of the devil, you enemy of all righteousness, full of all deceit and villainy, will you not stop making crooked the straight paths of the Lord? [11] And now listen—the hand of the Lord is against you, and you will be blind for a while, unable to see the sun." Immediately mist and darkness came over him, and he went about groping for someone to lead him by the hand. [12] When the proconsul saw what had happened, he believed, for he was astonished at the teaching about the Lord.

[a] Other ancient authorities read *from*
[b] Gk *tetrarch*

mediately fell ill and died shortly thereafter. **22:** God punishes persons who think themselves equal to a god (Ezek 28.1–10). **23:** *Worms,* appropriate punishment for those who persecute God's people (e.g., Jdt 16.17; 2 Macc 9.9). **24:** Threats against the believers regularly fail (4.4; 5.42; 14.6–7,19–20; 16.23–34). **25:** See 11.29–30. *John . . . Mark,* see v. 12; 9.36n.

13.1–14.28: Paul's journey in Asia Minor. The narrative shifts to Paul's travels through Asia Minor and Greece (chs 13–20), his arrest in Jerusalem and defense before Roman and Jewish authorities (chs 21–27), and his journey to Rome (chs 27–28).

13.1–12: Paul travels to Cyprus. 1–3: The church in Antioch. 1: *Prophets,* see 11.27. *Barnabas,* 4.36n. *Herod the ruler,* Gk "tetrarch," meaning Herod Antipas, son of Herod I and tetrarch of Galilee and Perea 6–37 CE, not Herod Agrippa. On Luke's presentation of Antipas, see Lk 23.8–11. **2:** *Holy Spirit,* 8.29; 10.19; 13.4; 16.6,7. **3:** *Praying they laid their hands,* actions sanctioning ministerial appointment (cf. 6.6; 1 Tim 4.14; 2 Tim 1.6). **4–12: Preaching on Cyprus. 4:** *Seleucia,* seaport near Antioch. *Cyprus,* other Christians preceded Paul and Barnabas there (11.19). **5:** *Salamis,* seaport on eastern side of Cyprus. *Synagogues of the Jews,* Paul regularly preaches in synagogues (13.14; 14.1; 16.13; 17.1,10,17; 18.4,19; 19.8). **6:** *Paphos,* seat of Roman administration on Cyprus, on the southwest coast. *Magician,* see Peter's meeting with Simon (8.14–24). *Bar-Jesus,* the Aramaic name means Son of Jesus/Joshua, a common Jewish name. **7:** *Proconsul, Sergius Paulus,* representing the Roman emperor (18.12; 24.22–27; 25.14). A "proconsul" was the governor of a province, usually for a fixed term of one year, by appointment of the emperor. **8:** *Elymas,* meaning uncertain, not a translation of Bar-Jesus. **9:** *Saul, also known as Paul,* here, and for most of the rest of Acts, the name Paul is used. Luke may have preferred the Hebrew name Saul to this point to emphasize Paul's Jewish background. *Intently,* see 3.4. **10:** *Son of the devil,* Elymas is the son not of Jesus but of Satan (cf. Jn 8.44). **11:** Paul often performs miracles (14.10; 19.11; 20.9–10; 28.3–6). Paul's ability to blind the magician reflects God's power to subdue Satan. **12:** *Lord,* here meaning Jesus.

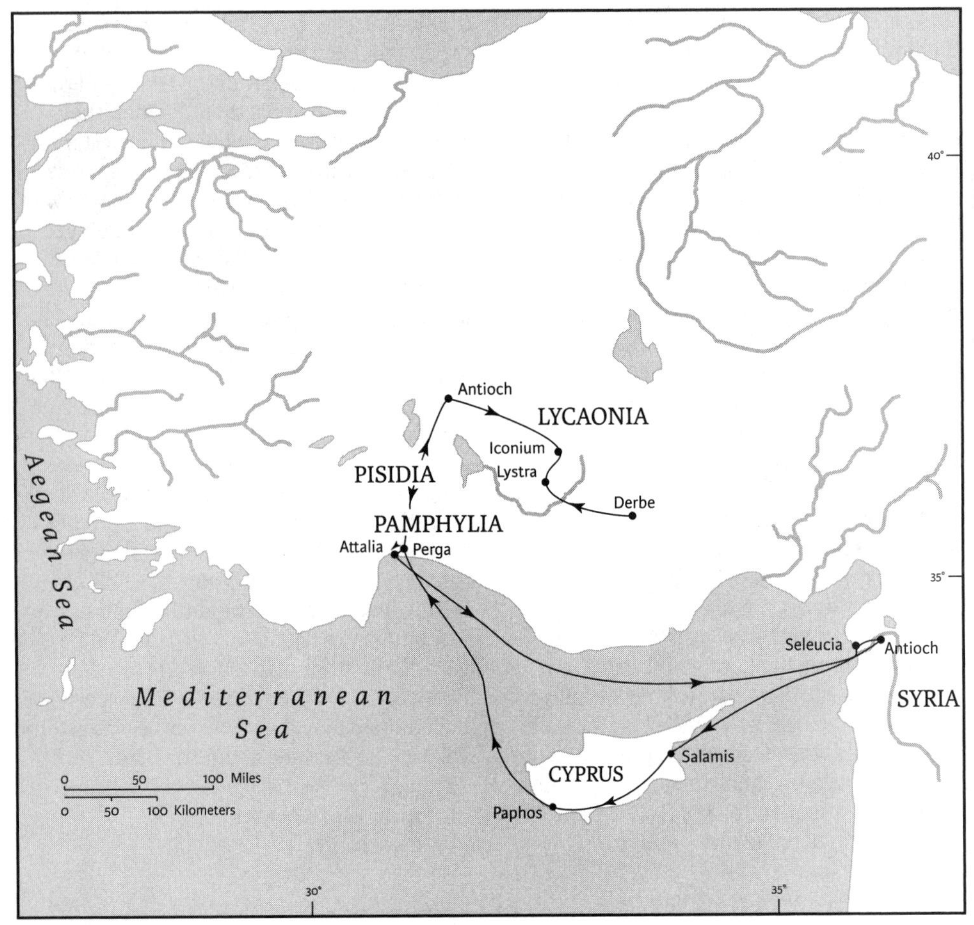

Chs 13–14: First missionary journey of Paul.

[13] Then Paul and his companions set sail from Paphos and came to Perga in Pamphylia. John, however, left them and returned to Jerusalem; [14] but they went on from Perga and came to Antioch in Pisidia. And on the sabbath day they went into the synagogue and sat down. [15] After the reading of the law and the prophets, the officials of the synagogue sent them a message, saying, "Brothers, if you have any word of exhortation for the people, give it." [16] So Paul stood up and with a gesture began to speak:

"You Israelites,[a] and others who fear God, listen. [17] The God of this people Israel chose our ancestors and made the people great dur-

[a] Gk *Men, Israelites*

13.13–52: Preaching in Pisidia. Paul's speech covers several central elements: Jesus is David's heir and the culmination of Israel's sacred narrative (vv. 17–25); his death and resurrection bring forgiveness and salvation to those who believe (vv. 26–41); Jews reject God's message and persecute Christians, while Gentiles become believers (vv. 44–52). **13:** *Perga in Pamphylia,* important seaport city in southern Asia Minor (present-day Turkey). *John,* 15.37–38. **14:** *Antioch in Pisidia,* Roman city approximately 100 mi (160 km) from Perga. *Sabbath day,* Jews regularly gathered on the Sabbath (seventh day, Saturday) to read scripture, both Torah (Pentateuch) and prophets (Philo, *Spec. Laws.* 2.60–62; Josephus, *J.W.* 2.289–92; *m. Meg.* 3.6). *Synagogue,* Paul's typical practice; see 13.5. **15:** *Officials,* Gk "archisynagōgos," commonly used for leaders in the Jewish community. **16:** *Others who fear God,* Gentiles are present in the synagogues (16.14; 17.4,12; 18.7). **17–25:** For Paul, Israel's story culminates with Jesus; cf. 7.2–5. *Chose our ancestors,* Deut 4.37; 7.6; 10.15. *Uplifted arm,* Ex 6.6; Deut 4.34; 26.8. **18:** *Put up*

ing their stay in the land of Egypt, and with uplifted arm he led them out of it. [18] For about forty years he put up with[a] them in the wilderness. [19] After he had destroyed seven nations in the land of Canaan, he gave them their land as an inheritance [20] for about four hundred fifty years. After that he gave them judges until the time of the prophet Samuel. [21] Then they asked for a king; and God gave them Saul son of Kish, a man of the tribe of Benjamin, who reigned for forty years. [22] When he had removed him, he made David their king. In his testimony about him he said, 'I have found David, son of Jesse, to be a man after my heart, who will carry out all my wishes.' [23] Of this man's posterity God has brought to Israel a Savior, Jesus, as he promised; [24] before his coming John had already proclaimed a baptism of repentance to all the people of Israel. [25] And as John was finishing his work, he said, 'What do you suppose that I am? I am not he. No, but one is coming after me; I am not worthy to untie the thong of the sandals[b] on his feet.'

[26] "My brothers, you descendants of Abraham's family, and others who fear God, to us[c] the message of this salvation has been sent. [27] Because the residents of Jerusalem and their leaders did not recognize him or understand the words of the prophets that are read every sabbath, they fulfilled those words by condemning him. [28] Even though they found no cause for a sentence of death, they asked Pilate to have him killed. [29] When they had carried out everything that was written about him, they took him down from the tree and laid him in a tomb. [30] But God raised him from the dead; [31] and for many days he appeared to those who came up with him from Galilee to Jerusalem, and they are now his witnesses to the people. [32] And we bring you the good news that what God promised to our ancestors [33] he has fulfilled for us, their children, by raising Jesus; as also it is written in the second psalm,

'You are my Son;
today I have begotten you.'

[34] As to his raising him from the dead, no more to return to corruption, he has spoken in this way,

'I will give you the holy promises made to David.'

[35] Therefore he has also said in another psalm,

'You will not let your Holy One experience corruption.'

[36] For David, after he had served the purpose of God in his own generation, died,[d] was laid beside his ancestors, and experienced corruption; [37] but he whom God raised up experienced no corruption. [38] Let it be known to you therefore, my brothers, that through this man forgiveness of sins is proclaimed to you; [39] by this Jesus[e] everyone who believes is set free from all those sins[f] from which you could not be freed by the law of Moses. [40] Beware, therefore, that what the prophets said does not happen to you:

[41] 'Look, you scoffers!
Be amazed and perish,
for in your days I am doing a work,
a work that you will never believe, even if someone tells you.'"

[a] Other ancient authorities read *cared for*
[b] Gk *untie the sandals*
[c] Other ancient authorities read *you*
[d] Gk *fell asleep*
[e] Gk *this*
[f] Gk *all*

with, other manuscripts read "cared for." The difference in the two Greek words is one letter. While both meanings fit the context, Stephen's speech (7.42) suggests Luke meant *put up with*. **19:** *Seven nations,* Deut 7.1. *Land as an inheritance,* Num 34.2; Deut 4.38; 26.1; Josh 14.1–2. **20:** *Four hundred fifty years,* this is not the length of time between the conquest and the judges; it may be that Paul is including 400 years before the Exodus (Gen 15.13), that is, from the time of Israel in Egypt. **21:** *Asked for a king,* 1 Sam 8.5,10; 10.21,24. *Forty years, Ant.* 6.378. **22:** A pastiche of citations (e.g., 1 Sam 13.14; Ps 89.24 [MT 89.25]). **23:** *Posterity,* Jesus' legal inheritance of Davidic descent according to Luke came through Joseph (Lk 3.23–38). **24:** *John,* Lk 3.3. **25:** See Lk 3.16. **27:** *Did not recognize him,* see 3.17. **28:** *No cause,* Lk 23.4,14–15,22,47. *Pilate,* see 3.13n. **29:** *Tree,* 5.30; 10.39. **30:** *God raised him,* 3.15; 4.10; 10.40. **31:** *Witnesses,* the primary responsibility of apostles (1.8n.; 2.32; 3.15; 5.32); Paul does so as well (23.11). **33:** Ps 2.7. **34:** Isa 55.3. **35:** Ps 16.10. **38:** *Forgiveness of sins,* forgiveness is tied to belief in Jesus (2.38; 5.31; 10.43; 26.18). **39:** *Set free,* Gk "justified"; on the relation between justification and the *law,* see Gal 3.23–25; Rom 3.28; 8.3. **40–41:** Hab 1.5. The quotation is from the LXX; *will never believe,* or "would not believe." For Luke, the

[42] As Paul and Barnabas[a] were going out, the people urged them to speak about these things again the next sabbath. [43] When the meeting of the synagogue broke up, many Jews and devout converts to Judaism followed Paul and Barnabas, who spoke to them and urged them to continue in the grace of God.

[44] The next sabbath almost the whole city gathered to hear the word of the Lord.[b] [45] But when the Jews saw the crowds, they were filled with jealousy; and blaspheming, they contradicted what was spoken by Paul. [46] Then both Paul and Barnabas spoke out boldly, saying, "It was necessary that the word of God should be spoken first to you. Since you reject it and judge yourselves to be unworthy of eternal life, we are now turning to the Gentiles. [47] For so the Lord has commanded us, saying,

'I have set you to be a light for the Gentiles,
so that you may bring salvation to the
ends of the earth.'"

[48] When the Gentiles heard this, they were glad and praised the word of the Lord; and as many as had been destined for eternal life became believers. [49] Thus the word of the Lord spread throughout the region. [50] But the Jews incited the devout women of high standing and the leading men of the city, and stirred up persecution against Paul and Barnabas, and drove them out of their region. [51] So they shook the dust off their feet in protest against them, and went to Iconium. [52] And the disciples were filled with joy and with the Holy Spirit.

14 The same thing occurred in Iconium, where Paul and Barnabas[a] went into the Jewish synagogue and spoke in such a way that a great number of both Jews and Greeks became believers. [2] But the unbelieving Jews stirred up the Gentiles and poisoned their minds against the brothers. [3] So they remained for a long time, speaking boldly for the Lord, who testified to the word of his grace by granting signs and wonders to be done through them. [4] But the residents of the city were divided; some sided with the Jews, and some with the apostles. [5] And when an attempt was made by both Gentiles and Jews, with their rulers, to mistreat them and to stone them, [6] the apostles[a] learned of it and fled to Lystra and Derbe, cities of Lycaonia, and to the surrounding country; [7] and there they continued proclaiming the good news.

[8] In Lystra there was a man sitting who could not use his feet and had never walked, for he had been crippled from birth. [9] He listened to Paul as he was speaking. And Paul, looking at him intently and seeing that he had faith to be healed, [10] said in a loud voice, "Stand upright on your feet." And the

a Gk *they*
b Other ancient authorities read *God*

prophets not only look forward to Jesus but also recognized the dire consequences for not believing in him. **43:** Many Jews respond positively (14.1; 17.4,11–12; 18.8). **45:** *The Jews,* Acts presents Jewish opposition as persistent (17.5,13; 18.12; 20.3,19) and irrational (5.17; 17.5). *Blaspheming,* perhaps meaning "swearing falsely." **46:** *Spoke out boldly,* see 4.13. Just as Jesus' death results from both divine will and Jewish malevolence, so the mission to the Gentiles results from God's plan (10.1–11.18) and Jewish rejection. **47:** Isa 49.6. Paul takes himself and his companions, rather than Israel (*T. Levi* 14.3; *Sib. Or.* 14.214), to be the light. **48:** *Destined for eternal life,* proven worthy of becoming part of God's kingdom. **50:** Jews are the source of enmity. **51:** *Shook the dust,* Lk 10.11; cf Mt 10.14. *Iconium,* present-day Konya, 75 mi (120 km) southeast of Antioch.

14.1–28: Preaching in Lycaonia. 1: *Iconium,* see 13.51n. *Synagogue,* despite announcing that he is turning to the Gentiles (13.46), Paul continues to preach to Jews (16.13; 17.1,10,17; 18.4,19,26; 19.8), some of whom continue to join the movement. *Jews,* see 13.43. *Greeks,* see 13.16. **3:** *Speaking boldly,* see 4.13. **4:** *Jews,* those not persuaded to join the movement of Jesus-followers. *Apostles,* title applied to Paul only here and v. 14. Paul claimed the title (Rom 1.1; 1 Cor 1.1; 9.1; 2 Cor 1.1; Gal 1.1), although some objected (1 Cor 9.2). **5:** *Rulers,* the leaders of each religious group (synagogue leaders for Jews, temple officials for Greeks). *Stone them,* uncertain whether legal punishment or mob action (cf. Stephen, 7.58). One of the accepted forms of punishment in the Tanakh (Lev 20.2; 24.14; Num 15.35–36; Deut 13.11; 17.5; 21.21) and rabbinic tradition (*b. Shabb.* 153b–154a; *b. B. Kamma* 44b; *b. Sanh.,* passim). **6:** *Lystra . . . Derbe,* smaller towns in Lycaonia. **8–20:** The healing parallels Peter's act (3.1–10). **9:** *Intently,* see 3.4. *Faith to be healed,* faith often accompanies healing (3.16; Lk 5.20; 7.50; 8.48). **10:** Paul often performs miracles (13.11; 19.11; 28.3–5).

man[a] sprang up and began to walk. [11] When the crowds saw what Paul had done, they shouted in the Lycaonian language, "The gods have come down to us in human form!" [12] Barnabas they called Zeus, and Paul they called Hermes, because he was the chief speaker. [13] The priest of Zeus, whose temple was just outside the city,[b] brought oxen and garlands to the gates; he and the crowds wanted to offer sacrifice. [14] When the apostles Barnabas and Paul heard of it, they tore their clothes and rushed out into the crowd, shouting, [15] "Friends,[c] why are you doing this? We are mortals just like you, and we bring you good news, that you should turn from these worthless things to the living God, who made the heaven and the earth and the sea and all that is in them. [16] In past generations he allowed all the nations to follow their own ways; [17] yet he has not left himself without a witness in doing good—giving you rains from heaven and fruitful seasons, and filling you with food and your hearts with joy." [18] Even with these words, they scarcely restrained the crowds from offering sacrifice to them.

[19] But Jews came there from Antioch and Iconium and won over the crowds. Then they stoned Paul and dragged him out of the city, supposing that he was dead. [20] But when the disciples surrounded him, he got up and went into the city. The next day he went on with Barnabas to Derbe.

[21] After they had proclaimed the good news to that city and had made many disciples, they returned to Lystra, then on to Iconium and Antioch. [22] There they strengthened the souls of the disciples and encouraged them to continue in the faith, saying, "It is through many persecutions that we must enter the kingdom of God." [23] And after they had appointed elders for them in each church, with prayer and fasting they entrusted them to the Lord in whom they had come to believe.

[24] Then they passed through Pisidia and came to Pamphylia. [25] When they had spoken the word in Perga, they went down to Attalia. [26] From there they sailed back to Antioch, where they had been commended to the grace of God for the work[d] that they had completed. [27] When they arrived, they called the church together and related all that God had done with them, and how he had opened a door of faith for the Gentiles. [28] And they stayed there with the disciples for some time.

15 Then certain individuals came down from Judea and were teaching the brothers, "Unless you are circumcised according to

[a] Gk *he*
[b] Or *The priest of Zeus-Outside-the-City*
[c] Gk *Men*
[d] Or *committed in the grace of God to the work*

11–12: *Lycaonian language,* if an independent language, it has not survived; it may also have been a local Greek dialect. That gods could appear in human form was widely accepted (Gen 18.2; Homer, *Od.* 17.483–487; Ovid, *Metam.* 8.611–724). **14:** *Tore their clothes,* showing deep distress (Gen 37.29; Judg 11.35; 2 Kings 2.12; Jdt 14.16; 1 Macc 13.45). **15:** *Worthless things,* idols (Isa 57.13; Ps 96.5; 97.7; Wis 13.10–19). *To the living God,* rejecting idols also required turning to the true God. **16:** Jews could express toleration of idols (Philo, *Spec. Laws* 1.53; *Life of Moses* 2.205; Josephus, *Ant.* 4.207; *Ag. Ap.* 2.237), and legitimize their use as ancestral customs (*b. Hul.* 13b). **17:** God cares for all and can be known by all; see 17.22–31. **19:** *Jews,* the presence of Jews from 100 miles away manifests Luke's view of their deep hatred for Paul. *Stoned,* see 2 Cor 11.25. **21–28:** Paul revisits the communities in Pisidia and Lycaonia where he had previously preached, and he ultimately returns to Jerusalem. **22:** *Strengthened the souls,* see 15.41; 16.5; 18.23; 20.2. Lk 21.12–19 attributes to Jesus teaching on suffering as a precursor to the kingdom of God; Jewish texts state that violence and suffering will accompany the end-time (Dan 11.32–35; *Sib. Or.* 3.635–51; *4 Ezra* 6.18–25; *2 Bar.* 70; *m. Sot.* 9.15). **23:** *Elders,* see 11.30. *Lord,* Jesus, see 1.21; 9.5. **25:** *Attalia,* seaport of Perga; see 13.13n. **27:** *Church,* assembly of believers. Although Paul had success among Jews, the story's interest remains with Gentile believers.

15.1–35: Jerusalem council. Gentiles have been accepted among the people of God (10.1–11.18; 13.1–14.28); now the church addresses the question of whether these believers should observe practices that the Torah commands for Israel. Luke presents this divisive issue as being easily and amicably resolved (cf. 6.1–6). Paul's letters offer a different picture (Gal 2.1–14). **1–5:** Gentile believers need to observe the law. **1:** *Circumcised,* Jews trace the practice to Abraham (Gen 17.9–14; see also Lev 12.3). Although circumcision was practiced by other peoples, it became a marker of Jewish identity (1 Macc 1.15; *Ant.* 1.192; Tacitus, *Hist.* 5.5.2). *Saved,* see 2.40n.

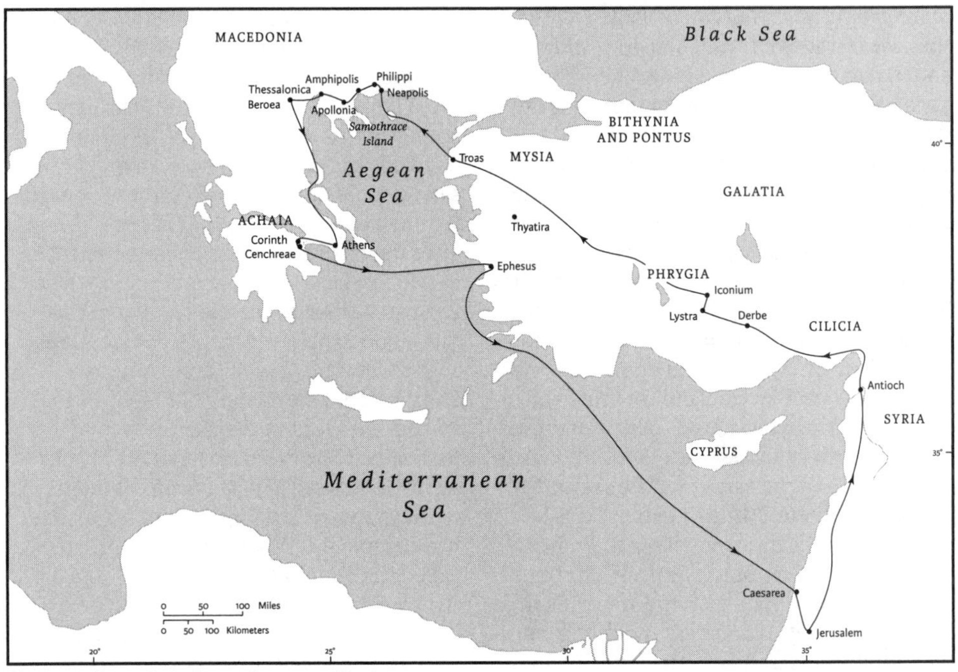

Chs 15–18: Second missionary journey of Paul.

the custom of Moses, you cannot be saved." [2] And after Paul and Barnabas had no small dissension and debate with them, Paul and Barnabas and some of the others were appointed to go up to Jerusalem to discuss this question with the apostles and the elders. [3] So they were sent on their way by the church, and as they passed through both Phoenicia and Samaria, they reported the conversion of the Gentiles, and brought great joy to all the believers.[a] [4] When they came to Jerusalem, they were welcomed by the church and the apostles and the elders, and they reported all that God had done with them. [5] But some believers who belonged to the sect of the Pharisees stood up and said, "It is necessary for them to be circumcised and ordered to keep the law of Moses."

[6] The apostles and the elders met together to consider this matter. [7] After there had been much debate, Peter stood up and said to them, "My brothers,[b] you know that in the early days God made a choice among you, that I should be the one through whom the Gentiles would hear the message of the good news and become believers. [8] And God, who knows the human heart, testified to them by giving them the Holy Spirit, just as he did to us; [9] and in cleansing their hearts by faith he has made no distinction between them and us. [10] Now therefore why are you putting God to the test by placing on the neck of the dis-

[a] Gk *brothers*
[b] Gk *Men, brothers*

An important objective in Acts (2.21; 4.12; 11.14; 16.30–31). **2:** *Appointed to go up,* Paul describes the decision as coming from a revelation (Gal 2.2), rather than a committee meeting. **4:** *Elders,* see 11.30. **5:** *Pharisees,* dedicated observers of Jewish law (Gal 1.14; Josephus, *J.W.* 1.110). *Keep the law of Moses,* clarifies what is implied by v. 1. Luke presents Pharisees as largely sympathetic with Christians. These Pharisees, however, understand believers in Jesus to be Jews, and therefore in need of circumcision. **6–11:** Peter, Paul, Barnabas, and James, also appear in Paul's account (Gal 2.1,9). In his previous appearance in Acts, Peter mentions Cornelius (10.1–11.18), argues that Gentiles received the Holy Spirit, insists God makes no distinction, and asserts both that the law presents an unreasonable burden and that salvation comes through grace, all arguments familiar from Paul. **7:** *Much debate,* the absence of defense by the Pharisees makes the proceedings seem harmonious. **8:** 10.1–11.18.

ciples a yoke that neither our ancestors nor we have been able to bear? [11] On the contrary, we believe that we will be saved through the grace of the Lord Jesus, just as they will."

[12] The whole assembly kept silence, and listened to Barnabas and Paul as they told of all the signs and wonders that God had done through them among the Gentiles. [13] After they finished speaking, James replied, "My brothers,[a] listen to me. [14] Simeon has related how God first looked favorably on the Gentiles, to take from among them a people for his name. [15] This agrees with the words of the prophets, as it is written,

[16] 'After this I will return,
and I will rebuild the dwelling of David,
which has fallen;
from its ruins I will rebuild it,
and I will set it up,
[17] so that all other peoples may seek the Lord—
even all the Gentiles over whom my name has been called.
Thus says the Lord, who has been making these things [18] known from long ago.'[b]

[19] Therefore I have reached the decision that we should not trouble those Gentiles who are turning to God, [20] but we should write to them to abstain only from things polluted by idols and from fornication and from whatever has been strangled[c] and from blood. [21] For in every city, for generations past, Moses has had those who proclaim him, for he has been read aloud every sabbath in the synagogues."

[22] Then the apostles and the elders, with the consent of the whole church, decided to choose men from among their members[d] and to send them to Antioch with Paul and Barnabas. They sent Judas called Barsabbas, and Silas, leaders among the brothers, [23] with the following letter: "The brothers, both the apostles and the elders, to the believers[e] of Gentile origin in Antioch and Syria and

a Gk *Men, brothers*
b Other ancient authorities read *things.* [18] *Known to God from of old are all his works.'*
c Other ancient authorities lack *and from whatever has been strangled*
d Gk *from among them*
e Gk *brothers*

9: *Cleansing their hearts,* see Ps 51.10 (Heb v. 12). *No distinction,* 10.34. **10:** *Putting God to the test,* 5.9; Ex 17.2; Ps 78.41. *Yoke,* Gk "zygos" in LXX often for Heb "'ol," lit., "yoke" as neckpiece on a draft animal; metaphorically, many texts in the Tanakh use the image of a yoke to express hardship, especially foreign oppression (Deut 28.48; Isa 14.25; Jer 27.12; Sir 40.1; 1 Macc 13.41). In rabbinic writings it represents proper acceptance of God's sovereignty (*m. Ber.* 2.2; *b. Seb.* 13a; *b. Ker.* 7a; *Ex. Rab.* 30.5), which extends blessings to those who wear it (*m. Avot* 3.5). **11:** *Saved through the grace,* another instance of similar phrasing in Paul's letters (e.g., Rom 3.21–26). The contrast between the faith that Jews possess and that of Jesus' followers, expressed here as "yoke/law" and "grace," is not borne out in Tanakh, e.g., Ex 34.6; Hos 11.3–4,8–9; Ps 51.1 (Heb v. 3). **12:** *Signs and wonders,* see 13.11; 14.8–10. **13–21:** James adds scriptural support for the inclusion of Gentiles. **13:** *James,* brother of Jesus; see 12.17; *Ant.* 20.200. **14:** *Simeon,* Semitic form of Simon, Peter's given name. *People for his name,* a term normally used to describe Israel (3.12; 4.10; 5.34; Lk 7.16; 19.47; 21.23). **16–18:** Am 9.11–12. The Hebrew version speaks of Israel's possessing other nations. The Septuagint, which in Luke's version here is what James quotes, refers to God's act of restoration of all peoples, Jews and Gentiles. **20:** James proposes a set of requirements for Gentiles: although not certain, it is likely the four elements relate to participation in pagan worship. *Things polluted by idols,* presumably foods sacrificed to idols; see v. 29; Ex 34.15; Dan 1.8; 1 Cor 8; 10.18–22. *Fornication,* improper sexual activity (Lev 18.6–30; 1 Cor 5.1; 6.18). *Strangled,* possibly a requirement that meat come only from animals slaughtered in the ritually correct manner (Lev 7.24; 17.15; Deut 14.21), so that the blood is drained from them. *Blood,* Lev 7.26–27; 17.10–16; Deut 12.23–25, possibly a reference to murder (i.e., bloodshed). Jewish texts set forth similar requirements for righteous Gentiles (*Jub.* 7.20); the Noachide Laws (an expansion of the covenant with Noah in Gen 9.1–17, which according to Jewish understanding is thereby incumbent on all human beings) require Gentiles to refrain from idolatry, blasphemy, murder, incest, stealing, and consuming flesh from a living creature, and to establish justice in an orderly legal system (*t. Avodah Zara* 8.4; *b. Sanh.* 52b; *Gen. Rab.* 16.6). See "The Law," p. 515. Leviticus makes similar declarations regarding strangers dwelling in the land (Lev 17–18). **21:** James suggests both that the Torah justifies his decision and that Gentile converts, having heard the Torah, would agree with it. **22:** *Barsabbas,* see 1.23. Nothing else is reported of him. *Silas,* Paul's frequent traveling

Cilicia, greetings. [24] Since we have heard that certain persons who have gone out from us, though with no instructions from us, have said things to disturb you and have unsettled your minds,[a] [25] we have decided unanimously to choose representatives[b] and send them to you, along with our beloved Barnabas and Paul, [26] who have risked their lives for the sake of our Lord Jesus Christ. [27] We have therefore sent Judas and Silas, who themselves will tell you the same things by word of mouth. [28] For it has seemed good to the Holy Spirit and to us to impose on you no further burden than these essentials: [29] that you abstain from what has been sacrificed to idols and from blood and from what is strangled[c] and from fornication. If you keep yourselves from these, you will do well. Farewell."

[30] So they were sent off and went down to Antioch. When they gathered the congregation together, they delivered the letter. [31] When its members[d] read it, they rejoiced at the exhortation. [32] Judas and Silas, who were themselves prophets, said much to encourage and strengthen the believers.[e] [33] After they had been there for some time, they were sent off in peace by the believers[e] to those who had sent them.[f] [35] But Paul and Barnabas remained in Antioch, and there, with many others, they taught and proclaimed the word of the Lord.

[36] After some days Paul said to Barnabas, "Come, let us return and visit the believers[e] in every city where we proclaimed the word of the Lord and see how they are doing." [37] Barnabas wanted to take with them John called Mark. [38] But Paul decided not to take with them one who had deserted them in Pamphylia and had not accompanied them in the work. [39] The disagreement became so sharp that they parted company; Barnabas took Mark with him and sailed away to Cyprus. [40] But Paul chose Silas and set out, the believers[e] commending him to the grace of the Lord. [41] He went through Syria and Cilicia, strengthening the churches.

16 Paul[g] went on also to Derbe and to Lystra, where there was a disciple named Timothy, the son of a Jewish woman who was a believer; but his father was a Greek. [2] He was well spoken of by the believers[e] in Lystra and Iconium. [3] Paul wanted Timothy to accompany him; and he took him and had him circumcised because of the Jews who were in those places, for they all knew that his father was a Greek. [4] As they went from town to town, they delivered to them for observance the decisions that had been reached by the apostles and elders who were in Jerusalem. [5] So the churches were strengthened in the faith and increased in numbers daily.

[a] Other ancient authorities add *saying, 'You must be circumcised and keep the law,'*
[b] Gk *men*
[c] Other ancient authorities lack *and from what is strangled*
[d] Gk *When they*
[e] Gk *brothers*
[f] Other ancient authorities add verse 34, *But it seemed good to Silas to remain there*
[g] Gk *He*

companion (16.16–18.17). **23–29: Letter to the church. 24:** The Jerusalem leaders repudiate any association with those requiring Gentiles to observe the law. **29:** See v. 20. **30–35: Paul and Barnabas return to Antioch.** The story ends where it began with Paul and Barnabas preaching in Antioch. **32:** *Prophets*, see 11.27.

15.36–18.23: Paul's journey to and in Greece.

15.36–16.10: Paul travels to Greece. 15.37–39: Paul and Barnabas disagreed over Jews and Gentiles sharing table fellowship (Gal 2.11–14). **37:** *John . . . Mark*, 12.12,25; 13.5,13,24,25. **38:** See 13.13. **39:** Barnabas is from Cyprus (4.36). **41:** *Strengthening the churches*, see 14.22. **16.1:** Paul returns to Derbe and Lystra. **1–3:** *Son of a Jewish woman . . . father was a Greek*, matrilineal descent may not have been established at this time; Timothy was not circumcised eight days after his birth, so because of his mixed parentage he was not raised as a Jew. He was Paul's valued companion (Rom 16.21; 1 Cor 4.17; 16.10; 2 Cor 1.1,19; Phil 1.1; 2.19,22; 1 Thess 1.1; 3.2,6). His family is mentioned in 2 Tim 1.5. Timothy's circumcision seems contrary to the conclusion of the Jerusalem council (15.19) and Paul's teaching (e.g., Gal 2.3–4; 5.2–11), but the actions fit Luke's larger portrayal of Paul as someone against whom Jews have no legitimate reason to object (cf. 21.21). **5:** *Churches were strengthened*, see 14.22. A summary depicting the expansion of believers (2.42–47; 4.32–35; 5.12–16; 6.7; 9.31; 16.5; 19.20). **6–7:** The Spirit directs Paul's movements to Greece (cf.

[6] They went through the region of Phrygia and Galatia, having been forbidden by the Holy Spirit to speak the word in Asia. [7] When they had come opposite Mysia, they attempted to go into Bithynia, but the Spirit of Jesus did not allow them; [8] so, passing by Mysia, they went down to Troas. [9] During the night Paul had a vision: there stood a man of Macedonia pleading with him and saying, "Come over to Macedonia and help us." [10] When he had seen the vision, we immediately tried to cross over to Macedonia, being convinced that God had called us to proclaim the good news to them.

[11] We set sail from Troas and took a straight course to Samothrace, the following day to Neapolis, [12] and from there to Philippi, which is a leading city of the district[a] of Macedonia and a Roman colony. We remained in this city for some days. [13] On the sabbath day we went outside the gate by the river, where we supposed there was a place of prayer; and we sat down and spoke to the women who had gathered there. [14] A certain woman named Lydia, a worshiper of God, was listening to us; she was from the city of Thyatira and a dealer in purple cloth. The Lord opened her heart to listen eagerly to what was said by Paul. [15] When she and her household were baptized, she urged us, saying, "If you have judged me to be faithful to the Lord, come and stay at my home." And she prevailed upon us.

[16] One day, as we were going to the place of prayer, we met a slave-girl who had a spirit of divination and brought her owners a great deal of money by fortune-telling. [17] While she followed Paul and us, she would cry out, "These men are slaves of the Most High God, who proclaim to you[b] a way of salvation." [18] She kept doing this for many days. But Paul, very much annoyed, turned and said to the spirit, "I order you in the name of Jesus Christ to come out of her." And it came out that very hour.

[19] But when her owners saw that their hope of making money was gone, they seized Paul and Silas and dragged them into the marketplace before the authorities. [20] When they had brought them before the magistrates, they said, "These men are disturbing our city; they are Jews [21] and are advocating customs that are not lawful for us as Romans to adopt or observe." [22] The crowd joined in attacking them, and the magistrates had them stripped of their clothing and ordered them to be beaten with rods. [23] After they had given them a severe flogging, they threw them into prison and ordered the jailer to keep them securely. [24] Following these instructions, he put them in the innermost cell and fastened their feet in the stocks.

[25] About midnight Paul and Silas were praying and singing hymns to God, and the prisoners were listening to them. [26] Suddenly there was an earthquake, so violent that

[a] Other authorities read *a city of the first district*
[b] Other ancient authorities read *to us*

8.26; 10.19–20; 13.4). **8.** *Troas,* Alexandria Troas in northwest Asia Minor (present-day Turkey). **9–10:** *Vision,* divine guidance often comes through visions; see 9.10. **10:** *Macedonia,* Roman province in northern Greece. *We,* the use of the first-person plural continues intermittently until the end of the book (vv. 10–17; 20.5–15; 21.1–18; 27.1–28.16), and may reflect either Luke's use of an eyewitness source or his desire to create that impression.

16.11–40: Events in Philippi. Paul was instrumental in establishing a Christian community in Philippi and wrote at least one letter to the church there. *Samothrace . . . Neapolis,* Paul travels westward along the coast of Thrace and Macedonia. **12:** *Philippi,* Greek city and later Roman colony in Macedonia. **13:** Paul seeks out the local Jewish community (13.5,14; 14.1; 17.1,10,17; 18.4,19; 19.8) gathered on the Sabbath (13.14; 17.2; 18.4). *Place of prayer,* Gk "proseuchē," can designate a synagogue building. **14:** *Lydia, a worshiper of God,* the phrase indicates that she is a Gentile involved in a Jewish community or expressing an interest in Judaism (10.2; 13.16,26; 18.7). *Thyatira,* city in the region of Lydia in western Asia Minor, known for its production of and trade in dyed cloth. **15:** See 11.14. *My home,* an indication that she is established and prosperous. **17:** *Most High God,* see Ps 57.2; 78.56; Dan 3.26; Jdt 13.18; Sir 7.9; 24.23; 3 Macc 7.9; also applied to pagan deities, thus recognizable by non-Jews. *Way of salvation,* see 2.40n.; 2.47; 4.12; 11.14; 13.26; 15.11; 16.30,31; 28.28. **18:** *In the name of Jesus Christ,* healings are performed using this language (3.6; 4.10). **19:** Acts disparages religious activities that yield financial gain (8.18; 19.19,25; 20.33). **20–21:** While Roman magistrates might condemn anyone for offending public order or morality, there was no general policy against Jews teaching non-Roman customs. The charge implies that Jewish customs, and perhaps therefore Jews, are incompatible with Roman life. **26:** *Earthquake,* understood as a divine

the foundations of the prison were shaken; and immediately all the doors were opened and everyone's chains were unfastened. [27] When the jailer woke up and saw the prison doors wide open, he drew his sword and was about to kill himself, since he supposed that the prisoners had escaped. [28] But Paul shouted in a loud voice, "Do not harm yourself, for we are all here." [29] The jailer[a] called for lights, and rushing in, he fell down trembling before Paul and Silas. [30] Then he brought them outside and said, "Sirs, what must I do to be saved?" [31] They answered, "Believe on the Lord Jesus, and you will be saved, you and your household." [32] They spoke the word of the Lord[b] to him and to all who were in his house. [33] At the same hour of the night he took them and washed their wounds; then he and his entire family were baptized without delay. [34] He brought them up into the house and set food before them; and he and his entire household rejoiced that he had become a believer in God.

[35] When morning came, the magistrates sent the police, saying, "Let those men go." [36] And the jailer reported the message to Paul, saying, "The magistrates sent word to let you go; therefore come out now and go in peace." [37] But Paul replied, "They have beaten us in public, uncondemned, men who are Roman citizens, and have thrown us into prison; and now are they going to discharge us in secret? Certainly not! Let them come and take us out themselves." [38] The police reported these words to the magistrates, and they were afraid when they heard that they were Roman citizens; [39] so they came and apologized to them. And they took them out and asked them to leave the city. [40] After leaving the prison they went to Lydia's home; and when they had seen and encouraged the brothers and sisters[c] there, they departed.

17 After Paul and Silas[d] had passed through Amphipolis and Apollonia, they came to Thessalonica, where there was a synagogue of the Jews. [2] And Paul went in, as was his custom, and on three sabbath days argued with them from the scriptures, [3] explaining and proving that it was necessary for the Messiah[e] to suffer and to rise from the dead, and saying, "This is the Messiah,[e] Jesus whom I am proclaiming to you." [4] Some of them were persuaded and joined Paul and Silas, as did a great many of the devout Greeks and not a few of the leading women. [5] But the Jews became jealous, and with the help of some ruffians in the marketplaces they formed a mob and set the city in an uproar. While they were searching for Paul and Silas to bring them out to the assembly, they attacked Jason's house. [6] When they could not find them, they dragged Jason and some believers[c] before the city authorities,[f] shouting, "These people who have been turning the world upside down have come here also, [7] and Jason has entertained them as guests.

[a] Gk *He*
[b] Other ancient authorities read *word of God*
[c] Gk *brothers*
[d] Gk *they*
[e] Or *the Christ*
[f] Gk *politarchs*

act; on miraculous escapes from prison, see 5.17–21; 12.6–11. **27:** Following Peter's escape, Herod executed the guards (12.19). **30–31:** *What must I do to be saved,* salvation requires acknowledging Jesus as Lord (2.21,38; 4.12). See 2.40n. **33:** See v. 15. **37:** *Roman citizens,* the first mention of Paul's citizenship, not confirmed in Paul's letters. **38–39:** Cities could be punished for mistreating Roman citizens (Tacitus, *Ann.* 12.58; Suetonius, *Aug.* 47; Cassius Dio 54.7.6). **40:** The episode ends as it began with Paul in the company of Lydia.

17.1–9: Events in Thessalonica. Paul was instrumental is establishing the Christian community in Thessalonica and wrote at least one letter to the church there. **1:** *Amphipolis and Apollonia* lie along the Via Egnatia, the main east–west road across Macedonia. *Thessalonica,* major city in Macedonia. *Synagogue,* see 13.5,14; 14.1; 16.13; 17.1,10,17; 18.4,19; 19.8. **2:** *Sabbath,* see 13.14; 18.4. **3:** *Necessary for the Messiah to suffer,* unclear what passages Luke had in mind. The suffering and resurrection of the Messiah are common themes in Luke-Acts (1.16; 3.18; 9.16; Lk 2.49; 24.7,26,46), but absent in the Tanakh and contemporary Jewish tradition. **4:** Both Jews and Gentiles become believers (13.43,50; 14.1–2). *Devout Greeks,* Gentiles who demonstrate interest in Judaism and involvement in the Jewish community (10.2; 13.16,26; 16.14; 17.12; 18.7; Lk 7.1–10). **5:** *Jealous,* 5.17; 13.45; 17.5; on negative responses to Christian preaching, see 9.22; 18.5–6,28. Although Paul was charged with disturbing the

They are all acting contrary to the decrees of the emperor, saying that there is another king named Jesus." [8] The people and the city officials were disturbed when they heard this, [9] and after they had taken bail from Jason and the others, they let them go.

[10] That very night the believers[a] sent Paul and Silas off to Beroea; and when they arrived, they went to the Jewish synagogue. [11] These Jews were more receptive than those in Thessalonica, for they welcomed the message very eagerly and examined the scriptures every day to see whether these things were so. [12] Many of them therefore believed, including not a few Greek women and men of high standing. [13] But when the Jews of Thessalonica learned that the word of God had been proclaimed by Paul in Beroea as well, they came there too, to stir up and incite the crowds. [14] Then the believers[a] immediately sent Paul away to the coast, but Silas and Timothy remained behind. [15] Those who conducted Paul brought him as far as Athens; and after receiving instructions to have Silas and Timothy join him as soon as possible, they left him.

[16] While Paul was waiting for them in Athens, he was deeply distressed to see that the city was full of idols. [17] So he argued in the synagogue with the Jews and the devout persons, and also in the marketplace[b] every day with those who happened to be there. [18] Also some Epicurean and Stoic philosophers debated with him. Some said, "What does this babbler want to say?" Others said, "He seems to be a proclaimer of foreign divinities." (This was because he was telling the good news about Jesus and the resurrection.) [19] So they took him and brought him to the Areopagus and asked him, "May we know what this new teaching is that you are presenting? [20] It sounds rather strange to us, so we would like to know what it means." [21] Now all the Athenians and the foreigners living there would spend their time in nothing but telling or hearing something new.

[22] Then Paul stood in front of the Areopagus and said, "Athenians, I see how extremely religious you are in every way. [23] For as I went through the city and looked carefully at the objects of your worship, I found among them an altar with the inscription, 'To an unknown god.' What therefore you worship as unknown, this I proclaim to you. [24] The God who made the world and everything in it, he who is Lord of heaven and earth, does not live in shrines made by human hands, [25] nor is he served by human hands, as though he needed anything, since he himself gives to all mortals life and breath and all things. [26] From one ancestor[c] he made all nations to inhabit the whole earth, and he allotted the times of their existence and the boundaries of the places where they would live, [27] so that they would search for God[d] and perhaps grope for him and find him—though

[a] Gk *brothers*
[b] Or *civic center*; Gk *agora*
[c] Gk *From one*; other ancient authorities read *From one blood*
[d] Other ancient authorities read *the Lord*

city (16.20; cf. 19.26–39; 24.5), Acts represents Jews as the disturbers. **7:** *Contrary to the decrees of the emperor,* 16.21; cf. 24.5. *Another king,* in the Gospel of Luke, Jews lodge a similar accusation against Jesus (23.2).

17.10–15: Events in Beroea. Paul and Silas turn off the Via Egnatia. **10:** *Synagogue,* see v. 1. **11:** *Examined the scriptures,* see v. 2. **12:** *Greek women and men of high standing,* Gentiles, including women, who participate in the life of the Jewish community; see v. 4. **13:** Only Jews are identified as opposing Paul.

17.16–34: Events in Athens. While Paul initially follows his pattern of preaching in a synagogue (see v. 1) to Jews and devout Greeks (see v. 4), the episode focuses on his engagement with Gentiles, particularly representatives of major philosophical schools. **17:** *Market place,* Gk "agora," the main social area in a city. **18:** *Epicurean,* a philosophical school that maintained that deities played no role in human affairs. *Stoic,* maintained that humans should use reason to live a life of virtue and to develop a will in accordance with nature. *Babbler,* a derogatory term representing Paul as one who has picked up scraps of new ideas. *Foreign divinities,* similar to the charge against Socrates (Plato, *Apol.* 24b–c). *Resurrection,* Gk "anastasis," which the bystanders take to be the name of a deity. **19:** *Areopagus,* Mars Hill, near the Acropolis and the city's chief administrative council. **21:** Athenians were known for being intellectually curious (Strabo, *Geogr.* 9.1.16; Livy, 45.27.11; Josephus, *Ag. Ap.* 2.130; Pausanias, *Descr.* 1.17.1). **22:** *Extremely religious,* ancient speeches often began by praising the audience, although the Greek phrase can connote superstitious belief, making Paul's words perhaps sarcastic. **24–25:** Paul's description of God as sole, self-sufficient creator not confined

indeed he is not far from each one of us. [28] For 'In him we live and move and have our being'; as even some of your own poets have said,

'For we too are his offspring.'

[29] Since we are God's offspring, we ought not to think that the deity is like gold, or silver, or stone, an image formed by the art and imagination of mortals. [30] While God has overlooked the times of human ignorance, now he commands all people everywhere to repent, [31] because he has fixed a day on which he will have the world judged in righteousness by a man whom he has appointed, and of this he has given assurance to all by raising him from the dead."

[32] When they heard of the resurrection of the dead, some scoffed; but others said, "We will hear you again about this." [33] At that point Paul left them. [34] But some of them joined him and became believers, including Dionysius the Areopagite and a woman named Damaris, and others with them.

18 After this Paul[a] left Athens and went to Corinth. [2] There he found a Jew named Aquila, a native of Pontus, who had recently come from Italy with his wife Priscilla, because Claudius had ordered all Jews to leave Rome. Paul[b] went to see them, [3] and, because he was of the same trade, he stayed with them, and they worked together—by trade they were tentmakers. [4] Every sabbath he would argue in the synagogue and would try to convince Jews and Greeks.

[5] When Silas and Timothy arrived from Macedonia, Paul was occupied with proclaiming the word,[c] testifying to the Jews that the Messiah[d] was Jesus. [6] When they opposed and reviled him, in protest he shook the dust from his clothes[e] and said to them, "Your blood be on your own heads! I am innocent. From now on I will go to the Gentiles." [7] Then he left the synagogue[f] and went to the house

[a] Gk *he*
[b] Gk *He*
[c] Gk *with the word*
[d] Or *the Christ*
[e] Gk *reviled him, he shook out his clothes*
[f] Gk *left there*

to any sanctuary was shared by Jews and others philosophically informed. **28:** *In him . . . being,* there is no known text with this quotation; it resembles the writing of Posidonius, a Platonist. *We too are his offspring,* Aratus, third century BCE poet (*Phaen.* 5). **29:** Jews (Isa 44.9–20; Wis 13.10; Philo, *Decalogue* 66; *Spec. Laws* 1.21) and philosophers (Seneca, *Ep.* 31.11; Plutarch, *Superst.* 6) commonly condemned idolatry. **30–31:** Paul moves to distinctly Christian arguments (although he does not name Jesus explicitly), some based on concepts from the Tanakh. Just as God is creator of all (v. 24) and humans are descended from a single ancestor (v. 26), so God's judgment applies to all persons (v. 30) and everywhere (v. 31), and proof comes from the resurrection. **32–34:** The response to Paul is divided, but with less intensity than previous occasions (13.43,45; 14.4,11; 17.4–5). **32:** *Scoffed,* the idea of bodily resurrection was contrary to most Greek notions of life after death that spoke of spiritual immortality. **34:** *Dionysius . . . Damaris,* both unknown. The pairing of male and female characters follows a pattern in the Gospel and Acts (Lk 2.25–38; 6.6–11; 13.10–17; 15.3–10; Acts 5.1–11). *Areopagite,* a member of the court that met at the Areopagus.

18.1–17: Events in Corinth. Paul was instrumental in establishing a Christian community in Corinth, and wrote at least two letters to the church there. **1:** *Corinth,* Roman administrative center in the province of Achaia (present-day Greece). A sizeable Jewish community existed in the city (Philo, *Leg. Gai.* 281). **2:** *Aquila . . . Priscilla,* 18.18. Paul mentions both as known to the Corinthian Christians (1 Cor 16.19) and at certain times present in Rome (Rom 16.3–4). *Pontus,* a province in northern Asia Minor (present-day Turkey). *Claudius had ordered all Jews to leave Rome,* the Roman historian Suetonius confirms this information, and adds that Jews were causing disturbances at the instigation of Chrestus (*Claud.* 25), which may be a corruption of "Christ"; the account may reflect tensions created by the proclamations of Jesus' followers. **3:** *Tentmakers,* Paul engaged in manual labor; see 1 Cor 4.12. **4:** Paul follows the typical pattern of teaching on Sabbath (see 17.2) in a synagogue (see 17.1) to Jews and Gentiles (see 17.4). **5:** *Silas and Timothy,* see 17.10–15. *The Messiah was Jesus,* the claim provokes a harsh response from Jews (9.22; 17.3–5; 18.28). **6:** *Shook the dust,* symbolizing separation; see 13.51. *Your blood,* 2 Sam 1.16; Mt 27.25. Acts emphasizes that Jews bear the responsibility for failing to acknowledge Jesus as the Messiah. *Innocent,* not responsible for their failure to enter the messianic kingdom. *Go to the Gentiles,* see 13.46; 28.28. **7:** *Titius Justus,* Acts highlights Gentile adherents to Judaism, e.g., the Ethiopian official (8.26–28), Cornelius (10.1), Lydia (16.14); see also the unnamed Roman centurion in the Gospel (Lk 7.1–5). **8:** *Crispus,* 1 Cor 1.14. *Official of the synagogue,* see 13.15. *Household,* see 11.14. **9:** *Vision,* see 9.10.

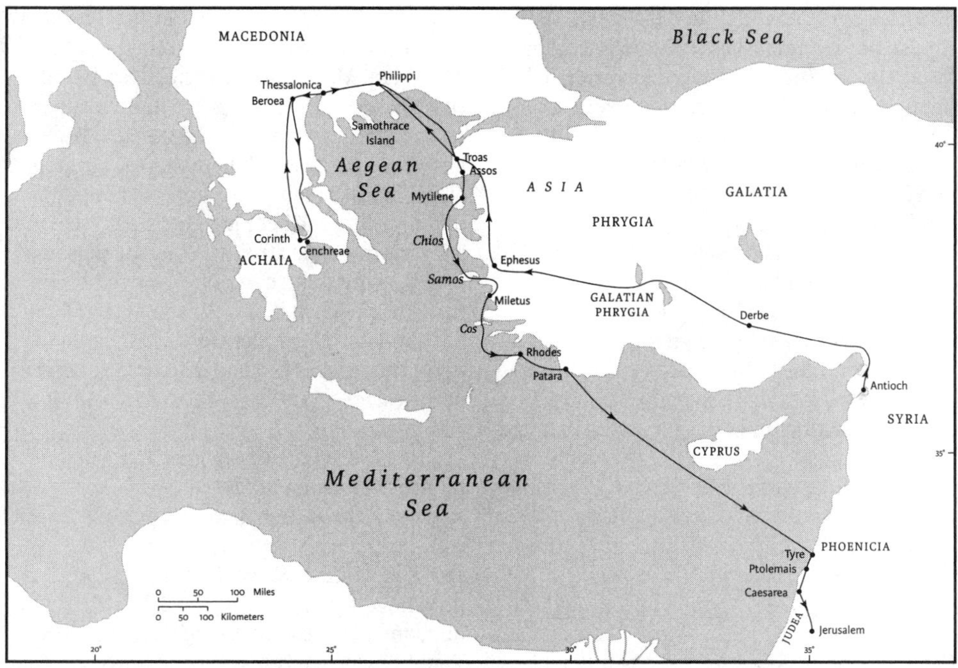

Chs 18–21: Third missionary journey of Paul.

of a man named Titius[a] Justus, a worshiper of God; his house was next door to the synagogue. [8] Crispus, the official of the synagogue, became a believer in the Lord, together with all his household; and many of the Corinthians who heard Paul became believers and were baptized. [9] One night the Lord said to Paul in a vision, "Do not be afraid, but speak and do not be silent; [10] for I am with you, and no one will lay a hand on you to harm you, for there are many in this city who are my people." [11] He stayed there a year and six months, teaching the word of God among them.

[12] But when Gallio was proconsul of Achaia, the Jews made a united attack on Paul and brought him before the tribunal. [13] They said, "This man is persuading people to worship God in ways that are contrary to the law." [14] Just as Paul was about to speak, Gallio said to the Jews, "If it were a matter of crime or serious villainy, I would be justified in accepting the complaint of you Jews; [15] but since it is a matter of questions about words and names and your own law, see to it yourselves; I do not wish to be a judge of these matters." [16] And he dismissed them from the tribunal. [17] Then all of them[b] seized Sosthenes, the official of the synagogue, and beat him in front of the tribunal. But Gallio paid no attention to any of these things.

[18] After staying there for a considerable time, Paul said farewell to the believers[c] and

[a] Other ancient authorities read *Titus*
[b] Other ancient authorities read *all the Greeks*
[c] Gk *brothers*

10: *I am with you,* Ex 3.12; Isa 43.5. *My people,* including Jews and Gentiles. **12:** *Gallio,* L. Junius Gallio Annaeanus was proconsul (chief Roman magistrate) in Achaia ca. 51–52. See 13.7n. *Jews,* Jews are singled out as Paul's opponents (13.45; 17.5,13; 20.3,19). **13:** *The law,* either Jewish law (as Gallio understands the accusation, v. 15; cf. 21.21) or Roman law (16.21; 17.7). **15:** *See to it yourselves,* Roman government granted Jewish communities permission to practice their own law (*Ant.* 16.163; 19.290) and to decide matters concerning their own customs (*Ant.* 14.195; 235, 260). **17:** *Sosthenes,* a Christian by this name was known to the Corinthian church (1 Cor 1.1). *Official of the synagogue,* see 13.15.

18.18–23: Paul concludes the journey. 18: *Priscilla and Aquila,* v. 2. *Cenchreae,* eastern port of Corinth. *Hair cut,* the act that completes the Nazirite vow (Num 6.1–21). Acts portrays Paul as observant of Jewish law.

sailed for Syria, accompanied by Priscilla and Aquila. At Cenchreae he had his hair cut, for he was under a vow. [19] When they reached Ephesus, he left them there, but first he himself went into the synagogue and had a discussion with the Jews. [20] When they asked him to stay longer, he declined; [21] but on taking leave of them, he said, "I[a] will return to you, if God wills." Then he set sail from Ephesus.

[22] When he had landed at Caesarea, he went up to Jerusalem[b] and greeted the church, and then went down to Antioch. [23] After spending some time there he departed and went from place to place through the region of Galatia[c] and Phrygia, strengthening all the disciples.

[24] Now there came to Ephesus a Jew named Apollos, a native of Alexandria. He was an eloquent man, well-versed in the scriptures. [25] He had been instructed in the Way of the Lord; and he spoke with burning enthusiasm and taught accurately the things concerning Jesus, though he knew only the baptism of John. [26] He began to speak boldly in the synagogue; but when Priscilla and Aquila heard him, they took him aside and explained the Way of God to him more accurately. [27] And when he wished to cross over to Achaia, the believers[d] encouraged him and wrote to the disciples to welcome him. On his arrival he greatly helped those who through grace had become believers, [28] for he powerfully refuted the Jews in public, showing by the scriptures that the Messiah[e] is Jesus.

19 While Apollos was in Corinth, Paul passed through the interior regions and came to Ephesus, where he found some disciples. [2] He said to them, "Did you receive the Holy Spirit when you became believers?" They replied, "No, we have not even heard that there is a Holy Spirit." [3] Then he said, "Into what then were you baptized?" They answered, "Into John's baptism." [4] Paul said, "John baptized with the baptism of repentance, telling the people to believe in the one who was to come after him, that is, in Jesus." [5] On hearing this, they were baptized in the name of the Lord Jesus. [6] When Paul had laid his hands on them, the Holy Spirit came upon them, and they spoke in tongues and prophesied— [7] altogether there were about twelve of them.

[8] He entered the synagogue and for three months spoke out boldly, and argued persuasively about the kingdom of God. [9] When some stubbornly refused to believe and spoke evil of the Way before the congregation, he left them, taking the disciples with him, and argued daily in the lecture hall of Tyrannus.[f] [10] This continued for two years, so that all the residents of Asia, both Jews and Greeks, heard the word of the Lord.

[11] God did extraordinary miracles through Paul, [12] so that when the handkerchiefs

[a] Other ancient authorities read *I must at all costs keep the approaching festival in Jerusalem, but I*
[b] Gk *went up*
[c] Gk *the Galatian region*
[d] Gk *brothers*
[e] Or *the Christ*
[f] Other ancient authorities read *of a certain Tyrannus, from eleven o'clock in the morning to four in the afternoon*

19: *Ephesus,* administrative seat of the province of Asia. *Synagogue,* see 13.5. **21:** *I will return,* Paul does so on his next journey (19.1–41). **22:** *Caesarea,* see 8.40. **23:** *Galatia and Phrygia,* see 16.6. *Strengthening all the disciples,* see 14.22.

18.24–20.38: Paul's return journey to Asia Minor and Greece. Paul embarks on a third journey, beginning in Asia Minor.

18.24–28: Apollos. 24: *Apollos,* an important figure in the Corinthian church (19.1; 1 Cor 1.12; 3.4–6,22; 4.6; 16.12). *Alexandria* was a noted center of learning with a large Jewish community. **25:** *Way,* see 9.2. *Baptism of John,* see 13.24. Possibly a ritual performed by a follower of John the Baptist, here presented as a rival messianic sect. **26:** *Speak boldly,* see 4.13n. *Priscilla and Aquila,* see v. 2n. **28:** *The Messiah is Jesus,* see 9.22.

19.1–41: Paul's return to Ephesus. Paul's return shows God's continuing involvement in his work (18.21). **3:** *John's baptism,* see 18.25. **4:** Paul summarizes John's preaching, Lk 3.16–17. **5:** *Baptized in the name,* see 2.38; 8.16; 10.48. **6:** *Laid . . . hands,* see 8.17; 9.12. *Spoke in tongues,* see 2.4,11; 10.46. **8:** *Synagogue,* see 13.5. *Spoke out boldly,* 4.13n. *Kingdom of God,* see 8.12. **9:** The motif of Jewish disbelief continues. *Way,* see 9.2; 18.25. *Lecture hall of Tyrannus,* the exact nature or location of the hall is unknown. **11–20: Seven Sons of Sceva.** Paul's miraculous

or aprons that had touched his skin were brought to the sick, their diseases left them, and the evil spirits came out of them. [13] Then some itinerant Jewish exorcists tried to use the name of the Lord Jesus over those who had evil spirits, saying, "I adjure you by the Jesus whom Paul proclaims." [14] Seven sons of a Jewish high priest named Sceva were doing this. [15] But the evil spirit said to them in reply, "Jesus I know, and Paul I know; but who are you?" [16] Then the man with the evil spirit leaped on them, mastered them all, and so overpowered them that they fled out of the house naked and wounded. [17] When this became known to all residents of Ephesus, both Jews and Greeks, everyone was awestruck; and the name of the Lord Jesus was praised. [18] Also many of those who became believers confessed and disclosed their practices. [19] A number of those who practiced magic collected their books and burned them publicly; when the value of these books[a] was calculated, it was found to come to fifty thousand silver coins. [20] So the word of the Lord grew mightily and prevailed.

[21] Now after these things had been accomplished, Paul resolved in the Spirit to go through Macedonia and Achaia, and then to go on to Jerusalem. He said, "After I have gone there, I must also see Rome." [22] So he sent two of his helpers, Timothy and Erastus, to Macedonia, while he himself stayed for some time longer in Asia.

[23] About that time no little disturbance broke out concerning the Way. [24] A man named Demetrius, a silversmith who made silver shrines of Artemis, brought no little business to the artisans. [25] These he gathered together, with the workers of the same trade, and said, "Men, you know that we get our wealth from this business. [26] You also see and hear that not only in Ephesus but in almost the whole of Asia this Paul has persuaded and drawn away a considerable number of people by saying that gods made with hands are not gods. [27] And there is danger not only that this trade of ours may come into disrepute but also that the temple of the great goddess Artemis will be scorned, and she will be deprived of her majesty that brought all Asia and the world to worship her."

[28] When they heard this, they were enraged and shouted, "Great is Artemis of the Ephesians!" [29] The city was filled with the confusion; and people[b] rushed together to the theater, dragging with them Gaius and Aristarchus, Macedonians who were Paul's travel companions. [30] Paul wished to go into

[a] Gk *them*
[b] Gk *they*

deeds stand in contrast to the ineptitude of the Jewish exorcists. **11:** On Paul's miracles, see 13.11; 14.10; 20.9–10; 28.3–6. **13:** *Jewish exorcists,* see *Ant.* 8.45–49. *I adjure you,* standard formula in magical texts, thus marking them as magicians. Non-Christians used Jesus' name for their purposes (e.g., *Greek Magical Papyri* 4.3019–20), but non-Christians cannot compel the power of Jesus' name by incantations. **14:** *Sceva,* no contemporary source attests a high priest by this Latin name. **15:** *Who are you,* only Christians have authority and ability to employ the power of Jesus' name (3.6; 4.10,30; 16.18). The demon humiliates and injures the Jewish would-be exorcists. **17:** The failure of the Jewish exorcists prompts belief in Jesus; see 13.6–12. **18:** *Confessed,* made verbal acknowledgment; used of sin, e.g., Mk 1.5. **19:** See 16.19n. (8.18; 20.33). **20:** *Word of the Lord grew mightily,* typical summary statement (2.41,47; 4.32–35; 5.12–16; 6.11; 9.31; 16.5). **21–41: Riot in Ephesus. 21:** First mention of Rome, the imperial capital and Acts' geographic goal (1.8). **22:** *Timothy,* see 16.1,3; 17.14–15; 18.5; 20.4. *Erastus,* see Rom 16.23; 2 Tim 4.20. **23:** *Way,* see 9.1–2. **24:** *Silver shrines,* used as votive offerings or souvenirs. *Artemis,* the city's principal deity, goddess of the hunt and wild animals, worshiped at a famous and opulent temple. *Brought no little business,* brought much business; "litotes," a figure of speech negating the opposite of what is meant, emphasizes by understatement. **26:** *Gods made with hands,* see 17.29. **27:** *Artemis will be scorned,* the temple of Artemis brought the city significant prestige and economic benefit. *Brought all Asia and the world to worship her,* Ephesus was responsible for the empire-wide dissemination of the worship of Artemis. **28:** *Great is Artemis of the Ephesians,* also v. 34. Well-known acclamation (Xenophon, *Ephesian Tale* 1.11.5). **29:** *Theater,* theaters were often used for large civic gatherings (Philo, *Flaccus* 41; Josephus, *J.W.* 7.107; Dio Chrys., *Or.* 7.24; Tacitus, *Hist.* 2.80). *Gaius* (20.4; Rom 16.23; 1 Cor 1.14) and *Aristarchus* (20.4; 27.2; Philem 24), close companions

the crowd, but the disciples would not let him; [31] even some officials of the province of Asia,[a] who were friendly to him, sent him a message urging him not to venture into the theater. [32] Meanwhile, some were shouting one thing, some another; for the assembly was in confusion, and most of them did not know why they had come together. [33] Some of the crowd gave instructions to Alexander, whom the Jews had pushed forward. And Alexander motioned for silence and tried to make a defense before the people. [34] But when they recognized that he was a Jew, for about two hours all of them shouted in unison, "Great is Artemis of the Ephesians!" [35] But when the town clerk had quieted the crowd, he said, "Citizens of Ephesus, who is there that does not know that the city of the Ephesians is the temple keeper of the great Artemis and of the statue that fell from heaven?[b] [36] Since these things cannot be denied, you ought to be quiet and do nothing rash. [37] You have brought these men here who are neither temple robbers nor blasphemers of our[c] goddess. [38] If therefore Demetrius and the artisans with him have a complaint against anyone, the courts are open, and there are proconsuls; let them bring charges there against one another. [39] If there is anything further[d] you want to know, it must be settled in the regular assembly. [40] For we are in danger of being charged with rioting today, since there is no cause that we can give to justify this commotion." [41] When he had said this, he dismissed the assembly.

20 After the uproar had ceased, Paul sent for the disciples; and after encouraging them and saying farewell, he left for Macedonia. [2] When he had gone through those regions and had given the believers[e] much encouragement, he came to Greece, [3] where he stayed for three months. He was about to set sail for Syria when a plot was made against him by the Jews, and so he decided to return through Macedonia. [4] He was accompanied by Sopater son of Pyrrhus from Beroea, by Aristarchus and Secundus from Thessalonica, by Gaius from Derbe, and by Timothy, as well as by Tychicus and Trophimus from Asia. [5] They went ahead and were waiting for us in Troas; [6] but we sailed from Philippi after the days of Unleavened Bread, and in five days we joined them in Troas, where we stayed for seven days.

[7] On the first day of the week, when we met to break bread, Paul was holding a discussion with them; since he intended to leave the next day, he continued speaking until midnight. [8] There were many lamps in the room upstairs where we were meeting. [9] A young man named Eutychus, who was sitting in the window, began to sink off into a deep sleep while Paul talked still longer. Overcome by sleep, he fell to the ground three floors

[a] Gk *some of the Asiarchs*
[b] Meaning of Gk uncertain
[c] Other ancient authorities read *your*
[d] Other ancient authorities read *about other matters*
[e] Gk *given them*

of Paul. **31:** *Officials of the province of Asia,* civic officials in Asia Minor, some of whom were connected with the worship of the emperor. Local officials and other elite persons often assist Paul or become believers (13.12,50; 16.35; 17.12,34; 18.15–16). **34:** *Great . . . Ephesians,* see v. 28n. **35:** *Town clerk,* a leading civic office. *Temple keeper,* title used by cities that built temples to the Roman emperor or patron deity. *Statue that fell from heaven,* refutes the claim that Ephesians worship a deity made with hands (v. 26). **37–38:** The accusation that Christians cause disturbance (16.20; 17.6; 24.5) is shown to be false. *Proconsuls,* see 13.7n.

20.1–38: Paul's return to Macedonia and Greece. 2: *Encouragement,* see 14.22. **3:** *Plot . . . by the Jews,* Acts often portrays Jews as Paul's leading opponents (see 18.12). **4:** *Sopater,* possibly Sosipater of Rom 16.21. *Beroea,* see 17.10–15. *Aristarchus,* see 19.29. *Secundus from Thessalonica,* otherwise unknown. On Thessalonica, see 17.1–9. *Gaius,* another companion by that name came from Macedonia (19.29). *Derbe,* see 14.6,20–21; 16.1. *Timothy,* see 16.1,3; 17.14–15; 18.5; 19.22. *Tychicus,* see Eph 6.21; Col. 4.7; 2 Tim 4.12; Titus 3.12. *Trophimus,* accompanies Paul to Jerusalem (21.29). **5:** *Us,* use of the first-person plural resumes (16.10–17). *Troas,* see 16.8–10. **6:** *Unleavened Bread,* in Luke's Gospel, Passover frames the time of Jesus' death (Lk 22.1); here the reference comes when the narrative turns to Paul's arrest. **7–12: Paul revives Eutychus.** On Paul's miraculous powers, see 13.11; 14.10; 19.11; 28.3–6. Luke attributes similar acts of resuscitation to Peter (9.36–43) and Jesus (Lk 7.11–17; 8.41–42,49–56). **7:** *First day of the week,* after the Sabbath; Sunday or possibly Saturday evening. **9:** *Eutychus,* the name means

below and was picked up dead. [10] But Paul went down, and bending over him took him in his arms, and said, "Do not be alarmed, for his life is in him." [11] Then Paul went upstairs, and after he had broken bread and eaten, he continued to converse with them until dawn; then he left. [12] Meanwhile they had taken the boy away alive and were not a little comforted.

[13] We went ahead to the ship and set sail for Assos, intending to take Paul on board there; for he had made this arrangement, intending to go by land himself. [14] When he met us in Assos, we took him on board and went to Mitylene. [15] We sailed from there, and on the following day we arrived opposite Chios. The next day we touched at Samos, and[a] the day after that we came to Miletus. [16] For Paul had decided to sail past Ephesus, so that he might not have to spend time in Asia; he was eager to be in Jerusalem, if possible, on the day of Pentecost.

[17] From Miletus he sent a message to Ephesus, asking the elders of the church to meet him. [18] When they came to him, he said to them:

"You yourselves know how I lived among you the entire time from the first day that I set foot in Asia, [19] serving the Lord with all humility and with tears, enduring the trials that came to me through the plots of the Jews. [20] I did not shrink from doing anything helpful, proclaiming the message to you and teaching you publicly and from house to house, [21] as I testified to both Jews and Greeks about repentance toward God and faith toward our Lord Jesus. [22] And now, as a captive to the Spirit,[b] I am on my way to Jerusalem, not knowing what will happen to me there, [23] except that the Holy Spirit testifies to me in every city that imprisonment and persecutions are waiting for me. [24] But I do not count my life of any value to myself, if only I may finish my course and the ministry that I received from the Lord Jesus, to testify to the good news of God's grace.

[25] "And now I know that none of you, among whom I have gone about proclaiming the kingdom, will ever see my face again. [26] Therefore I declare to you this day that I am not responsible for the blood of any of you, [27] for I did not shrink from declaring to you the whole purpose of God. [28] Keep watch over yourselves and over all the flock, of which the Holy Spirit has made you overseers, to shepherd the church of God[c] that he obtained with the blood of his own Son.[d] [29] I know that after I have gone, savage wolves will come in among you, not sparing the flock. [30] Some

[a] Other ancient authorities add *after remaining at Trogyllium*

[b] Or *And now, bound in the spirit*

[c] Other ancient authorities read *of the Lord*

[d] Or *with his own blood*; Gk *with the blood of his Own*

"fortunate." It might be a slave-name, not a given name ("Lucky"). **12:** The response is uncharacteristically underwhelming (see 19.24n., "litotes") (3.10; 5.16; 9.35; 14.11). **13–16: Journey to Miletus.** From Assos Paul travels south by boat in the eastern Aegean Sea to Miletus. **13:** *Assos*, northwest coast of Asia Minor. **14:** *Mitylene*, major city on the island of Lesbos (in the Aegean Sea), south of Assos. **15:** *Chios*, island south of Lesbos. *Samos*, island southeast of Chios. *Miletus*, prominent seaport city on the west coast of Asia Minor (present-day Turkey). **16:** *Eager to be in Jerusalem*, see 19.21. *Pentecost*, the Jewish festival of Shavuot (2.1), one of the three pilgrimage festivals. Paul's desire to be in Jerusalem reflects his observance of Jewish law and custom. **17–38: Paul's speech to the Ephesian elders.** Paul's speech provides a suitable conclusion to his missionary journeys. In it he looks back to his previous work and forward to the dangers that await him in Jerusalem, exhorts his listeners to remain faithful, and defends his actions among them. **17:** *Ephesus*, about thirty miles north of Miletus. *Elders*, see 11.30; 14.23; 15.2; 16.4. **19:** *Plots of the Jews*, Jews are singled out as opponents of Paul (13.45; 17.5,13; 18.12; 20.3). **23:** *Imprisonment and persecutions*, see 9.16; 16.23; 21.11,33. His sufferings were foreshadowed (9.16). **25:** *Kingdom*, see 8.12. **26:** *Not responsible for the blood*, having heard the gospel, all should affirm Jesus (3.17; 17.30; Lk 23.34) and thus be saved. **27:** *Purpose of God*, see 2.23; 4.28; 5.38–39; 13.36. **28:** *Overseers*, Gk "episkopoi," from which "bishop" is derived; here it is identified with "elders" (v. 17), Gk "presbyteroi," showing that the division of Christian offices in some denominations (bishop, deacon) was not yet firm. *Flock . . . shepherd*, pastoral images often applied to Israel and its leaders; see Jer 3.15; 23.1–4; Ezek 34.1–24; Ps 74.2; 78.52; 95.7. *Blood*, see Rom 3.25; Eph 1.7; Heb 9.12; 1 Jn 1.7; Rev 1.5. **29–30:** *Savage wolves*, admonitions against false teaching become common in early Christian writing; see Mt 7.15; 1 Tim 1.3–7; 4.1–3; 2 Tim 2.14–18, Ignatius, *Philad.* 2.1–2.

even from your own group will come distorting the truth in order to entice the disciples to follow them. [31] Therefore be alert, remembering that for three years I did not cease night or day to warn everyone with tears. [32] And now I commend you to God and to the message of his grace, a message that is able to build you up and to give you the inheritance among all who are sanctified. [33] I coveted no one's silver or gold or clothing. [34] You know for yourselves that I worked with my own hands to support myself and my companions. [35] In all this I have given you an example that by such work we must support the weak, remembering the words of the Lord Jesus, for he himself said, 'It is more blessed to give than to receive.'"

[36] When he had finished speaking, he knelt down with them all and prayed. [37] There was much weeping among them all; they embraced Paul and kissed him, [38] grieving especially because of what he had said, that they would not see him again. Then they brought him to the ship.

21 When we had parted from them and set sail, we came by a straight course to Cos, and the next day to Rhodes, and from there to Patara.[a] [2] When we found a ship bound for Phoenicia, we went on board and set sail. [3] We came in sight of Cyprus; and leaving it on our left, we sailed to Syria and landed at Tyre, because the ship was to unload its cargo there. [4] We looked up the disciples and stayed there for seven days. Through the Spirit they told Paul not to go on to Jerusalem. [5] When our days there were ended, we left and proceeded on our journey; and all of them, with wives and children, escorted us outside the city. There we knelt down on the beach and prayed [6] and said farewell to one another. Then we went on board the ship, and they returned home.

[7] When we had finished[b] the voyage from Tyre, we arrived at Ptolemais; and we greeted the believers[c] and stayed with them for one day. [8] The next day we left and came to Caesarea; and we went into the house of Philip the evangelist, one of the seven, and stayed with him. [9] He had four unmarried daughters[d] who had the gift of prophecy. [10] While we were staying there for several days, a prophet named Agabus came down from Judea. [11] He came to us and took Paul's belt, bound his own feet and hands with it, and said, "Thus says the Holy Spirit, 'This is the way the Jews in Jerusalem will bind the man who owns this belt and will hand him over to the Gentiles.'" [12] When we heard this, we and the people there urged him not to go up to Jerusalem. [13] Then Paul answered, "What are you doing, weeping and breaking my heart? For I am ready not only to be bound but even to die in Jerusalem for the name of the Lord Jesus." [14] Since he would not be persuaded, we remained silent except to say, "The Lord's will be done."

[15] After these days we got ready and started to go up to Jerusalem. [16] Some of the disciples from Caesarea also came along

[a] Other ancient authorities add *and Myra*
[b] Or *continued*
[c] Gk *brothers*
[d] Gk *four daughters, virgins,*

33: See 16.19n. (8.18; 19.25). **34:** *Worked with my own hands,* see 18.3; 1 Cor 4.12; 1 Thess 2.9. **35:** The saying does not appear in the Gospels, but versions were well known in Greek literature (Thucydides, *Hist.* 2.97.4; Seneca, *Ep.* 81.17; Plutarch, *Mor.* 173d).

21.1–26.32: Paul in Jerusalem.

21.1–36: Paul's arrival and arrest in Jerusalem. 1–16: Paul travels to Jerusalem. 1: *We,* the first-person plural narrative resumes and continues until Paul's arrival in Jerusalem (v. 18). The route begins off the coast of southwest Asia Minor and proceeds eastward along the southern coast to the Phoenician coastal city of Tyre. *Cos,* off the southwest coast of Asia Minor (present-day Turkey). *Rhodes,* a larger island south and east of Cos. *Patara,* port on the southern coast. **2:** *Phoenicia,* at the eastern end of the Mediterranean. **4:** *Spirit,* the Spirit frequently directs the action (8.39; 10.19; 11.12; 13.2,4; 15.28; 16.6,7; 28.25). **7:** *Ptolemais,* modern-day Akko/Acre in present-day Israel; coastal city twenty-two miles south of Tyre. **8:** *Caesarea,* see 8.40; 10.1. Philip traveled here following the conversion of the Ethiopian official (8.40). *One of the seven,* see 6.1–6. **9:** *Prophecy,* see 2.16; 3.18; 7.37; 10.43; 11.27; 13.1; 15.32; 19.6. *Daughters,* on women and prophetic powers, see 2 Kings 22.14; *T. Job* 46–52; *Ex. Rab.* 1.1. **10:** *Agabus,* see 11.28. **13:** *Die . . . for the name of the Lord Jesus,* see 5.41; 9.16. **14:** *The Lord's will be done,* Lk 22.42 attributes a similar statement to Jesus shortly before his arrest. **16:**

and brought us to the house of Mnason of Cyprus, an early disciple, with whom we were to stay.

[17] When we arrived in Jerusalem, the brothers welcomed us warmly. [18] The next day Paul went with us to visit James; and all the elders were present. [19] After greeting them, he related one by one the things that God had done among the Gentiles through his ministry. [20] When they heard it, they praised God. Then they said to him, "You see, brother, how many thousands of believers there are among the Jews, and they are all zealous for the law. [21] They have been told about you that you teach all the Jews living among the Gentiles to forsake Moses, and that you tell them not to circumcise their children or observe the customs. [22] What then is to be done? They will certainly hear that you have come. [23] So do what we tell you. We have four men who are under a vow. [24] Join these men, go through the rite of purification with them, and pay for the shaving of their heads. Thus all will know that there is nothing in what they have been told about you, but that you yourself observe and guard the law. [25] But as for the Gentiles who have become believers, we have sent a letter with our judgment that they should abstain from what has been sacrificed to idols and from blood and from what is strangled[a] and from fornication." [26] Then Paul took the men, and the next day, having purified himself, he entered the temple with them, making public the completion of the days of purification when the sacrifice would be made for each of them.

[27] When the seven days were almost completed, the Jews from Asia, who had seen him in the temple, stirred up the whole crowd. They seized him, [28] shouting, "Fellow Israelites, help! This is the man who is teaching everyone everywhere against our people, our law, and this place; more than that, he has actually brought Greeks into the temple and has defiled this holy place." [29] For they had previously seen Trophimus the Ephesian with him in the city, and they supposed that Paul had brought him into the temple. [30] Then all the city was aroused, and the people rushed together. They seized Paul and dragged him out of the temple, and immediately the doors were shut. [31] While they were trying to kill him, word came to the tribune of the cohort that all Jerusalem was in an uproar. [32] Immediately he took soldiers and centurions and ran down to them. When they saw the tribune and the soldiers, they stopped beating Paul. [33] Then the tribune came, arrested him, and ordered him to be bound with two chains; he inquired who he was and what he had done. [34] Some in the crowd shouted one thing, some another; and as he could not learn the facts because of the uproar, he ordered him to be brought into the barracks. [35] When Paul[b] came to the steps, the violence of the mob was so great that he had to be carried by the soldiers. [36] The crowd that followed kept shouting, "Away with him!"

[a] Other ancient authorities lack *and from what is strangled*

[b] Gk *he*

Mnason, otherwise unknown. Regarding Christianity on Cyprus, see 4.36; 11.19–20; 13.4–12. **17–26: Paul meets with James.** James's speech foreshadows Paul's troubles (20.23; 21.11) and defends Paul by pointing out that he has remained Torah-observant. **17:** *Welcomed us warmly,* Acts emphasizes the harmony among early Christians, especially between Paul and the leaders of the Jerusalem church. **18:** *James,* see 12.17. *Elders,* see 11.30. **19:** *Gentiles,* Acts often portrays Paul working among Gentiles, although his efforts result in converting Jews as well (13.43; 17.11; 18.8). **20–26:** Acts repeatedly defends Paul against the charge that he advocates that Jews abandon Torah observance (16.3; 18.18; 20.16). **23:** *Four men . . . under a vow,* possibly a Nazirite vow; see 18.18; Num 6.1–21. Agrippa I assumed payment for others who fulfilled the Nazirite vow (*Ant.* 19.294). **25:** *Gentiles . . . should abstain,* 15.20,29. **27–36: Paul's arrest in the Temple. 27:** *Jews from Asia,* see 20.19. **28:** Charges resemble those made against Stephen (6.13). *Brought Greeks into the temple,* Gentiles were prohibited from approaching the Temple beyond the Court of the Gentiles (Josephus, *J.W.* 5.193–94; 6.124–26; *Ant.* 15.417). **29:** *Trophimus,* see 20.4. **30–31:** The mob riot recalls actions against Stephen (7.54–60) and Paul in Ephesus (19.28–32). **31:** *Tribune,* later identified as Claudius Lysias (23.26). **36:** *Away with him,* see Lk 23.18. Luke depicts the Jewish crowd as frenzied and violent, the Romans as calm and orderly.

[37] Just as Paul was about to be brought into the barracks, he said to the tribune, "May I say something to you?" The tribune[a] replied, "Do you know Greek? [38] Then you are not the Egyptian who recently stirred up a revolt and led the four thousand assassins out into the wilderness?" [39] Paul replied, "I am a Jew, from Tarsus in Cilicia, a citizen of an important city; I beg you, let me speak to the people." [40] When he had given him permission, Paul stood on the steps and motioned to the people for silence; and when there was a great hush, he addressed them in the Hebrew[b] language, saying:

22 "Brothers and fathers, listen to the defense that I now make before you."

[2] When they heard him addressing them in Hebrew,[b] they became even more quiet. Then he said:

[3] "I am a Jew, born in Tarsus in Cilicia, but brought up in this city at the feet of Gamaliel, educated strictly according to our ancestral law, being zealous for God, just as all of you are today. [4] I persecuted this Way up to the point of death by binding both men and women and putting them in prison, [5] as the high priest and the whole council of elders can testify about me. From them I also received letters to the brothers in Damascus, and I went there in order to bind those who were there and to bring them back to Jerusalem for punishment.

[6] "While I was on my way and approaching Damascus, about noon a great light from heaven suddenly shone about me. [7] I fell to the ground and heard a voice saying to me, 'Saul, Saul, why are you persecuting me?' [8] I answered, 'Who are you, Lord?' Then he said to me, 'I am Jesus of Nazareth[c] whom you are persecuting.' [9] Now those who were with me saw the light but did not hear the voice of the one who was speaking to me. [10] I asked, 'What am I to do, Lord?' The Lord said to me, 'Get up and go to Damascus; there you will be told everything that has been assigned to you to do.' [11] Since I could not see because of the brightness of that light, those who were with me took my hand and led me to Damascus.

[12] "A certain Ananias, who was a devout man according to the law and well spoken of by all the Jews living there, [13] came to me; and standing beside me, he said, 'Brother Saul, regain your sight!' In that very hour I regained my sight and saw him. [14] Then he said, 'The God of our ancestors has chosen you to know his will, to see the Righteous One and to hear his own voice; [15] for you will be his witness to all the world of what you have seen and heard. [16] And now why do you delay? Get up, be baptized, and have your sins washed away, calling on his name.'

[17] "After I had returned to Jerusalem and while I was praying in the temple, I fell into a trance [18] and saw Jesus[d] saying to me, 'Hurry and get out of Jerusalem quickly, because they will not accept your testimony about me.' [19] And I said, 'Lord, they themselves know that in every synagogue I imprisoned and beat those who believed in you. [20] And while the blood of your witness Stephen was shed, I myself was standing by, approving and keeping the coats of those who killed him.' [21] Then he said to me, 'Go, for I will send you far away to the Gentiles.'"

[22] Up to this point they listened to him, but then they shouted, "Away with such a fellow from the earth! For he should not be allowed to live." [23] And while they were shouting, throwing off their cloaks, and tossing dust into the air, [24] the tribune directed that he was to be brought into the barracks, and ordered

[a] Gk *He*
[b] That is, *Aramaic*
[c] Gk *the Nazorean*
[d] Gk *him*

21.37–22.29: Paul's defense and reaction. 38: *Egyptian,* sometime during 52–58 CE he attempted to capture Jerusalem from Roman control (Josephus, *J.W.* 2.259–260; *Ant.* 20.167–72). Josephus claims he had 30,000 followers (*J.W.* 2.261). **40:** *Hebrew,* Aramaic (see translators' note *b*); see also 22.2. **22.1–21: Paul rehearses the events related to his becoming a believer in Jesus** (see 9.1–31; 26.9–18). **3:** *Tarsus,* see 9.11. *Gamaliel,* see 5.34. **4:** *Way,* see 9.2. **5:** *Letters,* 9.1–2. **6–11:** See 9.3–6. **9:** In the original report Paul's companions heard the voice (9.7). **12–16:** See 9.10–19. Previously identified as a disciple (9.10), here Ananias is described in a fashion similar to Paul, as an observant and well-respected Jew. **13:** *Regained my sight,* see 9.18. **14:** *God of our ancestors,* further identifying Paul as a faithful Jew (cf. 18.18). *Righteous One,* see 3.14; 7.52. **15:** *Witness to all the world,* see 1.8; 9.15. **16:** *Be baptized,* see 9.18. On the relation between baptism and removal of sins, see 2.38. **17–21:** The vision is not mentioned in the other accounts. **20:** *Blood*

PAUL AND THE JEWS

Paul first appears as consenting to the death of Stephen (8.1). After his vision of the resurrected Jesus (ch 9), he becomes one of the most important preachers of the gospel, particularly among Gentiles. His preaching often produces hostile reactions from Jews. In Pisidian Antioch (13.50) Jews drive Paul out of the district; in Iconium Jews seek to stone Paul (14.5); in Thessalonica, the jealousy of Jews leads them to set the city in an uproar (17.1–9); in Corinth Jews attack Paul and bring him before Gallio the proconsul of the region (18.1–13); in Achaea he disputes with Jews in public (18.28); in Greece he was apparently the target of a plot (20.3); in Jerusalem some Jews from Asia Minor accuse Paul of teaching against the Temple and the law (21.27–30). While in Jerusalem he is arrested for bringing disorder and speaking treason against the emperor (17.6–7), causing people to worship contrary to the law and the Temple (18.13; 21.28; 24.6), and for being an agitator (24.5). According to the presentation in Acts, these accusations are unfounded and often inspired by jealousy and antagonism toward the preaching about Jesus.

him to be examined by flogging, to find out the reason for this outcry against him. [25] But when they had tied him up with thongs,[a] Paul said to the centurion who was standing by, "Is it legal for you to flog a Roman citizen who is uncondemned?" [26] When the centurion heard that, he went to the tribune and said to him, "What are you about to do? This man is a Roman citizen." [27] The tribune came and asked Paul,[b] "Tell me, are you a Roman citizen?" And he said, "Yes." [28] The tribune answered, "It cost me a large sum of money to get my citizenship." Paul said, "But I was born a citizen." [29] Immediately those who were about to examine him drew back from him; and the tribune also was afraid, for he realized that Paul was a Roman citizen and that he had bound him.

[30] Since he wanted to find out what Paul[c] was being accused of by the Jews, the next day he released him and ordered the chief priests and the entire council to meet. He brought Paul down and had him stand before them.

23 While Paul was looking intently at the council he said, "Brothers,[d] up to this day I have lived my life with a clear conscience before God." [2] Then the high priest Ananias ordered those standing near him to strike him on the mouth. [3] At this Paul said to him, "God will strike you, you whitewashed wall! Are you sitting there to judge me according to the law, and yet in violation of the law you order me to be struck?" [4] Those standing nearby said, "Do you dare to insult God's high priest?" [5] And Paul said, "I did not realize, brothers, that he was high priest; for it is written, 'You shall not speak evil of a leader of your people.'"

[6] When Paul noticed that some were Sadducees and others were Pharisees, he called out in the council, "Brothers, I am a Pharisee, a son of Pharisees. I am on trial concerning the hope of the resurrection[e] of the dead." [7] When he said this, a dissension began between the Pharisees and the Sadducees, and the assembly was divided. [8] (The Sadducees say that there is no resurrection, or angel, or spirit; but the Pharisees acknowledge all three.) [9] Then a great clamor arose, and certain scribes of the Pharisees' group stood up and contended, "We

[a] Or *up for the lashes*
[b] Gk *him*
[c] Gk *he*
[d] Gk *Men, brothers*
[e] Gk *concerning hope and resurrection*

of... Stephen, see 7.60–8.1. **25:** *Roman citizen,* Paul's claim to be a citizen protects him against torture (see 16.37). **28:** *Born a citizen,* Paul is more "Roman" than the Roman tribune who had to buy his citizenship. Acts does not say how Paul's family would have acquired citizenship.

22.30–23.11: Paul appears before the Jewish council. 23.1: *Council,* the Sanhedrin. **2:** *Ananias,* high priest ca. 48–59 CE, who continued to remain an influential figure until the Revolt against Rome (66–70). **3:** *Whitewashed wall,* Ezek 13.10–16; Mt 23.27. Acts contrasts Paul and other believers in Jesus who follow the law with Jews and Jewish authorities who do not. It is not clear what *law* the high priest is *in violation of.* **5:** *Paul,* citing Ex 22.28 [Heb 27], affirms his obedience to Torah. **6:** On Paul's claim to be a Pharisee, see Phil 3.5. *Hope of the resurrection,* resurrection is a central tenet of Acts (2.32; 4.33; 5.30). **8:** Josephus notes that Sadducees rejected belief in bodily resurrection while Pharisees accepted it (*J.W.* 2.163–66; *Ant.* 18.12–17). **9:** The scribes' declaration of innocence

find nothing wrong with this man. What if a spirit or an angel has spoken to him?" [10] When the dissension became violent, the tribune, fearing that they would tear Paul to pieces, ordered the soldiers to go down, take him by force, and bring him into the barracks.

[11] That night the Lord stood near him and said, "Keep up your courage! For just as you have testified for me in Jerusalem, so you must bear witness also in Rome."

[12] In the morning the Jews joined in a conspiracy and bound themselves by an oath neither to eat nor drink until they had killed Paul. [13] There were more than forty who joined in this conspiracy. [14] They went to the chief priests and elders and said, "We have strictly bound ourselves by an oath to taste no food until we have killed Paul. [15] Now then, you and the council must notify the tribune to bring him down to you, on the pretext that you want to make a more thorough examination of his case. And we are ready to do away with him before he arrives."

[16] Now the son of Paul's sister heard about the ambush; so he went and gained entrance to the barracks and told Paul. [17] Paul called one of the centurions and said, "Take this young man to the tribune, for he has something to report to him." [18] So he took him, brought him to the tribune, and said, "The prisoner Paul called me and asked me to bring this young man to you; he has something to tell you." [19] The tribune took him by the hand, drew him aside privately, and asked, "What is it that you have to report to me?" [20] He answered, "The Jews have agreed to ask you to bring Paul down to the council tomorrow, as though they were going to inquire more thoroughly into his case. [21] But do not be persuaded by them, for more than forty of their men are lying in ambush for him. They have bound themselves by an oath neither to eat nor drink until they kill him. They are ready now and are waiting for your consent." [22] So the tribune dismissed the young man, ordering him, "Tell no one that you have informed me of this."

[23] Then he summoned two of the centurions and said, "Get ready to leave by nine o'clock tonight for Caesarea with two hundred soldiers, seventy horsemen, and two hundred spearmen. [24] Also provide mounts for Paul to ride, and take him safely to Felix the governor." [25] He wrote a letter to this effect:

[26] "Claudius Lysias to his Excellency the governor Felix, greetings. [27] This man was seized by the Jews and was about to be killed by them, but when I had learned that he was a Roman citizen, I came with the guard and rescued him. [28] Since I wanted to know the charge for which they accused him, I had him brought to their council. [29] I found that he was accused concerning questions of their law, but was charged with nothing deserving death or imprisonment. [30] When I was informed that there would be a plot against the man, I sent him to you at once, ordering his accusers also to state before you what they have against him.[a]"

[31] So the soldiers, according to their instructions, took Paul and brought him during the night to Antipatris. [32] The next day they let the horsemen go on with him, while they returned to the barracks. [33] When they came to Caesarea and delivered the letter to the governor, they presented Paul also before him. [34] On reading the letter, he asked what province he belonged to, and when he learned that he was from Cilicia, [35] he said,

[a] Other ancient authorities add *Farewell*

presents, as did Gamaliel (5.33–39), an implicit censure of Jews who condemn Paul. **10:** Acts presents even the Jewish legislature as violence-prone.

23.12–35: Paul transferred to Caesarea. The Jews' plot against Paul prompts the tribune to transfer him to the custody of the Roman procurator. **16:** No other biblical source refers to members of Paul's family. **22:** *Tell no one,* so that he can move Paul out of the city before the conspirators find out about the change in venue. **23:** *Caesarea,* the residence of the Roman governor. The numbers depict a large force accompanying Paul. **24:** *Felix,* Antonius Felix, a freedman, was procurator of Judea in the mid to late 50s, and possibly as late as 60. **26–30:** The tribune's letter describes previous events (21.27–23.23), omitting details such as his own hostile treatment of Paul (22.24). **29:** *Nothing deserving death,* several figures announce Paul's innocence (25.25; 26.31); the Gospel of Luke has Pilate express a similar opinion about Jesus (Lk 23.15). **31:** *Antipatris,* city on the road to Caesarea. **35:** *Herod's headquarters,* the palace built by Herod I and taken over by the Roman government.

"I will give you a hearing when your accusers arrive." Then he ordered that he be kept under guard in Herod's headquarters.[a]

24 Five days later the high priest Ananias came down with some elders and an attorney, a certain Tertullus, and they reported their case against Paul to the governor. [2] When Paul[b] had been summoned, Tertullus began to accuse him, saying:

"Your Excellency,[c] because of you we have long enjoyed peace, and reforms have been made for this people because of your foresight. [3] We welcome this in every way and everywhere with utmost gratitude. [4] But, to detain you no further, I beg you to hear us briefly with your customary graciousness. [5] We have, in fact, found this man a pestilent fellow, an agitator among all the Jews throughout the world, and a ringleader of the sect of the Nazarenes.[d] [6] He even tried to profane the temple, and so we seized him.[e] [8] By examining him yourself you will be able to learn from him concerning everything of which we accuse him."

[9] The Jews also joined in the charge by asserting that all this was true.

[10] When the governor motioned to him to speak, Paul replied:

"I cheerfully make my defense, knowing that for many years you have been a judge over this nation. [11] As you can find out, it is not more than twelve days since I went up to worship in Jerusalem. [12] They did not find me disputing with anyone in the temple or stirring up a crowd either in the synagogues or throughout the city. [13] Neither can they prove to you the charge that they now bring against me. [14] But this I admit to you, that according to the Way, which they call a sect, I worship the God of our ancestors, believing everything laid down according to the law or written in the prophets. [15] I have a hope in God—a hope that they themselves also accept—that there will be a resurrection of both[f] the righteous and the unrighteous. [16] Therefore I do my best always to have a clear conscience toward God and all people. [17] Now after some years I came to bring alms to my nation and to offer sacrifices. [18] While I was doing this, they found me in the temple, completing the rite of purification, without any crowd or disturbance. [19] But there were some Jews from Asia—they ought to be here before you to make an accusation, if they have anything against me. [20] Or let these men here tell what crime they had found when I stood before the council, [21] unless it was this one sentence that I called out while standing before them, 'It is about the resurrection of the dead that I am on trial before you today.'"

[22] But Felix, who was rather well informed about the Way, adjourned the hearing with the comment, "When Lysias the tribune comes down, I will decide your case." [23] Then he

[a] Gk *praetorium*
[b] Gk *he*
[c] Gk lacks *Your Excellency*
[d] Gk *Nazoreans*
[e] Other ancient authorities add *and we would have judged him according to our law. [7] But the chief captain Lysias came and with great violence took him out of our hands, [8] commanding his accusers to come before you.*
[f] Other ancient authorities read *of the dead, both of*

24.1–25.12: Paul appears before Roman governors.

24.1–27: Paul and Felix. 1: *Ananias,* see 23.2. *Tertullus,* the otherwise unknown person bears a Latin name. **2–4:** The speech begins conventionally by praising the governor for accomplishments and virtues. **5:** *Agitator,* a serious charge of fomenting rebellion (16.20; 17.6; 19.40). *Sect,* Gk "hairesis" carries the connotation of "party" or "school"; Josephus uses it to describe Pharisees, Sadducees, and Essenes, which denotes a distinct group (cf. 26.5). *Nazarenes,* Acts frequently uses "Nazarene" for Jesus (2.22; 3.6; 4.10; 6.14; 22.8; 26.9), but only here, in the plural, for Christians. **6:** *Profane the temple,* see 21.28–29. Such an act could have caused an uprising, which would have been a concern of the Roman government. **10–21:** Paul refutes each charge. **10:** *Cheerfully,* lit., "with a good spirit," willingly. **14–16:** Paul presents himself as a faithful and observant Jew; see 22.3; 25.4–5. **14:** *Way,* see 9.2. Paul prefers this term because of the implication that Christianity is the true way of God, rather than a sect (see v. 5n.). *Law . . . prophets,* the Tanakh. **15:** *Resurrection of both the righteous and the unrighteous,* see Dan 12.2. **17:** *Bring alms,* possibly a continuation of Paul's self-presentation as a pious Jew, or a reference to a collection of funds, send from Paul's Gentile congregations to the Jerusalem church (not explicitly mentioned in Acts but described in Paul's letters: Rom 15.25–29; 1 Cor 16.1–4; Gal 2.10). **19:** *Some Jews from Asia,* see 21.27. **21:** *Resurrection,* see 23.6. **22:** *Lysias,* see 23.26.

ordered the centurion to keep him in custody, but to let him have some liberty and not to prevent any of his friends from taking care of his needs.

[24] Some days later when Felix came with his wife Drusilla, who was Jewish, he sent for Paul and heard him speak concerning faith in Christ Jesus. [25] And as he discussed justice, self-control, and the coming judgment, Felix became frightened and said, "Go away for the present; when I have an opportunity, I will send for you." [26] At the same time he hoped that money would be given him by Paul, and for that reason he used to send for him very often and converse with him.

[27] After two years had passed, Felix was succeeded by Porcius Festus; and since he wanted to grant the Jews a favor, Felix left Paul in prison.

25 Three days after Festus had arrived in the province, he went up from Caesarea to Jerusalem [2] where the chief priests and the leaders of the Jews gave him a report against Paul. They appealed to him [3] and requested, as a favor to them against Paul,[a] to have him transferred to Jerusalem. They were, in fact, planning an ambush to kill him along the way. [4] Festus replied that Paul was being kept at Caesarea, and that he himself intended to go there shortly. [5] "So," he said, "let those of you who have the authority come down with me, and if there is anything wrong about the man, let them accuse him."

[6] After he had stayed among them not more than eight or ten days, he went down to Caesarea; the next day he took his seat on the tribunal and ordered Paul to be brought. [7] When he arrived, the Jews who had gone down from Jerusalem surrounded him, bringing many serious charges against him, which they could not prove. [8] Paul said in his defense, "I have in no way committed an offense against the law of the Jews, or against the temple, or against the emperor." [9] But Festus, wishing to do the Jews a favor, asked Paul, "Do you wish to go up to Jerusalem and be tried there before me on these charges?" [10] Paul said, "I am appealing to the emperor's tribunal; this is where I should be tried. I have done no wrong to the Jews, as you very well know. [11] Now if I am in the wrong and have committed something for which I deserve to die, I am not trying to escape death; but if there is nothing to their charges against me, no one can turn me over to them. I appeal to the emperor." [12] Then Festus, after he had conferred with his council, replied, "You have appealed to the emperor; to the emperor you will go."

[13] After several days had passed, King Agrippa and Bernice arrived at Caesarea to welcome Festus. [14] Since they were staying there several days, Festus laid Paul's case before the king, saying, "There is a man here

[a] Gk *him*

24: *Drusilla,* Julia Drusilla, daughter of Agrippa I (see 12.1n.); known for her beauty, she had been previously married to Azizus, king of Syrian Emesa, who had himself circumcised (*Ant.* 20.139). **26:** Felix had a reputation for corruption and cruelty (*Ant.* 20.160–65; Tacitus, *Ann.* 12.54; *Hist.* 5.9). **27:** *Porcius Festus,* procurator of Judea, in office from the late 50s until 62. *Grant the Jews a favor,* his successor, Festus, acts from the same motivation; see 25.9.

25.1–12: Paul and Festus. 1: *Caesarea,* see 8.40n. **3:** *Ambush,* Jewish leaders renew a previous plot against Paul; see 23.12–35. Once again, Luke presents Jews as conspiring to commit violence. **8:** Paul defends himself, as before, against charges that he violated Torah, the sanctity of the Temple, and public order (22.1–21; 23.1,6; 24.10–21). **9:** *Favor,* see 24.27. The "favor" is presumably aimed at keeping the local populace quiet. **10:** *Emperor's tribunal,* trial according to Roman law and under Roman jurisdiction. Paul does not want to be tried by a Jewish court. This appeal also serves Acts' narrative need to get Paul to Rome.

25.13–26.32: Paul and Agrippa. The sequence of Paul's appearances before the Jewish council (22.30–23.11), Roman governor (24.1–23; 25.1–12), and Jewish king (25.23–26.32) parallels Jesus' appearances before the Jewish council (Lk 22.66–71), Pilate (23.1–5), and Antipas (23.6–12). **13:** *King Agrippa,* Marcus Julius Agrippa (Agrippa II), son of Agrippa I (see 12.1n.), appointed ruler of Syrian Chalcis, and later the Decapolis, Galilee, and Perea (53–ca. 93 CE). *Bernice,* Julia Berenice, daughter of Agrippa I, sister of Agrippa II and Drusilla (24.24), rumored to have carried on romantic liaisons with the future Roman emperor Titus. **14–21:** Festus summarizes the events previously narrated in 24.27–25.12, adding that the dispute centered on religious matters and Jesus (v. 19; cf. 25.7–8),

who was left in prison by Felix. [15] When I was in Jerusalem, the chief priests and the elders of the Jews informed me about him and asked for a sentence against him. [16] I told them that it was not the custom of the Romans to hand over anyone before the accused had met the accusers face to face and had been given an opportunity to make a defense against the charge. [17] So when they met here, I lost no time, but on the next day took my seat on the tribunal and ordered the man to be brought. [18] When the accusers stood up, they did not charge him with any of the crimes[a] that I was expecting. [19] Instead they had certain points of disagreement with him about their own religion and about a certain Jesus, who had died, but whom Paul asserted to be alive. [20] Since I was at a loss how to investigate these questions, I asked whether he wished to go to Jerusalem and be tried there on these charges.[b] [21] But when Paul had appealed to be kept in custody for the decision of his Imperial Majesty, I ordered him to be held until I could send him to the emperor." [22] Agrippa said to Festus, "I would like to hear the man myself." "Tomorrow," he said, "you will hear him."

[23] So on the next day Agrippa and Bernice came with great pomp, and they entered the audience hall with the military tribunes and the prominent men of the city. Then Festus gave the order and Paul was brought in. [24] And Festus said, "King Agrippa and all here present with us, you see this man about whom the whole Jewish community petitioned me, both in Jerusalem and here, shouting that he ought not to live any longer. [25] But I found that he had done nothing deserving death; and when he appealed to his Imperial Majesty, I decided to send him. [26] But I have nothing definite to write to our sovereign about him. Therefore I have brought him before all of you, and especially before you, King Agrippa, so that, after we have examined him, I may have something to write— [27] for it seems to me unreasonable to send a prisoner without indicating the charges against him."

26 Agrippa said to Paul, "You have permission to speak for yourself." Then Paul stretched out his hand and began to defend himself:

[2] "I consider myself fortunate that it is before you, King Agrippa, I am to make my defense today against all the accusations of the Jews, [3] because you are especially familiar with all the customs and controversies of the Jews; therefore I beg of you to listen to me patiently.

[4] "All the Jews know my way of life from my youth, a life spent from the beginning among my own people and in Jerusalem. [5] They have known for a long time, if they are willing to testify, that I have belonged to the strictest sect of our religion and lived as a Pharisee. [6] And now I stand here on trial on account of my hope in the promise made by God to our ancestors, [7] a promise that our twelve tribes hope to attain, as they earnestly worship day and night. It is for this hope, your Excellency,[c] that I am accused by Jews! [8] Why is it thought incredible by any of you that God raises the dead?

[9] "Indeed, I myself was convinced that I ought to do many things against the name of Jesus of Nazareth.[d] [10] And that is what I did in Jerusalem; with authority received from

[a] Other ancient authorities read *with anything*
[b] Gk *on them*
[c] Gk *O king*
[d] Gk *the Nazorean*

and omitting mention of political charges (24.5; 25.9). **21:** *Imperial Majesty*, Gk "sebastos," the standard title for the Roman emperor, equivalent to Latin "Augustus." **25:** *Nothing deserving death*, see 23.29.

26.1–32: Paul's final defense (cf. 22.1–21; 24.10–21). Paul responds to charges brought by Jews (vv. 2–8), describes his conversion (vv. 9–18), summarizes his preaching (vv. 19–23), and appeals to Agrippa II (vv. 24–29). **1:** *Stretched out his hand*, common gesture (12.17; 13.16; 21.40). **2–4:** Paul opens with standard words of praise; see 24.2–4. **3:** *Customs . . . of the Jews*, the assumption that Agrippa practices Judaism. **4–5:** Acts represents Paul as an observant Jew; see 22.3; 24.15–16. **6–8:** Paul presents resurrection, the defining Christian belief according to Acts (23.6), as the fulfillment of God's promise to Israel and the constant hope of Jews. The *promise* to Abraham in Tanakh was descendants (Gen 15.5), not resurrection. **9–18:** Paul's conversion (see also 9.1–19; 22.3–21). **9–11:** Unlike previous reports (9.1–2; 22.4–5), Paul describes his actions against believers in Jesus as widespread and

the chief priests, I not only locked up many of the saints in prison, but I also cast my vote against them when they were being condemned to death. [11] By punishing them often in all the synagogues I tried to force them to blaspheme; and since I was so furiously enraged at them, I pursued them even to foreign cities.

[12] "With this in mind, I was traveling to Damascus with the authority and commission of the chief priests, [13] when at midday along the road, your Excellency,[a] I saw a light from heaven, brighter than the sun, shining around me and my companions. [14] When we had all fallen to the ground, I heard a voice saying to me in the Hebrew[b] language, 'Saul, Saul, why are you persecuting me? It hurts you to kick against the goads.' [15] I asked, 'Who are you, Lord?' The Lord answered, 'I am Jesus whom you are persecuting. [16] But get up and stand on your feet; for I have appeared to you for this purpose, to appoint you to serve and testify to the things in which you have seen me[c] and to those in which I will appear to you. [17] I will rescue you from your people and from the Gentiles—to whom I am sending you [18] to open their eyes so that they may turn from darkness to light and from the power of Satan to God, so that they may receive forgiveness of sins and a place among those who are sanctified by faith in me.'

[19] "After that, King Agrippa, I was not disobedient to the heavenly vision, [20] but declared first to those in Damascus, then in Jerusalem and throughout the countryside of Judea, and also to the Gentiles, that they should repent and turn to God and do deeds consistent with repentance. [21] For this reason the Jews seized me in the temple and tried to kill me. [22] To this day I have had help from God, and so I stand here, testifying to both small and great, saying nothing but what the prophets and Moses said would take place: [23] that the Messiah[d] must suffer, and that, by being the first to rise from the dead, he would proclaim light both to our people and to the Gentiles."

[24] While he was making this defense, Festus exclaimed, "You are out of your mind, Paul! Too much learning is driving you insane!" [25] But Paul said, "I am not out of my mind, most excellent Festus, but I am speaking the sober truth. [26] Indeed the king knows about these things, and to him I speak freely; for I am certain that none of these things has escaped his notice, for this was not done in a corner. [27] King Agrippa, do you believe the prophets? I know that you believe." [28] Agrippa said to Paul, "Are you so quickly persuading me to become a Christian?"[e] [29] Paul replied, "Whether quickly or not, I pray to God that not only you but also all who are listening to me today might become such as I am—except for these chains."

[30] Then the king got up, and with him the governor and Bernice and those who had

[a] Gk *O king*
[b] That is, *Aramaic*
[c] Other ancient authorities read *the things that you have seen*
[d] Or *the Christ*
[e] Or *Quickly you will persuade me to play the Christian*

extremely aggressive. **10:** *Saints,* see 9.13n. **14:** *In the Hebrew language,* a detail not mentioned previously. *It hurts you to kick against the goads,* a proverbial expression, not previously quoted, depicting Paul as resisting the pressure of God's plan by comparing him to a draft animal kicking the pointed stick used to move it in the desired direction. The saying is frequently attested in Greek literature (e.g., Euripides, *Bacch.* 795). **18:** *From darkness to light,* an image for those who acknowledge God and in this context conversion (13.47; Is 42.16; Lk 1.79; 2.32). *Satan,* conversion is more than a cognitive change; it marks the moving away from the powers of evil. The implication in Luke's rendering may be that Jews who resist such conversion are under Satan's control. *Forgiveness of sins* comes about only with belief in Jesus (2.38; 5.31; 10.43; 13.38). **20:** *Repent,* Paul calls for all to repent (17.30; 20.21). **21:** See 21.27–36. **22:** Paul's claim that his instruction comes from the prophets and Moses authenticates his status as a Jew (see 24.14–16), and establishes the Christian message as consistent with biblical teaching. **23:** *Messiah must suffer,* common understanding in Luke-Acts of messianic identity; see 3.18,21–25; 8.32–35; 9.16; 17.3; Lk 2.49; 24.7,26,46. *Light,* see v. 18. **24:** Festus confirms that Paul's views are based on knowledge and not ignorance, but that their results, or possibly Paul's zeal for them, show them to be *insane.* **27:** *Do you believe,* Paul's question implies that anyone who believes in the prophets should believe in Jesus. **31:** *Doing*

been seated with them; [31] and as they were leaving, they said to one another, "This man is doing nothing to deserve death or imprisonment." [32] Agrippa said to Festus, "This man could have been set free if he had not appealed to the emperor."

27 When it was decided that we were to sail for Italy, they transferred Paul and some other prisoners to a centurion of the Augustan Cohort, named Julius. [2] Embarking on a ship of Adramyttium that was about to set sail to the ports along the coast of Asia, we put to sea, accompanied by Aristarchus, a Macedonian from Thessalonica. [3] The next day we put in at Sidon; and Julius treated Paul kindly, and allowed him to go to his friends to be cared for. [4] Putting out to sea from there, we sailed under the lee of Cyprus, because the winds were against us. [5] After we had sailed across the sea that is off Cilicia and Pamphylia, we came to Myra in Lycia. [6] There the centurion found an Alexandrian ship bound for Italy and put us on board. [7] We sailed slowly for a number of days and arrived with difficulty off Cnidus, and as the wind was against us, we sailed under the lee of Crete off Salmone. [8] Sailing past it with difficulty, we came to a place called Fair Havens, near the city of Lasea.

[9] Since much time had been lost and sailing was now dangerous, because even the Fast had already gone by, Paul advised them, [10] saying, "Sirs, I can see that the voyage will be with danger and much heavy loss, not only of the cargo and the ship, but also of our lives." [11] But the centurion paid more attention to the pilot and to the owner of the ship than to what Paul said. [12] Since the harbor was not suitable for spending the winter, the majority was in favor of putting to sea from there, on the chance that somehow they could reach Phoenix, where they could spend the winter. It was a harbor of Crete, facing southwest and northwest.

[13] When a moderate south wind began to blow, they thought they could achieve their purpose; so they weighed anchor and began to sail past Crete, close to the shore. [14] But soon a violent wind, called the northeaster, rushed down from Crete.[a] [15] Since the ship was caught and could not be turned head-on into the wind, we gave way to it and were driven. [16] By running under the lee of a small island called Cauda[b] we were scarcely able to get the ship's boat under control. [17] After hoisting it up they took measures[c] to undergird the ship; then, fearing that they would run on the Syrtis, they lowered the sea anchor and so were driven. [18] We were being pounded by the storm so violently that on the next day they began to throw the cargo overboard, [19] and on the third day with their own hands they threw the ship's tackle overboard. [20] When neither sun nor stars appeared for many days, and no small tempest raged, all hope of our being saved was at last abandoned.

[21] Since they had been without food for a long time, Paul then stood up among them and said, "Men, you should have listened to me and not have set sail from Crete and thereby avoided this damage and loss. [22] I

[a] Gk *it*
[b] Other ancient authorities read *Clauda*
[c] Gk *helps*

nothing to deserve death, see 23.29. **32:** *Appealed to the emperor*, see 25.11; the process, once started, apparently cannot be stopped.

27.1–28.31: Paul's travel to Rome. 1–44: Sea voyage to Rome. Paul's sea voyage to Rome contains many elements common in contemporaneous literature: detailed itineraries, violent storms, shipwrecks, the crew's flight. Neither human resistance nor forces of nature can prevent Paul from reaching his divinely appointed end (19.21; 23.11). **1:** The first-person plural "we" resumes and continues through 28.16. *Augustan Cohort*, a military unit stationed in Syria, representing the imperial power. **2:** *Adramyttium*, port city in northwest Asia Minor (present-day Turkey). *Aristarchus*, see 19.29. **3–5:** The ship sailed north and west along the coast of Asia Minor. **6:** *Alexandrian ship*, the city of Rome relied for much of its grain on shipments from Egypt. **7:** *Cnidus*, southwest Asia Minor (present-day Turkey). *Salmone*, the northeast coast of Crete. **8:** *Fair Havens* and *Lasea*, the southern coast of Crete. **9:** *Fast*, Yom Kippur or the Day of Atonement, in late September/early October. From this time of year until early spring sailing in open waters was considered dangerous. **16:** *Cauda*, close to the southern shore of Crete. **17:** *Syrtis*, waters along the north coast of Africa, between Cyrene and Carthage, known as dangerous to shipping. **18:** A standard practice during violent storms; see Jon 1.5; Josephus, *J.W.* 1.1.280. **21:** *Listened to me*, see v. 10.

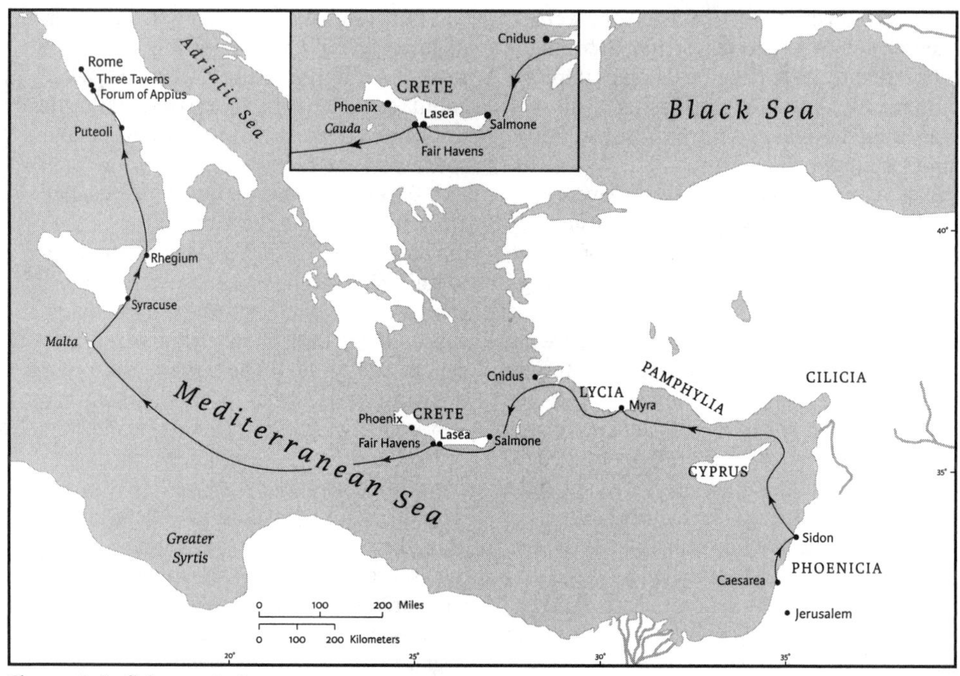

Chs 27–28: Paul's journey to Rome.

urge you now to keep up your courage, for there will be no loss of life among you, but only of the ship. [23] For last night there stood by me an angel of the God to whom I belong and whom I worship, [24] and he said, 'Do not be afraid, Paul; you must stand before the emperor; and indeed, God has granted safety to all those who are sailing with you.' [25] So keep up your courage, men, for I have faith in God that it will be exactly as I have been told. [26] But we will have to run aground on some island."

[27] When the fourteenth night had come, as we were drifting across the sea of Adria, about midnight the sailors suspected that they were nearing land. [28] So they took soundings and found twenty fathoms; a little farther on they took soundings again and found fifteen fathoms. [29] Fearing that we might run on the rocks, they let down four anchors from the stern and prayed for day to come. [30] But when the sailors tried to escape from the ship and had lowered the boat into the sea, on the pretext of putting out anchors from the bow, [31] Paul said to the centurion and the soldiers, "Unless these men stay in the ship, you cannot be saved." [32] Then the soldiers cut away the ropes of the boat and set it adrift.

[33] Just before daybreak, Paul urged all of them to take some food, saying, "Today is the fourteenth day that you have been in suspense and remaining without food, having eaten nothing. [34] Therefore I urge you to take some food, for it will help you survive; for none of you will lose a hair from your heads." [35] After he had said this, he took bread; and giving thanks to God in the presence of all, he broke it and began to eat. [36] Then all of them were encouraged and took food for themselves. [37] (We were in all two hundred seventy-six[a] persons in the ship.) [38] After they had satisfied their hunger, they lightened the ship by throwing the wheat into the sea.

[a] Other ancient authorities read *seventy-six*; others, *about seventy-six*

24: *Stand before the emperor*, see 9.15; 19.21; 23.11. **26:** *Have to run aground*, Paul's prediction is fulfilled; see v. 41. **27:** *Sea of Adria*, Adriatic Sea. **35:** By reciting a blessing before eating, Paul shows himself to be an observant Jew; see 22.3; 24.14–16. The benediction, now known as "Birchat ha-motsi" or "Blessing of the Bread" ("Bread" as

[39] In the morning they did not recognize the land, but they noticed a bay with a beach, on which they planned to run the ship ashore, if they could. [40] So they cast off the anchors and left them in the sea. At the same time they loosened the ropes that tied the steering-oars; then hoisting the foresail to the wind, they made for the beach. [41] But striking a reef,[a] they ran the ship aground; the bow stuck and remained immovable, but the stern was being broken up by the force of the waves. [42] The soldiers' plan was to kill the prisoners, so that none might swim away and escape; [43] but the centurion, wishing to save Paul, kept them from carrying out their plan. He ordered those who could swim to jump overboard first and make for the land, [44] and the rest to follow, some on planks and others on pieces of the ship. And so it was that all were brought safely to land.

28 After we had reached safety, we then learned that the island was called Malta. [2] The natives showed us unusual kindness. Since it had begun to rain and was cold, they kindled a fire and welcomed all of us around it. [3] Paul had gathered a bundle of brushwood and was putting it on the fire, when a viper, driven out by the heat, fastened itself on his hand. [4] When the natives saw the creature hanging from his hand, they said to one another, "This man must be a murderer; though he has escaped from the sea, justice has not allowed him to live." [5] He, however, shook off the creature into the fire and suffered no harm. [6] They were expecting him to swell up or drop dead, but after they had waited a long time and saw that nothing unusual had happened to him, they changed their minds and began to say that he was a god.

[7] Now in the neighborhood of that place were lands belonging to the leading man of the island, named Publius, who received us and entertained us hospitably for three days. [8] It so happened that the father of Publius lay sick in bed with fever and dysentery. Paul visited him and cured him by praying and putting his hands on him. [9] After this happened, the rest of the people on the island who had diseases also came and were cured. [10] They bestowed many honors on us, and when we were about to sail, they put on board all the provisions we needed.

[11] Three months later we set sail on a ship that had wintered at the island, an Alexandrian ship with the Twin Brothers as its figurehead. [12] We put in at Syracuse and stayed there for three days; [13] then we weighed anchor and came to Rhegium. After one day there a south wind sprang up, and on the second day we came to Puteoli. [14] There we found believers[b] and were invited to stay with them for seven days. And so we came to Rome. [15] The believers[b] from there, when they heard of us, came as far as the Forum of Appius and Three Taverns to meet us. On seeing them, Paul thanked God and took courage.

[16] When we came into Rome, Paul was allowed to live by himself, with the soldier who was guarding him.

[17] Three days later he called together the local leaders of the Jews. When they had assembled, he said to them, "Brothers, though

[a] Gk *place of two seas*
[b] Gk *brothers*

representing food in general) is a brief prayer said before eating; the standard benediction, "Birchat ha-mason," is said after eating. The action has Eucharistic overtones (Lk 22.19). **41:** See v. 26.

28.1–10: Paul on Malta. Paul is shown to have miraculous abilities to escape death and heal others (13.9–11; 14.9–11; 20.9–12). **1:** *Malta,* island off the southern coast of Sicily. **4:** *Justice,* possibly a personification, the deity Justice, seen as exacting retribution. **6:** *Say that he was a god,* in Iconium Paul's healing of a paralytic prompts the residents to refer to him as Hermes (14.12). **8:** *Putting his hands,* see 9.12; 14.3; 19.6; Lk 4.40; 13.11–13.

11–31: Paul in Rome. 11: *Alexandrian ship,* see 27.6. *Twin Brothers,* Dioscuri, the brothers Castor and Pollux, often considered as helpers to sailors in need. **12–14:** The final part of the journey takes Paul along the eastern coast of Sicily (*Syracuse*) to *Rhegium,* the port on the Italian peninsula opposite Sicily, and up the western coast of Italy to the port of *Puteoli,* near Naples, and finally to Rome. **15:** *Forum of Appius,* town forty-three miles south of Rome. *Three Taverns,* resting spot thirty-three miles south of Rome. **16:** *Live by himself,* under house arrest. **17–20:** Paul's remarks to the Jewish leaders summarize his position: he is loyal to Judaism and the Jewish people

I had done nothing against our people or the customs of our ancestors, yet I was arrested in Jerusalem and handed over to the Romans. [18] When they had examined me, the Romans[a] wanted to release me, because there was no reason for the death penalty in my case. [19] But when the Jews objected, I was compelled to appeal to the emperor—even though I had no charge to bring against my nation. [20] For this reason therefore I have asked to see you and speak with you,[b] since it is for the sake of the hope of Israel that I am bound with this chain." [21] They replied, "We have received no letters from Judea about you, and none of the brothers coming here has reported or spoken anything evil about you. [22] But we would like to hear from you what you think, for with regard to this sect we know that everywhere it is spoken against."

[23] After they had set a day to meet with him, they came to him at his lodgings in great numbers. From morning until evening he explained the matter to them, testifying to the kingdom of God and trying to convince them about Jesus both from the law of Moses and from the prophets. [24] Some were convinced by what he had said, while others refused to believe. [25] So they disagreed with each other; and as they were leaving, Paul made one further statement: "The Holy Spirit was right in saying to your ancestors through the prophet Isaiah,

[26] 'Go to this people and say,
You will indeed listen, but never understand,
and you will indeed look, but never perceive.
[27] For this people's heart has grown dull,
and their ears are hard of hearing,
and they have shut their eyes;
so that they might not look with their eyes,
and listen with their ears,
and understand with their heart and turn—
and I would heal them.'

[28] Let it be known to you then that this salvation of God has been sent to the Gentiles; they will listen." [c]

[30] He lived there two whole years at his own expense[d] and welcomed all who came to him, [31] proclaiming the kingdom of God and teaching about the Lord Jesus Christ with all boldness and without hindrance.

[a] Gk *they*
[b] Or *I have asked you to see me and speak with me*
[c] Other ancient authorities add verse 29, *And when he had said these words, the Jews departed, arguing vigorously among themselves*
[d] Or *in his own hired dwelling*

(22.3); he has committed no crimes against Rome (22.3–21; 24.11–13); Jesus is the fulfillment of Israel's traditions (23.6; 24.15; 26.6–8). **19:** *Appeal to the emperor*, see 25.11. *No charge to bring against my nation*, no accusation against the Jewish leadership that caused Paul's appeal to Rome. **22:** *Sect*, 9.2; 24.14. **23–29:** The final scene dramatically presents the related themes that the failure of the Jews to receive salvation both was foretold by the prophets and is a consequence of their own rejection of Jesus (13.12,45–46). **23:** *Law of Moses and from the prophets*, 26.22. **26:** Isa 6.9–10; cf. 13.46–48; 18.5–6. **28:** *Gentiles*, at least by anticipation of what developed later, if not in reality by the time represented in the narrative (mid-60s CE), the mission to the Jews is over. **30–31:** Acts ends without narrating Paul's death, although the text often alludes to it (19.21; 20.22–25; 23.11; 26.32; 27.24). **31:** *Kingdom of God*, see 8.12. *Boldness*, see 4.13.

THE LETTER OF PAUL TO THE ROMANS

TITLE, MEANING, AND AUTHORSHIP

Romans, the longest, and thus the first, of the epistles as they are traditionally arranged—although it is one of Paul's latest letters—is enormously influential for the development of Christian ideals and identity. It is equally important for Christian conceptualizations of Jews and Judaism as inferior to Christians and Christianity. Romans 11, which explains God's commitment to Jews because of the irrevocable promises made to the fathers, is a key text for those seeking to reverse the legacy of contempt for Jews and Judaism.

The traditional view of Romans, and of Paul's thought generally, is that as a "convert" to the new religious movement himself, he acted as have many converts before and since, and denigrated his previous religious commitment. In this view, Paul is the great evangelist of Christianity (anachronistically seen as a separate religion already in his time) as the movement of liberation from the bonds of legalism and "works-righteousness" that according to this conception characterized Judaism. Historically, this view has been reinforced by some Protestant Reformation theologians, such as Martin Luther, who saw medieval Roman Catholicism as a "works-righteousness" religion, one that emphasized the deeds of the faithful as necessary to earn their way into God's grace. He projected this view onto Judaism through his interpretation of the context for Paul's opposition, a context he likened to his own opposition to this development in the Roman Catholicism of that time. This view thus contrasted Christianity, and especially Protestant Christianity, as a "religion of grace" with Judaism (and Roman Catholicism) as "religions of law." Augustine, who was instrumental in the development of Roman Catholicism, had similarly attributed to Judaism the "works-righteousness" he challenged in the rival Christian groups of his own time. These caricatures of Judaism did not arise from the study of Judaism but from decisions made about how to apply their interpretations of Paul to their own contemporary cases of inter-Christian conflict.

Most scholars now reject this view as overly simplistic and mistaken, both in its treatment of Judaism at the time of Paul and in its characterization of Roman Catholicism and of other Christian rivals. The understanding of Paul's thought that is behind this view, however, has proven more tenacious. The understanding presented here, and in the related essay "Paul and Judaism" on p. 551, is intended in part to give an alternative and more nuanced analysis of Paul's thought and what he was trying to do within Judaism.

LITERARY HISTORY

It is crucial to attend to the mid-first-century, Greco-Roman cultural and political contexts of Romans' audience as well as the dynamics of that period's minority Jewish community. The minority Christ-following subgroups (*ekklēsiai* = assemblies, usually translated "churches") faced tensions with other Jewish communities (*synagōgai* = assemblies, usually translated "synagogues") in Rome (these are synonymous terms in Gk, not contrastive). Paul was a Jew who saw the subgroup as an authentic expression of Judaism and understood his mission to be one of bringing about the fullness of the aspirations of the Jewish people for the benefit of all people; he was not seeking to found a new religion. He engaged in an outreach to the "members from the other nations/peoples" (i.e., the *ethnē/goyim*/"Gentiles") because he believed that in Jesus the awaited age of God's restoration and rule, beginning with the Jewish community (i.e., Israel), had dawned.

The letter's intended audience was Christ-following Gentiles. These Gentiles needed to understand how they should live as well as how they should interact with the Jewish community, which was larger than their own subgroup, although the Jewish community itself was a minority in Rome. Paul explained how, although they did not practice proselyte conversion (he refers to this rite by terms such as "circumcision" and "works of law" [or "tradition's actions," "tradition's rites"]), they must understand themselves to be full members of the Jewish communities even though they had not become Jews, and even though many Jews were not welcoming them as more than guests if they did not become proselytes. In other words, Paul encouraged them to practice Judaism (the Jewish communal way of life) without becoming Jews. Paul also explains that their turning from idols to the worship of the One God alongside Israelites but remaining representatives from the other nations, as Israelites expected to occur at the end of the ages, would trigger the restoration of "all Israel."

INTERPRETATION

Since Paul cannot get to Rome until he has brought to Jerusalem the collection he has been gathering from among the nations in the Greek east, he writes to prevent further deterioration in the relationships between Christ-follower Gentiles, who are resentful that their claims for full inclusion are not accepted, and the Jews who refuse to accept them. These Gentiles are tempted to presume that they are replacing some Israelites, as if those Jews have lost God's favor. Instead of helping the gospel to succeed, Paul claims their attitudes threaten to undermine God's designs, and Paul writes to change their attitudes. Now that they have accepted the gospel, and thus have acknowledged the God of Israel—without going through the process of becoming Jews/Israelites by undertaking the rite of proselyte conversion ("circumcision" of males)—these non-Jewish followers will help persuade his fellow Jews to see that God's plan for the salvation of all is being fulfilled in Paul's ministry to the nations without the Jews' participation in this privileged task, entrusted to all Israelites at the end of the ages. When they see these non-Jews turning from sin to righteousness, as expected in the awaited day to come, his fellow Jews will then want to emulate him in proclaiming the good news ("gospel") of the arrival of that day to the nations. Thus the salvation of the Gentiles is in part contingent on the original "not persuaded" response to the mission expressed by some Jews, and the salvation of all Israel is contingent on the Gentiles' humble and respectful attitude toward that Jewish community, thereby validating Paul's claim to be carrying out Israel's awaited role of turning all humankind to the One Creator God worshiped among the Jewish people.

Mark D. Nanos

1 Paul, a servant[a] of Jesus Christ, called to be an apostle, set apart for the gospel of God, [2] which he promised beforehand through his prophets in the holy scriptures, [3] the gospel concerning his Son, who was descended from David according to the flesh [4] and was declared to be Son of God with power according to the spirit[b] of holiness by resurrection from the dead, Jesus Christ our Lord, [5] through whom we have received grace and apostleship to bring about the obedience of faith among all the Gentiles for the sake of his name, [6] includ-

[a] Gk *slave*
[b] Or *Spirit*

1.1–15: Salutation, thanksgiving, introduction of issues. Paul introduces his occupation as a herald of God's good news about Jesus Christ, the descendant of David who is the Messiah awaited by Israel. Christ will also rescue the nations, as promised in scripture. The letter opening represents formal features of Roman diplomatic correspondence, clarifying sender, who is represented, by what authority, and to whom written. **1–2:** *An apostle*, lit., "one sent"; i.e., herald; *gospel*, lit., "message of good news"; Paul is *set apart* to declare God's victory, cf. Isa 6.8; 49.1; 52.7–10; 61.1–9; Jer 1.5; *Pss. Sol.* 11.1; 1QH 18.14. **3:** *Son*, Jesus is defined as Christ and Lord/Master; sonship involves an obligation to reign righteously or be disciplined. Cf. 2 Sam 7.8–16; Ps 2.7 of the Davidic king; Israel is also the son of God (Ex 4.22–23; Hos 11.1) as are angels (Gen 6.2,4; Deut 32.8 [LXX]). This royal claim has political implications for the Jewish people (Ps 2.8; Acts 2.36; 13.33; *Pss. Sol.* 17.3,21), and involves an implicit challenge to a Roman emperor being the "son of a god" (e.g., Claudius, Nero), as well as to his client kings in Judea (e.g., Herod Agrippa II). **4:** *Son of God* is a Judaic notion of royal as well as priestly authority, here appealed to in order to demonstrate Jesus Christ as their Lord and Son of God with power as set apart by the spirit (or Spirit) of holiness. This stands in direct contrast to the apotheosis of the caesars to demonstrate their claims to be gods upon death, and thus, their heirs to the throne thereafter to be known as "sons of god." That Jesus is the anointed one (as "mashiaḥ" = anointed one) is witnessed by both heaven (spirit = divine empowerment) and earth (flesh = human, Davidic descent, v. 3). Resurrection bears witness to God's action in a way that defies the nature of the present age, declaring thereby that the age to come has begun in the present age, the dawning of the awaited age of the Creator God's reign on earth over all the nations, through Israel's king. **5:** *Grace* (Gk "charis" = lovingkindness; or benefaction/favor; Heb "ḥesed"); *obedience of faith* (or faithful obedience); both words overlap in meaning: "hypakoē" translates the Heb "shema" ("to hear/listen," in the sense of "to obey").

FAITH (1.8)

Paul uses the word *pistis* and cognates throughout the letter. It is usually translated "faith," but the alternative "faithfulness" is a better translation for the Pauline epistles. In 3.3, the NRSV recognizes that *pistis tou theou* is not "faith of God" but "faithfulness of God"; cf. 1 Thess 1.8–9. *Pistis* does not signify mere acknowledgment of a truth claim, or stand, in contrast to works. Rather, like Heb *'emunah*, it signifies loyalty and trust, which include appropriate behavior; hence, faithfulness. Where Paul contrasts faithfulness to deeds, he is actually contrasting two different propositions for two different groups (non-Jews or Jews), and thus two different ways of being faithful (by non-Jews, apart from circumcision and thus not under Mosaic covenant obligations because they do not become Jews/Israelites; by Jews, including circumcision and concomitant Mosaic covenant obligations). Paul opposes the idea that the faithfulness of Christ-following Gentiles should be measured by the obligation of faithfulness to proselyte conversion, which he indicates generally by reference to "circumcision" or "works of law." Later, in the argument of Romans, especially chs 6–8; 11–15, Paul defines the faithful lifestyle expected of Gentiles.

ing yourselves who are called to belong to Jesus Christ,

[7] To all God's beloved in Rome, who are called to be saints:

Grace to you and peace from God our Father and the Lord Jesus Christ.

[8] First, I thank my God through Jesus Christ for all of you, because your faith is proclaimed throughout the world. [9] For God, whom I serve with my spirit by announcing the gospel[a] of his Son, is my witness that without ceasing I remember you always in my prayers, [10] asking that by God's will I may somehow at last succeed in coming to you. [11] For I am longing to see you so that I may share with you some spiritual gift to strengthen you— [12] or rather so that we may be mutually encouraged by each other's faith, both yours and mine. [13] I want you to know, brothers and sisters,[b] that I have often intended to come to you (but thus far have been prevented), in order that I may reap some harvest among you as I have among the rest of the Gentiles. [14] I am a debtor both to Greeks and to barbarians, both to the wise and to the foolish [15]—hence my eagerness to proclaim the gospel to you also who are in Rome.

[16] For I am not ashamed of the gospel; it is the power of God for salvation to everyone

[a] Gk *my spirit in the gospel*
[b] Gk *brothers*

Greek "ethnē," often translated *Gentiles,* literally refers to "peoples/nations," usually to the groups of people or nations (Heb "goyim") other than Israel, although the word can refer to Israel, which is a people/nation as well. Hence, when being contrasted with Israel/Israelites/Jews, the reference is to "the people of the other nations." **7:** *Saints* (Gk "hagioi," those set apart [to God]/holy ones). Note that Paul does not use "Christians" here, an indication that the term was not in use yet, and neither was there a separate institutional identity of Christianity. **7:** *Father,* cf. Ps 103.13. **8:** *Faith,* or "faithfulness." **11:** *To strengthen,* lit., "to establish, settle." The *spiritual gift* Paul longs to impart is likely his apostolic proclamation of the gospel to the Jew first and then the Greek, making plain to them how they fit into God's plan for the nations as a part of God's plan for Israel. Lack of this understanding is a root cause of the problems he perceives among them that the letter seeks to address until he can arrive. **13–15:** Cf. 15.28. **13:** *Brothers and sisters,* Gk "adelphoi" can extend beyond masculine referents. **14:** *Barbarians,* i.e., those who do not speak Greek.

1.16–32: The evil of humankind. Paul begins to explain the gospel and his commitment to its success in spite of obstacles, especially the failure of humankind to obey God. God's faithfulness is demonstrated in the faithfulness of Christ, which rescues everyone. Paul refers to Hab 2.4 to declare that "the righteous (or just) live by their faith." In Habakkuk, this likely refers to Israelites standing together loyally in the face of adversity. The wicked behavior described may represent stereotypes of Roman rulers, who undermine the values they claim to represent. From this point through ch 3, the obligation of non-Jews to do what is right/just and their culpability for failing to do so, even though they do not have the Torah, are central aspects of Paul's argument. **16:** Paul claims he is *not ashamed* of the gospel's power to save (rescue) everyone who is faithful to this message,

who has faith, to the Jew first and also to the Greek. [17] For in it the righteousness of God is revealed through faith for faith; as it is written, "The one who is righteous will live by faith."[a]

[18] For the wrath of God is revealed from heaven against all ungodliness and wickedness of those who by their wickedness suppress the truth. [19] For what can be known about God is plain to them, because God has shown it to them. [20] Ever since the creation of the world his eternal power and divine nature, invisible though they are, have been understood and seen through the things he has made. So they are without excuse; [21] for though they knew God, they did not honor him as God or give thanks to him, but they became futile in their thinking, and their senseless minds were darkened. [22] Claiming to be wise, they became fools; [23] and they exchanged the glory of the immortal God for images resembling a mortal human being or birds or four-footed animals or reptiles.

[24] Therefore God gave them up in the lusts of their hearts to impurity, to the degrading of their bodies among themselves, [25] because they exchanged the truth about God for a lie and worshiped and served the creature rather than the Creator, who is blessed forever! Amen.

[26] For this reason God gave them up to degrading passions. Their women exchanged

[a] Or *The one who is righteous through faith will live*

the Jew first and also . . . the Greek; this suggests that he is engaged in apologetics, in resolving a theodicy. His audience may have been wavering about whether the gospel's proposition had failed to accomplish its claims, or they were perhaps being pressed to answer the suspicions of others. Paul hereafter would seem to be (re)asserting the gospel proposition that the tiny subject-nation of Israel has produced the Lord of the world instead of Rome. The theme of Jews first and then the rest of the peoples/nations continues throughout the letter and can communicate both chronological developments and prioritization, but also that, ultimately, everyone will answer to the gospel proposition. *Salvation,* (or rescue/restoration) from oppressive forces of the present evil age, and the appearance that the judgments of the Roman regime represent justice according to the gods. *Who has faith,* or who is being faithful. **17:** Hab 2.4, which can also be translated "But the righteous/just one out of faithfulness will live," could refer to believers living faithfully, or to Christ as the "righteous one who lives out faithfulness." To this faithfulness Jews and Gentiles are obliged to respond in faithful obedience. Cf. Isa 51.4–5; 52.10; Ps 98.2–3; Rom 5.18–19. *Righteousness,* or justice; i.e., one who keeps covenant faithfulness; Heb "tzedek." **18–19:** The alternative to living faithfully is suppressing the truth about God being and doing what is right. The *wrath of God* is revealed by the ones who live unjustly, mirroring how the justice of God is revealed by the ones who live faithfully. **20–32:** The plain truth about the *Creator* has been subverted by the worship of created beings. Cf. Wis 13.1–9. The likely contrast is to the Roman regime; cf. 1QpHab 3–7, for a similar Qumran community indictment of Rome, also appealing to Habakkuk. Many of the specific elements may signify behavior associated with recent emperors as representatives of stereotypes of non-Jewish cultural norms; see Suetonius, *Gaius* 22–58; *Nero* 26–35; Philo, *Leg. Gai.* 14–15; 89–90; 97; 107; 118. **21:** *Honor,* lit., "glorify"; cf. Heb "kavod." *They became,* lit., "they were made." **24:** *Gave them up,* lit., "handed them over." **26–27:** Paul's discourse apparently reflects contemporary Greco-Roman as well as Jewish moralists' cultural ideals for the male's domination of the female. A man was not to take the passive (soft) role of the subordinate or a woman to take the penetrating role of the superior, an arrangement that was undermined in same-sex relations, but equally of concern in heterosexual relations; cf. Diod. Sic. 32.10.4.9; 32.10.9.3; Cicero, *Verr.* 2.1.140; *Philipp.* 6.4; *Cael.* 32, 67; *Clu.* 18; Dio Chrys., *Or.* (*Euboicus*) 7.133–52; Philo, *Spec. Laws* 1.50; 3.37–42; *T. Abr.* 135–37; Pseudo-Phocylides, *Sent.* 190–93.; Wis 14.16; see Lev 18.22; 20.13. Alternatively, Paul could be appealing to the command in Gen 1.28 to procreate as that which is natural, and thus censoring uncontrolled sexual desire in marriage, noncoital relations in marriage, or same-sex relations, because in each of these cases the "proper-natural" desire to procreate is subverted. **26–32:** Thus God handed over idolaters (including those making rival claims to be sons of the gods) to unrighteous lifestyles, such as are listed, making manifest their foolishness and weakness instead of ostensible wisdom and power. That things will not turn out as they presently might appear to be is witnessed even in the unrighteous behavior to which the just God has handed them over. For indictments of this kind of depraved behavior, including insatiable sexual lust by Gaius Caligula, see Suetonius, *Gaius* 22–58 (for a Roman report), and Philo, *Leg. Gai.* 14–15; 89–90; 97; 107; 118 (for a Jewish report); for Nero, see Suetonius, *Nero* 26–35.

DIATRIBE (2.1)

Paul employs the rhetorical technique of diatribe here and throughout Romans. Like character portrayals in a drama, diatribe, which is speech-in-character, creates attitudes to which the audience is expected to relate, whether positively or negatively. Changes of voice from singular to plural and first to second or third person are regular characteristics. Thus, Paul may be asking the questions, or putting them in the mouth of the interlocutor (or interlocutors), or some of each. The diatribe form presents the interpreter with several problems, including separating Paul's views from those he attributes to his interlocutors. The original letter was probably delivered by a letter carrier (Phoebe; cf. 16.1) in a way that included acting out the parts.

natural intercourse for unnatural, [27] and in the same way also the men, giving up natural intercourse with women, were consumed with passion for one another. Men committed shameless acts with men and received in their own persons the due penalty for their error.

[28] And since they did not see fit to acknowledge God, God gave them up to a debased mind and to things that should not be done. [29] They were filled with every kind of wickedness, evil, covetousness, malice. Full of envy, murder, strife, deceit, craftiness, they are gossips, [30] slanderers, God-haters,[a] insolent, haughty, boastful, inventors of evil, rebellious toward parents, [31] foolish, faithless, heartless, ruthless. [32] They know God's decree, that those who practice such things deserve to die—yet they not only do them but even applaud others who practice them.

2 Therefore you have no excuse, whoever you are, when you judge others; for in passing judgment on another you condemn yourself, because you, the judge, are doing the very same things. [2] You say,[b] "We know that God's judgment on those who do such things is in accordance with truth." [3] Do you imagine, whoever you are, that when you judge those who do such things and yet do them yourself, you will escape the judgment of God? [4] Or do you despise the riches of his kindness and forbearance and patience? Do you not realize that God's kindness is meant to lead you to repentance? [5] But by your hard and impenitent heart you are storing up wrath for yourself on the day of wrath, when God's righteous judgment will be revealed. [6] For he will repay according to each one's deeds: [7] to those who by patiently doing good seek for glory and honor and immortality, he will give eternal life; [8] while for those who are self-seeking and who obey not the truth but wickedness, there will be wrath and fury. [9] There will be anguish and distress for everyone who does evil, the Jew first and also the Greek, [10] but glory and honor and peace for everyone who does

[a] Or *God-hated*
[b] Gk lacks *You say*

2.1–16: Human responsibility and divine judgment. This ch is framed as dialogues with a hypothetical Gentile's response and a Jewish teacher of Gentiles' reponse to the gospel's condemnation of unrighteous intentions and behavior; it claims that judging the unrighteous is not the congregation's place. That they themselves recognize a standard to which all should be held is itself a demonstration of their culpability, not their superiority. Those who know that God is just should be concerned with their own intention to do what is right rather than seeking to justify their behavior by the failures of others to live rightly. This difference may not always be evident in comparative social terms, but those who use legal means to subvert what is right, as well as those who outright reject doing right, will be judged by the Righteous One, just as will be those who seek to do right in all things. There is no reason to question whether God's righteousness is demonstrated by the unfaithful as well as the faithful: God is benevolent and holds everyone accountable. The ch as a whole undermines any notion that Paul separates responsibility to behave faithfully from the act of faith itself. **2:** *You say,* not in Gk. **4:** *Kindness . . . lead you to repentance,* see e.g., Num 14.18; Prov 3.11–12. **5:** *Day of wrath,* see Isa 2.12; 13.9,13; Zeph 1.15. **6:** Ps 62.12 [Heb 13], which brings up the topic of "deeds." **6–8:** Cf. Hab 2.3; 3.16–19. **7:** *Eternal life,* or an end-of-ages way of life lived in the present age. **8:** *Self-seeking,* or promoting strife/judging; *but wickedness,* or persuading to unrighteousness. **9:** *Who does evil,* lit., "for every soul of a human who oppresses the wronged."

LAW (2.12)

Nomos is usually translated "law" and often understood to mean Torah, "Teaching/Instruction." (See "The Law," p. 515.) But in many cases, Paul may be referring to the law of a particular people, whether Jewish, Roman, Greek, etc. In some cases, such as in ch 4, Paul uses *nomos* to refer to circumcision, but not to Torah more broadly. He also uses *nomos* in chs 7 and 8 to refer to the bond of marriage and of sin and death as well as of faith, life, and Christ.

good, the Jew first and also the Greek. [11] For God shows no partiality.

[12] All who have sinned apart from the law will also perish apart from the law, and all who have sinned under the law will be judged by the law. [13] For it is not the hearers of the law who are righteous in God's sight, but the doers of the law who will be justified. [14] When Gentiles, who do not possess the law, do instinctively what the law requires, these, though not having the law, are a law to themselves. [15] They show that what the law requires is written on their hearts, to which their own conscience also bears witness; and their conflicting thoughts will accuse or perhaps excuse them [16] on the day when, according to my gospel, God, through Jesus Christ, will judge the secret thoughts of all.

[17] But if you call yourself a Jew and rely on the law and boast of your relation to God [18] and know his will and determine what is best because you are instructed in the law, [19] and if you are sure that you are a guide to the blind, a light to those who are in darkness, [20] a corrector of the foolish, a teacher of children, having in the law the embodiment of knowledge and truth, [21] you, then, that teach others, will you not teach yourself? While you preach against stealing, do you steal? [22] You that forbid adultery, do you commit adultery? You that abhor idols, do you rob temples? [23] You that boast in the law, do you dishonor God by breaking the law? [24] For, as it is written, "The name of God is blasphemed among the Gentiles because of you."

[25] Circumcision indeed is of value if you obey the law; but if you break the law, your circumcision has become uncircumcision. [26] So, if those

11: Cf. Deut 10.17. **12:** Or as many as sinned (erred) lawlessly (Gk "anomōs," lawbreakers), will perish lawlessly, and as many as sinned by law (Gk "en nomos," law manipulators, those who use a law in ways that violate the ideals of that law), will be judged through law. **13:** *Justified*, lit., "made righteous," legitimated. **15–16:** Cf. Eccl 12.13–14. *Hearts* signifies real intentions; *secret thoughts of all*, lit., "hidden (intentions) of humans."

2.17–29: The responsibility of Jewish teachers. Turning from a dialogue with a hypothetical non-Jew's response to the gospel's condemnation of unrighteous intentions and behavior versus reward for righteous intentions and behavior, Paul enters into a hypothetical dialogue with a fictive Jewish teacher of Gentiles. Since Paul's target audience is Gentile Christ-followers, this turn to an imaginary Jewish interlocutor may serve as a rhetorical gambit to emphasize the message that no instructors, not even Jewish teachers, are above the judgment of the all-knowing God—nor would they be expected to claim to be. It is not Jewishness but pretentiousness and hypocrisy that are at issue. The overall message is that God always does right and seeks representatives among Israel and the nations who are fully committed to living by as well as teaching those values, and not masking either intentions or behavior behind mere appearances, which can perhaps hide hypocrisy from each other but not from God. It is not clear that there is any such Jew among Paul's audience; this is a rhetorical device to teach non-Jews Jewish values, not to criticize Jewish values, although traditional interpretations suggest otherwise. **17–24:** Epictetus, the Stoic-Cynic, offers similar criticism of those who call themselves philosophers but do not live accordingly—with which any philosopher would be expected to agree (*Diatr.* 2.19.19; 3.7.17; 3.22.93–94; 3.24.40–43; 4.8–9). **17:** The phrasing is theoretical ("if"), and ambiguous. The fictive interlocutor is portrayed as if claiming the title of Jew and as if a teacher of Gentiles. *Boast of your relation to God*, lit., "boast/exult in God"; "of your relation to" not in Gk. **18–20:** The point is not that one should not exult in God, or that Torah is at fault, but that it is self-evident that those who teach it should observe it. **23:** *Boast*, or "glory." **24:** Altered form of Isa 52.5 LXX. Isaiah was indicting the nations, not Israel or even, as Paul adapts it, certain hypocritical Israelites. Paul describes the opposite outcome from what should result when Israelites announce God's righteousness to the Gentiles. **25:** *Is of value*, lit., "helps"; *break*, lit., "stand beside"; *uncircumcision*, lit.,

CIRCUMCISION AND "WORKS OF LAW" (2.25)

"Circumcision" is a marker in males. For eight-day-old boys born to Jews, it signifies their identity within a Jewish family. For non-Jews, whom Paul is usually discussing when referring to circumcision, it signifies (male) completion of the rite of transformation into Jewish identity, i.e., proselyte conversion. Paul refers to this rite as *ergōn nomou*, which is usually translated "works of law." Paul uses the phrase to indicate the completion of the "actions" or "rites" involved in this identity transformation process, i.e., "actions/rites according to convention/tradition" or "tradition's actions/rites" for non-Jews to become Jews. It is this particular matter that Paul disputes with the contrast between faithfulness and works of law, for he upholds that Gentiles who turn to God because of the faithfulness of Christ are to remain non-Israelites, and that is the faithful way to live. In contrast, Paul expects Jews to circumcise their sons as the faithful way to live. Similarly, for Paul, the Torah was given to Israel to guide behavior, to demonstrate the righteousness of God to the nations, but it was not given to the nations. Paul argues from the viewpoint that circumcision is an advantage for (male) Jews, because it marks them as dedicated to God's righteousness, and thus also they are deeply aware of sin and the need for God's mercy and forgiveness (cf. 3.1–2,20).

who are uncircumcised keep the requirements of the law, will not their uncircumcision be regarded as circumcision? [27] Then those who are physically uncircumcised but keep the law will condemn you that have the written code and circumcision but break the law. [28] For a person is not a Jew who is one outwardly, nor is true circumcision something external and physical. [29] Rather, a person is a Jew who is one inwardly, and real circumcision is a matter of the heart—it is spiritual and not literal. Such a person receives praise not from others but from God.

3 Then what advantage has the Jew? Or what is the value of circumcision? [2] Much, in every way. For in the first place the Jews[a] were entrusted with the oracles of God. [3] What if some were unfaithful? Will their faithlessness nullify the faithfulness of God? [4] By no means! Although everyone is a liar, let God be proved true, as it is written,

[a] Gk *they*

"foreskin." The point of this statement is not to accuse Jews of hypocrisy but to help non-Jews carry out the Jewish value of avoiding hypocrisy.

Paul does not write "uncircumcision" and cognates, but "foreskin" and cognates throughout. **26:** If—without the benefit of Torah, or circumcision, which signifies commitment to Torah—a Gentile observed the intent of Torah by observing comparable laws of moral and civil behavior, that would signify what circumcision is meant to signify. Paul makes the same point as in 2.14–16. Paul affirms that the requirements of Torah are righteous, although this inference in the Gk is omitted in the translation. **27:** Therefore an intentionally righteous Gentile accomplishing the intention of Torah, yet without the benefit of circumcision or Torah guidance, would logically stand in judgment of an intentionally hypocritical (male) Jew. *Physically uncircumcised,* lit., "foreskinned from birth"; i.e., not circumcised at eight days of age, as are (male) Jews; *keep,* lit., "accomplish the goal." **28:** Paul refers to the ideals to which circumcised flesh for Jewish males bears witness: *For a person is not a Jew who is one outwardly,* lit., "for the Jew is not (ultimately) the one conspicuously known to be (a Jew)"; *nor is true* (Gk lacks "true") *circumcision something external and physical,* lit., "nor is the one known to be circumcised in the flesh thereby necessarily the ideal Jew." **29:** Paul's point is not that Gentiles are the true Jews, or that the foreskinned are the true or real circumcision; quite the opposite: the terms "Jew" and "circumcision" are reserved for Israelites. *Real circumcision* (Gk lacks "real"); *it is spiritual and not literal,* lit., "by spirit (made manifest in the way one lives), not by inscription (i.e., not [merely] by a cut into the flesh)." Thus this verse could be translated: Rather, the deepest character of the Jew, even the purpose of circumcision, is about the spirit, the intentions of the heart (at work through the way one lives who is so marked), not (merely) inscribed (in flesh) (as if a mark alone fully defined who one is).

3.1–26: God is just, and the one who justifies. 1: The diatribe continues. The interlocutor does not appear to be a Jew, since Jews are referred to in v. 2 as "they." **2:** *The Jews,* lit., "they." The *oracles* or words/prophecies of God; see discussions in 9.30–10.21. **4–5:** God is defended by appeal to Ps 51.6 (LXX 50.6). See also Ps 116.11 (LXX 115.2); 1QS 11.9–14. *Liar . . . true,* even if we all have to be shown to be lying, God will be shown to be true. *Injustice . . . jus-*

CIRCUMCISION OF THE HEART (2.29)

The idea that Israelites require a circumcision of the heart in addition to that of the body is a long-standing Jewish ideal; see Deut 10.16; 30.6; Jer 4.4; 9.25–26; 38.33; Ezek 44.7 (note also Philo, *Spec. Laws* 1.6; *QG* 3.46–52). In the case of Jer 9.25–26, it is specifically the Israelites who are punished for not having circumcised hearts. Paul seems to be working with the same distinction here: it is a special Jewish responsibility to live according to the ideals of being circumcised in the body, that is, to be circumcised in the heart and thus focused on walking humbly in accord with God's will. Such a Jewish person must be intentionally dedicated to righteousness (circumcised heart), and not simply to making an outward show.

GOD IS ONE FOR ALL HUMANITY (3.30)

Paul develops his argument around the oneness of God as upheld in the Shema Israel ("Hear, O Israel, the LORD is our God, the LORD is one"; Deut 6.4; see Rom 10.12–13), to make this case for the creator God as the only God of all humankind. The point is that God is the God of Israel specifically (the LORD is *our* God), yet not "only" the God of Israel, because if God is God alone (one), then there is no other god for the other nations who turn to God in Christ. Israel's God is God of both Israel and the members of the other nations who turn to the one God, and Jesus Christ has been faithful to both simultaneously; thus they remain thereafter identified differently as Jews (circumcised), and members of the nations other than Israel (foreskinned). Cf. *Sifre Deut.* 6.4 (piska 31); Rashi on Deut 6.4.

"So that you may be justified in your
words,
and prevail in your judging."[a]

[5] But if our injustice serves to confirm the justice of God, what should we say? That God is unjust to inflict wrath on us? (I speak in a human way.) [6] By no means! For then how could God judge the world? [7] But if through my falsehood God's truthfulness abounds to his glory, why am I still being condemned as a sinner? [8] And why not say (as some people slander us by saying that we say), "Let us do evil so that good may come"? Their condemnation is deserved!

[9] What then? Are we any better off?[b] No, not at all; for we have already charged that all, both Jews and Greeks, are under the power of sin, [10] as it is written:

"There is no one who is righteous, not
even one;
[11] there is no one who has
understanding,
there is no one who seeks God.
[12] All have turned aside, together they have
become worthless;
there is no one who shows kindness,
there is not even one."
[13] "Their throats are opened graves;
they use their tongues to deceive."
"The venom of vipers is under their lips."
[14] "Their mouths are full of cursing and
bitterness."
[15] "Their feet are swift to shed blood;
[16] ruin and misery are in their paths,
[17] and the way of peace they have not
known."
[18] "There is no fear of God before their
eyes."

[19] Now we know that whatever the law says, it speaks to those who are under the law, so that every mouth may be silenced, and the whole world may be held accountable to God. [20] For "no human being will be justified in

[a] Gk *when you are being judged*
[b] Or *at any disadvantage?*

tice, the fact that our actions or lives are shown to be unjust validates the very idea of justice, since we accept the standard by which we are being judged: *the justice of God.* **9:** *Are under the power of sin,* lit., "are under sin." *Sin* (or error) can dominate human beings; see 6.23. **10:** Eccl 7.20. See also Ps 14.3; 53.4; 1QH 9.14. **11:** Ps 14.2; cf. 53.3. **12:** Ps 14.3. **13–14:** Ps 5.9; 140.3; 10.7. **15–17:** Isa 59.7–8; cf. Prov 1.16. **18:** Ps 36.1. **19:** *It speaks to those who are under the law* (i.e., to Israel, entrusted to announce God's words to the nations), *so that every mouth may be silenced,* thus no one has the right to speak against God's righteousness/justice. **20:** Paul develops the humility of the psalmist's appeal

his sight" by deeds prescribed by the law, for through the law comes the knowledge of sin.

[21] But now, apart from law, the righteousness of God has been disclosed, and is attested by the law and the prophets, [22] the righteousness of God through faith in Jesus Christ[a] for all who believe. For there is no distinction, [23] since all have sinned and fall short of the glory of God; [24] they are now justified by his grace as a gift, through the redemption that is in Christ Jesus, [25] whom God put forward as a sacrifice of atonement[b] by his blood, effective through faith. He did this to show his righteousness, because in his divine forbearance he had passed over the sins previously committed; [26] it was to prove at the present time that he himself is righteous and that he justifies the one who has faith in Jesus.[c]

[27] Then what becomes of boasting? It is excluded. By what law? By that of works? No, but by the law of faith. [28] For we hold that a person is justified by faith apart from works prescribed by the law. [29] Or is God the God of Jews only? Is he not the God of Gentiles also? Yes, of Gentiles also, [30] since God is one; and he will justify the circumcised on the ground of faith and the uncircumcised through that same faith. [31] Do we then overthrow the law by this faith? By no means! On the contrary, we uphold the law.

4 What then are we to say was gained by[d] Abraham, our ancestor according to

[a] Or *through the faith of Jesus Christ*
[b] Or *a place of atonement*
[c] Or *who has the faith of Jesus*
[d] Other ancient authorities read *say about*

to God's righteousness, not his own, in Ps 143.2, and [of the psalmist's appeal] to God's faithfulness in 143.1; cf. *1 En.* 81.5–6; 1QS 11. *By deeds prescribed by the law*, lit., "by works of law," i.e., circumcision (for marking the people of God). An alternative translation is: "Because as a result of (completing transformation by) actions (prescribed by) Torah ["ergōn nomou," "works of law" or "tradition's actions/rites," i.e., the rite of circumcision] not all flesh will be made righteous before him," for through (completing) circumcision comes knowledge of sin (i.e., after becoming dedicated to God's righteousness by the rite of circumcision, one becomes aware when not living according to the conventions of righteousness under Torah, creating awareness of the need for God's forgiveness)." **21:** *Apart from law*, or in addition to a convention (of circumcised, Israelite identity); *attested by the law and the prophets*, i.e., by the "oracles/words of God" which the Jews are to declare to the nations, 3.2; 10.14–15. **22:** Or "the righteousness of God through Jesus Christ's faithfulness for all who are faithful (to it)." *For there is no distinction*, or utterance; i.e., "outcry" against God's justice. "Utterance" for "diastolē," rather than *distinction* (the verb can mean both "distinguish" and "command"; cf. Heb 12.20) brings out the point of v. 19, that everyone is "silenced," i.e., everyone is culpable; cf. 10.12. **24:** *They are now justified by his grace as a gift*, lit., "they are being justified freely by his benefaction." **25:** *Sacrifice of atonement*, lit., "as a place of expiation," draws upon the language of Yom Kippur (Lev 16.13–15; Heb "mercy seat ["kapōret"]"). *By his blood*, lit., "in his blood"; *effective* not in Gk; *through faith*, or through faithfulness. **26:** *And that he justifies the one who has faith in Jesus*, or "and that he [God] because of the faithfulness of Jesus justifies [every]one [i.e., whether Jew or Greek]."

3.27–31: God's faithfulness is for all. The issue throughout these chs is that the faithfulness of God includes non-Jews (foreskinned) as well as Jews (circumcised) among the righteous ones. There is no basis for judging each other inferior, for Jews and Gentiles are equal recipients of God's benefaction in Christ. **27:** *Then what becomes of boasting*, i.e., before other people for being identified as one of the righteous ones. *By that of works*, i.e., by being circumcised. *No, but by the law of faith*, or by faithfulness. **28:** *By faith*, or by faithfulness; *apart from works prescribed by the law*, without circumcision (in this case proselyte conversion); "prescribed by the" is not in Gk. Gentiles are justified by faithfulness to God's revelation in Christ apart from becoming members of Israel. **31:** *Do we then overthrow* (or make obsolete) *the law* (i.e., of circumcision, i.e., by which Israel has been marked and entrusted to announce God's word to the nations) *by this faith*? *We uphold* (establish) *the law* (i.e., the ideal of the circumcision of Israelites is an advantage for Israelites). For the Jew, Christ is the goal of Torah righteousness directly; for the one who is not a Jew, Christ is the goal of Torah righteousness indirectly, for Israel announces Torah righteousness for Jew and non-Jew; see 10.4.

4.1–25: The faithfulness of Abraham, and his descendants. The question now arises: If Gentiles enjoy through Christ the same benefaction as do Jews, without becoming members of Israel, why was Abraham circumcised? Paul argues that although Gentiles do not become children of Israel and thus under Torah, they do

the flesh? [2] For if Abraham was justified by works, he has something to boast about, but not before God. [3] For what does the scripture say? "Abraham believed God, and it was reckoned to him as righteousness." [4] Now to one who works, wages are not reckoned as a gift but as something due. [5] But to one who without works trusts him who justifies the ungodly, such faith is reckoned as righteousness. [6] So also David speaks of the blessedness of those to whom God reckons righteousness apart from works:

[7] "Blessed are those whose iniquities are
forgiven,
and whose sins are covered;
[8] blessed is the one against whom the Lord
will not reckon sin."

[9] Is this blessedness, then, pronounced only on the circumcised, or also on the uncircumcised? We say, "Faith was reckoned to Abraham as righteousness." [10] How then was it reckoned to him? Was it before or after he had been circumcised? It was not after, but before he was circumcised. [11] He received the sign of circumcision as a seal of the righteousness that he had by faith while he was still uncircumcised. The purpose was to make him the ancestor of all who believe without being circumcised and who thus have righteousness reckoned to them, [12] and likewise the ancestor of the circumcised who are not only circumcised but who also follow the example of the faith that our ancestor Abraham had before he was circumcised.

[13] For the promise that he would inherit the world did not come to Abraham or to his descendants through the law but through the righteousness of faith. [14] If it is the adherents of the law who are to be the heirs, faith is null and the promise is void. [15] For the law brings wrath; but where there is no law, neither is there violation.

[16] For this reason it depends on faith, in order that the promise may rest on grace and be guaranteed to all his descendants, not only to the adherents of the law but also to those who share the faith of Abraham (for he is the father of all of us, [17] as it is written, "I have made you the father of many nations")—in the presence of the God in whom he believed,

become children of Abraham, for Abraham was faithful and received the promise of children from many nations before he received circumcision as the sign of that faithfulness for himself and his ethnic descendants. His ethnic descendants know that they are responsible to undertake faithfulness to inherit the promises made to Abraham. They have a special benefaction before those from the other nations, but that does not warrant judging; instead, it involves responsibility to serve. Gentiles who are faithful to the descendant promised to Abraham to restore the world are children of Abraham, on the same ideal terms of faithfulness. Now both groups of descendants are called to live faithfully **2:** *By works,* by deeds; i.e., circumcision of himself and the males of his extended household. *Boast about,* because he is marked as set apart to God. **3:** Gen 15.6. *Abraham believed God,* or Abraham was faithful to God. **5:** *Without works,* lit., "without working"; i.e., without circumcision. **7–8:** Ps 32.1–2. The psalm ends with praise of an upright heart. "Without works/deeds" is not without Torah, but the failure to observe Torah fully, i.e., failure to do right even when one has an upright heart (cf. Ps 32.11); see 3.23. *Iniquities,* lit., "lawbreakings." **9:** Gen 15.6; *pronounced only on the circumcised,* "pronounced" not in Gk. *Faith,* or faithfulness. **12:** Lit., "and father of circumcision not only for those from circumcision, but also for those walking in the footsteps of the one in foreskin, our faithful father Abraham." **13:** See Gen 12.6–7; 15.5; 17.4–5; Isa 54.1–3; Philo, *Rewards.* 158. Paul answers the question posed in 4.1. *Law* ("nomos") does not refer to Torah here but the "convention" of circumcision. "Promise" is a new element in his argument, and it was made to Abraham before the commandment to be circumcised in Gen 17. Cf. Sir 44.19–21. *Descendants,* lit., "seeds." *Through the law,* or through a convention; i.e., circumcision; no article in Gk. **14:** Or for if the heirs are (merely) from a law/convention (i.e., of circumcision). **15:** For the convention (of circumcision) brings contempt for those who seem to be flaunting this God-given convention; but where no convention exists, neither does (the judgment) of sidestepping the work of circumcision (on the part of these non-Jews). **16–17:** Those who follow Abraham's example of trusting God at God's word, i.e., who are faithful, are the very descendants he was promised. Cf. 2 Macc 7.28. Here Paul works with the concept of the "merit of the fathers" (cf. 11.28–29; Lev 26.40–45), that is, with Abraham inheriting what was promised, which for Paul includes those from the other nations who are now turning to God in Christ as well as those who have been faithful to God as Israelites all along. **16:** *It,* i.e., the promised inheritance; *faith,* or faithfulness. *Descendants,* lit., "seed"; *adherents of the law,* "adherents" not in Gk. **17:** Gen 17.5. *In whom he believed,* or to whom

who gives life to the dead and calls into existence the things that do not exist. [18] Hoping against hope, he believed that he would become "the father of many nations," according to what was said, "So numerous shall your descendants be." [19] He did not weaken in faith when he considered his own body, which was already[a] as good as dead (for he was about a hundred years old), or when he considered the barrenness of Sarah's womb. [20] No distrust made him waver concerning the promise of God, but he grew strong in his faith as he gave glory to God, [21] being fully convinced that God was able to do what he had promised. [22] Therefore his faith[b] "was reckoned to him as righteousness." [23] Now the words, "it was reckoned to him," were written not for his sake alone, [24] but for ours also. It will be reckoned to us who believe in him who raised Jesus our Lord from the dead, [25] who was handed over to death for our trespasses and was raised for our justification.

5 Therefore, since we are justified by faith, we[c] have peace with God through our Lord Jesus Christ, [2] through whom we have obtained access[d] to this grace in which we stand; and we[e] boast in our hope of sharing the glory of God. [3] And not only that, but we[e] also boast in our sufferings, knowing that suffering produces endurance, [4] and endurance produces character, and character produces hope, [5] and hope does not disappoint us, because God's love has been poured into our hearts through the Holy Spirit that has been given to us.

[6] For while we were still weak, at the right time Christ died for the ungodly. [7] Indeed, rarely will anyone die for a righteous person—though perhaps for a good person someone might actually dare to die. [8] But God proves his love for us in that while we still were sinners Christ died for us. [9] Much more surely then, now that we have been justified by his blood, will we be saved through him from the wrath of God.[f] [10] For if while we were enemies, we were reconciled to God through

[a] Other ancient authorities lack *already*
[b] Gk *Therefore it*
[c] Other ancient authorities read *let us*
[d] Other ancient authorities add *by faith*
[e] Or *let us*
[f] Gk *the wrath*

he was being faithful. **18–19:** Gen 15.5; 17.2–7, and drawing from vv. 15–27. Abraham was faithful to hope what was "promised" would take place; see Gen 21.1–8. **20–21:** *Faith* (Gk "pistis"), the translation should highlight the meaning "faithfulness" rather than "faith," because Paul is defining a continuum of decisions and concomitant actions based on trust in God's promises. See Gen 17.1,17–22. Paul may be alluding to Abraham's willingness to be circumcised as an act of faithfulness toward being able to father this promised child. *Waver,* or quarrel; *strong,* or able. **22:** *His faith,* not in Gk. Gen 15.6, referring back to Rom 4.3. **24:** *But for ours also,* or but also because of us, making the analogy between Abraham's faith and that of Paul's contemporaries among the followers of Jesus. *Who believe in him,* or who are faithful to him [God]. **25:** *To death,* not in Gk.

5.1–21: The faithfulness of God in Christ. The privileges now gained by these Gentiles should lead to celebration and service rather than judging others. God's Spirit will enable those dedicated to this way of life even if they are not circumcised. Christ (through resurrection) broke a chain of death that began with Adam; now those in Christ are to live responsibly according to a new chain of life, not groping for self-satisfaction, but assured that God will provide. **1–11:** This passage appears to be the voice of a Christ-following Gentile dialogue partner ("we" and "us"), drawing conclusions from what Paul has argued about their equal standing with Jews to this point, or of Paul speaking inclusively for them. Paul explains who they are and how they are to walk in the footsteps of Abraham when he was not yet circumcised (i.e., before circumcision [or Torah]; 4.12). **1:** *We have,* or let us have; see translators' note *c*. **2:** *Grace,* or favor/benefaction. The concept of benefaction revolves around a reciprocal relationship involving a patron having the resources to give to clients gifts (such as work) beyond the means of those receiving them to repay precisely in kind; instead they repay from their means, including by the expression of loyalty (faithfulness), making known the honor and good deeds of the patron, etc. *And we,* other ancient authorities add "by faith/faithfulness." **3:** *But we,* other ancient authorities have "but let us." **5:** *Does not disappoint us,* lit., "is not ashamed." *Holy Spirit,* capitalized to indicate its divine origin (see 1.4; 8.2). The later Christian doctrine of the Holy Spirit as a "person" in the Trinity is not necessarily implied here. **9:** *Wrath of God,* "of God," not in Gk. **10:** *Enemies,* lit., "alienated

the death of his Son, much more surely, having been reconciled, will we be saved by his life. [11] But more than that, we even boast in God through our Lord Jesus Christ, through whom we have now received reconciliation.

[12] Therefore, just as sin came into the world through one man, and death came through sin, and so death spread to all because all have sinned— [13] sin was indeed in the world before the law, but sin is not reckoned when there is no law. [14] Yet death exercised dominion from Adam to Moses, even over those whose sins were not like the transgression of Adam, who is a type of the one who was to come.

[15] But the free gift is not like the trespass. For if the many died through the one man's trespass, much more surely have the grace of God and the free gift in the grace of the one man, Jesus Christ, abounded for the many. [16] And the free gift is not like the effect of the one man's sin. For the judgment following one trespass brought condemnation, but the free gift following many trespasses brings justification. [17] If, because of the one man's trespass, death exercised dominion through that one, much more surely will those who receive the abundance of grace and the free gift of righteousness exercise dominion in life through the one man, Jesus Christ.

[18] Therefore just as one man's trespass led to condemnation for all, so one man's act of righteousness leads to justification and life for all. [19] For just as by the one man's disobedience the many were made sinners, so by the one man's obedience the many will be made righteous. [20] But law came in, with the result that the trespass multiplied; but where sin increased, grace abounded all the more, [21] so that, just as sin exercised dominion in death, so grace might also exercise dominion through justification[a] leading to eternal life through Jesus Christ our Lord.

6 What then are we to say? Should we continue in sin in order that grace may abound? [2] By no means! How can we who died to sin go on living in it? [3] Do you not

[a] Or *righteousness*

ones." *Saved,* or rescued. These non-Jews were formerly alienated from God, worshipping idols, the state of the nations Paul described in 1.18–32. **12–17:** Adam as sinner (similarly, see Wis 2.24; 2 Esd 3.21,26; *2 Bar.* 54.15), vs. Christ as obedient. *Law* ("nomos"), here does not likely refer to Torah, which was not given until Moses. The principle is that one cannot "miss the mark" (sin/err; Heb "ḥt'") until a mark has been set by a convention ("nomos"), and once it has been set and missed, the consequence is distance (death) from the one the convention's ideals express (God). Once Adam sinned, death became a reality for all his descendants, whether they sinned like Adam, or not (e.g., Christ). Adam illustrates the results of sin, i.e., failure to trust the reality of God's command not to eat of the tree of knowledge, and thus he brought about death for all his descendants, just as Christ illustrates the results of faithfulness, trusting God, and thus gaining justification/righteousness for all his spiritual descendants. **13:** *Sin . . . law,* there was, in fact, sin (errors made) even when moral conventions had not yet been established, but it was not possible to take note of sin when moral conventions were not present. *Before the law,* no article in Gk; or before convention; *no law,* or no convention. **14:** *Transgression,* or sidestepping; Gentiles are [metaphorically] sidestepping circumcision yet becoming members of Abraham's family. *A type,* a model. **15–18:** *Free gift,* benefaction; "free" not in Gk. *Trespass,* misstep. *Grace,* or favor. **18:** *Led to condemnation,* led to a sentence of death. *Justification and life,* "and" not in Gk; lit., "justified living." **21:** *Eternal life,* see 2.7n.

6.1–23: The faithful obedience of life in Christ. The argument is continued in diatribe style, though the particular speakers are sometimes not clear (see "Diatribe," p. 257). Gentiles who have turned to God because of the faithfulness of Christ are obliged to live faithfully to the new life; although they are technically not under Torah since they are not Israelites/Jews, they are to dedicate themselves to righteousness. It is self-evident that those from the nations who have turned to God because of the faithfulness of Christ are obliged to be faithful to the new life that this initiates, a life no longer dominated by the judgmentalism of sin and death but by the service of doing what is right. Just as those from the other nations lived in Adam, now they are to live in Christ. Although these ones faithful to Christ are not under Torah, since they are from the other nations and not circumcised, they are to dedicate themselves to righteousness. It is possible that the issue revolves around how these males are to signify their standing as righteous ones apart from circumcision. Thus, in euphemistic

know that all of us who have been baptized into Christ Jesus were baptized into his death? [4] Therefore we have been buried with him by baptism into death, so that, just as Christ was raised from the dead by the glory of the Father, so we too might walk in newness of life.

[5] For if we have been united with him in a death like his, we will certainly be united with him in a resurrection like his. [6] We know that our old self was crucified with him so that the body of sin might be destroyed, and we might no longer be enslaved to sin. [7] For whoever has died is freed from sin. [8] But if we have died with Christ, we believe that we will also live with him. [9] We know that Christ, being raised from the dead, will never die again; death no longer has dominion over him. [10] The death he died, he died to sin, once for all; but the life he lives, he lives to God. [11] So you also must consider yourselves dead to sin and alive to God in Christ Jesus.

[12] Therefore, do not let sin exercise dominion in your mortal bodies, to make you obey their passions. [13] No longer present your members to sin as instruments[a] of wickedness, but present yourselves to God as those who have been brought from death to life, and present your members to God as instruments[a] of righteousness. [14] For sin will have no dominion over you, since you are not under law but under grace.

[15] What then? Should we sin because we are not under law but under grace? By no means! [16] Do you not know that if you present yourselves to anyone as obedient slaves, you are slaves of the one whom you obey, either of sin, which leads to death, or of obedience, which leads to righteousness? [17] But thanks be to God that you, having once been slaves of sin, have become obedient from the heart to the form of teaching to which you were entrusted, [18] and that you, having been set free from sin, have become slaves of righteousness. [19] I am speaking in human terms because of your natural limitations.[b] For just as you once presented your members as slaves to impurity and to greater and greater iniquity, so now present your members as slaves to righteousness for sanctification.

[20] When you were slaves of sin, you were free in regard to righteousness. [21] So what advantage did you then get from the things of which you now are ashamed? The end of those things is death. [22] But now that you have been freed from sin and enslaved to God, the advantage you get is sanctification. The end is eternal life. [23] For the wages of sin is death, but the free gift of God is eternal life in Christ Jesus our Lord.

[a] Or *weapons*
[b] Gk *the weakness of your flesh*

terms, even though foreskinned, they are responsible to dedicate their limbs not to the patterns of sin and death described in 1.18–32, for they are set apart to God and to righteous living. **1:** It may be that the Gentile interlocutor responds to Paul's argument in ch 5. **3:** *Death*, presumably death to sin. **5:** *For if*, or for since. **7:** *Freed*, lit., "justified." **8:** *Believe*, or trust. **10:** *Died to sin . . . lives to God*, perhaps meaning that as far as sin is concerned, Christ is as if dead and therefore impervious; as far as God is concerned, Christ is alive. *Once for all*, though the death was a singular event in the past, it is operative (in a way not specified) on behalf of anyone and everyone now. **11:** Cf. 4 Macc 7.19. **12:** *To make you obey their passions*, or, to listen obediently [to] its covetousnesses/intense lusts. Paul thinks the body needs to be tamed. **13:** *Members*, lit., "limbs"; by extension, organs (1 Cor 12.14). Paul may be personifying the "limbs" to refer to the penis that has been in dispute, and thus, to the implications for Gentiles: see Philo, *Migr.* 92: "because the rite of circumcision is an emblem of the excision of pleasures and of all the passions"; *Spec. Laws* 1.8–10; *Virtues* 214. **16:** *Slaves*, the choice is not whether to be slaves or free; the choice is which master one is going to belong to. **17:** Paul may be alluding to a specific code of conduct applicable to Gentile Christ-followers, such as the "Apostolic Decree," in lieu of the instruction that would have applied to them if they had undertaken proselyte conversion; see Acts 15.19–21,27–32; 16.4–5. *From the heart*, with deep intention. **19:** *In human terms*, using an analogy to the human institution of slavery. *Your natural limitations*, lit., "the weakness of your flesh." *Iniquity*, lit., "lawlessness," as described in 1.18–32. **20–23:** *Slaves*, see v. 16n. *Advantage*, lit., "fruit." *End*, goal, outcome, prize." *Enslaved to God*, Lev 25.55. *Sanctification*, being set apart to God, therefore not behaving according to other cultural norms. *Eternal life*, see 2.7n. *Free gift*, benefaction; "free" not in Gk.

7 Do you not know, brothers and sisters[a]—for I am speaking to those who know the law—that the law is binding on a person only during that person's lifetime? [2] Thus a married woman is bound by the law to her husband as long as he lives; but if her husband dies, she is discharged from the law concerning the husband. [3] Accordingly, she will be called an adulteress if she lives with another man while her husband is alive. But if her husband dies, she is free from that law, and if she marries another man, she is not an adulteress.

[4] In the same way, my friends,[a] you have died to the law through the body of Christ, so that you may belong to another, to him who has been raised from the dead in order that we may bear fruit for God. [5] While we were living in the flesh, our sinful passions, aroused by the law, were at work in our members to bear fruit for death. [6] But now we are discharged from the law, dead to that which held us captive, so that we are slaves not under the old written code but in the new life of the Spirit.

[7] What then should we say? That the law is sin? By no means! Yet, if it had not been for the law, I would not have known sin. I would not have known what it is to covet if the law had not said, "You shall not covet." [8] But sin, seizing an opportunity in the commandment, produced in me all kinds of covetousness. Apart from the law sin lies dead. [9] I was once alive apart from the law, but when the com-

[a] Gk *brothers*

7.1–25: Freedom from sin and death, enabled to live rightly. Paul begins with an analogy to the law/convention of marriage and how it no longer binds a spouse to that partner once the other party has died; likewise, the convention since Adam of children of the nations being slaves of sin no longer binds the audience. They are now bound to a new life in Christ. The language is very difficult to follow: the same terms are used but with different referents and implications along the way, and the prevailing psychological interpretations are themselves suspect. The goal of the argument is evident by the end of it, and in keeping with that which has been argued in the previous chs: it is that these members from the other nations who have turned to God in Christ are not bound to live according to the limitations of their previous identity in Adam, in sin leading to death, but in righteousness, because they now live in Christ. They are not circumcised and so not under Torah, because they are not Israelites, but they are nevertheless now free from the law of sin to live a life such as Torah describes, a life lived according to God's standards, and not those of sin and death. The next ch seeks to explain how to be enabled to live this righteous way of life, although still living with the conflicts that the body creates between what one approves of as right and what one nevertheless desires passionately to have that is not right. **1:** The previous argument is continued. *The law* or a convention; no article in Gk. "Nomos" (law) is not restricted to Jewish, Roman, or any other specific law in ch 7. Although translated "law" throughout in the NRSV, the referent changes throughout this argument. **2–3:** As the wife is no longer bound to her deceased husband, these Gentiles are no longer bound to Adam, but to Christ. **2:** *Is bound by the law*, a convention [i.e., of marriage]; no article in Gk. **3:** *She is not an adulteress*, i.e., sidestepper of that law/convention, since it no longer applies to her. **4:** *You have died to the law*, i.e., of sin, binding you to Adam. The law or convention from which they are freed was not Torah, for they were slaves to the law of sin, bound to Adam (6.16–21). The convention or law of sin is what 1.18–32 had spelled out, which had brought death to Adam's descendants. **5:** *Aroused by the law*, i.e., of sin, active for those bound to Adam. *Members*, lit., "limbs." **6:** *Discharged from the law*, i.e., of sin as descendants of Adam. *So that we are slaves not under the old written code*, or in order to serve as slaves in newness of spirit and not [as slaves] to an ancient inscription [i.e., a cut in the body]. Compare Philo discussing conversion as the change of life from old customs ("fabulous inventions") to becoming servants of God (e.g., *Spec. Laws* 1.51–53, 308–14; *Virtues* 214). **7–12:** Presuming that the voice in this section picks up from v. 4, we have the case of the wife introduced in vv. 1–4. Should the wife uncontrollably desire another man while her husband is still alive, acting on that desire would express what the "do not covet" commandment forbids. Paul's argument here is difficult to follow: this difficulty is partly due to the conflicted nature of the predicament to which the argument drives. On the centrality of covetousness as "the source of all evils," see Philo, *Spec. Laws* 4.79–99, and Epictetus, *Diatr.* 24.84–118. **7:** *If the law had not said* appears to refer to God's command to Adam; cf. Gen 2.16–17; 3.1–24. *Covet*, i.e., overwhelming desire for what is not yours. **8:** *An opportunity*, or a pretext. *In me*, i.e., in Adam and thus his descendants. *Apart from the law sin lies dead*, lit., "For without (a) law sin is dead" (there must be a norm in order to err according to it). *Commandment*, i.e., do not covet (Ex 20.17; Deut 5.21). **9:** Lit., "Now I was alive without the law formerly, but arrival of the commandment (see v. 7) enlivens the sin." In other words, the very existence of a prohibition can cause one

mandment came, sin revived [10] and I died, and the very commandment that promised life proved to be death to me. [11] For sin, seizing an opportunity in the commandment, deceived me and through it killed me. [12] So the law is holy, and the commandment is holy and just and good.

[13] Did what is good, then, bring death to me? By no means! It was sin, working death in me through what is good, in order that sin might be shown to be sin, and through the commandment might become sinful beyond measure.

[14] For we know that the law is spiritual; but I am of the flesh, sold into slavery under sin.[a] [15] I do not understand my own actions. For I do not do what I want, but I do the very thing I hate. [16] Now if I do what I do not want, I agree that the law is good. [17] But in fact it is no longer I that do it, but sin that dwells within me. [18] For I know that nothing good dwells within me, that is, in my flesh. I can will what is right, but I cannot do it. [19] For I do not do the good I want, but the evil I do not want is what I do. [20] Now if I do what I do not want, it is no longer I that do it, but sin that dwells within me.

[21] So I find it to be a law that when I want to do what is good, evil lies close at hand. [22] For I delight in the law of God in my inmost self, [23] but I see in my members another law at war with the law of my mind, making me captive to the law of sin that dwells in my members. [24] Wretched man that I am! Who will rescue me from this body of death? [25] Thanks be to God through Jesus Christ our Lord!

So then, with my mind I am a slave to the law of God, but with my flesh I am a slave to the law of sin.

8 There is therefore now no condemnation for those who are in Christ Jesus. [2] For the law of the Spirit[b] of life in Christ

[a] Gk *sold under sin*
[b] Or *spirit*

to recognize the wrongfulness of the prohibited act. **10:** Lit., "and the commandment that is (to lead) into life [possibly Gen 3.22–23; see also Lev 18.5; Deut 30.6], is being discovered by me (to lead) into death." **11–12:** It is not the action of the commandment that leads to death, but the reaction of the one who receives the commandment. *And through it killed me*, "me" not in Gk. **13–25:** Continuation of the argument for the power of sin at work in the body, even for the one who wills in the mind to do right. **13:** This leads to the next logical question: Should the "good" commandment not then be given? Would Adam have been better off if not told to refrain from eating of the tree? The answer is an unequivocal no. It revealed sin to be bringing about death, which would have otherwise gone unrealized, and thus not clearly to be avoided at all costs. **14:** *Spiritual*, possibly having to do with spiritual matters, e.g., honesty, righteousness, etc. *Of the flesh*, lit., "fleshly." *Sold into slavery under sin*, lit., "sold to being under sin (error)"; "into slavery" not in Gk. Cf. Isa 50.1; 11QPs[a] 19.9–10. **15–23:** The rabbis (*Sifre Deut.* 32) identify these conflicting impulses as "yetzer ha-tov" (the good inclination) and "yetzer ha-ra" (the evil inclination). Similar struggles are discussed in 1QS 3.15–4.26; Epictetus, *Diatr.* 2.26.4. **21–23:** Paul refers to the "nomos" arising from distinct sources, all in the sense of "principle" or "norm," rather than to signify Torah. He draws on his argument in 1.18–2.29, and thereafter, that everyone is aware of what is right before God, and thus responsible for intending and doing what is right—for instance, responsible for self-control instead of covetousness—and no one is excused from carrying out the intention of lawbreaking, including by the exploiting of law to do so, i.e., legally. **24:** The *I* seeks rescue not from Torah but from the body. **25:** *A slave to the law of God*, i.e., a member of God's family and principles for living. *A slave to the law of sin*, i.e., a member of the human family descended from Adam and the principles of sin and death. See 1QS 11.9–15; 1QH 4.30–38.

8.1–39: The Spirit-enabled life. Continuing the argument from chs 5–7, Paul explains that although still living in the body and thus subject to human limitations, the Spirit of God is in the lives of those who set their minds on the things of the Spirit in faithfulness to Christ, which will enable them to live the life of righteousness. It will not be without continued conflict between spiritual conventions and human limitations, for they are still living in bodies (i.e., in the present age), but victory is assured, not only for themselves but for all of creation, which will be rescued according to God's design (i.e., when the awaited age arrives fully). Thus rather than allowing fear of dissatisfaction and death to lead them into selfish choices, they are free to be indebted to pursuing what is right for everyone, for all of God's creation. In other words, they are to be committed to faithfully living according to the values of the age to come during the present age. **1:** The ch continues the change of direction begun in 7.25, and the overall argument of ch 7. **2:** For

Jesus has set you[a] free from the law of sin and of death. [3] For God has done what the law, weakened by the flesh, could not do: by sending his own Son in the likeness of sinful flesh, and to deal with sin,[b] he condemned sin in the flesh, [4] so that the just requirement of the law might be fulfilled in us, who walk not according to the flesh but according to the Spirit.[c] [5] For those who live according to the flesh set their minds on the things of the flesh, but those who live according to the Spirit[c] set their minds on the things of the Spirit.[c] [6] To set the mind on the flesh is death, but to set the mind on the Spirit[c] is life and peace. [7] For this reason the mind that is set on the flesh is hostile to God; it does not submit to God's law—indeed it cannot, [8] and those who are in the flesh cannot please God.

[9] But you are not in the flesh; you are in the Spirit,[c] since the Spirit of God dwells in you. Anyone who does not have the Spirit of Christ does not belong to him. [10] But if Christ is in you, though the body is dead because of sin, the Spirit[c] is life because of righteousness. [11] If the Spirit of him who raised Jesus from the dead dwells in you, he who raised Christ[d] from the dead will give life to your mortal bodies also through[e] his Spirit that dwells in you.

[12] So then, brothers and sisters,[f] we are debtors, not to the flesh, to live according to the flesh— [13] for if you live according to the flesh, you will die; but if by the Spirit you put to death the deeds of the body, you will live. [14] For all who are led by the Spirit of God are children of God. [15] For you did not receive a spirit of slavery to fall back into fear, but you have received a spirit of

[a] Here the Greek word *you* is singular number; other ancient authorities read *me* or *us*
[b] Or *and as a sin offering*
[c] Or *spirit*
[d] Other ancient authorities read *the Christ* or *Christ Jesus* or *Jesus Christ*
[e] Other ancient authorities read *on account of*
[f] Gk *brothers*

"pneuma," *spirit* or "breath," see Gen 1.2; Ezek 37; Ps 139.7; the *Spirit of life* is thus the presence of the divine righteousness and life, working through *Christ Jesus*, to *free* the followers of Jesus from *the law* (i.e., the principle) *of sin and of death. Law of the Spirit . . . of sin and of death,* Gk "nomos tou pneumatos," "hamartias . . . thanatou," "the law/principle of the spirit" as opposed to that "of error and death." The rightness of the law/principle is confirmed, not dismissed, by those who are now enabled to fulfill it by conducting their lives according to the spirit of life in Christ Jesus instead of, with Adam, in the spirit of death in sin. **3:** *The law, weakened by the flesh,* the moral convention or principle that provoked the very actions it was prohibiting because of human limitations/desires, as children of Adam. In the Hebrew Bible, *flesh* ("basar") can mean the body (Job 19.26); all of humankind (Isa 66.16); the weaker side of human nature (Ezek 35.26); weakness (Isa 31.3); and food (Dan 7.5). *To deal with sin,* lit., "concerning sin" or and on behalf of (being) a sin-offering (see translators' note *b*). The "sin-offering" (better, "purification offering") as set out in Lev chs 4; 12; 14; 15 was the means by which the Temple was cleansed so that God's presence could continue there; it was accomplished by the sprinkling of blood. **4–6:** Paul moves from declaring a state of change already accomplished to a conditional state that one can accomplish in a new way, but one that requires "walking" or "norms for living" (i.e., "halakh") to accomplish it. *Just requirement of the law,* God's principle/norm. *Spirit,* i.e., divine capability, in contrast to human limitations/desires (*flesh*). **8–9:** *In the flesh . . . not in the flesh,* the contrast is between those who are focused on how they are constrained by human limitations and those who are enabled by God's Spirit. Those having the spirit of Christ are said not to be in the flesh, although they are in "bodies" or "mortal bodies." They are said to be dead because of sin, yet now in a new way of living in the body, through the spirit that raised up Christ. They are not simply spiritual beings, but people with bodies, and bodies involve the role of flesh, both in the sense of the part of the body it constitutes, in terms of being known to look a certain way, and in terms of social reputation. This may be an allusion to resurrection. Cf. Ezek 37.14. They are not to be constrained by their foreskinned state to living lives of sin, but freed by God's Spirit at work in and among them to live the life to which Torah points, even though they, as Gentiles, are not technically under Torah. **14:** *Children,* lit., "sons," both Jews and Gentiles. Gentiles can understand their new identity apart from circumcision as nevertheless set apart to God in a way that represents what circumcision also represents ideally — a spiritual way of living, and not just in

adoption. When we cry, "Abba![a] Father!" [16] it is that very Spirit bearing witness[b] with our spirit that we are children of God, [17] and if children, then heirs, heirs of God and joint heirs with Christ—if, in fact, we suffer with him so that we may also be glorified with him.

[18] I consider that the sufferings of this present time are not worth comparing with the glory about to be revealed to us. [19] For the creation waits with eager longing for the revealing of the children of God; [20] for the creation was subjected to futility, not of its own will but by the will of the one who subjected it, in hope [21] that the creation itself will be set free from its bondage to decay and will obtain the freedom of the glory of the children of God. [22] We know that the whole creation has been groaning in labor pains until now; [23] and not only the creation, but we ourselves, who have the first fruits of the Spirit, groan inwardly while we wait for adoption, the redemption of our bodies. [24] For in[c] hope we were saved. Now hope that is seen is not hope. For who hopes[d] for what is seen? [25] But if we hope for what we do not see, we wait for it with patience.

[26] Likewise the Spirit helps us in our weakness; for we do not know how to pray as we

[a] Aramaic for *Father*

[b] Or [15] *a spirit of adoption, by which we cry, "Abba! Father!"* [16] *The Spirit itself bears witness*

[c] Or *by*

[d] Other ancient authorities read *awaits*

terms of the status conferred by the fleshly marker indicating dedication to that life. Gentiles are members of the family by adoption, but this does not mean the natural, circumcised children are not members of the family. **15:** *For you*, Gentiles. *When we*, whether Jew or Greek. *Abba*, Aramaic for "Father," i.e., that which Jews say. *Father*, Gk "Patēr," that which Gentiles say. Together they all call upon the same father, albeit in different languages (since they are from different nations). **16:** *We*, whether Jew or Greek. **17:** The idea parallels the Torah concept of Israelites being led by God from slavery in Egypt toward the promised land (e.g., Deut 1–12), including the concept of being God's child among the nations (Ex 4.22; also see Hos 1.10). Note the conditional clause in v. 17 that wraps up the argument: *if . . . we suffer with him*, presumably that suffering is what is endured for identification with Christ and the claims and lifestyle that this entails. There is also awareness of the penalties to which the Christ-following Gentiles are subjected: for example, from the Romans who control the standards of identity and lifestyle in the present age, as described in ch 1, or from the gatekeepers of the Jewish community who are enforcing their community norms and rejecting the claims of these Gentiles for full membership without proselyte conversion. **18–39:** Paul's argument now turns to the present-age suffering yet hope of the Christ-believer and of creation. Allusions to Gen 3 abound. It seems that the assertions of delivery from the body of death are now qualified (in v. 15 adoption is a present reality; in v. 23 it is still awaited). Thus it is not clear how the reality claimed in Christ has changed for the Christ-following Gentiles in the present age from that articulated in ch 7 because for the one in Adam; suffering continues, including suffering weakness in the body that requires intercession by the Spirit. The role of hope—of anticipation of that which has been promised—and thus living in a way that is both faithful to that reality rather than to present appearances, and that is also reliant on God's Spirit to enable that life (e.g., Isa 32.15–17; 44; Ezek 36.24–38; 37; Ps 139.7), were already central to the way of living valued by the righteous ones of Israel before Christ, and since. For examples from Qumran literature of dependence upon the Spirit, see 1QH 7.6; 12.11–12; 13.18–19; 16.11–12. The reality of the age to come that is being claimed by the Christ-believer involves a struggle with present age challenges from within and without, yet ultimate victory is claimed for those who intentionally (from the heart, which is searched) remain faithful to God's Spirit and promise in their lifestyles, and for all of creation which is suffering death since the sin of Adam. Suffering, as well as the Spirit, bear witness to the glory to be revealed. **20–21:** *Creation*, the natural world. *Subjected to futility*, perhaps as a consequence of the disobedience of Adam. *By the will of*, "the will" not in Gk. *The one who subjected it*, or because of the one submitting, i.e., Adam submitting to or giving in to sin. **22:** *Groaning in labor*, see Isa 42.14, where it is God who is in labor. **23:** Cf. Ps 43.26 LXX; *for adoption*, omitted in some of the best manuscripts. *Redemption of our bodies*, i.e., restoration at the place where human desire leading to defeat takes place. **24:** *Saved*, from idolatry. **26–27:** See Ps 7.11; 139.1. The Spirit articulates the needs of *the saints* better than they can themselves. *And God*, lit., "But the one."

ought, but that very Spirit intercedes[a] with sighs too deep for words. [27] And God,[b] who searches the heart, knows what is the mind of the Spirit, because the Spirit[c] intercedes for the saints according to the will of God.[d]

[28] We know that all things work together for good[e] for those who love God, who are called according to his purpose. [29] For those whom he foreknew he also predestined to be conformed to the image of his Son, in order that he might be the firstborn within a large family.[f] [30] And those whom he predestined he also called; and those whom he called he also justified; and those whom he justified he also glorified.

[31] What then are we to say about these things? If God is for us, who is against us? [32] He who did not withhold his own Son, but gave him up for all of us, will he not with him also give us everything else? [33] Who will bring any charge against God's elect? It is God who justifies. [34] Who is to condemn? It is Christ Jesus, who died, yes, who was raised, who is at the right hand of God, who indeed intercedes for us.[g] [35] Who will separate us from the love of Christ? Will hardship, or distress, or persecution, or famine, or nakedness, or peril, or sword? [36] As it is written,

"For your sake we are being killed all day long;
we are accounted as sheep to be slaughtered."

[37] No, in all these things we are more than conquerors through him who loved us. [38] For I am convinced that neither death, nor life, nor angels, nor rulers, nor things present, nor things to come, nor powers, [39] nor height, nor depth, nor anything else in all creation, will be able to separate us from the love of God in Christ Jesus our Lord.

a Other ancient authorities add *for us*
b Gk *the one*
c Gk *he* or *it*
d Gk *according to God*
e Other ancient authorities read *God makes all things work together for good*, or *in all things God works for good*
f Gk *among many brothers*
g Or *Is it Christ Jesus . . . for us?*

Searches the heart, probes the innermost thoughts; see, e.g., Jer 17.10; Ps 139.23; 1 Chr 28.9. *The Spirit* is not in Gk; lit., "because it/he." *According to the will of God*, lit., "according to God." **28:** *For good*, see Sir 39.25–27. *Love God*, see Ex 20.6; Deut 5.10; 6.5; 7.9; 10.12; Ps 31.24; 97.10. For similar statements, see *Pss. Sol.* 4.25; Plato, *Resp.* 10.12 (612e–613a). *To his purpose*, lit., "to a design." **29:** Cf. 1QS 3.15–16; 11.10–11,17–20; 1QH 1.7–8; CD 2.8. *Foreknew*, a characterization of God's sovereignty over the future, and not on the existence of free choice among human beings; see 9.10–13n. *Within a large family*, lit., among many brothers (and sisters) (see translators' note *f*). Jesus Christ is the firstborn of those who are raised from the dead (for non-Pauline expression of this idea, see Col 1.15,18). **30:** Cf. 1QM 3.2; 4.10–11. *Justified*, made righteous, conformed to righteousness. *Glorified*, presented in redeemed/resurrected body. Paul speaks as though these things had already been accomplished; since God intends them, they are as good as done. **31:** See Ps 118, esp. vv. 5–9. Diatribe style through v. 39, often with the negating answer implied. **32:** Cf. Gen 22.16, the "Akedah" (binding of Isaac). See Rom 3.24–25; 5.6–11; 11.28–29; 15.8–9. **33:** Cf. Isa 50.7–9. *Elect*, chosen. **34:** *Right hand*, an application of Ps 110.1, referring to the Davidic king, Jesus Christ. This sentence may be a question. *Intercedes*, prays for, appeals on behalf of. **35:** It is not clear if this relates to a specific situation in Rome or is more general; cf. Deut 28; 1 Chr 21.11–12; 2 Chr 20.9; 32.11. **36:** Ps 44.22; Paul applies the Psalm to the context of his argument about present suffering, in the style of pesher: the point in Ps 44 is that, for God's sake, faithful Israel suffers.

9.1–33: The place of Israel in God's overall purpose. Paul explains the state of Jews who do not share his convictions about Christ or about the responsibility to announce his message to the nations. God has designed the pattern so that not all Israelites will immediately take part in this task. Some Jews stumble over any announcement of salvation to the nations prior to proselyte conversion. This refusal Paul sees as seeking their own righteousness, that is, the righteousness of Israelites alone to receive the awaited rescue, and not those from the other nations, apart from joining Israel. Paul claims not to fault them (although his viewpoint expresses judgment). **1–3:** Change of focus from situation of non-Jews and Christ-followers (who nevertheless remain as the audience Paul has in view), to the situation of non-Christ-following Jews. If, as Paul has argued, this "good news"

9 I am speaking the truth in Christ—I am not lying; my conscience confirms it by the Holy Spirit—[2] I have great sorrow and unceasing anguish in my heart. [3] For I could wish that I myself were accursed and cut off from Christ for the sake of my own people,[a] my kindred according to the flesh. [4] They are Israelites, and to them belong the adoption, the glory, the covenants, the giving of the law, the worship, and the promises; [5] to them belong the patriarchs, and from them, according to the flesh, comes the Messiah,[b] who is over all, God blessed forever.[c] Amen.

[6] It is not as though the word of God had failed. For not all Israelites truly belong to Israel, [7] and not all of Abraham's children are his true descendants; but "It is through Isaac that descendants shall be named for you." [8] This means that it is not the children of the flesh who are the children of God, but the children of the promise are counted as descendants. [9] For this is what the promise said, "About this time I will return and Sarah shall have a son." [10] Nor is that all; something similar happened to Rebecca when she had conceived children by one husband, our ancestor Isaac. [11] Even before they had been born or had done anything good or bad (so that God's purpose of election might continue, [12] not by works but by his call) she was told, "The elder shall serve the younger." [13] As it is written,

"I have loved Jacob,
but I have hated Esau."

[14] What then are we to say? Is there injustice on God's part? By no means! [15] For he says to Moses,

"I will have mercy on whom I have mercy,
and I will have compassion on whom I have compassion."

[a] Gk *my brothers*
[b] Or *the Christ*
[c] Or *Messiah, who is God over all, blessed forever*; or *Messiah. May he who is God over all be blessed forever*

is foretold in scripture, then why have not all Jews embraced it? Note the parallel with Moses' vicarious offer in Ex 32.32. *My own people*, lit., "brethren"; i.e., fellow Israelites. *Flesh*, here and in v. 5 refers to shared ethnic identification, including by proselyte conversion; cf. vv. 7–8; 1.3. *Cut off*, perhaps a pun on the issue of circumcision. **4:** *To them belong*, lit., "of whom are." *Adoption*, lit., "sonship"; the Israelites are prior to the Gentiles in being members of God's family. *The glory*, God's presence (Heb "kavod"). *The covenants*, or covenant. *The giving of the law*, lit., "the legislation," probably implying the Mosaic Torah. *The worship*; i.e., Temple sacrificial system [Heb "avodah"]. **5:** *To them belong*, lit., "of whom [are]." *The patriarchs*, or fathers. *According to the flesh*, by ethnic descent. *Amen*, "it is so," "let it be so," indicating acceptance of what has been stated. **6:** Gk begins "But." *Had failed*, lit., "has fallen." *Truly* is not in Gk. *Belong to Israel*, or But are not all those Israel, who are from Israel? **7–9:** Ethnic descent is not denied, but the right to the inheritance is qualified. "Seed" remains singular throughout. **7:** Gen 21.12. *True* is not in Gk. **8:** *Flesh*, ethnic descent. *Descendants*, lit., "seed." **9:** Conflation of Gen 18.10,14. **10–13:** Paul's response to questions continues with the matter of discrimination between the two offspring of Isaac's seed: only one of the two—Jacob, who becomes Israel—will be the select one through which the divine promise to Abraham would be kept. Thus, not only could such divine discrimination occur because of the children produced by two different spouses, such as in Abraham's case of children through Hagar and Sarah, but also in the case of one spouse, such as Isaac and Rebecca, who had twins. Moreover, it occurred in her womb, so that it cannot demonstrate anything except God's plan in action. This argument tells against reading Paul's language of foreknowledge or predestination to imply that God knows what different people will do, and thus decides the outcome in advance. Rather, here it is God's sovereign choice that is exalted, albeit about a particular matter, the promised seed, and it does not claim that either child could not behave righteously, whether chosen as the seed or not. The choice occurred before either could commit good or evil; by implication, before God knew how Jacob and Esau would behave. It is neither a punishment nor a reward, but God's own design at work. Thus, implicitly, those of Israel not "yet" faithful to Christ are not at fault, which will raise a question to come. Contrast Philo, *Virtues* 207–9; *Rewards* 58–60; *Leg. all.* 3.75–88, who attributes their being chosen or rejected as God's response to their future behavior. **10:** Gen 25.21. **11:** *Bad*, Gk "phaulos" can also be translated "petty," in keeping with the Genesis narrative, wherein Esau values a meal over his birthright, and also "mean." *Election*, choice. **12:** Gen 25.23. **13:** Mal 1.2–3. *Hated* is hyperbolic to sharpen comparison with the one chosen. The choice of Jacob over Esau does not mean that the Jesus community, as the "younger," is preferable to Judaism, as the "elder"; instead, it is a pattern from Tanakh that demonstrates the precarious state of humans, for God does the unexpected. **15:** Ex 33.19.

[16] So it depends not on human will or exertion, but on God who shows mercy. [17] For the scripture says to Pharaoh, "I have raised you up for the very purpose of showing my power in you, so that my name may be proclaimed in all the earth." [18] So then he has mercy on whomever he chooses, and he hardens the heart of whomever he chooses.

[19] You will say to me then, "Why then does he still find fault? For who can resist his will?" [20] But who indeed are you, a human being, to argue with God? Will what is molded say to the one who molds it, "Why have you made me like this?" [21] Has the potter no right over the clay, to make out of the same lump one object for special use and another for ordinary use? [22] What if God, desiring to show his wrath and to make known his power, has endured with much patience the objects of wrath that are made for destruction; [23] and what if he has done so in order to make known the riches of his glory for the objects of mercy, which he has prepared beforehand for glory— [24] including us whom he has called, not from the Jews only but also from the Gentiles? [25] As indeed he says in Hosea,

"Those who were not my people I will call
'my people,'
and her who was not beloved I will call
'beloved.'"
[26] "And in the very place where it was said
to them, 'You are not my people,'
there they shall be called children of
the living God."

[27] And Isaiah cries out concerning Israel, "Though the number of the children of Israel were like the sand of the sea, only a remnant of them will be saved; [28] for the Lord will execute his sentence on the earth quickly and decisively." [a] [29] And as Isaiah predicted,

"If the Lord of hosts had not left survivors[b]
to us,
we would have fared like Sodom
and been made like Gomorrah."

[30] What then are we to say? Gentiles, who did not strive for righteousness, have at-

[a] Other ancient authorities read *for he will finish his work and cut it short in righteousness, because the Lord will make the sentence shortened on the earth*

[b] Or *descendants*; Gk *seed*

16: *It*, God's choice, a choice among Israelites. *Exertion*, lit., "running." The literal term here is significant, since the theme is Israel's role as herald of God's news of good to the nations, and Paul seeks to explain why some Israelites are not presently joining Paul in the task that, in his view, should be undertaken. Note that God's choice here is not between family members and nonfamily members, but among family members; not Israelites vs. non-Israelites, but among Israelites, as the argument began in 9.1–6. See 9.30–33. **17:** Ex 9.16. The purpose for Pharaoh was the proclamation of God's name among the nations. **18:** *Chooses*, or wills/wants among Israelites as well as among the Gentiles. *Hardens the heart*, makes resistant to change. **20–24:** See Isa 29.16; 45.9; 64.8; Jer 18.1–11; Wis 15.7; also Jer 50.25, for vessels of wrath. **20:** *Argue with God*, for contrasting views of this, see Abraham, Gen 18.22–33, and Job 42.1–6. **21:** *Same lump*, i.e., same descent group. *Object*, or vessel; *special use*, lit., "honor"; *ordinary use*, lit., "dishonor." **22–24:** *What if*, lit., "But if"; *his power*, or his capability. *Endured*, or brought forth; i.e., threw, as in pottery; or fashioned. *Objects*, or vessels; or "fashioned with much patience the vessels of wrath fit for destruction." **23:** *And what*, not in Gk. **25–26:** Hos 2.23; the first part of this verse in LXX, which Paul does not cite, is about "sowing," i.e., "seed"; see vv. 27–29. **26:** Hos 1.10. Hosea refers to the dispersed northern tribes of Israel in contrast to the Judeans. Paul speaks of the division between the remnant such as himself (i.e., Judea), and those Israelites who are stumbling (the northern tribes). He anticipates 11.26, the declaration that all Israel will be restored. **27–29:** Proofs continue; the theme of hope continues: the remnant will be saved from among those punished. **27:** Isa 10.22 conflated with Hos 1.10, following from v. 26. *Children of Israel were*, "are" or "will be"; no verb in Gk. *Only*, not in Gk. *Saved*, restored/rescued from destruction, restored to the task of declaring the good news, albeit presently under some kind of disciplinary state. **28:** Isa 10.23 conflated with Isa 28.22. **29:** Isa 1.9, *survivors*, lit., "seed." NRSV here translates according to the meaning of Isaiah in Heb, where the reference is to the remnant from among those now living, not to their descendants ("seed"), as in Paul's text. **30–33:** A diatribe in elliptical language, leaving out critical verbs and nouns: NRSV supplies *have attained it, that is . . . that is based . . . succeed in . . . strive for it on the basis . . . as if it were based.* Some heralds from Israel have not carried out their task of proclaiming the good news to the nations, while some Gentiles have come to know the news, an unexpected development (cf. 3.1–2; 11.17–26). **30:** *Who did not strive for*, lit., "who are not pursuing." **31:** *Did not succeed in fulfilling that law*, lit., "did not arrive sooner"; but

tained it, that is, righteousness through faith; [31] but Israel, who did strive for the righteousness that is based on the law, did not succeed in fulfilling that law. [32] Why not? Because they did not strive for it on the basis of faith, but as if it were based on works. They have stumbled over the stumbling stone, [33] as it is written,

"See, I am laying in Zion a stone that will
make people stumble, a rock that will
make them fall,
and whoever believes in him[a] will not
be put to shame."

10 Brothers and sisters,[b] my heart's desire and prayer to God for them is that they may be saved. [2] I can testify that they have a zeal for God, but it is not enlightened. [3] For, being ignorant of the righteousness that comes from God, and seeking to establish their own, they have not submitted to God's righteousness. [4] For Christ is the end of the law so that there may be righteousness for everyone who believes.

[5] Moses writes concerning the righteousness that comes from the law, that "the person who does these things will live by them." [6] But the righteousness that comes from faith says, "Do not say in your heart, 'Who will ascend into heaven?'" (that is, to bring Christ down) [7] "or 'Who will descend into the abyss?'" (that is, to bring Christ up from the dead). [8] But what does it say?

[a] Or *trusts in it*
[b] Gk *Brothers*

Israel, with a convention of delineating the family of righteousness by circumcision, in fact missed the point of the convention, which some Gentiles nevertheless grasped. **32:** *On works*, the action of circumcision for Gentiles completing proselyte conversion. Those Israelites confuse the sign of inclusion (circumcision) with the reason for inclusion, not recognizing the claims of Gentiles based on faithfulness to Christ. **33:** Isa 28.16 (also in 10.11), that God has put an obstruction in the path (see also Isa 8, esp. v. 14). The stone aimed not to cause failure but, ironically, to help them by slowing them down so that they did not miss the righteousness they were to declare. The stone could be Christ, or the proclamation of the gospel, or the inclusion of Gentiles apart from circumcision. Implicitly, they will regain their step and properly achieve the aim of the message, righteousness, albeit by way of faithfulness to the proclamation of the faithfulness of Christ. *A rock that will make them fall*, lit., "a rock of offense"; "fall" is not in the Gk, and goes against the argument, cf. 11.11. *And whoever believes*, whoever is faithful; *in him*, or to it; i.e., the stone.

10.1–21: Some Israelites do not comprehend the times. Paul continues at least through v. 5 to defend Israelites who have not joined him as heralds. The degree of current culpability Paul intends to communicate is difficult to assess. **1–5:** Continuation of argument and elliptical style from 9.30–33. **1:** *Them*, Israelites not sharing Paul's view. Paul's language, while involving a critique of fellow Jews, sees these "brothers/sisters" still being righteous ones on a course set for them but in need of stabilization; the comparison (9.32–33) is to messengers running but some tripping, and those need to be stabilized so they do not fall but return to running on the course to achieve the goal. *That they may be saved*, lit., "for their restoration." **2:** *Not enlightened*, lit., "not possessing complete information/comprehension." **3:** Not realizing God's righteousness (in Christ), they attend to the righteousness signified by their special signifier of righteousness, as if circumcision was required to be counted among the righteous. *Their own*, "their own righteousness" in some manuscripts, i.e., Israelite identity and thus circumcision as the necessary signifier of the righteous ones of God. **4:** *Law* ("nomos"), here signifying circumcision. Paul's message resonates with Deut 9.4–6 (Paul cites 9.4 in v. 6), in that Israel's entering the land is not on account of Israel's righteousness, but the covenant promise of God. *End*, as in the "goal." Christ is the goal toward which the circumcised righteous ones strive: they are to announce to the nations the words God has entrusted to them about Christ: "For the goal of a convention (of circumcision) is Christ [providing] righteousness to everyone who is being faithful." **5:** Lev 18.5, but the language is closely linked with Deut 30, which Paul develops in the next verses. Paul argues that observing Torah involves being faithful to the revelation of Christ (he is not arguing for the abolition of Torah but for recognizing its ideal goals). Cf. Sir 17.11; Philo, *Prelim. Studies* 84–85. *Person*, i.e., Israelite. **6–8:** A paraphrase of Deut 30.11–14 (the first clause is from Deut 9.4; cf. Deut 8.17). **6:** Christ would be brought down to make this case clear. *Faith*, or, faithfulness. **7:** *Abyss*, i.e., "depths of the sea," here meaning the underworld, Heb "Sheol" or Gk "Hades," but Deut 30.13 simply refers to crossing the "sea." This version is attested in Ps 107.26 (LXX "abyssos") and *Tg. Neof.* 1. The desire to have news brought back from the dead is attested by Homer, *Od.*, 10.487–574; 11.163–65, and see Lk 16.19–31. **8:** Deut 30.14.

THE SOURCE OF AUTHORITY IN INTERPRETATION (10.6–8)

Philo adapted Deut 30.12–13, albeit to different conclusions, in *Posterity* 84–85; Bar 3.29–30 also uses the passage. "Wisdom" is adapted and personified for the commandment in a way similar to Paul's introduction of "Christ." Philo used it for argumentation about similar topics, including proclamation to the nations; he had a positive assessment of those from the nations who turn to the One God, and the instructions for a virtuous life for those who join the people of God, including the claim that this is not too hard to achieve; see *Virtues* 175–86 (esp. 183); *Rewards* 79–84 (esp. 80; note that 83–84 includes a foot-race comparison); *Names* 235–39; *Dreams* 2.180; *Good Person* 68. Cf. *b. B. Metz.* 59b, where Deut 30.10–11 is similarly employed in intra-Jewish disputes to assert that the answer is near at hand, in this case, the rabbinic majority decision.

"The word is near you,
 on your lips and in your heart"
(that is, the word of faith that we proclaim); [9] because[a] if you confess with your lips that Jesus is Lord and believe in your heart that God raised him from the dead, you will be saved. [10] For one believes with the heart and so is justified, and one confesses with the mouth and so is saved. [11] The scripture says, "No one who believes in him will be put to shame." [12] For there is no distinction between Jew and Greek; the same Lord is Lord of all and is generous to all who call on him. [13] For, "Everyone who calls on the name of the Lord shall be saved."

[14] But how are they to call on one in whom they have not believed? And how are they to believe in one of whom they have never heard? And how are they to hear without someone to proclaim him? [15] And how are they to proclaim him unless they are sent? As it is written, "How beautiful are the feet of those who bring good news!" [16] But not all have obeyed the good news;[b] for Isaiah says, "Lord, who has believed our message?" [17] So faith comes from what is heard, and what is heard comes through the word of Christ.[c]

[18] But I ask, have they not heard? Indeed they have; for

a Or *namely, that*
b Or *gospel*
c Or *about Christ*; other ancient authorities read *of God*

9: *If you*, Gk implies "would." *Confess with your lips*, proclamation is the theme throughout; that which is at issue is that some Israelites are not proclaiming this news. It is part of the news to announce to the nations that the end of the ages has begun in the present age, since resurrection from the dead is an expectation of the age to come, not a present reality. **10:** *Heart . . . justified*, righteousness is an expression of one's intentional activity, of doing right for the right reasons. *Confesses . . . saved*, the manifestation of this righteousness in the effort to proclaim it to others. Paul is playing off of the elements of heart and mouth in the citations from Deut 30. If speaking to a herald he believes to be stumbling, the two aspects in view are the intention to behave faithfully to what God has revealed in Christ, and the profession of that message to the nations. He may even be drawing a graphic contrast for Israelites between faithfulness, which results in righteousness (standing upright after stumbling), and proclamation, which results in restoration (to running the course once stabilized). There may be a contrast with declaring Caesar as Lord. **11:** Isa 28.16, cited above in 9.33; the original meaning of trust in God to avoid fear here becomes a promise of vindication. **13:** Joel 2.32 (Heb 3.5). **14–21:** Similar to the issues in ch 3. The topic that was implicit in the adaptation of Deut 30.11–14 in vv. 6–8 is now addressed: What is the proof that this message is known to Israel now? Throughout there is a play on Gk "akouō" (vb, "hear") and "akoē" (noun, "what is heard"). This corresponds to Heb "shema," signifying obedient hearing. Paul plays on the citation of Isa 53.1 in v. 16. **15:** Isa 52.7 serves as the proof of the validity of the line of questioning, or alternatively, as an answer. In Isa 52 the heralds run to bring news of deliverance from Babylon, the return of God's reign, and the restoration to the land in spite of the fact that Jerusalem is in ruins. The nations will then see God acting to restore Israel (Isa 52.10). *Beautiful*, or timely. **16:** Isa 53.1. *Obeyed*, lit., "listened [obediently]." **17:** Or "Therefore faithfulness [results] from [responding faithfully to] a report." *Word of Christ*, "God" in some Mss. **18:** Ps 19.4 (LXX 18.5), a psalm that declares that apart from speech, the heavens declare the glory of God; in vv. 5–6, the sun is represented as a bridegroom coming out of its chamber to run its course, so that nothing is hidden. Verse

"Their voice has gone out to all the earth,
and their words to the ends of the world."

[19] Again I ask, did Israel not understand? First Moses says,

"I will make you jealous of those who are not a nation;
with a foolish nation I will make you angry."

[20] Then Isaiah is so bold as to say,

"I have been found by those who did not seek me;
I have shown myself to those who did not ask for me."

[21] But of Israel he says, "All day long I have held out my hands to a disobedient and contrary people."

11 I ask, then, has God rejected his people? By no means! I myself am an Israelite, a descendant of Abraham, a member of the tribe of Benjamin. [2] God has not rejected his people whom he foreknew. Do you not know what the scripture says of Elijah, how he pleads with God against Israel? [3] "Lord, they have killed your prophets, they have demolished your altars; I alone am left, and they are seeking my life." [4] But what is the divine reply to him? "I have kept for myself seven thousand who have not bowed the knee to Baal." [5] So too at the present time there is a remnant, chosen by grace. [6] But if it is by grace, it is no longer on the basis of works, otherwise grace would no longer be grace.[a]

[7] What then? Israel failed to obtain what it was seeking. The elect obtained it, but the rest were hardened, [8] as it is written,

[a] Other ancient authorities add *But if it is by works, it is no longer on the basis of grace, otherwise work would no longer be work*

14 calls the Lord "rock and redeemer," which may connect to Paul's stumbling stone image. **19:** Deut 32.21, the Song of Moses. **20:** Isa 65.1. **21:** Isa 65.2. *Disobedient*, lit., "noncomplying." In all of these citations, Paul is recontextualizing earlier verses that had a different meaning in their original historical context. Part of what Paul is doing is pesher-like: their "real" meaning is only fulfilled later, and perhaps even the original prophet did not understand their full meaning.

11.1–16: The restoration of Israel and the inclusion of the nations. Nonbelieving Jews are not rejected, but in God's design they have not yet been persuaded. However inscrutable this design or its purpose might be, it will result in the restoration of all Israel. Gentiles who respond faithfully fulfill their own responsibility to the success of this design. Paul now discusses the state of divided Israel, continuing the allegory of heralds to the nations, some running successfully while others stumble. But the real thrust of the argument shows non-Jews how their anomalous inclusion in God's plan for Israel's restoration is proceeding. Paul hopes to provoke empathy for those Israelites suffering now. He creates an allegorical image of grafting a wild shoot onto an olive tree, some of whose branches have been broken (bent), to explain the precarious place of these non-Jews in God's design. The broken branches are being protected by a callus until the wild shoot's graft is made, and then all of the natural branches will be healed. The present alienation of some Israelites serves to bring about the inclusion of these non-Jews. Based on the promises of God to the fathers, even the stumbling Israelites are beloved and their restoration is assured. **1:** Diatribe style continues with a question whether Israel has been "pushed back," which Paul denies (cf. Ps 94.14). The implication of Paul's argument since 9.30 is that Israel has (i.e., some Israelites have) stumbled and not reached the goal to which Torah pointed, that of being heralds of the news of Christ. In effect, Paul argues, some in Israel are not carrying out their task before some non-Jews have become Christ-believers; therefore, rather than *rejected* (Gk "apōsato"), "pushed back," is preferable, keeping the idea that though it may come later than God had planned, the Jewish people as a whole will be included in the coming kingdom (see vv. 11–12). Paul points to himself as proof that one cannot deny Israel's inclusion, for he is an Israelite, a seed of Abraham (i.e., one who was a circumcised as a child), and even declares his tribe. **2–5:** Cf. 1 Sam 12.22; Amos 3.2. **2:** *Foreknew*, here "knew from before," not "knew in advance." **3:** 1 Kings 19.10; note that Elijah does not plead against Israel, but for his own safety from certain unfaithful Israelites. **4:** 1 Kings 19.18. **5:** Cf. 9.29; 2 Kings 19.4; 1QS 8.6. **6:** The Israelites who are faithfully proclaiming the gospel, like Paul, were not chosen to do so because their deeds were better than those stumbling Israelites; this is the result of God's choice for how things should unfold; cf. 9.16. *Grace*, a gift of benefaction. **7:** See 9.6. *Failed*, not in Gk. *Were hardened*, lit., "were being callused, or wounded." See v. 25n. **8:** Loose citation of Deut 29.4 conflated with Isa 29.10. Deut 29.2–6 tells of Israel not yet recognizing the mysterious way that God used Pharaoh. "This day" signals the

GRAFTING THE OLIVE BRANCH (11.17–24)

The olive tree allegory is not designed to describe Israel per se, but the precarious place of the wild shoot among Israelites. Since it suggests that these Israelites have been cut off in order to make the a fortiori case that this wild shoot is all the more vulnerable to being cut off, this comparison conflicts with that of some heralds stumbling, though they have not fallen, and the overall message that all Israel will be restored. In vv. 17–21, Paul uses *ekklaō* to refer to the "broken" branches; however, unless specifically referred to as "broken *off*," *ekklaō* can refer to something broken, "dislocated" or "bent, but not severed"; see Lev 1.17; Pausanias, *Descr.* 8.40.2. In v. 22, when Paul warns the wild branch that it could be severed if it looks arrogantly upon the broken branches, Paul switches to *ekkoptō*, "cut off," and he again uses *ekkoptō* in v. 24. That leads to the impression that Paul regards some branches as broken off, although that is an inference that does not seem to be intended when he begins the allegory; it is rather an inference to rebuke the wild shoot, which has been cut off from its tree to be grafted in, and thus is in a precarious place compared to the natural branches. Cf. Isa 27.2–11. Note too, that the tree is not described as Israel, and Paul does not draw the inference that non-Israelites become members of Israel. The tree appears to represent all who are in the family of God, Israelite branches as well as ones from other nations.

"God gave them a sluggish spirit,
eyes that would not see
and ears that would not hear,
down to this very day."

[9] And David says,

"Let their table become a snare and a trap,
a stumbling block and a retribution for them;
[10] let their eyes be darkened so that they cannot see,
and keep their backs forever bent."

[11] So I ask, have they stumbled so as to fall? By no means! But through their stumbling[a] salvation has come to the Gentiles, so as to make Israel[b] jealous. [12] Now if their stumbling[a] means riches for the world, and if their defeat means riches for Gentiles, how much more will their full inclusion mean!

[13] Now I am speaking to you Gentiles. Inasmuch then as I am an apostle to the Gentiles, I glorify my ministry [14] in order to make my own people[a] jealous, and thus save some of them. [15] For if their rejection is the

[a] Gk *transgression*
[b] Gk *them*

end of the lack of perception. Isa 29 expresses a similar theme about Judah's prophets failing to perceive Judah's initial deliverance from the nations (Isa 29.9–14), while deaf and blind Israelites understand (Isa 29.17–21), with a message of restoration of those who have erred or grumbled (Isa 29.22–24). **10:** *Forever*, or continually. **11:** The quotations of judgment in vv. 8–10 provoke the diatribe question of whether these Israelites ("the rest") have stumbled (been unfaithful) and thus will not reach the goal of proclaiming God's righteousness to the nations. This picture draws heavily on Isa 8; 28; see Rom 9.30–33. *To make Israel*, lit., "them"; "Israel" not in Gk. **11–16:** Paul addresses the non-Jewish audience of the letter directly, not via diatribe, on the basis of his responsibility to them as members of the nations. He explains that he declares the glory of his ministry as a herald to the nations in the hope that he will provoke his fellow, currently stumbling, Israelites to be jealous of his ministry, so that they will want to emulate him by joining him in declaring this message of Christ to the nations. Note that it is neither the salvation of the non-Jews per se that he seeks to declare, nor is it jealousy of the non-Jews that Paul seeks to stir; rather, it is his own success among the non-Jews that he magnifies, and thus he seeks to provoke jealousy of his ministry among the nations. Note too, that Paul thinks of the fellow Israelites who are stumbling as his own flesh; how he knows himself is inseparable from his embodiment with them as Israel. Whether Paul calculated this or even realized the implications, the non-Jews might feel slighted by this statement, both because this expression ("my flesh") keeps alive the idea that the Gentile followers are not a part of Israel or fellow-members with Paul; even his ministry among them is in the service of a goal beyond themselves, although certainly it is for them too. The verbs are subjunctive in v. 14, and follow a conditional conjunction: this is the outcome that Paul hopes will result from this strategy, but he is not certain of it. **12:** *Defeat*, or slow down. *Full inclusion*, or completion (of the course). **14:** Lit., "if somehow I might make my flesh (i.e.,

reconciliation of the world, what will their acceptance be but life from the dead! [16] If the part of the dough offered as first fruits is holy, then the whole batch is holy; and if the root is holy, then the branches also are holy.

[17] But if some of the branches were broken off, and you, a wild olive shoot, were grafted in their place to share the rich root[b] of the olive tree, [18] do not boast over the branches. If you do boast, remember that it is not you that support the root, but the root that supports you. [19] You will say, "Branches were broken off so that I might be grafted in." [20] That is true. They were broken off because of their unbelief, but you stand only through faith. So do not become proud, but stand in awe. [21] For if God did not spare the natural branches, perhaps he will not spare you.[c] [22] Note then the kindness and the severity of God: severity toward those who have fallen, but God's kindness toward you, provided you continue in his kindness; otherwise you also will be cut off. [23] And even those of Israel,[d] if they do not persist in unbelief, will be grafted in, for God has the power to graft them in again. [24] For if you have been cut from what is by nature a wild olive tree and grafted, contrary to nature, into a cultivated olive tree, how much more will these natural branches be grafted back into their own olive tree.

[25] So that you may not claim to be wiser than you are, brothers and sisters,[e] I want you to understand this mystery: a hardening has come upon part of Israel, until the full

[a] Gk *my flesh*
[b] Other ancient authorities read *the richness*
[c] Other ancient authorities read *neither will he spare you*
[d] Gk lacks *of Israel*
[e] Gk *brothers*

those sharing my ethnic descent) jealous." **15:** *Rejection*, or present nonparticipation. *What will their acceptance be*, lit., "what [results from] gaining of them [back to participation]." **16:** These two comparisons—of the meal offering and of the root and branches—to the whole of Israel serve as a transition to the olive tree allegory. Paul has been working until this point with an image of heralds sent out to reach the nations, some having tripped along the way—so we have three comparisons at work in this ch. The first allegory is not developed after it is introduced. Lev 23.14 refers to the idea that offering the first of the dough makes the rest of the dough holy; Num 15.17–18 explains that when a cake made from the first of the dough is offered, then the rest of the cakes can be served to others who are profane, i.e., not priests. Paul uses it to say that holiness of the first part offered extends to the whole. This appears to imply that the whole (Israel) is made holy, i.e., set apart to God, by the dedicated first part, although he does not say who that is (e.g., the ancestors [cf. v. 28], or the remnant [cf. v. 5], or the presently stumbling [cf. v. 11]). The second allegory will be developed in the olive tree comparison that follows. The image seems to be more like a vine than a tree. Paul does not define the root or the branches, but simply makes the point that if the root is set apart to God, then so too are the branches that grow from it.

11.17–24: The olive tree allegory. This allegory is confronting any temptation of arrogance among the Christ-following non-Jewish audience toward the Israelites who are not Christ-proclaimers. **17:** The wild *shoot* is singular. *Were broken off*, lit., "were broken/bent." *Were grafted in their place*, lit., "being grafted among them"; "in their place," not in Gk. **18:** *Remember that* is not in Gk. **19:** In Isa 10.5–15 and 37.24–25,30–32, using tree metaphors, the king of Assyria expresses similar presumptuousness, which will be turned against him. *Broken off*, lit., "broken/bent." **20:** *That is true*, lit., "Well" (i.e., "it is well"). *Broken off*, lit., "they were being broken to [represent] the unfaithful, but you were established to [represent] the faithful." **21:** *Perhaps*, not in some manuscripts. **22:** The natural branches begin to be described as "cut off ["ekklaō"]," rather than merely "broken ["ekkoptō"]." This change highlights the severity of the fate of the wild shoot if it should be filled with presumptuous pride. **23:** Isa 59, in the midst of plant and tree metaphors, portrays God miraculously restoring Israel. *And even those*, lit., "but also they." *Of Israel* not in Gk. *If they do not persist in unbelief*, lit., "if they would not continue to [represent] the unfaithfulness [of not proclaiming the message to Gentiles]." *Has the power*, lit., "is able."

11.25–36: Further reflections on the cryptic process by which God is accomplishing the restoration of Israel and salvation of the nations. 25–26: Paul changes to direct instruction to the Christ-believing non-Jews, urging them not to be arrogant but instead to recognize that the grace with which they have been blessed should be internalized and turned to regard the suffering others with a spirit of benefaction or grace. **25:** *Part of Israel* has been "callused" ["pōrōsis"], usually translated "hardened"; broken branches experience the

RESTORATION OF ISRAEL (11.26–27)

Paul adapts and conflates elements from Isa 59.20–21 (closer to LXX than MT) with 27.9 for the last clause. Isa 59–61 are full of plant metaphors, as are Isa 27–28. The context of Isa 59 is God coming to the rescue of Israel when no one else does. The context of Isa 27 is the gathering of Israelites from the dispersion (vv. 12–13 involved the announcement of regathering). See 27.6: "in days to come Jacob shall take root, Israel shall blossom and put forth shoots, and fill the whole world with fruit." The verb (*sōthēsetai*) "will be restored/healed" or "will be saved," is also a common description of tree life, of being restored so as to produce fruit, in this case, as Israelites restore the nations to the Creator God. All Israel, whose divided state among Israelites has been the topic, refers to empirical Israel, Jews, not "spiritual Israel" or the Jesus followers inclusive of Gentiles. In metaphorical terms, the wild shoot does not become a natural branch, even though it will draw from the same root (God).

number of the Gentiles has come in. [26] And so all Israel will be saved; as it is written,

"Out of Zion will come the Deliverer;
he will banish ungodliness from Jacob."
[27] "And this is my covenant with them,
when I take away their sins."

[28] As regards the gospel they are enemies of God[a] for your sake; but as regards election they are beloved, for the sake of their ancestors; [29] for the gifts and the calling of God are irrevocable. [30] Just as you were once disobedient to God but have now received mercy because of their disobedience, [31] so they have now been disobedient in order that, by the mercy shown to you, they too may now[b] receive mercy. [32] For God has imprisoned all in disobedience so that he may be merciful to all.

[33] O the depth of the riches and wisdom and knowledge of God! How unsearchable are his judgments and how inscrutable his ways!

[34] "For who has known the mind of the Lord?
Or who has been his counselor?"
[35] "Or who has given a gift to him,
to receive a gift in return?"

[a] Gk lacks *of God*
[b] Other ancient authorities lack *now*

protective and healing process of growing a callus from the sap (cf. v. 17, which implies the broken branches are still drawing from the root). The noun here is not a cognate of the verb used to refer to Pharaoh having a hardened ("sklērynō") heart in 9.17–18, or in Exodus. *A hardening has come upon part of Israel,* or, a part of Israel has become callused, or, for a while a callus has developed for [to protect] Israel; *until the full number of the Gentiles has come in/commenced,* i.e., a part of Israel has become callused temporarily, until the fullness of the nations might commence. **26–27:** *And so,* lit., "And in this way"; or And then. *Will be saved,* or will be restored/rescued from stumbling, healed, restored as messengers. Paul's argument is based not on being in need of restoration to the covenant, but of being disciplined because they have not undertaken the covenant obligation of being entrusted with God's oracles to the nations. Paul writes "out of/from Zion" instead of LXX "to Zion," or MT "for the sake of Zion"; this may reflect the Diaspora situation in Rome. *He will banish,* lit., "he will turn away." **28–29:** Paul appeals to the faithfulness (or merit) of the fathers (cf. 8.32; Gen 22.16–17). **28:** *Enemies of God,* ("of God" not in Gk); lit., an adj.: "enemied"; i.e, alienated *for your sake.* **29:** *Irrevocable,* lit., "not regretted." **30:** *Disobedient to God,* lit., "not-persuaded with respect to God"; *because of their disobedience,* lit., "with respect to the not-being-persuaded-state of these ones." Paul does not write "disobey" in the sense "know and reject"; he writes "not persuaded yet." **32:** *Has imprisoned,* or has joined together; *all in disobedience,* lit., "everyone into a not-being-persuaded-state"; *so that he may be merciful to all,* or in order that everyone might be [equally in need of being] shown mercy. **33:** *Judgments,* or decisions. **34:** Adapted from Isa 40.13 LXX. **35:** Cf. Job 35.7; 41.1,3. *Given,* lit., "first given." *To receive a gift in return,* lit., "and [or, even] it will be repaid to him."

12.1–21: Living faithfully, "therefore." Paul explains how Gentiles are to live faithfully as Christ-followers in the midst of the Jewish communities of Rome. In disclosing how God is working through those Israelites who are bringing the message to the nations as well as those who are not, Paul *therefore* exhorts the non-Jewish Christ-followers to change their mind-set and behavior to fulfill their responsibilities in this

[36] For from him and through him and to him are all things. To him be the glory forever. Amen.

12

I appeal to you therefore, brothers and sisters,[a] by the mercies of God, to present your bodies as a living sacrifice, holy and acceptable to God, which is your spiritual[b] worship. [2] Do not be conformed to this world,[c] but be transformed by the renewing of your minds, so that you may discern what is the will of God—what is good and acceptable and perfect.[d]

[3] For by the grace given to me I say to everyone among you not to think of yourself more highly than you ought to think, but to think with sober judgment, each according to the measure of faith that God has assigned. [4] For as in one body we have many members, and not all the members have the same function, [5] so we, who are many, are one body in Christ, and individually we are members one of another. [6] We have gifts that differ according to the grace given to us: prophecy, in proportion to faith; [7] ministry, in ministering; the teacher, in teaching; [8] the exhorter, in exhortation; the giver, in generosity; the leader, in diligence; the compassionate, in cheerfulness.

[9] Let love be genuine; hate what is evil, hold fast to what is good; [10] love one another with mutual affection; outdo one another in showing honor. [11] Do not lag in zeal, be ardent in spirit, serve the Lord.[e] [12] Rejoice in hope, be patient in suffering, persevere in prayer. [13] Contribute to the needs of the saints; extend hospitality to strangers.

[14] Bless those who persecute you; bless and do not curse them. [15] Rejoice with those who rejoice, weep with those who weep. [16] Live in harmony with one another; do not be haughty,

[a] Gk *brothers*
[b] Or *reasonable*
[c] Gk *age*
[d] Or *what is the good and acceptable and perfect will of God*
[e] Other ancient authorities read *serve the opportune time*

design. Rather than respond on the basis of present appearances, they are to live according to that which has been revealed, for they play an important role in the completion of God's rescue of everyone. Most of this chapter gives general instructions for how to live with respect and consideration toward everyone in their lives, including those who may oppose them and their claims. This they can do if they work together and look to God's empowerment, since God is the just judge who indeed knows the intentions and actions of everyone. Their responsibility is instead to serve the other, and they are to realize that they only play a small part, however important, in the midst of all of humanity, so they must learn to live on behalf of everyone, even on behalf of those who may seem to be obstacles to their own success or happiness. As he argued in ch 2, things (and people) may not be as they seem; leave the judging to God. Most of the specific instructions for how to carry this out are attested in Tanakh and other wisdom literature of the time (see annotations). **1:** *Therefore*, in view of what Paul has just argued about the role of these Gentiles in God's plan, including how their interests are related to how God is working with Israelites, he offers in chs 12 to 15 the following exhortation for how these Gentiles ought to behave. *Mercies*, or, compassions. *Living sacrifice*, dedicating one's body and mind to God (cf. 15.16; Isa 1.10–17; 66.18–20; 1QS 8.5–10; 9.3–5; 4QFlor. 1.2–7; *Odes Sol.* 20.1–5). *Which is your spiritual worship*, or which is a logical expression of your worship [or service]; cf. *b. Sanh.* 43b. **2:** See 6.4. *To this world*, to this age. *Renewing . . . minds*, cf. Isa 1.18. **3:** *Each according to the measure of faith that God has assigned*, lit., "as God distributed to each person a measure of faithfulness." Cf. 1QS 4.2–6; 24–25. **4–5:** *Members*, or parts. Paul (and other NT writers) used this imagery about the community of Jesus followers, e.g., 1 Cor 12.12–30; Eph 4.16; 5.30. **6:** *Prophecy*, not predicting the future but speaking the present word of God to the community. **8:** Gives can also mean shares; Job 31.17 [LXX]; giving cheerfully, cf. Prov 22.9; 2 Cor 9.7; Sir 35.9; Philo, *Spec. Laws* 7.74; *Lev. Rab.* 34.9. **9:** *Be genuine*, lit., "without hypocrisy." Cf. Lev 19.33–34; Amos 5.15; Ps 97.10; 1QS 1.4–5; *T. Benj.* 8.1. **10:** *Love*, or be devoted to. Cf. Lev 19.18; 1QS 2.24–25; Jn 13.34; *m. Avot* 4.15. **11:** *Do not lag in zeal*, cf. Prov 6.6,9; 20.4. **12:** *Persevere*, or persist, devote yourself to prayer; cf. Isa 56.7; Prov 15.8. **13:** *Saints*, see 1.7n. *Hospitality*, see Gen 18; Job 31.32; Philo, *Abr.* 107–14; *Ant.* 1.196; Mk 1.29–31; 6.8–11; 14.3; Lk 10.38–42. **14:** Cf. Mt 5.44; Lk 6.28; contrast Gal 1.8–9; 5.11–12; 1 Thess 2.14–16. **15:** Cf. Job 30.25; Eccl 3.4–5; Sir 7.34; Epictetus, *Diatr.* 2.5.23. **16:** Cf. Isa 5.21; Prov 3.7. *Lowly*, or humble, weak; it can refer to social standing or poverty. Cf. Judg 6.15; Isa 14.32; Ps 10.18;

but associate with the lowly;[a] do not claim to be wiser than you are. [17] Do not repay anyone evil for evil, but take thought for what is noble in the sight of all. [18] If it is possible, so far as it depends on you, live peaceably with all. [19] Beloved, never avenge yourselves, but leave room for the wrath of God;[b] for it is written, "Vengeance is mine, I will repay, says the Lord." [20] No, "if your enemies are hungry, feed them; if they are thirsty, give them something to drink; for by doing this you will heap burning coals on their heads." [21] Do not be overcome by evil, but overcome evil with good.

13 Let every person be subject to the governing authorities; for there is no authority except from God, and those authorities that exist have been instituted by God. [2] Therefore whoever resists authority resists what God has appointed, and those who resist will incur judgment. [3] For rulers are not a terror to good conduct, but to bad. Do you wish to have no fear of the authority? Then do what is good, and you will receive

[a] Or *give yourselves to humble tasks*
[b] Gk *the wrath*

18.27; 34.18; 131.1–3; Prov 3.34; Job 5.11; Sir 3.20; 10.15. **17:** Cf. Prov 3.4; 20.22; 24.29. **18:** Ps 34.14 (LXX 33.15); Mk 13.22; Lk 6.27–36; 2 Cor 8.21. *Ant.* 4.310. **19:** Deut 32.35; cf. Lev 19.18. *Wrath of God*, "of God" not in Gk. The echoes of Proverbs in this section reflect similar concern to exhort to righteous living. **20:** *Heap burning coals*, drawn from Prov 25.22, perhaps indicates the blood rising for one who is shamed by the receipt of kindness from one to whom the recipient has been unkind; cf. 2 Kings 6.22; 1QS 10.17–20 similarly develops Prov 25.22; 9.21–22; 4 *Ezra* 16.54; *Tg. Prov.* 25.21–23. **21:** *Overcome evil with good*, cf. Lk 6.27–36; 1QS 10.17–18; *b. Ber.* 10a.

13.1–14: Subordination to higher authorities enjoined. The traditional view of this chapter is that it exhorts the community to obey or subject themselves to the empire or state. Some interpreters see it as referring to subordination rather than obedience per se (i.e., willing to pay the consequences for resistance to unethical demands). It could also be understood to be an ironic or "hidden" transcript; that is, in view of the instructions just given in ch 12, and what comes immediately after in the rest of ch 13, the audience can understand it as signifying compliance, yet not for the reasons offered, in case the letter became known to Roman authorities (since it was sent to Rome). The person or institution to which the community should subordinate itself is not specified. It could refer to synagogue rulers, also called "archontes," the word translated "rulers" in v. 3 (cf. Lk 8.41; 12.11; 18.18; 23.13,35; 24.20; Acts 7.27,35; 14.5; *C.I.J.* 1.347). That would follow the general line of instruction, concerned with how these non-Jews were to behave among those who did not share their convictions, and who perhaps were in a position to bring pressure on them to alter those convictions (as "enemies"; see 11.28n.). Resistance to synagogue communal authorities and membership obligations (such as the Temple tax) might well be expected from non-Jews, if the legitimacy of their claims and social needs were being questioned, or rebuffed, provoking such an instruction. That would be in keeping with Paul's continued concern to challenge any temptations toward resentment, most explicit in ch 11, now in the more practical matters of institutional behavior. Thus one of the ways that these Gentiles are instructed to live respectfully toward Jews is to accept the authority of the Jewish communal leaders. This includes the payment of the Temple tax for those who would claim full membership in Israel, such as these Gentile Christ-followers do. They are not under Torah on the same terms as Jews, but faithfulness for them similarly means living according to the righteous lifestyle and concern for the other that express the ideals of Torah. They are from the other nations, but now, because they are Christ-followers, they are called to a new way of expressing what that means in the world. See *Ant.* 14.110; 16.160–73; Cicero, *Flac.*, 28.66–69. Tacitus, *Hist.* 5.5.1. See also v. 2n. **1:** *Governing authorities*, or protective/higher powers; i.e., synagogue leaders; no article in Gk. It is difficult to understand how, if the traditional interpretation here is assumed, Paul would sanction either the Roman Empire or its administration as instituted, or as the alternative suggests, "arranged by God"; the present age is "night," and thus "darkness" (13.12) and "evil" according to Paul, one from which people need to be freed (cf. Gal 1.4; 1 Thess 5.3; 2 Thess 2.6ff.). **2:** The critique of the role of Israel's kings and other authorities, including religious leaders such as priests and prophets, is a significant part of Israelite ideals, and all the more, of the rulers of other nations and their gods, who are often used to discipline the unrighteous but who are also guilty of harming the righteous; they will be punished, and are frequently resisted in acts of faithful righteousness (cf. e.g., Deut 17.14–20; 1 Sam 8; Isa 47; Jer 29; Dan 3; 2 Macc 7; Wis 6.3–5). **3:** *Approval*, lit., "praise for behaving righteously," even when their identity claims are resisted. **4:**

its approval; [4] for it is God's servant for your good. But if you do what is wrong, you should be afraid, for the authority[a] does not bear the sword in vain! It is the servant of God to execute wrath on the wrongdoer. [5] Therefore one must be subject, not only because of wrath but also because of conscience. [6] For the same reason you also pay taxes, for the authorities are God's servants, busy with this very thing. [7] Pay to all what is due them—taxes to whom taxes are due, revenue to whom revenue is due, respect to whom respect is due, honor to whom honor is due.

[8] Owe no one anything, except to love one another; for the one who loves another has fulfilled the law. [9] The commandments, "You shall not commit adultery; You shall not murder; You shall not steal; You shall not covet"; and any other commandment, are summed up in this word, "Love your neighbor as yourself." [10] Love does no wrong to a neighbor; therefore, love is the fulfilling of the law.

[11] Besides this, you know what time it is, how it is now the moment for you to wake from sleep. For salvation is nearer to us now than when we became believers; [12] the night is far gone, the day is near. Let us then lay aside the works of darkness and put on the armor of light; [13] let us live honorably as in the day, not in reveling and drunkenness, not in debauchery and licentiousness, not in

[a] Gk *it*

It is not likely that Paul means to say that the rulers of the Roman Empire were just, or the Empire was God's servant. The *sword* ("machaira") was a small one that represented police-like and judicial authority ("ius gladii"), which is descriptive of the synagogue communal leader's rights and obligations to police among Jews, under the authority of the Empire, e.g., the responsibility to collect taxes and keep order. The sword signifies these same kinds of responsibilities for authorities of the empire in general, but not literally. Note that Paul says he has been punished (including physical measures) by synagogue authorities (2 Cor 11.23–26; Acts 14.5,19; 16.22–23), and moreover that he had, previously, sought to harm Christ-believers under some kind of Jewish communal police-like rights (cf. Gal 1.13–15,23; Acts 8.1; 9.1–2; 22.4–5), a case which also brings into question any assertion that Paul would claim that justice is always carried out even by Jewish authorities. **5:** Anticipates the argument of chs 14–15. *Conscience*, the sense of what is right. **6:** *Taxes*, cf. Mk 12.17. The reference to *authorities* as *God's servants* here is Gk "leitourgoi"; this could refer to priests, as opposed to "diakonos" ("servant") in v. 4. "Leitourgos" often signifies a more cult-oriented activity (cf. 15.16; Isa 61.6; Neh 10.39; *4 Ezra* 7.24), which would be a more likely view for Paul to hold toward collecting funds for the sacrificial cult activities in Jerusalem than toward the tax collectors of the empire. **7:** *Due them*, not in Gk. **8:** *For the one who loves another has fulfilled the law*, lit., "for loving the other fulfills Torah." Cf. Lev 19.18; Mt 5.43; 19.19; Gal 5.6,13–14. **9:** Drawn from the Decalogue in Ex 20.13–17; Deut 5.17–21. **10:** *Love is the fulfilling of the law*, lit., "love is the fullness of Torah"; no article with "nomos" in Gk. Similarly stated in negative terms by Hillel, *b. Shabb.* 31a: "What is hateful to you, do not do to your neighbor"; moreover, he continues, "this is the whole Torah, the rest is commentary; now go and learn!" Note that Paul plays off of the word translated "work" in his choice of verb: love does not "work" harm to a neighbor. "Fullness" ("plērōma") can indicate completeness or full measure, which accentuates that Torah ("nomos") is not a negative category, but one with ideal values, which can be subverted instead of carried out as ideally intended (cf. 2.12–13; 7.12). **11–14:** The call to live in the full light of the impending day. **11–12:** Cf. Prov 4.16–19; Job 29.14; Wis 17.1–18.4; 2 Cor 6.7; Eph 4.22–24; 6.13–17; Col 3.9–14; 1 Thess 5.8. The contrast of light and dark is central in the DSS, see 1QS 2.7; 3.20–4.1; 1QM 15.9. Note the ambiguity of the time being defined, a time when night is over and yet the new day has not yet dawned but is drawing near, which mirrors Paul's overall message that something is in the process of changing but not completed. He thus seeks to help his audience to think and act in this time based not on how things might appear, but on what God has promised the outcome will be. "Works" versus "armor" is not an equivalent contrast; the instruction is based on "armor" likewise being "works," how one walks, i.e., behaves. The point is to commit to certain behavior, eschewing other behavior. Note that the initial conjunction of v. 11, Gk "kai" ("and") suggests continuity with the point of v. 10, i.e., that one can love in that way because one knows that the day of restoration is close, that day when justice will be served. **11:** *Salvation*, or restoration/rescue. *Believers*, or faithful. Cf. 2 Cor 6.7; 10.4; Eph 6.11. **13:** The verb for "walking" used here corresponds to the verb "halakh", related to "halakhah" in Heb. The point is to behave as if everything is observed fully by God and humankind, rather than as if something can be gotten away with as if unseen. *Live honorably*, lit., "walk properly."

quarreling and jealousy. [14] Instead, put on the Lord Jesus Christ, and make no provision for the flesh, to gratify its desires.

14 Welcome those who are weak in faith,[a] but not for the purpose of quarreling over opinions. [2] Some believe in eating anything, while the weak eat only vegetables. [3] Those who eat must not despise those who abstain, and those who abstain must not pass judgment on those who eat; for God has welcomed them. [4] Who are you to pass judgment on servants of another? It is before their own lord that they stand or fall. And they will be upheld, for the Lord[b] is able to make them stand.

[5] Some judge one day to be better than another, while others judge all days to be alike. Let all be fully convinced in their own minds. [6] Those who observe the day, observe it in honor of the Lord. Also those who eat, eat in honor of the Lord, since they give thanks to God; while those who abstain, abstain in honor of the Lord and give thanks to God.

[7] We do not live to ourselves, and we do not die to ourselves. [8] If we live, we live to the Lord, and if we die, we die to the Lord; so then, whether we live or whether we die, we are the Lord's. [9] For to this end Christ died and lived again, so that he might be Lord of both the dead and the living.

[10] Why do you pass judgment on your brother or sister?[c] Or you, why do you despise your brother or sister?[c] For we will all stand before the judgment seat of God.[d] [11] For it is written,

"As I live, says the Lord, every knee shall
bow to me,
and every tongue shall give praise to[e]
God."

a Or *conviction*
b Other ancient authorities read *for God*
c Gk *brother*
d Other ancient authorities read *of Christ*
e Or *confess*

14: *For the flesh, to gratify its desires,* or for covetousnesses [i.e., intense desires] of the flesh; "to gratify" not in Gk. Cf. Job 29.14; Gal 3.27. This statement recalls the argument of ch 7, but now Paul enjoins freedom from the snare of covetousness, although ch 7 seems to claim that this state has already been realized. How is it to be accomplished? By making no provision for satisfying that which is craved, even though the principle ("nomos") to which Paul calls his audience admits that covetousness is still present in their lives, and must be combated.

14.1–23: God's faithfulness proclaimed in community. Paul continues to instruct these non-Jews on how they should live within the Jewish communities of Rome, specifically the way that they should respect the sensibilities of those Jews who do not share their convictions about the meaning of Christ. Paul refers to those Jews as "weak" or "stumbling" in faithfulness to the revelation of Christ, versus themselves and Jews such as Paul who are "strong" or "able" to express faithfulness to this message. The thrust of the exhortation is that these Christ-following Gentiles are to comply with the expectations of righteousness for themselves as non-Jews as well as to respect the expressions of righteousness incumbent upon Jews with whom they are in contact. Otherwise, they risk harming the very ones for whom they should be living graciously in faithfulness to Christ, who died on their behalf as well. Their rescue depends, at least in part, on the audience's service to these Israelites. **1:** The instruction is stronger than merely "accept" or "welcome"; it carries the sense of "bring in as a partner," "fetch," or "take hold of." A close association between "being weak/sick/disabled" and "stumbling/offense" (lit., "trap") is evident in LXX, where the Gk "astheneō" and cognates were used to translate the Heb "kashal" and cognates (Jer 6.21; 18.15,23; Hos 4.5; 5.5; 14.1,9; Ps 9.3; 26.2 LXX; 106.12 LXX; Dan 11.14,19,33–35; cf. 1QH 9.25–27, where it is also contrasted with "might/power" ["g-b-r"] in a way similar to the contrast Paul is drawing with cognates of Gk "dynamai"; see also Judg 5.31; 2 Kings 18.20; 1 Chr 29.11). This translation maintains the image Paul has been working with since 9.32–33 to explain how these Gentiles are to view the fellow Jews who are not Christ-followers. *Weak in faith,* Jews who are stumbling with respect to faithfulness [i.e., to Christ]. **2:** Torah-observant Jews might eat vegetables when the meat available is deemed inappropriate (Dan 1.8–16; 10.3; Tob 1.10–11; Jdt 10.5; 12.1–2; 2 Macc 5.27; Josephus, *Life* 14); see v. 14 below. The meat might be seen as contaminated by idolatry, or as not having been properly slaughtered or prepared. **6–8:** The *day* is not specified; it could be the Sabbath or other feast days, but also could be disputes about what day things should be observed based on differing calendars. **9:** *So that he might be Lord of both the dead and the living,* i.e., ruler of all, since he has conquered death. **10:** Cf. 2.1–16. **11:** Paul conflates and adapts Isa 49.18 and 45.23. *Shall give praise,* or, shall confess. **13:** This motif—not putting a *stumbling*

FOOD THAT IS "PROFANE" (14.14)

Paul recognizes that all things are by nature not created profane (*koinon*, "common," 1 Macc 1.47,62), for the creation was pronounced good (Gen 1). Whether food is common/profane versus holy (or alternatively, impure/contaminated/unclean versus pure/clean, in v. 20) is not intrinsic to the food source itself; rather, its valuation is imputed by each personal or community convention (*nomos*). According to Jews, God sets out for Israel what is profane and what is to be set apart (holy) to God, so that it is no longer common/profane (Lev 11.41–45; 19.2; 20.25–26). This distinction does not invalidate the purity laws of Judaism; indeed, it is recognized in Scripture (Ps 24.1; 50.1, which Paul cites in 1 Cor 10.26 to make a similar point), and in rabbinic literature (*Gen. Rab.* 44.1; *Sifra Aharei* 93d). Paul is not abrogating Torah. Instead, Paul is making halakhic decisions for Gentile Christ-followers.

[12] So then, each of us will be accountable to God.[a]

[13] Let us therefore no longer pass judgment on one another, but resolve instead never to put a stumbling block or hindrance in the way of another.[b] [14] I know and am persuaded in the Lord Jesus that nothing is unclean in itself; but it is unclean for anyone who thinks it unclean. [15] If your brother or sister[c] is being injured by what you eat, you are no longer walking in love. Do not let what you eat cause the ruin of one for whom Christ died. [16] So do not let your good be spoken of as evil. [17] For the kingdom of God is not food and drink but righteousness and peace and joy in the Holy Spirit. [18] The one who thus serves Christ is acceptable to God and has human approval. [19] Let us then pursue what makes for peace and for mutual upbuilding. [20] Do not, for the sake of food, destroy the work of God. Everything is indeed clean, but it is wrong for you to make others fall by what you eat; [21] it is good not to eat meat or drink wine or do anything that makes your brother or sister[c] stumble.[d] [22] The faith that you have, have as your own conviction before God. Blessed are those who have no reason to condemn themselves because of what they approve. [23] But those who have doubts are condemned if they eat, because they do not act from faith;[e] for whatever does not proceed from faith[f] is sin.[g]

15 We who are strong ought to put up with the failings of the weak, and not to please ourselves. [2] Each of us must

a Other ancient authorities lack *to God*
b Gk *of a brother*
c Gk *brother*
d Other ancient authorities add *or be upset or be weakened*
e Or *conviction*
f Or *conviction*
g Other authorities, some ancient, add here 16.25-27

block in another's *way*—is often associated with avoiding idolatry; see Ex 23.33; 34.12; Judg 2.3; 8.27; Jer 3.3; Hos 4.17; Zeph 1.3; Ps 106.36 (105.36 LXX); Wis 14.11; 1QS 2.11–12,17. It is part of the love focus in Lev 19.14 that one shall not "place a stumbling block before the blind," developed in *y. Demai* 3.23 (cf. Rom 11.7–10). *In the way of another*, lit., "in the way of the brother (or sister)." **14:** *Unclean*, lit., "profane/common." **15:** Cf. Lev 19.14. *Is being injured*, or is being harassed. **16:** *Be spoken of as evil*, lit., "be blasphemed." **17:** The epistle's only mention of the kingdom of God (cf. 1 Cor 4.20). **19:** Cf. Ps 34.14; *m. Avot* 1.12. **20:** *Clean*, or pure. *Fall*, lit., "stumble." **21:** Wine might be feared to have been involved with idolatry in production (because there are idolatrous activities involved in the production) or by a libation offered to the gods before it was served (Deut 32.38; Dan 1.8; 5.4,23; *m. Avodah Zara* 30b, 31a, 36a). **23:** Some manuscripts insert here the doxology in 16.25–27. *Have doubts*, lit. "cause disputes."

15.1–33: Living in view of God's faithfulness. The argument from ch 14 continues, calling for gracious service toward these Jews in Rome, following the model of Christ's suffering even for those who rejected him, and invoking a vision of these Gentiles worshiping within the congregation of Israel, as scripture foretold. God's faithfulness to all Israel is thereby shown in fulfillment of the promises to the fathers and in the mercy extended to the Gentiles. **1:** Lit., "but we, the able, are obligated to support the stumbling of the unable (ones)." For the first time we have a reference to the audience, together with Paul, as the ones who are "able/strong," and the others, the *neighbors* (v. 2), as "unable." There may be ironic insult involved in this turn of phrase: how "able" are they if they are "unable" to understand that faithfulness involves caring for the neighbor's interests, not their own in ways

please our neighbor for the good purpose of building up the neighbor. [3] For Christ did not please himself; but, as it is written, "The insults of those who insult you have fallen on me." [4] For whatever was written in former days was written for our instruction, so that by steadfastness and by the encouragement of the scriptures we might have hope. [5] May the God of steadfastness and encouragement grant you to live in harmony with one another, in accordance with Christ Jesus, [6] so that together you may with one voice glorify the God and Father of our Lord Jesus Christ.

[7] Welcome one another, therefore, just as Christ has welcomed you, for the glory of God. [8] For I tell you that Christ has become a servant of the circumcised on behalf of the truth of God in order that he might confirm the promises given to the patriarchs, [9] and in order that the Gentiles might glorify God for his mercy. As it is written,

"Therefore I will confess[a] you among the Gentiles,
and sing praises to your name";

[10] and again he says,

"Rejoice, O Gentiles, with his people";

[11] and again,

"Praise the Lord, all you Gentiles,
and let all the peoples praise him";

[12] and again Isaiah says,

"The root of Jesse shall come,
the one who rises to rule the Gentiles;
in him the Gentiles shall hope."

[a] Or *thank*

that harm their neighbor, who is already suffering the weaknesses of being unable. The interpreter must fill in a specific reference for the ability or inability. The NRSV, *the failings of the weak*, reverses the phrase. But Paul does not write of the inabilities of the weak ones; rather, he writes of the weaknesses of the unable ones. The NRSV alternative would perhaps lend support to the traditional view that the weak are unable to trust God enough to abandon the conviction that faithfulness includes Torah observance. But the latter alternative, which reflects what Paul writes, supports the idea that because the weak were unable to proclaim the faithfulness of Christ, they were thereby disabled; that is, in Paul's metaphorical terms, because they were unable to understand that Christ was the goal of Torah for righteousness for the nations as well as Israel, they were thus stumbling over the proclamation of Christ to the nations, and the positive response of Paul's addressees in Rome to that message. *Put up with*, Gk "bastazō" has a more positive sense here: Paul has already taught his audience not to cause stumbling or to dispute; now he exhorts them to *please* the neighbors (v. 2). The translation alternative keeps in view the positive nature of this instruction, to "support," that is, to take responsibility to help the stumbling to be able to stand (or the weak to be enabled); in terms of stumbling, "hold up" might be even better. Since Paul here identifies himself among the "able," it is significant how one defines what it is that separated the able from the unable throughout this argument. Traditionally, this has been understood to point to Paul as Torah-free, able to move "beyond" Torah in Christ; thus, the "weak" are as yet unable to give up Torah as Paul believes they should. He nonetheless calls those, like him, who are free to tolerate the immaturity of "the weak." The suggested interpretation is that Paul, the Israelite and Torah-observant, shares with his non-Israelite audience the "ability" to believe that God has granted righteousness through the faithfulness of Christ to all of the nations, and at the same time, he maintains a responsibility to live as slaves holding up those Israelites who are not similarly persuaded. Therefore, these unpersuaded ones are characterized presently as weak/disabled/stumbling until they regain their step and take up, with Paul, the announcing of this good news. **3:** Ps 69.9, which Paul has cited in 11.9. Cf. Phil 2.1–18. **4:** Cf. 1 Macc 12.9. As Paul has just applied scripture to instruct them, so too they are to learn to draw from scripture to muster the required endurance for taking the posture of slaves in the service of others, and they are to be encouraged (or exhorted) by those who have similarly suffered in the present age, but in hope trusted in God's promise of justice and restoration. **6:** *Voice*, lit., "mouth." **8–12:** Paul concludes this section by reiterating the dynamic enunciated in the concluding remarks of 11.30–32, about the interwoven destinies of Jews and Gentiles. The promise was that all the nations would be blessed, or bless themselves, by the circumcised seed (e.g., 11.28–29; Gen 22.16–17). This declaration is followed by citations that form a proof for it. (Note that Heb "'ammim" "peoples," and "goyim" "nations," can both include Israel [e.g., Ex 19.6]). **9:** Ps 18.49 (17.50 LXX; also 2 Sam 22.50 LXX). Vv. 8–9 probably draw from the next verse of Ps 18.50 (LXX 17.51), which declares that God "is showing mercy to his anointed one, to David and his seed forever." The psalm describes David confessing God among the nations. That is how Paul understands himself. *Sing praises*, lit., "sing psalms." **10:** Deut 32.43. **11:** Ps 117.1; mercy is mentioned in the next verse

[13] May the God of hope fill you with all joy and peace in believing, so that you may abound in hope by the power of the Holy Spirit.

[14] I myself feel confident about you, my brothers and sisters,[a] that you yourselves are full of goodness, filled with all knowledge, and able to instruct one another. [15] Nevertheless on some points I have written to you rather boldly by way of reminder, because of the grace given me by God [16] to be a minister of Christ Jesus to the Gentiles in the priestly service of the gospel of God, so that the offering of the Gentiles may be acceptable, sanctified by the Holy Spirit. [17] In Christ Jesus, then, I have reason to boast of my work for God. [18] For I will not venture to speak of anything except what Christ has accomplished[b] through me to win obedience from the Gentiles, by word and deed, [19] by the power of signs and wonders, by the power of the Spirit of God,[c] so that from Jerusalem and as far around as Illyricum I have fully proclaimed the good news[d] of Christ. [20] Thus I make it my ambition to proclaim the good news,[d] not where Christ has already been named, so that I do not build on someone else's foundation, [21] but as it is written,

"Those who have never been told of him
shall see,
and those who have never heard of him
shall understand."

[22] This is the reason that I have so often been hindered from coming to you. [23] But now, with no further place for me in these regions, I desire, as I have for many years, to come to you [24] when I go to Spain. For I do hope to see you on my journey and to be sent on by you, once I have enjoyed your company for a little while. [25] At present, however, I am going to Jerusalem in a ministry to the saints; [26] for Macedonia and Achaia have been pleased to share their resources with the poor among the saints at Jerusalem. [27] They were pleased to do this, and indeed they owe it to them; for if the Gentiles have come to share in their spiritual blessings, they ought also to be of service to them in material things. [28] So, when I have completed this, and have delivered to them what has been collected,[e] I will set out by way of you to Spain; [29] and I know that when I come to you, I will come in the fullness of the blessing[f] of Christ.

[30] I appeal to you, brothers and sisters,[a] by our Lord Jesus Christ and by the love of the Spirit, to join me in earnest prayer to God on my behalf, [31] that I may be rescued from the unbelievers in Judea, and that my ministry[g] to Jerusalem may be acceptable to the saints, [32] so that by God's will I may come to you with joy and be refreshed in your company. [33] The God of peace be with all of you.[h] Amen.

16 I commend to you our sister Phoebe, a deacon[i] of the church at Cenchreae, [2] so that you may welcome her in the Lord as is fitting for the saints, and help her in whatever she may require from you, for she has been a benefactor of many and of myself as well.

[3] Greet Prisca and Aquila, who work with me in Christ Jesus, [4] and who risked their necks for my life, to whom not only I give thanks, but also all the churches of the Gentiles. [5] Greet

a Gk *brothers*
b Gk *speak of those things that Christ has not accomplished*
c Other ancient authorities read *of the Spirit* or *of the Holy Spirit*
d Or *gospel*
e Gk *have sealed to them this fruit*
f Other ancient authorities add *of the gospel*
g Other ancient authorities read *my bringing of a gift*
h One ancient authority adds 16.25-27 here
i Or *minister*

of the psalm (v. 2; 116.2 LXX). **12:** Isa 11.10 (cf. Rom 14.17). **16:** Perhaps inspired by Isa 66.19–23, Paul sees himself like a priest preparing pure sacrifices (cf. Ex 28.35,43; Phil 2.17). Alternatively, he may be referring to the offering from the nations (vv. 25–32). **19:** *Of the Spirit of God*, "of God" not in some Mss. **21:** Isa 52.15 LXX. *Of him*, not in Gk. **27:** *They ought*, lit., "they are obligated." **28:** *What has been collected*, lit., "this fruit." **31:** *The unbelievers*, lit., "the ones not-being-persuaded." **33:** *The God of peace be with all of you*, some Mss add 16.25–27 here.

16.1–27: Commendation, greetings, and closing. Although he has not been to Rome, Paul knows of many members of the community by name, or household, or service. **1:** *Phoebe* likely carried and presented this letter. *Deacon*, Gk "diakonos," servant. *Church*, or assembly. *Cenchreae*, the port for Corinth. **2:** *Saints*, see 1.7n. *Benefactor*, one who has used wealth to help the less fortunate. **3:** *Prisca and Aquila*, Acts 18.2; 1 Cor 16.19; 2 Tim 4.19. **5:**

also the church in their house. Greet my beloved Epaenetus, who was the first convert[a] in Asia for Christ. [6]Greet Mary, who has worked very hard among you. [7]Greet Andronicus and Junia,[b] my relatives[c] who were in prison with me; they are prominent among the apostles, and they were in Christ before I was. [8]Greet Ampliatus, my beloved in the Lord. [9]Greet Urbanus, our co-worker in Christ, and my beloved Stachys. [10]Greet Apelles, who is approved in Christ. Greet those who belong to the family of Aristobulus. [11]Greet my relative[d] Herodion. Greet those in the Lord who belong to the family of Narcissus. [12]Greet those workers in the Lord, Tryphaena and Tryphosa. Greet the beloved Persis, who has worked hard in the Lord. [13]Greet Rufus, chosen in the Lord; and greet his mother—a mother to me also. [14]Greet Asyncritus, Phlegon, Hermes, Patrobas, Hermas, and the brothers and sisters[e] who are with them. [15]Greet Philologus, Julia, Nereus and his sister, and Olympas, and all the saints who are with them. [16]Greet one another with a holy kiss. All the churches of Christ greet you.

[17]I urge you, brothers and sisters,[e] to keep an eye on those who cause dissensions and offenses, in opposition to the teaching that you have learned; avoid them. [18]For such people do not serve our Lord Christ, but their own appetites,[f] and by smooth talk and flattery they deceive the hearts of the simple-minded. [19]For while your obedience is known to all, so that I rejoice over you, I want you to be wise in what is good and guileless in what is evil. [20]The God of peace will shortly crush Satan under your feet. The grace of our Lord Jesus Christ be with you.[g]

[21]Timothy, my co-worker, greets you; so do Lucius and Jason and Sosipater, my relatives.[c]

[22]I Tertius, the writer of this letter, greet you in the Lord.[h]

[23]Gaius, who is host to me and to the whole church, greets you. Erastus, the city treasurer, and our brother Quartus, greet you.[i]

[25]Now to God[j] who is able to strengthen you according to my gospel and the proclamation of Jesus Christ, according to the revelation of the mystery that was kept secret for long ages [26]but is now disclosed, and through the prophetic writings is made known to all the Gentiles, according to the command of the eternal God, to bring about the obedience of faith— [27]to the only wise God, through Jesus Christ, to whom[k] be the glory forever! Amen.[l]

a Gk *first fruits*
b Or *Junias*; other ancient authorities read *Julia*
c Or *compatriots*
d Or *compatriot*
e Gk *brothers*
f Gk *their own belly*
g Other ancient authorities lack this sentence
h Or *I Tertius, writing this letter in the Lord, greet you*
i Other ancient authorities add verse 24, *The grace of our Lord Jesus Christ be with all of you. Amen.*
j Gk *the one*
k Other ancient authorities lack *to whom*. The verse then reads, *to the only wise God be the glory through Jesus Christ forever. Amen.*
l Other ancient authorities lack 16.25-27 or include it after 14.23 or 15.33; others put verse 24 after verse 27

First convert, lit., "first fruit." **7:** *Apostles*, "those sent out," early ones dispersed to testify to the life, death, and resurrection of Jesus. **10:** *Approved*, lit., "a tested one." **17:** The word translated *offenses* is the same word used in Paul's citation of Isa 28.16 in 9.33, Ps 69.22 in 11.9, and in the instruction not to put such a thing in the way of another in 14.13. *Avoid them*, lit., "bend (turn) away from them." **18:** *Appetites*, lit., "belly." *The simple-minded*, or naïve, unsuspecting. The accusation that they are slaves of their belly rather than Christ, coupled with mention of a specific teaching that they oppose, may indicate that they oppose the accommodation of dietary norms for which Paul calls in 14.1–15.7. In this sense, one might think of them as just the kind of "gentilizers" that Paul's letter seeks to prevent from having further influence in Rome. Vv. 17–20 echo the imagery of the serpent of Gen 2–3. **19:** Cf. 1.5,8; 15.14–19; 16.26. **20:** Cf. Gen 3.14–15. *Satan*, or the adversary. **21:** *Timothy*, 1 Cor 4.17; 16.10; 2 Cor 1.1,19; Phil 1.1; 1 Thess 1.1; Philem 1; cf. ; Acts 16.1–3; Col 1.1; 2 Thess 1.1; 2 Tim 1.5. *Lucius*, cf. Acts 13.1; Col 4.14; 2 Tim 4.11; Philem 24; *Jason*, cf. Acts 17.5–9; *Sosipater*, cf. Acts 20.4. **22:** *Tertius*, the amanuensis who wrote Romans for Paul; many letters were dictated to a professional scribe. **23:** *Gaius*, cf. 1 Cor 1.14; Acts 19.29. *Erastus*, cf. 2 Tim 4.20; Acts 19.22. There is a Roman government officer, an "aedile," Erastus, memorialized as a benefactor for laying a pavement stone near the theater in Corinth. **24–27:** These verses represent a useful summary, although they are absent from many manuscripts and are widely regarded as a later addition. **25:** *For long ages*, lit., "eternal ages."

THE FIRST LETTER OF PAUL TO THE CORINTHIANS

Paul's poem, "Love is patient; love is kind" (1 Cor 13.4–13), his recitation of one of the earliest proclamations of the gospel message of Jesus' death on behalf of sinners and his resurrection (15.3–5), and his statement of a basic formula for celebration of the Lord's Supper (11.23b–25), make 1 Corinthians one of the New Testament's most important books. This letter, written in the mid-50s, reveals the divisions facing the Pauline churches over such central concepts as the Holy Spirit (ch 2), marital and sexual norms (chs 5–7; 11), relation with the Gentile world (chs 6; 8), worship practices (ch 12), women's roles (ch 14), and resurrection (ch 15).

Corinth, a prominent trade center boasting two ports, was the heart of Roman imperial culture in Greece. It contained temples to Aphrodite and Asclepius (the god of healing), in which worshipers could also dine after performing sacrifices, and a theater. The city also hosted athletic contests. Philo, the first-century Alexandrian Jewish philosopher, notes that Corinth contains a "Jewish colony" (*Leg. Gai.* 281–82). By the mid-first century the city probably had Jewish assemblies (Acts 18.4), both in private homes and public buildings, yet Paul never uses the word *synagōgē* in his correspondence. When he uses the Greek *ekklēsia* ("church" = Heb *qahal;* see LXX Deut. 31.30) to describe assemblies of Jesus-followers in Cenchreae and Corinth (1 Cor 1.2; Rom 16.1), he is likely distinguishing them from other assemblies of Jews and Greeks (1 Cor 10.32). The famous fragmentary inscription reading "Synagogue of the Hebrews," found in Corinth in 1898, dates not from the time of Paul but from the mid-to-late second century.

Arriving in Corinth ca. 50, Paul spent over a year organizing several house-assemblies (Acts 18). His letter, written from Ephesus within a few years, responds to problems facing these nascent congregations. The second letter Paul wrote to this church (1 Cor 5.9–12) mentions earlier correspondence. Paul will again write to this church (2 Cor), but the factionalism Paul seeks to mend continued to plague the congregation, as attested by the late first-century Christian letter *1 Clem.* (47.3).

According to 12.2 (cf. Rom 16.4) and Acts 18.4, the Corinthian congregants were mostly Gentile, with a few Jews, including some who relocated to Corinth after their expulsion from Rome toward the end of the Emperor Claudius's reign (Rom 16.3–4; Suetonius, *Claud.* 25.4). The letter addresses issues concerning Gentile rather than Jewish congregants, such as eating meat offered to idols in pagan temples. It mentions "Jews" (*Ioudaioi*) only four times (1.22–24; 9.20; 10.32; 12.13), each time in relation to the gospel's universal import. The letter also frequently references the Scriptures of Israel without explanation, such as the paschal offering (5.7) and the Sabbath (16.2); for the Gentile Corinthians, Israel's Scriptures are theirs as well.

LITERARY HISTORY

Corinthian Gentiles participated in the cultic activities of Greek, Roman, Egyptian, and Eastern deities, either in public, citywide festivals or in private assemblies. Even private dinner parties could involve religious rites, such as libation offerings. Many Jews considered such activities idolatrous, and some saw idolatry along with sexual immorality as quintessentially Gentile practices (Wis 14.11–31; *Sib. Or.* 3.694, 751–52; *Jub.* 1.8; *T. Moses* 10). Accordingly, Paul singles out idolatry as the principal feature his Corinthian converts had abandoned (12.2).

First Corinthians is an authentic letter. Only 14.34–35 (perhaps also v. 36), has attracted attention as a possible post-Pauline interpolation, largely because its content—the silencing of women in the *ekklēsia*—contradicts 11.5. Since the later Pastoral Epistles (1 Tim 2.11–12; Titus 2.5) advocate women's subordination, the same group responsible for the Pastorals may have inserted the passage in this epistle.

Paul inhabits an apocalyptic Jewish world known from Second Temple texts (e.g., Dan 7–12; *1 En.*; 1QM). For this former Pharisee (Phil 3.5), the Messiah has redeemed his followers from Satan's authority and death's power. The "saints" (Gk *hagioi*, lit., "holy ones"; Paul's term for church members) have been *justified*—made righteous in relation to God—because of their participation in Jesus' death and resurrection through baptism (6.11; cf. *1 En.* 48–51). They anticipate the near arrival of the messianic kingdom, when their mortal bodies will be transformed (15.53–55).

INTERPRETATION

Paul instructs his churches to bear witness to the power and authority of the Christ by the way they live. Although God's Spirit dwells in them, the Corinthians' moral failings and organizational chaos belie the gospel message. Paul instructs the congregation to let God's Spirit goad them to repentance, because only those who are reconciled with God and neighbor and who manifest love (Gk *agapē*) can remain in the unified *ekklēsia*.

Shira Lander

1

Paul, called to be an apostle of Christ Jesus by the will of God, and our brother Sosthenes,

[2] To the church of God that is in Corinth, to those who are sanctified in Christ Jesus, called to be saints, together with all those who in every place call on the name of our Lord Jesus Christ, both their Lord[a] and ours:

[3] Grace to you and peace from God our Father and the Lord Jesus Christ.

[4] I give thanks to my[b] God always for you because of the grace of God that has been given you in Christ Jesus, [5] for in every way you have been enriched in him, in speech and knowledge of every kind— [6] just as the testimony of[c] Christ has been strengthened among you— [7] so that you are not lacking in any spiritual gift as you wait for the revealing of our Lord Jesus Christ. [8] He will also strengthen you to the end, so that you may be blameless on the day of our Lord Jesus Christ. [9] God is faithful; by him you were called into the fellowship of his Son, Jesus Christ our Lord.

[10] Now I appeal to you, brothers and sisters,[d] by the name of our Lord Jesus Christ, that all of you be in agreement and that there be no divisions among you, but that you be united in the same mind and the same

a Gk *theirs*
b Other ancient authorities lack *my*
c Or *to*
d Gk *brothers*

1.1–3: Salutation. 1: *Apostle*, "one sent out"; not all regard Paul as such (9.2; see also 12.28; 15.9). *Sosthenes*, perhaps the synagogue ruler in Acts 18.17. **2:** *Church* ("ekklēsia") *of God*, compare Israel as the "assembly of God" (Heb "qahal") in Deut 4.10; Judg 20.2; 1 Kings 8.14; etc. *Sanctified . . . saints*, church members as set apart or elected (see 6.11; Lev 11.44–45). *Called*, suggesting election. *Call on the name*, see Gen 4.26; Joel 2.32 (Heb 3.5); Ps 99.6; 105.1. *Lord*, the *Christ* (Gk for "mashiaḥ") who sanctifies (LXX Lev 20.8). Jewish uses of "Lord" for the messiah are rare (see *Pss. Sol.* 17.32), and absent in the Hebrew Bible. **3:** *Grace . . . peace*, standard Pauline invocations (see Num 6.24–26; along with glory, Ps 84[LXX 83].12; Prov 3.34). Invocations for well-being were common in ancient letter-writing (e.g., 2 Macc 1.1); Paul also conveys eschatological blessings (v. 4). *Father*, an increasingly common Jewish usage (Isa 63.16; 64.8; Tob 13.4 [*Sinaiticus* A]; Jdt 9.12; Wis 14.3; Sir 23.1,4; 3 Macc 2.21; *Ant.* 7.380; *b. Ta'an.* 25b; Philo, *Decalogue* 64; *Rewards* 166), familiar today from the "Avinu Malkeinu" ("Our Father, Our King") prayer recited on high holy days and other occasions, and other prayers.

1.4–9: Thanksgiving. 4: *Give thanks*, standard epistolary greeting. *Grace* ("charis"; Heb "ḥen"), God's covenantal favor. **5:** *Speech and knowledge*, speaking in tongues (14.2) and claiming special knowledge ("gnōsis," 8.1) created factions. Paul's thanksgiving is ironic. **6:** *Testimony* about God's saving power. **7:** *Spiritual gift* ("charisma"), e.g., prophecy, speaking in tongues (see 12.1–31) caused by spirit-possession. *Revealing* ("apokalypsis"—whence "apocalypse"), referring to eschatological revelation. **8:** *Blameless* or unimpeachable, a rare usage (3 Macc 5.31). *Day of our Lord*, compare the "day of the LORD," referring to the eschaton, in Isa 13.6,9; Jer 25.33 [LXX 32.33]; Am 5.18,20; and elsewhere. **9:** *Faithful*, Jewish literature emphasizes God's fidelity (e.g., Deut 7.9; 32.4). *Fellowship* ("koinonia") or communion, the community's experiences and values. Philo uses the same word for the sharing of sacrificial meat at the Jerusalem Temple and to describe Essene fellowship (*Spec. Laws* 1.221; *Good Person* 84, 91; see also *Ant.* 14.214). The related Heb terms, "yaḥad" ("oneness, unity") (1QS 5.1) and "ḥavurah" ("companionship, friendship") (*m. Demai* 2.2–3) can indicate shared meals.

1.10–17: Unity. 10: *Brothers [and sisters]*, the letter is replete with kinship language. *Name*, perhaps a reference to baptism and thus an implicit appeal for unity (see 1.13). **11:** *Chloe's people*, family, slaves and/or em-

purpose. [11] For it has been reported to me by Chloe's people that there are quarrels among you, my brothers and sisters.[a] [12] What I mean is that each of you says, "I belong to Paul," or "I belong to Apollos," or "I belong to Cephas," or "I belong to Christ." [13] Has Christ been divided? Was Paul crucified for you? Or were you baptized in the name of Paul? [14] I thank God[b] that I baptized none of you except Crispus and Gaius, [15] so that no one can say that you were baptized in my name. [16] (I did baptize also the household of Stephanas; beyond that, I do not know whether I baptized anyone else.) [17] For Christ did not send me to baptize but to proclaim the gospel, and not with eloquent wisdom, so that the cross of Christ might not be emptied of its power.

[18] For the message about the cross is foolishness to those who are perishing, but to us who are being saved it is the power of God. [19] For it is written,

"I will destroy the wisdom of the wise,
and the discernment of the discerning I will thwart."

[20] Where is the one who is wise? Where is the scribe? Where is the debater of this age? Has not God made foolish the wisdom of the world? [21] For since, in the wisdom of God, the world did not know God through wisdom, God decided, through the foolishness of our proclamation, to save those who believe. [22] For Jews demand signs and Greeks desire wisdom, [23] but we proclaim Christ crucified, a stumbling block to Jews and foolishness to Gentiles, [24] but to those who are the called, both Jews and Greeks, Christ the power of God and the wisdom of God. [25] For God's

a Gk *my brothers*
b Other ancient authorities read *I am thankful*

ployees of a female-headed household. **12:** *Apollos*, an Alexandrian Jew Paul sent to Corinth (Acts 18.24–19.1; 1 Cor 3.4–6; 3.22; 4.6; 6.12). *Cephas*, Aramaic for "rock," Gk "Peter" (see Mt 16.18). **13:** *Baptized*, Gk term meaning "dip," "immerse" (see Mt 28.19; Acts 8.16). The Qumran fellowship immersed for purification (1QS 3.4–5,9) and believed that water conveyed the divine presence (4Q504 1–2, l.15). *In the name*, a Semitic expression, perhaps coming from Aramaic-speaking Jesus-followers. **14:** *Crispus*, a Jew with a Latin name, a synagogue ruler (Act 18.8). *Gaius*, a wealthy Roman, often identified with Titius Justus (Acts 18.7), who provided the venue for the Corinthian church (Rom 16.23). **16:** *Household*, including slaves. *Stephanas*, see 16.15. **17:** *Gospel* ("euangelion," "good news"), often used for political announcements (e.g., of a tax relief), and by Jesus' followers to announce God's message. In the Hebrew Bible "good news" (Heb "besorah tovah" or simply "besorah") indicates welcome tidings (2 Sam 18.27; 2 Kings 7.9; Isa 52.7). *Eloquent wisdom*, philosophical speculation or clever speech.

1.18–31: Divine vs. human wisdom. 18: *Are being saved*, Paul's authentic epistles regard salvation as a future event. **19:** *It is written*, standard Jewish formula to cite scripture. Paul cites LXX Isa 29.14 (see Mt 15.8–9; Mk 7.6–7), God's promise to rescue Israel despite false counsel by *the wise*, but reinterprets Isaiah's "amazing things" as related to the Christ. The Isaiah Pesher (4Q163 frags. 16–17) and *L.A.B.* 53.13 also interpret Isa 29.13–16 eschatologically. **20:** Paraphrasing Isa 19.12; 33.18; 44.25. *This age*, Jewish tradition (e.g., *m. Avot* 2.7) distinguished this age ("olam ha-zeh") from the age to come ("olam ha-ba"). **21:** Paul denigrates human wisdom as opposed to the *wisdom of God*, Christ (see 1.24). In postbiblical Judaism, divine wisdom (Gk "sophia") is often equated with Torah or natural law (Bar 3.9–14; 4.1; Sir 1.26; 4.24; 6.37; 19.20; Philo, *Dreams 1*, 167–77; *Gen. Rab.* 1.1). In Stoic philosophy, "sophia" can refer to a divine aspect mystically accessible to humans seeking immortality (Wis 1.6; 6.9–23; 7.23–28). *Foolishness* ("mōrainō," whence "moronic"), to make salvation a matter of belief in the gospel (*those who believe*) rather than of philosophy or human wisdom (see 2.5). **22:** *Signs*, miraculous events (*1 En.* 82.16; *Sib. Or.* 3.335). Characterization of Jews seeking signs supported medieval stereotypes of Jews as blind to Christian truth (Aquinas, *Summa Theologica* 3.47.5; see 3.1–3n.). In Torah, signs include circumcision, Shabbat, human warnings, and miracles (Gen 17.11; Ex 15.11; Num 21.8–9). Signs can refer to prophecy, whether true (1 Sam 10.7,9; 2 Kings 20.8–9; Isa 7.11,14) or false (Isa 44.25). There is some ambivalence in the Bible about whether it is good to seek divine signs (see Isa 7.1–17). Messianic sign lists appear in early Jewish texts (4Q521; *b. Sanh.* 97a–98b). **23:** *Stumbling block* ("skandalon," whence "scandal"; see Rom 9.33; 11.1–10; Ps 69), because they rejected a crucified and raised messiah (compare the later dying messiah ben Joseph in 2 Esd [4 *Ezra*] 7.29; *b. Sukk.* 52a). *Foolishness*, Gentiles expected kings to overcome enemies. **24:** *Called*, see 1.2n. **25–31:** Jewish wisdom literature commonly contrasts human foolishness and wisdom (e.g., Prov 10.1;

foolishness is wiser than human wisdom, and God's weakness is stronger than human strength.

[26] Consider your own call, brothers and sisters:[a] not many of you were wise by human standards,[b] not many were powerful, not many were of noble birth. [27] But God chose what is foolish in the world to shame the wise; God chose what is weak in the world to shame the strong; [28] God chose what is low and despised in the world, things that are not, to reduce to nothing things that are, [29] so that no one[c] might boast in the presence of God. [30] He is the source of your life in Christ Jesus, who became for us wisdom from God, and righteousness and sanctification and redemption, [31] in order that, as it is written, "Let the one who boasts, boast in[d] the Lord."

2 When I came to you, brothers and sisters,[a] I did not come proclaiming the mystery[e] of God to you in lofty words or wisdom. [2] For I decided to know nothing among you except Jesus Christ, and him crucified. [3] And I came to you in weakness and in fear and in much trembling. [4] My speech and my proclamation were not with plausible words of wisdom,[f] but with a demonstration of the Spirit and of power, [5] so that your faith might rest not on human wisdom but on the power of God.

[6] Yet among the mature we do speak wisdom, though it is not a wisdom of this age or of the rulers of this age, who are doomed to perish. [7] But we speak God's wisdom, secret and hidden, which God decreed before the ages for our glory. [8] None of the rulers of this age understood this; for if they had, they would not have crucified the Lord of glory. [9] But, as it is written,

"What no eye has seen, nor ear heard,
 nor the human heart conceived,
what God has prepared for those who love
  him"—

a Gk *brothers*
b Gk *according to the flesh*
c Gk *no flesh*
d Or *of*
e Other ancient authorities read *testimony*
f Other ancient authorities read *the persuasiveness of wisdom*

Sir 20.31), and notes that divine wisdom trumps human plans (Prov 19.21). **25–26:** God's kingdom inverts hierarchies (Hannah's prayer, as expanded in the Greek (LXX 1 Kings (2 Sam) 2.8–10=4QSam[a]; Mt 19.30; 1QH[a] 9.35–39; *Lev. Rab.* 1.5; see also Jer 9.22–3). **26:** Paul suggests most Corinthians were uneducated, non-elite, and lacked social influence. **27:** *To shame,* see Ps 6.10 (Heb v. 11); 31.17; 35.4; etc., where God shames enemies. **29:** *No one,* lit., "all flesh" (Heb "kol basar"), all humanity. *Boast,* a Pauline concern (see also 1.31; 3.21; 4.7; 13.3; 15.31). Paul, like the Tanakh (see esp. Jer 9.22–23, quoted below, and in *T. Jud.* 13.2; Pseudo-Phocylides, *Sent.* 53; Philo, *Spec. Laws* 1.311), condemns boasting. **30:** *He,* God. *Life,* eternal life *in Christ Jesus,* God's incarnate *wisdom. Righteousness,* justification (see 6.11); *sanctification,* holiness; *redemption,* the rare word ("apolutrōsis") that conveys rescue from death by resurrection (see Rom 8.23). Paul invokes Jer 9.23–24 (love, justice, righteousness). **31:** Jer 9.23 (see also LXX 1 Kings 2.10).

2.1–5: Paul's gospel. Paul uses his own actions to illustrate the inverted roles of wisdom and foolishness (1.18–31). **1:** *Mystery,* the gospel. **3:** *Fear and . . . trembling,* see LXX Ex 15.16; Deut 2.25; 11.25; Jdt 2.28, and elsewhere, suggesting reaction to a hostile situation. **4:** *Words of wisdom,* philosophy, mere sophistry (see 1.17). *Spirit and . . . power,* i.e., of God, demonstrated through both Jesus' resurrection and charismatic gifts.

2.6–16: Divine wisdom. 6: *Mature,* cf. 3.1. Human development was a common metaphor for intellectual and spiritual progress (Philo, *Dreams* 2.234). *Rulers,* political leaders or angelic beings (see Bar 3; 2 Cor 4.4). For human vs. divine wisdom, see also Dan 2. **7:** *Hidden,* primordially (see Deut 29.29). The idea that God's eschatological plans were *decreed before the ages* appears in apocalyptic (see Dan 12.9) and rabbinic literature (*Tanhuma, Naso* 11). On the primordial creation of wisdom see, e.g., Prov 8.22; Sir 1.4; Wis 9.9. **8:** Jesus' crucifixion resulted from Jewish leaders' ignorance (see 1 Thess 2.14–15). While the "glory of the Lord" is common, *Lord of Glory,* perhaps reflecting "el ha-kavod" in Ps 28.3, is unique to this letter (cf. Acts 7.2). **9:** Similar to Isa 52.15; 64.3 (see also *b. Sanh.* 99a; *L.A.B.* 26.13), this saying is attributed to Jesus in the *Gos. Thom.* (17) and appears in Muslim tradition (*Sahih Bukhari* 9.93.589; *Sahih Muslim* 4.6783). Elsewhere, Paul only uses *as it is written* to introduce scriptural passages (Rom 1.17; 2 Cor 8.15). The Heb version of "as it was written," "kakatuv," is used to cite authoritative earlier sources in places such as Josh 8.31; 1 Kings 2.3; 21.11; 2 Kings 14.6; Ezra 3.2; Dan 9.13; 1QS 5.17; 8.14; CD 7.19, and frequently in rabbinic literature (Aram "dichtiv"). *Love* ("agapē") unites the community (see 13.1–13).

[10] these things God has revealed to us through the Spirit; for the Spirit searches everything, even the depths of God. [11] For what human being knows what is truly human except the human spirit that is within? So also no one comprehends what is truly God's except the Spirit of God. [12] Now we have received not the spirit of the world, but the Spirit that is from God, so that we may understand the gifts bestowed on us by God. [13] And we speak of these things in words not taught by human wisdom but taught by the Spirit, interpreting spiritual things to those who are spiritual.[a]

[14] Those who are unspiritual[b] do not receive the gifts of God's Spirit, for they are foolishness to them, and they are unable to understand them because they are spiritually discerned. [15] Those who are spiritual discern all things, and they are themselves subject to no one else's scrutiny.

[16] "For who has known the mind of the
Lord
so as to instruct him?"
But we have the mind of Christ.

3 And so, brothers and sisters,[c] I could not speak to you as spiritual people, but rather as people of the flesh, as infants in Christ. [2] I fed you with milk, not solid food, for you were not ready for solid food. Even now you are still not ready, [3] for you are still of the flesh. For as long as there is jealousy and quarreling among you, are you not of the flesh, and behaving according to human inclinations? [4] For when one says, "I belong to Paul," and another, "I belong to Apollos," are you not merely human?

[5] What then is Apollos? What is Paul? Servants through whom you came to believe, as the Lord assigned to each. [6] I planted, Apollos watered, but God gave the growth. [7] So neither the one who plants nor the one who waters is anything, but only God who gives the growth. [8] The one who plants and the one who waters have a common purpose, and each will receive wages according to the labor of each. [9] For we are God's servants, working together; you are God's field, God's building.

[a] Or *interpreting spiritual things in spiritual language*, or *comparing spiritual things with spiritual*
[b] Or *natural*
[c] Gk *brothers*

10: *Spirit*, the presence of God transforms believers through their union with Christ; Spirit is identified with wisdom (e.g., Ex 31.3), which encompasses *the depths of God*. The *Spirit* is therefore to God as (ideally) one's inner life is to one's self-knowledge. **12:** *Spirit of the world*, the term does not appear elsewhere in the LXX or NT. *Gifts*, lit., "things graciously given," include spirit-filled activities (12.1–31), forgiveness of sins (15.3), promise of resurrection (6.14), and salvation (15.2). **13:** *Not taught by human wisdom*, on human vs. divine speech, see Philo, *Worse* 39, 44, 133. **14:** *Unspiritual* ("psychikos," breath-formed, or merely a living being) vs. *spiritual* ("pneumatikos," or spirit-formed; see 15.45 on the "first man, Adam . . . and the last Adam"). The contrast evokes both Gen 2.7 and philosophical distinctions between air/breath/soul and heaven/spirit/mind (see Philo, *Dreams* 1.16, 20, 30). **15:** *Discern*, a pun also meaning "interrogate" or "examine." Holy ones, or saints, act as judges in the context of *interpreting spiritual things* (2.13). **16:** *Mind*, see LXX Isa 40.13, the sole instance of Heb "ruaḥ" rendered as Gk "nous"; see also Wis 9.13; Rom 11.34. Paul equates knowing the *mind of the Lord* with having the *mind of Christ*.

3.1–4: Mother and infants. 1: *The flesh*, the lowest spiritual state (*infants*, see Gal 4.3) with respect to the gospel. Later Christian writers applied this contrast of "flesh" vs. "spirit" to Jews, whose rejection of Christ was portrayed as manifest by their nonspiritual, carnal nature (see Augustine's treatment of 1 Cor 9.19–21, *Op. mon.* 12, and Aelfric [eleventh century], *De Populo Israhel* 297–99). **2:** Images of nursing leaders, teachers, and even God appear in Jewish literature (Num 11.12; Isa 28.9; 60.16; 66.11; 1QH[a] 15.21–22; Philo, *On Agriculture* 9; *Good Person* 160; see also 1 Thess 2.7–8; Gal 4.19; *b. Yoma* 75a, *Pesiq. Rav Kah.* 12). **3:** The association of baser moral instincts with *the flesh* and ethical behavior with the spirit or mind appears in Jewish philosophical literature (e.g., Philo, *Leg. all.* 2.50). *Behaving*, lit., "walking around." **4:** *Paul . . . Apollos*, see 1.12n.

3.5–9: Farmer and plants. 5: *Servants* ("diakonoi," whence "deacons"), a biblical image for those who convey God's message. **6–8:** Agricultural images for God's relationship to the community (e.g., Isa 5.5–7; 32.15; 61.3; Jer 32.41; Ps 1; CD 1.7; 1QS 8.5; *Jub.* 1.16; 16.26; Philo, *On Agriculture* 9; see also 1 Cor 15.36–41). **8:** *Wages*, the reward for being righteous, a common metaphor (Jer 17.10; LXX Ps 61.13 ; Plutarch, *Mor.* 183D; *Ant.* 1.183; 18.309). **9:** *Servants* (Gk "synergoi"), lit., "co-workers." *God's field, God's building*, images of Israel as God's plantings are found

[10] According to the grace of God given to me, like a skilled master builder I laid a foundation, and someone else is building on it. Each builder must choose with care how to build on it. [11] For no one can lay any foundation other than the one that has been laid; that foundation is Jesus Christ. [12] Now if anyone builds on the foundation with gold, silver, precious stones, wood, hay, straw— [13] the work of each builder will become visible, for the Day will disclose it, because it will be revealed with fire, and the fire will test what sort of work each has done. [14] If what has been built on the foundation survives, the builder will receive a reward. [15] If the work is burned up, the builder will suffer loss; the builder will be saved, but only as through fire.

[16] Do you not know that you are God's temple and that God's Spirit dwells in you?[a] [17] If anyone destroys God's temple, God will destroy that person. For God's temple is holy, and you are that temple.

[18] Do not deceive yourselves. If you think that you are wise in this age, you should become fools so that you may become wise. [19] For the wisdom of this world is foolishness with God. For it is written,

"He catches the wise in their craftiness,"

[20] and again,

"The Lord knows the thoughts of the wise,
that they are futile."

[21] So let no one boast about human leaders. For all things are yours, [22] whether Paul or Apollos or Cephas or the world or life or death or the present or the future—all belong to you, [23] and you belong to Christ, and Christ belongs to God.

4 Think of us in this way, as servants of Christ and stewards of God's mysteries. [2] Moreover, it is required of stewards that they be found trustworthy. [3] But with me it is a very small thing that I should be judged by you or by any human court. I do not even judge myself. [4] I am not aware of anything against myself, but I am not thereby acquitted. It is the Lord who judges me. [5] Therefore do not pronounce judgment before the time,

[a] In verses 16 and 17 the Greek word for *you* is plural

in the Hebrew Bible (e.g., Jer 24.6; Ezek 16.7) and also as God's temple in Qumran literature (1QS 8.5–9; 11.8); they underlie parables describing God's relationship to Israel in agricultural and architectural terms (e.g., Mt 20.1–16; 7.21–28; *m. Avot* 2.15; *b. Ber.* 64a; *y. Ber.* 2.8; *Avot de R. Natan A* 24.1).

3.10–17: Builder and buildings. 3.10: *Skilled master builder*, lit., "wise architect" ("sophos architecton"), a common metaphor (see, e.g., Philo, *Dreams* 2.8). **13:** *The Day*, judgment day, "Day of the Lord," a common motif in Second Temple literature (*1 En.* 96.2; *Sib. Or.* 3.55,741; 4Q163 frags. 6–7; 2.11; see also Rom 13.12; 1 Cor 5.5; 1 Thess 5.4). In prophetic texts (e.g., Isa 13.6; Joel 1.15; Am 9.11), "the Day of the LORD" (Heb "yom YHWH"), sometimes called "the day," "that day," or "those days," is a technical term referring to God's judgment, sometimes of Israel, sometimes of the nations. *Fire*, not hellfire but metaphorically, testing, a biblical, Second Temple, and rabbinic metaphor (e.g., Num 31.22–23; Isa 43.2; Ezek 22.18–22; Mal 3.3; Ps 12.7; 66.10–12; Wis 3.4–6; *Sib. Or.* 3.85; *L.A.B.* 25.13; *T. Abr.* 13.11–14; *b. Sanh.* 93a). **14:** *Reward*, wages (see 3.8n.). **15:** *Through fire*, see Dan 3.50; 1 Pet 4.12–17; *L.A.B.* 6.16–18. **16–17:** *You*, plural. "Ekklēsia" constitutes *God's temple* as a corporate entity, which Paul identifies with the "body of Christ" (12.27). Paul uses "naos" (lit., "sanctuary") for the *temple*, also used for the Jerusalem Temple (LXX 1 Sam 1.9; identified as holy throughout the Psalms, e.g., LXX Ps 5.8); 1 Cor 6.19 uses "temple" (without the definite article) to refer to each member of the community. The Qumran community referred to itself as a sanctuary ("biet qodesh," 1QS 8.5–9; *T. Levi*[ar] "Aramaic Testament of Levi" Bodleian Col. b 19).

3.18–23: Reversal of standards. 19: Job 5.12–13. **20:** Ps 94.11. Paul modifies the biblical verses to fit his rhetorical needs. See also 1.19n. Juxtaposing biblical passages is a common rabbinic hermeneutical method. **21:** *Boast*, see 1.29n. **22:** See 1.12n. *All things are yours*, lit., "all are yours," a Stoic slogan. **23:** *Belongs to*, is subject to. See "Paul and the Trinity," p. 293, and 15.28.

4.1–5: Eschatological judgment. 1: *Servants* ("hupēretēs," lit., "under-rowers," those on the bottom deck) ... *stewards* ("oikonomos," "one who oversees the household"), see 3.5,9. **3–4:** *Judge*, human verdicts are a *small thing*, as opposed to final judgment (see 3.13n.; 11.31–2). Paul uses juridical language also in 6.1–8; 9.13–14. For the beginning of the verse, see also Job 27.6. *I am not aware ... not thereby acquitted*, Paul makes clear here that one's insight into one's own actions or character must give way to the *Lord who judges*; see his comments in

PAUL AND THE TRINITY

Once Christianity developed the doctrine of the Trinity, the triune nature of God, concerns arose over early Christian writings that seemed to understand God differently. First Corinthians 15.28 expresses Paul's end-time theology most fully, yet it is obscure. Paul's use of God (*theos*) more than 100 times in this epistle, compared with 64 occurrences of Christ, is noteworthy. He may be addressing some Corinthians' failure to recognize the implications of the gospel for God's power and sovereignty as revealed fully in the end of days (see 1.12,30), perhaps those who say, "I belong to Christ." This passage illustrates Paul's understanding that Christ (the messiah) is not God, even though Christ incarnates God's wisdom and power (1.24), imparts the Holy Spirit (6.17), and is the conduit for all existence (8.6); ultimately, "Christ belongs to God" (3.23), who is both the source of all that exists in the universe as well as its purpose. This view is termed "subordinationism," although many Christians would reject such characterization of Paul's theology.

before the Lord comes, who will bring to light the things now hidden in darkness and will disclose the purposes of the heart. Then each one will receive commendation from God.

[6] I have applied all this to Apollos and myself for your benefit, brothers and sisters,[a] so that you may learn through us the meaning of the saying, "Nothing beyond what is written," so that none of you will be puffed up in favor of one against another. [7] For who sees anything different in you?[b] What do you have that you did not receive? And if you received it, why do you boast as if it were not a gift?

[8] Already you have all you want! Already you have become rich! Quite apart from us you have become kings! Indeed, I wish that you had become kings, so that we might be kings with you! [9] For I think that God has exhibited us apostles as last of all, as though sentenced to death, because we have become a spectacle to the world, to angels and to mortals. [10] We are fools for the sake of Christ, but you are wise in Christ. We are weak, but you are strong. You are held in honor, but we in disrepute. [11] To the present hour we are hungry and thirsty, we are poorly clothed and beaten and homeless, [12] and we grow weary from the work of our own hands. When reviled, we bless; when

[a] Gk *brothers*
[b] Or *Who makes you different from another?*

Rom 7.15,18–19,23. **5:** *Do not pronounce judgment*, see Mt 7.1; Lk 6.37. *Bring to light*, reveal the *hidden* eschatological scenario. *Disclose*, relating to God's far superior knowledge (see Ps 44.21 [Heb v. 22]; Prov 24.12). *Purposes of the heart*, see Jer 11.20.

4.6–21: Apostolic admonitions. 6: The Greek is enigmatic. *Apollos*, see 1.12n.; 3.4–6,11,22; 16.12. *Nothing beyond*, perhaps invoked to remind the Corinthians that Paul and Apollos derive their teaching from scripture, unlike "false" apostles (2 Cor 11.13) who teach secret knowledge *beyond* the text (see *1 En.* 104.10–11). *Puffed up*, or "inflated" (4.18–19; 5.2; 8.1; 13.4), arrogance based on knowledge (see Rom 15.4; Philo, *Leg. Gai.* 86; 4QCatena[a] frag. 5; *Sib. Or.* 3.738–39). **7:** *Sees anything different*, "distinguishes between" or "renders judgment about," employing a form of the same verb ("diakrinō") used in 6.5; 11.29,31; 14.29. Paul scolds the Corinthians for judging others and touting knowledge as earned rather than as a *gift*. **8:** *Rich*, possibly the wealth of the gospel, whose benefits the Corinthians have already enjoyed as holy ones who have won favorable judgments. For wealth as representing wisdom and righteousness either simply or metaphorically, see Prov 14.24; Tob 4.21; Sir 30.15; *m. Avot* 4.1. Paul is being ironic: the Corinthians presume they are *kings*, when the kingdom has not yet come. See Wis 6.21. **9:** *Death . . . spectacle*, the public nature of the apostles' work exposed them to ridicule and assaults (4.11), like criminals tortured and killed in the amphitheatre. *To angels*, Paul imagines a cosmic arena (see 11.10n.). **10:** *Fools*, used both ironically (1.21,25; 2.14; 3.18–19) as here, and straightforwardly (1.18,23,27). Contrast 1.27–28: the Corinthians' hubris is antithetical to God's call. **11–13:** Lists of tribulations are common rhetorical devices attesting the admirable steadfastness of the sufferer (Plutarch, *Mor.* 326 D-E; *2 En.* 66.6; Josephus, *J.W.* 2.151–53; *m. Pesah.* 10.5; *m. B. Kamma* 1.1,4). See also Isa 53; Mt 5.3–11,39–45; 2 Cor 4.7–12. **12:** *Work of our own hands*, the Bible commends handiwork, and rabbis were to have trades (*m. Avot* 2.2; 4.5; *t. Qidd.* 1.11; *b. Qidd.*

persecuted, we endure; [13] when slandered, we speak kindly. We have become like the rubbish of the world, the dregs of all things, to this very day.

[14] I am not writing this to make you ashamed, but to admonish you as my beloved children. [15] For though you might have ten thousand guardians in Christ, you do not have many fathers. Indeed, in Christ Jesus I became your father through the gospel. [16] I appeal to you, then, be imitators of me. [17] For this reason I sent[a] you Timothy, who is my beloved and faithful child in the Lord, to remind you of my ways in Christ Jesus, as I teach them everywhere in every church. [18] But some of you, thinking that I am not coming to you, have become arrogant. [19] But I will come to you soon, if the Lord wills, and I will find out not the talk of these arrogant people but their power. [20] For the kingdom of God depends not on talk but on power. [21] What would you prefer? Am I to come to you with a stick, or with love in a spirit of gentleness?

5 It is actually reported that there is sexual immorality among you, and of a kind that is not found even among pagans; for a man is living with his father's wife. [2] And you are arrogant! Should you not rather have mourned, so that he who has done this would have been removed from among you?

[3] For though absent in body, I am present in spirit; and as if present I have already pronounced judgment [4] in the name of the Lord Jesus on the man who has done such a thing.[b] When you are assembled, and my spirit is present with the power of our Lord Jesus, [5] you are to hand this man over to Satan for the destruction of the flesh, so that his spirit may be saved in the day of the Lord.[c]

[6] Your boasting is not a good thing. Do you not know that a little yeast leavens the whole batch of dough? [7] Clean out the old yeast so

a Or *am sending*
b Or *on the man who has done such a thing in the name of the Lord Jesus*
c Other ancient authorities add *Jesus*

29a; for Paul, see 16.19; Acts 18.1–3); generally, the Greek elite disparaged manual labor. **14:** *Children*, common term for disciples (see Deut 14.1; Ps. 103.13; Prov. 22.6; *m. B. Metz.* 2.11). **15:** *Guardians* ("paidagōgous," whence "pedagogue") of young children, see Gal 3.24–25. *Father* ("pater"; see 1 Thess 2.11–12; Philem 10), evoking the responsibilities of the Roman "paterfamilias," including shaping his children's moral character. Deut 6.7; Prov 3.12; *b. Qidd.* 22a; 29a; etc. include moral instruction among a father's duties. *B. Sanh.* 19b compares teaching Torah to fathering a child. **16:** *Imitators*, Jewish and Greek teachers encouraged "mimesis" or "imitation" for their disciples (Xenophon, *Mem.* 1.6.3; *b. Ber.* 62a; see also Lk 6.40). **17:** *Timothy*, 16.10–11; Acts 16.3; Rom 16.21; 2 Cor 1.1,19; Phil 1.1; 2.19,22; 1 Thess 1.1; 3.2,6; and the addressee of 1 and 2 Timothy. *Child*, continuing the familial metaphor (Phil 2.22; 1 Tim 1.2; 2 Tim 1.2). *Ways*, see Jer 21.8–14; Sir 15.11–17; *Did.* 1, 5–6. **18:** *Arrogant*, see 4.6n. **19–20:** *Talk*, philosophical rhetoric vs. God's *power.* **21:** *Stick*, for pedagogical discipline, Prov 13.24; Diogenes Laertius (third century), *Vit. Phil.* 6.

5.1–8: Community purity. 1: *Sexual immorality* ("porneia") . . . *among pagans*, Paul scolds the Corinthian community for tolerating behavior that even idolaters would condemn regarding the case in question; on associating sexual immorality with idolatry see e.g., Ezek 6.9; 23.37; Rom 1.14–27; *Sib. Or.* 3.37–8. *Living with his father's wife*, Roman (Gaius, *Inst.* 1.63) and Jewish law (Lev 18.7–8; Pseudo-Phocylides, *Sent.* 179; 11Q19 66.12; Philo, *Spec. Laws* 3.20–28; *m. Ker.* 1.1) prohibited sexual relations between stepson and stepmother. **2:** *Arrogant*, see 4.6n. *Mourned*, because of the punishment for sin (Ezra 10.6; Neh 1.4). *Removed*, expelled (Deut 17.7, quoted in v. 13), see Ezra 7.26; Mt 18.15–18; 1 Tim 1.18–20; 1QS 7.1–2. **3–4:** Paul "in absentia" judged the sinner guilty. **5:** *Satan* (see 1 Cor 7.5; 2 Cor 12.17; 1 Tim 1.20), God's agent, as in Job 2.6. In rabbinic literature, Satan preys on human weakness and prosecutes sinners in the heavenly court (*b. Git.* 52a; *Pesiq. Rab.* 185b–186a); according to *1 En.* 53.3, he is the angel who destroys the wicked at the last judgment. *Destruction of the flesh*, bodily decay preceding the *day of the Lord. Saved*, rescued from damnation. *Day of the Lord*, see 1.8n.; 3.13. **6:** *Boasting*, see 1.29n., 4.7. *Leavens*, that which puffs up or causes *boasting* (Hos 7.4; Mt 16.6; Gal 5.9; *Mek. Beshallah* 3 on Ex 14.11). **7–8:** *Clean out*, removing leaven in preparation for Passover (Ex 12.15; 13.7). *Unleavened*, evoking the bread eaten at Passover with the *paschal lamb*, interpreted as Christ *sacrificed* at Passover (see Ex 12.8,21; Jn 1.29; Acts 8.32; 1 Pet 1.19; Rev 5.6). *Festival*, the communal meal of the "ekklēsia" (see *2 En.* 68.9). *Old yeast*, a metaphor for evil (*b. Ber.* 17a).

that you may be a new batch, as you really are unleavened. For our paschal lamb, Christ, has been sacrificed. [8] Therefore, let us celebrate the festival, not with the old yeast, the yeast of malice and evil, but with the unleavened bread of sincerity and truth.

[9] I wrote to you in my letter not to associate with sexually immoral persons— [10] not at all meaning the immoral of this world, or the greedy and robbers, or idolaters, since you would then need to go out of the world. [11] But now I am writing to you not to associate with anyone who bears the name of brother or sister[a] who is sexually immoral or greedy, or is an idolater, reviler, drunkard, or robber. Do not even eat with such a one. [12] For what have I to do with judging those outside? Is it not those who are inside that you are to judge? [13] God will judge those outside. "Drive out the wicked person from among you."

6

When any of you has a grievance against another, do you dare to take it to court before the unrighteous, instead of taking it before the saints? [2] Do you not know that the saints will judge the world? And if the world is to be judged by you, are you incompetent to try trivial cases? [3] Do you not know that we are to judge angels—to say nothing of ordinary matters? [4] If you have ordinary cases, then, do you appoint as judges those who have no standing in the church? [5] I say this to your shame. Can it be that there is no one among you wise enough to decide between one believer[a] and another, [6] but a believer[a] goes to court against a believer[a]—and before unbelievers at that?

[7] In fact, to have lawsuits at all with one another is already a defeat for you. Why not rather be wronged? Why not rather be defrauded? [8] But you yourselves wrong and defraud—and believers[b] at that.

[9] Do you not know that wrongdoers will not inherit the kingdom of God? Do not be deceived! Fornicators, idolaters, adulterers, male prostitutes, sodomites, [10] thieves, the greedy, drunkards, revilers, robbers—none of

[a] Gk *brother*
[b] Gk *brothers*

5.9–13: Eschewing evil. 9: This *letter* is no longer extant; parts may be contained in 2 Cor. See 7.1. *Not to associate*, see Ps 1.1–2; 101. *Sexually immoral*, see 5.1n. **11:** *Eat*, table fellowship includes only those who maintain their holy status (see Josephus, *J.W.* 2.129–33; 1QS 6.2–5,16–17,20–21, vs. Mk 2.16). Vice lists were common rhetorical devices, e.g., 6.9–10; Jer 7.9; Hos 4.2; Wis 14.24–27; Mk 7.21–23; Rom 1.29–31; 2 Cor 12.20–21; Gal 5.19–21; 1QS 4.9–11; Philo, *Sacr.* 5 [32]; *Apoc. Abr.* 24.6–25.3; *1 En.* 10.20; 91.6–7; *Jub.* 7.20–21; 21.21; 23.14. **12–13:** *Inside*, believers only judge other insiders. Judgment of *those outside* is God's purview (see 5.4n.). Paul quotes Deut 13.5; 17.7, and other passages (applying to idolatry and other misdeeds) to justify expulsion for immoral behavior; he is not, however, advocating capital punishment.

6.1–8: Lawsuits and grievances. 1: *Saints* (see 1.2n.) are accountable to the "law of Christ" (9.21), not Roman law. *Court*, Jewish communities outside Judea constituted semi-autonomous legal bodies (see Phil 3.20) that adjudicated noncapital offenses. However, there is no evidence for such a court in Corinth. Halakhic literature suggests Jews were expected to settle noncapital intra-Jewish violations of Jewish norms in local Jewish courts, yet Egyptian papyri suggest that some Jews did take divorce cases to Gentile courts (*m. Sanh.* 1–3; *b. Git.* 88b). **2:** *Judge*, i.e., in the final judgment (see LXX Dan 7.22; Wis 3.8; 9.12; Sir 4.15; 1QpHab 5.4). In some Jewish accounts, Israel judges the Gentiles (*Jub.* 32.19; *T. Abr.* 13.6; see also Dan 7.21–22; Rabbi David Kimchi on Isa 11.14 and 14.1). **3:** *Angels* are subject to the saints' judgment (Dan 4.14; 2 Pet 2.4; Jude 1.6–15; *1 En.* 14.21–24; 15; 19; 21; 41.9; 46.7; *y. Shabb.* 6.10 [8d]; *b. Sanh.* 38b). **4:** *Those . . . no standing*, pagans. **6:** *Believer*, lit., "brother"; pagan philosophers were also appalled that siblings would sue each other (see Plutarch, *Mor.* 481B). **7–8:** Paul accuses church members of wronging each other by their appeals to the Roman judiciary system.

6.9–11: Vice lists. See 5.11n. *Fornicators* ("pornoi"), translated as "sexually immoral persons" (see 5.1,9–11). *Male prostitutes* ("malakoi"), lit., "soft," referring to moral and physical weakness, and perhaps also to being sexually submissive or coerced; *sodomites* ("arsenokoitai," a term of uncertain meaning combining "male" and "bed"), perhaps those guilty of coercing others sexually. The translation is not a good one, since the original reference has nothing to do with Sodom (Gen 19) and the term "sodomite" does not appear in the Hebrew Bible, even in reference simply to residents of Sodom. See also 1 Tim 1.10; *Sib. Or.* 2.73; Lev 18.20; 20.13. **10:** *Inherit the kingdom*, see 15.50; Mt 25.34; 19.29; Mk 10.17; Lk 10.25; 18.18; Gal 5.21.

FREEDOM FROM THE LAW

Greek philosophers such as Dio Chrysostom (first century CE) discussed the relationship of kings to the law of the state (Dio Chrys., *Or.* 3.10; 14.7–18; 62.2). Kings could choose to follow the law without being subject to it. Similarly, Cynics and Essenes flouted cultural norms or obeyed them in extreme; in either case, they were demonstrating their freedom from the power of the bodily passions (Diogenes Laertius, *Vit. Phil.* 6.72–73; Philo, *Hypoth.* 11.3). For Jews, obedience to the law, or Torah, became the rallying cry of freedom, the vehicle for maintaining the divine covenant, and a demonstration of faithfulness to God, as reflected in the rabbinic aphorism "only one who engages in Torah study is truly liberated" (*m. Avot* 6.2; see also 1 Macc 2.20–27; 2 Macc 6.18–7.42; *T. Moses* 9.6). Paul did not understand the freedom vis-à-vis the law obtained in Christ as a license to immorality, as others did (see Rom 2.12–14; 6.15–18; 8.2; Gal 5.1), but portrayed freedom from sin as slavery "to righteousness" (Rom 6.18).

Slaves were neither subject to nor protected by imperial law; thus they were vulnerable to abuse and exploitation. Freed persons were subject to certain laws but were denied the full range of protections and privileges, while citizens were bound to and protected by the laws of the state. In Paul's allegorical schema of the old Mosaic covenant in the pre-Christ age, Gentiles were slaves and Jews were citizens. Christ freed Gentiles from sin so that they would no longer be slaves but free (7.22), transforming the exclusively Jewish Torah covenant into Gentile-inclusive *Christ's law* (9.21). Some Jews predicted that all the commandments would be rendered obsolete in the end-time (*b. Nidd.* 61b).

these will inherit the kingdom of God. [11] And this is what some of you used to be. But you were washed, you were sanctified, you were justified in the name of the Lord Jesus Christ and in the Spirit of our God.

[12] "All things are lawful for me," but not all things are beneficial. "All things are lawful for me," but I will not be dominated by anything. [13] "Food is meant for the stomach and the stomach for food,"[a] and God will destroy both one and the other. The body is meant not for fornication but for the Lord, and the Lord for the body. [14] And God raised the Lord and will also raise us by his power. [15] Do you not know that your bodies are members of Christ? Should I therefore take the members of Christ and make them members of a prostitute? Never! [16] Do you not know that whoever is united to a prostitute becomes one body with her? For it is said, "The two shall be one flesh." [17] But anyone united to the Lord becomes one spirit with him. [18] Shun fornication! Every sin that a person commits is outside the body; but the fornicator sins against the body itself. [19] Or do you not know that

[a] The quotation may extend to the word *other*

11: *Used to be,* their pagan immorality should have been expunged by their being *washed* (baptized). *Sanctified,* purified from sinful ways and set apart from idolatrous Gentiles; the Gk ("hēgiathēte") corresponds to the Heb "qidash" or rarely "kipper" (Ex 19.14; 29.36; Lev 11.44; see also 1.30 and 2.16). *Justified* (Heb "tzadaq"), vindicated or acquitted before God; the term draws on Roman juridical and Jewish prophetic language (Isa 43.9,26; Mic 6.11).

6.12–20: The body. 12: *All things are lawful,* a Corinthian slogan (see 7.1; 10.23), consistent with some Greek philosophical views (Epictetus, *Diatr.* 41.1; Dio Chrys., *Or.* 3.10). **13:** *Food is meant for the stomach . . . food,* this may be another Corinthian slogan; the claim may have developed as a reaction against Jewish dietary laws (see Mk 7.9). *Destroy,* in the resurrection. *Fornication* ("porneia"), sexual immorality. Paul is concerned that once polluted by fornication, the spiritual body would be unfit for resurrection (6.14; *1 En.* 15.3–7 notes the incommensurability of spiritual and physical bodies). **14:** See 15.51–52; Paul and contemporary Jewish literature see resurrection as both preceding final judgment (1 Cor 6.2; *T. Benj.* 10.7–10), and as referring to eternal life after the judgment (Rom 2.7 and 1 Cor 4.4; *Pss. Sol.* 3.12). **15:** The church is the "body of Christ" (see 12.12–27). Jewish literature often portrays Israel as a body (Isa 10.18; *y. Ned.* 9.4; *Mek. R. Shimon bar Yohai* on Ex 19.6). **16:** *The two,* in LXX Gen 2.24 but not in the Heb. Like Philo (*Giants* 13.58–15.65), Paul interprets the effects of immoral intercourse on the body described here as corrupting a person's divine nature. **17:** *United,* still echoing Gen 2.24. **18:** *Shun fornication,* see Prov 5.3; 6.23–7.27; Sir 9.6; 19.2; *T. Reuben* 5.5. An allusion to Gen 39 is also possible. *Against the body itself,* which Paul relates to the "spiritual" body to be resurrected. **19:** *Temple* (see 3.16–17n.), container for God's

your body is a temple[a] of the Holy Spirit within you, which you have from God, and that you are not your own? [20] For you were bought with a price; therefore glorify God in your body.

7 Now concerning the matters about which you wrote: "It is well for a man not to touch a woman." [2] But because of cases of sexual immorality, each man should have his own wife and each woman her own husband. [3] The husband should give to his wife her conjugal rights, and likewise the wife to her husband. [4] For the wife does not have authority over her own body, but the husband does; likewise the husband does not have authority over his own body, but the wife does. [5] Do not deprive one another except perhaps by agreement for a set time, to devote yourselves to prayer, and then come together again, so that Satan may not tempt you because of your lack of self-control. [6] This I say by way of concession, not of command. [7] I wish that all were as I myself am. But each has a particular gift from God, one having one kind and another a different kind.

[8] To the unmarried and the widows I say that it is well for them to remain unmarried as I am. [9] But if they are not practicing self-control, they should marry. For it is better to marry than to be aflame with passion.

[10] To the married I give this command—not I but the Lord—that the wife should not separate from her husband [11] (but if she does separate, let her remain unmarried or else be reconciled to her husband), and that the husband should not divorce his wife.

[12] To the rest I say—I and not the Lord—that if any believer[b] has a wife who is an unbeliever, and she consents to live with him, he should not divorce her. [13] And if any woman has a husband who is an unbeliever, and he consents to live with her, she should not divorce him. [14] For the unbelieving husband is made holy through his wife, and the unbelieving wife is made holy through her husband. Otherwise, your children would be unclean, but as it is, they are holy. [15] But if the

[a] Or *sanctuary*
[b] Gk *brother*

Holy Spirit. **20:** *Bought,* redeemed from their captivity to sin (see Isa 50.1). *Price,* Jesus' crucifixion (see 1.30; 15.3), a pun on "timē" ("honor," "[granting] appropriate worth [to]"), which also means "worship" or "glorify" (see LXX Ps 8.6); see 1 Cor 7.23. *Glorify God* by remaining pure *in your body.*

7.1–7: Sexuality in marriage. 1: "*It is well . . . ,*" another Corinthian slogan (see 6.12n.); their asceticism may have been influenced by Isis worship, teachings associated with Jesus (Mt 19.12), Paul himself (7.7), or eschatological concerns. **2:** *His own wife . . . her own husband,* marriage helps avoid immorality (see Tob 4.12; *T. Levi* 9.9–10). Monogamous marriage, in this view, is the only permitted relationship. **3:** *Conjugal rights,* Jewish tradition mandates a certain frequency of sexual intercourse according to a man's profession; it also discusses limited periods of voluntary abstinence (see *m. Ketub.* 5.6; *t. Ned.* 5.6). **5:** *Deprive . . . set time,* for example, abstaining from sexual intercourse before prayer or other contact with the Divine (Ex 19.15; *T. Naph.* 8.8; Philo, *Life of Moses* 2.68–9; *Sifre Num.* on Num 12.1 [99]; *Ex. Rab.* 19; 46.3; *Avot de R. Natan* 9.39; *Tanh.* 111.46, *b. Pesah.* 87b; *b. Shabb.* 87a; *Sylloge Inscriptionum Graecarum* 3.982). *Lack of self-control,* see 1 Thess 4.3–6: Paul regards sexual license as part of Gentile culture. **6:** *Concession,* celibacy is preferable to marriage. **7:** *As I myself am,* Paul is celibate. There is no evidence that Paul married. *Gift,* see 3.5–9; 7.17–24; 10–13.

7.8–16: On divorce. 9: *Self-control* over sexual desire, a philosophical discipline cultivated by Neoplatonists, Aristotelians, Stoics, Cynics, Philo, and rabbis (Philo, *On the Creation* 164; *Avot de R. Natan* 16). **10:** *Lord,* Jesus (see Mk 10.9 and "Sexual Mores," p. 298). **11:** *Unmarried or else be reconciled,* as opposed to marrying another. Paul glosses Jesus' command (Mt 5.31–32) regarding divorce. **12:** Fearing idolatrous influences, moral corruption, and/or defilement of Israel's holy seed, some Jews banned exogamy (1 Kings 11.1–10; Ezra 9.1–2; Tob 4.12; *Jub.* 30.7; 4Q397 "Halakhic Letter" MMT frags. 5+6, 6; *T. Levi* 9.10; *T. Job* 45.3; Philo, *Spec.Laws* 3.29; *L.A.B.* 9.5; 21.1) although there is ample evidence for intermarriage (*Ant.* 8.7.5 [191–93]; 16.7.6 [225]; 18.5.1 [109]; 18.5.4 [139–140]; 20.7.1–3 [139–147]). *B. Qidd.* 68b and *b. Yebam.* 45a regard intermarriages as invalid. **14:** *Holy,* elevated to a status of sanctity. Paul's view that unbelievers do not defile believers aligns with rabbinic opinion that regards sexual contact with Gentiles as neutral (*Sifra Pereq Zavim* 1.1). In Paul's time, Jews regarded children of intermarriages as Jewish as long as their fathers were Jewish (see the children of Joseph and Moses, and 2 Sam 3.3, concerning Absalom; *Ant.* [see 7.12n.]). Although rabbinic opinions diverged, matrilineal

SEXUAL MORES

Sexual behavior attracted legal attention in antiquity. The Emperor Augustus's attempt to regulate adultery mandated that an unfaithful wife be divorced, but it did not punish husbands who had sexual relations with unmarried women (*Lex Julia* 123). Jewish law of the time defined adultery in terms of the wife's infidelity but not the husband's (as long as his sexual partner was unmarried [*Ant.* 3.12.1(274)]), since polygyny (a man marrying several women) was allowed. The husband's *authority* over the wife's body was presumed by Roman law, but not the wife's *authority* over the husband's body, the position advanced by Paul. Rabbinic law accorded women some authority over her husband's body, namely, the right to sexual relations (*m. Ketub.* 5.6). The late first-century historian Plutarch advocated an ethic similar to Paul's (*Mor.* 144b), as did the first century Stoic philosopher Musonius Rufus (frag. 9.5, 7).

Divorce was easily available and widely tolerated by Roman citizens. Conversely, Mk 10.2–12 bans divorce under any circumstances, while Mt 5.31–32 (and see Mt 1.9; Lk 16.18) permits divorce only in cases of "porneia," sexual impropriety (see Deut 24.1). Jewish attitudes toward divorce were not homogeneous, as illustrated by the divergent rulings attributed to the two first-century sages Hillel and Shammai (*m. Git.* 9.10). King Herod's sister Salome granted her own divorce, while Pharisees apparently forbade women from initiating divorce (*Ant.* 4.8.23 [253]; 15.7.10 [259]; see also Philo, *Spec. Laws* 3.5 [30–31]).

There is evidence for polygyny among Second Temple period Jews, yet the practice is condemned by the Essenes and Roman law (Josephus, *Ant.* 12.4.6 [186–89]; 17.1.2 [14]; *J.W.* 1.24.2 [477], *m. Yebam.* 4.11; CD 4.20–21; 11Q19 57.17–18; third century *Cod. Just.* 5.5.2, and *Digest* 48.5.12.12).

Celibacy was cultivated by some Essenes (Josephus, *J.W.* 2.8.2 [119]) and, according to Philo, the Therapeutae, a Jewish enclave in Egypt (*Cont. Life* 68). Jesus praises those who "make themselves eunuchs" for the kingdom of heaven (Mt 19.12), and the book of Revelation identifies the first who are saved in the final judgment as male *virgins* (Rev 14.4). In light of his expectation of the Christ's imminent return, Paul was more concerned about *changes* in marital status than marital status per se. Nonetheless, Paul's teachings inspired a second-century movement of Christian celibacy (*Acts of Paul and Thecla* 3.5), and virginity was esteemed as a Christian virtue (Tertullian, *Exh. cast.*). The practice did not survive among Jews, perhaps in part because it was so emphasized by the early church. Christians began mandating celibacy for priests in the fourth century (Council of Elvira, canon 33). While the tradition of clerical celibacy continued in the Roman Catholic Church, the Eastern Church permitted clergy to remain married if they were already married at the time of their ordination (Council of Trullo, canon 13). After the Protestant Reformation, nearly all protestant churches abolished compulsory celibacy for clergy, though some sectarian movements (the Shakers) reintroduced it, and there were revivals of monastic orders in non-Roman Catholic churches (Anglicans).

unbelieving partner separates, let it be so; in such a case the brother or sister is not bound. It is to peace that God has called you.[a] [16] Wife, for all you know, you might save your husband. Husband, for all you know, you might save your wife.

[17] However that may be, let each of you lead the life that the Lord has assigned, to which God called you. This is my rule in all the churches. [18] Was anyone at the time of his call already circumcised? Let him not seek to remove the marks of circumcision. Was anyone at the time of his call uncircumcised? Let him not seek circumcision. [19] Circumcision

[a] Other ancient authorities read *us*

descent eventually became normative in Judaism (*m. Qidd.* 3.12, *m. Yebam.* 2.5; 7.5, *t. Qidd.* 4.16). **16:** *Save*, at the final judgment (see 7.14).

7.17–24: Eschatological urgency and social stability. 18: *Remove the marks*, epispasm, or foreskin reconstruction, likely inspired by the embarrassment of nude athletic competitions and public bathing (see 1 Macc 1.15; *Ant.* 12.241; *T. Moses* 8.3). *Circumcised*, some Jesus-followers advocated circumcision for Gentiles (Gal 2.3–12). *Not seek circumcision*, in Rom 3.1–2 Paul notes benefits associated with circumcision (i.e., being a member of the Jewish people). **19:** *Nothing*, since the eschatological "new covenant" (11.25) privileged the moral *commandments* (e.g., prohibitions of idolatry, sexual immorality, theft, greed, murder [Rom 13.9; Eph 5.3–5; 1 Cor 6.18])

is nothing, and uncircumcision is nothing; but obeying the commandments of God is everything. [20] Let each of you remain in the condition in which you were called.

[21] Were you a slave when called? Do not be concerned about it. Even if you can gain your freedom, make use of your present condition now more than ever.[a] [22] For whoever was called in the Lord as a slave is a freed person belonging to the Lord, just as whoever was free when called is a slave of Christ. [23] You were bought with a price; do not become slaves of human masters. [24] In whatever condition you were called, brothers and sisters,[b] there remain with God.

[25] Now concerning virgins, I have no command of the Lord, but I give my opinion as one who by the Lord's mercy is trustworthy. [26] I think that, in view of the impending[c] crisis, it is well for you to remain as you are. [27] Are you bound to a wife? Do not seek to be free. Are you free from a wife? Do not seek a wife. [28] But if you marry, you do not sin, and if a virgin marries, she does not sin. Yet those who marry will experience distress in this life,[d] and I would spare you that. [29] I mean, brothers and sisters,[b] the appointed time has grown short; from now on, let even those who have wives be as though they had none, [30] and those who mourn as though they were not mourning, and those who rejoice as though they were not rejoicing, and those who buy as though they had no possessions, [31] and those who deal with the world as though they had no dealings with it. For the present form of this world is passing away.

[32] I want you to be free from anxieties. The unmarried man is anxious about the affairs of the Lord, how to please the Lord; [33] but the married man is anxious about the affairs of the world, how to please his wife, [34] and his interests are divided. And the unmarried woman and the virgin are anxious about the affairs of the Lord, so that they may be holy in body and spirit; but the married woman is anxious about the affairs of the world, how to please her husband. [35] I say this for your own benefit, not to put any restraint upon you, but to promote good order and unhindered devotion to the Lord.

[36] If anyone thinks that he is not behaving properly toward his fiancée,[e] if his passions are strong, and so it has to be, let him marry as he wishes; it is no sin. Let them marry. [37] But if someone stands firm in his resolve, being under no necessity but having his own desire under control, and has determined in his own mind to keep her as his fiancée,[e] he will do well. [38] So then, he who marries his fiancée[e] does well; and he who refrains from marriage will do better.

[39] A wife is bound as long as her husband lives. But if the husband dies,[f] she is free to marry anyone she wishes, only in the Lord. [40] But in my judgment she is more blessed if she remains as she is. And I think that I too have the Spirit of God.

8 Now concerning food sacrificed to idols: we know that "all of us possess knowledge." Knowledge puffs up, but love builds

[a] Or *avail yourself of the opportunity*
[b] Gk *brothers*
[c] Or *present*
[d] Gk *in the flesh*
[e] Gk *virgin*
[f] Gk *falls asleep*

over circumcision. **21:** *Present condition,* as slaves. The Greek could be read either as encouraging slaves to obtain their freedom or as making the best of their status as slaves. **22:** *Slave . . . freed person,* Paul plays on the terms' Roman legal usage and their metaphoric sense in relation to Christ. **23:** *Bought,* see 6.20n.

7.25–40: Unmarried believers. 25: *Virgins,* never-married women. *Trustworthy,* Paul's authority derives from his mystical infusion of the Spirit of *the Lord's mercy* (see 2 Cor 3.3–6). **26:** *Impending crisis,* imminent eschaton. **27:** *Seek to be free,* see 7.11. **28:** *Distress,* demands of marriage and family (7.33–34). **29:** *Be . . . had none,* practice abstinence. **30–31:** Mourners, celebrants, and patrons acting contrary to their normal state, indicating eschatological transformation (compare 2 Esd [4 *Ezra*] 3.24; 4.26; 16.42–45). **32:** *Anxieties,* see 7.28. **36:** *Fiancée,* lit., "his virgin"; Jewish and Roman marriage consisted of two stages, betrothal (engagement) and nuptials. **37:** *Keep her,* without consummation. **39:** *In the Lord,* within the church, further circumscribing the Jewish desideratum of endogamy (see 7.12n.).

8.1–13: Dietary concerns. 1: *Food sacrificed to idols,* a derogatory word ("eidōlothutos") used by Jews and Christians for pagan sacrifices. Some congregants may have eaten the food in order to gain or retain social

up. [2] Anyone who claims to know something does not yet have the necessary knowledge; [3] but anyone who loves God is known by him.

[4] Hence, as to the eating of food offered to idols, we know that "no idol in the world really exists," and that "there is no God but one." [5] Indeed, even though there may be so-called gods in heaven or on earth—as in fact there are many gods and many lords— [6] yet for us there is one God, the Father, from whom are all things and for whom we exist, and one Lord, Jesus Christ, through whom are all things and through whom we exist.

[7] It is not everyone, however, who has this knowledge. Since some have become so accustomed to idols until now, they still think of the food they eat as food offered to an idol; and their conscience, being weak, is defiled. [8] "Food will not bring us close to God."[a] We are no worse off if we do not eat, and no better off if we do. [9] But take care that this liberty of yours does not somehow become a stumbling block to the weak. [10] For if others see you, who possess knowledge, eating in the temple of an idol, might they not, since their conscience is weak, be encouraged to the point of eating food sacrificed to idols? [11] So by your knowledge those weak believers for whom Christ died are destroyed.[b] [12] But when you thus sin against members of your family,[c] and wound their conscience when it is weak, you sin against Christ. [13] Therefore, if food is a cause of their falling,[d] I will never eat meat, so that I may not cause one of them[e] to fall.

9 Am I not free? Am I not an apostle? Have I not seen Jesus our Lord? Are you not my work in the Lord? [2] If I am not an apostle

[a] The quotation may extend to the end of the verse
[b] Gk *the weak brother . . . is destroyed*
[c] Gk *against the brothers*
[d] Gk *my brother's falling*
[e] Gk *cause my brother*

status and familial connections. Jews generally avoided such food; they had permission to bring their own meat into local marketplaces (*Ant.* 14.259–61). Philo condemned Jewish participation in pagan ceremonial meals (*Dreams* 2.123; *Joseph* 154; *Spec. Laws* 3.126, and elsewhere). *All of us possess knowledge*, see 1.5n.; the phrase is likely another Corinthian slogan. *Puffs up*, see 5.6n.; Isa 2.11–12,17 construes idolatry as hubris. *Love* ("agapē") *builds up* rather than fractures communities (see 8.10). *Love* epitomizes the law (Rom 13.8,10; Gal 5.14; see Mt 22.37–40). **2:** *Know* from scripture (see 8.4). *Knowledge* of the one God (see 8.7n.; Dan 12.3). **4:** *No idol . . . exists*, see Jon 2.8; Ps 115; 2 Chr 13.9; Wis 13. *There is no God but one*, in late biblical religion, this became a core Jewish belief (Deut 4.35; 6.4; 1 Kings 18.39; Mk 12.29). Following prophetic tradition (e.g., Jer 2.28), Paul combines the scriptural prohibitions against idolatry and polytheism (Ex 20.3–4). Thus he is concerned about the Corinthians partaking in Greco-Roman cultic meals on two counts: the statues are merely empty vessels (8.7), and the many gods that pagans worship are false because there is only one God (8.5). **5:** *In fact*, better translated "as if"; Paul denies their existence. *Many gods and many lords*, titles given to the *so-called gods* of the Gentiles. **6:** *Father*, see 1.3n. *Exist*, we were created by God and it is for God's sake that we live. Jesus is the vehicle by which *all things . . . exist*, some Jewish literature understood wisdom as the attribute of God through which the world was created (Prov 8.22; Sir 1.4; Philo, *Drunkenness* 30–31). For a NT passage probably not by Paul, see Col 1.15–17, perhaps recapitulating Wis 7.22–8.1. **7:** *Knowledge* of the one God and therefore that *idols* are not gods. *Defiled*, see Ezek 20.18; 23.30. **8–9:** Paul favorably quotes the Corinthian viewpoint that food has no bearing on one's relationship *to God*. The Hebrew Bible has a variety of attitudes toward sacrifice; it is fundamental to the priestly worldview, but ranked second to mercy elsewhere (e.g. Isa 1.10–17; Hos 6.6; Ps 51.16–17 [Heb vv. 18–19]). *Stumbling block*, since sharing in the Lord's Supper affirmed belief in Jesus (11.20–34), the weak might be misled by pagan meal-sharing into affirming pagan deities. **10:** *Temple of an idol* ("eidōleion"), banquet areas within temple complexes. *Conscience*, awareness of God and conviction that idols are not gods. Rabbinic strictures prohibited even the appearance of misconduct because of its potential influence on others (Heb "mar'it 'ayin," see *y. Demai* 6.2). **12:** *Sin*, mislead believers (Isa 9.16; Ezek 13.9–10; Mic 3.5). **13:** *Never eat meat*, since meat sold in the marketplace was associated with pagan sacrifice, Corinthians could avoid sin by abstaining from meat. Paul's theory parallels the rabbinic concept of "lifnei meshurat ha-din," going beyond the boundaries of the law to ensure fidelity (*b. B. Metz.* 24b).

9.1–18: Rights of an Apostle. **1:** *Apostle*, see 1.1n. *Seen Jesus*, see 15.8–10. **2:** *Seal*, a means of fastening a document with softened wax, lead, or clay impressed with a stamp, used to ensure the authenticity of what was thus

to others, at least I am to you; for you are the seal of my apostleship in the Lord.

[3] This is my defense to those who would examine me. [4] Do we not have the right to our food and drink? [5] Do we not have the right to be accompanied by a believing wife,[a] as do the other apostles and the brothers of the Lord and Cephas? [6] Or is it only Barnabas and I who have no right to refrain from working for a living? [7] Who at any time pays the expenses for doing military service? Who plants a vineyard and does not eat any of its fruit? Or who tends a flock and does not get any of its milk?

[8] Do I say this on human authority? Does not the law also say the same? [9] For it is written in the law of Moses, "You shall not muzzle an ox while it is treading out the grain." Is it for oxen that God is concerned? [10] Or does he not speak entirely for our sake? It was indeed written for our sake, for whoever plows should plow in hope and whoever threshes should thresh in hope of a share in the crop. [11] If we have sown spiritual good among you, is it too much if we reap your material benefits? [12] If others share this rightful claim on you, do not we still more?

Nevertheless, we have not made use of this right, but we endure anything rather than put an obstacle in the way of the gospel of Christ. [13] Do you not know that those who are employed in the temple service get their food from the temple, and those who serve at the altar share in what is sacrificed on the altar? [14] In the same way, the Lord commanded that those who proclaim the gospel should get their living by the gospel.

[15] But I have made no use of any of these rights, nor am I writing this so that they may be applied in my case. Indeed, I would rather die than that—no one will deprive me of my ground for boasting! [16] If I proclaim the gospel, this gives me no ground for boasting, for an obligation is laid on me, and woe to me if I do not proclaim the gospel! [17] For if I do this of my own will, I have a reward; but if not of my own will, I am entrusted with a commission. [18] What then is my reward? Just this: that in my proclamation I may make the gospel free of charge, so as not to make full use of my rights in the gospel.

[19] For though I am free with respect to all, I have made myself a slave to all, so that I

[a] Gk *a sister as wife*

sealed; used metaphorically: since Paul founded the community, the community authenticated his apostolic role. **3:** *Defense*, Gk "apologia." **4:** *Right*, apostles expected church support. **5:** *Believing*, lit., "sister" ("adelphē"), a member of the church, such as Priscilla and Aquila (16.19; Rom 16.3). Paul has remained celibate (9.12). *Brothers of the Lord*, see Mt 12.46–49; 13.55; 28.10; Mk 3.31–34; Lk 8.19–21; Jn 2.12; 7.3–10; 20.17; Gal 1.19). *Cephas*, Peter. See 1.12; 3.22; 15.5; according to Mt 8.14–15; Mk 1.29–31; Lk 4.38–39, Jesus healed Cephas's mother-in-law; the NT does not name his wife. **6:** *Barnabas*, Aram for "son of encouragement"; see Acts 4.36; 9.27; 11.27–30; 13.8–13; 15.38–40; Gal 2.1–14. *Working for a living*, see 4.12n. **8:** *Law* of Moses (v. 9). **9–11:** *The law*, Deut 25.4; the *ox* represents apostles, *plows* and *threshes* refer to evangelizing, *treading out* to the apostles' ability to enjoy *material benefits* while teaching. Several texts relate Deut 25.4 to leaving fallen harvest for gleaners (Lev 19.9, Deut 24.19; *Ant.* 4.8.21 [233]). Paul uses a form of argument similar to rabbinic-type Jewish "qal vahomer" (from the lesser to the greater) argument: if oxen can eat, so can apostles (compare *m. B. Metz.* 7.2). This form of argument was also established within Greco-Roman thought (as in the argument "a fortiori"). Alternatively, this comparison can be read allegorically. **12:** *This rightful claim*, i.e., to food and a wife from within the church. *Obstacle*, Paul worried that the financial burden of his support might discourage ecclesial participation. **13:** *Temple* ("hieron") can also refer to pagan shrines (e.g., LXX Jdt 4.1; Bel 8, Bel [Theodotion] 22). Jewish and pagan priests were sustained by temple sacrifices (Num 18.8–32; Deut 18.1–5; *Ant.* 3.224–36). **14:** *The Lord*, Jesus (Mt 10.10; Lk 10.7). **15–16:** *Boasting*, see 5.6. **17:** Two motivations for proclaiming the gospel: free will and compulsion (see Gal 1.15; Jer 1.5). **18:** *Reward*, Paul eschews apostolic rights in order to teach *free of charge*, paralleling the rabbinic notion of "sekhar mitzvah mitzvah," the performance of a divine imperative is its own reward (*m. Avot* 4.2).

9.19–23: Slave to all. The argument here can be misunderstood. Paul is not presenting himself as a dissembler who pretends to be something he is not in order to persuade people under false pretenses to become members of the community. Rather, as the parenthetical clause in v. 21 suggests, he is speaking to differing groups in terms that they can understand. **19:** *Free with respect to all*, belonging to no one. *Slave* ("doulos"), devoted to the well-being of others in the service of God (LXX Jer 7.25; 25.4; Ezek 38.17; Joel 2.29; Am 3.7; Zech 1.6).

might win more of them. [20] To the Jews I became as a Jew, in order to win Jews. To those under the law I became as one under the law (though I myself am not under the law) so that I might win those under the law. [21] To those outside the law I became as one outside the law (though I am not free from God's law but am under Christ's law) so that I might win those outside the law. [22] To the weak I became weak, so that I might win the weak. I have become all things to all people, that I might by all means save some. [23] I do it all for the sake of the gospel, so that I may share in its blessings.

[24] Do you not know that in a race the runners all compete, but only one receives the prize? Run in such a way that you may win it. [25] Athletes exercise self-control in all things; they do it to receive a perishable wreath, but we an imperishable one. [26] So I do not run aimlessly, nor do I box as though beating the air; [27] but I punish my body and enslave it, so that after proclaiming to others I myself should not be disqualified.

10 I do not want you to be unaware, brothers and sisters,[a] that our ancestors were all under the cloud, and all passed through the sea, [2] and all were baptized into Moses in the cloud and in the sea, [3] and all ate the same spiritual food, [4] and all drank the same spiritual drink. For they drank from the spiritual rock that followed them, and the rock was Christ. [5] Nevertheless, God was not pleased with most of them, and they were struck down in the wilderness.

[6] Now these things occurred as examples for us, so that we might not desire evil as they did. [7] Do not become idolaters as some of them did; as it is written, "The people sat down to eat and drink, and they rose up to play." [8] We must not indulge in sexual immorality as some of them did, and twenty-three thousand fell in a single day. [9] We must not put Christ[b] to the test, as some of them did,

[a] Gk *brothers*
[b] Other ancient authorities read *the Lord*

20: *As a Jew,* Paul argued from the perspective of Jewish interlocutors. *Under the law,* Paul argued from the perspective of following Mosaic Law. **21:** *Outside the law,* the perspective of Gentiles neither bound nor protected by Torah. *Under Christ's law,* the Gk preposition "en" is better translated "in" rather than *under* (see Gal 6.2). Paul never forbids Jews in the church from following Torah. See" Freedom from the Law," p. 296. **22:** *Weak,* see 1.27; 2.3; 4.10; 8.7–12; 12.22. **23:** *Blessings,* full promises of the kingdom.

9.24–27: The good race. 24–25: *Only one . . . perishable wreath,* in Greek athletic competitions the winner received a wreath; the race for the kingdom has many victors who receive an *imperishable* prize, a resurrected body; a rare metaphor in Second Temple literature (Philo, *Confusion* 181; *On Agriculture* 42). **27:** *Disqualified* from the kingdom.

10.1–13: Israel's negative examples. 1: *Ancestors,* Israelites, the Corinthians' spiritual forebears (Gal 3.7). *Cloud,* divine presence protecting Israelites in the desert (Ex 13.21; 14.19–22), seen as God's wisdom (Wis 10.17; Philo, *Heir* (42) 203–4; *Mek. Beshallah* 1 on Ex 13.17–22), which Paul identifies as Christ (1.20–21). **2:** *Baptized,* infused with the *cloud*'s Spirit and immersed in the *sea* (at the Exodus). Jewish tradition does not see this event as "baptism," but does regard it as both present and proleptic salvation (*Mek. Beshallah* on Ex 14.13; 15.2). **3:** *Spiritual food,* manna, "bread from heaven" (Ex 16.4–36; Num 11.6–9; see Jn 6.31–32), the "bread of angels" (Ps 78.24–25). **4:** *Spiritual drink,* water (Ex 17.1–7; Num 20.1–13) that Moses drew from the *rock* at Horeb. Paul identifies the *rock* with *Christ,* since it *followed them* and sustained them (see *t. Sukk.* 3.3, 11; *b. Ta'an.* 9a). Philo, *Leg. all.* 2.86, and *L.A.B.* 10.7 see the rock as representing Wisdom; water as a metaphor for Torah and Wisdom frequently appears in Jewish texts (Wis 11.4; Philo, *Dreams* 2.221–22; *b. B. Kamma* 82a; *Song Rab.* 1.19; see Am 8.11). **5:** Some biblical texts idealize the period of wandering (see esp. Jer 2.2), while others (e.g., Ps 106), like Paul, see it as a period of unending apostasy. **6:** *Examples,* counterexamples, since the pattern of faithlessness and condemnation culminates with the eschaton (see Neh 9.11–21). *Desire evil,* see Num 11. **7:** LXX Ex 32.6 . *Idolaters,* golden calf worshipers punished by death (Ex 32.27–28), just as those who are unfaithful will be condemned in the final judgment. **8:** *Sexual immorality,* Num 25.1–2 portrays idolatry as a consequence of intercourse with Moabites. *Twenty-three thousand* likely is a variant of the 24,000 of Num 25.9 (see also Num 26.62). **9:** *Christ,* Some manuscripts have "the Lord," paraphrasing Deut 6.16 (see Ex 17.7; Mt 4.7). *Test* ("ekpeirazō"), the limits of Christ's forgiveness; the same word names the place where the Israelites demanded Moses bring water from the rock (LXX Ex 17.7; see also LXX Ps 77.18,41,56; Heb "Masah"). *Serpents,* Num 21.7, where Israel is punished for

and were destroyed by serpents. [10] And do not complain as some of them did, and were destroyed by the destroyer. [11] These things happened to them to serve as an example, and they were written down to instruct us, on whom the ends of the ages have come. [12] So if you think you are standing, watch out that you do not fall. [13] No testing has overtaken you that is not common to everyone. God is faithful, and he will not let you be tested beyond your strength, but with the testing he will also provide the way out so that you may be able to endure it.

[14] Therefore, my dear friends,[a] flee from the worship of idols. [15] I speak as to sensible people; judge for yourselves what I say. [16] The cup of blessing that we bless, is it not a sharing in the blood of Christ? The bread that we break, is it not a sharing in the body of Christ? [17] Because there is one bread, we who are many are one body, for we all partake of the one bread. [18] Consider the people of Israel;[b] are not those who eat the sacrifices partners in the altar? [19] What do I imply then? That food sacrificed to idols is anything, or that an idol is anything? [20] No, I imply that what pagans sacrifice, they sacrifice to demons and not to God. I do not want you to be partners with demons. [21] You cannot drink the cup of the Lord and the cup of demons. You cannot partake of the table of the Lord and the table of demons. [22] Or are we provoking the Lord to jealousy? Are we stronger than he?

[23] "All things are lawful," but not all things are beneficial. "All things are lawful," but not all things build up. [24] Do not seek your own advantage, but that of the other. [25] Eat whatever is sold in the meat market without raising any question on the ground of conscience, [26] for "the earth and its fullness are the Lord's." [27] If an unbeliever invites you to a meal and you are disposed to go, eat whatever is set before you without raising any question on the ground of conscience. [28] But if someone says to you, "This has been offered in sacrifice," then do not eat it, out of consideration for the one who informed you, and for the sake of conscience— [29] I mean the other's conscience, not your own. For why should my liberty be subject to the judgment of someone else's conscience? [30] If I partake with thankfulness, why should I be denounced because of that for which I give thanks?

[31] So, whether you eat or drink, or whatever you do, do everything for the glory of God. [32] Give no offense to Jews or to Greeks or

[a] Gk *my beloved*
[b] Gk *Israel according to the flesh*

"speaking against the LORD." **10:** *Destroyer*, see 5.5n., likely an angel (Ex 12.23; 2 Sam 24.16; Wis 18.25; *T. Abr.* A 8.12; 16.1–16; *3 Bar.* 4.8; 9.7; *Deut. Rab.* 11.10; *Midr. Tanh.* on Gen 39.1; *b. Avodah Zara* 20b). **12:** *Standing*, the position of the righteous and redeemed. *Falling*, the position of the condemned (Ex 14.13; 32.28). **13:** *Faithful*, see 1.9n. *Beyond your strength*, the motif of testing appears in rabbinic literature in the suffering of the righteous (*Gen. Rab.* 40.3, *b. Ber.* 5a–b "yisurin shel 'ahavah" [chastisements of love]). *Way out*, believers survive *testing* by remaining faithful to God (see Zech 13.9).

10.14–22: Idolatry vs. fidelity. 14: *Friends* ("agapētos"), lit., "beloved" (4.14; 15.58). **16:** *Cup*, wine shared in the Lord's Supper (see Introduction), representing Christ's *blood*. *Bread*, representing *the body of Christ*. *Sharing* ("koinonia"), lit., "fellowship, communion." **17:** *One*, uniting believers with each other and with Christ. Blessing wine and bread was fundamental to Jewish festival meals (see *m. Ber.* 6.1). *Y. Ber.* 7.3 speaks of a blessing recited over the cup at the end of a meal. *Body*, see 12.12–26. **18:** *People of Israel*, lit., "Israel according to the flesh." *Eat the sacrifices*, communal events like the Passover created fellowship, making Israelites *partners in the altar* (see 1.9n.; Lev 7.5–8; Deut 18.1–5). **20:** *Pagans*, not in the Greek. *They sacrifice . . . to God*, LXX Deut 32.17. *Demons* ("daimones"), a general term for noncorporeal or spiritual powers that later came to mean only malevolent ones. Jewish folk-belief in such powers lasted beyond the Middle Ages (Tob 8.3; Bar 4.7; *Jub.* 2.1–2; 10.7–9; *b. Ber.* 6a; *b. Eruv.* 100b; *b. Nidd.* 24b; *b. Pesah.* 109b–112a; *b. Sukk.* 28a; *Gen. Rab.* 20; *Pirqe R. El.* 34; *Num. Rab.* 11.5; *Eccl. Rab.* 2.6; Nachmanides on Lev. 27.7; *Zohar* 3.229b; *Shulchan Arukh, Orech Chaim*, 4.2; 90.6; 181.2; *Yoreh De'ah*, 116.5; 179.16, 19). Paul uses the term to refer to pagan deities, whose existence he denies (8.4–5). **21:** *Lord*, Christ. **22:** *Jealousy*, see Deut 32.21.

10.23–11.1: More dietary concerns. 23: See 6.12n. **25:** *Market*, see 8.13n. *Conscience*, see 8.10n. **26:** Ps 24.1 (LXX 23.1). **27:** *Without raising any question*, assume the food has not been sacrificed to idols. **32:** *Offense to Jews*, by

to the church of God, [33]just as I try to please everyone in everything I do, not seeking my own advantage, but that of many, so that they may be saved.

11 [1]Be imitators of me, as I am of Christ.

[2]I commend you because you remember me in everything and maintain the traditions just as I handed them on to you. [3]But I want you to understand that Christ is the head of every man, and the husband[a] is the head of his wife,[b] and God is the head of Christ. [4]Any man who prays or prophesies with something on his head disgraces his head, [5]but any woman who prays or prophesies with her head unveiled disgraces her head—it is one and the same thing as having her head shaved. [6]For if a woman will not veil herself, then she should cut off her hair; but if it is disgraceful for a woman to have her hair cut off or to be shaved, she should wear a veil. [7]For a man ought not to have his head veiled, since he is the image and reflection[c] of God; but woman is the reflection[c] of man. [8]Indeed, man was not made from woman, but woman from man. [9]Neither was man created for the sake of woman, but woman for the sake of man. [10]For this reason a woman ought to have a symbol of[d] authority on her head,[e] because of the angels. [11]Nevertheless, in the Lord woman is not independent of man or man independent of woman. [12]For just as woman came from man, so man comes through woman; but all things come from God. [13]Judge for yourselves: is it proper for a woman to pray to God with her head unveiled? [14]Does not nature itself teach you that if a man wears long hair, it is degrading to him, [15]but if a woman has long hair, it is her glory? For her hair is given to her for a covering. [16]But if anyone is disposed to be contentious—we have no such custom, nor do the churches of God.

[17]Now in the following instructions I do not commend you, because when you come

a The same Greek word means *man* or *husband*
b Or *head of the woman*
c Or *glory*
d Gk lacks *a symbol of*
e Or *have freedom of choice regarding her head*

flaunting the consumption of food offered to idols. **33:** *Saved,* see 5.5n.; 15.2n. **11.1:** *Imitators,* see 4.16n. This verse concludes this section, where Paul discusses his own behavior (10.30,33). The idea of imitating God is prevalent in rabbinic thought (*Mek. Shirah* 3; *Sifra* 19.2; *b. Sot.* 14a).

11.2–16: Gender roles. 2: *Handed them,* Jews understood the conveying of tradition as a chain of transmission (*Ant.* 13.10.6 [297]; *m. Avot* 1.1). **3:** *Head,* authority or source, referring to Paul's image of believers as the body of Christ (3.23) or to the order suggested by Gen 2.18–25; 3.16 (see 11.8n.). Philo, citing Plato, understands the head to be the body's most divine part, its master (*On the Creation* 119; see Plato, *Tim.* 45a; *Leg.* 12.942e). **4:** *Disgraces his head,* see "Headcovering," p. 305. **5:** The Talmud counts seven female prophets (Sarah, Miriam, Deborah, Hannah, Abigail, Huldah, and Esther [*b. Meg.* 14a]); Neh 6.14 mentions a (false) female prophet, Noadiah. *Shaved,* signaling shame (Aristophanes, *Thesm.* 837; Tacitus, *Germ.* 19; *T. Job* 23.7–10; 24.10) or pagan cultic practices. **6:** *Cut off her hair,* to discourage sexual attraction, particularly from angels (see 11.10n.). *Disgraceful,* in Germany and Cyprus, adulteresses were shorn (Tacitus, *Germ.* 19, Dio Chrys., *Or.* 64.3). **7:** *Image,* Gen 5.1 describes Adam but not Eve as a physical likeness of God (see 11.8n.; contrast Gen 1.26–27). *Reflection* ("doxa," in LXX for "kavod," "glory" [e.g., Ex 16.7]), lit., "glory." (The Gk term has a root meaning of "[good] repute.") God's "glory" as resting on men's heads like a crown (Ps 8.5 LXX 8.6; Bar 5.2; see 15.40) was a common Jewish image (4Q491 frag. 11; *1 En.* 62:15–16, *b. Ber.* 17b; *b. Sanh.* 111b; *b. Meg.* 15b). For woman as the *reflection of man* see *y. Ketub.* 11.3 in reference to a wife in an unhappy marriage. **8:** Gen 2.21–23. As God was the prototype for Adam, Adam was the prototype for Eve (Philo, *QG* 1, 4, 27–28). Adam was the perfect original; Eve was derivative (Philo, following Plato, *On the Creation* 46 [134]; *Leg. all.* 1.12 [31–33]; 2.13 [44]; *QG* 1, 25, 43; see also *Gen. Rab.* 8.9; 12; 17.4; 18.2; *b. Nidd.* 31b). **9:** *For the sake of,* Gen 2.18,20,24. **10:** *Angels,* to avoid the lust of the "watchers" (*1 En.* 6–11; *T. Naph.* 3.5; *Tg. Ps.-J.* to Gen 6.2). **11:** *Man,* or husband ("anēr"). *Woman,* or wife ("gynē"), see 7.3–4. **12:** *Comes through,* is birthed by. **14–15:** *Nature,* creation's established order, corresponding to Roman social order (see 11.3n.; Ovid, *Ars* 1.505, 518; Cicero, *Cat.* 2.22–24; Seneca the Elder, *Controversiae.* 2, preface 2; Martial, *Epigrams* 10.65.8). *Degrading,* see Philo, *Spec. Laws* 3.37–38; Pseudo-Phocylides, *Sent.* 210–12. **15:** *Covering,* long enough to cover her bosom (see *m. Sot.* 1.5; *Tg. Ps.-J.* to Gen 6.2).

HEADCOVERING

Roman women covered their hair in public (except during mourning, weddings, and certain festivals) as a sign of modesty and to indicate their respectable status and as protection against solicitation. Veiling was also normative for married women in Jewish culture (Sus 32 [Theodotion]; *m. Ketub.* 2.1; 7.4; *Avot de R. Natan* B 9.25; 42.117; *b. Ketub.* 72a–b). Uncovering or shaving a woman's head were forms of shaming, punishment, or mourning in biblical and later culture (Num 5.18; Isa 3.17–24; 3 Macc 4.6; *m. Sot.* 1.5). Paul recommends customs consonant with both Jewish and Roman social attitudes: what is appropriate for women is inappropriate for men and vice versa (11.14–15). Roman and Jewish priests traditionally covered their heads when in the divine presence (Plutarch, *Quaest. rom.* 10; *Mor.* 266C; Ex 28.36–40; Ezek 44.18–20). However, non-priests did not cover their heads when viewing (or in the case of Romans, performing) sacrifices. Paul mandated this non-priestly practice for all males (11.4), perhaps to preserve a sense of unity or to avoid pagan ritual associations. Rabbinic tradition describes male headcovering (Heb "sudara") as signifying the "fear of heaven" and as a "crown of glory" (*b. Ber.* 60b, quoting Ps 8.5; *b. Shabb.* 156b; see also *b. Qidd.* 31a). Widespread wearing of head coverings by Jewish men was a post-Talmudic custom.

together it is not for the better but for the worse. [18] For, to begin with, when you come together as a church, I hear that there are divisions among you; and to some extent I believe it. [19] Indeed, there have to be factions among you, for only so will it become clear who among you are genuine. [20] When you come together, it is not really to eat the Lord's supper. [21] For when the time comes to eat, each of you goes ahead with your own supper, and one goes hungry and another becomes drunk. [22] What! Do you not have homes to eat and drink in? Or do you show contempt for the church of God and humiliate those who have nothing? What should I say to you? Should I commend you? In this matter I do not commend you!

[23] For I received from the Lord what I also handed on to you, that the Lord Jesus on the night when he was betrayed took a loaf of bread, [24] and when he had given thanks, he broke it and said, "This is my body that is for[a] you. Do this in remembrance of me." [25] In the same way he took the cup also, after supper, saying, "This cup is the new covenant in my blood. Do this, as often as you drink it, in remembrance of me." [26] For as often as you eat this bread and drink the cup, you proclaim the Lord's death until he comes.

[27] Whoever, therefore, eats the bread or drinks the cup of the Lord in an unworthy manner will be answerable for the body and

[a] Other ancient authorities read *is broken for*

11.17–34: The Lord's Supper. 17: *Come together* to share the Lord's Supper. **18:** *Divisions*, in Roman culture, the richest, powerful guests received the best seats along with the finest food and drink; the poorest and least influential were relegated to auxiliary courtyards. **19:** *Genuine* ("dokimos"), proved righteous. **23:** *Received . . . handed on*, see 11.2n. *Betrayed* ("paradidōmi"), lit., "handed over," referring to God's handing over Jesus to death (Rom 4.25; 8.32). Death as vicarious atonement appears in Isa 53; 4 Macc 6.27–29; 17.20–22; *T. Benj.* 3.8; 1QS 5.6; 8.3; 9.4; *Mek. Pisḥa* 1 on Ex 12.1, and elsewhere. **24:** *Thanks*, blessing before the meal (cf. Lk 22.19). In Jewish practice, blessing before the meal ("birchat ha-motsi," "benediction on bringing out") is complemented by the blessing after the meal ("birchat ha-mason," "benediction on nourishment") (see v. 25n.; the requirements for this latter blessing are in *m. Ber.* 7.1–5). *This is my body*, 5.7n.; 10.3,16–17n.; Mt 26.26; Mk 14.22; Lk 22.19; cf. Jn 6.51, 54–55. **25:** *After supper*, blessing after meals (*Jub.* 22.6–9, Philo, *Cont. Life* 10 [79–80], Josephus, *J.W.* 2.8.5 [131]). *New covenant*, see Jer 31.31; LXX 38.31; in the letter to the Hebrews (8.13; 9.15; 12.24), Jesus' covenant supersedes the "first one"; in 2 Cor 3.6 the phrase is used to contrast the "letter" of the law vs. the "spirit"; see also Lk 22.20. Covenants were sometimes sealed with blood sacrifices (see Gen 15.10–18; Ex 24.8; Ps 50.5). Rabbinic literature links the redemptive aspect of the blood of circumcision to that of the blood of the paschal lamb based on a reinterpretation of Ezek 16.6, "in your blood, live!" recited during both circumcision ceremonies and Passover seders (*b. Eruv.* 19a; *Tg. Neb.* Ezek 16.6). *In remembrance of me*, see Lk 22.19, compare Heb "l'zikkaron" ("reminder"), used in Ex 13.9 of the "tefillin" or phylacteries.

EUCHARIST AND PASSOVER

Whether the Last Supper was a Passover meal (Mk 14.12–25 indicates that it is; Jn 13.1–2; 18.28; 19.14,31 indicate that it took place on the day before Passover began), the commemoration of Israel's exodus from Egypt forms the background for understanding the significance of the Lord's Supper, later referred to as "Eucharist" (lit., "thanksgiving") or "Communion." Remembrance is foundational to both the Lord's Supper and Passover: "In every generation, each must see himself as if he went forth from Egypt" (*m. Pesah.* 10.5). Jews acknowledge the continuing saving power of God by recalling the Exodus in the wine sanctification or Kiddush of every Sabbath, as commanded in Ex 13.3, "Remember this day on which you came out of Egypt," and the rabbis interpret the Decalogue in Ex 20.8 as ordaining the recitation of this blessing (*Mek. Bahodesh* 7; *b. Pesah.* 106a; 117b).

blood of the Lord. [28] Examine yourselves, and only then eat of the bread and drink of the cup. [29] For all who eat and drink[a] without discerning the body,[b] eat and drink judgment against themselves. [30] For this reason many of you are weak and ill, and some have died.[c] [31] But if we judged ourselves, we would not be judged. [32] But when we are judged by the Lord, we are disciplined[d] so that we may not be condemned along with the world.

[33] So then, my brothers and sisters,[e] when you come together to eat, wait for one another. [34] If you are hungry, eat at home, so that when you come together, it will not be for your condemnation. About the other things I will give instructions when I come.

12 Now concerning spiritual gifts,[f] brothers and sisters,[e] I do not want you to be uninformed. [2] You know that when you were pagans, you were enticed and led astray to idols that could not speak. [3] Therefore I want you to understand that no one speaking by the Spirit of God ever says "Let Jesus be cursed!" and no one can say "Jesus is Lord" except by the Holy Spirit.

[4] Now there are varieties of gifts, but the same Spirit; [5] and there are varieties of services, but the same Lord; [6] and there are varieties of activities, but it is the same God who activates all of them in everyone. [7] To each is given the manifestation of the Spirit for the common good. [8] To one is given through the Spirit the utterance of wisdom, and to another the utterance of knowledge according to the same Spirit, [9] to another faith by the same Spirit, to another gifts of healing by the one Spirit, [10] to another the

a Other ancient authorities add *in an unworthy manner,*
b Other ancient authorities read *the Lord's body*
c Gk *fallen asleep*
d Or *When we are judged, we are being disciplined by the Lord*
e Gk *brothers*
f Or *spiritual persons*

28: *Examine* in the legal sense of determining the truth (see 3.13; 16.3; 2 Cor 8.8). **29:** *Discerning,* distinguishing between regular eating and the Lord's Supper. **30:** *Reason,* improper observance incurs sickness and death. **31:** *Judged ourselves,* See 5.12–6.11. **32:** *Disciplined,* prodded to repent. *Condemned,* eternally punished (Wis 3.5–6).

12.1–11: Spiritual gifts. ("pneumatika," "spiritual ones"). *Gifts,* supplied by the translation; see translators' note *f,* behaviors enabled by the Holy Spirit, such as speaking in tongues and prophesying. The Dead Sea Scrolls attribute "prudence, insight, and wonderful wisdom" to God's Spirit (1QS 4.3). Although rabbinic literature understands prophecy as having ended in the early Second Temple period, Qumran, Josephus, and Jewish apocalyptic literature attest to its perceived continuation (*b. Sanh.* 11a; 1QpHab 7.4–6; *2 Bar.* 1.1). Some rabbinic sages performing miracles, and "hekhalot" ("palaces") mystics practiced glossolalia (*b. Ta'an.* 24b, *b. Pesah.* 112b; *b. B. Kamma* 50a; *Otsar ha-Geonim, Hagigah, Teshuvoth* 14–15). **2:** *Idols that could not speak,* see 10.14; 1 Kings 18.26–29; Hab 2.18–19; Ps 115.5; Bar 6.7; 3 Macc 4.16; *Jos. Asen.* 13.11. **3:** *Spirit,* speech was understood as breath flowing through the body. *By,* infused with. **4–7:** Diverse *gifts* ("charismata," "graced things"; see 1.7), *services* and *activities* reflect a common purpose for the church. **11:** *Chooses,* gifts are allocated by the Spirit, and are not based on merit or skill.

CURSING JESUS

Let Jesus be cursed! (12.3) may allude to Paul's discussion of Deut 21.23 (see Gal 3.13). Second-century Roman authorities demanded that Christians blaspheme Christ; those who resisted were martyred (*Mart. Pol.* 9.3). Polycarp's younger contemporary, Justin Martyr (ca. 160), claimed that Jews cursed Christ (*Dial.* 137.2), although no ancient Jewish sources attest this practice. Origen attributed this curse to Jews who blasphemed Jesus to avoid anti-Christian persecution (*Hom. Ps.* 37 [36]). Medieval Jewish apostates may have proven their return to the fold by reciting such formulas publicly (Agobard of Lyons, *On the Insolence of the Jews to Louis the Pious*). Alternatively, in the tradition of ancient malediction formulae, the phrase could be translated, "May Jesus curse . . .," which Paul cautions would only be efficacious if recited *by the Holy Spirit* (12.3) and not in the name of pagan deities. Paul advises the former pagan Corinthians to use the name "Jesus" in place of underworld deities like Hecate and Persephone, which are mere *idols* (12.2). Paul himself invokes a curse on opponents of *the Lord* (16.22).

SPIRITUAL GIFTS (12.8–10)

Paul lists nine activities manifesting the Spirit's work: (1) *wisdom utterance*: pronouncements of God's wisdom revealed in the death and resurrection of Jesus (see 1.30; 2.7–10); (2) *knowledge utterance*: proclamations about the divine nature (see 1.5; 8.7,11; Rom 15.14); (3) *faith*: trustworthy words as opposed to deceitful utterances (see LXX Prov 12.17); (4) *healing*: Jewish traditions mention the healing powers of the patriarchs, Moses, Solomon, and various prophets and rabbis; the traditions also saw healing as a manifestation of God's power (Gen 20.17; Num 12.13; 2 Chr 30.20; *Sir* 38.4–8; 48.23, *T. Reuben* 1.7; Philo, *On Agriculture* 95–8; *Ant.* 8.42; 4QPrNab ar; *b. Ber.* 34b); (5) *miracles*: attributed to patriarchs, Solomon, various prophets and rabbis, e.g., Ḥoni the Circle Drawer who elicited rainfall (*m. Ta'an.* 3.8); (6) *prophecy*: speech with eschatological, ethical, or mystical insight; (7) *discernment of spirits*: deciding whether a spirit manifested in gifts is demonic or angelic (5.12–6.11); Qumran texts mention "interrogating (*drsh*) their spirits (*ruaḥ*)" (1QS 5.20–21,23–24; 6.14; 1QSa 2.10); (8) *tongues*: speaking in foreign languages, including the unintelligible language of angels (see 13.1,8; 14.2; Isa 28.11 [xenolalia], Acts 2.4,11; 10.46; 2 Esd 14.40–41; *Gen. Rab.* 28.6; *T. Job* 48–50; *1 En.* 71.11); (9) *interpretation of tongues*: *Mek.Bahodesh* 9 on Ex 20.15; Plutarch, *Pyth. orac.* 24–25.

working of miracles, to another prophecy, to another the discernment of spirits, to another various kinds of tongues, to another the interpretation of tongues. [11] All these are activated by one and the same Spirit, who allots to each one individually just as the Spirit chooses.

[12] For just as the body is one and has many members, and all the members of the body, though many, are one body, so it is with Christ. [13] For in the one Spirit we were all baptized into one body—Jews or Greeks, slaves or free—and we were all made to drink of one Spirit.

[14] Indeed, the body does not consist of one member but of many. [15] If the foot would say, "Because I am not a hand, I do not belong to the body," that would not make it any less a part of the body. [16] And if the ear would say, "Because I am not an eye, I do not belong to the body," that would not make it any less a part of the body. [17] If the whole body were an eye, where would the hearing be? If the whole body were hearing, where would the sense of smell be? [18] But as it is, God arranged the members in the body, each one of them, as he chose. [19] If all were a single member, where would the body be? [20] As it is, there are many members, yet one body. [21] The eye cannot say to the hand, "I have no need of you," nor again the head to the feet, "I have no need of you." [22] On the contrary, the members of the body that seem to be weaker are indispensable, [23] and those members of the body that we think less honorable we clothe with greater honor, and our less respectable

12.12–26: The body. 12: Paul's *body* metaphor inverts Roman popular usage that supports the empire's class system. For the body as a metaphor for the people Israel see e.g., Isa 1.5–6; Philo, *Spec. Laws* 3.131. **13:**

members are treated with greater respect; [24] whereas our more respectable members do not need this. But God has so arranged the body, giving the greater honor to the inferior member, [25] that there may be no dissension within the body, but the members may have the same care for one another. [26] If one member suffers, all suffer together with it; if one member is honored, all rejoice together with it.

[27] Now you are the body of Christ and individually members of it. [28] And God has appointed in the church first apostles, second prophets, third teachers; then deeds of power, then gifts of healing, forms of assistance, forms of leadership, various kinds of tongues. [29] Are all apostles? Are all prophets? Are all teachers? Do all work miracles? [30] Do all possess gifts of healing? Do all speak in tongues? Do all interpret? [31] But strive for the greater gifts. And I will show you a still more excellent way.

13 If I speak in the tongues of mortals and of angels, but do not have love, I am a noisy gong or a clanging cymbal. [2] And if I have prophetic powers, and understand all mysteries and all knowledge, and if I have all faith, so as to remove mountains, but do not have love, I am nothing. [3] If I give away all my possessions, and if I hand over my body so that I may boast,[a] but do not have love, I gain nothing.

[4] Love is patient; love is kind; love is not envious or boastful or arrogant [5] or rude. It does not insist on its own way; it is not irritable or resentful; [6] it does not rejoice in wrongdoing, but rejoices in the truth. [7] It bears all things, believes all things, hopes all things, endures all things.

[8] Love never ends. But as for prophecies, they will come to an end; as for tongues, they will cease; as for knowledge, it will come to an end. [9] For we know only in part, and we prophesy only in part; [10] but when the complete comes, the partial will come to an end. [11] When I was a child, I spoke like a child, I thought like a child, I reasoned like a child; when I became an adult, I put an end to childish ways. [12] For now we see in a mirror, dimly,[b] but then we will see face to face. Now I know only in part; then I will know fully, even as I have been fully known. [13] And now faith, hope, and love abide, these three; and the greatest of these is love.

[a] Other ancient authorities read *body to be burned*

[b] Gk *in a riddle*

See Gal 3.28. **15–25:** The body relies on each part fulfilling its proper role. **26:** *All suffer*, see 11.23n.; 15.3n. Vicarious suffering and reward appears in prophetic and later Jewish literature (Isa 53; *b. Shabb.* 39a, *Lev. Rab.* 4.6).

12.27–31: Distribution of gifts. 28: *First . . . second . . . third*, in order of authority or perhaps chronology. **31:** *But strive*, better: "Yet you strive," a challenge to overcome jealousy of others' *gifts* and embrace a *more excellent way* of sustaining the community (see 13.1–2).

13.1–13: Love. Paul's great evocation of love first recalls his discounting of eloquence (1.17; 2.1) and wisdom (1.20–25), before turning to spiritual gifts and insisting that if they are not grounded in the effort to bring about the best for those in the community, if they do not aim to reveal the reality of love, they amount to nothing at all. **1:** *Love* ("agapē") of God and neighbor, the *more excellent way* of 12.31 (LXX Lev 19.18; LXX Deut 6.5, which Jesus summarizes as the "greatest commandment" in Mt 22.36–40; Mk 12.31; see also Lk 10.25–28). The Psalms LXX associate "agapē" with righteous worship (LXX Ps 30.23; 39.16; 68.35; 96.10; 144.20). In Isa 56.6, the likely background for Paul's discussion, this worship includes the Gentiles and Jerusalem's restoration (*1 En.* 108.12). *Tongues . . . of angels*, see *T. Job* 48.3; 49.2; 50.1–2; *1 En.* 71.11. *Clanging cymbal* of both pagan and Jewish worship (Ovid, *Metam.* 4.38, Strabo, *Geogr.* 10.3.7,13,15; LXX Ps 150.5; *Ant.* 7.306). **2:** *Knowledge . . . faith*, see 12.8–9. *Mysteries*, see 15.51n. **3:** *Give away*, extreme generosity was a hallmark of the "ekklēsia" (see Acts 2.45) and perhaps part of Jesus' agenda (Mt 19.21; Mk 10.21; Lk 12.23; 18.22). *Boast* about hardships. Other manuscripts have "burned," punished (see 4.9–13). **11:** *Child*, see 2.6n., 3.1n. **12:** *Face to face*, like Moses' encounter with God (Num 12.8; Deut 34.10; Philo, *Heir* 262, uses the same contrast). **13:** *Faith, hope, and love* will outlast spiritual gifts, but *love* is eternal. In the fulfillment of the kingdom, *love* will embrace all (see Wis 3.9; *T. Gad* 4.7 on love as a gift of the Spirit). Rabbinic tradition ties faith in God to hope for the world-to-come (*Mek. Beshallah* 7 on Ex 14.31).

14 Pursue love and strive for the spiritual gifts, and especially that you may prophesy. [2] For those who speak in a tongue do not speak to other people but to God; for nobody understands them, since they are speaking mysteries in the Spirit. [3] On the other hand, those who prophesy speak to other people for their upbuilding and encouragement and consolation. [4] Those who speak in a tongue build up themselves, but those who prophesy build up the church. [5] Now I would like all of you to speak in tongues, but even more to prophesy. One who prophesies is greater than one who speaks in tongues, unless someone interprets, so that the church may be built up.

[6] Now, brothers and sisters,[a] if I come to you speaking in tongues, how will I benefit you unless I speak to you in some revelation or knowledge or prophecy or teaching? [7] It is the same way with lifeless instruments that produce sound, such as the flute or the harp. If they do not give distinct notes, how will anyone know what is being played? [8] And if the bugle gives an indistinct sound, who will get ready for battle? [9] So with yourselves; if in a tongue you utter speech that is not intelligible, how will anyone know what is being said? For you will be speaking into the air. [10] There are doubtless many different kinds of sounds in the world, and nothing is without sound. [11] If then I do not know the meaning of a sound, I will be a foreigner to the speaker and the speaker a foreigner to me. [12] So with yourselves; since you are eager for spiritual gifts, strive to excel in them for building up the church.

[13] Therefore, one who speaks in a tongue should pray for the power to interpret. [14] For if I pray in a tongue, my spirit prays but my mind is unproductive. [15] What should I do then? I will pray with the spirit, but I will pray with the mind also; I will sing praise with the spirit, but I will sing praise with the mind also. [16] Otherwise, if you say a blessing with the spirit, how can anyone in the position of an outsider say the "Amen" to your thanksgiving, since the outsider does not know what you are saying? [17] For you may give thanks well enough, but the other person is not built up. [18] I thank God that I speak in tongues more than all of you; [19] nevertheless, in church I would rather speak five words with my mind, in order to instruct others also, than ten thousand words in a tongue.

[20] Brothers and sisters,[a] do not be children in your thinking; rather, be infants in evil, but in thinking be adults. [21] In the law it is written,

"By people of strange tongues
and by the lips of foreigners
I will speak to this people;
yet even then they will not listen
to me,"

says the Lord. [22] Tongues, then, are a sign not for believers but for unbelievers, while prophecy is not for unbelievers but for believers. [23] If, therefore, the whole church comes together and all speak in tongues, and outsiders or unbelievers enter, will they not say that you are out of your mind? [24] But if all prophesy, an unbeliever or outsider who enters is reproved by all and called to account by all. [25] After the secrets of the unbeliever's

[a] Gk *brothers*

14.1–40: Prophecy and tongues. 1: *Spiritual gifts* ("pneumatika"), see 12.1–11n. and "Spiritual Gifts," p. 307. **2:** *Speaking mysteries*, talking in incomprehensible language about hidden heavenly secrets. **3:** Prophecy enlightens more than tongues because it is immediately comprehensible; see 12.8; Wis 14.28; *Sib. Or.* 3.163, 298, 491; Plutarch, *Pyth. orac.* 24–25. **8:** Roman army musicians signaled maneuvers with instruments; see also Num 10.2–9; Josh 6.4–20; 4Q491 frag. 11, col. 2.1–7; frag. 13.1–6. **14:** *Mind*, awareness. **15:** *Sing praise*, chanting of psalms or hymns acclaiming God's accomplishments. **16:** *Blessing*, thanksgiving, requiring assent of other believers by proclaiming *the "Amen"* (Heb "truly"; see Ps 106.48; Neh 5.13; 1 Chr 16.36; *m. Ber.* 8.8; *m. Ta'an.* 2.5; *t. Rosh Ha-Shanah* 2.14). *Outsider*, or unlearned ("idiotēs") in the Gospel. **20:** *Children*, see 2.6n.; 3.1n.; 13.11. **21:** Isa 28.11–12, in a version different from both the Masoretic and extant Greek. *Law*, Jewish Scriptures (see 9.8n.; 9.9n.; Rom 3.19). Paul considers prophetic writing as well as the Torah to be authoritative, as does rabbinic tradition (*b. Git.* 36a). **22:** *Not for unbelievers* because it is alienating. The idea that the same instrument can have opposite effects appears in Wis 11.5. **23:** *Out of your mind*, as with some Greek ecstatic utterances (Wis 14.28). *Outsiders*, see 14.6n. **25:** Isa 45.14; see also 3.16; Ezek 39.21;

heart are disclosed, that person will bow down before God and worship him, declaring, "God is really among you."

[26] What should be done then, my friends?[a] When you come together, each one has a hymn, a lesson, a revelation, a tongue, or an interpretation. Let all things be done for building up. [27] If anyone speaks in a tongue, let there be only two or at most three, and each in turn; and let one interpret. [28] But if there is no one to interpret, let them be silent in church and speak to themselves and to God. [29] Let two or three prophets speak, and let the others weigh what is said. [30] If a revelation is made to someone else sitting nearby, let the first person be silent. [31] For you can all prophesy one by one, so that all may learn and all be encouraged. [32] And the spirits of prophets are subject to the prophets, [33] for God is a God not of disorder but of peace.

(As in all the churches of the saints, [34] women should be silent in the churches. For they are not permitted to speak, but should be subordinate, as the law also says. [35] If there is anything they desire to know, let them ask their husbands at home. For it is shameful for a woman to speak in church.[b] [36] Or did the word of God originate with you? Or are you the only ones it has reached?)

[37] Anyone who claims to be a prophet, or to have spiritual powers, must acknowledge that what I am writing to you is a command of the Lord. [38] Anyone who does not recognize this is not to be recognized. [39] So, my friends,[c] be eager to prophesy, and do not forbid speaking in tongues; [40] but all things should be done decently and in order.

15 Now I would remind you, brothers and sisters,[a] of the good news[d] that I proclaimed to you, which you in turn received, in which also you stand, [2] through which also you are being saved, if you hold firmly to the message that I proclaimed to you—unless you have come to believe in vain.

[3] For I handed on to you as of first importance what I in turn had received: that Christ died for our sins in accordance with the scriptures, [4] and that he was buried, and that he was raised on the third day in accordance with the scriptures, [5] and that he appeared to Cephas, then to the twelve. [6] Then he appeared to more than five hundred brothers and sisters[a] at one time, most of whom are still alive, though some have died.[e] [7] Then he appeared to James, then to all the apostles. [8] Last of all, as to one untimely born, he

a Gk *brothers*
b Other ancient authorities put verses 34-35 after verse 40
c Gk *my brothers*
d Or *gospel*
e Gk *fallen asleep*

Zech 8.23. **26:** *Lesson,* instruction (see LXX Ps 59.1; Sir 9.1). *Revelation,* wisdom utterance or prophecy (see 14.6; 12.8–10). *Tongue,* see 12.10; 13.1. *Interpretation,* see 12.10; 14.13. **29:** *Weigh what is said,* see Deut 18.22. **33b–36:** Some scholars consider this passage an interpolation: it appears to contradict 11.5; its position varies among manuscripts; it is easily removed without disrupting the rhetoric. **34:** *Women* ("gynaikes"), could be translated "wives" (see 12.10,28,30; 14.2,4–6,13,27–28); a husband who interprets his wife's utterance would be subordinate to her (see 12.30), contravening 11.8–9. *The law,* perhaps *the law* of creation, that a "husband is the head of his wife" (11.3; see also LXX Gen 3.16). Readings that attribute Paul's injunction to an imagined normative misogynist "rabbinic background" lack any basis. Jewish women spoke publicly in their capacity as civil leaders (*Ant.* 13.405, e.g.) and leaders of synagogues (*CIJ* 741, e.g.). **39:** *Friends* ("adelphoi"), lit., "brothers." **40:** *Decently,* decorously. *In order,* according to the divine, cosmic order delineated in the previous two chapters.

15.1–11: The tradition. 1: *Good news,* gospel. **2:** *Saved,* from sin and eternal death. **3:** *Handed on . . . received,* see 11.2n. *For our sins,* vicarious atonement, expiatory sacrifice, or propitiatory sacrifice have scriptural resonance (Isa 53; Ps 22; LXX Dan 3.40; 4 Macc 6.27–29; 17.20–22; *T. Benj.* 3.8, *Mek. Pisha* 1 on Ex 12.1). **3–4:** *For our sins,* perhaps evoking Isa 53.5; see *Tg. Neb.* Isa 53. *Scriptures,* which passages Paul invokes are unclear: suggestions include LXX Jer 23.5; LXX Hos 6.2 (the Targum adds "In the day of the resurrection of the dead" to this verse); Dan 7.25; Jon 1.17 (LXX 2.1). See also 1 Thess 4.14. **4:** *Was raised,* by God. **5:** *Cephas,* see 1.12n.; Lk 24.34. *The twelve,* Paul never mentions Judas. **6:** *Appeared,* the sole attestation for this appearance to 500. **7:** *James,* the

appeared also to me. [9] For I am the least of the apostles, unfit to be called an apostle, because I persecuted the church of God. [10] But by the grace of God I am what I am, and his grace toward me has not been in vain. On the contrary, I worked harder than any of them—though it was not I, but the grace of God that is with me. [11] Whether then it was I or they, so we proclaim and so you have come to believe.

[12] Now if Christ is proclaimed as raised from the dead, how can some of you say there is no resurrection of the dead? [13] If there is no resurrection of the dead, then Christ has not been raised; [14] and if Christ has not been raised, then our proclamation has been in vain and your faith has been in vain. [15] We are even found to be misrepresenting God, because we testified of God that he raised Christ—whom he did not raise if it is true that the dead are not raised. [16] For if the dead are not raised, then Christ has not been raised. [17] If Christ has not been raised, your faith is futile and you are still in your sins. [18] Then those also who have died[a] in Christ have perished. [19] If for this life only we have hoped in Christ, we are of all people most to be pitied.

[20] But in fact Christ has been raised from the dead, the first fruits of those who have died.[a] [21] For since death came through a human being, the resurrection of the dead has also come through a human being; [22] for as all die in Adam, so all will be made alive in Christ. [23] But each in his own order: Christ the first fruits, then at his coming those who belong to Christ. [24] Then comes the end,[b] when he hands over the kingdom to God the Father, after he has destroyed every ruler and every authority and power. [25] For he must reign until he has put all his enemies under his feet. [26] The last enemy to be destroyed is death. [27] For "God[c] has put all things in subjection under his feet." But when it says, "All things are put in subjection," it is plain that this does not include the one who put all things in subjection under him. [28] When all things are subjected to him, then the Son himself will also be subjected to the one who put all things in subjection under him, so that God may be all in all.

[a] Gk *fallen asleep*
[b] Or *Then come the rest*
[c] Gk *he*

"brother of the Lord [Jesus]" (9.5; Gal 1.18–19; Mk 6.3). *Apostles*, see 1.1n. **8–9:** *Untimely born*, like a stillbirth, referring to either Paul's physical appearance or early hostility to the gospel (Gal 1.13; Phil 3.6; see also Acts 8.1–3; 9.1–5; 22.4; 26.9–11). **10:** *Grace*, see "spiritual gifts," 12.1. **11:** *I or they*, other apostles. *Proclaim*, 2.4; see also LXX Isa 61.1; Joel 2.1; Jon 1.2; 3.2; Zech 9.9; Prov 1.21; Dan 3.4.

15.12–19: Centrality of the resurrection. *No resurrection*, denial of bodily resurrection (vs. immortality of the soul), a misunderstanding of Jesus' resurrection as a one-time event rather than as the inauguration of the general resurrection (15.20), or the belief that those baptized were already resurrected and so no longer bound by rules regarding the sanctity of the body. Pharisees, but not all Jewish groups of the Second Temple, expected bodily resurrection. **14:** *Proclamation*, that Christ "was raised on the third day" (15.4). *Faith* in their own resurrection. **17:** *In your sins*, unable to be reconciled with God (15.3). **18:** *Died in Christ*, deceased church members (see 1 Thess 4.16). **19:** *For this life*, to receive only this-world benefits (see *2 Bar.* 21.13).

15.20–28: Christ's victory. 20: *First fruits*, the first of many; the sign of the anticipated general resurrection. **21:** *Human*, Adam, who brought sin and death into the world (15.22n.; 45–47); Jesus removed them (see 1.7–8; 11.26). On the messiah as an anti-type to Adam see Rom 5.14–15; *Gen. Rab.* 8.1. **22:** *All die*, Adam's sin introduced mortality (see Gen 3.19), a widespread interpretation (Wis 2.24; *1 En.* 69.11; *L.A.E.* 44.1; *Apoc. Mos.* 14.2; *L.A.B.* 13.8; *Gen. Rab.* 8.11; 16.6; *Sifra* 27a). *Made alive*, resurrected, (Dan 12.2; 2 Macc 7.9ff.; *T. Sim.* 6.7; *T. Jud.* 25.1, 4; *T. Zeb.* 10.2; *T. Benj.* 10.7; *1 En.* 51.1–2, *Pss. Sol.* 2.31; 3.12; *m. Sanh.* 10.1; *b. Sanh.* 90b–91a; Maimonides, *Commentary on the Mishneh, Sanhedrin* 10.1). **23:** *At his coming*, when Christ returns (see 1.7–8). **24:** *Hands over*, God assumes sovereignty after the messiah has *destroyed every ruler* (*1 En.* 53.5; 55.4; *Pss. Sol.* 2.30) *and every authority* (or dominion) *and power*, earthly and demonic forces (Isa 24.21–22; *1 En.* 54.5). **25:** Rabbinic tradition similarly distinguishes between the messianic era and the world to come (*b. Ber.* 34b). *Under his feet*, Ps 110.1. **26:** *Death*, perhaps personified, God's enemy (see *Pss. Sol.* 7.4; *L.A.B.* 3.10; 33.3). In Isa 25.8 (Heb), God "will swallow up death forever," but in LXX "Death . . . swallowed them [the nations] up," at which point God will take away their tears. *Destroyed*, through resurrection. **27:** Ps 8.6. *In subjection*, to the messiah (see 3.22). **28:** *To him*, the messiah. *The one*, God. See "Paul and the Trinity," p. 293.

[29] Otherwise, what will those people do who receive baptism on behalf of the dead? If the dead are not raised at all, why are people baptized on their behalf?

[30] And why are we putting ourselves in danger every hour? [31] I die every day! That is as certain, brothers and sisters,[a] as my boasting of you—a boast that I make in Christ Jesus our Lord. [32] If with merely human hopes I fought with wild animals at Ephesus, what would I have gained by it? If the dead are not raised,

"Let us eat and drink,
for tomorrow we die."

[33] Do not be deceived:

"Bad company ruins good morals."

[34] Come to a sober and right mind, and sin no more; for some people have no knowledge of God. I say this to your shame.

[35] But someone will ask, "How are the dead raised? With what kind of body do they come?" [36] Fool! What you sow does not come to life unless it dies. [37] And as for what you sow, you do not sow the body that is to be, but a bare seed, perhaps of wheat or of some other grain. [38] But God gives it a body as he has chosen, and to each kind of seed its own body. [39] Not all flesh is alike, but there is one flesh for human beings, another for animals, another for birds, and another for fish. [40] There are both heavenly bodies and earthly bodies, but the glory of the heavenly is one thing, and that of the earthly is another. [41] There is one glory of the sun, and another glory of the moon, and another glory of the stars; indeed, star differs from star in glory.

[42] So it is with the resurrection of the dead. What is sown is perishable, what is raised is imperishable. [43] It is sown in dishonor, it is raised in glory. It is sown in weakness, it is raised in power. [44] It is sown a physical body, it is raised a spiritual body. If there is a physical body, there is also a spiritual body. [45] Thus it is written, "The first man, Adam, became a living being"; the last Adam became a life-giving spirit. [46] But it is not the spiritual that is first, but the physical, and then the spiritual. [47] The first man was from the earth, a man of dust; the second man is[b] from heaven. [48] As was the man of dust, so are those who are of the dust; and as is the man of heaven, so are those who are of heaven. [49] Just as we have borne the im-

[a] Gk *brothers*
[b] Other ancient authorities add *the Lord*

15.29–34: Exhortations to correct belief. 29: *On behalf of the dead,* interpreted as washing the dead, posthumous baptism, or martyrdom, the phrase can be translated "for the sake of the dead"; Mormons cite this verse in support of posthumous baptisms (*Doctrine and Covenants* 128.15–16). **30:** *Danger,* hardships experienced by apostles. **32:** *Merely human hopes,* or "in human terms." *Wild animals,* Paul's opposition (see 16.8). *Let us eat,* Isa 22.13, invoked sarcastically and caricaturing Epicureanism. **33:** *Deceived,* by fatalistic philosophies. *Bad company,* quoting the playwright Menander (d. 292 BCE; *Thaïs,* frag. 218) to impugn the source of resurrection-denial.

15.35–58: The resurrected body. 35: Rabbinic literature speculates about the form of the resurrected body; Roman-period Jewish epitaphs suggest that some understood resurrection as non-bodily (*b. Sanh.* 90b–91a; *b. Ketub.* 11a–b; *y. Kil.* 12.3; *Gen. Rab.* 14.5; *Eccl. Rab.* 1.4; *BS* 2.130, *CIJ* 788). **36–38:** *Seed,* see 3.8–9; *dies,* for the same resurrection metaphor, see Jn 12.24; *b. Sanh.* 90b. Greco-Roman biology thought both human and plant seeds ("sperma") contained a fully formed embryo. **39:** See Gen 1.11–12. **40:** *Heavenly,* of celestial material. *Earthly,* of terrestrial substance. *Glory* (see 11.7n.), radiance, often depicted as a garment (see 15.53; Rom 13.14; 2 Cor 5.4; Phil 3.21; *1 En.* 62.15; *Pss. Sol.* 11.7). Some Jewish literature depicts astral objects as bodies encased in light; one midrash describes Adam and Eve's clothing (Gen 3.21) as "garments of light," based on a pun of "garments of skin ('or')" and "light ('or)" (*1 En.* 18.13–16; 21.3–6; Philo, *Planting* 3 [12]; *Gen. Rab.* 20.12). **41:** Belief that human essence consisted of the same ethereal, luminous substance as celestial bodies led to the idea that souls become stars (see Cicero, *Somn. Scip.* 3; Dan 12.2–3). **42:** *Sown,* the body in which one is born. *Imperishable,* unsusceptible to disease, death, and decay. **43:** *Dishonor,* correlating conception and birth with death or *weakness* (Philo, *Heir* 52–58). *Power,* both God's power, namely Christ (1.24; 2.5), and the manifestation of that power by believers (2.4; 12.10). **44:** *Physical* ("psychikon") . . . *spiritual* ("pneumatikon"), see 2.14, which contrasts these terms. **45:** Gen 2.7. God infused Adam with earthly breath-matter ("pnoē"), not heavenly spirit ("pneuma"). *Life-giving,* enlivening believers with divine *spirit.* **46:** *Physical . . . then the spiritual,* reversing the order of creation (see 15.47; Plato, *Tim.* 29b–31a; Philo, *On the Creation* 134, 141). **47:** Philo, familiar with Platonic ideas, also understands Gen 2 as describing "earthly man" and Gen 1 as describing the "heavenly man" (*Leg. all.* 1.31; see also *Dreams* 1.33). Some rabbinic literature portrays

age of the man of dust, we will[a] also bear the image of the man of heaven.

[50] What I am saying, brothers and sisters,[b] is this: flesh and blood cannot inherit the kingdom of God, nor does the perishable inherit the imperishable. [51] Listen, I will tell you a mystery! We will not all die,[c] but we will all be changed, [52] in a moment, in the twinkling of an eye, at the last trumpet. For the trumpet will sound, and the dead will be raised imperishable, and we will be changed. [53] For this perishable body must put on imperishability, and this mortal body must put on immortality. [54] When this perishable body puts on imperishability, and this mortal body puts on immortality, then the saying that is written will be fulfilled:

"Death has been swallowed up in victory."
[55] "Where, O death, is your victory?
Where, O death, is your sting?"

[56] The sting of death is sin, and the power of sin is the law. [57] But thanks be to God, who gives us the victory through our Lord Jesus Christ.

[58] Therefore, my beloved,[d] be steadfast, immovable, always excelling in the work of the Lord, because you know that in the Lord your labor is not in vain.

16 Now concerning the collection for the saints: you should follow the directions I gave to the churches of Galatia. [2] On the first day of every week, each of you is to put aside and save whatever extra you earn, so that collections need not be taken when I come. [3] And when I arrive, I will send any whom you approve with letters to take your gift to Jerusalem. [4] If it seems advisable that I should go also, they will accompany me.

[5] I will visit you after passing through Macedonia—for I intend to pass through Macedonia— [6] and perhaps I will stay with you or even spend the winter, so that you may send me on my way, wherever I go. [7] I do not want to see you now just in passing, for I hope to spend some time with you, if the Lord permits. [8] But I will stay in Ephesus until Pentecost, [9] for a wide door for effective work has opened to me, and there are many adversaries.

[10] If Timothy comes, see that he has nothing to fear among you, for he is doing the work of the Lord just as I am; [11] therefore let no one despise him. Send him on his way in peace, so that he may come to me; for I am expecting him with the brothers.

[12] Now concerning our brother Apollos, I strongly urged him to visit you with the other brothers, but he was not at all willing[e] to come now. He will come when he has the opportunity.

[13] Keep alert, stand firm in your faith, be courageous, be strong. [14] Let all that you do be done in love.

[a] Other ancient authorities read *let us*
[b] Gk *brothers*
[c] Gk *fall asleep*
[d] Gk *beloved brothers*
[e] Or *it was not at all God's will for him*

the first human as having two natures, one heavenly and one earthly (*Gen. Rab.* 8.11). **49:** *Image*, in rabbinic literature, the image of God refers either to humanity's spiritual nature or physical resemblance to God (*t. Ber.* 4.1; *Gen. Rab.* 8.9; *Lev. Rab.* 34.3; *Deut. Rab.* 11.3). **50:** *Flesh and blood*, a common postbiblical term for the human body (Sir 14.18; Philo, *Heir* 12 [57]; *b. Sanh.* 91a). The resurrected body is compositionally different from the mortal body (see 15.42n.). The Talmud considers how God refashions a body from decomposed flesh and blood (*b. Sanh.* 90b–91a). **51–52:** *Mystery*, see 2.1n.; Rom 16.25; 1Q27 frag. 1, col. 1; 1QH[a] 9.21–25. *Die*, believers will have their earthly bodies *changed* into spiritual bodies. *Trumpet*, Joel 2.1, referring to the impending "day of the LORD," connected to the resurrection in *Pss. Sol.* 11.1; 4Q496 col. 4 frag. 11.3–4; *b. Rosh Ha-Shanah* 16b; *Tg. Ps.-J.* to Ex 20.15; see 3.13n.; 1 Thess 4.13–18; 2 Cor 5.1–5. **53:** *Put on*, see 15.40n.; Rom 13.12,14; Gal 3.27. **54:** Compare Isa 25.7. **55:** Compare Hos 13.14. **56:** *Sin*, rebellion against God, which introduced *death*. *Law*, because it reveals sin and specifies punishments. **57:** *Victory*, God's vanquishing sin and death by Jesus' death and resurrection (see 1.24).

16.1–4: The collection. 1: *Collection*, for the Jerusalem church (see Gal 2.10; 2 Cor 8–9). By accepting this offering, Jerusalem church leaders would signal their recognition of Paul's Gentile congregations. Jerusalem remained central to the early church as it was for non-apocalyptic Jews, as evidenced by diaspora Jewish communities' right to export money for their Temple contribution. **2:** *First day*, Sunday.

16.5–24: Plans and farewells. 8: *Pentecost*, Feast of Weeks (Heb "Shavuot"); for the church, the giving of the Holy Spirit (Acts 2.1–42). **10:** *Timothy*, see 4.17. **12:** *Apollos*, see 1.12. **13:** *Courageous . . . strong*, these verbs appear

[15] Now, brothers and sisters,[a] you know that members of the household of Stephanas were the first converts in Achaia, and they have devoted themselves to the service of the saints; [16] I urge you to put yourselves at the service of such people, and of everyone who works and toils with them. [17] I rejoice at the coming of Stephanas and Fortunatus and Achaicus, because they have made up for your absence; [18] for they refreshed my spirit as well as yours. So give recognition to such persons.

[19] The churches of Asia send greetings. Aquila and Prisca, together with the church in their house, greet you warmly in the Lord. [20] All the brothers and sisters[a] send greetings. Greet one another with a holy kiss.

[21] I, Paul, write this greeting with my own hand. [22] Let anyone be accursed who has no love for the Lord. Our Lord, come![b] [23] The grace of the Lord Jesus be with you. [24] My love be with all of you in Christ Jesus.[c]

[a] Gk *brothers*
[b] Gk *Marana tha.* These Aramaic words can also be read *Maran atha,* meaning *Our Lord has come*
[c] Other ancient authorities add *Amen*

in LXX 2 Sam 10.12; Ps 27.14; 31.25 (compare LXX Deut 31.6; Josh 1.6–7). **15:** *Stephanus,* see 1.16. *Achaia,* Greek province whose capital was Corinth. **17:** *Coming,* visiting Paul in Ephesus. *Fortunatus and Achaicus,* Romans with church authority. **19:** *Aquila and Prisca,* married couple expelled from Rome when the emperor Claudius expelled the Jews, perhaps for disturbances regarding the proclamation of Jesus (Rom 16.3–4; Suetonius, *Claud.* 25.4). They were co-founders of the Corinthian church (Acts 18.2). *House* or household, see 1.16. **20:** *Holy kiss,* greeting exchanged at the Lord's Supper. **22:** *Accursed,* Jer 17.5; *Ep. Arist.* 311; *Jub.* 23.30; *1 En.* 5.5–7; *Pss. Sol.* 4.14–22; *Sib. Or.* 3.295–349, 492–519; 1QS 2.4–9; Mt 23.13–27. *Love,* brotherly love ("phileō"), used by Paul only here (contrast 2.9,13). *Our Lord, come,* transliterated Aram into Gk "marana tha," an invocation of judgment upon unbelievers (*1 En.* 9.1; *Did.* 10.6).

THE SECOND LETTER OF PAUL TO THE CORINTHIANS

NAME, AUTHORSHIP

Paul writes to persuade the Corinthian church, which he had founded, to maintain its exclusive relationship with him as an apostle and with the gospel of Jesus he proclaimed. After an earlier dispute with the Corinthians about Paul's fund-raising for the Jerusalem church, a new group of missionaries—apparently distinguished by exceptional rhetorical and spiritual gifts—has led church members to reject Paul's leadership and message. Paul reacts by restating his historical relationship to the Corinthian church, explaining the travels that have taken him away from them, and, most importantly, rearticulating the style of leadership and the singular message that characterize his gospel and that distinguish him as a true apostle of Jesus Christ.

LITERARY HISTORY AND INTERPRETATION

Paul's argument is twofold. First, he challenges his opponents' desire that the Corinthians observe those elements of Jewish law (*halakhah*) that distinguish Jews from Gentiles (e.g., dietary regulations, male circumcision). Paul characterizes the law as an aspect only of the "old" and deficient covenant that God made with the Jews, a covenant entirely superseded by the "new" covenant God has made available to those who believe in Jesus. Second, Paul strives to buttress his apostolic status. In contrast to the newcomers, whom he derisively calls "super-apostles" (11.5; 12.11), Paul portrays himself as humble and lacking in oratorical skill. In a recurrent theme, he argues that his weaknesses are signs of his strength and of his gospel. Paul thus contrasts himself with the "super-apostles" who express power through shows of mystical abilities. Even as he announces that he has similar skills, Paul depicts his opponents' actions as *self*-promotion rather than promotion of the gospel. Paul's ironic message is that, in Christ, weakness is power.

Perhaps because of the distinct tasks Paul sets for himself, or perhaps because 2 Corinthians combines several originally separate Pauline writings, the letter rapidly switches topics and tone. If there are independent sources, their precise extent and relative chronology are uncertain (see notes on 2.13; 6.14–7.1; 8.1–9.15; 10.1–18). A conciliatory passage and introduction to Paul's travels (2.5–13) are interrupted by an initial self-defense (2.14–5.21). In the manner of a midrashic exegesis, Paul interprets Moses' veil in Ex 34 (3.1–18) as showing that the law is obsolete and not a path to true knowledge of God. This discussion ends with an anxious appeal for reconciliation (6.1–13; 7.2–4 [6.14–7.1 appears parenthetical]), followed by the resumption of the travelogue, which picks up where Paul left off at 2.13.

Chapters 8 and 9, on the collection for the poor of Jerusalem, may be separate solicitation letters, and these are followed by a highly charged polemical conclusion (10.1–13.10), which returns to Paul's main focus: Paul has the same powers as the "super-apostles," but he knows that to boast of such things is to be a fool. To regain the Corinthians' support, Paul brags of his own strengths even as he ironically rejects the value of that bragging. Weakness, not extravagant power, Paul says, authenticates true ministry, and for this reason he allowed himself to boast only of his afflictions.

READING GUIDE

Despite these varying topics and shifting rhetorical styles, the letter presents certain recurring motifs. The relationship between affliction and consolation, raised in 1.3–11, is the backbone of the arguments in 4.7–10; 4.16–5.10; and 12.7–10. The twin themes of boasting and confidence intimated in 1.12–14 feature prominently in 3.4–18; 8.1–7,24; 9.1–5; and all of 10–13. The paradox of power in weakness informs the whole letter. Even if 2 Corinthians is a composite, the different letters were composed within a brief period to address specific controversial issues.

The second letter to the Corinthians offers no extended reflection on any specific idea taken from Judaism, and in it Paul evidences no distinctive knowledge of Jewish thought or practice. Nevertheless, alongside his dependence on the Septuagint, which he constantly quotes and interprets, Paul reflects his Jewish intellectual and religious milieu. His exegetical technique resembles the style of rabbinic midrash that begins to emerge shortly after his day. His declarations regarding the nature of God reflect common Jewish liturgical themes, and his depiction of his personal heavenly journey (12.2–11) evidences a type of heavenly ascent familiar from Jewish writings of this same period. Even the places in which Paul differs from Jewish thinking—his negative attitude toward the law; his distinctive use of the concept of Satan (11.14)—suggest that he consistently thinks within a Jewish framework. It is one more irony of this letter that in order to deny the validity of the "old" covenant of the flesh that God made with the Jews, Paul depends for proof on those biblical writings that embody that covenant, through which he loudly and proudly proclaims his own Jewish heritage.

Alan J. Avery-Peck

1 Paul, an apostle of Christ Jesus by the will of God, and Timothy our brother,

To the church of God that is in Corinth, including all the saints throughout Achaia:

[2] Grace to you and peace from God our Father and the Lord Jesus Christ.

[3] Blessed be the God and Father of our Lord Jesus Christ, the Father of mercies and the God of all consolation, [4] who consoles us in all our affliction, so that we may be able to console those who are in any affliction with the consolation with which we ourselves are consoled by God. [5] For just as the sufferings of Christ are abundant for us, so also our consolation is abundant through Christ. [6] If we are being afflicted, it is for your consolation and salvation; if we are being consoled, it is for your consolation, which you experience when you patiently endure the same sufferings that we are also suffering. [7] Our hope for you is unshaken; for we know that as you share in our sufferings, so also you share in our consolation.

[8] We do not want you to be unaware, brothers and sisters,[a] of the affliction we experienced in Asia; for we were so utterly, unbearably crushed that we despaired of life itself. [9] Indeed, we felt that we had received

[a] Gk *brothers*

1.1–2.13: Opening. Salutation and statement of Paul's bond with the Corinthians.

1.1–2: Salutation. A greeting formula (1 Cor 1.1; Gal 1.1) reminds the Corinthians that Paul was appointed *by* (lit., "through") *the will of God*. Paul's status resembles that of Hebrew prophets, appointed directly by God. In rabbinic Judaism, the status of rabbi is a product of an individual's study and personal commitment, a process in which anyone can (and is encouraged to) engage. *Timothy*, with Silvanus, accompanied Paul at the founding of the Corinthian congregation (v. 19; Acts 18.5) and acted as Paul's representative (1 Cor 4.17; 16.10–11; cf. Acts 19.22). *Brother*, a title of respect used, though infrequently, by rabbis; e.g., *b. B. Metz.* 107a, "My brother Rabin!" *Saints*, followers of Christ. *Achaia*, Roman senatorial province of which *Corinth* was the capital. **2:** *Grace to you and peace . . .* , a standard Pauline greeting (except 1 Thess 1.1) and familiar from Jewish sources (e.g., 1 Chr 12.18; 1 Sam 25.6). *Father*, as a term of reference for God is commonplace in Jewish sources (e.g., 1QH 15, 20–24; 4Q372; 3 Macc 6.2–3; Philo, *Leg. all.* 114–15, 292–93; *m. Yoma* 8.9; *b. Ta'an.* 25b). See 1.3–7n. on "Father of mercies."

1.3–7: Paul blesses God for rescuing him and consoling his afflictions. Paul stresses his relationship with the recipients (e.g., Phil 1.3–11; 1 Thess 1.2–10) by a blessing emphasizing God's mercy and compassion (Rom 12.1; Phil 2.1). These divine traits appear especially in Psalms (e.g., 86.15), and prominently in Jewish liturgy, which refers to God as "Father of mercies" (Heb "av ha-raḥamim") in the prayer for the rebuilding of Jerusalem based on Ps 51.18, recited on Sabbath and festival mornings immediately before the "Shema Yisrael." **3–4:** *God of all consolation*, the phrase does not appear in early Jewish sources, but God as a consoling figure does (e.g., *b. Ber.* 48b). **5:** *Sufferings of Christ*, *b. Sukk.* 52a refers to a Messiah ben Joseph, who will die prior to the Davidic messiah's arrival. R. Dosa says that this event is reflected in Zech 12.10–12's prophecy of Jerusalem grieving as for a firstborn son. **6:** *Afflicted*, see 12.10. The nature of this affliction is unclear.

1.8–11: God delivers Paul. 8: *Asia*, Roman senatorial province (modern western Turkey) that included Ephesus. *Unbearably crushed . . . sentence of death*, the specific ordeal is unclear. See Phil 1.19–24 and 1 Cor 15.32. **9:** While Paul's expectation for resurrection is shaped by his experience of Jesus' resurrection, his language follows Jewish liturgical formulas. *We would rely not on ourselves* resembles the early Aramaic prayer, found in *Zohar*, "VeYakhel,"

the sentence of death so that we would rely not on ourselves but on God who raises the dead. [10] He who rescued us from so deadly a peril will continue to rescue us; on him we have set our hope that he will rescue us again, [11] as you also join in helping us by your prayers, so that many will give thanks on our[a] behalf for the blessing granted us through the prayers of many.

[12] Indeed, this is our boast, the testimony of our conscience: we have behaved in the world with frankness[b] and godly sincerity, not by earthly wisdom but by the grace of God—and all the more toward you. [13] For we write you nothing other than what you can read and also understand; I hope you will understand until the end— [14] as you have already understood us in part—that on the day of the Lord Jesus we are your boast even as you are our boast.

[15] Since I was sure of this, I wanted to come to you first, so that you might have a double favor;[c] [16] I wanted to visit you on my way to Macedonia, and to come back to you from Macedonia and have you send me on to Judea. [17] Was I vacillating when I wanted to do this? Do I make my plans according to ordinary human standards,[d] ready to say "Yes, yes" and "No, no" at the same time? [18] As surely as God is faithful, our word to you has not been "Yes and No." [19] For the Son of God, Jesus Christ, whom we proclaimed among you, Silvanus and Timothy and I, was not "Yes and No"; but in him it is always "Yes." [20] For in him every one of God's promises

[a] Other ancient authorities read *your*
[b] Other ancient authorities read *holiness*
[c] Other ancient authorities read *pleasure*
[d] Gk *according to the flesh*

accompanying the removal of the Torah scroll from the ark on the Sabbath ("Not on mortals do I rely . . . but on the God of the universe"). *God who raises the dead,* a Jewish commonplace, e.g., the second benediction of the "Amidah," known from the Mishnah (*m. Sot.* 9.15; *m. Sanh.* 10.1). **10:** *Deadly peril,* see 1.8n. *On him we have set our hope,* the same wording appears in the Aramaic prayer just cited. **11:** *Your prayers,* praying for the welfare of others, especially those in peril, is well established in the Jewish liturgy (e.g., the Morning Blessings).

1.12–2.13: Paul stresses his bond with the Corinthians. Paul recounts his past dealings with the Corinthians and his plans to visit.

1.12–14: Paul's conduct is a basis of solidarity. 12: *Boast,* or confidence, a Pauline theme (e.g., 1 Thess 2.19) especially in 1 and 2 Corinthians. *Conscience,* the term has no Hebrew equivalent but the Talmudic expression "his heart knocks him," e.g., *b. B. Bat.* 8a, suggests the same idea. *Earthly wisdom,* considerations of expediency and personal gain, contrasted with the truth that emerges when one is *frank* and *sincere.* Paul insists that such truth is gained through God's *grace,* an idea roughly equivalent to the Hebrew concepts "ḥen" or "ḥesed" which, in the Tanakh (e.g., Ps 31.16,21 [Heb vv. 17,22]) and later Jewish literatures (see, e.g., *Gen. Rab.* 33.3; 78.13; *Ex. Rab.* 12.2), refer to God's compassionate kindness even toward those who do not merit it. **13:** *Until the end* can mean "completely," in contrast to "in part" in 1.14. **14:** *Day of the Lord,* Jesus' second coming (1 Cor 5.5; Phil 1.6,10). The phrase in Amos (e.g., 5.18–20) evokes fear of judgment, not the welcome of vindication.

1.15–2.4: Paul responds to misunderstandings caused by his canceled visit. 16: *Macedonia,* a Roman province in northern Greece that included Philippi and Thessalonica. *Send me on* (Gk "propempein"), a technical term for provisioning (Rom 15.24; 1 Cor 16.6,11; cf. Acts 15.3; 20.38; 21.5; Titus 3.13; 3 Jn 6), including finance, escorts, letters of recommendation. *Judea,* not just southern Palestine but especially Jerusalem. The visit relates to delivering the collection for the poor (2 Cor 8.1–9.15n.; Rom 15.25–26). The Talmud notes rabbis who traveled from Israel to the Babylonian academies to present legal rulings (e.g., *b. Ber.* 22a). **17:** *Vacillating,* lit., "trifling." Paul defends against charges that he and his co-workers changed their minds frivolously and claims that his actions cannot be evaluated according to human standards. **18:** *God is faithful,* God's faithfulness (Heb ḥesed), especially to covenantal promises, features prominently in Jewish sources. For example, the second benediction of the "Amidah" asserts God's faithfulness: "You revive the dead." *Yes and No,* indicating equivocation; see Mt 5.37; Jas 5.12. **19:** *Son of God,* denoting Jesus' divine nature. In Jewish texts, the phrase used by God to refer to the people of Israel (Ex 4.22; Jer 31.20; Hos 11.1), to David (2 Sam 7.14; Ps 2.7; 89.26–27), and eventually to any Israelite ruler, including, especially in the Dead Sea Scrolls (see, e.g., 4Q246; *Aram. Apoc.* 50.9–51.1), the Davidic messiah. In postbiblical Judaism, the term commonly applies to the just (Sir 4.10; Wis 2.17–18; *Jub.* 1.24–25). *Silvanus,* or Silas, Paul's companion (Acts 15.40–18.5; 1 Thess 1.1; 2 Thess 1.1); see 1.1n. **20:** *Amen,* Hebrew, "cer-

is a "Yes." For this reason it is through him that we say the "Amen," to the glory of God. [21] But it is God who establishes us with you in Christ and has anointed us, [22] by putting his seal on us and giving us his Spirit in our hearts as a first installment.

[23] But I call on God as witness against me: it was to spare you that I did not come again to Corinth. [24] I do not mean to imply that we lord it over your faith; rather, we are workers with you for your joy, because you stand firm

2 in the faith. [1] So I made up my mind not to make you another painful visit. [2] For if I cause you pain, who is there to make me glad but the one whom I have pained? [3] And I wrote as I did, so that when I came, I might not suffer pain from those who should have made me rejoice; for I am confident about all of you, that my joy would be the joy of all of you. [4] For I wrote you out of much distress and anguish of heart and with many tears, not to cause you pain, but to let you know the abundant love that I have for you.

[5] But if anyone has caused pain, he has caused it not to me, but to some extent—not to exaggerate it—to all of you. [6] This punishment by the majority is enough for such a person; [7] so now instead you should forgive and console him, so that he may not be overwhelmed by excessive sorrow. [8] So I urge you to reaffirm your love for him. [9] I wrote for this reason: to test you and to know whether you are obedient in everything. [10] Anyone whom you forgive, I also forgive. What I have forgiven, if I have forgiven anything, has been for your sake in the presence of Christ. [11] And we do this so that we may not be outwitted by Satan; for we are not ignorant of his designs.

[12] When I came to Troas to proclaim the good news of Christ, a door was opened for me in the Lord; [13] but my mind could not rest

tainly" or "let it be so;" an affirmation or response to a prayer; see Deut 27.14–26; 1 Chr 16.36; Neh 5.13; 8.6. The rabbis (*b. Shabb.* 119b; *b. Sanh.* 111a) understand the consonants in amen to be an acronym for the declaration, "God, faithful king," a declaration an individual makes before reciting the Shema when praying apart from a prayer quorum ("minyan"). *Glory of God*, a common idiom referring to God's manifestation in the world (e.g., Isa 6.3). **21:** *Anointed*, in the Tanakh, a commission, especially kingship (e.g., 1 Sam 24.6). In postbiblical Judaism "anointing" develops eschatological significance (*2 Bar.* 29, 30, 72; *4 Ezra* 12). In Talmudic literature (see, e.g., *b. Hor.* 7a), the high priest is anointed; here the term lacks messianic connotations. **22:** Receiving the *Spirit* as *first installment* (the same Gk word is translated "guarantee" in 5.5) proves that God's promises will be fulfilled (v. 20). **23:** *I call on God as witness*, see Gen 31.50; Mic 1.2. *I did not come again* refers to the canceled double visit (1.15–16). **24:** *Workers*, Paul is a partner, not an overseer or manager. The metaphor of *workers* in faith does not appear in early Judaism. *Joy*, Psalms and Isaiah especially depict knowledge of and closeness to God with "joy" (e.g., Ps 43.3; Isa 35.10; 51.11). **2.1:** The *painful visit* may be mentioned in 13.2, during which some church members offended Paul (see 2.5–11; 7.12). A third visit is anticipated in 12.14,21; 13.1. **3–4:** *I wrote as I did. . . . with many tears* (also v. 9), the "letter of tears," written shortly after the "painful visit"; see 7.8,12. See Introduction. The combination of *tears* and *joy* is reminiscent of Ps 126.12. The letter is either lost or portions of it are preserved in chs 10–13. **4:** *Abundant love*, familiar from the benediction immediately preceding the liturgical recitation of the Shema ("Barukh 'atah Adonai, ha-boḥer be'amo Yisrael be'ahavah," "Blessed are You, O Lord, who in your [his] love choose your [his] people Israel").

2.5–13: The "letter of tears" well received. Paul pleads that the offender be forgiven (v. 7) since the congregation has meted out appropriate punishment (v. 6). **6:** *Such a person* remains unknown; see 7.12. **7:** *Forgive and console*, both are Jewish virtues; Judaism demands that people request forgiveness from neighbors they have wronged (e.g., *b. Yoma* 87a) and requires consoling the needy (e.g., Ps 34.18 [Heb v. 19]). **9:** *To test you*, a common idea in Judaism, where masters might test their disciples' loyalty (*b. Eruv.* 62b). **10:** *I also forgive*, see Mt 6.12; 18.21–35. Jewish sources call people to be like God in forgiving (e.g., Sir 28.2). **11:** *Satan*, see 11.14; 12.7. Second Corinthians also calls this figure "the god of this world" (4.4), "Beliar" (6.15—a variant of Belial), and "serpent" (11.3). In Jewish sources, the term, generally interpreted "accuser," refers to a heavenly being who challenges God to test humans (as Job) and who tempts individuals to sin; see *b. Yoma* 20a (Satan has power to accuse humans before God every day except Yom Kippur). **12:** *Troas*, Roman colony in northwest Turkey, a short sea-voyage to Philippi; see Acts 16.8–11. *Good news*, Gk "euangelion," usually translated "gospel." **13:** *Titus*, a co-worker like Timothy and Silvanus, likely the carrier of the "letter of tears" (2.3–4; 7.8).

because I did not find my brother Titus there. So I said farewell to them and went on to Macedonia.

[14] But thanks be to God, who in Christ always leads us in triumphal procession, and through us spreads in every place the fragrance that comes from knowing him. [15] For we are the aroma of Christ to God among those who are being saved and among those who are perishing; [16] to the one a fragrance from death to death, to the other a fragrance from life to life. Who is sufficient for these things? [17] For we are not peddlers of God's word like so many;[a] but in Christ we speak as persons of sincerity, as persons sent from God and standing in his presence.

3 Are we beginning to commend ourselves again? Surely we do not need, as some do, letters of recommendation to you or from you, do we? [2] You yourselves are our letter, written on our[b] hearts, to be known and read by all; [3] and you show that you are a letter of Christ, prepared by us, written not with ink but with the Spirit of the living God, not on tablets of stone but on tablets of human hearts.

[4] Such is the confidence that we have through Christ toward God. [5] Not that we are competent of ourselves to claim anything as coming from us; our competence is from God, [6] who has made us competent to be ministers of a new covenant, not of letter but of spirit; for the letter kills, but the Spirit gives life.

[7] Now if the ministry of death, chiseled in letters on stone tablets,[c] came in glory so that the people of Israel could not gaze at Moses'

[a] Other ancient authorities read *like the others*
[b] Other ancient authorities read *your*
[c] Gk *on stones*

2.14–4.6: The ministry of glory.

2.14–17: God equips competent ministers. 14: *Thanks be to God,* the expression is absent from Jewish sources, but the commonplace idea is reflected in obligations to recite benedictions thanking God for all that one experiences (see *b. Ber.* 59b). *Triumphal procession,* an image of God the victor leading Paul as captive. *Fragrance,* and *aroma* (v. 15), could allude to the execution of prisoners, thus combining Roman customs with biblical sacrificial language (e.g., Lev 1.9). It could also allude to the sweet scent of divine wisdom (Sir 24.15). **15–16:** *Saved . . . perishing,* different effects Paul's preaching has on hearers. Early Judaism imagines God's judgment to result in one's being sealed for eternal life or for Gehenna (e.g., *t. Sanh.* 13.1–12 and the long excurses in *b. Rosh Ha-Shanah* 16b–17a). *Sufficient,* or competent, suggests that only God equips competent ministers; see 3.5–6. **17:** Paul disdainfully calls his opponents *peddlers of God's word,* probably alluding to their acceptance and Paul's refusal of financial support; see 11.8–9n. Judaism insists that one should not profit from knowledge of Torah (e.g., *y. B. Metz.* 2.5 [8b], where Samuel bar Sursetai risks beheading rather than act in a way that suggests he fears anyone but God and so benefits from doing what the law demands). *Sincerity* anticipates charges of falsehood and cunning (see 4.2).

3.1–12: Ministers of the new covenant. 1: *Letters of recommendation,* introductions to the writer's friends and wider circles for missionaries; see Acts 18.27. Paul's lack of such letters is seen as a weakness; see 5.12. **2–3:** *Spirit* recalls the Corinthians' conversion; see Gal 3.2–3. *Tablets of stone . . . tablets of human hearts,* contrasts the Ten Commandments (Ex 20.1–17; 24.12; 31.18; 34.1) with a "new covenant" through which God says, "I will put my law within them, and I will write it on their hearts" (Jer 31.31–33); Ezek 36.26–27 contrasts "heart of stone" with "heart of flesh" and the spirit of God that will be poured into the people. Talmudic rabbis similarly found a powerful metaphor in the idea of God's law being in the people's hearts (e.g., "Study with all your heart and with all your soul to know my ways. . . . Keep my Torah in your heart and have awe of me before your eyes" (*b. Ber.* 17a). **4:** *Confidence,* see v. 12 and 1.12–14n. **5–6:** *Competence,* see 2.15–16n. In these verses the adjective, noun, and verb forms of Gk "hikanos" ("fitting," "qualified") indicate that God equips *us* for serving the *new covenant;* see 3.2–3n. *Spirit,* the Holy Spirit, recalls v. 3 and anticipates vv. 17–18. In Paul's binary thinking, since *the Spirit gives life,* i.e., raises to resurrected life (Rom 4.17; 8.11; 1 Cor 15.22,36,45; Gal 3.21; cf. Jn 5.21; 6.63; 1 Pet 3.18), its opposite, *the letter,* i.e., the written code, must mean death. **7–11:** The controlling imagery is Moses' radiant countenance (Ex 34.29–35). Paul uses a rabbinic argument, from the lesser to the greater ("qal vahomer"): *if the ministry of* (that brought) *death* [the lesser covenant written in stone] . . . *came in glory* [Moses' radiant face] . . . *how much more will the ministry of the Spirit* [greater] *come in glory.* The Talmud (*y. Sanh.* 7.11) lists this interpretative technique as the first of seven exegetical principles set out by Hillel. **7:** *Ministry of death,* the old covenant's fading glory. **12:** *Boldness,* fearlessness of appearing before God in the end-time (v. 4; 1.12–14n.).

PAUL AND THE RABBIS ON MOSES' RADIANT FACE (2 COR 3.12–18; EX 34.29–35)

According to Ex 34, when Moses descended Mount Sinai with the tablets of the Torah, "the skin of his face was shining" (34.30) because "he had been talking with God" (34.31). Because this transfiguration of their leader made the people afraid, Moses would veil his face while he spoke with them, but in direct conversation with God he would remove the veil. Paul reads this text midrashically to suggest that Moses "put a veil over his face to keep the people of Israel from gazing at the end of the glory"—Paul here refers to the Torah—"that was being set aside" (3.13).

Rabbinic commentators hundreds of years after Paul found no need to respond to Paul's dismissal of Torah. According to *b. Ber.* 7a, the emanating glow was Moses' reward for hiding his face from the presence of God at the burning bush (Ex 3.7). The rabbis also took practical lessons from Moses' experience: that Moses did not know his face was glowing (Ex 34.29) proves that one need not inform a gift's recipient of the gift (*b. Shabb.* 10b); that Moses wrote out the covenant and God repaid him with a radiant face teaches that the bridegroom pays the cost of preparing the marriage contract (*Deut. Rab.* 3.12).

Only one passage somewhat relates Moses' radiant face directly to Torah. *Ex. Rab.* 33.1 states that individuals can determine the worth of merchandise from the value of the commission paid the broker. In this way, Moses' glowing face reveals the value of Torah.

face because of the glory of his face, a glory now set aside, [8] how much more will the ministry of the Spirit come in glory? [9] For if there was glory in the ministry of condemnation, much more does the ministry of justification abound in glory! [10] Indeed, what once had glory has lost its glory because of the greater glory; [11] for if what was set aside came through glory, much more has the permanent come in glory!

[12] Since, then, we have such a hope, we act with great boldness, [13] not like Moses, who put a veil over his face to keep the people of Israel from gazing at the end of the glory that[a] was being set aside. [14] But their minds were hardened. Indeed, to this very day, when they hear the reading of the old covenant, that same veil is still there, since only in Christ is it set aside. [15] Indeed, to this very day whenever Moses is read, a veil lies over their minds; [16] but when one turns to the Lord, the veil is removed. [17] Now the Lord is the Spirit, and where the Spirit of the Lord is, there is freedom. [18] And all of us, with unveiled faces, seeing the glory of the Lord as though reflected in a mirror, are being transformed into the same image from one degree of glory to another; for this comes from the Lord, the Spirit.

4 Therefore, since it is by God's mercy that we are engaged in this ministry, we do not lose heart. [2] We have renounced the shameful things that one hides; we refuse to practice cunning or to falsify God's word; but by the open statement of the truth we com-

[a] Gk *of what*

3.13–18: Moses' veil. Paul interprets Moses' *veil* (Ex 34.33–35) as covering the transitory *glory that was being set aside,* lit., "abolished." **14–15:** Paul reads the passage regarding Moses' veil as a series of metaphors, creating a rabbinic-style parable ("mashal"). The *veil* represents lack of enlightenment. *Old covenant* refers to Mosaic (Sinaitic) law. It is debatable whether Paul is only insisting that the law is not obligatory for Gentiles, or whether he denies its applicability to Jews as well. **15:** *Moses* signifies the Torah (see 2 Chr 25.4; Mk 12.26; Acts 15.21). **16:** Ex 34.34 states that Moses would remove the veil. Paul deletes "Moses" and changes "removed" to "is removed," resulting in *the Lord* removing *the veil,* in contrast to veiled "minds" (14–15). **17:** Paul adds that "the Lord" refers to *the Spirit,* which guarantees freedom. **18:** *Glory of the Lord* parallels *the Lord, the Spirit* (16–17). *Being transformed,* a fundamental change in those who remove their veils. *Image,* see Rom 8.29; 1 Cor 15.49; Col 3.10. *One degree of glory to another* reflects the Greco-Roman belief that an encounter with the divine transforms the beholder into its image. Conversely, Rabbinic interpretation (*b. Ber.* 7a) understands the transformation of Moses' face to have been a divine reward for Moses' having turned his face away from the vision of God at the burning bush (Ex 3.6).

4.1–6: Climax of Paul's self-defense. Paul returns to the question of competence raised in 2.16. **1:** *God's mercy,* see 1.3–7n. **2–3:** Answers to charges; see 2.17. *Cunning,* lit., "crafty"; see 11.3; 12.16. *Conscience,* see 1.12n.

mend ourselves to the conscience of everyone in the sight of God. [3] And even if our gospel is veiled, it is veiled to those who are perishing. [4] In their case the god of this world has blinded the minds of the unbelievers, to keep them from seeing the light of the gospel of the glory of Christ, who is the image of God. [5] For we do not proclaim ourselves; we proclaim Jesus Christ as Lord and ourselves as your slaves for Jesus' sake. [6] For it is the God who said, "Let light shine out of darkness," who has shone in our hearts to give the light of the knowledge of the glory of God in the face of Jesus Christ.

[7] But we have this treasure in clay jars, so that it may be made clear that this extraordinary power belongs to God and does not come from us. [8] We are afflicted in every way, but not crushed; perplexed, but not driven to despair; [9] persecuted, but not forsaken; struck down, but not destroyed; [10] always carrying in the body the death of Jesus, so that the life of Jesus may also be made visible in our bodies. [11] For while we live, we are always being given up to death for Jesus' sake, so that the life of Jesus may be made visible in our mortal flesh. [12] So death is at work in us, but life in you.

[13] But just as we have the same spirit of faith that is in accordance with scripture—"I believed, and so I spoke"—we also believe, and so we speak, [14] because we know that the one who raised the Lord Jesus will raise us also with Jesus, and will bring us with you into his presence. [15] Yes, everything is for your sake, so that grace, as it extends to more and more people, may increase thanksgiving, to the glory of God.

[16] So we do not lose heart. Even though our outer nature is wasting away, our inner nature is being renewed day by day. [17] For this slight momentary affliction is preparing us for an eternal weight of glory beyond all measure, [18] because we look not at what can be seen but at what cannot be seen; for what can be seen is temporary, but what cannot be seen is eternal.

5 For we know that if the earthly tent we live in is destroyed, we have a building from God, a house not made with hands, eternal in the heavens. [2] For in this tent we groan, longing to be clothed with our heavenly dwelling— [3] if indeed, when we have taken it off[a] we will not be found naked. [4] For while we are still in this tent, we groan under our

[a] Other ancient authorities read *put it on*

4: *This world,* see 1 Cor 3.19; 5.10; 7.31 (twice), Paul's synonym for "the present age" (Gal 1.4) and "the present time" (Rom 3.26; 8.18; 11.5). *God of this world,* see "rulers of this age" (1 Cor 2.6,8; Eph 2.2) and 2.11n. Early Jewish sources similarly distinguish "this world" from a messianic "world to come" but without the negative attitude that Paul expresses toward current life. See, e.g., Rabbi Jacob's statement at *m. Avot* 4.17: "Better is a single moment spent in penitence and good deeds in this world than the whole of the world to come." *Light* as a metaphor for God's teaching is common (e.g., Isa 2.5; Ps 43.3; 118.27; Prov 6.23) and later Jewish sources (see, e.g., *Eccl. Rab.* 11.6; 12.7). **6:** Paraphrase of Gen 1.3; Isa 9.2; Ps 112.4.

4.7–5.10: Ministry of hardship. Affliction and consolation, first raised in 1.3–11, are elaborated: weakness and suffering signal God's empowering presence; *b. Ber.* 5 following Prov 3.12 depicts suffering and affliction in the absence of sin as evidence of God's love. **7:** Broken *clay jars* cannot be mended but must be discarded. The contrast with *treasure* demonstrates God's power. **8–9:** Catalogue of hardships formulated as antithetical pairs to show the incomparability of God's glory. See 6.4–10; 11.23–27; 12.10; Rom 8.35,38–39; 1 Cor 4.11–13; Phil 4.12. Stoics used such catalogues to demonstrate their indifference to adversity; for Paul adversity demonstrates the vessels' unworthiness and the overcoming of adversity documents divine power. Rabbinic Judaism carried the idea a step farther: the suffering of those God loves assures their greatest possible reward in the world-to-come (see, e.g., *Sifre Deut.* 32.5–11; *b. Hor.* 11a). **10–11:** *Carrying . . . the death of Jesus,* Jesus' death is replicated in Paul's bodily sufferings, with the result that *the life of Jesus may also be made visible;* cf. Gal 2.20. **13:** Ps 116.10. **4.16–5.10:** Paul uses dualistic language to express the tension between present afflictions and ongoing renewal. **16:** *Lose heart,* see 4.1. The *outer nature* that is *wasting away* is that part that undergoes sufferings (vv. 8–9) and carries Jesus' death (vv. 10–11). The *inner nature* is that part *being renewed* daily; cf. Rom 12.2. **18:** *Temporary* and *eternal,* a distinction familiar in Jewish eschatological thinking (see, e.g., *b. Shabb.* 10a, 33b; *b. Ta'an.* 21a). **5.1:** Paul continues the temporary–permanent contrast with one between *earthly tent,* referring to the body (see Wis 9.15), and *building from God,* which is *eternal in the*

burden, because we wish not to be unclothed but to be further clothed, so that what is mortal may be swallowed up by life. [5] He who has prepared us for this very thing is God, who has given us the Spirit as a guarantee.

[6] So we are always confident; even though we know that while we are at home in the body we are away from the Lord— [7] for we walk by faith, not by sight. [8] Yes, we do have confidence, and we would rather be away from the body and at home with the Lord. [9] So whether we are at home or away, we make it our aim to please him. [10] For all of us must appear before the judgment seat of Christ, so that each may receive recompense for what has been done in the body, whether good or evil.

[11] Therefore, knowing the fear of the Lord, we try to persuade others; but we ourselves are well known to God, and I hope that we are also well known to your consciences. [12] We are not commending ourselves to you again, but giving you an opportunity to boast about us, so that you may be able to answer those who boast in outward appearance and not in the heart. [13] For if we are beside ourselves, it is for God; if we are in our right mind, it is for you. [14] For the love of Christ urges us on, because we are convinced that one has died for all; therefore all have died. [15] And he died for all, so that those who live might live no longer for themselves, but for him who died and was raised for them.

[16] From now on, therefore, we regard no one from a human point of view;[a] even though we once knew Christ from a human point of view,[a] we know him no longer in that way. [17] So if anyone is in Christ, there is a new creation: everything old has passed away; see, everything has become new! [18] All this is from God, who reconciled us to himself through Christ, and has given us the ministry of reconciliation; [19] that is, in Christ God was reconciling the world to himself,[b] not counting

[a] Gk *according to the flesh*
[b] Or *God was in Christ reconciling the world to himself*

heavens. **5:** *Guarantee,* see 1.22n. **6–8:** *While . . . in the body,* see Phil 1.21,23; the body is a barrier to being fully with Christ. Rabbinic Judaism is more positive about bodily life. Again, *m. Avot* 4.17 suggests the enigmatic relationship between bodily existence and eternal life: "Better is a single moment spent in penitence and good deeds in this world than the whole of the world-to-come. And better is a single moment of inner peace in the world-to-come than the whole of a lifetime spent in this world" (see above, 4.4). **10:** See Rom 14.10. Rabbinic sources also commonly speak of God's seat, or throne, of judgment (see, e.g., *b. Arak.* 10b, *Lev. Rab.* 29.3,4,6,9).

5.11–21: Ministry of reconciliation. 11–13: Paul recalls his relationship to the Corinthians. **11:** *Consciences,* a theme introduced at 1.12 and 4.2. **12:** *Commending,* see 3.1n. *Boast,* see 1.12n. and 3.12n. *Those who boast in outward appearance* may refer to opponents who advocated circumcision for non-Jewish church members. Early Jewish writings also distinguish between the content of one's heart and outer appearances: "one whose inside is not as his outside may not enter the school house" (*b. Ber.* 28a). **13:** Paul's opponents may have derided him for an apparent lack of ecstatic experiences (12.1,12); Paul answers by distinguishing between being *beside ourselves* (lit., "we are ecstatic") and being *in our right mind.* The former concerns God; the latter concerns his ministry; cf. 1 Cor 14.2–5,18–19,27–28. Paul's thinking parallels rabbinic Judaism's generally negative attitude toward ecstatic experiences (*m. Hag.* 2.1; *b. Hag.* 14b) and recalls the rabbis' focus upon leadership that promotes communal welfare (see, e.g., *b. B. Kamma* 80b; *b. Sanh.* 24b; *b. Arak.* 2b). **14–15:** *Love of Christ,* Christ's love for us. *Those who live . . . was raised,* Christ's death enlivens all who will die, so that they owe their lives to him; Gal 2.19–20; Rom 7.4; 14.7–9. As the source of life, the Christ serves the role that Torah serves for the rabbis; one "eats its fruits in this world even as the principal remains for the world-to-come" (*m. Qidd.* 4.14). **17:** The reality of *anyone* being *in Christ* documents the onset of the *new creation,* the eschatological reversal of the primordial fall. The *old* way of looking from a human point of view *has passed.* For new creation, see Gal 6.15; Eph 2.15; 2 Pet 3.13; Rev 21.1; cf. Rom 8.19–21. Paul reflects on a common theme in Isa (43.18–19; see also 65.17; 66.22). Rabbinic Judaism, by contrast, reads Isaiah to mean that former things become secondary to new things. All history will be eclipsed, but not forgotten, at the end of time (*b. Ber.* 13a). **18–19:** As a result of the Christ's undoing the damage caused by Adam and Eve's rebellion, *trespasses* are canceled (see Rom 4.8), and human beings are *reconciled* to God; Rom 5.10–11; Col 1.20. Rather than seeing human sinfulness as a result of Adam and Eve's rebellion and so as reversible, the rabbis understood sin, and especially what they describe as an inclination toward sin, as an in-

their trespasses against them, and entrusting the message of reconciliation to us. [20] So we are ambassadors for Christ, since God is making his appeal through us; we entreat you on behalf of Christ, be reconciled to God. [21] For our sake he made him to be sin who knew no sin, so that in him we might become the righteousness of God.

6 As we work together with him,[a] we urge you also not to accept the grace of God in vain. [2] For he says,

"At an acceptable time I have listened to you,
and on a day of salvation I have helped you."

See, now is the acceptable time; see, now is the day of salvation! [3] We are putting no obstacle in anyone's way, so that no fault may be found with our ministry, [4] but as servants of God we have commended ourselves in every way: through great endurance, in afflictions, hardships, calamities, [5] beatings, imprisonments, riots, labors, sleepless nights, hunger; [6] by purity, knowledge, patience, kindness, holiness of spirit, genuine love, [7] truthful speech, and the power of God; with the weapons of righteousness for the right hand and for the left; [8] in honor and dishonor, in ill repute and good repute. We are treated as impostors, and yet are true; [9] as unknown, and yet are well known; as dying, and see—we are alive; as punished, and yet not killed; [10] as sorrowful, yet always rejoicing; as poor, yet making many rich; as having nothing, and yet possessing everything.

[11] We have spoken frankly to you Corinthians; our heart is wide open to you. [12] There is no restriction in our affections, but only in yours. [13] In return—I speak as to children—open wide your hearts also.

[14] Do not be mismatched with unbelievers. For what partnership is there between righteousness and lawlessness? Or what fellowship is there between light and darkness? [15] What agreement does Christ have with Beliar? Or what does a believer share with an unbeliever? [16] What agreement has the temple of God with idols? For we[b] are the temple of the living God; as God said,

"I will live in them and walk among them,
and I will be their God,
and they shall be my people.

[a] Gk *As we work together*
[b] Other ancient authorities read *you*

nate and necessary part of human nature (see, e.g., *Gen. Rab.* 9.7). **21:** *Made him to be sin,* a difficult phrase that may refer to the Christ's identification with humanity. The saints can be so embraced by God's reconciliation that *we might become the righteousness of God;* see Rom 1.17; 3.5,21–22,25–26; 10.3 (twice); Phil 3.9; also Mt 6.33; Jas 1.20; 2 Pet 1.1.

6.1–10: Summary of defense. 2: Isa 49.8. Isaiah speaks of the end of the Babylonian exile, which began in 597 and 586 BCE and ended in 538 BCE with the edict of Cyrus permitting the Jewish people to return to Jerusalem. **4–5:** Catalogue of hardships; see 4.8–9n. **6–7:** Catalogue of virtues; see Gal 5.22–23; Phil 4.8. **8–10:** These seven contrasting pairs, *impostors, and yet are true . . . having nothing, and yet possessing everything,* are not paradoxes to show the imperturbability of an ideal sage (as in Stoic philosophy) but antitheses answering charges against Paul. This is a summary of his self-defense that began in 2.14. From a human view (5.16), Paul and his co-workers might be accused of being *impostors, unknown,* etc., but in the context of the new creation (5.17), they are *true, known,* etc.

6.11–7.4: Final appeal to the Corinthians. 6.11–13: *Frankly,* see 1.12n. **6.14–7.1:** An interruption of Paul's appeal, since 7.2–4 more naturally follows 6.11–13. This passage contains many words used nowhere else by Paul; the stark dualism is also uncharacteristic of him. **14:** *Mismatched,* lit., "misyoked," only here in the NT. The term may play upon the Tanakh's restriction against yoking different kinds of animals or creating unnatural mixtures (Lev 19.19). *Partnership* (only here in the NT), *fellowship,* and *share* (v. 15) are synonyms meaning "association." *Righteousness and lawlessness,* see Rom 6.19, where the second word is translated "iniquity." *Light and darkness* (see Rom 2.19; 13.12; 1 Cor 4.5; 1 Thess 5.4–5) undergirds the imagery of 4.3–6, where the contrast between "believers" and *unbelievers* (v. 15) is also found. The metaphorical distinction between light and dark is familiar from ancient Judaism, notably from 1QM's distinction of "sons of light" and "sons of darkness." **15:** *Beliar,* Satan; see 2.11n. **16a:** *Temple of the living God,* see 1 Cor 3.16. *Living God,* a common early Jewish phrase (see, e.g., Deut 5.26). **16b–18:** A chain of citations: Lev 26.12; Ezek 37.27; 2 Sam 7.14; Isa 52.11; Isa 43.6 indicat-

[17] Therefore come out from them,
and be separate from them, says the Lord,
and touch nothing unclean;
then I will welcome you,
[18] and I will be your father,
and you shall be my sons and daughters,
says the Lord Almighty."

7 Since we have these promises, beloved, let us cleanse ourselves from every defilement of body and of spirit, making holiness perfect in the fear of God.

[2] Make room in your hearts[a] for us; we have wronged no one, we have corrupted no one, we have taken advantage of no one. [3] I do not say this to condemn you, for I said before that you are in our hearts, to die together and to live together. [4] I often boast about you; I have great pride in you; I am filled with consolation; I am overjoyed in all our affliction.

[5] For even when we came into Macedonia, our bodies had no rest, but we were afflicted in every way—disputes without and fears within. [6] But God, who consoles the downcast, consoled us by the arrival of Titus, [7] and not only by his coming, but also by the consolation with which he was consoled about you, as he told us of your longing, your mourning, your zeal for me, so that I rejoiced still more. [8] For even if I made you sorry with my letter, I do not regret it (though I did regret it, for I see that I grieved you with that letter, though only briefly). [9] Now I rejoice, not because you were grieved, but because your grief led to repentance; for you felt a godly grief, so that you were not harmed in any way by us. [10] For godly grief produces a repentance that leads to salvation and brings no regret, but worldly grief produces death. [11] For see what earnestness this godly grief has produced in you, what eagerness to clear yourselves, what indignation, what alarm, what longing, what zeal, what punishment! At every point you have proved yourselves guiltless in the matter. [12] So although I wrote to you, it was not on account of the one who did the wrong, nor on account of the one who was wronged, but in order that your zeal for us might be made known to you before God. [13] In this we find comfort.

In addition to our own consolation, we rejoiced still more at the joy of Titus, because his mind has been set at rest by all of you. [14] For if I have been somewhat boastful about you to him, I was not disgraced; but just as everything we said to you was true, so our boasting to Titus has proved true as well. [15] And his heart goes out all the more to you, as he remembers the obedience of all of you, and how you welcomed him with fear and trembling. [16] I rejoice, because I have complete confidence in you.

8 We want you to know, brothers and sisters,[b] about the grace of God that has been granted to the churches of Macedonia;

[a] Gk lacks *in your hearts*
[b] Gk *brothers*

ing separation from defilement. **7.1:** *Body* and *spirit* are not in opposition here; contrast Gal 5.16–26. Like Paul, both the Tanakh and early rabbinic Judaism distinguish the physical body from the "soul" or "spirit," viewed as the life force. Associated with respiration, the "soul" was understood to derive from God's own "breath" (Gen 2.7). The rabbis see body and soul as closely connected and equally responsible for a person's choices. At the eschaton, the reunited body and soul will be judged together (*b. Sanh.* 90b–91a). *Fear of God* (see 5.11), a common Jewish conception (e.g., Prov 1.7), understood as the underpinning of piety. **2–4:** Resumption of appeal in 6.11–13. **3:** *Die . . . live,* Paul reverses the traditional declaration of friendship, "live . . . die," to emphasize his bond with the Corinthians through identification with Christ. **4:** *Boast,* see 1.12–14n. and 3.12n. *Consolation . . . affliction,* see 1.3–7n.

7.5–16: Resumption of travelogue (2.12–13). 6–8: *God, who consoles the downcast,* the Talmud (*b. Ketub.* 8b) refers to God as "Lord of consolation," who brings comfort to the bereaved. *Titus* (2.13n.) brought news that Paul's *letter* (2.3–4n.) was received favorably; see 2.5–11. **10:** This idea of repentance parallels the central theme of Yom Kippur, the Day of Atonement. **12:** *The one who did the wrong,* the offender of 2.6. *The one who was wronged,* Paul. **16:** *Confidence* concludes the narrative of vv. 5–16 and anticipates the appeal for the collection in chs 8–9.

[2] for during a severe ordeal of affliction, their abundant joy and their extreme poverty have overflowed in a wealth of generosity on their part. [3] For, as I can testify, they voluntarily gave according to their means, and even beyond their means, [4] begging us earnestly for the privilege[a] of sharing in this ministry to the saints— [5] and this, not merely as we expected; they gave themselves first to the Lord and, by the will of God, to us, [6] so that we might urge Titus that, as he had already made a beginning, so he should also complete this generous undertaking[b] among you. [7] Now as you excel in everything—in faith, in speech, in knowledge, in utmost eagerness, and in our love for you[c]—so we want you to excel also in this generous undertaking.[b]

[8] I do not say this as a command, but I am testing the genuineness of your love against the earnestness of others. [9] For you know the generous act[d] of our Lord Jesus Christ, that though he was rich, yet for your sakes he became poor, so that by his poverty you might become rich. [10] And in this matter I am giving my advice: it is appropriate for you who began last year not only to do something but even to desire to do something— [11] now finish doing it, so that your eagerness may be matched by completing it according to your means. [12] For if the eagerness is there, the gift is acceptable according to what one has—not according to what one does not have. [13] I do not mean that there should be relief for others and pressure on you, but it is a question of a fair balance between [14] your present abundance and their need, so that their abundance may be for your need, in order that there may be a fair balance. [15] As it is written,

"The one who had much did not have too much,
and the one who had little did not have too little."

[16] But thanks be to God who put in the heart of Titus the same eagerness for you that I myself have. [17] For he not only accepted our appeal, but since he is more eager than ever, he is going to you of his own accord. [18] With him we are sending the brother who is famous among all the churches for his proclaiming the good news;[e] [19] and not only that, but he has also been appointed by

[a] Gk *grace*
[b] Gk *this grace*
[c] Other ancient authorities read *your love for us*
[d] Gk *the grace*
[e] Or *the gospel*

8.1–7: Letter for the collection. The collection for the Jerusalem church was meant to bring economic relief and to show unity between it and the Gentile diaspora congregations; see Gal 2.10; 1 Cor 16.1–4; Rom 15.25–27. Acts does not mention the collection, and it is possible the Jerusalem church refused it. Chapters 8 and 9 are probably two separate letters to two different regions in Achaia; see 9.2n. The Macedonian churches are an example of generosity. **1:** *Grace* (Gk "charis"), used ten times in chs 8–9 to describe the collection, translated in 8.4 as "privilege"; in 8.6,7,19 as "generous undertaking"; in 8.9 as "generous act"; in 8.16 as "thanks"; in 9.8 as "blessing"; in 9.15 as "thanks." Other words used in this connection: Gk "eulogia," "bountiful gift" and "voluntary gift" (9.5); "bountifully" (9.6 twice); "ministry" (Gk "leitourgia"), 9.12; "sharing" (Gk "koinonia"), 8.4; 9.13. Paul thus attaches rich theological significance to the collection. Early Judaism understands support for the needy to be both an act of generosity (Heb "tzedekah," righteousness) and an obligation based on recognition of dependence upon God for sustenance (e.g., Deut 11.13–15). *Macedonia,* 1.16n. Principally the Philippian and Thessalonian churches, but see 9.2. **2:** *Severe ordeal,* possibly the event as in Phil 1.29–30. **4:** *Sharing* (Gk "koinonia"), here describing the collection (9.13; Rom 15.26); the term also refers to participation in the Eucharist (1 Cor 10.16) and in Christ's suffering (Phil 3.10); see 8.1n. *Saints,* here and in 9.1,12, refers to the Jerusalem believers. **6:** *Titus,* 2.13n.; 8.16–24.

8.8–15: Generosity in relation to the collection. 9: A close parallel of *though he was rich . . . he became poor* is 5.21, "He made him to be sin who knew no sin"; see also Phil 2.6–8. **11:** *Now finish doing it,* contrast *m. Avot* 2.16: "It is not your job to finish the work, but neither are you free to walk away from it." **12:** *According to what one has,* see Deut 16.17. **15:** *"The one . . . too little,"* Ex 16.18.

8.16–24: The sending. The sending of Titus and two *brothers* (vv. 18,22–23) might indicate that the collection is modeled after the Temple tax (Ex 30.13–15), the delivery of which, according to Philo, *Spec. Laws* 1.76–78 (referring to "first fruits" and "ransom"), was carried out by "sacred ambassadors selected on account of their virtue."

the churches to travel with us while we are administering this generous undertaking[a] for the glory of the Lord himself[b] and to show our goodwill. [20] We intend that no one should blame us about this generous gift that we are administering, [21] for we intend to do what is right not only in the Lord's sight but also in the sight of others. [22] And with them we are sending our brother whom we have often tested and found eager in many matters, but who is now more eager than ever because of his great confidence in you. [23] As for Titus, he is my partner and co-worker in your service; as for our brothers, they are messengers[c] of the churches, the glory of Christ. [24] Therefore openly before the churches, show them the proof of your love and of our reason for boasting about you.

9 Now it is not necessary for me to write you about the ministry to the saints, [2] for I know your eagerness, which is the subject of my boasting about you to the people of Macedonia, saying that Achaia has been ready since last year; and your zeal has stirred up most of them. [3] But I am sending the brothers in order that our boasting about you may not prove to have been empty in this case, so that you may be ready, as I said you would be; [4] otherwise, if some Macedonians come with me and find that you are not ready, we would be humiliated—to say nothing of you—in this undertaking.[d] [5] So I thought it necessary to urge the brothers to go on ahead to you, and arrange in advance for this bountiful gift that you have promised, so that it may be ready as a voluntary gift and not as an extortion.

[6] The point is this: the one who sows sparingly will also reap sparingly, and the one who sows bountifully will also reap bountifully. [7] Each of you must give as you have made up your mind, not reluctantly or under compulsion, for God loves a cheerful giver. [8] And God is able to provide you with every blessing in abundance, so that by always having enough of everything, you may share abundantly in every good work. [9] As it is written,

"He scatters abroad, he gives to the poor;
his righteousness[e] endures forever."

[10] He who supplies seed to the sower and bread for food will supply and multiply your seed for sowing and increase the harvest of your righteousness.[e] [11] You will be enriched in every way for your great generosity, which will produce thanksgiving to God through us; [12] for the rendering of this ministry not only supplies the needs of the saints but also overflows with many thanksgivings to God. [13] Through the testing of this ministry you glorify God by your obedience to the confession of the gospel of Christ and by the generosity of your sharing with them and with all others, [14] while they long for you and pray for you because of the surpassing grace of God that he has given you. [15] Thanks be to God for his indescribable gift!

10 I myself, Paul, appeal to you by the meekness and gentleness of Christ—I who am humble when face to face with you, but bold toward you when I am away!— [2] I

a Gk *this grace*
b Other ancient authorities lack *himself*
c Gk *apostles*
d Other ancient authorities add *of boasting*
e Or *benevolence*

9.1–15: A second letter concerning the collection. 1: Ch 9 starts the appeal afresh. **2:** *Macedonia,* compared to 8.1, now hears Paul's boasting that *Achaia has been ready since last year.* **3:** *Brothers,* also v. 5, are probably those mentioned in 8.18,22–23. **5:** *Bountiful gift* and *voluntary gift* both translate Gk "eulogia"; see 8.1n. **6:** *The one who sows bountifully will also reap bountifully,* cf. Hos 10.12; a similar idea appears throughout the rabbinic literature (see, e.g., *b. Avodah Zara* 5b, *b. Sukk.* 49b). **7:** *God loves a cheerful giver,* Prov 22.8. **8:** Abundance carries with it the responsibility of sharing. *Enough* (Gk "autarkeia"), see 1 Tim 6.6 ("contentment"). The word connotes the Hellenistic philosophical ideal of self-sufficiency. In contrast, Paul, taking up an idea familiar from Judaism (see 1.9n.), states that God is the basis for such sufficiency. See 12.9n. **9:** Ps 112.9. **10:** *Seed . . . food,* Isa 55.10. *Harvest of your righteousness,* Hos 10.12. **11–12:** One possible motive for Paul's working tirelessly on the collection is the apocalyptic vision of Gentiles pouring into Jerusalem (Isa 60.4–7; Mic 4.1–2), rendering overflowing *thanksgiving to God.*

ask that when I am present I need not show boldness by daring to oppose those who think we are acting according to human standards.[a] [3] Indeed, we live as human beings,[b] but we do not wage war according to human standards;[a] [4] for the weapons of our warfare are not merely human,[c] but they have divine power to destroy strongholds. We destroy arguments [5] and every proud obstacle raised up against the knowledge of God, and we take every thought captive to obey Christ. [6] We are ready to punish every disobedience when your obedience is complete.

[7] Look at what is before your eyes. If you are confident that you belong to Christ, remind yourself of this, that just as you belong to Christ, so also do we. [8] Now, even if I boast a little too much of our authority, which the Lord gave for building you up and not for tearing you down, I will not be ashamed of it. [9] I do not want to seem as though I am trying to frighten you with my letters. [10] For they say, "His letters are weighty and strong, but his bodily presence is weak, and his speech contemptible." [11] Let such people understand that what we say by letter when absent, we will also do when present.

[12] We do not dare to classify or compare ourselves with some of those who commend themselves. But when they measure themselves by one another, and compare themselves with one another, they do not show good sense. [13] We, however, will not boast beyond limits, but will keep within the field that God has assigned to us, to reach out even as far as you. [14] For we were not overstepping our limits when we reached you; we were the first to come all the way to you with the good news[d] of Christ. [15] We do not boast beyond limits, that is, in the labors of others; but our hope is that, as your faith increases, our sphere of action among you may be greatly enlarged, [16] so that we may proclaim the good news[d] in lands beyond you, without boasting of work already done in someone else's

[a] Gk *according to the flesh*
[b] Gk *in the flesh*
[c] Gk *fleshly*
[d] Or *the gospel*

10.1–13.13: Defense of apostolic authority. The ironic and polemical tone of chs 10–13 contrasts sharply with that of the preceding chapters. Paul no longer refers to his opponents indirectly (see 2.17n.; 5.12n.), but pointedly. For these reasons, many scholars think that chs 10–13 are from another letter (see Introduction).

10.1–18: Paul attacks his opponents. 1–6: Paul's opponents criticize him for lack of power, but he insists on the ironic idea that power is demonstrated through weakness; see 4.7–12n.; 11.30 (summarizing 11.21b–29); 12.9–10 (summarizing 12.1–8); 1 Cor 1.17–25. **1:** *Meekness and gentleness of Christ,* see 8.9; Phil 2.6–8. *I who am . . . when I am away,* alludes to the charge against him; see also v. 10. *Humble,* lit., "base" or "humiliated," see 11.7n. **2:** *Those who think . . . ,* opponents Paul addresses throughout only in the third person; see 10.10–12; 11.5,12–15,22–23,26; 12.11. **3–5:** *Not merely human, but . . . divine power,* Paul and those like him live as *human beings,* but his *weapons* have superhuman power. *We destroy arguments,* Paul characterizes his opponents as debaters; see 1 Cor 1.19–20. *Wage war . . . destroy,* and *take . . . captive,* warfare imagery applied to the religious debate. **6:** Paul hopes that the Corinthians' *obedience* may be *complete.* Paul's threat of "punishment" contrasts with his commendation in 7.15 for obedience; this lends support to the idea that chs 10–13 belong to a different letter. **7–11:** Paul answers specific charges. **7:** *Just as you belong to Christ, so also do we,* answers the opponents' boasting that they "belong to Christ." **8:** *Boast,* Paul normally boasts of the Corinthians; see 1.12n., 3.12n.; here he boasts of himself, only by claiming authority as their founder. The proper content of boasting is a matter of contention in chs 10–13. *Building you up . . . tearing you down,* cf. Jer 1.10; Eccl 3.3. **9–11:** *Letters* answer direct charges by the opponents (v. 10) that his appearances and speech, unlike his *weighty* letters, are unimpressive. *His speech contemptible,* see 11.6. **12–18:** The proper way to boast is within one's territory. **12:** *We do not dare to classify or compare,* standard rhetorical device of calling attention to one's praiseworthy acts in comparison with superior persons. Paul denounces the practice here but parodies it in his "fool's speech"; see 11.21b–12.10. **13–16:** *Field* (v. 13), lit., "(measure of) rule (Gk "kanon")" (also vv. 15,16), probably refers to the proper jurisdiction, i.e., the Gentiles, assigned to Paul and Barnabas (Gal 2.9). Paul reminds readers that he founded the congregation legitimately, *without boasting of work already done in someone else's sphere of action.* Paul thus accuses his opponents of overstepping their bounds. *In lands beyond you,* Paul wanted to use Corinth as a base for missionary work.

sphere of action. [17] "Let the one who boasts, boast in the Lord." [18] For it is not those who commend themselves that are approved, but those whom the Lord commends.

11 I wish you would bear with me in a little foolishness. Do bear with me! [2] I feel a divine jealousy for you, for I promised you in marriage to one husband, to present you as a chaste virgin to Christ. [3] But I am afraid that as the serpent deceived Eve by its cunning, your thoughts will be led astray from a sincere and pure[a] devotion to Christ. [4] For if someone comes and proclaims another Jesus than the one we proclaimed, or if you receive a different spirit from the one you received, or a different gospel from the one you accepted, you submit to it readily enough. [5] I think that I am not in the least inferior to these super-apostles. [6] I may be untrained in speech, but not in knowledge; certainly in every way and in all things we have made this evident to you.

[7] Did I commit a sin by humbling myself so that you might be exalted, because I proclaimed God's good news[b] to you free of charge? [8] I robbed other churches by accepting support from them in order to serve you. [9] And when I was with you and was in need, I did not burden anyone, for my needs were supplied by the friends[c] who came from Macedonia. So I refrained and will continue to refrain from burdening you in any way. [10] As the truth of Christ is in me, this boast of mine will not be silenced in the regions of Achaia. [11] And why? Because I do not love you? God knows I do!

[12] And what I do I will also continue to do, in order to deny an opportunity to those who want an opportunity to be recognized as our equals in what they boast about. [13] For such boasters are false apostles, deceitful workers, disguising themselves as apostles of Christ. [14] And no wonder! Even Satan disguises himself as an angel of light. [15] So it is not strange if his ministers also disguise themselves as ministers of righteousness. Their end will match their deeds.

[16] I repeat, let no one think that I am a fool; but if you do, then accept me as a fool, so that

[a] Other ancient authorities lack *and pure*
[b] Gk *the gospel of God*
[c] Gk *brothers*

17: Jer 9.23–24, also cited in 1 Cor 1.31. **18:** *It is not those who commend themselves that are approved,* see *m. Avot* 2.8: "If you have learned much Torah, do not take credit for yourself, since for this purpose you were created."

11.1–12.10: A fool's speech. Paul parodies his opponents' penchant for comparison after criticizing them for doing the same (10.12).

11.1–15: Appeal to the Corinthians as a fool. 1: *Foolishness* (Gk "aphrosynē") is the opposite of "moderation" or "sober-mindedness" (Gk "sophrosynē"); see "madman" (Gk "paraphronōn"), 11.23; 1 Cor 1–3 uses different words for "foolishness" (Gk "mōria," "mōros"), whose opposite is "wisdom" (Gk "sophia"). **2:** *I promised you in marriage,* Paul presents himself as father of the bride, that is, the founder of the congregation; see 1.19. **3:** *Serpent,* Satan; see 2.11; 11.14; 1 Cor 7.5. *Deceived Eve,* Gen 3.13. In connection with "marriage" and "virginity" (v. 2), Paul is probably thinking of the Jewish tradition that Satan sexually seduced Eve (see *2 En.* 31.6). **4–5:** *Another Jesus . . . different spirit . . . different gospel,* reminiscent of Gal 1.6–9; see 10.13–16n. Cf. Deut 13.1–5. **6:** *Untrained in speech,* see 10.10. **7:** *Humbling,* lit., "debasing"; see also 12.21; Phil 4.12. The adjective is used in 10.1. Phil 2.8 describes the Christ as "debased." Greco-Roman philosophers viewed craftsmen as debased, but the rabbis did not; the Talmudic literature contains no negative statements regarding craftsmen, and they are viewed positively at *b. Ber.* 58a, *b. Mo'ed Qat.* 13a, and *b. Arak.* 10b; craftsmen are, at the same time, in a different social class from rabbis, before whom they must stand and from whom they will remain separate even in the world-to-come (*b. Hul.* 54b, *Eccl. Rab.* 3.11); Paul's use of the word may refer to his work in self-support (see 1 Cor 4.12; 1 Thess 2.9. **9:** *I did not burden anyone,* see 12.13; 1 Cor 9 on self-support; see 1 Thess 2.9; Phil 4.16,18, for Macedonian support. Accepting support obligated the recipient (client) to the benefactor (patron). By refusing their support, Paul refuses the Corinthians the status and authority of patronage; by accepting Macedonian support, Paul is seen as slighting the Corinthian congregation; see 12.12–18n. **12–15:** Characterization of Paul's opponents. **14:** *Satan disguises himself,* see 2.11n. Jewish sources depict Satan's disguising himself as a woman to entangle in sin even such rabbis as Meir and Akiva, who declared that people can easily subdue their evil inclination (*b. Qidd.* 81a). The Talmudic literature does not imagine opponents as "ministers" of Satan.

I too may boast a little. [17] What I am saying in regard to this boastful confidence, I am saying not with the Lord's authority, but as a fool; [18] since many boast according to human standards,[a] I will also boast. [19] For you gladly put up with fools, being wise yourselves! [20] For you put up with it when someone makes slaves of you, or preys upon you, or takes advantage of you, or puts on airs, or gives you a slap in the face. [21] To my shame, I must say, we were too weak for that!

But whatever anyone dares to boast of—I am speaking as a fool—I also dare to boast of that. [22] Are they Hebrews? So am I. Are they Israelites? So am I. Are they descendants of Abraham? So am I. [23] Are they ministers of Christ? I am talking like a madman—I am a better one: with far greater labors, far more imprisonments, with countless floggings, and often near death. [24] Five times I have received from the Jews the forty lashes minus one. [25] Three times I was beaten with rods. Once I received a stoning. Three times I was shipwrecked; for a night and a day I was adrift at sea; [26] on frequent journeys, in danger from rivers, danger from bandits, danger from my own people, danger from Gentiles, danger in the city, danger in the wilderness, danger at sea, danger from false brothers and sisters;[b] [27] in toil and hardship, through many a sleepless night, hungry and thirsty, often without food, cold and naked. [28] And, besides other things, I am under daily pressure because of my anxiety for all the churches. [29] Who is weak, and I am not weak? Who is made to stumble, and I am not indignant?

[30] If I must boast, I will boast of the things that show my weakness. [31] The God and Father of the Lord Jesus (blessed be he forever!) knows that I do not lie. [32] In Damascus, the governor[c] under King Aretas guarded the city of Damascus in order to[d] seize me, [33] but I was let down in a basket through a window in the wall,[e] and escaped from his hands.

12 It is necessary to boast; nothing is to be gained by it, but I will go on to visions and revelations of the Lord. [2] I know a person in Christ who fourteen years ago was caught up to the third heaven—whether in the body or out of the body I do not know; God knows.

[a] Gk *according to the flesh*
[b] Gk *brothers*
[c] Gk *ethnarch*
[d] Other ancient authorities read *and wanted to*
[e] Gk *through the wall*

11.16–12.10: Paul compares himself to his opponents. Paul's hardships validate his apostolic authenticity. **16–21:** *Fool,* see 11.1n. One who boasts of human accomplishments is a fool, for these things are meaningless compared to the true life offered to believers in the Christ. Paul, responding to those who claim they are greater than he, ironically lists his achievements. He announces that he will accordingly speak as a fool and boast *according to human standards.* **22:** *Hebrews . . . Israelites . . . descendants of Abraham,* suggests that Paul's opponents boast of their Jewish pedigree. Paul declares his own Jewish heritage whenever the situation requires it; see Rom 9.4; 11.1; Gal 1.13; Phil 3.5, but cf. 11.24n. **23a:** *Madman,* see 11.1n. **23b–27:** Catalogue of hardships used ironically to show Paul's afflictions; see annotations on 1.3–7; 4.8–9; 10.1. **24:** *Forty lashes minus one,* see Deut 25.3 which the rabbis interpreted as 39. In the Hebrew Bible (e.g., Deut 25.1–3) and rabbinic literature (*m. Makk.* 1.3 and throughout), lashes are a judicial punishment imposed by a court for violations of communal norms. *From the Jews,* Paul, who just spoke proudly of his Jewish heritage, now depicts himself as an outsider to the Jewish community, a common tactic in his writings (see, e.g., Rom 15.30; 1 Cor 9.19–22; Gal 5.11). **25:** *Beaten with rods,* Roman, not Jewish, punishment. *Stoning,* not the punishment described by Jewish sources, where stoning is a form of capital punishment in which the convicted person is pushed off of a high place and then, if he is still alive, crushed with a single, heavy boulder that is dropped on him (*m. Sanh.* 6.1–4). **32–33:** See Acts 9.23–25. *Aretas* IV ruled the Nabateans from 9 BCE until his death ca. 41 CE. The Nabateans took Damascus in 37 CE, soon after which Paul escaped from the city *in a basket.* **12.1–10:** Paul relates an out-of-body experience, since his opponents claim such experiences as validation of their spiritual prowess; see 5.13n. **1:** *Visions and revelations,* extrasensory events that endow the seer with power and status; see v. 7; 1 Cor 9.1; 15.5–8; Gal 1.12; 2.1–2. **2–3:** *I know a person* (also v. 5), an oblique self-reference, following the apocalyptic convention of anonymous authorship; see vv. 7–9. In rabbinic anecdotes, similarly, the narrator may refer to himself in the third person, generally as "that man" (see, e.g., *b. Mo'ed Qat.* 17a). *Third heaven,* i.e., *Paradise* (v. 4), where, according to mystical Judaism

[3] And I know that such a person—whether in the body or out of the body I do not know; God knows— [4] was caught up into Paradise and heard things that are not to be told, that no mortal is permitted to repeat. [5] On behalf of such a one I will boast, but on my own behalf I will not boast, except of my weaknesses. [6] But if I wish to boast, I will not be a fool, for I will be speaking the truth. But I refrain from it, so that no one may think better of me than what is seen in me or heard from me, [7] even considering the exceptional character of the revelations. Therefore, to keep[a] me from being too elated, a thorn was given me in the flesh, a messenger of Satan to torment me, to keep me from being too elated.[b] [8] Three times I appealed to the Lord about this, that it would leave me, [9] but he said to me, "My grace is sufficient for you, for power[c] is made perfect in weakness." So, I will boast all the more gladly of my weaknesses, so that the power of Christ may dwell in me. [10] Therefore I am content with weaknesses, insults, hardships, persecutions, and calamities for the sake of Christ; for whenever I am weak, then I am strong.

[11] I have been a fool! You forced me to it. Indeed you should have been the ones commending me, for I am not at all inferior to these super-apostles, even though I am nothing. [12] The signs of a true apostle were performed among you with utmost patience, signs and wonders and mighty works. [13] How have you been worse off than the other churches, except that I myself did not burden you? Forgive me this wrong!

[14] Here I am, ready to come to you this third time. And I will not be a burden, because I do not want what is yours but you; for children ought not to lay up for their parents, but parents for their children. [15] I will most gladly spend and be spent for you. If I love you more, am I to be loved less? [16] Let it be assumed that I did not burden you. Nevertheless (you say) since I was crafty, I took you in by deceit. [17] Did I take advantage of you through any of those whom I sent to you? [18] I urged Titus to go, and sent the brother with him. Titus did not take advantage of you, did he? Did we not conduct ourselves with the same spirit? Did we not take the same steps?

[19] Have you been thinking all along that we have been defending ourselves before you? We are speaking in Christ before God. Everything we do, beloved, is for the sake

[a] Other ancient authorities read *To keep*

[b] Other ancient authorities lack *to keep me from being too elated*

[c] Other ancient authorities read *my power*

(see, e.g., *Ex. Rab.* 25.7–8; 45.6, and, esp., *b. Hag.* 14b), one obtains a vision of God. The earliest portions of *1 En.* 14 depict a three-tiered cosmology. By Paul's time, seven tiers were more common. Paul is either unfamiliar with the later conception or, dismissing triumphant mystical enthusiasm, he presents himself as a failed mystic, a point that emerges in v. 7. Again, Paul ironically boasts that he is as great in spiritual matters as his adversaries even as he maintains that, for one in Christ, power is represented in weakness. Cf. vv. 9–11. **4:** That the content of mystical revelations is to be kept secret is commonplace. See especially *m. Hag.* 2.1. **7:** The nature of the *thorn* is unknown. **9–11:** Participation in angelic worship is acceptable only when it is characterized by Christlike humility, vulnerability, and reliance on God. Paul's strength is evidenced in his failure to become exalted. He rejects spiritual experiences that detract from the central message of faith. Note the similar rabbinic treatment of Ḥoni the Circle Drawer (*m. Ta'an.* 3.8); the rabbis praise his spiritual power and closeness to God even as they assert that anyone else who acts has Ḥoni does would be subject to excommunication (see "Jewish Miracle Workers," p. 536). **9:** *Sufficient,* unlike the Hellenistic ideal of sufficiency that transcends hardships (see 9.8), Paul accepts these hardships as real, because in their *weakness* they manifest God's *power*; see 10.1n.

12.11–13: Conclusion of the "fool's speech." 11: *Commending,* see 3.1n. *Super-apostles,* see 10.2n. **12:** Again decrying having acted as a fool by boasting, Paul is not above reminding the Corinthians that he too performed miracles. **13:** See 11.9n.

12.14–21: Paul prepares for a third visit. 14–18: Paul answers charges that he has been enriching himself through the collection (chs 8–9). **14:** *Third* visit (also v. 21; 13.1), see 2.1n. for the second "painful visit." *I will not be a burden,* see 11.9n. *Parents,* for Paul as father to his converts, see 11.2. **16:** *I took you in by deceit,* some Corinthians evidently accused Paul of skimming the collection funds. **18:** Paul sent *Titus* to oversee the collection (8.6,16,23); see also 2.13n. *The brother,* sent to accompany Titus (8.22–23); not the "brother" elected by the

of building you up. [20] For I fear that when I come, I may find you not as I wish, and that you may find me not as you wish; I fear that there may perhaps be quarreling, jealousy, anger, selfishness, slander, gossip, conceit, and disorder. [21] I fear that when I come again, my God may humble me before you, and that I may have to mourn over many who previously sinned and have not repented of the impurity, sexual immorality, and licentiousness that they have practiced.

13 This is the third time I am coming to you. "Any charge must be sustained by the evidence of two or three witnesses." [2] I warned those who sinned previously and all the others, and I warn them now while absent, as I did when present on my second visit, that if I come again, I will not be lenient— [3] since you desire proof that Christ is speaking in me. He is not weak in dealing with you, but is powerful in you. [4] For he was crucified in weakness, but lives by the power of God. For we are weak in him,[a] but in dealing with you we will live with him by the power of God.

[5] Examine yourselves to see whether you are living in the faith. Test yourselves. Do you not realize that Jesus Christ is in you?—unless, indeed, you fail to meet the test! [6] I hope you will find out that we have not failed. [7] But we pray to God that you may not do anything wrong—not that we may appear to have met the test, but that you may do what is right, though we may seem to have failed. [8] For we cannot do anything against the truth, but only for the truth. [9] For we rejoice when we are weak and you are strong. This is what we pray for, that you may become perfect. [10] So I write these things while I am away from you, so that when I come, I may not have to be severe in using the authority that the Lord has given me for building up and not for tearing down.

[11] Finally, brothers and sisters,[b] farewell.[c] Put things in order, listen to my appeal,[d] agree with one another, live in peace; and the God of love and peace will be with you. [12] Greet one another with a holy kiss. All the saints greet you.

[13] The grace of the Lord Jesus Christ, the love of God, and the communion of[e] the Holy Spirit be with all of you.

[a] Other ancient authorities read *with him*
[b] Gk *brothers*
[c] Or *rejoice*
[d] Or *encourage one another*
[e] Or *and the sharing in*

congregations in 8.18. **19:** *Building you up,* see 10.8; 13.10. **20–21:** Catalogue of vices, see Rom 1.29–31; 13.13; 1 Cor 5.10–11; 6.9–10; Gal 5.19–21. **21:** Ironic use of *humble,* here meaning "humiliate"; see 11.7n.

13.1–10: Previous themes resume in a warning of harsh discipline. 1: *Third* visit, see 12.14n. *"Any . . . witnesses,"* Deut 19.15. **3–4:** *Christ . . . is not weak . . . but is powerful,* the weakness–powerful paradox summarized; see 10.1n.; 12.10n. **5:** *Examine yourselves . . . test yourselves,* a central rabbinic theme, e.g., *b. Ber.* 5a: "If a person sees that sufferings afflict him, let him examine his deeds." **10:** Strong warning while *away,* so that Paul will not have to resort to *severe* discipline, precisely what the opponents accused Paul of doing (10.10–11). **10:** Paul reminds the Corinthians that this is so for the purpose of *building up,* not *tearing down;* see 10.8; 12.19.

13.11–13: Final benediction. 11: *Finally,* a standard device to conclude a discussion. *Farewell* (or "rejoice") *. . . put . . . listen . . . agree . . . live . . .,* a series of parting exhortations. *God of love and peace,* the exact formulation does not appear in Jewish sources, although midrashic literature and liturgy routinely characterize the relationship between God and Israel as one of mutual love (see 2.4n.). God's role in bringing peace is also a central theme. The final benediction of the "Amidah" praises God for blessing the people of Israel with peace. **12:** *Holy kiss,* see Rom 16.16; 1 Cor 16.20; 1 Thess 5.26. Cf. *Gen. Rab.* 70.12, "All kissing is indecent, except in three instances: the kiss of high office, the kiss of reunion, and the kiss of separation." **13:** A full triadic benediction found nowhere else in Paul's letters.

THE LETTER OF PAUL TO THE GALATIANS

NAME, DATE, AND AUTHORSHIP

The Roman province of Galatia in central Asia Minor (modern Turkey) extended from the Black Sea in the north to the Mediterranean in the south. There is much scholarly debate about the location of Paul's "churches of Galatia" (1.2), whether in the north or the south and whether this letter dates from the late 40s or mid 50s CE. Paul's own location when writing this letter is not known. This letter shares language and themes with Romans and Corinthians, but the relative sequence of these letters is uncertain.

STRUCTURE

Following an autobiographical defense of his views, Paul forthrightly states his thesis: "a person is justified not by works of law but through faith in Jesus Christ" (2.16; cf. 2.21; 3.2; 5.2). To clarify this opposition between works and faith, Paul then appeals to other oppositions: flesh vs. spirit (3.3; 4.29; 5.16–25; 6.8), flesh vs. promise (4.23), slave vs. free (4.23,30), present Jerusalem vs. heavenly Jerusalem (4.26). Paul's point is that faith does not supplement Torah piety but replaces it (5.2).

INTERPRETATION

Paul's negative assessment of the Torah and those who follow it is striking: he insists that the Torah does not come from God (3.19–20); no longer has a salvific role, and perhaps never did (3.21–22); and its observance is akin to the worship of the Greek gods (4.9–10). He furthermore claims that the Jewish people are neither the true seed of Abraham (3.16) nor the Israel of God (6.16). In perhaps the letter's most famous verse, Paul writes that distinctions between Jew and Greek are effaced because all are one in Christ (3.28).

In Romans, Paul addresses these same issues, but his positions there are far more nuanced. Competition prompted this extreme negativity toward the Torah and Jewish distinctiveness. Rival apostles in Galatia sought to convince Paul's converts that Christian faith required Torah piety, and they insisted that (male) Christians undergo circumcision in consonance with God's instructions to Abraham in Gen 17. Paul angrily accuses these teachers of perverting the gospel (1.6–9), of being unprincipled and of demanding circumcision merely to avoid persecution (6.12), and to provide an occasion for boasting (6.13). Because these rivals attacked Paul's apostolic credibility, Paul not only responds in kind, but offers an autobiographical defense of his beginnings in the faith and his relations with the pillars of the Jerusalem church (1.10–2.14). He also provides empirical proof for his legitimacy: after believing in Christ as Paul taught them, the Galatian Christians received the Holy Spirit and the ability to do miracles, gifts they did not receive by observing works of law (3.2–5).

This letter, prompted by the specific situation of the churches in Galatia, contains some of the most enduring and influential formulations of the Christian faith. Later Christians learned from this letter that Judaism, that is, the observance of the commandments of the Torah and the refusal to believe in Jesus as the son of God, had and has no value. In the sixteenth century this letter gave Protestant reformers the rhetoric of "faith vs. works" that they would turn against both Judaism and Roman Catholicism. In recent times scholars have softened the polemical edge of this letter by observing that Paul's attack on the law was addressed to Gentile believers in Christ; his primary concern was to make sure that they did not begin to observe the Torah. Nowhere in his letters, either in Galatians or elsewhere, does Paul attempt to convince Jews to abandon the Torah.

Shaye J. D. Cohen

1 Paul an apostle—sent neither by human commission nor from human authorities, but through Jesus Christ and God the Father, who raised him from the dead— [2] and all the members of God's family[a] who are with me,

To the churches of Galatia:

[3] Grace to you and peace from God our Father and the Lord Jesus Christ, [4] who gave himself for our sins to set us free from the present evil age, according to the will of our God and Father, [5] to whom be the glory forever and ever. Amen.

[6] I am astonished that you are so quickly deserting the one who called you in the grace of Christ and are turning to a different gospel— [7] not that there is another gospel, but there are some who are confusing you and want to pervert the gospel of Christ. [8] But even if we or an angel[b] from heaven should proclaim to you a gospel contrary to what we proclaimed to you, let that one be accursed! [9] As we have said before, so now I repeat, if anyone proclaims to you a gospel contrary to what you received, let that one be accursed!

[10] Am I now seeking human approval, or God's approval? Or am I trying to please people? If I were still pleasing people, I would not be a servant[c] of Christ.

[11] For I want you to know, brothers and sisters,[d] that the gospel that was proclaimed by me is not of human origin; [12] for I did not receive it from a human source, nor was I taught it, but I received it through a revelation of Jesus Christ.

[13] You have heard, no doubt, of my earlier life in Judaism. I was violently persecut-

[a] Gk *all the brothers*
[b] Or *a messenger*
[c] Gk *slave*
[d] Gk *brothers*

1.1-5: Salutation. Paul's salutations typically combine autobiography with theology. Paul perceives himself as sent by God (1.15; Acts 9.3–6; 1 Cor 15.8). Rabbinic literature similarly mentions emissaries (Heb "sheliḥim") sent by some central authority to the hinterlands of Judea or the Diaspora (*m. Rosh Ha-Shanah* 1.3). **1:** *Jesus Christ and God the Father,* Paul regularly refers to God as "father," "our father," or "father of the Lord" (e.g., v. 3, Rom 15.6; 2 Cor 1.3; Phil 2.11). Jesus is "Lord" or "our Lord" (e.g., Rom 1.4; 4.24; 1 Cor 15.57). *Who raised him from the dead,* Jesus' crucifixion and resurrection are for Paul the only important facts of Jesus' biography. **2:** *Members of God's family,* lit., "brothers," a common early Christian address. *Churches* (Gk "ekklēsiai"), places of worship or congregations (see v. 3). Believers in Jesus called their assemblies "ekklēsiai" to distinguish them from "synagōgai." **3:** *Grace,* a Greek salutation, *and peace,* reflecting the Hebrew salutation "shalom" (Rom 1.7; 1 Cor 1.3; 2 Cor 1.2; 1 Thess 1.1). **4:** *For our sins,* perhaps alluding to Isa 53.5–6. *Set us free,* remove us *from the present evil age,* controlled by evil or demonic forces (4.3) but soon to be either destroyed or radically transformed. Christ's death rescues humanity from these forces. **5:** This is the only Pauline letter whose salutation ends with a doxology, the attribution of "glory" (Gk "doxa") to God under the influence of such verses as Ezek 3.12; Ps 29.1–2, and especially 104.31. Glory (Heb "kavod") is a common attribute of God in the Tanakh (e.g., Ex 16.10; 24.16).

1.6–9: Paul rebukes the Galatians. Unlike other Pauline epistles, Galatians lacks a thanksgiving section. **6:** *The one who called you,* in Paul's letters, the subject of "to call" (Gk "kalein") is always God. Cf. 1.15; 5.8. Some manuscripts omit *of Christ,* confirming that the one who has called is God. *Different gospel,* cf. 2 Cor 11.4. "Other" or "different" meaning "wrong, illegitimate" appears in rabbinic literature too: a wrong view is "another way" (Heb "derekh 'aḥeret", *t. Ber.* 6.6), idolaters are sometimes called "other ones, different ones" ("'aḥerim," *Mek. Neziqin* 12), the arch-heretic Elisha ben Abuyah was known as "the other one" ("'aḥer," *b. Hag.* 14b). *Gospel* ("evangelion"), lit., "good tidings," translation of Heb "besorah." The root "b-s-r" is used in Deutero-Isaiah's prophecies of redemption (40.9; 52.7; 60.6; 61.1).**8:** *Angel* ("angelos"), lit., "messenger." Compare Deut 13.1–6, concerning false prophets who mislead people. **9:** *What you received,* via teaching and tradition; cf. 1 Cor 15.1–3. The rabbinic equivalent is "qibbel" (*m. Avot* 1.1). *Let that one be accursed,* lit., "let him be 'anathema,'" the Gk translation of biblical "ḥerem" (Deut 7.26; Josh 6.17).

1.10–12: Paul's independence. 12: *A revelation of Jesus Christ,* claiming his "gospel" derives directly from God (cf. 1 Cor 11.23; 15.3), Paul stresses his independence.

1.13–14: Paul's life in Judaism. 13: *Judaism* appears in the NT only here and v. 14; "judaize" and "judaicly" only in 2.14. (The adjective "judaic" appears in Titus 1.14.) The Greek term connotes the distinctive ways and manners, customs and beliefs of the Judean people, cf. Phil 3.5. (See "Paul and Judaism," p. 551; "Judaism and

Places mentioned in Galatians 1–2.

ing the church of God and was trying to destroy it. [14] I advanced in Judaism beyond many among my people of the same age, for I was far more zealous for the traditions of my ancestors. [15] But when God, who had set me apart before I was born and called me

Jewishness," p. 513.) Paul's *earlier life* was *in Judaism*, but his current life, after he received his revelation from God (1.15–16), is not. *Violently persecuting*, Acts 8–9; 22.4–5. *Church of God*, see 1.2n. **14:** *Zealous*, the language of "zeal" had currency in first-century Jewish circles; the revolutionaries whom Josephus calls "Zealots" probably depicted themselves as zealots for God and Torah, inspired by such verses as Num 25.11 and 1 Kings 19.10,14. Here the word means "a devotee of." *Traditions of my ancestors*, "traditions of the ancestors" (lit., "fathers"), a quintessentially Pharisaic concept (see Phil 3.5). Josephus writes: "the Pharisees handed down to the people certain observances by succession from their fathers, which are not written in the laws of Moses" (*Ant.* 13.10.6 [297]). Cf. Mk 7.3–4. Rabbinic literature also refers to the sages of old as "fathers" (*m. Ed.* 1.4), but does not use the phrase "traditions of the fathers." When the Mishnah refers to an ancient tradition it uses the term "devar soferim," "a word of the scribes" (*m. Yebam.* 2.4, *m. Sanh.* 11.3).

1.15–17: Paul's call. 15: *Before I was born*, lit., "from the womb of my mother," see Jer 1.5; Isa 49.1. **16:** *Son*, Paul regularly refers to Jesus as "Son of God" (e.g., 4.4; Rom 8.3; 2 Cor 1.19; 1 Thess 1.10), even if he was also

through his grace, was pleased [16] to reveal his Son to me,[a] so that I might proclaim him among the Gentiles, I did not confer with any human being, [17] nor did I go up to Jerusalem to those who were already apostles before me, but I went away at once into Arabia, and afterwards I returned to Damascus.

[18] Then after three years I did go up to Jerusalem to visit Cephas and stayed with him fifteen days; [19] but I did not see any other apostle except James the Lord's brother. [20] In what I am writing to you, before God, I do not lie! [21] Then I went into the regions of Syria and Cilicia, [22] and I was still unknown by sight to the churches of Judea that are in Christ; [23] they only heard it said, "The one who formerly was persecuting us is now proclaiming the faith he once tried to destroy." [24] And they glorified God because of me.

2 Then after fourteen years I went up again to Jerusalem with Barnabas, taking Titus along with me. [2] I went up in response to a revelation. Then I laid before them (though only in a private meeting with the acknowledged leaders) the gospel that I proclaim among the Gentiles, in order to make sure that I was not running, or had not run, in vain. [3] But even Titus, who was with me, was not compelled to be circumcised, though he was a Greek. [4] But because of false believers[b] secretly brought in, who slipped in to spy on the freedom we have in Christ Jesus, so that they might enslave us— [5] we did not submit to them even for a moment, so that the truth of the gospel might always remain with you. [6] And from those who were supposed to be acknowledged leaders (what they actually were makes no difference to me; God shows no partiality)—those leaders contributed nothing to me. [7] On the contrary, when they saw that I had been entrusted with the gospel

[a] Gk *in me*
[b] Gk *false brothers*

"of the line of David according to the flesh" (Rom 1.3). *To me*, lit., "in me" parallel to "in the Gentiles." *Gentiles* (Gk "ethnē"), lit. "nations" (Heb "goyyim"). Following biblical usage, Paul divides humanity between Jews (or "Israel") and Gentiles/the "nations" (e.g., 2.2) or "Greeks" (e.g., 2.3). *Any human being*, lit., "flesh and blood," a frequent rabbinic expression for humans. Paul denies that his teaching has a human source; apparently his opponents accused him as lacking independent knowledge of God or Christ. Cf. 1.20n. **17:** *Go up to Jerusalem*, one ascends to Jerusalem (v. 18; 2.1), then the church's headquarters, cf. 2.1. *Apostles before me*, who knew Jesus. Paul argues that his God-given authority is equal to theirs. *Arabia*, the Transjordan and the Negev. *Returned to Damascus*, Acts 9.8–25; 2 Cor 11.32–33.

1.18–24: Paul's independence. 18: *Three years*, whether beginning with Paul's revelation (1.15-16) or return to Damascus (1.17). *Visit Cephas*, not to study with him. Cephas, (Aram for "rock"), Paul's usual name for Peter (Gk for "rock"). Paul too had a Semitic and a Greek name (Acts 13.9). *Fifteen days*, a brief period. Acts 9.26–30 has a different version of this visit. **19:** *James* (lit., "Jacob"), leader of the Jerusalem church (2.9; Acts 15.13; 21.18). Josephus describes his death (*Ant.* 20.9.1 [200]). **20:** Similar affirmations of veracity are in 1 Thess 2.5; 2 Cor 1.23; 11.31. Paul's opponents apparently argued that Paul was subordinate to the Jerusalem apostles. **21:** *Syria and Cilicia*, far from Jerusalem. Tarsus, Paul's hometown (Acts 9.11), is in Cilicia. **22:** *Churches*, see 1.2n.

2.1–10: Paul meets with the apostles. Acts 15 gives a different account of these events. **1:** *After fourteen years*, the date from which this is to be reckoned is not clear; cf. 1.18n. Paul again claims apostolic independence. *Jerusalem*, see 1.17n. *Barnabas*, Paul's Jewish companion (Acts 4.36; 9.27; 11.22–30; 12.25; 13.1–15.39; 1 Cor 9.6). *Titus*, Paul brings Titus (2.3) to test the Jerusalem church's acceptance of uncircumcised Gentiles. **2:** *Revelation*, either his original revelation (1.12), or a subsequent one; Paul clarifies that he was not summoned by the Jerusalem church. *Acknowledged leaders*, lit., "those who seem," "those who are esteemed," James, Cephas, and John, cf. 2.6,9. **3:** *Titus . . . was not compelled*, vindicating Paul's insistence that Gentile believers need not follow Torah. *Greek*, Gentile. Cf. 3.28. **4:** *False believers*, lit., "false brothers," cf. 2 Cor 11.26, who insisted that Gentile believers must be circumcised. *Secretly brought in*, lit., "intrusive, alien." The Gk implies not stealth but inappropriateness or foreignness. *Freedom* enjoyed by believers is a major theme here (ch 5) and elsewhere (1 Cor 10.29; 2 Cor 3.17). The slavery (5.1; 1 Cor 7.22; 9.19) entails following Torah commandments. **5:** *We did not submit*, some versions omit "not"; this reading might explain Paul's circumcision of Timothy (Acts 16.1–3) and the rumor Paul denies at 5.11. **6:** *Shows no partiality*, lit., "does not take the face of a person," a biblical idiom describing the ideal judge, whether mortal or divine (e.g., Lev 19.15; Deut 10.17; 2 Chr 19.7; cf.

for the uncircumcised, just as Peter had been entrusted with the gospel for the circumcised [8](for he who worked through Peter making him an apostle to the circumcised also worked through me in sending me to the Gentiles), [9]and when James and Cephas and John, who were acknowledged pillars, recognized the grace that had been given to me, they gave to Barnabas and me the right hand of fellowship, agreeing that we should go to the Gentiles and they to the circumcised. [10]They asked only one thing, that we remember the poor, which was actually what I was[a] eager to do.

[11]But when Cephas came to Antioch, I opposed him to his face, because he stood self-condemned; [12]for until certain people came from James, he used to eat with the Gentiles. But after they came, he drew back and kept himself separate for fear of the circumcision faction. [13]And the other Jews joined him in this hypocrisy, so that even Barnabas was led astray by their hypocrisy. [14]But when I saw that they were not acting consistently with the truth of the gospel, I said to Cephas before them all, "If you, though a Jew, live like a Gentile and not like a Jew, how can you compel the Gentiles to live like Jews?"[b]

[15]We ourselves are Jews by birth and not Gentile sinners; [16]yet we know that a person is justified[c] not by the works of the law but through faith in Jesus Christ.[d] And we have come to believe in Christ Jesus, so that we might be justified by faith in Christ,[e] and not by doing the works of the law, because no one will be justified by the works of the law.

[a] Or *had been*
[b] Some interpreters hold that the quotation extends into the following paragraph
[c] Or *reckoned as righteous;* and so elsewhere
[d] Or *the faith of Jesus Christ*
[e] Or *the faith of Christ*

Rom 2.11). *Contributed nothing,* perhaps "did not confer with me" (same word as in 1.16). **7:** *Had been entrusted* by God (2.8). *The uncircumcised,* lit., "the foreskinhood," those who have a foreskin, Gentiles (cf. 5.6). *The circumcised,* lit., "the circumcision," Jews. Cf. Eph 2.11, lit.,"Gentiles in the flesh, called 'the foreskin' by what is called 'the circumcision.'" *M. Ned.* 3.11 presents the same contrast. Acts 10 depicts Peter as bringing the Gospel to Gentiles (cf. Mt 28.19), and Acts 13 depicts Paul as first evangelizing Jews. **9:** *John,* the son of Zebedee (Mk 1.19), Peter's associate (Acts 3–4), not elsewhere mentioned by Paul. *Pillars,* a metaphor also found in rabbinic literature (*b. Ber.* 28b). *Right hand of fellowship,* our "shaking hands," a gesture attested in 2 Kings 10.15; Ezra 10.19. **10:** *Asked only one thing,* the great compromise of Acts 15.20,29 is conspicuously missing. *Remember the poor,* Paul raises money for the Jerusalem "poor" (Rom 15.25–29; 1 Cor 16.1–3; 2 Cor 8–9), the church's self-designation. The use of the plural term "the poor" as a self-designation may have its origins in the Psalms; see e.g., Ps 34.3; 147.6; 149.4. Giving money to the poor and raising money for the poor are paramount virtues in rabbinic piety (*t. Pe'ah* 4.18–21; *Lev. Rab.* 5.4).

2.11–14: Paul confronts Peter at Antioch. 12: *James,* see 1.19n. *Eat with Gentiles,* on table-fellowship, see "Food and Table Fellowship," p. 521. *Fear of the circumcision faction,* lit., "fear of those from the circumcised," that is, Jews. **13:** *Other Jews,* most likely, Jewish believers of the church in Antioch. *Barnabas,* see 2.1n. **14:** *Cephas,* see 1.18n. *Live like a Gentile,* there are no other reports that Peter abandoned Torah Law, although Acts 10 can be understood as Peter's rejecting dietary laws. *Live like Jews,* lit., "judaize," to follow Jewish practices, see 1.13n. Paul interprets Peter's refusal to dine with Gentile Christians as an effort to compel them to observe Torah Law.

2.15–21: Faith vs. law. 15: *We,* Paul and Peter. *By birth,* or "by nature"; cf. Rom 2.27; 11.21–24. *Gentiles* are *sinners* because they worship idols and do not follow the Torah. Since Paul believes that Gentiles, even in their Gentile state, can be justified before God (see next verse), either he is speaking ironically or is citing the view of his traditionalist opponents. **16:** *Justified* ("dikaiosynē"), or "reckoned as righteous." The LXX uses the Gk to translate Heb "tzedaqah," especially in Gen 15.6, a significant verse for Paul (cf. 3.6; Rom 4.3). *Works of the law,* lit., "works of law," legal observances (see 3.2; Rom 3.28). With the definite article (see 4.21n.) the phrase would be equivalent to "ma'asei ha-Torah," lit., "works of the Torah," which appears at Qumran (e.g., 4QMMT). Greek-speaking Jews used "nomos" to translate "Torah." *Faith* ("pistis"), like Heb "'emunah," connotes "trust, confidence"; it does not refer to belief in something irrational. *Faith in Jesus Christ* means confidence in Christ. The alternative translation, "faith of Jesus Christ," means that Jesus had confidence in God. The phrase is usually understood in the former sense (cf. 3.26, which is unambiguous), but the latter is

[17] But if, in our effort to be justified in Christ, we ourselves have been found to be sinners, is Christ then a servant of sin? Certainly not! [18] But if I build up again the very things that I once tore down, then I demonstrate that I am a transgressor. [19] For through the law I died to the law, so that I might live to God. I have been crucified with Christ; [20] and it is no longer I who live, but it is Christ who lives in me. And the life I now live in the flesh I live by faith in the Son of God,[a] who loved me and gave himself for me. [21] I do not nullify the grace of God; for if justification[b] comes through the law, then Christ died for nothing.

3 You foolish Galatians! Who has bewitched you? It was before your eyes that Jesus Christ was publicly exhibited as crucified! [2] The only thing I want to learn from you is this: Did you receive the Spirit by doing the works of the law or by believing what you heard? [3] Are you so foolish? Having started with the Spirit, are you now ending with the flesh? [4] Did you experience so much for nothing?—if it really was for nothing. [5] Well then, does God[c] supply you with the Spirit and work miracles among you by your doing the works of the law, or by your believing what you heard?

[6] Just as Abraham "believed God, and it was reckoned to him as righteousness," [7] so, you see, those who believe are the descendants of Abraham. [8] And the scripture, foreseeing that God would justify the Gentiles by faith, declared the gospel beforehand to Abraham, saying, "All the Gentiles shall be blessed in you." [9] For this reason, those who believe are blessed with Abraham who believed.

[10] For all who rely on the works of the law are under a curse; for it is written, "Cursed is everyone who does not observe and obey all the things written in the book of the law." [11] Now it is evident that no one is justified before God by the law; for "The one who is

[a] Or *by the faith of the Son of God*
[b] Or *righteousness*
[c] Gk *he*

possible. *No one will be justified,* Ps 143.2. Paul adds *by the works of the law,* cf. Rom 3.20. **17:** *We ourselves have been found to be sinners,* according to you, Peter; because you separated from Gentiles, implying that table-fellowship with them was sinful. *Certainly not,* because faith in Christ frees us from Torah observance. **18:** *The very things,* the very aspects of Torah piety, including separation from Gentiles. **19:** *Crucified with Christ,* a Pauline tenet: 5.24; 6.14; Rom 6.5–11; 2 Cor 4.7–12. **20:** *Christ who lives in me,* another central tenet: Rom 8.9–11; 2 Cor 13.5; cf. Col 1.27. *I live by faith* or "I live in the faith," cf. 2.16n. **21:** By rejecting works of law, Paul might be thought to be *nullifying the grace of God,* who gave Israel the Torah. Paul denies he is doing this. He discusses why God gave the Torah in 3.19–25.

3.1–5: Faith vs. works. 2: *By doing the works of the law or by believing what you heard,* lit., "by works of law or by hearing of faith" (also v. 5). In Acts possession by the Holy Spirit, especially in relation to baptism (2.38) or the laying on of hands (8.15–16; 19.5–6), evinces the efficacy of faith (2.4; 10.44). **3:** *Spirit . . . flesh,* an important contrast (4.29; 5.16–25; 6.8; Rom 2.28–29; 8.4–17; 1 Cor 5.5). *Flesh* may allude to circumcision. **5:** *Miracles,* charismatic activity attesting to the Spirit's presence.

3.6–9: Abraham the model of faith. 3.6–4.31 centers on Abraham. Paul's opponents likely adduced Abraham, because the Torah declares circumcision an everlasting covenant between God and Abraham's descendants; the uncircumcised as "cut off" (Gen 17.9–14). **6:** Gen 15.6. Paul states that Abraham, before his circumcision in Gen 17, was declared righteous through faith (or trust; 2.16n.). **7:** Hence those *who believe* become "*descendants* [lit., "sons," the better translation given the allusion to circumcision] *of Abraham,*" "blessed with Abraham" (v. 9, cf. 3.14), and "offspring of Abraham" (3.29). See also Rom 2–4. **8:** *Scripture* ("graphē"), usually referring to a specific verse, corresponding to the rabbinic "ha-katuv," "what is written." *All the Gentiles shall be blessed in you* (Gen 12.3, cf. 18.18). The Heb is ambiguous. Paul understands *in you* to mean "through you": following Abraham's example the nations attain God's blessing. Jewish exegesis understands *in you* as "by you." Rashi on Gen 12.3 explains that even Gentiles will say "may God bless you as he blessed Abraham" ("by you" = "by invoking you"). *Gen. Rab.* on Gen 12.3 explains that God tells Abraham that the blessings of nature will reach all humanity "by you" = "on your account. "

3.10–14: The curse of the law. 10: *Cursed is everyone,* Deut 27.26. Paul's citation differs slightly (by adding "the book") from the Heb or Gk. **11:** *The one who is righteous,* the Heb of Hab 2.4 (cf. Rom 1.17) should probably

righteous will live by faith."[a] [12] But the law does not rest on faith; on the contrary, "Whoever does the works of the law[b] will live by them." [13] Christ redeemed us from the curse of the law by becoming a curse for us—for it is written, "Cursed is everyone who hangs on a tree"— [14] in order that in Christ Jesus the blessing of Abraham might come to the Gentiles, so that we might receive the promise of the Spirit through faith.

[15] Brothers and sisters,[c] I give an example from daily life: once a person's will[d] has been ratified, no one adds to it or annuls it. [16] Now the promises were made to Abraham and to his offspring;[e] it does not say, "And to offsprings,"[f] as of many; but it says, "And to your offspring,"[e] that is, to one person, who is Christ. [17] My point is this: the law, which came four hundred thirty years later, does not annul a covenant previously ratified by God, so as to nullify the promise. [18] For if the inheritance comes from the law, it no longer comes from the promise; but God granted it to Abraham through the promise.

[19] Why then the law? It was added because of transgressions, until the offspring[e] would come to whom the promise had been made; and it was ordained through angels by a mediator. [20] Now a mediator involves more than one party; but God is one.

[21] Is the law then opposed to the promises of God? Certainly not! For if a law had been given that could make alive, then righteousness would indeed come through the law. [22] But the scripture has imprisoned all things under the power of sin, so that what was promised through faith in Jesus Christ[g] might be given to those who believe.

[23] Now before faith came, we were imprisoned and guarded under the law until faith

[a] Or *The one who is righteous through faith will live*
[b] Gk *does them*
[c] Gk *Brothers*
[d] Or *covenant* (as in verse 17)
[e] Gk *seed*
[f] Gk *seeds*
[g] Or *through the faith of Jesus Christ*

be translated "The one who is righteous shall live by his faith," but Paul's argument implies "The one who is righteous by faith shall live." For Paul, Gen 15.6 and Hab 2.4 prove righteousness is attained through faith (confidence, trust, see 2.16n.), not "works of the law." For the Talmud, Hab 2.4 demonstrates the opposite: the Torah contains 613 commandments, but Habakkuk concentrated them in one, "the righteous one shall live by his faith" (*b. Makk.* 24a). **12:** Lev 18.5. **13:** Deut 21.23 [LXX], which Paul cites to create a parallel to Deut 27.26 cited in 3.10. Deut 21.23 speaks of hanging (exposing) the corpse of an executed criminal; for Paul *tree* means "cross," and the verse speaks of the execution. The *curse* is pronounced against all those who cannot observe the entire Torah. 11QSTemple and 4QpNahum also understand Deut 21.23 as referring to crucifixion.

3.15–18: Covenant and law. God's *covenant* (Heb "berit," Gk "diathēkē") with Abraham included a *promise* or *promises* of an inheritance. **15:** *Has been ratified,* Mosaic Torah does not nullify the earlier Abrahamic covenant, see v. 17. **16:** *Offspring* ("sperma," lit., "seed"), Gen 12.7; 15.5; 17.8; 22.17, singular in Heb. For Genesis, "seed" is a collective noun referring to the people of Israel. Paul reads the noun as a singular, referring to Christ. **17:** Ex 12.40 (Heb) places the Israelites in Egypt *four hundred thirty years.* Paul, following the Septuagint, has those four hundred and thirty years begin with Abraham's sojourn in Canaan. Rabbinic chronology agrees (*Seder Olam Rab.* 3), claiming that Israel's sojourn in Egypt was 210 years. **18:** Paul posits a mutually exclusive relationship between the covenant, *the promise,* and *the inheritance* on one side, and *law* on the other.

3.19–22: The purpose of the law. Cf. Rom 7. **19:** *Because of transgressions,* either the law restrains sin (vv. 23–24), brings knowledge of sin (Rom 3.20; 7.7), or provokes sin (Rom 5.20). *Offspring,* see v. 16n. For *angels* having a role in the revelation of Torah see Deut 33.2 LXX; Acts 7.38,53; Heb 2.2; *Ant.* 15.136. Paul's point is that Torah, ordained by angels, is of lesser status than Abraham's covenant, which came from God. *By,* lit., "by the hand of"; perhaps a Hebraism (Lev 26.46; Num 36.13), perhaps to be taken literally (Ex 32.19). *Mediator,* Moses (Deut 5.5). Philo (*Life of Moses* 2.166) calls Moses a mediator. In Heb 8.6; 9.15; 12.24; 1 Tim 2.5, Jesus is the mediator. **20:** *More than one party,* thus the law did not come directly from God. **21:** The logic of the argument implies that the law is opposed to divine promises, but Paul is unwilling to draw this conclusion (see Rom 11.1). **21–22:** The law was to *imprison* or confine *all things under the power of sin,* not to *make alive. Faith in Jesus Christ,* see 2.16n.

would be revealed. [24] Therefore the law was our disciplinarian until Christ came, so that we might be justified by faith. [25] But now that faith has come, we are no longer subject to a disciplinarian, [26] for in Christ Jesus you are all children of God through faith. [27] As many of you as were baptized into Christ have clothed yourselves with Christ. [28] There is no longer Jew or Greek, there is no longer slave or free, there is no longer male and female; for all of you are one in Christ Jesus. [29] And if you belong to Christ, then you are Abraham's offspring,[a] heirs according to the promise.

4 My point is this: heirs, as long as they are minors, are no better than slaves, though they are the owners of all the property; [2] but they remain under guardians and trustees until the date set by the father. [3] So with us; while we were minors, we were enslaved to the elemental spirits[b] of the world. [4] But when the fullness of time had come, God sent his Son, born of a woman, born under the law, [5] in order to redeem those who were under the law, so that we might receive

[a] Gk *seed*
[b] Or *the rudiments*

3.23–29: Children of God through faith. 24–25: *Disciplinarian* ("pedagogue"), a household slave charged with keeping the master's son out of trouble and escorting him outside the house. Calling the law a pedagogue indicates its temporary role and the immaturity of its wards. **27:** *Were baptized into Christ,* immersion of converts to Judaism is not securely attested in pre-rabbinic texts, so there is much debate whether Christian baptism of converts derives from Jewish practice. In Christian baptism, the convert is baptized "in" or "in the name of" Christ (Mt 28.19; Acts 8.16; 19.3,5; Rom 6.3; 1 Cor 1.13,15); the Jewish conversion ritual has no baptizer and no "in the name of" language (*b. Yebam.* 47a–b). Verse 27 has suggested to scholars that v. 28 is a baptismal formula. *Clothed yourselves,* Rom 13.14. **28:** The law in general, and circumcision in particular, maintain social distinctions. According to Diogenes Laertius, a historian of the second century CE, Socrates (or some other Greek sage) said he had three blessings: "that I was born a human being and not a beast, a man and not a woman, a Greek and not a barbarian" (*Vit. Phil.* 1.33). According to *t. Ber.* 6.18, R. Judah says that a man is obligated daily to recite: "Blessed is God who has not made me a Gentile, who has not made me a boor, who has not made me a woman." *B. Men.* 43b–44a substitutes "slave" for "boor," and these three separate blessings—"Blessed is God who has not made me a Gentile . . . a slave . . . a woman"—still appear in the Orthodox prayerbook. (In fourteenth-century Spain the custom arose for women to recite "who has made me according to his will" instead of simply skipping "who has not made me a woman," and this custom is still followed in Orthodox circles.) These three benedictions have raised much controversy in modern times. Some Jewish movements have done away with them altogether, or have converted the negative into a positive: "Blessed is God who has made me an Israelite (or Jew) . . . a free-person . . . a human being (or in some versions: in his image)." Some modern Christians have tried to read Paul as a liberation theologian, as if Paul, anticipating the struggles of our time, was opposed to the power structures of his time. But this reading of Paul is most unlikely. On the contrary, Paul and the Pauline tradition counsel women to remain subject to their husbands (1 Cor 11.3; 14.34–35; cf. Eph 5.22–24; Col 3.18; 1 Tim 2.12; Titus 2.4–5; 1 Pet 3.1–5). Paul's acceptance of slavery is evident in Philemon. The phrase in Gal 3.28 recurs in somewhat different form in Rom 10.12; 1 Cor 12.13, and Col 3.11, but the only distinction that appears in all four is that between Jew and Greek (Gentile), because the effacement of that distinction is the one that matters to Paul. **29:** *Abraham's offspring* (or "seed"), united with Christ, believers receive Christ's status as Abraham's offspring (see 3.16n.). In rabbinic Judaism, by accepting the Torah converts are deemed to be the offspring of Abraham, and consequently permitted to join native Jews in praying to "Our God and God of our fathers" (*y. Bik.* 1.4.64a).

4.1–7: Sons and heirs. 1: *Heirs . . . minors . . . slaves . . . owners,* all these nouns are singular in the original (see 3.23–29). **2:** *Guardians* ("epitropoi," sing. "epitropos"), a Gk word meaning "guardian" or "trustee," appearing frequently in rabbinic literature for a guardian of a child. **3:** *Elemental spirits* (or "the rudiments"), polytheistic piety previously observed by the Gentile Galatians (4.8–9) and possibly also Torah observance. Paul's implicit equation of the two is striking. See also Col 2.8,20. **4:** *Fullness of time,* cf. Mk 1.15; Eph 1.10. Many rabbis believed that the messiah would arrive at a time predetermined by God (*b. Ketub.* 111a; *b. Sanh.* 97b). *Born of a woman,* not necessarily implying divine paternity, cf. Job 14.1; Mt 11.11. *Under the law,* lit., "under law," i.e., as a Jew. **5:** *Those who were under the law,* cf. 4.21n. This phrase would seem to refer to Jews, but Paul goes on to say *we,*

adoption as children. [6] And because you are children, God has sent the Spirit of his Son into our[a] hearts, crying, "Abba![b] Father!" [7] So you are no longer a slave but a child, and if a child then also an heir, through God.[c]

[8] Formerly, when you did not know God, you were enslaved to beings that by nature are not gods. [9] Now, however, that you have come to know God, or rather to be known by God, how can you turn back again to the weak and beggarly elemental spirits?[d] How can you want to be enslaved to them again? [10] You are observing special days, and months, and seasons, and years. [11] I am afraid that my work for you may have been wasted.

[12] Friends,[e] I beg you, become as I am, for I also have become as you are. You have done me no wrong. [13] You know that it was because of a physical infirmity that I first announced the gospel to you; [14] though my condition put you to the test, you did not scorn or despise me, but welcomed me as an angel of God, as Christ Jesus. [15] What has become of the goodwill you felt? For I testify that, had it been possible, you would have torn out your eyes and given them to me. [16] Have I now become your enemy by telling you the truth? [17] They make much of you, but for no good purpose; they want to exclude you, so that you may make much of them. [18] It is good to be made much of for a good purpose at all times, and not only when I am present with you. [19] My little children, for whom I am again in the pain of childbirth until Christ is formed in you, [20] I wish I were present with you now and could change my tone, for I am perplexed about you.

[21] Tell me, you who desire to be subject to the law, will you not listen to the law? [22] For

[a] Other ancient authorities read *your*
[b] Aramaic for *Father*
[c] Other ancient authorities read *an heir of God through Christ*
[d] Or *beggarly rudiments*
[e] Gk *Brothers*

indicating "we humans," cf. 3.26; 4.3. *Adoption,* Paul changes his metaphor, from becoming adults (4.1–2) to being adopted (cf. Rom 8.14–17). An alternative translation is "sonship" (as in Rom 9.4) denoting the relationship between God and his special people. **6:** *Spirit of his son,* Paul distinguishes between Christ and God (1.1n.; 1 Cor 8.6), but not between the Spirit and Christ (Rom 8.9–10). In the fourth century the Nicene Creed distinguished God the Father, God the Son (Christ), and the God the Spirit. This Trinitarian conception is unknown to Paul and is barely attested in the NT (Mt 28.19). *Abba! Father,* cf. Mk 14.36; Rom 8.15. Rabbinic theology, following biblical precedent (Deut 14.1 and Jer 31.20), often conceived of God as father and Israel as son or sons. Still, although rabbinic prayers were sometimes directed to "our father in heaven" (e.g., *m. Sot.* 9.15) or "our father our king" (e.g., *b. Ta'an.* 25b), no rabbinic prayers invoke God as *Abba,* which affects a level of intimacy with the divine that made the rabbis uncomfortable (see *m. Ta'an.* 3.8).

4.8–11: Avoiding the pagan past. 8–9: *Beings . . . elemental spirits,* see 4.3n. Paul accuses the Galatians of wanting to return to pagan worship and juxtaposes this accusation to an attack on Torah observance, suggesting that these are the same. **10:** *Days . . . years,* usually understood as referring to Jewish calendrical observance. Cf. Rom 14.5–6; Col 2.16.

4.12–20: Paul as exemplar. 13: *Physical infirmity,* v. 15 may suggest eye trouble. *Gospel,* see 1.6n. *First,* or "on the prior" occasion, suggesting Paul visited Galatia twice (see Acts 16.6; 18.23). **14:** *Though my condition put you to the test, you did not scorn or despise me,* lit., "and that which was a temptation to you in my flesh, you did not reject or despise." Because of Paul's ailment the Galatians might have rejected him, cf. Ps 22.25. *As an angel of God, as Christ Jesus,* the Galatians showed Paul the same respect they would have shown to a heavenly representative. **17–18:** *They,* Paul's opponents, who teach Torah observance and exclude the non law-observant, cf. 2.12. *Make much,* or "seek out." **19:** *Pain of childbirth,* Paul, like Moses (Num 11.12; cf. 1 Thess 2.7) imagines himself a mother in labor. In 1 Cor 4.15 and 1 Thess 2.11 he calls himself a father. Paul regularly refers to his followers as "children" (1 Cor 4.14; 2 Cor 6.13; 1 Thess 2.11). *Until Christ is formed in you,* the Galatians too are "pregnant"!

4.21–5.1: Allegory of Hagar and Sarah. 21: The Greek distinguishes *subject to the law,* lit., "subject to law," without the definite article, from *listen to the law,* with the definite article (see Rom 3.21). Without the definite article, *law* ("nomos") usually means something general like "legal observances" as in the phrase "subject to law" or "under law" (3.23; 4.4–5; 5.18; Rom 6.14–15). With the article *the law* usually refers to the Bible, specifically Torah (3.10,19; 5.3). Similarly in rabbinic idiom "the Torah" ("ha-Torah") usually refers to the Written Torah,

it is written that Abraham had two sons, one by a slave woman and the other by a free woman. [23] One, the child of the slave, was born according to the flesh; the other, the child of the free woman, was born through the promise. [24] Now this is an allegory: these women are two covenants. One woman, in fact, is Hagar, from Mount Sinai, bearing children for slavery. [25] Now Hagar is Mount Sinai in Arabia[a] and corresponds to the present Jerusalem, for she is in slavery with her children. [26] But the other woman corresponds to the Jerusalem above; she is free, and she is our mother. [27] For it is written,

"Rejoice, you childless one, you who bear
no children,
burst into song and shout, you who
endure no birth pangs;
for the children of the desolate woman are
more numerous
than the children of the one who is
married."

[28] Now you,[b] my friends,[c] are children of the promise, like Isaac. [29] But just as at that time the child who was born according to the flesh persecuted the child who was born according to the Spirit, so it is now also. [30] But what does the scripture say? "Drive out the slave and her child; for the child of the slave will not share the inheritance with the child of the free woman." [31] So then, friends,[c] we are children, not of the slave but of the free

5 woman. [1] For freedom Christ has set us free. Stand firm, therefore, and do not submit again to a yoke of slavery.

[2] Listen! I, Paul, am telling you that if you let yourselves be circumcised, Christ will be of no benefit to you. [3] Once again I testify to every man who lets himself be circumcised that he is obliged to obey the entire law. [4] You who want to be justified by the law have cut yourselves off from Christ; you have fallen away from grace. [5] For through the Spirit,

a Other ancient authorities read *For Sinai is a mountain in Arabia*
b Other ancient authorities read *we*
c Gk *brothers*

while "Torah" refers to something much broader, Oral Torah. Cf. *m. Avot* 1.1 "Moses received Torah (not "the Torah") at Sinai." *Listen to the law*, listen to what scripture says. **22:** *It is written*, Gen 16; 21. **24:** In an *allegory*, literal meaning is not the real meaning. Allegories typically represent moral qualities or philosophical concepts as concrete entities such as persons, or places. Allegories are present in the Hebrew Bible (see e.g., Isa 5). Philo, the Alexandrian Jewish philosopher, Paul's older contemporary, understands many biblical stories as allegories. For example, Abram's journey from Chaldea to Canaan (Gen 12) represents the soul's ascent from the world of matter to that of the spirit. For Philo, allegorical meanings complement or supplement literal meanings; Paul's language suggests that the allegorical meaning negates the literal meaning. Numerous rabbinic texts (e.g., *Gen. Rab.* 65.21) understand the conflict between Esau and Jacob (Gen 25–33) as representing the conflict between Israel (Jacob) and Rome (Edom, Esau). Hagar, a slave who bears children into slavery, represents the Sinaitic covenant. **25–26:** *Jerusalem . . . with her children*, on Zion as mother, see Isa 49.14–23; 66.8. Textual variants show that ancient readers were not sure how to understand Paul's identification of Hagar with Sinai. **25–26:** *Jerusalem*, when speaking of Jerusalem as a symbol, Paul uses the Hebrew ("Ierousalēm"); speaking of the actual place (1.17–18; 2.1), he uses the Gk ("Hierosolyma"). *Present Jerusalem . . . Jerusalem above*, various biblical verses depict God as building the Jerusalem Temple (Ex 15.17; Ps 78.69) or Jerusalem itself (Ps 147.2; perhaps Ps 87). This Pauline passage seems to be the earliest attestation of the idea that a heavenly Jerusalem corresponds to the earthly one, the former built by God, the latter built by humans . After the Temple's destruction in 70 CE, this idea takes on a consolatory function: earthly Jerusalem is destroyed but heavenly Jerusalem endures (*4 Ezra* [2 Esd] 7.26; Rev 3.12; 21.1–3; *b. Ta'an.* 5a). Paul understands the relationship between earthly and heavenly Jerusalem to be not complementary but adversarial. Contrast Heb 12.22. **27:** Isa 54.1. **29:** That Ishmael *persecuted* Isaac is based on a midrashic reading of Gen 21.9. **30:** Gen 21.10. **5.1:** *Yoke of slavery*, Torah observance and pagan worship. Cf. Acts 15.10. Rabbinic literature, too, occasionally refers to Torah piety as the "yoke of the commandments" (*m. Ber.* 2.2; *Sifra* on Lev 11.43) or "the yoke of the kingdom of heaven" (*m. Ber.* 2.2; *b. Ber.* 14b), but for the rabbis this rhetoric serves to justify not the rejection of the commandments, as in Paul, but their affirmation.

5.2–12: Resisting circumcision. Paul asserts, but does not explain, that seeking righteousness through the law, by means of circumcision, takes away the benefit of salvation through Christ. **2:** *I, Paul*, emphatic (2 Cor 10.1; 1 Thess 2.18). **3:** *Obliged to obey the entire law*, 6.13n. **4:** *Have cut yourselves*, this bad pun is absent from the

by faith, we eagerly wait for the hope of righteousness. [6] For in Christ Jesus neither circumcision nor uncircumcision counts for anything; the only thing that counts is faith working[a] through love.

[7] You were running well; who prevented you from obeying the truth? [8] Such persuasion does not come from the one who calls you. [9] A little yeast leavens the whole batch of dough. [10] I am confident about you in the Lord that you will not think otherwise. But whoever it is that is confusing you will pay the penalty. [11] But my friends,[b] why am I still being persecuted if I am still preaching circumcision? In that case the offense of the cross has been removed. [12] I wish those who unsettle you would castrate themselves!

[13] For you were called to freedom, brothers and sisters;[b] only do not use your freedom as an opportunity for self-indulgence,[c] but through love become slaves to one another. [14] For the whole law is summed up in a single commandment, "You shall love your neighbor as yourself." [15] If, however, you bite and devour one another, take care that you are not consumed by one another.

[16] Live by the Spirit, I say, and do not gratify the desires of the flesh. [17] For what the flesh desires is opposed to the Spirit, and what the Spirit desires is opposed to the flesh; for these are opposed to each other, to prevent you from doing what you want. [18] But if you are led by the Spirit, you are not subject to the law. [19] Now the works of the flesh are obvious: fornication, impurity, licentiousness, [20] idolatry, sorcery, enmities, strife, jealousy, anger, quarrels, dissensions, factions, [21] envy,[d] drunkenness, carousing, and things like these. I am warning you, as I warned you before: those who do such things will not inherit the kingdom of God.

[22] By contrast, the fruit of the Spirit is love, joy, peace, patience, kindness, generosity,

a Or *made effective*
b Gk *brothers*
c Gk *the flesh*
d Other ancient authorities add *murder*

Greek; lit., "you have become estranged," or "you have been released from an association." **6:** *Circumcision nor uncircumcision* (lit., "foreskinhood," cf. 2.7n.), this does not contradict 5.2. To those who are not circumcised, Paul preaches that they should not accept circumcision; to those who are already circumcised, Paul preaches that they should not remove the marks of circumcision (1 Cor 7.19). See 6.15. *Faith working through love,* faith is a main topic of this epistle, but love is not, although it is significant in some of Paul's other writings (most notably, 1 Cor 13). Love ("agapē") here anticipates 5.13–14,22 and echoes 2.20. The phrase appears to mean "faith/trust/confidence in God/Christ, made effective by love of God/Christ." **7:** *Running,* see 2.2. **8:** *One who calls,* God, cf. 1.6n. **9:** 1 Cor 5.6 records the same proverb. Agents of change can be effective even if small. Since leaven can be a symbol of corruption (Mt 16.5–12; 1 Cor 5.7; *b. Ber.* 17a), the proverb might have a negative valence. However, by itself the proverb is neutral. Rabbinic sages also observed that a little bit of leaven goes a long way (*b. Ber.* 34a). **11:** *Still being persecuted* by fellow Jews (cf. 6.12n.). *If I am still preaching circumcision,* apparently Paul's opponents alleged that he did not really oppose circumcision, and that therefore the Galatian Christians should become circumcised. *Offense* ("skandalon," lit., "stumbling block"), Jesus' crucifixion is an offense to Jews because of the freedom from the law that believers claimed as its effect; were the Galatians to submit to circumcision/the law, then the offense to Jews would end. Cf. 1 Cor 1.23. **12:** *Would castrate themselves,* lit., "cut off," "mutilate." Cf. Phil 3.2. The Romans sometimes regarded circumcision as a kind of castration; one cause of the Bar Kochba rebellion (132–135 CE) was a Roman ban against Jewish circumcision, an extension of a ban against castration (*Historia Augusta,* "Vita Hadriani" 14.2).

5.13–15: Summarizing Torah. Although not under the law, the Galatians should not abuse that freedom by yielding to temptation or strife. **14:** *Summed up,* lit., "fulfilled," cf. Rom 8.4. *Love your neighbor as yourself,* Lev 19.18; cf. Rom 13.8–10; Mt 22.34–40. Rabbinic literature attributes a similar statement to Hillel (*b. Shabb.* 31a) (see "The Concept of Neighbor" p. 540).

5.16–26: Living by the Spirit. On *flesh* vs. *Spirit* see 3.3n. **18:** *Subject to the law,* see 4.21n. **19–21:** Vice lists are common in Paul's letters (Rom 1.29–31; 1 Cor 6.9–10; 2 Cor 12.20). Cf. *m. Avot* 2.7 (virtues and vices). **21:** *Kingdom of God,* 1 Cor 15.50 suggests that this is an eschatological idea, cf. 1 Cor 6.9–10; Rom 14.17 suggests that the kingdom presently exists. In rabbinic usage "kingdom of heaven" is not eschatological but refers to the acknowledgement of God's suzerainty in this world; cf. 5.1n. **22–23:** Catalogue of virtues: 2 Cor 6.6–7; Phil 4.8.

faithfulness, [23] gentleness, and self-control. There is no law against such things. [24] And those who belong to Christ Jesus have crucified the flesh with its passions and desires. [25] If we live by the Spirit, let us also be guided by the Spirit. [26] Let us not become conceited, competing against one another, envying one another.

6 My friends,[a] if anyone is detected in a transgression, you who have received the Spirit should restore such a one in a spirit of gentleness. Take care that you yourselves are not tempted. [2] Bear one another's burdens, and in this way you will fulfill[b] the law of Christ. [3] For if those who are nothing think they are something, they deceive themselves. [4] All must test their own work; then that work, rather than their neighbor's work, will become a cause for pride. [5] For all must carry their own loads.

[6] Those who are taught the word must share in all good things with their teacher.

[7] Do not be deceived; God is not mocked, for you reap whatever you sow. [8] If you sow to your own flesh, you will reap corruption from the flesh; but if you sow to the Spirit, you will reap eternal life from the Spirit. [9] So let us not grow weary in doing what is right, for we will reap at harvest time, if we do not give up. [10] So then, whenever we have an opportunity, let us work for the good of all, and especially for those of the family of faith.

[11] See what large letters I make when I am writing in my own hand! [12] It is those who want to make a good showing in the flesh that try to compel you to be circumcised—only that they may not be persecuted for the cross of Christ. [13] Even the circumcised do not themselves obey the law, but they want you to be circumcised so that they may boast about your flesh. [14] May I never boast of anything except the cross of our Lord Jesus Christ, by which[c] the world has been crucified to me, and I to the world. [15] For[d] neither circumcision nor uncircumcision is anything; but a new creation is everything!

a Gk *Brothers*
b Other ancient authorities read *in this way fulfill*
c Or *through whom*
d Other ancient authorities add *in Christ Jesus*

Cf. *m. Avot* 2.7 (virtues and vices); 3.17; 6.6. **24:** *Crucified the flesh,* Christians participate in Jesus' crucifixion (see 2.19n.), which in turn represents the mortification of the body (cf. 6.14; Rom 8.13). Philo interpreted circumcision as "the excision of excessive and superfluous pleasure" (*Spec. Laws* 1.1–11). Paul transfers the metaphor from circumcision to crucifixion.

6.1–10: Concluding exhortations. 1: *Anyone,* lit., "a person," here a fellow Christian. **2:** Paul cites Jesus' teachings (1 Cor 7.10; 9.14; 11.23; perhaps 1 Thess 4.15–17), which may constitute *the law of Christ.* Perhaps Paul means the Christian life animated by Christ's spirit, cf. 1 Cor 9.21; Rom 8.2. **6:** *Word,* presumably the word of God, either scripture or the lessons derived from scripture. A *teacher* (1 Cor 12.28; Eph 4.11; 1 Tim 5.17) is entitled to compensation from students (1 Cor 9.4–14; Phil 4.14–19; cf. Mt 10.9–11). The Mishnah disagrees (*m. Ned.* 4.3). **7:** *You reap whatever you sow,* proverbial expression found in classical literature (e.g., Cicero, *De or.* 2.65) as well as Hos 8.7; 10.12; Prov 22.8; Job 4.8. Cf. 2 Cor 9.6. **8:** *Eternal life,* from Dan 12.2. Cf. Rom 2.7; 5.21; 6.22–23. See Rom 8.5–8. **10:** *Those of the family* (lit., "household"), Paul has various images to express Christian unity: temple of God (1 Cor 3.16–17; 2 Cor 6.16); house (or building) of God (1 Cor 3.9); body of Christ (1 Cor 12.12–27). Here Paul conceives of the Christian community as a household *of faith;* cf. Eph 2.19; 1 Tim 3.15; 1 Pet 4.17. Hence all Christians are siblings: 1.2n.

6.11–18: Postscript. 11: Paul dictated this letter to a secretary, but adds the postscript in his *own hand,* cf. 1 Cor 16.21; Col 4.18; 2 Thess 3.17; Philem 19. **12:** *Persecuted* by fellow Jews *for the cross:* Jews who do not believe in Christ are persecuting (what exactly this means is unclear) Jews who do believe in Christ, presumably because the former suspect the latter of rejecting the Torah. Hence to avoid persecution the Christian Jews demonstrate their loyalty to the Torah by demanding circumcision of the Galatian Gentiles who believe in Christ. Cf. 5.11n. **13:** *Even the circumcised,* lit., "even those who are being circumcised," Galatian Christians who follow Paul's opponents. The variant, "even those who have been circumcised," may refer to Jewish Christians. *Do not themselves obey the law,* if referring to circumcised Galatian Christians, the verse implies that they did not, and apparently were not expected to, observe the entire Torah (see 5.3); if to Jewish believers in Christ, perhaps Paul is alluding to Peter's alleged failure to observe the law (2.14) or something similar. Paul reprises his argument that those subordinate to the law must observe the entire law, which is impossible (3.10–14; 5.3). **15:** See 5.6; 1 Cor 7.19. *New*

[16] As for those who will follow this rule—peace be upon them, and mercy, and upon the Israel of God.

[17] From now on, let no one make trouble for me; for I carry the marks of Jesus branded on my body.

[18] May the grace of our Lord Jesus Christ be with your spirit, brothers and sisters.[a] Amen.

[a] Gk *brothers*

creation, Isa 65.17; 66.22; 2 Cor 5.17. **16:** *This rule,* the rule or principle of v. 15, that circumcision does not matter; only new creation in Christ matters. *Peace be upon them, and mercy, and upon the Israel of God,* Paul adapts the traditional "peace be upon Israel" (Ps 125.5; 128.6). The NRSV translation invokes a double blessing (cf. 1.3n.) upon two groups, those who live according to the rule of v. 15, and the Israel of God. An alternative translation, "Peace be upon them, and mercy upon the Israel of God," suggests that he invokes peace on the former and mercy on the latter. However, reading the Gk as "Peace and mercy be upon them, that is to say, upon the Israel of God," Paul invokes a double blessing on only one group. At stake is what *Israel of God* means. This is the first time Galatians uses *Israel,* and the only time anywhere that Paul qualifies Israel with *of God,* a locution never found in the Hebrew Bible. Elsewhere Paul argues that "not all Israelites truly belong to Israel" (Rom 9.6); "Israel according to the flesh" (Gk, 1 Cor 10.18) is not the same as the "real" Israel, what Paul here calls *the Israel of God.* Presumably Paul's opponents argued that if the Galatian Christians wish to be part of God's chosen, the people Israel, they need to be circumcised and observe the Torah. Paul argues that the old distinction between circumcision and foreskin, between ethnic Israel and ethnic Gentile, no longer obtains (3.28), because the true Israel, the Israel of God, consists of all those who are a new creation in Christ (cf. Rom 2.29; Phil 3.3). **17:** *Marks of Jesus branded on my body,* lit., "For I carry the scars ("stigmata") of Jesus on my body" ("branded" is not in the Gk). "Stigmata" can indicate branding (as of a slave) or tattooing (as of a religious devotee). Paul's scars are the result of his beatings (2 Cor 6.4–6; 11.23–27) which he understands to mirror Jesus' sufferings (2 Cor 4.7–10). Alternatively, the scars may be metaphorical (cf. 1 Cor 15.32, whose reference to "fighting beasts" might be literal or metaphorical). **18:** This is the only Pauline letter in whose closing benediction Paul refers to his addressees as *brothers*; Paul wishes to end on an irenic note.

THE LETTER OF PAUL TO THE EPHESIANS

NAME

The letter to the Ephesians emphasizes the "mystery of God's will" (1.9; 3.3–4,9; 5.32; 6.19) that Christ breaks down the "wall" of hostility between Jews and Gentiles (2.14). The text's theme is unity, articulated in both cosmic terms and descriptions of Christian households.

AUTHORSHIP, LITERARY HISTORY, AND DATE

Traditionally, the letters to the Ephesians, Philippians, Colossians, and Philemon were assumed to have been written by Paul during his imprisonment in Rome (Acts 28.16–31), and were consequently called "captivity epistles." The attribution of all of these to Paul, and the recognition that references to imprisonment and the imperial guard (e.g., Phil 1.7,13) do not necessarily mean imprisonment in Rome because there were detachments of the emperor's guards at various places, have led most scholars to abandon this interpretation.

Despite the traditional title, therefore, and the references to sender and recipient in 1.1 (with further reference to the sender in 3.1), most scholars doubt that Ephesians is by Paul, and many doubt that it is in fact a letter. The similarity of this text to the letter to the Colossians, which is also of uncertain Pauline authorship, suggests a false attribution of authorship (known as pseudepigraphy); in addition, its theology and vocabulary do not reflect Paul's concerns, especially in presenting resurrection as a current rather than a future event (2.1–2,6; cf. Rom 6.5–8; Phil 3.10–11). It mentions "heavenly places" (1.3,20; 2.6; 3.10; 6.12) and speaks of Christ as "the head" of the church, which is "his body" (1.22–23; 4.11,15–16), key theological expressions absent from the undisputed Pauline epistles. Nor does it deal with the relationship of the community to Torah, a major focus of Paul's writings in Galatians and Romans. The text's connection to Ephesus is also problematic: the words "in Ephesus" (1.1) are absent from some of the best early manuscripts. Defenders of Pauline authorship argue that the letter was written late in Paul's ministry for a different audience (Marcion, a second-century Christian thinker, later condemned for heresy, suggested the Laodiceans). Without the opening and closing sections (1.1–2 and 6.21–24) the letter reads more like a sermon or exhortation addressed to Christian communities in general, rather than a letter specifically dealing with the problems and concerns of one community in particular.

HISTORICAL CONTEXT

More than in the undisputed Pauline letters but like Colossians, the Pastorals, and the Catholic Epistles, Ephesians delineates models for a new social order. Gentiles are to reject their previous lawlessness (e.g., 1.11; 2.3,19; 4.17) and, expressed in a more muted fashion, Jews are to reject insularity or legalism (e.g., 2.1–2,15). Wives must submit to their husbands, and husbands are to treat their wives kindly; children are to respect their parents, and parents are to love their children; conventional but respectful relations are encouraged between masters and slaves.

Imagery familiar from Jewish apocalyptic literature appears especially in reference to this age and the age to come (1.21; 2.7; see, e.g., *Jub.* 1.29; 23.26–29; *1 En.* 10.16–22; 11; 45.3–6; *T. 12 Patr.* 18.2–14); the distinction between the children or pathways of light and those of darkness (1.18; 2.1–2; 5.8–14; compare 1QS 3.13–4.14); and the anticipation of the end-time (1.10; 3.10). See the annotations for more specific references to biblical and extra-biblical texts.

STRUCTURE

Ephesians falls into two more or less equal parts: chs 1–3 contain the theological teachings, and chs 4–6 consist of exhortations to more upright behavior befitting the hearers' new life in Christ.

Maxine Grossman

1 Paul, an apostle of Christ Jesus by the will of God,

To the saints who are in Ephesus and are faithful[a] in Christ Jesus:

[2] Grace to you and peace from God our Father and the Lord Jesus Christ.

[3] Blessed be the God and Father of our Lord Jesus Christ, who has blessed us in Christ with every spiritual blessing in the heavenly places, [4] just as he chose us in Christ[b] before the foundation of the world to be holy and blameless before him in love. [5] He destined us for adoption as his children through Jesus Christ, according to the good pleasure of his will, [6] to the praise of his glorious grace that he freely bestowed on us in the Beloved. [7] In him we have redemption through his blood, the forgiveness of our trespasses, according to the riches of his grace [8] that he lavished on us. With all wisdom and insight [9] he has made known to us the mystery of his will, according to his good pleasure that he set forth in Christ, [10] as a plan for the fullness of time, to gather up all things in him, things in heaven and things on earth. [11] In Christ we have also obtained an inheritance,[c] having been destined according to the purpose of him who accomplishes all things according to his counsel and will, [12] so that we, who were the first to set our hope on Christ, might live for the praise of his glory.

a Other ancient authorities lack *in Ephesus*, reading *saints who are also faithful*
b Gk *in him*
c Or *been made a heritage*

1.1–14: Salutation and blessing. Praising God who grants believers an inheritance as part of the cosmic order. **1–2:** Salutation, cf. Col 1.1–2. **1:** *Apostle*, Gk "one who is sent," someone acting as representative or ambassador for another. *Saints*, Gk "hagioi," "holy ones," those set apart and sanctified by God through faith in Christ. In the Torah, Israel is "a holy people" sanctified by the covenant (Ex 19.6; Deut 7.6). *In Ephesus*, the absence of this phrase from some textual witnesses suggests the epistle might have been intended for general circulation. For Ephesus, see Acts 18.19–21; 19; 1 Cor 16.8. **2:** *Father*, cf. 1.3,17; 2.18; 3.14; 4.6; 5.20; 6.23. The term was often used by Jesus' followers, describing their relationship to God as father (Mt 6.9; Mk 11.25; Lk 11.2; Rom 8.15–17; Gal 4.6–7). The image was infrequent, but not unknown, in the Hebrew Bible (Isa 63.16; 64.8; Jer 3.4,19; Ps 68.5; 89.26; 103.13). **3:** *Blessed be . . .*, reminiscent of Jewish blessing formulas, e.g., 1 Kings 8.15,56; Ps 103.48; 1 Chr 16.36; cf. 2 Cor. 1.3; 1 Pet 1.3. *Spiritual blessing*, sanctification, being made holy or being set apart in the Holy Spirit. *Heavenly places*, unseen realms cf. 1.20; 2.6; 3.10; 6.12 but in this sense nowhere else in the NT. **4:** *Chose us . . . before the foundation of the world* (cf. Col 1.15–17). The Damascus Document (CD 2.2–13) makes a similar claim. On Christ's preexistence, see Jn 1.1–5; Wisdom, which *Gen. Rab.* 1.1 understands as Torah, plays this role in Prov 8.22–31. *Blameless*, lit., "without blemish," like priests in the Temple (Lev 21.16–23) or sacrificial animals (Lev 22.17–25). Cf. 5.27; Col 1.22. *In love*, God liberates Israel because "the LORD loved you and kept the oath that he swore to your ancestors" (Deut 7.8). **5–6:** *Adoption* as God's children, being granted status as heirs; cf. 2.19. By adoption one becomes a full family member, with all rights and responsibilities. *Grace* (Gk "charis," Heb "ḥen"), favor (see Gen 6.8; Prov 3.4).*Freely bestowed* by God; see Rom 8.14–17; Gal 4.1–7. Torah's treatment of Israel as God's "firstborn son" suggests adoption; see Ex 4.22; Jer 31.9; Hos 11.1. *Beloved*, cf. Mk 1.11; Col 1.13. **7:** *Redemption* (cf. 1.14; 4.30; Col 1.14), as in freeing a slave or returning a captive; *through his blood*, Mt 26.27–28; Mk 10.45; Lk 22.20; Heb 9.14,20. In the biblical tradition blood is life (Gen 9.4; Deut 12.23); here it is the sacrifice of Christ's life poured out for *redemption*. *Forgiveness of our trespasses*, see Mt 6.14–15. The Jewish tradition, especially concerning Yom Kippur, stresses both human and divine forgiveness (*b. Yoma* 85b; Maimonides, *Rules of Repentance* 2.9–10; Karo, *Code of Jewish Law* ["Orech Chaim," "Laws of Prayer"] 606). **9:** *Mystery of his will*, that Jews and Gentiles alike are part of God's chosen people. The Dead Sea literature frequently refers to mysteries ("raz"), and "raz nihyeh" ("mystery of existence" or "mystery of what is to come") is prominent in 4QInstruction (4Q415–418c, 4Q423; see also 1Q26). **10:** *Fullness*, or completeness; cf. 1.23; 3.19; 4.10,13. *Fullness of time*, referring in 4.4 to Christ's return. Jewish apocalyptic tradition anticipates a "completion of time," sometimes accompanied by a final judgment or general resurrection (Dan 12; *1 En.* 50; *Jub.* 1.26; CD 2.2–13). **11:** *Inheritance*, cf. Rom 8.17; Gal 4.7; Col 1.12. **12:** *Praise of his glory*, see 1.6; cf. 1.14; possibly referring to a liturgical refrain. *Glory*, reflecting "kavod" in the Hebrew Bible, is mostly used for the divine manifestation of God in the Tabernacle and the Temple. **13:** *You*, Gentiles (2.11; 3.1). *Word of truth*, as the following phrases indicate, the *word* is both the *gospel* and Christ (*believed in him*); see Jn 1.14. *Seal*, symbolizing ownership or authenticity. *Holy Spirit*, not the giver of charismatic gifts but the way to enter the being and wisdom of God. **14:** *Pledge*, guarantee of salvation (cf. 2 Cor 1.22; 5.5).

[13] In him you also, when you had heard the word of truth, the gospel of your salvation, and had believed in him, were marked with the seal of the promised Holy Spirit; [14] this[a] is the pledge of our inheritance toward redemption as God's own people, to the praise of his glory.

[15] I have heard of your faith in the Lord Jesus and your love[b] toward all the saints, and for this reason [16] I do not cease to give thanks for you as I remember you in my prayers. [17] I pray that the God of our Lord Jesus Christ, the Father of glory, may give you a spirit of wisdom and revelation as you come to know him, [18] so that, with the eyes of your heart enlightened, you may know what is the hope to which he has called you, what are the riches of his glorious inheritance among the saints, [19] and what is the immeasurable greatness of his power for us who believe, according to the working of his great power. [20] God[c] put this power to work in Christ when he raised him from the dead and seated him at his right hand in the heavenly places, [21] far above all rule and authority and power and dominion, and above every name that is named, not only in this age but also in the age to come. [22] And he has put all things under his feet and has made him the head over all things for the church, [23] which is his body, the fullness of him who fills all in all.

2 You were dead through the trespasses and sins [2] in which you once lived, following the course of this world, following the ruler of the power of the air, the spirit that is now at work among those who are disobedient. [3] All of us once lived among them in the passions of our flesh, following the desires of flesh and senses, and we were by nature children of wrath, like everyone else. [4] But God, who is rich in mercy, out of the great love with which he loved us [5] even when we were dead through our trespasses, made us alive together with Christ[d]—by grace you have been saved— [6] and raised us up with him and seated us with him in the heavenly places in Christ Jesus, [7] so that in the ages to come he might show the immeasurable riches of his grace in kindness toward us in Christ Jesus. [8] For by grace you have been saved through faith, and this is not your own doing; it is the gift of God— [9] not the result of works, so

[a] Other ancient authorities read *who*
[b] Other ancient authorities lack *and your love*
[c] Gk *He*
[d] Other ancient authorities read *in Christ*

1.15–23: Thanksgiving. 15: *Saints,* see 1.1n. **17:** *Father of glory,* see 1.2 and 1.6, and Ps 24.7–10, "king of glory" (Heb "melekh ha-kavod"). *Spirit of wisdom and revelation,* recalls prophecies of the charismatic Davidic ruler in Isa 11.2. **18:** *Enlightened,* contrast 4.18. *Hope to which he has called you,* the *inheritance* as of an heir (see 1.5–6n.), resurrection (as developed in following verses). *Inheritance,* see 1.11n. *Saints,* 1.1n. **20:** *Raised him from the dead,* see Mt 22.23–33; Mk 12.18–27; Lk 20.27–40; Jn 11.20–27; Acts 23.6–8; Josephus, *J.W.* 2.153–158,162–165; *Ant.* 18.13–18. *At his right hand,* see Ps 110.1; Mt 22.41–46; Mk 12.35–37; Lk 20.41–44; Acts 2.34–36; Heb 1.13; 10.12–13. *Heavenly places,* 1.3n. **21:** *Rule and authority and power and dominion,* see Dan 7.14; 1 Cor 15.24–25. Jesus receives the *name* "Lord" and is exalted, cf. 3.10; 6.12; Rom 8.38; Phil 2.6–11; Col 1.16; 2.10,15; 1 Pet 3.22. *This age . . . age to come,* see 1.1. **22–23:** *Under his feet,* see Ps 8.6; 110.1. Cf. 1 Cor 15.15–28. Christ is *the head,* and *the church* is *his body,* cf. 4.11,15–16, extending the metaphor of the fellowship of the followers of Jesus as "body" in 1 Cor 12.12–28; Rom 12.5.

2.1–10: Rebirth from sin. 1–2: *Ruler of the power of the air,* a cosmic force of disobedience. Cf. 4.27; 6.11. In the book of Enoch, the fallen angels appear in such a role; see *1 En.* 6.3,7, where the angel Semyaz appears as their "ruler." *The spirit . . . now at work,* the Holy Spirit and a spirit of transgression compete. In 1QS 3.13–4.14 rival spirits of truth and falsehood are represented by a prince of lights (1QS 3.20) and an angel of darkness (1QS 1.20–21). Although Christ rules (cf. 1.21), the spirits continue to influence humanity. **3:** *By nature,* by birth or in the ordinary course. Compare rabbinic idea of "impulse of evil" ("yetzer ha-ra"), *m. Ber.* 9.5. *Children of wrath,* cf. Rom 1.18–32; see also 5.6; Col 3.6. **4:** *Rich in mercy* (Heb "rav ḥesed," "greatness of loving kindness"); cf. Num 14.18; Joel 2.13; Jon 4.2; Ps 86.5; 103.8; Neh 9.17. **5:** *Have been saved,* salvation is not a present reality but a future possibility in Paul's undisputed epistles (Rom 5.9,10; 6.5; 13.11; 1 Cor 15.21–23; Phil 3.10–11; 1 Thess 5.8). **6:** *Raised us up,* Christ's resurrection is the context for believers' resurrection. *Heavenly places,* 1.3n. **7:** *Ages to come,* 1.10n; 2.2. It is not clear why "ages" is plural here; perhaps it indicates the limitless character of God's *grace.* **8–9:** *Saved through faith,* faith in Christ leads to salvation *by* God's *grace,* not human initiative (*works*). *No one may boast,* cf. Rom 3.27; 4.2; 1 Cor 1.29–31. See Deut 9.4–6. **10:** *Prepared beforehand,* see 1.4. *Good works,* see Col 1.10;

that no one may boast. [10] For we are what he has made us, created in Christ Jesus for good works, which God prepared beforehand to be our way of life.

[11] So then, remember that at one time you Gentiles by birth,[a] called "the uncircumcision" by those who are called "the circumcision"—a physical circumcision made in the flesh by human hands— [12] remember that you were at that time without Christ, being aliens from the commonwealth of Israel, and strangers to the covenants of promise, having no hope and without God in the world. [13] But now in Christ Jesus you who once were far off have been brought near by the blood of Christ. [14] For he is our peace; in his flesh he has made both groups into one and has broken down the dividing wall, that is, the hostility between us. [15] He has abolished the law with its commandments and ordinances, that he might create in himself one new humanity in place of the two, thus making peace, [16] and might reconcile both groups to God in one body[b] through the cross, thus putting to death that hostility through it.[c] [17] So he came and proclaimed peace to you who were far off and peace to those who were near; [18] for through him both of us have access in one Spirit to the Father. [19] So then you are no longer strangers and aliens, but you are citizens with the saints and also members of the household of God, [20] built upon the foundation of the apostles and prophets, with Christ Jesus himself as the cornerstone.[d] [21] In him the whole structure is joined together and grows into a holy temple in the Lord; [22] in whom you also are built together spiritually[e] into a dwelling place for God.

3 This is the reason that I Paul am a prisoner for[f] Christ Jesus for the sake of you Gentiles— [2] for surely you have already heard of the commission of God's grace that was given me for you, [3] and how the mystery was

[a] Gk *in the flesh*
[b] Or *reconcile both of us in one body for God*
[c] Or *in him,* or *in himself*
[d] Or *keystone*
[e] Gk *in the Spirit*
[f] Or *of*

believers are to do good works, not to earn salvation but because of the salvation they receive. *Way of life,* comparable to "halakhah."

2.11–22: Uniting of Jews and Gentiles in Christ. 11: *By birth,* lit., "in the flesh." **12–13:** *Aliens . . . and strangers,* Judaism urges ethical treatment of strangers (Ex 22.21). Ephesians emphasizes alienation between Jews and Gentiles to highlight unity found in Christ. *Covenants of promise,* Gen 12.2 and elsewhere. Rom 9.1–5 treats *covenants* and *promises* as Israel's unique possessions, where Paul defines "Israel," not as "the children of the flesh" but "the children of the promise" (Rom 9.6–8), Jews and Gentiles who have accepted Christ. *Far off . . . brought near,* cf. 2.17; Isa 57.19. *Blood,* see 1.7. **14:** *Peace,* see 1.2; 2.15,17; 4.3; 6.15. *In his flesh,* through his crucifixion and resurrection. *Dividing wall* symbolizes the *hostility* between Jews and Gentiles, and may also allude to the Jerusalem Temple, where Gentiles were excluded from the place where Jewish males could worship. Josephus mentions Greek and Latin signs warning Gentiles not to go past the outer court (*Ant.* 12.145; 15.417; *J.W.* 5.194); two such Greek inscriptions on limestone blocks were discovered in Jerusalem. Given that this letter likely was composed after 70 CE, the claim that the crucifixion broke *down the dividing wall,* like the imagery of the torn curtain (Mk 15.38) and the transformation of sacrificial offerings (Heb 9.1–28; 10.19–20), appropriates the Jewish sacerdotal tradition for the church. **15:** *Abolished the law,* rejecting Jewish practice such as circumcision and dietary regulations. **17:** *Far off . . . near,* Gentiles, who were not *near* the covenant, and Jews, who were. **18:** *Spirit,* see 1.13n.; *Father,* see 1.2n. **19:** *Strangers and aliens,* see 2.12. *Citizens,* enfranchised members of God's *household;* cf. 3.15; 5.21–6.4; 1 Tim 3.15; 1 Pet 4.17. **20:** *Foundation,* cf. 1 Cor 3.11. *Apostles,* see 1.1n.; *prophets,* those who speak in God's name or deliver a divinely inspired message to the assembly of believers. *Cornerstone* (or "keystone"), cf. Isa 28.16; Ps 118.22; Mt 21.42; 1 Pet 2.6–8. Rabbinic and Jewish mystical traditions envision the cosmic founding of the world upon a foundation stone in the Holy of Holies in the Jerusalem Temple; see *m. Yoma* 5.2; *t. Yoma* 2.14; *b. Yoma* 54b; *Lev. Rab.* 20.4; *Pesiq. Rav Kah.* 26.4; *Zohar* 1.231a–b. **21–22:** *A holy temple . . . a dwelling place.* Cf. Ex 25.8; 29.43–46; 2 Sam 7.1–16. The new construction built *in* Christ replaces the Jerusalem Temple (see 2.14n.); cf. 1 Cor 3.16–17; 6.19; 1 Pet 2.4–6.

3.1–21: Revelation of the mystery and the gospel. 1: *Prisoner,* of Rome, because of missionary activity (Acts 21.27–33; 2 Cor 6.5; 11.23; Phil 1.13–14; Col 4.3,18; Philem 1,9). **2:** *Commission,* cf. 1 Cor 9.17; Col 1.25; Paul was called

made known to me by revelation, as I wrote above in a few words, [4] a reading of which will enable you to perceive my understanding of the mystery of Christ. [5] In former generations this mystery[a] was not made known to humankind, as it has now been revealed to his holy apostles and prophets by the Spirit: [6] that is, the Gentiles have become fellow heirs, members of the same body, and sharers in the promise in Christ Jesus through the gospel.

[7] Of this gospel I have become a servant according to the gift of God's grace that was given me by the working of his power. [8] Although I am the very least of all the saints, this grace was given to me to bring to the Gentiles the news of the boundless riches of Christ, [9] and to make everyone see[b] what is the plan of the mystery hidden for ages in[c] God who created all things; [10] so that through the church the wisdom of God in its rich variety might now be made known to the rulers and authorities in the heavenly places. [11] This was in accordance with the eternal purpose that he has carried out in Christ Jesus our Lord, [12] in whom we have access to God in boldness and confidence through faith in him.[d] [13] I pray therefore that you[e] may not lose heart over my sufferings for you; they are your glory.

[14] For this reason I bow my knees before the Father,[f] [15] from whom every family[g] in heaven and on earth takes its name. [16] I pray that, according to the riches of his glory, he may grant that you may be strengthened in your inner being with power through his Spirit, [17] and that Christ may dwell in your hearts through faith, as you are being rooted and grounded in love. [18] I pray that you may have the power to comprehend, with all the saints, what is the breadth and length and height and depth, [19] and to know the love of Christ that surpasses knowledge, so that you may be filled with all the fullness of God.

[20] Now to him who by the power at work within us is able to accomplish abundantly far more than all we can ask or imagine, [21] to him be glory in the church and in Christ Jesus to all generations, forever and ever. Amen.

4 I therefore, the prisoner in the Lord, beg you to lead a life worthy of the calling to which you have been called, [2] with all humility and gentleness, with patience, bearing with one another in love, [3] making every effort to maintain the unity of the Spirit in the bond of peace. [4] There is one body and

a Gk *it*
b Other ancient authorities read *to bring to light*
c Or *by*
d Or *the faith of him*
e Or *I*
f Other ancient authorities add *of our Lord Jesus Christ*
g Gk *fatherhood*

to evangelize Gentiles (Gal 1.15–16; 2.7–9). **3–4:** *Mystery*, this word, which meant a spiritual teaching revealed only to those who were initiated into a particular religion, Paul uses to describe his teaching that Gentiles share in Christ's resurrection (see 1.9). **5:** *Not made known*, cf. Rom 16.25 (see Dan 8.26; 12.4). *Apostles*, ones sent out on a mission; see 1.1n. *Prophets*, see 2.20n. **7:** *Servant*, cf. 1 Cor 3.5; Col 1.23,25. *Grace*, cf. 1.6; 2.8–9. **8:** *Least of all the saints*, see 1.1n.; cf. 1 Cor 15.9. *To the Gentiles*, see 3.2n. **9:** *Plan of the mystery*, 1.9–10; 3.3–5. **10:** *Church*, the community of believers; cf. Rom. 16.4–5,16; Philem 2. *Wisdom of God*, here probably not meant as the personified Wisdom of Prov 8 and Wis 7.22–8.1, but rather the plan that God has for all people. *Rulers and authorities*, see 1.3,20–21; 2.2. **12:** *Access to God*, through Christ as mediator. **13:** *My sufferings*, see Rom 5.3; 8.35–36; 2 Cor 11.23–28. *Your glory*, brought about by *my sufferings* on your behalf. **14–15:** *Bow my knees*, opening of a prayer; cf. Phil 2.10. Prayers were recited in this position; see e.g., 1 Kings 8.54; Heb "bless" ("b-r-k") is related to the word knee ("berek[h]"). *Family*, Gk "patria," from the same root as "father"; on the fatherhood of God see 1.2n.; 5.21–6.9. **16:** *Glory*, see 1.12n. *Inner being*, cf. Rom 7.22, as opposed to the body. **18–19:** *Saints*, see 1.1n. *Surpasses knowledge*, perhaps both "is greater than (human) intellect" and an assertion that one's personal relationship to Christ is more important than the factual knowledge one might have about who Christ is. **21:** *Church*, see 1.22–23n.

4.1–16: Unity of believers in Christ. This section expands on 1.22–23; 2.14–16,18. **1:** *Prisoner*, see 3.1n. *Worthy*, see Col 1.10; 1 Thess 2.12. *Calling*, from God; nevertheless, despite the divine act of grace, the believer is responsible to *lead a life worthy* of that grace. **2–3:** 1 Cor 13.4–13 (cf. Col 3.12–13) offers a similar delineation of virtues, framed around *love*. **4–6:** *One body . . . one Spirit . . . one baptism*, seven forms of unity culminate in the

one Spirit, just as you were called to the one hope of your calling, [5] one Lord, one faith, one baptism, [6] one God and Father of all, who is above all and through all and in all.

[7] But each of us was given grace according to the measure of Christ's gift. [8] Therefore it is said,

"When he ascended on high he made
captivity itself a captive;
he gave gifts to his people."

[9] (When it says, "He ascended," what does it mean but that he had also descended[a] into the lower parts of the earth? [10] He who descended is the same one who ascended far above all the heavens, so that he might fill all things.) [11] The gifts he gave were that some would be apostles, some prophets, some evangelists, some pastors and teachers, [12] to equip the saints for the work of ministry, for building up the body of Christ, [13] until all of us come to the unity of the faith and of the knowledge of the Son of God, to maturity, to the measure of the full stature of Christ. [14] We must no longer be children, tossed to and fro and blown about by every wind of doctrine, by people's trickery, by their craftiness in deceitful scheming. [15] But speaking the truth in love, we must grow up in every way into him who is the head, into Christ, [16] from whom the whole body, joined and knit together by every ligament with which it is equipped, as each part is working properly, promotes the body's growth in building itself up in love.

[17] Now this I affirm and insist on in the Lord: you must no longer live as the Gentiles live, in the futility of their minds. [18] They are darkened in their understanding, alienated from the life of God because of their ignorance and hardness of heart. [19] They have lost all sensitivity and have abandoned themselves to licentiousness, greedy to practice every kind of impurity. [20] That is not the way you learned Christ! [21] For surely you have heard about him and were taught in him, as truth is in Jesus. [22] You were taught to put away your former way of life, your old self, corrupt and deluded by its lusts, [23] and to be renewed in the spirit of your minds, [24] and to clothe yourselves with the new self, created according to the likeness of God in true righteousness and holiness.

[25] So then, putting away falsehood, let all of us speak the truth to our neighbors, for

[a] Other ancient authorities add *first*

omnipresence of God. In order to promote the unity of Jews and Gentiles in the Christian community, the text reframes Deut 6.4 ("the LORD . . . is one" KJV), which in this period became an important prayer (the Shema). *Body*, the church congregation; see 1.22–23n.; *baptism*, immersion in water as a rite of initiation, here regarded as one of the bases of unity for the congregation. *Father*, see 1.2n. **7:** *Grace*, see 1.6n. *The measure of Christ's gift*, as explained in vv. 11–12, varying gifts are meant to build up the community. **8–10:** Ps 68.18. The passage originally referred to God's triumph in battle; Ps 68.20 includes salvation and escape from death. *Descended*, perhaps referring to descent into the underworld (the "harrowing of hell"); cf. Mt 12.40; Rom 10:6–8; 1 Pet 3.19. Rabbinic midrash understands the chariots in Ps 68.18 in reference to Ezek 1.15–28, framing the giving of the Torah in terms of God's descent in a chariot, or "merkavah" (*Midr. Tanh. Yitro* [Buber]; cf. *Pesiq. Rav Kah.* 12.22) or the ascent of Moses through the heavenly spheres (*Pesiq. Rab.* 20). **11–12:** *Gifts* (cf. Rom 12.6–8; 1 Cor 12.28–30) refer to leadership and teaching; charismatic abilities such as speaking in tongues and healing go unmentioned. *Saints*, 1.1n. *Body of Christ*, 1.22–23n. **13–14:** *Maturity*, as opposed to remaining *children*; cf. 1 Cor 3.1–3; 13.11; 14.20; Phil 3.15; Col 1.28. *Children*, in rabbinic tradition (*m. Nidd.* 5.6) girls of twelve years and a day and boys of thirteen years and a day are adults in the sense of being fully responsible to fulfill the mitzvot. **15–16:** *Head*, see 1.22–23. Each organ has distinct responsibilities; cf. 1 Cor 12.14–18. *In love . . . in love*, see 1.4; 3.18–19. Metaphors of body, household, and cosmos point to new social order.

4.17–5.20: Community standards. 17: *As the Gentiles live*; cf. Rom 1.20–25. **18:** *Ignorance*, not only of God's commandments and covenant but also of their misperceptions (idolatry is viewed as a kind of ignorance in Isa 44.9–17). *Hardness of heart*, see Ex 7.13–14. **19:** *Greedy to practice . . . impurity*, sexual sin, seen here in terms of uncleanness (Lev 17–26). **22–24:** *Former way of life*, reflects the absolute demarcation separating each community member's past and present existence. **24:** *Clothe yourselves*, cf. Gal 3.27; Col 3.10. A *new self, created according to the likeness of God*; recapitulation of Gen 1.26–27; see esp. Col 3.10. **25:** *Speak the truth*, Zech 8.16. *Neighbors*, fellow believers; see Lev 19.13–18 and "The Concept of Neighbor" p. 540. *Members of one another*,

we are members of one another. [26] Be angry but do not sin; do not let the sun go down on your anger, [27] and do not make room for the devil. [28] Thieves must give up stealing; rather let them labor and work honestly with their own hands, so as to have something to share with the needy. [29] Let no evil talk come out of your mouths, but only what is useful for building up,[a] as there is need, so that your words may give grace to those who hear. [30] And do not grieve the Holy Spirit of God, with which you were marked with a seal for the day of redemption. [31] Put away from you all bitterness and wrath and anger and wrangling and slander, together with all malice, [32] and be kind to one another, tenderhearted, forgiving one another, as God in Christ has forgiven you.[b]

5 [1] Therefore be imitators of God, as beloved children, [2] and live in love, as Christ loved us[c] and gave himself up for us, a fragrant offering and sacrifice to God.

[3] But fornication and impurity of any kind, or greed, must not even be mentioned among you, as is proper among saints. [4] Entirely out of place is obscene, silly, and vulgar talk; but instead, let there be thanksgiving. [5] Be sure of this, that no fornicator or impure person, or one who is greedy (that is, an idolater), has any inheritance in the kingdom of Christ and of God.

[6] Let no one deceive you with empty words, for because of these things the wrath of God comes on those who are disobedient. [7] Therefore do not be associated with them. [8] For once you were darkness, but now in the Lord you are light. Live as children of light— [9] for the fruit of the light is found in all that is good and right and true. [10] Try to find out what is pleasing to the Lord. [11] Take no part in the unfruitful works of darkness, but instead expose them. [12] For it is shameful even to mention what such people do secretly; [13] but everything exposed by the light becomes visible, [14] for everything that becomes visible is light. Therefore it says,

"Sleeper, awake!
Rise from the dead,
and Christ will shine on you."

[15] Be careful then how you live, not as unwise people but as wise, [16] making the most of the time, because the days are evil. [17] So do not be foolish, but understand what the will of the Lord is. [18] Do not get drunk with wine, for that is debauchery; but be filled with the

[a] Other ancient authorities read *building up faith*
[b] Other ancient authorities read *us*
[c] Other ancient authorities read *you*

part of the same body; see 1.22–23n. **26:** *Be angry but do not sin,* cf. Lev 19.18a; Ps 4.4 LXX. *Let the sun go down . . . ,* a commonplace (Plutarch states the same of the Pythagoreans [*On Brotherly Love* 488B]). **27:** *Devil,* a cosmic force of wickedness (cf., e.g., Mt 4.1–11; Lk 4.1–13; Jude 9). In the Septuagint this term translates the Heb "satan," as "adversary" who is in dialogue with God (Job 1.6); works as a bad influence among humans (1 Chr 21.1), or serves as an accuser of the people (Zech 3.1); cf. 6.11. **28:** *Give up stealing,* past misbehaviors do not preclude church membership. **29:** *Evil talk,* cf. Ex 20.7,16; Prov 6.16–19; 10.8. The Talmud regularly warns against a "wicked tongue" ("lashon ha-ra"), malicious gossip (*b. Arak.* 15b; *b. Sanh.* 31a). The Community Rule (1QS 7.2–9) forbids speaking in anger against the community leaders, lying, insulting one's companions, or speaking foolishly. **30:** *Holy Spirit . . . marked,* cf. 1.13. *Day of redemption,* cf. 1.14; day of the general resurrection. **32:** *Forgiving one another,* cf. Mt 6.12; Lk 11.4. **5.1:** *Imitators of God,* following Lev 19.2, though less common in the NT than "imitators of Christ" (see Mt 5.44–45,48). *B. Shabb.* 133b states that humans should be merciful in imitation of God's mercy. Paul urges his audience to imitate him in faithfulness (e.g., 1 Cor 4.16; 11.1; Phil 3.17). **2:** *Fragrant offering and sacrifice,* as in Ex 29.18; Lev 1.9, and elsewhere; the crucifixion is a sacrifice, and believers are to be similarly self-sacrificial, cf. Rom 12.1; Phil 4.18. **3:** *Saints,* cf. 1.1n.,15; 3.8. **4–5:** Lists of vices; cf. Rom 1.29–31; 1 Cor 6.9–10; Gal 5.19–21, and other places. Such lists of vices and virtues were common. *Vulgar talk,* cf. 4.29. **5:** *Fornicator . . . greedy,* cf. 4.19. Prophetic literature links idolatry to adultery; cf. Isa 57; Hos 1.2. *Inheritance,* see 1.5–6n.; 1.11n. **6:** *Wrath of God,* cf. Rom 1.18; Col 3.6; Rev 19.15. **7:** *Do not be associated,* cf. 2 Cor 6.14; see also 1 Cor 5.9–14; 7.12–16. **8–14:** Extended metaphor of darkness and light, cf. 1.18; 2.1–2; 4.18. **8:** *Children of light,* cf. Mt 5.16; Lk 16.8; Jn 12.36; 1 Thess 5.5; 1QM, and 1QS 3.13–4.14. **10:** *Pleasing to the Lord,* cf. 5.17. **14:** Possibly from a Christian hymn. Imagery of death as sleep, and the dead awakening, appears in Isa 26.19 and continues in later Jewish texts. This passage echoes Isa 60.1, with *Christ* in the position of "the glory of the LORD." **16:** *Days are evil,* cf. 2.1–2; cf. Acts 2.40; Gal 1.4. **17:** *Will of the Lord,* see Deut 10.12–13; Mic 6.8.

Spirit, [19] as you sing psalms and hymns and spiritual songs among yourselves, singing and making melody to the Lord in your hearts, [20] giving thanks to God the Father at all times and for everything in the name of our Lord Jesus Christ.

[21] Be subject to one another out of reverence for Christ.

[22] Wives, be subject to your husbands as you are to the Lord. [23] For the husband is the head of the wife just as Christ is the head of the church, the body of which he is the Savior. [24] Just as the church is subject to Christ, so also wives ought to be, in everything, to their husbands.

[25] Husbands, love your wives, just as Christ loved the church and gave himself up for her, [26] in order to make her holy by cleansing her with the washing of water by the word, [27] so as to present the church to himself in splendor, without a spot or wrinkle or anything of the kind—yes, so that she may be holy and without blemish. [28] In the same way, husbands should love their wives as they do their own bodies. He who loves his wife loves himself. [29] For no one ever hates his own body, but he nourishes and tenderly cares for it, just as Christ does for the church, [30] because we are members of his body.[a] [31] "For this reason a man will leave his father and mother and be joined to his wife, and the two will become one flesh." [32] This is a great mystery, and I am applying it to Christ and the church. [33] Each of you, however, should love his wife as himself, and a wife should respect her husband.

6 Children, obey your parents in the Lord,[b] for this is right. [2] "Honor your father and mother"—this is the first commandment with a promise: [3] "so that it may be well with you and you may live long on the earth."

[4] And, fathers, do not provoke your children to anger, but bring them up in the discipline and instruction of the Lord.

[5] Slaves, obey your earthly masters with fear and trembling, in singleness of heart, as you obey Christ; [6] not only while being watched, and in order to please them, but as slaves of Christ, doing the will of God from the heart. [7] Render service with enthusiasm, as to the Lord and not to men and women, [8] knowing that whatever good we do, we

a Other ancient authorities add *of his flesh and of his bones*

b Other ancient authorities lack *in the Lord*

18–20: *Drunk with wine*, see Isa 28.7–8; Hos 4.11; Prov 20.1; 23.19–21,29–35. *Melody to the Lord*, for psalms and hymns see esp. Ps 145–150. Philo's description of the Therapeutae (*Cont. Life* 40,64–90) emphasizes both their sobriety and their joyful songs that praise God.

5.21–6.9: The household code. The threefold hierarchy of husband/wife, parent/child, and master/slave is conventional (e.g., Aristotle, *Pol.* 1259A; Seneca, *Ep.* 94–1–3; Pseudo-Phocylides, *Sent.* 195–227; Josephus, *Ag. Ap.* 2.189–214). **21:** All are *subject to* one another; cf. 1 Pet 5.5. **22–33:** A shorter household code, upon which this passage is likely based, appears at Col 3.18–19. **22:** *Wives* are subject both to their husbands and to the Lord. 1 Pet 3.1–7 presents a more extreme expression of wifely submission. **23:** Cf. 1 Cor 11.3. *Head . . . body*, see 1.22–23; 4.15–16. **24:** *Subject . . . in everything*, see 1 Cor 11. **25:** *Gave himself up for her*, husbands are to imitate Christ's sacrificial love. **26:** *Cleansing her with the washing of water*, a baptismal image. Husbands are responsible for their wives' purity and instruction. **27:** *Present the church*, husbands are compared to the Christ, wives to the church. *Holy and without blemish*, cf. 1.1; 2.21–22; see also Phil 1.10. **28–29:** *Their own bodies*, cf. 5.24. *B. B. Metz.* 59a presents arguments both that husbands should respect their wives' opinions and that such a view leads to damnation. **30:** *Members of his body*, see 1.22–23n. **31:** Gen 2.24; see Mt 19.3–6; 1 Cor 6.16. The passage in Genesis is a proof text for prohibiting marriage after divorce in CD 4.20–21. **32:** *Great mystery*, cf. 1.9; 3.3–4. *Applying it*, as a metaphor, to *Christ and the church*. Marital imagery for the relationship of God and people is a commonplace of biblical prophecy (cf. 5.5n.); see also rabbinic and patristic treatments of the Song of Songs as another example (cf. *Song. Rab.*). **33:** *Love . . . respect*, wives and husbands have a hierarchical relationship of mutuality. **6.1:** *Children . . . parents*, see Col 3.20–21. **2:** *Honor your father and mother*, Ex 20.12; Deut 5.16; cf. Prov 1.8–9. **3:** *So that it may be well*, Deut 5.16 connects morality to possessing the land of Israel; this quotation shifts the meaning to general well-being. **4:** *Discipline and instruction*, cf. Heb 12.7–11; Sir 7.23. **5:** Cf. Col 3.22–4.1; 1 Tim 6.1–2; Titus 2.9–10; 1 Pet 2.18–25. **6:** *Slaves of Christ*, Rom 1.1; 1 Cor 7.22; Phil 1.1. The slave's obedience is *doing the will of God*. **7:** *With enthusiasm*, the rabbis envision devoted slaves (e.g., Gamaliel mourning the death of his

will receive the same again from the Lord, whether we are slaves or free.

[9] And, masters, do the same to them. Stop threatening them, for you know that both of you have the same Master in heaven, and with him there is no partiality.

[10] Finally, be strong in the Lord and in the strength of his power. [11] Put on the whole armor of God, so that you may be able to stand against the wiles of the devil. [12] For our[a] struggle is not against enemies of blood and flesh, but against the rulers, against the authorities, against the cosmic powers of this present darkness, against the spiritual forces of evil in the heavenly places. [13] Therefore take up the whole armor of God, so that you may be able to withstand on that evil day, and having done everything, to stand firm. [14] Stand therefore, and fasten the belt of truth around your waist, and put on the breastplate of righteousness. [15] As shoes for your feet put on whatever will make you ready to proclaim the gospel of peace. [16] With all of these,[b] take the shield of faith, with which you will be able to quench all the flaming arrows of the evil one. [17] Take the helmet of salvation, and the sword of the Spirit, which is the word of God.

[18] Pray in the Spirit at all times in every prayer and supplication. To that end keep alert and always persevere in supplication for all the saints. [19] Pray also for me, so that when I speak, a message may be given to me to make known with boldness the mystery of the gospel,[c] [20] for which I am an ambassador in chains. Pray that I may declare it boldly, as I must speak.

[21] So that you also may know how I am and what I am doing, Tychicus will tell you everything. He is a dear brother and a faithful minister in the Lord. [22] I am sending him to you for this very purpose, to let you know how we are, and to encourage your hearts.

[23] Peace be to the whole community,[d] and love with faith, from God the Father and the Lord Jesus Christ. [24] Grace be with all who have an undying love for our Lord Jesus Christ.[e]

a Other ancient authorities read *your*
b Or *In all circumstances*
c Other ancient authorities lack *of the gospel*
d Gk *to the brothers*
e Other ancient authorities add *Amen*

slave, Tabi, *m. Ber.* 2.7). **8:** *Whether we are slaves or free*, contrast Gal 3.28 and see 1 Cor 7.22. **9:** *No partiality*, contrast 1 Pet 2.18–25, in which no constraints are put on the behavior of masters, while unjustly punished slaves are to follow Christ's suffering. Lev 25.39–40 similarly enjoins that slaves should be treated well, as hirelings.

6.10–17: The armor of God. 10: *Be strong in the Lord*, cf. Josh 1.6. **11:** *Armor of God*, see Isa 11.5; 59.17; Wis 5.17–20; 2 Cor 6.7; 1 Thess 5.8. *Wiles of the devil* (Gk "diabolos"), cf. 4.27n. **12–13:** *Rulers . . . authorities*, cf. 3.10. *Present darkness*, cf. 5.8–14. *Heavenly places*, cf. 1.3,20; 2.6; 3.10. *Evil day*, the final clash between God's forces and the *cosmic powers of this present darkness*. **14:** *Belt of truth*, see Isa 11.5. **15:** *Gospel*, the "good news" *of peace*, cf. 1.13; 2.14–17; 3.6–7; 6.19. See also Isa 52.7. **16:** *Flaming arrows*, Ps 76.4 (Heb v. 3); Prov 26.18. *Evil one*, see v. 11.

6.18–24: Concluding exhortations and blessing. 18: *Pray in the Spirit*, implying both the Jewish concept of "kavvanah" (mindfulness in worship) and the understanding of the Holy Spirit as a force enabling believers to become conscious of divine power. *Keep alert*, perhaps a veiled reference to the return of Christ; see Mk 13.35; perhaps also an exhortation to beware of temptation; see Mk 14.38. **19:** *Pray also for me*, as in Job 42.10. **20:** *Ambassador in chains*, see 3.1; 4.1. **21:** *Tychicus*, cf. Col 4.7–9. *Minister*, lit., "servant" (Gk "diakonos"). **23–24:** *Peace . . . love . . . grace*, authentic Pauline epistles end similarly.

THE LETTER OF PAUL TO THE PHILIPPIANS

TITLE AND AUTHORSHIP

Philippians is Paul's epistle to the first church that he established on European soil. In 50/51 CE, he sailed from Asia Minor (Turkey) to Macedonia, in northern Greece (Acts 16.11–40). A ten-mile access road from the Aegean Sea brought him to Philippi, named for its founder, Philip II (father of Alexander the Great).

DATE AND HISTORICAL CONTEXT

Dating Philippians is problematic because, while stating that he is in prison, Paul does not indicate where. Christian tradition presumes Rome in the early 60s (cf. Acts 28.16). But the many messages and trips (past and anticipated) that the letter presupposes between Philippi and Paul's prison site (2.19,23–30; 4.18) cannot be squared with Philippi's formidable distance from Rome—exceeding seven hundred land-miles, nine hundred by sea. While some scholars opt for an earlier Pauline captivity in the late 50s in Caesarea Maritima (Acts 23.23,33; 25.24), Caesarea is even farther from Philippi than is Rome. Increasingly, recent scholarship has gravitated to a mid-50s dating at Ephesus, only four hundred miles south-southeast of Philippi. While we know of no Pauline incarceration there, Paul alludes to "far more imprisonments" (2 Cor 11.23; cf. 6.5), and Paul's ministry in Ephesus lasted three years. As chief city of Rome's Asia province, Ephesus also hosted contingents of both imperial soldiers (1.13) and Caesar's administrative staff (4.22). Further, Timothy, mentioned alongside Paul in the letter's salutation (1.1; 2.19–24), was with Paul at Ephesus (1 Cor 4.17; 16.10; cf. Acts 19.22).

Despite the Philippians' poverty (2 Cor 8.1–5), they had sent Paul sustenance several times (4.10,15–16; cf. 2 Cor 11.7–9), most recently through Epaphroditus. Since Epaphroditus has just recovered from a life-threatening illness, Paul now dispatches him homeward, bearing this letter. Paul warmly thanks the Philippians, assesses his circumstances and prospects for release, and advises the Philippians on their problems (which he likely learned from Epaphroditus directly).

LITERARY HISTORY

Due to an abrupt transition as ch 3 opens, and arguably a disorderly sequencing of the Epistle's themes, some conclude that Philippians is a composite of two or more Pauline writings fastened together: one encompassing 1.1–3.1a concluded by 4.21–23; a second, 3.1b–4.20 (with 4.10–20 as yet a possible third). Others see no decisive reason to deny Philippians' literary unity—with the proviso that Paul likely drew the Christ hymn (2.6–11) from elsewhere.

CONTENT

Paul affirms his capacity to persevere in joyful proclamation of the gospel even when confronting opposition, suffering, and possible death (1.12,18,30). He then draws an analogy between this ability and what the Philippians themselves must achieve vis-à-vis their own opponents and trials. Humility and unity are vital in this regard. Accordingly, the Philippians should strive to match the mind-set of Christ who showed that the way to achieve God's exaltation is not by preoccupation with status—grasping at a higher place—but by becoming humbly obedient and looking to the interests of others.

Warranting special attention are descriptions of Paul's opponents (1.15–17) and those of the Philippians (1.28; 3.2–4,18–19); the moving Christ hymn (2.6–11); the litany of Paul's autobiographical details (3.5–6); and Paul's reasons (stated or not) for delaying Timothy's visit to Philippi (2.19,25).

MATTERS BEARING ON A JEWISH READING

One may consider whether Jewish themes underlie the Christ hymn (2.6–11). Another topic concerns the vehemence of Paul's opposition to adult male circumcision for Gentile Christians. Finally, readers may wonder how they should view Paul's devaluation of his superlative Jewish credentials (3.7–8).

Michael Cook

1 Paul and Timothy, servants[a] of Christ Jesus,

To all the saints in Christ Jesus who are in Philippi, with the bishops[b] and deacons:[c]

[2] Grace to you and peace from God our Father and the Lord Jesus Christ.

[3] I thank my God every time I remember you, [4] constantly praying with joy in every one of my prayers for all of you, [5] because of your sharing in the gospel from the first day until now. [6] I am confident of this, that the one who began a good work among you will bring it to completion by the day of Jesus Christ. [7] It is right for me to think this way about all of you, because you hold me in your heart,[d] for all of you share in God's grace[e] with me, both in my imprisonment and in the defense and confirmation of the gospel. [8] For God is my witness, how I long for all of you with the compassion of Christ Jesus. [9] And this is my prayer, that your love may overflow more and more with knowledge and full insight [10] to help you to determine what is best, so that in the day of Christ you may be pure and blameless, [11] having produced the harvest of righteousness that comes through Jesus Christ for the glory and praise of God.

[12] I want you to know, beloved,[f] that what has happened to me has actually helped to spread the gospel, [13] so that it has become known throughout the whole imperial guard[g] and to everyone else that my imprisonment is for Christ; [14] and most of the brothers and sisters,[f] having been made confident in the Lord by my imprisonment, dare to speak the word[h] with greater boldness and without fear.

[15] Some proclaim Christ from envy and rivalry, but others from goodwill. [16] These proclaim Christ out of love, knowing that I have been put here for the defense of the gospel; [17] the others proclaim Christ out of selfish ambition, not sincerely but intending to increase my suffering in my imprisonment. [18] What does it matter? Just this, that Christ is proclaimed in every way, whether out of false motives or true; and in that I rejoice.

Yes, and I will continue to rejoice, [19] for I know that through your prayers and the help of the Spirit of Jesus Christ this will turn out for my deliverance. [20] It is my eager expectation and hope that I will not be put to shame in any way, but that by my speaking with all boldness, Christ will be exalted now as always in my body, whether by life or by death. [21] For to me, living is Christ and dying is gain. [22] If I am to live in the flesh, that means fruitful labor for me; and I do not know which I prefer. [23] I am hard pressed between the two: my desire is to depart and be with Christ, for that is far better; [24] but to remain in the flesh is more necessary for you. [25] Since I am con-

a Gk *slaves*
b Or *overseers*
c Or *overseers and helpers*
d Or *because I hold you in my heart*
e Gk *in grace*
f Gk *brothers*
g Gk *whole praetorium*
h Other ancient authorities read *word of God*

1.1–2: Salutation. 1: *Timothy* assisted in founding the church and remains popular among its members. *Servants,* lit., "slaves" (see translators' note *a*: "douloi," in LXX for Heb. " 'ebed," but rarely as a description of relation to God; see Jer 2.14). *Bishops and deacons,* overseers and assistants (see notes *b* and *c*). The exact functions of those with these titles was yet to be settled. **2:** *Grace . . . peace,* standard opening for a letter (see, e.g., 1 Cor 1.3; Gal 1.3). *Lord* (Gk "kyrios," used in LXX for "adonai/YHWH" but also a simple title of respect), Paul's usual title for Jesus given as a part of the standard opening but also used as occasional variation for reference to Christ (e.g., 1 Cor 11.27; 2 Cor 2.12; 4.5).

1.3–11: Thanksgiving and prayer. 5: *The first day,* of Paul's preaching at Philippi. **6:** *Day of Jesus Christ,* of his return and the close of this age (cf. 1.10; 2.16). **9:** *Prayer* (for others), see Job 42.8. **11:** *Harvest,* a standard image in Jesus' teaching (e.g., Mt 9.37; cf. Jas 3.18), but also in Hebrew prophets (Jer 2.3).

1.12–26: Paul's prison circumstances and outlook. 13: *Imperial guard,* a local contingent of this soldiery. *For Christ,* for preaching Christ. **15:** *Envy . . . rivalry,* Paul condemns not his opponents' message but their efforts to outdo him. **17:** *Increase my suffering,* their freedom makes Paul feel his captivity more acutely. See also, e.g., Ps 22.3–5 for hope that the faithful not be put to shame. **21:** *Living . . . gain,* Paul cares only about Christ, not about the outcome of his own life. **25:** *Convinced,* Paul rationalizes that God will spare him execution so that he can assist the Philippians further. **26:** *Come to you again,* whether this happened is unknown.

vinced of this, I know that I will remain and continue with all of you for your progress and joy in faith, [26] so that I may share abundantly in your boasting in Christ Jesus when I come to you again.

[27] Only, live your life in a manner worthy of the gospel of Christ, so that, whether I come and see you or am absent and hear about you, I will know that you are standing firm in one spirit, striving side by side with one mind for the faith of the gospel, [28] and are in no way intimidated by your opponents. For them this is evidence of their destruction, but of your salvation. And this is God's doing. [29] For he has graciously granted you the privilege not only of believing in Christ, but of suffering for him as well— [30] since you are having the same struggle that you saw I had and now hear that I still have.

2 If then there is any encouragement in Christ, any consolation from love, any sharing in the Spirit, any compassion and sympathy, [2] make my joy complete: be of the same mind, having the same love, being in full accord and of one mind. [3] Do nothing from selfish ambition or conceit, but in humility regard others as better than yourselves. [4] Let each of you look not to your own interests, but to the interests of others. [5] Let the same mind be in you that was[a] in Christ Jesus,

[6] who, though he was in the form of God,
did not regard equality with God
as something to be exploited,
[7] but emptied himself,
taking the form of a slave,
being born in human likeness.
And being found in human form,
[8] he humbled himself
and became obedient to the point of death—
even death on a cross.

[9] Therefore God also highly exalted him
and gave him the name
that is above every name,
[10] so that at the name of Jesus
every knee should bend,
in heaven and on earth and under the earth,
[11] and every tongue should confess
that Jesus Christ is Lord,
to the glory of God the Father.

[12] Therefore, my beloved, just as you have always obeyed me, not only in my presence,

[a] Or *that you have*

1.27–2.18: Exhortations to unity and humility. 28: *Your opponents,* inside Philippi but outside its church. **29:** *Privilege . . . of suffering,* Tanakh sources that reflect suffering do not glorify it (e.g., Ps 13; 69; Job passim). **30:** *The same struggle* that Paul had undergone when founding this church (cf. 1 Thess 2.2). *Still have,* Paul's imprisonment. **2.5:** *The same mind,* the mind-set of humility. **6:** *Though he was,* preexistent before his activity in v. 7 (see, "Christ Hymn," p. 357). *Form of God,* not visibly but in essential, divine nature. *Something to be exploited,* and never relinquished. **7:** *Emptied himself* (from Gk "kenosis," "emptiness"), the pre-incarnate Christ could have asserted his advantageous status of equality with God. *Form of a slave,* by assuming the lowly form of humanity. **8:** *Humbled himself,* for service. *Even death on a cross,* a phrase Paul possibly added to the received hymn to dramatize how Christ's humiliation was that reserved for a malefactor (cf. Deut 21.23)—a fall to the lowest imaginable low from a pre-incarnate highest imaginable high. **9:** *Highly exalted him,* reminiscent of enthronement (Ps 47; 93; 95–99). Entailed here is, first, Christ's being raised from the dead, and then his ascension to installation in the highest place of honor, the seat of power and might (cf. Eph 4.10). *Name . . . above every name,* parallels his exaltation to a place above any other. If meant literally, "name" is Lord rather than Jesus or Jesus Christ (despite vv. 10–11). But more likely "name" is here meant metaphorically (Eph 1.21; cf. 4.10; Heb 1.4), signifying rank, office, dignity, or glory of person, as in "seated at the right hand of God" (see Acts 2.33; 5.31; 7.56). **10–11:** *Every knee . . . every tongue,* drawing on Isa 45.23 (as does Rom 14.11 and, centuries later, the Hebrew "Aleinu" prayer, the prayer of congregational praise in the synagogue that begins "It is incumbent upon us to praise the Lord" and includes "all humanity shall call upon your name" and "to [God] every knee must bend, every tongue vow loyalty"); in Isa 45.24, "LORD" (as distinct from "God") became typically construed by Christians as the second person of the Trinity (i.e., Christ the Son of God). **12–13:** *Work out . . . own salvation,* the salvation process, while accomplishable solely by God, also activates a drive for human self-betterment that completes God's work; hence: *God . . . at work in you, enabling you . . . to will and*

CHRIST HYMN (2.6–11)

This early Christological hymn portrays the preexistent Christ as graciously laying aside his extraordinary position of equality with God, emptying himself by incarnation—taking on the form of a servant. For this humility, God exalted Christ by giving him the divine name, taking "name" not in the modern sense of a generally arbitrary label but in the biblical sense of that which truly expresses character, power, and status (e.g., Ps 8.2 [Heb 8.1]; 20.2 [Heb 20.1]). This hymn Paul interweaves with his exhortation to humility, thereby challenging the Philippians: If the one in the "form of God" could humbly abdicate the dignity of his original status so as to suffer in order to show love for humankind, can the Philippians refrain from following his conduct?

The hymn may draw on several Jewish sources:

» The contrasts here conjured up between the *first* Adam (Gen 2.15–3.24) and imagery concerning a *last* Adam (1 Cor 15.20–22,45–49; Rom 5.12–21): while the Adam of Genesis was created in the image of God but, by ambitiously trying to go *higher*, went lower through his sin (and so death), Christ, the last Adam, was the very image of God but, choosing to go *lower* (and so dying), thereby became exalted (cf. Mt 23.12; Lk 14.11). Because the doctrine of the Christ as the *second* Adam appears distinctively Pauline, it was likely Paul himself who introduced it into the Church.

» The motif of the suffering servant who (Isa 53.12) "poured out himself to death" (cf. 45.22–23; and, broadly, 52.13–53.12).

» The preexistent figure of divine Wisdom created by, or proceeding from, God who came down to dwell among humans, offering them knowledge of the Divine (Prov 1.20–33; 8–9; Wis 7.22–10.21; Sir 24).

Akin in function to the liturgical use of Hebrew biblical psalms and other poetry, the Christ hymn presupposes a Christian cultus practicing religious devotion (perhaps being set at baptism or the Eucharist). Attesting to early use of hymns in Christianity are Acts 16.25; Eph 5.19; Col 3.16; and Lk 1.46–55,67–70; 2.14; cf. also Pliny, *Letters* 10.96–97 (here, to the Emperor Trajan): Christians "were accustomed to meet on a fixed day before dawn and sing responsively a hymn to Christ as to a god." The Christ hymn likewise lent itself to responsive singing.

As the earliest extant material underpinning later Christology, the Christ hymn's closest New Testament approximations are Col 1.15–20; 1 Tim 3.6; and 1 Pet 3.18–22; cf. Jn 1.1–5. The Christ hymn seems *pre*-Pauline because it is easily detachable from its current context, and its superlative style makes it difficult to envision Paul composing it, extemporaneously, amidst the flow of dictating the wider epistle. Rather, he likely incorporated this known hymn as apt for buttressing his admonitions to the Philippians. It is unlikely that Paul composed it himself earlier and only now incorporated it since it lacks a key Pauline motif: the redemptive significance of Christ's death.

but much more now in my absence, work out your own salvation with fear and trembling; [13] for it is God who is at work in you, enabling you both to will and to work for his good pleasure.

[14] Do all things without murmuring and arguing, [15] so that you may be blameless and innocent, children of God without blemish in the midst of a crooked and perverse generation, in which you shine like stars in the world. [16] It is by your holding fast to the word of life that I can boast on the day of Christ that I did not run in vain or labor in vain. [17] But even if I am being poured out as a libation over the sacrifice and the offering of your faith, I am glad and rejoice with all of

to work for his . . . pleasure (cf. Rom 6.12ff.). **15:** *Blameless and innocent,* repeating Paul's concern (1.10) that the Philippians will be found "blameless." *Without blemish,* in contrast to those "no longer [God's] children because of their blemish" (quoting here Deut 32.5). *Crooked . . . perverse generation,* while Deut 32.5 designates Israel as "blameworthy," Paul here substitutes pagans in Philippi. **17:** *Poured out,* possibly intended to parallel Christ's emptying himself (v. 7). The imagery casts the Philippians (with Paul now adding himself to them) as priests offering their faith as a sacrifice to God, with Paul's present suffering, even potential death sentence (Phil 1.20–25; cf. 2 Tim 4.6), a wine libation willingly poured out beside the altar (a standard culmination of the sacrificial ceremony); thereby the ebbing away of Paul's own life will meld Paul into the perfection of the Philippians' own sacrifice. Cf. Rom 12.1; Heb 13.15.

you— [18] and in the same way you also must be glad and rejoice with me.

[19] I hope in the Lord Jesus to send Timothy to you soon, so that I may be cheered by news of you. [20] I have no one like him who will be genuinely concerned for your welfare. [21] All of them are seeking their own interests, not those of Jesus Christ. [22] But Timothy's[a] worth you know, how like a son with a father he has served with me in the work of the gospel. [23] I hope therefore to send him as soon as I see how things go with me; [24] and I trust in the Lord that I will also come soon.

[25] Still, I think it necessary to send to you Epaphroditus—my brother and co-worker and fellow soldier, your messenger[b] and minister to my need; [26] for he has been longing for[c] all of you, and has been distressed because you heard that he was ill. [27] He was indeed so ill that he nearly died. But God had mercy on him, and not only on him but on me also, so that I would not have one sorrow after another. [28] I am the more eager to send him, therefore, in order that you may rejoice at seeing him again, and that I may be less anxious. [29] Welcome him then in the Lord with all joy, and honor such people, [30] because he came close to death for the work of Christ,[d] risking his life to make up for those services that you could not give me.

3 Finally, my brothers and sisters,[e] rejoice[f] in the Lord.

To write the same things to you is not troublesome to me, and for you it is a safeguard.

[2] Beware of the dogs, beware of the evil workers, beware of those who mutilate the flesh![g] [3] For it is we who are the circumcision, who worship in the Spirit of God[h] and boast in Christ Jesus and have no confidence in the flesh— [4] even though I, too, have reason for confidence in the flesh.

If anyone else has reason to be confident in the flesh, I have more: [5] circumcised on the eighth day, a member of the people of Israel, of the tribe of Benjamin, a Hebrew born of Hebrews; as to the law, a Pharisee; [6] as to zeal,

a Gk *his*
b Gk *apostle*
c Other ancient authorities read *longing to see*
d Other ancient authorities read *of the Lord*
e Gk *my brothers*
f Or *farewell*
g Gk *the mutilation*
h Other ancient authorities read *worship God in spirit*

2.19–3.1a: Planning travels for Timothy and Epaphroditus. 19: *Cheered by news of you,* Paul may mean "cheered" only if Timothy confirms that the Philippians have heeded his advice in 1.27–2.18; 3.2ff.,17ff.; 4.2ff. **23:** *How things go,* what the verdict regarding Paul will be. **25:** *Still, I think it necessary to send . . . Epaphroditus,* Paul softens the news that he is sending Epaphroditus first and alone, and only later Timothy—whom Paul knows they have been awaiting (see 2.19n.). **26:** *Because you heard that he was ill,* how they heard is unspecified. **30:** *Came close to death,* underscoring v. 27 so as to motivate the Philippians to welcome Epaphroditus enthusiastically. *Risking his life . . . you could not give me,* it is unclear what Paul is alluding to, but it may be a further commendation of Epaphroditus's willingness to die for his faith. **3.1a:** *Finally,* seen by some to indicate that one letter ended here.

3.1b–11: Warnings against false teachers. 1b: *The same things,* of which Paul had warned others (cf. Gal 6.12–15), possibly even the Philippians—as in another letter. **2:** *Dogs* (see "Beware of the Dogs," p. 359). **3:** *We . . . are the circumcision,* suggests that the Philippians are Gentiles. This one full verse essentially summarizes the core of Paul's epistle to the Galatians. Cf. Rom 2.28–29, echoing Deut 30.6. **4:** *I have more,* Paul is a truer son of Israel than are his opponents, so he cannot only refute but preempt their contention that observing the law will bring salvation from the bondage to sin. **5:** *Circumcised on the eighth day,* not in his maturity (as with male proselytes). *Of the people of Israel,* not grafted in. *Of the tribe of Benjamin,* source of Israel's first king (Saul) and the sole tribe remaining loyal to Judah when the Northern Kingdom broke away (1 Kings 12.21–23). *Hebrew . . . of Hebrews,* from Hebrew parentage (unlike proselytes). *Pharisee,* far more expert in the law than his opponents. **6:** *Persecutor,* an expression of Paul's zeal before his conversion (cf. 1 Cor 15.9; Gal 1.13). *Blameless,* upstaging Paul's opponents who champion the law instead of faith; i.e., the reason Paul is a follower of Jesus cannot be due to any incapacity on his part to fulfill Torah. Rather, one could be justified not by fulfilling works of the law but only by righteousness based on faith in Christ's

"BEWARE OF THE DOGS" (3.2–9)

These adversaries from outside Philippi who *might* someday soon arrive were evidently different from opponents mentioned earlier in 1.15–18 and 1.28. They were either Jewish-Christians (or Gentile-Christians partial to the law, or conceivably even Jewish agitators bent on winning back Gentile god-fearers). Customarily, they falsely argued that Gentile males must be circumcised. Paul sarcastically terms them "mutilators" (perhaps obliquely referring to the self-inflicted wounds by the prophets of Baal [cf. 1 Kings 18] or to devotees of the Phrygian mystery goddess, Cybele, who would slash themselves amid religious frenzy).

Paul was wary because of his own past experiences with this danger elsewhere (cf. Gal 2.1–16; 5.2–6,12) and likely also because Philippi's vulnerable location near the Egnatian Way rendered this church susceptible to such subversives showing up. The bitterness of his tirade is a measure of his conviction that believers in Christ should not emphasize the flesh lest they nullify their new freedom, thereby hindering God's plans for Gentile salvation and clouding their perception that justification comes solely by the grace of God through faith in Christ's shed blood. Indeed, if one could become righteous by one's own works, then Christ would not have needed to die (Gal 2.21b).

Instead, the Philippians should heed Paul who is himself qualified not only to refute but to preempt his enemies—given his own consummate possession of the very privileges of which his adversaries boast (see 3.3–6nn.). Expert in appraising his impeccable privileges at their true value (namely, as less than nothing), Paul gladly relinquished them in favor of the extreme gain of knowing Christ Jesus as Lord.

Paul depreciates his Jewish background only in the context of his polemic against the "dogs"" who seek to discredit him. "Dog" in the ancient world was an insulting term; see 1 Sam 17.43; Rev 22.15; also the Greek "cynics" (from "kyon, kynarion," "dog") were so called because their deliberately uninhibited public behavior was regarded as shameful. We should, therefore, contrast this invective with Rom 9.4–5, where Paul declares that "to them [the Israelites] belong the adoption, the glory, the covenants, the giving of the law, the worship, and the promises; . . . the patriarchs, and from them, according to the flesh, comes the Messiah."

a persecutor of the church; as to righteousness under the law, blameless.

[7] Yet whatever gains I had, these I have come to regard as loss because of Christ. [8] More than that, I regard everything as loss because of the surpassing value of knowing Christ Jesus my Lord. For his sake I have suffered the loss of all things, and I regard them as rubbish, in order that I may gain Christ [9] and be found in him, not having a righteousness of my own that comes from the law, but one that comes through faith in Christ,[a] the righteousness from God based on faith. [10] I want to know Christ[b] and the power of his resurrection and the sharing of his sufferings by becoming like him in his death, [11] if somehow I may attain the resurrection from the dead.

[12] Not that I have already obtained this or have already reached the goal;[c] but I press on to make it my own, because Christ Jesus has made me his own. [13] Beloved,[d] I do not consider that I have made it my own;[e] but this one thing I do: forgetting what lies behind and straining forward to what lies ahead, [14] I press on toward the goal for the prize of the heavenly[f] call of God in Christ Jesus. [15] Let those of us then who are mature be of the same mind; and if you think differently about anything, this too God will reveal to you. [16] Only let us hold fast to what we have attained.

[17] Brothers and sisters,[d] join in imitating me, and observe those who live according to

[a] Or *through the faith of Christ*
[b] Gk *him*
[c] Or *have already been made perfect*
[d] Gk *Brothers*
[e] Other ancient authorities read *my own yet*
[f] Gk *upward*

sacrifice as the only means to accomplish forgiveness of humanity's sinfulness. **11:** *If somehow*, expresses humility, not doubt. *Attain the resurrection from the dead*, to become accounted worthy of, and possessing the sure hope of, securing the reward of resurrection from among the dead (Lk 20.35; cf. 1 Pet 1.3) at Christ's coming (1 Cor 15.23; 1 Thess 4.15).

the example you have in us. [18] For many live as enemies of the cross of Christ; I have often told you of them, and now I tell you even with tears. [19] Their end is destruction; their god is the belly; and their glory is in their shame; their minds are set on earthly things. [20] But our citizenship[a] is in heaven, and it is from there that we are expecting a Savior, the Lord Jesus Christ. [21] He will transform the body of our humiliation[b] that it may be conformed to the body of his glory,[c] by the power that also enables him to make all

4 things subject to himself. [1] Therefore, my brothers and sisters,[d] whom I love and long for, my joy and crown, stand firm in the Lord in this way, my beloved.

[2] I urge Euodia and I urge Syntyche to be of the same mind in the Lord. [3] Yes, and I ask you also, my loyal companion,[e] help these women, for they have struggled beside me in the work of the gospel, together with Clement and the rest of my co-workers, whose names are in the book of life.

[4] Rejoice[f] in the Lord always; again I will say, Rejoice.[f] [5] Let your gentleness be known to everyone. The Lord is near. [6] Do not worry about anything, but in everything by prayer and supplication with thanksgiving let your requests be made known to God. [7] And the peace of God, which surpasses all understanding, will guard your hearts and your minds in Christ Jesus.

[8] Finally, beloved,[g] whatever is true, whatever is honorable, whatever is just, whatever is pure, whatever is pleasing, whatever is commendable, if there is any excellence and if there is anything worthy of praise, think about[h] these things. [9] Keep on doing the things that you have learned and received and heard and seen in me, and the God of peace will be with you.

[10] I rejoice[i] in the Lord greatly that now at last you have revived your concern for me; indeed, you were concerned for me, but had no opportunity to show it.[j] [11] Not that I am referring to being in need; for I have learned to be content with whatever I have. [12] I know what it is to have little, and I know what it is to have plenty. In any and all circumstances I have learned the secret of being well-fed and of going hungry, of having plenty and of being in need. [13] I can do all things through him who strengthens me. [14] In any case, it was kind of you to share my distress.

[15] You Philippians indeed know that in the early days of the gospel, when I left Macedonia, no church shared with me in the matter of giving and receiving, except you alone. [16] For even when I was in Thessalonica, you sent me help for my needs more than once. [17] Not that I seek the gift, but I seek the profit that accumulates to your account. [18] I have been paid in full and have more than enough; I am fully satisfied, now that I have received from Epaphroditus the gifts you sent, a fragrant offering, a sacrifice acceptable and pleasing to God. [19] And my God will

[a] Or *commonwealth*
[b] Or *our humble bodies*
[c] Or *his glorious body*
[d] Gk *my brothers*
[e] Or *loyal Syzygus*
[f] Or *Farewell*
[g] Gk *brothers*
[h] Gk *take account of*
[i] Gk *I rejoiced*
[j] Gk lacks *to show it*

3.12–4.1: Confession and further exhortation. **18:** *Even with tears*, possibly because the Philippians were back. **19:** *Is the belly*, likely libertines pandering to sensual pleasures (cf. Rom 16.18). **21:** *Conformed to*, fashioned in the manner of. *Body of his glory*, spiritual, upon resurrection (cf. 1 Cor 15.44).

4.2–9: Final appeals. **2:** *Euodia ... Syntyche*, whose dissension could destabilize this church, especially given the considerable social esteem accorded Macedonian women; cf. Paul's earlier emphasis on unity (1.27; 2.2). **3:** *My loyal companion*, either some Philippian leader; or possibly a proper name (i.e., my loyal "Syzygus"); or, plausibly, Epaphroditus—who now hears himself directly charged to settle this quarrel. *Beside me*, as co-evangelists with Paul in founding this church. *Book of life*, cf. Ex 32.32; Ps 69.28; Lk 10.20; Rev 3.5.

4.10–20: Thanking the Philippians. **14:** *Kind of you*, lest, in declaring his independence, Paul appear unappreciative of their gift. **15:** *Except you alone*, cf. 2 Cor 11.9. **18:** *Paid in full*, releasing them from further obligation. *Fragrant offering ... sacrifice acceptable and pleasing*, cf. Lev 1.3–4,9.

fully satisfy every need of yours according to his riches in glory in Christ Jesus. [20] To our God and Father be glory forever and ever. Amen.

[21] Greet every saint in Christ Jesus. The friends[a] who are with me greet you. [22] All the saints greet you, especially those of the emperor's household.

[23] The grace of the Lord Jesus Christ be with your spirit.[b]

[a] Gk *brothers*
[b] Other ancient authorities add *Amen*

4.21–23: Closing greetings. *Emperor's household,* soldiers and staff whom Paul had successfully evangelized (cf. 1.13n.). *The grace . . . spirit,* similar to the ending of Galatians (6.18).

THE LETTER OF PAUL TO THE COLOSSIANS

NAME, AUTHORSHIP, AND CANONICAL STATUS

While Colossians presents itself as a letter of Paul (1.1,23; 4.8), much critical scholarship concludes that the letter is written at least one generation after Paul by one of his followers and is thus "Deutero-Pauline," the sort of fictive authorship that Paul himself refers to in 2 Thess 2.2, "letter, as though from us." The author of Colossians sets the letter against the backdrop of Philippians and Philemon, and constructs yet another "captivity letter," written by Paul from prison (but cf. 4.3n.,10n.).

Scholars suggest that Colossians is inauthentic to Paul on several counts. While its author knows Paul's distinctive theological vocabulary (e.g. "principalities and powers," "love" [agapē], "justification," "body of Christ"), he puts this vocabulary in service to a Christology and eschatology distinct from that of Paul's authentic letters. The authentic epistles speak of "justification" and "sanctification" in the present (see Rom 6.4–5) but reserve "salvation" for the future; for Colossians, salvation is a present reality (3.1–4), and justification has no place at all. A stronger argument against the authenticity of Colossians lies in its inclusion (3.22–4.1)—the earliest in the New Testament—of the hierarchical description of household relations called, since Martin Luther, "Haustafeln," or "household codes." In his authentic letters, Paul's description of marital relationships is remarkably nonhierarchical (cf. 1 Cor 7.1–4, where husbands and wives each serve the other); he was an antagonist to the kind of marital hierarchy promulgated in the household codes of both Deutero-Pauline letters, the pastoral letter Titus, and 1 Peter, all products of the second or third generation of New Testament writers. Such codes (also found in Eph 6.5–9; 1 Tim 6.1–2; and 1 Pet 2.18–21), are likely the products of the second or third generation of New Testament writers, aware that the second coming of Jesus is not likely to occur in the near future, and needing to provide guidelines on how his followers should live. Colossians also shares multiple phrases with Ephesians, another Deutero-Pauline letter (see "Colossians and Ephesians: Parallels," p. 365). If Paul did write the letter, he wrote under circumstances that forced him to adopt theological and social ideas strongly at variance with those we find in letters we know to be authentic.

HISTORICAL CONTEXT, LITERARY HISTORY

The author writes to the church in Colossae, east of Ephesus and near Laodicea and Hierapolis, a church he claims to have been founded by Epaphras (Col 1.7; 4.12) a claim perhaps based on Paul's mention of this fellow apostle in Philem 23. The author has never visited Colossae (1.4; 2.1) but rather responds to new teachings there regarding both belief and practice. The theologians of this young church have placed the Christ ("the Anointed One") on the same level as angels (2.18), the "elemental spirits of the universe" (2.8), and "rulers and authorities" (2.15), and have insisted on particular practices regarding food and drink, asceticism, and Sabbath and new moon observances (2.16,20–23). The search for a single set of thinkers who promoted both ascetic practices and the rituals surrounding the Jewish calendar has prompted a great deal of speculation regarding Jewish sectarian groups such as the Essenes, but it is also possible that these diverse ideas represent two competing groups (cf. 2.18n.).

To the challenges of these Colossian thinkers, the author offers a new and important Christology: the Christ's preeminent, cosmic role. Borrowing the most famous ecclesiological metaphor from Paul, the church as the body of Christ (1 Cor 12.27), the author insists that the Christ is the head of the church (1.18), with the members comprising his body. As in the Platonic thought-world of another post-Pauline letter, Hebrews, the author belittles his opponents' favorite ritual observances as "shadows" whereas the Christ is what is real (2.17; cf. Heb. 8.5; 10.1). The Christological hymn in 1.15–20, which sounds some of the same themes as the hymns in Jn 1.1–18 and Phil 2.6–11, praises the Christ's preeminence, role in creation, and the role of his death in reconciling God and humankind. This preeminence relieves believers of the need to placate spirits (2.15) or to engage in asceticism or any ritual practices other than baptism. The letter imitates 1 Corinthians in urging its readers to put aside the sinfulness of their pre-baptismal lives and devote themselves to virtue (3.1–17).

GUIDE TO READING

Comparing this letter with an authentic Pauline epistle on the subject of Jewish ritual is instructive. When Paul wrote Galatians, whether Gentile believers needed to observe distinctive Jewish rituals (especially circumcision, but also dietary regulations, purity codes, and Sabbath observance) was subject to debate in the churches; Paul himself considers Jews to be obliged to observe the Torah (cf. Gal 5.3) but insists that Gentile believers are not to become Jews and are not to follow practices that mark Jews as distinct. In Colossians, the author takes church members' interest in observing such rituals as antagonistic to the rule of the Christ; he has moved beyond the point where Jewish observance is an option for anyone within the churches. In Galatians, as in most of his authentic letters, Paul can argue from scripture to illustrate his points, and so connects even his Gentile readers with what he considers to be their biblical past. Not so in Colossians: Its few references to the Tanakh are echoes, not quotations. The letter is a window on a period in the history of Christianity when church leaders turned away from Judaism, even while some church members continued to find Jewish practice meaningful.

Peter Zaas

1 Paul, an apostle of Christ Jesus by the will of God, and Timothy our brother,

[2] To the saints and faithful brothers and sisters[a] in Christ in Colossae:

Grace to you and peace from God our Father.

[3] In our prayers for you we always thank God, the Father of our Lord Jesus Christ, [4] for we have heard of your faith in Christ Jesus and of the love that you have for all the saints, [5] because of the hope laid up for you in heaven. You have heard of this hope before in the word of the truth, the gospel [6] that has come to you. Just as it is bearing fruit and growing in the whole world, so it has been bearing fruit among yourselves from the

[a] Gk *brothers*

1.1–2: Salutation. Colossians follows Paul's salutation formula. **1:** *Apostle*, lit., "one sent" (cf. Heb "shaliaḥ"). *Timothy*, all of Paul's authentic letters except Romans have multiple senders; Timothy is listed as co-sender of all except Galatians. Timothy is Paul's chief lieutenant, whom he mentions more frequently than any other person except Jesus in his authentic letters. See also Acts 16; he was so prominent in the second century CE that the Pastoral Epistles of 1 and 2 Timothy are addressed to him. *Brother*, an address for unrelated members of a number of religious communities, including the Essenes (cf. Josephus, *J.W.* 2.122) and the followers of the Greco-Egyptian god Serapis (*Paris Papyrus* [second century BCE] 20). **2:** *Saints*, lit., "holy ones," Paul's most common designation for "believers" in his authentic letters; the term is more frequent in Ephesians and Colossians than in the authentic Pauline letters. *Brothers and sisters*, the plural of the Gk word for "brother" ("adelphos/adelphoi") may refer to "brothers and sisters" (see translators' note *a*). *Colossae*, city in the Lycus valley, east of Ephesus, substantially destroyed by an earthquake in 60 CE. *Grace . . . peace*, Paul adapted the standard Greek letter greeting ("chairein," "greetings") to the similar-sounding theological term "charis," "grace," and included the Jewish epistolary greeting "shalom," "peace" (Gk "eirēnē"). Ephesians and the Pastoral Epistles follow the same practice.

1.3–7: Thanksgiving. Ancient Greek letters conventionally included a thanksgiving formula following the salutation, in which the sender offered the recipient good wishes. All of Paul's authentic letters except Galatians include a thanksgiving (the thanksgiving of 1 Thess is the first three chs of the letter), which mentions the main themes of the letter. In Colossians and Ephesians the author thanks his audience for their faith, love, and hope, standard virtues in the church, as if the letter had no particular epistolary situation. **3–5:** *Faith . . . love . . . hope*, imitating Paul's triumvirate of virtues ("pistis," "faith" occurs nearly a hundred times in the authentic letters). The three appear together in 1 Thess 1.3; 5.8; 1 Cor. 13.13. **3:** *Lord*, Jesus' followers referred to him as "kyrios," "Lord, master." Paul, in his authentic letters, only once uses the term in a secular sense, as the master of a slave (Gal 4.1), and once ironically (1 Cor 8.5). All other 208 occasions refer to Jesus. In the Deutero-Pauline letters the authors refer to Jesus as "Lord" in the typical manner, but in the "Haustafeln" the word serves both functions: for Jesus, and for slave-owners, as in Col 3.22, where it means both. **4:** *Faith*, both trust and trustworthiness, often in the economic sphere, like the Heb "'emunah." For "agapē," "love," see 2.2n. **5:** *Gospel* (Gk "euangelion," "good news"), the standard expression for the narrative about the messiahship of Jesus. **6:** *Bear-*

day you heard it and truly comprehended the grace of God. [7] This you learned from Epaphras, our beloved fellow servant.[a] He is a faithful minister of Christ on your[b] behalf, [8] and he has made known to us your love in the Spirit.

[9] For this reason, since the day we heard it, we have not ceased praying for you and asking that you may be filled with the knowledge of God's[c] will in all spiritual wisdom and understanding, [10] so that you may lead lives worthy of the Lord, fully pleasing to him, as you bear fruit in every good work and as you grow in the knowledge of God. [11] May you be made strong with all the strength that comes from his glorious power, and may you be prepared to endure everything with patience, while joyfully [12] giving thanks to the Father, who has enabled[d] you[e] to share in the inheritance of the saints in the light. [13] He has rescued us from the power of darkness and transferred us into the kingdom of his

a Gk *slave*
b Other ancient authorities read *our*
c Gk *his*
d Other ancient authorities read *called*
e Other ancient authorities read *us*

ing fruit, growth of knowledge and right action (vv. 9–10), probably in imitation of Gal 5.22. **7:** *Epaphras*, first apostle to Colossae, so far as this letter is concerned, who is with the author as he writes (4.12–13; see Philem 23). *Fellow servant* (Gk "syndoulos," "fellow-slave"), a term appearing in NT letters here and 4.7. *Minister*, Gk "diakonos," "server"; these were the first officers in the church. The term in Acts 6 still carries with it its original connotation of "waiter" or "server," inasmuch as the seven men who were appointed as "diakonoi" were to obviate the apostles from having to wait on tables (Acts 6.2). Whether the term carries that connotation for Phoebe, "a deacon of the church at Cenchreae" (Rom 16.1), or Apollos (1 Cor 3.5), the church officials named as deacons in the earliest NT texts, or for Epaphras here, arguably the last person named as a deacon in the NT, remains uncertain.

1.8: Apostolic visitation. As the author cannot pretend that Paul was in Colossae, he merges the thanksgiving (Epaphras brought back news of the church's virtues) with the apostolic "parousia," Gk "coming," a typical section in Paul's letters where he remembers, usually fondly, his experiences while visiting the church.

1.9–14: Prayer for spiritual wisdom. 9–11: The prayer concludes the thanksgiving (v. 12). The author prays his audience excel in "sophia kai sunesei pneumatikē," *spiritual wisdom and understanding*. In 1 Cor, chs 1–4, Paul contrasts the negative attributes of wisdom and understanding—which he associates not with virtue but with cleverness in argumentation—with "pneumatika," "spiritual things," which he considers the goal of life. The author of Colossians takes Paul's moral vocabulary but reverses it: Wisdom, here positive, involves *knowledge* (v. 9), right living (v. 10), and *patience* (v. 11). **9:** *God's will*, this phrase is common in both Paul's authentic letters (nineteen examples) and in the Deutero-Pauline letters (four examples), but extremely rare in Jewish Scriptures, appearing in the LXX only in 1 Esd 8.16. In the DSS, however, the phrase "retzon 'el," "will of God," conventionally contrasts divine with human will. *Spiritual wisdom* (Gk "sophia," LXX for Heb "hokhmah," "wisdom," e.g., Prov 1.2) *and understanding* (Gk "synesis," LXX for Heb "binah," "understanding, discernment," e.g., Prov 1.2, where it is also used with "hokhmah"), a major theme of the letter (1.25–28; 2.2–4,9–15). Paul uses the noun "sophia" or the adjective thirty-four times in his authentic letters, but only twice as a positive attribute (in Rom 11.33 and 16.27, both as descriptions of God). The author of Colossians follows in the tradition of the wisdom literature of the Tanakh, using the term five times, only positively. **10:** *Pleasing* (Gk "ariskeia," "desire to please"), only here in the NT. **11:** *Endure* (Gk "hypomonē," "endurance"), a common theme of the Pauline letters (e.g., 1 Cor 4.12; 9.12; 2 Cor 1.6) and NT letters generally (e.g., Heb 12.7; 1 Pet 2.19–20). The paired virtues "endurance" and "patience" occur together in 2 Tim 3.10. **12–13:** *Light . . . darkness*, a common image for moral dualism. The second-century *Teaching of the Twelve Apostles* (*Did.*) calls it "the Two Ways." It appears in Deut 30.19; Jer 21.8 and throughout the NT (1 Thess 5.5; John [many occurrences, e.g., 3.19]; 1 Pet 2.9; Eph 5.8), and less definitively, here. The trope is found in Greek texts (*Prodicus Judgment of Heracles* [*Mem.* 2.1.21]). It is fully developed in the DSS (see 1QM and 1QS 3.13–4.26), the *Did.*, and the *Ep. Barn.* (also possibly second century). **12:** *Giving thanks*, the thanksgiving section continues, probably to the end of the hymn (vv. 15–20). **13:** *Power of darkness*, continuing the theme of v. 12. **14:** *Redemption . . . forgiveness*, the extent to which these familiar Christian theological terms reflect Jewish ideas of redemption is questionable.

COLOSSIANS AND EPHESIANS: PARALLELS

Eph 1.1–2	Col 1.1–2	Eph 5.22	Col 3.18
Eph 1.7	Col 1.14	Eph 5.25,33	Col 3.19
Eph 3.2	Col 1.25	Eph 6.1	Col 3.20
Eph 3.9	Col 1.26	Eph 6.5	Col 3.22–25
Eph 4.16	Col 2.19	Eph 6.9	Col 4.1
Eph 5.3	Col 3.6	Eph 6.21–22	Col 4.7–8

beloved Son, [14] in whom we have redemption, the forgiveness of sins.[a]

[15] He is the image of the invisible God, the firstborn of all creation; [16] for in[b] him all things in heaven and on earth were created, things visible and invisible, whether thrones or dominions or rulers or powers—all things have been created through him and for him. [17] He himself is before all things, and in[b] him all things hold together. [18] He is the head of the body, the church; he is the beginning, the firstborn from the dead, so that he might come to have first place in everything. [19] For in him all the fullness of God was pleased to dwell, [20] and through him God was pleased

[a] Other ancient authorities add *through his blood*
[b] Or *by*

Although Jewish texts in the intertestamental period begin to talk of redemption from sin, the more common biblical expression involves redemption from exile; Judaism rarely allied itself with the idea of inborn or original sin, from which a person needed to be rescued (though some may see a hint of this in Ps 51.1–5 [Heb vv. 3–7]). Gk "apolutrosis," "ransoming," translated in the NRSV as *redemption*, appears in the LXX only in Dan 4.34; but see, e.g., "lutrōtēs," "redeemer," Ps 19.14 [Heb v. 15, "go'el"; LXX Ps 18.15]); the term is relatively rare in Paul (Rom 3.24; 8.23; 1 Cor 1.30) but relatively common in the Deutero-Pauline letters (Eph 1.7,14; 4.30, and here). "Aphesis," *forgiveness*, never appears in Paul but is found in both Colossians and Ephesians. The notion is relatively popular in the DSS (e.g., 1QS 2.8).

1.15–20: Hymn to the Christ. The thanksgiving section concludes with a developed Christology, borrowing themes from both Paul and the Septuagint, perhaps from the Fourth Gospel, offered in terms accessible to the letter's Gentile readers. The Christ more than rules the world: he is both the first thing created and the principle of creation (vv. 15–17), the head of the world and head of the church (vv. 18–20). This Christology is perhaps the "highest" (i.e., the farthest along a spectrum from "the Christ is fully human" to "the Christ is fully divine") of any NT source. It resembles the description of personified Wisdom in Prov 8.22–31, present with God at creation; here the Christ has a much greater role than does Wisdom in Proverbs (see also Wis 7.22b–8.1). **15–20:** *Image of the invisible God,* Gk "aoratos," "invisible," echoes Rom 1.20, but there Paul alludes to LXX Gen 1.2, "aoratos kai akataskeuastos," "invisible and disorganized," reflecting Heb "tohu va-vohu," "formless void" (NRSV). For Col 1.15–16, an invisible God creates invisible things. Cf. 1 Tim 1.17; Heb 11.27. The Christ is both the *firstborn of all creation* (v. 15) and the *firstborn from the dead* (v. 18), that is, the first person raised from the dead. "Firstborn," used only once in Paul (Rom 8.29), occurs in the LXX 132 times. In Hebrews, it refers once to the Christ (1.6), once to the firstborn sons of Egypt, killed by the angel of death (11.28), once to the Israelites in Egypt who were not slain (also 11.28), and once to the believers in the author's own generation (12.23). See also Acts 26.2; Rev 1.5. Biblical law (e.g., Deut 21.15–17) affirms the superior inheritance right of firstborn sons, though some rabbinic legislators argued for a more equal distribution of estates (cf. *b. Shabb.* 10b) **16:** *Thrones . . . powers,* to Paul's apocalyptic image of the "archai" (*rulers*) and "exousiai" ("authorities"), the spiritual forces that rule the world, the author adds the non-Pauline "thronoi" (*thrones*), indicating any concentration of power, secular, demonic, or divine (cf. Eph 1.21; 3.10). **17–20:** The Christ is the organizing principle of creation as in Jn 1.1ff. **18:** *Head,* the Christ is the head of the body, the church, echoing 1 Cor 12.18–31. For Paul, the members of the church are limbs (or organs) of the Christ's body, and therefore should function in harmony, each with different roles. *The body, the church,* here and in 1.24, "ekklēsia," "church" means something larger than the believers gathered in a particular location, the meaning in Paul's letters. **19:** *Fullness of God,* probably an echo of Ps 24 (LXX Ps 23), "the earth is the LORD's and its fullness" (NRSV "and all that is in it").

to reconcile to himself all things, whether on earth or in heaven, by making peace through the blood of his cross.

[21] And you who were once estranged and hostile in mind, doing evil deeds, [22] he has now reconciled[a] in his fleshly body[b] through death, so as to present you holy and blameless and irreproachable before him— [23] provided that you continue securely established and steadfast in the faith, without shifting from the hope promised by the gospel that you heard, which has been proclaimed to every creature under heaven. I, Paul, became a servant of this gospel.

[24] I am now rejoicing in my sufferings for your sake, and in my flesh I am completing what is lacking in Christ's afflictions for the sake of his body, that is, the church. [25] I became its servant according to God's commission that was given to me for you, to make the word of God fully known, [26] the mystery that has been hidden throughout the ages and generations but has now been revealed to his saints. [27] To them God chose to make known how great among the Gentiles are the riches of the glory of this mystery, which is Christ in you, the hope of glory. [28] It is he whom we proclaim, warning everyone and teaching everyone in all wisdom, so that we may present everyone mature in Christ. [29] For this I toil and struggle with all the energy that he powerfully inspires within me.

2 For I want you to know how much I am struggling for you, and for those in Laodicea, and for all who have not seen me face to face. [2] I want their hearts to be encouraged and united in love, so that they may have all the riches of assured understanding and have the knowledge of God's mystery, that is, Christ himself,[c] [3] in whom are hidden all the treasures of wisdom and knowledge. [4] I am saying this so that no one may deceive you with plausible arguments. [5] For though I am absent in body, yet I am with you in spirit, and I rejoice to see your morale and the firmness of your faith in Christ.

a Other ancient authorities read *you have now been reconciled*

b Gk *in the body of his flesh*

c Other ancient authorities read *of the mystery of God, both of the Father and of Christ*

20: *Reconcile . . . making peace*, "apokatallasso," "reconcile," appears only in the Deutero-Pauline letters (Eph 2.16; Col 1.20,22). Paul uses "katallagē/ katallasso," "reconciliation/reconcile" (cf. Rom 5.10); the vocabulary is different, but the notion is similar: God's power is manifested in the reconciliation of former enemies.

1.21–23: Assurance and exhortation. 21: *Estranged*, Gentiles separated from Israel's God before they heard the good news about the Christ. The Gk word occurs in the NT only in the Deutero-Pauline letters (Eph 2.12; 4.18, and here). **22:** *Fleshly body*, see Jn 1.14; 1 Cor. 15.35ff. *To present you . . . before him*, reconciliation here exists in a juridical context; it entails judgment (v. 28). **23:** *The faith*, for the Deutero-Pauline letters, "pistis" shifts from "trust" or "trustworthiness" to "belief." *Proclaimed to every creature*, hyperbole indicating that the author, a generation or more after Paul, knows about the spread of the gospel. *Servants*, v. 25; cf. v. 7n.

1.24–29: Witness and mission. Only once in his authentic letters, outside of opening and closing greetings, does Paul use his name in first-person discourse, and there (Gal 5.2) he is emphatic. The authors of Colossians and Ephesians, borrowing Paul's identity, insert an extra mention of his name, thus attempting to establish Pauline authorship (cf. Eph 3.1). **24:** *Sufferings*, the author follows Paul in calling for imitating the Christ in his suffering (e.g., 2 Cor 4.7–12; 11.23–28). *Body*, see 1.18n. **26–27:** *Mystery*, lit., "secret revealed to initiates." The term is more than twice as frequent in the Deutero-Pauline letters as in other NT books. The secret here is God's election of the Gentiles (2.2; 4.3). *Saints*, see 1.2n. *Gentiles*, Colossians, like Paul's authentic letters, addresses a Gentile audience. **28:** *Mature in Christ*, in 1 Cor 3.1–2, Paul complains that congregants are too immature to receive the full measure of the gospel; in Colossians he frequently expresses hopes that the congregants might be presented as mature (cf. 4.12). The Gk can also mean "perfect" (Mt 5.48).

2.1–5: Pastoral concerns. *Laodicea*, a neighboring city; see 4.13n.; Rev 3.14–22. Josephus records several letters regarding a petition from the Jewish high-priest Hyrcanus (ca. 76–40 BCE) to the proconsul that the Jews of Laodicea be allowed to observe their ancestral laws and to manage their lands according to the Torah (*Ant.* 14.241ff.) **2:** *Love* (Gk "agapē"), Paul's term for the virtue that holds diverse parts in a harmonious whole (1 Cor 13), becomes ubiquitous in post-Pauline letters, appearing ten times in Ephesians, and five more in Colossians (1.4,8,13; 2.2; 3.14). *Mystery*, see 1.26–27n. **5:** *Firmness* (Gk "stereoma"), normally refers to the "firmament" of creation, but in conjunction with "taxis" ("order," NRSV "morale") the image is military.

[6] As you therefore have received Christ Jesus the Lord, continue to live your lives[a] in him, [7] rooted and built up in him and established in the faith, just as you were taught, abounding in thanksgiving.

[8] See to it that no one takes you captive through philosophy and empty deceit, according to human tradition, according to the elemental spirits of the universe,[b] and not according to Christ. [9] For in him the whole fullness of deity dwells bodily, [10] and you have come to fullness in him, who is the head of every ruler and authority. [11] In him also you were circumcised with a spiritual circumcision,[c] by putting off the body of the flesh in the circumcision of Christ; [12] when you were buried with him in baptism, you were also raised with him through faith in the power of God, who raised him from the dead. [13] And when you were dead in trespasses and the uncircumcision of your flesh, God[d] made you[e] alive together with him, when he forgave us all our trespasses, [14] erasing the record that stood against us with its legal demands. He set this aside, nailing it to the cross. [15] He disarmed[f] the rulers and authorities and made a public example of them, triumphing over them in it.

[16] Therefore do not let anyone condemn you in matters of food and drink or of ob-

a Gk *to walk*
b Or *the rudiments of the world*
c Gk *a circumcision made without hands*
d Gk *he*
e Other ancient authorities read *made us*; others, *made*
f Or *divested himself of*

2.6–15: Proper understanding of the crucifixion. 6–7: The letter's major concern is to promote a particular ecclesiology (understanding of the nature of the church or Christian community) and to oppose other views. **7:** *The faith,* see 1.23n. **8:** *No one,* the author likely is opposing church members interested in exploring new philosophical and religious traditions. *Philosophy,* except for 4 Macc (1.1; 5.11,22; 7.9,21), where the word occurs five times, this is the only use of the term in the Bible. Here philosophy is a negative concept, what Paul called "human wisdom" (1 Cor 2.5), and Colossians associates it with "human tradition" and "elemental spirits of the world." *Human tradition,* the charge Jesus makes against Pharisees (Mk 7.8); *elemental spirits of the universe* occurs only here and in Gal 4.3, where it describes the powers that enslaved the Gentile Galatians before they received the good news about the Christ. The author thus simultaneously condemns Greek philosophical traditions, Jewish legal teaching, and pagan worship. **9–10:** *Fullness,* see 1.19n. *Head,* see 1.18n. **11:** *Circumcision,* the author of Colossians, like Paul in Galatians, faces community members who want to observe "brit milah," the sign for males of inclusion in God's covenant. These church members want to behave like Jews, whether or not they want to be full-fledged members of the Jewish community. *Spiritual circumcision,* lit., "circumcision not done by hands." *By putting off . . . flesh,* the author labors to draw analogies between baptism and circumcision, urging the former and forbidding the latter. *Putting off* (Gk "apekdusis"; cognate verb "apekduomai") appears in Col 2.11,15; 3.9, but nowhere else in the NT; the NRSV translates each appearance differently. The words mean "undressing" as in NRSV 3.9, "stripped off the old self." **12:** *You were buried . . . also raised,* unlike Paul's authentic letters, Colossians speaks of resurrection in the present. **13:** *Uncircumcision* (Gk "akrobustia," lit., "foreskin"), a traditional rendering, translates an indelicate word delicately. Paul (1 Cor 7.18) is the only biblical author to use the correct medical term for "uncircumcision." Gentiles were dead with respect to baptism, and men among them were dead with respect to circumcision, i.e., their foreskins were intact. *Forgave us all our trespasses,* reminiscent of Mt 6.12; Lk 11.4. **14:** *Record . . . demands* (Gk "cheirographon"), normally refers to a bill, as in Tob 5.3 and 9.5; cf. Philem 19. Jesus' crucifixion erased the believers' debts. **15:** *Rulers and authorities,* see 1.16n. *Disarmed . . . triumphing,* a parade of vanquished enemies, an image familiar to Roman residents. *Disarmed,* better "stripped naked" (cf. 2.11n.).

2.16–23: Warnings against Jewish observance. 16: The author complains about the Colossians' observance of Jewish dietary laws and calendar rituals. Arguments about dietary laws divided his churches (see Rom 14.15,17,20; 1 Cor 8.1–13). The Colossians want to eat, drink, and sanctify time like Jews. *Food and drink* probably imitates Rom 14.17. *Festivals* (Gk "heortē"; used in LXX chiefly for Heb "ḥag," e.g., Ex 10.9), refers in general to a Jewish festival or to a specific one, Pesach (Mt 26.5) or Sukkot (Jn 7.8); it appears in no other NT letter. *New moons, or sabbaths,* one of this letter's few direct echoes of the LXX (e.g. Ezek 4.17; Hos 2.11). Jewish rituals for "rosh chodesh," the first day of the month (cf. Num 28.11) are never mentioned in the NT but are well known to Josephus (cf. *Ant* 3.238) and

serving festivals, new moons, or sabbaths. [17] These are only a shadow of what is to come, but the substance belongs to Christ. [18] Do not let anyone disqualify you, insisting on self-abasement and worship of angels, dwelling[a] on visions,[b] puffed up without cause by a human way of thinking,[c] [19] and not holding fast to the head, from whom the whole body, nourished and held together by its ligaments and sinews, grows with a growth that is from God.

[20] If with Christ you died to the elemental spirits of the universe,[d] why do you live as if you still belonged to the world? Why do you submit to regulations, [21] "Do not handle, Do not taste, Do not touch"? [22] All these regulations refer to things that perish with use; they are simply human commands and teachings. [23] These have indeed an appearance of wisdom in promoting self-imposed piety, humility, and severe treatment of the body, but they are of no value in checking self-indulgence.[e]

3 So if you have been raised with Christ, seek the things that are above, where Christ is, seated at the right hand of God. [2] Set your minds on things that are above, not on things that are on earth, [3] for you have died, and your life is hidden with Christ in God. [4] When Christ who is your[f] life is revealed, then you also will be revealed with him in glory.

[5] Put to death, therefore, whatever in you is earthly: fornication, impurity, passion, evil

[a] Other ancient authorities read *not dwelling*
[b] Meaning of Gk uncertain
[c] Gk *by the mind of his flesh*
[d] Or *the rudiments of the world*
[e] Or *are of no value, serving only to indulge the flesh*
[f] Other authorities read *our*

the DSS (cf. 11Q5 27.7; 11Q19 43.20). In contrast to the Tanakh, Mishnaic references largely focus on legal questions involving the observation of the new moon, vital to establishing festival dates, rather than on special observance for the new moon festival, although *m. Zeb.* 10.1 describes "rosh chodesh" sacrifices in conjunction with Shabbat sacrifices. Paul never mentions Sabbath or "rosh chodesh" observance in his authentic letters; Gal 4.10 refers to pagan, not Jewish, ritual. For Paul, the church is a Gentile congregation gathering on the Lord's Day ("the first day of the week" [1 Cor 16.2]). **17:** *Shadow . . . substance,* despite its negative view of philosophy, Colossians shares with Hebrews and Philo the Platonic view that perceptible reality is a shadow of ultimate reality (see e.g., Heb 8.5n.; 10.1; Philo, *Leg. all.* 3.96ff.). **18:** *Self-abasement,* if it refers to ascetic practice, this is the only place in the NT where it does so; in 2.23 the word means a degree of humility with which our author is uncomfortable, an outcome of following the Jews' human traditions (cf. 3.12; Eph 4.2; Phil 2.3). *Worship of angels,* both Paul and the authors of the DSS believed that angels were present during the congregation's worship (1 Cor 11.10; 1QSa 2.9; see "Divine Beings," p. 544). *Visions,* glimpses of the heavenly realm (see 2 Cor 12.1–10). *Puffed up,* see 1 Cor 4.6,18,19, etc. **19:** *Head . . . body,* see 1.18n. **20:** *Died to the elemental spirits,* no longer under their authority (vv. 8–15). See 2.8n. *As if . . . world,* continues the idea that believers are under the Christ's rule, nonbelievers under the authority of heavenly powers that govern this world (cf. 1 Cor 15.12–28). **21:** *Handle . . . taste . . . touch,* the author mocks Jewish impurity laws as trivial. Paul had issues with the Torah but never viewed it as trivial. **22:** *Human commands and teachings,* another rare LXX reference (Isa 29.13), although a more proximate source for the quotation is Mk 7.7 || Mt. 15.9. Colossians does not record the other part of Jesus' legal ruling, that followers should observe only biblical laws, not human tradition. **23:** *Humility,* the same word translated "self-abasement" (see 2.18n.). *Self-indulgence* (Gk "plēsmonē"), a crux for translators, who have difficulty explaining how piety and humility fail to check self-indulgence. It is best to take the sentence as ironic, maintaining the mocking tone of the section.

3.1–4.6: Paraenesis (moral exhortation). NT letters, like other Greek letters, typically include moral exhortation, more or less tied to the letter's situation. The epistolary situation of Colossians is very thin, and the moralizing therefore not especially particular to Colossae. In the authentic Pauline epistles, the paraeneses (exhortations) always refer to the situation at hand.

3.1–4: Baptism confers new moral life. The paraenesis picks up the theme of 2.12–14, that baptism allows believers to start a new life free of the debt of sin. **1–3:** *Seated at the right hand,* possibly an echo of Ps 110.1, although this idea is already a NT motif, appearing twenty-five times (cf. Mk 12.36; 14.62; Acts 2.33–34; Rom 8.34; Eph 1.20; Heb 10.12). *Died,* see 2.20n. *Hidden,* a formulation, unique to the NT, whereby believers will be revealed at the fullness of time with the Christ.

desire, and greed (which is idolatry). [6] On account of these the wrath of God is coming on those who are disobedient.[a] [7] These are the ways you also once followed, when you were living that life.[b] [8] But now you must get rid of all such things—anger, wrath, malice, slander, and abusive[c] language from your mouth. [9] Do not lie to one another, seeing that you have stripped off the old self with its practices [10] and have clothed yourselves with the new self, which is being renewed in knowledge according to the image of its creator. [11] In that renewal[d] there is no longer Greek and Jew, circumcised and uncircumcised, barbarian, Scythian, slave and free; but Christ is all and in all!

[12] As God's chosen ones, holy and beloved, clothe yourselves with compassion, kindness, humility, meekness, and patience. [13] Bear with one another and, if anyone has a complaint against another, forgive each other; just as the Lord[e] has forgiven you, so you also must forgive. [14] Above all, clothe yourselves with love, which binds everything together in perfect harmony. [15] And let the peace of Christ rule in your hearts, to which indeed you were called in the one body. And be thankful. [16] Let the word of Christ[f] dwell in you richly; teach and admonish one another in all wisdom; and with gratitude in your hearts sing psalms,

a Other ancient authorities lack *on those who are disobedient* (Gk *the children of disobedience*)
b Or *living among such people*
c Or *filthy*
d Gk *its creator,* [11]*where*
e Other ancient authorities read *just as Christ*
f Other ancient authorities read *of God*, or *of the Lord*

3.5–11: The old life. 5: The author describes the pre-baptismal life of his audience in a vice-catalogue, a form of moral instruction common in the NT (Rom 1.29ff.; 1 Cor 5.10,11; 6.9ff.; Gal 5.19ff.; Eph 4.32; 1 Tim 1.9ff.; 2 Tim 3.2ff.; Titus 3.3; 1 Pet 2.1; (Mk 7.21ff. || Mt 15.19; Rev 21.8), but not in Q (the posited sayings source that presumably provided the words attributed to Jesus that are common to Mt and Lk but not found in Mk) or in the Johannine tradition (Jn and 1, 2, and 3 John). They are a feature of the moral instruction in 1QS 4.9ff. and Philo, *Spec. Laws* 1.281, as well as Stoic catalogues of virtues and vices (e.g., Chrysippus, *Stoicorum Veterum Fragmenta* 3.397). *Fornication*, prohibited sexual intercourse. *Idolatry*, connected to sexual vices (e.g., 1 Cor 10.7–8 and in Tanakh, e.g., Hos 1.2), but Col and Eph 5.5 emphatically connect it with greed. **6:** *Wrath*, a particular formulation describing God's final judgment (see Rom 1.18; 5.9; etc., and 1 Thess 1.10; 2.16; 5.9). The idea of a "day of wrath" or a "day of YHWH" is at least as old as the pre-exilic Hebrew prophets (cf. Am 5.18–20). **8:** *Anger . . . abusive language*, there is no hint that the particular vices mentioned relate to the situation in Colossae. **9–10:** *Stripped off . . . clothed*, this metaphor may indicate a baptismal context, or may remind the audience of their baptism, or may, given its frequency in this letter, be a metaphor for the new life brought by the gospel. Paul uses the verb "enduo," "dress," in a baptismal context (Gal 3.27), but also of putting on armor (Rom 13.12,14) and to describe believers dressing themselves in their new resurrection bodies (1 Cor 15.53ff.). *Old self . . . new self . . . image of its creator*, the power of the gospel or of baptism, causes believers to become new creations; an allusion to Gen 1.26. **11:** *Greek and Jew, circumcised and uncircumcised*, for this letter, these distinctions are different. Apparently (cf. 2.11n.) some (Gentile) members of the Colossian church want to become circumcised or have already become so. *Barbarian*, a person who speaks no Greek. *Scythian*, in Greek literature, the epitome of an uncivilized person; it is difficult to see the antithesis that the author intends. Taking "Scythian" as synonymous with "slave" only compounds the difficulty. The antitheses echo Gal 3.28 and 1 Cor 7.19, but, as they serve here to introduce the household codes (3.18–24), they lack the social leveling that Paul intends.

3.12–17: Living the new life. 12: *Chosen ones* (Gk "eklektoi"), that Israel is God's chosen people (Heb "baḥir"), a common expression in Deutero-Isaiah and related texts (e.g., Isa 45.4), becomes even more common as a label for believers in the NT (see Rom 8.33; Mk 13.20,22; Lk 18.7; 2 Tim 2.10; Titus 1.1; Rev 17.14). The Qumran sectarians saw themselves as the chosen of the chosen (cf. CD 4.3). The author of this letter reminds readers that chosenness confers obligations, an idea that the later rabbis would agree with. *Compassion . . . patience*, a catalogue of virtues to balance the vice catalogue of 3.8. As the Colossians were to strip off the vices, they are to dress themselves in virtues. The virtues are also generic. **13:** *Forgive*, perhaps an echo of Mt 6.12,14–15, or of 1 Cor 6.1–8. Cf. Eph 4.32. **14–15:** *Love* (Gk "agapē"), the highest virtue in which the congregants should dress. See 2.2n.; 1 Cor 13. *Body*, see 1.18n. **16:** *Word of Christ*, unique to Col, where it seems to be equivalent to "good news

hymns, and spiritual songs to God.[a] [17] And whatever you do, in word or deed, do everything in the name of the Lord Jesus, giving thanks to God the Father through him.

[18] Wives, be subject to your husbands, as is fitting in the Lord. [19] Husbands, love your wives and never treat them harshly.

[20] Children, obey your parents in everything, for this is your acceptable duty in the Lord. [21] Fathers, do not provoke your children, or they may lose heart. [22] Slaves, obey your earthly masters[b] in everything, not only while being watched and in order to please them, but wholeheartedly, fearing the Lord.[b] [23] Whatever your task, put yourselves into it, as done for the Lord and not for your masters,[c] [24] since you know that from the Lord you will receive the inheritance as your reward; you serve[d] the Lord Christ. [25] For the wrongdoer will be paid back for whatever wrong has been done, and there is no partiality. **4** [1] Masters, treat your slaves justly and fairly, for you know that you also have a Master in heaven.

[2] Devote yourselves to prayer, keeping alert in it with thanksgiving. [3] At the same time pray for us as well that God will open to us a door for the word, that we may declare the mystery of Christ, for which I am in prison, [4] so that I may reveal it clearly, as I should.

[5] Conduct yourselves wisely toward outsiders, making the most of the time.[e] [6] Let your speech always be gracious, seasoned with salt, so that you may know how you ought to answer everyone.

[7] Tychicus will tell you all the news about me; he is a beloved brother, a faithful minister, and a fellow servant[f] in the Lord. [8] I have sent him to you for this very purpose, so that you may know how we are[g] and that he may encourage your hearts; [9] he is coming with Onesimus, the faithful and beloved brother, who is one of you. They will tell you about everything here.

[10] Aristarchus my fellow prisoner greets you, as does Mark the cousin of Barnabas,

[a] Other ancient authorities read *to the Lord*
[b] In Greek the same word is used for *master* and *Lord*
[c] Gk *not for men*
[d] Or *you are slaves of*, or *be slaves of*
[e] Or *opportunity*
[f] Gk *slave*
[g] Other authorities read *that I may know how you are*

of the Christ." **17:** *God the Father,* the Tanakh rarely addresses God as father, preferring "God of our ancestors ["Fathers"]," although see Isa 63.16; Ps 89.26. The usage is known, but not common, at Qumran (see 4Q460, "'avi va'doni," "my father and my lord" [91.6]).

3.18–4.1: Household codes. The "Haustafeln" (see Introduction) governing the patriarchal family appear also in Eph 5.22–6.9 and 1 Pet 2.18–3.7. *Husbands . . . fathers . . . masters* are exhorted to behavior that undercuts the social leveling implied by the new hegemony of the Christ (cf. 3.11n.). **18–19:** *Be subject* (Gk "hypotasso"), accept the husband's authority; see 1 Cor 14.34 ("women . . . should be subordinate"), for which strong manuscript indications now show most probably to be an interpolation. Colossians names at least one woman, Nympha (see 4.15n.), with substantial authority, whether or not she was submissive to her husband. **20–21:** See Eph 6.1–4 and annotations. **3.22–4.1:** See Eph 6.5–9. For Paul, as for the author of Colossians, slave owners and slaves are both subject to the Christ, but neither author condemns the institution of slavery (cf. 3.11; see also Philem).

4.2–6: Final admonitions. 3: *Door for the word,* Paul uses this expression (1 Cor 16.9; 2 Cor 2.12) for an opportunity to travel to proclaim the gospel. *Mystery,* see 1.26–27n.; here a synonym for "word of the Christ," 3.16. *Prison,* see 4.10. **5:** *Making the most* (Gk "exagorazomenoi"), a word from the realm of commerce ("agora," "forum, marketplace") meaning "redeem" or "buy back." The phrase occurs only in the Deutero-Paulines (here and Eph 5.16), whose audiences have been given an opportunity (see translators' note *e*); they can improve their lot in the final judgment by behaving appropriately now. **6:** *Seasoned with salt,* to make speech more interesting or witty (as in Plutarch, *On Talkativeness* 514ff., who is not entirely enamored of the quality).

4.7–18: Closing greetings. The author mentions names from Paul's authentic letters, especially Philem, and Acts. **7:** *Tychicus,* see Eph 6.21; 2 Tim 4.12; Titus 3.12; Acts 20.4, which might have suggested him to the authors of Eph and Col. *Fellow servant,* lit., "fellow-slave"; see 1.7n. **9:** *Onesimus,* main character in Philem. **10:** *Aristarchus,* mentioned in Acts 19.29; 20.4; 27.2, and Philem 24. *Fellow prisoner,* Paul uses the term twice, in

concerning whom you have received instructions—if he comes to you, welcome him. [11] And Jesus who is called Justus greets you. These are the only ones of the circumcision among my co-workers for the kingdom of God, and they have been a comfort to me. [12] Epaphras, who is one of you, a servant[a] of Christ Jesus, greets you. He is always wrestling in his prayers on your behalf, so that you may stand mature and fully assured in everything that God wills. [13] For I testify for him that he has worked hard for you and for those in Laodicea and in Hierapolis. [14] Luke, the beloved physician, and Demas greet you. [15] Give my greetings to the brothers and sisters[b] in Laodicea, and to Nympha and the church in her house. [16] And when this letter has been read among you, have it read also in the church of the Laodiceans; and see that you read also the letter from Laodicea. [17] And say to Archippus, "See that you complete the task that you have received in the Lord."

[18] I, Paul, write this greeting with my own hand. Remember my chains. Grace be with you.[c]

[a] Gk *slave*
[b] Gk *brothers*
[c] Other ancient authorities add *Amen*

Philem 23 to describe Epaphras and Rom 16.7 to describe Andronicus and Junia, who may have been imprisoned with him. *Mark*, Philem 24; see also Acts 12.12,25; perhaps 13.13; 15.37–39; possibly 1 Pet 5.13. *Cousin*, Acts closely associates Mark with Barnabas; the author of Colossians concludes that they were cousins. Christian tradition, via Papias of Hierapolis (second century), makes him Peter's disciple and author of the second Gospel. *Barnabas*, Paul's mentor (see Acts 9.27; 11.22,30; 14.12); both Acts 15.36ff. and Gal 2.13 suggest he and Paul parted ways on poor terms; Colossians, with its theme of reconciliation, presents them in fellowship. **11:** *Jesus . . . Justus*, double names (one Heb, one Gk or Lat) elsewhere in the NT: Saul ("Sha'ul") and Paul (Acts 13.9); John ("Ioannēn/Yoḥanan") and Mark ("Marcus") (Acts 12.12). *The circumcision*, Jewish members of the Jesus movement. Colossians distinguishes Jew from Greek, and circumcision from foreskin (cf. 2.11n.). **12:** *Epaphras*, see 1.7n. In Philem 23, Epaphras is Paul's "fellow prisoner"; here that distinction goes to Aristarchus. *Servant* (Gk "doulos"), slave. *Mature*, see 1.28n. **13:** *Laodicea . . . Hierapolis*, cities near Colossae. **14:** *Luke*, 2 Tim 4.11; Philem 24. This verse is the source for identifying him as a doctor. *Demas*, Philem 24; 2 Tim 4.10. **15:** *Nympha*, the owner of the house church, the dwelling where worship services were conducted for the local congregants (see Rom 16.5; 1 Cor 16.9). *Nympha*, "bride," sounds generic, but see *CIJ* 651–52, noting two Jewish women in Sicily in the fourth–fifth century CE with the name. **16:** *Letter from Laodicea*, not known; identifying it with the Epistle to the Ephesians, whose source and destination are even more unclear than Colossians, is as good a supposition as any. **17:** *Archippus*, in Philem 2, Paul called Archippus "fellow soldier." Colossians makes him the recipient of a private message, "See that you complete the task. . . ." **18:** As ancient letters were normally dictated to a scribe (see Rom 16.22), the author adds his handwritten signature (cf. 1 Cor 16.21; Gal 6.11; 2 Thess 3.17–18). *Chains*, or "imprisonment," cf. Phil 1.7,13ff. and 4.3n.,10n.

THE FIRST LETTER OF PAUL TO THE THESSALONIANS

AUTHORSHIP, DATE

Paul's first letter to the Thessalonians, written ca. 50 CE, is the earliest of Paul's extant writings and, therefore the New Testament's oldest book. During Paul's second missionary journey (see map, p. 228), he traveled to Macedonia and Greece, where he founded a Gentile community in Thessalonica, the capital of the Roman province of Macedonia. Paul writes this letter several months after leaving Thessalonica. Although he mentions his fellow missionaries, Silvanus and Timothy, Paul likely wrote the letter himself (with the possible exception of 2.12–16). Paul was practiced in the conventions of Greco-Roman letter writing, which he adapted to fit his purposes; the letter demonstrates a well-developed epistolary style. It follows standard patterns of letter-writing, opening with the names of the sender and recipients and including a greeting in the form of a blessing (1.1). It closes with another greeting and final blessing (5.25–28). It also shows that Paul has been reflecting on the theology of his message in his efforts to answer the questions from the Thessalonian community.

Two main sources help determine the letter's date and circumstances. One is the letter's first major section (1.2–3.13), in which Paul comments on his experience during the Macedonian mission (cf. Phil 4.16). The second, Acts 17.1–10, recounts Paul's activity in Thessalonica. Acts and 1 Thessalonians disagree on several key points, including the length of Paul's stay in Thessalonica and his outreach to the Jewish community, which Acts describes as a regular part of Paul's missionary strategy but which the letter does not mention. This and other discrepancies between Paul's writing and Acts—and the presumption that Paul writing about his own actions is more likely to be accurate than the author of Acts reporting about him—raise questions about the historical reliability of Acts. Both Acts and 1 Thessalonians, however, report Paul's difficulties during his mission in Macedonia as well as his desire to support the churches he founded.

INTERPRETATION

The epistle first describes Paul's general concern, perhaps exacerbated by his trials (2.18; 3.4,7), about how the church has fared since he left Thessalonica. After the formal address, Paul devotes three chapters to reviewing his relationship with the Thessalonians. He thanks God and praises the Thessalonians for their faithfulness. He reminds them of their time together and expresses how he had worried about them. Driven by lack of information and unable to go himself, he sends Timothy to the new church. Paul mentions Athens in 3.1, perhaps indicating that he wrote from there. However, it is more likely that he was in Athens when he dispatched Timothy, and then traveled to Corinth, where Timothy rejoined him. Timothy returns with a positive report (3.6–7), and Paul immediately writes this letter, primarily to encourage the Thessalonians to remain steadfast in their faith as they await the parousia (the "second coming" or return of Jesus to judge and rule) and, secondarily, to clarify and reinforce the matters of belief and conduct that Timothy has noted.

Paul's relief on hearing good news from Timothy sets the stage for chs 4–5, in which Paul looks to the future and instructs the Thessalonians regarding the behavior that will enable believers to be saved when Jesus returns. Paul encourages the Thessalonians to continue to live according to God's demands. He focuses on sexual morality, sobriety, and the maintenance of good relations both within the Thessalonian community and with other churches. He also urges them to live a simple and unobtrusive life.

Paul then turns to a number of questions about the parousia. Members of the church had died before Jesus' return: if they were dead, how could they experience salvation? Paul reassures the Thessalonians that believers who had died would be resurrected on the "day of the Lord"—the new age when the kingdom of God would be established—to participate in the promised salvation. Paul then warns readers to avoid speculation about the date of the second coming, to live according to God's will, and to trust that they will be saved because of their faith. The letter closes with a prayer for the salvation of the Thessalonians. A few months later, Paul writes a second letter to the Thessalonians.

David Fox Sandmel

1 Paul, Silvanus, and Timothy,
To the church of the Thessalonians in God the Father and the Lord Jesus Christ:
Grace to you and peace.

[2] We always give thanks to God for all of you and mention you in our prayers, constantly [3] remembering before our God and Father your work of faith and labor of love and steadfastness of hope in our Lord Jesus Christ. [4] For we know, brothers and sisters[a] beloved by God, that he has chosen you, [5] because our message of the gospel came to you not in word only, but also in power and in the Holy Spirit and with full conviction; just as you know what kind of persons we proved to be among you for your sake. [6] And you became imitators of us and of the Lord, for in spite of persecution you received the word with joy inspired by the Holy Spirit, [7] so that you became an example to all the believers in Macedonia and in Achaia. [8] For the word of the Lord has sounded forth from you not only in Macedonia and Achaia, but in every place your faith in God has become known, so that we have no need to speak about it. [9] For the people of those regions[b] report about us what kind of welcome we had among you, and how you turned to God from idols, to serve a living and true God, [10] and to wait for his Son from heaven, whom he raised from the dead—Jesus, who rescues us from the wrath that is coming.

2 You yourselves know, brothers and sisters,[a] that our coming to you was not in vain, [2] but though we had already suffered and been shamefully mistreated at Philippi, as you know, we had courage in our God to declare to you the gospel of God in spite of great opposition. [3] For our appeal does not spring from deceit or impure motives or trickery, [4] but just as we have been approved by God to be entrusted with the message of the gospel, even so we speak, not to please mortals, but to please God who tests our hearts. [5] As you know and as God is our witness, we never came with words of flattery or with a pretext for greed; [6] nor did we seek praise from mortals, whether from you or from others, [7] though we might have made demands as apostles of Christ. But we were gentle[c] among you, like a nurse tenderly caring for her own children. [8] So deeply do we care for you that we are determined to share with you not only the gospel of God but also our own selves, because you have become very dear to us.

[a] Gk *brothers*
[b] Gk *For they*
[c] Other ancient authorities read *infants*

1.1: Address and salutation. Unlike most of his letters, Paul does not identify himself as an apostle. In antiquity *church* ("ekklēsia"), like synagogue ("synagōgē"), denoted primarily a community or assembly of people, not a building.

1.2–2.16: Paul gives thanks for the Thessalonians' faith.

1.2–10: Opening thanksgiving. Paul uses several strategies for encouraging the Thessalonians, all of which undergird the instruction in chs 4–5. He recalls their time together and his dedication to them. He praises them for their faith and acknowledges their present difficulties. **3:** *Faith . . . love . . . hope*, a standard Pauline linkage of these three terms; see, e.g., 1 Cor 13. **4:** *Chosen*, or "picked out"; perhaps the same concept that indicates the choice of Israel (Deut 7.6). **5:** *Holy Spirit*, see also 4.8. The later development of ideas about the spirit of God (see Rom 15.19; cf. Jn 14–16) may go beyond Paul's statement here. **6:** *Persecution* (Gk "thlipsis"), used in LXX to describe the suffering of God's people, and elsewhere in the NT (Mt 24.9,21,29; Rev 1.9) in an eschatological context. In antiquity, as today, new religions provoked suspicion if not violence from the larger community; family and friends often rejected converts. **7:** *Macedonia*, the northern province of the Greek peninsula, where Thessalonica was located. *Achaia*, the southern province of Greece, location of Corinth and Athens. **9:** *From idols*, the converts were Gentiles. **10:** *Wrath that is coming*, Paul believed he was living during that period of upheaval preceding the end of days, an idea found in the prophets and developed in Second Temple Judaism and early Christianity (e.g., Ezek 38.18–23; 1QM; Rev 16.12–16). The same word as used above for "persecution" (Gk "thlipsis") is used in Rev 7.14 (translated "ordeal" in NRSV) for the final "tribulation" of the Christian community.

2.1–12: Paul recalls his time with the Thessalonians. 2: Cf. Phil 1.29–30; Acts 16.19ff. **7:** *Apostles*, those "sent out," ambassadors with a message. *Nurse*, i.e., a wet nurse, one who feeds infants from her breast, an unusual image of pastoral care (but see Num 11.12). **8:** *Our own selves*, Paul intends to visit the Thessalonians, not merely to

DIATRIBE AGAINST THE JEWS

This passage (2.14–16) reflects Paul's perspective on the tension between Jews who did not accept Jesus as messiah and the early followers of Jesus, whether Jews or Gentiles. These verses present a succinct summary of classical Christian anti-Judaism: the Jews killed Jesus, persecuted his followers, and threw them out of the synagogues; they are xenophobic and sinners, and God has rejected and punished them. The harshness of these words raises questions about Paul's attitude toward his fellow Jews.

Because the Greek word for Jews, "Ioudaioi," means both "Jews" and "Judeans," Paul's wrath may be directed at this geographically limited group. (See essay, "Ioudaios," p. 524.) Even were this Paul's intention, neither the Thessalonian Gentile Christians nor later readers would grasp this distinction.

Some scholars argue that these verses are an interpolation: they are not consistent with Paul's comments about Jews in Romans 9–11 nor are they integral to the letter; were they excised, the narrative flow would not be affected. However, no ancient manuscript excludes these verses, and they fit logically and stylistically into the epistle's context. Paul elsewhere uses strong language about his opponents consistent with his apocalyptic worldview of the struggle between good and evil (e.g., Gal 5.2–26; 2 Thess 1.5–12). Thus, Pauline authorship of these verses should be presumed.

This passage has implications for the emergence of anti-Judaism in the Christian tradition. If Paul wrote these words, then he is inextricably associated with the promulgation of anti-Judaism, regardless of his intentions. The debate over Pauline authorship does not alter the role these verses have played in forming Christian attitudes towards Jews.

[9] You remember our labor and toil, brothers and sisters;[a] we worked night and day, so that we might not burden any of you while we proclaimed to you the gospel of God. [10] You are witnesses, and God also, how pure, upright, and blameless our conduct was toward you believers. [11] As you know, we dealt with each one of you like a father with his children, [12] urging and encouraging you and pleading that you lead a life worthy of God, who calls you into his own kingdom and glory.

[13] We also constantly give thanks to God for this, that when you received the word of God that you heard from us, you accepted it not as a human word but as what it really is, God's word, which is also at work in you believers. [14] For you, brothers and sisters,[a] became imitators of the churches of God in Christ Jesus that are in Judea, for you suffered the same things from your own compatriots as they did from the Jews, [15] who killed both the Lord Jesus and the prophets,[b] and drove us out; they displease God and oppose everyone [16] by hindering us from speaking to the Gentiles so that they may be saved. Thus they have constantly been filling up the measure of their sins; but God's wrath has overtaken them at last.[c]

[17] As for us, brothers and sisters,[a] when, for a short time, we were made orphans by being separated from you—in person, not in heart—we longed with great eagerness to see you face to face. [18] For we wanted to come to

[a] Gk *brothers*
[b] Other ancient authorities read *their own prophets*
[c] Or *completely* or *forever*

send messages. **9:** Paul reminds the Thessalonians that he supported himself by manual *labor*, a lowly occupation (he was a tent-maker; see Acts 18.3), to demonstrate his humility and serve as an example of filial love. See 4.9–12.

2.13–16: The churches in Judea. 15: *Killed . . . prophets*, see Lk 11.47; 13.34; Acts 7.52. The Hebrew Bible does narrate the killing of a prophet (Uriah son of Shemaiah, Jer 26.20–23), but it is more usual for prophets to be persecuted short of death (e.g., Jer 20.1–2). Postbiblical literature understands that many prophets were persecuted to death (see Heb 11.36-38n.).

2.17–3.10: Paul's concern for the Thessalonians.

2.17–20: Paul's anguish over being separated from the Thessalonians. 18: Paul does not indicate precisely how *Satan* hindered him; however, he mentions Satan often in connection with his time in Corinth (e.g., 1 Cor 5.5; 7.5; 10.10; 2 Cor 2.11; 4.4; 6.15; 12.7). In 3.5 he again refers to Satan, calling him the "tempter," a role he plays in rabbinic literature as well; however, neither Paul nor the rabbis portray Satan as the embodiment of evil. Paul interpreted his difficulties during his mission in terms of the eschatological struggle between good and evil

you—certainly I, Paul, wanted to again and again—but Satan blocked our way. [19] For what is our hope or joy or crown of boasting before our Lord Jesus at his coming? Is it not you? [20] Yes, you are our glory and joy!

3 Therefore when we could bear it no longer, we decided to be left alone in Athens; [2] and we sent Timothy, our brother and co-worker for God in proclaiming[a] the gospel of Christ, to strengthen and encourage you for the sake of your faith, [3] so that no one would be shaken by these persecutions. Indeed, you yourselves know that this is what we are destined for. [4] In fact, when we were with you, we told you beforehand that we were to suffer persecution; so it turned out, as you know. [5] For this reason, when I could bear it no longer, I sent to find out about your faith; I was afraid that somehow the tempter had tempted you and that our labor had been in vain.

[6] But Timothy has just now come to us from you, and has brought us the good news of your faith and love. He has told us also that you always remember us kindly and long to see us—just as we long to see you. [7] For this reason, brothers and sisters,[b] during all our distress and persecution we have been encouraged about you through your faith. [8] For we now live, if you continue to stand firm in the Lord. [9] How can we thank God enough for you in return for all the joy that we feel before our God because of you? [10] Night and day we pray most earnestly that we may see you face to face and restore whatever is lacking in your faith.

[11] Now may our God and Father himself and our Lord Jesus direct our way to you. [12] And may the Lord make you increase and abound in love for one another and for all, just as we abound in love for you. [13] And may he so strengthen your hearts in holiness that you may be blameless before our God and Father at the coming of our Lord Jesus with all his saints.

4 Finally, brothers and sisters,[b] we ask and urge you in the Lord Jesus that, as you learned from us how you ought to live and to please God (as, in fact, you are doing), you should do so more and more. [2] For you know what instructions we gave you through the Lord Jesus. [3] For this is the will of God, your sanctification: that you abstain from fornication; [4] that each one of you know how to control your own body[c] in holiness and honor, [5] not with lustful passion, like the

a Gk lacks *proclaiming*

b Gk *brothers*

c Or *how to take a wife for himself*

(cf. 5.5). Paul does not refer to a physical encounter with Satan, but means rather a struggle characteristic of a world during the period immediately before the new age begins.

3.1–5: Timothy's mission to the Thessalonians. 1: *Athens*, see Acts 17.15–18.1. **4:** Paul again invokes persecution; *suffer persecution* (Gk "thlibesthai") could be translated "undergo tribulation." See 1.10n. **5:** *Tempter . . . tempted*, the Gk word means "test, put to the proof." Paul's fear was that the Thessalonians had failed to withstand the test, whatever it was.

3.6–10: Paul expresses his relief and elation. On hearing Timothy's positive report, he reiterates his desire to visit (v. 6) to help the Thessalonians strengthen their faith (v. 10). **10:** Likely Timothy brought a letter to Paul from the Thessalonians containing questions that arose in the community; such questions may indicate what Paul understands to be *lacking in your faith*. Paul now turns from the past to the future, setting the stage for the exhortation in chs 4–5.

3.11–13: Prayer concluding first part of the letter. The themes in the following chs—sanctification (4.3–8), love (4.9–12), and the return of the Messiah (4.15–5.11)—are first mentioned in this prayer. *Coming . . . saints*, believers who have already died (see 4.14).

4.1–5.22: Exhortation: Paul instructs the community on doctrine and behavior as it awaits Jesus' return.

4.1–2: Paul's introduction to the letter's exhortatory section. Paul presupposes what he has previously taught. **1:** *Live*, lit., "walk," Heb "halakh," related to "halakhah," an echo of a Hebrew Bible expression (e.g., Ps 1.1, "Happy the one who has not walked ["halakh"] in the counsel of the wicked").

4.3–8: Paul stresses the importance of sexual morality. 3–4: *Sanctification*, or "holiness" (same word in vv. 4,7); believers are called to be "set apart" (Heb "qadosh") by their conduct (Lev 19.2). *Abstain . . . control your own body*, Paul encourages marriage (the expression is lit., "control your own vessel," which could mean either the sexual organ specifically or one's spouse; see translators' note *c*) and warns against adultery. **5:** *Lustful passion . . . Gentiles*,

Gentiles who do not know God; [6] that no one wrong or exploit a brother or sister[a] in this matter, because the Lord is an avenger in all these things, just as we have already told you beforehand and solemnly warned you. [7] For God did not call us to impurity but in holiness. [8] Therefore whoever rejects this rejects not human authority but God, who also gives his Holy Spirit to you.

[9] Now concerning love of the brothers and sisters,[b] you do not need to have anyone write to you, for you yourselves have been taught by God to love one another; [10] and indeed you do love all the brothers and sisters[b] throughout Macedonia. But we urge you, beloved,[b] to do so more and more, [11] to aspire to live quietly, to mind your own affairs, and to work with your hands, as we directed you, [12] so that you may behave properly toward outsiders and be dependent on no one.

[13] But we do not want you to be uninformed, brothers and sisters,[b] about those who have died,[c] so that you may not grieve as others do who have no hope. [14] For since we believe that Jesus died and rose again, even so, through Jesus, God will bring with him those who have died.[c] [15] For this we declare to you by the word of the Lord, that we who are alive, who are left until the coming of the Lord, will by no means precede those who have died.[c] [16] For the Lord himself, with a cry of command, with the archangel's call and with the sound of God's trumpet, will descend from heaven, and the dead in Christ will rise first. [17] Then we who are alive, who are left, will be caught up in the clouds together with them to meet the Lord in the air; and so we will be with the Lord forever. [18] Therefore encourage one another with these words.

5 Now concerning the times and the seasons, brothers and sisters,[b] you do not need to have anything written to you. [2] For you yourselves know very well that the day of the Lord will come like a thief in the night. [3] When they say, "There is peace and security," then sudden destruction will come upon them, as labor pains come upon a pregnant woman, and there will be no escape! [4] But you, beloved,[b] are not in darkness, for that day to surprise you like a thief; [5] for you are all children of light and children of the day;

a Gk *brother*
b Gk *brothers*
c Gk *fallen asleep*

Roman sexual licentiousness was notorious (see Rom 1.28–32; Gal 5.19–21; 1 Tim 1.9–10). The comment applies to nonbelievers, though it may also serve to remind the Thessalonians what they have left behind (see 1 Cor 6.9–11). **8:** *Holy Spirit*, see 1.4n.

4.9–12: Paul commends self-sufficiency. See 2.8–9. Self-sufficiency is a form of filial love. **11:** *Aspire to live quietly* (Gk "philotimesthai hēsychazein," lit., "be emulous [or ambitious] to rest, to live in quiet"), Paul's phrasing may be meant to distinguish the community from an Epicurean assembly. Some Epicureans withdrew from society in pursuing their ideal of "ataraxia," "freedom from disturbance." Paul did not want to encourage withdrawal from society, and he wished to distinguish a quiet life of responsible work from the effort to avoid the disturbances of life entirely; nor did he want the church confused with the Epicureans, who were generally disparaged. *Work with your hands*, in emulation of Paul (2.9).

4.13–18: Questions about the salvation of those believers who have died and about the coming of the Lord. The Thessalonians had apparently sent Paul questions about the fate of those among them who had died before the return ("parousia") of the messiah in glory. **15:** *The word of the Lord*, Paul may be referring to a prophecy that he understood as coming from God; the Gospels record no such teaching. These verses are the primary source (see also Mt 24.29–31) of the "Rapture," part of a method of scriptural interpretation that arose in the late nineteenth and early twentieth centuries, and that spells out a detailed "end times" scenario. The Rapture, associated with the Tribulation (see 1.10n.; 3.4n.), suggests that Jesus' followers who have died will be resurrected and, along with living Christians, will literally ascend to heaven. (The Rapture has become a significant component of some contemporary conservative Protestant eschatology.) Paul, however, is less concerned to provide details about the events of the messiah's return; he is rather trying to reassure those Thessalonians who are concerned about the ultimate fate of their fellow-believers.

5.1–11: The timing of the Lord's return. Paul instructs the Thessalonians how to prepare for the *day of the Lord*, a phrase appearing often in the Prophets (e.g., Isa 2.12–17; Joel 2.1; Am 5.18,20; Zeph 1.7), who use it to

we are not of the night or of darkness. [6] So then let us not fall asleep as others do, but let us keep awake and be sober; [7] for those who sleep sleep at night, and those who are drunk get drunk at night. [8] But since we belong to the day, let us be sober, and put on the breastplate of faith and love, and for a helmet the hope of salvation. [9] For God has destined us not for wrath but for obtaining salvation through our Lord Jesus Christ, [10] who died for us, so that whether we are awake or asleep we may live with him. [11] Therefore encourage one another and build up each other, as indeed you are doing.

[12] But we appeal to you, brothers and sisters,[a] to respect those who labor among you, and have charge of you in the Lord and admonish you; [13] esteem them very highly in love because of their work. Be at peace among yourselves. [14] And we urge you, beloved,[a] to admonish the idlers, encourage the faint-hearted, help the weak, be patient with all of them. [15] See that none of you repays evil for evil, but always seek to do good to one another and to all. [16] Rejoice always, [17] pray without ceasing, [18] give thanks in all circumstances; for this is the will of God in Christ Jesus for you. [19] Do not quench the Spirit. [20] Do not despise the words of prophets,[b] [21] but test everything; hold fast to what is good; [22] abstain from every form of evil.

[23] May the God of peace himself sanctify you entirely; and may your spirit and soul and body be kept sound[c] and blameless at the coming of our Lord Jesus Christ. [24] The one who calls you is faithful, and he will do this.

[25] Beloved,[d] pray for us.

[26] Greet all the brothers and sisters[a] with a holy kiss. [27] I solemnly command you by the Lord that this letter be read to all of them.[e]

[28] The grace of our Lord Jesus Christ be with you.[f]

a Gk *brothers*
b Gk *despise prophecies*
c Or *complete*
d Gk *Brothers*
e Gk *to all the brothers*
f Other ancient authorities add *Amen*

describe divine action including: God's retribution against foreign nations that oppressed Israel; God's punishment of Israel, Judah, or the Jewish people, and vindication of the oppressed; God's reestablishment of Israel, Judah or the Jewish people under the rule and justice of God. Some texts specifically mention a messiah or Davidic king (e.g. Jer 23.5–6; Am 9.11) while others include the redemption of Gentile nations or all creation (e.g. Isa 2.2–4; Mic 4.1–3). New Testament writers use it, or variations of it (e.g., 1 Cor 1.8; 5.5; 2 Tim 1.18; Heb 9.28; 10.5), to refer to Jesus' return. **1:** *Times and the seasons*, the end of days (see Dan 2.21). **2–5:** *Thief*, see Lk 12.39–40. *Labor pains . . . pregnant woman*, see Isa 42.14; 66.7; Rom 8.22. *Children of light*, see Lk 16.8; Jn 12.36; Eph 5.8; cf. 1 Jn 2.8–11. See also Jn 1.4–5,7–9; 3.19–21; 8.12; 12.46. Apocalyptic writers describe the cosmic battle between good and evil in terms of light and dark. This imagery appears in the Hebrew Bible (e.g., light is associated with Torah [Isa 2.5], darkness with evil [Prov 2.13]; God is pictured as light [Ps 104.2]). In the DSS, humankind is divided into the "sons of light" and the "sons of darkness" (see esp. 1QM, which depicts the final battle between "the sons of light and the sons of darkness," and 1QS). **6–8:** *Awake . . . breastplate . . . helmet*, see Rom 13.11–13; Eph 6.13–17.

5.12–15: Behavior within the community. 14: *Idlers*, lit., "disorderly ones" (Gk "ataktos").

5.16–22: Closing exhortations and warnings. 19–21: Paul warns the community not to *quench* words of prophecy, but nonetheless to *test* for false prophets. Prophecy here means words spoken, usually during worship, as from the Lord to the community by inspired members of the assembly.

5.23–28: Conclusion and final benediction. 26: *Holy kiss*, see also Rom 16.16; 1 Cor 16.20; 2 Cor 16.12. It was a chaste expression of the familial love ("agapē") that characterized nascent Christian communities. It may have been part of early liturgy, or Paul was encouraging Christians to greet each other in this manner. **27:** *Command . . . that this letter be read to all*, the concluding section (beginning perhaps with v. 15) may have been written to be read to the assembly during worship. **28:** A standard close to Paul's letters; see Rom 16.20; 1 Cor 16.23. *Grace*, (Gk "charis"), favor bestowed; here *Jesus Christ* is seen as the bestower, a god-like action.

THE SECOND LETTER OF PAUL TO THE THESSALONIANS

NAME AND CANONICAL STATUS

The book of 2 Thessalonians appears to be a letter by Paul (1.1; 3.7) to an all-Gentile church in the Greek city of Thessalonica.

AUTHORSHIP, DATE

As early as the second century CE, Christians accepted Paul's authorship of the letter. Some modern scholars agree. Accepting 1 Thessalonians as authentic, they claim that 2 Thessalonians was written to correct misunderstandings in the first letter (2.2). They note references to an earlier work (2.15; 3.17), and parallels between the letters in language, structure, and subjects addressed, especially eschatology. However, many modern scholars, perhaps most, doubt Pauline authorship; accepting 1 Thessalonians as authentic, they note differences in eschatological scenarios. They contrast the imminence and unpredictability of the end in 1 Thessalonians with the futuristic, drawn-out scenario of 2 Thessalonians. Other indications of non-Pauline authorship include the harsher tone of the second letter (3.4–12; cf. 1 Thess 1–3) and self-conscious insistence on Pauline authorship (3.17). The appeal to Paul's authority (3.4–12) and demand for faithfulness to earlier tradition (2.15; 3.6) may also fit a post-Pauline period.

With no certainty about authorship and little specific information on setting (e.g., the description of persecution in 1.4 is vague), date and context are unknown. If Pauline, the letter was probably written shortly after 1 Thessalonians, in the early 50s. If inauthentic, a late first-century date seems likely. A later author may have crafted a letter appealing to Paul's authority to squelch fervor about the end of days.

Even though the context is murky, the problems raised in the letter are clear: persecution, disagreements about the end-times, and refusal to work. The author alternately consoles and reproves. He exhorts his congregation to accept his interpretations and avoid false teachings (2.3,10; 3.6). Facing internal divisions, he insists that they adhere to his traditions. Against those preaching that the end is imminent, he offers an alternative scenario. A series of steps must occur, including a painful period of increasing wickedness (2.3–12). Against those "living in idleness," perhaps believing the end has arrived, he insists that they work (3.11).

The language is dualistic, dividing insiders from outsiders (including dissenting followers of Jesus). The author criticizes those without faith or understanding (3.2,14) and welcomes God's destruction of opponents (1.8–9). The counterpart to denunciation is insistence that God protects believers. In a parallel to Jewish ideas of God's election of Israel (e.g., Deut 7.6), he insists on believers' chosenness (1.11; 2.13–14). Though they suffer now, God will soon send them relief (1.7).

HISTORICAL CONTEXT, LITERARY HISTORY

Although the letter generally received less attention from later Christians, the section on eschatology did interest some commentators. Its vagueness led to speculation, for example, about who or what held back the "lawless one"; some even said the Roman Empire, by maintaining social order, prevented his arrival (Tertullian, *Apol.* 32; J. Chrys., *Hom. 2 Thess.* 4). Others reapplied the letter to contemporary contexts: Gnostics found evidence of a second god in 2.4 (Irenaeus, *Adv. Haer.* 3.6.5), and Reformation-era polemicists denounced both Luther and the pope as the "lawless one." It was a resource for church leaders, because its portrait of a confident, even authoritarian Paul offered a model of a strong bishop (Caesarius of Arles, Sermon 232). Also, the demand for faithfulness to tradition buttressed later opponents of views deemed novel or heretical.

The author addresses Gentiles. He says nothing about Jews or Judaism and quotes no biblical verses. However, he is deeply indebted to Jewish thought, and allusions to biblical and postbiblical texts abound. The author draws ideas from scenarios about divine deliverance for oppressed and suffering Jews (e.g., Dan 7–12; *1,2 En.*; *4 Ezra*; *2 Bar.*). These scenarios include often-enigmatic human and supernatural antagonists, and furnish the author with relevant imagery; e.g., "the lawless one" (2.3), "Satan" (2.9), and one who "exalts himself"

(2.4). The tension between the view that the end has arrived, and yet the final consummation is still to come, is present in Jewish texts (cf. DSS, esp. 1QH).

The author also appropriates Jewish theological concepts and images. He affirms God's election of the community (1.11; 2.13–14) and promises divine vengeance on opponents of God's people (1.5–10). For these claims, he employs biblical images of sacrifice (2.13) and angels (1.7). Notably, he avoids supersessionism (i.e., he does not reject the Jews); rather, the Jews are simply ignored. If the author is *not* Paul, his background is unknown, though like Paul he has a thorough grounding in Jewish thought.

Adam Gregerman

1 Paul, Silvanus, and Timothy,
To the church of the Thessalonians in God our Father and the Lord Jesus Christ:

[2] Grace to you and peace from God our[a] Father and the Lord Jesus Christ.

[3] We must always give thanks to God for you, brothers and sisters,[b] as is right, because your faith is growing abundantly, and the love of every one of you for one another is increasing. [4] Therefore we ourselves boast of you among the churches of God for your steadfastness and faith during all your persecutions and the afflictions that you are enduring.

[5] This is evidence of the righteous judgment of God, and is intended to make you worthy of the kingdom of God, for which you are also suffering. [6] For it is indeed just of God to repay with affliction those who afflict you, [7] and to give relief to the afflicted as well as to us, when the Lord Jesus is revealed from heaven with his mighty angels [8] in flaming fire, inflicting vengeance on those who do not know God and on those who do not obey the

[a] Other ancient authorities read *the*
[b] Gk *brothers*

1.1–3: Greeting and first thanksgiving. Parallels 1 Thess 1.1. **1:** *Silvanus*, or Silas; Acts 15.22,40; 17.1. *Timothy*, Paul's co-worker and emissary; 1 Cor 16.10–11; Phil 2.19–24. **3:** *Love . . . for one another*, believers' solidarity is praised, dividing them from outsiders (Jn 13.34; Phil 1.9; 1QS 5.1–20). Some rabbinic texts encourage tight bonds among the learned and separation from the unlearned (*b. Pesah.* 49b).

1.4–10: God's righteous judgment. The author, influenced by Jewish apocalypticism, assures persecuted readers of divine justice. **4:** *Among the churches of God*, the community is connected with other Christian communities, suggesting a broad network of Gentile churches (1.7; Rom 16.4,16; 2 Cor 8.1; 1 Thess 1.7,9). *Steadfastness and faith*, emphasizing not the content of their faith but devotion despite suffering; Job 2.9–10; *b. Ber.* 61b, on commitment to God and Torah despite Roman persecution. *Persecutions . . . afflictions*, external evidence for mid-to-late first century persecution is limited. Persecution need not be violent; ostracism might provoke pain and anger. **5:** *This is evidence*, an ambiguous phrase, but *this* might refer to *steadfastness and faith*. When linked with God's *righteous judgment*, God is seen to be the source of their devotion; Phil 1.28. Alternately, *this* might be believers' *afflictions*. Rather than undermining confidence in God, their afflictions are temporary chastenings for sins by a *righteous* God (even they have fallen short; Rom 2.5–11). Soon, however, they will receive rewards in God's *kingdom*, while persecutors will be punished. Jewish texts offer a similar theodicy of present suffering and future reward; *Pss. Sol.* 13.9–10; 2 Macc 6.12–16; *2 Bar.* 13.3–10; *Gen. Rab.* 33.1. **7–9:** The author uses vivid, traditional Jewish images of divine justice. On *mighty angels* see Zech 14.5; Ps 78.49; *1 En.* 54.6; 61.10; 1QM 1.10–11; on *flaming fire* see Isa 66.15; Dan 7.9–10. Along with belief in an afterlife, *eternal destruction* (v. 9) emerges (as a form of divine punishment) in some late Second Temple period texts; Dan 12.2; 4 Macc 10.15; 1QM 1.5; 1QS 2.14–15; 5.10–13. **7:** *The Lord Jesus is revealed*, he is the agent of divine justice; Rom 2.5. Similar expectations of a divinely sent redeemer who will punish Israel's oppressors appear in Jewish texts; *1 En.* 48.1–49.4; *4 Ezra* 7.28; 13.32. **8:** *Vengeance*, reminiscent of Jewish texts, often sectarian, forecasting God's destruction of opponents and even nonmembers; *Jub.* 21.21–24; 1QS 10.20; 4Q511 1–8; CD 8.1–19; *2 Bar.* 54.14–22. *Those who do not know God . . . those who do not obey the gospel*, perhaps two groups of opponents: pagans (both Christians and Jews said they *do not know God*; Jer 10.25; Gal 4.8; 1 Thess 4.5) and Jews (who know but *do not obey* Christian teaching; Rom 10.16–21). No accusations of hostility from Jews (or Jewish-Christians) appear in 2 Thessalonians, but do elsewhere: Mt 10.23; Acts 13.50; 2 Cor 11.24; 1 Thess 2.14–16; *Mart. Pol.* 12–13; Justin, *Apol.* 1. 31.

gospel of our Lord Jesus. [9]These will suffer the punishment of eternal destruction, separated from the presence of the Lord and from the glory of his might, [10]when he comes to be glorified by his saints and to be marveled at on that day among all who have believed, because our testimony to you was believed. [11]To this end we always pray for you, asking that our God will make you worthy of his call and will fulfill by his power every good resolve and work of faith, [12]so that the name of our Lord Jesus may be glorified in you, and you in him, according to the grace of our God and the Lord Jesus Christ.

2 As to the coming of our Lord Jesus Christ and our being gathered together to him, we beg you, brothers and sisters,[a] [2]not to be quickly shaken in mind or alarmed, either by spirit or by word or by letter, as though from us, to the effect that the day of the Lord is already here. [3]Let no one deceive you in any way; for that day will not come unless the rebellion comes first and the lawless one[b] is revealed, the one destined for destruction.[c] [4]He opposes and exalts himself above every so-called god or object of worship, so that he takes his seat in the temple of God, declaring himself to be God. [5]Do you not remember that I told you these things when I was still with you? [6]And you know what is now restraining him, so that he may be revealed when his time comes. [7]For the mystery of lawlessness is already at work, but only until the one who now restrains it is removed. [8]And then the lawless one will be revealed, whom the Lord Jesus[d] will destroy[e] with the breath of his mouth,

a Gk *brothers*
b Gk *the man of lawlessness*; other ancient authorities read *the man of sin*
c Gk *the son of destruction*
d Other ancient authorities lack *Jesus*
e Other ancient authorities read *consume*

1.11–12: Prayer. 11: *Worthy of his call*, Jewish election language; Deut 7.6; 26.17; Isa 41.9; *Jub.* 2.9; 15.30–31; Rom 9.6–7; 11.29; Eph 1.18; 1 Pet 2.9; cf. 2.13. The author recalls the believers' (past) chosenness by God in order to demand (future) good works and faith. Jewish texts link election with demands for Torah-obedience; Josh 24.22; Ps 105.45; *Pss. Sol.* 9–11; *Jub.* 2.17–22; *m. Avot* 3.18, on the demand that Israel, as the beloved of God, not forsake the Torah. **12:** *Name*, possibly referring to Isa 66.5 [LXX], and substituting Jesus' name for God's.

2.1–12: The day of the Lord. The central argument, dispelling belief in the imminence of the end; cf. 1 Thess 5.1–3. **1–3:** The author fears his authority is threatened by misrepresentation of his views (a forged letter) or others' teachings. **1:** *Coming*, see 2.8; Mt 24.3; 1 Cor 15.23; 1 Thess 3.13. **2:** *Spirit . . . word . . . letter*, the reference seems to be to information given by any means: a message from Paul or another, a reading during worship, or a message (prophecy) given to a member of the community by spiritual means. *Day of the Lord*, an expression from the Hebrew prophets; Isa 13.6; Joel 2.1; Am 5.18. **3:** *Rebellion*, better, "apostasy": religious transgression will occur first; Ezek 38–39; Joel 2–3; *Jub.* 23.14–23; *4 Ezra* 14.14–16; *b. Sanh.* 97b, on scenarios of future wars and upheaval; cf. Mk 13.7–27. It is symbolized by the coming of an unidentified *lawless one*; *Pss. Sol.* 17.11; 1QM 13.2–5; *Sib. Or.* 3.63–74. This may be a false teacher or a Roman emperor claiming divine status. **4:** He insolently challenges God and *exalts himself*. This figure is modeled on foreign oppressors of Israel like Antiochus IV (second century BCE) and Pompey (first century BCE); Dan 11.24–45; *Pss. Sol.* 2.1–2; 17.11. Just as they violated the Jerusalem Temple, he will sit *in the temple*, an image presumably shocking not just to Jews but even to Gentile converts who did not participate in Temple worship. The emphasis in the statement, therefore, falls on the phrase *declaring himself to be God* (as Roman emperors did). **6–7:** Readers may know the unidentified restrainer's identity (*what is now restraining him*). Confusingly, the text uses both neutral (*what*) and masculine (*who*) participles. The scenario is clearer: *already* there is *lawlessness*, and restraint on it will soon be *removed*. *Only until . . . removed*, presumably not applied to *already at work* but rather to the *mystery* or implied hiddenness of the "lawless one" that will end when *he* [is] *revealed*. Unlike the undoubtedly authentic Pauline epistles, "law" here does not refer to the commands of the Torah but to apostasy and false teachings (cf. Rom 10.4–5; Gal 2.16). Present suffering foreshadows future turmoil. **8:** *Jesus'* triumph, described in Jewish images of victory (*breath* that "consumes" [see translators' note *e*—the same verb is translated "consume" in Lk 9.54; Gal 5.15]) by God or a Davidic messiah; Isa 11.4; *Pss. Sol.* 17.24; *1 En.* 62.2; *4 Ezra* 13.10; cf. Rev 19.11–21. **9–12:** The author returns to the present. *Satan*, though subordinate to God, is blamed for the *deception* of the believers; Zech 3.1–2; Job 1.6–2.7; 1 Chr 21.1; *b. B. Bat.* 16a, on God's being deceived—seemingly "against his better judgment"—by Satan. In the Bible, God also sometimes deceives

annihilating him by the manifestation of his coming. [9] The coming of the lawless one is apparent in the working of Satan, who uses all power, signs, lying wonders, [10] and every kind of wicked deception for those who are perishing, because they refused to love the truth and so be saved. [11] For this reason God sends them a powerful delusion, leading them to believe what is false, [12] so that all who have not believed the truth but took pleasure in unrighteousness will be condemned.

[13] But we must always give thanks to God for you, brothers and sisters[a] beloved by the Lord, because God chose you as the first fruits[b] for salvation through sanctification by the Spirit and through belief in the truth. [14] For this purpose he called you through our proclamation of the good news,[c] so that you may obtain the glory of our Lord Jesus Christ. [15] So then, brothers and sisters,[a] stand firm and hold fast to the traditions that you were taught by us, either by word of mouth or by our letter.

[16] Now may our Lord Jesus Christ himself and God our Father, who loved us and through grace gave us eternal comfort and good hope, [17] comfort your hearts and strengthen them in every good work and word.

3 Finally, brothers and sisters,[a] pray for us, so that the word of the Lord may spread rapidly and be glorified everywhere, just as it is among you, [2] and that we may be rescued from wicked and evil people; for not all have faith. [3] But the Lord is faithful; he will strengthen you and guard you from the evil one.[d] [4] And we have confidence in the Lord concerning you, that you are doing and will go on doing the things that we command. [5] May the Lord direct your hearts to the love of God and to the steadfastness of Christ.

[6] Now we command you, beloved,[a] in the name of our Lord Jesus Christ, to keep away from believers who are[e] living in idleness and not according to the tradition that they[f] received from us. [7] For you yourselves know how you ought to imitate us; we were not idle when we were with you, [8] and we did not eat anyone's bread without paying for it; but with toil and labor we worked night and day, so that we might not burden any of you. [9] This was not because we do not have that right,

[a] Gk *brothers*
[b] Other ancient authorities read *from the beginning*
[c] Or *through our gospel*
[d] Or *from evil*
[e] Gk *from every brother who is*
[f] Other ancient authorities read *you*

people; 1 Kings 22.23 (false prophets); Isa 6.10 (Israel); cf. Rom 11.7–8. **10:** *Truth*, not a generic term, it refers specifically to the "traditions" they were taught; 2.15. *Saved*, recalls the rewards in 1.5,7,9.

2.13–17: Second thanksgiving. Parallels 1 Thess 2.13, though not necessarily evidence that either letter is composite. **13:** *First fruits*, if correct (see translators' note *b*), believers are likened to a Temple offering (Jer 2.3) affirming God's faithfulness to biblical promises; Rom 8.23; 1 Cor 15.20. *Sanctification*, "making holy" or being set apart *by the Spirit* as a worthy offering. **15:** Summarizing his response to all threats—of persecution, confusion, and dissension—the author demands that readers accept his *traditions*; 3.4; 1 Thess 3.8. On faithfulness to tradition, see Deut 5.32–33; Josephus, *Ag. Ap.* 2.22; *m. Avot* 3.17. **16–17:** See 1 Thess 3.2,11–13.

3.1–5: Prayer and encouragement. **1:** *Spread rapidly and be glorified*, reflects Christian missionary impulse: successful preaching leads to glorification of God; Mt 5.16; Acts 13.48; Rom 15.9. **3:** *The evil one* may be Satan in 2.9. **5:** *Direct your hearts*, Jewish language of religious intention; Ps 10.17; 1 Chr 29.18; *m. Men.* 13.11; *b. Ber.* 17a: regardless of one's level of learning, what is most important is that "one directs one's heart to heaven."

3.6–13: Denunciation of idleness. **6:** *Living in idleness*, perhaps because they believed the end had arrived, though the connection to 2.2 is not explicit; 1 Thess 4.11. *Name*, see 3.12; 1 Cor 5.4; Eph 4.17; 1 Thess 4.1. **6 (also 10,12):** *Command*, stern language, demonstrating the seriousness of the threat. **7, 9:** *Imitate*, 1 Cor 4.16; 11.1; Phil 3.17; *b. Ber.* 62a, on imitating the actions of the rabbis in all areas of life. **8:** *Toil and labor*, Jews and Christians praised labor; Prov 10.4; 1 Thess 2.9; 5.12–14; *Did.* 12.4–5; *Mek. Ex.* 20.9; *m. Avot* 2.2 praises combining Torah study and labor, though not all rabbis worked. Some were wealthy, and others were paid a fee for teaching or expected to be supported by the community; cf. Sir 38.24. Idleness may have been unseemly in the eyes of non-Christian neighbors, though some pagans disdained labor, at least by the learned; 1 Thess 4.12. **9:** *Right*, see 1 Cor 9.4–15.

but in order to give you an example to imitate. [10] For even when we were with you, we gave you this command: Anyone unwilling to work should not eat. [11] For we hear that some of you are living in idleness, mere busybodies, not doing any work. [12] Now such persons we command and exhort in the Lord Jesus Christ to do their work quietly and to earn their own living. [13] Brothers and sisters,[a] do not be weary in doing what is right.

[14] Take note of those who do not obey what we say in this letter; have nothing to do with them, so that they may be ashamed. [15] Do not regard them as enemies, but warn them as believers.[b]

[16] Now may the Lord of peace himself give you peace at all times in all ways. The Lord be with all of you.

[17] I, Paul, write this greeting with my own hand. This is the mark in every letter of mine; it is the way I write. [18] The grace of our Lord Jesus Christ be with all of you.[c]

[a] Gk *Brothers*
[b] Gk *a brother*
[c] Other ancient authorities add *Amen*

3.14–15: Warning the disobedient. 14–15: Readers should *have nothing to do with them,* perhaps ejecting them from communal meals; 3.10; Mt 18.17; 1 Cor 5.3; 2 Jn 1.10; 1QS 6–8. However, they are not to *regard them as enemies.* This appears contradictory, and no specific policies are offered, though the emphasis is on faithfulness to tradition, not rules for membership. Compare the example of Rabbi Eliezer, who was shunned by his colleagues after a legal dispute; *b. B. Metz.* 59b.

3.16–18: Closing. Parallels 1 Thess 5.23–28. See a similar blessing, Num 6.24–26. **17:** *Own hand,* see 1 Cor 16.21; Col 4.18. The strong claim here may reflect the fear in 2.2.

THE FIRST LETTER OF PAUL TO TIMOTHY

INTRODUCTION

First and Second Timothy, along with Titus, are known as the "Pastoral Epistles"; despite differences among them, they are commonly grouped together. The term "Pastoral Epistles," though it is not used in the letters themselves, has been used for these three letters because they are concerned mostly with the life and rules governing individual Christian communities. Although presented as a short, personal letter written by the apostle Paul to Timothy, a co-missionary who remained in Ephesus to guide the nascent community, 1 Timothy's Pauline authorship is doubted. The themes and issues are different from Paul's concerns with justification and are more focused on matters of dissent within the communities. The concept of faith presented here—that of "sound teaching" (4.6)—differs from that in the genuine letters of Paul, for instance Gal 3.6–9. The tone and vocabulary of these epistles differ from Paul's undisputed letters. On the one hand they share commonality with popular Greek ethical writings, and on the other they speak of Jesus' epiphany, moral uprightness, and community traditions to be kept, rather than Jesus' second coming, justification, and trust in God. It is therefore more likely, in the view of scholars, that these letters are attributed to Paul but not written by him. The attribution of letters and other texts to past worthies was known in various contexts: Jewish (e.g., *1 Enoch*), pagan (e.g., the so-called *Homeric Hymns*, odes to the gods in the style of Homer but almost certainly not by him), as well as in early Christian history (e.g., the *Gospel of Thomas*), and it is possible the Pastorals represent the views of late first- or early second-century Christians who appealed to Paul for their authority.

According to Acts (16.1) Timothy is the son of a Jewish mother and a Greek father. If pseudonymous, the letter's choice of Timothy (rather than some other disciple) makes sense, for Timothy, who encountered Paul in Lystra, accompanied the apostle in some cities, represented him in others, and often co-signed his letters (e.g., 2 Cor 1.1; Phil 1.1; 1 Thess 1.1; Philem 1).

INTERPRETATION

Paul sought to prepare his churches for Jesus' imminent return (see 1 Thess 4). In some of his undisputed letters, and particularly in later legendary stories (such as the apocryphal second-century *Acts of Paul and Thecla*), Paul can be understood as erasing the distinctions between slave and free and between male and female (see Gal 3.28) as well as advocating celibacy (see 1 Cor 7.7). This understanding led some of his followers to refuse the social conventions of slavery and marriage. The delay of the "coming of the Lord" (1 Thess 4.15) prompted others to insist on conformity to prevailing Roman social values: slaves were to be obedient to their masters; women and men were to marry and procreate; husbands and fathers were to rule their homes. In this corrective mode, the Pastoral Epistles present Paul as supporting the status quo.

Naomi Koltun-Fromm

1 Paul, an apostle of Christ Jesus by the command of God our Savior and of Christ Jesus our hope,

[2] To Timothy, my loyal child in the faith:

Grace, mercy, and peace from God the Father and Christ Jesus our Lord.

[3] I urge you, as I did when I was on my way to Macedonia, to remain in Ephesus so that you may instruct certain people not to teach any different doctrine, [4] and not to occupy themselves with myths and endless genealogies that promote speculations rather than the divine training[a] that is known by faith. [5] But the aim of such instruction is love that comes from a pure heart, a good conscience, and sincere faith. [6] Some people have deviated from these and turned to meaningless talk, [7] desiring to be teachers of the law, without understanding either what they are saying or the things about which they make assertions.

[8] Now we know that the law is good, if one uses it legitimately. [9] This means understanding that the law is laid down not for the innocent but for the lawless and disobedient, for the godless and sinful, for the unholy and profane, for those who kill their father or mother, for murderers, [10] fornicators, sodomites, slave traders, liars, perjurers, and whatever else is contrary to the sound teaching [11] that conforms to the glorious gospel of the blessed God, which he entrusted to me.

[12] I am grateful to Christ Jesus our Lord, who has strengthened me, because he judged me faithful and appointed me to his service, [13] even though I was formerly a blasphemer, a persecutor, and a man of violence. But I received mercy because I had acted ignorantly in unbelief, [14] and the grace of our Lord overflowed for me with the faith and love that are in Christ Jesus. [15] The saying is sure and worthy of full acceptance, that Christ Jesus came into the world to save sinners—of whom I am the foremost. [16] But for that very reason I received mercy, so that in me, as the foremost, Jesus Christ might display the utmost patience, making me an example to those who would come to believe in him for eternal life. [17] To the King of the ages, immortal, invisible, the only God, be honor and glory forever and ever.[b] Amen.

a Or *plan*
b Gk *to the ages of the ages*

1.1–2: Opening greeting. *Paul*, teacher and mentor, writes to his disciple and co-worker, *Timothy*, to encourage him in his work. *God our Savior*, presumably through *Christ* ["mashiaḥ"]. *Jesus our hope*, "savior" or "deliverer" (Gk "sotēr," Heb "yisha‘," e.g., Ps 24.5 [LXX 23.5]) is a divine title. *Loyal child*, a term of endearment (as also 2 Tim 1.2), not a designation of kinship. *Grace*, Gk "charis," "favor, thanks"; *mercy*, Gk "eleos," in LXX for Heb "ḥesed" (e.g., Ps 85.10 [Heb 85.11; LXX 84.11]), "lovingkindness"; *peace*, Gk "eirēnē," in LXX for Heb "shalom." The salutation combines Greek and Hebrew (Jewish) greetings. *God the Father*, occasionally used in the Hebrew Bible (e.g., Ps 68.5; Jer 3.4). In Christian usage increasingly it meant the believers' union with Jesus as God's (adoptive) children, e.g., Rom 8.15.

1.3–11: Countering false teaching. The author argues for a consistent doctrine, supported by his own authority, in distinction to the teachings of rival Christians. **4–5:** *Myths and endless genealogies*, the author dismisses all opponents as "myth-makers" rather than true teachers. There is no consensus on the specific content of these teachings, though they may indicate some form of fanciful reading of biblical texts; see also 4.7; Titus 1.14; 3.9. *Faith* here has as much to do with correct beliefs or teachings as it does with trust. *Conscience* (Gk "syneidēsis"), the self-awareness that comes with moral maturity (cf. Rom 2.15); see 1.19; 3.9; 4.2; 2 Tim 1.3. **7–8:** *Law* here is seen as a *good* if subordinate part of the teaching. The writer presumably means "Torah," not secular, civil law. **9–11:** The list of sins is conventional (see 1 Cor 6.9–10; Mk 7.21–23; Gal 5.19–20) and may be loosely tied to the Decalogue, the Holiness Code of Leviticus (Lev 18–19), and a general fear of immorality, although vice lists are common (e.g., Col 3.5–9; see also, e.g., Tob 4.12; *Jub*. 7.20), especially in later NT writings. *Sound teaching* is the key both to *the glorious gospel* and to proper action.

1.12–20: Paul's experience as lesson. 13–14. *Formerly a blasphemer*, in 1 Cor 15.9 (cf. Acts 8.1; 9.1–2) Paul cites his own past as a persecutor of the early Jesus followers. *Mercy . . . grace* (Gk "eleos," "compassion"; Heb "ḥesed"; Gk "charis," "grace," "favor"; Heb "ḥen"), the loving actions of God to which the believer responds with *faith and love . . . in Christ Jesus*. **16:** *An example*, a standard exhortation, to imitate one's teachers as they in turn imitate Christ (1 Cor 11.1). **17:** *King of the ages* (Gk "basilei tōn aiōnōn"), perhaps a rendering of Heb "melekh

[18] I am giving you these instructions, Timothy, my child, in accordance with the prophecies made earlier about you, so that by following them you may fight the good fight, [19] having faith and a good conscience. By rejecting conscience, certain persons have suffered shipwreck in the faith; [20] among them are Hymenaeus and Alexander, whom I have turned over to Satan, so that they may learn not to blaspheme.

2 First of all, then, I urge that supplications, prayers, intercessions, and thanksgivings be made for everyone, [2] for kings and all who are in high positions, so that we may lead a quiet and peaceable life in all godliness and dignity. [3] This is right and is acceptable in the sight of God our Savior, [4] who desires everyone to be saved and to come to the knowledge of the truth. [5] For

there is one God;
there is also one mediator between God and humankind,
Christ Jesus, himself human,
[6] who gave himself a ransom for all —

this was attested at the right time. [7] For this I was appointed a herald and an apostle (I am telling the truth,[a] I am not lying), a teacher of the Gentiles in faith and truth.

[8] I desire, then, that in every place the men should pray, lifting up holy hands without anger or argument; [9] also that the women should dress themselves modestly and decently in suitable clothing, not with their hair braided, or with gold, pearls, or expensive clothes, [10] but with good works, as is proper for women who profess reverence for God. [11] Let a woman[b] learn in silence with full submission. [12] I permit no woman[b] to teach or to have authority over a man;[c] she is to keep silent. [13] For Adam was formed first, then Eve; [14] and Adam was not deceived, but the woman was deceived and became a transgressor. [15] Yet she will be saved through childbearing, provided they continue in faith and love and holiness, with modesty.

[a] Other ancient authorities add *in Christ*
[b] Or *wife*
[c] Or *her husband*

ha-olam," "king of the universe/king of eternity/king forever." See Ps 10.16. **18:** *Prophecies*, see 4.14; these are not predictions of the future but words presumed to be from God, spoken during worship, in this case concerning the ministry for which Timothy is being set aside. **19:** *Conscience*, see 1.4–5n. **20:** *Turned over to Satan*, for correction leading to amendment of life (1 Cor 5.5) or for punishment (3.6–7; 2 Tim 2.26). The devil is seen as one who leads believers astray (5.15).

2.1–15: Social order and creation. 2.1–2: One should pray for the welfare of the government (see Jer 29.7; Rom 13.1–7). The goal of such accommodation is *a quiet and peaceable life* in which believers can exist with *godliness and dignity*. This suggestion follows common practice throughout the Second Temple period in which a sacrifice on behalf of the emperor's health was offered in the Jerusalem Temple. Both Paul (Rom 13.1–2) and the rabbis (e.g., *b. Ned.* 28a) advocated deference to the governing authority. **3–4:** Paul supports this position by claiming both that his God is universal and that through his gift of Jesus, God wants everyone to participate in salvation. *God our savior*, see 1.1n. *Saved . . . knowledge of the truth*, in the writer's view, salvation is clearly linked with right doctrine. **5–6:** The passage is set in poetical form to indicate that it might be an extract from a hymn. *Ransom* (Gk "antilutron," only place in NT where this form occurs; "lutron" in LXX for "pidyon," "ge'ulah," "kofer," payment as for a life [Ex 21.30] or for freeing slaves [Lev 19.20]), a payment for redemption or liberation, presumably here from sin; see Mk 10.45; Mt 20.28. **8:** *Lifting up holy hands*, a gesture of prayer (Ps 28.2; 63.4 [Heb v. 5]; 134.2; 141.2). **9–10:** *Modestly . . . reverence for God*, concern for female modesty is elsewhere in the Pastorals (e.g., 5.11–15; Titus 2.5). **11–15:** This strong gender differentiation contradicts Gal 3.28, in which gender differentiation is abrogated, and Rom 16.1–3,7, which depict women in leadership roles. The passage is, however, consistent with 1 Cor 14.33b–36, which many scholars regard as a non-Pauline addition to that letter. **13–15:** One could claim that 1 Cor 14.33b–36 is specific to the Corinthian church, but 1 Timothy grounds female subordination in creation. For the author, Adam knowingly gave up Eden for the sake of his deceived wife. *Through childbearing*, i.e., by keeping busy with household tasks, these women will be kept from giving in to worldly temptation (see 5.14–15). By stating that women's salvation is based on bearing children, however, the author condemns women, including married women, who choose celibacy as part of their Christian calling. The view that women are subordinate to men and that the subordination derives from Genesis appears in later Jewish circles and is native to some rabbinic understanding of womanhood (e.g., *b. Ber.* 61a).

3 The saying is sure:[a] whoever aspires to the office of bishop[b] desires a noble task. [2] Now a bishop[c] must be above reproach, married only once,[d] temperate, sensible, respectable, hospitable, an apt teacher, [3] not a drunkard, not violent but gentle, not quarrelsome, and not a lover of money. [4] He must manage his own household well, keeping his children submissive and respectful in every way— [5] for if someone does not know how to manage his own household, how can he take care of God's church? [6] He must not be a recent convert, or he may be puffed up with conceit and fall into the condemnation of the devil. [7] Moreover, he must be well thought of by outsiders, so that he may not fall into disgrace and the snare of the devil.

[8] Deacons likewise must be serious, not double-tongued, not indulging in much wine, not greedy for money; [9] they must hold fast to the mystery of the faith with a clear conscience. [10] And let them first be tested; then, if they prove themselves blameless, let them serve as deacons. [11] Women[e] likewise must be serious, not slanderers, but temperate, faithful in all things. [12] Let deacons be married only once,[f] and let them manage their children and their households well; [13] for those who serve well as deacons gain a good standing for themselves and great boldness in the faith that is in Christ Jesus.

[14] I hope to come to you soon, but I am writing these instructions to you so that, [15] if I am delayed, you may know how one ought to behave in the household of God, which is the church of the living God, the pillar and bulwark of the truth. [16] Without any doubt, the mystery of our religion is great:

He[g] was revealed in flesh,
vindicated[h] in spirit,[i]
seen by angels,
proclaimed among Gentiles,
believed in throughout the world,
taken up in glory.

[a] Some interpreters place these words at the end of the previous paragraph. Other ancient authorities read *The saying is commonly accepted*
[b] Or *overseer*
[c] Or *an overseer*
[d] Gk *the husband of one wife*
[e] Or *Their wives*, or *Women deacons*
[f] Gk *be husbands of one wife*
[g] Gk *Who*; other ancient authorities read *God*; others, *Which*
[h] Or *justified*
[i] Or *by the Spirit*

3.1–16: Church leaders. Church leaders should be blameless in personal conduct and prove themselves through their well-managed households, for the church is the household of God. In the Mishnah, worship of God is moved from the Temple (which no longer existed) into the home. In both cases, the issue is that behavior in religious settings is seen as the standard for behavior in daily life. **1–7:** Qualifications for a bishop. **1:** *Bishop* (Gk "episkopos," "one who oversees," "supervisor"), the bishop was the head of a local church. Later (second century CE and following) the bishop became the chief pastor of a geographical area that could include a number of local congregations. **2:** The author points to single marriage (only one spouse, no remarriage). If this statement refers to divorce, it could be based on Mt 19.3–12; see also 1 Thess 4.4, if it is translated "each one of you [should] know how to take a wife for himself in holiness and honor." If it means no remarriage after the loss of a spouse through death, it would contradict 1 Cor 7.39. It probably reflects a reaction to Roman society, which sanctioned divorce. **4:** *Submissive*, Gk "hypotagē," "under subjection," i.e., subordinate to the parent. **7:** *Well thought of*, lit., "a good witness" (Gk "kalēn martyrian"); *by outsiders*, those not members of the community. **8–13:** Qualifications for deacons. **8:** A *deacon* (Gk "diakonos") was "one who serves," but not necessarily a slave (Gk "doulos"). **9:** *Mystery of the faith*, the (presumably secret) instruction for those newly joining the community; the deacons were apparently those responsible for such instruction, so they must *hold fast* to it both in the sense of keeping it safe and in adhering to it themselves. **10:** *Tested*, lit., "proved genuine" (Gk "dokimazō," "to assay [as metal]," "try"). **11:** *Women*, the text is ambiguous; it is possible but not certain that the writer means "women deacons"; see translators' note *e*. See also Rom 16.1. **14–16:** Further exhortation about proper behavior. **15:** *Household . . . church*, behavior should be consistent no matter where the believer is. **16:** *Mystery*, see v. 9n. *Religion*, lit., "good (or proper) reverence" (Gk "eusebeia"). *Revealed . . . glory*, presumably a fragment of an early Christian hymn that expresses the teaching conveyed to members of the community when they are initiated. *Vindicated in spirit*, or "justified by the Spirit" (see translators' notes *h* and *i*): either proved worthy by resurrection or shown to be right by the later manifestation of the Spirit in Christian communities.

4 Now the Spirit expressly says that in later[a] times some will renounce the faith by paying attention to deceitful spirits and teachings of demons, [2] through the hypocrisy of liars whose consciences are seared with a hot iron. [3] They forbid marriage and demand abstinence from foods, which God created to be received with thanksgiving by those who believe and know the truth. [4] For everything created by God is good, and nothing is to be rejected, provided it is received with thanksgiving; [5] for it is sanctified by God's word and by prayer.

[6] If you put these instructions before the brothers and sisters,[b] you will be a good servant[c] of Christ Jesus, nourished on the words of the faith and of the sound teaching that you have followed. [7] Have nothing to do with profane myths and old wives' tales. Train yourself in godliness, [8] for, while physical training is of some value, godliness is valuable in every way, holding promise for both the present life and the life to come. [9] The saying is sure and worthy of full acceptance. [10] For to this end we toil and struggle,[d] because we have our hope set on the living God, who is the Savior of all people, especially of those who believe.

[11] These are the things you must insist on and teach. [12] Let no one despise your youth, but set the believers an example in speech and conduct, in love, in faith, in purity. [13] Until I arrive, give attention to the public reading of scripture,[e] to exhorting, to teaching. [14] Do not neglect the gift that is in you, which was given to you through prophecy with the laying on of hands by the council of elders.[f] [15] Put these things into practice, devote yourself to them, so that all may see your progress. [16] Pay close attention to yourself and to your teaching; continue in these things, for in doing this you will save both yourself and your hearers.

5 Do not speak harshly to an older man,[g] but speak to him as to a father, to younger men as brothers, [2] to older women as mothers, to younger women as sisters—with absolute purity.

[a] Or *the last*
[b] Gk *brothers*
[c] Or *deacon*
[d] Other ancient authorities read *suffer reproach*
[e] Gk *to the reading*
[f] Gk *by the presbytery*
[g] Or *an elder*, or *a presbyter*

4.1–16: Practice. 1–5: Paul returns to creation theology to counter asceticism: there is no reason to reject either marriage or food when both were created and deemed good by God. **1:** *The Spirit expressly says*, perhaps a reference to words of prophecy (i.e., purported messages from God) delivered during worship. *Later times*, or "the last times" (see translators' note *a*), the times leading up to the end of the age and the inauguration of the new era. **4–5:** *Everything . . . sanctified*, all foods are licit (cf. Mk 7.19; Acts 10.15). *Sanctified*, lit., "made holy"; things holy are set apart for God, *by God's word and by prayer*. God's word (command) is the means by which all that God created was good (Gen 1.31). **6–7:** The author contrasts *the words of the faith* and *sound teaching* with those of his opponents, which are nothing but *myths* (see 1.4–5n.) and *old wives' tales* (the Gk phrase is lit., "profane [things] and old-womanish myths"), or worse, demonic (v. 1). Labeling one's opponents' teachings "demonic" or "false" was a known first-century Greco-Roman, Jewish, and Christian practice (e.g., 1QpHab 14.22; Wis 14.22–28; Mt 23; Jn 8.44–47). *Godliness*, lit., "good (or proper) reverence" (Gk "eusebeia"); the same word is translated "religion" in 3.16. **8:** *Physical training* was a Greco-Roman cultural ideal, part of the good life; the point here is that spiritual training is of value not only in *the present life* but also in *the life to come*. **10:** The notion that the God of Israel is the savior of all people follows from the notice in Gen (cf. 2.5) that all God's creations are good. It also appears in prophetic texts such as Isa 45.22–23. **13:** *The public reading of scripture*, see Lk 4.16–20; Neh 7.73b–8.8. "Qeri'at ha-Torah," "reading of the Torah," became standard Jewish practice in the Second Temple period (Neh 8.8) and was taken over in Christian settings. **14:** *Prophecy . . . elders*, a brief description of the practice in which a ministry was authorized and initiated (see Acts 6.6; 2 Tim 1.6). See also 4.1n. *Elders* (Gk "presbyteroi") were, along with the bishop ("episkopos," "overseer"; see 3.1n.) the leaders of a local congregation; they may in fact have originally been elders. Jewish Diaspora communities had "archisynagōgoi" or "rulers of the synagogue" (see e.g., Mk 5.22), but it is not clear what their roles were.

5.1–6.2: Charity and life in community. 5.1–2: *Father . . . purity*, respect for elders (Ex 20.12; Lev 19.32) is combined with exhortations to treat those younger—either of the same age or lesser is not clear—with

[3] Honor widows who are really widows. [4] If a widow has children or grandchildren, they should first learn their religious duty to their own family and make some repayment to their parents; for this is pleasing in God's sight. [5] The real widow, left alone, has set her hope on God and continues in supplications and prayers night and day; [6] but the widow[a] who lives for pleasure is dead even while she lives. [7] Give these commands as well, so that they may be above reproach. [8] And whoever does not provide for relatives, and especially for family members, has denied the faith and is worse than an unbeliever.

[9] Let a widow be put on the list if she is not less than sixty years old and has been married only once;[b] [10] she must be well attested for her good works, as one who has brought up children, shown hospitality, washed the saints' feet, helped the afflicted, and devoted herself to doing good in every way. [11] But refuse to put younger widows on the list; for when their sensual desires alienate them from Christ, they want to marry, [12] and so they incur condemnation for having violated their first pledge. [13] Besides that, they learn to be idle, gadding about from house to house; and they are not merely idle, but also gossips and busybodies, saying what they should not say. [14] So I would have younger widows marry, bear children, and manage their households, so as to give the adversary no occasion to revile us. [15] For some have already turned away to follow Satan. [16] If any believing woman[c] has relatives who are really widows, let her assist them; let the church not be burdened, so that it can assist those who are real widows.

[17] Let the elders who rule well be considered worthy of double honor,[d] especially those who labor in preaching and teaching; [18] for the scripture says, "You shall not muzzle an ox while it is treading out the grain," and, "The laborer deserves to be paid." [19] Never accept any accusation against an elder except on the evidence of two or three witnesses. [20] As for those who persist in sin, rebuke them in the presence of all, so that the rest also may stand in fear. [21] In the presence of God and of Christ Jesus and of the elect angels, I warn you to keep these instructions without prejudice, doing nothing on the basis of partiality. [22] Do not ordain[e] anyone hastily, and do not participate in the sins of others; keep yourself pure.

[23] No longer drink only water, but take a little wine for the sake of your stomach and your frequent ailments.

[24] The sins of some people are conspicuous and precede them to judgment, while the sins of others follow them there. [25] So also good works are conspicuous; and even when they are not, they cannot remain hidden.

a Gk *she*

b Gk *the wife of one husband*

c Other ancient authorities read *believing man or woman*; others, *believing man*

d Or *compensation*

e Gk *Do not lay hands on*

equal propriety. *Purity* would seem to mean treating everyone in the community as members of one's family, and not, for instance, treating younger women as potential marital partners. **3–16:** The writer here addresses the charitable functions of the community, particularly in reference to widows. The Torah mandates care for the poor, widows, and orphans (e.g., Deut 24.17–22; Tob 14.8–11). M. Pe'ah deals with rights of the poor. Because the community should not support all widows, the author recommends that they should take care of their own; only those absolutely in need should receive community support. **5:** A *real widow* is one without any family to support her and who has thus turned to God in constant *supplications and prayers*. **6:** *Lives for pleasure*, lit., "lives luxuriously"; see Jas 5.5. **9:** *Put on the list*, presumably for material support from the community. *Sixty years old* would have been an advanced age for the time (see "Jewish Family Life," p. 537). **10:** *Washed the saints' feet*, shown willingness to perform humble service (see Lk 7.36–50; Jn 13.1–16). **11–15:** *Younger widows*, the catalogue here contains stereotypical language about young women whose *sensual desires* mean they will not remain as widows (*their first pledge*), and whose idleness can lead them astray. The solution is to let them marry—thereby disqualifying them from ever being put on the support list (v. 9)—and keep them busy and out of trouble with household tasks. **17–25:** Leadership advice. **18:** The text's only direct Torah citation: Deut 25.4 (see also Mt 10.10). **19:** *Two or three witnesses*, see Deut 19.15. **21:** *In the presence . . . elect angels*, the proceedings are conducted as if the heavenly court is present.

6

Let all who are under the yoke of slavery regard their masters as worthy of all honor, so that the name of God and the teaching may not be blasphemed. [2] Those who have believing masters must not be disrespectful to them on the ground that they are members of the church;[a] rather they must serve them all the more, since those who benefit by their service are believers and beloved.[b]

Teach and urge these duties. [3] Whoever teaches otherwise and does not agree with the sound words of our Lord Jesus Christ and the teaching that is in accordance with godliness, [4] is conceited, understanding nothing, and has a morbid craving for controversy and for disputes about words. From these come envy, dissension, slander, base suspicions, [5] and wrangling among those who are depraved in mind and bereft of the truth, imagining that godliness is a means of gain.[c] [6] Of course, there is great gain in godliness combined with contentment; [7] for we brought nothing into the world, so that[d] we can take nothing out of it; [8] but if we have food and clothing, we will be content with these. [9] But those who want to be rich fall into temptation and are trapped by many senseless and harmful desires that plunge people into ruin and destruction. [10] For the love of money is a root of all kinds of evil, and in their eagerness to be rich some have wandered away from the faith and pierced themselves with many pains.

[11] But as for you, man of God, shun all this; pursue righteousness, godliness, faith, love, endurance, gentleness. [12] Fight the good fight of the faith; take hold of the eternal life, to which you were called and for which you made[e] the good confession in the presence of many witnesses. [13] In the presence of God, who gives life to all things, and of Christ Jesus, who in his testimony before Pontius Pilate made the good confession, I charge you [14] to keep the commandment without spot or blame until the manifestation of our Lord Jesus Christ, [15] which he will bring about at the right time—he who is the blessed and only Sovereign, the King of kings and Lord of lords. [16] It is he alone who has immortality and dwells in unapproachable light, whom no one has ever seen or can see; to him be honor and eternal dominion. Amen.

[a] Gk *are brothers*
[b] Or *since they are believers and beloved, who devote themselves to good deeds*
[c] Other ancient authorities add *Withdraw yourself from such people*
[d] Other ancient authorities read *world—it is certain that*
[e] Gk *confessed*

6.1–2: The writer urges those in the community to accommodate themselves to their lowly status; see Eph 6.5–9; Col 3.22–4.1, but note that unlike those exhortations, this passage does not include a corresponding stricture for the masters. For the Hebrew Bible's view of the relations between *slaves* and *masters*, see e.g., Lev 25.39–43; Deut 15.12–17. Slaves, like women according to this teaching, need to remember their place in this world, even if they will be better off in the next. The polemical rhetoric reflects common Greco-Roman moral discourse, used to discredit the opponent, and can be found among Jewish apologists as well (e.g., Philo, *Confusion* 106; Josephus, *Ag. Ap.* 1.15).

6.3–21: True and false teaching and final benediction. 3: *Godliness*, lit., "good (or proper) reverence" (Gk "eusebeia"); the same word is translated "religion" in 3.16. See also vv. 5,6; 4.7. **6:** *Contentment*, lit., "self-sufficiency" (Gk "autarkeia"). **7:** A possible allusion to Job 1.21 or Eccl 5.15. **9–10:** *Rich . . . love of money*, a warning not against social injustice but rather an exhortation to avoid peril to one's own well-being. The Wisdom of Ben Sirach likewise warns of the dangers of wealth (14.3–10; 31.5–11) or at least the duty to use it well (3.30–4.10; 29.1–20). **12:** *Eternal life*, or "life of the coming age" (Gk "aiōn"). *Good confession*, or "good acknowledgment," "good assent." Timothy acknowledged the "sound teaching" (4.6). **13:** *Pontius Pilate*, the only NT reference to him outside the Gospel accounts. *Good confession*, here the acknowledgment (Jn 18.33–38) or the refusal to deny (Mt 27.11–13) that Jesus is the messiah. **14:** *Commandment* or "injunction" (Gk "entolē"), what one has undertaken to see through. This may be a reference to Timothy's profession of faith (v. 12). **15:** *King of kings, and Lord of lords*, see Deut 10.17; Dan 2.37; 2 Macc 13.4; 3 Macc 5.35; *4 Ezra* 7.12; Philo, *Spec. Laws* 1.18, as well as Rev 17.14; 19.16. **16:** *Dwells in unapproachable light*, God's dwelling as light is a common metaphor in the Hebrew Bible; see e.g., Ps 36.9; see also 1 Jn 1.5; Philo, *Life of Moses* 2.70. That God should not be approached, see Ex 19.12;

[17] As for those who in the present age are rich, command them not to be haughty, or to set their hopes on the uncertainty of riches, but rather on God who richly provides us with everything for our enjoyment. [18] They are to do good, to be rich in good works, generous, and ready to share, [19] thus storing up for themselves the treasure of a good foundation for the future, so that they may take hold of the life that really is life.

[20] Timothy, guard what has been entrusted to you. Avoid the profane chatter and contradictions of what is falsely called knowledge; [21] by professing it some have missed the mark as regards the faith.

Grace be with you.[a]

[a] The Greek word for *you* here is plural; in other ancient authorities it is singular. Other ancient authorities add *Amen*

Lev 22.2. *No one has ever seen*, see 1 Jn 4.12. **18–19:** *Storing up . . . treasure*, see Mt 6.19–20; *m. Pe'ah* 1.1 ("capital in the world to come" as the fruit of righteous acts now); *T. Levi* 13.5. The wider concept of receiving one's reward in heaven may indicate that expectations of the beginning of a new age, in which justice will be established under the rule of God, have receded in this later generation of Christ-followers. **20:** *Falsely called knowledge*, perhaps a reference to a Gnostic form of teaching, in which secret knowledge imparted to the believer is the key to salvation. **21:** *Grace*, see 1.1–2n.

THE SECOND LETTER OF PAUL TO TIMOTHY

Although 2 Timothy states that this is a letter composed by the apostle Paul (1.1) while imprisoned in Rome (1,8,16; 2.9) and awaiting execution (4.6), written to his closest disciple, Timothy, in Ephesus (2.17), most scholars now doubt Pauline authorship. Indications that Timothy is a "third generation" Christian (1.5) combined with an emphasis on "right teaching" (e.g., 2.2,15) lead to the conclusion that the letter is responding to post–Pauline conditions.

The Pastoral Epistles—2 Timothy, 1 Timothy, and Titus—were probably composed at the beginning of the second century, perhaps in Asia Minor (modern Turkey; see Introduction to 1 Timothy). They primarily address Christian doctrine and church leadership. Their attribution to Paul—a common practice in ancient writing in which "writings falsely ascribed," or "pseudepigrapha," are attributed to known authors—is intended to give them apostolic authority.

In this letter the writer urges Timothy to leave all and come to him in Rome (4.9). The New Testament elsewhere tells us that Paul met Timothy in Lystra in Asia Minor and then chose him as a travel companion (Acts 16.1–3). Other letters (2 Cor 1.1; Phil 1.1; 2 Thess 1.1; Philem 1) all mention Timothy as co-author of the letters. Paul presents him as his messenger to the budding Christian communities (e.g., 1 Cor 4.7). According to Acts 16.1–3, Timothy had a Jewish mother but a Greek father, and he was uncircumcised until Paul circumcised him (Acts 16.1–3). In the opening paragraph of the letter, Paul reminds Timothy of his pious (apparently Jewish) mother, Eunice, and grandmother Lois. He omits mention of Timothy's Gentile father.

In ch 2 the author complains about persons who deny the relevance of the doctrine of resurrection (2.18), and in ch 3 he describes those with opposing opinions as evil men (3.3–5), who have won over the ears and hearts of sinful and lustful women (3.6–7). The question of resurrection may relate to various early Christian views about the nature of Jesus' body. Paul's statement in 1 Cor 15.50 that "flesh and blood cannot inherit the kingdom of God" coupled with early docetic views, which maintained that Jesus only "seemed" (Gk *dokeō*, "to seem, appear") to be human, suggested the divine Jesus never actually died and thus was not resurrected (see 1 Cor 15.12–20). This view motivated the church to emphasize the physical nature of Jesus' resurrection. In Second Temple Jewish circles, however, the question of the belief in the resurrection was already being hotly debated. While the Pharisees and Essenes apparently endorsed it, the Sadducees flatly denied it, as becomes clear both from the writings of the historian Josephus (*J.W.* 2.163–65; *Ant.* 18.14,16,18), the New Testament (Acts 23.6–8) and even from rabbinic texts (*Avot de R. Natan (A)*A 5; B 10). By the time 2 Timothy was composed, the Sadducees and their school had ceased to exist, and Jews held opinions similar to those of the Christians on this issue. Another problem discussed in the letter is that of women as being influenced by new Christian doctrine. That new doctrine and the place of women were real concerns in Christian circles is confirmed by the various Apocryphal Acts of the Apostles (e.g., *Acts of Paul and Thecla, Acts of Thomas, Acts of John*), dated to about the time of this letter in the late first century or early second century CE, which usually view women's celibacy positively. The issue of women being influenced by various sects is also documented in Jewish sources from the Second Temple period. Thus Josephus reports that women were strongly influenced by the Pharisees (*Ant.* 17.41–43) and rabbinic sources seem to confirm this assertion (*b. Nidd.* 5.2).

It is difficult to discern how Jewish, or how informed about anything Jewish, the author of 2 Timothy was. Jewishness is not an issue in the letter. In 3.15 the author refers to Timothy's acquaintance with scripture, although to what scripture the author refers remains unclear. In 2.8 we read that Jesus was a descendant of David: "Remember Jesus Christ, raised from the dead, a descendant of David—that is my gospel." This probably implies, however, that the author's knowledge of Jesus' illustrious descent derives from his knowledge of Paul's views (Rom 1.3) and not necessarily from the Tanakh or its Greek translation, the Septuagint.

The best location to test whether the author of 2 Timothy is acquainted with the Tanakh is in 3.8. Here the author compares the persons who, in his view, are leading his community astray with false doctrines, to Moses' two opponents—Pharaoh's magicians (see annotations). Yet the author is certainly referring not to what we would recognize as the biblical account but rather to an apocryphal retelling of the story of Moses. In the Tanakh, the multiple Egyptian magicians are nameless (Ex 7.11–12), but a long apocryphal tradition focuses on two named magicians, Jannes and Jambres, and details their exploits. Fragments of a Greek composition named *Jannes and Jambres* have surfaced on two Egyptian papyri, but it is hard to decide whether this composition was written by Christians (inspired by this verse in 2 Timothy) or whether this is an old Jewish apocryphal text. The Qumran Damascus Document, where the magicians Moses bested are Johana and his brother (5.18–19), supports the claim that 2 Timothy is referring to a Jewish tradition. Jannes, the protagonist of the apocryphal papyrus, is viewed as Jambres's brother, and his name can be explained as a Greek rendering of the Qumranic Johana. Another possibility, however, is to view Jannes and Jambres as belonging to an Exodus countertradition, as related by the Egyptians. Fragments of this very negative, anti-Jewish tradition have been preserved in many sources, such as Hecataeus of Abdera (preserved in Diod. Sic., 40.3), Manetho (as e.g., in Josephus, *Ag. Ap.* 1.237–51) and Apion (preserved in Josephus, *Ag. Ap.* 2.16–17, 20–21). The invention of Jannes and Jambres as part of this tradition can be found in the mention of Jannes (and another Egyptian magician named Lotapes) in the writing of Pliny the Elder, who is not elsewhere familiar with biblical traditions (*Nat.* 30.11). It is evident from Tacitus (*Hist.* 5 3.1) that a counter-Egyptian Exodus tradition was in vogue in Rome at that time. Thus, 2 Timothy's knowledge of the Moses tradition in this form does not help place this epistle: the tradition is derived either from a non-Jewish, most likely anti-Jewish tradition (as represented by Pliny) or from the writings of a Jewish group removed from mainstream Judaism (as represented by the writings from the CD) or even from a Jewish apocryphal composition so marginal that it has been preserved only in fragments, and by Christians (the papyri—if indeed these were not actually composed by Christians, inspired by the reference in 2 Timothy). Obviously this reference does not show an acquaintance with Jewish scripture as such.

Tal Ilan

1 Paul, an apostle of Christ Jesus by the will of God, for the sake of the promise of life that is in Christ Jesus,

[2] To Timothy, my beloved child:

Grace, mercy, and peace from God the Father and Christ Jesus our Lord.

[3] I am grateful to God—whom I worship with a clear conscience, as my ancestors did—when I remember you constantly in my prayers night and day. [4] Recalling your tears, I long to see you so that I may be filled with joy. [5] I am reminded of your sincere faith, a faith that lived first in your grandmother Lois and your mother Eunice and now, I am sure, lives in you. [6] For this reason I remind you to rekindle the gift of God that is within you through the laying on of my hands; [7] for God did not give us a spirit of cowardice, but rather a spirit of power and of love and of self-discipline.

[8] Do not be ashamed, then, of the testimony about our Lord or of me his prisoner, but join with me in suffering for the gospel, relying on the power of God, [9] who saved us and called us with a holy calling, not according to our works but according to his own purpose and grace. This grace was given to us in Christ Jesus before the ages began, [10] but it has now been revealed through the appearing of our

1.1–2. Salutation. 1: Rom 1.1–7; 1 Cor 1.1; 1 Tim 1.1. *Life,* see Col 3.4; 1 Tim 4.8. **2:** *Child,* a term of endearment, not blood relationship. *Grace,* Gk "charis," standard in Pauline greetings; *mercy,* Gk "eleos," in LXX for Heb "ḥesed" (e.g. Ps 85.10 [Heb 85.11; LXX 84.11]), "lovingkindness"; *peace,* Gk "eirēnē," in LXX for Heb "shalom."

1.3–18: Exhortations to remain faithful in suffering. 3: *Ancestors,* Paul's Jewish predecessors; see Phil 3.4–6. **5:** *Grandmother . . . mother,* Timothy is thus a third-generation Christian, an indication that the letter is post-apostolic. *Eunice* (Gk "good victory"); Acts 16.1 states that she was Jewish. **6–7:** *Gift,* his commission, received by *laying on . . . hands,* a gesture of healing and dedication; see e.g., Acts 6.6; 9.12. Such dedication—although not healing, for which it is not used in the Hebrew Bible—follows Jewish practice (e.g., Num 8.10,12). *Spirit of cowardice . . . self-discipline,* see Sir 34.14–16; re-dedication leads to fortitude. **8:** *Do not be ashamed,* one of the letter's themes (see vv. 12,16; 2.15): the exhortation to *rekindle* (v. 6) commitment is expressed in bold testifying. *Prisoner,* ostensibly a second prison term, following that of Philippians, Colossians and Philemon. See 1.17; 4.6–8. *Gospel,* the "good news" of Jesus (see 1.10). **9:** *Saved us,* Paul's authentic letters typically regard salvation as a future event. *Not according to our works . . . grace,* a leading theme in Paul's authentic letters (e.g., Rom 3.21–27; Gal 2.15–21). *Before the*

Savior Christ Jesus, who abolished death and brought life and immortality to light through the gospel. [11] For this gospel I was appointed a herald and an apostle and a teacher,[a] [12] and for this reason I suffer as I do. But I am not ashamed, for I know the one in whom I have put my trust, and I am sure that he is able to guard until that day what I have entrusted to him.[b] [13] Hold to the standard of sound teaching that you have heard from me, in the faith and love that are in Christ Jesus. [14] Guard the good treasure entrusted to you, with the help of the Holy Spirit living in us.

[15] You are aware that all who are in Asia have turned away from me, including Phygelus and Hermogenes. [16] May the Lord grant mercy to the household of Onesiphorus, because he often refreshed me and was not ashamed of my chain; [17] when he arrived in Rome, he eagerly[c] searched for me and found me [18]—may the Lord grant that he will find mercy from the Lord on that day! And you know very well how much service he rendered in Ephesus.

2 You then, my child, be strong in the grace that is in Christ Jesus; [2] and what you have heard from me through many witnesses entrust to faithful people who will be able to teach others as well. [3] Share in suffering like a good soldier of Christ Jesus. [4] No one serving in the army gets entangled in everyday affairs; the soldier's aim is to please the enlisting officer. [5] And in the case of an athlete, no one is crowned without competing according to the rules. [6] It is the farmer who does the work who ought to have the first share of the crops. [7] Think over what I say, for the Lord will give you understanding in all things.

[8] Remember Jesus Christ, raised from the dead, a descendant of David—that is my gospel, [9] for which I suffer hardship, even to the point of being chained like a criminal. But the word of God is not chained. [10] Therefore I endure everything for the sake of the elect, so that they may also obtain the salvation that is in Christ Jesus, with eternal glory. [11] The saying is sure:

If we have died with him, we will also live
with him;
[12] if we endure, we will also reign with him;
if we deny him, he will also deny us;
[13] if we are faithless, he remains faithful—
for he cannot deny himself.

[14] Remind them of this, and warn them before God[d] that they are to avoid wrangling over words, which does no good but only

[a] Other ancient authorities add *of the Gentiles*
[b] Or *what has been entrusted to me*
[c] Or *promptly*
[d] Other ancient authorities read *the Lord*

ages, see Eph 1.4. **10:** *Appearing,* Jesus' earthly life. **11:** *Herald,* Gk "kēryx," "proclaimer"; the message proclaimed is "kērygma." *Apostle,* lit., "one sent out," the title of those who witnessed Jesus' life and resurrection (e.g., Acts 1.15–26). *Teacher,* some manuscripts read "teacher of the Gentiles," reflecting 1 Tim 2.7. **12:** *Suffer,* a Pauline theme, especially in the captivity epistles (Eph, Phil, Col, Philem). **13–14:** *Sound teaching . . . faith . . . treasure,* faith is equated not with trust but with assent to doctrine. **15:** *Phygelus and Hermogenes,* not mentioned elsewhere. **16:** *Onesiphorus,* apparently the leader of a house church (4.19). *Chain,* sign of his arrest (see Acts 28.20). **18:** *Lord . . . Lord,* entreating the Lord for the Lord's own mercy; cf. Ps 84.11 (Heb v. 12). *Mercy,* Gk "eleos," in LXX for Heb "ḥesed," "steadfast love"; see e.g., Ps 103.17. *That day,* the coming of Christ in glory as judge (cf. 4.1).

2.1–13: Further exhortations to endurance. 3–6: Three comparisons—*soldier, athlete, farmer*—make the point that perseverance and dedication to purpose are necessary to complete one's task, no matter how arduous. Two of these themes are found in genuine Pauline epistles. On the former see 1 Cor 3.6. On the *athlete,* see 1 Cor 8.24. For a parallel Jewish text, see the description of the martyr Eleazar in 4 Macc 6.10. **7:** *The Lord will give you understanding,* see Prov 2.6. **8:** *Jesus Christ, raised . . . descendant of David,* a summary of belief: Jesus the Messiah, the resurrection, the royal ruler. **9:** *Chained,* see 1.16. **10:** *Elect,* Gk "chosen," those in the community. In the Tanakh the people of Israel are the chosen; see, e.g., Deut 7.6; in the Second Temple literature of Qumran, the sect is implied; see, e.g., 1QS 4.22. *Eternal glory,* lit., "glory of the ages"; cf. Isa 54.8, "everlasting love" (Heb "ḥesed 'olam"). **11–13:** A brief hymn encouraging endurance. **11:** *Saying is sure,* a phrase characteristic of the Pastoral Epistles (1 Tim 1.15; 3.1; 4.9; Titus 3.8).

2.14–26: Further warnings. 14: *Wrangling,* arguing uselessly. **15:** *Worker . . . explaining the word of truth,* the task is to present established teaching clearly. **16:** *Profane chatter,* conversation about worldly concerns (see

ruins those who are listening. [15] Do your best to present yourself to God as one approved by him, a worker who has no need to be ashamed, rightly explaining the word of truth. [16] Avoid profane chatter, for it will lead people into more and more impiety, [17] and their talk will spread like gangrene. Among them are Hymenaeus and Philetus, [18] who have swerved from the truth by claiming that the resurrection has already taken place. They are upsetting the faith of some. [19] But God's firm foundation stands, bearing this inscription: "The Lord knows those who are his," and, "Let everyone who calls on the name of the Lord turn away from wickedness."

[20] In a large house there are utensils not only of gold and silver but also of wood and clay, some for special use, some for ordinary. [21] All who cleanse themselves of the things I have mentioned[a] will become special utensils, dedicated and useful to the owner of the house, ready for every good work. [22] Shun youthful passions and pursue righteousness, faith, love, and peace, along with those who call on the Lord from a pure heart. [23] Have nothing to do with stupid and senseless controversies; you know that they breed quarrels. [24] And the Lord's servant[b] must not be quarrelsome but kindly to everyone, an apt teacher, patient, [25] correcting opponents with gentleness. God may perhaps grant that they will repent and come to know the truth, [26] and that they may escape from the snare of the devil, having been held captive by him to do his will.[c]

3 You must understand this, that in the last days distressing times will come. [2] For people will be lovers of themselves, lovers of money, boasters, arrogant, abusive, disobedient to their parents, ungrateful, unholy, [3] inhuman, implacable, slanderers, profligates, brutes, haters of good, [4] treacherous, reckless, swollen with conceit, lovers of pleasure rather than lovers of God, [5] holding to the outward form of godliness but denying its power. Avoid them! [6] For among them are those who make their way into households and captivate silly women, overwhelmed by their sins and swayed by all kinds of desires,

[a] Gk *of these things*
[b] Gk *slave*
[c] Or *by him, to do his* (that is, God's) *will*

1 Tim 6.20–21). Cf. also *m. Avot* 3.14, "a fence around wisdom is silence," based on earlier biblical Wisdom ideals (e.g., Prov 17.28). **17–18:** *Gangrene,* the metaphor implies that the loss of believers through false teaching is the same as the loss of a limb from lack of blood. *Hymenaeus,* subject to criticism as a false teacher also in 1 Tim 1.20. *Philetus,* not otherwise mentioned. *Resurrection . . . already taken place,* apparently a form of apocalyptic belief maintaining that believers had already achieved their destiny in the present *resurrection* of the believers, not of Jesus. **19:** *Firm foundation,* see 1 Tim 6.19, where it is charitable giving; here it probably refers to scripture generally. *The Lord . . . who are his,* quotation from Num 16.5, concerning the rebellion of Korah the Levite and his followers against Moses. Although this is a direct quotation from LXX, this is another use of a Pauline theme; cf. 1 Cor 10.10. *Let everyone who calls . . . ,* combining phrases from Isa 26.13; Job 36.10; Sir 17.26. **20–21:** *Utensils . . . work,* whatever the material out of which the *utensils* are made, it is those who *cleanse themselves* who will become *ready for every good work.* The argument is against drawing conclusions on the basis of distinctions within the community. **22:** *Shun . . . pursue,* what "cleansing" means. *Pure heart,* see Ps 51.10 (Heb v. 12; LXX Ps 50.12): Heb "lebh tahor," "clean heart" or "pure heart"; Gk "katharas kardias," in LXX "kardian katharan," "cleansed heart." **24–26:** *Lord's servant,* anyone in the church. Right teaching and *gentleness* in *correcting opponents* may help them *escape from the snare of the devil,* here not wrong action but following incorrect teaching. See also *m. Avot* 3.13, "Receive all men cheerfully"; also *m. Avot* 4.3, "Despise no man . . . for there is not a man that has not his hour."

3.1–17: Endurance in the present and during the last days. **1–5:** *Last days,* the close of the present age and beginning of the reign of God. Moral depravity, an eschatological sign, suggests the end-times have begun. *Lovers of themselves . . . Avoid them,* a "vice list" of the characteristics that the outsiders were expected to exhibit, and those who remain faithful were to avoid. For other examples, see 1 Tim 1.9–10; Rom 1.29–31; 1 Cor 5.11; 6.9–10; Gal 5.19–21. **6–9:** Warnings against false teaching. *Silly women,* the writer does not think women capable of leadership or intellectual activity (see 1 Tim 5.11–15). *Jannes and Jambres,* names given to Pharaoh's magicians (Ex 7.11–12,22) in the CD (5.17–19); see discussion in the Introduction. **10–17:** The writer testifies to

[7] who are always being instructed and can never arrive at a knowledge of the truth. [8] As Jannes and Jambres opposed Moses, so these people, of corrupt mind and counterfeit faith, also oppose the truth. [9] But they will not make much progress, because, as in the case of those two men,[a] their folly will become plain to everyone.

[10] Now you have observed my teaching, my conduct, my aim in life, my faith, my patience, my love, my steadfastness, [11] my persecutions, and my suffering the things that happened to me in Antioch, Iconium, and Lystra. What persecutions I endured! Yet the Lord rescued me from all of them. [12] Indeed, all who want to live a godly life in Christ Jesus will be persecuted. [13] But wicked people and impostors will go from bad to worse, deceiving others and being deceived. [14] But as for you, continue in what you have learned and firmly believed, knowing from whom you learned it, [15] and how from childhood you have known the sacred writings that are able to instruct you for salvation through faith in Christ Jesus. [16] All scripture is inspired by God and is[b] useful for teaching, for reproof, for correction, and for training in righteousness, [17] so that everyone who belongs to God may be proficient, equipped for every good work.

4 In the presence of God and of Christ Jesus, who is to judge the living and the dead, and in view of his appearing and his kingdom, I solemnly urge you: [2] proclaim the message; be persistent whether the time is favorable or unfavorable; convince, rebuke, and encourage, with the utmost patience in teaching. [3] For the time is coming when people will not put up with sound doctrine, but having itching ears, they will accumulate for themselves teachers to suit their own desires, [4] and will turn away from listening to the truth and wander away to myths. [5] As for you, always be sober, endure suffering, do the work of an evangelist, carry out your ministry fully.

[6] As for me, I am already being poured out as a libation, and the time of my departure has come. [7] I have fought the good fight, I have finished the race, I have kept the faith. [8] From now on there is reserved for me the crown of righteousness, which the Lord, the righteous judge, will give me on that day, and not only to me but also to all who have longed for his appearing.

[9] Do your best to come to me soon, [10] for Demas, in love with this present world, has deserted me and gone to Thessalonica; Crescens has gone to Galatia,[c] Titus to Dalmatia. [11] Only Luke is with me. Get Mark and bring him with you, for he is useful in my ministry. [12] I have sent Tychicus to Ephesus. [13] When you come, bring the cloak that I left with Carpus at Troas, also the books, and above all the parchments. [14] Alexander the coppersmith did me great harm; the Lord will

[a] Gk lacks *two men*
[b] Or *Every scripture inspired by God is also*
[c] Other ancient authorities read *Gaul*

his own exemplary experience, using a list of virtues (vv. 10–11), advice (vv. 12–13), and further exhortations (vv. 14–17). **11:** *Antioch, Iconium, and Lystra,* see Acts 13.14–14.23. **12:** *Persecuted,* a NT theme concerning apostolic witness (see e.g., Mt 5.11,44; 10.23; Lk 11.49; 21.12; Jn 15.20; Acts 7.52). **15–16:** *Sacred writings . . . scripture,* the Septuagint. *Inspired by God,* lit., "God-inspirited" (Gk "theopneustos"; "pneuma" can mean "wind," "breath," or "spirit" [similar to Heb "ruaḥ"]), conveying right teaching, as shown in the list of what the writings are useful for. Although the characteristics, such as usefulness, are not exalted, this verse serves as the proof text for some who claim that the Bible is divinely inspired and thus inerrant. See also 2 Pet 1.20–21.

4.1–18: Final exhortations. 1: *Judge the living and the dead,* Jesus' eschatological role (see Acts 10.42; 1 Pet 4.5). **2–5:** The characteristics of sound teaching, necessary to counter the false teaching in *myths.* For the Pastorals, unlike Paul's genuine epistles, the opponents are false teachers within the church rather than non-messianic pagans or Jews. *Itching ears,* insatiable curiosity. *Evangelist,* one who proclaims the "gospel" (Gk "euangelion"). **6–8:** The writer, anticipating his martyrdom, presents himself as a sacrifice (Phil 2.17) and an athlete, who wins a *crown* (see 2.5; 1 Cor 9.25 and 4 Macc 6.10) when he finishes first in a *race.* **9–10:** *Demas . . . Titus,* see Eph 6.21; Col 4.7,10,14; Titus 3.12; Philem 24. **11:** *Luke,* see Col 4.14; Philem 24; the book of Acts, written by the same author as the Gospel of Luke, presents the author as Paul's companion. *Mark,* see Acts 12.12,25; 15.37,39; Col 4.10, Philem 24; 1 Pet 5.13. Papias of Hierapolis (ca. 70–155 CE) associates this Mark with the Gospel bearing

pay him back for his deeds. [15] You also must beware of him, for he strongly opposed our message.

[16] At my first defense no one came to my support, but all deserted me. May it not be counted against them! [17] But the Lord stood by me and gave me strength, so that through me the message might be fully proclaimed and all the Gentiles might hear it. So I was rescued from the lion's mouth. [18] The Lord will rescue me from every evil attack and save me for his heavenly kingdom. To him be the glory forever and ever. Amen.

[19] Greet Prisca and Aquila, and the household of Onesiphorus. [20] Erastus remained in Corinth; Trophimus I left ill in Miletus. [21] Do your best to come before winter. Eubulus sends greetings to you, as do Pudens and Linus and Claudia and all the brothers and sisters.[a]

[22] The Lord be with your spirit. Grace be with you.[b]

[a] Gk *all the brothers*

[b] The Greek word for *you* here is plural. Other ancient authorities add *Amen*

his name. *Books . . . parchments,* both words mean "scrolls." **14:** *Alexander,* see 1 Tim 1.20. **16:** *First defense,* the first opportunity the accused has to offer an explanation (Gk "apologia," here rendered "defense"). **17:** *Gentiles might hear,* Paul regarded himself as the apostle to the Gentiles (see Rom 11.13; 15.16; Gal 2.8–9; Eph 3.8). *Lion's mouth,* see Am 5.19; Dan 6.1–24.

4.19–22: Concluding greetings. 19: *Prisca and Aquila,* see Acts 18.2–3,18; Rom 16.3; 1 Cor 16.19. *Onesiphorus,* see 1.16–17. **20:** *Erastus,* see Acts 19.22; Rom 16.23. A man with the same name was the city treasurer of Corinth. *Trophimus,* see Acts 20.4–5; 21.29. **21:** *Eubulus . . . Claudia,* not mentioned elsewhere. *Linus and Claudia,* the fourth-century Christian "Apostolic Constitutions" identify Linus as Peter's successor in Rome and Claudia as his mother. Apparently, there were a number of people with the writer, despite v. 11 above. **22:** *Your* is singular; *you* is plural.

THE LETTER OF PAUL TO TITUS

NAME, AUTHORSHIP, AND BACKGROUND

The Letter to Titus, along with 1 and 2 Timothy, constitute the Pastoral Epistles, so named because they impart practical advice to believers, including requirements for leadership. For further background on these letters, see the introduction to 1 Timothy. The letter purports to be written by Paul to Titus, a co-worker who acted as an emissary in Paul's correspondence with the Corinthians (2 Cor 8.23) and accompanied Paul to Jerusalem (Gal 2.1).

Based on analyses of language and content, the oldest extant fragment of Titus dates from the second century CE. The Pastoral Epistles are also mentioned by many of the early Christian theologians (often referred to as the "church fathers"), including Polycarp, Tertullian, and Jerome; some accept their authenticity, others question it. By the fourth century, Titus was widely accepted as Pauline. In the eighteenth and nineteenth centuries, scholars revisited the question of Pauline authorship. Currently, the consensus is that Titus is pseudonymous—an anonymous Christian leader wrote the letter in Paul's name to direct a community struggling with issues of definition and organization.

STRUCTURE AND INTERPRETATION

After greeting Titus (1.1–4), the author sketches ways in which the community should be organized and outlines the qualifications for elders and bishops (1.5–9). The author then launches into a denunciation of certain community members (1.10–16; see also 3.8b–11). The nascent communities sought to define their theology and thus establish institutions that would preserve orthodoxy. The author warns his followers to avoid alternative teachings and even advises shunning those who remain divisive.

The epistle addresses not only community structure but also household order and obedience, including the paramount values of self-control and perfect submission of women and slaves, which reflect Hellenistic ideals (2.1–10). Since churches developed out of gatherings in private homes, and since in the Roman world the family was seen as a microcosm of the state, the family and the community reflected one another. Social organization is thus linked to ethical behavior and given theological significance. The epistle then connects good behavior with salvific actions of God (2.11–3.8a).

A distinguishing characteristic of Titus is the title "savior" to describe both God and Jesus. In a key phrase, the letter speaks of waiting for "the manifestation of the glory of our great God and Savior, Jesus Christ" (2.13). The words "manifestation" (*epiphaneia*) and "savior" (*soteros*) are borrowed from the Hellenistic context where they are applied to deities and emperors. For example, an Ephesian inscription calls Julius Caesar "god made manifest, of Ares and Aphrodite, the common savior of human life." The explicit equation between Jesus and God is rare in the New Testament, although it is suggested by other passages such as John 1, and it becomes a central Christian doctrine, articulated by the Councils of Nicaea (325 CE) and Chalcedon (451 CE).

GUIDE TO READING

Titus emerges out of a confluence of Hellenistic culture and Jewish Scriptures. "Paul" calls himself a "servant of God" who labors for "God's elect" (1.1). The title "servant of God" appears frequently in the Septuagint in reference to the patriarchs, Moses, Elijah, David, and Jonah, among others. The phrase "God's elect" also draws on themes from the Jewish Scriptures. Jesus' followers, regardless of background, saw themselves as the true inheritors of the Jewish covenant.

The letter identifies the rebellious group as "of the circumcision" (1.10) and accuses them of propagating "Jewish myths" and "commandments of those who reject the truth" (1.14). The passage continues with the language of purity and defilement (1.15–16), perhaps alluding to the irrelevance of dietary regulations (as in Rom 14.14,20) or asceticism and celibacy (as expressed in 1 Tim 4.3–4). Whereas Paul's epistles (especially Galatians) address challenges from "Judaizers" (those, whether Jewish or Gentile in origin, who believed that followers of Jesus should also follow Torah's ritual as well as moral laws), the Pastorals show little engagement with this issue (see also 1 Tim 1.7). The letter closes by adding "genealogies" and "quarrels about the law" to the list of disagreeable beliefs and behaviors (3.9). These genealogies may be the generational lists that appear in the

Jewish Scriptures (Gen 10; 11.10–32; 1 Chr 1–9), and the speculations about them may be similar to those found among the Dead Sea Scrolls (1QapGen). Alternatively, the genealogies may be of Jesus himself, of which two conflicting ones are extant (Mt 1 and Lk 3). The extent to which Mosaic legislation was still binding on those who believed in Jesus as the Christ was a hotly debated issue in several New Testament epistles (see especially Galatians, which also identifies an antagonistic group as "of the circumcision" in 2.12).

It is difficult to determine the ways in which the letter reflects social and historical realities. There may be differences between Jewish and Gentile community members over the interpretation of scripture and living out its teachings. However, "those from the circumcision" are not necessarily Jewish believers in Jesus, since there were Jews who did not advocate circumcision for inclusion in the community (most notably, Paul); there were Gentiles who did want to follow Torah, or at least believed that circumcision was an essential mark of the covenant, whether "old" or "new" (some Gentiles in Galatia were circumcised). In addition to these complexities, the rhetoric of the letter is harsh, likening the writer's opponents to animals, and including an ethnic slur against Cretans (1.11–12). Such polemical language makes determining the views of those the author condemns difficult, since it indicates that the author is relying more on name-calling than reasoned argument to discredit his opponents. Thus, the letter may reflect a time in the developing church when simply associating a teaching with Judaism was to mark it as unacceptable, whether or not the teaching really had such a connection.

Jennifer L. Koosed

1 Paul, a servant[a] of God and an apostle of Jesus Christ, for the sake of the faith of God's elect and the knowledge of the truth that is in accordance with godliness, [2] in the hope of eternal life that God, who never lies, promised before the ages began— [3] in due time he revealed his word through the proclamation with which I have been entrusted by the command of God our Savior,

[4] To Titus, my loyal child in the faith we share:

Grace[b] and peace from God the Father and Christ Jesus our Savior.

[5] I left you behind in Crete for this reason, so that you should put in order what re-

[a] Gk *slave*
[b] Other ancient authorities read *Grace, mercy,*

1.1–4: Salutation. The longest opening of any Pastoral Epistle, the passage may have been intended to introduce all three letters. **1:** *Servant,* lit., "slave" ("doulos"), *of God,* a frequent title in Jewish literature; see 2 Sam 3.18; Jer 7.25; Ps 19.11,13; 27.9; Ezra 5.11; 9.11; Neh 1.6,11; and Jon 1.9 LXX. *Apostle,* "messenger," is used seventy-nine times in the NT but only once in the LXX (I Kings 14.6). *God's elect* alludes to the election of Israel (see Isa 65.9, which also links election to servanthood) although the LXX does not use the exact phrase; through faith and discipleship, Christ's followers are "elect" (e.g., Mt. 22.14; Mk 13.20–27; Titus 1.1; 1 Pet 1.2; 2.9–10). *Knowledge of the truth,* God's revelation through Christ; the phrase has an almost formulaic meaning in the Pastorals (1 Tim 2.4; 2 Tim 2.25; 3.7). *Godliness,* living in accordance with truth, an important virtue in both Hellenistic Jewish (Philo) and Gentile (Epictetus) literature. **2:** *Eternal life,* Dan 12.2; *Pss. Sol.* 3.12; and Wis 5.15 where it refers to the resurrection of the righteous. *Never lies,* God's fidelity and honesty are central in the Jewish Scriptures (Num 23.19; 1 Sam 15.29). **4:** *The faith,* a communal confession about God's revelation through Christ; the definite article makes it a technical term, unlike Paul's use of "faith" ("pistis"), which connotes relationship rather than doctrine (see Rom 3.22). *Savior* ("soteros"), used once in the undisputed Pauline corpus (Phil 3.20) but ten times in the Pastorals. Savior language is never associated with hopes for a messiah in Jewish literature, except in the NT, where God's saving actions are made manifest through Jesus (whose name means "God saves"). Salvation has multiple dimensions, including present-oriented righteous living and future-oriented eternal life.

1.5–9: Qualifications for elders. 5: Only canonical reference to a Pauline mission to *Crete.* Tacitus (*Hist.* 5.2) states Crete had a sizeable Jewish community. *Elders* ("presbyteroi"), an early church office (see Acts 20.17,28) that may have developed among the Jewish Jesus-followers in Jerusalem (see Acts 11.30; 15.4). A fourth-century CE epitaph from Crete identifies as Jewish a woman named Sophia; she is both "elder" ("presbyter") and "synagogue leader" ("archisynagogos"). The position of "elder" in Titus parallels leadership positions in Judaism,

mained to be done, and should appoint elders in every town, as I directed you: [6] someone who is blameless, married only once,[a] whose children are believers, not accused of debauchery and not rebellious. [7] For a bishop,[b] as God's steward, must be blameless; he must not be arrogant or quick-tempered or addicted to wine or violent or greedy for gain; [8] but he must be hospitable, a lover of goodness, prudent, upright, devout, and self-controlled. [9] He must have a firm grasp of the word that is trustworthy in accordance with the teaching, so that he may be able both to preach with sound doctrine and to refute those who contradict it.

[10] There are also many rebellious people, idle talkers and deceivers, especially those of the circumcision; [11] they must be silenced, since they are upsetting whole families by teaching for sordid gain what it is not right to teach. [12] It was one of them, their very own prophet, who said,

"Cretans are always liars, vicious brutes,
lazy gluttons."

[13] That testimony is true. For this reason rebuke them sharply, so that they may become sound in the faith, [14] not paying attention to Jewish myths or to commandments of those who reject the truth. [15] To the pure all things are pure, but to the corrupt and unbelieving nothing is pure. Their very minds and consciences are corrupted. [16] They profess to know God, but they deny him by their actions. They are detestable, disobedient, unfit for any good work.

2 But as for you, teach what is consistent with sound doctrine. [2] Tell the older men to be temperate, serious, prudent, and sound in faith, in love, and in endurance.

[3] Likewise, tell the older women to be reverent in behavior, not to be slanderers or slaves to drink; they are to teach what is good, [4] so that they may encourage the young women to love their husbands, to love their children, [5] to be self-controlled, chaste, good managers of the household, kind, being submissive to their husbands, so that the word of God may not be discredited.

[6] Likewise, urge the younger men to be self-controlled. [7] Show yourself in all respects

[a] Gk *husband of one wife*
[b] Or *an overseer*

where elders (usually older men) were respected for piety and wisdom (Ex 3.16; Num 11.16; see also Jdt 8.10; Sus 1.5); the NT frequently lists elders with chief priests (Mt 16.21; Lk 9.22). **6:** *Married only once*, marriage was an important qualification for Jewish community leaders because of the emphasis on family (see Gen 1.28), although some early apocalyptic communities advocated celibacy or separation from one's spouse after the commandment to procreate had been fulfilled (1QSa 1.6–13; 1QM 7.2–4). Only in the Middle Ages did the Roman Catholic Church require celibacy for clergy (see Mt 19.12; 1 Cor 7.7,32–35). **7:** *Bishop* ("episkopos"), lit., "overseer," an early Christian office (Phil 1.1; 1 Tim 3.1–7; 5.17–22). Titus equates bishop and elder. It is possible that in the older church 1 Timothy represents, bishops evolved from a larger group of elders, gaining preeminence as teachers (1 Tim 3.1; 5.17), while in the younger churches Titus mentions, such distinctions had not appeared.

1.10–16: Community controversies. 10: *Of the circumcision*, a reference to Jewish followers of Jesus and/or Gentile followers who submitted to circumcision; see Acts 11.2; 15.5; Gal 2.12; Rom 2:25–29; 1 Cor 7.18–19; Col 4.11. **11:** *Silenced*, lit., "reined in," refers to the muzzling of horses. **12:** The proverb is attributed to Epimenides, a sixth-century Cretan. In its original context, it was a mind teaser. Paul quotes Epimenides in Acts 17.28. **14:** *Jewish* (Gk "Ioudaikos") occurs only here in the NT (in the LXX, only in 2 Macc 8.11; 13.21), although both Josephus and Philo use the adjective. *Myths... commandments*, disparaging reference to interpretations of stories ("haggadah") and law ("halakhah"). On *myths* see 1 Tim 1.4; 4.7; 2 Tim 4.4; 2 Pet 1.16. The reference is probably to midrashic and pseudepigraphical stories. **15:** *Pure*, possible reference to Jewish purity codes, especially concerning food (Lev 11). *Consciences*, see Acts 23.1; 24.16; 1 Tim 1.5,19; 3.9; 4.2; 2 Tim 1.3; Heb 10.22; 13.18; 1 Pet 3.16,21. **16:** *Actions*, indicators of proper belief, as in 1.1 where "knowledge of the truth" is linked to "godliness."

2.1–10: Household rules. Household codes ("Haustafeln") appear also in Col 3.18–4.1; Eph 5.21–6.9; 1 Pet 3.1–7, except without the reciprocal duties of the male householder. The originally Greek form was adopted by Jewish writers (Philo, *Hypoth.* 7.14; Josephus, *Ag. Ap.* 2.23–29). **1:** *Sound* (lit., "healthy") *doctrine*, a particular concern of the Pastorals (1.9; 1 Tim 1.10; 2 Tim 4.3). **2:** See 1 Tim 3.2,8. **3:** Cf. 1 Tim 3.11. **4:** See 1 Tim 2.11–15. **5–6:** *Self-controlled*, one of the four cardinal virtues, advocated by both Jewish and Gentile writers (Aristotle, Homer,

a model of good works, and in your teaching show integrity, gravity, [8] and sound speech that cannot be censured; then any opponent will be put to shame, having nothing evil to say of us.

[9] Tell slaves to be submissive to their masters and to give satisfaction in every respect; they are not to talk back, [10] not to pilfer, but to show complete and perfect fidelity, so that in everything they may be an ornament to the doctrine of God our Savior.

[11] For the grace of God has appeared, bringing salvation to all,[a] [12] training us to renounce impiety and worldly passions, and in the present age to live lives that are self-controlled, upright, and godly, [13] while we wait for the blessed hope and the manifestation of the glory of our great God and Savior,[b] Jesus Christ. [14] He it is who gave himself for us that he might redeem us from all iniquity and purify for himself a people of his own who are zealous for good deeds.

[15] Declare these things; exhort and reprove with all authority.[c] Let no one look down on you.

3 Remind them to be subject to rulers and authorities, to be obedient, to be ready for every good work, [2] to speak evil of no one, to avoid quarreling, to be gentle, and to show every courtesy to everyone. [3] For we ourselves were once foolish, disobedient, led astray, slaves to various passions and pleasures, passing our days in malice and envy, despicable, hating one another. [4] But when the goodness and loving kindness of God our Savior appeared, [5] he saved us, not because of any works of righteousness that we had done, but according to his mercy, through the water[d] of rebirth and renewal by the Holy Spirit. [6] This Spirit he poured out on us richly through Jesus Christ our Savior, [7] so that, having been justified by his grace, we might become heirs according to the hope of eternal life. [8] The saying is sure.

I desire that you insist on these things, so that those who have come to believe in God may be careful to devote themselves to good works; these things are excellent and

[a] Or *has appeared to all, bringing salvation*
[b] Or *of the great God and our Savior*
[c] Gk *commandment*
[d] Gk *washing*

Philo, Josephus). **7:** *Good works*, those consistent with the author's values (see 3.1; 1 Tim 2.10). **9:** 1 Tim 6.1–2. *Slaves*, integral to Hellenistic households, perhaps constituted a majority in some urban areas. Jewish and Gentile writers rarely question the institution, although Philo mentions a few Jewish communities that rejected slavery, including the Essenes (*Good Person* 79). Some slaves were baptized as part of the household, while others joined on their own accord.

2.11–3.8a: Salvation and exhortations. 11: *Grace* ("charis"), lit., "favor, beneficence." *Grace of God* never appears in LXX, though believers frequently "find grace" before God (see Gen 6.8). *Salvation*, see 1.14n. and 3.5n. **12:** Exhortations reflecting Hellenistic moral philosophy, specifically Stoic concerns with self-control; see 2.5–6n. **13:** *Great God and Savior*, language related to Roman emperor cult describes Jesus as God (see Jn 1.14; 20.28; Heb 1.8). **14:** Perhaps quoting from an early Christian hymn. *Redeem*, from sin as slaves are manumitted (see Ex 6.6; Ps 130.8 [129.8 LXX]). *People of his own*, lit., "chosen people" ("laon periousion"), only here in the NT but five times in the LXX (Ex 19.5; 23.22; Deut 7.6; 14.2; 26.18; see also Ezek 37.23) to refer to Israel's election. The (predominantly Gentile) church sees itself in continuity with Israel. **3.1:** *Rulers and authorities*, governmental leaders; a warning against civil disobedience (see Rom 13.1–7; 1 Tim 2.1–2; 1 Pet 2.13–14). **4–7:** A single sentence in Greek, perhaps a baptismal formula. **5:** *Saved us*, God's salvation, indicated by Christ's actions and believers' moral transformation, is a completed action; by contrast, in the authentic Pauline epistles, salvation is completed by future resurrection. For salvation as moral conversion see Philo, *Rewards* 163. *Not because of any works* reflects Pauline language (Rom 3.28; Gal 2.16; see also Deut 9.5), where Paul refers specifically to "works of the law." *Mercy* ("eleos") is a central attribute of the divine in Jewish Scriptures (see Ex 34.6–7; Num 14.18; Ps 86.5,15 [LXX 85.5,15]) where it also describes a God of love and compassion (Heb "ḥesed"). *Water of rebirth and renewal by the Holy Spirit*, baptism. *Rebirth and renewal* draw on a rich complex of meanings that connects God's past act of creation to God's present act of the transformation of the believer's heart, to God's future re-creation or bodily resurrection. See 1QH 11–12. *The Holy Spirit*, God at work in the world; the Greek lacks the definite article. **7:** *Justified*, brought into right relationship with God. Paul stresses justification outside of the law (see Rom 3.24; Gal 2.16; compare Jas 2.21–25).

profitable to everyone. [9] But avoid stupid controversies, genealogies, dissensions, and quarrels about the law, for they are unprofitable and worthless. [10] After a first and second admonition, have nothing more to do with anyone who causes divisions, [11] since you know that such a person is perverted and sinful, being self-condemned.

[12] When I send Artemas to you, or Tychicus, do your best to come to me at Nicopolis, for I have decided to spend the winter there. [13] Make every effort to send Zenas the lawyer and Apollos on their way, and see that they lack nothing. [14] And let people learn to devote themselves to good works in order to meet urgent needs, so that they may not be unproductive.

[15] All who are with me send greetings to you. Greet those who love us in the faith.

Grace be with all of you.[a]

[a] Other ancient authorities add *Amen*

3.8b–11: Community controversies. 8: *Good works*, see 2.7n.; 3.5n. **9:** 1 Tim 1.4,6–7. *Genealogies*, either generational lists in the Jewish Scriptures or genealogies of Jesus (Gen 10; 1 Chr 1–9; Mt 1.1–17; Lk 3.23–38). *Quarrels about the law*, see 1.14n. **10:** *Admonition*, Mt 18.15–17 and the DSS (1QS), and CD enjoin similar methods for addressing disputes.

3.12–15: Farewell. 12: *Tychicus*, Paul's companion (Acts 20.4; Eph 6.21; Col 4.7–9; 2 Tim 4.12). *Nicopolis*, city on Greece's western coast. **13:** *Apollos*, see Acts 18.24–28; 1 Cor 3.4–6; 16.12. **14:** *Good works*, see 3.5n.

THE LETTER OF PAUL TO PHILEMON

NAME AND AUTHORSHIP

This letter, one of Paul's undisputed writings, takes its name from its first-mentioned addressee, Philemon (v.1). The shortest of the Pauline letters at 335 words in Greek, Philemon has been the subject of voluminous debate due both to the many uncertainties concerning its historical context and purpose and to its presentation. It is unique among the New Testament writings in naming a slave in a Christian household.

Paul writes the letter from prison (vv. 1,9–10,13,23) but does not mention the location of his imprisonment. Possibilities include Rome (see Acts 28.16) and Caesarea Maritima (Acts 23.23,33). Today many favor Ephesus, given Paul's lengthy stay and missionary activities there and the city's relative proximity to Colossae, the likely location of the letter's addressees. Colossae or its environs is suggested by the mention of Archippus (v. 2), the slave Onesimus (v. 10), and the co-workers who send greetings (vv. 23–24) in the later Letter to the Colossians (see Col 4.9–10,12,14,17). If written from Rome, the date of Philemon is ca. 61–63; if from Ephesus, an earlier date in the mid-50s is likely. Philemon has traditionally been grouped with two other letters, Philippians (a genuine Pauline letter) and Colossians (a letter attributed to Paul but probably not by him) into a group known as the "captivity epistles," because they all claim to have been written from jail.

STRUCTURE AND CONTENTS

The broad structure of the letter is consistent with Pauline epistolary style, which is generally also that of other known Greek letters. It begins with an introduction (vv. 1–3), including senders, recipients, and an opening greeting. Then follow words of thanksgiving (vv. 4–7) in which Paul expresses his gratitude to Philemon for his faith and his support of a community of early believers. The body of the letter (vv. 8–22) appeals to Philemon concerning his slave Onesimus. The section closes with an instruction to prepare for a visit from Paul. The letter concludes (vv. 23–25) with final greetings and a benediction.

INTERPRETATION

In terms of the circumstances prompting the letter, this much is clear: Philemon's slave, Onesimus, had encountered Paul in prison. Paul converted him and is now sending him back to Philemon. Since the late fourth century, most commentators have interpreted Onesimus to be a runaway slave, but this is not certain. It is possible that Onesimus had sought Paul, as his master's friend, to act as a mediator between the two, or perhaps Philemon had sent Onesimus to Paul to serve him while in prison, similar to the Philippian church's sending Epaphroditus to Paul (Phil 2.25–30). Because the circumstances of Onesimus's status cannot be precisely determined, neither can we determine Paul's intent in writing. Is he seeking Onesimus's continued service for himself (vv. 13–14), is he seeking to ensure that Philemon receive his returned slave with welcome and forgiveness (vv. 17–18), and perhaps "even more" (v. 21), is he suggesting Philemon manumit Onesimus (release him from servitude), since he is now a "beloved brother" to both Paul and Philemon in the church (vv. 16,21)? Although the appeal is directed to an individual, the letter is also a kind of public correspondence whose recipients include "the church in your house" (v. 1). Its private and communal character is singular among Paul's writings; it may have functioned not only to apply pressure to Philemon in the context of a specific situation involving him and Onesimus but also to impart to the entire community Paul's conviction that all members of the church should be treated by one another with forgiveness and love.

What is known of Onesimus, except for a reference in Col 4.9, comes from the Letter of Ignatius, bishop of Antioch, to the church at Ephesus, written probably in the year 107, when Ignatius, under arrest, was on his way to Rome to martyrdom. He refers (ch 1) to the bishop of the church at Ephesus, Onesimus, and tradition has held that this is the same Onesimus as in Philemon.

In the antebellum United States, both proslavery advocates and abolitionists appropriated the letter to support their views of slavery. Some of the former argued that Paul had indeed returned the slave Onesimus to Philemon, and that Philemon himself was both a Christian and a slaveholder. Conversely, some abolitionists argued that Paul, as a Jew, could not possibly have returned a fugitive slave to his owner. They cited Deut 23.15 with its injunction that "slaves who have escaped to you from their owners shall not be given back to them," as well as other texts from the Hebrew Bible (see "Slavery in the Roman Empire," p. 404) which set limits on the duration of enslavement.

Roman law and practice, even if not directly pertinent to the situation described in Philemon, is valuable in broadly contextualizing the letter. Throughout the centuries of the Roman Empire, legal and other texts from a variety of locations provide evidence of a great concern on the part of government as well as individual slaveholders that fugitive slaves be returned to their owners. Legislation also provided stipulations for the manumission of slaves. Thus Paul's return of Onesimus to Philemon and the possibility of Onesimus's manumission would have been consistent with Roman practice.

Paul writes of slaves and slavery, both literally and metaphorically, in a number of his letters. For example, concerning the latter, he signifies his obedience and submission to Christ in describing himself at the opening of Romans and Philippians as a slave of Christ (Rom 1.1; Phil 1.1). Elsewhere, he likens life under the law to slavery (Gal 4.8–11; 4.21–5.1). Although Paul does not seek the manumission of slaves, he envisions them as free and equal in their status as believers within the church (see 1 Cor 7.21–24; Gal 3.28).

The household codes ("Haustafeln") of Colossians and Ephesians are rooted in the Graeco-Roman ideal of the household and its role as the foundation of the larger community. They lack the ambiguity of the authentic writings of Paul in their treatment of slavery, demanding the obedience of wives to husbands and children to parents, as well as slaves to masters (Eph 6.1–9; Col 3.18–4.1). Similarly, 1 Timothy and Titus require that slaves serve their masters (1 Tim 6.1–2; Titus 2.9–10). Like Colossians and Ephesians, 1 Timothy and Titus, while attributed to Paul, are considered by most modern scholars to be non-Pauline in authorship and post-Pauline in date.

Many readers, past and present, have turned to Philemon to understand Paul's view of slavery. However, the puzzling nature of the letter and its focus on a specific situation concerning Onesimus, Philemon, and Paul are such that it does not yield any clear conclusions. Additionally, it is uncertain what impact Philemon's authorship by a Jew had on its content. The letter is exceptional in the New Testament corpus in its absence of concern with issues around the relationship of the Jesus Movement to other forms of Judaism.

Barbara Geller

[1] Paul, a prisoner of Christ Jesus, and Timothy our brother,[a]

To Philemon our dear friend and coworker, [2] to Apphia our sister,[b] to Archippus our fellow soldier, and to the church in your house:

[3] Grace to you and peace from God our Father and the Lord Jesus Christ.

[4] When I remember you[c] in my prayers, I always thank my God [5] because I hear of your love for all the saints and your faith toward the Lord Jesus. [6] I pray that the sharing of your

[a] Gk *the brother*
[b] Gk *the sister*
[c] From verse 4 through verse 21, *you* is singular

1–3: Introduction. 1: *Timothy*, a co-sender also of 2 Corinthians, Philippians, and 1 Thessalonians. **2:** *Apphia* is mentioned only here; she may have been Philemon's wife or perhaps was prominent in the community, since she is singled out for notice. *Archippus*, see Col 4.17; *fellow soldier*, co-worker (see also Philem 2.25). *In your house*, presumably the community met in Philemon's house; this was common in the early years of the movement. **3:** *Grace . . . and peace . . . Lord Jesus Christ*, standard Pauline salutation (see, e.g., Rom 1.7). *Our Father*, following Jesus' example (e.g., Mt 6.9). The Tanakh does not usually refer to God this way, but see Isa 63.16; Ps 89.26 [Heb v. 27].

4–7: Thanksgiving. Paul uses the singular for "you" in vv. 4–22a; most commentators hold it to refer to Philemon although a few argue for Archippus. **4:** *Remember*, the remembrance of people appears in ancient Jewish prayers and letters (e.g., 1 Macc 12.11; 2 Macc 1.2–6), frequently in the form of a petitioner beseeching God to "remember" and to deliver him or his people (e.g., Jer 15.15; Ps. 106.4). Remembrance is an important theme in later rabbinic liturgies, including "Yizkor" (lit., "remembrance") in memory of the dead. **5:** *Saints*, Gk "hagioi," "holy ones," Paul's usual characterization of believers (e.g., Rom 1.7; 1 Cor 1.2; etc.). It suggests persons and objects set apart for service to God (e.g., Lev 11.44–45). **6:** *Good that we* (or "you"; see translators' note *a* on next p.) *may do*, presumably by bringing others into the community of believers.

SLAVERY IN THE ROMAN EMPIRE

Chattel slavery, in which the slave-owner had absolute or nearly absolute control over the slave, was widespread in the Roman Empire. Although some, especially Stoics (e.g., Epictetus, *Diatr.* 1.13), wrote of the fundamental humanity of slaves and advocated that slaves be treated humanely, none rejected the institution. Roman slavery was not race based: individuals were enslaved primarily through captivity in war or birth to a slave mother. Slaves could be freed and become Roman citizens. Nonetheless, Roman slaves lived with the possibility of losing their families and with physical violence or the threat of it.

There is not much information about slavery in Jewish communities. The writings of Philo and Josephus as well as early rabbinic literature take it for granted, even as they advocate humane treatment and posit common humanity. Both Philo (*Good Person* 12.79; *Hypoth.* 11.4) and Josephus (*Ant.* 18 1.5) claim that the Essenes do not practice slavery; Josephus says that the Essenes believe the ownership of slaves contributes to injustice, and Philo states that the Essenes view slave ownership as unjust and as destroying nature's ordinances of equality. However, mentions of slaves in the Cairo Damascus Document suggest some practice of slavery (CD 11.12; 12.10). Jews were themselves enslaved in the Roman-Jewish wars.

The Mishnah integrates slaves into its overall system. Nearly all the texts ignore the Tanakh's distinctions between the Israelite and non-Israelite slave, the former having more protections from the power of the slave-owner and also a fixed period of six years of enslavement, more like an indentured servant, where the foreign slave was more like a chattel slave (see Ex 21.1–11; Lev 25.39–55; Deut 15.12–18). In the Mishnah, slaves enter the Israelite household having lost their prior nationhood and ethnicity. The texts are consistent with sources such as the writings of Josephus and the New Testament in assuming the existence of slavery in the Jewish community. The Mishnah and later texts write of Rabbi Gamaliel and his slave, Tabi, as an ideal master-slave pair. Gamaliel, the Torah sage, is kind, considerate, and respectful of Tabi. Tabi embodies Gamaliel's values and follows the teachings of Torah. (See, for example, *m. Sukk.* 2.1.) Overall, rabbinic law and Roman law reflect common concerns about the regulation of slaves ranging from their punishment to their manumission. Rabbinic law, like earlier biblical law, had greater restraints on the power of the slave-owner over the slave than did Roman law.

Paul envisioned slaves as free and equal in the church while not seeking the abolition of slavery. The Gospels assume that slaves are part of the social order. Jesus heals a centurion's slave (Mt 8.5–13), and the slave of the high priest is in the crowd of those who arrest Jesus (Mk 14.47). Slaves figure in some of the parables, echoing Roman stereotypes of the good and bad slave, and hinting at the violence to which a slave might be subject as well as his subordinate social position (Mt 25.14–30; Mk 12.1–11; see also Lk 17.7–10). The household codes mandate obedience: Eph 6.5–8 combines a negative stereotype with a hint of the threat of violence to which slaves were subject, and then frames it in the context of the teachings of the church in which God will reward both slaves and free for the good that they do. The Jesus Movement and contemporary Jewish groups shared the Graeco-Roman practice of slavery but differed from it due to religious teachings and social conditions. Neither the institutions of pagan Rome nor those of Judaism and Christianity offered a fundamental challenge to the practice of slavery.

faith may become effective when you perceive all the good that we[a] may do for Christ. [7] I have indeed received much joy and encouragement from your love, because the hearts of the saints have been refreshed through you, my brother.

[8] For this reason, though I am bold enough in Christ to command you to do your duty, [9] yet I would rather appeal to you on the basis

[a] Other ancient authorities read *you* (plural)

7: *Hearts*, lit., "viscera," inner organs, the site of the emotions; see also vv. 12,20. *Brother*, one of Paul's usual names for his colleagues (e.g., Rom 16.23). Such kinship terminology appears in ancient Jewish letters from the early Arad letters (e.g., Arad 16) that antedate the Babylonian invasion of 597 BCE to the letters associated with the War of Bar Kochba (132–135 CE; e.g., Murabba'at 43). Brother/s appears frequently in the Tanakh and later rabbinic writings to refer to the 'family' of Israel (e.g., Ps 133.1).

8–22: Paul's appeal to Philemon. 9: *Old man*, Paul is characterized as "young" in Acts 7.58, describing events perhaps two or three decades before the date of this letter. His expectation that he would be treated

of love—and I, Paul, do this as an old man, and now also as a prisoner of Christ Jesus.[a] [10] I am appealing to you for my child, Onesimus, whose father I have become during my imprisonment. [11] Formerly he was useless to you, but now he is indeed useful[b] both to you and to me. [12] I am sending him, that is, my own heart, back to you. [13] I wanted to keep him with me, so that he might be of service to me in your place during my imprisonment for the gospel; [14] but I preferred to do nothing without your consent, in order that your good deed might be voluntary and not something forced. [15] Perhaps this is the reason he was separated from you for a while, so that you might have him back forever, [16] no longer as a slave but more than a slave, a beloved brother—especially to me but how much more to you, both in the flesh and in the Lord.

[17] So if you consider me your partner, welcome him as you would welcome me. [18] If he has wronged you in any way, or owes you anything, charge that to my account. [19] I, Paul, am writing this with my own hand: I will repay it. I say nothing about your owing me even your own self. [20] Yes, brother, let me have this benefit from you in the Lord! Refresh my heart in Christ. [21] Confident of your obedience, I am writing to you, knowing that you will do even more than I say.

[22] One thing more—prepare a guest room for me, for I am hoping through your prayers to be restored to you.

[23] Epaphras, my fellow prisoner in Christ Jesus, sends greetings to you,[c] [24] and so do Mark, Aristarchus, Demas, and Luke, my fellow workers.

[25] The grace of the Lord Jesus Christ be with your spirit.[d]

a Or *as an ambassador of Christ Jesus, and now also his prisoner*
b The name Onesimus means *useful* or (compare verse 20) *beneficial*
c Here *you* is singular
d Other ancient authorities add *Amen*

with respect also recalls the use of "elder" as a title in the community of believers (e.g., Acts 20.17). Ancient Judaism had a deeply rooted tradition of respect for elders (e.g., Lev 19.32). **10:** *Onesimus,* see Col 4.9; Ignatius, *Eph.* 1; see Introduction. *Whose father I have become,* see 1 Cor 4.15. On the use of familial language in ancient Jewish texts to describe the relationship of teachers to disciples, see, for example, 1QH 15.20–21 from Qumran and, from later rabbinic literature, *b. Sanh.* 19b. **11:** *Useful,* a pun on Onesimus's name, which means "useful"; it is not clear if this was his name or was given to him when he was taken as a slave (as if nicknaming him "Handy"). **13:** *Be of service,* although the verb "diakoneō" is related to "diakonia," "ministry" and to "diakonos," "servant, deacon," it almost always means household service, not religious service (e.g., Lk 22.27). *Gospel,* here the preaching of the message of salvation through Jesus, which is the cause of his *imprisonment.* **15:** *Was separated,* referring to Onesimus's absence; the use of the passive may be a way of softening the fact of Onesimus's flight. **16:** *No longer as a slave . . . a beloved brother,* although this verse describes a transformed relationship among Philemon and Paul and the converted Onesimus—they are now beloved brothers—it is not clear what this portends for Onesimus's slave status. Paul may be asking Philemon to free Onesimus, or he may be referring solely to Onesimus's changed status in the context of the church. The use of the word "brother" to refer to a slave, who is also a community member, appears as well in Deut 15.12. The latter mandates that a Hebrew slave, after six years of servitude, must be freed in the seventh year. **18:** *If he has wronged you . . . or owes you anything,* Onesimus may have caused Philemon financial loss, either by stealing or by the loss of service consequent on his absence, which Paul offers to repay. Alternatively, this may be one of Paul's rhetorical strategies to put himself in the position of benefactor rather than supplicant. **19:** *Writing this with my own hand,* see 1 Cor 16.21; Gal 6.11; Paul's letters were usually dictated to a scribe. *Owing me even your own self,* a probable reference to Paul's conversion of Philemon. **21:** *You will do even more than I say,* perhaps Paul's plea that Philemon give Onesimus his freedom. **22:** *Guest room,* Gk "xenia," lodging place for strangers (i.e., those not of the house). *Restored to you,* lit., "be bestowed on you."

23–25: Conclusion. 23–24: *Epaphras . . . Mark, Aristarchus, Demas, and Luke,* greetings from co-workers, all of whom are named in Col 4.10–14; for Epaphras, see also Col 1.7. **25:** *Your spirit,* a blessing on the recipient's inmost being.

THE LETTER TO THE HEBREWS

Hebrews stands out from other New Testament literature in three ways: it is the only document that contains a sustained argument on the nature of Christ; its origin is unknown and thus its connections to other early Christian writings are unclear; and it is often perceived as the New Testament's most anti-Jewish text.

AUTHORSHIP AND LITERARY HISTORY

Although pre-modern commentators assumed that Paul wrote Hebrews, virtually all scholars today agree that Paul was not the author. The document circulated anonymously in antiquity, and the title "To the Hebrews" was added when it was collected together with Paul's letters. Although there are some resonances between Hebrews and Paul's genuine writings (for example, references to "dead works" [6.1; 9.14]), the language, style, and purpose of Hebrews is different. Although it has traditionally been considered a letter, 13.22 identifies the work as a "word of exhortation," implying that it was a sermon. Some interpreters have compared Hebrews to other ancient Jewish sermons, and one scholar has even suggested that Hebrews was a synagogue homily delivered on the ninth of the month of Ab, the day that commemorates the destruction of the First and Second Temple (*m. Ta'an.* 4.6).

Scholars debate whether Hebrews was written before or after the destruction of the Jerusalem Temple in 70 CE. Those arguing for a pre-70 date observe that Hebrews nowhere mentions the destruction. Because of the text's supersessionist perspective—namely, the temple cult is superseded by the one-time sacrifice of Jesus—an appeal to the destruction of the Temple would have greatly bolstered the argument that the Levitical sacrifices have become obsolete (chs 8–10). Those advocating a post-70 date argue that the text assumes the reality of the Temple's destruction and that its supersessionism is a response to the catastrophe.

Hebrews' geographical setting is also debated. The title "To the Hebrews" indicates that early readers thought that the intended audience was Jewish, and that led to postulating a Jerusalem setting. Many commentators, both ancient and modern, believe the author writes to Jewish-Christians tempted to "backslide" into non-messianic Judaism. But the text displays no knowledge of the Jerusalem Temple, focusing instead on the wilderness Tabernacle (Ex 25.1–31.11; 36.1–40.38). Because Hebrews has a Platonic philosophical orientation resembling that of Philo of Alexandria—for example, both Hebrews and Philo conceptualize the Jerusalem Temple as the physical form of an immaterial temple (8.1–5; 9.23–24; Philo, *Heir* 75, 112–13; *Prelim. Studies* 116–17)—an Alexandrian setting is possible. (There is no clear evidence, however, that the author of Hebrews was familiar with the writings of Philo.) Still others posit a Roman setting because Heb 13.24 extends greetings to "those from Italy" and because the earliest mention of Hebrews comes from the early Christian text, *1 Clement*, written from Rome. Whatever the setting of the author or the audience, Hebrews does not appear to be addressing local circumstances as do the Pauline letters.

STRUCTURE AND CONTENTS

Hebrews has the New Testament's most sophisticated Greek, marked by rhythmic cadences, alliteration, and other poetic devices. Although hard to detect in English, its first four verses form a poetic chain of syllabically balanced clauses, and the opening line resounds with alliteration and assonance. Creating an alliterative rhythm, the phrase "by faith" introduces each figure named in the list of biblical heroes in ch 11.

A good portion of Hebrews is taken up with explicating scripture cited from the Greek translation of the Bible (the Septuagint). The author demonstrates sophisticated scriptural interpretation and often expounds a single word or phrase at great length (see, e.g., Ps 95.11 in ch 4 or Ps 110.1 in ch 7). The purpose of such citations is almost always to demonstrate the superiority of Christ.

Hebrews offers a distinct and elevated Christology. As the son of God, Jesus is superior to all other beings, including angels—he is uncreated, immortal, and permanent. He is also superior to all biblical heroes, including Moses and Abraham, as well as institutions like the Levitical priesthood. As both perfect sacrifice and heavenly priest who intercedes for humans, Jesus supersedes the Jewish sacrificial system, rendering it obsolete. Indeed, the text states that sacrifices performed by the Levitical priests are ineffective precisely because they had to be repeated (10.1–5), while Jesus' sacrifice was only offered once. Yet, for Hebrews, Jesus is also fully human: although sinless (4.15), he died to atone for the sins of others.

GUIDE TO READING

Because Hebrews argues for Jesus' superiority over all else, Hebrews can be read as supersessionist. Drawing on Jeremiah's reference (31.31) to a "new covenant," the author calls Mosaic Law "only a shadow of the good things to come" (10.1) and insists that "in speaking of 'a new covenant,' he has made the first one obsolete. And what is obsolete and growing old will soon disappear" (8.13). Such language helped foster the view that Judaism was an inferior religion, a temporary guide prior to Christ. In recent years, scholars have made efforts to address the problem of anti-Judaism in Hebrews and have attempted to offer alternative understandings of these key verses.

Pamela Eisenbaum

1 Long ago God spoke to our ancestors in many and various ways by the prophets, [2] but in these last days he has spoken to us by a Son,[a] whom he appointed heir of all things, through whom he also created the worlds. [3] He is the reflection of God's glory and the exact imprint of God's very being, and he sustains[b] all things by his powerful word. When he had made purification for sins, he sat down at the right hand of the Majesty on high, [4] having become as much superior to angels as the name he has inherited is more excellent than theirs.

[5] For to which of the angels did God ever say,

"You are my Son;
today I have begotten you"?

Or again,

"I will be his Father,
and he will be my Son"?

[6] And again, when he brings the firstborn into the world, he says,

"Let all God's angels worship him."

[7] Of the angels he says,

"He makes his angels winds,
and his servants flames of fire."

[8] But of the Son he says,

"Your throne, O God, is[c] forever and ever,
and the righteous scepter is the scepter of your[d] kingdom.
[9] You have loved righteousness and hated wickedness;
therefore God, your God, has anointed you
with the oil of gladness beyond your companions."

[10] And,

"In the beginning, Lord, you founded the earth,
and the heavens are the work of your hands;

a Or *the Son*
b Or *bears along*
c Or *God is your throne*
d Other ancient authorities read *his*

1.1–3: Introduction. A poetic presentation of the main theme: the superiority of Christ, called *Son* to emphasize his unique status. The plural "sons of God" refers to angels in Gen 6.1–4 (cf. Ps 82.1,6). **1–2:** *Long ago . . . but in these last days*, contrasts of differing periods of divine revelation anticipate the contrast between old and new covenants (8.6–13). **2:** *Created the worlds*, see traditions about Wisdom's presence at creation (Prov 8.22; Sir 1.4; Wis 9.9). Philo says similar things about the "logos," "divine reason" (*On the Creation* 5.20; 8.30–31). See "John's Prologue as Midrash," p. 546. *Last days*, the end of the present age, awaiting the beginning of the new era. **3:** *Reflection of God's glory and the exact imprint of God's very being*, see Prov 8.22–31; Wis 7.25–26; 9.9; Philo, *QG* 1.57. Wisdom was seen as working alongside God at creation; *reflection* (as of an object that returns light exactly as it received it) and *imprint* (as of a coin that exactly reproduces the contours of its originating mold) are ways of expressing the Son's transmission of God's nature without any flaw. *Glory*, Heb "kavod," was a quality frequently attributed to God (e.g., Ex 16.10; Isa 6.3; Ps 19.1; and many other places). *Purification*, see 9.14n.

1.4–14: Superior to angels. The audience may have understood Jesus as an angel analogous to Michael or Raphael. **4:** *Name*, perhaps "Lord" (see Phil 2.9–11). **5:** Ps 2.7; 2 Sam 7.14. These texts appear together in two Qumran collections of biblical quotations used messianically (4QTest; 4QFlor 1.10–19). **6:** Deut 32.43 LXX; the line ("worship him, all you gods") is not in the received Hebrew text (MT), but it is preserved in a Deut Ms from Qumran. *Firstborn*, Jesus. **7:** Ps 104.4 LXX. In the psalm, the praise is to God; here God speaks of angels. **8–9:** Ps 45.6–7, a royal wedding hymn that calls the Davidic king "God"; here, it is applied to Jesus.

PERFECTION THROUGH SUFFERING

Pervasive in Hebrews, the language of perfection refers to more advanced teachings (6.1), the condition of those who follow Jesus (10.1,14; 11.40; 12.23), what the law lacks but what Jesus achieves (7.11,19; 9.9), and what Jesus achieves for himself through his suffering (2.10; 5.9). The term itself, "teleios," connotes maturity, fulfillment, moral perfection, wholeness, and holiness. In cultic contexts it refers to the unblemished state of sacrificial animals and the condition of the priest who makes the sacrifice (*m. Midd.* 5.4). Many exhortations to be perfect before God appear in the Tanakh (Gen 20.5; Deut 18.13; Judg 9.16,19). Philo, like the author of Hebrews, favors perfection terminology, and uses it to name the goal of the virtuous individual (*Leg. all.* 1.94; 3.74; *Names* 24) as well as the state of the person who achieves a vision of the divine (*Leg. all.* 3.74). Finally, according to Hebrews, Jesus is perfected through his suffering. Similar ideas appear in Jewish Hellenistic literature, developing the concept that one's sufferings, if undergone in the right way, can bring one to maturity and completion. In Wis 4.13, the righteous man who dies before reaching old age is said to have been "perfected," even though his life was brief; in 4 Macc 7.15, Eleazer's martyrdom is said to have rendered him "perfect." In the latter case, the language of perfection describes a pious man's suffering to death.

[11] they will perish, but you remain;
they will all wear out like clothing;
[12] like a cloak you will roll them up,
and like clothing[a] they will be changed.
But you are the same,
and your years will never end."
[13] But to which of the angels has he ever said,
"Sit at my right hand
until I make your enemies a footstool
for your feet"?
[14] Are not all angels[b] spirits in the divine service, sent to serve for the sake of those who are to inherit salvation?

2 Therefore we must pay greater attention to what we have heard, so that we do not drift away from it. [2] For if the message declared through angels was valid, and every transgression or disobedience received a just penalty, [3] how can we escape if we neglect so great a salvation? It was declared at first through the Lord, and it was attested to us by those who heard him, [4] while God added his testimony by signs and wonders and various miracles, and by gifts of the Holy Spirit, distributed according to his will.

[5] Now God[c] did not subject the coming world, about which we are speaking, to angels. [6] But someone has testified somewhere,
"What are human beings that you are
mindful of them,[d]
or mortals, that you care for them?[e]

[a] Other ancient authorities lack *like clothing*
[b] Gk *all of them*
[c] Gk *he*
[d] Gk *What is man that you are mindful of him?*
[e] Gk *or the son of man that you care for him?* In the Hebrew of Psalm 8.4-6 both *man* and *son of man* refer to all humankind

10–12: Ps 102.25–27. **13:** Ps 110.1, frequently cited as a prophecy about Jesus (see also Mk 12.35–37; Acts 2.34; 1 Cor 15.25).

2.1–4: Exhortation to attention. 2: *Declared through angels,* see Acts 7.53; Gal 3.19; *Ant.* 15.5.3. Angels are frequently present in rabbinic recountings about the giving of the Torah at Sinai (and in many other biblical events), but they are not there teachers or mediators of the divine word as in *Jubilees. Transgression . . . received a just penalty* refers to the Sinaitic covenant (e.g., Ex 20.22–23.33) that specifies penalties for sins. **3:** *Escape,* evade the coming judgment. *Lord,* Jesus. *By those who heard him,* evidence for dating Hebrews at least a generation after Jesus. **4:** *Signs and wonders,* referring to miracles performed by Moses and Aaron (Ex 7.3; Deut 4.34; 6.22) and by Jesus and the apostles (Acts 2.43; 15.12). *Gifts of the Holy Spirit,* unspecified, but perhaps including ecstatic experiences like speaking in tongues (1 Cor 12.4–11), or increased wisdom, discernment, and understanding (Wis 7.22–8.1).

2.5–9: Jesus exalted. 5: *Coming world,* a new world wherein Jesus reigns. Ps 110.1, quoted in 1.13, functions as a summary statement of this reign. **6–7:** Ps 8.4–8. *Human beings . . . them* ("anthropos . . . auton"), the terms, singular in Gk (reproducing Heb singular nouns as well), are understood to be about Jesus. *A little while,* in the MT this phrase is meant spatially not temporally, while the LXX is ambiguous. Hebrews interprets it temporally

[7] You have made them for a little while
lower[a] than the angels;
you have crowned them with glory and
honor,[b]
[8] subjecting all things under their feet."
Now in subjecting all things to them, God[c] left nothing outside their control. As it is, we do not yet see everything in subjection to them, [9] but we do see Jesus, who for a little while was made lower[d] than the angels, now crowned with glory and honor because of the suffering of death, so that by the grace of God[e] he might taste death for everyone.

[10] It was fitting that God,[c] for whom and through whom all things exist, in bringing many children to glory, should make the pioneer of their salvation perfect through sufferings. [11] For the one who sanctifies and those who are sanctified all have one Father.[f] For this reason Jesus[c] is not ashamed to call them brothers and sisters,[g] [12] saying,
"I will proclaim your name to my brothers
and sisters,[g]
in the midst of the congregation I will
praise you."
[13] And again,
"I will put my trust in him."
And again,
"Here am I and the children whom God
has given me."

[14] Since, therefore, the children share flesh and blood, he himself likewise shared the same things, so that through death he might destroy the one who has the power of death, that is, the devil, [15] and free those who all their lives were held in slavery by the fear of death. [16] For it is clear that he did not come to help angels, but the descendants of Abraham. [17] Therefore he had to become like his brothers and sisters[g] in every respect, so that he might be a merciful and faithful high priest in the service of God, to make a sacrifice of atonement for the sins of the people. [18] Because he himself was tested by what he suffered, he is able to help those who are being tested.

3 Therefore, brothers and sisters,[g] holy partners in a heavenly calling, consider that Jesus, the apostle and high priest of our confession, [2] was faithful to the one who appointed him, just as Moses also "was faithful

[a] Or *them only a little lower*
[b] Other ancient authorities add *and set them over the works of your hands*
[c] Gk *he*
[d] Or *who was made a little lower*
[e] Other ancient authorities read *apart from God*
[f] Gk *are all of one*
[g] Gk *brothers*

as referring to the time of Jesus' earthly life. **9:** *Made lower*, took on human form (see Phil 2.6). *Taste death for everyone*, share completely in the experience of human existence.

2.10–18: Jesus' humanity. 10: *Pioneer*, Jesus. *Perfect*, see "Perfection through Suffering," p. 408. See also 5.8; 7.28; 10.14; 12.2. **11:** *Sanctifies*, makes holy. *Father*, although the title "Son" applies uniquely to Jesus (1.1), God is father to all humanity insofar as God created humanity. On paternal language for God in relation to the Davidic king, see 2 Sam 7.14; Ps 2.7; 89.26–27; Mt 6.9; Lk 11.2. **12:** Ps 22.22. The psalm is used to describe Jesus' suffering and death in Mt 27.46; Mk 15.34. In Hebrews, the citation highlights Jesus' role as mediator between God and humans. The psalm originally speaks in the voice of a supplicant in prayer. **13:** Isa 8.17–18. Isaiah speaks in the first person, whereas Hebrews understands the speaker as Jesus. **14:** For the idea that the devil brought death into the world, see Wis 2.24; although the idea appears in rabbinic literature, it is often minimized or refuted, perhaps due to anti-Christian polemic; see *t. Sot.* 4.17; *b. B. Bat.* 16a. **16:** *Descendants of Abraham*, followers of Jesus are heirs of the Abrahamic promises (see ch 11). **17:** *In every respect*, for Hebrews, Jesus is both fully human and fully divine (see 4.14–15; 1 Cor 15.20–28). This thesis was debated in early Christianity but became Christian doctrine in 325 at the Council of Nicaea and was definitively formulated at the Council of Chalcedon in 451. Jesus as *high priest* is unique to Hebrews (see 4.14–5.10; 7.1–8.7; 9.11–14). Paradoxically, Jesus is both perfect priest and perfect sacrifice. *Atonement*, the author accepts the traditional view that atonement requires sacrifices, and the Yom Kippur sacrifices can be offered only by the high priest (Lev 16). **18:** *Tested*, see Ex 15.25; Deut 8.2,16. Suffering was sometimes interpreted as a test from God (see Prov 3.11–12; 2 Macc 6.12–16).

3.1–6: Jesus compared to Moses. As with angels (1.5–14), so with Moses: Jesus is the superior intermediary. **1:** *Apostle*, "the one sent." This is the only time the NT applies the term "apostle" to Jesus. **2:** *Faithful*, persever-

in all[a] God's[b] house." [3] Yet Jesus[c] is worthy of more glory than Moses, just as the builder of a house has more honor than the house itself. [4] (For every house is built by someone, but the builder of all things is God.) [5] Now Moses was faithful in all God's[b] house as a servant, to testify to the things that would be spoken later. [6] Christ, however, was faithful over God's[b] house as a son, and we are his house if we hold firm[d] the confidence and the pride that belong to hope.

[7] Therefore, as the Holy Spirit says,
"Today, if you hear his voice,
[8] do not harden your hearts as in the
rebellion,
as on the day of testing in the
wilderness,
[9] where your ancestors put me to the test,
though they had seen my works [10] for
forty years.
Therefore I was angry with that
generation,
and I said, 'They always go astray in their
hearts,
and they have not known my ways.'
[11] As in my anger I swore,
'They will not enter my rest.'"

[12] Take care, brothers and sisters,[e] that none of you may have an evil, unbelieving heart that turns away from the living God. [13] But exhort one another every day, as long as it is called "today," so that none of you may be hardened by the deceitfulness of sin. [14] For we have become partners of Christ, if only we hold our first confidence firm to the end. [15] As it is said,
"Today, if you hear his voice,
do not harden your hearts as in the
rebellion."

[16] Now who were they who heard and yet were rebellious? Was it not all those who left Egypt under the leadership of Moses? [17] But with whom was he angry forty years? Was it not those who sinned, whose bodies fell in the wilderness? [18] And to whom did he swear that they would not enter his rest, if not to those who were disobedient? [19] So we see that they were unable to enter because of unbelief.

4 Therefore, while the promise of entering his rest is still open, let us take care that none of you should seem to have failed to reach it. [2] For indeed the good news came to us just as to them; but the message they heard did not benefit them, because they were not united by faith with those who listened.[f] [3] For we who have believed enter that rest, just as God[g] has said,
"As in my anger I swore,

[a] Other ancient authorities lack *all*
[b] Gk *his*
[c] Gk *this one*
[d] Other ancient authorities add *to the end*
[e] Gk *brothers*
[f] Other ancient authorities read *it did not meet with faith in those who listened*
[g] Gk *he*

ing. The quotation is Num 12.7–8 (LXX). **5:** *Servant* (Gk "therapon") connotes a priest or a healer. *Testify to the things . . . spoken later*, Moses functions as an inferior prototype of Jesus.

3.7–19: Leaving the wilderness and entering God's rest. 7–11: Ps 95.7–11. **7:** *Holy Spirit*, presumed inspiration behind the biblical authors; see 9.8; 10.15. **8:** The *rebellion* in the *wilderness* (Ex 17.1–7) was the "quarrel" (Heb "merivah") the people had with God; the "testing" (Heb "masah") was the demand for water (which God provided). *Testing*, same word used in 2.18. **10:** *Forty years* seen as preceding the rebellion, whereas the Tanakh reverses the order. **11:** *Rest*, for the psalm—settlement in Canaan; for Hebrews—salvation. See 4.1–11n. **12:** *Living God*, a traditional way of referring to God meant initially to contrast the God of Israel to idols; see Deut 5.26; Josh 3.10; 2 Kings 19.4,16; Isa 37.4,17; Jer 10.10; 23.36; Dan 6.20,26; 4 Macc 5.24; Acts 14.15; 2 Cor 3.3; 1 Thess 1.9; Heb 10.31; 12.22; Rev 7.2. **13:** *Today* makes the warnings immediate for the audience of Hebrews, as it was immediate for the audience of Israelites for whom the psalm was written. See 4.6–7n. **15:** Ps 95.7. **17:** *Fell in the wilderness*, see Num 14.29. **19:** *Unbelief*, lack of persevering faith.

4.1–11: Promise of rest. 1–8: Because Gen 2.2 uses the verb *rest* to describe God's rest on the seventh day, the author expands its meaning in Ps 95 to include a divine utopia. **1:** *Still open*, since the promise went unfulfilled, those faithful to Christ can obtain it. **2:** *Good news*, gospel message. *Not united by faith with those who listened*, were not diligent in obeying what they heard; see Num 13.30–14.10. **3:** Again quoting Ps 95.11. *Foundation of the world*, at creation. **4–5:** Gen 2.2 and Ps 95.11. *My rest* in the psalm is the land of Israel, God's resting place.

'They shall not enter my rest,'"
though his works were finished at the foundation of the world. [4] For in one place it speaks about the seventh day as follows, "And God rested on the seventh day from all his works." [5] And again in this place it says, "They shall not enter my rest." [6] Since therefore it remains open for some to enter it, and those who formerly received the good news failed to enter because of disobedience, [7] again he sets a certain day—"today"—saying through David much later, in the words already quoted,

"Today, if you hear his voice,
do not harden your hearts."

[8] For if Joshua had given them rest, God[a] would not speak later about another day. [9] So then, a sabbath rest still remains for the people of God; [10] for those who enter God's rest also cease from their labors as God did from his. [11] Let us therefore make every effort to enter that rest, so that no one may fall through such disobedience as theirs.

[12] Indeed, the word of God is living and active, sharper than any two-edged sword, piercing until it divides soul from spirit, joints from marrow; it is able to judge the thoughts and intentions of the heart. [13] And before him no creature is hidden, but all are naked and laid bare to the eyes of the one to whom we must render an account.

[14] Since, then, we have a great high priest who has passed through the heavens, Jesus, the Son of God, let us hold fast to our confession. [15] For we do not have a high priest who is unable to sympathize with our weaknesses, but we have one who in every respect has been tested[b] as we are, yet without sin. [16] Let us therefore approach the throne of grace with boldness, so that we may receive mercy and find grace to help in time of need.

5 Every high priest chosen from among mortals is put in charge of things pertaining to God on their behalf, to offer gifts and sacrifices for sins. [2] He is able to deal gently with the ignorant and wayward, since he himself is subject to weakness; [3] and because of this he must offer sacrifice for his own

[a] Gk *he*
[b] Or *tempted*

6–7: *Today*, both David's time and the time of the writing of Hebrews. Cf. *b. Sanh.* 98a, which evokes Ps 95.7 in the context of messianic expectation. *David,* the Psalm's traditional author. *Much later*, David lived centuries after Joshua; therefore, the settlement of Canaan did not fulfill the promise of rest. **9:** *Sabbath rest*, Qumran's 4QShirShabb[a] portrays the heavenly host (together with the Dead Sea community) as celebrating a heavenly Sabbath. *M. Tamid* 7.4 describes messianic age as a Sabbath. *People of God*, designating Israel in Judg 40.2; 2 Sam 14.13. Gk "laos," "people," often refers to Israel in the LXX (e.g., Ex 33.13,16; Deut 7.6; Hos 4.6,8,12), and is used of Christians in the NT (Acts 15.14; 18.10; Rom 9.25; 1 Pet 2.10).

4.12–16: Divine judgment. 12: *Word of God* as *sword*, see Eph 6.17; Rev 1.16; 2.12. *Soul from spirit*, the word can separate what is seemingly indivisible. There may be an allusion to Prov 20.27. **13:** *Hidden*, no one can hide from God; see Ps 139.7–12; *4 Ezra* 16.62–63. *Account*, Gk "logos," rendered "word" in v. 12. **14:** *Passed through the heavens*, see 1.3–4. Special individuals like Enoch (Gen 5.24) and Elijah (2 Kings 2.1–12) experienced heavenly journeys; Ezekiel and Daniel have visions of heavenly journeys (Ezek 1; Dan 7). Heavenly journeys appear frequently in extra-biblical texts; the best-known is *1 En.* 1–36. In later Jewish mysticism, "merkavah" or "chariot" mysticism (derived from interpretations of Ezekiel's vision) became a recognized form for the visionary to relate a heavenly journey. *Confession*, faith or confidence in Jesus; see 10.23. **15:** See 2.17; 5.2. No other NT text emphasizes Jesus' sinlessness to the degree of Hebrews, but the idea is mentioned elsewhere; 2 Cor 5.21; 1 Pet 2.22 (citing Isa 53.9b); 1 Jn 3.5. **16:** *Throne of grace,* on the divine throne, see 1 Kings 22.19; Isa 6.1; Ezek 1.26; Dan 7.9; 4 Macc 17.18; *1 En.* 14. Here it is not clear if the *throne* belongs to God or Christ. The expression does not occur elsewhere; more usual is "throne of glory" (e.g., Jer 14.21; Mt 19.28) expressing majesty or power. It therefore may mean God's (or Christ's) reign as expressing merciful forgiveness.

5.1–6: High priestly qualifications. 1: *Chosen*, in the first century the high priest was chosen by political authorities and served at their pleasure; thus, many were politically corrupt. See "The High Priest in Jewish Tradition," p. 412. **2:** *Weakness*, the Mishnah prescribes actions to guard against the high priest's falling asleep before the time of sacrifice on Yom Kippur (*m. Yoma* 1.4,7). **3:** *For his own sins*, see Lev 16.6–17 on Yom Kippur sacrifices. *Sacrifice*, after the temple was destroyed, some rabbis believed prayer, repentance, and

THE HIGH PRIEST IN JEWISH TRADITION

Understanding of the high priest in Hebrews is predicated on the high priest's distinctive role in Jewish tradition. Ex 29.1–35 and Lev 8–9 recount the establishment of the priesthood, where Moses ordains Aaron as the first high priest. In theory all high priests were to be descendents of Aaron, although later sources indicate that the high priestly line passed to Zadok (2 Sam 8.17; 1 Kings 2.27,35). During the monarchy, the high priest's status was secondary to that of the king and his authority was limited to the religious sphere, but beginning in the Persian period, and more especially during the Hellenistic period, the authority of the high priest extended to the political arena. The Maccabees' authority lies in their having installed themselves in the high priest's position (1 Macc 10.15–21). Genealogical lineage was not required once civil authorities gained the right to appoint the high priest. Indeed, Herod the Great appointed six high priests.

Given the corrupt appointment procedure, speculation developed about heavenly and messianic priests. A few texts from Qumran speak of two messiahs, one kingly and one priestly (1QS 9.11: "the anointed one of Aaron"; see also "Melchizedek," p. 415). Despite the political and religious importance of the high priest during the Second Temple period, there is no evidence that Hebrews depends on any specific extra-biblical sources.

sins as well as for those of the people. [4] And one does not presume to take this honor, but takes it only when called by God, just as Aaron was.

[5] So also Christ did not glorify himself in becoming a high priest, but was appointed by the one who said to him,

"You are my Son,
today I have begotten you";

[6] as he says also in another place,

"You are a priest forever,
according to the order of Melchizedek."

[7] In the days of his flesh, Jesus[a] offered up prayers and supplications, with loud cries and tears, to the one who was able to save him from death, and he was heard because of his reverent submission. [8] Although he was a Son, he learned obedience through what he suffered; [9] and having been made perfect, he became the source of eternal salvation for all who obey him, [10] having been designated by God a high priest according to the order of Melchizedek.

[11] About this[b] we have much to say that is hard to explain, since you have become dull in understanding. [12] For though by this time you ought to be teachers, you need someone to teach you again the basic elements of the oracles of God. You need milk,

[a] Gk *he*
[b] Or *him*

alms-giving achieve atonement (see, e.g., *b. Sukk.* 49b; *Avot de R. Natan* 4.5). According to the Mishnah, the daily prayers substitute for the temple sacrifice (see *b. Ber.* 1.1; see also Heb 13.15–16n.). **4:** *Aaron*, Ex 29.1–30.10. **5:** Ps 2.7 (see 1.5). **6:** Ps 110.4 (see 1.13). *Order of Melchizedek*, there is no special priestly branch known as "the order of Melchizedek"; here the order includes only Melchizedek and Jesus. Jesus' connection to Melchizedek emphasizes that Jesus is not a biological descendant of Aaron. On the connection between the two figures, see 7.1–22.

5.7–10: Jesus' perfection. 7: Most likely a reference to Jesus in Gethsemane (Mt 26.36–46; Mk 14.32–42; Lk 22.40–46). **8:** *Learned obedience . . . suffered*, the idea that steadfastness in suffering results in redemption appears in 2 Macc 6.12–16; 4 Macc 17.11–12. See also *b. Ta'an.* 5.11, where Moses prays that he might be redeemed by suffering for his sins; Heb 12.5–11n. **9:** *Made perfect*, see "Perfection through Suffering," p. 408. See also 2.10; 5.8; 7.28; 10.14; 12.2. *Source of eternal salvation*, the idea that a martyr's death atones for others is prominent in 4 Macc, a popular text in Christian circles. *Obey him*, follow Jesus. **10:** *Order of Melchizedek*, see v. 6n.

5.11–6.3: Elementary teaching. 12: *Oracles of God*, scripture; cf. Rom 3.1. *Milk . . . solid food*, see 1 Cor 3.1–3; Philo, *On Agriculture* 9. The imagery is common in Hellenistic rhetoric. **13–14:** *Word of righteousness*, ethical discernment. *Trained*, Gk "gymnao," lit., "exercise naked," commonly in Greek sources as a metaphor for education. *Distinguish good from evil*, like their Greco-Roman counterparts, Jewish Hellenistic writers believed that education was not only for the purpose of wisdom, but also for the attainment of virtue; see Philo, *Confusion*

not solid food; [13] for everyone who lives on milk, being still an infant, is unskilled in the word of righteousness. [14] But solid food is for the mature, for those whose faculties have been trained by practice to distinguish good from evil.

6 Therefore let us go on toward perfection,[a] leaving behind the basic teaching about Christ, and not laying again the foundation: repentance from dead works and faith toward God, [2] instruction about baptisms, laying on of hands, resurrection of the dead, and eternal judgment. [3] And we will do[b] this, if God permits. [4] For it is impossible to restore again to repentance those who have once been enlightened, and have tasted the heavenly gift, and have shared in the Holy Spirit, [5] and have tasted the goodness of the word of God and the powers of the age to come, [6] and then have fallen away, since on their own they are crucifying again the Son of God and are holding him up to contempt. [7] Ground that drinks up the rain falling on it repeatedly, and that produces a crop useful to those for whom it is cultivated, receives a blessing from God. [8] But if it produces thorns and thistles, it is worthless and on the verge of being cursed; its end is to be burned over.

[9] Even though we speak in this way, beloved, we are confident of better things in your case, things that belong to salvation. [10] For God is not unjust; he will not overlook your work and the love that you showed for his sake[c] in serving the saints, as you still do. [11] And we want each one of you to show the same diligence so as to realize the full assurance of hope to the very end, [12] so that you may not become sluggish, but imitators of those who through faith and patience inherit the promises.

[13] When God made a promise to Abraham, because he had no one greater by whom to swear, he swore by himself, [14] saying, "I will surely bless you and multiply you." [15] And thus Abraham,[d] having patiently endured, obtained the promise. [16] Human beings, of course, swear by someone greater than themselves, and an oath given as confirmation puts an end to all dispute. [17] In the same way, when God desired to show even more clearly to the heirs of the promise the unchangeable

[a] Or *toward maturity*
[b] Other ancient authorities read *let us do*
[c] Gk *for his name*
[d] Gk *he*

181; *On Agriculture* 42. **6.1:** *Perfection,* Gk "teleiotes," lit., "maturity" (see translators' footnote *a*), appears only here and in Col 3.14 among NT texts. The *basic teaching* has not been discussed. The items listed collectively in vv. 1–2 show that nothing is as important as understanding the significance of Jesus. *Dead works,* activities that do not serve God. **2:** *Baptisms,* "washings," most likely not the Christian practice of baptism, but exactly what the author has in mind is not clear. *Laying on of hands* occurs during healings and the conferral of special status; it can both convey the gift of the spirit (Acts 8.17; 19.6) and initiate a commission (Acts 6.6; 1 Tim 4.14). *Resurrection of the dead,* a belief held by both Pharisees and Christians; see *m. Sot.* 9.15; *m. Sanh.* 10.1. *Eternal judgment,* an idea common in Jewish and Christians sources; see Ezek 34.17–22; Dan 7.26; *4 Ezra* 7.33–44; Mt 25.31–46. The Mishnah speaks of the unrighteous going to Gehenna, but it is never described as eternal; see *m. Qidd.* 14.4; *m. Ed.* 2.10; *m. Avot* 1.5; 5.19,20.

6.4–8: Warning against apostasy. 4–6: A baptized member who has *fallen away* has no opportunity for repentance; apostasy results in expulsion. The claim resembles the "karet" ("cut off") punishment, where those who commit certain violations of the Torah, such as idolatry and incest, are excluded from the community (Ex 12.15,19; Lev 18.29; 20.3; 23.29). For the Qumran community, violations of the "Community Rule" sometimes resulted in expulsion (1QS 7.23–24; 8.21–24). Christians held different views on how to treat sin after baptism (cf. Mk 3.29; 1 Jn 3.6; Herm., *Vis.* 5.7). While some later interpreters took Heb 6.4–6 literally (see also 10.26–31), others argued that apostates should be permitted to return and that Hebrews prohibits only a second baptism. **7–8:** Cf. Isa 5.2–7.

6.9–20: Divine fidelity. 10: *Love* for God is a central Tanakh idea (Deut 6.5). *Saints,* lit., "holy ones," referring to Jesus' followers generally in 1 Cor 1.2; 2 Cor 1.1; Phil 1.1. To whom it refers here is unclear. **12:** *Imitators of those who . . . inherit the promises,* see ch 11. **13–14:** *Promise to Abraham* included progeny, land, and an eternal covenant; see Gen 12.2–3; 15.5; 17.5. **15:** *Patiently endured,* Abraham waited until he was one hundred years old for the fulfillment of the *promise* of his son Isaac. **17:** *Heirs of the promise,* the descendants of Abraham, extended

character of his purpose, he guaranteed it by an oath, [18] so that through two unchangeable things, in which it is impossible that God would prove false, we who have taken refuge might be strongly encouraged to seize the hope set before us. [19] We have this hope, a sure and steadfast anchor of the soul, a hope that enters the inner shrine behind the curtain, [20] where Jesus, a forerunner on our behalf, has entered, having become a high priest forever according to the order of Melchizedek.

7 This "King Melchizedek of Salem, priest of the Most High God, met Abraham as he was returning from defeating the kings and blessed him"; [2] and to him Abraham apportioned "one-tenth of everything." His name, in the first place, means "king of righteousness"; next he is also king of Salem, that is, "king of peace." [3] Without father, without mother, without genealogy, having neither beginning of days nor end of life, but resembling the Son of God, he remains a priest forever.

[4] See how great he is! Even[a] Abraham the patriarch gave him a tenth of the spoils. [5] And those descendants of Levi who receive the priestly office have a commandment in the law to collect tithes[b] from the people, that is, from their kindred,[c] though these also are descended from Abraham. [6] But this man, who does not belong to their ancestry, collected tithes[b] from Abraham and blessed him who had received the promises. [7] It is beyond dispute that the inferior is blessed by the superior. [8] In the one case, tithes are received by those who are mortal; in the other, by one of whom it is testified that he lives. [9] One might even say that Levi himself, who receives tithes, paid tithes through Abraham, [10] for he was still in the loins of his ancestor when Melchizedek met him.

[11] Now if perfection had been attainable through the levitical priesthood—for the people received the law under this priesthood—what further need would there have been to speak of another priest arising according to the order of Melchizedek, rather than one according to the order of Aaron? [12] For when there is a change in the priesthood, there is necessarily a change in the law as well. [13] Now the one of whom these things are spoken belonged to another tribe, from which no one has ever served at the altar. [14] For it is evident that our Lord was descended from Judah, and in connection with that tribe Moses said nothing about priests.

[15] It is even more obvious when another priest arises, resembling Melchizedek, [16] one who has become a priest, not through a legal requirement concerning physical descent, but

[a] Other ancient authorities lack *Even*
[b] Or *a tenth*
[c] Gk *brothers*

to mean the members of the Christian community. *Guaranteed it by an oath*, Gen 22.17; see Philo, *Migr.* 273, for a similar argument. **18:** *Two unchangeable things*, God's promise and oath. **19:** *Inner shrine*, the Holy of Holies, which only the high priest may enter on Yom Kippur; see 9.3; Lev 16.2. *Curtain*, see Ex 26.31–35; see also Mk 15.38, which claims the curtain tore at Jesus' death. **20:** *Melchizedek*, see 5.6n.

7.1–17: Melchizedek's superiority to the Levitical priesthood. 1–2: A paraphrase of the encounter between Abraham and the priest-king Melchizedek (Gen 14.17–20); see 5.6n. *Salem*, understood as from Heb "peace" ("shalom"), identified with Jerusalem; it may have originally been a name of a Canaanite god, Shalim. Philo also offers an etymology connected to peace (*Leg. all.* 3.15.79). *King of*, Heb "malki-," from "melek," "king." *Righteousness*, from Heb "tzedek." **3:** *Without father*, except for Gen 14 and Ps 110.4, early scripture says nothing of Melchizedek. In the apocryphal *2 En.*, Melchizedek is miraculously born from his dead mother, is a priest from birth, and is kept safe from the flood in order to be the priest in the post-flood generation (23.15–41). *Son of God*, Jesus. *Priest forever*, Ps 110.4 (see 5.6). **4:** *A tenth of the spoils*, Gen 14.20; 28.22. **5:** *Descendants of Levi* are entitled *to collect tithes*, see Num 18.21–32. **7:** *Inferior is blessed by the superior*, the reverse is frequent; Melchizedek himself blesses "God Most High" (Gen 14.20). **9–11:** As if Levi tithed to Melchizedek because Levi descended from Abraham. As Melchizedek is superior to Abraham and so to Levi, so Jesus, the priest in the *order of Melchizedek*, is superior to the Jewish priesthood. *Perfection*, see 2.10; 5.8; 7.28; 10.14; 12.2. **12:** *Change in the law*, it is unclear why the author makes this argument; perhaps he builds on the idea that priests were repositories of law (see Jer 18.18; Ezek 7.26). Like Plato, the author sees permanence as perfection and change as undesirable. **13:** *Ever served*, only Levi's descendants could serve as priests; see Ex 32.25–29; Deut 10.8. **14:** *Judah*, Jesus was seen as of

MELCHIZEDEK

Although Melchizedek is mentioned only briefly (Gen 14.18–20 and Ps 110.4), this ancient personage received substantial attention from later commentators who recognized his special status as a priest-king (Philo, *Migr.* 235; *Leg. all.* 3.79–82; Josephus, *Ant.* 1.177–82). Among the DSS, an entire work is devoted to him (11QMelch); there he becomes a superhuman figure, who executes divine judgment. The text does not describe him as a priest, but he is described as having priestly functions (11QMelch 2.6). In rabbinic tradition, Melchizedek bestows the priesthood on Abraham, who then becomes a "priest forever" (*b. Ned.* 32b; *Lev. Rab.* 25.6). Some rabbinic texts identify Melchizedek as descended from Noah's son Shem, which may be a polemic against Hebrews' claim that Melchizedek lacks human genealogy (*b. Ned.* 32b; *Num. Rab.* 4.8; *Pirqe R. El.* 27.3). *2 En.* 71–72 describes Melchizedek's miraculous birth to Nir, the wife of Noah's brother. Melchizedek is chosen to be saved from the flood so that he might continue the priestly lineage inaugurated by Seth (see 71.29, 32).

through the power of an indestructible life. [17] For it is attested of him,

"You are a priest forever,
according to the order of Melchizedek."

[18] There is, on the one hand, the abrogation of an earlier commandment because it was weak and ineffectual [19] (for the law made nothing perfect); there is, on the other hand, the introduction of a better hope, through which we approach God.

[20] This was confirmed with an oath; for others who became priests took their office without an oath, [21] but this one became a priest with an oath, because of the one who said to him,

"The Lord has sworn
and will not change his mind,
'You are a priest forever'"—

[22] accordingly Jesus has also become the guarantee of a better covenant.

[23] Furthermore, the former priests were many in number, because they were prevented by death from continuing in office; [24] but he holds his priesthood permanently, because he continues forever. [25] Consequently he is able for all time to save[a] those who approach God through him, since he always lives to make intercession for them.

[26] For it was fitting that we should have such a high priest, holy, blameless, undefiled, separated from sinners, and exalted above the heavens. [27] Unlike the other[b] high priests, he has no need to offer sacrifices day after day, first for his own sins, and then for those of the people; this he did once for all when he offered himself. [28] For the law appoints as high priests those who are subject to weakness, but the word of the oath, which came later than the law, appoints a Son who has been made perfect forever.

8 Now the main point in what we are saying is this: we have such a high priest, one who is seated at the right hand of the throne of the Majesty in the heavens, [2] a min-

[a] Or *able to save completely*
[b] Gk lacks *other*

Davidic descent, and thus of the tribe of Judah; see Mt 1.6; Lk 3.31; Rom 1.3. Thus, he is here connected typologically to Melchizedek rather than genealogically to Aaron. **17:** *Forever*, here understood in reference to personal life, not to the dynasty. Ps 110.4, cited also in 5.6; 6.20; 7.21.

7.18–28: Jesus the high priest. 18: *Abrogation*, because Jesus is not descended from Aaron or Levi and not appointed according to Ex 29.1–35; Lev 8–9. **19:** *The Law made nothing perfect*, although Hebrews sees the Torah as given by God, it cannot be *perfect*, because it is a human institution that exists in the material realm. Although the Tanakh rarely uses language of perfection for Torah, Ps 119 idealizes Torah as God-like. Jewish mystical traditions describe the Torah as the pre-existent blueprint for creation; *Gen. Rab.* 1.1; *Zohar* "Terumah" 61. **20–21:** Ps 110.4. For the divine promise as *oath* see 6.17–18. **22:** *Guarantee*, promise. *Better covenant*, a theme developed in chs 8–10. **25:** *To make intercession*; see Job 33.23. **28:** *Word of the oath*, referring to Ps 110.4 (5.6; 7.17,21). *A Son*, Jesus (see 1.2). Because God speaks the oath through David in the psalm, it comes *later than the law*, the Sinaitic covenant.

8.1–13: Mediator of a better covenant. 1: *Seated at the right hand . . . of the Majesty* alludes to Ps 110.1. **2:** *Sanctuary*, plural in Gk, "the holy places." *Tent*, the tabernacle, Ex 25.1–27.21; 36.1–40.38. The idea that the earthly

ister in the sanctuary and the true tent[a] that the Lord, and not any mortal, has set up. [3] For every high priest is appointed to offer gifts and sacrifices; hence it is necessary for this priest also to have something to offer. [4] Now if he were on earth, he would not be a priest at all, since there are priests who offer gifts according to the law. [5] They offer worship in a sanctuary that is a sketch and shadow of the heavenly one; for Moses, when he was about to erect the tent,[a] was warned, "See that you make everything according to the pattern that was shown you on the mountain." [6] But Jesus[b] has now obtained a more excellent ministry, and to that degree he is the mediator of a better covenant, which has been enacted through better promises. [7] For if that first covenant had been faultless, there would have been no need to look for a second one.

[8] God[c] finds fault with them when he says:
"The days are surely coming, says the Lord,
when I will establish a new covenant with the house of Israel
and with the house of Judah;
[9] not like the covenant that I made with their ancestors,
on the day when I took them by the hand to lead them out of the land of Egypt;
for they did not continue in my covenant,
and so I had no concern for them, says the Lord.
[10] This is the covenant that I will make with the house of Israel
after those days, says the Lord:
I will put my laws in their minds,
and write them on their hearts,
and I will be their God,
and they shall be my people.
[11] And they shall not teach one another
or say to each other, 'Know the Lord,'
for they shall all know me,
from the least of them to the greatest.
[12] For I will be merciful toward their iniquities,
and I will remember their sins no more."

[13] In speaking of "a new covenant," he has made the first one obsolete. And what is obsolete and growing old will soon disappear.

9 Now even the first covenant had regulations for worship and an earthly sanctuary. [2] For a tent[a] was constructed, the first one, in which were the lampstand, the table, and the bread of the Presence;[d] this is called the Holy Place. [3] Behind the second curtain was a tent[a] called the Holy of Holies. [4] In it stood the golden altar of incense and the ark of the covenant overlaid on all sides with gold, in which there were a golden urn holding the manna, and Aaron's rod that budded,

[a] Or *tabernacle*
[b] Gk *he*
[c] Gk *He*
[d] Gk *the presentation of the loaves*

Temple has a heavenly counterpart may perhaps be found in the Tanakh (see e.g., Isa 6), and becomes common in early Jewish writings; see *1 En.* 14.9–23; *T. Levi* 3.2–4; *2 Bar.* 4.5; Wis 9.8; Philo, *Heir* 112. See Rev 3.12; 11.19; 15.5. **5:** Ex 25.9,40. *Shadow*, cf. 10.1. God's instructions for the Tabernacle (Ex 25.1–27.21) suggest the divine ideal; the description of its construction (Ex 36.1–40.38) suggests the material form. Philo makes a similar argument (*Leg. all.* 3.102). **6–7:** A supersessionist theology. Not only is Jesus the *mediator of a better covenant*, but the first covenant was faulty because it failed to create the perfect relationship between humans and God. **8–12:** Jer 31.31–34 (Jer 38 LXX). There are some notable differences between the MT and the LXX; most significantly in 31.32, where the LXX has "I had no concern for them," while the MT has "I was their husband" (v. 9). In its original context, Jeremiah was suggesting that the Torah would be renewed after the Babylonian exile by being implanted in people's hearts or minds, so they could instinctively observe it; therefore they would not any longer sin, and so there would not be another exile. *Remember their sins no more;* that atonement in the new covenant is permanent is essential to the argument; see 10.26. **13:** The term for *covenant* does not appear in this verse (the Gk reads lit., "new one" and "first one"), but the author is clearly referring to the *covenant* in Jer 8.8–12, where it refers to the Mosaic covenant. Heb 9.16–18 offers an interpretation of the word "covenant" (Gk "diathēkē"). For the idea that the new covenant renders the old obsolete see also 2 Cor 3.7–14.

9.1–10: Inadequacies of the first covenant. 1–5: The description is based on Ex 25.8–31.11; 36.1–40.38. **2:** *The first one*, the sanctuary's outer court. *Holy Place*, plural in Gk, "places." **3:** *Holy of Holies*, see 6.19n. **4:** *Urn holding*

and the tablets of the covenant; [5] above it were the cherubim of glory overshadowing the mercy seat.[a] Of these things we cannot speak now in detail.

[6] Such preparations having been made, the priests go continually into the first tent[b] to carry out their ritual duties; [7] but only the high priest goes into the second, and he but once a year, and not without taking the blood that he offers for himself and for the sins committed unintentionally by the people. [8] By this the Holy Spirit indicates that the way into the sanctuary has not yet been disclosed as long as the first tent[b] is still standing. [9] This is a symbol[c] of the present time, during which gifts and sacrifices are offered that cannot perfect the conscience of the worshiper, [10] but deal only with food and drink and various baptisms, regulations for the body imposed until the time comes to set things right.

[11] But when Christ came as a high priest of the good things that have come,[d] then through the greater and perfect[e] tent[b] (not made with hands, that is, not of this creation), [12] he entered once for all into the Holy Place, not with the blood of goats and calves, but with his own blood, thus obtaining eternal redemption. [13] For if the blood of goats and bulls, with the sprinkling of the ashes of a heifer, sanctifies those who have been defiled so that their flesh is purified, [14] how much more will the blood of Christ, who through the eternal Spirit[f] offered himself without blemish to God, purify our[g] conscience from dead works to worship the living God!

[15] For this reason he is the mediator of a new covenant, so that those who are called may receive the promised eternal inheritance, because a death has occurred that redeems them from the transgressions under the first covenant.[h] [16] Where a will[h] is involved, the death of the one who

a Or *the place of atonement*
b Or *tabernacle*
c Gk *parable*
d Other ancient authorities read *good things to come*
e Gk *more perfect*
f Other ancient authorities read *Holy Spirit*
g Other ancient authorities read *your*
h The Greek word used here means both *covenant* and *will*

the manna, Ex 16.33–34; *Aaron's rod*, Num 17.25. *Tablets*, Ex 40.20; 1 Kings 8.9. **5:** *Cherubim*, composite creatures with features from eagles, lions, etc.; in the Bible, they served as God's throne in the Temple (Ex 25.17–22). *Mercy seat* (Gk "hilasterion" in LXX for Heb "kapporet," "cover," e.g., Num 7.89), where atonement can be effected. The term occurs elsewhere in NT only in Rom 3.25 ("sacrifice of atonement"), and in 4 Macc 17.22 ("atoning sacrifice"). **7:** *Once a year*, on Yom Kippur, the Day of Atonement. **8:** *Holy Spirit*, Hebrews sometimes speaks of the *Holy Spirit* as the speaker of scripture; see 3.7. *Has not yet been disclosed*, although the high priest has access to the inner sanctuary, the focus here is not on access, but on the exclusion of others from that space. **9:** *Conscience of the worshiper*, relief from the burden of guilt; cf. Wis 17.10. **10:** At best the sacrifices deal with minor matters of purification. See 10.1–3n. In Jewish tradition, sacrifice has many functions, including worship, commemoration, inauguration, purification, as well as expiation.

9.11–28: Christ's better covenant. 11: *Good things that have come* may refer to the new covenant; the phrase could be translated "good things to come" and so refer to the promise of salvation Jesus' followers inherit; see ch 4; 5.9; 6.5. *Not made with hands*, see Acts 7.48; 17.24. **12:** *Holy Place*, likely the Holy of Holies (see 9.2). *Eternal redemption*, permanent atonement (see 7.27–28). **13:** *Ashes of a heifer*, an allusion to the burning of the red heifer in Num 19, a ritual distinct from Yom Kippur. **14:** *How much more* introduces what rabbinic texts call a "qal vahomer" argument, an argument (similar to the argument "a fortiori," "how much more so") from the minor to the major. *Blood of Christ*, see 9.25–28. *Eternal spirit*, emphasizing the immaterial nature of Christ's sacrifice. *Without blemish*, sacrificial animals were required to be without blemish. Here it means that Christ was without sin. *Dead works*, see 6.1. *Living God*, see 3.12n. **15–22:** The author's logic rests on the word "diathēkē," meaning either "covenant" or "will" in the sense of one's last will and testament. Both a "will" and a "covenant" require a death to take effect. Blood was necessary for inauguration of the Mosaic covenant; Christ's blood is similarly necessary to inaugurate the *new covenant*. Paul makes a similar wordplay with "diathēkē" in Gal 3.15–18. **15:** *New covenant*, see 8.6–7; 10.9–10. *Eternal inheritance*, salvation; see 1.14; 6.12,17; also Rom 8.15–17; Gal 3.29; 4.6–7. *Transgressions under the first covenant*, sins. **16–17:** *Will* ("diathēkē"), the same term

made it must be established. [17] For a will[a] takes effect only at death, since it is not in force as long as the one who made it is alive. [18] Hence not even the first covenant was inaugurated without blood. [19] For when every commandment had been told to all the people by Moses in accordance with the law, he took the blood of calves and goats,[b] with water and scarlet wool and hyssop, and sprinkled both the scroll itself and all the people, [20] saying, "This is the blood of the covenant that God has ordained for you." [21] And in the same way he sprinkled with the blood both the tent[c] and all the vessels used in worship. [22] Indeed, under the law almost everything is purified with blood, and without the shedding of blood there is no forgiveness of sins.

[23] Thus it was necessary for the sketches of the heavenly things to be purified with these rites, but the heavenly things themselves need better sacrifices than these. [24] For Christ did not enter a sanctuary made by human hands, a mere copy of the true one, but he entered into heaven itself, now to appear in the presence of God on our behalf. [25] Nor was it to offer himself again and again, as the high priest enters the Holy Place year after year with blood that is not his own; [26] for then he would have had to suffer again and again since the foundation of the world. But as it is, he has appeared once for all at the end of the age to remove sin by the sacrifice of himself. [27] And just as it is appointed for mortals to die once, and after that the judgment, [28] so Christ, having been offered once to bear the sins of many, will appear a second time, not to deal with sin, but to save those who are eagerly waiting for him.

10 Since the law has only a shadow of the good things to come and not the true form of these realities, it[d] can never, by the same sacrifices that are continually offered year after year, make perfect those who approach. [2] Otherwise, would they not have ceased being offered, since the worshipers, cleansed once for all, would no longer have any consciousness of sin? [3] But in these sacrifices there is a reminder of sin year after year. [4] For it is impossible for the blood of bulls and goats to take away sins. [5] Consequently, when Christ[e] came into the world, he said,

"Sacrifices and offerings you have not desired,
but a body you have prepared for me;
[6] in burnt offerings and sin offerings

[a] The Greek word used here means both *covenant* and *will*
[b] Other ancient authorities lack *and goats*
[c] Or *tabernacle*
[d] Other ancient authorities read *they*
[e] Gk *he*

as for "covenant." **18:** *Blood*, see Ex 24.4–8. **19–21:** Hebrews conflates different rituals and the objects they require. See Lev 14.2–6; Num 19.9,18,20. **20:** See Ex 24.8. **21:** *Sprinkled with the blood*, in Ex 24.8 Moses sprinkles the people, not the tent, though in Lev 8.15,19 Moses sprinkles blood on the altar when ordaining Aaron. **22:** *Purified with blood*, the efficacy of sacrifice. **23:** *Sketches of the heavenly things*, the early sanctuary and its rituals. *Heavenly things*, perhaps meaning that the world is cleansed from the cosmic force of sin, or that the consciences of worshipers have been purified (see 9.14). **24:** *Human hands*, see 9.11. *On our behalf*, see 7.25. **25–26:** See 10.1–18n. *End of the age*, the events surrounding Christ signal the end of time. **27:** *Judgment*, views of a collective judgment at the end of time were common among Jews of antiquity; see *Jub.* 5.10; 23.11; *1 En.* 10.4–16; 45.2; *T. Abr.* chs. 11–14; *Mekhilta Beshallah* 4, *Mekhilta Shirah* 6; Rev 20.12. In the Mishnah judgment is annual (*m. Rosh Ha-Shanah* 1.2). **28:** *Bear the sins of many* is from Isa 53.12, concerning the suffering servant; it is alluded to in Mk 10.45, and a different portion of the passage is quoted in Acts 8.32–35. *Second time*, see Mk 13.24–27; 1 Thess 3.13; 4.13–17. Jewish tradition combines the coming of the messiah with the messianic age; it requires no "second coming."

10.1–18: Christ, a single sacrifice for sin. Jesus' sacrifice is seen as curing people of sin. See 9.25–26; 10.11–14. **1:** *Shadow*, cf. 8.5. *Continually offered*, see 9.25. On why the law cannot achieve perfection, see 7.18–19,28; 9.9–10. **3–4:** Hebrews claims ritual sacrifice is only a *reminder of sin*, not the cure for it. Sin here means willful defiance of God, not simply errant behavior. **5–9:** Ps 40.6–8 (Heb 7–9), in its context a general statement, here applied to the arrival of Christ; Hebrews explains what is meant by "then"; for the idea that sacrifices do not substitute for repentance, see Isa 1.10–17; Jer 7.21–26; Hos 6.6; Ps 50.8–15. **5:** *Came into the world*, Jewish expression for birth; see *m. Rosh Ha-Shanah* 1.2; *Sifre Deut.* 312. *Body you have prepared for me* is only in the Septuagint.

you have taken no pleasure.
[7] Then I said, 'See, God, I have come to do
your will, O God'
(in the scroll of the book[a] it is written
of me)."

[8] When he said above, "You have neither desired nor taken pleasure in sacrifices and offerings and burnt offerings and sin offerings" (these are offered according to the law), [9] then he added, "See, I have come to do your will." He abolishes the first in order to establish the second. [10] And it is by God's will[b] that we have been sanctified through the offering of the body of Jesus Christ once for all.

[11] And every priest stands day after day at his service, offering again and again the same sacrifices that can never take away sins. [12] But when Christ[c] had offered for all time a single sacrifice for sins, "he sat down at the right hand of God," [13] and since then has been waiting "until his enemies would be made a footstool for his feet." [14] For by a single offering he has perfected for all time those who are sanctified. [15] And the Holy Spirit also testifies to us, for after saying,

[16] "This is the covenant that I will make
with them
after those days, says the Lord:
I will put my laws in their hearts,
and I will write them on their minds,"

[17] he also adds,

"I will remember[d] their sins and their
lawless deeds no more."

[18] Where there is forgiveness of these, there is no longer any offering for sin.

[19] Therefore, my friends,[e] since we have confidence to enter the sanctuary by the blood of Jesus, [20] by the new and living way that he opened for us through the curtain (that is, through his flesh), [21] and since we have a great priest over the house of God, [22] let us approach with a true heart in full assurance of faith, with our hearts sprinkled clean from an evil conscience and our bodies washed with pure water. [23] Let us hold fast to the confession of our hope without wavering, for he who has promised is faithful. [24] And let us consider how to provoke one another to love and good deeds, [25] not neglecting to meet together, as is the habit of some, but encouraging one another, and all the more as you see the Day approaching.

[26] For if we willfully persist in sin after having received the knowledge of the truth, there no longer remains a sacrifice for sins, [27] but a fearful prospect of judgment, and a fury of fire that will consume the adversaries. [28] Anyone who has violated the law of Moses dies without mercy "on the testimony of two or three witnesses." [29] How much worse punish-

[a] Meaning of Gk uncertain
[b] Gk *by that will*
[c] Gk *this one*
[d] Gk *on their minds and I will remember*
[e] Gk *Therefore, brothers*

Heb reads "ears you have dug for me" (Ps 40.7). Hebrews understands Jesus to be speaking (see 2.13n.). **9:** *First . . . second*, in reference to covenants established, respectively, by Moses and Jesus. **10:** *Sanctified*, cleansed of sin. **12–13:** Ps 110.1 (see 1.13; 8.1); in both the Hebrew Bible and its reuse here, making *enemies* into a *footstool* refers to vanquishing them. **14:** *Single offering*, see 9.25–26. *Perfected*, see 2.10; 5.8; 7.28; 12.2. **15:** *Holy Spirit*, see 3.7; 9.8. **16–17:** A paraphrase of Jer 31.33; see also 8.10. *With them* replaces "the house of Israel," and *their lawless deeds* is added.

10.19–25: Exhortation to faithful endurance. 19: *Friends* ("adelphoi"), lit., "brothers." *Sanctuary*, see 9.24. **20:** Cf. 9.8. *Curtain*, see 6.19; 9.3. *His flesh* refers to Jesus' sacrificial death. **21:** *Great priest*, see 4.14. *House of God*, see 3.5. **22:** *Washed with pure water*, perhaps a baptismal allusion. Cleansing with water is a common practice for achieving purity in order to receive the divine presence. **23:** *Confession of our hope*, faith, not confession of sin; see 3.1; 4.14. *He who has promised*, referring to God. **25:** *Meet together*, perhaps gathering for worship; the Greek is "episynagōgē," same root as "synagogue," though it refers to the congregation, not a building. *Day*, Jesus' return, related to traditions of the Day of the Lord; see Isa 2.12; Joel 1.15; 3.14; Zech 14.1; 1 Thess 5.4; 2 Pet 3.12; Rev 16.14.

10.26–39: Warning about the day of judgment. 26–27: See 6.4–6n. **26:** *Willfully persist*, there is a long tradition of distinguishing between willful and unwitting sinning; see Lev 4.1–5.13; Num 15.22–31; 2 Macc 14.3; Philo, *Cher.* 75; *m. Shabb.* 7.1; 11.6; *m. Ker.* 1.2. **27:** *Fury of fire*, such language is often associated with God's condemnation of the wicked; see 12.29; also Deut 4.24; Isa 26.11; 66.15–16; Zeph 1.18; Rev 20.9. **28–29:** *Witnesses*,

ment do you think will be deserved by those who have spurned the Son of God, profaned the blood of the covenant by which they were sanctified, and outraged the Spirit of grace? [30] For we know the one who said, "Vengeance is mine, I will repay." And again, "The Lord will judge his people." [31] It is a fearful thing to fall into the hands of the living God.

[32] But recall those earlier days when, after you had been enlightened, you endured a hard struggle with sufferings, [33] sometimes being publicly exposed to abuse and persecution, and sometimes being partners with those so treated. [34] For you had compassion for those who were in prison, and you cheerfully accepted the plundering of your possessions, knowing that you yourselves possessed something better and more lasting. [35] Do not, therefore, abandon that confidence of yours; it brings a great reward. [36] For you need endurance, so that when you have done the will of God, you may receive what was promised. [37] For yet

"in a very little while,
the one who is coming will come and will not delay;
[38] but my righteous one will live by faith.
My soul takes no pleasure in anyone who shrinks back."

[39] But we are not among those who shrink back and so are lost, but among those who have faith and so are saved.

11 Now faith is the assurance of things hoped for, the conviction of things not seen. [2] Indeed, by faith[a] our ancestors received approval. [3] By faith we understand that the worlds were prepared by the word of God, so that what is seen was made from things that are not visible.[b]

[4] By faith Abel offered to God a more acceptable[c] sacrifice than Cain's. Through this he received approval as righteous, God himself giving approval to his gifts; he died, but through his faith[d] he still speaks. [5] By faith Enoch was taken so that he did not experience death; and "he was not found, because God had taken him." For it was attested before he was taken away that "he had pleased God." [6] And without faith it is impossible to please God, for whoever would approach him must believe that he exists and that he rewards those who seek him. [7] By faith Noah, warned by God about events as yet unseen,

a Gk *by this*
b Or *was not made out of visible things*
c Gk *greater*
d Gk *through it*

Deut 17.6; 19.15. **29:** *How much worse* refers not to Jews who have rejected Jesus, but to Christians who commit apostasy; the form of this argument is "qal vahomer"; see 9.14n. *Profaned the blood of the covenant,* not referring to profaning the Eucharist but metaphorically to spurning Jesus. **30:** Deut 32.35–36. **31:** *Living God,* see 3.12. **33:** *Persecution,* no empirewide persecution of Christians occured until 250–51. **34:** *Prison,* some early Christians were imprisoned; see Acts 12; 16; Phil 2.25; 4.14–18. Prisoners relied on friends and family to bring them provisions. **36:** *Promised,* see 11.13,39–40. Cf. Maimonides, who said it was a Jew's obligation to wait for the messiah (*Mishneh Torah, Laws of Kings* 11). **37–38:** A paraphrase of Hab 2.3–4 (see also Rom 1.17; Gal 3.11). *My* is not in Heb or LXX. **39:** *Are saved,* from the coming judgment.

11.1–40: Heroes of faith. The list of biblical heroes functions to encourage hope in salvation, even though present circumstances appear to justify despair. Similar lists appear in an array of postbiblical literature (see "Heroes of the Faith," p. 421). **1:** *Faith* carries overtones of endurance, trust, and insight into spiritual reality. *Assurance,* Gk "hypostasis," "substance, steadiness, firmness"; in 1.3 the same word is translated "very being." *Conviction,* Gk "elengchos," "proof, test." **3:** Creation by *the word of God* is a common theme; see Gen 1.3; Ps 33.6; Jn 1.1–3; Wis 9.1; *2 Bar.* 14.17; Philo, *Sacr.* 65. The idea of creation by divine speech both supports the claim that the visible is made from what is *not visible* and connects to the idea of divine promise of future reward, a major theme in what follows. **4:** Gen 4.1–16. *Abel,* viewed as the first martyr and judge of souls; see Mt 23.35; *1 En.* 22.7; *T. Abr.* 13. *Still speaks,* see Gen 4.10; Heb 12.24. **5:** Gen 5.24. *Enoch* became a figure of great legend in extra-canonical literature because the words "God had taken him" were interpreted as a heavenly exaltation; see *1* and *2 En.*; *Jub.* 4.23; 19.24–27; Philo, *Names* 38; *Ant.* 1.3.4 and 85; *Tg. Onq.* Gen 5.24; *Gen. Rab.* 25.1. Because Enoch *pleased God* (Gen 5.22 LXX), he was seen as exemplary for his repentance (see Sir 44.16; Philo, *Migr.* 17–26). **7:** Gen 6.9–9.28. *Condemned the world,* legend has it that *Noah* preached repentance to his generation; *Mekhilta Shirah* 5; *Sifre Num.* 43; *b. Sanh.* 108a–b; *Pirqe R. El.* 22. *Righteousness,* Noah is the first

HEROES OF THE FAITH

The list of heroes resembles lists of biblical heroes in Jewish literature (Sir 44.1–49.16; Wis 10.1–21; 1 Macc 1.51–60; 4 Macc 18.11–19; 4 *Ezra* 7.105–111), but it reflects some unusual choices. Except for a passing mention of David at the end (11.32), the author includes no priests or kings. Certain expected highlights do not appear, and unexpected ones do. For example, no mention is made of God's covenant with Abraham from Gen 17, nor is Sinai mentioned despite the attention given to Moses. Instead of focusing on the heroes' leadership roles, Hebrews emphasizes the characters as largely set apart from the people. Generally speaking, the heroes in Hebrews have three characteristics: (1) Near-death experience: Noah would have perished in the flood; Moses would have died as an infant; (2) Ability to see the future and act faithfully in light of that knowledge: Noah receives an oracle about the flood and builds the ark; Abraham receives a promise about Isaac, and very late in his life that promise is realized; (3) Alienation: The heroes are portrayed as alienated from the people of their generation. Abraham lived in the land "as in a foreign land," and Moses was not really one of his people, because he was raised by Pharaoh's daughter. The heroes are not distinguished *by* their comrades, as those depicted in Sir 44–50; they are distinguished *from* them. The list functions as a kind of genealogy for the community; it creates a lineage independent from the people of Israel because the heroes are portrayed as outsiders and includes non-Israelites. Hebrews 11 set the stage for the way in which Christians would eventually come to understand the Old Testament as a precursor to the New Testament.

respected the warning and built an ark to save his household; by this he condemned the world and became an heir to the righteousness that is in accordance with faith.

[8] By faith Abraham obeyed when he was called to set out for a place that he was to receive as an inheritance; and he set out, not knowing where he was going. [9] By faith he stayed for a time in the land he had been promised, as in a foreign land, living in tents, as did Isaac and Jacob, who were heirs with him of the same promise. [10] For he looked forward to the city that has foundations, whose architect and builder is God. [11] By faith he received power of procreation, even though he was too old—and Sarah herself was barren—because he considered him faithful who had promised.[a] [12] Therefore from one person, and this one as good as dead, descendants were born, "as many as the stars of heaven and as the innumerable grains of sand by the seashore."

[13] All of these died in faith without having received the promises, but from a distance they saw and greeted them. They confessed that they were strangers and foreigners on the earth, [14] for people who speak in this way make it clear that they are seeking a homeland. [15] If they had been thinking of the land that they had left behind, they would have had opportunity to return. [16] But as it is, they desire a better country, that is, a heavenly one. Therefore God is not ashamed to be called their God; indeed, he has prepared a city for them.

[a] Or *By faith Sarah herself, though barren, received power to conceive, even when she was too old, because she considered him faithful who had promised.*

person scripture calls righteous (Gen 6.9). **8–19:** *Abraham* is the premier example of faith in Jewish tradition; see Sir 44.19–21; 1 Macc 2.52; *Jub.* 11.14–17; 12.1–5; 17.15–18; *Ant.* 1.7; Philo, *Migr.* 16–17; *Gen. Rab.* 43; *Mekhilta Mishpatim* 18. **8:** *Abraham obeyed*, Gen 12.1–9. Jewish interpreters highlight Abraham's immediate response as a sign of great faith; see Philo, *Migr.* 66. Jesus' exemplary status is also predicated on obedience; see 5.7. *Place*, Canaan, the land of Israel. *Not knowing where*, God's command to Abraham is to go to a "land that I will show you" (Gen 12.1). **9–10:** *Land he had been promised, as in a foreign land*, Hebrews emphasizes Abraham's faith as future-oriented, since Abraham does not live to see his descendants inherit the land (see v. 13). Interpreters frequently highlight Abraham's patient faith in wandering (*Jub.* 19.8–9), but here the focus is on Abraham's displacement. **10:** *City*, the heavenly Jerusalem. **11:** Gen 18.9–15; 21.1–8. **12:** Gen 22.17. *As good as dead*, see Rom 4.19. **13:** *Died in faith*, therefore their reward still awaits them (see 11.39–40). *Strangers and foreigners*, Gen 23.4. **14–16:** *Homeland . . . better country*, a heavenly dwelling; see 12.22–28. *City*, heavenly Jerusalem.

[17] By faith Abraham, when put to the test, offered up Isaac. He who had received the promises was ready to offer up his only son, [18] of whom he had been told, "It is through Isaac that descendants shall be named for you." [19] He considered the fact that God is able even to raise someone from the dead—and figuratively speaking, he did receive him back. [20] By faith Isaac invoked blessings for the future on Jacob and Esau. [21] By faith Jacob, when dying, blessed each of the sons of Joseph, "bowing in worship over the top of his staff." [22] By faith Joseph, at the end of his life, made mention of the exodus of the Israelites and gave instructions about his burial.[a]

[23] By faith Moses was hidden by his parents for three months after his birth, because they saw that the child was beautiful; and they were not afraid of the king's edict.[b] [24] By faith Moses, when he was grown up, refused to be called a son of Pharaoh's daughter, [25] choosing rather to share ill-treatment with the people of God than to enjoy the fleeting pleasures of sin. [26] He considered abuse suffered for the Christ[c] to be greater wealth than the treasures of Egypt, for he was looking ahead to the reward. [27] By faith he left Egypt, unafraid of the king's anger; for he persevered as though[d] he saw him who is invisible. [28] By faith he kept the Passover and the sprinkling of blood, so that the destroyer of the firstborn would not touch the firstborn of Israel.[e]

[29] By faith the people passed through the Red Sea as if it were dry land, but when the Egyptians attempted to do so they were drowned. [30] By faith the walls of Jericho fell after they had been encircled for seven days. [31] By faith Rahab the prostitute did not perish with those who were disobedient,[f] because she had received the spies in peace.

[32] And what more should I say? For time would fail me to tell of Gideon, Barak, Samson, Jephthah, of David and Samuel and the prophets— [33] who through faith conquered kingdoms, administered justice, obtained promises, shut the mouths of lions, [34] quenched raging fire, escaped the edge of

a Gk *his bones*
b Other ancient authorities add *By faith Moses, when he was grown up, killed the Egyptian, because he observed the humiliation of his people* (Gk *brothers*)
c Or *the Messiah*
d Or *because*
e Gk *would not touch them*
f Or *unbelieving*

17–19: Rabbinic lore sees Abraham undergoing ten tests of faith, culminating with the "Akedah" ("binding" of Isaac) (Gen 22.1–19), which explicitly uses the word "test" or "try" (Gen 22.1); see *m. Avot* 4.3; *Avot de R. Natan* 33; *Pirqe R. El.* 26. **18:** Gen 21.12. **19:** *Raise someone from the dead, Pirqe R. El.* 31 draws a connection between resurrection and the "Akedah"; this is also found in the high holy day liturgy. *Figuratively speaking,* Gk "en parabolē," the same word used in 9.9 (there translated "symbol"); the event is symbolic of resurrection. **20:** Gen 27.1–40. **21:** *Sons of Joseph,* Ephraim and Manasseh; Gen 48.8–22. *Bowing in worship,* Gen 47.31 LXX. *Top of his staff* (LXX), "head of his bed" (Heb): Heb "matteh" "staff" and "mittah" "bed, couch" have the same consonants; LXX reads the former, MT reads the latter. **22:** Gen 50.24–25. The reburial of Joseph's bones in the promised land featured prominently in retellings of Joseph's story; see Sir 49.15; *Jub.* 46.5; *T. Sim.* 8.3–4; *Mekhilta Beshallah* 1.86–98. **23:** Ex 2.1–10. In the MT, only Moses' mother hides him; in the LXX both parents do; see also Philo, *Life of Moses* 1.8–11. **24–25:** Like the patriarchs (vv. 13–16), Moses is portrayed as alienated from his native land. Elaborations of Moses' switch of allegiance to the Israelites appear in Philo, *Life of Moses* 1.32–39; *Ant.* 2.10.1–2 §238–53. **25:** *Pleasures of sin,* characterizations of Egypt as a locus of sin are commonplace; see Lev 18.3; Wis 12.23–27; 17.1–21; Philo, *Decalogue* 16.76–81. **26:** *Abuse suffered for the Christ,* it is unlikely the author means that Moses envisioned Christ; rather he projects the current situation onto the past. **27:** Ex 2.11–15. *He saw him who was invisible,* Ex 33.11; Num 12.8. **28:** Ex 12.1–28; 12.43–13.10. *Destroyer,* parts of the Exodus narrative attribute the killing of the firstborn to the "destroyer" (Ex 12.23), other parts to God (12.12,29). **29:** See Ex 14.30; Josh 5. **31:** Josh 2.1–21; 6.17. Jewish and Christian traditions remember *Rahab,* in spite of the fact that she was a prostitute, as a heroine and the ancestor of other great biblical figures; see *Sifre Num.* 78; *Num. Rab.* 8; *b. Meg.* 14b; Mt 1.5; Jas 2.25. **32:** *Gideon,* Judg 6–8; *Barak,* Judg 4–5; *Samson,* Judg 13–16; *Jephthah,* Judg 11–12. This incomplete list of judges leaves out Ehud and Deborah, among others (see 1 Sam 12.11). *David* and *Samuel,* 1, 2 Samuel passim. **33:** *Shut the mouths of lions,* stories of heroes defeating lions occur in Judg 14.6; Dan 6.19–23. **34:** *Quenched raging fire,* see Dan 3; *Pr. Azar.* 26–27. *Escaped the edge of the sword . . . foreign armies to flight,* these descriptions

the sword, won strength out of weakness, became mighty in war, put foreign armies to flight. [35] Women received their dead by resurrection. Others were tortured, refusing to accept release, in order to obtain a better resurrection. [36] Others suffered mocking and flogging, and even chains and imprisonment. [37] They were stoned to death, they were sawn in two,[a] they were killed by the sword; they went about in skins of sheep and goats, destitute, persecuted, tormented— [38] of whom the world was not worthy. They wandered in deserts and mountains, and in caves and holes in the ground.

[39] Yet all these, though they were commended for their faith, did not receive what was promised, [40] since God had provided something better so that they would not, apart from us, be made perfect.

12 Therefore, since we are surrounded by so great a cloud of witnesses, let us also lay aside every weight and the sin that clings so closely,[b] and let us run with perseverance the race that is set before us, [2] looking to Jesus the pioneer and perfecter of our faith, who for the sake of[c] the joy that was set before him endured the cross, disregarding its shame, and has taken his seat at the right hand of the throne of God.

[3] Consider him who endured such hostility against himself from sinners,[d] so that you may not grow weary or lose heart. [4] In your struggle against sin you have not yet resisted to the point of shedding your blood. [5] And you have forgotten the exhortation that addresses you as children—

"My child, do not regard lightly the
discipline of the Lord,
or lose heart when you are punished by
him;
[6] for the Lord disciplines those whom he
loves,
and chastises every child whom he
accepts."

[7] Endure trials for the sake of discipline. God is treating you as children; for what child is there whom a parent does not discipline? [8] If you do not have that discipline in which all children share, then you are illegitimate and not his children. [9] Moreover, we had human parents to discipline us, and we respected them. Should we not be even more willing to be subject to the Father of spirits and live? [10] For they disciplined us for a short time as seemed best to them, but he disciplines us for our good, in order that we may share his holi-

[a] Other ancient authorities add *they were tempted*
[b] Other ancient authorities read *sin that easily distracts*
[c] Or *who instead of*
[d] Other ancient authorities read *such hostility from sinners against themselves*

could refer to several different figures, including Elijah. **35:** *Women received their dead by resurrection*, i.e., the dead persons were restored to life and presented to the *women* (mothers); 1 Kings 17.17–24; 2 Kings 4.18–37. *Others were tortured* likely refers to 2 Macc 6.18–7.42. In contrast to resuscitation, *a better resurrection* refers to eternal life. **36–38:** Sufferings of various prophets: *Stoned to death* refers either to Zechariah (2 Chr 24.21) or to legends about Jeremiah (Tertullian, *Scorp.* 8); 2 Kings 21.16, concerning the murderous King Manasseh, who was often accused of killing prophets; see *Seder Olam Rab.*20. *Sawn in two*, the fate of Isaiah according to Jewish, Christian, and Islamic legend; see *Mart. Isa.* 5.11–14; Justin, *Dial.* 120; *b. Yebam.* 49b; *y. Sanh.* 10. *Skins of sheep and goats* evokes the garb of Elijah and Elisha (1 Kings 19.13,19 LXX). *Wandered . . . holes in the ground* evokes the trials of Elijah and Elisha (1 Kings 17.1–7; 19.3–9; 2 Kings 2.25). **39:** *Did not receive what was promised*, see 11.13. **40:** *Made perfect*, see 2.10; 5.8; 7.28; 10.14; 12.2.

12.1–13: Divine discipline. 1: *Cloud* is a common metaphor for "crowd" in Greco-Roman literature. *Witnesses*, Gk "martyron," origin of the term "martyr." *Weight . . . sin*, an occasional comparison found in the Hebrew Bible (e.g., Ps 38.4). *Race*, a common metaphor in NT exhortations ; see 1 Cor 9.24–27; Gal 2.2; Phil 2.16; 2 Tim 4.7. **2:** *Pioneer and perfecter*, see 2.10. *Seat at the right hand of the throne*, see Ps 110.1; also 1.3,13; 8.1; 10.12. **3–4:** *Endured . . . hostility . . . resisted . . . shedding your blood*, continuing with the comparison between the audience and Jesus, the writer points out that Jesus endured mockery (Mk 15.16–20; cf. Isa 53.3; Ps 22.7) and was martyred by crucifixion. **5–11:** Suffering is understood as instructional *discipline* administered by God; cf. 2 Macc 6.12–17; *Sifre Deut.* 311. This peripheral idea in the Hebrew Bible became mainstream in rabbinic literature, perhaps under the influence of the Hadrianic persecutions (132–135 CE), where it is called "yisurin shel ahavah," "chastisements of love"; *Mek. Bahodesh* 10; *b. Ber.* 5a; *b. Sanh.* 101a; *Gen. Rab.* 42.1; cf. Heb 5.8. **5–6:** Prov 3.11–12. **8:** *Illegitimate*, bastards. **9:** *Human*

ness. [11] Now, discipline always seems painful rather than pleasant at the time, but later it yields the peaceful fruit of righteousness to those who have been trained by it.

[12] Therefore lift your drooping hands and strengthen your weak knees, [13] and make straight paths for your feet, so that what is lame may not be put out of joint, but rather be healed.

[14] Pursue peace with everyone, and the holiness without which no one will see the Lord. [15] See to it that no one fails to obtain the grace of God; that no root of bitterness springs up and causes trouble, and through it many become defiled. [16] See to it that no one becomes like Esau, an immoral and godless person, who sold his birthright for a single meal. [17] You know that later, when he wanted to inherit the blessing, he was rejected, for he found no chance to repent,[a] even though he sought the blessing[b] with tears.

[18] You have not come to something[c] that can be touched, a blazing fire, and darkness, and gloom, and a tempest, [19] and the sound of a trumpet, and a voice whose words made the hearers beg that not another word be spoken to them. [20] (For they could not endure the order that was given, "If even an animal touches the mountain, it shall be stoned to death." [21] Indeed, so terrifying was the sight that Moses said, "I tremble with fear.") [22] But you have come to Mount Zion and to the city of the living God, the heavenly Jerusalem, and to innumerable angels in festal gathering, [23] and to the assembly[d] of the firstborn who are enrolled in heaven, and to God the judge of all, and to the spirits of the righteous made perfect, [24] and to Jesus, the mediator of a new covenant, and to the sprinkled blood that speaks a better word than the blood of Abel.

[25] See that you do not refuse the one who is speaking; for if they did not escape when they refused the one who warned them on earth, how much less will we escape if we reject the one who warns from heaven! [26] At that time his voice shook the earth; but now he has promised, "Yet once more I will shake not only the earth but also the heaven." [27] This phrase, "Yet once more," indicates the removal of what is

a Or *no chance to change his father's mind*
b Gk *it*
c Other ancient authorities read *a mountain*
d Or *angels, and to the festal gathering* [23]*and assembly*

parents, lit., "fathers of our flesh." *Father of spirits*, God; father of human spirits, contrasts with "fathers of our flesh." **12:** See Isa 35.3.

12.14–29: Final warnings. 14: *Pursue peace*, a common exhortation; see Ps 34.14 (Heb v. 15); Rom 14.19; *m. Avot* 1.12. *See the Lord*, achieve salvation. **15:** *Grace of God*, perhaps referring to God's action through Jesus; cf. 2.9. *Root of bitterness*, possibly an allusion to Deut 29.17 LXX. **16:** *Birthright*, see Gen 25.29–34. *Immoral*, Gk "pornos," meaning sexually *immoral*. Postbiblical traditions portray Esau as more wicked than depicted in the Tanakh, the opposite of his brother Jacob, though none describe him as "pornos"; see Philo, *Virtues* 208; *Sacr.* 120; *b. Sanh.* 101b; *Gen. Rab.* 37, 40, 43, 45. **17:** *Inherit the blessing*, Gen 27. *Found no chance to repent*, see 6.4–8; 10.26–31. *With tears*, Gen 27.38. **18–21:** Sinaitic imagery; see Ex 19; Deut 4.10–15. **19:** *Voice*, in contrast to Heb 12.19, Maimonides claimed that Israel's experiencing of the divine voice guaranteed that the Torah was of divine origin (see *Mishneh Torah, Hilcot Yesodei ha-Torah* 8.1), see also *Mek. Bahodesh* 4, comment on Ex 19.19. **20:** Ex 19.12–13. **21:** Deut 9.19. **22:** *Mount Zion*, the mountain in Jerusalem where God dwells; the image is in contrast to descriptions of Sinai in vv. 18–21; cf. Gal 4.21–31. *Living God*, see 3.12; 9.14; 10.31. *Heavenly Jerusalem*, although *Jerusalem* is not earlier named explicitly, the heavenly city was mentioned; see 11.10,16. *Innumerable angels*, angels are often part of theophanies; see Deut 33.2 (referring specifically to Sinai); Dan 7.10; Rev 5.11; *1 En.* 13.8; 14.18–21; 20; 39.4–5; in 4QShirShabb[a] angels singing God's praise assemble in heaven for Sabbath worship. **23:** *Firstborn*, though possibly meaning the angels, it most likely refers to humans (cf. 1.5–6). *Enrolled*, in Greco-Roman cities, citizens were registered shortly after birth to record their status and thus insure their legal and social privileges; following a Mesopotamian model, Jewish tradition sometimes describes the righteous as "inscribed" in a heavenly book; see Ex 32.32; Ps 69.29; Dan 12.1. The image is ubiquitous in the Rosh Ha-Shanah and Yom Kippur liturgy. **24:** *Mediator of a new covenant*, see chs 8–9. *Sprinkled blood*, see 9.11–28; Ex 24.4–8. *Blood of Abel*, see Gen 4.10; 11.4. **25:** *One who is speaking*, most likely God (not Christ); so 1.1. *They did not escape*, the wilderness generation. *One who warned them*, most likely Moses, so vv. 18–21. **26–27:** Hag 2.6 LXX. *Yet once more* implies *removal* because Hebrews takes "once" to mean that God's shaking of heaven and earth happens only once; cf. 6.4. **27:**

shaken—that is, created things—so that what cannot be shaken may remain. [28] Therefore, since we are receiving a kingdom that cannot be shaken, let us give thanks, by which we offer to God an acceptable worship with reverence and awe; [29] for indeed our God is a consuming fire.

13 Let mutual love continue. [2] Do not neglect to show hospitality to strangers, for by doing that some have entertained angels without knowing it. [3] Remember those who are in prison, as though you were in prison with them; those who are being tortured, as though you yourselves were being tortured.[a] [4] Let marriage be held in honor by all, and let the marriage bed be kept undefiled; for God will judge fornicators and adulterers. [5] Keep your lives free from the love of money, and be content with what you have; for he has said, "I will never leave you or forsake you." [6] So we can say with confidence,

"The Lord is my helper;
I will not be afraid.
What can anyone do to me?"

[7] Remember your leaders, those who spoke the word of God to you; consider the outcome of their way of life, and imitate their faith. [8] Jesus Christ is the same yesterday and today and forever. [9] Do not be carried away by all kinds of strange teachings; for it is well for the heart to be strengthened by grace, not by regulations about food,[b] which have not benefited those who observe them. [10] We have an altar from which those who officiate in the tent[c] have no right to eat. [11] For the bodies of those animals whose blood is brought into the sanctuary by the high priest as a sacrifice for sin are burned outside the camp. [12] Therefore Jesus also suffered outside the city gate in order to sanctify the people by his own blood. [13] Let us then go to him outside the camp and bear the abuse he endured. [14] For here we have no lasting city, but we are looking for the city that is to come. [15] Through him, then, let us continually offer a sacrifice of praise to God, that is, the fruit of lips that confess his name. [16] Do not neglect to do good and to share what you have, for such sacrifices are pleasing to God.

[17] Obey your leaders and submit to them, for they are keeping watch over your souls and will give an account. Let them do this with joy and not with sighing—for that would be harmful to you.

[18] Pray for us; we are sure that we have a clear conscience, desiring to act honorably in all things. [19] I urge you all the more to do this, so that I may be restored to you very soon.

[20] Now may the God of peace, who

[a] Gk *were in the body*
[b] Gk *not by foods*
[c] Or *tabernacle*

What cannot be shaken, the heavenly realm, what remains once the material world passes away. **29:** *Consuming fire,* citing Deut 4.24 and 9.3, but here evoking burnt offerings.

13.1–25: Final exhortations. 1: *Mutual love,* Gk "philadelphia," most commonly used of affection between siblings. **2:** *Hospitality to strangers* (Gk "philoxenia") was a virtue throughout the ancient Mediterranean; see Gen 19.1–3; Judg 19.19–21; Job 31.32; Rom 12.13; 1 Pet 4.9; *Did.* 12.1–2. *Entertained angels,* Gen 18.1–15. **3:** *Prison . . . tortured,* 10.32–34. **4–5:** *Marriage . . . money,* commonplace moralisms among Jews and Christians; see Josephus, *Ag. Ap.* 2.199–203; Mt 19.4–5; Mk 10.6–8; Eph 5.22–23. *Never . . . forsake,* see Deut 31.6,8; Josh 1.5. **6:** Ps 118.6. *Lord,* God. **7:** *Leaders,* never named. *Imitate,* resembles Paul's language; see 1 Cor 4.16; 11.1; Gal 4.12; Phil 3.17; 4.9; 1 Thess 1.6–7. **8:** *Same . . . forever,* intended as a reassurance that Christ's redeeming power would never wane. **9:** *Strange teachings,* see Eph 4.14; Col 2.8; 1 Tim 1.3–7. *Regulations about food,* perhaps a reference to Jewish dietary laws or to the issue of meat offered to idols (see Acts 15; 1 Cor 8). **10:** *Altar,* site of Christ's sacrifice in the heavenly temple. **11:** The Yom Kippur and red heifer sacrifices were *burned outside the camp*; see Lev 16.27; Num 19.2–3. **12:** *Outside the city gate,* see Jn 19.17–20. *Sanctify the people,* see 9.13–14; 10.10,14,29. **13:** *Bear the abuse he endured,* share in his sufferings by our own witness (including the possibility of death). **14:** *No lasting city,* see 11.13–16; 12.22–29. *City that is to come,* the heavenly Jerusalem; see 11.10,16; 12.22. **15–16:** Prayer, hymns, and good works are described as forms of sacrifice in Ps 27.6; 50.14,23; 51.17 [Heb v. 19]; 107.22; Tob 4.11; Sir 3.3,20; Philo, *Spec. Laws* 1.253, 271–72, 277, 289–90; *Avot de R. Natan* 4. In rabbinic writings, the daily prayers replace the daily sacrifices; see 5.3n. **17:** *Obey your leaders,* see 13.7. **18:** *Clear conscience,* see 10.22. **19–25:** The closing includes typical elements of letters: mention of travel plans, a benediction, final exhortations, and final greetings; cf. Rom 16; 1 Cor 16.13–24. **19:** *Restored to you,* reunited. **20–21:** Concluding benediction. *God of peace,* similar

brought back from the dead our Lord Jesus, the great shepherd of the sheep, by the blood of the eternal covenant, [21] make you complete in everything good so that you may do his will, working among us[a] that which is pleasing in his sight, through Jesus Christ, to whom be the glory forever and ever. Amen.

[22] I appeal to you, brothers and sisters,[b] bear with my word of exhortation, for I have written to you briefly. [23] I want you to know that our brother Timothy has been set free; and if he comes in time, he will be with me when I see you. [24] Greet all your leaders and all the saints. Those from Italy send you greetings. [25] Grace be with all of you.[c]

a Other ancient authorities read *you*

b Gk *brothers*

c Other ancient authorities add *Amen*

language is found in Paul; see Rom 15.33; 16.20; 2 Cor 13.11; Phil 4.9; 1 Thess 5.23. **20:** *Great shepherd,* following ancient Mesopotamian and Jewish models, a popular epithet for Jesus as the ideal leader; see Mt 26.31; Jn 10.11; 1 Pet 5.4; Rev 7.17, building upon the idea that the Davidic king and God are called "shepherd" in the Hebrew Bible (e.g. Ezek 34; Ps 23). *Eternal covenant,* God's covenant with Israel is described as eternal; see 2 Sam 7.13,16; Isa 55:13. **23:** *Timothy,* Paul's companion, see 1 Cor 4.17; 2 Cor 1.1; Phil 1.1; 1 Thess 1.1; also the recipient of two disputed Pauline letters, 1 and 2 Timothy. Acts 16.1–3 reports that his mother was Jewish. **24:** *Saints,* see 3.1; 6.10. *Those from Italy,* most likely Italians living abroad. Paul's Letter to the Romans points to a sizable community of Jesus-followers in Rome by the mid-first century. Some use this verse to suggest that the Romans were the original addressees; see the Introduction.

THE LETTER OF JAMES

The letter of James takes its name from the attribution of authorship in 1.1; the letter itself does not otherwise identify its author. Some commentators suggest that the author is the brother of Jesus (Mt 13.55; Mk 6.3) and the head of the church in Jerusalem (Acts 12.17; 15.13–21; Gal 1.19). If that attribution is correct, the letter would have to have been written before 62 CE, when James was executed (*Ant.* 20.9.1; Eusebius, *Hist. eccl.* 2.23).

The excellent Greek of the text leads many scholars to doubt this traditional attribution of authorship. It would, they argue, be unlikely that a rural Galilean would be capable of such expression. Defenders have argued that the letter incorporates genuine material from James, perhaps a sermon that was reworked by a follower trained in Greek rhetoric. The address "to the twelve tribes in the Dispersion" (Gk "diaspora") suggests that the recipients identified with the people of Israel and perhaps were Jewish followers of Jesus (see 1 Pet 1.1).

CONTENT AND STRUCTURE

The text appears to be responding to the views of Paul, particularly with regard to the relationship of faith and works. (Cf. Jas 2.18–26 with Rom 4.1–5.) It also stresses ethics: the virtues of self-discipline and disdain of wealth, efficacy of prayer, and repentance in anticipation of the final judgment. Motifs shared with Jewish sources are frequent. James is particularly conversant with the Torah but also with the wisdom tradition, and the text displays echoes of both the Hebrew scriptures and the Greek writings in the apocryphal/deuterocanonical books preserved in the Septuagint and retained in some versions of the Christian Old Testament.

Of all the texts in the New Testament, the letter of James has the least specific focus on Jesus of Nazareth. With the two references (1.1; 2.1) removed, the text could function as an address to synagogue communities in the Diaspora. On the other hand, it has numerous echoes of the Gospel tradition, especially Matthew.

GUIDE TO READING

The letter of James is sometimes read as a sermon or a piece of wisdom literature like Proverbs or Sirach to which an epistolary opening, but no closing, has been added. This letter was placed among the "catholic" or universal letters, sometimes also called "General Epistles," because it is seen as addressed to the early church generally and not to one specific community or person.

Herbert Basser

1 James, a servant[a] of God and of the Lord Jesus Christ,
To the twelve tribes in the Dispersion:
Greetings.

[2] My brothers and sisters,[b] whenever you face trials of any kind, consider it nothing but joy, [3] because you know that the testing of your faith produces endurance; [4] and let endurance have its full effect, so that you may be mature and complete, lacking in nothing.

[5] If any of you is lacking in wisdom, ask God, who gives to all generously and ungrudgingly, and it will be given you. [6] But ask in faith, never doubting, for the one who doubts is like a wave of the sea, driven and tossed by the wind; [7, 8] for the doubter, being double-minded and unstable in every way, must not expect to receive anything from the Lord.

[9] Let the believer[c] who is lowly boast in being raised up, [10] and the rich in being brought low, because the rich will disappear like a flower in the field. [11] For the sun rises with its scorching heat and withers the field; its flower falls, and its beauty perishes. It is the

[a] Gk *slave*
[b] Gk *brothers*
[c] Gk *brother*

1.1–8: Importance of faith. 1: *James,* Gk "Iakobos" from Heb "Ya'aqov." *Servant of God* (lit., "slave"; see translators' note *a*), a title, e.g., Deut 34.5. *Sifre Deut.* 3.24 identifies by name those who (presumptuously) gave themselves the title and those who received the title from God. *Lord* (Gk "kurios"), meaning master, like the Hebrew "Adonai," substituted for the tetragrammaton. James uses a standardized opening formula identifying author and addressee(s); see, e.g., Phil 1.1. *And of the Lord Jesus Christ,* joining "Jesus Christ" to "the Lord" breaches later Jewish ideas of monotheism (*b. Sanh.* 63a) but may not, according to later Jewish sources, constitute idolatry; James approves the belief that "God is one" (2.19). *Twelve tribes,* the followers of Jesus, appropriating imagery from Israelite history, pictured the messianic ideal of the return of the exiled tribes as referring to the Christian present (Acts 15.15–21), as opposed to (unredeemed) Israel whose tribes remain in captivity. *Dispersion,* Gk "diaspora," Heb "galut," "golah," Jewish communities in Gentile lands. *Greetings* (lit., "rejoice," Phil 3.1), a frequent opening for a letter (see Acts 15.23); see also Gamaliel's epistle in *b. Sanh.* 11b: "To our brothers, inhabitants of the Dispersion. . . . Great be your peace always." **2:** *My brothers* (see translators' note *b*), the opening address of a moral sermon as in *m. Ta'an.* 2.1. *Trials,* see Mt 5.10–12. **3:** *Testing . . . endurance,* in *Tanh. Num.* "beha'alotekha" 8 names many righteous people who withstood tests of faith, including Levites who martyred themselves to preserve their faith and law (Deut 33.9) and cites Ps 11.5 (God "tests the righteous"). **4:** *Let endurance, m. Avot* 1.1, "be patient/temperate in judgment," both in experiencing divine judgment and in adjudicating human justice. *B. Ber.* 17a explains the positive side of Prov 15.1 by adding to "a temperate/soft expression turns away wrath" the phrase "and increases wholeness/peace between relatives and friends and all humanity and even foreigners come-to-market: thus will one be beloved above, and endeared below, and be welcomed by all." *Be . . . complete, Gen. Rab.* 79.5, "'Complete' means in body, in property, in wisdom, and in children." **5:** *Wisdom . . . given you, y. Ber.* 4.4, "Grace us with wisdom" (followed by) "You have graced us with wisdom." See Ps 16 praising constancy of faith and Prov 16.33 on all things coming from God. The "Amidah" or "standing" prayer that opens Jewish worship calls attention to "God on high [who] fully gives tender goodness" (" 'El 'elyon gomel ḥasadim tovim"). **6:** *Like . . . sea,* an image of inconstancy (cf. the waves in *Midr. Min.,* 305). *Midr. Ps.* 119.46 describes those tossed around "who grasp the rope by both ends" looking for salvation, like those wavering between God and Baal (1 Kings 18.21). See Ps 34.4–6 (Heb vv. 5–7) for the power of faith. **7–8:** *Double-minded, Midr. Mishle* 12.20, refers to two minds (lit., "two kidneys") that will bend a person toward good but also away from it; two hearts are both good and evil advisers (Eccl 10.12; Ps 32.10 [Heb v. 11]). Anything of "two kinds" (Deut 22.9–11) represents lack of wholeness; thus James is urging his audience to integrity of being.

1.9–11: Poor and rich. 9: *Lowly . . . up, Num. Rab.* 22 states that God judges, lowering one and raising another (Ps 75.7 [Heb v. 8]). In this world, the true social order is often reversed (*b. Pesah.* 50a). In the next world the righteous bask in their "crowns" of spiritual attainments and in "seeing God" (*b. Ber.* 17a). See also Lk 1.52–53; 6.20–25. **10–11:** *And the rich . . . low,* see 1 Sam 2.7–8 and *Tanh. Vay.* 10, citing Ps 35.5. *Because the rich will disappear,* cf. Job 14; Ps 34. *Sifre Deut. piska* 43 shows cases where abundance led to sin and perdition, as in the generation of Noah.

IMPLANTED WORD

Perhaps this phrase (v. 21) is a reference to Deut 30.14, "The word is very near to you; it is in your mouth and in your heart for you to observe." Conversely, Paul interprets Deut 30.14 (in Rom 10.8–10): "'The word is near you, on your lips and in your heart' . . . because if you confess with your lips that Jesus is Lord and believe in your heart that God raised him from the dead, you will be saved. For one believes with the heart and so is justified, and one confesses with the mouth and so is saved." Paul understands the "word" to refer to "Lord Jesus." "Heart," for him, refers to "belief"; "mouth" refers to confessing that belief. But Paul omits to say what "observe" indicates, and James fills this in. By "implanted word," then, James means God's natural law of mercy "in the mouth and heart," the law that needs to be observed (see v. 22).

same way with the rich; in the midst of a busy life, they will wither away.

[12] Blessed is anyone who endures temptation. Such a one has stood the test and will receive the crown of life that the Lord[a] has promised to those who love him. [13] No one, when tempted, should say, "I am being tempted by God"; for God cannot be tempted by evil and he himself tempts no one. [14] But one is tempted by one's own desire, being lured and enticed by it; [15] then, when that desire has conceived, it gives birth to sin, and that sin, when it is fully grown, gives birth to death. [16] Do not be deceived, my beloved.[b]

[17] Every generous act of giving, with every perfect gift, is from above, coming down from the Father of lights, with whom there is no variation or shadow due to change.[c] [18] In fulfillment of his own purpose he gave us birth by the word of truth, so that we would become a kind of first fruits of his creatures.

[19] You must understand this, my beloved:[b] let everyone be quick to listen, slow to speak, slow to anger; [20] for your anger does not produce God's righteousness. [21] Therefore rid yourselves of all sordidness and rank growth of wickedness, and welcome with meekness the implanted word that has the power to save your souls.

a Gk *he*; other ancient authorities read *God*
b Gk *my beloved brothers*
c Other ancient authorities read *variation due to a shadow of turning*

1.12–18: Temptation and good deeds. 12: *Blessed . . . temptation,* see Ps 1.1, "blessed [or "favored"] the man" (Heb "'ashrei ha'ish," Gk "makarios anēr"). This formula appears in biblical (1 Kings 10.8) and Talmudic (*m. Yoma* 8.9) literature, DSS (1QS 525.1–4), and the Gospels (Mt 5.3–12). *Temptation* (Gk "peirasmos") is used in Jas 1.2 (NRSV translates "trials"); see Mt 6.13; 26.41, and elsewhere. *Midr. Tann.* to Deut 23.15 shows how self-control leads to eternal life. *Crown,* a wreath given to athletes, soldiers, and leaders. **13:** Num 15.39–40 warns against following personal lusts and temptations, while the commandments of God are meant to prevent sin. **14–15:** *Desire . . . sin . . . death, Kallah Rabbati* 2.6 remarks that lustful thoughts lead to sinful actions and sin kills (also, *b. Ber.* 33a); it is not the serpent that kills, but sin. Rabbinic literature contains many references to "temptation" and the "evil desire." For example, *b. Sukk.* 52a compares the righteous winning their struggle against temptation to one who conquers a mountain; *b. Sukk.* 52b advises that one can melt and smash the evil urge by engaging in Torah study. God will help defeat it. *B. B. Bat.* 16b equates the "evil urge," "satan," and "the angel of death." **17–18:** *From . . . Father of lights,* this epithet for God ("Father of Light" as divine power) is found in the sectarian writings of the DSS (1QM 13.10; 1QS 3.20; cf. CD A 5.18). *With whom there is no variation,* James, like Mal 3.6, speaks of God's unchanging faithfulness. *Birth . . . truth, Gen. Rab.* 8 (to Gen 1.26) says God convened a committee ("us") to oversee humanity's creation, initially comprised of Truth, Mercy, Righteousness, and Peace. Truth and Peace, foreseeing humanity's true nature, objected to the creation of humans, and Truth was for a period cast out from the divine counselors (see Ps 85.10–11 [Heb vv.11–12]). On (new) *birth* see Jn 3.5–6. *First fruits,* the first word of Gen 1.1 ("bereshit") when read as "for the first" rather than "in the beginning" is taken (*Lev. Rab.* 36.4) to refer to "first fruits" ("reshit," Ex 34.26) in the sense by which Jer 2.3 metaphorically defines Israel as God's first fruits ("reshit"), the choicest of the nations.

1.19–27: Ears, eyes, hands, mouths. 19: *Let everyone . . . speak,* see Sir. 5.11 ("Be quick to hear, but deliberate in answering"); cf. *m. Avot* 1.15, "say little and do much." *Slow to anger, m. Avot* 5.11 stresses, "be slow to anger; quick to pacify." **21:** *Implanted word,* see "Implanted Word" above. **22:** *But be doers of the word,* for Jews, "doers"

[22] But be doers of the word, and not merely hearers who deceive themselves. [23] For if any are hearers of the word and not doers, they are like those who look at themselves[a] in a mirror; [24] for they look at themselves and, on going away, immediately forget what they were like. [25] But those who look into the perfect law, the law of liberty, and persevere, being not hearers who forget but doers who act—they will be blessed in their doing.

[26] If any think they are religious, and do not bridle their tongues but deceive their hearts, their religion is worthless. [27] Religion that is pure and undefiled before God, the Father, is this: to care for orphans and widows in their distress, and to keep oneself unstained by the world.

2 My brothers and sisters,[b] do you with your acts of favoritism really believe in our glorious Lord Jesus Christ?[c] [2] For if a person with gold rings and in fine clothes comes into your assembly, and if a poor person in dirty clothes also comes in, [3] and if you take notice of the one wearing the fine clothes and say, "Have a seat here, please," while to the one who is poor you say, "Stand there," or, "Sit at my feet,"[d] [4] have you not made distinctions among yourselves, and become judges with evil thoughts? [5] Listen, my beloved brothers and sisters.[e] Has not God chosen the poor in the world to be rich in faith and to be heirs of the kingdom that he has promised to those who love him? [6] But you have dishonored the poor. Is it not the rich who oppress you? Is it not they who drag you into court? [7] Is it not they who blaspheme the excellent name that was invoked over you?

a Gk *at the face of his birth*
b Gk *My brothers*
c Or *hold the faith of our glorious Lord Jesus Christ without acts of favoritism*
d Gk *Sit under my footstool*
e Gk *brothers*

refers to performing Torah. Some rabbis (*b. Shabb.* 88a) linked "we will do and we will hear" at Sinai (Ex 24.7) to "doers of his word" and "hearers of his word" (Ps 103.18–21). James restricts the "implanted word" command to the law of mercy (1.27). **23–24:** *Immediately forget, Avot de R. Natan* A 22.2 states that the saintly Hanina ben Dosa counseled that if one's thoughts were of greater focus than one's deeds, the former would eventually perish. Ps 36 condemns the boastfulness of sinners. **25:** *But those who look . . . perfect law . . . liberty*, for James to *look* is to meditate on moral laws. *B. Men.* 99b finds great reward for those who constantly meditate on Torah. Ps 19.7 (Heb v. 8) states: "The law of the LORD is perfect, reviving the soul." The law of liberty (2.12) means that the way individuals act toward others impacts how God acts toward the individuals (*m. Sot.* 1.7). *The perfect law* is later called "the royal law" (2.8), the law that teaches compassion. *B. Eruv.* 54a, referring to Ex 32.16 describing the tablets of the law as God's writing "engraved," reads "engraved" [Heb "ḥarut"] law as if it said "freedom" [Heb "ḥeirut"] law, suggesting that the law of Sinai itself is a law of freedom. **26:** *Bridle their tongues*, see Prov 11.13 for the danger of gossip; see also on 3.6. **27:** *God, the Father*, lit., "before the God and father." The implication is that God has a son. Jews would say "our Father" as in *b. Ta'an.* 25b (see also Mt 6.9 and the salutations of various Pauline epistles). *Care for orphans . . . distress*, James restricts the implanted word/command to the law of mercy. *M. Ta'an.* 2.1 says, "God saw their works" (Jon 3.10) not their mourning rituals. Likewise for James, without acts of loving-kindness, confessing beliefs is worthless. See e.g., Deut 10.18. *Unstained by the world*, an expression of freedom from the earthly, unspiritual side of human existence based on bodily desires and jealousies; see 4.4. James worries about "pagan" mores and assimilation as do *b. Mo'ed Qat.* 16b and *b. Ber.* 59a, where God weeps over his children assimilating among the pagan nations.

2.1–7: Favoring the rich. 1–4: *Midr. Tann.* explains Deut 16.19, on the qualities necessary for judges: "Do not say this one is rich while this one is poor . . . this one [qualified yet destitute] should sit beneath [me], and do not have it that the poor stand and that the rich sit . . . God stands with the poor and not with those who oppress them." *Assembly*, lit., "synagogue." **5:** *Chosen the poor . . . heirs of the kingdom*, this is a Christian formulation (Mt 5.3; Lk 6.20) referring to the eschaton, the end of the current age and beginning of the new one. See also Mt 5.5 and compare Ps 37.11, which refers to the meek inheriting the land. As for Jews, all Israel, with few exceptions, have a share in the next world (*m. Sanh.* 10.1). **6:** *Who drag you into court*, Ex 23.3 and Lev 19.15 warn judges against favoring the poor (or rich) in a law suit. James addresses judges who show favoritism and persecute the poor. **7:** *Blaspheme*, perhaps referring to the denigration of God's special care for the poor and oppressed, or to the disrespectful way some rich people referred to followers of Jesus.

[8] You do well if you really fulfill the royal law according to the scripture, "You shall love your neighbor as yourself." [9] But if you show partiality, you commit sin and are convicted by the law as transgressors. [10] For whoever keeps the whole law but fails in one point has become accountable for all of it. [11] For the one who said, "You shall not commit adultery," also said, "You shall not murder." Now if you do not commit adultery but if you murder, you have become a transgressor of the law. [12] So speak and so act as those who are to be judged by the law of liberty. [13] For judgment will be without mercy to anyone who has shown no mercy; mercy triumphs over judgment.

[14] What good is it, my brothers and sisters,[a] if you say you have faith but do not have works? Can faith save you? [15] If a brother or sister is naked and lacks daily food, [16] and one of you says to them, "Go in peace; keep warm and eat your fill," and yet you do not supply their bodily needs, what is the good of that? [17] So faith by itself, if it has no works, is dead.

[18] But someone will say, "You have faith and I have works." Show me your faith apart from your works, and I by my works will show you my faith. [19] You believe that God is one; you do well. Even the demons believe—and shudder. [20] Do you want to be shown, you senseless person, that faith apart from works is barren? [21] Was not our ancestor Abraham justified by works when he offered his son Isaac on the altar? [22] You see that faith was active along with his works, and faith was brought to completion by the works. [23] Thus the scripture was fulfilled that says, "Abraham believed God, and it was reckoned to him as righteousness," and he was called the friend of God. [24] You see that a person is justified by works and not by faith alone. [25] Likewise, was not Rahab the prostitute also justified by works when she welcomed the messengers and sent them out by another road? [26] For just as the body

[a] Gk *brothers*

2.8–13: Wholeness under the law. 8: *Royal law*, in quoting Lev 19.18 on love of one's neighbor and characterizing it as "royal," James is in agreement with *Midr. Sifra* to Lev 19.18, which calls this commandment "the supreme rule" that is served by all of scripture's tenets. (See "The Concept of Neighbor," p. 540.) For Lev 19.18 see also Mt 22.39; Mk 12.31; Lk 10.27. **9:** *Partiality*, favoring one law or litigant and neglecting another (see Lev 19.15). **10–11:** *Fails in one point . . . transgressor*, by neglecting any part of the law, they show disbelief in God. *T. Sebu.* 3.6 offers an almost identical list of transgressions and concludes: "[Who is a complete lawbreaker?] . . . One does not do even one transgression without denying the One who commanded it." Like James, *Midr. Pitaron Torah Kedoshim* claims one fulfills "love of neighbor" every time one refrains from breaking an ethical injunction in Torah. **12:** *The law of liberty*, see 1.25n. The point of the law is to free humanity from the domination of evil powers. As one chooses, so God rewards and punishes. **13:** *For judgment will be . . . no mercy*, rabbis called this "measure for measure," and it is the major principle of divine justice (see *b. Sanh.* 90a). *Mercy triumphs over judgment*, mercy conquers (Heb "kovesh") judgment (*Sifre Num.* 134; e.g., Num 14.18–19); the proof text is Mic 7.19–20. "Mercy" is a major theme in Tobit, Wisdom, and Sirach; see also Mt 5.7; 18.33.

2.14–26: Faith as expressed in works. 14: *Faith*, declared only in words will not help anyone. **18:** *I by my works will show you my faith*, only by works can one demonstrate trust in God's ordering of life. This section can be seen as a correction of those who understood Paul (Rom 4.5–6) as dismissing the importance of works. James mentions ethical rather than ritual laws in his examples, and it might be that for him this is the substance of "works." **19:** *Even the demons believe*, belief simply in the existence of the one God means little. This is not true faith since demons also believe in God. For later rabbinic Jews, praising the name of Jesus together with God's name is a breach of strict monotheism (*b. Sanh.* 63a). **21–24:** Abraham is *justified* (lit., "made righteous") *by works* in his willingness to sacrifice Isaac (see Gen 22); his *faith* (trust) in God *was brought to completion by the works. Our ancestor Abraham . . . Isaac on the altar*, Nachmanides (on Gen 15.5–6) observes that Gen 22.15–17 completes the demonstration of Abraham's faith so Abraham could now receive the promise of numerous descendants. "Faith" is dependent on works. See also 1 Macc 2.5. **23:** *Friend of God*, see Isa 41.8; 2 Chr 20.7. **25:** *Rahab the prostitute*, her acts showed the faith she declared in Josh 2.11. According to Talmudic tradition (*b. Meg.* 14a–b) she reformed and married Joshua, the successor of Moses; see also Mt 1.5. **26:** *Body . . . spirit*, see Gen 2.7 (human life is dependent on spirit/breath). Also, for the rabbis, the body needs the soul to live (*b. Ber.* 10a and *b. Mo'ed*

without the spirit is dead, so faith without works is also dead.

3 Not many of you should become teachers, my brothers and sisters,[a] for you know that we who teach will be judged with greater strictness. [2] For all of us make many mistakes. Anyone who makes no mistakes in speaking is perfect, able to keep the whole body in check with a bridle. [3] If we put bits into the mouths of horses to make them obey us, we guide their whole bodies. [4] Or look at ships: though they are so large that it takes strong winds to drive them, yet they are guided by a very small rudder wherever the will of the pilot directs. [5] So also the tongue is a small member, yet it boasts of great exploits.

How great a forest is set ablaze by a small fire! [6] And the tongue is a fire. The tongue is placed among our members as a world of iniquity; it stains the whole body, sets on fire the cycle of nature,[b] and is itself set on fire by hell.[c] [7] For every species of beast and bird, of reptile and sea creature, can be tamed and has been tamed by the human species, [8] but no one can tame the tongue—a restless evil, full of deadly poison. [9] With it we bless the Lord and Father, and with it we curse those who are made in the likeness of God. [10] From the same mouth come blessing and cursing. My brothers and sisters,[d] this ought not to be so. [11] Does a spring pour forth from the same opening both fresh and brackish water? [12] Can a fig tree, my brothers and sisters,[e] yield olives, or a grapevine figs? No more can salt water yield fresh.

[13] Who is wise and understanding among you? Show by your good life that your works are done with gentleness born of wisdom. [14] But if you have bitter envy and selfish ambition in your hearts, do not be boastful and false to the truth. [15] Such wisdom does

[a] Gk *brothers*
[b] Or *wheel of birth*
[c] Gk *Gehenna*
[d] Gk *My brothers*
[e] Gk *my brothers*

Qat. 28b–29a). The body without any life, a corpse, is ritually unclean (Num 19.14–22), as is anyone who comes in contact with it; so, according to James, is *faith without works.*

3.1–12: Importance of guarding speech. 1: *Teachers*, a slight error will be compounded by students, who in turn will teach nonsense that will lead their students to seek foreign values (*Avot de R. Natan* A.11). See Acts 13.1; 1 Cor 12.28–29; Eph 4.11; 1 Tim 1.7. **2:** *Perfect* here means those who are so in control of thoughts and actions that they do not misspeak, let alone misbehave. Ps 39.1 speaks of bridling the tongue; Prov 10.31 speaks of the mouth of the just; Sir 5.11–6.1 (cf. 28.12–26) warns against being "double-tongued." Jewish sages (*m. Avot* 1.17), following Tanakh traditions, concluded the best medicine for the body's welfare is silence. **5:** *Tongue . . . exploits*, the tongue wreaks havoc. It is worse than the worst of sins (*Midr. Tanh. Lev.*, "Metzora" 4–5). **6:** *Fire*, cf. Ps 120.3–4 (Heb vv. 4–5): "Deceitful tongue . . . arrows . . . glowing coals." According to Sir 28.11–12, a quarrel is like a fire: "If you blow on a spark, it will glow; if you spit on it, it will be put out; yet both come out of your mouth." Therefore take care what—incitement or calmness—comes out of your mouth. **9:** *Bless . . . curse, Midr. Tann.* to Deut 11.26–28, "blessing and curse," finds this lesson for lovers of good and lovers of evil ("Death and life") in an exposition of Prov 18.21.

3.13–18: Dangers of envy. 15: *Wisdom, Avot de R. Natan* B. 43 contrasts divine, gentle wisdom and earthly, wicked wisdoms. **16–18:** *Envy . . . peace*, for the rabbis, the heavenly realms are devoid of envy, hatred, and ambition. Everyone requires peace (*Deut. Rab.* 5.12 on Sabbath observance). Many passages (e.g., *Num. Rab.* 11.7; *Sifre Num.* 42) extol peace, the reward for righteousness, using the imagery of Isa 32.17.

4.1–10: Friend of the world, enemy of God. 1–2: *Those conflicts*, rabbis speak of "maḥloket" ("dispute, argument") and "qetatah" ("quarreling"). *M. Avot* 5.3: Whoever thinks, "Yours is mine" is a Sodomite; *b. Ber.* 16b suggests that humanity wants to do God's will but self-aggrandizement and Roman oppression prevent it. The early church faced numerous conflicts created by factionalism; see esp. 1 Cor and the Johannine letters. **3–4:** *Ask wrongly*, prayer is the proper way to gain money for needs, not for worldly pleasures. See Ps 37, especially v. 4. *Adulterers*, a standard denunciation of idolatry, or putting some other being or object in the place of God (e.g., Hos 1–3; Jer 3.2). *Friendship with the world*, not ordinary life activities but an orientation toward accepting material goods as the highest value, and consequently denigrating spiritual values and actions such as care for the neighbor (cf. 2.15–16). *Enmity with God*, Ps 6.8–10 [Heb 9–11]. In 1 Kings 18, Elijah is zealous for God, while in ch 21

not come down from above, but is earthly, unspiritual, devilish. [16] For where there is envy and selfish ambition, there will also be disorder and wickedness of every kind. [17] But the wisdom from above is first pure, then peaceable, gentle, willing to yield, full of mercy and good fruits, without a trace of partiality or hypocrisy. [18] And a harvest of righteousness is sown in peace for[a] those who make peace.

4 Those conflicts and disputes among you, where do they come from? Do they not come from your cravings that are at war within you? [2] You want something and do not have it; so you commit murder. And you covet[b] something and cannot obtain it; so you engage in disputes and conflicts. You do not have, because you do not ask. [3] You ask and do not receive, because you ask wrongly, in order to spend what you get on your pleasures. [4] Adulterers! Do you not know that friendship with the world is enmity with God? Therefore whoever wishes to be a friend of the world becomes an enemy of God. [5] Or do you suppose that it is for nothing that the scripture says, "God[c] yearns jealously for the spirit that he has made to dwell in us"? [6] But he gives all the more grace; therefore it says,

"God opposes the proud,
but gives grace to the humble."

[7] Submit yourselves therefore to God. Resist the devil, and he will flee from you. [8] Draw near to God, and he will draw near to you. Cleanse your hands, you sinners, and purify your hearts, you double-minded. [9] Lament and mourn and weep. Let your laughter be turned into mourning and your joy into dejection. [10] Humble yourselves before the Lord, and he will exalt you.

[11] Do not speak evil against one another, brothers and sisters.[d] Whoever speaks evil against another or judges another, speaks evil against the law and judges the law; but if you judge the law, you are not a doer of the law but a judge. [12] There is one lawgiver and judge who is able to save and to destroy. So who, then, are you to judge your neighbor?

[13] Come now, you who say, "Today or tomorrow we will go to such and such a town and spend a year there, doing business and making money." [14] Yet you do not even know what tomorrow will bring. What is your life? For you are a mist that appears for a little while and then vanishes. [15] Instead you ought to say, "If the Lord wishes, we will live and do this or that." [16] As it is, you boast in your arrogance; all such boasting is evil. [17] Anyone, then, who knows the right thing to do and fails to do it, commits sin.

[a] Or *by*
[b] Or *you murder and you covet*
[c] Gk *He*
[d] Gk *brothers*

he prophesies the destruction of God's enemy. **5:** *Scripture says,* James may be citing an unknown text, or referring to general biblical statements. *God yearns jealously,* Deut 6.5 speaks of loving God with "heart," "soul," and goods (Heb "me'odekha," not really "might," *m. Ber.* 9.5); *Zohar* 2 (Ex, Terumah) 162b claims God's gift of the soul enables one to accomplish such love. **6:** *Grace to the humble,* Prov 3.34 (LXX). **7–8:** *Submit . . . he will draw near, m. Avot* 2.4 says "Make your will God's will that he may make his will your will. *B. Ber.* 5a counsels Torah study to stifle temptation. *Cleanse your hands . . . hearts,* the imagery is from Ps 24.4–5 (Heb vv. 3–4). *Y. Ber.* 9.5 cites a lost work, the Scroll of the Pious: "Depart from me one day and I will depart from you two [days]." See also Deut 30.2–3 on returning to God and then God returning to you. **10:** *Humble . . . exalt,* see Mic 6.8; Ps 107.41; 113.7.

4.11–17: Evil and careless speech. 11: *Do not speak evil . . . judges the law, y. Pe'ah* 1.1 relates that the speaker of evil denies divine justice. **12:** *There is one . . . judge,* cf. *m. Avot* 4.8. God alone has the right to judge, since God gave the law and will judge in accordance with it. **13–16:** An extended paraphrase of Prov 27.1. **14:** *What tomorrow will bring,* building on this image, the sages counsel against imagining the future (*b. Ber.* 9b). See also Eccl 10.14. *What is your life,* see *b. Yoma* 87b for the expression, "What is our life?" The next sentence gives the implied answer. *A mist . . . vanishes,* see Ps 103.15 (Heb v. 16); Job 7.9; Eccl 12.7. **15–16:** *If the Lord wishes . . . boasting is evil, b. Sanh.* 98a—while "God willing" is rare in talmudic literature (*b. B. Bat.* 55a has "with the help of heaven"), it becomes frequent in the spoken word of Jews ("im Yertz[eh] ha-Shem," "If God [lit., 'the Name'] wills it"). The paraphrase of Prov 27.1 now ends. **17:** *Anyone . . . commits sin,* the rabbis had harsher expressions (following Eccl 6.3): better such a one had been stillborn! (*Midr. Tanh. ki tavo* 4 to Deut 11.13–17).

5 Come now, you rich people, weep and wail for the miseries that are coming to you. [2] Your riches have rotted, and your clothes are moth-eaten. [3] Your gold and silver have rusted, and their rust will be evidence against you, and it will eat your flesh like fire. You have laid up treasure[a] for the last days. [4] Listen! The wages of the laborers who mowed your fields, which you kept back by fraud, cry out, and the cries of the harvesters have reached the ears of the Lord of hosts. [5] You have lived on the earth in luxury and in pleasure; you have fattened your hearts in a day of slaughter. [6] You have condemned and murdered the righteous one, who does not resist you.

[7] Be patient, therefore, beloved,[b] until the coming of the Lord. The farmer waits for the precious crop from the earth, being patient with it until it receives the early and the late rains. [8] You also must be patient. Strengthen your hearts, for the coming of the Lord is near.[c] [9] Beloved,[d] do not grumble against one another, so that you may not be judged. See, the Judge is standing at the doors! [10] As an example of suffering and patience, beloved,[b] take the prophets who spoke in the name of the Lord. [11] Indeed we call blessed those who showed endurance. You have heard of the endurance of Job, and you have seen the purpose of the Lord, how the Lord is compassionate and merciful.

[12] Above all, my beloved,[b] do not swear, either by heaven or by earth or by any other oath, but let your "Yes" be yes and your "No" be no, so that you may not fall under condemnation.

[13] Are any among you suffering? They should pray. Are any cheerful? They should sing songs of praise. [14] Are any among you sick? They should call for the elders of the church and have them pray over them, anointing them with oil in the name of the Lord. [15] The prayer of faith will save the sick, and the Lord will raise them up; and anyone who has committed sins will be forgiven. [16] Therefore confess your sins to

[a] Or *will eat your flesh, since you have stored up fire*
[b] Gk *brothers*
[c] Or *is at hand*
[d] Gk *Brothers*

5.1–6: The emptiness of riches. 1: *Rich,* see *Sifre Deut.* 318 to Deut 32.15, wealth always leads to corruption. *Miseries . . . coming to you,* riches are of no use at the end, whether one sees this as one's individual death or as the day of judgment (cf. Mt 19.23). **2–3:** *Riches . . . rotted . . . gold and silver . . . rusted,* see Mt 6.19–21. *Treasure for the last days,* cf. *y. Pe'ah* 1.1: treasure of deeds is for the next world, that of wealth for this world. **4:** *The wages . . . cry out,* see Deut 24.14–15. The oppressed and exploited cry for justice (Gen 4.10). **5:** *You have fattened . . . slaughter,* see Deut 32.15 for indulgence leading to rebellion. "Fat" is occasionally a metaphor for intransigent wickedness, e.g., Ps 119.70. **6:** *Murdered the righteous one,* the poor, righteous person is condemned by the protected rich; see Wis 2.10–20.

5.7–12: Patience and care in speaking. 7–8: *The coming of the Lord,* the time must be ripe and the ground prepared for Jesus' return. *The early and the late rains* (Deut 11.14; Jer 5.24; Joel 2.23) are in October and April. **9:** *Do not . . . judged,* see *m. Sot.* 1.7 and *b. Shabb.* 27b for the same idea phrased positively: God is the judge (Gen 18.25) whose verdict is final. *The Judge is standing at the doors,* here probably Jesus, since the coming of the Lord was just mentioned. **10–11:** *The prophets . . . Job,* prophets (e.g., Jer 38) were persecuted for delivering unwelcome messages. Job has faith in his own righteousness. James refers to Job as he is shown in the first two and final chapters of that book. *M. Ta'an.* 2.4 gives a list of prophets and holy people who endured suffering and were saved. *Compassionate and merciful,* e.g., Ex 34.6; Ps 103.8. **12:** James returns to the topic of careful speech. *"Yes" be yes . . . ,* see Mt 5.34–37 and *b. B. Metz.* 49a; also see Eccl 5.4.

5.13–20: Prayer, praise, and following the truth. 13: *Suffering . . . pray . . . cheerful . . . praise,* speech should be appropriate to the circumstance. **14:** *Elders* (Gk "presbyteroi"), see Acts 15; 1 Tim 5.17,19; Titus 1.5; 1 Pet 5.1,5; 2 Jn 1; 3 Jn 1. *Anointing,* in the Hebrew Bible anointing was a sign of consecration or of installation of a priest or king; in the NT it is occasionally used in healing, as here and Mk 6.13. *Name of the Lord,* invoking the name of Jesus to heal (see Mk 16.17–18). *Y. Ma'as. S.* 2.1 refers to healing the sick by intoning (perhaps Ex 15.26) and anointing with oil. **15:** *The prayer of faith will save the sick . . . raise them up . . . be forgiven,* catalogues of blessings were common (e.g., 4Q521 ["Messianic Apocalypse"] 2 lines 8–13) and the synagogue "Amidah" prayer states: "Lord . . . you uphold the falling . . . heal the sick . . . free those in bondage." **16:** *Confess your sins to one another,* Jewish

one another, and pray for one another, so that you may be healed. The prayer of the righteous is powerful and effective. [17] Elijah was a human being like us, and he prayed fervently that it might not rain, and for three years and six months it did not rain on the earth. [18] Then he prayed again, and the heaven gave rain and the earth yielded its harvest.

[19] My brothers and sisters,[a] if anyone among you wanders from the truth and is brought back by another, [20] you should know that whoever brings back a sinner from wandering will save the sinner's[b] soul from death and will cover a multitude of sins.

[a] Gk *My brothers*
[b] Gk *his*

sources only know of confession to God (Ps 38.15–18). *And pray for one another*, when you ask for another, your needs are given (*b. B. Kamma* 92a based on Job 42.10). *The prayer of the righteous*, *b. Ta'an.* 8a recommends having a pious person pray for you. **17–18:** *Elijah . . . harvest*, see 1 Kings 17–18, although the account does not quote Elijah praying that there should be no rain. **19–20:** *Brings back a sinner*, the message concludes by stressing the benefits of repentance, a major Jewish theme; for "covering" sin, see Ps 32.1.

THE FIRST LETTER OF PETER

AUTHORSHIP, DATE, AND LITERARY HISTORY

This work is included as one of the seven "catholic" letters mentioned by the fourth-century church historian Eusebius [*Hist. eccl.* 2.23.25]; "catholic" (Gk "for the whole" or universal) indicates a text that spoke to the whole church. Its form is a letter by Peter, the most prominent of the twelve men in Jesus' inner circle, written from prison in Rome (the "Babylon" in 5.13) to believers in Asia Minor (modern Turkey). More likely one of Peter's followers wrote this epistle, imitating Paul's letter form, after Peter's death in 64 CE. Reasons for doubting Peter's authorship include the letter's excellent literary Greek, which would be surprising from a Galilean fisherman; the salutation from Peter, a nickname, rather than his given name Simon or Simon bar Jonah; the use of "Babylon" for Rome, which became common in Jewish and Christian literature only after Rome destroyed the Jerusalem Temple in 70 CE; and the use of terms such as "presbyteros" ("elder," 5.1), which were in use at a later stage of church development.

The letter is addressed to Gentiles, suggested by references that they formerly were ignorant of God (1.14), were not God's people (1.18; 2.10), and engaged in idolatry, drunkenness, and sexual immorality (4.2–4).

PETER IN CHRISTIAN TRADITION

If Peter did not write the work, it nevertheless remains "Petrine" in that it gathers traditions associated with him. Peter is the only one of the Twelve to whom the Gospels accord significant speaking parts and actions (although John's Gospel reveres the unspecified "beloved disciple"). Readers often warm to him because he shows human weakness in his failure to understand Jesus (Mk 8.31–33) and his denial of Jesus at his arrest (Mk 14.66–72 and parallels) despite his promise of fidelity (Mk 14.29). Flawed as he is, Peter is the "rock" (Gk "petra") upon which Jesus builds his church, to whom he gives the keys to the kingdom and the power to forgive sins (Mt 16.17–19). Early Christian tradition, such as *1 Clem.* 5.1–4 (written ca. 90 CE from Rome) reports that Peter died a martyr's death, probably in the persecutions by Nero in the 60s.

Peter is quickly appropriated by others. Acts of the Apostles, probably written in the early second century, shows that Peter has already developed a powerful image in the church as a preacher, healer, and wonder-worker. He is also depicted as preaching to Gentiles (Acts 10.1–11.1; see also Mt 28.19), accepting them into the church. The legend that he dispatched the fraudulent magician Simon Magus (Acts 8.9–24) continues in the apocryphal *Acts of Peter* (second–third century). Peter is put forward by Christians who continued to observe a form of Jewish law that emphasized purity regulations and ritual immersion as related in *The Pseudo-Clementines.* Peter and James are early church heroes in this literature, against Paul, who preached the law-free gospel. Even some Gnostic works (e.g., *Apocalypse of Peter*) claim him. Peter is appropriated by every group as a symbol of legitimacy and connection to the historical Jesus.

READING GUIDE

The believers addressed are not at ease or well understood by the surrounding society. They suffer a lack of social status, but the writer uses Israel's history and traditions—through creative use of verses from the Septuagint—to make sense of their separateness and suffering. The chain or catena of connected verses is reminiscent of rabbinic midrash and the Dead Sea Scrolls. The addressees are, like the Jews, a kingdom of priests and a holy people who live within a broader society, which rejects their theology, their morality, and their history.

JEWISH/CHRISTIAN/PAGAN RELATIONS

First Peter shows the shaky status of Christians in the Roman Empire. They could no longer trade on the antiquity of the Jews nor on the limited privileges Rome granted the Jews. As a disparaged group, believers in Jesus created an alternative identity as "the household of God." They looked to biblical Israel as a model. Although aliens, wanderers, and outsiders, Israelites (identified as the addressees of 1 Peter) are the people of God. The author deftly claims the identity of Israel for all believers in Jesus.

Claudia Setzer

1 Peter, an apostle of Jesus Christ,
To the exiles of the Dispersion in Pontus, Galatia, Cappadocia, Asia, and Bithynia, [2] who have been chosen and destined by God the Father and sanctified by the Spirit to be obedient to Jesus Christ and to be sprinkled with his blood:

May grace and peace be yours in abundance.

[3] Blessed be the God and Father of our Lord Jesus Christ! By his great mercy he has given us a new birth into a living hope through the resurrection of Jesus Christ from the dead, [4] and into an inheritance that is imperishable, undefiled, and unfading, kept in heaven for you, [5] who are being protected by the power of God through faith for a salvation ready to be revealed in the last time. [6] In this you rejoice,[a] even if now for a little while you have had to suffer various trials, [7] so that the genuineness of your faith—being more precious than gold that, though perishable, is tested by fire—may be found to result in praise and glory and honor when Jesus Christ is revealed. [8] Although you have not seen[b] him, you love him; and even though you do not see him now, you believe in him and rejoice with an indescribable and glorious joy, [9] for you are receiving the outcome of your faith, the salvation of your souls.

[10] Concerning this salvation, the prophets who prophesied of the grace that was to be yours made careful search and inquiry, [11] inquiring about the person or time that the Spirit of Christ within them indicated when it testified in advance to the sufferings destined for Christ and the subsequent glory. [12] It was revealed to them that they were serving not themselves but you, in regard to the things that have now been announced to you through those who brought you good news by the Holy Spirit sent from heaven—things into which angels long to look!

[13] Therefore prepare your minds for action;[c] discipline yourselves; set all your hope on the grace that Jesus Christ will bring you when he is revealed. [14] Like obedient children, do not be conformed to the desires that you formerly had in ignorance. [15] Instead, as he who called you is holy, be holy yourselves in all your conduct; [16] for it is written, "You shall be holy, for I am holy."

a Or *Rejoice in this*
b Other ancient authorities read *known*
c Gk *gird up the loins of your mind*

1.1–2: Greeting. 1: *Exiles of the Dispersion,* lit., "the elect sojourning in the Diaspora." The Diaspora began with the deportations of 597 and 586 BCE, when many Judeans were exiled to Babylon. Even after the return of some exiles from Babylon, Israel as a people was not fully restored, suffering further expulsions after the destruction of the Second Temple in 70 CE and after the Bar Kochba Revolt in 132–135 CE. The word "diaspora" evokes the image of Israel, the chosen people, scattered among but not absorbed into the nations. "Sojourning" ("parepidēmos") is the word the Septuagint applies to Abraham (Gen 23.4). For the author of 1 Peter, diaspora is not geographical, but social and theological. Believers are "in" the earthly realm, but not truly "of" it. **2:** *Chosen and destined by God the Father,* lit., "known beforehand by God." Rabbinic midrash (*Gen. Rab.* 1.4) shows the election of Israel as known by God before the creation of the world. *Sprinkled with his blood,* on the Day of Atonement, the high priest purifies the sanctuary and atones for the people by sprinkling the blood of a bull and goat before the tent of meeting (Lev 16.11–16). In this work (1.19; see Heb 9.13–14) Jesus' death purifies and redeems.

1.3–12: Blessing. Christians experience trials and testing but expect reward. As early as the second century BCE, Jewish texts like *Testament of Judah* and *1 Enoch* (*Book of the Watchers*) speak of final judgment and reward for the righteous. Referring to the persecution under Antiochus Epiphanes, 2 Macc 7 identifies the reward of the righteous as the reward for martyrs. **3:** *New birth,* Paul uses the image of the baptized believer as a "new creation" that erases distinctions between Jew and Gentile (Gal 6.15; 2 Cor 5.17; cf. Gal 3.28). **10:** *Prophets who prophesied of the grace,* early Christian proclamation understood Jesus' life, death, and resurrection as predicted in the Hebrew Bible (1 Cor 15.3).

1.13–2.3: Encouragement to holiness. 13: *When he is revealed,* a reference to the return of the Messiah in glory (Mk 14.62; 1 Thess 4.15–16). **14:** *Desires that you formerly had,* suggests a pagan audience. Some early Christian sources (e.g., *Ep. Barn.* 4.7–8; 14.4) accused Jews of blindness and willfulness but not ignorance of God. **15:** *As he who called you is holy,* invokes the holiness God commends to Israel (Lev 19.2), a virtue that carries the idea of

SUFFERING UNDER PERSECUTION

The letter makes numerous references to alienation and unjust suffering. Nero killed Christians in 64 to deflect blame for Rome's burning. Even Tacitus, no admirer of Christians, is repelled by his cruelty (*Ann.* 15.44): Nero crucified some and burned others alive as human torches. According to early church tradition, Peter is martyred (Jn 21.18–19) at Rome under Nero. *First Clement* 4–5, written about the same time as 1 Peter, indicates Peter and Paul are martyred, while Eusebius, a third-century church historian, adds that Peter is killed in Rome in the Neronic persecutions (*Hist. eccl.* 2.25). There is no empirewide persecution of Christians until the mid-third century.

The audience's suffering probably comes not from Roman officials but from neighbors. Followers of Jesus had become an irritant: because they emerged from a Jewish group, adhered to its scriptures (in Gk translation, the LXX), and had Jewish members, they inherited many of the stereotypes associated with the Jews. Believers in Jesus were said to worship an ass (or in one graffito on the wall of the Imperial Palace on Rome's Palatine Hill, a crucified ass). Like the Jews, they were accused of *odium humani generis*, hatred of humanity (Tacitus, *Ann.* 15.44). Christian separatism at different points included avoiding Roman spectacles and festivals, or avoiding certain professions like the military, and therefore looked to outsiders like misanthropy. Like the Jews, they were considered unpatriotic because they refused to sacrifice to the Roman gods and emperors (Jews were exempt, thanks to an earlier decree from Julius Caesar). City deities needed to be mollified, lest they send misfortune. Like the Jews, Christians were accused of strange rituals, of being oversexed, and of engaging in lewd acts (Tacitus, *Hist.* 5.1–13 [Jews]; Athenagoras, *Plea* 36.1; Minucius Felix, *Octavius* 9.4–6; Tertullian, *Apol.* 2.1; 4.1–2).

[17] If you invoke as Father the one who judges all people impartially according to their deeds, live in reverent fear during the time of your exile. [18] You know that you were ransomed from the futile ways inherited from your ancestors, not with perishable things like silver or gold, [19] but with the precious blood of Christ, like that of a lamb without defect or blemish. [20] He was destined before the foundation of the world, but was revealed at the end of the ages for your sake. [21] Through him you have come to trust in God, who raised him from the dead and gave him glory, so that your faith and hope are set on God.

[22] Now that you have purified your souls by your obedience to the truth[a] so that you have genuine mutual love, love one another deeply[b] from the heart.[c] [23] You have been born anew, not of perishable but of imperishable seed, through the living and enduring word of God.[d] [24] For

"All flesh is like grass
and all its glory like the flower of grass.
The grass withers,
and the flower falls,
[25] but the word of the Lord endures
forever."

That word is the good news that was announced to you.

2 Rid yourselves, therefore, of all malice, and all guile, insincerity, envy, and all slander. [2] Like newborn infants, long for the pure, spiritual milk, so that by it you may grow into salvation— [3] if indeed you have tasted that the Lord is good.

[4] Come to him, a living stone, though rejected by mortals yet chosen and precious in God's sight, and [5] like living stones, let your-

[a] Other ancient authorities add *through the Spirit*
[b] Or *constantly*
[c] Other ancient authorities read *a pure heart*
[d] Or *through the word of the living and enduring God*

separation. **17:** *Your exile,* like Israel, believers are aliens in the surrounding society. **18:** *The futile ways inherited from your ancestors,* another typical way of referring to non-Jews. **19:** *A lamb without defect or blemish,* Jesus is identified as the Lamb of God in Jn 1.29–36. This reference also recalls the suffering servant of Isa 53.6–7 who is like a lamb, as well as the lamb sacrificed at Passover (Ex 12.5). The emphasis of perfection and lack of blemish indicates the context of Temple sacrifice (Lev 3.1). **23:** *You have been born anew,* in Jn 3.3–5, Jesus tells the Pharisee Nicodemus one must be "born from above," which may also be translated "born anew." **24:** The author cites Ps 34.8 to distinguish the perishable from the imperishable.

USE OF ISRAEL'S SCRIPTURE

Christian identification with biblical Israel became so familiar that by the second century, the apologist Justin Martyr declared Christians the "true Israel" (*Dial.* 11.5; 123.6–9; 135.3). An unfortunate corollary for some Christian interpreters was that "old Israel" lost the covenant (so the *Epistle of Barnabas*, which is included in some early Christian canonical listings). The stage was set for an anti-Jewish reading of Israel's Scripture and the denial of Jews as a covenant people.

In ch 2 of 1 Peter the author marshals verses from the Septuagint much as rabbinic literature uses biblical verses as proof texts. The aim is clear: Christians assume the identity of Israel, the people of God, through faith in Jesus. In becoming Israel, these Christians may suffer as the Exodus people, and like Israel, they will be rescued. What has happened to the Jews, the former Israel, the author does not say. So thorough is the church's identification with biblical Israel that non-Christians are now called "Gentiles" (2.12), and the hostile world is the "diaspora."

selves be built[a] into a spiritual house, to be a holy priesthood, to offer spiritual sacrifices acceptable to God through Jesus Christ. [6] For it stands in scripture:

"See, I am laying in Zion a stone,
a cornerstone chosen and precious;
and whoever believes in him[b] will not be put to shame."

[7] To you then who believe, he is precious; but for those who do not believe,

"The stone that the builders rejected
has become the very head of the corner,"

[8] and

"A stone that makes them stumble,
and a rock that makes them fall."

They stumble because they disobey the word, as they were destined to do.

[9] But you are a chosen race, a royal priesthood, a holy nation, God's own people,[c] in order that you may proclaim the mighty acts of him who called you out of darkness into his marvelous light.

[10] Once you were not a people,
but now you are God's people;
once you had not received mercy,
but now you have received mercy.

[11] Beloved, I urge you as aliens and exiles to abstain from the desires of the flesh that wage war against the soul. [12] Conduct yourselves honorably among the Gentiles, so that, though they malign you as evildoers, they may see your honorable deeds and glorify God when he comes to judge.[d]

[13] For the Lord's sake accept the authority of every human institution,[e] whether of the emperor as supreme, [14] or of governors, as sent by him to punish those who do wrong and to praise those who do right. [15] For it is God's will that by doing right you should silence the ignorance of the foolish. [16] As servants[f] of God, live as free people, yet do not use your freedom as a pretext for evil. [17] Honor everyone. Love the family of believers.[g] Fear God. Honor the emperor.

[18] Slaves, accept the authority of your masters with all deference, not only those who are kind and gentle but also those who are

a Or *you yourselves are being built*
b Or *it*
c Gk *a people for his possession*
d Gk *God on the day of visitation*
e Or *every institution ordained for human beings*
f Gk *slaves*
g Gk *Love the brotherhood*

2.4–10: God's own people. *Come to him, a living stone, though rejected by mortals*, a catena (chain or linkage) of texts (Ex 19.6; Isa 28.16; 43.20–21; Hos 2.23; Ps 118.22) is woven together to prove the community has acquired privileges formerly granted to Israel.

2.11–4.11: Believers as aliens. 11: *Aliens and exiles*, as "resident aliens" ("paroikos," lit., "one who lives beside"; the Septuagint uses this word to translate the Heb "ger" or "ger toshav" in Gen 12.10; 15.13; Ex 12.45; Lev 25.35; Deut 23.7). Christians were not at home in society. Ancient lists of city residents show resident aliens possess a social standing below citizens but above strangers, freed slaves, and slaves. First Peter sees its addressees as alienated from, but living among, residents of the Roman Empire. They suffer from negative views, ranging from suspicion to violence. Their behavior must be blameless, as it reflects on the community as a whole. **2.18–3.7:** *Slaves, accept*

harsh. [19] For it is a credit to you if, being aware of God, you endure pain while suffering unjustly. [20] If you endure when you are beaten for doing wrong, what credit is that? But if you endure when you do right and suffer for it, you have God's approval. [21] For to this you have been called, because Christ also suffered for you, leaving you an example, so that you should follow in his steps.

[22] "He committed no sin,
and no deceit was found in his mouth."

[23] When he was abused, he did not return abuse; when he suffered, he did not threaten; but he entrusted himself to the one who judges justly. [24] He himself bore our sins in his body on the cross,[a] so that, free from sins, we might live for righteousness; by his wounds[b] you have been healed. [25] For you were going astray like sheep, but now you have returned to the shepherd and guardian of your souls.

3 Wives, in the same way, accept the authority of your husbands, so that, even if some of them do not obey the word, they may be won over without a word by their wives' conduct, [2] when they see the purity and reverence of your lives. [3] Do not adorn yourselves outwardly by braiding your hair, and by wearing gold ornaments or fine clothing; [4] rather, let your adornment be the inner self with the lasting beauty of a gentle and quiet spirit, which is very precious in God's sight. [5] It was in this way long ago that the holy women who hoped in God used to adorn themselves by accepting the authority of their husbands. [6] Thus Sarah obeyed Abraham and called him lord. You have become her daughters as long as you do what is good and never let fears alarm you.

[7] Husbands, in the same way, show consideration for your wives in your life together, paying honor to the woman as the weaker sex,[c] since they too are also heirs of the gracious gift of life—so that nothing may hinder your prayers.

[8] Finally, all of you, have unity of spirit, sympathy, love for one another, a tender heart, and a humble mind. [9] Do not repay evil for evil or abuse for abuse; but, on the contrary, repay with a blessing. It is for this that you were called—that you might inherit a blessing. [10] For

"Those who desire life
and desire to see good days,
let them keep their tongues from evil
and their lips from speaking deceit;
[11] let them turn away from evil and do good;
let them seek peace and pursue it.
[12] For the eyes of the Lord are on the righteous,
and his ears are open to their prayer.
But the face of the Lord is against those who do evil."

[13] Now who will harm you if you are eager to do what is good? [14] But even if you do suffer for doing what is right, you are blessed. Do not fear what they fear,[d] and do not be intimidated, [15] but in your hearts sanctify Christ as Lord. Always be ready to make your defense to anyone who demands from you an accounting for the hope that is in you; [16] yet do it with gentleness and reverence.[e] Keep your conscience clear, so that, when you are maligned, those who abuse you for your good conduct in Christ may be put to shame. [17] For it is better to suffer for doing good, if suffering should be God's will, than to suffer

[a] Or *carried up our sins in his body to the tree*
[b] Gk *bruise*
[c] Gk *vessel*
[d] Gk *their fear*
[e] Or *respect*

the authority of your masters, begins a "household code" ("Haustafeln"), a set of rules for the Roman household (see also Eph 5.22–6.9; Col 3.18–4.1). **2.22–25:** The text weaves in images from Isa 53.3–9, where Israel is like the sacrificial lamb, suffering on behalf of others who are straying *like sheep.* Probably emerging from the period after Israel's exile, the passage gives meaning to Israel's suffering as redemptive or instructive. **3.1–6:** *Wives, . . . accept the authority of your husbands* is an ideal of the deferential woman, modest in dress and behavior; the type occurs throughout Greco-Roman literature. Christian women married to non-Christian men are urged to promote the faith through pious example. *Called him lord,* Sarah never calls Abraham "Lord" in the Hebrew Bible but she does in the Septuagint (Gen 18.12); see also the Jewish noncanonical *Testament of Abraham,* where Sarah is a model of wifely obedience. **10–12:** A citation of Ps 34.12–16. The Jewish prayer "Elohai Netzor," recited after the "Amidah," a central prayer in

for doing evil. [18] For Christ also suffered[a] for sins once for all, the righteous for the unrighteous, in order to bring you[b] to God. He was put to death in the flesh, but made alive in the spirit, [19] in which also he went and made a proclamation to the spirits in prison, [20] who in former times did not obey, when God waited patiently in the days of Noah, during the building of the ark, in which a few, that is, eight persons, were saved through water. [21] And baptism, which this prefigured, now saves you—not as a removal of dirt from the body, but as an appeal to God for[c] a good conscience, through the resurrection of Jesus Christ, [22] who has gone into heaven and is at the right hand of God, with angels, authorities, and powers made subject to him.

4 Since therefore Christ suffered in the flesh,[d] arm yourselves also with the same intention (for whoever has suffered in the flesh has finished with sin), [2] so as to live for the rest of your earthly life[e] no longer by human desires but by the will of God. [3] You have already spent enough time in doing what the Gentiles like to do, living in licentiousness, passions, drunkenness, revels, carousing, and lawless idolatry. [4] They are surprised that you no longer join them in the same excesses of dissipation, and so they blaspheme.[f] [5] But they will have to give an accounting to him who stands ready to judge the living and the dead. [6] For this is the reason the gospel was proclaimed even to the dead, so that, though they had been judged in the flesh as everyone is judged, they might live in the spirit as God does.

[7] The end of all things is near;[g] therefore be serious and discipline yourselves for the sake of your prayers. [8] Above all, maintain constant love for one another, for love covers a multitude of sins. [9] Be hospitable to one another without complaining. [10] Like good stewards of the manifold grace of God, serve one another with whatever gift each of you has received. [11] Whoever speaks must do so as one speaking the very words of God; whoever serves must do so with the strength that God supplies, so that God may be glorified in all things through Jesus Christ. To him belong the glory and the power forever and ever. Amen.

[12] Beloved, do not be surprised at the fiery ordeal that is taking place among you to test you, as though something strange were happening to you. [13] But rejoice insofar as you are sharing Christ's sufferings, so that you may also be glad and shout for joy when his glory is revealed. [14] If you are reviled for the name of Christ, you are blessed, because the spirit of glory,[h] which is the Spirit of God, is resting on you.[i] [15] But let none of you suffer as a murderer, a thief, a criminal, or even as a mischief maker. [16] Yet if any of you suffers as a Christian, do not consider it a disgrace, but glorify God because you bear this name. [17] For the time has come for judgment to begin with the household of God; if it begins with us,

[a] Other ancient authorities read *died*
[b] Other ancient authorities read *us*
[c] Or *a pledge to God from*
[d] Other ancient authorities add *for us*; others, *for you*
[e] Gk *rest of the time in the flesh*
[f] Or *they malign you*
[g] Or *is at hand*
[h] Other ancient authorities add *and of power*
[i] Other ancient authorities add *On their part he is blasphemed, but on your part he is glorified*

Jewish liturgy, draws from the same verse as 10b, as well as promoting the idea of non-retaliation for injury. **19–20:** *Proclamation to the spirits in prison,* perhaps those who died in the flood (Gen –9); perhaps rebellious angels (see Gen 6.4; *1 En.* 6–36; *2 En.* 7.1–5). The author argues that just as Noah saved people from the water, Jesus saves through the water of baptism. **4.6:** *Proclaimed even to the dead,* the idea that Jesus descended into hell after his death (Rom 10.7; Eph 4.9), where he redeemed the saints (Eph 4.8) or defeated the evil angels (Phil 2.10; Col 2.15; cf. the second-century *Ascen. Isa.* 9–11, where he defeats the angel of death and Satan and the angels worship him, and *Odes Sol.* 17.9; 42.15 where he frees the dead). **8:** *Maintain constant love for one another,* the stress on Christian love ("agapē") as the love that builds up community flows from Prov 10.12b.

4.12–5.11: Suffering as a Christian. 12: *Test,* the same word is used in Mt 6.13, "do not bring us to the time of trial." **16:** *Suffers as a Christian,* the Maccabean martyrs (2, 4 Macc) are models of piety and their suffering and noble deaths present turning points in the restoration of the Jewish nation, the defeat of her oppressors, and a return to obedience to Torah. Similarly, the suffering of Christians will be rewarded. **17:** *Household of God,* im-

what will be the end for those who do not obey the gospel of God? [18] And

"If it is hard for the righteous to be saved,
what will become of the ungodly and
the sinners?"

[19] Therefore, let those suffering in accordance with God's will entrust themselves to a faithful Creator, while continuing to do good.

5 Now as an elder myself and a witness of the sufferings of Christ, as well as one who shares in the glory to be revealed, I exhort the elders among you [2] to tend the flock of God that is in your charge, exercising the oversight,[a] not under compulsion but willingly, as God would have you do it[b]—not for sordid gain but eagerly. [3] Do not lord it over those in your charge, but be examples to the flock. [4] And when the chief shepherd appears, you will win the crown of glory that never fades away. [5] In the same way, you who are younger must accept the authority of the elders.[c] And all of you must clothe yourselves with humility in your dealings with one another, for

"God opposes the proud,
but gives grace to the humble."

[6] Humble yourselves therefore under the mighty hand of God, so that he may exalt you in due time. [7] Cast all your anxiety on him, because he cares for you. [8] Discipline yourselves, keep alert.[d] Like a roaring lion your adversary the devil prowls around, looking for someone to devour. [9] Resist him, steadfast in your faith, for you know that your brothers and sisters[e] in all the world are undergoing the same kinds of suffering. [10] And after you have suffered for a little while, the God of all grace, who has called you to his eternal glory in Christ, will himself restore, support, strengthen, and establish you. [11] To him be the power forever and ever. Amen.

[12] Through Silvanus, whom I consider a faithful brother, I have written this short letter to encourage you and to testify that this is the true grace of God. Stand fast in it. [13] Your sister church[f] in Babylon, chosen together with you, sends you greetings; and so does my son Mark. [14] Greet one another with a kiss of love.

Peace to all of you who are in Christ.[g]

[a] Other ancient authorities lack *exercising the oversight*
[b] Other ancient authorities lack *as God would have you do it*
[c] Or *of those who are older*
[d] Or *be vigilant*
[e] Gk *your brotherhood*
[f] Gk *She who is*
[g] Other ancient authorities add *Amen*

agery evokes the idea of the "house of Israel," while responding to the institution of the Roman household. **18:** Prov 11.31. **5.1:** *Elder . . . elders,* title of a church official (Acts 14.23; Jas 5.14). **4:** *Chief shepherd,* image for the king (Ps 78.71) and for God (Ps 23.1); applied to Jesus (e.g., Jn 10.11). **5:** Prov 3.34. **9:** *Your brothers and sisters,* lit., "your brotherhood," one of the earliest self-designations the believers had for one another.

5.12–14: Farewell blessings. 13: *In Babylon,* "Babylon" refers to Rome in Jewish literature (*4 Ezra; 2 Bar.; Sib. Or.* 5) and Revelation; Babylon destroyed the first Jerusalem Temple in 586 BCE, as Rome destroyed the second in 70 CE. **13:** *My son Mark,* most likely John Mark, a Jewish believer and former companion of Paul, who knew Peter in Jerusalem and became helpful to Peter, perhaps his student and scribe (Acts 12.12,25; 13.13; 15.37–39; Col 4.10; 2 Tim 4.11; Philem 24).

THE SECOND LETTER OF PETER

NAME, AUTHORSHIP, AND DATE

Second Peter purports to be the second letter written by the apostle Peter (3.1), whom Jesus names as the foundation of his church (Mt 16.18), whom Paul names as one of the three "pillars" of the church (Gal 2.9), and who, in church tradition (Irenaeus, *Adv. Haer.* 3.3.2), founded the Christian community in Rome. Most scholars today, however, argue that the letter was written not by Peter but by a second-century Christian writing in Peter's name. The epistle maintains the guise of Petrine authorship by presenting a purported "testament" or final address of Peter (1.12–15), a claim to have been an eyewitness to Jesus' transfiguration (1.16–18; see Mt 17.1–8; Mk 9.2–8; Lk 9.28–36), and an allusion to having authored 1 Peter, which it regards as a genuine letter of the apostle (3.1).

HISTORICAL CONTEXT

Evidence for a late date of composition, possibly as late as the second quarter of the second century, includes the letter's heavy borrowing from the epistle of Jude (compare 2 Pet 2.1–2,4,6,10b–17 to Jude 4,6–13) while at the same time identifying Jude's "ungodly" persons (Jude 4) as "false teachers among you" (2 Pet 2.1); its implication of a developing Christian orthodoxy (1.20–21); the assumption that the earliest generation of Christian teachers is dead (3.2); and the reference to a collection of Pauline epistles as "scriptures" (3.15–16), that is, equal in authority with the Jewish Scriptures. Finally, the sophisticated Greek of the letter is unlikely to have been written by a presumably uneducated Galilean fisherman whose primary language was Aramaic. The letter's skillful blending of allusions to the Hebrew Bible (Tanakh) with allusions to Greco-Roman literature and the religious language of the Hellenistic world suggest an author at home in both Jewish and Greek traditions. Origen (ca. 185–ca. 254), the first church father to mention the letter, indicates that its Petrine authorship was already disputed (Eusebius, *Hist. eccl.* 6.25.8). The earliest existing manuscript of the epistle is Bodmer papyrus P.72, which dates to ca. third or fourth century. Peter himself is most closely associated with Rome, and the letter could have originated there. The introduction, however, names no specific recipients, and 3.1 implies that the recipients are the same as those of 1 Peter, which is addressed to several regions in Asia Minor (modern Turkey). If the "to you" in 3.15 refers to a specific church rather than the more general "those who have received a faith" (1.1b), then one of the churches associated with Paul's letters may be meant.

GUIDE TO READING

The author's opponents are members or former members of the author's Christian community (2.1,20–22). The letter charges that they are "forgetful of the cleansing of past sins" (1.9), "follow cleverly devised myths" (1.16), and are "false teachers" who behave licentiously (2.1–2,10,14,18). They deny both that Jesus will return and that there will be a last judgment (3.3–7). In a final charge, the author claims that his opponents twist the meaning of Paul's letters and "the other scriptures" (3.15–16). Comforting and assuring the readers that these false teachers will be punished (2.9,12b–13a,17b,21–22) and that Jesus will return, the author reminds them that God's time is not like human time (3.8–10) and that they will indeed enjoy the rewards of "new heavens and a new earth" (3.13).

Although denial of a final judgment (3.3–6) has prompted some commentators to identify the opponents of 2 Peter as Epicureans, references to "cleverly devised myths" (1.16) and the twisting of scriptures (3.16) have led many more to suggest opponents sympathetic to what are broadly described as Gnostic views. The Epicureans were followers of Epicurus, the third-century BCE philosopher who denied the concept of divine providence; by the early second century CE, this philosophy had apparently begun to affect both church and synagogue, since the Mishnah (*m. Sanh.* 10.1) speaks of an *apikoros*, the rabbinic term for "apostate," which derives from "Epicurean," as one who does not have a share in the world to come. Gnostics included those who claimed, for example, that the God revealed in the Jewish Scriptures, the Christian "Old Testament," was flawed and that the Christ was sent by the true God to bring humanity knowledge (Gk *gnōsis*) of its true origins.

Michael R. Greenwald

1 Simeon[a] Peter, a servant[b] and apostle of Jesus Christ,

To those who have received a faith as precious as ours through the righteousness of our God and Savior Jesus Christ:[c]

[2] May grace and peace be yours in abundance in the knowledge of God and of Jesus our Lord.

[3] His divine power has given us everything needed for life and godliness, through the knowledge of him who called us by[d] his own glory and goodness. [4] Thus he has given us, through these things, his precious and very great promises, so that through them you may escape from the corruption that is in the world because of lust, and may become participants of the divine nature. [5] For this very reason, you must make every effort to support your faith with goodness, and goodness with knowledge, [6] and knowledge with self-control, and self-control with endurance, and endurance with godliness, [7] and godliness with mutual[e] affection, and mutual[e] affection with love. [8] For if these things are yours and are increasing among you, they keep you from being ineffective and unfruitful in the knowledge of our Lord Jesus Christ. [9] For anyone who lacks these things is short-sighted and blind, and is forgetful of the cleansing of past sins. [10] Therefore, brothers and sisters,[f] be all the more eager to confirm your call and election, for if you do this, you will never stumble. [11] For in this way, entry into the eternal kingdom of our Lord and Savior Jesus Christ will be richly provided for you.

[12] Therefore I intend to keep on reminding you of these things, though you know them already and are established in the truth that has come to you. [13] I think it right, as long as I am in this body,[g] to refresh your memory, [14] since I know that my death[h] will come soon, as indeed our Lord Jesus Christ has made clear to me. [15] And I will make every effort so that after my departure you may be able at any time to recall these things.

[16] For we did not follow cleverly devised myths when we made known to you the power and coming of our Lord Jesus Christ, but we had been eyewitnesses of his majesty. [17] For he received honor and glory from God the Father when that voice was conveyed to

a Other ancient authorities read *Simon*
b Gk *slave*
c Or *of our God and the Savior Jesus Christ*
d Other ancient authorities read *through*
e Gk *brotherly*
f Gk *brothers*
g Gk *tent*
h Gk *the putting off of my tent*

1.1–2: Greeting and invocation. 1: *Simeon,* Gk rendition of Heb "Shim'on" or "Sim'on." This spelling, as opposed to the more common "Simon," appears in the NT only here and in Acts 15.14. *Peter* (Gk "Petros," from "petra," "rock") translates Aram "Cephas," "rock" (see Mt 16.18; Gal 1.18–2.14). *Faith,* here not "trust" but rather teaching or doctrine and right action, associated with "knowledge" (vv. 3,6,8), "goodness" (v. 5), and "self-control" (v. 6). *Our God and Savior* may be an early, and if so, unusual, instance of the equation of God with Jesus. **2:** *Grace and peace,* as in Paul's epistles, the traditional Hellenistic salutation "greetings" ("chairein," "rejoicing, joy") is modified to the Christian "grace" (Gk "charis," "favor") and combined with the Jewish "shalom," Gk "eirēnē," "peace."

1.3–11: Exhortation to virtuous behavior. 3: *Knowledge* (Gk "epignōsis," lit "full knowledge") is a major theme (see 1.2,8; 2.20; use of related term "gnōsis," see 1.5,6; 3.18). *Goodness* (Gk "aretē"), virtue, courage; in LXX for Heb "hod," "majesty" (e.g., Hab 3.3). **4:** *Participants of the divine nature,* language of popular Greek mystery religions. **5–7:** The virtues progress from *faith* to *love.* **9:** *Short-sighted and blind,* probable reference to the author's opponents. *Cleansing of past sins,* by forgetting, the believers forsake their knowledge of Jesus Christ, which has rescued them from a life enslaved to sin (see 2.20). **10:** *Call and election,* similar to terms used to describe God's choice of Israel; see, e.g., Isa 41.9. **11:** *Eternal kingdom,* the life that begins with the new age. *Lord and Savior,* note that it is *Jesus Christ* who is so characterized.

1.12–15: Peter's testament. The author follows the "testament" form, cf. Gen 49; Deut 32–33; Josh 23–24; and the noncanonical *Testament of the 12 Patriarchs.*

1.16–19a: Peter's authority. 16: *Myths,* the beliefs that the author is combating by invoking the authority of *eyewitnesses.* The content of these false beliefs is not specified. *Coming* (Gk "parousia"), the technical term for the "second coming" (the return of Jesus). *Eyewitnesses* (Gk "epoptai"), the only place in either the Septuagint

him by the Majestic Glory, saying, "This is my Son, my Beloved,[a] with whom I am well pleased." [18] We ourselves heard this voice come from heaven, while we were with him on the holy mountain.

[19] So we have the prophetic message more fully confirmed. You will do well to be attentive to this as to a lamp shining in a dark place, until the day dawns and the morning star rises in your hearts. [20] First of all you must understand this, that no prophecy of scripture is a matter of one's own interpretation, [21] because no prophecy ever came by human will, but men and women moved by the Holy Spirit spoke from God.[b]

2 But false prophets also arose among the people, just as there will be false teachers among you, who will secretly bring in destructive opinions. They will even deny the Master who bought them—bringing swift destruction on themselves. [2] Even so, many will follow their licentious ways, and because of these teachers[c] the way of truth will be maligned. [3] And in their greed they will exploit you with deceptive words. Their condemnation, pronounced against them long ago, has not been idle, and their destruction is not asleep.

[4] For if God did not spare the angels when they sinned, but cast them into hell[d] and committed them to chains[e] of deepest darkness to be kept until the judgment; [5] and if he did not spare the ancient world, even though he saved Noah, a herald of righteousness, with seven others, when he brought a flood on a world of the ungodly; [6] and if by turning the cities of Sodom and Gomorrah to ashes he condemned them to extinction[f] and made them an example of what is coming to the ungodly;[g] [7] and if he rescued Lot, a righteous man greatly distressed by the licentiousness of the lawless [8] (for that righteous man, living among them day after day, was tormented in his righteous soul by their lawless deeds that he saw and heard), [9] then the Lord knows how to rescue the godly from trial, and to keep the unrighteous under punishment until the day of judgment [10]—especially those who indulge their flesh in depraved lust, and who despise authority.

[a] Other ancient authorities read *my beloved Son*
[b] Other ancient authorities read *but moved by the Holy Spirit saints of God spoke*
[c] Gk *because of them*
[d] Gk *Tartaros*
[e] Other ancient authorities read *pits*
[f] Other ancient authorities lack *to extinction*
[g] Other ancient authorities read *an example to those who were to be ungodly*

or the NT where this word refers to a human being. The term was commonly used in Hellenistic literature for "initiates" into the mystery religions (cf. Plutarch, *Alc.* 22). **17–18:** *This is my Son . . . holy mountain*, an allusion to the Transfiguration (Mt 17.1–8; Mk 9.2–8; Lk 9.28–36), according to the Synoptic Gospels, witnessed by Peter, James, and John; the quotation is closest to Mt 17.5, itself an allusion to Ps 2.7b.

1.19b–21: Exhortation to hope. 19: *Prophetic message,* this could mean either the message of the Hebrew Bible prophets that was fulfilled in Jesus (as in v. 20) or a message from God by the Holy Spirit given (usually during worship) by a believer (as perhaps in v. 21); on the latter, see 1 Cor 12.27–30; 14.37–40. *Lamp,* see Mt 5.14–16; 6.22–23; see also Ps 119.105. *Morning star* refers to Christ in Rev 2.28; the star motif from Num 24.17 was also used by Shimon "Bar Kochba" (Aram "son of the star"), a messianic claimant and leader of the second Jewish rebellion against Rome, 132–35 CE. **20:** *One's own interpretation* implies a developing orthodox reading of scripture. **21:** *Moved by the Holy Spirit* suggests a developing concept of divine inspiration. See also *m. Sot.* 9.15: "saintliness leads to the Holy Spirit, and the Holy Spirit leads to the resurrection of the dead."

2.1–22: False prophets. 1: *False prophets,* the term is never used in the Tanakh but is in LXX at Jer 6.13; Zech 13.2. The author, in the guise of Peter, "predicts" what has occurred. *Deny the Master,* cf. Jude 4. *Master,* Gk "despotēs," "lord" (often in correlation to "slave, servant"); here refers to Jesus. **2:** *Licentious ways,* a standard invective; the opponents perhaps misunderstand Paul's position on the Law (cf. Rom. 3:8; 1 Cor. 6:12). *Way of truth,* see Ps 25.5; 86.11. **4:** *Angels,* see Gen 6.1–4; *1 En.* 6–16, detailing the fall of the angels, their union with human women, their offspring the Nephilim, and the ultimate judgment that will befall them. *Hell,* Gk "Tartaros," which evokes the images of Zeus casting the Titans to Tartaros in Hesiod's *Theogony* (ll. 687–819). **5:** *Noah,* Gen. 6.5–9.28. *Seven others,* Noah's wife, three sons, and their wives. The author substitutes the more universal "Noah" for Jude's "Israelites." See Jude 5–7; 1 Pet. 3.20. **6:** *Sodom and Gomorrah,* see Gen 19; pertains to the sin of violation of hospitality, not homosexuality as often supposed; cf. Judg 19. **9–10a:** See Jude 8–13. *Day of judgment,* the eschatological or final

Bold and willful, they are not afraid to slander the glorious ones,[a] [11] whereas angels, though greater in might and power, do not bring against them a slanderous judgment from the Lord.[b] [12] These people, however, are like irrational animals, mere creatures of instinct, born to be caught and killed. They slander what they do not understand, and when those creatures are destroyed,[c] they also will be destroyed, [13] suffering[d] the penalty for doing wrong. They count it a pleasure to revel in the daytime. They are blots and blemishes, reveling in their dissipation[e] while they feast with you. [14] They have eyes full of adultery, insatiable for sin. They entice unsteady souls. They have hearts trained in greed. Accursed children! [15] They have left the straight road and have gone astray, following the road of Balaam son of Bosor,[f] who loved the wages of doing wrong, [16] but was rebuked for his own transgression; a speechless donkey spoke with a human voice and restrained the prophet's madness.

[17] These are waterless springs and mists driven by a storm; for them the deepest darkness has been reserved. [18] For they speak bombastic nonsense, and with licentious desires of the flesh they entice people who have just[g] escaped from those who live in error. [19] They promise them freedom, but they themselves are slaves of corruption; for people are slaves to whatever masters them. [20] For if, after they have escaped the defilements of the world through the knowledge of our Lord and Savior Jesus Christ, they are again entangled in them and overpowered, the last state has become worse for them than the first. [21] For it would have been better for them never to have known the way of righteousness than, after knowing it, to turn back from the holy commandment that was passed on to them. [22] It has happened to them according to the true proverb,

"The dog turns back to its own vomit,"

and,

"The sow is washed only to wallow in the
mud."

3 This is now, beloved, the second letter I am writing to you; in them I am trying to arouse your sincere intention by reminding you [2] that you should remember the words spoken in the past by the holy prophets, and the commandment of the Lord and Savior spoken through your apostles. [3] First of all you must understand this, that in the last days scoffers will come, scoffing and indulging their own lusts [4] and saying, "Where is the promise of his coming? For ever since our ancestors died,[h] all things continue as they were from the beginning of creation!" [5] They deliberately ignore this fact, that by the word of God heavens existed long ago and an earth was formed out of water and by means of water, [6] through which the world of that time was deluged with water and perished. [7] But by

[a] Or *angels*; Gk *glories*
[b] Other ancient authorities read *before the Lord*; others lack the phrase
[c] Gk *in their destruction*
[d] Other ancient authorities read *receiving*
[e] Other ancient authorities read *love-feasts*
[f] Other ancient authorities read *Beor*
[g] Other ancient authorities read *actually*
[h] Gk *our fathers fell asleep*

assessment. *Depraved lust,* in the context of human sexual relations with angels (see v. 4n.), this probably refers to such relationships. **10b–22:** Author returns to the condemnation of the false prophets in 2.1–3. Cf. Jude 8–13. *Glorious ones,* lit., "glories," another reference to angels. **15–16:** *Balaam, son of Bosor,* hired to curse Israel (Num 22.21–35). Cf. Jude 11. **17:** Cf. Jude 12. Tartaros (see v. 4n.) was depicted as utterly dark. **19:** *Slaves,* see Rom 6.6,16. **20–21:** *After they have escaped,* opponents, who had been part of the author's community, mistake licentiousness for "freedom." *Holy commandment,* probably not one commandment but a reference to the entirety of faith or of the Tanakh. **22:** Prov 26.11 and a common saying occur here in place of the citation of *1 En.* 1.9 in Jude 14.

3.1–13: Reassurance of Christ's return. 1: *Beloved,* common term of endearment among Christians, 1 Cor 4.14; as here, in addressing audience, 1 Cor 10.14. *Second letter,* reference to 1 Peter. **2:** *Holy prophets,* of the Tanakh; the author assumes that the prophets of the Tanakh predict Jesus' return. *Savior,* see 1.1,11; 2.20. *Apostles,* "those sent," ambassadors or representatives, whom the author sees in an authoritative line with the prophets. **3–4:** *Scoffers will come,* another "vaticinium ex eventu" ("prophecy from the event") prediction (see 2.1n.). The theme of the delay of God's justice appears also in Plutarch's "On the Delays of the Divine Vengeance" in *Mor.* 548D;

the same word the present heavens and earth have been reserved for fire, being kept until the day of judgment and destruction of the godless.

[8] But do not ignore this one fact, beloved, that with the Lord one day is like a thousand years, and a thousand years are like one day. [9] The Lord is not slow about his promise, as some think of slowness, but is patient with you,[a] not wanting any to perish, but all to come to repentance. [10] But the day of the Lord will come like a thief, and then the heavens will pass away with a loud noise, and the elements will be dissolved with fire, and the earth and everything that is done on it will be disclosed.[b]

[11] Since all these things are to be dissolved in this way, what sort of persons ought you to be in leading lives of holiness and godliness, [12] waiting for and hastening[c] the coming of the day of God, because of which the heavens will be set ablaze and dissolved, and the elements will melt with fire? [13] But, in accordance with his promise, we wait for new heavens and a new earth, where righteousness is at home.

[14] Therefore, beloved, while you are waiting for these things, strive to be found by him at peace, without spot or blemish; [15] and regard the patience of our Lord as salvation. So also our beloved brother Paul wrote to you according to the wisdom given him, [16] speaking of this as he does in all his letters. There are some things in them hard to understand, which the ignorant and unstable twist to their own destruction, as they do the other scriptures. [17] You therefore, beloved, since you are forewarned, beware that you are not carried away with the error of the lawless and lose your own stability. [18] But grow in the grace and knowledge of our Lord and Savior Jesus Christ. To him be the glory both now and to the day of eternity. Amen.[d]

[a] Other ancient authorities read *on your account*
[b] Other ancient authorities read *will be burned up*
[c] Or *earnestly desiring*
[d] Other ancient authorities lack *Amen*

549D. Cf. 2.1. **5:** *Word of God,* See Gen ch 1. **6:** *Deluged,* see Gen 6–9. **7:** *Fire,* instrument of judgment in *T. Abr.* 10.11; 12.4. **8:** *Day is like a thousand years,* based on Ps. 90.4. **9:** *Not slow,* see Deut 7.10; *all to come to repentance,* the delay of the parousia allows for universal repentance. Cf. Rom 11.25. **10:** *The day of the Lord,* see Joel 2.2–32; Am 5.18–20; 1 Thess 5.2. **13:** *New heavens and a new earth,* Isa 65.17; 66.22; Rev 21.1 (though there is no evidence that the author of 2 Peter knows Revelation).

3.14–17: Exhortation for patience and righteousness. 14: *Beloved,* see 3.1n. *Spot or blemish,* in Tanakh an animal offered for sacrifice must be without blemish (Lev 21.17; same root word in LXX as here). **15:** *Patience . . . salvation,* reiteration of the idea in 3.9. See Rom 2.4; 9.22. **16:** *Other scriptures,* Paul's letters are considered scripture equal with the Tanakh. If 2 Peter antedates Marcion (fl. 140–144), this is the earliest mention of scriptural status being assigned to Paul's epistles. **17:** *Beloved,* see 3.1n. *Error of the lawless* refers back to the false teachers of 2.1 and 3.3–7 who deny that Jesus will return or that there will be a last judgment.

3.18: Doxology. *Knowledge,* return to the theme begun in 1.2. *Day of eternity,* lit "day of ages," a reference to the coming new age.

THE FIRST LETTER OF JOHN

AUTHORSHIP AND DATE

First John is the traditional title of one of three documents collectively called the "Johannine Letters." Even though the author is not named in any of the three, and they do not claim to have been written by the author of the Gospel of John, the title reflects the understanding that there is a relationship among the three documents, and between them and the Gospel of John.

CANONICAL STATUS

The text shares much of the vocabulary, and a number of themes, with John's Gospel (e.g., light and darkness [1 Jn 1.5–7; 2.9–11; cf. Jn 8.12; 12.46]; abiding in Christ [1 Jn 2.27–28; cf. Jn 13.34–35, also Jn 15.5]; new commandment [1 Jn 2.7–8; Jn 13.34–35]; eternal life [1 Jn 1.2; 2.25; 3.15; etc., and Jn 3.16]). However, given the significant differences in style and content between the letter and the Gospel, most modern scholars do not believe that 1 John was written by the author of the Fourth Gospel. Rather than attributing the responsibility for the writing of both the letters of John and the Gospel to a single author, they propose a "Johannine school" or "Johannine community" that shared a common vocabulary and theological outlook.

The earliest attestation of 1 John occurs in the letter of the Christian author Polycarp, *Phil.* 7.1, dated to ca. 117–120. While some argue that 1 John predates the Gospel of John (ca. 90–100 CE) the majority of experts place its composition to sometime after the writing of the gospel, therefore putting its date of composition at approximately 100–110. Likewise, the location of the community to which 1 John is written cannot be firmly ascertained. The majority of scholars place the Johannine community in western Asia Minor (modern Turkey), in Ephesus, which is the location most often named by tradition. Recently, however, Syria has gained supporters as a possibility.

HISTORICAL CONTEXT AND LITERARY HISTORY

In contrast to 2 and 3 John, 1 John lacks the elements typically found in a letter (e.g., salutation, identification of recipients and senders, greetings to local persons); hence it is more accurately described as a persuasive essay or exhortation. Its author wished to encourage and instruct his fellow believers when the community was reeling from a recent acrimonious schism (see 2.19).

What is not certain, however, is precisely what created the rift. This letter reflects a tension between two distinct views regarding Jesus, and this issue may lie at the heart of the schism. The author asserts that Jesus "has come in the flesh" (4.2). Others—perhaps those who had split from the community—deny this claim. They may represent a theology known as "Docetism." This term is derived from the Greek word ("dokeō") meaning "to seem," and according to docetic belief, Jesus only *seemed* to be human but was fully, and only, divine. This perspective may have derived from the philosophical principle that God, as spirit, cannot suffer pain and death. The author associates this docetic view with the "spirit of the antichrist" (4.3). This term refers not to a supernatural agent, but to false teachers, and the author appears to be concerned that other members of his community may find the docetic perspective appealing, hence his repeated encouragement that they are the children of God (3.2; 4.4,6; 5.19), with the implication being that the others are not.

INTERPRETATION

In contrast to the Gospel of John, 1 John does not reflect a polemical attitude toward Jews. In 1 John 2.7, the author states: "I am writing you no new commandment, but an old commandment that you have had from the beginning," but in v. 8 he asserts: "Yet I am writing you a new commandment that is true in him and in you" and continues by explaining that loving one's brothers and sisters is more consistent with "liv[ing] in the light" than hating them (9–11). The reference here to "a new commandment" likely refers to the "new commandment" introduced by Jesus in the Gospel of John 13.34: "I give you a new commandment, that you love one another. Just as I have loved you, you also should love one another," and is not a reference to a new set of precepts that would replace the Torah. Indeed, the idea of loving one's brothers and sisters and neighbors is one of the central tenets of Judaism expressed in the Hebrew Bible (e.g., Lev 19.18), and in later Jewish sources as well. A version of this "golden rule" teaching is expounded by one of Judaism's most distinguished first-century CE teachers, Hillel, in response to a request from a non-Jew that Hillel teach him "all" Jewish traditions, values, and practices while standing on one foot. Hillel's response, found in the *b. Shabb.* 31a, is: "What is hateful to you, do not do to your neighbor. All the rest is commentary; go and learn." The well-known Rabbi Akiva, who lived approximately one hundred years after Jesus, is said to have declared, "Love your neighbor as yourself—this is the major principle of the Torah" (*y. Ned.* 9.4). Other Jewish documents dated to around this time likewise reflect the importance of loving one's neighbor in connection with loving God (e.g., *T. Iss.* 5.2). If there is anything "new" about the commandment to love one another in the Gospel of John or in 1 John 2.8, it might be the last part of the statement from the Gospel: "Just as I have loved you." (See "The Concept of Neighbor," p. 540.) First John's use of images of light and darkness (1.5–7; 2.9–11), which reflect the Gospel of John's influence (Jn 8.12; 12.46), appear as well in Jewish writings from late antiquity. The Dead Sea Scrolls, for example, denounce competing groups by labeling them "sons of darkness" who are led by an "Angel of Darkness," while their own supporters are identified as "sons of light" who are followers of the "Prince of Light" (IQS 3.10–21; 1QM).

Michele Murray

1 We declare to you what was from the beginning, what we have heard, what we have seen with our eyes, what we have looked at and touched with our hands, concerning the word of life— [2] this life was revealed, and we have seen it and testify to it, and declare to you the eternal life that was with the Father and was revealed to us— [3] we declare to you what we have seen and heard so that you also may have fellowship with us; and truly our fellowship is with the Father and with his Son Jesus Christ. [4] We are writing these things so that our[a] joy may be complete.

[5] This is the message we have heard from him and proclaim to you, that God is light and in him there is no darkness at all. [6] If we say that we have fellowship with him while we are walking in darkness, we lie and do not do what is true; [7] but if we walk in the light as he himself is in the light, we have fellowship with one another, and the blood of Jesus his Son cleanses us from all sin. [8] If we say that we have no sin, we deceive ourselves, and the truth is not in us. [9] If we confess our sins, he who is faithful and just will forgive us our sins and cleanse us from all unrighteousness. [10] If we say that we have not sinned, we make him a liar, and his word is not in us.

[a] Other ancient authorities read *your*

1.1–4: Entering community fellowship. 1: *From the beginning*, see 2.13,14; Jn 1.1. *Touched with our hands*, the Gospels of Luke and (especially) John are the only ones to contain a post-resurrection event in which Jesus invites disciples to touch him. *Concerning the word*, the prologue of the Gospel of John (1.1–14) introduces the concept of word (Gk "logos"). The phrase *from the beginning* as well as the *word* here suggest that the author of 1 John was borrowing from the Gospel. **2:** *We have seen it*, the author states three times in the first three verses that he was an eyewitness to Jesus' ministry.

1.5–2.28: The core of belief. 1.5: The theme of *light* and *darkness* appears also in Jn 1.4,5,9; 3.19–21; 8.12; 9.5; 12.35–36,46. It is a theme repeated in the first two chs of 1 John and is common in sectarian literature from Qumran. **6:** *Fellowship*, (Gk "koinonia," the community of fellow-believers). It is not possible to participate in the community of light while *walking in darkness* (cf. Isa 9.1). **7:** *Blood . . . cleanses*, a reference to sacrificial practice; see Lev 4. **8–10:** *Sin*, etmologically falling short or missing a goal; to deny one's sin is to *deceive* oneself and deny God's truth. *Confess*, acknowledge the existence of. *Unrighteousness*, to be righteous or *just* is to be in accord with God's will, which is *faithful*. Judaism does not generally teach the concept of "original sin" (but see Ps 51.5 [Heb v. 7]); thus Jews do not believe that humans are born into a context in which they are estranged from God and must repair a rift. There is, however, an understanding within Judaism that humans do sin; confessing sin directly to God in prayer with a repentant attitude, therefore, is a Jewish practice. Confession of one's shortcomings often occurs in a communal setting, for example on Yom Kippur (Day of Atonement) in a synagogue, but can also be expressed in personal prayer, at any time, in or out of the synagogue. Jews believe that God is compassionate and will forgive a contrite sinner. **2.1:** *Little children*, perhaps a wisdom allusion (e.g., Prov 1.4,8), but may also mean "newest members" of

2 My little children, I am writing these things to you so that you may not sin. But if anyone does sin, we have an advocate with the Father, Jesus Christ the righteous; [2] and he is the atoning sacrifice for our sins, and not for ours only but also for the sins of the whole world.

[3] Now by this we may be sure that we know him, if we obey his commandments. [4] Whoever says, "I have come to know him," but does not obey his commandments, is a liar, and in such a person the truth does not exist; [5] but whoever obeys his word, truly in this person the love of God has reached perfection. By this we may be sure that we are in him: [6] whoever says, "I abide in him," ought to walk just as he walked.

[7] Beloved, I am writing you no new commandment, but an old commandment that you have had from the beginning; the old commandment is the word that you have heard. [8] Yet I am writing you a new commandment that is true in him and in you, because[a] the darkness is passing away and the true light is already shining. [9] Whoever says, "I am in the light," while hating a brother or sister,[b] is still in the darkness. [10] Whoever loves a brother or sister[c] lives in the light, and in such a person[d] there is no cause for stumbling. [11] But whoever hates another believer[e] is in the darkness, walks in the darkness, and does not know the way to go, because the darkness has brought on blindness.

[12] I am writing to you, little children,
because your sins are forgiven on
account of his name.
[13] I am writing to you, fathers,
because you know him who is from the
beginning.
I am writing to you, young people,
because you have conquered the evil one.
[14] I write to you, children,
because you know the Father.
I write to you, fathers,
because you know him who is from the
beginning.
I write to you, young people,
because you are strong
and the word of God abides in you,
and you have overcome the evil one.

[15] Do not love the world or the things in the world. The love of the Father is not in those who love the world; [16] for all that is in the world—the desire of the flesh, the desire of the eyes, the pride in riches—comes not

a Or *that*
b Gk *hating a brother*
c Gk *loves a brother*
d Or *in it*
e Gk *hates a brother*

the community. *Advocate* (Gk "paraklētos," lit., "one who stands alongside"), this term is found only here and in Jn 14.16,26; 15.26; 16.7 (where it refers to the coming of the Spirit). It can mean "one who speaks on behalf of another" or "one who offers aid to another." It can also be translated "comforter" or "counselor." *Righteous*, or "one who is just." **2:** *Atoning sacrifice* (Gk "hilasmos"), see 4.10; these are the only places in the NT where this word is used; in LXX it appears, e.g., in Lev 25.9; Num 5.8 (translated "atonement"). The sacrifice of atonement is one that reestablishes the relationship between God and human beings. **3:** *Know*, a favorite Johannine term, here alluding to the personal knowledge of God that leads one to love other members of the community (Jn 13.34). **4–6:** *Obey*, in conforming one's behavior one exemplifies *the love of God*. *Abide in*, participate in the life of. *Walk*, live one's life; cf. e.g., Ps 1.1; 15.2. **7:** *New commandment*, see Jn 13.34; 2 Jn 5. **11:** *Believer*, lit., "brother" (see translators' note *e*), this presumably applies to relationships within the community, not to those with outsiders. **12–14:** A rhythmic series of phrases repeating the threefold *children . . . fathers . . . young people* characterizes of the various groups within the community, perhaps as a way of making the exhortation memorable. *Sins . . . name*, forgiveness is from God; the *name* is not an arbitrary label but the expression of the person, including the person's innate authority. **13–14:** *Evil one* (Gk "poneros"), see also Mt 6.13, "rescue us from evil" or "the evil one"; Jn 17.15. *You have conquered*, perhaps through *the word of God*. **15:** Johannine literature often uses *world* (Gk "kosmos") as representing the sphere of opposition to God (see e.g., Jn 15.18–19, but note Jn 3.16: "God so loved the world"). **18:** *Antichrist*, this term is found in the NT only in these two letters (also 2.22; 4.3) and 2 Jn 7. The noun "christos" means "anointed one" or "messiah"; the prefix "anti-" can mean either "against" or "in place of." The antichrist is the adversary of God and Christ that comes in the end times. Antecedents to this idea can be found in Jewish literature and other sources (e.g., Dan 7.19–27; 8.9–11,23–25; 9.27; CD 8.2; 1QM 17.5–8; 11QMelch 2.12–13; and *Sib. Or.* 3.75–92, 611–15). In 1 John the sign of the (or an) antichrist seems to be false teaching, the denial of Jesus' messiahship, and the denial of the relation

from the Father but from the world. [17] And the world and its desire[a] are passing away, but those who do the will of God live forever.

[18] Children, it is the last hour! As you have heard that antichrist is coming, so now many antichrists have come. From this we know that it is the last hour. [19] They went out from us, but they did not belong to us; for if they had belonged to us, they would have remained with us. But by going out they made it plain that none of them belongs to us. [20] But you have been anointed by the Holy One, and all of you have knowledge.[b] [21] I write to you, not because you do not know the truth, but because you know it, and you know that no lie comes from the truth. [22] Who is the liar but the one who denies that Jesus is the Christ?[c] This is the antichrist, the one who denies the Father and the Son. [23] No one who denies the Son has the Father; everyone who confesses the Son has the Father also. [24] Let what you heard from the beginning abide in you. If what you heard from the beginning abides in you, then you will abide in the Son and in the Father. [25] And this is what he has promised us,[d] eternal life.

[26] I write these things to you concerning those who would deceive you. [27] As for you, the anointing that you received from him abides in you, and so you do not need anyone to teach you. But as his anointing teaches you about all things, and is true and is not a lie, and just as it has taught you, abide in him.[e]

[28] And now, little children, abide in him, so that when he is revealed we may have confidence and not be put to shame before him at his coming.

[29] If you know that he is righteous, you may be sure that everyone who does right has

3 been born of him. [1] See what love the Father has given us, that we should be called children of God; and that is what we are. The reason the world does not know us is that it did not know him. [2] Beloved, we are God's children now; what we will be has not yet been revealed. What we do know is this: when he[e] is revealed, we will be like him, for we will see him as he is. [3] And all who have this hope in him purify themselves, just as he is pure.

[4] Everyone who commits sin is guilty of lawlessness; sin is lawlessness. [5] You know that he was revealed to take away sins, and in him there is no sin. [6] No one who abides in him sins; no one who sins has either seen him or known him. [7] Little children, let no one deceive you. Everyone who does what

[a] Or *the desire for it*
[b] Other ancient authorities read *you know all things*
[c] Or *the Messiah*
[d] Other ancient authorities read *you*
[e] Or *it*

between God the Father and the Son. *Last hour*, the apocalyptic worldview is that God's intervention into human history and the ultimate defeat of evil are expected at any time. This is not an end of time, but an end of an era. **19:** *They went out from us*, the recent schism resulted in the withdrawal from the community of those who taught opposing views. **20:** *Anointed by the Holy One*, anointing (marking with oil) is an indication of the beginning of a new task or taking on a new situation; the one who has marked the members of the community is the Spirit. **23:** *Denies the Son*, possibly a reference to non-messianic Jews. **25:** *Eternal life*, the life of, or from, God, who is the only eternal being. **27:** *Abide in him*, or "abide in it," referring to the anointing. **28:** *Coming* (Gk "parousia"), the judgment consequent on the Messiah's return (see e.g., Mal 3.2 [referring to the "messenger" who precedes the coming of God]; 1 Cor 15.23; 1 Thess 2.19; 3.13; 4.15; 2 Thess 2.1).

2.29–3.24: Behaving as the children of God. 3.2: *We are God's children* (also 3.1; 4.4; 5.19), perhaps by this repeated theme the author seeks to assure readers of their status. *We will be like him*, believers become Christ-like in the resurrection (Jn 1.12–13; 13.15). Jews frequently are referred to as God's children in the Hebrew Bible (e.g., Deut 14.1–2) and in rabbinic literature (e.g., *m. Avot* 3.12). This imagery is used to convey the special, intimate nature of the relationship between God and the Jews—and how this special consecrated (or holy) status places certain moral and behavioral expectations upon the house of Israel, such as following dietary laws (Deut 14.3-21), and providing agricultural tithes that support the poor (Deut 14.28-29), which distinguish Israel from other nations. **3:** *Purify . . . pure*, necessary for coming into contact with God; see Isa 6.5–7; Mal 3.2. **4:** *Sin . . . lawlessness*, Gk "anomia" may imply the doctrine that believers can do without "nomos" ("law," the LXX translation of "Torah"), a view that Paul also combated (see e.g., Rom 3.31; 6.15ff.). **5:** *No sin*, see also Heb 4.15: Jesus shared all human experience except those arising from human sin. **6–10:** *No one who abides in him sins*, the author sets a

is right is righteous, just as he is righteous. [8] Everyone who commits sin is a child of the devil; for the devil has been sinning from the beginning. The Son of God was revealed for this purpose, to destroy the works of the devil. [9] Those who have been born of God do not sin, because God's seed abides in them;[a] they cannot sin, because they have been born of God. [10] The children of God and the children of the devil are revealed in this way: all who do not do what is right are not from God, nor are those who do not love their brothers and sisters.[b]

[11] For this is the message you have heard from the beginning, that we should love one another. [12] We must not be like Cain who was from the evil one and murdered his brother. And why did he murder him? Because his own deeds were evil and his brother's righteous. [13] Do not be astonished, brothers and sisters,[c] that the world hates you. [14] We know that we have passed from death to life because we love one another. Whoever does not love abides in death. [15] All who hate a brother or sister[b] are murderers, and you know that murderers do not have eternal life abiding in them. [16] We know love by this, that he laid down his life for us—and we ought to lay down our lives for one another. [17] How does God's love abide in anyone who has the world's goods and sees a brother or sister[d] in need and yet refuses help?

[18] Little children, let us love, not in word or speech, but in truth and action. [19] And by this we will know that we are from the truth and will reassure our hearts before him [20] whenever our hearts condemn us; for God is greater than our hearts, and he knows everything. [21] Beloved, if our hearts do not condemn us, we have boldness before God; [22] and we receive from him whatever we ask, because we obey his commandments and do what pleases him.

[a] Or *because the children of God abide in him*
[b] Gk *his brother*
[c] Gk *brothers*
[d] Gk *brother*

very high standard of behavior (see vv. 8–10). The main forms of sin, however, seem to be the failure to *love their brothers and sisters* and denial of God and the Son (2.22). **8:** *Child of the devil*, perhaps a reference to those who withdrew (2.19); there is no indication here of the identification of Jews as children of the devil, as in Jn 8.44. **9:** *Seed*, perhaps the Holy Spirit; one's "seed" is one's offspring, here the deeds of love and faith in God. **11:** *Love one another* (see 3.14,16,18), love is one of the frequent themes of the Johannine literature (see Jn 13.34–35). **12:** *We must not be like Cain*, Cain was the first murderer (see Gen 4). The Hebrew Bible does not explain why God preferred Abel's offering to that of Cain's—an episode that prompted Cain's feelings of hostility for Abel. One suggestion is that when comparing Gen 4.4, which describes Abel as bringing "the choicest of the firstlings of his flock," with Gen 4.3, in which Cain brings "an offering . . . from the fruits of his soil," it may be understood that Abel's offer was the better, and more pious, of the two. Another explanation is that Abel was chosen over Cain because of the brothers' different lifestyles. Abel was a shepherd, Cain a farmer, and numerous times in the Bible God shows a preference for the seminomadic, pastoral lifestyle of the shepherd (e.g., Moses [Ex 3.1] and David [1 Sam 16.11; 2 Sam 7.8] were shepherds before they were chosen by God to be leaders, and each was a younger brother as well). Various attempts to explain why Cain murdered Abel are found in Jewish postbiblical traditions. **13:** *The world hates you*, see Jn 15.18–19. **16:** *Laid down his life*, the rabbinic term "kiddush ha-Shem" denotes martyrdom, in particular, the willingness to die a martyr in order to sanctify ("kiddush") God's name ("ha-Shem"). Though the term is rabbinic, the concept is biblical, based on Lev 22.32, which states, "You shall not profane my holy name, that I may be sanctified among the people of Israel." Choosing death was considered mandatory by the rabbis if life meant transgressing three commandments against idolatry, unchastity (including incest, adultery, and, under certain circumstances, any infraction of the code of sexual morality), and murder (*b. Sanh.* 74a). **19–21:** *Hearts*, the Hebrew Bible views the heart as the seat of the emotional and intellectual inner life of a human being; the Hebrew word for heart, "lev(av)," was used metaphorically to refer to the source of the intellectual activities of a person (e.g., 1 Kings 8.48; Isa 10.7; Ezek 36.26). The laws of God were considered to have been written on the heart of humans (Ps 37.31). The rabbis also adopted the view that the heart was the seat of the emotions and intellect; most rabbinic references to the heart pertain to the sphere of ethics (e.g., *m. Avot* 2.9), and prayer is understood to be the "service of the heart" (*y. Ber.* 4.1; 7a). **21:** *Boldness* (Gk "parresia," the confidence to speak one's mind), see 2.28, "confidence"; 4.17, "boldness" resulting from

Cardinal Newman's Prayer

May He support us all the day long,
Till the shadows lengthen
And the evening comes,
And the busy world is hushed
And the fever of life is over
And our work is done.

Then in His mercy may He grant us
A safe lodging and
A holy rest and
Peace at the last.

Amen

Cardinal John Henry Newman

[23] And this is his commandment, that we should believe in the name of his Son Jesus Christ and love one another, just as he has commanded us. [24] All who obey his commandments abide in him, and he abides in them. And by this we know that he abides in us, by the Spirit that he has given us.

4 Beloved, do not believe every spirit, but test the spirits to see whether they are from God; for many false prophets have gone out into the world. [2] By this you know the Spirit of God: every spirit that confesses that Jesus Christ has come in the flesh is from God, [3] and every spirit that does not confess Jesus[a] is not from God. And this is the spirit of the antichrist, of which you have heard that it is coming; and now it is already in the world. [4] Little children, you are from God, and have conquered them; for the one who is in you is greater than the one who is in the world. [5] They are from the world; therefore what they say is from the world, and the world listens to them. [6] We are from God. Whoever knows God listens to us, and whoever is not from God does not listen to us. From this we know the spirit of truth and the spirit of error.

[7] Beloved, let us love one another, because love is from God; everyone who loves is born of God and knows God. [8] Whoever does not love does not know God, for God is love. [9] God's love was revealed among us in this way: God sent his only Son into the world so that we might live through him. [10] In this is love, not that we loved God but that he loved us and sent his Son to be the atoning sacrifice for our sins. [11] Beloved, since God loved us so much, we also ought to love one another. [12] No one has ever seen God; if we love one another, God lives in us, and his love is perfected in us.

[13] By this we know that we abide in him and he in us, because he has given us of his Spirit. [14] And we have seen and do testify that the Father has sent his Son as the Savior of the world. [15] God abides in those who confess that Jesus is the Son of God, and they abide in God. [16] So we have known and believe the love that God has for us.

God is love, and those who abide in love abide in God, and God abides in them. [17] Love

[a] Other ancient authorities read *does away with Jesus* (Gk *dissolves Jesus*)

knowledge of the love of God; 5.14, "boldness" in asking "according to [God's] will." **23:** *Name*, one's essential nature, including inherent authority; see 2.12–14n.

4.1–5.12: Identifying children of God. 4.1–2: *Test the spirits*, the author warns his community to be vigilant against *false prophets*, who may speak a word as if from God but propagate false teaching (see Deut 13.1–5; Jer 14.13–16); the "test" is the confession of *Jesus Christ . . . in the flesh* (i.e., not an illusion of being a human person). This statement implies that the opponents, presumably those who have recently separated, do *not* believe that Jesus came in the flesh. In the Tanakh, being able to distinguish between true and false prophets was a perplexing issue. Deut 18.20–22 attempts to provide two criteria: (1) true prophets speak only on behalf of the God of Israel alone (i.e., not on behalf of other gods), and (2) a true prophecy will come to pass. These criteria were not fail-safe; for example, if a false prophet is recognized as such by the failure of his or her prophecy, how is one to decide in the present? The rabbis likewise were concerned about the distinction between true and false prophets; they warned, for example, that false prophets would entice Jews to transgress Mosaic law by promising great rewards (e.g., *Pesiq. Rav Kah.* 24.15). Rabbis were particularly concerned about the relationship between prophecy and law, and which had more authority: "Until now [in the age of Alexander the Great] the prophets prophesied through the medium of the Holy Spirit; from now on, incline your ear and hearken to the words of the sages" (*Seder Olam Rab.* 30). **5:** *From the world*, the area of opposition to God; see 2.15n. **6:** *Spirit of truth . . . error*, the Holy Spirit contrasted with the spirit of the world or the devil (3.10). In the DSS there are references to two competing spirits, one good, and one bad. The good spirit, at times called the "spirit of truth," is associated with light, truth, and righteousness, and the bad spirit, sometimes labeled the "spirit of deceit" or "Belial" (lit., "of no worth") is associated with darkness, sin, and evil (1QS 3.17–21; 4.7–25). **7–12:** *Let us love one another*, see 3.11. The *love* that the members of the community have for each other is participation in God's love, shown when *God sent his only Son . . . to be the atoning sacrifice* (see 2.2n.). **12:** *No one has ever seen God*, Jn 1.18; visions of God (Moses, Ex 34.5–6; Isa 6.1; Ezek 1) are presumably either partial (back, lower body) or manifestations of visibility only for purposes of communication, not what God "really" is. **13:** *Spirit*, here capitalized to indicate that translators read it as being God's Spirit. **14:** *Savior of the world*, see Jn 4.42; the purport is that the Son is the (potential) Savior of all, not of a particular group. **17:** *Day of judgment*, this expression is

has been perfected among us in this: that we may have boldness on the day of judgment, because as he is, so are we in this world. [18] There is no fear in love, but perfect love casts out fear; for fear has to do with punishment, and whoever fears has not reached perfection in love. [19] We love[a] because he first loved us. [20] Those who say, "I love God," and hate their brothers or sisters,[b] are liars; for those who do not love a brother or sister[c] whom they have seen, cannot love God whom they have not seen. [21] The commandment we have from him is this: those who love God must love their brothers and sisters[b] also.

5 Everyone who believes that Jesus is the Christ[d] has been born of God, and everyone who loves the parent loves the child. [2] By this we know that we love the children of God, when we love God and obey his commandments. [3] For the love of God is this, that we obey his commandments. And his commandments are not burdensome, [4] for whatever is born of God conquers the world. And this is the victory that conquers the world, our faith. [5] Who is it that conquers the world but the one who believes that Jesus is the Son of God?

[6] This is the one who came by water and blood, Jesus Christ, not with the water only but with the water and the blood. And the Spirit is the one that testifies, for the Spirit is the truth. [7] There are three that testify:[e] [8] the Spirit and the water and the blood, and these three agree. [9] If we receive human testimony, the testimony of God is greater; for this is the testimony of God that he has testified to his Son. [10] Those who believe in the Son of God have the testimony in their hearts. Those who do not believe in God[f] have made him a liar by not believing in the testimony that God has given concerning his Son. [11] And this is the testimony: God gave us eternal life, and this life is in his Son. [12] Whoever has the Son has life; whoever does not have the Son of God does not have life.

[13] I write these things to you who believe in the name of the Son of God, so that you may know that you have eternal life.

[14] And this is the boldness we have in him, that if we ask anything according to his will, he hears us. [15] And if we know that he hears us in whatever we ask, we know that we have

a Other ancient authorities add *him*; others add *God*
b Gk *brothers*
c Gk *brother*
d Or *the Messiah*
e A few other authorities read (with variations) [7]*There are three that testify in heaven, the Father, the Word, and the Holy Spirit, and these three are one.* [8]*And there are three that testify on earth:*
f Other ancient authorities read *in the Son*

not found in the Tanakh. Instead "day of the LORD" is used (e.g., Isa 13.6–13; Joel 1.15; 2.1; 3.4; 4.14; Am 5.18–20; Ob 15; Zeph 1.17–18; Mal 3.23), a somewhat vague phrase understood to refer to a future point in time in which the wicked will be punished and justice will be achieved; it is strongly associated with the motifs of darkness and doom. The images connected with the "day of the LORD" contributed to the subsequent development of the day of judgment and its eschatology. Within Jewish tradition, the concept or term "day of judgment" appears in texts written during the Greco-Roman period (such as Dan 7.9–27 [the term is not used here]; Jdt 16.17; *Jub.* 5.10–14; *T. Levi* 3.2–3). **5.1:** *Born of God*, remade in the image of God (Gen 1.26–27; Jn 1.12–13: "born, not of blood or of the will of the flesh or of the will of man, but of God"). **2–3:** *We . . . obey his commandments*, see Jn 14.15–17. **4–5:** *Conquers*, overcomes, is no longer subject to the power of (the world). The rabbis understood that human beings were engaged in a constant internal struggle between following their "evil inclination" ("yetzer ha-ra") or following their "good inclination" ("yetzer ha-tov"). Righteous behavior and following the law were keys to "conquering" (kovesh) the evil inclination, but it was possible to receive forgiveness if one periodically faltered and allowed the evil inclination to prevail (*b. Sanh.* 43b: "R. Joshua b. Levi said: He who sacrifices his [evil] inclination and confesses [his sin] over it , Scripture imputes it to him as though he had honored the Holy One, blessed be He, in both worlds, this world and the next; for it is written, Whoso offereth the sacrifice of confession honoreth me." **6–8:** *Water . . . blood . . . Spirit*, probably another connection with the Gospel of John, which refers (19.34) to a spear being thrust into Jesus' side, from which blood and water emerge. *Water* is baptism, in the sense of cleansing from impurity (see, e.g., Lev 14.9); *blood* is sacrifice (e.g., Lev 4); the *Spirit* is the true witness (Jn 16.13).

5.13–21: Sin and eternal life. 16–17: *There is sin that is mortal*, the author's precise meaning is not clear, but possibly *mortal* refers to sin that prevents one from attaining eternal life (see 2.25n.). **18:** *Those who are born of*

obtained the requests made of him. [16] If you see your brother or sister[a] committing what is not a mortal sin, you will ask, and God[b] will give life to such a one—to those whose sin is not mortal. There is sin that is mortal; I do not say that you should pray about that. [17] All wrongdoing is sin, but there is sin that is not mortal.

[18] We know that those who are born of God do not sin, but the one who was born of God protects them, and the evil one does not touch them. [19] We know that we are God's children, and that the whole world lies under the power of the evil one. [20] And we know that the Son of God has come and has given us understanding so that we may know him who is true;[c] and we are in him who is true, in his Son Jesus Christ. He is the true God and eternal life.

[21] Little children, keep yourselves from idols.[d]

a Gk *your brother*
b Gk *he*
c Other ancient authorities read *know the true God*
d Other ancient authorities add *Amen*

God do not sin, see 1.8. **20–21:** *Him who is true*, the "true" and only God, in contrast to *keep yourselves from idols*, This abrupt concluding statement suggests that the author understands that at least some of his readers (and perhaps the majority) are of pagan backgrounds.

THE SECOND LETTER OF JOHN

TITLE, AUTHORSHIP, AND DATE

The brief letter known as 2 John is included in the "Johannine" letters because its vocabulary and themes overlap substantially with those of 1 and 3 John, which in turn share themes with the Gospel of John. (For a fuller discussion of these shared themes and vocabulary, and of the Johannine literature, see the Introduction to 1 John.) Like 3 John, 2 John is written by someone calling himself "the elder" (Gk "presbyteros"). The early second-century Christian writer Papias (Eusebius, *Hist. eccl.* 3.39.17) refers to an elder named John, and since at least that time the letter has been attributed to "John the elder," that is, a different John from the disciple traditionally credited with writing the Gospel. The term "presbyter" can designate either an aged (and thus presumably venerable) person, or a leader, regardless of age. It commonly translates the Hebrew "zaqen," which has a similar range of meanings (see Lev 19.32; Job 32.6–9; and the debate on who qualifies as a "zaqen" in *b. Qidd.* 32b, in which the argument turns on whether honor to an aged person ["hoary head"] depends only on the fact of age, or also on a quality sometimes acquired with age, such as wisdom).

This "elder," apparently a leader of local importance, is in a position to advise another congregation—"the elect lady and her children," a reference either to the leader and her community or a personification of the community as a "lady." Like the author of Proverbs (e.g., 1.8,10) and other ancient Near Eastern literature, the elder refers to his readers as children for whom he is responsible.

The letter of 2 John was probably produced in the same circles responsible for the other Johannine literature, in Asia Minor, sometime around the year 100. The letters rely on the Gospel of John for many concepts, as noted above, but the controversy with, and critical attitude toward, Jews that characterize the Gospel is not present in the letters; many scholars therefore conclude that the letters are later than the Gospel (which dates from the 90s), and are concerned with matters of false belief about the nature of Christ rather than with the conflict with Jewish opponents.

CONTENTS

The situation is similar to that addressed in 1 John, in that the congregation is warned against missionaries proclaiming a false gospel. But whereas in 1 John the deceitful missionaries have defected from the author's congregation, in 2 John the author warns the "elect lady" against the arrival of these "deceivers."

Throughout the letter, the elder emphasizes the idea of truth: he loves the believers in truth, they know the truth, the truth abides in them, and they walk in the truth. The conflict with the "deceivers" is apparently due to competing truth-claims regarding belief. For 2 John, belief that Jesus is the Christ is insufficient; equally important is correct belief about Jesus.

The opponents "do not confess that Jesus Christ [is coming] in the flesh" (v. 7; the NRSV translates the present participle as "has come"), and therefore do not "have God" (v. 9). By contrast, those who agree with the elder have "both the Father and the Son." The opponents' claim has been understood as (1) a denial that Jesus was truly human (a belief known as "docetism," from Gk "dokeō," "to seem, appear"); (2) a denial that he was truly divine (therefore those who think so do not "have God"); and (3) a denial that Jesus will return to earth in the flesh. If 2 John were written in the same community that produced 1 John and the Fourth Gospel, the opponents probably object to the elevation of Jesus to divine status, that is, an increasingly close identification of "the Father and the Son."

Julie Galambush

[1]The elder to the elect lady and her children, whom I love in the truth, and not only I but also all who know the truth, [2]because of the truth that abides in us and will be with us forever:

[3]Grace, mercy, and peace will be with us from God the Father and from[a] Jesus Christ, the Father's Son, in truth and love.

[4]I was overjoyed to find some of your children walking in the truth, just as we have been commanded by the Father. [5]But now, dear lady, I ask you, not as though I were writing you a new commandment, but one we have had from the beginning, let us love one another. [6]And this is love, that we walk according to his commandments; this is the commandment just as you have heard it from the beginning—you must walk in it.

[7]Many deceivers have gone out into the world, those who do not confess that Jesus Christ has come in the flesh; any such person is the deceiver and the antichrist! [8]Be on your guard, so that you do not lose what we[b] have worked for, but may receive a full reward. [9]Everyone who does not abide in the teaching of Christ, but goes beyond it, does not have God; whoever abides in the teaching has both the Father and the Son. [10]Do not receive into the house or welcome anyone who comes to you and does not bring this teaching; [11]for to welcome is to participate in the evil deeds of such a person.

[12]Although I have much to write to you, I would rather not use paper and ink; instead I hope to come to you and talk with you face to face, so that our joy may be complete.

[13]The children of your elect sister send you their greetings.[c]

[a] Other ancient authorities add *the Lord*
[b] Other ancient authorities read *you*
[c] Other ancient authorities add *Amen*

1–3: Opening. 1: *The elect lady,* the personification of the community as a woman (Gk "kyria," in LXX for "geveret," "mistress," is the feminine form of "kyrios," "lord" or "master"), and its members as her children, parallels the practice of personifying Jerusalem as a woman (see, e.g., Isa 54). The Greek "eklektos" (*elect*) is frequently used in the Septuagint to translate "beḥir," "chosen," in reference to Israel. The congregation is thus addressed as part of the covenant community (see also 1 Pet 2.9). **3:** *The Father's Son,* the author stresses the close relationship between Jesus and "the Father."

4–6: Mutual love. 4: The image of *walking* in good (or evil) paths echoes Prov (1.15; 2.20) and Ps (1.1,6), where path represents moral orientation. *Walking in the truth,* see Ps 25.5; 86.11. Here 2 John defines the "right" path not as a moral choice but as correct belief. **5:** The commandment to *love one another* reflects Jn 13.34; 1 Jn 2.7–11; 3.11. It is addressed to the community; the issue of care for outsiders is not dealt with here. The stress on mutual love may derive from Lev 19.18, "love your neighbor as yourself." **6:** To *walk according to his commandments* probably refers not to "halakhah," the way or path that one should follow with specific reference to the commands in the Tanakh, but to Jesus' commandment (Jn 13.34). In Tanakh there is no opposition between loving God and observing the commandments, and both are equated with walking in God's ways (see Deut 30.16).

7–11: Warning against deceivers. 7: The identity of the *deceivers* is not known to us; what it means to deny that *Jesus Christ has come in the flesh* is also unclear. The term *antichrist* is a neologism, used only here and in 1 Jn 2.18; 4.3 to indicate that the opponents are literally "against the Messiah." The term does not suggest (as it does in later Christian literature [see Cyril of Jerusalem, *Catechetical Lectures* 15.11–15]) that the opponents are satanic agents. **8–9:** *Reward . . . has both the Father and the Son,* this implies that the goal of the community's life is not an external goal but rather life in God's love. This also echoes 1 Jn 2.22–23, which claims that the antichrist, who denies that Jesus is the Christ, denies both Father and Son. **10–11:** The prohibition against giving hospitality to deceivers is supported on moral grounds: to share hospitality is to *participate in* their *evil deeds.* Both Greco-Roman and Jewish traditions considered hospitality a primary virtue. The NT word for "hospitality" ("philoxenia," lit., "love of the stranger" in e.g., Rom 12.13) is not used here, where congregants are warned that they incur "guilt by association" if they *welcome* (Gk "chairein," "greet with joy") sinners (cf. *Avot de R. Natan* 30: "He who joins himself to those who commit transgressions, though he does not do what they do, will nevertheless receive punishment as one of them").

12–13: Closing and greetings.

THE THIRD LETTER OF JOHN

The shortest document in the New Testament (at 219 words), lacking any reference to scripture, 3 John is a private letter probably written near the end of the first century. Its author, "the elder" (Gk "presbyteros"), a leading figure in the Johannine community, most likely wrote 2 John and is presumed to have written 1 John as well. Although some early Christians, like the church father Origen (ca. 185–254), cast doubt on whether the same "John" who wrote the Gospel and the first two letters attributed to him also wrote 3 John, the general view was that John, the son of Zebedee (see e.g., Mt 4.21; Mk 1.19; Lk 5.10; Jn 21.2; Gal 2.9) was the author. Scholarly consensus now holds that the author of any of the Fourth Gospel is not the same as the author of the epistles, yet there are thematic connections among the three letters and the Fourth Gospel. This Johannine community, founded by the "beloved disciple" mentioned in John's Gospel (21.24), faced challenges both from Jews who did not believe in Jesus' messiahship and from its own members. Some in this nascent community resisted an increasing focus on the divinity of Jesus; others may have questioned the terms of the mission to Gentiles; still others rejected certain claimants for church leadership.

Scholars presume that the writing of John's Gospel and the three letters occurred at different stages in the history of the community. In this light, 3 John is relatively early, when the majority were still ethnically Jewish but were extending their mission to Gentiles, and when rivalries were beginning but before the increasingly acrimonious divisions attested in 1 and 2 John. This letter, which conforms to the genre known today as a "letter of recommendation" (see 2 Cor 3.1–3), commends the loving behavior of Gaius and Demetrius. Diotrephes, a fellow church member, appears to have rejected the elder's leadership. None of these named characters is known apart from this letter.

The elder seems to view himself and his audience as ethnically Jewish, since he differentiates his audience from the "Gentiles" (Gk "ton ethnikon"), translated "nonbelievers" in the NRSV, v. 7. Nevertheless, his identity and that of his community, as he understands it, rests *primarily in their shared belief*, as opposed to shared observance of distinctively Jewish ritual practices, which he does not mention. They are all "brothers" who "testify" to, "walk in," and are "co-workers in" the same "truth" (3–4,8,12). The language of "truth" and "love" in 3 John warrants its association with the early communities who produced the Gospel of John and 1–2 John, though v. 7 suggests that it reflects an earlier stage in the Johannine community when its ethnically Jewish believers in Christ proselytized to Gentiles.

Although the NRSV translates "for the sake of the name" as "for the sake of Christ," v. 7 (following most Christian commentators; see Acts 5.41; 1 Jn 2.12; 3.23; 5.13), some suggest that the phrase means "for the sake of the name [of God]." Underlying this construction may be the Jewish circumlocution "ha-Shem" (Heb for "the Name") used infrequently for the name of God (the tetragrammaton) in the Tanakh (Lev 24.11; Deut 28.58), but very frequent in rabbinic texts (as in the Heb expression "kiddush ha-Shem," ["sanctification of the Name"], in e.g., *b. Avodah Zara* 27b; *b. Sanh.* 74a,b). Thus, 3 John does not explicitly mention Jesus or the Christ.

Jonathan Brumberg-Kraus

[1] The elder to the beloved Gaius, whom I love in truth.

[2] Beloved, I pray that all may go well with you and that you may be in good health, just as it is well with your soul. [3] I was overjoyed when some of the friends[a] arrived and testified to your faithfulness to the truth, namely how you walk in the truth. [4] I have no greater joy than this, to hear that my children are walking in the truth.

[5] Beloved, you do faithfully whatever you do for the friends,[a] even though they are strangers to you; [6] they have testified to your love before the church. You will do well to send them on in a manner worthy of God; [7] for they began their journey for the sake of Christ,[b] accepting no support from nonbelievers.[c] [8] Therefore we ought to support such people, so that we may become co-workers with the truth.

[9] I have written something to the church; but Diotrephes, who likes to put himself first, does not acknowledge our authority. [10] So if I come, I will call attention to what he is doing in spreading false charges against us. And not content with those charges, he refuses to welcome the friends,[a] and even prevents those who want to do so and expels them from the church.

[11] Beloved, do not imitate what is evil but imitate what is good. Whoever does good is from God; whoever does evil has not seen God. [12] Everyone has testified favorably about Demetrius, and so has the truth itself. We also testify for him,[d] and you know that our testimony is true.

[13] I have much to write to you, but I would rather not write with pen and ink; [14] instead I hope to see you soon, and we will talk together face to face.

[15] Peace to you. The friends send you their greetings. Greet the friends there, each by name.

a Gk *brothers*
b Gk *for the sake of the name*
c Gk *the Gentiles*
d Gk lacks *for him*

1: Greeting. *Elder,* Gk "presbyter"; the term can refer to a church office (e.g., Acts 15; Titus 1.5; Jas 5.14; 1 Pet 5.1; 2 Jn 1), but it also means "old man" (e.g., Acts 2.17; 1 Tim 5.1). *Beloved,* a frequent epithet in Christian texts (vv. 2,5,11 and e.g., Rom 12.19; 16.5,8,9,12; 1 Cor 15.58; 2 Cor 12.19; Phil 1.12). *Gaius,* the addressee, is a member of a Johannine community, probably not identical to the Gaiuses mentioned in Acts 19.29; 20.4; Rom 16.23; 1 Cor 1.14. *Truth,* a major motif of the letter, related to a theme of John's Gospel and perhaps a reference to Jesus (see, e.g., Jn 1.14; 4.23–24; 5.33; 8.32; 14.17).

2-8: Gaius commended for his hospitality. 2: *Soul,* the inmost and spiritual being; it is not necessary to suppose the Greek belief in the immortality of the soul. **3:** *Friends,* Gk "adelphoi," lit., "brothers": the term members of the group use to refer to one another (also vv. 5,10); *testified,* Gk "martyroō," "bore witness to," the verbal form of the Gk word on which English "martyr" is based. The theme of testifying, or bearing witness (also vv. 6,12) is a Johannine motif. **4:** *My children* may refer to believers the elder converted; it does not have the dualistic connotation it has in other Johannine literature, like the "children of God" vs. the "children of the devil" (1 Jn 3.10). Nor does the elder assert his authority over his children. He appears to have no official role. **6:** *Church,* Gk "ekklēsia," referring to the assembly of believers. *Send them on,* likely, provide financial support. **7:** Lit., "for they went out for the sake of the Name accepting no support from the Gentiles" (see Introduction). *Support,* see 1 Cor 9.3–12.

9-12: Diotrephes and Demetrius. 9: *Diotrephes,* one in the community who snubbed the elder. *Does not acknowledge our authority,* lit., "does not welcome us," the same verb used in v. 10. The breach of hospitality contravened social conventions. Perhaps Diotrephes rejected the elder's teaching (see 2 Jn 9–11). **10:** *False charges,* rivalry between Christian leaders was not uncommon (e.g., 1 Cor 11.5; 12.11; Rev 2.14,20–23). *He refuses to welcome the friends,* his hostile behavior to the elder and his associates proves that he is not "walking in the truth" (see 2 Jn 4–6); *expels,* removes from the community (see Mt 18.17). **11:** *Imitate,* Gk "mimēsis," a form of instruction (see 2 Thess 3.7,9; Heb 13.7). **12:** *Demetrius,* otherwise unknown, may be the bearer of the letter.

13-15: Closing. 13–14: *Rather not write with pen and ink* (lit., "ink and reed"), the elder may not be referring to his need for an amanuensis (see 2 Jn 12–13),but rather declaring his preference for *face to face* conversation (cf. 2 Jn 12, "that our joy may be complete") over long distance communication. **15:** *Peace to you,* a Semitic rather than conventional Greek blessing, found in other Christian letters (Eph 6.23; 1 Pet 5.14; 2 Jn 3). *Friends,* a Christian address (see Jn 15.15), likely referring to the elder's supporters.

THE LETTER OF JUDE

AUTHOR AND DATE

This last letter of the New Testament claims to be written by Jude (or Judas) "brother of James." Mark 3.6 lists both Judas and James as brothers of Jesus. By the second century, Judas Didymus Thomas (Didymus and Thomas mean "twin" in Greek and Aramaic, respectively) was associated with extra-canonical documents such as the *Gospel of Thomas* and *Acts of Thomas* (the latter sees him as Jesus' twin brother; e.g., 11, 34, 45). By referring so obliquely to a Judas who may be Jesus' brother, this letter's author may have been attempting to reclaim the figure of Jude from other Christian groups who claimed his authority. Some scholars suggest that the epistle may actually have been written by Jesus' brother in the 50s. Others insist that the letter is later (perhaps early second century) and pseudonymous; the reference (v. 17) to "the apostles" as established authorities suggests institutional hierarchies already in place.

CONTEXT

The letter warns of immoral "intruders" whose laxity challenges institutional authority. Echoes of Paul's opponents in Corinth (see 1–2 Cor) and Gnostic libertine groups suggest ongoing conflicts over how to understand God's gift of salvation from sin ("grace," v. 4). Some Christians taught that, thanks to God's salvation, they were no longer bound to earthly authority and morality. Thus they could not imperil their salvation by any action, since spiritually they were safe.

It is also possible that vague and stereotypical accusations of "licentiousness" rhetorically echo prophetic literature, which equated sexual license with impiety generally (see, in a well-known passage, Ezek 16).

CULTURAL INFLUENCES

The letter draws heavily on popular, late Second Temple Jewish cosmic narratives (e.g., *1 Enoch*) to shape its understanding of the moral order of the universe. The Torah was elaborated in this period by creative narratives filling in the words and deeds of the patriarchs and great leaders of the Israelites (for instance, in *Jubilees*, which consists mostly of instructions to Moses from an angelic presence on the mountain at the time of the giving of the Torah). The author refers, for instance, to a story of the angel Michael and the devil battling over Moses' corpse. Particularly the focus on angels as historical and moral agents (vv. 6,8–9) ties this letter to patterns of thought common among first-century Jews. The vast collection of stories known as *1 Enoch*, cited directly in v. 14, created an elaborate angelology and promoted apocalyptic expectations. This book interpreted the "sons of God" in Gen 6.2 as fallen angels whose interactions with humanity initiated a division between godly and godless humans, which would last until the end of the world. The author of Jude couples this Jewish apocalyptic worldview with the more stabilizing "predictions of the apostles of our Lord Jesus Christ" (v. 17), thereby linking it to Christian tradition. Nonetheless, the prophetic language and angelic outlook of this letter attach it closely, almost intimately, to the Jesus movement's Jewish roots.

The author of 2 Peter used substantial portions of Jude, particularly the idea that present-day religious divisions are simply the latest act in a cosmic drama pitting the pious against their devious and immoral opponents. Jude and 2 Peter remain certain that, as in the past, present, and future, participants in this struggle will receive appropriate rewards and punishments.

Andrew S. Jacobs

[1] Jude,[a] a servant[b] of Jesus Christ and brother of James,

To those who are called, who are beloved[c] in[d] God the Father and kept safe for[d] Jesus Christ:

[2] May mercy, peace, and love be yours in abundance.

[3] Beloved, while eagerly preparing to write to you about the salvation we share, I find it necessary to write and appeal to you to contend for the faith that was once for all entrusted to the saints. [4] For certain intruders have stolen in among you, people who long ago were designated for this condemnation as ungodly, who pervert the grace of our God into licentiousness and deny our only Master and Lord, Jesus Christ.[e]

[5] Now I desire to remind you, though you are fully informed, that the Lord, who once for all saved[f] a people out of the land of Egypt, afterward destroyed those who did not believe. [6] And the angels who did not keep their own position, but left their proper dwelling, he has kept in eternal chains in deepest darkness for the judgment of the great day. [7] Likewise, Sodom and Gomorrah and the surrounding cities, which, in the same manner as they, indulged in sexual immorality and pursued unnatural lust,[g] serve as an example by undergoing a punishment of eternal fire.

[8] Yet in the same way these dreamers also defile the flesh, reject authority, and slander the glorious ones.[h] [9] But when the archangel Michael contended with the devil and

[a] Gk *Judas*
[b] Gk *slave*
[c] Other ancient authorities read *sanctified*
[d] Or *by*
[e] Or *the only Master and our Lord Jesus Christ*
[f] Other ancient authorities read *though you were once for all fully informed, that Jesus* (or *Joshua*) *who saved*
[g] Gk *went after other flesh*
[h] Or *angels*; Gk *glories*

1–2: Salutation. *Jude* (Heb "Yehudah"), lit., "Jewish man" or "Judean," the name of several NT figures, including Judas Iscariot (Mk 3.19) and another "Judas" who, along with *James*, is listed as one of the brothers of Jesus (Mk 6.3). Lk 6.16 and Acts 1.13 refer to "Judas son of James"; although this phrase is normally understood as "son of James" it could also be translated as *brother of James*, if *James* is a sufficiently well-known figure. The letter-writer refers to himself only as the *servant* (lit., "slave") of Jesus; yet since *James* was well known as "the Lord's brother" (Gal 1.19) and leader of the Christians in Jerusalem (Gal 4; Acts 15), it is likely the author is also indirectly claiming to be Jesus' brother. *Beloved . . . kept safe . . . love,* the standard letter salutation is expanded with blessings and prayers for well-being of the recipients.

3–4: Reason for the letter. An otherwise commendable community must be warned against devious *intruders*. The community is "saved" from being *ungodly* and from *licentiousness*, but also *for the faith . . . entrusted to the saints. Salvation we share,* communal salvation was a hope shared in this period by Jews (whose covenant bound them through history) and followers of Jesus (who understood God's saving acts as binding them together as a new people). *Long ago . . . designated for this condemnation,* as in many apocalyptic communities, like that at Qumran (which divided humanity into "children of light" and "children of darkness," 1QS 1.9–11), humanity has already been divided into camps of saved and condemned. *Licentiousness,* accusations against the *intruders* are vague but suggest sexual immorality.

5–7: Disobedience is punished. Reminders of divine punishment from sacred history; cf. 2 Pet 2.4–6. **5:** *Destroyed those who did not believe,* see Num 14.35. **6:** *And the angels,* refers to common legends of the "fall of angels" based on Gen 6.1–4 (see Introduction). **7:** *Sodom and Gomorrah,* Gen 19.4–11, ties disobedience to licentiousness and fiery *punishment*. Although this passage has traditionally been taken as a condemnation of homosexuality, it may in fact be a further denunciation of unhealthy spiritual practices; *unnatural lust,* Gk "sarkos heteras," "other flesh" (see translators' note *g*), referring to those who had, or wish to have, intercourse with angels. In the Tanakh, the "sin of Sodom" was seen as injustice and economic exploitation (e.g., Ezek 16.49).

8–13: Accusations against intruders. 8: *Dreamers* might imply that the false teachers have replaced apostolic authority (see v. 17) with personal visions and revelation. *Glorious ones* (or "glories"), possibly angels, understood as intermediaries (e.g., Dan 9.20–22) between the divine and human realms, and conveyors of insight, moral exhortation, and steadfastness among Second Temple Jews. **9:** *Michael contended with the devil,* the story of Moses' body probably drawn from the *T. Moses*, an incomplete text giving Moses' last words to Joshua. As it stands the text does

disputed about the body of Moses, he did not dare to bring a condemnation of slander[a] against him, but said, "The Lord rebuke you!" [10] But these people slander whatever they do not understand, and they are destroyed by those things that, like irrational animals, they know by instinct. [11] Woe to them! For they go the way of Cain, and abandon themselves to Balaam's error for the sake of gain, and perish in Korah's rebellion. [12] These are blemishes[b] on your love-feasts, while they feast with you without fear, feeding themselves.[c] They are waterless clouds carried along by the winds; autumn trees without fruit, twice dead, uprooted; [13] wild waves of the sea, casting up the foam of their own shame; wandering stars, for whom the deepest darkness has been reserved forever.

[14] It was also about these that Enoch, in the seventh generation from Adam, prophesied, saying, "See, the Lord is coming[d] with ten thousands of his holy ones, [15] to execute judgment on all, and to convict everyone of all the deeds of ungodliness that they have committed in such an ungodly way, and of all the harsh things that ungodly sinners have spoken against him." [16] These are grumblers and malcontents; they indulge their own lusts; they are bombastic in speech, flattering people to their own advantage.

[17] But you, beloved, must remember the predictions of the apostles of our Lord Jesus Christ; [18] for they said to you, "In the last time there will be scoffers, indulging their own ungodly lusts." [19] It is these worldly people, devoid of the Spirit, who are causing divisions. [20] But you, beloved, build yourselves up on your most holy faith; pray in the Holy Spirit; [21] keep yourselves in the love of God; look forward to the mercy of our Lord Jesus Christ that leads to[e] eternal life. [22] And have mercy on some who are wavering; [23] save others by snatching them out of the fire; and have mercy on still others with fear, hating even the tunic defiled by their bodies.[f]

[24] Now to him who is able to keep you from falling, and to make you stand without blemish in the presence of his glory with rejoicing, [25] to the only God our Savior, through Jesus Christ our Lord, be glory, majesty, power, and authority, before all time and now and forever. Amen.

[a] Or *condemnation for blasphemy*
[b] Or *reefs*
[c] Or *without fear. They are shepherds who care only for themselves*
[d] Gk *came*
[e] Gk *Christ to*
[f] Gk *by the flesh.* The Greek text of verses 22-23 is uncertain at several points

not depict the assumption, that is, taking Moses bodily into heaven. The legend that the angel Michael and the devil fought over Moses' body has no known clear source. It is used here to combine references to good and bad angels (see vv. 6,8) with overall concern for authority, morality, and truth. **11:** Three villains from the Tanakh: *Cain*, fratricide (Gen 4.1–16), also considered in Jewish midrash (*Tg. Ps.-J.*; Gen 4.1) a son of Eve and the devil; *Balaam* (Num 22), a false prophet; *Korah* (Num 16), a rebel against Moses. **12–13:** These intruders are selfish *blemishes*, fruitless, destructive, and misleading; cf. 2 Pet 2.17–18. *Love-feasts*, eucharists that may have included meals for the community (cf. 1 Cor 11.20–21); they were presumably intended to increase the bonds of love in the community. *Twice dead*, those baptized who have fallen away; they have died once in baptism (cf. Rom 6.3), and again by betraying their faith.

14–19: Intruders foretold. 14: *Enoch*, descendant of Adam (Gen 5.18–24); his prophecy comes from *1 En.* 1.9. Jude takes "the Lord" to be Jesus. **17–18:** *Predictions of the apostles*, otherwise unattested (though perhaps meaning those such as 2 Thess 2.3); *the last time* reinforces the author's apocalyptic worldview (cf. 2 Pet 3.3).

20–23: Exhortation. The recipients should hold firm, trust in their reward, and keep those *wavering* from following the defiling teaching of the enemies. **20:** *Faith*, the teaching of the community, not a relationship of trust. *Pray in the Holy Spirit*, perhaps a reference to the worship practice of ecstatic utterance of words presumed to be from God (cf. 1 Cor 12.3,10). **21–22:** *Mercy . . . eternal life*, the *love of God* as expressed in the compassion of *Jesus* brings the believers into the kingdom (*eternal life*, the life of God). *Have mercy*, show mercy as you are yourselves shown mercy.

24–25: Doxology. An extended, concluding praise of God (cf. Rom 16.27). *Without blemish*, language of sacrifice, in which both those serving in the Temple (Lev 21.17–18) and the offered animal (Lev 22.20–21) must be free from defect. *God . . . Savior, through Jesus Christ*, God saves by the agency of Jesus; the text may reflect views of the status of the messiah that do not yet see him as divine.

THE REVELATION TO JOHN

This writing, attributed to an otherwise unknown prophet "John" in Asia Minor, calls itself both an *apocalypsis*, a literary disclosure of heavenly secrets, and a prophecy, an oral communication of divine intentions. One of the tantalizing features of the book is its creative combination of these two genres.

While the author's name and the title "Lamb" for the risen Christ might suggest some relationship to the "Johannine tradition" represented by the Gospel, epistles, and the extra-canonical *Acts of John*, the language and interests of Revelation bear little in common with these other texts.

Revelation has been dated to various points in the second half of the first century, based on the author's interest in the emperor Nero (see annotations on 13.3 and 13.18), who was assassinated in 68; while his bitterness toward Rome (17–18) and elevation of blood-martyrdom (6.9–11; 20.4) might suggest imperial persecution of Jesus-believers. One period favored by scholars is the reign of the emperor Domitian (81–96), depicted as especially horrendous by the fourth-century historian Eusebius (*Hist. eccl.* 3.17–18), who also quotes the second-century church father Irenaeus (*Adv. Haer.* 5.30.3) as attributing Revelation to late in Domitian's reign. Yet modern historians have found little evidence that Domitian instigated any greater degree of persecution than other first-century emperors. The scenes of eschatological battles (19.11–21; 20.7–9) might reflect the Jewish revolt of 66–70 CE, while the image of a holy city without a Temple (21.22) could imply a date after the historical Temple's destruction in 70 CE.

Some critics have sought to reconcile the range of possible dates by proposing a series of literary stages: an original apocalypse composed at about the time of the death of Nero (68), which was re-edited with an "epistolary" introduction (chs 1–3) in the later first century. But there has been no agreement on what such a "proto-apocalypse" would have looked like.

LITERARY HISTORY

While Revelation's striking juxtapositions of vision and letter, song and list, oracle and narrative might suggest stages of compilation, and certain phrases seem to represent an editor's glossing of an earlier text (11.14; 13.6c,18; 14.12), early manuscripts provide no evidence of prior versions. Revelation is best seen, like so many ancient documents, as a complex composition of one author, stimulated by his literary and historical context, with perhaps another's additions soon afterwards.

OUTLINE

I. Introductory vision (1.1–20)
II. Heavenly letters dictated to seven congregations (2.1–3.22)
III. Vision of heavenly throne (4.1–11)
IV. Delivery of the scroll with seven seals to the Lamb (5.1–14)
V. Opening of the first six seals (6.1–17)
    A. Seals of destruction (6.1–8)
    B. Seals of judgment (6.9–17)
VI. Vision of the 144, 000 sealed (7.1–17)
VII. Opening of the seventh seal and emergence of seven trumpeter angels (8.1–11.19)
    A. Trumpets 1–6 and the eschatological woes they cause (8.1–9.21)
    B. Appearance of new angel to herald the final trumpet (10.1–11)
    C. Excursus: measurement of the current temple and the eschatological appearance and acts of Moses and Elijah. (11.1–14)
    D. Seventh trumpet declares the new reign (11.15–19)
VIII. Vision of the heavenly woman and child and dragon (12.1–18)
IX. Emergence of eschatological chaos-monsters (13.1–18)
    A. From the sea (13.1–10)
    B. From the earth (13.11–18)
X. Visions of heavenly beings preparing for eschatological destruction (14.1–20)
XI. Priestly angels with seven bowls (15.1–16.21)

XII. Vision and destruction of the great whore Babylon (17.1–19.6)
XIII. Avenging warrior and marriage supper (19.7–18)
XIV. Millenial rule and last judgment (19.19–20.15)
XV. Revelation of heavenly Jerusalem (21.1–22.5)
XVI. Oracles of eschatological imminence and closing (22.6–21)

INTERPRETATION

Revelation is foremost visionary literature, belonging to a tradition that reaches back to Isa 6, the books of Ezekiel and Daniel, *1* and *2 Enoch*, and forward to the various apocalypses in "John's" own time composed under the names of *Ezra* and *Baruch*. Such books combine narratives of their heroes' visionary experiences (through a journey to heaven or some mystical disciplines) with vivid depictions of a heavenly world, populated with frightening angelic beings and in many cases cryptic revelations of events to come. If the text is attributed to a hero of the past, then historical events known to the readers would be first revealed as if prophecy, followed by events that the real author imagines will happen (cf. Dan 11–12, in which history turns to fantasy in verse 11.40). Revelation is somewhat unusual in its self-attribution to an otherwise unknown Jewish seer, "John," but there were other ancient apocalyptic documents that likewise presented visions in the names of lesser-known seers: Dositheus, Hermas, Mani, among others. The point of all such apocalyptic texts lay in revealing the heavenly world, not as a paradisal delight but as a paradigmatic super-reality, attention to which allowed the working out of crises and frustrations in this world. With this purpose Revelation details the multiple eschatological sufferings of sinners, to excite audiences with the prospect of their enemies' and rivals' downfall.

It has long been customary among Christian exegetes to attribute the vindictiveness of this imagery, and the violence of the text overall, to some putative persecution that the author and his intended audience were suffering: Domitian's policies, local pogroms, a particular efflorescence of the emperor cult, or Roman imperial rule in general. This tendency in historical interpretation manages to turn violently vindictive fantasy into righteous political critique. In fact, this apologetic justification for Revelation's violence has had the unfortunate effect of blaming Jews as well as Romans for persecution of Christians. The text's criticism of those who call themselves Jews and their "synagogues of Satan" (2.9; 3.9) has typically been taken as referring to real Jews (who, it follows, were persecuting John's "Christians"). Yet this interpretation plainly fails in view of the fact that in these verses John criticizes those who are *not* Jews but only label themselves so. More importantly, Revelation shows no sense of a Christianity, or even of a Jesus-devotion, unmoored from Judaism.

The earliest uses of Revelation understood it as unrelated to any particular historical context. In second-century Asia Minor and third-century upper Egypt, for example, the book was read as sanction for an imminent millennium on earth. It is only with the fourth-century author Eusebius of Caesarea that Revelation came to be linked with the putative sufferings of John of Patmos himself, and thus interpreted in relation to a developing martyrological tradition in Christianity that elevated blood and suffering as instructive spectacles.

READING GUIDE

John's concern is to represent his visionary authority as superior to that of rivals in the same religious movement (see, e.g., 2.14,19–23). It is in regard to John's claim that the text should serve as prophecy in writing that we can understand his special emulation of Ezekiel as visionary model, from his image of the divine throne and its "living creatures" (cf. Ezek 1) to the precise layout of the heavenly city (11.1–2; 21; cf. Ezek 40–42), his notion of the pure in a doomed city saved by divine "seals" (14.1–5; cf. Ezek 9), and his overall priestly image of angelic liturgy. Furthermore, John's image of women as containers, instigators, and embodiments of sexual impurity (2.20–22; 14.4; 17–19), as well as the vindictive fantasy of violence against such women (2.22–23; 17.16; 18.8–10), stand in explicit imitation of Ezekiel (23) and thus represent a resurgence of one of the less savory features of biblical tradition. We are prompted to ask, as have many anthropologists, how a concern for ritual purity, its antithesis, and its restoration can be translated so readily into misogynistic symbolism.

The text also invites attention to the transcendent orderliness of the heavenly cult, its trumpets, bowls, and incense, a theme reflected in other Jewish apocalyptic literature (*1, 2 Enoch, 2 Baruch*) but here imagined as the source of cosmic catastrophe. Indeed, the surrealism of this heavenly world allows revelations of the risen Christ's true nature that are quite far from the human Jesus of the Gospels. Here he appears as a seven-eyed Lamb (5.6), as a luminescent old man with flaming eyes (1.12–16), and as a mounted warrior with a sword emerging from his mouth (19.11–16). He is that alternately enthroned, glorified, and militant aspect of God on which Jewish apocalyptic authors had been speculating since Ezekiel (1), Daniel (7), and *Enoch* (40–71).

READING REVELATION AS A JEWISH TEXT

Revelation provides an important witness to a variety of traditions central to Jews in the first-century eastern Diaspora. *Kashrut* is far more critical to John's sense of religious purity (2.14,20) than Paul's (1 Cor 8); and the text's focus on images of sexual impurity (2.20–22; 17; 22.13) suggest that sexual purity could—even in the Diaspora—carry strict interpretations in the effort to define community. The brief glorification of celibacy (14.4), coupled with a reference to the "camp" of the righteous (20.9), allies this text with the holy-war ideology of the Qumran scrolls. The central symbols of priesthood (1.6; 5.10; 20.6b), the twelve tribes of Israel (7), and the Holy City (with or without a Temple: 11.1–2; 21–22.5) show the abiding value of these themes for Jews outside Judea and Galilee, and even after the destruction of Jerusalem. In these ways we can speak of the text as having a fundamentally Jewish frame of reference.

The various, kaleidoscopic appearances of Christ do not mitigate this Jewishness, any more than the appearances of the angel Metatron or the "Son of Man" mitigate the Jewishness of *Enoch* or *hekhalot* texts. The elevation of the executed Jesus to heavenly status is hardly more extreme than the ways many Hasidic leaders have been celebrated by their followers, and it certainly represented no departure from Judaism for the author. Thus, increasingly, scholars are looking at Revelation as a Jewish text that reveals a heavenly Christ rather than a Christian text with Jewish attributes.

In this light we must query two verses that have long been invoked as condemnations of Judaism: 2.9 and 3.9, in which John assails "those who say that they are Jews and are not, but are a synagogue of Satan." Interpreters who assume the text is Christian naturally take these "so-called Jews" as real Jews, local Jews; they are "so-called" because they don't believe in Jesus. But for John it is not Christ-belief that is the arbiter of Judaism; it is purity that is the arbiter of sainthood. Interpreted in context, as a Jewish text, it is more likely that these pretenders are—as John says—*non-Jews* claiming some Jewish identity. The most likely constituency would be Pauline Gentile God-fearers, who sought Jewish salvation through a hybrid variation on Jewish practices and who might well pose an intrinsic threat to the *purity* of Jewish Christ-veneration.

David Frankfurter

1 The revelation of Jesus Christ, which God gave him to show his servants[a] what must soon take place; he made[b] it known by sending his angel to his servant[c] John, [2] who testified to the word of God and to the testimony of Jesus Christ, even to all that he saw.

[3] Blessed is the one who reads aloud the words of the prophecy, and blessed are those who hear and who keep what is written in it; for the time is near.

[4] John to the seven churches that are in Asia:

Grace to you and peace from him who is and who was and who is to come, and from the seven spirits who are before his throne, [5] and from Jesus Christ, the faithful witness,

a Gk *slaves*
b Gk *and he made*
c Gk *slave*

1.1–3: Introduction. 1: The text is designated a *revelation* (Gk "apocalypsis," equivalent to Lat "revelatio," "take away the veil, uncover") rather than a letter or account or book. It is focused on imminent events. As with many sacred texts, its special authority comes from its angelic origin. The term "apocalypse" gives its name to a literary genre usually characterized by heavenly visions of highly symbolic images with angelic mediation (see Introduction). *Servants*, Gk "douloi," "slaves," members of the community. **2:** *Testified*, bore witness (Gk "martyroō"). **3:** *Blessed*, Gk "makarios," for Heb "'ashrei," "happy, fortunate" in LXX, e.g., Ps 1.1. *Prophecy*, word from God, here in written form that should be conveyed orally, not privately or secretly. *Time is near*, Gk "kairos," critical hour or day, referring to the time of the new age.

1.4–8: Opening doxology. 4: The text now becomes a letter, with a traditional epistolary greeting (see, e.g., 1 Cor 1.3; Phil 1.2; etc.). *Seven churches*, representing all of the Christian community. *Asia*, the Roman province

ORAL AND WRITTEN PROPHECY

By designating his work as a prophecy, not just a revelation, that recipients should hear (1.3), John situates this text in a social world that held prophets in high regard—not only such legendary authors as Ezekiel and Isaiah but also living embodiments of the divine word. John is, of course, a scribe of God's heavenly revelations much like Enoch and Ezekiel (10.3–4; 21.5; see "John, a New Ezekiel," p. 473), and the prophecies he offers his audience are supposed to originate in heavenly writing (10.1–11; 22.7,10). Yet in its anxious divine utterances (16.15; 22.7,10,12–13,16,20) Revelation clearly means to be a prophecy, a vehicle of the divine voice itself.

There is much evidence for a resurgence of prophet figures in first- and second-century Judaism and its Christian offshoots (Acts 5.36–37; 13.6; 21.38; Josephus, *J.W.* 2.58–63; *Ant.* 20.167–72; Origen, *Cels.* 7.9; Eusebius, *Hist. eccl.* 5.16–17), and John's negative appraisal of certain rival prophets in his own milieu (2.20; cf. 13.11–15) suggests his active involvement in a world in which congregations depended on such charismatic figures for direction and interpretation of the times. He has also prefaced his revelation with an epistolary introduction (1.4–6) and seven letters, all bearing the authority of God himself and the risen Christ (1.8,17–19). He or a subsequent editor also shows particular concern at the end of the book for the exact and inerrant transmission of his prophecy, with a curse on anyone who might change specific passages (22.18–19). Revelation thus oscillates between text and prophetic voice, alternately claiming the distinctive authority of each.

Do these features of Revelation reflect a historical situation in which letters had gained a certain religious cachet and in which authors and speakers both might justly be concerned for the accuracy of their messages' transmission? Could the increasing authority of Paul's letters have stimulated John's composition (or a subsequent edition of it)? Paul, after all, wrote on human authority but in grandiose terms (Gal 1.1; 1 Cor 1.1) and promoted dilutions of Jewish purity laws that John seems to have adamantly rejected (2.14,20; see "The Letters to the Seven Congregations," p. 468).

the firstborn of the dead, and the ruler of the kings of the earth.

To him who loves us and freed[a] us from our sins by his blood, [6] and made[b] us to be a kingdom, priests serving[c] his God and Father, to him be glory and dominion forever and ever. Amen.

[7] Look! He is coming with the clouds;
  every eye will see him,
 even those who pierced him;
  and on his account all the tribes of the
   earth will wail.
So it is to be. Amen.

[8] "I am the Alpha and the Omega," says the Lord God, who is and who was and who is to come, the Almighty.

[9] I, John, your brother who share with you in Jesus the persecution and the kingdom and the patient endurance, was on the island called Patmos because of the word of God and the testimony of Jesus.[d] [10] I was in the spirit[e] on the Lord's day, and I heard behind me a loud voice like a trumpet [11] saying, "Write in a book what you see and send it to the seven churches, to Ephesus, to Smyrna, to

a Other ancient authorities read *washed*
b Gk *and he made*
c Gk *priests to*
d Or *testimony to Jesus*
e Or *in the Spirit*

of Asia Minor, present-day Turkey. *Grace . . . peace*, the standard Gk salutation "chairete," "be joyful, happy," adapted to Christian use with "charis," "grace, favor" (from God) and adding the Jewish salutation "peace," Gk "eirēnē," Heb "shalom." *Is . . . was . . . and is to come*, Gk "the being and the was and the coming," unusual phrasing indicating past, present, and imminent future in God; *seven spirits*, an apparent reference to the seven angels who are agents of God (*1 En.* 20.1–8). **5:** *Witness*, Gk "martys, martyros," from which comes English "martyr." *Firstborn of the dead*, Gk "prōtotokos" in LXX for Heb "beckhor," "firstborn" either literally or figuratively; e.g., Ps 89.27 [Heb v. 28; LXX 88.28], implying that Jesus' resurrection was the first of an imminent general resurrection. **6:** Christ transforms his devotees into a *kingdom* and *priests*—symbols of eschatological perfection paralleled at Qumran (1QSa), *Jubilees*, and echoed throughout Revelation (5.10; 20.6; cf. Ex 19.6; Isa 61.6). **8:** *Alpha and the Omega*, first and last letters of the Gk alphabet, meaning "beginning and end."

1.9–20: The heavenly call. *John*, an otherwise unknown early Christian writer; he is not the author of John's Gospel or of the Letters of John. *Patmos*, an island off the western coast of Asia Minor (in the eastern Aegean

CHRIST AS MANIFESTATION OF GOD

John expresses his principal devotion to the Jewish Lord, God of heaven and earth (e.g., 1.8; 15.3–4; 19.5–6), whose wrath will cause eschatological destruction. But the book also reveals various heavenly roles for the risen Christ: as God's own spirit of prophecy (19.10), as the seven-eyed Lamb that will reign with God in the eschatological Jerusalem (5.6; 21.22–22.5), and perhaps most importantly as the "Son of Man" in the beginning, whose unearthly voice dictates the letters to the seven congregations. How can we understand Christ as fitting into John's Jewish cosmology?

Most apocalypses since Ezekiel had revealed simultaneously God's inconceivability and at least one chief angelic mediator through whose visible or embodied appearance one might contemplate divine agency and understand biblical references to God's human-like appearance (e.g., Ps 18; Isa 6.1). This figure was often called "the human-like one" in Semitic phraseology, "one like a son of man" (Dan 7.13–14; *1 En.* 46,48,62,69–70) or as enthroned bearer of God's holy name, the tetragrammaton YHWH, called "Lord" (*4 Ezra* [2 Esd 3–14] 13.51; 14.19) or even "Jao-El" (*Apoc. Abr.* 10.9). In the later Jewish visionary traditions called *hekhalot* ("palaces," presenting a vision of heaven as a mansion with many rooms), these angelic representatives were described in frighteningly monstrous guises. Some texts even proposed that the most righteous among humans, like Enoch or Jacob, had become assimilated to this heavenly mediator angel (*1 En.* 71; *Pr. Jos.*). It is in this sense that we might understand the "Son of Man" in ch 1, who is an explicit composite of the two heavenly figure in Dan 7 but who is also identified as a form of the risen Christ (1.18). This figure bears the cosmic and vengeful aspects and titles of God, but in visible and communicative form.

Revelation, of course, displays other heavenly hypostases (manifestations of divine functions): God's *vengeance*, in the form of a rider (19.11–16), and the prophetic voice of imminent judgment, in the form of a rainbow-headed angel descending on the shore (ch 10), with neither of whom is Christ assimilated. As an apocalyptic visionary John is particular about those hypostases or heavenly attributes with which Christ has merged. Indeed, the initial "Son of Man" figure further subdivides into a series of seven discrete epithets that address the seven congregations in chs 2–3. Then, after the opening "Son of Man" figure, we are especially directed to the slaughtered and triumphant Lamb (ch 5). Incorporating both risen Christ and God's messianic agent, indeed, God's throne-mate (5.13; 22.1), the seven-eyed, scroll-wielding Lamb is meant to serve as the true heavenly form of God's regent.

Apocalyptic visions of the heavenly world involved an awesome, even terrifying sequence of unearthly sounds, polymorphic beings, and shifting appearances; in this document John departs utterly from traditions of the earthly Jesus and his resurrection to reveal the beings with which Christ came to be incorporated in heaven, and in which form he would imminently return.

Pergamum, to Thyatira, to Sardis, to Philadelphia, and to Laodicea."

[12] Then I turned to see whose voice it was that spoke to me, and on turning I saw seven golden lampstands, [13] and in the midst of the lampstands I saw one like the Son of Man, clothed with a long robe and with a golden sash across his chest. [14] His head and his hair were white as white wool, white as snow; his eyes were like a flame of fire, [15] his feet were

Sea). It is fated that John be there, although not necessarily because of exile. He declares his participation with Jesus in both *kingdom* and "thlipsis," *persecution* or "affliction." **10–11:** *In the spirit*, a state of prophetic ecstasy initially brings an aural theophany; the divine voice immediately assigns John to a scribal role, typical of apocalyptic seers (*4 Ezra* 14; cf. Ezek 2.8–3.3). **11:** *Ephesus . . . Laodicea*, the *seven churches* in western Asia Minor (see map, p. 470). **12–16:** This initial vision of the angelic mediator is constructed from several biblical visions of God and his chief manifesting forms (Dan 7; Ezek 1), augmented with new symbols like the lampstands, suggestive of the Temple. By attributing his revelations to such a figure, John thus claims a superlative heavenly source. **12:** *Lampstands*, Gk "lychnia," Heb "menorah," the lamps in the Temple near the altar (Ex 37.17–24), here an attribute of the revealing Christ. **13:** *Son of Man*, Dan 7.13–14; *1 En.* 46–48,62,69–71, the human-like embodiment or representative of God's rule. *Golden sash*, Dan 10.5, probably a badge of rank or honor. **14:** *White*, Dan 7.9, representing both venerable age and purity. *Flame of fire*, Dan 7.9; 10.6. Fire was a purifying agent. **15:** *Bronze*, Dan 10.6. *Many waters*, a simile for loudness but also a comparison for the divine voice, which overcomes the

THE LETTERS TO THE SEVEN CONGREGATIONS

Each letter in chs 2–3 is addressed in standard epistolary form, from one of the divine epithets of the "Son of Man" figure John has just encountered, to a congregation or group of Christ-devotees in a city in Asia Minor (*ekklēsia* in this era is best not translated "church"). Each letter consists of historically obscure prophetic allusions, and cryptic threats and promises, from none of which it is possible to reconstruct a convincing background scenario. Nor is it possible to know John's precise relationship to, or authority in, the congregations he addresses. What is apparent, however, is a general crisis of authority over the strict observance of Jewish purity, with the prophet John vilifying those who would dilute *halakhah* as he sees it (2.9,14; 3.9). What evidence we have of Jewish life in first-century Asia Minor shows much intermingling with Greco-Roman culture, even as the communities for which we have evidence seem to have maintained basic Jewish institutions like Sabbath, prayer, and some meal-purity practices. John stands well to the right of this fluid Jewish world, as a kind of reformer, seeking a rigorous *priestly* purity for the congregations of the end-times.

like burnished bronze, refined as in a furnace, and his voice was like the sound of many waters. [16] In his right hand he held seven stars, and from his mouth came a sharp, two-edged sword, and his face was like the sun shining with full force.

[17] When I saw him, I fell at his feet as though dead. But he placed his right hand on me, saying, "Do not be afraid; I am the first and the last, [18] and the living one. I was dead, and see, I am alive forever and ever; and I have the keys of Death and of Hades. [19] Now write what you have seen, what is, and what is to take place after this. [20] As for the mystery of the seven stars that you saw in my right hand, and the seven golden lampstands: the seven stars are the angels of the seven churches, and the seven lampstands are the seven churches.

2 "To the angel of the church in Ephesus write: These are the words of him who holds the seven stars in his right hand, who walks among the seven golden lampstands:

[2] "I know your works, your toil and your patient endurance. I know that you cannot tolerate evildoers; you have tested those who claim to be apostles but are not, and have found them to be false. [3] I also know that you are enduring patiently and bearing up for the sake of my name, and that you have not grown weary. [4] But I have this against you, that you have abandoned the love you had at first. [5] Remember then from what you have fallen; repent, and do the works you did at first. If not, I will come to you and remove your lampstand from its place, unless you repent. [6] Yet this is to your credit: you hate the works of the Nicolaitans, which I also hate. [7] Let anyone who has an ear listen to what the Spirit is saying to the churches. To everyone who conquers, I will give permission to eat from the tree of life that is in the paradise of God.

sound of storm or cataract as God overcomes the waters in creation (Gen 1); compare Ezek 1.24; 43.2; Ps 29.3; 93.4. **16:** *Seven stars,* the *angels* that are the guardians of the communities (see v. 20). *Two-edged sword,* God's word in the mouth of a prophet (see Isa 49.2). **17:** *As though dead,* John's terror is typical of prophetic visions and calls: Isa 6.5; Dan 7.15; *4 Ezra* 5.14; 10.29–30. *First and last,* see v. 8n. **18:** *Keys of Death and of Hades,* the abode of the dead, which will be opened up in the last judgment, ch 20. **19:** Hab 2.2. **20:** *Angels,* see v. 16n.

2.1–3.22: Letters dictated to seven congregations.

2.1–7: Ephesus. 1: *Ephesus,* a major port city on the Asia Minor coast, known especially for a temple to a famous local form of the goddess Artemis. Evidence points to a robust Jewish community there (cf. Josephus, *Ag. Ap.* 2.439; *Ant.* 14.10.25.263–65; Acts 19). *Seven stars,* see 1.16n. **2:** *Apostles,* "ones sent out," representatives or ambassadors for the community. **6:** The author judges positively the efforts of this congregation to discern true and false apostles and to resist the practices of the *Nicolaitans,* an unknown group. **7:** The repeated phrase *Let anyone who has an ear . . . ,* probably referred to the traditions of Jesus' own words (cf. Mk 4.9,23, etc.), although here it is meant to sanction the voice of the risen Christ's spirit. *Tree of life that is in the paradise of God,* the tree of Gen 2 is here assumed to be located in heaven (see *1 En.* 24–25,32).

SO-CALLED JEWS AND THEIR SYNAGOGUES OF SATAN

Who are "those who say that they are Jews and are not," who are rather a "synagogue of Satan" (2.9; 3.9)? Interpreters have customarily assumed that John, a "Christian," would have viewed true Judaism as Christ-devoted, and thus that these so-called Jews must be Jews who ignored or denied Christ. John would then, in effect, be pitting himself against the (non-Christ-devoted) Jewish community as radically as against the Roman Empire (chs 17–18). Some Christian exegetes have proposed, in fact, collusion between Roman authorities and Jews in persecuting Jesus-believers, for which there is no reliable evidence.

It is important to recognize that nowhere in this text does John juxtapose himself to Judaism or Jewish traditions. Indeed, his specific opponents in this part of the book appear to espouse not Jewish teachings but rather the diluted interpretations of meal and sexual purity laws we associate with Paul of Tarsus (2.14,20; cf. 1 Cor 7–8), and even the mega-enemy, Rome, is described in terms of female sexual pollution (17.4–6). Elsewhere John adheres to the strictest concepts of Jewish purity, those associated with the Temple priesthood and comparable to the laws of the Qumran Essene community (12.17; 14.4; 21.27; 22.14). As we consider John's profound commitment to Jewish purity in combination with the increasing popularity of Pauline teachings among Gentile God-fearers in Asia Minor over the later first century, it begins to make more sense to take John's polemic against so-called Jews in plain terms. Thus, he declares that those Gentile God-fearers claiming an affiliation with Judaism as a basis for Christ's salvation (cf. Rom 2.17–24,28–29) are in fact not Jews at all. "Synagogue of Satan" in this case refers generally to an assembly (Heb *edah*) rather than a building or institution, and was often used to denote a collective opponent, as at Qumran (1QS 5.1–2, 10–20; CD 1.12; 1QM 1.1). Thus, notwithstanding the phrase's anti-Semitic history as a condemnation of Judaism, John means "synagogue of Satan" only as a rejection of those pretending to be Jews. The real Jews are the ones who, like John and his confederates, cleave to a strict, priestly interpretation of purity laws.

[8] "And to the angel of the church in Smyrna write: These are the words of the first and the last, who was dead and came to life:

[9] "I know your affliction and your poverty, even though you are rich. I know the slander on the part of those who say that they are Jews and are not, but are a synagogue of Satan. [10] Do not fear what you are about to suffer. Beware, the devil is about to throw some of you into prison so that you may be tested, and for ten days you will have affliction. Be faithful until death, and I will give you the crown of life. [11] Let anyone who has an ear listen to what the Spirit is saying to the churches. Whoever conquers will not be harmed by the second death.

[12] "And to the angel of the church in Pergamum write: These are the words of him who has the sharp two-edged sword:

[13] "I know where you are living, where Satan's throne is. Yet you are holding fast to my name, and you did not deny your faith in me[a] even in the days of Antipas my witness, my faithful one, who was killed among you, where Satan lives.

[a] Or *deny my faith*

2.8–11: Smyrna. 8: *Smyrna*, another seaport on the Asia Minor coast, about whose Jewish community nothing is known. *First and the last*, see 1.17; 1.8n. **9–11:** *Slander*, see "So-Called Jews and Their Synagogues of Satan" above. *Synagogue* (i.e., assembly), a common Gk term for religious or social assembly. *Of Satan*, in context, Gentile members of Pauline congregations (see Introduction); the traditional view, that this is a condemnation of practicing Jews who do not believe in Jesus, is not supported if Revelation is read as a Jewish text. It was, of course, possible for Jews to criticize other Jews as demonically inspired; see 1QH 2.22, calling apostate (from the Essene perspective) Jews "a congregation of Belial." **10:** *Devil*, seen as the author of testing. Cf. Job, where the adversary (Heb "ha-satan") provokes a test of Job (chs 1–2). *Ten days*, a limited period (Dan 1.12). *Crown of life*, Jas 1.12; 1 Pet 5.4. The *crown* was given to a victor in a contest (2 Tim 2.5); here it means those who triumph through death. **11:** *Second death*, final condemnation (see 20.14).

2.12–17: Pergamum. 12: *Pergamum*, a major city in Asia Minor, notable for its elaborate acropolis with a temple to the Roman emperor. *Two-edged sword*, see 1.16n. **13:** *Satan's throne*, often identified as the imperial altar on the acropolis. *Holding . . . my name*, commitment to central tenets of Christ according to this author. *Antipas*

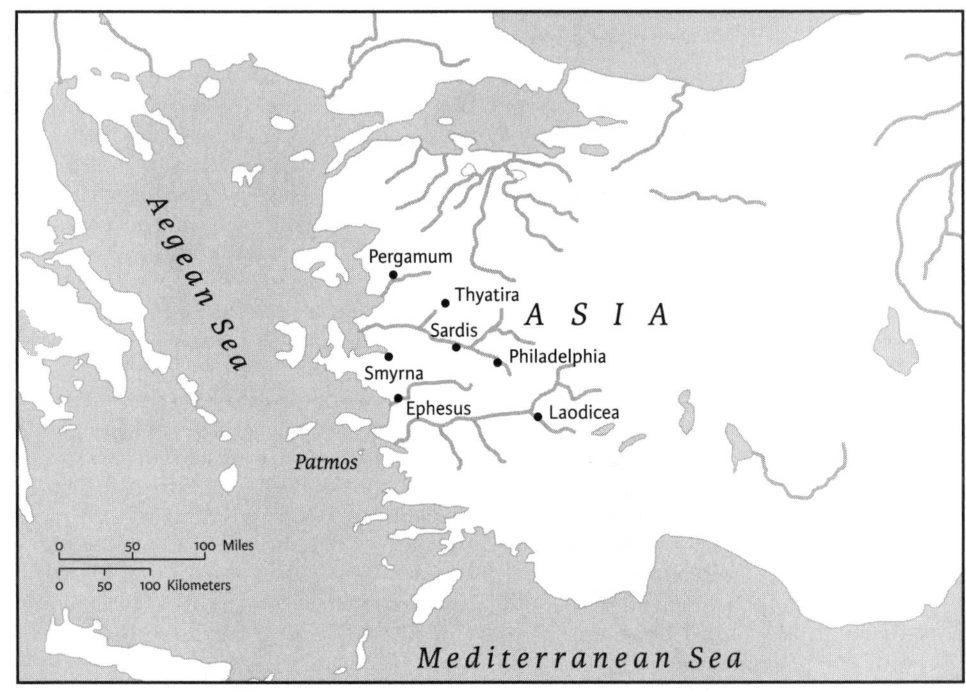

Chs 2–3: The seven churches.

[14] But I have a few things against you: you have some there who hold to the teaching of Balaam, who taught Balak to put a stumbling block before the people of Israel, so that they would eat food sacrificed to idols and practice fornication. [15] So you also have some who hold to the teaching of the Nicolaitans. [16] Repent then. If not, I will come to you soon and make war against them with the sword of my mouth. [17] Let anyone who has an ear listen to what the Spirit is saying to the churches. To everyone who conquers I will give some of the hidden manna, and I will give a white stone, and on the white stone is written a new name that no one knows except the one who receives it.

[18] "And to the angel of the church in Thyatira write: These are the words of the Son of God, who has eyes like a flame of fire, and whose feet are like burnished bronze:

[19] "I know your works—your love, faith, service, and patient endurance. I know that your last works are greater than the first. [20] But I have this against you: you tolerate that

my witness, Revelation's only named martyr. **14:** *Balaam*, seer who led Israel to intermarriage and idolatry (Num 22.15–24.25); used here as a pseudonym for a rival prophet who permits the eating of "eidōlothuta," food ritually dedicated to idols, and unregulated sexuality ("porneuō"), both likely caricatures of the Pauline mission (cf. Acts 15.29; 1 Cor 7–8). Both would be seen as polluting to a halakhically concerned prophet like John. John identifies the true community as faithful to Jewish law. **15:** *Nicolaitans*, see 2.6n. **16:** *Sword*, see 1.16n. **17:** *Hidden manna*, heavenly food (Ex 16.31). *White stone*, amulet with a secret divine name, not unlike the magical gems purveyed around the Roman world at this time. Millennialist movements often develop new forms of magical protection.

2.18–29: Thyatira. 18: *Thyatira*, a town of little significance in the first century, known best for many influential trade-guilds and its religious diversity; Acts 16.14 describes its Jewish population as welcoming godfearers. *Eyes like a flame*, Dan 10.6. **20–21:** *Jezebel*, King Ahab's queen, who patronized the Baal-cult (1 Kings 16.31; 19.1–2); like Balaam (2.14), a pseudonym for a prophet who allows nonkosher food and some loosening of sexual restrictions that John deems essential for sexual purity. John sees her gender and her sexual teachings

woman Jezebel, who calls herself a prophet and is teaching and beguiling my servants[a] to practice fornication and to eat food sacrificed to idols. [21] I gave her time to repent, but she refuses to repent of her fornication. [22] Beware, I am throwing her on a bed, and those who commit adultery with her I am throwing into great distress, unless they repent of her doings; [23] and I will strike her children dead. And all the churches will know that I am the one who searches minds and hearts, and I will give to each of you as your works deserve. [24] But to the rest of you in Thyatira, who do not hold this teaching, who have not learned what some call 'the deep things of Satan,' to you I say, I do not lay on you any other burden; [25] only hold fast to what you have until I come. [26] To everyone who conquers and continues to do my works to the end,

I will give authority over the nations;
[27] to rule[b] them with an iron rod,
as when clay pots are shattered—

[28] even as I also received authority from my Father. To the one who conquers I will also give the morning star. [29] Let anyone who has an ear listen to what the Spirit is saying to the churches.

3 "And to the angel of the church in Sardis write: These are the words of him who has the seven spirits of God and the seven stars:

"I know your works; you have a name of being alive, but you are dead. [2] Wake up, and strengthen what remains and is on the point of death, for I have not found your works perfect in the sight of my God. [3] Remember then what you received and heard; obey it, and repent. If you do not wake up, I will come like a thief, and you will not know at what hour I will come to you. [4] Yet you have still a few persons in Sardis who have not soiled their clothes; they will walk with me, dressed in white, for they are worthy. [5] If you conquer, you will be clothed like them in white robes, and I will not blot your name out of the book of life; I will confess your name before my Father and before his angels. [6] Let anyone who has an ear listen to what the Spirit is saying to the churches.

[7] "And to the angel of the church in Philadelphia write:

These are the words of the holy one, the true one,
who has the key of David,
who opens and no one will shut,
who shuts and no one opens:

[8] "I know your works. Look, I have set before you an open door, which no one is able to shut. I know that you have but little power, and yet you have kept my word and have not denied my name. [9] I will make those of the synagogue of Satan who say that they are Jews and are not, but are lying—I will make them

[a] Gk *slaves*
[b] Or *to shepherd*

(which may be Pauline; cf. 1 Cor 7.5–10) as inextricably polluting (see "Woman and the Symbolism of Pollution," p. 489). Her *fornication* is less likely a literal charge than John's metaphor to describe her positive relations with Greco-Roman society. **22:** *Bed* (Gk "klinē") suggests illness, not rape. *Adultery*, a metaphor for idolatry (cf. Jer 3.6–11). **24:** *Deep things of Satan* is likely an ironic reference to misguided teaching that presents itself as profound. **27:** See Ps 2.8–9, which is here broadened from the Davidic king to all who follow Christ. **28:** *Morning star*, Jesus, see 22.16; Num 24.17.

3.1–6: Sardis. 1: *Sardis*, a wealthy inland city; *Ant.* 14.235, 259–61, describes the success of its Jewish community, later reflected in its enormous synagogue, built and expanded over the third through seventh centuries CE. Sardis Jews seem to have had good relations with non-Jews. *Seven spirits*, see 1.4n. *Seven stars*, see 1.16n.; 1.20. **3:** *Thief*, likely reference to an aphorism of Jesus about the surprise of the eschaton's arrival, Mt 24.42–44. **4:** *Soiled* garments (cf. 22.11) that might be replaced with clean ones (cf. 3.18; 7.14; 19.14); John regards the congregation as impure in a moral, not necessarily cultic, sense. **5:** *White robes*, see 1.14n. *Book of life*, Ps. 69.28; Dan 12.1; the list of those who are redeemed. See also 13.8; 17.8; 20.12,15.

3.7–13: Philadelphia. 7: *Philadelphia*, a hill-town in western Asia Minor, known for its trade-guilds; it suffered a terrible earthquake in 17 CE and more thereafter (Pliny, *Nat.* 2.86.200; Strabo, *Geogr.* 12.8.18; 13.4.10). There is no evidence predating the third century CE of Jews there, though their presence before that time cannot be ruled out. *Key of David . . . shut*, Isa 22.22. As in Mt 16.9; 18.18, the key is a symbol of authority. **8:** *Open door . . . shut*, an opportunity that no one can prevent them from acting on. **9:** *Synagogue of Satan*, see "So-Called

come and bow down before your feet, and they will learn that I have loved you. [10] Because you have kept my word of patient endurance, I will keep you from the hour of trial that is coming on the whole world to test the inhabitants of the earth. [11] I am coming soon; hold fast to what you have, so that no one may seize your crown. [12] If you conquer, I will make you a pillar in the temple of my God; you will never go out of it. I will write on you the name of my God, and the name of the city of my God, the new Jerusalem that comes down from my God out of heaven, and my own new name. [13] Let anyone who has an ear listen to what the Spirit is saying to the churches.

[14] "And to the angel of the church in Laodicea write: The words of the Amen, the faithful and true witness, the origin[a] of God's creation:

[15] "I know your works; you are neither cold nor hot. I wish that you were either cold or hot. [16] So, because you are lukewarm, and neither cold nor hot, I am about to spit you out of my mouth. [17] For you say, 'I am rich, I have prospered, and I need nothing.' You do not realize that you are wretched, pitiable, poor, blind, and naked. [18] Therefore I counsel you to buy from me gold refined by fire so that you may be rich; and white robes to clothe you and to keep the shame of your nakedness from being seen; and salve to anoint your eyes so that you may see. [19] I reprove and discipline those whom I love. Be earnest, therefore, and repent. [20] Listen! I am standing at the door, knocking; if you hear my voice and open the door, I will come in to you and eat with you, and you with me. [21] To the one who conquers I will give a place with me on my throne, just as I myself conquered and sat down with my Father on his throne. [22] Let anyone who has an ear listen to what the Spirit is saying to the churches."

4 After this I looked, and there in heaven a door stood open! And the first voice, which I had heard speaking to me like a trumpet, said, "Come up here, and I will show you what must take place after this." [2] At once I was in the spirit,[b] and there in heaven stood a throne, with one seated on the throne! [3] And the one seated there looks like jasper and carnelian, and around the throne is a rainbow that looks like an emerald. [4] Around the throne are twenty-four thrones, and seated on the thrones are twenty-four elders, dressed in white robes, with golden crowns on their heads. [5] Coming from the throne are flashes of lightning, and rumblings and peals of thunder, and in front of the throne burn seven flaming torches, which are the seven spirits of God; [6] and in front of the throne there is something like a sea of glass, like crystal.

[a] Or *beginning*
[b] Or *in the Spirit*

Jews and Their Synagogues of Satan," p. 469. **11:** *Crown*, symbol of achievement, as in the crown of victory for the winner of a race (see 2.10n.) **12:** *Pillar in the temple*, symbol of permanence. Revelation refers often to the symbolic value of the heavenly temple furniture and infrastructure: 4.5; 11.4. *New Jerusalem*, see chs 21–22, cf. Ezek 40–48. *New name*, see 2.17n.

3.14–22: Laodicea. 14: *Laodicea*, an important regional city that suffered earthquakes in 60 CE; it had a considerable Jewish community (*Ant.* 12.147–53). *Amen*, Heb assent to prayer; used as a title for Jesus, 2 Cor 1.20, meaning the definitive acceptance of God's will. *Origin of God's creation*, or "beginning" (see translators' note *a*); cf. Jn 1.1–3. **18:** *Gold refined by fire*, a metaphor for purifying from sin; see Prov 27.21. *White robes*, see 1.14n.

4.1–11: Vision of heavenly throne. 1–2: John is again in or still assumed into an ecstatic state (*in the spirit*). His ascent to the heavenly throne room is immediate and unmediated, unlike other apocalyptic ascent narratives such as Daniel, *1 Enoch*, and the *Testament of Levi*. **3:** The vague *one seated there* and the mineralogical similes recall Ezek 1.16,26–27; Dan 10.6. **4:** *Elders* are John's obscure innovation, unparalleled in any other apocalyptic vision. It is unclear whether they represent a rank of angel, ascended patriarchs, members of the Jewish Jesus Movement, or some synthesis of any of these alternatives, but they subsequently serve as guides to and commenters on what is happening (11.16; 19.4). *White robes . . . crowns*, 1.14n.; 2.10n. **5:** Storm imagery recalls Ezek 1.4–14 and characterized visions of God in Jewish apocalyptic literature (*4 Ezra* 13.1–11; *Apoc. Abr.* 17–18; *1 En.* 14); it draws on ancient Canaanite and Israelite traditions of storm theophanies (Ex 19; Isa 6.1–4; Ps 29; Dan 7.9). *Seven spirits*, 1.4n. **6:** *Sea of glass*, the heavenly sea became a standard motif in Jewish ascent narratives (*1 En.* 14.10), and may be related to the

JOHN, A NEW EZEKIEL

New Testament scholars have often noted that Revelation is unusual among Jewish apocalypses for keeping the real name of its seer, John. Most other apocalypses, from Daniel and *Enoch* through those ascribed to Ezra and Abraham, couched their revelations as the experiences of Jewish heroes legendary for their piety, purity, or intimacy with the divine world. Who is this John, scholars ask, that such an outlandish book should depend on his authority? Did the Jesus Movement itself change the terms in which apocalyptic visions were transmitted?

Of course, Revelation does emerge from a milieu of prophetic mediation in which John may well have had some historical authority, and in any event the book gained its credibility in early Christianity not as the visions of "some" John but rather of *the* John who allegedly wrote the Gospel and Letters. But the authority of this book for its audiences would not have depended on the legend of its implied author so much as on the very familiarity of its materials, which echo revered biblical texts: Exodus (7–11; cf. Rev 8–9; 16), Isaiah (6; cf. Rev 4.8), Jeremiah (51; cf. Rev 18), and most importantly, the book of Ezekiel.

John's debt to Ezekiel appears already in the description of the four "living creatures [Heb *chai'im*]" by the throne of God in ch 4 (cf. Ezek 1.5–11). The idea of divine marks or seals that afford the bearer protection from divine judgment (Rev 7; 9) depends fundamentally on Ezekiel's secret vision of the destruction of Jerusalem and the marking of the righteous (Ezek 8–9). The instruction to John to eat the rainbow-angel's scroll, and his description of its sweet taste and bitter digestion (Rev 10.8–11), borrow the vivid symbols for literary prophecy of Ezek 3. The defeat of the mysterious enemies Gog and Magog (Rev 19.17; 20.7) depends on Ezekiel's vengeful description of these two people's destruction (Ezek 38–39), while the feminized and sexualized downfall of the *pornē* Rome (Rev 18) draws from Ezekiel's nearly pornographic tale of the shaming of the two sisters, Oholah and Oholibah (Ezek 23), as well as this same author's sarcastic dirge over the city of Tyre (Ezek 27). Finally, John's divine instructions to *measure* Jerusalem before and after its destruction (11.1–2; 21), thus assuring his audience of the city's heavenly dimensions, follows Ezekiel's similar actions with the heavenly temple (Ezek 40–42).

These are all quite central features of the book of Revelation, its images of woe, divine vengeance, and heavenly secrets, and no listener would have missed their echoes of Ezekiel. The Ezekelian heaven and prophetic imagery would have endowed John's Revelation with authority: visions of heaven that cleaved to recognizable traditions. And it may not have been an arbitrary source of material, for Ezekiel in his world, like John in his own, was formulating a notion of prophecy that was not simply spontaneous utterance or oracle but rather suggested the authority of heavenly books and writing. John thus presents himself as a new Ezekiel for these latter days of eschatological imminence.

Around the throne, and on each side of the throne, are four living creatures, full of eyes in front and behind: [7] the first living creature like a lion, the second living creature like an ox, the third living creature with a face like a human face, and the fourth living creature like a flying eagle. [8] And the four living creatures, each of them with six wings, are full of eyes all around and inside. Day and night without ceasing they sing,

"Holy, holy, holy,
the Lord God the Almighty,
who was and is and is to come."

[9] And whenever the living creatures give glory and honor and thanks to the one who is seated on the throne, who lives forever and ever, [10] the twenty-four elders fall before the one who is seated on the throne and worship the one who lives forever and ever; they cast their crowns before the throne, singing,

[11] "You are worthy, our Lord and God,
to receive glory and honor and power,
for you created all things,
and by your will they existed and were created."

dome or "raqia" in Ezek 1.22 (cf. Gen 1.6). *Living creatures* (Heb "chai'im"; Gk "zōa") replicate those of Ezek 1.5–11. **8:** By imagining the *creatures* with *six wings*, singing a version of the "Kedushah" (Isa 6.1–3), John incorporates Isaiah's vision; multiple *eyes* evoke the wheels on the "merkavah" (heavenly chariot-throne) of Ezek 1.18. **9–11:** Heavenly *glory* and perfection are revealed in liturgical drama and responsive praise-songs, reminiscent of the "Sabbath Songs" of Qumran (4QShirShabb[a]). See Dan 7.9–10.

5 Then I saw in the right hand of the one seated on the throne a scroll written on the inside and on the back, sealed[a] with seven seals; [2] and I saw a mighty angel proclaiming with a loud voice, "Who is worthy to open the scroll and break its seals?" [3] And no one in heaven or on earth or under the earth was able to open the scroll or to look into it. [4] And I began to weep bitterly because no one was found worthy to open the scroll or to look into it. [5] Then one of the elders said to me, "Do not weep. See, the Lion of the tribe of Judah, the Root of David, has conquered, so that he can open the scroll and its seven seals."

[6] Then I saw between the throne and the four living creatures and among the elders a Lamb standing as if it had been slaughtered, having seven horns and seven eyes, which are the seven spirits of God sent out into all the earth. [7] He went and took the scroll from the right hand of the one who was seated on the throne. [8] When he had taken the scroll, the four living creatures and the twenty-four elders fell before the Lamb, each holding a harp and golden bowls full of incense, which are the prayers of the saints. [9] They sing a new song:

"You are worthy to take the scroll
and to open its seals,
for you were slaughtered and by your blood you ransomed for God
saints from[b] every tribe and language and people and nation;
[10] you have made them to be a kingdom
and priests serving[c] our God,
and they will reign on earth."

[11] Then I looked, and I heard the voice of many angels surrounding the throne and the living creatures and the elders; they numbered myriads of myriads and thousands of thousands, [12] singing with full voice,

"Worthy is the Lamb that was slaughtered
to receive power and wealth and wisdom and might
and honor and glory and blessing!"

[13] Then I heard every creature in heaven and on earth and under the earth and in the sea, and all that is in them, singing,

"To the one seated on the throne and to the Lamb
be blessing and honor and glory and might
forever and ever!"

[14] And the four living creatures said, "Amen!" And the elders fell down and worshiped.

6 Then I saw the Lamb open one of the seven seals, and I heard one of the four living creatures call out, as with a voice of thunder, "Come!"[d] [2] I looked, and there was a

[a] Or *written on the inside, and sealed on the back*
[b] Gk *ransomed for God from*
[c] Gk *priests to*
[d] Or *"Go!"*

5.1–14: Delivery of the scroll with seven seals to the Lamb. 1–4: Like Ezekiel (2.9–11; see "John, a New Ezekiel," p. 473), John receives a heavenly scroll whose contents are so foreboding no heavenly being will assume its responsibility. **1:** *Seven seals*, completely sealed. **5:** *Lion of the tribe of Judah*, Gen 49.9–10; here, a messianic title. *Root of David*, Isa 11.1–10. The messiah is the one to open the scroll. *Has conquered*, overcome death and sin by sacrifice and resurrection. **6–7:** *Lamb . . . as if . . . slaughtered*, the crucified messiah in risen, heavenly form (cf. v. 9; 11.8). The lamb was also the main Passover sacrifice while the Temple stood (Ex 12.21; cf. 1 Cor 5.7; Jn 1.29,36). The correspondence of its sevenfold attributes to seven spirits (see 1.4n.), congregations, and seals signifies the perfection of all things radiating from heaven. *Right hand*, the hand of power (e.g., Ps 89.13 [Heb v. 14]), favor (Ps 80.15 [Heb v. 16]), and blessing (Gen 48.17). **8:** *Incense . . . prayers*, incense was a Temple offering (Ex 30.6) and was taken to symbolize prayer (Ps 141.2). *Saints*, members of the community. **9:** *New song*, a way of indicating a new beginning or a new era; Isa 42.10; Ps 33.3; 40.3 [Heb v. 4]. *Every tribe*, the ecumenical image of those included in kingdom and priesthood presupposes their Jewish observance (cf. Tob 13.11–17; *2 Bar.* 51.7–15). The liturgy suggests heavenly enthronement and a new cosmic era (cf. *Ascen. Isa.* 7–10). **10:** *Kingdom and priests*, Ex 19.6 is here democratized from Israel to all people (cf. 1 Pet 2.9). *Reign on earth*, the eschatological age will be established in earthly rule. **11:** *Myriads*, Dan 7.10; Jewish apocalyptic visions of the heavenly throne room often envisioned the innumerability of angels around the throne. **12–13:** The heavenly song makes a clear distinction between the enthroned one and the sacrificial Lamb.

6.1–17: The first six seals. In the interconnected world of heavenly symbols, the seals holding the scroll closed each release an angel of vengeance or catastrophe. **1:** *Lamb*, see 5.6–7n. **2:** *White horse*, John introduces horses first

THE NUMEROLOGY OF REVELATION

In antiquity certain numbers implied perfection in the cosmos or experience, and different cultures entertained different assortments of such perfect numbers. The Torah itself offers different types of numerological perfection in seven (Gen 2.1–3; 7.2–4) and twelve (Gen 35), while four signified (as in most cultures) the cardinal directions, and forty conveyed an enormous but limited period.

Apocalyptic texts regarded these numbers as based in heaven, linked intrinsically to God's own perfection. Enoch's tours of the cosmos revealed four very different regions of heavenly activity (*1 En.* 17–36), and Ezekiel beheld four "living creatures" surrounding God's throne, while many texts presumed four principal archangels and seven or twelve heavens. The periodizations of history that some apocalypses offered to explain the alternation of fortune and misfortune in Jewish experiences usually unrolled according to some perfect number: 490 (= 7 x 70, Dan 9) or fourteen (= 12 + 1 + 1, *2 Bar.* 53–74). By the second century some Christians envisioned their four most popular Gospels as expressing the perfection of the divine number four, even connecting them to Ezekiel's four living creatures (Irenaeus, *Adv. Haer.* 3.11.8).

Revelation is especially interested in the unfolding potentiality of the number seven as God's heavenly number. The main sevenfold entities consist of temple materials (1.12) and angelic servants of the heavenly temple (8–9; 16), although this heavenly number is extended to the congregations to which the heavenly Christ, himself holding seven stars (1.16), addresses his letters (2–3) and to the number of seals on the mysterious scroll of judgment (6). In this way the nature of the Jesus-congregations in John's world becomes an intrinsic extension of the perfect order of the heavenly world.

John also develops the symbolism of the number twelve, which signifies the special perfection of Jewish heritage (Gen 35), but probably had also acquired astrological associations by the Roman period (see Rev 12.1). The blessed of Israel are organized in twelve groups of twelve thousand each (where the word "thousand" signifies a sufficient enormity, 7.4–8; 12.1), and the mysterious "elders" John finds in heaven are themselves numbered at twenty-four (4.4). Recalling the perfection of measurements in Ezekiel (40–48) and the Dead Sea Temple Scroll, the structure of John's eschatological Jerusalem reflects the twelvefold perfection of Israel (21.12–14,16–17).

Revelation also offers three forms of "negative" numerology. The period designated for the rampage of the nations and the activity of the two martyrs in ch 11 is limited to forty-two months, precisely half of seven years and so an indication of incompleteness. The association of the dragon and the polymorphic beast with the numbers seven and ten (12.3; 13.1; 17.7–12) may indicate these creatures' deceptive pretenses to holiness. On the other hand, the "number of the beast," 666 (13.18), is merely the calculation of the numerical equivalents of the Hebrew letters that would spell "Nero Caesar." This calculation reflects an ancient Jewish practice called "gematria": exploring the mysteries of words through their corresponding numbers (on the assumption that Hebrew letters themselves had a divine origin). By itself, however, 666 (or 616 in some manuscripts) had no special numerological significance.

white horse! Its rider had a bow; a crown was given to him, and he came out conquering and to conquer.

[3] When he opened the second seal, I heard the second living creature call out, "Come!"[a] [4] And out came[b] another horse, bright red; its rider was permitted to take peace from the earth, so that people would slaughter one another; and he was given a great sword.

[5] When he opened the third seal, I heard the third living creature call out, "Come!"[a] I looked, and there was a black horse! Its rider held a pair of scales in his hand, [6] and I heard what seemed to be a voice in the midst of the four living creatures saying, "A quart of wheat for a day's pay,[c]

[a] Or *"Go!"*
[b] Or *went*
[c] Gk *a denarius*

(2,4,5b,8a). Horses in the Mediterranean world, associated with Greek and Roman armies, signified raw military power (see also *1 En.* 86.4; 88.3). The four horsemen represent conquest (v. 2), internecine violence (v. 4), famine and inflation (v. 6), and death (v. 8). **5–6:** *Scales* and inflated pricing signify economic breakdown. The famine

and three quarts of barley for a day's pay,[a] but do not damage the olive oil and the wine!"

[7] When he opened the fourth seal, I heard the voice of the fourth living creature call out, "Come!"[b] [8] I looked and there was a pale green horse! Its rider's name was Death, and Hades followed with him; they were given authority over a fourth of the earth, to kill with sword, famine, and pestilence, and by the wild animals of the earth.

[9] When he opened the fifth seal, I saw under the altar the souls of those who had been slaughtered for the word of God and for the testimony they had given; [10] they cried out with a loud voice, "Sovereign Lord, holy and true, how long will it be before you judge and avenge our blood on the inhabitants of the earth?" [11] They were each given a white robe and told to rest a little longer, until the number would be complete both of their fellow servants[c] and of their brothers and sisters,[d] who were soon to be killed as they themselves had been killed.

[12] When he opened the sixth seal, I looked, and there came a great earthquake; the sun became black as sackcloth, the full moon became like blood, [13] and the stars of the sky fell to the earth as the fig tree drops its winter fruit when shaken by a gale. [14] The sky vanished like a scroll rolling itself up, and every mountain and island was removed from its place. [15] Then the kings of the earth and the magnates and the generals and the rich and the powerful, and everyone, slave and free, hid in the caves and among the rocks of the mountains, [16] calling to the mountains and rocks, "Fall on us and hide us from the face of the one seated on the throne and from the wrath of the Lamb; [17] for the great day of their wrath has come, and who is able to stand?"

7 After this I saw four angels standing at the four corners of the earth, holding back the four winds of the earth so that no wind could blow on earth or sea or against any tree. [2] I saw another angel ascending from the rising of the sun, having the seal of the living God, and he called with a loud voice to the four angels who had been given power to damage earth and sea, [3] saying, "Do not damage the earth or the sea or the trees, until we have marked the servants[c] of our God with a seal on their foreheads."

[4] And I heard the number of those who were sealed, one hundred forty-four thousand, sealed out of every tribe of the people of Israel:

[a] Gk *a denarius*
[b] Or *"Go!"*
[c] Gk *slaves*
[d] Gk *brothers*

is short lived, however; it affects *wheat* and *barley*. **8:** *Death* (Gk "thanatos," recalling Heb "Mot," a northwest Semitic deity of death [Hab 2.5]) is accompanied by *Hades*, the Greek underworld. Their coupling may reflect the parallelism of "Mot" and "Sheol" in ancient Hebrew poetry (Isa 28.15,18; Ps 18.5; 49.14; 116.3). **9:** The heavenly *altar*, a privileged sight in apocalyptic literature, reminiscent of apocalyptic topographies of the afterlife, like *1 En.* 22 and *Apoc. Zeph.* Martyrs appear in Jewish literature in 2 Macc 7 and 4 Macc. **10:** The slaughtered righteous cry out to *avenge our blood*, following a theme in Jewish apocalyptic literature (cf. *1 En.* 47). **11:** *White robe*, see 1.14n. *Number*, speculation on such divine plans for the number of righteous dead was common in early Jewish and Christian apocalyptic: *1 En.* 47.4; *4 Ezra* 4.35–37; *2 Bar.* 23.5; cf. Rom 11.25; *5 Ezra* [2 Esd 1–2] 2.38–41. **12–14:** John envisions the utter collapse of the cosmos (see also, Joel 2.30–32 [Heb 3.4]). **17:** The *day of their wrath* (see Zeph 1.14–16) will impel suicide.

7.1–8: The 144,000 sealed. The visionary sequence alternates between images of cosmic cataclysm and images of spectacular glory. **1–3:** *Angels* of *the four winds* (cf. *1 En.* 18.1–5; 72) and an angel who rises with *the sun* declare a temporary reprieve from destruction until the sealing of righteous is completed. *Marked the . . . foreheads,* following the scene in Ezek 9, the righteous are sealed on the forehead, reflecting amuletic practices like the placement of "tefillin" (Deut 6.8; cf. Rev 13.16–17; Ezek 9.4). **4–8:** The twelve tribes of Israel (not including Dan and Ephraim), multiplied by twelve thousand, this "census" of the righteous resembles military lists like those in 1QM. John's eschatology revolves around the restoration of the tribes of Israel, as in Ezek 37.15–22; cf. Tob 13.13; *4 Ezra* 13.13, 39–47; *2 Bar.* 78.4–7, and affirming the fundamentally ethnic ideology of this book (cf. 7.4b). In 14.1–5 this same *144,000* are credited with a special degree of purity that involved celibacy, perhaps reflecting priestly rules for holy war (Ex 19.15; 1 Sam 21.4).

[5] From the tribe of Judah twelve thousand sealed,
from the tribe of Reuben twelve thousand,
from the tribe of Gad twelve thousand,
[6] from the tribe of Asher twelve thousand,
from the tribe of Naphtali twelve thousand,
from the tribe of Manasseh twelve thousand,
[7] from the tribe of Simeon twelve thousand,
from the tribe of Levi twelve thousand,
from the tribe of Issachar twelve thousand,
[8] from the tribe of Zebulun twelve thousand,
from the tribe of Joseph twelve thousand,
from the tribe of Benjamin twelve thousand sealed.

[9] After this I looked, and there was a great multitude that no one could count, from every nation, from all tribes and peoples and languages, standing before the throne and before the Lamb, robed in white, with palm branches in their hands. [10] They cried out in a loud voice, saying,

"Salvation belongs to our God who is seated on the throne, and to the Lamb!"

[11] And all the angels stood around the throne and around the elders and the four living creatures, and they fell on their faces before the throne and worshiped God, [12] singing,

"Amen! Blessing and glory and wisdom
and thanksgiving and honor
and power and might
be to our God forever and ever! Amen."

[13] Then one of the elders addressed me, saying, "Who are these, robed in white, and where have they come from?" [14] I said to him, "Sir, you are the one that knows." Then he said to me, "These are they who have come out of the great ordeal; they have washed their robes and made them white in the blood of the Lamb.

[15] For this reason they are before the throne of God,
and worship him day and night within his temple,
and the one who is seated on the throne will shelter them.
[16] They will hunger no more, and thirst no more;
the sun will not strike them,
nor any scorching heat;
[17] for the Lamb at the center of the throne will be their shepherd,
and he will guide them to springs of the water of life,
and God will wipe away every tear from their eyes."

8 When the Lamb opened the seventh seal, there was silence in heaven for about half an hour. [2] And I saw the seven angels who stand before God, and seven trumpets were given to them.

[3] Another angel with a golden censer came and stood at the altar; he was given a great quantity of incense to offer with the prayers of all the saints on the golden altar

7.9–12: Universal worship. 9: *Great multitude*, Gentiles who have devoted themselves to purity (white robes) and to the God and messiah of Judaism (cf. 15.3–4; Tob 13.11). *Palm branches*, cf. Mt 21.8; Mk 11.8; 1 Macc 13.51. **11:** *Elders and . . . living creatures*, see 4.4n.; 4.6n.

7.13–17: Reward for fidelity during the tribulation. The idea of purification by means of martyrdom may be inspired by Dan 11.35; the motif of a great tribulation (Gk "thlipsis") became a common feature among early Jesus-believers (Mk 13.19, 24;2 Thess 1; etc.). Gentiles thus sanctified become like priests, servants before the heavenly throne and within the heavenly temple. **14:** *You are the one that knows*, see Zech 4.5. *Blood of the lamb*, see 5.6–7n., and "Names Inscribed on the Body," p. 485. **16:** John refers to Isa 49.10, which originally concerned the return from the Babylonian exile, in depicting the blessed status of the sanctified Gentiles. **17:** The Lamb's status *at the center of the throne* does not imply a merging with God but rather anticipates its eschatological status on Mount Zion (14.1) and at the center of the new Jerusalem (21.22–23); the continuation of the verse cites the eschatological Isa 25.8.

8.1: The seventh seal. The *silence* provides an aural break between the heavenly liturgy of the righteous and the sequence of acts initiated with the opening of the *seventh seal*.

8.2–10.11: The seven trumpets. 2: *Trumpets* recall priestly duties at festivals and the changing of times, at the Temple, and especially in holy war (cf. Num 10.1–10; 1QM cols. 7–9, 17–18; cf. Isa 27.13). **3–4:** *Censer*, incense-

THE HEAVENLY TEMPLE CULT

One of the functions of Jewish apocalyptic literature was to reveal a temple cult that prospered in heaven, by God's very throne, by the hands of angels, according to the stringent precepts of the Torah, regardless of the historical abominations that might be afflicting the Temple in Jerusalem. Stimulated by such ancient blueprints for Jewish liturgical perfection as the desert tabernacle (Ex 25–31; 36–39) and Ezekiel's heavenly temple (Ezek 40–48), authors of the Enoch and Levi apocalypses (for example), which were composed over the Hellenistic and early Roman periods, incorporated specific details of heavenly and liturgical procedure both to reassure readers and to signify the priestly functions of the angels in heaven. The Qumran Essenes saw themselves as active participants in this heavenly cult through their Sabbath Songs (11QShirShabb), which were supposed to call into action the priestly angels and perhaps even substitute for animal offerings. Neither the final destruction of the Jerusalem Temple nor Jesus-belief eliminated such esoteric interests in a heavenly cult, as we see in Christian texts like the *Testament of Levi* and the Letter to the Hebrews.

Revelation offers remarkably detailed images of this heavenly temple cult, from the blowing of trumpets and pouring of bowls in chs 6–9, details that would also have conjured sights of non-Jewish civic ritual in Asia Minor cities, to the use of incense at the altar (8.1–3). The heavenly temple of John's apocalypse functions not just as the site of angelic service (cf. 16.17) but also as the spectacle of divine power, alternately veiled (15.8) and visible (11.19) according to the stages of the liturgical process through which the eschaton unfolds. Most importantly, both the angels (including the mysterious twenty-four elders, 4.10–11) and the righteous function primarily as priests and liturgical choristers (4–7; 15.2–8; 20.6), and as at Qumran, the eschatological status of the righteous depends fundamentally on their absolute priestly purity (14.4; 21.7; 22.3–4).

Modern readers might find an uncomfortable paradox between the holy angels' heavenly ministrations and the horrific cataclysms that each liturgical act causes on earth. But ancient audiences most likely found a reassuring perfection in the scenes of heavenly cult and a satisfying clarity in the extreme forms of divine judgment that John envisioned.

that is before the throne. [4] And the smoke of the incense, with the prayers of the saints, rose before God from the hand of the angel. [5] Then the angel took the censer and filled it with fire from the altar and threw it on the earth; and there were peals of thunder, rumblings, flashes of lightning, and an earthquake.

[6] Now the seven angels who had the seven trumpets made ready to blow them.

[7] The first angel blew his trumpet, and there came hail and fire, mixed with blood, and they were hurled to the earth; and a third of the earth was burned up, and a third of the trees were burned up, and all green grass was burned up.

[8] The second angel blew his trumpet, and something like a great mountain, burning with fire, was thrown into the sea. [9] A third of the sea became blood, a third of the living creatures in the sea died, and a third of the ships were destroyed.

[10] The third angel blew his trumpet, and a great star fell from heaven, blazing like a torch, and it fell on a third of the rivers and on the springs of water. [11] The name of the star is Wormwood. A third of the waters became wormwood, and many died from the water, because it was made bitter.

[12] The fourth angel blew his trumpet, and a third of the sun was struck, and a third of the moon, and a third of the stars, so that a

offering by the altar before God's throne affirms the *trumpets'* priestly, liturgical character. See Lev 16.12–13. **5:** *Fire* on the altar suggests that the heavenly worship replicates in every way the Temple in Jerusalem. Angelic trumpets, symbols of proper priestly function in heaven, result paradoxically in destruction on earth (inspired generally by the ten plagues [Ex 7–11]).

8.6–13: Trumpets 1–4. 7: *Hail and fire*, and *blood* from the *first* trumpet recall the seventh plague upon the Egyptians (Ex 9.23–25). The limitation of destruction to a third allows room for still greater catastrophe later. **8–9:** The *second* trumpet (*sea became blood*) recalls the first plague (Ex 7.20–21) but applies the destruction also to maritime culture. **10–11:** *Great star*, cf. Lk 10.18. *Wormwood*, a bitter herb; in Jer 9.15; 23.15 it is punishment for

third of their light was darkened; a third of the day was kept from shining, and likewise the night.

[13] Then I looked, and I heard an eagle crying with a loud voice as it flew in midheaven, "Woe, woe, woe to the inhabitants of the earth, at the blasts of the other trumpets that the three angels are about to blow!"

9 And the fifth angel blew his trumpet, and I saw a star that had fallen from heaven to earth, and he was given the key to the shaft of the bottomless pit; [2] he opened the shaft of the bottomless pit, and from the shaft rose smoke like the smoke of a great furnace, and the sun and the air were darkened with the smoke from the shaft. [3] Then from the smoke came locusts on the earth, and they were given authority like the authority of scorpions of the earth. [4] They were told not to damage the grass of the earth or any green growth or any tree, but only those people who do not have the seal of God on their foreheads. [5] They were allowed to torture them for five months, but not to kill them, and their torture was like the torture of a scorpion when it stings someone. [6] And in those days people will seek death but will not find it; they will long to die, but death will flee from them.

[7] In appearance the locusts were like horses equipped for battle. On their heads were what looked like crowns of gold; their faces were like human faces, [8] their hair like women's hair, and their teeth like lions' teeth; [9] they had scales like iron breastplates, and the noise of their wings was like the noise of many chariots with horses rushing into battle. [10] They have tails like scorpions, with stingers, and in their tails is their power to harm people for five months. [11] They have as king over them the angel of the bottomless pit; his name in Hebrew is Abaddon,[a] and in Greek he is called Apollyon.[b]

[12] The first woe has passed. There are still two woes to come.

[13] Then the sixth angel blew his trumpet, and I heard a voice from the four[c] horns of the golden altar before God, [14] saying to the sixth angel who had the trumpet, "Release the four angels who are bound at the great river Euphrates." [15] So the four angels were released, who had been held ready for the hour, the day, the month, and the year, to kill a third of humankind. [16] The number of the troops of cavalry was two hundred million; I heard their number. [17] And this was how I saw the horses in my vision: the riders wore breastplates the color of fire and of sapphire[d] and of sulfur; the heads of the horses were like lions' heads, and fire and smoke and sulfur came out of their mouths. [18] By these three plagues a third of humankind was killed, by the fire and smoke and sulfur coming out of their mouths. [19] For the power

a That is, *Destruction*
b That is, *Destroyer*
c Other ancient authorities lack *four*
d Gk *hyacinth*

idolatry. **12:** The *fourth* trumpet's effects recall the ninth plague (Ex 10.21–23) as well as many depictions of the darkness of the Day of the LORD (e.g., Joel 3.14). **13:** *Eagle,* usually a symbol of Rome; here used ironically as the herald of Rome's destruction. *Woe, woe, woe,* the next three trumpets are woes (9.12).

9.1–12: The fifth trumpet. 1: The *star that had fallen from heaven* is charged with opening temporarily the portal of the underworld, allowing the limited escape of underworld demons; see 8.11. *Bottomless pit,* the source of evil (11.7; 17.8). **3:** *Locusts,* if inspired by the eighth plague (cf. Ex 10.12–15), John has magnified the horror from mere agricultural threat (cf. 9.4) to monstrous danger to humans (9.5–10), recalling military vehicles (9.9). **7–8:** The *appearance* of the *locusts* recalls Joel 1–2. As in Ezekiel's vision of the punishment of Jerusalem (Ezek 9.4–9), the locusts do not harm the 144,000 bearing the seal of God. **11:** *Abaddon,* angelic king of the *bottomless pit,* the Abyss, Abbadon/*Apollyon,* personifying an ancient Hebrew parallel to Sheol: Prov 15.11; Job 26.6; 1QH 3.16–19. In the Tanakh, Abaddon usually refers to the place where the dead live, a synonym for Sheol (e.g., Ps 88.12), though in Job 28.22, as here, it refers to a demon of death.

9.13–21: The sixth trumpet. 13: *Horns of . . . altar,* quarter-round protuberances in Israelite and other ancient altars; see Ex 27.2. **14–15:** Unlike more traditional stories of the binding of demons in distant places (cf. Tob 8.3; Dan 10.13), the angel *releases* four vengeance angels. *Euphrates,* at the time the eastern border of the Roman Empire, marking the boundary between that and the Parthian Empire. **16–19:** John envisions the angels' armies as cavalries, whose terror lies in monstrous *horses.* The *fire and smoke and sulfur* from their mouths constitute

of the horses is in their mouths and in their tails; their tails are like serpents, having heads; and with them they inflict harm.

[20] The rest of humankind, who were not killed by these plagues, did not repent of the works of their hands or give up worshiping demons and idols of gold and silver and bronze and stone and wood, which cannot see or hear or walk. [21] And they did not repent of their murders or their sorceries or their fornication or their thefts.

10 And I saw another mighty angel coming down from heaven, wrapped in a cloud, with a rainbow over his head; his face was like the sun, and his legs like pillars of fire. [2] He held a little scroll open in his hand. Setting his right foot on the sea and his left foot on the land, [3] he gave a great shout, like a lion roaring. And when he shouted, the seven thunders sounded. [4] And when the seven thunders had sounded, I was about to write, but I heard a voice from heaven saying, "Seal up what the seven thunders have said, and do not write it down." [5] Then the angel whom I saw standing on the sea and the land

raised his right hand to heaven
[6] and swore by him who lives forever
and ever,

who created heaven and what is in it, the earth and what is in it, and the sea and what is in it: "There will be no more delay, [7] but in the days when the seventh angel is to blow his trumpet, the mystery of God will be fulfilled, as he announced to his servants[a] the prophets."

[8] Then the voice that I had heard from heaven spoke to me again, saying, "Go, take the scroll that is open in the hand of the angel who is standing on the sea and on the land." [9] So I went to the angel and told him to give me the little scroll; and he said to me, "Take it, and eat; it will be bitter to your stomach, but sweet as honey in your mouth." [10] So I took the little scroll from the hand of the angel and ate it; it was sweet as honey in my mouth, but when I had eaten it, my stomach was made bitter.

[11] Then they said to me, "You must prophesy again about many peoples and nations and languages and kings."

11 Then I was given a measuring rod like a staff, and I was told, "Come and measure the temple of God and the altar and those who worship there, [2] but do not measure the court outside the temple; leave that out, for it is given over to the nations, and they will trample over the holy city for forty-two months. [3] And I will grant my two witnesses authority to prophesy for one

[a] Gk *slaves*

three plagues. **20–21:** The allusion to idolatry as well as bodily sins recalls Ezekiel's vision of the punishment of Jerusalem (Ezek 8–9, cf. Ps 115; Isa 44.9–20). **21:** *Sorceries . . . thefts*, crimes associated with idolatry (Wis 12.3–11).

10.1–11: Appearance of new angel to herald the final trumpet. The *mighty angel*'s descent to declare the imminence of the seventh trumpet functions paradoxically to draw out the completion of the eschatological catastrophes. **1–3:** The *cloud* and *seven thunders* are traditional imagery of storm theophany (cf. Ps 18.6–15; 29), and suggest the pillars of cloud and fire of Ex 13.21–23. The angel straddles *land* and *sea* to signify God's dominion and judgment over both zones (cf. 10.6; 20.13). **4:** It is unclear what John was going to transcribe; it may be related to the ultimate revelation of "the mystery of God" (v. 7). **6:** *Lives forever*, God as source of eternal life (cf. Neh 9.5–6). **7:** *Mystery of God*, cf. Rom 16.25–26. *The prophets*, here including John the author. **8–11:** In close imitation of Ezekiel (2.8–3.4), John receives a *scroll* to *eat*, allowing God's (written) warnings to come from his mouth. As with Ezekiel's scroll, the sweetness of its divine origin turns into the bitterness of the vengeful decrees he must announce.

11.1–14: Interlude: Measurement of the current Temple and the eschatological acts of Moses and Elijah, the two witnesses. 1–2: As in Ezekiel's vision of the new Temple (Ezek 40–42), measurement denotes the appreciation of divine perfection, although here it is the seer, not an angel, who measures (cf. Ezek 40.3; Rev 21.9–21). That only the outer court of Gentiles is consigned to desecration could mean the vision originated before 70 CE. *Forty-two months*, equal to three and a half years, half of seven years, indicating a lengthy time but not one of total desecration. It also equals 1,260 days. **3:** *Two witnesses* typically identified as Moses and Elijah for their miraculous powers (11.5–6), which recall the legends of these figures (Ex 7–12; 1 Kings 17–21; 2 Kings 1). *Sackcloth*, a rough fabric (often made from goat or camel hair) similar to burlap, worn next to the skin as a sign

thousand two hundred sixty days, wearing sackcloth."

[4] These are the two olive trees and the two lampstands that stand before the Lord of the earth. [5] And if anyone wants to harm them, fire pours from their mouth and consumes their foes; anyone who wants to harm them must be killed in this manner. [6] They have authority to shut the sky, so that no rain may fall during the days of their prophesying, and they have authority over the waters to turn them into blood, and to strike the earth with every kind of plague, as often as they desire.

[7] When they have finished their testimony, the beast that comes up from the bottomless pit will make war on them and conquer them and kill them, [8] and their dead bodies will lie in the street of the great city that is prophetically[a] called Sodom and Egypt, where also their Lord was crucified. [9] For three and a half days members of the peoples and tribes and languages and nations will gaze at their dead bodies and refuse to let them be placed in a tomb; [10] and the inhabitants of the earth will gloat over them and celebrate and exchange presents, because these two prophets had been a torment to the inhabitants of the earth.

[11] But after the three and a half days, the breath[b] of life from God entered them, and they stood on their feet, and those who saw them were terrified. [12] Then they[c] heard a loud voice from heaven saying to them, "Come up here!" And they went up to heaven in a cloud while their enemies watched them. [13] At that moment there was a great earthquake, and a tenth of the city fell; seven thousand people were killed in the earthquake, and the rest were terrified and gave glory to the God of heaven.

[14] The second woe has passed. The third woe is coming very soon.

[15] Then the seventh angel blew his trumpet, and there were loud voices in heaven, saying,

"The kingdom of the world has become
the kingdom of our Lord
and of his Messiah,[d]
and he will reign forever and ever."

[16] Then the twenty-four elders who sit on their thrones before God fell on their faces and worshiped God, [17] singing,

"We give you thanks, Lord God Almighty,
who are and who were,
for you have taken your great power
and begun to reign.
[18] The nations raged,
but your wrath has come,
and the time for judging the dead,
for rewarding your servants,[e] the prophets
and saints and all who fear your name,
both small and great,
and for destroying those who destroy the
earth."

[19] Then God's temple in heaven was opened, and the ark of his covenant was seen

a Or *allegorically*; Gk *spiritually*
b Or *the spirit*
c Other ancient authorities read *I*
d Gk *Christ*
e Gk *slaves*

of mourning and repentance (Jon 3.5–6,8; Isa 50.3). **4:** *Olive trees*, source of oil for Temple lamps (Zech 4.3–14). *Lampstands*, see 1.12n. **6:** *Shut the sky*, bring a drought as Elijah did (1 Kings 17.1). *Blood . . . plague*, as in the Exodus tradition (see 8.7–9nn.). **7:** *Beast*, see 13.1; 17.8. A monster from the Abyss (cf. 9.2–3) symbolizing evil. **8:** *Great city*, Jerusalem, as indicated by the reference to Jesus' crucifixion. This is one of the very few references to the historical Jesus in Revelation. *Sodom* is applied to Jerusalem in Ezek 16.46–56 (cf. Isa 1.10; Jer 23.14), an analogy to the city of violence and fornication of Gen 19. *Egypt*, the place of slavery. **9:** *Three and a half days*, cf. 11.1–2. *Peoples and tribes*, Jerusalem seen as overrun with Gentiles and with little care for dead bodies (cf. Ps 79.1–3; Tob 1–2). **10:** *Exchange presents*, parody of celebration. **11:** *Breath of life from God*, cf. Ezek 37.5,10, resurrection. **12:** *Come up here*, an ascension. *Cloud*, traditional means of heavenly transport (see Ezek 1.4; Ps 18.11–12; Dan 7.13; *4 Ezra* 13.3; Mk 13.26).

11.15–19: The seventh trumpet declares the new reign. The seventh trumpet initiates a liturgical declaration of a shift in "kingdoms," from worldly to divine dominion. Verb tenses describe God's assumption of dominion as a completed, victorious act. **15:** *Kingdom of the world*, the earthly rulers. *Our Lord and of his Messiah*, the kingdom of God. *He will reign*, Ex 15.18. **18:** See Ps 2.1–3. **19:** *Temple in heaven*, see 4.1–11, and "The Heavenly Temple Cult," p. 478. *Flashes of lightning*, another storm theophany (cf. 4.5; 8.5; 10.3).

within his temple; and there were flashes of lightning, rumblings, peals of thunder, an earthquake, and heavy hail.

12 A great portent appeared in heaven: a woman clothed with the sun, with the moon under her feet, and on her head a crown of twelve stars. [2] She was pregnant and was crying out in birth pangs, in the agony of giving birth. [3] Then another portent appeared in heaven: a great red dragon, with seven heads and ten horns, and seven diadems on his heads. [4] His tail swept down a third of the stars of heaven and threw them to the earth. Then the dragon stood before the woman who was about to bear a child, so that he might devour her child as soon as it was born. [5] And she gave birth to a son, a male child, who is to rule[a] all the nations with a rod of iron. But her child was snatched away and taken to God and to his throne; [6] and the woman fled into the wilderness, where she has a place prepared by God, so that there she can be nourished for one thousand two hundred sixty days.

[7] And war broke out in heaven; Michael and his angels fought against the dragon. The dragon and his angels fought back, [8] but they were defeated, and there was no longer any place for them in heaven. [9] The great dragon was thrown down, that ancient serpent, who is called the Devil and Satan, the deceiver of the whole world—he was thrown down to the earth, and his angels were thrown down with him.

[10] Then I heard a loud voice in heaven, proclaiming,

"Now have come the salvation and the power
and the kingdom of our God
and the authority of his Messiah,[b]
for the accuser of our comrades[c] has been thrown down,
who accuses them day and night before our God.
[11] But they have conquered him by the blood of the Lamb
and by the word of their testimony,
for they did not cling to life even in the face of death.
[12] Rejoice then, you heavens
and those who dwell in them!

[a] Or *to shepherd*
[b] Gk *Christ*
[c] Gk *brothers*

12.1–6: The woman clothed with the sun. 1–2: The vivid drama of the *pregnant* woman and the dragon is a portent or sign ("semeion") rather than a specific heavenly being. The woman is comparable to other symbolic women in apocalyptic visions (*4 Ezra* 9.38–10.54; Herm. *Vis.*) rather than identified as Mary (with whom she came eventually to be linked). She also recalls cosmic goddesses of the author's time, like Isis and Astarte. *Twelve stars*, if the woman is Israel, from whom the messiah is born, these would be the twelve tribes. *Birth pangs*, draws on the prophetic metaphor of childbirth (Isa 7.14; 21.3; 26.17; 66.7; Jer 4.31; 6.24; 13.21). **3–4a:** *Dragon*, soon to be identified in v. 9 as "Devil, Satan, and deceiver," recalls in its *seven heads* and cosmic destructiveness the ancient Semitic chaos-monster Leviathan, portrayed in some ancient art with seven heads (cf. Ps 74.13–14; Job 40.25). *Ten horns*, possibly a reference to various rulers, but specific identification is not possible. **4b:** John imagines the dragon receiving the infant directly from the woman's womb into its mouth. **5:** *Rule all the nations*, *Pss. Sol.* 17.22–24; *rod of iron*, Ps 2.9 (see 11.18n.). **6:** *Wilderness*, here a place of safety. *1,260 days*, forty-six months or three and a half years; see 11.1–2n. The motif of the pregnant woman chased by the dragon, here and in vv. 13–17, recalls the story of Leto (and her child, Apollo), pursued by Python. It is not surprising that a Jewish author from Asia Minor might draw out a vision rooted in prophetic oracles by means of regional mythology.

12.7–9: War in heaven. Like the great primordial theomachies (divine battles) of Titans versus gods, and Yahweh versus dragon (Isa 27.1; 51.9–10; Ps 74.12–15), the dragon and his angelic army battle Michael, God's military angel (Dan 10; 12), and his host. The idea of armies amassing in heaven in preparation for eschatological battle is presumed in 2 Macc 3.25–26; 1QM; and Mt 26.53; see also Job 25.2–3. **9:** *Thrown down*, as were the Watchers in *1 En.* 6–21. *Ancient serpent*, usually taken to refer to that of Gen 3.1–7. *Devil . . . Satan*, compare Lk 10.18.

12.10–12: Victorious declaration of Satan's fall. The text credits God and the Lamb rather than Michael's forces, perhaps suggesting a later editorial addition to the vision itself. **10:** *Accuser*, referring to Satan (Heb "adversary, accuser"; see Job 1.6–12). **11:** *Blood of the Lamb*, see 5.6–7n. **12:** *Rejoice*, Isa 44.23; 49.13; Ps 96.11. *Woe to the earth and sea* may herald the arrival of beasts, ch 13.

CHAOS MONSTERS

The bizarre polymorphic beasts that arise in ch 13 to threaten and delude the earth belong to the most archaic biblical traditions of creation and would have been easily recognized as such by early audiences. The idea that the God of Israel, like other Canaanite gods, defeated and bound the monsters Leviathan/Rahab and Behemoth—respectively sea- and land-monsters—at the beginning of time is invoked in such disparate biblical sources as Ps 74 and Job 41, and Isaiah calls for its reenactment, to perfect the earth once again (Isa 27.1; 51.9–10). While many sources from John's own period still refer to these primordial beasts by name (*1 En.* 60.7–9; *2 Bar.* 29.4; *4 Ezra* 6.49–52), the book of Daniel had begun a tradition of imagining their anonymous reappearance in horrific forms that reflected the imperial powers of history (Dan 7), and it is this visionary tradition that John draws upon in ch 13. *We* know they are primordial chaos monsters, but John just beholds them fearfully.

Other frightening beasts in Revelation draw on the same archaic traditions of chaos in creation. The seven-headed Satan-dragon (ch 12) owes much to early images of Leviathan (cf. Isa 27.1), even while its harassment of the woman and infant have been shown to follow more closely the Greek myth of Leto and the child Apollo, threatened by the monster Python, than ancient Canaanite mythology. Interestingly, the Satan-dragon is said to serve God's own eschatological designs (17.17) before its final destruction (20.9–10). So also the minor demon Death, a latter-day version of the ancient Canaanite drought-monster Mot, is introduced first as an agent of divine wrath (6.7–8) before its final destruction (20.14). This paradoxical status, instrument of God and enemy of God, pertains to many demonic figures in the ancient world.

Like many Jewish apocalyptic authors, John depicts the eschatological theater as a subtle and shifting balance between divine violence and a demonic—or at least initially extra-divine—violence, at the end of which is perfect peace and order.

But woe to the earth and the sea,
for the devil has come down to you
with great wrath,
because he knows that his time is
short!"

[13] So when the dragon saw that he had been thrown down to the earth, he pursued[a] the woman who had given birth to the male child. [14] But the woman was given the two wings of the great eagle, so that she could fly from the serpent into the wilderness, to her place where she is nourished for a time, and times, and half a time. [15] Then from his mouth the serpent poured water like a river after the woman, to sweep her away with the flood. [16] But the earth came to the help of the woman; it opened its mouth and swallowed the river that the dragon had poured from his mouth. [17] Then the dragon was angry with the woman, and went off to make war on the rest of her children, those who keep the commandments of God and hold the testimony of Jesus.

[18] Then the dragon[b] took his stand on the

13 sand of the seashore. [1] And I saw a beast rising out of the sea, having ten horns and seven heads; and on its horns were ten diadems, and on its heads were blasphemous names. [2] And the beast that I saw was like a leopard, its feet were like a bear's, and

[a] Or *persecuted*

[b] Gk *Then he*; other ancient authorities read *Then I stood*

12.13–18: The woman and the dragon. 14: *Great eagle*, perhaps that of 8.13; see Ex 19.4. *Time and times, and half a time*, three and a half times (see 11.1–2n.). **15–16:** The ancient Leviathan was associated with floods and uncontrollable waters (Ex 15.8; Ps 29.10). *Earth* (Gk "Gē," cf. Gaia), is here a helpful (female) force; cf. *2 Bar.* 6.8–9. **17:** *Her children*, those of whom John approves. *Commandments*, "mitzvot." John envisions those who keep Mosaic Torah.

13.1–10: The beast from the sea. 1: Dan 7 is the immediate inspiration for beasts arising from sea and land, but they ultimately derive from ancient Semitic traditions about the primal chaos-monsters Leviathan and Behemoth (see "Chaos Monsters" above). *Ten horns and seven heads*, see 12.3–4n. *Blasphemous names* represent a perversion of the holy names on the foreheads of the 144,000 followers of the Lamb (7.3; 9.4). **2:** As in Dan 7.4–6, the beast's polymorphic appearance indicates its monstrous nature, much as demons were imagined in

its mouth was like a lion's mouth. And the dragon gave it his power and his throne and great authority. [3] One of its heads seemed to have received a death-blow, but its mortal wound[a] had been healed. In amazement the whole earth followed the beast. [4] They worshiped the dragon, for he had given his authority to the beast, and they worshiped the beast, saying, "Who is like the beast, and who can fight against it?"

[5] The beast was given a mouth uttering haughty and blasphemous words, and it was allowed to exercise authority for forty-two months. [6] It opened its mouth to utter blasphemies against God, blaspheming his name and his dwelling, that is, those who dwell in heaven. [7] Also it was allowed to make war on the saints and to conquer them.[b] It was given authority over every tribe and people and language and nation, [8] and all the inhabitants of the earth will worship it, everyone whose name has not been written from the foundation of the world in the book of life of the Lamb that was slaughtered.[c]

[9] Let anyone who has an ear listen:
[10] If you are to be taken captive,
into captivity you go;
if you kill with the sword,
with the sword you must be killed.
Here is a call for the endurance and faith of the saints.

[11] Then I saw another beast that rose out of the earth; it had two horns like a lamb and it spoke like a dragon. [12] It exercises all the authority of the first beast on its behalf, and it makes the earth and its inhabitants worship the first beast, whose mortal wound[d] had been healed. [13] It performs great signs, even making fire come down from heaven to earth in the sight of all; [14] and by the signs that it is allowed to perform on behalf of the beast, it deceives the inhabitants of earth, telling them to make an image for the beast that had been wounded by the sword[e] and yet lived; [15] and it was allowed to give breath[f] to the image of the beast so that the image of the beast could even speak and cause those who would not worship the image of the beast to be killed. [16] Also it causes all, both small and great, both rich and poor, both free and slave, to be marked on the right hand or the forehead, [17] so that no one can buy or sell who does not have the mark, that is, the name of the beast or the number of its name. [18] This calls for wisdom: let anyone

[a] Gk *the plague of its death*
[b] Other ancient authorities lack this sentence
[c] Or *written in the book of life of the Lamb that was slaughtered from the foundation of the world*
[d] Gk *whose plague of its death*
[e] Or *that had received the plague of the sword*
[f] Or *spirit*

Jewish and Christian protective spells. *Dragon*, Satan. *Authority* (cf. v. 4) suggests that the beast's danger stems not just from its primal threat of chaos but also from a larger evil, as if all dangers are linked. **3:** *Death-blow* (or mortal wound), usually taken as a reference to the emperor Nero; following his 68 CE suicide by sword (Suetonius, *Nero* 49.3–4), popular traditions in the eastern Mediterranean imagined his resurrection and reconquering of Rome. Several "new Neros" appeared in the later first century. Jewish sources despised him (*Sib. Or.* 3.68–74). **4–7:** The beast is notable for inspiring general worship, *blaspheming* holy things, and persecuting the saints (cf. 12.17; 13.9–10), all ways that John imagines emperor veneration whether officially prescribed or not. These views of the emperor cult recall Dan 7.25; 11.36–39, referring to Antiochus IV Epiphanes. *Forty-two months*, three and a half years; see 11.1–2n. *Dwelling* (lit., "tent, tabernacle") recalls Dan 11.31–39 and reflects contemporaneous fears that eschatological evil would involve a foreign ruler's hubris in the Jerusalem Temple (see also 2 Thess 2.4, cf. Ezek 28.2; Isa 14.13–14). A later editor has clarified "dwelling" to refer to the saints. **8:** *Foundation of the world*, as translated this would imply that some are predestined to destruction; the phrase can also apply to *slaughtered* (see translators' note *c*), implying that the Lamb's sacrifice was performed at the beginning of creation. *Book of life*, see 3.5n.

13.11–18: The beast from the earth. The new behemoth is characterized chiefly by its deceptive qualities, resembling the Lamb (v. 11) and mimicking the thaumaturgy of the two prophets (vv. 13–14; cf. 11.5–6), but he encourages idolatry (vv. 14–15). **12:** *Mortal wound*, see v. 3n. **15:** *Image of the beast*, the notion of cult-images gaining "life" and thus "speaking" refers to statue oracles customary around the Greco-Roman world. Ritually infused with the god's spirit, such statues could "speak" through sounds and movements, and communities depended on them in crisis situations. **16–17:** The beast's deceptiveness extends to a parody of the divine marks

NAMES INSCRIBED ON THE BODY

In one of the most mysterious and distinctive features of this book, John imagines the righteous of Israel as "sealed [*sphragizein*]" on their foreheads with the name of God and the Lamb (7.3–4; 14.1; 22.4; cf. 4 *Ezra* 6.5), and the unrighteous, the dupes of the beast, as likewise receiving "marks [*charagma*]" on the forehead or right hand with the encrypted name of the beast (13.16–18). The great *pornē* of Babylon also has inscribed on her forehead a name—"a mystery," John asserts—that rather unmysteriously identifies her as "Babylon the great, mother of whores and of earth's abominations" (17.5).

Whether labeled seals, marks, or simply names, these forehead insignia clearly have functions beyond simply identifying their bearers. The sealing of the righteous follows quite explicitly from a scene in Ezekiel in which God calls a scribal angel to put a *taw* (or X-mark) on the foreheads of everyone in Jerusalem who rejected the desecration of the Temple, and it is those inscribed who alone escape the bloodbath of the executioner angels (Ezek 9). As with the doorpost marks that in the Passover story of Exodus, safeguarded the Israelites from the slaying of the firstborn (Ex 12.21–27), these forehead marks are *apotropaic,* magically protective of their bearers from supernatural dangers.

The magical force of seals with heavenly names or pedigrees to protect and empower their bearers appears in Greek ritual manuals from Roman Egypt (*Patrologia Graeca* [Migne] 3.226; 4.3039; 7.583; 36.39). In many Jewish and Christian apocalyptic texts the bearers of such seals are protected, during heavenly ascent, from dangerous mid-air demons and ambivalent lower angels (*Ascen. Isa.* 10.23–31; *Apoc. Eli.* 1.9–12; *Hekhalot Zutrati* 415–16; *Hekhalot Rabbati* 219–24). Some books, like the Gnostic *Books of Jeu*, even included diagrams of the seals to be drawn on the body or inscribed on metal or gemstone. Many museums hold large collections of such inscribed gems, many of which served as protective "seals." The gold "rosette [tzitz]" that the Jewish high priest was supposed to wear on the front of his turban, inscribed with "Holy to YHWH," reflects an earlier idealization of such amulets (Ex 28.36–38) and may have been in John's mind in the depiction of the people of the heavenly city (22.4). In Jewish tradition the tetragrammaton held special power to sanctify the bearer without diagrams, an idea that fed into the traditions that a golem could be activated through the inscription of a specific holy name.

What then of the number 666 on the unrighteous, which John carefully distinguishes as a *charagma* rather than a *sphragis* (13.16–17)? The number is, as John makes clear, a name, and while it certainly does not protect its bearers from divine judgment, it does protect their ability to buy and sell goods—to mark them as consecrated insiders of their own sorts—and thus serves as an effective parody of the seals on the followers of the Lamb (14.1).

with understanding calculate the number of the beast, for it is the number of a person. Its number is six hundred sixty-six.[a]

14 Then I looked, and there was the Lamb, standing on Mount Zion! And with him were one hundred forty-four thousand who had his name and his Father's name written on their foreheads. [2] And I heard a voice from heaven like the sound of many waters and like the sound of loud thunder; the voice I heard was like the sound of harpists playing on their harps, [3] and they sing a new song before the throne and before the four living creatures and before the elders. No one could learn that song except the one hundred forty-four thousand who have been redeemed from the earth. [4] It is these who have not

[a] Other ancient authorities read *six hundred sixteen*

on the 144,000 (see "The Numerology of Revelation," p. 475). **18:** *Six hundred sixty-six* represents a "gematria" [Jewish numerology] of the name Nero Caesar, using the numerical equivalents of the Heb letters underlying the Gk spelling of Nero's name: "Kaisar Nerōn" spelled in Heb is "qof-samek-resh" "nun-resh-vav-nun"; the numerical values are 100 + 60 + 200 + 50 + 200 + 6 + 50 = 666. (If the final "nun" is omitted, spelling "Nero" rather than "Neron," the numbers add up to 616 [see translators' note *a*].)

14.1–5: The 144,000. The unwholesome spectacle of the marked followers of the beast is balanced by the heavenly spectacle of the 144,000 with their divine marks (see "The Numerology of Revelation," p. 475). **1:** *Mount Zion*, Jerusalem. **2:** Heavenly perfection is expressed through the alternation of heavenly voices and chants. *Many waters*. see 1.15n. **3:** *Living creatures*, see 4.6n. **4:** *Defiled themselves*, the purity of the 144,000 is sig-

defiled themselves with women, for they are virgins; these follow the Lamb wherever he goes. They have been redeemed from humankind as first fruits for God and the Lamb, [5] and in their mouth no lie was found; they are blameless.

[6] Then I saw another angel flying in midheaven, with an eternal gospel to proclaim to those who live[a] on the earth—to every nation and tribe and language and people. [7] He said in a loud voice, "Fear God and give him glory, for the hour of his judgment has come; and worship him who made heaven and earth, the sea and the springs of water."

[8] Then another angel, a second, followed, saying, "Fallen, fallen is Babylon the great! She has made all nations drink of the wine of the wrath of her fornication."

[9] Then another angel, a third, followed them, crying with a loud voice, "Those who worship the beast and its image, and receive a mark on their foreheads or on their hands, [10] they will also drink the wine of God's wrath, poured unmixed into the cup of his anger, and they will be tormented with fire and sulfur in the presence of the holy angels and in the presence of the Lamb. [11] And the smoke of their torment goes up forever and ever. There is no rest day or night for those who worship the beast and its image and for anyone who receives the mark of its name."

[12] Here is a call for the endurance of the saints, those who keep the commandments of God and hold fast to the faith of[b] Jesus.

[13] And I heard a voice from heaven saying, "Write this: Blessed are the dead who from now on die in the Lord." "Yes," says the Spirit, "they will rest from their labors, for their deeds follow them."

[14] Then I looked, and there was a white cloud, and seated on the cloud was one like the Son of Man, with a golden crown on his head, and a sharp sickle in his hand! [15] Another angel came out of the temple, calling with a loud voice to the one who sat on the cloud, "Use your sickle and reap, for the hour to reap has come, because the harvest of the earth is fully ripe." [16] So the one who sat on the cloud swung his sickle over the earth, and the earth was reaped.

[17] Then another angel came out of the temple in heaven, and he too had a sharp

[a] Gk *sit*

[b] Or *to their faith in*

nified in their celibacy, which reflects Jewish holy-war practices (Ex 19.15; Deut 23.10–15; Rev 20.9; 1QM 7.3–7); *defiled themselves with women* recalls less the impure spilling of bodily substances (as in Deut 23) as the pollution that the Watchers incurred by joining with human women (*1 En.* 7.1; 9.8; 10.11; 15.3; 69.5). The implication is that the 144,000 are like angels, whose purity women threaten. *First fruits*, harvest offering meant to sanctify the totality of the harvest (see, e.g., Ex 23.19; 34.22; Lev 23.9–14), used in an apocalyptic sense to signify the first stage of eschatological redemption (see also 1 Cor 15.23).

14.6–11: Angelic announcements of judgment. 6: *Eternal gospel* (Gk "euangelion," as in Mk 1.1; 1 Cor 15.1) of proper obeisance to the God of creation; here the term preserves its more general meaning of "good news," lacking any particular reference to Jesus. **7:** *Fear God*, Deut 10.12–15. **8:** Based on Isa 21.9, this announcement foreshadows the vision of Babylon in 17–19. *Babylon* as Rome, see *4 Ezra* 3.1–2. *Wine of the wrath*, Jer 25.15–38. **9–13:** The third angel's declaration of imminent torment for the minions of the beast functions also as a curse, consigning them to eschatological torment. **9:** *Mark*, see 13.15–17. **10:** *Wine of God's wrath*, see v. 8n. *Unmixed*, wine was typically diluted with water in this period; unmixed wine was especially potent. *Fire and sulfur*, as in the destruction of Sodom and Gomorrah (Gen 19.24) and Gog and Magog (Ezek 38.22). The older name for *sulfur*, "brimstone," survives in the phrase "fire and brimstone" (as in the KJV).

14.12–13: Rewards of the saints. 12: *Commandments*, i.e., "mitzvot" (Gk "entolas"). Those who die in holiness will achieve a blessed state (cf. *4 Ezra* 7.35; 8.33). **13:** *Deeds follow them*, in early Jewish visions of final judgment people are often accompanied by their deeds, personified as witnesses to their earthly activities (see Wis 4.20).

14.14–20: Reaping of the earth. 14: *White cloud*, Dan 7.13. The one *like the Son of Man*, (cf. Dan 7.9–13) appears here as eschatological destroyer, perhaps inspired by Ps 110.5–6. **15–16:** The heavenly *temple* serves as the source of eschatological instructions delivered by angels. *Sickle and reap*, the horrific harvest imagery, inspired by Joel 3.13 [Heb 4.13] and Isa 63.1–6 (cf. Isa 17.4–6; 24.13; Jer 51.33) became a standard metaphor for eschatologi-

sickle. [18] Then another angel came out from the altar, the angel who has authority over fire, and he called with a loud voice to him who had the sharp sickle, "Use your sharp sickle and gather the clusters of the vine of the earth, for its grapes are ripe." [19] So the angel swung his sickle over the earth and gathered the vintage of the earth, and he threw it into the great wine press of the wrath of God. [20] And the wine press was trodden outside the city, and blood flowed from the wine press, as high as a horse's bridle, for a distance of about two hundred miles.[a]

15 Then I saw another portent in heaven, great and amazing: seven angels with seven plagues, which are the last, for with them the wrath of God is ended.

[2] And I saw what appeared to be a sea of glass mixed with fire, and those who had conquered the beast and its image and the number of its name, standing beside the sea of glass with harps of God in their hands. [3] And they sing the song of Moses, the servant[b] of God, and the song of the Lamb:

"Great and amazing are your deeds,
Lord God the Almighty!
Just and true are your ways,
King of the nations![c]
[4] Lord, who will not fear
and glorify your name?
For you alone are holy.
All nations will come
and worship before you,
for your judgments have been revealed."

[5] After this I looked, and the temple of the tent[d] of witness in heaven was opened, [6] and out of the temple came the seven angels with the seven plagues, robed in pure bright linen,[e] with golden sashes across their chests. [7] Then one of the four living creatures gave the seven angels seven golden bowls full of the wrath of God, who lives forever and ever; [8] and the temple was filled with smoke from the glory of God and from his power, and no one could enter the temple until the seven plagues of the seven angels were ended.

16 Then I heard a loud voice from the temple telling the seven angels, "Go and pour out on the earth the seven bowls of the wrath of God."

[2] So the first angel went and poured his bowl on the earth, and a foul and painful sore

[a] Gk *one thousand six hundred stadia*
[b] Gk *slave*
[c] Other ancient authorities read *the ages*
[d] Or *tabernacle*
[e] Other ancient authorities read *stone*

cal judgment by the early Roman period (*4 Ezra* 4.28–32; *2 Bar.* 70.2; Mt 13.24–30). **18:** *Authority over fire*, see 8.3–5. **19:** *Wine press*, Isa 63.1–6. **20:** *Outside the city*, where polluting activities take place (1 Kings 21.13; Heb 13.11–12). The image of torrents of blood from massacred sinners, already noted in Joel and Isaiah, becomes a common motif in Roman Jewish (and Jewish-Christian) texts: *1 En.* 100.3; *6 Ezra* [2 Esd 15–16] 15.35–36; cf. Josephus, *J.W.* 6.406 (innocents massacred by Romans). *Blood*, for wine as metaphor for blood, see Gen 49.11; Deut 32.14; Sir 39.26. *Horse's bridle*, see 19.15. *Two hundred miles*, Gk "1,600 stadia" (see translators' footnote *a*), a number equal to 4 x 4 x 10 x 10; four is the number of earth, and ten signifies completeness. The blood thus covers the whole earth, in a recapitulation of flood-imagery (Gen 7.17–24).

15.1–4: Universal acclamation. **1:** *Wrath . . . is ended*, cf. Gen 8.21–22; 9.11–17. **2:** *Sea of glass* stands before the throne (4.6). *Number of its name*, see 13.18n. **3:** *Song of Moses*, the scene evokes the Israelites before the Red Sea (Ex 14.30–15.19), where the first "Song of Moses" was sung. **4:** *All nations will come*, Isa 56.3–8; 60.3; Tob 13.11.

15.5–8: The heavenly temple. **5:** *Tent of witness*, Num 9.15. This moveable tabernacle accompanied the Israelites on their journey in the wilderness. **6–7:** The *plagues* proceed from *bowls* [Gk "phialai"], cultic utensils typical to most temple rituals in antiquity, including Jerusalem (*Ep. Arist.* 33, 42, 79; *L.A.E.* 33.4; *Ant.* 12.40, 82). *Linen . . . sashes*, garments that recall Aaron's vestments when offering the sacrifice of atonement (Lev 16.4). **8:** *Smoke*, Ex 19.18; Isa 6.1–4. Stormlike manifestations of God's *glory* and *power* refer to Ezek 1.28, in which divine attributes have become separate agencies (cf. Ex 24.6; 40.34–35).

16.1–21: The seven bowls. As in enumerations of the plagues on the Egyptians in Ex 7–12 and subsequent "aggadic" versions (as in the Haggadah of Pesach), the vindictive details offer readers both joy in the downfall of the unrighteous and warning to endure among the righteous. These plagues are only loosely based on those in Exodus (cf. Ezek 38.19–22), though it is noteworthy that Ps 78 and 105 likely depict seven plagues as well. **2:** *Sore*, cf. Ex

came on those who had the mark of the beast and who worshiped its image.

[3] The second angel poured his bowl into the sea, and it became like the blood of a corpse, and every living thing in the sea died.

[4] The third angel poured his bowl into the rivers and the springs of water, and they became blood. [5] And I heard the angel of the waters say,

"You are just, O Holy One, who are and were,
for you have judged these things;
[6] because they shed the blood of saints and prophets,
you have given them blood to drink.
It is what they deserve!"

[7] And I heard the altar respond,

"Yes, O Lord God, the Almighty,
your judgments are true and just!"

[8] The fourth angel poured his bowl on the sun, and it was allowed to scorch people with fire; [9] they were scorched by the fierce heat, but they cursed the name of God, who had authority over these plagues, and they did not repent and give him glory.

[10] The fifth angel poured his bowl on the throne of the beast, and its kingdom was plunged into darkness; people gnawed their tongues in agony, [11] and cursed the God of heaven because of their pains and sores, and they did not repent of their deeds.

[12] The sixth angel poured his bowl on the great river Euphrates, and its water was dried up in order to prepare the way for the kings from the east. [13] And I saw three foul spirits like frogs coming from the mouth of the dragon, from the mouth of the beast, and from the mouth of the false prophet. [14] These are demonic spirits, performing signs, who go abroad to the kings of the whole world, to assemble them for battle on the great day of God the Almighty. [15] ("See, I am coming like a thief! Blessed is the one who stays awake and is clothed,[a] not going about naked and exposed to shame.") [16] And they assembled them at the place that in Hebrew is called Harmagedon.

[17] The seventh angel poured his bowl into the air, and a loud voice came out of the temple, from the throne, saying, "It is done!" [18] And there came flashes of lightning, rumblings, peals of thunder, and a violent earthquake, such as had not occurred since people were upon the earth, so violent was that earthquake. [19] The great city was split into three parts, and the cities of the nations fell. God remembered great Babylon and gave her the wine-cup of the fury of his wrath. [20] And every island fled away, and no mountains were to be found; [21] and huge hailstones, each weighing about a hundred pounds,[b] dropped from heaven on people, until they cursed God for the plague of the hail, so fearful was that plague.

17 Then one of the seven angels who had the seven bowls came and said to me, "Come, I will show you the judgment of the

[a] Gk *and keeps his robes*
[b] Gk *weighing about a talent*

9.8–12. *Mark*, see 13.16–17. **3–4:** *Blood*, cf. 8.8–9; Ex 7.14–24. **5:** *Angel of the waters*, see 7.1–2, angels in control of the winds; 14.18, angel in control of fire. In *1 En.* 60.10–20, various angels have charge of natural phenomena. **6:** *Blood to drink*, Ezek 39.19; cf. Rev 17.6. **7:** As in 9.13, the *altar* (lit., "one from the altar") blesses God. In the Qumran Sabbath hymns, every part of the furniture of the heavenly temple participates in liturgy (4QShirShabb[f]). **9:** As with all the plagues, the suffering multitudes do not praise the God of judgment but curse him (cf. 9.20–21; 16.11,21). **10:** *Throne of the beast*, 13.2. *Darkness*, cf. 8.12; Ex 10.21. **12:** Drying of the *Euphrates* achieves the reverse of the Red Sea crossing in Ex 14.21–15.19, for it allows the invasion of *kings from the east*, as many apocalyptic texts imagined in end-time scenarios (*1 En.* 56; *Sib. Or.* 4.137–39; *6 Ezra* 15.28–45). **13:** If inspired by Ex 8.1–15, John reconceptualizes *frogs* as the form taken by the demonic spirits of false prophecy (hence false thaumaturgy, v. 14). *Dragon*, 12.3. Concern for the *false prophet* goes back to Deut 18.20–22 and preoccupied the early Jesus Movement (e.g., Mk 13.22; 2 Cor 11.13–15; 1 Jn 4.1–3). **14:** *Signs*, see 13.3. **15:** *Like a thief*, A prophetic oracle, in the voice of the risen Christ (see 3.30; Mt 24.42–43), here displays true prophecy (cf. Mk 13.11b). The abruptness of the oracle resembles those in ch 22. **16:** *Harmagedon* is probably biblical Megiddo, though this place has no parallels as an eschatological battlefield. The focus on a mountain (Heb "har") as site of eschatological war resembles traditions in Ezekiel (38.8; 39.2,4) and *4 Ezra* (13.34–35). **19:** *Great city*, Rome, here called *Babylon*. *Wine-cup*, see 14.10. **21:** *Hailstones*, Ex 9.13–35; Ps 18.13; Wis 5.22.

WOMAN AND THE SYMBOLISM OF POLLUTION

John of Patmos exhibits a concern with female sexuality that is unique among Jewish apocalypses. His rival "Jezebel," a teacher of what seem to be Pauline teachings (cf. 1 Cor 7–8), is accused of engaging in *porneia*, impure sexual activity, and her followers' attention to her John likens to adultery (2.20–22). His hatred of Rome/Babylon is subsumed into disgust for a giant *pornē* of kings' pleasure (17.2), whose polluting fornication is likened to a disgusting liquid she holds in a golden cup (17.4b). The horror of her liquid impurities (menses do not lie far from John's language here) is ramified through her drunkenness "with the blood of the saints" (17.6), an utter inversion of Jewish meal and sexual purity (cf. Gen 9.4–6; Lev 7.26–27; 15; 17.10–14; Deut 23.10).

John's horror of women as sexual bearers of pollution extends to a critical detail of the 144,000 saints: that "they have not defiled themselves with women, for they are virgins" (14.4). In transcending marriage and sexuality the 144,000 are to be like angels, a kind of apocalyptic celibacy that many Jesus-believers were embracing (1 Cor 7.1), comparable to the stringent sexual purity of the Qumran Essenes (CD 12.1–2). Yet it is not just ritual celibacy that John is enjoining here, for he specifically imagines women as a source of "defilement [*molunō*]." John's preoccupation with female fluids also emerges in the vision of the woman and the dragon (ch. 12). As the woman gives birth, almost directly into the dragon's mouth (12.4b), so the dragon expels a flood of water (12.15), which is swallowed in turn by the helpful (and female) earth. The alternation of fluids, expelling, and swallowing amounts to a nightmarish image of female reproduction.

Much Jewish literature from the Greek and Roman periods is preoccupied with the boundaries of the Jewish community, and the penetration or breaching of these boundaries through either intermarriage or cultural influences is invariably discussed in terms of impure sexuality: *zenut* (Hebrew) or *porneia*. The most vivid example, projected into antediluvian myth, is the seduction of the Watcher angels by human women, through whose impure sexual congress all kinds of foreign customs, magic, and divination practices entered human culture, thus polluting Judaism (*1 En.* 6–9; cf. *T. Reuben* 3.11–14). By the Roman period intermarriage and fornication had become the dominant language in sectarian Judaism for discussing priestly purity, Jewish communal purity, and the incorporation or rejection of foreign ideas and practices; and of course the image of women's bodies, their orifices and sexuality, never drifted far from these discussions (cf. Prov 7).

It is important to recognize John's preoccupations with female sexuality for what they are: one Jewish prophet's way of addressing the halakhic necessity for eschatological celibacy, to maintain purity and angelic status when the Jesus Movement was shifting in a more sexually tolerant direction (cf. 1 Cor 7.3–5,9). John comprehends this threat in the most graphic terms his tradition offers: the sexuality and fluids of women.

great whore who is seated on many waters, [2] with whom the kings of the earth have committed fornication, and with the wine of whose fornication the inhabitants of the earth have become drunk." [3] So he carried me away in the spirit[a] into a wilderness, and I saw a woman sitting on a scarlet beast that was full of blasphemous names, and it had seven heads and ten horns. [4] The woman was clothed in purple and scarlet, and adorned with gold and jewels and pearls, holding in her hand a golden cup full of abominations

[a] Or *in the Spirit*

17.1–19.6: Vision and destruction of the great whore Babylon. In counterpoint to the pregnant woman (ch 12), this spectacle of an alluring but perverse whore (Gk "pornē"), "Babylon," is inspired by the description of the two lustful sisters, Oholah (Samaria) and Oholibah (Jerusalem), in Ezek 23. John means this figure to represent Rome (17.2a,9), but the emphasis on her "fornication" (Gk "porneia") allows this figure to refract broader issues of purity and the body (cf. 2.20–22; 14.4; 22.15).

17.1–6: Her image. 1: *On many waters* suggests the enthronement of Canaanite gods. **2:** *Wine . . . drunk*, see 14.20n.; 16.6. **3–4:** *In the spirit*, in an ecstatic state (cf. 1.10; 4.2). *Purple and scarlet*, members of the Roman senate wore these colors. Her "throne" becomes a beast identical to the Satan-dragon of 12.3, signifying the diabolical power behind her authority; her attire suggests success in seduction (unlike the shameful nakedness of Oholah and Oholibah in Ezek 23.1,10,18,29, etc.). *Heads and . . . horns*, see 12.3. The *cup* recalls the cup of "derision and

and the impurities of her fornication; [5] and on her forehead was written a name, a mystery: "Babylon the great, mother of whores and of earth's abominations." [6] And I saw that the woman was drunk with the blood of the saints and the blood of the witnesses to Jesus.

When I saw her, I was greatly amazed. [7] But the angel said to me, "Why are you so amazed? I will tell you the mystery of the woman, and of the beast with seven heads and ten horns that carries her. [8] The beast that you saw was, and is not, and is about to ascend from the bottomless pit and go to destruction. And the inhabitants of the earth, whose names have not been written in the book of life from the foundation of the world, will be amazed when they see the beast, because it was and is not and is to come.

[9] "This calls for a mind that has wisdom: the seven heads are seven mountains on which the woman is seated; also, they are seven kings, [10] of whom five have fallen, one is living, and the other has not yet come; and when he comes, he must remain only a little while. [11] As for the beast that was and is not, it is an eighth but it belongs to the seven, and it goes to destruction. [12] And the ten horns that you saw are ten kings who have not yet received a kingdom, but they are to receive authority as kings for one hour, together with the beast. [13] These are united in yielding their power and authority to the beast; [14] they will make war on the Lamb, and the Lamb will conquer them, for he is Lord of lords and King of kings, and those with him are called and chosen and faithful."

[15] And he said to me, "The waters that you saw, where the whore is seated, are peoples and multitudes and nations and languages. [16] And the ten horns that you saw, they and the beast will hate the whore; they will make her desolate and naked; they will devour her flesh and burn her up with fire. [17] For God has put it into their hearts to carry out his purpose by agreeing to give their kingdom to the beast, until the words of God will be fulfilled. [18] The woman you saw is the great city that rules over the kings of the earth."

18 After this I saw another angel coming down from heaven, having great authority; and the earth was made bright with his splendor. [2] He called out with a mighty voice,

"Fallen, fallen is Babylon the great!
It has become a dwelling place of demons,
a haunt of every foul spirit,
a haunt of every foul bird,

scorn" handed to Oholibah (Ezek 23.31–34), here transformed into a symbol of liquid impurities, the flows of fornication (cf. Lev 15; Deut 23.10). **5:** *Written a name,* as with those imprinted with the Lamb and beast's marks, the name on her forehead pertains to her fate as well as her identity (cf. 9.9; 14.11). Alternately, this "name" can resemble a brand with which Roman criminals and slaves were marked. **6:** *Drunk with the blood of the saints* casts the "pornē" as a cannibalistic monster and extends the "impurities" in her cup to blood, inverting one of the main points of "kashrut" (Gen 9.4–6; Lev 7.26–27; 17.10–14).

17.7–18: Her interpretation. 7: As with many Jewish and Christian apocalyptic visions, the strange concatenation of figures and attributes constitutes a *mystery* that an angel must decode (e.g., Dan 8.15–25; *4 Ezra* 12.3–35; *2 Bar.* 55–56.2). **8:** *Was, and is not, and is about to ascend,* a threefold temporal status parodying the threefold temporal status of God (cf. 1.4,8; 4.8; etc.). *Bottomless pit,* see 9.1. *Book of life,* see 3.5n. **9:** *Mind that has wisdom* suggests that here the symbolism makes a direct translation to something in the real world (similar codes appear in Dan 7–8 and *4 Ezra* 12). *Seven mountains,* usually identified with the city of Rome. *Seven kings,* likely Roman emperors, although scholars disagree on which are meant. **11:** *Was and is not,* see v. 8. **14:** The text supposes that Roman political history culminates in eschatological *war* against the Lamb, here awarded traditional messianic titles, and his followers (*1 En.* 9.4; cf. Rev 19.16). This vision of eschatological war does not necessarily replicate that in 16.14–16. **16–17:** As in Ezekiel's story of Oholah and Oholibah, vengeance on the *whore* is performed by her lovers, who begin by stripping her *naked* (cf. Ezek 23.10,25–26,29) to condemn sexually the body that had been sexually alluring. Rather than being stabbed or stoned to death (cf. Ezek 23.10,47), this whore is devoured and burned (the punishment for sexual crimes, Gen 38.24; Lev 21.9). **17:** *Put it into their hearts,* in turning against the whore, even such an evil beast as the Satan-dragon is supposed to serve God's purpose.

18.1–19.6: Lament over the whore. This multivoiced dirge over the destruction of the whore Babylon/Rome is inspired by biblical taunt-songs, wherein a kingdom's past glories are rehearsed to sharpen the description of its downfall (see esp. Isa 14; 47; and Jer 30–31 on Babylon; cf. Isa 23; Ezek 26–27 on Tyre).

a haunt of every foul and hateful beast.[a]
[3] For all the nations have drunk[b]
of the wine of the wrath of her
fornication,
and the kings of the earth have committed
fornication with her,
and the merchants of the earth have
grown rich from the power[c] of her
luxury."

[4] Then I heard another voice from heaven saying,

"Come out of her, my people,
so that you do not take part in her sins,
and so that you do not share in her plagues;
[5] for her sins are heaped high as heaven,
and God has remembered her iniquities.
[6] Render to her as she herself has rendered,
and repay her double for her deeds;
mix a double draught for her in the cup
she mixed.
[7] As she glorified herself and lived
luxuriously,
so give her a like measure of torment
and grief.
Since in her heart she says,
'I rule as a queen;
I am no widow,
and I will never see grief,'
[8] therefore her plagues will come in a
single day—
pestilence and mourning and famine—
and she will be burned with fire;
for mighty is the Lord God who judges
her."

[9] And the kings of the earth, who committed fornication and lived in luxury with her, will weep and wail over her when they see the smoke of her burning; [10] they will stand far off, in fear of her torment, and say,

"Alas, alas, the great city,
Babylon, the mighty city!
For in one hour your judgment has come."

[11] And the merchants of the earth weep and mourn for her, since no one buys their cargo anymore, [12] cargo of gold, silver, jewels and pearls, fine linen, purple, silk and scarlet, all kinds of scented wood, all articles of ivory, all articles of costly wood, bronze, iron, and marble, [13] cinnamon, spice, incense, myrrh, frankincense, wine, olive oil, choice flour and wheat, cattle and sheep, horses and chariots, slaves—and human lives.[d]

[14] "The fruit for which your soul longed
has gone from you,
and all your dainties and your splendor
are lost to you,
never to be found again!"

[15] The merchants of these wares, who gained wealth from her, will stand far off, in fear of her torment, weeping and mourning aloud,

[16] "Alas, alas, the great city,
clothed in fine linen,
in purple and scarlet,
adorned with gold,
with jewels, and with pearls!
[17] For in one hour all this wealth has been
laid waste!"

And all shipmasters and seafarers, sailors and all whose trade is on the sea, stood far off [18] and cried out as they saw the smoke of her burning,

"What city was like the great city?"

[a] Other ancient authorities lack the words *a haunt of every foul beast* and attach the words *and hateful* to the previous line so as to read *a haunt of every foul and hateful bird*
[b] Other ancient authorities read *She has made all nations drink*
[c] Or *resources*
[d] Or *chariots, and human bodies and souls*

18.1–8: Hymn against Babylon. 2: *Demons,* believed to inhabit desolate cities, Isa 13.21–22; 34.14; Jer 9.11; 10.22; 51.37; Lam 5.18. **3:** *Wine . . . fornication,* see 14.8. **4:** Echoing Jer 51.45, John transmits a call to his readers to separate themselves from Babylon/Rome for their own safety. **5:** *Remembered her iniquities,* see Ezra 9.6 for similar hyperbole. **6:** *Render to her . . . repay her double,* see Isa 40.2. **7:** Personified Babylon/Rome gives a "hubris soliloquy," a prophetic form in which a great political power trumpets its infallibility to make the downfall seem the more ironic: cf. Isa 14.12–14; Ezek 28.2.

18.9–19: Mourning destroyed Babylon. Narrative digressions to the spectacle of the whore's burning body and the misery of those who loved her punctuate the dirge (also vv. 11,15,17b–18a). **9:** *Alas, alas,* see Zech 2.10; see also vv. 16,19 below. **11–19:** The precious trade-goods and attention to maritime merchants echo Ezekiel's dirge over Tyre (ch 27). **16:** *Purple and scarlet,* see 17.4n. **17:** *Shipmasters and seafarers,* see 17.15n.

[19] And they threw dust on their heads, as they wept and mourned, crying out,
"Alas, alas, the great city,
where all who had ships at sea
grew rich by her wealth!
For in one hour she has been laid waste."
[20] Rejoice over her, O heaven, you saints and apostles and prophets! For God has given judgment for you against her.
[21] Then a mighty angel took up a stone like a great millstone and threw it into the sea, saying,
"With such violence Babylon the great city
will be thrown down,
and will be found no more;
[22] and the sound of harpists and minstrels
and of flutists and trumpeters
will be heard in you no more;
and an artisan of any trade
will be found in you no more;
and the sound of the millstone
will be heard in you no more;
[23] and the light of a lamp
will shine in you no more;
and the voice of bridegroom and bride
will be heard in you no more;
for your merchants were the magnates of the earth,
and all nations were deceived by your sorcery.
[24] And in you[a] was found the blood of prophets and of saints,
and of all who have been slaughtered on earth."

19 After this I heard what seemed to be the loud voice of a great multitude in heaven, saying,
"Hallelujah!
Salvation and glory and power to our God,
[2] for his judgments are true and just;
he has judged the great whore
who corrupted the earth with her fornication,
and he has avenged on her the blood of his servants."[b]
[3] Once more they said,
"Hallelujah!
The smoke goes up from her forever and ever."
[4] And the twenty-four elders and the four living creatures fell down and worshiped God who is seated on the throne, saying,
"Amen. Hallelujah!"
[5] And from the throne came a voice saying,
"Praise our God,
all you his servants,[b]
and all who fear him,
small and great."
[6] Then I heard what seemed to be the voice of a great multitude, like the sound of many waters and like the sound of mighty thunderpeals, crying out,
"Hallelujah!
For the Lord our God
the Almighty reigns.
[7] Let us rejoice and exult
and give him the glory,
for the marriage of the Lamb has come,
and his bride has made herself ready;
[8] to her it has been granted to be clothed
with fine linen, bright and pure"—

[a] Gk *her*
[b] Gk *slaves*

19: *Dust on their heads*, an indication of mourning (Ezek 27.30; Job 2.12).

18.20–24: Hymnic response to Babylon's destruction. 21: This symbolic action reflects an ancient performative idiom by which prophets would demonstrate God's plans, cf. Jer 27–28; 51.63–64. **22:** Jer 25.10; Ezek 26.13; Lam 5.14–15. **23:** *Sorcery* ["pharmakeia"] is not meant metaphorically; protective rituals were part of state ceremony in biblical times (cf. Isa 47.9, where God overrides Babylon's sorceries), while unauthorized sorcery was a chief subversive crime in the Roman empire; for John, sorcery constituted the sorts of impure practices that demonic forces introduced to the world through fornication (with which sorcery is often paired): *1 En.* 8–9; cf. 2 Kings 9.22; Rev 21.8; 22.15. **24:** *Blood of prophets and of saints*, an allusion to Jer 51.49 but a contrast to the Gospel Sayings Source, which blamed the murder of prophets on Israel itself (Mt 23.34–36; Lk 11.49–51).

19.1–6: Heavenly celebration. The concluding glorification of God's judgment shifts the antiphonal chanting to heaven and the voices of beings at the throne of God. **2:** *Judgments . . . just*, Ps 19.9 [Heb v. 10]; *avenged . . . blood*, Ps 79.10. *Great whore*, see 17.1. *Fornication*, see 14.8. **4–5:** *Hallelujah*, Heb "praise Yah," Ps 146–150; 106.1; etc. That the voice *from the throne* calls for praises to *our God* implies that its source (on or in the throne) is not God but another aspect of God.

for the fine linen is the righteous deeds of the saints.

[9] And the angel said[a] to me, "Write this: Blessed are those who are invited to the marriage supper of the Lamb." And he said to me, "These are true words of God." [10] Then I fell down at his feet to worship him, but he said to me, "You must not do that! I am a fellow servant[b] with you and your comrades[c] who hold the testimony of Jesus.[d] Worship God! For the testimony of Jesus[d] is the spirit of prophecy."

[11] Then I saw heaven opened, and there was a white horse! Its rider is called Faithful and True, and in righteousness he judges and makes war. [12] His eyes are like a flame of fire, and on his head are many diadems; and he has a name inscribed that no one knows but himself. [13] He is clothed in a robe dipped in[e] blood, and his name is called The Word of God. [14] And the armies of heaven, wearing fine linen, white and pure, were following him on white horses. [15] From his mouth comes a sharp sword with which to strike down the nations, and he will rule[f] them with a rod of iron; he will tread the wine press of the fury of the wrath of God the Almighty. [16] On his robe and on his thigh he has a name inscribed, "King of kings and Lord of lords."

[17] Then I saw an angel standing in the sun, and with a loud voice he called to all the birds that fly in midheaven, "Come, gather for the great supper of God, [18] to eat the flesh of kings, the flesh of captains, the flesh of the mighty, the flesh of horses and their riders—flesh of all, both free and slave, both small and great." [19] Then I saw the beast and the kings of the earth with their armies gathered to make war against the rider on the horse and against his army. [20] And the beast was captured, and with it the false prophet who had performed in its presence the signs by which he deceived those who had received the mark of the beast and those who worshiped its image. These two were thrown alive into the lake of fire that burns with sulfur. [21] And the rest were killed by the sword of the rider on the horse, the sword that came from his mouth; and all the birds were gorged with their flesh.

20 Then I saw an angel coming down from heaven, holding in his hand the

a Gk *he said*
b Gk *slave*
c Gk *brothers*
d Or *to Jesus*
e Other ancient authorities read *sprinkled with*
f Or *will shepherd*

19.7–10: Announcement of the marriage supper. The heavenly antiphony shifts from the destruction of the *whore* (v. 2), the image of abomination and pollution, to the celebration of the marriage of the Lamb to his pure bride Jerusalem. **8:** *Fine linen*, see 15.6–7n. *Deeds*, see 14.13n.; 16.15n. **9:** *Blessed are*, see 1.3n. *Supper*, often interpreted as the great eschatological feast for the righteous to which some Jewish apocalyptic texts allude (cf. Isa 25.6–8; *2 Bar.* 29.4; *4 Ezra* 6.52; *1 En.* 62.14), but the horrible nature of this feast is soon revealed, 19.17–18; **10:** Cf. 22.8–9. *To worship him*, seers privy to extraordinary visions of heaven often misunderstand who is God and who is an angel or secondary expression of God. If in earlier times the mistake went unnoticed (cf. Tob 12.16–22), the recurrence of the motif in Jewish-Christian texts of the first and second centuries suggests that questions about the concept of monotheism were quite pressing in such quarters (cf. *Apoc. Zeph.* 6.11–15; *Ascen. Isa.* 4.2–14). It is God, not the Lamb/Jesus, who is to be worshiped. *Testimony* about Jesus is the *spirit of prophecy* that communicates from God to John.

19.11–16: The avenging warrior. 11: *White horse . . . rider*, the personification of God's Word as a militant warrior, an expression of vengeance, appears in contemporaneous Jewish texts (esp. Wis 18.15–16); the imagery draws on such traditions as Isa 63.1–3; *Pss. Sol.* 17.24; and *4 Ezra* 13.4–11. **13:** *Robe dipped in blood* could designate military efficacy (cf. Isa 63.3), purity (cf. Rev 7.14), or, least likely, identification with Christ. **14:** *Armies of heaven*, see e.g., 2 Kings 2.12; Judg 5.20. **15:** *Mouth . . . sword*, see 1.16n. *Rod of iron*, see 12.5n. *Wine press*, see 14.19n.; 14.20n. The enemies imagined here are *the nations* (Gentiles). **16:** *King . . .lords*, cf. Deut 10.17.

19.17–18: The perverse marriage supper. Cf. v. 9. **17:** *The great supper* is for all the birds', not the saints', delectation; it vividly recalls Ezekiel's invocation of birds and beasts to feast on the forces of the defeated Gog (Ezek 39.17–20); cf. Isa 34.5–7. **18:** *Eat the flesh of kings*, a parody of the supper of the Lord (v. 9n.).

19.19–20.3: Punishment of beast, false prophet, and Satan. 19.19–20: *Beast*, see 13.1; 17.8. *False prophet*, see 16.13n. *Mark*, see 7.3n.; 13.16–17n. *Lake of fire . . . sulfur*, see 14.10n. **20.1:** *Bottomless pit*, the Satan-dragon from

key to the bottomless pit and a great chain. [2] He seized the dragon, that ancient serpent, who is the Devil and Satan, and bound him for a thousand years, [3] and threw him into the pit, and locked and sealed it over him, so that he would deceive the nations no more, until the thousand years were ended. After that he must be let out for a little while.

[4] Then I saw thrones, and those seated on them were given authority to judge. I also saw the souls of those who had been beheaded for their testimony to Jesus[a] and for the word of God. They had not worshiped the beast or its image and had not received its mark on their foreheads or their hands. They came to life and reigned with Christ a thousand years. [5] (The rest of the dead did not come to life until the thousand years were ended.) This is the first resurrection. [6] Blessed and holy are those who share in the first resurrection. Over these the second death has no power, but they will be priests of God and of Christ, and they will reign with him a thousand years.

[7] When the thousand years are ended, Satan will be released from his prison [8] and will come out to deceive the nations at the four corners of the earth, Gog and Magog, in order to gather them for battle; they are as numerous as the sands of the sea. [9] They marched up over the breadth of the earth and surrounded the camp of the saints and the beloved city. And fire came down from heaven[b] and consumed them. [10] And the devil who had deceived them was thrown into the lake of fire and sulfur, where the beast and the false prophet were, and they will be tormented day and night forever and ever.

[11] Then I saw a great white throne and the one who sat on it; the earth and the heaven fled from his presence, and no place was found for them. [12] And I saw the dead, great and small, standing before the throne, and

[a] Or *for the testimony of Jesus*

[b] Other ancient authorities read *from God, out of heaven*, or *out of heaven from God*

ch 12 is bound, like most great demons, in a pit (cf. Tob 8.3; *1 En.* 10.3–6; 14.5; 18.16; 21.3–6; *Jub.* 10.7–11; cf. Mk 3.27). See 9.1n.; 9.11n. **2:** *Dragon*, see 12.1–2n.; 12.3–4n. *Thousand years*, while *1 Enoch* specifies the period of the fallen angels' binding with an incalculably huge number, 10, 000 years (21.6), John envisions the Satan-dragon's thousand-year imprisonment as a temporary reprieve for the world. **3:** *He must be let out for a little while*, the dragon's release (20.7–10) reignites a great eschatological war echoing Ezekiel's vision of Gog's defeat.

20.4–6: First resurrection and thousand-year reign of witnesses. 4: *Thrones*, symbols of authority (see chs 4–5). *Beheaded*, reflects both Roman execution style and an incipient martyrological tradition that focuses on the torments of the righteous (2.13; 6.9–10; cf. 2 Macc 7; *Ascen. Isa.* 5). This new detail does not require that any systematic legal persecution of Jesus-believers had taken place in the author's time. **5–6:** *First resurrection*, John's innovation of a dual resurrection, first of the saints and then (v. 12) of the rest of humanity, maintains the distinctive glory of the saints, whose holiness allows them the privilege of reigning a thousand years longer than those redeemed at the final judgment (vv. 13,15) and guarantees their immunity from further punishment or "second death." *Priests*, a quality of the heavenly state achieved by the beheaded martyrs, cf. 1.6; 5.10.

20.7–10: The end of the millennial rule. That *Satan will be released* does not result in a theomachy (divine battle), as in 12.7–9 (cf. Isa 27.1; 51.9–10; Ps 74.12–15) but rather a great amassing of armies, recalling the war against Gog and Magog in Ezek 38–39 (cf. Rev 19.17–21). The Satan-dragon serves as the instrument of deception behind the armies rather than as the opponent himself (cf. 16.13–16). Large-scale eschatological war often takes precedence in Jewish apocalyptic tradition over heroic theomachy (Dan 11.40–12.1; Mk 13.7–8; 1QM), although sometimes the traditions are combined: Dan 12.1; *4 Ezra* 13. **8:** *Gog and Magog*, see Ezek 38–39; the names refer to kings seen as archetypal enemies of God and the people of God. **9:** *Camp* [Gk "parembolē"; Heb "machaneh"], cf. Deut 23.10–14, reflects the holy-war context for John's notion of sainthood, purity, and conflict (cf. Rev 14.4). *Beloved city*, Jerusalem. **10:** *Devil*, see 2.10n.; 12.3–4n. *Lake of fire*, 19.19–20n.; 14.10n. Eternally *tormented*, cf. *1 En.* 21.6–10; see also Dan 12.2.

20.11–15: Last judgment. 11: *White throne*, symbolizing both purity and authority. *One who sat on it*, God. *The earth and the heaven fled*, see 6.14; creation begins to come to an end in the presence of the creator; cf. Mt 24.25,39. **12:** John's interest in heavenly *books* (see 1.3; 6.14; 10.8–11; 22.7,18–19) reflects a broader Jewish tradi-

books were opened. Also another book was opened, the book of life. And the dead were judged according to their works, as recorded in the books. [13] And the sea gave up the dead that were in it, Death and Hades gave up the dead that were in them, and all were judged according to what they had done. [14] Then Death and Hades were thrown into the lake of fire. This is the second death, the lake of fire; [15] and anyone whose name was not found written in the book of life was thrown into the lake of fire.

21 Then I saw a new heaven and a new earth; for the first heaven and the first earth had passed away, and the sea was no more. [2] And I saw the holy city, the new Jerusalem, coming down out of heaven from God, prepared as a bride adorned for her husband. [3] And I heard a loud voice from the throne saying,

"See, the home[a] of God is among mortals.
He will dwell[b] with them;
they will be his peoples,[c]
and God himself will be with them;[d]
[4] he will wipe every tear from their eyes.
Death will be no more;
mourning and crying and pain will be no more,
for the first things have passed away."

[5] And the one who was seated on the throne said, "See, I am making all things new." Also he said, "Write this, for these words are trustworthy and true." [6] Then he said to me, "It is done! I am the Alpha and the Omega, the beginning and the end. To the thirsty I will give water as a gift from the spring of the water of life. [7] Those who conquer will inherit these things, and I will be their God and they will be my children. [8] But as for the cowardly, the faithless,[e] the polluted, the murderers, the fornicators, the sorcerers, the idolaters, and all liars, their place will be in the lake that burns with fire and sulfur, which is the second death."

[9] Then one of the seven angels who had the seven bowls full of the seven last plagues came and said to me, "Come, I will show you the bride, the wife of the Lamb." [10] And in the spirit[f] he carried me away to a great, high mountain and showed me the holy city Jerusalem coming down out of heaven from God. [11] It has the glory of God and a radiance like a very rare jewel, like jasper, clear as crystal. [12] It has a great, high wall with twelve gates, and at the gates twelve angels, and on the gates are inscribed the names of the twelve tribes of the Israelites; [13] on the east three gates, on the north three gates, on the south

[a] Gk *the tabernacle*
[b] Gk *will tabernacle*
[c] Other ancient authorities read *people*
[d] Other ancient authorities add *and be their God*
[e] Or *the unbelieving*
[f] Or *in the Spirit*

tion (e.g., Dan 7.10; *1 En.* 47.3; *4 Ezra* 6.20). *Book of life*, see 3.5n. **13–15:** *The sea* as the place of lost bodies reflects John's attention to maritime culture (cf. 8.9; 18.11–20). *Death and Hades*, hitherto presented as mounted agents of God's vengeance (6.7–8), are themselves consigned to eternal punishment as demonic forces. *Lake of fire*, 19.19–20n.; 14.10n.

21.1–8: New world and new Jerusalem. 1: *New heaven and a new earth*, cf. Isa 65.17; 66.22. **2:** *New Jerusalem*, cf. 19.7–9. *Prepared as a bride*, see 19.7–10n. **3:**The descent of the heavenly city signifies God's *home* [Gk "skēnē"; Heb "mishkan," "tent/dwelling"] among people, following Ezek 37.27 (cf. *4 Ezra* 7.26). A similar passage about God's holy dwelling among the pure, probably also of Jewish origin, appears in 2 Cor 6.16–18. See also Ex 25.8. **4:** *Every tear . . . Death will be no more*, 7.17; cf. Isa 25.8; 35.10. **5:** John continues to interpose divine declarations reminiscent of Isa 65–66 and Ezek 37 with the distinctive divine attributes introduced in 1.8,17–18. *Seated on the throne*, God. **6:** *It is done*, cf. Jn 19.30. *Alpha and the Omega*, see 1.8n. *Water of life*, the river that runs through the Edenic Jerusalem (22.1–2; cf. Ezek 47.1–12). **7:** *Conquer*, see conclusions to letters, chs 2–3. **8:** The list of evildoers may be meant to characterize the Greco-Roman city. *Lake . . . with fire*, 19.19–20n.; 14.10n.

21.9–21: Vision of the city: walls and gates. The systematic description of the city's architecture recalls Ezekiel's tour of God's heavenly temple (chs 40–42), likewise on a tall mountain (40.2). **9:** That one of the *angels* with a bowl of the *last plagues* (see 15.1) now serves as an "angelus interpres," or "tour-angel," signifies that the functions of heavenly ministry have shifted from execution of judgment to revelation of the pure world. **10:** *In the spirit*, 1.10. **11:** *Glory* (Gk "doxa"; Heb "kavod") of God, an aspect of the enthroned presence: Ezek 1.28; 43.4; cf. 15.8

A HOLY CITY WITHOUT A HOLY TEMPLE

How can the eschatological city lack a physical temple (21.22)? Given the apparent inextricability of temple space and divine presence in biblical tradition (Ps 24; 84; Ex 15.17–18), it is no surprise that texts from Ezekiel and Deutero-Isaiah to *Enoch* and the Dead Sea Scrolls all imagined a great, eternal temple as the centerpiece of God's new creation (Isa 66.20; Ezek 40–48; *1 En.* 90.28–29; *Jub.* 1.27–28; 11QTemple). In deliberately noting its absence, John seems to specify that such a structure will not exist. Is he reflecting on the Roman destruction of the Jerusalem Temple in 70 CE, that God thus indicated such a structure to be an anachronism? Or, as Christian interpreters have been fond of suggesting, does John mean that with Christ's death the Temple, its barriers and priestly privileges, were superfluous obstacles to the divine presence (cf. Mk 15.38)?

But much like Ezekiel's eschatological temple, John's holy city stringently excludes all impurities (21.27; 22.3,15); and its holiness is manifest in its divisions and gates (21.12–21) as much as the light and presence of God and Lamb (21.11,22–23; 22.5). Indeed, when we read these two details in light of Ezekiel and the Temple Scroll from Qumran, both of which imagined temples (or temple rules) covering virtually the entirety of their eschatological cities, it seems clear that the boundaries of John's holy city constitute the perfection that allows the divine presence to dwell. In fact, as surprised as John claims to be in a temple's absence, the infrastructure of the eschatological Jerusalem was a topic of quite diverse thinking in apocalyptic literature: from meticulous reestablishments of temple cult (Ezekiel; 11QTemple; cf. *2 Bar.* 6.7–9), to far more abstract notions of a space for God's eternal dwelling (*4 Ezra* 10.27, 44–54; *T. Benj.* 9.2; *T. Levi* 18; cf. 2 Macc 5.19). Indeed, even in the Psalms YHWH is celebrated as dwelling in a city or a mountain, not just a physical sanctuary (Ps 48; 87; cf. Jer 3.16–17). Thus John's combined interests in purity, architecture, and divine presence can be situated easily in this continuum of Jewish ideas.

three gates, and on the west three gates. [14] And the wall of the city has twelve foundations, and on them are the twelve names of the twelve apostles of the Lamb.

[15] The angel[a] who talked to me had a measuring rod of gold to measure the city and its gates and walls. [16] The city lies foursquare, its length the same as its width; and he measured the city with his rod, fifteen hundred miles;[b] its length and width and height are equal. [17] He also measured its wall, one hundred forty-four cubits[c] by human measurement, which the angel was using. [18] The wall is built of jasper, while the city is pure gold, clear as glass. [19] The foundations of the wall of the city are adorned with every jewel; the first was jasper, the second sapphire, the third agate, the fourth emerald, [20] the fifth onyx, the sixth carnelian, the seventh chrysolite, the eighth beryl, the ninth topaz, the tenth chrysoprase, the eleventh jacinth, the twelfth amethyst. [21] And the twelve gates are twelve pearls, each of the gates is a single pearl, and the street of the city is pure gold, transparent as glass.

[22] I saw no temple in the city, for its temple is the Lord God the Almighty and the Lamb. [23] And the city has no need of sun or moon to shine on it, for the glory of God is its light, and

[a] Gk *He*
[b] Gk *twelve thousand stadia*
[c] That is, almost seventy-five yards

and 21.23b. **12:** Names of the twelve tribes inscribed on *gates*, cf. Ezek 48.30–35. **14:** An odd addition, perhaps by a later editor (cf. Eph 2.20), since *twelve foundations* is unclear, and in Revelation *Lamb* is not used as a title for the historical Jesus pre-crucifixion (cf. 11.8). **15–17:** As in Ezek 40–42, measuring with an angel's help reveals the perfection of heavenly symmetry as well as the incalculable enormity of a divine structure. Unlike most Mediterranean cities of John's time, God's city is a perfect square (v. 16). *One hundred forty-four cubits*, 12 x 12 cubits, symbolizing the completeness of God's people (cf. 7.4n.); a cubit was approximately 18 inches. **18–21:** Perhaps inspired by Isaiah's verses about a bejeweled Jerusalem (54.11–12), John transposes the full panoply of jewels from the breastplate of the high priest (Ex 28.17–21; 39.10–13) onto the walls of the heavenly city, as if to combine two visual spectacles of divine perfection. Cf. Qumran 11Q18 JN ("Jerusalem nouvelle"); *Jos. Asen.* 18.6; Isa 61.10.

21.22–27: The holy city. **22:** *No temple*, that John *saw* the absence of a temple means that it would have been expected (see "A Holy City without a Holy Temple," above). **23–26:** John draws out the image of eternal

its lamp is the Lamb. [24] The nations will walk by its light, and the kings of the earth will bring their glory into it. [25] Its gates will never be shut by day—and there will be no night there. [26] People will bring into it the glory and the honor of the nations. [27] But nothing unclean will enter it, nor anyone who practices abomination or falsehood, but only those who are written in the Lamb's book of life.

22 Then the angel[a] showed me the river of the water of life, bright as crystal, flowing from the throne of God and of the Lamb [2] through the middle of the street of the city. On either side of the river is the tree of life[b] with its twelve kinds of fruit, producing its fruit each month; and the leaves of the tree are for the healing of the nations. [3] Nothing accursed will be found there any more. But the throne of God and of the Lamb will be in it, and his servants[c] will worship him; [4] they will see his face, and his name will be on their foreheads. [5] And there will be no more night; they need no light of lamp or sun, for the Lord God will be their light, and they will reign forever and ever.

[6] And he said to me, "These words are trustworthy and true, for the Lord, the God of the spirits of the prophets, has sent his angel to show his servants[c] what must soon take place."

[7] "See, I am coming soon! Blessed is the one who keeps the words of the prophecy of this book."

[8] I, John, am the one who heard and saw these things. And when I heard and saw them, I fell down to worship at the feet of the angel who showed them to me; [9] but he said to me, "You must not do that! I am a fellow servant[d] with you and your comrades[e] the prophets, and with those who keep the words of this book. Worship God!"

[10] And he said to me, "Do not seal up the words of the prophecy of this book, for the

a Gk *he*

b *Or the Lamb. [2]In the middle of the street of the city, and on either side of the river, is the tree of life*

c Gk *slaves*

d Gk *slave*

e Gk *brothers*

intimacy between God and holy city through the metaphor of light (cf. Ps 132.17). As with most biblical and Second Temple depictions of the eschatological city, the city serves as a beacon to all nations (cf. Jer. 3.17; Isa 60.1–11; Tob 13.11). John's imagery of ecumenical devotion to the new sanctified Jerusalem is inspired by such biblical poetry rather than consistency with the preceding judgment scenes (cf. 19.17–20; 20.7–9), with whose vengeance on Gentile kingdoms it conflicts. **25:** *Gates will never be shut*, in the new creation there will be no need for boundaries against the outside. *There will be no night there*, a reversal of creation (cf. Gen 1.3–5,14–18) to restore an undifferentiated divine presence (cf. 22.5). **27:** The heavenly purity of the city is reasserted through the exclusion of the *unclean* [Gk "koinon" can also mean "common"] and polluting (cf. 21.8; 22.15; Lev 15; 21; Deut 23.9–14; Isa 52.1; 11QTemple 47.3–18).

22.1–2: River of the water of life. 1: Anticipated in 21.6, the depiction of a pure *river* extending from beneath the throne of God is an ancient Near Eastern image (even found on early Babylonian cylinder seals) and conjures the rivers of Eden (Gen 2.10). Transposed to the eschatological temple/city, the image recalls most directly Ezek 47.1–12 and has a parallel in 11QTemple (cf. Sir 24.30–39). *Throne*, this symbol of authority now becomes the source of life. **2:** *Tree of life*, see Gen 3.22. *Twelve kinds of fruit*, the trees are perpetually fruitful. *Healing*, the leaves are medicinal, like herbal remedies. Jewish eschatology often imagined the promulgation of healing powers and remedies in the messianic era: Isa 35.5–6; Mk 7.37; Lk 7.22.

22.3–5 Intimacy between God and the saints. 3: *Accursed*, any such are consigned to the lake of fire (20.14–15). **4:** *See his face*, represents the greatest privilege in Jewish visionary literature (see *2 En.* 22; 39), one not granted to Isaiah (6.1), Ezekiel (ch 1), or Enoch (*1 En.* 14.21; cf. *1 En.* 46.1)—perhaps following God's own proscription in Ex 33.20–23 (cf. Gen 32.31)—but promised as an eschatological reward in *Jub.* 1.28; *4 Ezra* 7.98. *Name . . . foreheads*, recalls the mark on the followers of the Lamb (14.1), representing the opposite of the mark of the beast (13.16); (see "Names Inscribed on the Body," p. 485). **5:** *No more night*, cf. 21.25n.

22.6–17: Oracles of eschatological imminence. 6: *God of the spirits of the prophets*, see 1QH 20.11–13. *His angel*, cf. 21.9,15, referring back to 1.1. **7:** Word of the risen Christ (also in 16.15), referring back to 1.3. *I am coming soon*, this announcement occurs twice more (vv. 12,20), affirming the prophetic nature of this text. *Blessed*, see 1.3n. **8–9:** See 19.10n. **10:** While many Jewish apocalypses charged their scribes to keep revelations secret

time is near. [11] Let the evildoer still do evil, and the filthy still be filthy, and the righteous still do right, and the holy still be holy."

[12] "See, I am coming soon; my reward is with me, to repay according to everyone's work. [13] I am the Alpha and the Omega, the first and the last, the beginning and the end."

[14] Blessed are those who wash their robes,[a] so that they will have the right to the tree of life and may enter the city by the gates. [15] Outside are the dogs and sorcerers and fornicators and murderers and idolaters, and everyone who loves and practices falsehood.

[16] "It is I, Jesus, who sent my angel to you with this testimony for the churches. I am the root and the descendant of David, the bright morning star."

[17] The Spirit and the bride say, "Come."
And let everyone who hears say, "Come."
And let everyone who is thirsty come.
Let anyone who wishes take the water of
life as a gift.

[18] I warn everyone who hears the words of the prophecy of this book: if anyone adds to them, God will add to that person the plagues described in this book; [19] if anyone takes away from the words of the book of this prophecy, God will take away that person's share in the tree of life and in the holy city, which are described in this book.

[20] The one who testifies to these things says, "Surely I am coming soon."

Amen. Come, Lord Jesus!

[21] The grace of the Lord Jesus be with all the saints. Amen.[b]

a Other ancient authorities read *do his commandments*

b Other ancient authorities lack *all*; others lack *the saints*; others lack *Amen*

(Dan 8.26; 12.4; 4 *Ezra* 14.45–48), Revelation charges that its visions be kept open, since the end *is near*. **11:** The idea that all people should remain as they are in anticipation of the eschaton is a common theme in the early Jesus Movement (1 Cor 7.17–24), but the statement here has less to do with social position (slave, married) and more with inner nature, as in the Qumran teachings on the portions of darkness and their works (1QS 4.15–26; 4Q186). **12:** Another oracle of the risen Christ, referring to 1.8. **13:** *Alpha and the Omega*, see 1.8n. **14:** The two possible readings, blessing "those who wash . . . robes" [Gk "plunontes tas stolas"] and "those who do . . . commandments" [Gk "poiountes tas entolas"] look similar in Greek. *Tree of life*, 22.2n. **15:** See 21.8. 4QMMT proscribes dogs from entering the holy camp, as animals that bring corpse-pollution (61–65). **16:** Oracle of the risen Christ using traditional Jewish messianic titles (Isa 11.2,10). **17:** Invitations to be part of the holy city. The invocation to *come* anticipates the invocation to Christ in v. 20b. *Water of life*, see 22.1–2n.

22.18–19: Final warnings. John or a later editor specifies that "keeping the words of the prophecy" (1.3; 22.7,9) means not changing a word (cf. Deut 4.2 and 13.1) under threat of eschatological curse. The text is meant to appear as unchanged from the time of its revelation. *Tree of life*, see 22.2n.

22.20–21: Closing. *Come, Lord Jesus*, translating Aram "maranatha" (cf. 1 Cor 16.22; *Did*. 10.6), may serve as an audience response to the preceding prophetic oracle, but its ritual function was to usher Christ's eschatological return.

Essays

Tables

Glossary

Index

BEARING FALSE WITNESS
COMMON ERRORS MADE ABOUT EARLY JUDAISM

Amy-Jill Levine

There are numerous Church guidelines on how to present Jews and Judaism (e.g., Vatican Commission for Religious Relations with the Jews, "Notes on the Correct Way to Present the Jews and Judaism in Preaching and Catechesis in the Roman Catholic Church" [1985]; National Conference of Catholic Bishops, "God's Mercy Endures Forever: Guidelines on the Presentation of Jews and Judaism in Catholic Preaching" [1988]; General Convention of the Episcopal Church, "Guidelines for Christian-Jewish Relations" [1988]; Evangelical Lutheran Church in America, "Guidelines for Lutheran-Jewish Relations" [1988]). However, out of ignorance many pastors and religious educators strip Jesus from his Jewish context and depict that context in false and noxious stereotypes. This volume represents an effort to redress this significant problem.

There are five major reasons for this problem. First, most Christian seminaries and divinity schools do not offer detailed education about Judaism, whether at the time of Jesus or subsequently. The Association of Theological Schools in the United States and Canada, the accrediting organization for these institutions, does not as of 2011 recommend that candidates studying for the Christian ministry receive formal instruction in how to avoid anti-Jewish preaching and teaching.

Second, whereas a number of churches have guidelines on the presentation of Jews and Judaism, not all clergy know the guidelines. Even clergy who receive some education about Judaism need refresher courses: people forget what they have learned in graduate and professional schools, and these understandings change as research progresses. But too few church bodies sponsor continuing education programs on Judaism, on Jewish-Christian relations, and specifically on anti-Jewish biblical interpretation, and too few clergy attend the programs that are offered.

Third, as church demographics shift increasingly to Asia and Africa, new forms of anti-Jewish biblical interpretations develop. Christians from these areas lack direct memory of the Shoah, the Holocaust, and so may be less sensitized to the dangers of detaching of Jesus from his Jewish tradition. Any negative stereotype flourishes more easily when there are no personal contacts to combat it, when there is limited access to Jews and Jewish resources, and when the challenge to anti-Jewish teaching—such as might be raised by a Jewish Board of Deputies or the Anti-Defamation League—is not part of the culture.

Fourth, biblical studies does, appropriately, speak to contemporary issues. In the effort to deploy the biblical text for purposes of liberation, interpreters insensitive to the issue of anti-Jewish teaching sometimes present Jesus as the liberator from his social context, namely Judaism, which they depict as analogous to present-day social ills. The motivations of such politicized readings are profound and laudable: social justice, alleviation of poverty, and cessation of ethnic strife, and the like; the real difficulties facing these interpreters must be acknowledged. However the means by which their argument is made are sometimes unintentionally anti-Jewish.

Fifth, and perhaps most pernicious, the problem of ahistorical, anti-Jewish interpretation is not always acknowledged. Fortunately, most ministers and religious educators take care in addressing the obviously difficult passages (e.g., the "blood cry" of Mt 27.25 that depicts "the people as a whole" [Gk *pas ho laos*] saying, "His blood be on us and on our children!"; Jn 8.44a, where Jesus accuses the "Jews": "You are from your father the devil, and you choose to do your father's desires"). But problems enter when homilists or teachers do not know Jewish history or theology and out of ignorance construct a negative Judaism over and against which they position Jesus, or when they presume that Jesus' numerous insightful and inspirational comments are original to him rather than part of his Jewish identity.

Anti-Jewish stereotypes remain in some Christian preaching and teaching in the following ten areas. (For additional details, see annotations to the NT passages that this essay references.)

First, as part of a broader theological view that contrasts Jewish "law" with Christian "grace," some Christians may believe that the Law (Torah) is impossible to follow, "a yoke that neither our ancestors nor we have been able to bear" (Acts 15.10), as opposed to Jesus' "easy yoke" (see Mt 11.29–30). In actuality, Jews, then and now, did not find Torah observance any more burdensome than citizens in most countries find their country's laws today. As Deut 30.11a states, "surely, this commandment that I am commanding you today is not too hard for you." Furthermore, modern states have more laws than there are in all the ancient Jewish sources combined. In fact,

Jesus sometimes makes observance more stringent: Torah forbids murder (Ex 20.13; Deut 5.17), but Jesus forbids anger (Mt 5.22); Torah forbids adultery (Ex 20.14; Deut 5.18), and Jesus expands the definition of adultery to encompass both lust (Mt 5.28) and remarriage after divorce (Mt 19.9; Mk 10.11–12; Lk 16.18).

Jesus himself was halakhically obedient: he wears fringes (*tzitzit*—see Num 15.38–39; Deut 22.12) to remind him of the Torah (Mt 9.20; Lk 8.44; Mt 14.36; Mk 6.56); he honors the Sabbath and keeps it holy; he argues with fellow Jews about appropriate observance (one does not debate something in which one has no investment). It is from Torah that he takes his "Great Commandment" (Mt 22.36–40): love of God (Deut 6.5) and love of neighbor (Lev 18.19).

A second misconception, and correlate to the first, is the view that Jews follow Torah in order to earn God's love or a place in heaven. Therefore, Judaism is a religion of "works righteousness" rather than of grace. This view fails to observe that the election of Israel is based on grace, not merit or works. Jews do not follow Torah in order to "earn" divine love or salvation; the Mishnah (*m. Sanh.* 10.1) states that "all Israel has a share in the world to come"—it is part of the covenant. Divine love is already present; it is not earned. Some texts contemporaneous with the New Testament (e.g., the Dead Sea Scroll text 4QMMT) can be read to suggest a works-righteousness model, but this is by no means the majority view, at least as can be determined by the literature of the period.

A third misconception connected to Torah is the view that purity laws were both burdensome and unjust. For example, numerous commentators explain that the priest and the Levite of the parable of the good Samaritan (Lk 10.30–37) bypass a wounded traveler because they are commanded by Jewish law to avoid touching a corpse. The parable, however, does not give this as the rationale for the priest and the Levite's behavior. Indeed, it could not have been the rationale, since the priest is "going down" from Jerusalem (Lk 10.31), not "up" to it, where purity in the Temple would have been an issue. Although Lev. 21.1–2 forbids priests from contact with corpses save for those of near relatives, no such injunction applies to the Levites. In rabbinic literature, the responsibility to save a life supersedes other commandments (e.g., *b. Yoma* 846). Next, Samaritans had the same purity laws as did Jews. Josephus (*Ag. Ap.* 2.30.211) insists that Jews are "not to let anyone lie unburied; the Mishnah (*m. Naz.* 7.1) mandates that even a high priest must assure an unattended corpse receives proper burial. Consequently, Jews would have expected the priest and Levite to provide care, and part of the shock of the parable is that they do not. The parable mentions priest and Levite for rhetorical, not legal reasons: it leads listeners to expect to hear "Israelite," the typical third member of the priest-Levite-Israelite trio, and thus listeners are shocked again when the third person is revealed to be a Samaritan.

Similarly, many sermons claim, incorrectly, that by touching a woman suffering from hemorrhages (Mt 9.20–22; Mk 5.25–34; Lk 8.43–48) and a corpse (Mt 9.23–26; Mk 5.35–43; Lk 8.49–56), Jesus violates purity laws or social taboos. First, Jesus does not touch the woman; she touches him. Second, hands do not convey menstrual impurity. The point of the healing is that Jesus restores a woman to health (and to ritual purity), not that impurity, which is a natural part of the world-order, is evil. Regarding the corpse: again, no law forbids touching a corpse; although corpses convey serious ritual impurity, being in a ritually impure state is not prohibited unless one is going to the Temple. In fact, attending to a corpse is an important *mitzvah* (commandment) in the book of Tobit (2.1–7), in rabbinic literature, and in the New Testament, as we see, for example, when the disciples of John the Baptist claim their teacher's body (Mk 6.29; Mt 14.12), when Joseph of Arimathea claims Jesus' body (Mk 15.43–46), and when the women visit the tomb (Mk 16.1; Lk 24.1).

Women who have just given birth are ritually impure, but Elizabeth, the mother of John the Baptist, and Mary, the mother of Jesus, were not marginalized or demeaned following parturition. Ritual purity along with Sabbath observance, avoiding certain foods such as pork, making sure meat was slaughtered in an appropriate manner, and tithing certain agricultural products also helped Jews resist assimilation, served as a sign of Jewish identity, helped support the poor, and otherwise reminded them that they were Israel, the covenant community. For additional details, see The "Law," p. 515.

The fourth misconception is the view that early Judaism was so misogynistic that it made the Taliban look progressive by comparison, and that Jesus liberated women from this oppressive system. For example, numerous commentators express surprise that Jesus would have permitted Mary to sit at his feet (Lk 10.38–42), because "rabbis" were forbidden to talk to women. This idea of a "feminist" Jesus amid a retrograde Judaism serves several expedient purposes. Since Jesus is not proactive concerning women (e.g., no women are appointed among the twelve apostles; no women are explicitly mentioned as being present at the Transfiguration, the Last Supper, or Gethsemane), then if Jewish women could be depicted as no better than property, any interaction Jesus had with a woman would be seen as progressive. The case for describing women as oppressed by Judaism was then made by very selective citations of rabbinic statements, ignoring significant counterexamples (e.g., Beruriah, the well-educated wife of Rabbi Meir, whose legal rulings are authoritative), and ignoring the role of patrons and guests in private homes.

The New Testament, as well as other Jewish literature of the period, from the deuterocanonical texts to Josephus and Philo to inscriptional evidence to early rabbinic sources, tells us that Jewish women owned their own homes (see Lk 10.38 [Martha]; Acts 12.12 [Mary the mother of John called Mark]); served as patrons (Lk 8.1–3); appeared in the Temple (which had a dedicated "Court of the Women") and in synagogues; had use of their own property (from the poor widow who puts her coins in the Temple treasury [Mk 12.42; Lk 21.2] to the rich woman who anoints Jesus, whether on the head [Mt 26.6–13 || Mk 14.3–9] or on his feet [Lk 7.36–50; John 12.1–3]); had freedom of travel (as with the women from Galilee who accompany Jesus to Judea); appear in public; and so on. Clearly it was not because of Jewish oppression that women joined Jesus. Perhaps some women outside of marital situations (widows, single women, divorced women) were particularly attracted to Jesus' movement given its possible focus on celibacy (see Mt 19.12), non-privileging of child-bearing (Lk 11.27–28), and alternative family structures (see Mt 12.50 || Mk 3.35).

The fifth misconception, related to the fourth, is that Jesus forbids divorce in order to protect women, because "the rabbis" stated that men would divorce their wives for the flimsiest of reasons (see *m. Git.*). This view fails to note that in addition to some liberal rabbinic divorce comments, we find much more stringent ones that restrict divorce to cases of adultery; this view also fails to note that the Jewish wife had a marriage contract (Heb *ketubah*) that protected her financially in case of divorce. Jesus' concern is not the protection of women, but theological. Mark 10.6–9 explains: "From the beginning of creation, 'God made them male and female.' 'For this reason a man shall leave his father and mother and be joined to his wife, and the two shall become one flesh.' So they are no longer two, but one flesh. Therefore what God has joined together, let no one separate."

The sixth problem is a matter substantially of vague rhetoric: the claim that Jesus ministers to the "outcasts" and "marginals." Many pastors and teachers do not explain: Cast out by whom? Cast out from what? Marginal to what? For example, that Jesus eats with "sinners and tax collectors" (e.g., Mk 2.16) is seen as an example of his ministering to the "cast out." Groups ranging from the sick, the women, and the Gentiles (such as centurions) to children and the poor are seen as "marginal." This is historically inaccurate. Sinners and tax collectors are not "cast out"; rather, they are people who violate the welfare of the community and who have deliberately removed themselves from the common good. Nor are they "cast out" of anything: to the contrary, Luke 18.10 locates a "tax collector" and "sinner" in the Jerusalem Temple. Second, the majority of people suffering from diseases in the Gospels are part of larger familial or social groups. Women are not cast out or marginal, and children are so loved that their parents and care-givers bring them to Jesus for a blessing. Nor are Gentiles "cast out"; Luke reports that a Gentile centurion built a synagogue in Capernaum, and depicts the Jewish elders as pleading on his behalf to Jesus (Lk 7.1–10). Gentiles were welcome in the Jerusalem Temple and in synagogues. Judaism of this period was not an egalitarian or universalist utopia, but nor was it in general a system that "cast out" women, children, the poor and sick, and so on. It is therefore important that pastors and teachers be more cautious when they use terms like "marginal" and "outcast."

The seventh misconception is the view that all Jews wanted a militant messiah and therefore rejected Jesus because he proclaimed love of enemies. First-century Judaism had no single messianic blueprint. Some Jews expected a priestly messiah, others a shepherd, still others thought John the Baptist was the messiah. And still others had no such expectations. Missing from this view of the pacifistic Jesus vs. militant Judaism is also contrary evidence from the New Testament. For example, Jesus' followers are armed, as we see in the attempts to prevent his arrest in Gethsemane. Jesus instructs his disciples, "The one who has a purse must take it, and likewise a bag. And the one who has no sword must sell his cloak and buy one" (Lk 22.36b) and disciples respond: "Lord, look, here are two swords" (22.38).

Eighth is the view that for early Judaism, God had become a transcendent, distant king, and that Jesus invented the idea of a heavenly "father"; connected to this view is the still-heard claim that when Jesus addressed God as "abba" (Mk 14.36; see also Rom 8.15; Gal 4.6) that he used an intimate term meaning "daddy" that would have been offensive to his fellow Jews. These claims miss the numerous biblical and postbiblical uses of "father" for the divine, including Ps 68.5 [Heb v. 6]; 89.26 [Heb v. 27]; Isa 64.8; Jer 31.9; *Ant.* 7.380, etc.; 1QH; *b. Ta'an.* 23b (on the grandson of Ḥoni the Circle Drawer); and *b. Ta'an.* 25b (*avinu malkeinu*—"our father our king").

Ninth is the insistence that Jesus objected to the "temple domination system" that overtaxed the population, forced upon them oppressive purity laws (see above), and functioned as an elitist institution in cooperation with Rome. Thus we have the common stereotype that the "money changers" were overcharging pilgrims. Jesus never makes this charge, although there are rabbinic notices that the high priests would sometimes take the tithes due to the poorer priests. Nor have we evidence that the Temple oppressed the peasants or overtaxed them. The vast majority of the Jewish people loved the Temple, visited it on pilgrimage festivals, protected it from Roman profanation, and mourned its destruction. According to the book of Acts, Jesus' followers, including Paul, continued to worship there. When in the first revolt against Rome, the Zealot factions gained control of Jerusalem, they did burn the Temple debt records, but they also appointed their own high priest. To some extent, the idea of the temple domination system stems from Jesus' comment about the "den of robbers" (Mt 21.13) ; however, "den of robbers" is a quotation from the Hebrew Bible, from Jer 7.11, and it refers not to where people steal but where thieves go to feel safe.

Tenth is the claim that early Judaism was narrow, clannish, and exclusivistic and that Jesus invented universalism. For example, in Acts 10.28a, Peter states, "it is unlawful for a Jew to associate with or to visit a Gentile." The claim is false, as the Gospel of Luke itself indicates (see Lk 7.1–10), as the Court of the Gentiles in the Temple proves, and as the presence of God-fearers and the conversion of pagans to Judaism in the first century all indicate. Yes, some Jews were narrow (the Qumran scroll 1QM, which divides the world into the "Sons of Light" and the "Sons of Darkness" is hardly a model of ecumenical and interfaith alliance); others were not. Universalism has important precedents in the Hebrew Bible, especially in texts describing the ideal future ("the messianic age"; see, e.g., Isa 2.1–4), and such ideas continued in rabbinic texts as well.

These common stereotypes, and there are others, can be addressed by reading and teaching the entire New Testament carefully within its context. The commentaries and essays in this volume should provide for readers not only a greater appreciation for the Scriptures of the Christian Church but should also prevent the false teaching that deforms the "good news" of Jesus.

THE NEW TESTAMENT BETWEEN THE HEBREW BIBLE (TANAKH) AND RABBINIC LITERATURE

Marc Zvi Brettler

It is impossible to read the New Testament aptly without knowledge of the Jewish Bible, the Tanakh (an acronym for Torah, Nevi'im [Prophets], and Ketuvim [Writings], what the church calls the "Old Testament," and what is sometimes called the "Hebrew Bible"). Most of the books that comprise the New Testament presume the background of that collection of writings—usually in its Greek translation, the Septuagint (see "The Septuagint," p. 562); they quote it, allude to it, use its thought forms and concepts, and in general rely upon it as a source of ideas, history, and religious meaning.

But such appreciation of the Hebrew Bible is not enough for a full understanding of how the New Testament discerns this earlier biblical material. Informed reading of the New Testament must also take account of the development of Jewish thought, including Jewish biblical interpretation, through the time of Jesus of Nazareth and his early followers. Of the approximately 8,000 verses in the New Testament, more than 250 quote the Tanakh, and perhaps twice as many directly allude to it; if verses with more distant allusions are included, the number is far greater. For example, in Matthew 2.2, the magis' question—"Where is the child who has been born king of the Jews? For we observed his star at its rising, and have come to pay him homage"—likely alludes to Numbers 24.17, "a star shall come out of Jacob, and a scepter shall rise out of Israel."

The New Testament authors also find significant continuity between the Scriptures of Israel and the story of Jesus: Jesus is portrayed as a new Moses in Matthew 2–7 (both savior figures are rescued when children around them are slaughtered by royal decree; both descend to Egypt, cross water, endure temptation in the wilderness, ascend a mountain, and deliver a law); the depiction of the crucified Jesus as an offering whose blood atones (Heb 9.11–28; cf. Mk 10.45) evokes the Priestly writings (Lev 16.1–19; Num 19.1–10). Gospel accounts, such as the multiplication of food (e.g., Mk 6.30–44) or bringing a child back to life (Mk 5.22–24,35–43) recall the prophetic stories of Elijah (see 1 Kings 17.8–16,17–24); similar multiplication of food, and cleansing from leprosy (Mk 1.40–42) bring to mind those of Elisha (2 Kings 4.1–7; 5.1–19). (To a lesser extent, such miracle stories are found about a small number of rabbinic sages, such as Ḥoni the Circle Drawer [see *b. Ta'an.* 19a]; see "Jewish Miracle Workers,"

p. 536). A wide variety of other stories, beginning with the creation narratives, are recalled (see e.g., 1 Tim 2.13). The New Testament frequently quotes or alludes to Israel's laws (e.g., Lev 19.18 and Deut 6.5 in Lk 10.25–28, where Jesus elicits the references from a lawyer; in Mk 12.28–31 and Mt 13.16–17, Jesus quotes the verses himself). The Christian texts frequently appeal to the book of Psalms, and sometimes regard them as prophecies (e.g., Ps 16.8–11 in Acts 2.25–28; Ps 2.7; 104.4; 45.6–7; 102.25–27; 110.1 in Heb 1.5,7,8,10–12,13); much of the description of Jesus' crucifixion, especially as presented in the Gospels of Matthew and Mark, draws upon Psalm 22. Some of Jesus' aphorisms (e.g., Mt 6.27,34) are continuous with the Israelite wisdom tradition in Proverbs 10–31, and the Prologue to the Gospel of John (1.1–5,10–18) is based on the idea of wisdom personified at the beginning of Proverbs (1.19–20; 8.22–31). Revelation, the last book of the New Testament, depends on the similarly apocalyptic Daniel, to which it frequently alludes (compare e.g., Rev 2.18 with Dan 10.6); it is by far the most allusive New Testament writing, with hundreds of allusions to many books of the Tanakh, although with no exact direct quotations.

Both the Tanakh and New Testament incorporate multiple, contradictory traditions, as we see when the same story is narrated in Kings and Chronicles, or among the four Gospels. This is very different from modern books, which typically, especially when they deal with the past, take a single viewpoint. The variety of opinions on crucial ideas in the Tanakh (Is God corporeal? Are people essentially good? Is there intergenerational punishment?) anticipates the variety of ideas in the New Testament (Is the new age imminent or has it been delayed? Should Jesus' followers marry or live singly? Is Jesus an incarnate divine being or an adopted son of God? Does early Christianity mean to replace the law?). Both the Tanakh and the New Testament do not participate in the either/or world of the twenty-first century.

And yet there is much in the New Testament that is not anticipated in the Tanakh, such as the core idea of a divine messiah who brings redemption by dying for Israel's sins. Some of these ideas exist separately in the Hebrew Bible—a messiah (though that term is never used there of the future ideal Davidic king), a future ideal king who has some supernatural or at least hyperbolically described characteristics (see Isa 11.1–5), though he is never called divine, and a suffering servant (see esp. Isa 53), though the identity of this servant is very unclear, and it is uncertain if the Hebrew Bible intends an individual or a group, and if this servant lives in the past, present, or future.

Thus, some of what is new in the New Testament reflects a bringing together of separate ideas found in the Tanakh. Some of the New Testament's themes draw not directly upon the Tanakh but upon Hellenistic Jewish literature. For example, the concept of the martyr, put to death by the state, whose sacrifice has salvific meaning for fellow Jews, begins to be developed in the apocryphal book 2 Maccabees (a book in the Roman Catholic and Orthodox but not the Protestant versions of the Old Testament). The shift of Satan from a member of the heavenly court to a personification of evil likewise developed in this milieu.

There is also, of course, material in the New Testament that is not anticipated in the Tanakh; the best examples of this are the epistles, letters written to individuals or to congregations. Nor does the Tanakh offer "Gospels" in the sense of a focused biography of an individual, although the stories of Moses and David, are developed in detail. Furthermore, the Hebrew materials tend to point out the flaws of even the principal figures discussed; no figure in the Tanakh is depicted as perfect or sinless.

Much of what is new is found in the Jewish texts from approximately the same period of the New Testament. For example, the formula used to introduce many citations from the Scriptures of Israel in the New Testament is "(as) it is written" (e.g., Mk 1.2), like the rabbinic formula *kakatuv* (see, e.g., the Aleinu prayer, where *kakatuv* introduces the citation of Deut 4.39). (This term is also used in some the latest texts in the Hebrew Bible, such as Ezra 3.4, which are closer in time to the NT.) There are also forms of argument well attested in rabbinic texts, such as the argument from the minor to the major, also known the *qal vahomer* (lit., "light and heavy"; see the seven principles of Hillel, found at the beginning of the rabbinic midrash *Sifra*), found several times in the New Testament using the phrase "how much more so" (e.g., Mt 12.12). Rabbinic readings of the biblical text are often fanciful and decontextualize the text from its original historical setting—a feature of the New Testament as well. For example, Matthew 13.14–15 and its parallels quote Isaiah 6.9–10, which in its original context is about Isaiah's generation in the eighth century BCE, yet the Gospels understand these verses as being fulfilled in the period of Jesus. This is no different from the way similar prophetic texts were understood by the rabbis and the Dead Sea Scrolls community as being fulfilled centuries after they were first recorded (see esp. the pesher texts from the Dead Sea Scrolls, or R. Akiva's understanding that Num 24.17 was fulfilled with Bar Kochba [see *y. Ta'an.* 4.8]).

Reflecting on how rabbinic Judaism appropriates and interprets the Tanakh can also help readers understand more deeply the relation between the New Testament and the Tanakh. A Jewish reader might say the suffering servant passage in Isaiah 53, emphasized by a variety of New Testament texts (see e.g., Mk 10.45 in relation to Isa 53.12), is peripheral to the Tanakh, which generally emphasizes personal responsibility rather than vicarious punishment. Thus, the New Testament reading of this passage of the Tanakh could be seen as a distortion. But in the same way, rabbinic Judaism does not represent the Hebrew Bible in a proportionate fashion, and it can emphasize relatively marginal passages. For example, the notion of "chastisement of love," that righteous people are punished as a sign of divine love and should accept this punishment with love, is found only rarely in the Tanakh (most clearly Prov 3.12). Yet within rabbinic Judaism, it becomes much more central, probably as a result of the Hadrianic persecutions of 132–35 CE (the Bar Kochba revolt), in which many righteous Jews were killed while and for observing the Torah (e.g., *b. Sanh.* 101a). For both rabbinic Judaism and the New Testament, the Tanakh should be seen as a sourcebook, where the later traditions pick particular themes or ideas to emphasize and interpret, and consequently de-emphasize others.

The rabbis and the New Testament authors do not interpret their respective texts (the Hebrew Bible for the rabbis, the Septuagint, usually, for the NT authors) in a straightforward fashion. The casual reader of the Tanakh would not imagine that the phrase "You shall not boil a kid in its mother's milk" (Ex 23.19; 34.26; Deut 14.21) suggests that no milk and meat products may be eaten or cooked together, as the rabbis adduced (*b. Hul.* 115b). Nor would the casual reader of Jeremiah assume that

> The days are surely coming, says the LORD, when I will make a new covenant with the house of Israel and the house of Judah. It will not be like the covenant that I made with their ancestors when I took them by the hand to bring them out of the land of Egypt—a covenant that they broke, though I was their husband, says the LORD. But this is the covenant that I will make with the house of Israel after those days, says the LORD: I will put my law within them, and I will write it on their hearts; and I will be their God, and they shall be my people. (Jer 31.31–33)

refers to an entirely new revelation that replaces the old, as suggested in Hebrews:

> But Jesus has now obtained a more excellent ministry, and to that degree he is the mediator of a better covenant, which has been enacted through better promises. For if that first covenant had been faultless, there would have been no need to look for a second one.
> God finds fault with them when he says:
> "The days are surely coming, says the Lord,
> when I will establish a new covenant with the house of Israel
> and with the house of Judah;
> not like the covenant that I made with their ancestors,
> on the day when I took them by the hand to lead them out of the land of Egypt;
> for they did not continue in my covenant,
> and so I had no concern for them, says the Lord.
> This is the covenant that I will make with the house of Israel
> after those days, says the Lord:
> I will put my laws in their minds,
> and write them on their hearts,
> and I will be their God,
> and they shall be my people.
> And they shall not teach one another
> or say to each other, 'Know the Lord,'
> for they shall all know me,
> from the least of them to the greatest.
> For I will be merciful toward their iniquities,
> and I will remember their sins no more."
> In speaking of "a new covenant," he has made the first one obsolete. And what is obsolete and growing old will soon disappear. (Heb 8.6–13)

The latest books of the Hebrew Bible, including Daniel, are usually understood to have been written in the second century BCE, although biblical ideas continued to flourish later, while the first rabbinic book, the Mishnah, is dated to approximately 200 CE, although it incorporates earlier traditions. From a chronological perspective, these two corpora—the Tanakh and rabbinic literature—form bookends around the New Testament and offer much context that clarifies its meaning. The New Testament is a Christian book—the final part of a Scripture of a community that had come, by the time these books were regarded as a distinct collection, to view itself as separate from the Jewish community. Nevertheless, the Hebrew Bible and rabbinic literature, as well as the Jewish literature contemporaneous with the New Testament, offer an important context for any reader who is trying to understand it. In turn, reading the New Testament provides additional lenses by which we might understand the lives, the ideas, and the practices of many Jews, both those who chose to follow Jesus of Nazareth and those who chose the various other paths that comprised late Second Temple Judaism. In that sense, the New Testament is very much part of Jewish history.

JEWISH HISTORY, 331 BCE–135 CE

Martin Goodman

FROM ALEXANDER THE GREAT TO THE MACCABEAN REVOLT

Alexander of Macedon, known as "the Great," conquered the Near East in a rapid series of campaigns beginning in 331 BCE and so wrested the land of Israel from the Persians; by the time of his death in 323, he had gained control not only of parts of Europe but also of Syria, Egypt, Mesopotamia, and the entire Persian Empire. In his wake, the Jewish populations in the land of Israel and in the Diaspora, like other peoples whom Alexander ruled, came firmly under the influence of Greek thought and the Greek language. Scholars have given the name "Hellenism" to the synthesis Alexander encouraged between the indigenous cultures of his empire and his Greek-Macedonian ethos. In Judea and Galilee, Aramaic and Hebrew remained in general use, but in most Diaspora communities apart from Babylon, Greek came to be the preferred language and Hebrew was in some cases unknown.

In Alexander's time, the only large Jewish Diaspora population was in Babylon; this population was descended from the Judahites taken into exile by the Babylonians in the sixth century BCE. But by the first century BCE Jewish communities existed far beyond Judea's borders: from Rome and Greece to Cyrene in Libya, to the Anatolian plateau in Western Asia Minor (now Turkey), and to Syria and Egypt. The largest Diaspora communities were in Alexandria in Egypt and in Syrian Antioch. Some of these Jews were descendants of slaves taken captive in the numerous wars following Alexander's death; others were the heirs of Jews employed by various Hellenistic rulers as soldiers for hire. Some Jews relocated from Judea because of overpopulation. Jewish numbers also increased in the Diaspora because of proselytes: while Jews did not actively campaign to gain converts, they did welcome Gentile affiliates.

Following Alexander's death, his generals divided the conquered lands. Of the dynasties these generals formed, two—the Ptolemies of Egypt and the Seleucids of Syria-Mesopotamia—would determine the fate of the land of Israel for the next 200 years. From 301 BCE to 198 BCE, the land formed part of the Ptolemaic state, although Seleucid authorities continued to dispute Jerusalem's ownership. After six unsuccessful attempts at seizing the land of Israel from Ptolemaic control, the Seleucid king Antiochus III annexed the Jewish homeland to his empire at the battle of Paneas in 198.

This shift in state control signaled more than the direction in which taxes would flow; it also created new cultural and political opportunities. The Ptolemaic government had the structure of a large bureaucracy, in part necessitated by Egypt's reliance on state-controlled irrigation for agriculture. When Egypt gained colonial conquests, it extended its bureaucratic governmental system as well. Thus there was little room for local populations to exercise extensive political power. The Seleucids, on the other hand, substantially ruled through cooperation with elite members of the conquered populations, to whom they provided financial and political incentives. Consequently, under the Seleucid system, there was greater room for political advancement provided that non-Greek elites were completely loyal to the Syrian rulers and were sufficiently Hellenized. While some members of Jerusalem's ruling elite—principally the high priestly families—did not embrace Hellenistic culture, others did. The first quarter of the second century BCE witnessed Jewish high priests with Greek names such as Menelaus and Jason, the occasional practice of epispasm (the removal, or attempt to remove, the mark of circumcision through surgery), and Jews undergoing a gymnasium education. The adoption of some elements of Greek culture need not in itself have weakened Jewish identification, as the writings of the highly Hellenized first-century CE Jewish philosopher Philo indicate; *enforced* acculturation, however, would have ended the Jews' distinctive beliefs and practices.

In 167 BCE, the Seleucid ruler Antiochus IV Epiphanes, with the collaboration of the Hellenized ruling elite in Jerusalem, ordered the conversion of the Jerusalem Temple into a pagan shrine. According to 1 Maccabees, the Hellenization program encompassed more than the Temple system; it was also designed to eradicate distinct Jewish practice.

> Then the king wrote to his whole kingdom that all should be one people, and that all should give up their particular customs. All the Gentiles accepted the command of the king. Many even from Israel gladly adopted his religion; they sacrificed to idols and profaned the sabbath. . . . They were to make themselves abominable by everything unclean and profane, so that they would forget the law and change all the ordinances. He added, "And whoever does not obey the command of the king shall die." (1 Macc 1.41–50)

Such a move to dismantle the ancestral religion of a conquered nation was unprecedented in either Ptolemaic or Seleucid history. The main sources describing this policy,

1 and 2 Maccabees, suggest that factionalism within the Jewish ruling class and, especially, the attempt by some within the high priestly circles to gain power via Hellenization prompted the innovation, but only in these books does an explicit contrast between Judaism and Hellenism surface. It is also possible that Antiochus, who had attempted to lay siege to Egypt but had been forced by the Romans to withdraw, was either seeking a firmer consolidation of his holdings or simply looting wealth from the Temple treasury.

THE HASMONEAN DYNASTY

Opposing this Hellenization, with its enforced transgression of Jewish practice, Mattathias, a priest from Modi'in northwest of Jerusalem, together with his five sons, led a guerrilla-style revolt against Seleucid rule. In 164, under the leadership of Mattathias's son Judah (Gk Judas) Maccabeus ("hammer"), they defeated the Syrian forces and purified and rededicated the Temple. This is the origin of the festival of Hanukkah, whose name means "dedication" (see Jn 10.22); 1 Maccabees 4.56–59 describes the eight-day celebration, but the story of the miraculous cruse of oil that lasted for eight days does not appear until the Babylonian Talmud (*b. Shabb.* 21a). A new high priest, Alcimus, who had been an associate of the previous priestly regime, served the restored Temple system, and Judah took over the government. The Syrian military defeat did not create peace in the area, however. Judah also repelled Syrian-Greek attacks on Jewish communities in the Transjordan and Galilee, and he attacked the Syrian troops stationed at the citadel at Acre. Alcimus also faced opposition, including from Judah; the high priest then sought support from the Syrian government, while Judah signed a treaty with Rome.

In 161 BCE Judah was killed in battle against Syrian-Greek forces; his brother Jonathan replaced him as political and military leader. Alcimus died in 159, and in 152 Jonathan arranged with his Seleucid allies to be appointed to the high priesthood. From 152 until 37 BCE, when Herod the Great gained control over Judea, all the high priests as well as the kings came from the family of Mattathias. Their dynasty took the name "Hasmonean," from an ancestor of Mattathias.

The early Hasmoneans were clients of the Syrian-Greek government. The Seleucids kept a garrison in Jerusalem until ca. 129 BCE, and the dynasty continued to interfere in local governance. But internal disintegration and external pressure from Rome, which had taken an increasing interest in the Eastern Mediterranean during the second century BCE, allowed the Hasmoneans greater autonomy. Jonathan took Ashkelon peacefully and Gaza by force, while his brother Simon, who received from the Seleucids vassal control over the coastal regions from Tyre to the Egyptian frontier, conquered the fortress of Beth-Zur.

It is in the context of Jonathan's high priesthood, ca. 145, that Josephus describes the "schools of thought" (Gk *haireseis*) of the Pharisees, Sadducees, and Essenes (*Ant.* 13.171–73). Some have argued that it was at this time, if not earlier, that a group of Jews, led by the "Teacher of Righteousness" mentioned in some of the Dead Sea Scrolls, rejected both the Temple and Jerusalem and eventually settled at Qumran, by the Dead Sea.

In 142 BCE, when the Seleucid general Diodotus Tryphon captured Jonathan and his children, Simon paid the ransom, but he also blocked the general from further movement. Diodotus Tryphon then executed Jonathan, and Simon became, in 141, both "prince" of Israel and high priest. The fate of Jonathan's children is not recorded, although one of his daughters was the ancestor of the first-century Jewish military leader and historian Josephus.

Simon ruled until 135 BCE, when his son-in-law arranged his assassination. Two of his sons were also killed, but the third son, John Hyrcanus, took both the throne and the high priesthood from 135 until 104. By the 120s, Hyrcanus had sufficient autonomy to expand the borders of his kingdom: in ca. 112 he brought the region of Idumea, south of Judea, under his control (*Ant.* 13.257–58). Included in Hyrcanus's expansion were Galilee, Samaria (where he destroyed the Samaritan Temple on Mount Gerizim), and the Transjordan. Hyrcanus's son Aristobulus, who ruled only one year, from 104 to 103, brought the Ituraeans under Judean control as well.

But under Aristobulus, known as "philhellene" ("lover of Greek culture"), Hasmonean power took a new step. Whereas his grandfather held the title of "prince" and his father "ethnarch" (lit., "ruler of a nation"; the term indicates a status below that of a king), Aristobulus declared himself "king." He and his successor, Alexander Jannaeus (103–76 BCE) then ruled as did other Hellenistic kings: they used mercenary soldiers to secure their rule and continued their expansionist policies. Jannaeus conquered Gaza and the Golan Heights, and he took over Nabatean trade routes. Internally, Jannaeus, who received support from the Sadducees, faced a rebellion from Pharisees and others. According to Josephus, while Jannaeus "was feasting with his concubines, in the sight of all the city, he ordered about eight hundred of [his opponents] to be crucified; and while they were living, he ordered the throats of their children and wives to be cut before their eyes" (*Ant.* 13.380). The dynasty that began as a defense of Judaism against Hellenism came to epitomize Hellenistic rule. When Jannaeus died, his wife Alexandra Jannaea Salome became queen (76–67 BCE); this type of inheritance was found elsewhere in the Hellenistic world, but having a legitimately recognized queen (in contrast to Athalya, the ninth-century BCE queen of Judah) was an innovation for Jews.

ROMAN RULE

The Hasmonean dynasty declined because of a combination of internal dissent and Roman ambition. In 67 BCE, Salome Alexandra's sons, Hyrcanus II and Aristobulus, vied for political control; Rome, which had in the 70s gained control of the remnants of the Seleucid empire, stepped into politics of Judea. In 63, the Roman general Pompey intervened, ostensibly on behalf of Hyrcanus, but he then put Jerusalem under siege and, appalling the Jewish population, entered the Temple's Holy of Holies. His motive was curiosity regarding the rumor that the sanctuary contained no cult object. For the Jews, however, the act was the height of transgression (cf. Lev 16). Pompey then took control over the Hasmonean areas of Judea, Galilee, Idumea, and Perea.

Typically, Rome utilized client kings for provincial rule, but this policy proved impossible in Judea in 40 BCE because of Parthian intervention. The Parthians—rulers of an empire based east of the boundaries of the Roman empire, roughly where modern Iran is located—took advantage of civil war in the Roman world to invade the eastern regions under Roman control, including Judea. They imprisoned Hyrcanus and replaced him with his nephew Antigonus. Antigonus then made sure that Hyrcanus would no longer serve as high priest by mutilating his ears (cf. Lev 21.17). The Romans—lacking both political control in Judea and their own suitable Hasmonean candidate for the throne—opted to back Herod. The young man had the powerful political connections: his grandfather, Antipater, was an Idumean and convert to Judaism whom Alexander Jannaeus had appointed *strategos* (in effect, military governor) over the recently incorporated Idumea. His father, also called Antipater, had sided with Pompey in the Roman capture of Jerusalem and then aided Hyrcanus II to regain the throne under Roman auspices. When Julius Caesar defeated Pompey in 48 BCE, he appointed Antipater the procurator of Judea and granted him Roman citizenship. In 47, Antipater in turn appointed Herod governor of Jerusalem.

Herod thus knew the political system and how to maintain it, but because he was of Idumean background and hence not of priestly descent, he could not hold the high priesthood. To gain Hasmonean support, in 42 BCE he became betrothed to Mariamme I, the granddaughter of both Hyrcanus II and Aristobulus, and in 37 he married her. However, the popularity of the Hasmoneans was itself a threat. Bowing to popular pressure, in 36 he appointed Mariamme's brother, Aristobulus III, to the high priesthood, but in 35 he had Aristobulus drowned, and in 27 he executed Mariamme herself. Aristobulus was the last high priest of Hasmonean descent. Herod appointed subsequent high priests from families of limited social clout. Thereby he was able to retain control of the Temple and prevent the high priesthood from becoming a source of revolt.

The main base of Herod's power was always the support of Rome. Upon being proclaimed "king of Judea, Galilee, and Perea" in 40 BCE in Rome by the Roman Senate, and with the support of both Mark Antony and Octavian (Augustus), Herod's first act was to offer a sacrifice to Jupiter. In 37, it was the Roman legions, with only marginal help from Herod, who defeated the Parthian troops that were backing Antigonus and who captured Jerusalem. Herod's main achievement in this campaign was to dissuade the Roman soldiers from looting the city.

Herod reigned until 4 BCE with a combination of repression, paranoia (some of which was justified), and skillful international negotiation. Enlarging Judea to the size it had been during the Hasmonean expansion, he turned the country into a regional power. For defense, he built fortresses at Masada, Machereus, and Herodium; for glory, his renovations to the Jerusalem Temple made it one of the most magnificent buildings of antiquity. Herod also rebuilt the Tomb of the Patriarchs in Hebron, constructed the city of Caesarea Maritima, including its new harbor, and rebuilt the capital of Samaria, which he named Sebaste. He increased Jerusalem's water supply and boosted the local economy by encouraging international pilgrimage to the city, much facilitated by the ease of travel possible under the *Pax Romana*.

While presenting himself as loyal to Judaism and apparently encouraging circulation of a false genealogy that depicted him as a descendant of a Judahite family taken into Babylonian exile, Herod also supported numerous Hellenized projects such as constructing a theater, amphitheater, and hippodrome in Jerusalem, serving as the patron of the Olympic games (either in 12 or in 8 BCE), and erecting a golden eagle over the Jerusalem Temple gate. According to Josephus, he felt "closer to the Greeks than to the Jews" (*Ant.* 19.329), and he built temples to pagan gods in Gentile areas under his control.

Dependent on Roman support, Herod imposed on his subjects a loyalty oath to Augustus. A number of Jews refused, and Herod executed them. According to Josephus, Jewish representatives in Rome complained to the emperor, that "the miseries which Herod, in the course of a few years, had inflicted on the Jews surpassed all that their ancestors had suffered during all the time since they left Babylon to return to their own country"

(*J.W.* 2.86). Although the "slaughter of the innocents" described in Matthew 2.1–18 is not confirmed by external sources, the report is consistent with Herod's reputation.

In 7 BCE, Herod arranged for the execution of Alexander and Aristobulus, his sons by Mariamme I; the ease with which he executed members of his family prompted a punning joke attributed to Augustus, "Better to be Herod's pig (*hus*) than his son (*huios*)" (Macrobius, *Saturnalia* 2.4.11). In other words, the king kept Jewish dietary practices, but he did not hesitate to murder. The son of this Aristobulus, Marcus Julius Agrippa, would three decades later become the Judean king Agrippa I.

When Herod died in 4 BCE, a number of small revolts broke out; Varus, the governor of Syria, quickly suppressed them, but they were harbingers of difficulties to come. Herod had changed his will so often that the final version was disputed, so Rome determined his heirs. Augustus appointed Archelaus, son of Herod and his Samaritan wife Malthace, ethnarch of Judea; his brother Antipas became the tetrarch (lit., "ruler of a quarter"; like "ethnarch," the title signals a status below that of "king") of Galilee. A third son, Herod Philip—whose mother was Herod's fifth wife (of ten), Cleopatra of Jerusalem—became the tetrarch of the predominantly Gentile region of Ituraea and part of the Transjordan (4 BCE–34 CE). He built Caesarea Philippi, famous for the site of Peter's confession of Jesus' messianic status (see Mk 8.22–26; Mt 16.13–28).

Archelaus was unable to impose the same repressive rule as his father, although he utilized similar techniques, such as deposing and appointing high priests (*Ant.* 17.33). In 6 CE Rome banished Archelaus to Vienne in southern Gaul. Even the Gospel of Matthew (2.20–23) explains that Joseph was afraid to live under Archelaus's rule. Instead of finding another client king, Rome placed a praefectus (prefect) of equestrian rank over Judea. The most famous of these, the fifth, is Pontius Pilate, who ruled from 26 to 36 CE. By 44 if not before, the status of the governor changed to "procurator."

Josephus states that Pilate "removed the army from Caesarea to Jerusalem, to take their winter quarters there, in order to abolish the Jewish laws. So he introduced Caesar's effigies, which were upon the ensigns, and brought them into the city; whereas our law forbids us the very making of images" (*Ant.* 18.55). When the Jews protested this transgression, Pilate first threatened the crowds with death but then relented and removed the offending ensigns. Josephus also recounts that Pilate raided the Temple treasury for funds to construct an aqueduct; when the population again protested, Pilate arranged for his soldiers to mingle among the crowds and then, at an appointed signal, massacre them (*Ant.* 18.60–62). According to Philo, who also describes the incident of the shields, Pilate was

> a man of a very inflexible disposition, and very merciless as well as very obstinate . . . in respect of his corruption, and his acts of insolence, and his rapine, and his habit of insulting people, and his cruelty, and his continual murders of people untried and uncondemned, and his never ending, and gratuitous, and most grievous inhumanity. (*Leg. Gai.* 301–2)

In Galilee, Antipas rebuilt Sepphoris and constructed alongside the Sea of Galilee a new capital, Tiberias. Although Sepphoris and Tiberias were the two largest cities in Galilee, strikingly the New Testament never mentions them. Josephus (*Ant.* 18.118–19) records that Antipas engaged in a preemptive strike against John the Baptist, whose popularity he feared. The Gospels attribute this execution to John's condemnation of Antipas's marriage to his niece (and sister-in-law) Herodias (Mt 14.3; Mk 6.7; Lk 3.19). According to Luke 23.6–12, Antipas heard Jesus speak and became friendly with Pilate.

This Herodian heir lost his throne because of his own greed. When Caligula appointed Agrippa I king of Judea in 37 CE, Antipas and his wife Herodias, who was Agrippa I's sister, went to Rome to request that Antipas also be appointed king. Agrippa I brought charges against his brother-in-law, and Caligula exiled him to Gaul as well. Although the emperor, learning that Herodias was Agrippa's sister, offered her back her property and her freedom, Herodias accompanied her husband into exile.

In 41 CE, the emperor Claudius confirmed Agrippa's rule over Philip's land as well as over Judea and Samaria. According to Luke (Acts 12.1–2), Agrippa was responsible for the execution of James, the son of Zebedee, and the arrest of Peter. By the time of Agrippa's death in 44 (described in Acts 12.22–23 and *Ant.* 19.343–50), the borders of his kingdom matched those of his grandfather Herod.

Because Agrippa's son, Agrippa II, was only sixteen at this time, Claudius returned the region to provincial status, and Judea came back into direct Roman rule. The next series of Roman governors exacerbated the increasingly tense relationship between Judea and Rome. Fadus (44–46) faced the revolt of Theudas; Tiberius Julius Alexander (46–48), Philo's nephew, put down the revolt of the sons of Judas the Galilean, a leader of the revolt over the census in 6 CE; Cumanus (48–52), who ignored growing enmity between Galileans and Samaritans, was removed by Claudius at Agrippa II's insistence.

The emperor's positive relationship with Agrippa II did not extend to the Jewish population in Rome. According to Suetonius (*Claud.* 25.4; see Acts 18.2), Claudius expelled the Jews from Rome because they "were constantly causing disturbances at the instigation of Chrestus." Theories that "Chrestus" stands for "Christ" and that the expulsion reflects something to do with Christian claims remain speculative.

In 50 CE, Claudius gave Agrippa II the kingdom of Chalcis. Nero, in 54, granted him Tiberias and Tarichaea and some further territory. Agrippa II also gained the right to appoint the high priest for the Jerusalem Temple. Josephus reports that Agrippa II deposed the Sadducee high priest Ananus when "leading men" (perhaps Pharisees) protested his execution of Jesus' brother James (*Ant.* 20.197–203). According to Acts 25.13–26.32, Agrippa II and his sister Berenice, who would later have an affair with the emperor Titus, heard Paul testify in Jerusalem. When Agrippa II died (either ca. 93 or ca. 100), Rome incorporated his holdings into the province of Syria and placed them under direct Roman rule.

Rome never restored Judea to the Herodian household, and during Agrippa's life Roman governors still controlled Judea. Felix (52–60 CE), whose relationship to Agrippa II's sister Drusilla is recorded both in Acts 24.24 and by Josephus (*Ant.* 20.141–44), faced several revolts including that of a messianic pretender called "the Egyptian." Festus (60–62), mentioned in Acts 25.12, by threatening to remove the wall that blocked the Temple from Agrippa's view, did not endear himself to the population either.

THE FIRST REVOLT

In 6 CE, when Rome imposed a census on Judea as part of their provincial organization, portions of the population had rebelled. The Jewish population again threatened a revolt in 40, when Gaius Caligula, one of Rome's less adept emperors, mandated that his statue be erected in the Jerusalem Temple. Josephus states: "Many tens of thousands of Jews with their wives and children came" to the Syrian governor "with petitions not to use force to make them transgress and violate their ancestral code"; they replied, "on no account would we fight . . . but we will sooner die than violate our laws" (*Ant.* 18.269–72). Caligula's assassination rescinded the order.

Yet Rome did not place numerous troops in Judea and did not, until 66, consider the population threatening. Josephus, who is admittedly prone to demographic exaggeration, asserts (*J.W.* 6.423–27) that in 65, more than 2,700,000 men (the number then must be increased to include women and children) participated in the Passover celebration in Jerusalem; no one appeared to expect a revolt. The military garrison of Judea, housed in Caesarea, consisted of only five cohorts and one cavalry unit.

Even in 66 CE, Rome first entered battle less to subdue a national revolt than to force the Jews to reinstate Temple sacrifice offered on behalf of the emperor. Josephus, upper-class priest and military commander of the Jewish troops in the Galilee, blamed the revolt on incompetent Roman officials and lower-class Jews, including "the sicarii [dagger-men], who left no word unspoken, no deed untried, to insult and destroy the objects of their foul plots" (*J.W.* 7.269). At fault were also the very elites Josephus represented, as his own involvement in the revolt demonstrates. Economic and other factors leading to the war included a shortage of public works after the completion of Herod's Temple in 64 left Jerusalem with a problem of unemployment; a surplus of funds in Jerusalem brought to the city from throughout the Roman world prompted impoverished peasants to relocate to the city; demographic pressure created by competition for limited resources in the countryside because Jews did not traditionally practice contraception, abortion, or infanticide; and strife between Jews and Gentiles in Caesarea increased local tensions. The upper class, weakened initially by Herod's manipulation of the priesthood and then by Roman rule, lacked sufficient prestige in the eyes of the general population to control the volatile political situation.

Eleazar, son of Ananias, the captain of the Temple, was the priest responsible in 66 CE for the cessation of sacrifices offered to the emperor. Eleazar was reacting to the incompetence of the Roman procurator, Gessius Florus, whose own reaction to the failure of the local elite to control the urban mob was to punish the elite. Rome's initial response to the stopping of the loyal sacrifices was a march on Jerusalem by the governor of Syria, Cestius Gallus. After a successful initial incursion, Gallus, while withdrawing from Jerusalem, was dramatically defeated by Jewish forces. In 67, Nero sent a new general, Vespasian, to stop the revolt. Vespasian entered Galilee, where Josephus not only surrendered but also (or so he later claimed) predicted the general's success. By 68, Vespasian took the area around Qumran. Following Nero's suicide in June 68, a series of three Roman generals seized power one after another. Finally, in July 69, Rome's army in the east declared Vespasian emperor. While Vespasian then concentrated on consolidating his control over the empire, his son Titus took control of the troops in Judea.

It is possible that neither Rome nor the Jews initially expected the siege of Jerusalem to be as extensive as it was. Large numbers of pilgrims still came to Jerusalem in the spring of 70 to celebrate the Passover. Moreover, the Jews in the city were divided into three factions led by Simon bar Gioras, John of Gischala, and the priest Eleazar ben Simeon. When Roman troops surrounded the city, the factions combined under the command of bar Gioras. Late rabbinic accounts (*b. Git.* 56b; *Avot de R.Natan* A.4) suggest that Yoḥanan ben Zakkai received Vespasian's permission to establish a school in Jamnia (Yavneh); according to Josephus, Yavneh was a Roman prison camp for those who left Jerusalem (*J.W.* 4.130, 444). Eusebius (*Hist. eccl.* 3.5) states that the Jerusalem-based church fled to Pella, across the Jordan.

In August 70, the Romans, engaging in military action of exceptional violence, burned down the Temple and reduced much of the city to rubble. By 73, they erased all pockets of resistance, including Masada. It is likely that Roman political needs prompted the strategy: Titus sought to gain the empire's respect for himself and his father, Vespasian, since the latter needed evidence of military success to be able to portray himself as a benefactor of the Roman people. This need for popular acclaim accounts for Titus's victory parade with its several hundred prisoners, the numerous monuments, including the famous Arch of Titus in Rome with its depiction of the Temple menorah and altar table, and the Judea Capta ("Captured Judea") coins with the vanquished country depicted as a mourning woman. Hundreds of thousands of Jews were killed or sold as slaves; members of the ruling class disappeared from history. Rome transformed the annual half-shekel/two denarii Temple contribution, which had been paid by adult Jewish males into a special penal tax (the *Fiscus Judaicus*, the "Jewish treasury") to be paid by all Jews, men and women alike, initially for the rebuilding of the temple of Jupiter in Rome (*J.W.* 7.218). To prevent further revolt, Rome stationed a legion in Jerusalem.

The destruction of the Temple, while a catastrophe, did not create universal Jewish despair. The Babylonians had destroyed Solomon's Temple in 586 BCE, but it was rebuilt, so there was every reason to expect a new temple to be erected. Moreover, it was standard Roman policy to allow temples to be rebuilt. The Jewish case became exceptional: most likely Rome refused to allow the Temple to be rebuilt because they did not want the population to have another rallying cry or centralized gathering point. The high priesthood, however, was now defunct, and Rome saw no need to appoint a new high priestly leader.

DIASPORA REVOLT

The years 115–117 witnessed an uprising of the Jewish populations in Cyprus, Cyrene, Asia Minor, and Egypt. It is possible that the Diaspora Jews, at least in part, rose up because their hope for the rebuilding of the Temple had collapsed. In 96, the elderly emperor Nerva, who succeeded the last of the Flavians, Domitian, may have planned to allow the rebuilding of the Temple. If so, the plan was stopped by Nerva's successor, Trajan, whose father had, two decades earlier, fought under Vespasian in the initial battles against the Jews.

More than religious reasons may have motivated the revolt. Trajan himself, who expanded Rome's borders in 115 by conquering Armenia and the western fringes of the Parthian empire, had overstretched his army on Rome's eastern frontiers, thus making revolts in Rome's older provinces possible.

According to the fourth-century church historian Eusebius, the revolt started in Cyprus. In Cyrene, the Jews destroyed the temples dedicated to Apollo, Artemis, Demeter, Zeus, and Isis. The Roman historian Cassius Dio, who like most ancient historians cannot be fully trusted with statistics, reports that the Jews killed 240,000 Greeks (Cassius Dio 68.32.1–3). When Lucius Quietus, the Roman general, stopped the revolt (hence probably the designation used in rabbinic texts for this uprising, the "War of Quietus"), Cyprus enacted legislation prohibiting Jews from living on the island, even in case of shipwreck. All record of the sizeable Egyptian Jewish community comes to an end after 117.

SECOND JUDEAN REVOLT

In 132, revolt broke out again in Judea, once more prompted by Roman action. In 130, Hadrian decided to rebuild Jerusalem as a Roman colony. The name "Jerusalem" would be replaced by "Aelia Capitolina" (Cassius Dio 69.12.1–2). It is uncertain whether prohibition of circumcision by the emperor, attested around this time, was also a cause. With coinage inscribed "For the Freedom of Jerusalem," the Jews rebelled under the leadership of Simon ben Kosiba. That some of the coinage ben Kosiba had minted records the name "Eleazar the priest" may suggest that he had appointed a new "high priest," although the evidence is too scant for a definitive answer. Ben Kosiba became known in some later rabbinic traditions as "bar Kochba," "son of a star," based on a messianic interpretation of Numbers 24.17. His letters, preserved in a cache discovered in the Judean desert, reveal his religious fidelity; one Aramaic papyrus describes preparations for the celebration of the holiday of Sukkot (Tabernacles, Booths).

Ben Kosiba's military strategy, according to Cassius Dio (69.12.3), was to use underground hiding complexes; some of these have recently been excavated. Although ben Kosiba, like his predecessors in 66–70, minted coinage featuring Jerusalem, it is not clear if he ever captured the city.

The revolt was eventually suppressed by Julius Severus. Cassius Dio reports that

> by intercepting small groups . . . and by depriving them of food and shutting them up he was able, rather slowly, to be sure, but with comparatively little danger, to crush, exhaust and exterminate them.

Very few Jews in fact survived. Fifty of their most important outposts and 985 better known villages were razed to the ground. 580,000 were killed in the various engagements or battles. As for the numbers who perished from starvation, disease or fire, that was impossible to establish. (69.13.2–3)

Hadrian renamed Judea "Syria Palaestina" and took the unusual step of banishing Jews from what had once been the city of Jerusalem. Rabbinic sources suggest that some refugees escaped north to Galilee, which for the rabbis became the new center of Jewish life in the homeland.

JUDAISM AND JEWISHNESS

Shaye J. D. Cohen

Greek-speaking Jews in antiquity regularly referred to themselves as *Ioudaioi*. As an ethnogeographical term, best translated "Judeans," it designates the members of the ethnic group inhabiting the district of Judea, or their descendants wherever they may be. It translates the Hebrew term *yehudim*, which appears in the Hebrew Bible in books of the exilic period (2 Kings, Jeremiah, Ezra-Nehemiah, Esther). In the course of the last centuries BCE and the first century CE the ethnogeographical meaning of *Ioudaioi* receded, and a new religious meaning came to take its place. As a religious term, best translated "Jews," it designates people of whatever ethnic or geographical origins who worship the God whose temple is (or, after 70 CE, had been) in Jerusalem. Modern translations, including the New Testament translation used in this volume, usually take *Ioudaioi* as a religious term ("Jews") rather than as an ethnogeographical term ("Judeans"), although this translation is not always certain or correct. See "Ioudaios," p. 524. In contrast, Hebrew and Aramaic speaking Jews in the last centuries BCE did not usually call themselves *yehudim* (for example, that term appears in the Qumran scrolls very rarely and in rabbinic literature only seldom, and there almost always in the mouths of Gentiles). The term *yahadut*, Judaism, does not appear until the Middle Ages.

In addition to adopting the term *Ioudaioi*, Greek-speaking Jews also used the word *Ioudaïsmos*, which is broader than our English word "Judaism." Greek *Ioudaïsmos* designates all the ways and manners, beliefs and mores, that make the *Ioudaioi* distinctive. In the conflict between the Hasmoneans and the Seleucid Greeks, the Jews had to consider exactly which beliefs and practices were essential to Jewish identity. Out of that clash came the word *Ioudaïsmos*, which appears for the first time in 2 Maccabees (written by a diaspora Jew in Greek ca. 100 BCE, referring to the events of the 160s BCE). Indeed, the main theme, explicit or not, of all of Graeco-Jewish literature is *Ioudaïsmos*, the distinctiveness of the Jews within their social and cultural environment.

We can begin to trace the idea of Judaism to Josephus's *Against Apion*, completed around 100 CE. This short work, a kind of supplement to his *Jewish Antiquities*, is a defense of Judaism and Jewish history—Josephus himself calls it an *apologia* (2.147). In the first three-quarters of the book, Josephus proves the falsehood of various slanders spread by Graeco-Egyptian writers against the Jews of Alexandria. The last quarter of the book is a panegyric on the constitution established by Moses, emphasizing its beauty, harmony, and perfection (2.145–296). This panegyric is the only work of Jewish antiquity that aims to give a précis of Judaism and Jewishness.

In this text Judaism first and foremost is a system of *laws*. The laws cover all aspects of life (2.173) and have endured unchanged since they were given by Moses (2.156); all Jews everywhere know and observe the laws (2.175–178); the laws inculcate the virtues of justice, temperance, endurance, and concord (2.170); the point of the laws is the worship of God (2.164–67, 188–90); in fact the political system established by Moses might rightly be called a *theocracy* (2.165; a word that Josephus may have coined). Second, Judaism is a *philosophy* teaching that God knows all, governs all, and has created all; God is uncreated and immutable; God cannot be represented in any material form; God is the beginning, middle, and end of all things (2.190–92). Third, at the heart of Jewish worship is the *temple*: "one temple for the one God" (2.193). Fourth, the laws teach kindness to foreigners so that "all who desire to come and live under the same laws with us" are to receive a gracious welcome, because affinity is established "not only by birth but also by choice in the manner of life" (2.210). In other words, the laws permit what we would call *conversion to Judaism*.

For all of its rhetorical and apologetic exaggerations, the portrait of Judaism in this text is remarkably consistent with the portraits that emerge from other Graeco-Jewish texts (e.g., *Ep. Arist.*; 2 Macc; 4 Macc; Philo, *Hypoth.*) and from references to Jews and Judaism in the writings of Greek and Latin authors. Let us look at these four points: laws, philosophy, temple, and conversion.

The observance of three laws in particular characterized the Jews of antiquity: circumcision, abstention from work on the Sabbath, and abstention from eating pork. Anyone in antiquity who knew anything about the Jews knew that Jewish men are circumcised. The Jews were not the only people in the ancient world who practiced male circumcision, but beginning in the second century BCE, circumcision became particularly associated with them, probably because the Jews themselves began to see circumcision as a sign of difference vis-à-vis the Greeks. No Jewish community in antiquity admitted uncircumcised males to membership.

Anyone who knew anything about the Jews knew that the Jews do not do any work every seventh day. Ancient cultures had holidays and festivals, good-luck days and bad-luck days, but no one else had a regularly recurring holy day like the Jewish Sabbath. Outsiders were contemptuous that the Jews devoted one-seventh of their lives to idleness. If a general wanted to attack Jerusalem, for instance, all he had to do was to attack on the seventh day, when the foolish Jews would not fight—or at least so ran a historiographical commonplace.

Anyone who knew anything about the Jews knew that the Jews do not eat pork. Every people and society had (and has) its own food taboos, but the Jewish abstention from pork struck outsiders as particularly odd. The essayist Plutarch (*Quaest. conv.* 4.5) records a conversation of scholars debating why the Jews abstain from pork: Is it because they venerate the pig or detest it? Plutarch leaves the matter open. (But see Lev 11.7–8 and Deut 14.3–8 for dietary laws.)

Some outsiders knew that the Jews believed that their distinctive laws derive from a sacred book attributed to Moses. Josephus is not the only Jewish writer to emphasize the regular study of the laws; the Dead Sea community emphasized continuous regular study of sacred texts, and some other sources suggest weekly study of the Torah in synagogue on the Sabbath. Prayer to God was also a regular part of these services. (See "The Synagogue," p. 519.)

The Jewish practice of worshiping God, whether in the Temple of Jerusalem or in synagogues, without images, was highly unusual in the ancient world, and it gained the approval of some philosophers who disapproved of the worship of the divine through images. Nevertheless, the worship of one God exclusively was seen as very odd. Even the emperor had to recognize that the Jews would pray *for* him but not *to* him, because the Jews could not acknowledge the emperor as a god. Only a mad emperor like Caligula would try to erect a statue of himself in the Temple. As a result of this theological exclusivity, many Jews refused to partake of the meat that was distributed at civic festivals, what the Jews called "meat sacrificed to idols" (cf. Acts 15.29; 1 Cor 8.1–13). The social separation of the Jews was manifest to all.

"One temple for the one God," says Josephus. Jews throughout the ancient world venerated the Temple of Jerusalem. They sent half-shekel donations each year (apparently beginning in the second half of the second century BCE), and especially after Herod rebuilt the Temple, providing it with a large forecourt and plaza, thousands of pilgrims would come at each of the three pilgrimage festivals. Diaspora Jews did not build competing temples, although beginning in the third century BCE they built synagogues. (Only one competing temple is known in this period, built in Leontopolis in Egypt by Onias, a high priest fleeing from the persecution of Antiochus IV in the 160s BCE. But this temple seems not to have had any impact upon, or following among, the Jews of Egypt; Philo never mentions it.) Some Diaspora Jews even went to Jerusalem to help protect the Temple against the Romans in the great war of 66–70 CE.

Josephus emphasizes the centrality of the Temple but not of the land; in his *Jewish Antiquities* he downplays biblical covenant theology, which posits a connection between God, the people Israel, and the land of Israel. This de-emphasis likely reflects the perspective of a diaspora apologist writing in Rome after the Temple's destruction. Similarly, although Philo refers (*Flaccus* 46) to Jerusalem as the "mother city" (Gk *mētropolis*) of the Jews, and although he went on pilgrimage once to the Jerusalem Temple (*Providence* 2.64), he too, as a diaspora Jew living in Alexandria, does not attribute any theological advantage to the holy land.

In emphasizing Judaism's openness to outsiders, Josephus is responding to the charge that the Jews are hostile to the rest of humanity (the charge of *misanthropia*). Josephus's near-contemporary, the Roman historian Tacitus, says in a memorable passage:

> The customs of the Jews are base and abominable, and owe their persistence to their depravity: for the worst rascals among other peoples, renouncing their ancestral religions, always kept sending tribute and contributing to Jerusalem . . . again, the Jews are extremely loyal toward one another, and always ready to show compassion, but toward every other people they feel only hate and enmity. They sit apart at meals and they sleep apart, and although as a race they are prone to lust, they abstain from intercourse with foreign women; yet among themselves nothing is unlawful. They adopted circumcision to distinguish themselves from other peoples by this difference.

> Those who are converted to their ways follow the same practice, and the earliest lesson they receive is to despise the gods, to disown their country, and to regard their parents, children, and brothers as of little account. (*Hist.* 5.5.1–2)

According to Tacitus, a hostile outsider, the Jews form boundaried communities with a clear sense of who is in and who is out, marked by social separation from general society: no sharing of food, no mixed marriage, and an attitude of hostility. Josephus does not deny that Jewish communities are marked by social separation, but he denies the charge of hostility. Tacitus sees converts to Judaism as an expression of social hostility; Josephus sees converts as proof of Judaism's openness and tolerance.

Tacitus knows and Josephus elsewhere confirms that the act of circumcision is the act of male conversion; when a Gentile is circumcised, he has converted to Judaism. This is exactly the attitude of Paul in his letter to the Galatians. Josephus explains (*Ag. Ap.* 2.210) that Gentiles can convert to Judaism because affinity is established "not only by birth but also by choice in the manner of life." In other words culture or religion can be changed even if birth cannot; achievement (changing one's beliefs and practices) trumps ascription (birth). This is an important principle that will become central to later Jewish thinking about conversion. Some scholars have argued that priestly conceptions of identity, which emphasized birth above all else, militated against the possibility of conversion in this period, but Josephus, although a priest himself, represents the viewpoint that would triumph. Within the Jewish communities of the Diaspora and the land of Israel, converts were accepted as members. Even without converting to Judaism some Gentiles befriended Jews, were benefactors of local Jewish communities, or participated in some aspect or another of communal life. Jews sometimes called such Gentiles "venerators of God" or "fearers of Heaven" (e.g., Acts 10.2).

Josephus, as an apologist, does not address apostasy, the mirror image of conversion. Just as there were Gentiles who were willing, even eager to join the Jewish community, there were Jews who were willing, even eager, to leave. There are only three named examples in the Second Temple period: Dositheus son of Drimylus, "a Jew by birth, who subsequently changed his religion and became estranged from his ancestral laws" (3 Macc 1.3); Tiberius Julius Alexander, the governor of Judea as well as the nephew of Philo, "who did not abide by the ancestral practices" (*Ant.* 20.5.2 100); and Antiochus of Ascalon, who publicly gave evidence of his "changeover [to the Greeks] and his hatred of the Jewish customs" (*J.W.* 7.3.3 50). This may suggest that the incidence of apostasy was relatively rare.

Although rabbinic law from approximately the second century CE on determined the status of the offspring of mixed marriage matrilineally (that is, the status follows the mother; see *b. Qidd.* 68b), this was not the accepted rule in either the biblical period or the Second Temple period. Josephus, Philo, the Qumran scrolls, the New Testament—none of these knows the rabbinic law. In Second Temple times the definitions of Jewishness were not yet firmly established, and the rabbinic rules were still centuries in the future.

THE LAW

Jonathan Klawans

When it comes to understanding the New Testament in its Jewish context, few topics are as controversial, confusing, or complicated as the Law. The topic is controversial because Jews and Christians have argued among themselves and against each other regarding the validity and force of biblical law. Traditional-minded Jews continue to practice many biblical (and Talmudic) laws, even as many modernizing or secular Jews reject the traditional laws partially or completely. Paul insisted that Gentile followers of Jesus did not need to practice circumcision (Gen 17.9–14; cf. Gal 5.2), Mark's Gospel rejects the dietary restrictions (Lev 11.1–47; Deut 14.4–21; cf. Mk 7.19b), and many modern Christians have difficulty understanding why any Jews still practice such laws at all. Indeed, the stereotypically negative charge of Jewish *legalism*—tedious adherence to ancient rituals mixed with a misguided fascination with legal minutiae—has not fully evaporated from Christian critiques of Judaism, whether popular or scholarly. Yet anyone familiar with contemporary Christianity knows that the Mosaic Law has not been completely displaced. The Ten Commandments (Ex 20.1–17; Deut 5.6–21) are perhaps the most famous of the legal passages from the Torah whose literal meanings continue to have binding legal force for many Christians. Biblical prohibitions of homosexuality (Lev 18.22; 20.13) have also resurfaced in public discourse as passages taken literally and seriously by many conservative Christians, much to the chagrin of Christian liberals.

These controversies are further complicated by terminological confusion. The term "the Law" (*nomos*) appears nearly two hundred times in the New Testament, but no single understanding of the term applies in all instances. Moreover, the texts use other terms as well, including "commandment" (*entolē*, "charge, order, command"; e.g., Lk 15.29) and "tradition" (*paradosis*, "handing over, transmission"; e.g., Mk 7.9). Indeed the Gospel of Mark never mentions the term "law," despite its numerous depictions of Jesus arguing with Pharisees about various biblical commandments and traditional ritual practices (e.g., Mk 7.1–23). The topic is further complicated by the fact that ancient Jewish and Christian sources attest that legal matters were subject to dispute and undergoing dramatic development throughout the period of the New Testament. Yet at the same time, there are some striking agreements among Jews and Christians when it comes to the Law—depending, however, on how the term is understood.

To bring some clarity to the situation, we do well to begin with the first (though not necessarily earliest) New Testament passage that mentions the Law: the Gospel of Matthew's Sermon on the Mount (5.17): "Do not think that I have come to abolish the law or the prophets; I have come not to abolish but to fulfill." Here "law" and "prophets" refer to the first two sections of the Hebrew Bible: the Torah (Pentateuch) and Nevi'im (Prophets).

The term "law" remains uncapitalized in the quotation above, as is the case throughout the New Revised Standard Version (NRSV). Jewish translators, however, often prefer to capitalize the words used to translate *torah*. In 1 Kings 2.3, for instance, the NRSV renders the Hebrew *torat moshe* as "the law of Moses." The New Jewish Publication Society (NJPS) translation, by contrast, reads: "the Teaching of Moses." The latter is in keeping both with the traditional Jewish reverence for the Torah, as well as a more nuanced meaning of the Hebrew word *torah*. The NJPS translation appropriately reflects the fact that the Pentateuch contains not only laws but also many narratives—teachings that are nonlegal in nature (e.g., Genesis, the beginnings of Exodus and Deuteronomy).

If the NRSV's lower-case "law" can be traced to non-Jewish sensibilities, it must be pointed out that the translation itself—"law" over "teaching"—can reliably be traced back to ancient Jewish authorities. With nearly perfect consistency, the Jewish translations of the Hebrew Bible into Greek (produced piecemeal throughout the Hellenistic period and collectively known as the Septuagint [LXX]) render the Hebrew word *torah* with the Greek term *nomos*, which means "law." At times, the word *torah* does mean "law" (e.g., Lev 11.46). But perhaps more significant is the fact that the Torah, though it has important nonlegal, narrative components, is chock-full of laws, statutes, and ordinances (cf. 1 Kings 2.3). For these reasons, Greek-speaking Jews likely adopted the name *Nomos* ("Law") for the Torah.

This is not to say that Torah and the Law were synonymous for ancient Jews. As the Gospels and other writers are aware (e.g., Mk 7.1–23; Josephus, *Ant.* 18.297), first-century Pharisaic Jews in particular also adhered to nonbiblical traditions, such as the rule advocating hand-washing before meals. The Dead Sea Scrolls attest to a number of laws not found in the Hebrew Bible, such as a ruling prohibiting divorce (CD 4.19–5.6). Later rabbinic Jews derived many other laws from biblical texts by means of exegesis—that is, by midrash. For example, the biblical prohibition against putting a stumbling block before the blind (Lev 19.14) is understood in rabbinic texts to prohibit various kinds of deception by word or deed (*Sifra Kedoshim*, on Lev 19.14). Eventually, rabbinic Judaism comes to articulate a firm belief that divine revelation occurred in both written and oral forms: In a famous Talmudic story, the sage Hillel patiently instructs the would-be proselyte who has begun to study with him that there are two Torahs: one written down and the other oral (*b. Shabb.* 31b). Once this belief in a dual divine revelation (written and oral) takes root, entire realms of Jewish practice concerning food, Sabbath, and the synagogue (among other matters) can develop with hardly any basis in scripture whatsoever. These rulings come to be justified not by an appeal to scripture but by the belief that they derive from the Oral Torah. So while the (Written) Torah can reasonably be called "the Law," not all traditional Jewish law appears in the (Written) Torah.

Because "the Law" (Torah) is not the only or final word on what Jews considered to be law, it becomes be clear why, in Matthew's sermon, Jesus on the one hand asserts his desire to "fulfill the law" and at the same time asserts that the plain sense of a given passage from the Torah is insufficient. Consider Matthew 5.38–39: "You have heard that it was said, 'An eye for an eye and a tooth for a tooth.' But I say to you, Do not resist an evildoer." Although early rabbinic law offers no precise parallel to the principle of nonresistance, its understanding of the law of the *talion* ("an eye for an eye"; Ex 21.24–25; Lev 24.17–19; Deut 19.21) controverts the plain meaning of these biblical passages no less than does Matthew 5.39. Where the Pentateuch literally mandates corporal punishment in equal measure, rabbinic law mandates payment of fines commensurate with the pain, suffering, and lost abilities of the injured party (*m. B. Kamma* 8.1; *Mekhilta de-Rabbi Ishmael, Nezikin 8*, on Ex 21.24–25).

Consider also Matthew 5.31–32: "It was also said, 'Whoever divorces his wife, let him give her a certificate of divorce' [the reference is to Deut 24.1]. But I say to you that anyone who divorces his wife, except on the ground of unchastity, causes her to commit adultery." A tradition preserved among the Dead Sea Scrolls (CD 4.19–5.6) also suggests that divorce results in adultery. Both traditions apparently contradict at least one way of understanding the permission to divorce and remarry ostensibly granted (in Deut 24.1–2) . These examples illustrate that ancient Jewish law is not defined by the plain, literal sense of any given passage from the Torah. Paradoxically, therefore, Jesus' *fulfillment* of "the law" as articulated in Matthew's Sermon on the Mount can question the plain meaning of passages from "the Law" (the Pentateuch), even as it reaches some conclusions that are commensurate with Jewish law generally speaking.

Consequently, virtually all of the statements attributed to Jesus on "the law" specifically, or matters of Jewish rituals or ethics in general, can be placed within the broad context of ancient Jewish thought and practice. This is obviously the case for those passages that depict Jesus as adhering to the law, such as his instruction to the man he healed of leprosy: "Go, show yourself to the priest, and offer for your cleansing what Moses commanded, as a testimony to them" (Mk 1.44; Mt 8.4; Lk 5.14; cf. Lev 14.2–32). But this assessment also holds for the more controversial passages, such as Jesus' declaration to a would-be disciple: "Let the dead bury their own dead" (Mt 8.22; Lk 9.60), as well as the narrative concerning the plucking of grain on the Sabbath (Mt 12.1–8; Mk 2.23–28; Lk 6.1–5). Burial of deceased parent is an important facet of Jewish piety, and the Gospels themselves suggest that plucking a grain on the Sabbath apparently violated the oral traditions of the Pharisees (cf. *b. Shabb.* 73b). But neither of these pronouncements constitutes an unambiguous rejection of Jewish law.

The reasons for this are twofold. First, due to our paucity of sources contemporaneous with the Gospels, we cannot always reconstruct what various groups of Jews thought about matters of legal practice raised in the New Testament. For instance, we know little about Jewish mourning rites in the Second Temple period, and we know less about how non-Pharisaic Jews viewed the matter of plucking grain on the Sabbath. But the details we do *not* know are supplemented by some generalities we do know: ancient Jewish sources attest to a great variety of approaches to Jewish law and the interpretation of the Torah. We have already noted the dispute between the Pharisees and the Sadducees regarding the former's adherence to extrabiblical oral traditions. Among the Dead Sea Scrolls, 4QMMT presents a list of legal disputes, apparently between the Qumran sect and the Temple authorities. And the Temple Scroll from Qumran (11QTemple) rewrites the legal material from the Torah, making it look as if God revealed the architectural plans of a future temple directly to the people of Israel long ago. Further, there are legal treatises and biblical summaries by authors such as Philo and Josephus that diverge from scripture in their own ways without necessarily agreeing with the scrolls, later rabbinic sources, or any other known writer or group. We also know of groups of Jews who, at various times in antiquity, rejected much or even all of Jewish law, while nevertheless maintaining their identity as Jews and presumably believing in the Torah. The "extreme allegorizers" Philo describes (*Migr.* 89) serve as one example; the radical reformers who played a key role in the events leading up to the Maccabean revolt (1 Macc 1.10–13; 2 Macc 4.7–22) were another. According to Mark, perhaps Jesus would be a third example, if we are to accept the clarifying assertion advanced in Mark 7.19b: "thus he declared all foods clean." Scholars are nearly unanimous in rejecting this passage's authenticity: if there were a firmly established teaching of Jesus abrogating food laws, it is difficult to explain why this continued to be a controversy among the early followers of Jesus (e.g., Acts 10.9–16). Nevertheless, the legal statements attributed to Jesus in the Gospels fit within the broad range of ancient Jewish discourse on the law, precisely because that discourse was wide-ranging and diverse. Therefore, even when we cannot identify a precise parallel to a particular legal statement or practice associated with Jesus, we can still place the great majority of Gospel traditions concerning these matters within the broad diversity of ancient Jewish legal discourse and practice.

The situation is somewhat more complicated when it comes to considering Paul's place within this arena. Certainly Paul did not reject "the Law," when we understand that term to mean "the Pentateuch." Even in Galatians where he declares that salvation is by faith and "not by works of the law" (2.16), what is rejected (as a means of Pauline "salvation") is not the Pentateuch per se but some set of practices articulated within it, such as circumcision (5.2). Paul's displacement of "the works of the law" nonetheless leaves Pentateuchal narratives concerning figures such as Abraham and Hagar (e.g., Gal 3.15–18; 4.21–5.1) in a place of importance. These Paul affirms as eternally valid.

When speaking of his own background, Paul tells us that he was "as to the law, a Pharisee" (Phil 3.5). The book of Acts depicts Paul as claiming to have been reared "at the feet of Gamaliel" (22.6) and to have lived according to Pharisaic law (26.5). Yet at some point for Paul there was a break: in his words, he "died to the law" so that he "might live to God" (Gal 2.19). Indeed, some scholars believe that Paul made a clean and complete break with Jewish law. But the problem is that the apparently rejectionist stance articulated in Galatians is softened elsewhere: "Do we then overthrow the law by means of this faith? By no means! On the contrary, we uphold the law" (Rom 3.31).

Scholars frequently introduce two distinctions to help make sense of Paul's comments on the law. The first is one that looms large especially in Paul's discussion of the law in Romans (2.12–3.31): the contrast between Jews and Gentiles. This particular distinction also operates in later rabbinic law. Building on passages such as Genesis 9.1–17 (and possibly postbiblical traditions such as *Jub.* 7.20), the rabbis developed a list of seven "Noachide Laws" that constitute the minimal legal obligations imposed on Gentiles. According to one Talmudic listing (*b. Sanh.* 56a), Gentiles are prohibited from cursing God, idolatry, sexual immorality, bloodshed, robbery, and eating a limb off of a living animal; they are obligated to establish and maintain courts of law. This concept may shed light on Paul's assertion that some "Gentiles, who do not possess the law, do instinctively what the law requires" (Rom 2.14; cf. 2.21–24). Presumably keeping kosher is not what came naturally to such Gentiles, but avoiding bloodshed, robbery, and perhaps even idolatry could have come naturally to those Paul has in mind.

A second distinction—between ritual and moral laws—has also been adduced to explain Paul's position. Some scholars believe that Paul rejected the Torah's ritual or ceremonial laws but maintained its ethical laws. The value of this position is that it focuses precisely on Paul's vociferous rejection of specific rituals such as circumcision and food laws (e.g., Gal 5.2; Rom 14.14), at the same time making sense of his insistence on moral and sexual ethics (e.g., Rom 6.1–23; 1 Cor 5.1–13). But Paul does not draw a clear distinction between ritual and ethics; neither does rabbinic literature or any other Jewish legal source from the Second Temple period. Moreover, it is not clear that Paul's ethical advice is entirely rooted in Jewish Scripture. While Paul recites four of the Ten Commandments in one passage (Rom 13.8–10), he offers ritual and ethical advice without quoting scripture in others (e.g., Rom 14.13–23). Understanding Paul's view of the Law has proven difficult. Still, we can say that at least some "works of the law"—especially certain rituals concerning food and the body—troubled the apostle, particularly when practiced by Gentiles.

In the generations following Jesus and Paul, Judaism and Christianity moved in two very different directions with regard to the observances that characterized Second Temple Judaism. Rabbinic Jews maintained circumcision and expanded the dietary and Sabbath laws. Rabbinic Judaism also developed fuller systems of law to deal with marriage, civil matters, and criminal law, all the while maintaining the memory of laws concerning matters of purity and sacrifice that were no longer practiced following the Temple's destruction. These come to be recorded in the first great literary monument of rabbinic Judaism, the law book known as the Mishnah. Christianity, by contrast, moved in the direction of Galatians 5.2 and Mark 7.19b: foods were declared clean, circumcision was disregarded, and the Jewish holy days, Sabbaths, and other observances were replaced by distinctive Christian rites such as baptism. The writings of the early church thinkers take on a tone that is entirely different from the legal style of the Mishnah. And Judaism comes to be seen by some Christians—unfairly—as a *legalistic* religion.

Yet with regard to "the Law," when understood to mean the Pentateuch (the Torah), Christianity and rabbinic Judaism share more than is commonly realized. Christians include the Torah in their canon and believe it to be part of the "Old Testament"—the first covenant. It is, in other words, an authentic divine teaching that requires the fulfillment found in the New Testament, even while certain select passages (such as the Ten Commandments—see the Romans passage cited above) maintain their original significance. Jews too supplemented the Pentateuch with oral traditions and exegetical explanations, such that the Written Torah of Moses finds its completion for rabbinic Jews in the Oral Torah preserved in the Mishnah, Talmud, and other rabbinic writings. To be sure, traditional Judaism teaches that the Oral Torah is co-eternal with the Written, while Christianity considers the *Old* Testament fulfilled by something *New*. Yet Christians and rabbinic Jews have come to agree on one very important matter regarding what Greek-speaking Jews long ago called "the Law": The Pentateuch does not stand on its own, and indeed is quite often insufficient in its plain sense. Neither Christians nor rabbinic Jews have come to abolish the Law. And traditionally, Christians and Jews have fulfilled the Torah/Pentateuch by finding its deeper meanings somewhere else, be it the New Testament for Christians, or the Oral Torah for Jews.

THE SYNAGOGUE

Lee I. Levine

The synagogue was a unique and innovative institution that played a central role in Jewish life in antiquity, leaving an indelible mark on Christianity and Islam as well. It was the most prominent public space in Jewish communities throughout the Greco-Roman world (excluding pre-70 CE Jerusalem and perhaps several Jewish cities in Galilee) and was always the largest and most monumental building, often located in the center of a town or village. After 70 CE, it came to replace the Temple in Jerusalem as the central religious institution in Jewish life, and was revolutionary in a number of ways:

(1) *Location.* Unlike the Temple, the synagogue was universal in nature and enabled Jews everywhere to organize their communal life and worship ritual.

(2) *Leadership.* Anyone could hold a leadership position in the synagogue; functionaries were not restricted to a specific socioreligious group, as was the case in the Temple, where only priests could officiate.

(3) *Worship.* The synagogue provided a context for forms of worship other than the sacrifices that had dominated the Temple ritual, eventually embracing a wide range of religious activities, including scriptural readings, *targum* (the Aramaic translation of Scriptures), communal prayers, hymns, sermons, and *piyyut* (religious poetry).

(4) *Participation.* The synagogue included a wide range of worshipers in its ritual, unlike the Jerusalem Temple setting, where almost everyone in attendance remained in the outer "Women's Court," unless they themselves were offering a sacrifice. Worshipers in the synagogue, both men and women, were present throughout the entire service. The term "synagogue" (Gk *synagōgē*, "assembly," originally referring to a collection of persons, things, or writings) was used in the Septuagint, the Greek translation of the Hebrew Bible, for *edah*, "congregation" (e.g., Ex 12.3) and *qahal*, "assembly" (e.g., Deut 5.22). Based in part on these usages, it eventually became the term for the *beit keneset*, the "house of meeting."

JUDEAN SYNAGOGUES IN THE LATE SECOND TEMPLE PERIOD

Synagogues in Judea are first attested in the first century BCE, and in one case (Modi'in) perhaps as early as the second century BCE. From its inception, the communal dimension was the building's most prominent feature, and those excavated to date reflect an architectural plan befitting such a community-oriented institution. Synagogue structures in Gamla (in the Golan), Migdal (in the Galilee), Masada and Herodium (in the Judean Desert), as well as Qiryat Sefer and Modi'in (in the western Judean foothills) were all square or rectangular spaces with columns and benches on four sides (Qiryat Sefer had benches on only three sides), an arrangement that facilitated communal participation in political, religious, and social activities. The model chosen for these settings approximated the Hellenistic *bouleutērion* ("council chamber") or *ecclesiastērion* ("place of assembly"), which likewise catered to a group of people gathering for multiple purposes.

The religious dimension was also a significant component of the synagogue's agenda in this early period, although it should be placed in proper perspective given the natural propensity of both Jewish and Christian literary sources to emphasize this particular aspect of the synagogue's activities. Archaeological remains provide an important corrective to this proclivity. The first-century synagogue buildings uncovered to date were neutral structures devoid of notable religious components, such as inscriptions, artistic representations (Migdal excepted), or a permanent place for a Torah shrine. Scrolls appear to have been introduced into the synagogue hall expressly for the Torah-reading ceremony and were then removed. Architecturally, these early synagogues did not have the decidedly religious profile that a synagogue would have in Late Antiquity (see below). The inclusion of the social-communal aspects of the synagogue, along with its religious-educational functions, is clearly evidenced in the Theodotos inscription from first-century CE Jerusalem, which notes both these components:

> Theodotos, the son of Vettenos, priest and *archisynagōgos*, grandson of an *archisynagogōgos*, built this synagogue for the reading of the Law (= Torah) and the study of the commandments, and a guesthouse and rooms and water installations for hosting those in need from abroad, it (= the synagogue) having been founded by his fathers, the presbyters, and Simonides.

Jewish society of the late Second Temple period, both in Judea and the Diaspora, witnessed two contrasting, yet complementary, developments. On the one hand, the Temple assumed an ever-more central role in Jewish religious life, both because of the growth of Jerusalem as an urban center and focus of pilgrimage, and because the Temple Mount was now providing a wide range of social, economic, religious, and political services for Judean society. On the other hand, the synagogue was concurrently evolving into a distinct and defined center of local communal activity. Although the Temple was universally recognized as the central institution in Jewish life prior to its destruction in 70 CE, the emerging synagogue had now become the pivotal institution within almost every individual Jewish community. This parallel development of centralization and decentralization in the first centuries BCE and CE was indeed fortuitous, and although no one could have foreseen the tragedy of 70, the fact remains that the seeds of Jewish communal and religious continuity had already been sown beforehand.

DIASPORA SYNAGOGUES IN THE PRE-70 ERA

First evidenced in third-century BCE Hellenistic Egypt, the Diaspora synagogue is known to us through varied sources. Within each of the three major types of sources available—literary, archaeological, and epigraphic—there are substantial differences in the nature of the evidence and its historical value with regard to this Diaspora institution. The literary material, for example, includes references in Philo's commentaries and treatises (e.g., *Life of Moses* 3.27), edicts cited by Josephus (that of Augustus concerning a "sabbath house" [*Ant.* 16.6.2]), and Acts' accounts of Paul's visits to synagogues in Asia Minor and Greece (e.g., 14.1; 17.1–2; 18.4,7); all attest to the presence of synagogues throughout the Mediterranean world, from Italy eastward to Greece, Asia Minor, and Syria, as well as Egypt and North Africa.

This wide range of primary sources attests to a number of features shared by the pre-70 Diaspora *synagōgē* or *proseuchē* ("place of prayer"; e.g., Acts 16.13)—both widely used terms at this time. They subscribe to the centrality of this institution among far-flung Jewish communities, and this is reinforced by the fact that no other Jewish communal institution or building by any other name is ever noted.

As a result, the synagogue was the setting for all facets of communal life. It was a sine qua non in Diaspora Jewry's quest to preserve its Jewish identity. The synagogue distinguished Jews from the surrounding society by providing a place for fulfilling their communal religious, educational, social, political, and economic needs. In this respect, the Diaspora synagogue paralleled its Judean counterpart.

Although linked by a distinct (though not always easily defined) religious and ethnic heritage, Diaspora communities exhibited a striking degree of diversity stemming primarily from the fact that the Jews had no models of a communal facility from which to draw inspiration. In addition, Diaspora communities were exposed to patterns and models of neighboring cultures, adopting or adapting them to meet their needs. For instance, the names appearing in synagogue inscriptions often imitated those popular on the local scene. The donation of a synagogue building in Acmonia, a city in Phrygia, Asia Minor (modern Turkey) by Julia Severa, a prominent pagan aristocrat, reflects a type of patronage that was typical of this region; the organization and operation of the Jewish *politeuma* ("government") in Berenice (Cyrenaica, modern Libya) seems to derive, in part at least, from local Cyrenian models; the type of building used by the Jews of Delos bore similarities to other buildings on that island; and the formulary components of synagogue manumission decrees from Bosporus are well known and unique to that particular region.

Pagan interest in the synagogue is indicative not only of the institution's prominence but also of its importance and centrality to the Jewish community. Evidence of pagan sympathizers (God-fearers or *sebomenoi*) and converts throughout the Diaspora is ample (Mt 23.15; Acts 17.4), and in many instances these people were actively involved in the local Jewish community. Also noteworthy is the attraction of women to Judaism, a phenomenon attested throughout the Roman world (see esp. the book of Acts, e.g., 17.10–12).

The Diaspora synagogue was a creative synthesis of Jewish tradition, the specific requirements of each community, and the influence of the surrounding culture. Far from constituting an isolated and insulated minority—or the opposite, a people on the threshold of assimilation—the Jews succeeded in creating an institution that answered their needs, both as individuals and as a community, doing so within the confines of the cultural and social contexts in which they found themselves.

For all its borrowing and diversity, the Diaspora synagogue remained quintessentially Jewish, serving that community and housing its rites and observances, which were influenced first and foremost (though far from exclusively) by a common Jewish past and present. The Jews brought to the Diaspora their own *patria*, i.e., cultural and religious tradition, that pagans could either respect, resent, or ignore. These Jews were committed to honoring and perpetuating this heritage, and Roman society was, for the most part, supportive of safeguarding and transmitting an ethnic or religious group's traditional customs. On the communal level, the synagogue was the main conduit for achieving these goals.

THE LITURGY OF THE EARLY SYNAGOGUE (FIRST AND SECOND CENTURIES)

The fundamental form of worship in synagogues at this time, the Torah-reading ceremony, is explicitly mentioned in almost every type of source from the first century CE in Judea and the Diaspora, in cities as well as villages. Josephus makes this point clearly:

> He [Moses] appointed the Law to be the most excellent and necessary form of instruction, ordaining not that it should be heard once for all or twice or on several occasions, but that every week men should abandon their other occupations and assemble to lis-

> ten to the Law and to obtain a thorough and accurate knowledge of it, a practice that all other legislators seem to have neglected. (*Ag. Ap.* 2.175)

The New Testament preserves several important accounts of first-century synagogue liturgy as well:

> When he [Jesus] came to Nazareth, where he had been brought up, he went to the synagogue on the sabbath day, as was his custom. He stood up to read, and the scroll of the prophet Isaiah was given to him. He unrolled the scroll and found the place where it was written. (Lk 4.16–17)

> But they [Paul and his companions] went on from Perga and came to Antioch in Pisidia. And on the sabbath day they went into the synagogue and sat down. After the reading of the law and the prophets, the officials of the synagogue sent them a message. (Acts 13.14–15)

Thus, there can be little doubt that by the first century CE, Torah reading had become the core of Jewish synagogue worship. Several related liturgical features, although not as well attested, accompanied the Torah reading. For example, both the Gospel of Luke and the book of Acts refer to readings from the Prophets (*haftarot*) and sermons that followed the scriptural reading.

This liturgy was unique to the ancient world, as no such form of worship featuring the recitation and study of a sacred text by an entire community on a regular basis was in evidence at this time; we know only of certain mystery cults in the Hellenistic-Roman world that produced sacred texts, which were read on occasion to initiates. The self-laudatory tone of the Jewish sources may indeed reflect their authors' desire to trumpet this unique form of worship that set the Jewish community apart from its neighbors.

THE SYNAGOGUE IN LATE ANTIQUITY (THIRD TO SEVENTH CENTURIES)

In the centuries leading up to the end of Late Antiquity, Jewish society underwent many transformations, and there is no more illustrative an example of these far-reaching changes than the ancient synagogue. While continuing to function as a communal center, the synagogue of Late Antiquity began to acquire a significantly enhanced measure of sanctity—through its orientation to Jerusalem, its religiously infused artistic representations, its expanded liturgy, and the permanent presence of a Torah shrine, although each community utilized these components differently. Two complementary factors were at work here: the religious dimension stimulated in part by the non-Jewish social and religious milieux (especially the rise of Christianity in the fourth century and thereafter); and the communal dimension, which remained the central factor in determining how the synagogue, as a local institution par excellence, looked and functioned. The tastes and proclivities of each and every community determined the physical, functional, cultural, and religious aspects of the local synagogue.

The synagogue of Late Antiquity's primary historical significance was that it constituted the core institution for Jews everywhere. Despite its geographical, linguistic, cultural, and religious diversity, this communal institution and the ongoing expansion of its religious component provided a common framework for all Jewish communities. In a sense, the function fulfilled by the central and unique Jerusalem Temple in the pre-70 era was now carried out, mutatis mutandis, by the locally based, yet universally present, synagogue. It was indeed a "diminished sanctuary" (Ezek 11.16; *b. Meg.* 29a), one that served Jewish communal and religious needs throughout Late Antiquity and beyond.

FOOD AND TABLE FELLOWSHIP

David M. Freidenreich

Food and table fellowship figure prominently in the New Testament. Many of Jesus' parables draw on food imagery, such as salt, yeast, mustard seeds, and banquets, and he speaks of bread and wine as his body and blood. Jesus miraculously feeds large crowds, and he draws criticism for dining with sinners as well as for the fact that his followers do not fast. Leaders within the Jesus movements use table fellowship to unite believers and promote a sense of collective distinctiveness. Familiarity with Jewish dining practices deepens our understanding of the New Testament and, by extension, the nascent Christian community.

FOOD RESTRICTIONS WITHIN THE JESUS MOVEMENTS

The Torah prohibits its followers from consuming various types of meat (Lev 11, Deut 14); the Jewish practice of abstaining from pork was well known, and often maligned, in the Second Temple period (e.g., Tacitus, *Hist.* 5.4.2). The *Letter of Aristeas*, a Jewish text probably written during the second century BCE, and the first-century Alexandrian Jewish philosopher Philo both explain that the Torah's dietary norms offer lessons in moral virtue whose observance sets Jews apart from their immoral Gentile neighbors (*Ep. Arist.* 139–69; Philo, *Spec. Laws* 4.101).

Jesus and his disciples adhered to these food restrictions. Although Mark reports that Jesus "declared all foods clean" (7.19), it is clear from the context of this passage and its parallels (Mt 15.1–20; Lk 11.37–44) that this phrase constitutes an historically inaccurate gloss. In these passages, Jesus does not reject the dietary laws of the Torah but rather the more stringent Pharisaic requirement that food be consumed in a ritually pure fashion. Jesus contests other food practices associated with Jewish sectarians as well, such as the refusal to eat with non-sectarians and the frequent observance of fasting (Mt 9.10–1; Mk 2.15–20; Lk 5.29–35); but these stances in no way indicate ambivalence toward dietary laws found in the Torah.

Unlike Jesus, Paul declares that "nothing is unclean in itself; but it is unclean for anyone who thinks it unclean" (Rom 14.14). In other words, believers in Christ need not adhere to Jewish dietary laws, but those who regard these laws as binding should continue to obey them. To promote "peace and . . . mutual upbuilding," Paul encourages those who eat all foods to accommodate those who abstain (14.19). A later letter pseudonymously ascribed to Paul, in contrast, condemns abstinence from foods (1 Tim 4.3–4). Early Christian writers (e.g., the *Letter of Barnabas* [ca. 130], ch 10) polemicize against the Jews and those who would follow Jewish practice for their literal adherence to the Torah's dietary laws, insisting that these statements are purely allegorical.

In a letter called the "Apostolic Decree" (Acts 15.23–29), James the brother of Jesus, who is the leader of the Jerusalem Church, enjoins Gentile members to "abstain from what has been sacrificed to idols and from blood and from what is strangled." The last of these terms refers to meat from animals slaughtered in a manner that does not allow their blood to drain out. James also forbids *porneia*, sexual impropriety. The Apostolic Decree exempts Gentile Christ-believers from most Jewish dietary laws but requires them to observe two fundamental Jewish food taboos. Jews of the Second Temple period regarded consumption of food offered to idols as tantamount to idolatrous worship itself, and some embraced martyrdom rather than engage in such behavior (2 Macc 6–7; 1 Macc 1.62–63; cf. 4 Macc). Various passages in the Torah and Prophets compare consumption of blood to murder and declare that all people, or all in the covenant community, must abstain from such activity (Gen 9.3–6; Lev 17.10–12; Ezek 33.25–26). Early Christian authorities uniformly interpret the decree literally.

A faction within the community of Corinth saw nothing wrong with eating meat offered to idols (1 Cor 8). Paul, in contrast, declares that "You cannot drink the cup of the Lord and the cup of demons. You cannot partake of the table of the Lord and the table of demons" (10.21). Paul does, however, allow Christ-believers to eat food purchased in the marketplace or served in the homes of non-believers so long as they do not know that this food had been offered to idols (10.25–29; cf. 5.9–10). In the Greco-Roman world, much of the meat available in the market came from sacrifices in local temples, and adherents of traditional Hellenistic religions regularly served sacrificial food at home. Paul's permissive stance regarding meat whose provenance is unknown finds parallels within early rabbinic literature, which does not subject such meat to the stringent prohibitions associated with idolatry either (*t. Hul.* 2.20).

THE LORD'S SUPPER

Paul's letters and Acts of the Apostles make clear that the commemoration of the final meal that Jesus shared with his followers, the Last Supper or Lord's Supper, constitutes the central ritual of the community. Because of its significance, Paul warns, those who participate must do so not to satisfy physical hunger but to unite in remembrance of Jesus' death. Paul reports that Jesus himself instituted this ritual during his last meal with the disciples (1 Cor 11.17–34). Matthew, Mark, and Luke associate the Last Supper with the Passover meal, in which Jews gathered in Jerusalem to consume the meat of their sacrificial lambs. (The seder is a later development after the destruction of the Temple, when the paschal lamb was no longer offered.) John, in contrast, portrays Jesus himself as the sacrificial lamb and dates the crucifixion to the time the Paschal lambs are sacrificed in the Temple, an event that precedes the Passover meal (19.14,31,36). Historically, John's dating has much to commend it. If the accounts of Jesus' trial before the Jewish authorities and then before the Roman procurator, Pontius Pilate (Mt 26.57–27.26; Mk 14.53–15.15; Lk 22.54–23.25), are an accurate reflection of the events, it is highly unlikely that they would have taken place once Passover had begun. The Temple authorities would more likely have put off any trials until after the festival, or at least until the first day had passed.

Paul treats bread and wine, staples in Mediterranean antiquity, as the primary elements—the "body" and "blood," respectively—of the Lord's Supper. In their later accounts, Mark and Matthew also associate these elements with Jesus' body and blood. "Those who eat my flesh and drink my blood have eternal life," Jesus declares in John 6.54. This statement both reinforces the significance of the Lord's Supper and alludes to the biblical motif of ingesting God's words (e.g., Ezek 3.1–3; Prov 24.13–14); John declares explicitly that Jesus is the Word incarnate (Jn 1.14).

Unlike the present-day celebration of the Lord's Supper (also known as the Eucharist, Holy Communion, the Mass, or the Divine Liturgy), the practice in the New Testament period was to serve a full meal, a Christian version of the Greco-Roman banquet. Communal worship, moreover, apparently occurred in the course of this banquet (see 1 Cor 11.17–34). Within the Greco-Roman world, the banquet (commonly but imprecisely called the symposium, which is a "drinking meal") constituted an especially important means of strengthening bonds within social groups. It is no surprise, therefore, that Paul employs exclusion from table fellowship as a means of disciplining sinful members (1 Cor 5.11). Paul and other leaders of the Jesus movements treat commensality, the act of eating together, as a proxy for their debates over the status of Gentiles as members of the Christ-believing community: if non-Jewish converts are included at the table, they are full-fledged members.

TABLE FELLOWSHIP BETWEEN JEWS AND GENTILES

Paul insists that membership in the church is open to Jews and Gentiles without distinction. For that reason, he sharply rebukes Peter (called Cephas) for withdrawing from commensality with Gentiles "for fear of the circumcision faction" (Gal 2.11–14). Paul may tolerate continued observance of other Jewish food practices (Rom 14), but he insists that all Christ-believers, Jewish and Gentile, can and ought to eat together as equals. Others within the church, whom Paul calls "the circumcision faction," affirm the ongoing relevance of the Jew/Gentile distinction and consequently object to commensality between Jews and Gentiles, even among those who believe in Christ. This objection conforms to norms found in numerous Jewish works from the Second Temple period: Jews ought not share meals with Gentiles or eat food prepared by them (Dan 1.8–12; Jdt 10–12; Tob 1.10.11; Add Esth C.26; *Jub.* 22.16).

Jesus himself reportedly adhered to these traditional norms. He eats with those among the Jewish populace who are socially derogated, the "tax collectors and sinners," comparing his behavior to a physician's focus on the sick (Mt 9.10–13; Mk 2.15–18; Lk 5.29–32). Jesus does not, however, eat with Gentiles nor, as a general rule, does he minister to them (see Mt 15.21–28; Mk 7.24–30 for a telling exception). Those around him take for granted that Jesus, a Jew, would not eat the food of Samaritans (Jn 4.9,33). Jesus envisions a time when faithful Gentiles will eat with Abraham, Isaac, and Jacob in the kingdom of heaven (Mt 8.11; cf. Lk 13.29), but the fact that no early Christian figure invoked Jesus' own practice in support of commensality with Gentiles indicates that they had no tradition of his engaging in such behavior.

Acts, which portrays "the breaking of bread" as a paradigmatic activity of Christ-believers (2.42), uses commensality as a motif to describe the process through which the community opened to Gentile participation. Peter, criticized by "circumcised believers" for his decision to "go to uncircumcised men and eat with them," justifies his willingness to convert the centurion Cornelius and his Gentile household on the basis of a vision he experienced (Acts 10–11). (The content of the vision suggests that Peter ought not distinguish between permitted and prohibited meat, but the message Peter takes from it is that he ought not distinguish between Jews and Gentiles.) When the apostles meet to consider whether Gentile Christ-believers must adhere to the Torah in order to join the community, Peter reminds them that God bestowed the Holy Spirit upon Cornelius and his associates even though they were not Jewish. The apostles rely on this precedent in ruling that Gentiles, so long as they adhere to the conditions listed in the Apostolic Decree, may become full-fledged members of the Christ-believing community (15.1–29).

Acts presents the Jerusalem council as a turning point in the history of the early Christ-believing community because it eases the way for Gentiles to join its ranks. The following chapters recount Paul's outreach efforts toward Gentiles, work that regularly involves shared meals (16.15,34). One incident is especially symbolic of the growing estrangement of Christ-believers from the Jewish community: when the Jews of Corinth spurn Paul's message, he leaves the synagogue and accepts the hospitality of a neighboring Gentile (18.6–7). On a ship lost at sea, Paul takes bread from the ship's provisions, gives thanks, and breaks bread with his fellow 276 passengers (27.33–37). Paul's actions allude to those of Jesus, who fed the multitudes in the same manner (Lk 9.16); unlike Jesus, however, Paul breaks bread with—and spreads the gospel to—Gentiles.

As the movement of Jesus' followers developed into a more institutional form of Christianity, it became necessary to define the identity and proper behavior of true Christians. Polemic against Jewish dietary practices played an important role in this process of self-definition.

The New Testament, however, reflects the degree to which Jesus and his immediate followers conformed to Jewish dietary practices. It highlights, moreover, efforts on the part of the first leaders of the new movement to accommodate both Jewish and Gentile followers within a single community.

IOUDAIOS

Joshua D. Garroway

Ioudaios (f. *Ioudaia*, pl. *Ioudaioi*) is the Greek word for "Jew" or "Judean." Translators usually prefer to render it in English as "Jew" when *Ioudaios* designates anyone adhering to Judaism, specifically the laws, customs, rituals, or beliefs associated with the God of Israel. "Judean" is used when the term refers in a strictly political or geographical sense to one living in or originating from the region of Judea. However, the translation of *Ioudaios* is contentious.

When Alexander the Great conquered the Persian Empire in the late fourth century BCE, one of the many lands he obtained was a small province, centered upon Jerusalem, called *Yehud* in Aramaic (Ezra 5.1; 5.8; 7.14). This name stemmed from the kingdom of Judah (Heb *Yehudah*)—the Southern Kingdom under the descendants of King David, who had ruled that land—after the separation from the Northern Kingdom of Israel in the late tenth century BCE, for more than three centuries before its occupation, first by the Babylonians (597–586 BCE), then by the Persians (539 BCE). Greek-speakers such as Clearchus of Soli (ca. 300 BCE) soon began referring to this region as *Ioudaia*, "Judea," and its inhabitants as *Ioudaioi*, "Judeans." This correspondence between the name of a region and its resident "people" (Gk *ethnos*) was common in Greek: Athenians lived in Athens, Egyptians in Egypt, and so, Judeans in Judea. Such ethno-geographic labels were maintained even when one resided abroad. People in Alexandria, for example, who were descended from *Ioudaioi* and lived according to their laws and customs, would be known as *Ioudaioi* even if their families had lived in Alexandria for generations. *Ioudaios* was rarely, if ever, a preferred self-designation. Among themselves *Ioudaioi* favored the older terms, known from the Tanakh: Israel, Israelites (*huioi Israel*, "sons of Israel" in LXX), or Hebrews (*Hebraioi*).

As with any term of identity, dispute and/or confusion at times emerged in antiquity over who properly should be called a *Ioudaios*. The problems began in the second century BCE, when an important development complicated the definition of the term *Ioudaios*. When the Hasmonean kings expanded Judean hegemony by conquering regions to the north and south of Judea—e.g., Samaria, Galilee, and Idumea—they imposed their laws on the native populations. As a result, many who previously had no ethnic or geographic connection to Judea became *Ioudaioi*, inasmuch as they resided on lands controlled by Judea and obeyed its laws. Yet, opinions varied regarding the extent to which one actually became a *Ioudaios* through such incorporation.

The Idumeans to the south provide a good example. They were conquered in 125 BCE by the Hasmonean king John Hyrcanus, who allowed them to stay on their land provided they adopted the laws of the *Ioudaioi*. According to the first-century CE historian Josephus (*Ant.* 13.257–58), those who did so became *Ioudaioi*. In contrast, a contemporary historian named Ptolemy (Ammonius, *De Adfinium Vocabulorum Differentia*, no. 243) stated that even though the Idumeans came to be called *Ioudaioi* once they submitted to the new way of life, they were nevertheless different from *Ioudaioi* because originally they constituted a separate ethnic group. This is one reason why Herod the Great, a descendant of Idumeans, faced objections to the legitimacy of his kingship over the *Ioudaioi*. Josephus (*Ant.* 14.403) reports that one of Herod's early rivals disputed his right to rule because, being an Idumean, he was only a *hemiioudaios*, a half- or partial-*Ioudaios*. Political incorporation of outsiders during the reign of the Hasmoneans thus broadened and complicated the parameters of the term *Ioudaios*.

A second important development was the emergence of conversion. While a process of conversion may be suggested by the Hebrew *mityahadim* in Esther 8.17 (fourth- or third-century BCE), it had become a well-attested practice by the first century BCE. The beliefs and way of life of the *Ioudaios* appeared attractive to many Gentiles. Some expressed their affection through benefactions to communities of *Ioudaioi*; others adopted certain of their rituals or beliefs; still others became proselytes, which meant confessing allegiance to the God of Israel, supporting God's Temple in Jerusalem, participating in a local synagogue, and living in accordance with the ancestral laws and customs of the *Ioudaioi*. Yet, it remains unclear to what extent proselytes became full-fledged *Ioudaioi* as a result of their conversion. The later rabbinic literature suggests that they did not. Even the most generous estimation of converts declares them to be "like an Israelite in all respects" (*b. Yebam.* 47b): *like* an Israelite but not a *native* Israelite, a distinction with ramifications in certain legal and liturgical contexts. For example, a female convert was forbidden from marrying a priest.

Evidence from non-rabbinic environments is more difficult to construe. Outsiders such as Epictetus (mid-first to mid-second century CE) (Arrian, *Dissertations of Epictetus* 2.19–21 [early- to mid-second century CE]) believed that proselytes became *Ioudaioi*. Certain of the Dead Sea Scrolls, however (e.g., 4QFlor; 11QSTemple), indicate that proselytes were distinguished from Israelites and were either forbidden to enter the Temple or allowed to pass only as far as the outer court. This evidence from Qumran, alongside an inscription from the Temple Mount barring entrance to the "foreign born" and a dispute between Simon and Agrippa reported by Josephus (*Ant.* 19.332–34), has led some to suppose that certain priestly circles believed native *Ioudaioi* should be distinguished from proselytes when it came to participation in sacrificial worship. Philo calls for legal equality for proselytes and praises their resolve, but he never says they become *Ioudaioi* (e.g., *Life of Moses* 1.147; *Virtues* 102–3). Josephus, on the other hand, does use the term *Ioudaios* when reporting the conversion of Queen Helena of Adiabene (*Ant.* 20.2–4), and the book of Judith says that Achior the Ammonite "joined the house of Israel" (Jdt 14.10). Thus, whether a proselyte was considered a full-fledged *Ioudaios* seems to have depended on the proselyte in question and the perspective of the observer.

The rise in the importance of conversion may be significant because it could point to a transformation in the meaning of the term *Ioudaios*, which in turn explains its traditional translation into English. Since conversion is understood to be a *religious* act, in which a change in belief prompts modifications in lifestyle, there must have arisen at least by the second century BCE a distinct cultural and religious aspect to the word *Ioudaios*. Many correlate this development to a parallel shift in the Greek term *Hellēn*, "Hellene," which in the centuries after Alexander came to signify not only a resident or descendant from Greece, but also anyone committed to Greek culture, thus *Hellenismos* or "Hellenism." *Ioudaios* likewise came to describe anyone devoted to the beliefs and practices of the *Ioudaioi*: *Ioudaïsmos* or "Judaism." Since the English word "Jew" captures this religious aspect better than "Judean" does, translators since the emergence of modern English in the sixteenth century have preferred it as a rendering of *Ioudaios* whenever the religious connotation is primary, reserving "Judean" only for those cases in which context demands specific emphasis on the ethno-geographic sense. When an author refers only to the *Ioudaioi* inhabiting Judea, for example, a translator would choose "Judean" instead of "Jew" (e.g., *Ant.* 11.173).

In recent years, some scholars have argued that translating *Ioudaios* with two terms—"Jew" for the religious connotation and "Judean" for the ethno-geographic one—is anachronistic. Only after the development of Christianity, these scholars maintain, did it become viable to speak of religion or religious identity as a discrete realm of human experience, separable from ethnicity or place of origin. What we understand to be "religion"—belief in God(s), customs associated with the worship of that God, and so on—was thought by the ancients to be integral to one's ethno-geographic affiliation. The term *Ioudaios* designated a person who was from or whose ancestors were from Judea, and for that reason worshiped the God of Judea. It was thoroughly an ethno-geographic term and thus, according to this scholarly view, should always be translated "Judean." Likewise, *Ioudaïsmos* should not be rendered as "Judaism," which conveys anachronistically the notion of a discrete religion, but rather as "Judeanism," "Judeanness," "Judean ways," or some other expression that captures the basic connection of the term to the land of Judea and its people. Conversion, on this view, was not a change in religion as we might understand it, but the adoption of beliefs, laws, and customs of another *ethnos*. Proselytes did not accept "Judaism," a religion, but rather the conventions of the people inhabiting Judea. Only in the wake of the rabbis is it possible to speak of *Ioudaioi* with the religious terms "Jew" and "Judaism," although it should be noted that rabbinic literature employs the Hebrew and Aramaic equivalents of "Jew" and "Judaism" sparingly, preferring the ancient self-designation "Israel."

Other scholars oppose the change in translation, insisting that *Ioudaios* indeed possesses a uniquely religious connotation in antiquity, which at times prevails over its ethno-geographic counterpart. They point to Acts 2, for example, which states that the *Ioudaioi* gathered in Jerusalem at Pentecost derive from "every nation (Gk *ethnos*) under heaven," and subsequently identifies them with explicit ethno-geographic labels: Parthian, Elamite, Cretan, Arab, and so on. This makes *Ioudaios* look more like a religious label, "Jew" rather than "Judean," in the modern sense. So, too, when Josephus refers to a certain Atomos as "a *Ioudaios*, but a Cyprian by birth" (*Ant.* 20.142), the former sounds like the designation of a religious identity, the latter his ethnicity or place of origin.

The issue of how to translate *Ioudaios* is not entirely academic. It holds ramifications for contemporary Jewish identity and Jewish-Christian relations as well. Translators of the term, particularly in New Testament texts, often justify their choice with moral as well as intellectual arguments. Some advocates for "Judean" claim that applying the term "Jew" to the *Ioudaioi* of antiquity is incorrect not only because it anachronistically attributes to them a uniquely religious identity, but also because it might lead to anti-Jewish prejudice: readers may associate today's Jews with the *Ioudaioi* of the New Testament, who are described as being "from . . . the devil" (Jn 8.44) or of having "killed both the Lord Jesus and the prophets" (1 Thess 2.15). The word "Judean" disassociates contemporary Jews from such harsh rebukes in the New Testament and makes it more difficult for anti-Judaism to find a scriptural foothold.

Those who prefer "Jew" say just the opposite. Purging "Jews" from New Testament texts by replacing them with "Judeans," even if well intentioned, too eerily resembles the efforts of outspoken anti-Semites, both past and present, who have tried to erase the Jewish origins of Jesus and Christianity. Much European scholarship in the nineteenth and early twentieth centuries held that since Jesus was from Galilee, rather than Judea, he was not a Jew but a Galilean. This trend climaxed in Nazi propaganda, which depicted Jesus as a racial Aryan who opposed Judaism vigorously. Jesus and Christianity were thus entirely free of Jewish taint.

The removal of the word "Jews" from ancient texts also undermines the Jews' own sense of continuity. Jews traditionally do not trace their roots only as far as the rabbinic period, as if this were the time when they ceased being ethno-geographic Judeans and became religious Jews. Rather, they understand themselves to be the latest link in an unbroken chain of tradition originating in the age of the Tanakh; and, with several obvious exceptions, such as Temple sacrifice and pilgrimage to Jerusalem for Passover, Shavuot (Weeks/Pentecost), and Sukkot (Booths), the characteristic practices of ancient *Ioudaioi* are still those kept by observant Jews today: Sabbath, circumcision, festivals, dietary laws, and so on. By the first century CE one could add to that list the veneration of the Torah, participation in synagogues, and the like. To suggest by way of terminology that contemporary Jews differ essentially from ancient Judeans disregards these crucial similarities. Moreover, even today the term "Jew" is not bereft of ethno-geographic content. Many Jews pray regularly for a return to the land of Israel and/or the rebuilding of the Temple, pray facing Jerusalem, send their children there on "Birthright" trips, and conclude the Passover Seder with the proclamation, "Next year in Jerusalem." They also reckon their identity according to birth and routinely speak of "peoplehood." In this respect, "Jew" might capture the connection between the ancient *Ioudaios* and his or her ancestral homeland just as well as "Judean."

In the end, then, it is prudent to be circumspect when reading in translation any ancient Greek text that mentions "Jews" or "Judeans." Underlying both terms is the Greek *Ioudaios*, and the translator's preference invariably reflects certain aims and assumptions.

JEWISH MOVEMENTS OF THE NEW TESTAMENT PERIOD

Daniel R. Schwartz

The development of Judaism from the fourth century BCE through the period covered by the New Testament (the first and second centuries CE) is a complex story that is still not fully understood. When early Judaism emerges from the fourth and third centuries BCE, which are hardly documented, into the second, the sources—now much more abundant—frequently refer to groups of Jews that bear distinct names and seem, therefore, to have had their own identities. Such groups as the *Asidaioi* ("pious people, religious ones") mentioned in 1 Macc 7.13 and 2 Macc 14.6, and the three schools of thought or "philosophies" (Pharisees, Sadducees, and Essenes) that Josephus (*Ant.* 13.171) says existed around the middle of the second century BCE, are sometimes termed "sects" by modern scholars, since none of the groups represents a majority or near-majority of Jews living at the time.

More evidence about these groups was supplied by the discovery, beginning in 1947, of a sectarian settlement and scrolls at Qumran, near the Dead Sea. These testify to a separatist group that called itself "the *Yaḥad*" ("togetherness") and referred to rival groups by such biblical sobriquets as "Ephraim," "Manasseh," and "Seekers of Smooth Things" (cf. Isa 30.10). Probably those names refer to the Sadducees and the Pharisees, condemning the former as if they were comparable to the northerners (Ephraim, Manasseh) who rebelled from the Davidic kingdom and set up a rival cult (1 Kings 12.25–33), and condemning the latter as if they held overly lenient and self-serving positions on Jewish law. The latter identification is especially attractive on the assumption that the denunciation of the "Seekers of Smooth Things" [*doreshei ḥalaqot*] was meant to mock a Pharisaic self-understanding as *doreshei halakhot*, "those who seek [to follow or determine] *halakhot* (religious laws)." The Qumran *Yaḥad* itself is apparently to be identified as those by Josephus and others called Essenes. Pliny, a Roman scholar of the first century, refers to an Essene settlement near the Dead Sea, thus offering strong support for that identification, although some controversy about it still persists.

The New Testament books do not mention the Essenes, but the Gospels and Acts refer to Pharisees and Sadducees and Paul, in one of his epistles (Phil 3.5), claims that he himself was a Pharisee. Moreover, the New Testament books additionally testify to the circles that formed around John the Baptist and Jesus, as well as some others (e.g., Acts 5.36–37; see "Messianic Movements," p. 530), and they also supply some references to yet another type of group—anti-Roman rebels known as Sicarii (Acts 21.38; see also 5.37). That Latin name means "dagger-men" and thus designates them as terrorists, reflecting a Roman point of view; Josephus (*Ant.* 18.9), who denounces the Sicarii for their violence and role in bringing about the final rebellion and destruction of the Temple, nonetheless terms them a "fourth philosophy" alongside his main trio of Pharisees, Sadducees, and Essenes.

The various testimonies to these groups, to which we may add the later evidence of rabbinic literature (see "Messianic Movements," p. 530), are sporadic and often tantalizingly brief or ambiguous. Moreover, even when they do furnish seemingly useful information it may reflect the interests and views of the ancient writers at least as much as those of the groups described. Thus, when speaking about the Pharisees and Sadducees, Luke focuses on their respective belief and disbelief concerning resurrection (Lk 20.27–40; Acts 23.6–8). This corresponds so well to the interests of the Christian historian that we may wonder how central that issue was for those two sects themselves, which also differed on many other more practical and immediate issues. Similarly, we may suspect that Josephus skewed his account of the Essenes to encourage Roman readers to view them with admiration as disciplinarians in their own image; his explanations that the Essenes were celibate because they thought women could not be faithful (*J.W.* 2.121), or because they thought marriage only led to quarrels (*Ant.* 18.21), may have more to do with his own experiences with women, which included two divorces (*Life* 415, 426), than with the Essenes' own considerations. In any case, most of our sources were written by outsiders and, even apart from their biases, they may not have been well informed about other groups. The following is an attempt, despite these difficulties, to summarize what we know about these sects and to suggest that we understand them all as responding to the fundamental issue that all Jews had to address in the Hellenistic and Roman periods: Could, and should, being Jewish remain natural, a product of one's birth—something most appropriate to life in Judea? Or was it, rather, to be something undertaken deliberately—an orientation more appropriate to a diaspora situation?

FROM PHARISEES VS. SADDUCEES TO RABBIS VS. PRIESTS

Of the two schools of thought that are most prominent, the Pharisees and the Sadducees, the former are treated in the sources primarily according to their orientation toward Torah. For example, Matthew 12 opens with a story about the Pharisees' insistence upon the Sabbath laws; Acts 5.34 mentions a law-teacher named Gamaliel as one of their leaders, just as Josephus, referring to the next generation, mentions one Simeon ben Gamaliel (son and successor of Gamaliel) as a leader of the Pharisees in a passage in which Josephus characterizes the Pharisees as noted for their precision in matters of Jewish law (*Life* 191). Paul similarly identified himself "as to the law, a Pharisee" (Phil 3.5). These texts correspond to the fact that rabbinic literature of the first several centuries of our era focuses on knowledge of the law and refers to Gamaliel and his son Simeon as early heroes of the rabbinic movement, just as it also frequently condemns the Sadducees and sides with the Pharisees in their disputes with the Sadducees. The Pharisees thus are likely a "proto-rabbinic" movement, although there were certainly differences between the Pharisees of the days of the Temple and the rabbis of the later period.

The Sadducees, in contrast, are often treated in connection with the high priesthood. At Acts 5.17 Luke glosses "the high priest . . . and all those who were with him" with "that is, the sect of the Sadducees." That jives quite well with the fact that the very name "Sadducee" derives from "Zadok," the name of the high priest in the days of David and Solomon; according to the Hebrew Bible (1 Chr 6.1–15; Ezra 3.2; Neh 12.10–11,22; cf. *Ant.* 20.234), Zadok founded the dynasty that provided high priests down to the second century BCE (see Sir 51 [Hebrew addition] "Give thanks to him who has chosen the sons of Zadok to be priests"); although at that point the Hasmoneans ("Maccabees") took over the high priesthood, the Zadokites/Sadducees nonetheless remained prominent thereafter. This high-priestly nexus is supported by various points in rabbinic literature (e.g., *b. Yoma* 19b;

53a) and also by Josephus, who reports that James, the brother of Jesus, was executed at the instigation of a Sadducean high priest (*Ant.* 20.199–200).

Recognition of the high-priestly nature of the Sadducees allows us to expand our understanding of them in two ways. First, just as the Pharisees' focus on Gamaliel and on law allowed us to align them with the later rabbis, the Sadducees' priestly orientation suggests a similarity to the Qumran sect, though with some tensions between the groups. The similarity rests in the fact that the Qumran sectarians too were very much occupied by priestly issues. Note, for example, their concern with ritual purity and with the laws focused on priestly matters in the Temple Scroll (11QSTemple), and that according to its most basic rules, the sect entrusted supreme authority to the priests: "only the sons of Aaron shall rule with regard to law and property, and according to their say shall decisions be made concerning all matters concerning the people of the *Yaḥad*" (1QS 9.7). Thus, although there were certainly differences and at times even hostility between the Sadducees and the Qumran sectarians, we may nevertheless view them both as priestly sects. Just as we may meaningfully contrast modern Protestants to Catholics even though there are differences among denominations of Protestants, so too should we view the Sadducees and the Qumran sect as "denominations" of priestly Judaism that may be contrasted with the Pharisaic/proto-rabbinic type of Judaism.

PRIESTS VS. RABBIS: INHERITED ROLES AND CHOSEN ROLES

The similarity of the Sadducees and the Qumran sect allows us to use the Dead Sea Scrolls as evidence for the nature of the Sadducees too and facilitates our understanding of what being "priestly" implied. Among Jews, priests are born, as sons of priests (Aaronites). Among Pharisees and rabbinic Jews, in contrast, those who excel in the study of the Torah became rabbis if and when their teachers and their communities decided to recognize them as such. This suggests that priestly Jews would tend to assume that the rules dealing with the sacred and with binding obligations are established by nature, whereas Pharisaic and rabbinic Jews would tend to think that human decisions play a much more important role. This was reinforced by the institutions within which priests and rabbis usually worked, and which granted them their status: for the priests religious life was focused upon the one Temple of Jerusalem, of which the location was determined (so the Bible teaches) by God; for the Pharisees and rabbis (even before the Temple was destroyed in 70 CE and certainly thereafter) were typically associated with houses of study and synagogues, which were founded at will by Jewish individuals and communities. (See "The Synagogue," p. 519.)

This distinction, between roles acquired by birth and those that are chosen, seems to have been at the heart of the distinction between these two types of Jews, and it had significant implications. For example, anyone who believes that religious status derives in the first place from the facts of birth is likely to have doubts about the possibility of conversion to Judaism. Indeed, several texts bespeak the priestly view that although Gentiles might associate themselves with the community, they cannot become Jews. Thus, Greek inscriptions on the Temple Mount forbade the entry of the *allogenēs* (person of non-Jewish birth) beyond a certain limit; cols. 39–40 of the Temple Scroll from Qumran forbids converts entry into the Temple's inner courts; and the Damascus Document (CD 14.3–6) treats converts as a fourth group alongside priests, Levites, and "Israel." Similarly, since a belief in immortality or resurrection entails the belief that there is a soul independent of the body, and there is tension between that and the definition of priests according to their birth with no regard to anything pertaining to their souls, it is no surprise that the priestly sects denied life after death, as is reported by Josephus (*Ant.* 18.16) and the New Testament (note esp. Mk 12.18–27 and parallels, also Acts 4.1–2 and 23.6–8). Again, Jews of a priestly orientation, whose religious life centered on the Temple of Jerusalem, will have found it somewhat difficult to take a synagogue seriously, since their own status was reinforced by the fact that they, but not those who do not share priestly birth, could enter into the Temple's sacred sphere and minister in the Temple service. Rather, priests tended to adhere to the notion of a natural law, that is, that the values inherent in nature ("written on their hearts . . . conscience," as Paul put it in Rom 2.15) are indeed binding, whereas Pharisees and rabbis preferred to hold that, just as with regard to the making of religious leaders and location of religious institutions, it is human decisions that endow things with their importance and their legal status.

Thus, for example, a central Qumran text insists that the calendar must correspond to the movements of the moon, with "no moving times up or moving holidays back" and with "no deviation right or left" (1QS 1.14–15), which is an allusion to Deut 17.11. The rabbis, in contrast, insisted that their court's decisions about the new moon must be accepted even if they were wrong astronomically (*m. Rosh Ha-Shana* 2.8), and on the basis of the same verse in Deuteronomy they argued that courts' decisions must be followed even if they declare the right to be left or the left to be right. On the other hand, the Mishnah reports (*m. Ketub.* 13.2) that since it is obviously natural and fair to expect that a man who traveled abroad will reimburse a neighbor who supported his family in his absence, "the sons of the high priests" held that such a husband was indeed required to do so. The rabbis, in contrast, held that the fact that the neighbor had not formulated the matter as a loan, via promissory note or the like, meant that it could not obligate the husband. That is, even at the expense of rejecting a demand that is obviously fair, the rabbis demonstratively held that it is decisions that matter. The things that matter, and oblige us, are not simply so; rather, they acquire that status because we decided to call them so. The rabbis, that is, held that months and debts are like rabbis: they are not natural, instead, they are created or determined by human decision. Priests, in contrast, held that months and debts were in effect "natural" occurrences created, like themselves, by nature.

THE OTHER GROUPS: FILLING OUT THE EXTREMES

At this point, we can place the other sects in relation to the Pharisees and Sadducees. Those two sects, we may assume, were fairly centrist. The Sadducees, who depended upon the values of sacred birth and sacred place, represent the nationalist position that reflects the basic ethnic values of a people living in its land. Even more traditional than the Sadducees (so somewhat to their "right") was the Qumran sect; if earlier we noted its priestly orientation, now we may add that it must have been more doctrinaire about it than were the Sadducees, for the latter remained well represented in Jerusalem, at the center of Jewish society, while the Qumran sectarians, unhappy about what they considered mismanagement of the Temple and corruption of the priesthood, chose a separatist and self-imposed exile. Still more doctrinaire, as far as nationalist beliefs are concerned, were the movements of anti-Roman rebels, such as the Sicarii, whose rebelliousness derived from their uncompromising devotion to the value of Holy Land—a value that was centered around the axis of priestly Judaism, the Temple, which, as what the Bible frequently terms "the house of God," was the linchpin of the Land's sanctity. The Romans' demand that Judea be ruled from Rome, not from Jerusalem, contradicted that biblical notion diametrically, and the Sicarii and other rebels were willing to risk all to terminate that anomaly. Indeed, in the end they rebelled and the anomaly was removed—but by the destruction of the Temple, not by the end of Roman rule in Judea.

The basic orientation of the Pharisees and proto-rabbis, namely, the ascription of importance to things we decide upon rather than givens, was, in contrast, the basic principle of diasporan existence. For if is natural for those in Judea to do like the Judeans and for those in Rome to do like the Romans, and they do it by default, the only way Judeans in Rome (or elsewhere in the Diaspora) could go on doing what Judeans do is for them to decide to do what is unnatural: although they could not adhere to Judea, they could adhere to Juda*ism*, if they chose to do so despite their natural circumstances. Moreover, Jews in the Diaspora were more exposed to and influenced by Hellenistic civilization than were their Judean cousins, and the whole premise of Hellenism—a universalist movement, which allowed people everywhere to become "Greeks" by virtue of their education and culture—is that what makes people what they are is their culture, i.e., their values and commitments, not their birth or their location. The Greek gymnasia around the East were schools that turned barbarians into Greeks—a process analogous to the processes that could turn Gentiles into Jews, run-of-the-mill Jews into rabbis, and profane sites into "holy places" because a community decided to build a synagogue upon it. Thus, the basic premises of Pharisaism and of Hellenistic culture were basically the same but were certainly felt more intensely in the Hellenistic Diaspora. For the purposes of this schematic survey the important point is that the Hellenistic Jews of the Diaspora were to the "left" of the Pharisees, even more willing than the Pharisees to place a premium upon choice rather than birth. Thus, if the Qumran sect and anti-Roman rebels were more Sadducean than the Sadducees, Jews of the Hellenistic Diaspora were more Pharisaic than the Pharisees.

That Hellenistic Diaspora was the context that produced Paul, in Tarsus, which was "no mean (Greek) *polis*" ("an important city," Acts 21.39), so too Paul, who proclaims so insistently that "there is no difference [in Christ] between Jew and Greek" (Rom 10.12; also Gal 3.28, echoed in Col 3.11). For Paul, God's presence is not limited to people of any particular pedigree or of any particular place like the Temple of Jerusalem, but is found within the heart of every believer and within every believing community (1 Cor 3.16; 6.19; 2 Cor 6.16; so too in a letter by one of Paul's disciples, Eph 2.19–22). These views are quite nonpriestly but quite easily paralleled by equally demonstrative statements in early rabbinic literature. Indeed, if we had to guess with whom someone like Paul would study upon coming to Jerusalem, it would in fact be, as the narrator of Acts tells us, a Pharisaic teacher, Gamaliel (Acts 22.3).

The conceptual scheme suggested here must be modified to allow for more nuance. First, note that Pharisaic religion left a good bit of room for choice by God too; what was important for them was that he made such choices independent of nature. For example,

CD 4.21–5.1 states the priestly view that since God created one man and one woman, polygamy is forbidden; but the Pharisees and the rabbis—just as they refused to collect a debt, which was only natural but not formulated as one, so too they allowed polygamy because there is no statement in the Torah that forbids it. Second, note that despite the basic similarity of Pharisaic Judaism of Palestine and Hellenistic Judaism of the Diaspora, the Pharisaic emphasis on observance of the law was harder to maintain in the societal conditions of the Hellenistic diaspora, and there we often find, instead, a tendency to interpret Jewish law allegorically. Third, similarly, there are basic differences between life in Jerusalem and life in the desert, and therefore, despite the basic similarity of the Sadducees and the Essenes as priestly sects, the fact that the latter lived, by choice, in "exile," out in the desert, led it to develop some nonpriestly characteristics reminiscent of those of Diaspora Judaism.

A well-known example: Various Qumran texts downplay the division of people in this world between priests and lay Israelites, substituting that between Sons of Light and Sons of Darkness, which are quite universalistic categories. There was serious tension between that view and the sect's basic priestly stance. If—as is often assumed, for good reason—there is a link between John the Baptist and Qumran, he was someone who took the sect's universalistic message to its logical conclusion, preaching a message of salvation "for all flesh" (Luke, later than Mark, extends the quotation from Isaiah 40 through v. 5) and belittling the importance of Jewish descent, arguing that God can turn even stones into sons of Abraham (Lk 3.6–8).

CONCLUSION

It is true that apart from the nature vs. choice issue there were other issues and influences at work, and that all historical personalities have their own special character. Nevertheless, it seems that the successful rise of Christianity was based on the transformation of a leader, Jesus of Nazareth—who came from an environment favorable to a nationalist movement and whom Pontius Pilate, the Roman governor, took to be the leader of such a movement—into the personification of a universalist mission aimed at all of humankind. The reader of this volume is left to ponder how the failure of a movement to restore Israel became instead a victory over death, and how the mission associated with Jesus changed from one devoted to national salvation to one focused on individual salvation.

MESSIANIC MOVEMENTS

David B. Levenson

The followers of Jesus of Nazareth founded an early Jewish movement centered on a charismatic figure who offered hope for an ideal future in which the power of the God of Israel would be dramatically manifested and universally recognized. The movement they began was not, however, the only one of its kind. Other such movements, dating from the first century BCE to the second century CE, promised a sudden end of the present age, which they regarded as evil and corrupt, and the inauguration of a new age in which God's people would see the wicked punished and the world ruled in righteousness.

THE MESSIAH IN EARLY JEWISH THOUGHT

The evidence for these movements is sparse and mostly derives from unsympathetic witnesses. The concept of a divinely appointed deliverer, however, is widely attested in Jewish apocalyptic literature of the period. Although no apocalyptic texts can be directly connected to these movements and their leaders, the end-time scenario they present provides an important context for understanding how followers might have understood such charismatic leaders and how those leaders might have understood themselves.

An ideal Davidic king is one of the most prominent types of eschatological redeemer. The mid-first century BCE *Psalms of Solomon* (17.21–24,26–27; 18.6–7) provides a classic description:

> Behold, O Lord, and raise up for them their king,
> the son of David, at the time which you choose,
> O God,
> to rule over Israel your servant.
> And gird him with strength, to shatter unjust rulers,
> to purge Jerusalem from nations that trample (her)
> down to destruction;
> in the wisdom of righteousness to thrust out
> sinners from the inheritance . . .
> to crush all their substance with a rod of iron;
> to destroy the lawless nations with the word of
> his mouth . . .
> And he will gather together a holy people,
> whom he will lead in righteousness . . .

And he will not allow injustice to lodge any more in their midst,
and no one knowing evil will dwell with them . . .
Blessed are the ones in those days,
in that they will see the good things of the Lord,
which he will perform for the generation that is to come,
under the rod of discipline of the Lord's anointed.

Here the future ideal Davidic king is the Lord's "anointed one," a designation also used for the figure who will conquer the nations and judge the world in *2 Baruch* and *4 Ezra* (2 Esd 3–14), two lengthy apocalypses composed after the destruction of the Second Temple in 70 CE (*2 Bar.* 29–30; 39–40; 72; *4 Ezra* 7 and 11–13). Notably, this king accomplishes his goals not by military might; his weapon is "the word of his mouth," based on Isaiah 11.4.

The term "anointed one" translates the Hebrew *mashiaḥ* (Gk *christos*). The Tanakh refers to human kings as "the LORD's anointed" (e.g., 1 Sam 12.3; Ps 2.2), because they were "anointed" (Heb *m-sh-ḥ*) with oil when they began their reigns (Judg 9.8–15; 2 Sam 5.3; 1 Kings 1.39). The "Anointed One" in *Psalms of Solomon* and *4 Ezra* is also called a descendant of David, reflecting the biblical tradition of God's promise to David that his descendants would occupy the throne forever (2 Sam 7.13; 22.51; Ps 89.4 [Heb v. 5]). During the time of the Davidic kingship, the hope was expressed that a new king would establish a kingdom like that of his ancestor David, whose reign was idealized as a time of peace, prosperity, and justice. After the termination of Davidic kings in the sixth century BCE, the hope for such an ideal ruler was projected into the future. (The genealogies in Mt 1.1–17 and Lk 3.23–38 do not agree on the names listed between David and Jesus; there are no other reliable genealogical lists from the period tracing Davidic ancestry.) This future hope was intensified in apocalyptic circles, likely comprised of scribes intimately familiar with the rich resources of Israel's literature; these writers saw foreign rulers such as the Hellenistic king Antiochus IV (175–164 BCE), best known today in relation to the festival of Hanukkah, and the succession of Roman rulers beginning in the first century BCE as oppressors of God's people, unjustly claiming for themselves the land of Israel. Some of these writers also regarded Jewish rulers such as the Hasmonean kings (142–63 BCE) and Herod the Great (40–4 BCE) as oppressors who would be overthrown by the agents of God.

One major function of the Messiah is to bring about God's justice by defeating all agents of oppression, human and superhuman (*Pss. Sol.* 17.24; *4 Ezra* 13.38). However, the focus of the texts is less on the messianic figure than on the messianic age, the time when God's justice, rather than Satan or Empire, would prevail. Apocalyptic texts such as *2 Baruch* and *4 Ezra* provide ample evidence of the supernatural character of the messianic age, such as a new Jerusalem descending from heaven (*4 Ezra* 7.26; *2 Bar* 32.4; see also Rev 21.2) and the resurrection of the dead (*4 Ezra* 7; *2 Bar.* 50–51). *4 Ezra* 7.29–32 also reports that the Messiah son of David will die seven days before the resurrection of the dead, final judgment, and the beginning of the new age.

Not only kings were anointed in ancient Israel, and therefore not all messiahs were Davidic kings. For example, Elijah is instructed to "anoint Jehu . . . as king over Israel" and "anoint Elisha . . . as prophet in your place" (1 Kings 19.16); in Isa 61.1 the prophet refers to himself as "anointed." Elijah became viewed as the one to announce "the day of the LORD" (Mal 4.5 [Heb 3.23]) because he never died (2 Kings 2.11).

Anointing was also part of ordination to priesthood (e.g., Ex 29.7), and the high priest could be referred to as the "anointed priest" (*ha-kohen ha-mashiaḥ:* Lev 4.3,5,16; 6.15 [Heb v. 7 in some other versions]). These texts undergird the development of prophetic and priestly eschatological messianic figures.

Finally, not all messianic figures—defined as agents of redemption and not necessarily as "anointed"—were human. In the book of Daniel, the angel Michael delivers the righteous at the end-time when the wicked king of the north (Antiochus IV) is about to attack Jerusalem (Dan 12.1; Michael might also be identified with the "the one like a son of man" [i.e., human being] in 7.13–14). In the *Similitudes of Enoch* (*1 En.* 37–71; first century CE), a preexisting heavenly Son of Man, reflecting the figure described in Daniel 7 (cf. *4 Ezra* 13.26), also called the "Chosen One," "Righteous One," and "Messiah," executes the final judgment (*1 En.* 46–53), punishing the wicked and rewarding the righteous (*1 En.* 62).

MESSIANIC LEADERS AND THEIR FOLLOWERS

The term "messiah" only rarely appears in the texts that describe "messianic" leaders and their movements. However, scholars often designate these leaders and movements as "messianic" because they proclaim a radical transformation of the world and the restoration of Israel's independence and security under the leadership of charismatic figures, often claiming to be agents of divine deliverance. These figures fit into the three main categories of prophets, kings, and priests.

Prophetic Figures

Josephus is the chief source for "messianic" figures. The most prominent type among these were those whom many Jews regarded as prophets, but whom Josephus consistently calls deceivers and *goētes* (Gk "charlatans, enchanters") and whom he associates with the various rebel groups, the chief villains in his history.

Josephus provides tantalizingly brief reports for six such individuals: (1) Under the Roman procurator Fadus (44–46 CE), a certain Theudas led a large multitude, who brought along their possessions, to the Jordan River, which he promised they could cross after the waters parted at his command. Many were massacred by a cavalry squadron sent by the procurator. Theudas was killed and his head was brought to Jerusalem (*Ant.* 20.97–99; cf. Acts 5.36). (2) In the time of Felix (52–60 CE), a man from Egypt led several thousand followers through the wilderness to the Mount of Olives; he promised them that at his command the walls of the city would fall and that they would enter the city where he would be installed as ruler. Roman soldiers killed 400 and took 200 prisoner, but their leader escaped (*J.W.* 2.261–63; *Ant.* 20.169–72; cf. "the Egyptian" in Acts 21.38). (3) Roman troops sent by Festus (60–62 CE) killed a man (whom Josephus does not name) and those who followed him into the wilderness, where he promised them they would find "salvation and rest from troubles" (*Ant.* 20.188). (4) In the last days of the Temple, a prophet proclaimed that God had commanded the people to go up to the Temple court to receive "the signs of their deliverance." Instead 6,000 were killed when the portico where they had taken refuge caught fire (*J.W.* 6.285). (5) In the period immediately after the destruction of Temple, a weaver named Jonathan, whom Josephus associates with the Sicarii (Gk "dagger men," rebels who assassinated those whom they saw as enemies of the Jews [*J.W.* 2.435; 7.432]), led a multitude of what Josephus describes as "the poor" of Cyrene into the wilderness, where he promised to show them "signs and apparitions." Although the provincial governor initially spared Jonathan and used his testimony to accuse the local Jewish aristocracy of sedition and confiscate their wealth, he was executed after an inquiry ordered by Vespasian (*J.W.* 7.437–450). (6) A Samaritan, perhaps connected with the expectation of an eschatological Mosaic prophet attested in later Samaritan texts, organized an armed multitude for an ascent of Mount Gerizim (see Jn 4.20–21), promising them he would show them the sacred vessels which Moses had buried there. Their slaughter by troops sent by Pilate (26–36 CE) was the occasion for the prefect's being recalled to Rome to face accusations the Samaritans leveled against him (*Ant.* 18.85–87).

Josephus's hostile reports tell us little about the content of these prophets' messages. They likely condemned the present situation and promised blessings for the elect who followed them. Some probably claimed the role of the prophet like Moses who, according to an interpretation of Deut 18.15–19 (cf. 1 Macc 14.41), they understood would arise at some future time. The wilderness recalls the place where the Israelites encountered God directly and from which they conquered the Promised Land. It was therefore an appropriate location from which to launch a new conquest that would purify the land from idolatrous foreign oppressors and corrupt Jewish leaders. The extent to which these figures planned or engaged in military action is hard to gauge. Josephus claims several did, and Rome's swift and brutal response might seem to support such a conclusion. But caution is in order; history provides many examples in the first century CE—most notably Christianity—of the violent suppression of groups critical of present governments and anticipating a new age, but who demonstrate their faith not by military means but by relying on the imminent arrival of supernatural change.

Another example of a nonviolent prophetic figure executed by political authorities is John the Baptist. According to Josephus, John

> had exhorted the Jews to join in baptism, practicing virtue and treating their fellows with righteousness and God with piety. For he said in this way indeed baptism would be acceptable to God, not by using it to gain pardon for some sins, but for the purification of the body, since the soul had already been thoroughly cleansed by righteousness. (*Ant.* 18.116–117)

In this view, baptism was a ritual of purification (see e.g., Lev 15; 16.4) that signified but did not effect forgiveness. The forgiveness of God followed from the cleansing of the inner life by the practice of virtue. But Josephus's benign portrait of John as a teacher of ethics, like his description of the Essenes and the other Jewish movements, is meant to appeal to an educated Roman audience. More historically probable is the Gospels' version of a prophetic Elijah figure demanding that Israel repent before the imminent judgment. Together with repentance, John's distinctive rite of baptism, with which he is most prominently identified (there were no people called in antiquity "Simon the Baptist" or "Martha the Baptist"), is apparently essential for the forgiveness of sins and protection from divine punishment.

Like several of the other prophets Josephus mentions, John attracted a following in the wilderness where he performed an action that would help bring deliverance. The fact that he had disciples, some of whom remained loyal to him, suggests that he was the founder of a movement composed of those who had undergone the rite, though not necessarily of an organized community.

According to Josephus (*Ant.* 18.118–19), Herod Antipas executed John because he feared that John's influence over the people might lead to sedition. The Gospel accounts state that John was executed for denouncing Herod's marriage to his brother's wife (Mt 13.4–6; Mk 6.17–18). The two motivations do not necessarily conflict.

The Gospels show John subordinating himself to Jesus. Historically, this is unlikely, given that John baptized Jesus and that John's followers remained loyal to him after Jesus appeared on the scene (cf. Mk 2.18; Acts 19.3). Had John thought Jesus to be the Messiah, he would not have retained his own disciples. The connection of John to Elijah also suggests that John was not, historically, Jesus' forerunner. In the Tanakh, Elijah's role is to prepare Israel for "the great and terrible day of the LORD" (Mal 4.5 [Heb 3.23]), not to announce another agent of God.

Josephus mentions several individuals who make predictions but who do not have followers (cf. *J.W.* 2.112–113; 6.300–309; *Ant.* 15.373–79; 17.345–48). Chief among these is the historian himself. Although he never directly calls himself a prophet, Josephus presents himself as having a prophetic mission and as being a divinely guided interpreter of the ancient prophets. He was convinced that he, like Jeremiah, understood that God decreed the destruction of the Temple for the people's sins and that those who claimed to be prophets promising security for God's people and Temple were offering false hopes. Josephus also insists that he recognized, through divine inspiration, that God chose Vespasian to rule the world (*J.W.* 3.351–54, 400–402; cf. Suetonius, *Vesp.* 4.5; 5.6; Tacitus, *Hist.*, 5.13.2).

Royal Figures

From the death of Herod the Great in 4 BCE to the second revolt against the Romans in 132–135 CE, a number of popular figures with substantial followings presented themselves as Jewish kings.

As part of his description of the political instability following Herod's death, Josephus mentions in succession three individuals, each of whom claimed kingship. Judas, the son of Ezechias, attacked the royal palace at Sepphoris, captured arms and possessions, and proceeded to plunder the wealth of the countryside in his zeal for "royal rank" (see Acts 5.37). Herod's slave Simon of Perea, noted for his size and strength, "dared to put on the diadem," and with his followers pillaged the royal palace in Jericho and "many other royal residences in many parts of the country." Finally, Athronges, a shepherd, like Simon "distinguished by great stature and feats of strength," ruled as a king, setting up a council and putting each of his four brothers, also known for their size and acts of valor, in charge of a band of fighters. Their targets were both Romans and Herodian troops (*J.W.* 2.56–65; *Ant.* 17.271–84).

For Josephus, these are all "brigands" who had neither the character nor the background to claim royal status. Yet behind Josephus's negative portrait may be the continuation of a biblical tradition of charismatic leaders such as the judges, Saul, and especially David, men who reach power through their physical stature and bravery and who act against political oppressors. Since David is the most prominent example of this type and since Josephus's account suggests the figures had some Davidic features (e.g., shepherd turned guerilla fighter), it is possible these charismatic figures identified with David, and that their supporters accepted that identification.

According to Josephus, two of the leaders of the First Revolt also claimed royal honors. At the beginning of the war, Menahem, the leader of the Sicarii, raided Masada to capture weapons, then entered Jerusalem "like a king," and became a leader of the insurrection (*J.W.* 2.433–34). Soon thereafter, he was attacked in the Temple, where he had gone to worship "arrayed in royal garments." He was subsequently tortured and killed by the supporters of the Temple captain Eleazar, one of the revolt's first leaders, and the son of the high priest Ananias whom Menahem's men had murdered (*J.W.* 2.443–48).

A religious background to Menahem's royal claims can be inferred from the report that his father Judas the Galilean had called for a revolt sixty years before. Judas declared that agreeing to a census, the Roman assessment of Jewish property, meant rejecting God as sole master (see Ex 30.12; 2 Sam 24) and that the people could expect divine help if they rebelled (*J.W.* 2.118, 443; *Ant.* 18.4, 23; cf. Lk 2.1–5; Acts 5.37).

Of all the warriors claiming kingship mentioned by Josephus, the most important was Simon bar Giora. A hero in the earlier stages of the war, he left Jerusalem as others took charge of the revolt, gathered a large force with which he returned to the city, and established himself as the leader of the Jewish rebels. His execution at the climax of the Roman victory celebration indicates that the Romans regarded him as the most prominent enemy general (*J.W.* 7.153–54). His royal self-understanding can be seen in his dramatic surrender: from the site where the Temple stood, he emerged dressed in white tunics and a purple mantle (*J.W.* 7.29–31).

The names of the leaders are among the few details recorded for the extensive Jewish revolts that swept through Cyrenaica, Egypt, and Cyprus in 115–117 CE during the reign of the emperor Trajan and that resulted in the annihilation of the well-established Jewish communities of these regions. The Roman historian Cassius Dio says that a certain Andreas led the revolt in Cyrenaica and

Egypt and Artemion in Cyprus (68.32). Eusebius gives the name of the leader of the revolt in Cyrenaica and Egypt as Lukuas to whom he ascribes the title king (*Hist. eccl.* 4.2). The extent of the revolt and the number of Jews participating in it, the attacks on Greek and Egyptian religious sites, and the title king, all raise the possibility that the leader(s) were viewed as agents of God.

According to rabbinic tradition, Akiva ben Joseph (ca. 50–135 CE), the most prominent rabbi of his generation, declared Simon bar Kosiba, the leader of the second revolt against the Romans in 132–135 CE, to be the Messiah (*y. Ta'an.* 4.8; *Lam. Rab.* 2.5). Rabbinic comments on bar Kosiba, however, are generally hostile, exemplified by the usual reference to him as Bar Koziba ("liar") and by Rabbi Yoḥanan ben Torta's retort to Akiva: "Grass will grow between your cheeks and he [the messiah] still will not have come." An association of bar Kosiba with Num 24.17 ("A star [Heb *kokhav*] shall go forth out of Jacob"), said to have been made by R. Akiva, gave rise to the nickname Bar Kochba ("son of a star"), which is also found in the Christian writer Justin (*1 Apol.* 1.31.6), who wrote shortly after the conclusion of the revolt.

Letters unearthed in 1960 establish that his actual name was Simon bar Kosiba and that he bore the title Nasi' of Israel, a word that can mean "leader" or "prince" but that refers to the future Davidic king in the latter part of Ezekiel (e.g., 34.23–24) and is associated with a Davidic messiah in several passages from the Dead Sea Scrolls (1QM 5; 4Q285; 4QpIsa[a]). The letters, though brief and fragmentary, present a person projecting great authority, who enforces strict military discipline, dispenses justice, and is extremely concerned about religious observance, even in the midst of difficult circumstances. Coins struck by the rebels with the image of the Temple, and some with the name "Eleazar the Priest," suggest that one of the goals of the revolt was capturing Jerusalem and rebuilding the Temple. Although the rebels inflicted heavy casualties on the Roman army, the war ended with a decisive defeat at Bethar. Jews were allowed to set foot in Jerusalem, refounded and renamed Aelia Capitolina, only on the ninth of Av to mourn the destruction of the Temple.

Among all these royal figures, there is no explicit claim to Davidic ancestry. The nature of the evidence and the short-lived and unsuccessful character of these movements also prevent us from getting any specific sense of the sort of world they hoped would replace the present age.

Priests

For much of the Second Temple period, the high priest served as the political as well as religious leader of the Jewish community in Judea. It is not surprising then that an ideal future might feature an ideal high priest who would serve in a purified Temple; one example of such a priest is Eleazar, associated with Simon bar Kosiba.

The best-documented group that viewed the ideal high priest as the most authoritative figure in the new age is the community reflected in documents from among the Dead Sea Scrolls. In the first-century CE, they looked back on their idealized priestly founder and leader, the Teacher of Righteousness (second or first century BCE), who transmitted inspired interpretations of the Torah and Prophets that formed the basis for their theology and practice (1QpHab 7). They also looked to an idealized future priest, sometimes designated "Messiah of Aaron" (1QS 9; CD 12, 14, and 19), who would stand at the head of the Children of Light in their final battle against the Children of Darkness (1QM 15) and would have precedence in the community council of the messianic age (1QSa 2). The scrolls also suggest an important place for a future prophet and a future warrior king, the Messiah of Israel (1QS 9.11), also called "Branch of David" [Heb *tzemaḥ david*; see esp. Jer 23.5; 33.15] and "Prince of the Congregation," [*nesi ha-edah*] but these are subordinated to the priestly leader, who is perhaps to be identified with the future "Interpreter of the Torah." (See "The Dead Sea Scrolls," p. 569.)

RABBINIC TRADITIONS

The vast corpus of rabbinic literature from the late second century CE and beyond does not offer a consistent or systematic presentation of messianic ideas. Many of the themes found in the apocalyptic writings are also found in rabbinic texts and in the liturgy transmitted and shaped by the rabbis. For example, the daily *Amidah* prayer (*Shemoneh Esreh* or "Eighteen Benedictions"), composed in the first centuries CE and still recited today, includes praise of God who resurrects the dead and brings a redeemer to the descendants of the patriarchs. It also contains petitions for the return of the dispersed exiles to the land of Israel, restoration of judges and counselors, rebuilding of Jerusalem and the Temple, restoration of the Temple service, and the establishment of the throne of David. The fifteenth blessing specifically mentions: "May you swiftly cause the sprout of David your servant to flourish, and may his horn be raised through your deliverance" (cf. Isa 11.1 and Jer 33.15).

A number of traditions shared with earlier apocalyptic texts are found in rabbinic literature: final battles against the nations of the world and against Gog and Magog (e.g., *m. Ed.* 2.10; *b. Shabb.* 118b; cf. 1QM 11.16; *Sib. Or.* 3.319–349; Rev 20.8–9), eschatological timetables culminating in the coming of the Messiah (e.g., *b. Sanh.* 97a; cf. *2 Bar.* 26–30), travails leading up to the messianic age (e.g., *m. Sot.* 9.15; *Mek., Vayassa* 5 [end]; *b. Sanh.* 98b; cf. *4 Ezra* 6.17–28; *2 Bar.* 70.2–8; Mk 13.8), spectacular prosperity during it (e.g., *b. Ketub.* 111b; cf. *2 Bar.* 29), and a distinction in some texts between the "Days of the Messiah" and a subsequent eternal Age to Come (Heb *'olam ha-ba'*) (e.g. *b. Sanh.* 99a; cf. *4 Ezra* 7.29–33; Rev 20–22).

At the same time, alternative traditions that are not reflected in Jewish apocalyptic texts or in the New Testament are frequently found, such as the ideas that the messiah will come in a generation that is either completely righteous or completely sinful (*b. Sanh.* 98a), or that the messiah will come either in glory on the clouds of heaven (Dan 7.13–14) if Israel has been faithful, or humbly riding on an ass, if it has not (Zech 9.9) (*b. Sanh.* 98a). Playful and ingenious interpretation of the Bible characterizes a number of traditions, such as the debate about the name of the messiah in which rabbis compete with each other in producing biblical verses that would identify the name of the messiah with the name of their teachers (*b. Sanh.* 98b). The last voice identifies the messiah as "the leper scholar," citing Isa 53.4, "Surely he has borne our infirmities and carried our diseases; yet we accounted him stricken [with disease], struck down by God, and afflicted" (cf. *b. Sanh.* 93b, where Isa 11.3 is interpreted to mean that the messiah will be loaded with good deeds and suffering). The connection of the messiah with people suffering from leprosy is also reported in *b. Sanh.* 98a, where R. Joshua b. Levi is said to have been told by Elijah that the messiah is present in the world, bandaging the sores of people with leprosy, yet ready for his mission at any moment. These passages could be a response to Christian associations of Jesus with the "suffering servant" of Isaiah 53 (see Mt 8.17; 1 Pet 2.22). A passage not found elsewhere, but likely based on a popular tradition, reports that the messiah son of David will be granted his request to bring back to life the slain messiah son of Joseph (*b. Sukk.* 52a; cf. Zech 12.10–12), who probably represents the ten northern tribes who were exiled by the Assyrian empire in 722/721 BCE. The slain and resurrected Messiah son of Joseph, however, is not identified as a suffering messiah. *Pesiqta Rabbati*, an early medieval text possibly influenced by Christianity, gives the name Ephraim (a son of Joseph) to the messiah, who suffers for the sins of Israel. Unlike the Messiah son of Joseph in *b. Sukk.* 52a, this figure does not die, and there is no mention of any additional messiah (chs 36 and 37).

Critiques of Messianic speculation are also voiced, such as the traditions attributed to R. Samuel b. R. Nahmani on the authority of R. Jonathan, "Blasted be the bones of those who calculate the end" (*b. Sanh.* 97b), or the saying of R. Yoḥanan b. Zakkai, "If you have a sapling in your hand, and it is said to you, 'Behold, there is the Messiah'—go on with your planting, and afterward go out and receive him (*Avot de R. Natan* B.11). There is even a rabbinic view reported that there will not be a future messiah, "since Israel enjoyed him in the days of Hezekiah" (*b. Sanh.* 99a), a tradition the medieval commentator Rashi (1040–1105) explains as derived from the idea that God alone will redeem Israel.

In evaluating the rabbinic evidence, it is important to keep in mind several things: (1) messianic themes represent only a small fraction of rabbinic literature, and much of the messianic material is concentrated in one lengthy passage (*b. Sanh.* 96b–99a); (2) all of these statements are from nonlegal material (*aggadah*), in which multiple traditions are often cited for the purpose of edification and even entertainment, with no interest in producing a single authoritative opinion; (3) while the expectation of a future redemption and belief in a resurrection of the dead and final accounting are fundamental principles of the rabbinic worldview, most rabbinic literature focuses on sanctifying this world by studying and keeping the commandments and repenting for sin by deeds of mercy and piety (see, for example, *b. B. Bat.* 10a, *b. Shabb.* 118b, and *b. Sanh.* 97b for statements that these, and not supernatural intervention, are the acts that will bring redemption). Finally, in no Jewish sources of antiquity—biblical texts, Dead Sea Scrolls, Apocrypha and Pseudepigrapha, Josephus, rabbinic writings—is the messianic figure ever either identified with God or worshiped.

MESSIANIC MOVEMENTS IN JEWISH HISTORY

Although intense interest in messianism has not been the norm in Jewish history, times of suffering have given rise to messianic literature and movements. For example, the wars among Byzantine, Persian, and Islamic armies in the Near East in the first part of the seventh century are the backdrop for Hebrew messianic speculations in the Hebrew apocalypses *Sefer Eliyyahu (Elijah)* and *Sefer Zerubbabel*, which combine the themes of classical apocalyptic literature with rabbinic traditions. The massacres of Jews in seventeenth-century Europe were a major factor in the rise and rapid expansion throughout the Jewish world of the movement centered on the messianic claims of Shabbetai Tzvi (1626–76). In our own times, intense messianic speculation has attracted a small minority of Jews, such as some adherents of the Chabad (Lubavitch) movement who believe their late leader (rebbe) Menahem Schneerson (1902–94) is the Messiah and will return soon. For the vast majority of Jews, however, messianic concerns are projected into a distant idealized future, if they are held at all. Since the nineteenth century, the Reform Movement, which represents a large percentage of American Jews, has rejected the concept of an individual messiah and other features of traditional Jewish eschatology in favor of the idea also found in the Bible (see Isa 2.1–5; Mic 4.1–5) of a messianic age of peace and justice achieved through human efforts.

JEWISH MIRACLE WORKERS IN THE LATE SECOND TEMPLE PERIOD

Geza Vermes

Jesus is portrayed in the Gospels as a charismatic miracle-worker who heals the sick, raises the dead, exorcizes the demon-possessed, and feeds the hungry. These features also appear in the broader context of prophetic-charismatic religion of biblical and early postbiblical Judaism.

The Bible attributes such phenomena to the influence of the Spirit of God or divine power. This power is the source of revelation, thaumaturgy, and ecstasy. The earliest scriptural events of this kind are associated with Moses, the performer of signs and wonders (Deut 34.10–12), and with the elders in the desert, especially Eldad and Medad (Num 11.24–29). Charismatic prophecy begins with Samuel: prophetic ecstasy in his day is regularly displayed by the "sons of the prophets," who, possessed by the Spirit, worked themselves up into ecstatic states that could be contagious and affect passersby like the first Israelite king, Saul (1 Sam 10.6,10).

The golden age of charismatic prophecy comes with Elijah and Elisha. These men of action were endowed with superhuman power. Elijah bested the prophets of Baal by calling down fire from heaven (1 Kings 18; see also 1 Chr 21.26; Lk 9.54) and eliminated two companies of soldiers sent to arrest him (2 Kings 1.9–12). Elisha routed the Syrian army that besieged Samaria (2 Kings 7.6). However, these prophets were mostly remembered for their beneficial miracles: healing (2 Kings 5.1–19), resuscitating (1 Kings 17.17–24; 2 Kings 4.11–37), bringing rain (1 Kings 18.41–46), wondrous feeding of the hungry (1 Kings 17.8–16; 2 Kings 4.1–7), and other prodigies.

Stories of such wonder-working prophets continue into later biblical and postbiblical Jewish writings as well as in Flavius Josephus and in the Mishnah, Talmud, and Midrash. Ben Sira in the second century BCE (Sir 48.1–14) recalls the "zeal," "wondrous deeds," "glory," and "marvels" of Elijah and Elisha. Josephus depicts Elisha as a doer of "paradoxical deeds" (*Ant.* 9.182), an expression used also in the *Testimonium Flavianum*, the passage about Jesus (*Ant.* 18.63), whose partial authenticity is recognized by many scholars. Josephus also mentions a Jewish contemporary, called Eleazar, who practiced exorcism before Vespasian and Titus (*Ant.* 8.46–48). (See "Josephus," p. 575.)

Thus the miracles and signs ascribed to Jesus in the Gospels and to his followers in the Acts of the Apostles are not anomalous in Jewish culture. Ecstatic behavior plays a significant part in the story of the giving of the Spirit at Pentecost (Acts 2), the descent of the Holy Spirit on new believers (e.g., Acts 4.31; 7.55; 8.17; 10.44; 19.6), and the charismatic activity outlined by Paul in 1 Cor 11.4–11 and 14.1–33.

The principal representatives of charismatic Judaism in the age of Jesus are Ḥoni, surnamed "ha-Me'agel," "the Circle Drawer" (because on one occasion when he prayed for rain and it did not commence, he drew a circle and stood inside it, saying he would not move until the rains came); Ḥoni's grandsons Abba Ḥilkiah and Ḥanan; and the Galilean holy man Ḥanina ben Dosa. Josephus mentions Ḥoni under the Hellenized name of Onias; all four figures appear in the Mishnah and the Talmud.

Josephus, who reports that Ḥoni was stoned to death by the supporters of Hyrcanus II for refusing to curse Aristobulus, the rival Hasmonean candidate for the throne, dates this wonder-worker to the period shortly before Pompey's conquest of Jerusalem in 63 BCE (*Ant.* 14.22–30). His grandsons must have lived in the second half of the first century BCE and the beginning of the Christian era. Ḥanina ben Dosa, probably a younger contemporary of Jesus, is described in the Talmud (*b. Ber.* 34b) as a disciple of Yoḥanan ben Zakkai and is linked to Rabban Gamaliel, possibly Gamaliel the Elder, (see Acts 5.34–39). All four were known for their miraculous rain-making power, which associated them with the prophet Elijah. Abba Ḥilkiah, who modestly attributed to God the arrival of the rain, was told by his rabbinic interlocutors: "We know that this rain has come *through you*" (*b. Ta'an.* 23ab).

In addition to rain making, Ḥanina ben Dosa was renowned for curing the sick, even curing the son of Rabban Gamaliel from a distance (*y. Ber.* 9d) as Jesus healed the servant of the Roman centurion without visiting him (see Mt 8.5–13; Lk 7.1–10; Jn 4.46–54). One legend (*m. Ber.* 5.1; see also *b. Ber.* 33a) uses Ḥanina's piety to illustrate the importance of the *Shemoneh Esreh* (the eighteen benedictions or *Amidah* prayer): "Once while he was reciting the Prayer, a poisonous lizard bit him, but he did not interrupt [his prayer]. His students went and found it dead at the entrance to its hole. They said, 'Woe to the man who is bitten by a lizard. Woe to the lizard that bit Ben Dosa.'" He is also celebrated as a saintly exorcist who controlled Igrat, the queen of the demons (*b. Pesah.* 112b).

Ḥanan "the hider" (so-called because he would hide when people came to ask him to make it rain) is accounted a wonder-worker. The Babylonian Talmud (*b. Ta'an.*

23b) reports that when the world needed rain, the sages would send schoolchildren to Ḥanan: the children would plead, "Abba, abba [father, father], give us rain," and Ḥanan would pray, "Master of the Universe, act for the sake of those who cannot distinguish between the Abba who gives rain and the abba who does not give rain."

Not surprisingly, traditionalists were occasionally critical of these wonder-workers, as they were suspicious of Jesus. For example, Simeon ben Shetaḥ, a Pharisaic leader, reproached Ḥoni for showing lack of respect for God and wanted to, but dared not, excommunicate him (*m. Ta'an.* 3.8). Ḥanina was implicitly charged with disregard toward the command of avoiding ritual impurity—he picked up a dead animal (*b. Ber.* 33a)—and with unseemly behavior by walking in the street unaccompanied at night (*b. Pesah.* 112b). The efficacy of his miraculous prayer was either questioned by rabbinic envoys or was attributed to the merits of the patriarchs and not to his closeness to God (*y. Ber.* 9d; *b. Ber.* 34b; *b. B. Kamma* 50a; *b. Yebam.* 121b).

With the destruction of the Jerusalem Temple in 70 CE and then the disaster of the Bar Kochba revolt against Rome (132–35 CE), the rabbis recognized the dangers of claiming direct heavenly commission or revelation. In their view, the age of prophecy was over: knowledge of the divine will would come from study of the Written and Oral Torahs, not visionary experience and not charismatic claims. Consequently, rabbinic holy men and miracle workers such as Ḥoni the Circle Drawer and Ḥanina ben Dosa are domesticated from charismatic prophets to faithful scholars.

For the rabbis, study of Torah was more important than visionary experience and charismatic action. Consequently, rabbinic texts bring miracle workers such as Ḥoni and Ḥanina into the realm of the study house (see e.g., *m. Avot* 3.9, which quotes Ḥanina: "He would say, 'Anyone whose deeds are more than his wisdom—his wisdom will endure, and anyone whose wisdom is more than his deeds—his wisdom will not endure'"). For rabbinic Judaism, community voice was more important than individual charismatic activity; study of Torah held preeminence over miracle working.

On the other hand, Josephus called Ḥoni "the Righteous" (*Ant.* 14.22), and Ḥanina became in rabbinic tradition the prototype of the "men of deeds" or performer of prodigies. Early rabbinic theology treats both of them as "sons of God," Ḥoni because his familiarity with God resembled the relationship between a beloved child and his doting father, and Ḥanina because a heavenly voice (*bat qol*, "daughter of the voice") called him "my son," a proclamation identical with that heard at the baptism and at the transfiguration of Jesus (*b. Ta'an.* 24b; see Mk 1.11 || Mt 3.17 || Lk 3.22; Mk 9.7 || Mt 17.5 || Lk 9.35). Furthermore, just as Jesus was seen by some of his contemporaries as the revived Elijah (Mk 8.28; Mt 16.14; Lk 9.8), so were both Ḥoni and Ḥanina (*Gen Rab.* 13.7; *b. Ber.* 34b, 61b). The rabbis even ascribe to Ḥanina's intervention the survival of the whole of humanity and attribute to his merits the creation of the world to come (*b. Ta'an.* 24b; *b. Ber.* 61b). Yet their domesticating of him and his fellow charismatic wonder-workers precluded these figures being identified as in any way "messianic" or "divine."

Although both Ḥoni and Ḥanina lose their importance in the post-Talmudic centuries, they do not vanish altogether. The great tenth-century luminary, Saadia Gaon, was thought to be of Ḥanina's lineage (*Sefer ha-Kabbalah*). The eleventh-century Spanish-Jewish convert to Christianity, Peter Alphonsi, violently attacked the credibility of Ḥanina's miracles, which in his mind detracted from the uniqueness of the miracles of Jesus (Migne, *Patrologia Latina* 157, col. 569).

JEWISH FAMILY LIFE IN THE FIRST CENTURY CE

Ross S. Kraemer

The topic "Jewish Family Life" is likely to strike many readers as straightforward and unproblematic. Yet what, exactly, was a "family" in the first century? Was Jewish family life homogeneous? Was it distinctive from the surrounding cultures? And perhaps most important, are our sources sufficient to answer these questions?

In recent years, scholars of the ancient Mediterranean world have drawn on a rich collection of law codes, personal correspondence, histories, biographies of illustrious men, epigrams, epitaphs, legal documents, and representations of families in plays and novels, all of which offer persuasive portraits of families and family life, both idealized and actual. For families in Roman-period Judea, we have much less evidence: the writings of Josephus and

Philo of Alexandria, some personal papyri from Egypt and the Judean desert (of which the Babatha archive—a trove of documents from the life of a second-century Jewish woman, Babatha, deposited in a cave around the time of the Bar Kochba revolt in 135 CE—is perhaps the richest), some burial inscriptions, and the depictions of families in late Hellenistic Jewish writings such as the book of Tobit and of Susanna, an addition to the book of Daniel. Each type of evidence presents particular challenges as we try to reconstruct the reality that lay behind it. Virtually all of the literary evidence comes from elite male authors: the voices of others, including elite women, are perceptible, if at all, only in some of the documentary evidence.

Families in ancient Judea, including the first century CE, seem similar in many ways to those of the larger Greco-Roman Mediterranean culture. With complex arrangements that might have seemed more familiar to Americans a century ago, many Judean households consisted of several generations: an older, free adult male, his wife, their grown sons, the wives of those sons, and the minor children of the second generation. Grown daughters of the older generation typically became part of the households of their own husbands and lived elsewhere; this could be as close as another courtyard in the same village or town, or much farther away. High maternal mortality rates also meant that households might consist of a free man, his children by one or more prior wives, one or more daughters-in-law, and grandchildren, one or more current wives, their children from a prior marriage, and the children of the most recent marriage.

The domestic arrangements depicted in the Tanakh, while rooted in earlier practices, illuminate various features of ancient Judean families, including polygyny (one man married to two or more women) and slavery. By the first century CE, few men were able to afford more than one wife and the attendant children, but polygynous marriage remained permissible under Mosaic Law (and in rabbinic thinking), and seems to have been practiced at least occasionally. Some members of the Herodian royal family may have participated in such marriages, and the early-second-century personal papers of Babatha of Ma'oza indicate that her second marriage was polygynous, (see *P. Yadin* 26). Slavery was licit throughout the ancient Mediterranean and widely practiced in the first century (and far beyond): Jews participated in these systems both as slaveholders and enslaved persons. The multigenerational, patriarchal household would regularly have included some enslaved persons.

These enslaved persons often had families, but their own biological relationships had no social significance or legal consequence. Considered part of the households of their owners, slaves lacked the legal capacity and agency to form their own families. Children born to enslaved women had no licit fathers, and their mothers had no rights to them (even free women had little if any legal control over their children). Enslaved children could be separated from their mothers and sold by their owners. Male slave-owners had the legal right to have sex with the persons they owned, both male and female, children and adults. A child born to an enslaved woman was automatically enslaved, even when, as often seems to have been the case, the child's father was the mother's owner. Male slave-owners did sometimes free female slaves with whom they wished to have licit children.

The demographics of ancient Jewish families seem to have been fairly similar to those of non-Jews. Free women seem to have married for the first time between the ages of about twelve and twenty, to men who were typically ten or even fifteen years older. Although rabbinic sources envision regular early first marriage for girls, the available demographic evidence (mostly from burial inscriptions, occasional personal documents that survive on papyrus, and infrequent literary accounts) suggest that this is an idealized construction. The Herodian princess Berenice was about sixteen when she was married to her paternal uncle, a second marriage, after a very brief first marriage. Berenice makes a brief appearance in Acts 25.13–26.32, where she and her brother, Agrippa II, preside at a hearing where Paul pleads his case. A burial inscription from Egypt in the second century BCE (*CPJ* 1513; *JIGRE* 36) memorializes a young Jewish woman of twenty who died on the eve of her marriage. First marriages were regularly a matter of family arrangements, often negotiated between the couple's fathers, or between the bride's father and her future husband (e.g., Tob 7.9–13). Subsequent marriage arrangements might often involve more active participation by the woman herself, particularly when her own father was no longer alive.

Many if not most free persons were married more than once, facilitated by the substantial age differential for many marriages and high maternal mortality rates. Some marriages terminated in divorce. Later rabbinic law, from the Mishnah (generally thought to be collated around 200 CE) and later sources, presumes that only husbands initiate divorce proceedings (e.g., *m. Git.*), but there is some evidence that Jewish women did occasionally initiate divorce proceedings in the first century. The wealth, Roman citizenship, and elite status of women in the royal Herodian family, for instance, may have enabled them to take actions unavailable to ordinary women. Josephus says that Salome, the sister of Herod the Great, gave her husband Castobarus a divorce decree, although he represents this as transgressive. Particularly intriguing is a controversial document from the Judean desert

[*P. Se'elim* 13, dated to the second century CE] that some scholars read to be a "*get*" (a divorce decree) from a woman named Shelamzion to her husband, Eleazar.

In the absence of other factors such as illness, diet, and infertility, women who were sexually active could expect to continue to become pregnant every two to three years. Women who did not die in childbirth, and who remained married throughout their childbearing years, might thus expect to give birth to many as eight children (not to mention miscarriages), several of whom would die either as infants or as young children. An optimally fertile family, then, might produce four or five children who lived to be adults.

In the ancient Mediterranean generally (as in many modern societies), much ordinary social life *was* family life: that is, social relations took place within kinship networks. Many men continued to live in close proximity to their parents, grown brothers, and younger siblings. Women, by contrast, regularly moved away from their natal families when they married, whether to the next courtyard, the next village, or a far distant town. Such practices also likely differed for those living in cities like Alexandria, Jerusalem, Antioch, or Rome, all places with substantial Jewish populations in the first century, and for those from elite families as opposed to those eking out a living.

Many ancient sources, Jewish and otherwise, idealize the love between parents and children; often these envision father-son relationships, and to a lesser extent, mother-son relationships. The realities, as always, were more complex. Although many families may have had an older patriarch at their head, the tendency of men to marry late, and remarry even later, often meant that sons (and daughters) lost their fathers at an early age. Jewish literature from this period says little about mother-daughter relationships, idealized or otherwise. As in many cultures, sons were generally more desired than daughters, a reality reinforced by marital practices that required potentially expensive dowries for daughters, and removed girls from their natal households at a relatively early age. Many daughters would have been closer in age to their mothers than sons (and daughters) to their fathers, although it is hard to know how, if at all, this would have affected mother-daughter relationships.

Many children may have had strong affective ties to their wet nurses, and perhaps others who raised them. Wet-nurse contracts apparently employing Jewish women survive in small numbers from Egypt in this period.

Demographic realities had other likely consequences, for Jews and non-Jews alike. A first-century wedding with four grandparents in attendance would have been a very rare event. While some men lived to see their grandchildren born, and even reach adulthood, most did not. Women had the best chance of seeing grandchildren from daughters but also from sons, especially sons they had borne relatively early. Men had a better chance of seeing grandchildren from daughters than from sons.

Sibling relationships might often have had the greatest social weight, especially those between sons of the same father, though significant evidence concerning this important question is largely lacking.

Demographics played a significant role in marital relationships. First marriages between girls in their early to late teens and men thirty or older would have been highly asymmetrical, even were both husband and wife from families of similar standing. Marriages, especially first ones, were often contracted with little regard for the affection between, or even acquaintance of, the prospective spouses. How much power daughters (or even sons) had to refuse these matches is difficult to determine. Nevertheless, Jewish (e.g., Tob 4.3–4) and non-Jewish (e.g., the writings of Plutarch) sources from the early Roman period idealize harmonious relations between husbands and wives, although frequently a harmonious marriage was taken to mean one in which the wife acquiesced to her husband's judgments, tastes, and values, deferred to his authority, and comported herself with modesty.

Ancient Mediterranean family life, Jewish and otherwise, was frequently gender-segregated, with men and women spending much of their time in various daily tasks with others of the same sex. Among the more elite classes, though, this may have been somewhat less the case. Daughters were raised at home and rarely educated, although elite women, again, were sometimes highly educated. The women of the Herodian family, some of them raised in the imperial court at Rome, were almost certainly educated, and multilingual. The Jewish philosopher Philo of Alexandria represents the women of a monastic community of contemplative philosophers as highly literate, able to spend their days reading allegorical treatises, and skilled at composition, although whether this is Philo's imagining of an ideal community (not unlike Plato's *Republic* in some respects) or an actual group, is unclear. Musonius Rufus, a Roman Stoic writer, appears to have written at least two short treatises arguing that training women in philosophy makes them better wives and mothers (and defending counterclaims that educating women masculinizes them). Some philosophical groups, such as the "Garden" of Epicurus, included women. Early rabbinic texts have very little to say about teaching women Torah: one of the only instances is actually a more narrow discussion of whether teaching women that meritorious deeds offset the effects of the punishment of the woman accused of adultery in Numbers 5.11–31 is a good idea, or encourages illicit sexuality (*m. Sot.* 3.4). Highly educated Jewish women are rare in rabbinic representation. A prominent exception is the figure of Beruriah, said in the Babylonian Talmud to have been the brilliant wife of Rabbi Meir, but there is no way to know whether Beruriah was a historical person, a rabbinic fiction, or some combination of the two. In any case, it is unwise to extrapolate from later rabbinic sources to the social realities of the first century.

In a few areas, at least, Jewish "family life" *might* have been distinctive. We do not have any real evidence for how many married couples observed the biblical restrictions on marital intercourse during and after menstruation (e.g., Lev 15.19–30; 18.19, let alone their elaboration in later rabbinic texts, such as *m. Nidd.* and *b. Nidd.*), but if these were widely practiced, they would have had some effect on marital relationships, and perhaps also on fertility rates. Tacitus claimed that Jews were unusual in that they raised all their children (*Hist.* 5.5), rather than abandoning unwanted babies at birth, or aborting unwanted pregnancies. If polygynous marriage, which was illegal under Roman law, was practiced by more than a few Jews, that would have been distinctive in the ancient Mediterranean, where serial marriage seems more the norm.

Some of the most evocative evidence for Jewish family life in the first century comes from the New Testament Gospels. Their often incidental vignettes of household life in the Galilee and Judea feature struggling widows (Lk 18.1–8), a household of unmarried, or possibly widowed, sisters (Lk 10.38–42), the occasional village wedding (Jn 2.1–10), a mother-in-law silently serving her son-in-law and his male guests (Mk 1.31), fathers and widowed or otherwise husbandless women desperately seeking healing for ill children (Mt 9.18–26; 15.21–28; 17.14–21; Mk 5.21–43; 7.24–30; 9.14–29; Lk 7.11–17; 8.40–56). They also depict relations between siblings, especially brothers, and strong mother-son ties. Adult fathers are generally absent from the Gospel narratives, as are grandparents and mother-daughter relationships; depictions of marital relations are also minimal. Peter, for instance, has a mother-in-law (Mk 1.30 and parallels), but there is never any mention of his wife, let alone any representation of interactions between them. Many followers of Jesus are depicted in ways that seem to detach them from larger family relationships. Some writings of the New Testament regularly construct the relationships between early Christians in terms of reconfigured kinship, especially that of siblings, although this language is more common in the letters of Paul and in Acts than it is in the Gospels, where sibling terminology often seems to designate persons with shared parents. Stories about Jesus and parables attributed to him might not reliably reflect the usual familial relations of the first century. For instance, by depicting individuals as detached from family ties, or at least by not presenting such ties, these stories and texts may authorize the kinds of new family arrangements associated with some of the teachings attributed to Jesus, which critique families based on ordinary kinship ties, and authorize, instead, new familial relations based on loyalty to Jesus.

One of the best exemplars of Jewish family demographics is the birth family of Jesus himself, at least as represented in the Synoptic Gospels of Mark, Matthew, and Luke. These portray Jesus as one of a large family of perhaps four other brothers (sometimes named as James, Joses or Joseph, Simon, and Judas [Mt 13.55]) and two or more unnamed sisters. The age difference between Jesus' mother, Mary, and her husband, Joseph, is never explicitly stated, but one way to understand the lack of any references to Joseph in the Gospel narratives, apart from the stories of Jesus' birth and childhood, is that Joseph died before Jesus' public career, consistent with the demographic pattern noted earlier. Neither Jesus nor any of his siblings appears to be married or to have children. We might, perhaps, imagine them all to be too young to be married yet, but this may also be another instance where the Gospel writers portray the family of Jesus in accord with their other interests.

THE CONCEPT OF NEIGHBOR IN JEWISH AND CHRISTIAN ETHICS

Michael Fagenblat

The commandment to "love your neighbor as yourself" (Lev 19.18) plays a central role in both Jewish and Christian ethics, yet it has also been the subject of Christian misunderstanding of Judaism. Two misunderstandings are paramount.

First, some Christian readers, influenced by the parable of the good Samaritan (Lk 10.25–38) and Jesus' exhortation to "love your enemies" (Mt 5.44; Lk 6.27–35), accuse Judaism of having an exclusivist ethic: Jews only love fellow Jews; Christians expand the definition of neighbor and are to love everyone, Jew and Gentile, friend and enemy. This mistaken view of Judaism is based on a misunderstanding of the role of Leviticus 19.18 in Jewish thought.

Second, some of Jesus' early followers understood his use of the commandment to love the neighbor, in conjunction with the commandment from Deuteronomy 4.6 to love God, as a substitute for the entire law. The understanding comes from Jesus' response to the question: "Which commandment is the first of all?" Jesus answered, "The first is, 'Hear, O Israel: the Lord our God, the Lord is one; you shall love the Lord your God with all your heart, and with all your soul, and with all your mind, and with all your strength.' The second is this, 'You shall love your neighbor as yourself.' There is no other commandment greater than these" (Mk 12.28–31; see also Mt 22.34–40; Lk 10.27). Early interpreters took this combination to mean that Jesus abrogated all the other commandments. Conversely, Jews regarded the command to "love your neighbor as yourself," as a principle for regulating other laws. In respect to both the definition of the "neighbor" as referring to a fellow Jew and the relation of Leviticus 19.18, to the rest of the law, the historical Jesus was probably closer to the Jewish position than to the interpretation advanced by later Christians.

The full range of the Tanakh's *rea*, "neighbor," is remarkably wide, like the English "fellow." It can designate any human being (Gen 11.3) or denote a person with whom one has an intimate relationship such as a friend (e.g., Ex 33.11; 1 Chr 27.33) or a lover (e.g., Hos 3.1; Song 5.16). Often *rea* refers to a person encountered in everyday life: Proverbs 3.29 explains that "your *rea*" is someone who "lives trustingly beside you"; in Jeremiah 9.1–5 the prophet berates his people for the widespread deception among neighbors. In Deuteronomy 19.14 and 27.17 *rea* refers to a landowner with whom one shares a boundary.

It is therefore not surprising that the term "neighbor" figures prominently in the legal literature of the Tanakh, for neighbors rely on laws to regulate their relationships. In the context of biblical law the term refers to a person with whom one has a legal relationship (e.g., Ex 22.25; Deut 4.42). Here it is perhaps analogous to "citizen" or "compatriot." This is the case for Leviticus 19.18.

In its literary context, as in later Jewish interpretations, the commandment to "love your neighbor" is restricted to members of the covenant community. It appears within a set of laws aimed at regulating judicial impartiality and cultivating fraternity within Israel. These are *this nation's particular laws* rather than a set of universal guidelines; in this context "neighbor" (*rea*) refers to a person encountered within the framework of covenantal relationships. Leviticus 19 opens with an imperative addressed "to all the congregation of the people of Israel . . . : You shall be holy, for I the LORD your God am holy" (19.2). It then proceeds to address this specific audience through various synonyms that reinforce Israel's covenantal fellowship: "your kinsfolk" (*aḥikha*), "your people" (*bnei 'amekha*), "your compatriot" (*amitkha*), and "your neighbor" (*re'akha*). The Greek term *plēsion*, by which the Septuagint translates *rea*, also refers to someone encountered nearby. Like *rea*, *plesion* can refer to any other human being and not only to fellow members of the covenant; however there is no evidence that pre-Christian Hellenistic Jews understood Leviticus 19.18 in this broader sense.

Thus, charging Jews with failing to interpret "the neighbor" in a universal sense amounts to charging them with failing to *mis*interpret the language of their own scriptures. Moreover, claiming that the Jewish reading is morally restrictive is like condemning a modern nation for legislating for its own citizens rather than for the whole world.

Early rabbinic literature retains this view of Leviticus 19 as a national charter. *Sifra*, a halakhic midrash on Leviticus from approximately the third century, states that Leviticus 19 was recited at *hakhel*, a national assembly held every seven years (see Deut 31.10–13). The rabbis accord this special status to Leviticus 19 because it commands "all . . . of Israel" to "be holy" and then enumerates laws that "most of the essentials of the Torah depend (lit., hang) on" (*Parashah Aleph*).

The fact that Jewish tradition understood Leviticus 19.18b in the context of national law and not as a universal moral principle, however, does not imply that Jews are legally obliged to love only each another. This view of ancient Judaism as restrictive ironically restricts Jewish ethics to one verse and neglects the full charter of Leviticus 19. The chapter goes on, in v. 34 (cf. Deut 10.19) to mandate: "The alien who resides with you shall be to you as the citizen among you; you shall love the alien as yourself, for you were aliens in the land of Egypt: I am the LORD your God." By using the same love language as Leviticus 19.18b, verse 34 equates the love prescribed to one's fellow Israelite with love for the stranger.

Moreover, biblical and Jewish ethics provide alternative avenues for cultivating a "universalistic" moral attitude. For example, Genesis 1.27; 5.1–2; 9.6 insist that all humanity is created in the image of God. The Noahide laws, fundamental principles that the rabbis regard as binding upon all people, include renouncing idolatry, establishing judicial systems, and prohibiting murder and theft (*t. Avodah Zara* 8.4; *b. Sanh.* 56a; cf. Acts 15.29). The first-century Jewish historian Josephus remarks that the function of Jewish law includes "mutual communion" among Jews as well as "a general love of mankind" (*Ag. Ap.* 2.15). Ancient Jews thus understood the Torah as implying not only laws for Israel but also universal moral precepts; they simply did not derive these precepts from Leviticus 19.18.

The significance of Lev 19.18 in Jewish tradition is also seen in its interpretation by the great Rabbi Akiva, who lived in Israel a century after Jesus and was, like Jesus, executed by the Roman state. Akiva claimed that love of the neighbor is "the great principle of the Torah" (*y. Ned.* 9,3,41; *Sifra Kedoshim* 4.12; *Gen Rab.* 24.27). For Akiva, this verse was the foundation for the rest of the Torah, and all other commandments are to be interpreted in its light. Rabbi Meir, Akiva's student, invokes Leviticus 19.18 to justify releasing a man from a vow when it has unforeseen consequences (*m. Ned.* 9.4). He reasons that had the man known that the oath would require him to transgress Leviticus 19.18, he never would have taken it. Another of Akiva's students, Rabbi Judah, cites that verse in a discussion of capital punishment. Opposing the view that execution by fire means burning the convicted felon alive, Rabbi Judah insists: "It says love your neighbor as yourself—select for him a good death" (*t. Sanh.* 9.1). As with Rabbi Meir, for Rabbi Judah the obligation to love the neighbor implies that one should interpret another law, in this case the law of execution, in a charitable way. While modern readers might have difficulty seeing "a good death [sentence]" as an expression of "love your neighbor," in a context where resurrection of the body was a fundamental belief, it was indeed an act of charity to ensure that the integrity of the body was maintained at death. Moreover, in this case the person to whom love is rendered has been convicted of a capital offense and is therefore a clear contender for an "enemy" who is being loved by means of a charitable interpretation of the law.

These observations help us to understand several New Testament passages. It is possible to see Jesus' command to "Love your enemies" as belonging to the same tradition as Rabbi Judah's ruling. Therefore, when Jesus states, according to Matthew 5.43, "You have heard that it was said, 'You shall love your neighbor and hate your enemy,'" he is not referring to a Pharisaic or proto-rabbinic view. More likely, he is referring to the composers of certain Dead Sea Scrolls, such as the Community Rule, who divide the world into those who follow "the path for the wise" and therefore merit love and those other "men of the pit" who deserve "eternal hatred" (1QS 9.21).

Further evidence points to this common ground between Jesus and the Pharisaic and later rabbinic tradition. While it is often thought that Jesus and his followers rejected the "restrictive" Jewish notion of the neighbor, it is more accurate to say that in place of restricting the term "neighbor" to fellow Israelites, the followers of Jesus redefined the term in their own "restrictive" sense. As in the Jewish sources, Matthew's Gospel glosses the broader context of Leviticus 19.18 to instruct *its particular community*, the church. Immediately before "You shall love your neighbor as yourself," Leviticus exhorts: "You shall not hate in your heart anyone of your kin; you shall reprove your neighbor, or you will incur guilt yourself. You shall not take vengeance or bear a grudge against any of your people" (19.17–18a). Matthew 18.15–17 states:

> If another member of the church [lit., "your brother"] sins against you, go and point out the fault when the two of you are alone. If the member [lit., "he"] listens to you, you have regained that one. But if you are not listened to, take one or two others along with you, so that every word may be confirmed by the evidence of two or three witnesses. If the member [lit., "he"] refuses to listen to them, tell it to the church; and if the offender [lit., "he"] refuses to listen even to the church, let such a one be to you as a Gentile and a tax collector.

Matthew's gloss on Leviticus 19.15–18 concerns reproach. But the neighbor is a "brother" who belongs to Matthew's community. The Johannine community likewise understood Jesus' commandment to love as applying to fellow community members (Jn 13.34–35; 1 Jn 3.11–17). While the commandment to love is at the center of Johannine theology, the evangelist never uses the term "neighbor" but consistently concentrates on love between those in the new community created by Jesus.

Jewish perspectives on Leviticus 19.18 can also help to elucidate Luke's parable of the good Samaritan. Jesus' interlocutor, the Jewish lawyer, holds a restrictive definition of "neighbor": his question, "Who is my neighbor?" presupposes that some people are not neighbors. Contrary to many interpretations, however, the parable neither redefines the term "neighbor" nor abolishes the distinction between Jew and Gentile. Jews did not regard Samaritans as Gentiles. There was certainly long-standing enmity between Samaritans and Jews: the two nations claimed different locations for the Temple, different versions of the Torah, and alternative lines of priests (2 Kings 17.24–41; *Ant.* 9.277–91). Despite this mutual enmity, which Josephus and the Gospels both attest (Lk 9.52f; Jn 4.9; *Ant.* 18.2.6–7, 20.6.1–3; *J.W.*

2.232–37), Jews in Galilee and Judea lived next door to Samaritans. Early tannaitic rabbis consider Samaritans to be Israelites (*b. Qidd.* 75b; *y. Ketub.* 3,1, 27a; minor tractate *Kutim* 1.1), and it is only later amoraic rabbis who regard them as Gentiles. The parable of the good Samaritan should therefore not be understood as redefining the category of "neighbor" so as to include Gentiles, for the parable makes no reference to Gentiles. The Samaritans were Israelites with entrenched opposition to the Jewish ways of understanding their shared tradition. A subtle but decisive shift at the end of story confirms that Jesus' point was not to redefine the category of "neighbor" to include Gentiles but to emphasize that neighbors are those who show love:

> "Which of these three, do you think, was a neighbor to the man who fell into the hands of the robbers?" [The lawyer] said, "The one who showed him mercy." Jesus said to him, "Go and do likewise." (Lk 10.36–37)

In the end, the parable does not answer the lawyer's question "Who is my neighbor?" but illustrates *how to love*. It shows the Jewish questioner what a neighbor *does* but does not redefine who a neighbor *is*.

The matter of how to *act* as neighbor relates to what is often called the "golden rule." The golden rule was a common teaching expressed in a wide range of pre-Christian Greek (Herodotus, Isocrates and many others) and Jewish (e.g., Tobit and *Aristeas*) texts, but Jesus may have been the first to connect the golden rule to the love commandment. Matthew, who records Jesus as saying that "the law and the prophets" "hang" or "depend" on Leviticus 19.18 (Mt 22.40), elsewhere quotes Jesus as making an analogous remark about the golden rule: "In everything do to others as you would have them do to you; for this is the law and the prophets" (7.12). Luke cites the golden rule and then explains it with what seems to be an allusion to the love command (Lk 6.31ff.). The *Didache*, another early Christian text, opens with a gloss on the two Great Commandments (Deut 6.5 and Lev 19.18) explained in terms of the golden rule (*Did.* 1.2). Paul may be combining the love commandment and the golden rule in Romans 13.10, "Love does no wrong to a neighbor; therefore, love is the fulfilling of the law" (cf. Gal 5.14). James likewise seems to allude to the golden rule, which he calls "the royal law," when he cites the love command (Jas 2.8). So far, none of this conflicts with Jewish teaching.

However, as the followers of Jesus continued their expansion into the Gentile world, the connotations they gave to the love command began to change. Leviticus 19.18 (along with Deut 6.5) became a substitute for—rather than the guiding principle for understanding—the laws of the Torah. In turn, they redefined the term "neighbor" to include those outside the community of Israel. Perhaps this transformation of the notion of "neighbor" was facilitated by the connection of the commandment to love your neighbor as yourself with the golden rule. When preaching to Gentiles, the followers of Jesus needed to express biblical injunctions in familiar language: Gentiles would have been familiar with the golden rule, but not necessarily with Leviticus 19. Paul's view became decisive: "the whole law is summed up in a single commandment, 'You shall love your neighbor as yourself'" (Gal 5.14). Here Leviticus 19.18 replaces the rest of the law and the term "neighbor" has been redefined to include Gentiles, though Paul also acknowledges that working "for the good of all" is not incompatible with giving priority to "those of the family of faith" (Gal 6.10).

Indeed, Jewish sages cited the golden rule in similar circumstances. When Hillel the elder, Jesus' contemporary, was confronted by a would-be convert who audaciously demanded to be taught the whole Torah while standing on one foot, the sage answered with the famous words: "What is hateful to you, do not do to your fellow. That is the whole Torah. The rest is commentary" (*b. Shabb.* 31a). Philo likewise calls on the golden rule in seeking to explain the rationality of biblical law to Gentiles (*Hypoth.* 7.6). But whereas for Paul, or at least certainly Paul's later Christian interpreters, the golden rule and the love command came to replace the rest of Torah, in Judaism, the concern for love remained the guiding principle by which Torah was to be interpreted.

If we think of the historical Jesus as one who kept Torah requirements (Mt 5.17–19), and as primarily concerned with a mission to Israel (Mt 10.5–6; 15.24), then his use of Leviticus 19.18 looks quite similar to Akiva's and quite dissimilar to the way it was understood by the later Christians. Like both his Pharisaic contemporaries and later rabbinic Jews, Jesus neither sought to redefine the category of the neighbor so that it includes Gentiles nor to replace all the laws of Judaism with one or two Great Commandments. Like Akiva and his students, he regarded Leviticus 19.18 as the greatest of the commandments in the sense that it should be used to interpret the rest of the law. Only later, during the Gentile mission, did his followers revise this position.

DIVINE BEINGS

Rebecca Lesses

Jews and Christians in the biblical period and Late Antiquity believed in a panoply of supernatural beings who partook in divine power and glory. While both groups claimed to be monotheistic, evidence from the Hebrew Bible (Tanakh), early postbiblical Jewish literature, and the New Testament demonstrates that divine qualities were found not only in the creator of the universe, but in a host of other beings known by various names: sons of God; the Angel of the LORD (a chief angel second only to God); Wisdom; named angels like Gabriel or Michael; the Son of Man; the divine Glory; and the *Logos* (Word; see "John's Prologue as Midrash," p. 546). Christians came to believe that Jesus, identified in the New Testament as the Son of Man, the Son of God, and the *Logos*, had a status equal to God's; for example Jn 1.1 says: "In the beginning was the Word [*Logos*], and the Word was with God, and the Word was God."

In the Tanakh, the God identified by the tetragrammaton YHWH is the creator and ruler of the universe who has made a covenant with the people of Israel, his special treasure (Ex 19.6). He appears to individuals (for example, Abraham in Gen 15) and to the people of Israel at Sinai. He bestows both reward and punishment on individuals and on nations. In the Tanakh, God is male; female imagery is rarely applied to him, and his grammatical gender is always male. However, both male and female are made in the divine image (Gen 1.26). The Tanakh occasionally refers to the gods of other nations, but always as objects of scorn, and many prophets strongly denounce Israelites who worship them. By the time of the Babylonian exile, an anonymous prophet teaches that there is only one God, and that the deities whom other nations worship do not exist (Isa 40–55).

The figure of Wisdom in the book of Proverbs (whose date is disputed) and in Second Temple Jewish literature is the only female figure that comes close to divine status. In Proverbs, Wisdom speaks about herself in the first person (8.22–23): "The LORD created me at the beginning of his work, the first of his acts of long ago. Ages ago I was set up, at the first, before the beginning of the earth." What is more, she participated in creation (8.30): "then I was beside him, like a master worker; and I was daily his delight, rejoicing before him always." The first-century BCE apocryphal work, the Wisdom of Solomon, exalts her status even more: she is the "fashioner of all things" (7.22), "a breath of the power of God, and a pure emanation of the glory of the Almighty" (7.25). She sits by the throne of God's glory (9.4,10), and is closely linked with the "all powerful word," who leaps from the royal throne to destroy the firstborn of the Egyptians (18.15). In a review of biblical events (Wis 10), she is the protector and guide of human beings from the beginnings of human history, playing a role the Tanakh gives to God or angels.

While according to Jewish belief God does not have a son, Genesis 6 and Job 1–2 refer to the "sons of God" (*bnei Elohim*). The term "sons of God" refers to a council of divine beings who advise God and carry out his commands. The divine council also appears in Ps 82.1, where its members are called "gods" (*elohim*). The adversary (*ha-satan* in Hebrew) in the book of Job is a member of this council, whose task it is to observe human beings. In 1 Kings 19, the prophet Micaiah is privileged to observe the meeting of the divine council. In Daniel 7, the members of the divine council are called "the holy ones of the Most High." The Septuagint and a Dead Sea Scroll also refer to sons of God at Deut 32.8. In Joshua 5.13–15, "the captain of the LORD's host" appears as a "man" with an unsheathed sword.

One notable angel in Tanakh is the Angel of the Lord, who is often indistinguishable from God himself. Sometimes, the Tanakh calls angels "man" or "men." For example, when three "men" (angels) visit Abraham (Gen 18), it is not obvious at first that one of them is God, but eventually, when he replies to Sarah's laughter at the news she will bear a son in her old age, his identity becomes clear. Exodus 23.20–21 refers to another angel in exalted terms—

> Behold, I send an angel in front of you, to guard you on the way and to bring you to the place that I have prepared. Be attentive to him and listen to his voice; do not rebel against him, for he will not pardon your transgression; for my Name is in him.

This angel bears God's essence, his name, and even though he is distinct from God he possesses divine authority. The later pseudepigraphic *Apocalypse of Abraham* (perhaps first-century CE) names this angel Yahoel; in early Jewish mystical literature he is called Metatron. The development in Jewish thought of this angel who bears the name of God into God's principal angel is an important component in the fashioning of early Christian ideas about the divinity of Jesus.

In rabbinic and mystical literature, the angel Metatron is identified as the *sar ha-panim*, the Prince of the (divine) Presence. He is the angel next to God in power and authority. In the later mystical work *3 Enoch* (dated to the sixth century CE), Metatron is identified with the translated Enoch (who in Gen 5.24 "walked with God and then was not, for God took him"). When Enoch enters the divine realm, he is challenged by the angels, but God takes him then and transforms him into an enormous fiery heavenly being with many wings and eyes whose status is higher than any of the other angels. In the third- or fourth-century CE rabbinic story of the four who entered the *pardes* (paradise), Elisha ben Avuyah (a second-century tannaitic rabbi) sees Metatron sitting in judgment of the world and cries out that there are "two powers" in the heavenly realm. For this statement the rabbinic story judged him a heretic; this indicates that any approach to teachings that could be seen as analogous to Christian doctrine were viewed negatively by some rabbinic authors.

YHWH can also be manifested in other forms, for example as the pillar of cloud or fire that led the Israelites in the desert (see, e.g., Ex 13.21–22). In Ex 16.10 the glory (Heb *kavod*) of the LORD appeared in the cloud to the people. The glory (*kavod*), seated on the divine throne, has a close relationship to the divine essence, and it is depicted especially in Priestly and related literature. In Ezekiel 1, the *kavod* is anthropomorphic, as the prophet sees their "appearance: they were of human form" (1.5) on the throne, which is the "appearance of the likeness of the glory of the LORD" (1.28). Daniel 10.5–6 depicts a similar figure:

> a man clothed in linen, with a belt of gold from Uphaz around his waist. His body was like beryl, his face like lightning, his eyes like flaming torches, his arms and legs like the gleam of burnished bronze, and the sound of his words like the roar of a multitude.

He may be identified as the angel Gabriel, who also appears in Daniel 8.15–26; 9.21. Named angels appear only in the book of Daniel and postbiblical books (for example, the angel Raphael is an important character in the book of Tobit). Michael is Israel's protector (Dan 12.1). Soon after the period in which Daniel was written (second century BCE), the number of angels, including named angels, proliferated in many Jewish sources.

One important role of angels in both the Tanakh and the New Testament is to announce to certain women that they will give birth to important sons. Along with the three "men" who announced that Sarah would have a son (Gen 18), the angel of the LORD informs Hagar, Abraham's second wife, that she will have a son whom she should name Ishmael (Gen 16.11). In Judges 13.3, an angel of the LORD appears to the wife of Manaoh and announces to her that she will "conceive and bear a son" (Samson); some later readers even believe that this angel impregnated her (see Gen 6.1–4). In Lk 1.11 "an angel of the Lord" appears in the Temple to the priest Zechariah to tell him that his wife will bear a son (John the Baptist). The angel is Gabriel (Lk 1.19), "who stand[s] in the presence of God." Gabriel also tells Mary that she will bear a child, whom she will name Jesus (Lk 1.31).

A very significant figure for developing messianic views appears in Daniel 7.9–14. Daniel sees that "thrones were set in place, and an Ancient One (lit., "Ancient of Days," a name for God) took his throne." Daniel then sees "one like a human being (lit., 'son of man') coming with the clouds of heaven," who came to the "Ancient One and was presented before him." (In Hebrew and Aramaic, "son" may refer to a biological male child, or to a member of a class, and thus the translations "son of man" and "human being" are both possible.) To him was given "dominion and glory and kingship, that all peoples, nations, and languages should serve him." This text distinguishes between "the son of man/the one like a human being" and God. Most early Jewish and Christian interpreters identified the "son of man" as the messiah. A first-century CE pseudepigraphic Jewish work, the *Similitudes of Enoch*, further developed the image of the "one like a human being" of Daniel 7, depicting him as a messianic figure who existed before the world was created: "even before the sun and the constellations were created, before the stars of heaven were made, his name was named before the Lord of Spirits" (*1 En.* 48.3) and: "from the beginning the Son of Man was hidden, and the Most High kept him in the presence of his power and revealed him only to the chosen" (62.8). Modern scholars disagree with the ancient interpretation, arguing that Daniel displays no interest in the Davidic dynasty and would not have applied the term "messiah" to the "one like a human being." For Daniel, this figure was likely a divine being subordinate to YHWH, perhaps Michael, the leader of the heavenly host of angels, who is called "the great prince, the protector of your people" (Dan 12.1).

The New Testament uses the term "Son of Man" in various ways. It is Jesus' preferred self-designation; sometimes he uses it to refer, cryptically, to an eschatological heavenly judge and advocate. For example, when Jesus heals a man who is paralyzed, he says to the skeptical scribes who question his actions (Mk 2.9–11),

> "Which is easier, to say to the paralytic, 'Your sins are forgiven,' or to say, 'Stand up and take your mat and walk?' But so that you may know that the Son of Man has authority on earth to forgive sins"—he said to the paralytic—"I say to you, stand up, take your mat, and go to your home."

Here, he identifies himself with the Son of Man who has the divine authority to forgive sins. In Mk 14.61–62, the high priest asks him, "Are you the Messiah, the Son of the Blessed One?" Jesus answers by saying, "I am; and 'you will see the Son of Man seated at the right hand of the Power,' and 'coming with the clouds of heaven.'" (Parallels in Mt 26.64 and Lk 22.70 have Jesus say, "You say [that I am]" in response to the question.) Jesus here quotes from Daniel 7.13, implying that his future role will be as ruler, seated at the right hand of God. John's Gospel uses "Son of Man" twice in sayings of Jesus to refer to the preexistent Christ: see Jn 3.13: "No one has ascended into heaven except the one who descended from heaven, the Son of Man." Eventually, in Christian usage, the title "son of man" for Jesus was replaced by the title "son of God."

Later Jewish rabbinic and mystical literature continued to develop earlier concepts about angels and lesser divine beings, ranging from the midrashic idea that God consulted the ministering angels when deciding whether to create human beings, to the portrayal in early mystical texts of a vast host of angels, organized in a hierarchy, who are responsible for all aspects of the world. Postbiblical Christian writers also continued to elaborate ideas about angels. In the early sixth century CE, a Christian writer known as Pseudo-Dionysius wrote *The Celestial Hierarchy*, which presented the angels in a threefold hierarchy, using terms known both from Tanakh and the New Testament. The highest order included seraphim, cherubim, and thrones; the second order consisted of dominions, authorities, and powers; the third order encompassed principalities, archangels, and angels. In the Middle Ages, the Jewish philosopher Maimonides also organized the angels into a hierarchy containing ten levels.

LOGOS, A JEWISH WORD
JOHN'S PROLOGUE AS MIDRASH

Daniel Boyarin

In the first centuries of the Christian era, the idea of the Word (Gk *Logos*) was known in some Greek philosophical circles as a link connecting the Transcendent/the Divine with humanity/the terrestrial. For Jews, the idea of this link between heaven and earth, whether called by the Greek *Logos* or *Sophia* ("wisdom") or by the Aramaic *Memra* ("word"), permeated first- and second-century thought. Although monotheistic, Jews nevertheless recognized other supernatural beings who communicated the divine will. The use of the *Logos* in John's Gospel ("In the Beginning was the Word/*Logos*, and the Word was with God, and the Word was God" [Jn 1.1]) is thus a thoroughly Jewish usage. It is even possible that the beginning of the idea of the Trinity occurred precisely in pre-Christian Jewish accounts of the second and visible God that we find in many early Jewish writings.

Philo, writing in first-century CE Alexandria for an audience of Jews devoted to the Bible, uses the idea of the *Logos* as if it were a commonplace. His writings make apparent that at least for some pre-Christian Judaism, there was nothing strange about a doctrine of a manifestation of God, even as a "second God"; the *Logos* did not conflict with Philo's idea of monotheism.

Philo and his Alexandrian Jewish community would have found the "Word of God" frequently in the Septuagint (LXX), where it creates, reveals, and redeems. For example, speaking of the exodus, Philo writes:

> whereas the voice of mortals is judged by hearing, the sacred oracles intimate that the *words of God* (*logoi*, the plural) are seen as light is seen, for we are told that *all of the people saw the Voice* [Ex 20.18], not that they heard it; for what was happening was not an impact of air made by the organs of mouth and tongue, but the radiating splendor of virtue indistinguishable from a fountain of reason.... But the voice of God which is not that of verbs and names yet seen by the eye of the soul, he [Moses] rightly introduces as "visible." (*Migr.* 47–48)

This text draws a close connection between the *Logos* and light, as in John 1.4–5: "In him was life, and the life was the light of all people. The light shines in the darkness, and the darkness did not overcome it."

Further, for Philo as for the Gospel of John, the *Logos* is both a part of God and also a separate being:

> To His Word (*Logos*), His chief messenger (*archangelos*), highest in age and honor, the Father (*Pater*) of all has given the special prerogative, to stand on the border and separate the creature from the Creator. This same [i.e., the Word] both pleads with the immortal as suppliant for afflicted mortality and acts as ambassador of the ruler to the subject. He glories in this prerogative and proudly proclaims, "and I stood between the LORD and you" [Deut 5.5], that is neither uncreated by God, nor created as you, but midway between the two extremes, a surety to both sides. (*Heir* 205–6)

Philo oscillates on the point of the ambiguity between separate existence of the *Logos*, God's Son, and its total incorporation within the godhead. Philo's *Logos* is neither just the Wisdom (Gk *sophia*; Heb *ḥokhmah*) of the Bible, nor is it quite the Platonic *logos*, nor the divine Word (Heb *davar*), but a new synthesis of all of these.

Although this particular synthesis is as far as we know original to Philo, he develops it, as is his wont, by biblical allegories:

> The Divine Word (*Theios Logos*) descends from the fountain of wisdom (*Sophia*) like a river to lave and water the olympian and celestial shoots and plants of virtue-loving souls which are as a garden. And this Holy Word (*Hieros Logos*) is separated into four heads, which means that it is split up into the four virtues. . . . It is this Word (*Logos*) which one of Moses' company compared to a river, when he said in the Psalms: "the river of God is full of water" (Ps 65.10); where surely it were absurd to use that word literally with reference to rivers of the earth. Instead, as it seems, he represents the Divine Word (*Theios Logos*) as full of the stream of wisdom (*Sophia*), with no part empty or devoid of itself . . . inundated through and through and lifted up on high by the continuity and unbroken sequence from that ever-flowing fountain. (*Dreams* 2.242–45)

Other versions of *Logos* theology, namely notions of the second god as personified Word or Wisdom of God, were present among Aramaic-, Hebrew-, and Syriac-speaking Jews as well. Hints of this idea appear in Jewish texts that are part of the Bible such as Proverbs 8.22–31, Job 28.12–28, as well as those not in the Hebrew Bible (but included in the Apocryphal/Deuterocanonical books): Sirach 24.1–34, Wisdom of Solomon 7.22–10.21, and Baruch 3.9–4.4. Especially common is the Aramaic word *Memra* ("Word") of God, appearing in the Targumim, the early Aramaic translations and paraphrases of the Bible (e.g., *Targum Onqelos*, *Targum Neofiti*), where it is used in contexts that are frequently identical to ones where the *Logos* has its home among Greek-speaking Jews.

Although official rabbinic theology sought to suppress all talk of the *Memra* or *Logos* by naming it the heresy of "Two Powers in Heaven" (*b. Hag.* 15a), before the rabbis, contemporaneously with them, and even among them, there were many Jews in both Palestine and the Diaspora who held on to a version of monotheistic theology that could accommodate this divine figure linking heaven and earth. Whereas Maimonides and his followers until today understood the *Memra*, along with the *Shekhinah* ("Presence"), as a means of avoiding anthropomorphisms in speaking of God, historical investigation suggests that in the first two centuries CE, the *Memra* was not a mere name, but an actual divine entity functioning as a mediator.

The following examples from the Targumim suggest that the *Memra* has many of the same roles as the *Logos*:

> *Creating:* Gen 1.3: "And the *Memra* of H' (a form of abbreviation for the Divine Name, the Tetragrammaton) said 'Let there be light' and there was light by his *Memra*." In each of the following verses, it is the *Memra*—intimated by the expression "and he said"—that performs all of the creative actions.
>
> *Speaking to humans*: Gen 3.8ff.: "And they heard the voice of the *Memra* of H'. . . . And the *Memra* of H' called out to the Man."
>
> *Revealing the Divine Self*: Gen 18.1: "And was revealed to him the *Memra* of H'."
>
> *Punishing the wicked*: Gen 19.24: "And the *Memra* of H' rained down on Sodom and Gomorrah."
>
> *Saving*: Ex 17.21: "And the *Memra* of H' was leading them during the day in a pillar of cloud."
>
> *Redeeming*: Deut 32.39: "When the *Memra* of H' shall be revealed to redeem his people."

These examples show that the *Memra* performs many, if not all, of the functions of the *Logos* of Christian theology (as well as of Wisdom).

In the Targumic tradition, the translation of Exodus 3.12–14, the theophany of the burning bush, offers an instructive illustration of the essence of the *Memra*. The Hebrew text reads, "God said to Moses: 'I am that I am,' and he said: 'Thus shall you say unto them, I am has sent me to you.'" "I am" is here a name of God. The *Palestinian Targum* translates: "And the *Memra* of H' said to Moses: He who said to the world from the beginning, Be there, and it was there, and who is to say [to it Be there, and it will be there]; and he said, Thus shall you say to the Israelites, He has sent me to you." In other words, the name "I am" is glossed in the Targumim by a reference to Genesis 1.3, "And God said: Let there be": the Word by which God brought the universe into being is the *Memra*.

In the next verse in the *Palestinian Targum*, this name for God, "He who said to the world 'Be there,'" becomes transformed into a divine being in its own right: "I, My *Memra*, will be with you: I, My *Memra*, will be a support for you."

Targum Neofiti (Ms. 1) confirms this connection between the divine being and the word. In Exodus 3.13, in answer to Moses' apprehension that he will not be up to the task of going to Pharaoh and persuading or forcing him to allow Moses to bring out the Israelites, God answers: "I will be with you." *Neofiti* reads: "I, My *Memra*, will be with you." The other Targumim maintain this interpretation but add the element of the *Memra* as supporter, thus: "And he said: Because my *Memra* will be for your support." From here we see how this *Memra*, revealed to Moses in the declaration "I am," supports him, redeems the Israelites, and all the rest of the saving activities. In the Targum, as in the *Logos* theology, this Word has been hypostasized, turned into an actual divine being.

The conclusive evidence for the connection of the Targumic *Memra* and the *Logos* of John appears in the Palestinian Targumic poetic homily on the "Four Nights," probably a liturgical text in which four special nights in sacred history are delineated:

> Four nights are written in the Book of Memories: The first night: when the Lord was revealed above the world to create it. The world was unformed and void and darkness was spread over the surface of the deep; *and through his* Memra *there was light and illumination* [italics added], and he called it the first night.

This text matches the first verses of John's Prologue, with its association of *Logos*, the Word, and light. The midrash of the "four nights" culminates in the coming of the Messiah, drawing even closer the connections between the Targum heard in the synagogue and John's Gospel. Moreover, the midrash of the "four nights" is most likely a fragment of Paschal liturgy, suggesting even more palpably its appropriateness as a text for comparison with John's Gospel, where Jesus is compared to the Paschal offering. In order to see this, however, we must pay attention to the formal characteristics of Midrash as a mode of reading Scripture (see "Midrash and Parables in the New Testament," p. 565). One of the most characteristic forms of Midrash is a homily on a scriptural passage or extract from the Pentateuch that invokes, explicitly or implicitly, texts from either the Prophets or the Hagiographa (Gk "holy writings": specifically, very frequently Psalms, Song of Songs, or Wisdom literature) as the framework of ideas and language that is used to interpret and expand the Pentateuchal text being preached. This interpretive practice is founded on a theological notion of the oneness of Scripture as a self-interpreting text, especially on the notion that the latter books are a form of interpretation of the Five Books of Moses. Gaps are not filled with philosophical ideas but with allusions to or citations of other texts.

The first five verses of the Prologue to the Fourth Gospel fit this form nearly perfectly. The verses being preached are the opening verses of Genesis, and the text that lies in the background as interpretive framework is Proverbs 8.22–31. The primacy of Genesis as text being interpreted explains why we have here *Logos* and not "Wisdom." In an intertextual interpretive practice such as a midrash, imagery and language may be drawn from a text other than the one under interpretation, but the controlling language of the discourse is naturally the text that is being interpreted and preached. The preacher of the Prologue to John had to speak of *Logos* here, because his homiletical effort is directed at the opening verses of Genesis, with their majestic: "And God said: Let there be light, and there was light." It is the "saying" of God that produces the light, and indeed through this saying, everything was made that was made.

Philo, like others, identifies Sophia and the *Logos* as a single entity. Consequently, nothing could be more natural than for a preacher, such as the composer of John 1, to draw from the book of Proverbs the figure, epithets, and qualities of the second God (second person), the companion of God and agent of God in creation; for the purposes of interpreting Genesis, however, the preacher would need to focus on the linguistic side of the coin, the *Logos*, which is alone mentioned explicitly in that text. In other words, the text being interpreted is Genesis, therefore the Word; the text from which the interpretive material is drawn is Proverbs, hence the characteristics of Wisdom:

1. In the beginning was the Word,
   And the Word was with God,
2. And the Word was God.
   He was in the beginning with God.
3. All things were made through him,
   and without him was not anything made that was made.
4. In him was life, and the life was the light of men.
5. The light shines in the darkness, and the darkness did not receive it.

The assertion that the Word was with God is easily related to Proverbs 8.30, "Then I [wisdom] was beside him," and even to Wisdom of Solomon 9.9, "With thee is wisdom." As is frequently the case in rabbinic midrash, the gloss on the verse being interpreted is dependent on a later biblical text that is alluded to but not explicitly cited. The Wisdom texts, especially Proverbs 8, had become commonplaces in the Jewish interpretive tradition of Genesis 1. Although, paradoxically, John 1.1–5 is our earliest example of this, the form is so abundant in late antique Jewish writing that it can best be read as the product of a common tradition shared by (some) messianic Jews and (some) non-messianic Jews. Thus the operation of John 1.1 can be compared with the Palestinian Targum to this very verse, which translates "In the beginning" by "With Wisdom God created," clearly also alluding to the Proverbs passage. "Beginning" is read in the Targumim sometimes as Wisdom, and sometimes as the *Logos, Memra*: By a Beginning—Wisdom—God created.

In light of this evidence, the Fourth Gospel is not a new departure in the history of Judaism in its use of *Logos* theology, but only, if even this, in its incarnational Christology. John 1.1–5 is not a hymn, but a midrash, that is, it is not a poem but a homily on Genesis 1.1–5. The very phrase that opens the Gospel, "In the beginning," shows that creation is the focus of the text. The rest of the Prologue shows that the midrash of the *Logos* is applied to the appearance of Jesus. Only from John 1.14, which announces that the "Word became flesh," does the Christian narrative begins to diverge from synagogue teaching. Until v. 14, the Johannine prologue is a piece of perfectly unexceptional non-Christian Jewish thought that has been seamlessly woven into the Christological narrative of the Johannine community.

AFTERLIFE AND RESURRECTION

Martha Himmelfarb

Writing toward the end of the first century CE, the Jewish historian Josephus tells us that of the three Jewish "philosophies," two, the Essenes and the Pharisees, embraced the idea of the immortality of the soul and an afterlife involving reward and punishment (*J.W.* 2.154–58,163; *Ant.* 18.14,18). Josephus does not mention a belief in resurrection, perhaps because immortality of the soul was a concept more familiar to his Roman audience, but some ancient Jews believed that the soul would be returned to its body at the time of the last judgment. Josephus's claim that the Pharisees believed in reincarnation (*J. W.* 2.163) may be an attempt to present this idea in a form more accessible to his audience.

According to Josephus, the Sadducees were the only Jewish group to reject the idea of the immortality of the soul and postmortem reward and punishment (*J. W.* 2.165; *Ant.* 18.16). Though they were in the minority, the Sadducees would have been right to remind other Jews that most of the writings that eventually became part of the Tanakh say nothing about reward and punishment after death. Rather, they envision the dead, righteous and wicked together, enduring a shadowy existence in Sheol, an inhospitable place often described as a miry pit (e.g., Isa 38.18), a widespread idea in the ancient Near East, similar to Hades in the Homeric poems. The blessings and curses that attach to Israel's covenant with God play a central role in the Torah and prophetic writings, but they are typically experienced collectively by the people of Israel as a group, and they take place in this world.

The only strand of the Tanakh to emphasize the reward and punishment of the individual is Wisdom literature, but these texts locate rewards and punishments in this life. The book of Proverbs, which may contain ancient material but probably reached its final form early in the Second Temple period, presents the optimistic side of the Wisdom tradition: "Long life is in [Wisdom's] right hand; in her left hand are riches and honor" (Prov 3.16). Human experience has always offered observers abundant evidence to the contrary, however, and other Wisdom works criticize the view that wise and righteous behavior leads to reward. The book of Job launches a frontal attack as the pious Job demands to know why God has inflicted so much suffering on him. The divine response appears in the final chapters of the book, where the LORD answers Job from a whirlwind with a poetic invocation of his awesome creative powers and rejects the message of the friends who insist that Job must have done something wrong to merit the evils that have befallen him. Ecclesiastes (Qohelet), likely written around the fourth century BCE, takes a less direct but perhaps even more subversive approach to the problem of why the righteous suffer and the wicked prosper: it juxtaposes sayings that describe the rewards of wisdom to sayings that claim that the wicked and righteous share a single fate.

Neither Job nor Ecclesiastes suggests the possibility of an afterlife as a venue for righting earthly wrongs. The first Jewish text to take that step is the *Book of the Watchers*, as scholars call the work preserved as *1 Enoch* 1–36. This work, which reached its final form by the end of the third century BCE, was extremely influential during the Second Temple period. In the last portion of the *Book of the Watchers*, the patriarch Enoch, mentioned briefly in Genesis 5.21–24, is taken on a tour of the earth in the company of the archangels. After seeing the fiery abyss in which the watchers of the title of the work, angels who descended to earth to marry women, are imprisoned (*1 En.* 21), Enoch comes to a mountain with four chambers. Three of the chambers are dark, but the fourth is light and has a fountain in its midst (*1 En.* 22). Although difficult, the passage suggests that the chambers house the souls of the dead, with the souls of the wicked consigned to the dark chambers while the souls of the righteous enjoy light and the fountain as they await their final disposition on the Day of Judgment. In at least one of the dark chambers the wicked souls are already undergoing punishment.

A little later in the tour Enoch arrives at the center of the earth where he sees a holy mountain and an accursed valley (*1 En.* 26–27). In keeping with the setting of the *Book of the Watchers* in the period before the flood, the place is not named as Jerusalem. Yet the holy mountain is Mount Zion, on which the Temple later stood, while the valley is the valley of Hinnom (Heb *Gehinnom*; Gk *Gehenna*), where Jerusalemites are said to have sacrificed their children as burnt offerings to the god Moloch (see, e.g., Jer 7.31–32). The angelic guide tells Enoch that at the last judgment, those who have cursed God will be gathered there, cursed forever. Later Jewish as well as Christian texts will detach Gehinnom/Gehenna from its geographical associations and use the designation as a name for hell.

By the end of the third century BCE, then, we have evidence that some Jews imagined the survival of the soul after death as an opportunity to reward the righteous and punish the wicked. It is possible that exposure to Greek culture, with its idea of the immortality of the soul, contributed to these developments, although there is nothing in the *Book of the Watchers* to suggest the strong body/soul dualism found in some strands of Greek thought.

It is difficult to gauge how quickly the new picture of the afterlife became widespread among Jews. It is not prominent among the sectarian writings of the Dead Sea community. There is no hint of it in the Wisdom of ben Sirach (Ecclesiasticus), written in the early second century BCE, not long after the composition of the *Book of the Watchers*. A little later the book of Daniel promises that at the last judgment

> Many of those who sleep in the dust of the earth shall awake, some to everlasting life, and some to shame and everlasting contempt. Those who are wise shall shine like the brightness of the sky, and those who lead many to righteousness, like the stars forever and ever. (Dan 12.2–3)

This picture differs significantly from that of the *Book of the Watchers*. Reward and punishment are administered only after the last judgment, and in the meantime the dead "sleep." Furthermore, not everyone will receive reward or punishment: "many" will awake, but not all. Finally, unlike the *Book of the Watchers*, Daniel describes the righteous who enjoy eternal life as like the stars.

Daniel's picture probably reflects concern for the deaths of some of the "wise"—as the book calls the pious elite to which its author belonged (Dan 11.33–35)—in the course of the Maccabean revolt (167–163 BCE). The martyrs who died for observing Torah in the face of prohibitions by Antiochus IV, the Seleucid king to whose empire Judea belonged, posed the problem of the suffering of the righteous in a new and acute way. They suffered and died not despite their righteousness but because of it. The many who awake are, presumably, the martyrs, the righteous who suffered in this life, and the wicked who flourished; those righteous who lived out the full measure of their days in peace and those wicked who received their just desserts in this world are not in need of postmortem redress.

The expectation of reward after death also plays a central role in the story of the mother and her seven sons martyred by Antiochus, preserved in 2 Maccabees (ch 7), an account written in Greek in the decades following the revolt. Because they refused the king's order to violate Torah by eating the meat of swine, the sons are tortured and put to death together with their mother, who urges them on in defying the king. A central theme of the words of both mother and sons is the certainty that God will reward them by returning them to their bodies for eternal life (7.23,36). This understanding of the afterlife as involving bodily resurrection stands in contrast to Daniel's picture of the righteous dead as stars.

Two centuries later, as Josephus testifies, belief in reward and punishment after death had become the dominant view among Jews, and the idea is central to rabbinic Judaism, which emerged in the aftermath of the destruction of the Second Temple in 70 CE. The Mishnah, the earliest document of rabbinic Judaism, completed early in the third century CE, insists that all Jews have a portion in the world to come as long as they do not forfeit it through particular forbidden beliefs and practices (*m. Sanh.* 10.1). This statement indicates both the centrality of the belief in an afterlife and the fact that not all accepted it. But the rabbis also remind Jews that they will be held to account for their deeds: "This world is like an antechamber before the world to come; prepare yourself in the antechamber so that you may enter the banquet hall" (*m. Avot* 4.16). The embrace of these ideas about the afterlife by Jews in the late Second Temple period and the early rabbinic era helps to explain why the New Testament takes them for granted. But even as reward and punishment after death became a central Jewish belief, there was a range of views about the precise contours of the afterlife. The differences in the sources discussed earlier over the status of the body in the afterlife, and the relationship between postmortem reward and punishment and the last judgment, were never definitively resolved. A consensus eventually emerged on some points, such as the bodily resurrection of the righteous, but the rabbis do not appear to have been worried about the lack of unanimity on this subject, which had no legal implications.

Early Jews and Christians were clearly fascinated with the specifics of postmortem reward and punishment. In the *Apocalypse of Peter*, a second-century Christian work, the apostle Peter is granted a vision in which he sees the rewards and punishments that begin after the Day of Judgment. The righteous inhabit a garden filled with beautiful, fruit-bearing trees and fragrant spices while the wicked endure terrible punishments, including fire, boiling mud, and wild beasts, as angels of torment supervise. Some of the punishments are appropriate for specific sins. For example, sinners hang by the sinful limb: the tongue for blasphemers, the hair for women who engaged in sexual sins, and the thighs for men who also did so. Such hanging punishments play an important role in Jewish visions of hell as well, and although no surviving Jewish text predates the *Apocalypse of Peter*, the work appears to have adapted the punishments from earlier Jewish works. In the centuries that followed the *Apocalypse of Peter*, the subject of postmortem reward and punishment was taken up by many other apocalyptic works, both Jewish and Christian. Virtually without exception these works give more attention to the punishments of hell than to the rewards of paradise.

The afterlife and the resurrection of the dead become a central aspect of Jewish thought in the rabbinic period and beyond. The opening paragraphs of the *Amidah*, the central prayer in the rabbinic liturgy, repeatedly praise God for bringing the dead back to life, and the passage from Mishnah *Sanhedrin* promising all Israel a portion in the world to come is recited before each chapter of *m. Avot* when it is read in the synagogue on Sabbath afternoons. Maimonides, the great philosopher and legal authority of the twelfth century, included the resurrection of the dead among his thirteen articles of faith. Where the traditional liturgy is in use and the classical texts of the Jewish tradition are studied, the idea remains very much alive.

PAUL AND JUDAISM

Mark D. Nanos

AUTHORSHIP AND DATE

Paul (Saul), author of many important New Testament letters (including Romans, 1 and 2 Corinthians, Galatians, Philippians, 1 and 2 Thessalonians, and Philemon [others attributed to him are disputed]) was born to a Jewish family, early in the first century CE. (All dates for Paul's life are conjectural but fall within the first sixty or so years of the first century CE.) At some point after the early Jesus-following subgroups became active, Paul (who had opposed these groups) had a change of heart about their merit following an experience while traveling toward Damascus to seek to stop these Jews from continuing on their course. From about the mid-40s CE he traveled and founded communities in the eastern Mediterranean area, writing to his congregations and to others. He was arrested by the Roman authorities and taken to Rome; there is no mention in the New Testament of his death, but tradition holds that he was beheaded during one of the persecutions of Christians by the emperor Nero, in the mid-60s. All that we know about Paul is what can be deduced from his letters, to which many features are traditionally added from the account of his ministry in Acts of the Apostles. Acts, however, was written some decades after Paul's presumed date of death and is a problematic source for a number of reasons, not least that it does not mention either that Paul wrote letters or that he was actively engaged in raising collections from the non-Jews of his communities for the benefit of poor Jewish followers of Jesus in Judea (Rom 15.25–32; 1 Cor 16.1–4; 2 Cor 9.1–15; Gal 1.10; Phil 1.15–19), both of which are otherwise central to what we learn from Paul firsthand.

Few would disagree that Paul was born and raised a Jew, or that he had practiced Judaism according to Pharisaic norms, all of which Paul acknowledges (Rom 9.1–5; 11.1; 2 Cor 11.22; Gal 1.13–16; Phil 3.4–6; cf. Acts 9.21–26). More controversial is whether he continued to practice Judaism *after* his change from being a persecutor of the followers of Jesus to becoming an apostle to the nations (i.e., the Gentiles). Paul has traditionally been portrayed as having converted from Judaism to Christianity, and thus as both the original apostate and a threat to the Jewish people and to Judaism. But that is not the only way to interpret Paul. During his time, Jews who accepted the proclamation that Jesus was the Messiah understood themselves (and were understood by many others) to be practicing Judaism, albeit as representatives of a new subgroup.

In Philippians 3.3–11 (cf. citations in the previous paragraph), Paul argues from his special status as an observant Jew, one who observed Torah "blamelessly" (Phil 3.6), to make the case that even though he has this standing and his Gentile audience does not, he is nevertheless no greater than they in their relationship to God through Jesus. Paul also held that those Jews who did not agree with him about proclaiming Jesus to the Gentiles were in a position of advantage: they (male) had circumcision to signify that they were set apart to observe God's Torah ("teaching"), and the "words" or "oracles" of God (Rom 3.1–2; 4.1,12; 15.8). These words from Moses and the Prophets not only informed Jews about what righteousness meant for themselves but were also the message they were privileged to announce to the nations, the task Paul understands himself to be undertaking (Rom 1.1–6). Indeed, Paul declared, the Torah overall was "holy and just and good," even "spiritual" as opposed to "of the flesh" (Rom 7.7–25). In Romans 11.28–29, Paul explained that the Jews who did not agree with him about Jesus' role were nevertheless "beloved for the sake of the patriarchs" of Israel, and thus will be restored, because "the gifts and calling of God are irrevocable" (11.26,30–32).

Paul set out some of these gifts in Rom 9.4–5:

> They are Israelites, and to them belong the adoption, the glory, the covenants, the giving of the law, the worship [i.e., the Temple sacrificial system], and the promises; to them belong the patriarchs, and from them, according to the flesh, comes the Messiah.

Paul speaks in the present tense of these privileges for Israelites and their continued covenant standing regardless of their current view of Jesus. Paul even informed the non-Jews to whom he wrote the letter that his own ministry among them was in part a vehicle to demonstrate to his fellow Jews his gospel proposition, that Gentiles would be admitted to membership in Abraham's people by way of Jesus (11.13–14).

INTERPRETATION

For Paul, those of his fellow Jews who did not share his persuasion were not outsiders to God's family. He saw them as temporarily mistaken, and thus outsiders to the Christ-following remnant—and that by God's design, but only until the message had begun to go out to the rest of the nations. Thereafter, he believed that his fellow Jews would join him in his convictions about Christ, and in the task of declaring this news to the nations (Rom 9–11). He also saw his role as fulfilling Torah, for he maintained that the promise to Abraham was not just of one nation, but that he would be "the father of many nations" (Gen 12.1–3,17; 22.15–18; Rom 4; Gal 3.6–9).

Paul saw himself wholly within Judaism, as one who was assigned a special role in the restoration of Israel and the nations (Rom 11.1–15; Gal 1.13–16). He was a reformer, one who sought to redress what he believed to be an oversight (his own, formerly, and that of his fellow Jews, still); he was not the founder of a new religion, even if things later turned out otherwise. When he related his calling, he explained that he thereafter no longer lived in Judaism in the same way that he had before (Gal 1.13–16). Indeed, he had been one seeking to stamp out this new movement, and now he became an unmatchable force in its success. Paul does not write that he no longer lives in Judaism, but that he has changed *the way* he lives Judaism.

Paul did not leave Judaism, neither the Jewish way of life nor Jewish communities. He rejected, however, his former opposition to the assertion of the nascent Christ-movement that non-Israelites became equal members of the family of Abraham without becoming members of the family of Israel. He now believed that what Judaism awaited, that day when the nations would turn from idols to worship Israel's God, had begun in the end-of-the-ages resurrection of Jesus. For Paul, the resurrection was a sign that the messianic age had been inaugurated.

Thus, Judaism, Paul believed, should announce that it was time for the nations to turn to Israel's God, the one and only God, through Jesus. The Gentiles do not become Israel when that day arrives; rather, they must remain members of the other nations, just as was expected (see Isa 2.2–4; chs 65–66). But they do become fellow members of the Jewish way of life, that is, of the Jewish communities and their religious practice of Judaism. Jews remain Jews in that day, which was so fundamentally obvious for Paul and his contemporaries that it was not even a topic of his discussions; it was simply assumed. It is evident in the logic of his instructions to non-Jews, e.g., in 1 Cor 7.17–24, when he says his "rule" in all his assemblies is for everyone to remain in the state one was in when called, the circumcised in a circumcised state, and the foreskinned in foreskinned state, but in whichever state one is in, it is essential that one "obey the commandments of God." When this instruction is coupled with Paul's attestation (Gal 5.3) that anyone in a circumcised state is obliged to observe the whole Torah, it is evident that Paul presumes all Jewish Christ-followers would remain faithful to their Jewish covenant identity by the observance of Torah.

Moreover, Paul's statement that he has been disciplined in the synagogue with forty lashes less one on five occasions (2 Cor 11.24) indicates that both he and the authorities who administer such punishment understood him to be under the jurisdiction of the Jewish communities. The infraction for which he was disciplined was likely his claim that his Gentile converts were full members of the family of Abraham, and not merely guests. Thus, adjustments (new *halakhot*) had to be made by these Jews to accommodate the non-Jews eating together with them as equals, such as how to arrange seating at meals without the usual hierarchical arrangements in order to demonstrate that the messianic banquet had begun for Israel *and* the nations.

This issue of table fellowship between Jews and Gentiles is at the center of the disagreement between Peter and Paul in Antioch. (See "Food and Table Fellowship," p. 521.) According to Paul (Gal 2.11–14), Peter (called "Cephas" here, the Aramaic word for "rock" that was the equivalent of "Peter") at first shared table fellowship with non-Jews but then, when representatives of the Jerusalem community came to visit, withdrew. Paul accuses Peter of withdrawing not because of the food served, but because of the way non-Jews were being treated as full members at the table apart from commitment to become Jews. The challenge does not come from the kosher menu committee, but from those who advocate circumcision (i.e., proselyte conversion) of these non-Jews if they are to be seated within this Jewish subgroup as full members of the Jewish community at large. The argument Paul makes is based on Peter's agreement about the gospel, the proposition that these non-Jews are now equal in standing before God with Jews like Peter and Paul, through their mutual commitment to the God who raised up Jesus. But Peter's withdrawal undermined what they both taught; thus Paul accused him of hypocrisy, thereby making these non-Jews question whether what they have been taught is in fact what these Jews believe, or whether it would be better to become proselytes and avoid such discrimination in the future. The issue was one of consistency in teaching and practice: if Gentiles wishing to join this Jewish subgroup community did not have to become Jews first, then Jews who were members of the community would of necessity treat them as equals, and not as those who were outside the community (Gal 2.14).

Paul's letters arguably indicate that he lived in a Torah-observant manner, including eating according to the prevailing halakhic conventions for an observant Jew. But that is not the way he has been most commonly interpreted. Rather, his urging of non-Jews to remain non-Jews, and his own self-deprecating comments about the supposed superiority of his standing as a Jew relative to their own questionable standing in the larger Jewish communities, has led many to suppose that Paul was demeaning the value of Jewish identity and behavior, of Torah as well as Israel. If, however, we look at the rhetorical context of his comments, we see that in all his extant letters they are directed to non-Jews. Such an audience is by definition not under Torah obligations as if they were Jews, and, Paul maintains, they are not to become Jews. This makes clear the highly situational nature of his arguments, which are actually based on citations from scripture and on the enduring value of Torah to guide their lives (cf. Rom 3.31; 15.4; 1 Cor 10.11; Gal 5.14). In order to facilitate this alternative, it is useful to add "for Christ-following non-Jews" to virtually all of his statements of instruction to non-Jews; otherwise, the universalizing of Paul's comments about circumcision and Torah-observance will appear to be inclusive of Jews, of everyone, and thereby miss his ethnically nuanced points. These provide for continued Jewish identity and Torah observance for Jesus-following Jews, alongside of Torah-respectful behavior for Jesus-following non-Jews.

Moreover, this understanding of Paul corrects the common view of 1 Cor 9.19–22:

> For though I am free with respect to all, I have made myself a slave to all, so that I might win more of them. To the Jews I became as a Jew, in order to win Jews. To those under the law I became as one under the law (though I myself am not under the law) so that I might win those under the law. To those outside the law [lawless ones] I became as one outside the law [as a lawless one] (though I am not free from God's law but am under Christ's law) so that I might win those outside the law [the lawless]. To the weak I became weak, so that I might win the weak. I have become all things to all people, that I might by all means save some.

This statement has overwhelmingly been read to mean that Paul compromised Torah-observance to "become like" non-Jews in order to gain them to Christ, as well as to mimic the behavior of Torah-observant Jews to win them. But Paul does not write that he *behaves* like each one he seeks to gain. Rather, he explains that he *relates rhetorically* to each according to the premises from which each works. Paul does not worship idols or eat idol food to "become like" Greeks in order to win them to Christ. That would be deceptive, mimicking another's propositional values if not actually sharing them, tricking someone into a move that will result in a new identity that is other than it was represented to be. This has often, and rightly, been pointed out, based on the traditional interpretation. Rather, we should look at it as we look at what is expected in a philosophical discussion: one philosopher seeking to persuade another will make a case based on that philosopher's premises, in an effort to show that they can lead to a very different conclusion. Paul does not seek to convince the "lawless" from Torah or Roman law or even the general principles of lawfulness, but from the principles to which the lawless would appeal to justify their behavior, and similarly, he seeks to convince the lawful from law, including, in the case of Torah-observing Jews, from Torah, and in the case of Roman-law-observing citizens, from Roman law.

An example from Acts, the earliest biographical sketch of Paul, though written several decades after his ministry, illustrates this point. In Acts 17.16–34, Luke describes a scene in which Paul sought to convince Greek philosophers in Athens about the God of Israel and Jesus. Whether the account in Acts accurately represents a historical event in Paul's life or not, it is pertinent to note that the author describes Paul relating to these worshipers of other gods in their own terms. He shows Paul beginning from these philosophers' own premises, even praising them for their religious inclinations, and then seeking to bring them to understand that there is a god not made with hands whom they should be worshiping. He includes criticism of the making of statues along the way, but that is after he has made the case from their premises. He quotes a Greek poet in this argument, but not anything from Torah (whereas, when speaking to Jews earlier in this chapter, Luke portrays Paul citing Torah; vv. 1–3; cf. 13.32–43). In contrast to the prevailing views of later interpreters of Paul, including those who denounce him as an apostate, this example supports the idea that an early interpreter of Paul understood him to continue to be faithful to Jewish practices, but to adjust his arguments to different audiences in order to win them to his understanding of the significance of Jesus.

Paul's theological basis for the policy of maintaining ethnic and gender and other forms of difference—but at the same time upholding that this difference does not legitimate discrimination in the assemblies of Christ—is based explicitly on the Shema (Deut 6.4: "Hear, O Israel: The LORD [is] our God, the LORD alone" or "The LORD [is] our God, the LORD [is] one"). Note that in translation "is" must be supplied (Hebrew does not require that each sentence contains a verb), so there is no tense in the original outside of context. Paul is arguing that up to the present God has been our (Israel's) God, but is from henceforth to be the one God of all the other nations with the arrival of the awaited day (so too *Sifre* on Deut 6.4 [*piska* 31]; Rashi on Deut 6.4 still maintains a similar interpretation roughly a millennium after Paul). Paul claimed this was a present reality: he believed that day had indeed dawned, and it was the responsibility of these groups to demonstrate the truth of that proposition by remaining different, yet equal: "since God is one" (Rom 3.29–31; 4.9–12; 15.5–12; 1 Cor 8.5–6; Gal 3.28–29). He believed the end of the ages that the prophets foretold, when the wolf will lie down with the lamb, not becoming a lamb but not eating the lamb either, was fulfilled when the members of the nations will join alongside of Israel in worship of the One God within the assemblies of Jesus-followers who are thus called to practice righteousness together (Isa 65.25; cf. 65–66; 2.2–4). This awaited time of "shalom," of concord within the community and relief from enemies, is what Paul claimed was now to take place, at least in the assemblies of followers of Christ.

Paul was, however, adamant that Christ-following non-Israelites must not become proselytes to Judaism (i.e., males must not be circumcised). That is, they must not become Jews or Israelites, but they nevertheless become co-participants with Jews/Israelites in the community of those set apart to the One God. (Similarly, for other Jewish teachers against proselyte conversion, albeit for different reasons, in rivalry with those who do teach it, see the discussion of King Izates in *Ant.* 20.38–42.) That nuanced position of difference without discrimination is easy to misunderstand, and thus could be largely responsible for the traditional portrayal of Paul as anti-Torah and anti-Judaism.

Humans can seldom live according to such utopian ideals, yet Paul appealed to his assemblies to rely upon God's Spirit in their way of life together (Rom 8; 1 Cor 2; 12; Gal 5.16–6.8). That, Paul believed, would bear witness to his fellow Jews who did not share his convictions (yet) that something had changed. Paul anticipated that these fellow Jews would thereafter join with him in declaring this news to the nations, undertaking with Paul Israel's special calling as God's heralds (Rom 11).

JUDAIZERS, JEWISH CHRISTIANS, AND OTHERS

Charlotte Elisheva Fonrobert

In recent years the so-called parting of the ways question—when and how did "Judaism" and "Christianity" turn into two distinct and separate phenomena—has been approached in new ways. We have learned to recognize more clearly how Christian and Jewish authorities were trying to secure clearer boundaries between the two traditions. We have also learned to differentiate the official position from how the people whom they were addressing may have behaved and believed. For instance, as late as 386 CE John Chrysostom, the Christian bishop and author of *Adversus Judaeos* (sermons "Against the Jews"), can thunder at his audience about the dangers of attending synagogues and succumbing to "the evils" of the Jewish holiday observances. This vitriolic attack is a clear indication that people in his Christian communities in Antioch on the Orontes were attracted to and frequented Jewish synagogues. While Chrysostom would have liked his flock to consider this as a dangerous blurring of boundaries, his audience—for all we know—may have considered attendance at synagogues as perfectly compatible with their Christian beliefs.

The more careful reading of the ancient texts has moved the supposed date of the actual separation between Judaism and Christianity from its initial dating at the end of the first century CE to the current one that places it at the end of Late Antiquity (ca. 200–700 CE), or later. Not even the Roman emperor Constantine's conversion in the early fourth century signals the end of Jewish and Christian enmeshing, since the Christianization of the empire and the institutional boundaries that this produced took centuries longer.

In this discussion, so-called hybrid groups variously labeled Jewish Christians, Christian Jews, Judaizers, and in early rabbinic texts *minim* (a generic Hebrew term for sectarians) play a central role. Such groups, we assume, blurred the boundaries between the two major religious traditions, much like the Antiochian Christian synagogue-goers that so enraged Chrysostom. The persisting problem with these labels, however, is that none of the people to whom they are applied would have recognized them or chosen them. In most cases, such terminology is used either by early Christian and rabbinic polemic writers, declaring those who do not follow their guidelines to be heretics, or by modern scholars who seek to clarify the story of Jewish and Christian identity formation. Furthermore, in many cases we cannot even be sure whether such a group or groups existed, since ancient authors may have concocted them in order to shore up their own control over their own presumed authentic and pure version of Christianity or Judaism. In other words, these terms cannot easily work as descriptive terms and thus may have outlived their usefulness.

The category of "Jewish Christian" is used often in the effort to understand the impact of Paul's mission to the Gentiles (Gk *ethnē*, lit., "nations"). The early Judean and Galilean followers of Jesus, minus Paul, might have formed nothing more than a group of Jews who believed that Jesus' life and death had significance for their lives, not much different from, say, Jews who followed the Jewish messianic pretender Sabbatai Zvi in the seventeenth century or other messiah figures in later Jewish history.

Paul differentiates between the "gospel for the circumcised," of which Peter, the "apostle to the circumcision" (Gal 2.8), is in charge, and the "gospel for the uncircumcised" (Gal 2.7). Equally, in the later book of Acts, the leaders of the earliest community of Jesus' followers in Jerusalem, James and his colleagues, address the newly established community of Antioch—with its many non-Jewish members—as "the brothers *of Gentile origin* in Antioch and Syria" (Acts 15.23, my emphasis), versus the "circumcised believers" (Acts 10.45; 11.2; etc.). Scholars subsequently restate this distinction by referring to the two types of early believers as Jewish (as opposed to Gentile) Christians. However, no New Testament author uses the terminology "Jewish Christian."

The Petrine mission, the "gospel for the circumcised," would appear to have produced Jewish Christians, Jews who are also Jesus-believers (and who may still understand themselves to be Jews). What about the people whom Paul seeks to convert, the "Gentiles"? Are these simply Gentile Christians, former "pagans" who have become followers of Christ, as opposed to the Jewish Christians that Peter produces? This distinction appears to be an ethnic one.

Things become messy, however, as the two groups merge to form one community, as is the case in Antioch. Initially, Peter and his "Jewish Christians" get along just fine with Paul and his "Gentile Christians," and share meals. But when James sends emissaries from Jerusalem to Antioch to check up on what is going on, Peter apparently prefers to draw a clearer line again, at least in Paul's account of the conflict, by "separating" himself and presumably his group from Paul's people during common meals. This is the only time the New Testament refers to "Judaizing," as Paul accuses Peter (Cephas) of wanting Paul's "Gentile Christians" to "Judaize" (Gk *ioudaizein*, Gal 2.14), literally, behave or live like Jews. This term is found in the Septuagint (Esth 8.17), in Josephus (*J.W.* 2.17.10 §454 and 2.18.2 §§462–63), and in Plutarch (*Cic.* 7.6) to refer to Jewish practices. Later Christian writers used the term in this way, such as Ignatius, the Antiochian bishop at the end of the first century CE, who provides a whole list of Sabbath observances that would be considered "Judaizing" (*Magn.* 9), down to John Chrysostom, who labels the attendance at or veneration of synagogues "Judaizing." It is generally used with reference to non-Jews who observe Jewish customs, *without thereby necessarily becoming Jewish*. Thus, given the context, Paul's complaint about Peter is that he seeks to turn Paul's Gentile Christians into Judaizers, namely "Jewish-acting Gentiles," presumably by modeling a behavior that aims to persuade them into following some kind of Jewish food rules.

When contemporary scholars describe James or Peter as Judaizers, they use the term inappropriately from a historical perspective, since James and Peter are Jews, in however complicated a way, and as such the term did not apply to them. Paul does not call Peter a Judaizer; he just blames him for turning the Gentiles in the Antiochean group into a Judaizing kind of people, rather than allowing them to be something else. Indeed, a description of James and Peter as Judaizers reflects the polemical use of the term in later Christian literature, namely as a label for people who inappropriately propagate Jewish behavior. Thus, by the time we get to Chrysostom's sermons against the Jews, the Judaizers among his audience, i.e., the Christians who frequent the synagogues, are described with military metaphors such as enemy infiltrators, or alternately with metaphors of disease, as people who infect the community with some Judaizing virus. Indeed, the polemical echo that this term bears renders it potentially offensive to contemporary Jewish ears. It cannot possibly operate as a culturally neutral term.

Compared to Judaizer and Judaizing, the term "Jewish Christian" may seem more straightforward. It may lack the polemical overtones that Judaizer has acquired, but whether it is descriptive is another question. The "Jewish" in "Jewish Christian" is not so easy to determine. If it is intended to serve as an ethnic term, how is this ethnic identity determined? A mere reference to birth seems insufficient, since at least with the onset of Diaspora, birth is not a self-evident means of establishing identity. For example, the earliest evidence for the matrilineal principle is found in the Mishnah at the end of the second century CE (e.g., *m. Qidd.* 4.1). A case that brings this problem to the fore is Paul's disciple Timothy, who is "the son of a Jewish woman, but [whose] father was a Greek" (Acts 16.1), and whom Paul has circumcised, ostensibly to placate local Jews.

Or, alternately, would the word "Jewish" in Jewish Christian refer to *practice*, to a certain level of observance of Jewish customs and law such as submitting to circumcision? Here also a host of follow-up questions emerges: is circumcision sufficient to establish Jewishness? Is a circumcised man unquestionably Jewish, regardless of other observances? What about observant (circumcised) Jews with beliefs such as holding Jesus to be the messiah, the Son of God, or the like? Does their observance keep them within the category of Jewish? Or are they now something other than Jewish?

Finally, is the criterion for determining Jewish identity recognition by other Jews, and if so by which Jews? Paul knew who the believers ("the church of God") were (Gal 1.13), and he persecuted them. Would he have considered them as heretical Jews or as Jewish Christians?

To add another level of complication, the term "Jewish Christian" is also used to describe the character of certain texts and interpretive practices. This particular use is perhaps the most fraught one, as it tends to make assumptions about patterns of thought as essentially Jewish. If an early Christian text uses a particular strategy that we assume might appeal to a supposedly more Jewish-oriented audience, such a text is easily considered as a Jewish Christian one. For instance, it is often suggested that the audience of the Gospel of Matthew consisted of, or at least contained, Jewish Christians, because (for example) this Gospel's author, more than the others, emphasizes that Jesus has come to fulfill biblical prophecies: Matthew quotes (the Septuagint's version of) prophetic texts and explains how Jesus has come to fulfill them. Is this Gospel therefore a Jewish Christian text, rather than a Christian text, or for that matter rather than a Jewish text? Is it aimed at Jewish Christians, because we assume that biblical quotations are for Jews who became Jesus followers (and of course, so this argument goes, all Jews know their Bible)? And can we extrapolate from a text to the social makeup of its audience or the identity of its writer? These questions are crucial, because the same kind of arguments are applied again and again to early Christian texts (after most or all of the New Testament writings are completed) that are more rule- or law-oriented, such as the *Didache* (end of first/early second century), and the *Didascalia Apostolorum* (third century). Since Jews, so the argument goes, have a predisposition toward law, the audience for these writings or the authors of such texts must be Jewish Christian. The point is not that this identification is necessarily wrong, but that we have to be aware of the assumptions that we make as we study the beginnings of Christianity.

The lesson we may learn is perhaps that there is no master narrative to be told with two clearly delineated characters, Christianity and Judaism, and then a third one that cannot decide what it is. In the past scholars have tried to consider "Jewish Christianity" as the third force in such a story, as a social group that eventually atrophied, with its own tradition and literature beginning with the Gospel of Matthew. In this version, all the people declared heretics of a Jewish Christian sort by our authoritative writers in early Christianity and Talmudic Judaism—groups with labels such as the rabbis' *minim*, the Ebionites mentioned by Irenaeus (at the end of the second century CE), Jerome's Nazarenes (who believed in Jesus in some way "but do not cease to observe the old law"), and more—were part of "Jewish Christianity." This understanding became largely discredited as we learned to identify the practice of heresiology (the effort of identifying heresy and heresies) as a rhetorical technique of polemic rather than as an ethnography of existing groups. It is easier to define boundaries of identity, Jewish or Christian, by invoking that which one is *not*. Thus, Christian beliefs that rely on biblically inspired ideas and Jewish views that include a belief in a messiah essentially remain implicated in each other in some way, and the early struggles for winning followers were acutely marked by figuring out where to draw the boundaries. Only the forces of institutionalization, with the church on one side and the study houses of the rabbinic sages that would formulate the Mishnah and the Talmud on the other, would allow for certain versions of Judaism and Christianity to win out. This process of institutionalization enabled structures of authority to produce and enforce canons of permitted and prohibited texts, which in turn shored up stronger boundaries between Judaism and Christianity as two very different religious traditions.

THE CANON OF THE NEW TESTAMENT

Michael R. Greenwald

The collection of documents that we today call "The New Testament" came into being over a prolonged period that extended from the second through the fourth centuries in the West of the Roman Empire and through the sixth century in the East. The word "canon" itself derives from a Greek word meaning "measuring rod," "rule," or "standard"; however, when applied to the Christian Bible, it has, since the fourth century CE, come to mean a list of books sanctioned by the majority Christian church as having divine authority and in which each book is understood in light of all of the others. For most of the period since the sixth century, the canon of the New Testament has been the same in every Christian tradition although Christian churches still differ about the contents of their Old Testament canons (see chart, p. 600). During the Protestant Reformation, though, the canon even of the New Testament was called into question and is, in some places, questioned again today.

The earliest collections of Christian documents were very probably small collections of Paul's epistles in various places in the Roman Empire. Clement of Rome (ca. 96) certainly had Romans, 1 Corinthians (which he cites in *1 Clem.* 47), and probably Ephesians. He also had the so-called Epistle (actually more an exhortation or sermon) to the Hebrews, but he shows no clear indication of having used any other specifically Christian documents. Similarly, Ignatius of Antioch (ca. 110–117), in his *Letter to the Ephesians* (Ignatius, *Eph.* 12.2) says, "Paul . . . mentions you in Christ in all his epistles." Furthermore, in both of these cases, the authority claimed is no more than that of the writer or perhaps of Paul himself. The second letter of Peter, probably the latest document in the New Testament (possibly as late as the second quarter of the second century) in what is almost certainly the first reference to Christian documents as "scripture," says, "the ignorant and unstable twist [the epistles of Paul] to their own destruction as they do the other scriptures" (3.16b), thereby attesting to a collection of Paul's epistles, albeit of unknown scope, that is now being accorded the status of "scripture," that is, equal to the Tanakh. Beyond this statement in 2 Peter, the first significant collection of Christian documents for which we have evidence is that of Marcion, who flourished in Rome ca. 140. Marcion rejected Christian use of the Tanakh and in its place, offered an abbreviated version of Luke's Gospel and a collection of ten Pauline epistles identical to our current collection minus Ephesians and the Pastoral Epistles (1 and 2 Timothy and Titus). In place of Ephesians, Marcion included an epistle to the Laodiceans, which the African church father Tertullian (late second/early third century) identified as our Ephesians.

Collections or even clear references to the Gospels begin to appear somewhat later. Nevertheless, our earliest actual fragment of New Testament writing is a small papyrus (P.52), dated ca. 125–150, containing John 18.31–33,37–38. Papias (fl. ca. 125–150), an early bishop of Hierapolis, mentions Mark and Matthew in what the church historian Eusebius (ca. 325 CE) says is a reference to the Gospels (*Hist. eccl.* 3.39.15–16). But Papias also says that he regards the authority of the words of Jesus as transmitted by the elders from the apostles themselves to be greater than that of any information from books (*Hist. eccl.* 3.39.4). Eusebius further tells us unambiguously that Papias "used quotations" from 1 John and 1 Peter (*Hist. eccl.* 3.39.17).

Ignatius of Antioch may show some familiarity with the same tradition that generated Matthew (compare his letter to Polycarp [Ignatius, *Pol.*] 2.2 with Mt 10.16 and Ignatius, *Eph.* 14.2 with Mt. 12.33) but shows no evidence of familiarity with the Gospel itself, and he is much more likely to have used a collection of the sayings of Jesus in much the same way that the authors of the Gospels themselves did. Similarly, Polycarp of Smyrna, in his *Epistle to the Philippians* (ca. 117–140), may allude to passages in Matthew and Luke, but as with Ignatius, it is possible that he too used a collection of Jesus' sayings. Nevertheless, it is after Polycarp that we begin to see introductory formulae like "as it is written," which heretofore had been used to introduce passages from the Tanakh (see "The New Testament between the Hebrew Bible [Tanakh] and Rabbinic Literature," p. 504), now being used to introduce quotations from Christian documents.

The earliest direct evidence for a collection of the Gospels comes from Justin Martyr (also the first to mention the Revelation of John, see *Dial.* 81.15), ca. 160, who makes direct reference to Matthew, Mark, Luke, and possibly John, and says that he permits the reading of "memoirs of the apostles or apostolic men" (*1 Apol.* 66–67) in worship, one sign that the Gospels too might now be considered Christian scripture. If Justin did in fact have John, this is also the first indication of a collection of the *four* Gospels. But the multiplicity of Gospels is now itself a problem for the church. Justin's student Tatian (ca. 175) attempted to solve this problem by combining the four Gospels into a single narrative that we call the *Diatessaron* (literally, "through the four"), a text used as scripture by the Syrian church into the fifth century.

The first Christian to argue for *limiting* the number of Gospels to four was Irenaeus of Lyons (ca. 180). Irenaeus argues further that certain other accounts may *not* be read because they are heretical. His implied "New Testament" (a term that he uses, but not clearly referring to texts) includes the four Gospels, Acts of the Apostles (the first evidence of its use), the thirteen epistles attributed to Paul, 1 Peter, 1 and 2 John, the Revelation of John, and also the *Shepherd of Hermas*, a work no longer part of the New Testament canon (see, e.g., *Adv. Haer.* 3.21.3–4.).

By the beginning of the third century, the contours of a "New Testament" as we know it begin to emerge. Clement of Alexandria and Tertullian in Carthage treat as authoritative a collection of Christian documents similar to that of Irenaeus. Both approve of Hebrews (Eusebius says that Irenaeus also used Hebrews, but that cannot be demonstrated from his surviving work) and both use the epistle of Jude. Tertullian treats as scripture both the *Shepherd of Hermas* and the *Epistle of Barnabas*, another work no longer part of the New Testament. He is, furthermore, the first to use the term "New Testament" in a clear reference to a collection of texts (*Prax.* 15). Clement of Alexandria includes the *Revelation of Peter* and calls *1 Clement*, the *Shepherd of Hermas*, the *Epistle of Barnabas*, and a late first/early second century work called the *Didache* "inspired." Furthermore, the Muratorian Fragment (some time between the second and fourth centuries CE), includes four Gospels (Matthew and Mark are missing, but this is a clear defect in the text), Acts, thirteen epistles of Paul, 1 and 2 John, Jude, the Revelation of John, and curiously, the Wisdom of Solomon. The author also hesitatingly accepts the *Revelation (Apocalypse) of Peter*. The Muratorian author rejects the *Shepherd of Hermas* as being too recent and epistles to the Laodiceans and Alexandrians as forgeries in the name of Paul. Hebrews is absent as is the otherwise early attested 1 Peter. While this list of documents is roughly congruent to usage at the end of the second century, and the heresies that it mentions are second-century heresies, it is, in form, somewhat similar to fourth-century canon lists.

Origen (ca. 185–254), whose words are preserved by Eusebius, stated that there are "four Gospels, which alone are unquestionable" (*Hist. eccl.* 6.25.4): Matthew, Mark, Luke, and John. Eusebius also says that Origen stated that Peter "left one acknowledged epistle, and it may be, a second also, for it is doubted," and that the author of the Fourth Gospel also wrote Revelation and at least one epistle (*Hist. eccl.* 6.25.8–10). Origen considers Acts and Hebrews to be scripture, although by this time the authorship of the latter was a matter of debate within in the church; Origen, though usually content to attribute it to Paul, at one point says, "But who the writer of the epistle was: in truth, God knows" (*Hist. eccl.* 25.14, citing Origen's *Homilies*). Origen is unclear, apparently deliberately so, concerning the status of James and Jude.

By the fourth century, the accepted list of books that were treated as the New Testament had not changed much, as we can see from Eusebius's *Ecclesiastical History*. Eusebius lists those books that everyone recognizes as scripture (*homologoumena*): four Gospels, Acts of the Apostles, fourteen epistles of Paul (the thirteen ascribed to him as well as Hebrews), 1 John, 1 Peter, and Revelation. Of the latter, he acknowledges that "some reject it, but others count it among the recognized books." Next are the "disputed books" (*antilegomena*): the epistles of James, Jude, 2 and 3 John, and 2 Peter (which he elsewhere rejects as not genuine [*Hist. eccl.* 3.3.4]). Next are the "illegitimate" or "not recognized" books: the *Acts of Paul*, the *Shepherd of Hermas*, the *Revelation of Peter*, the *Epistle of Barnabas*, the *Didache*, and perhaps also the Revelation of John, which he now says that some count among the recognized books. He then makes an additional, rather confusing comment that all of these books "according to the tradition of the church, are true, genuine, and recognized, and those which differ from them in that they are not in the testament, but rather are disputed, albeit known to most of the churches." Finally, he lists those works that he considers "entirely wicked and impious" because they are "forgeries of heretics." Among these he includes gospels under the names of Peter, Thomas, and Matthias, and Acts under the names of "Andrew, John, and the other apostle" (*Hist. eccl.* 3.25.1–7).

The emperor Constantine asked Eusebius to produce fifty copies of the Christian Bible. Unfortunately, none of these copies has survived, but Eusebius must have made decisions as to which texts to include. Two biblical codices (singular "codex") from the fourth century have survived. One of these, called *Sinaiticus* because it was discovered in St. Catherine's Monastery on Mount Sinai, is the oldest complete Old (Greek only) and New Testament. Its New Testament contains all the books of the modern New Testament plus the *Shepherd of Hermas* and the *Epistle of Barnabas*. The second codex, called *Vaticanus* because it was discovered in the library of the Vatican, is of nearly equal age, but it is complete only through Hebrews 9.14 (the epistles of Paul come at the end). The remainder of Hebrews is missing, as are Philemon, the Pastoral Epistles, and Revelation.

After Eusebius, canon lists, some using the term "canon," are drawn up in various places by various bishops or church synods. These list the books of the New Testament for the express purpose of saying "these books and no others." One of these, the Thirty-ninth Festal Letter of Bishop Athanasius of Alexandria, presents in 367, for the first time, a list of the twenty-seven books that are included in the modern New Testament. Many of the canon lists drawn up after that of Athanasius do not follow his list, and into the fifth century the Western churches still continued to challenge the canonicity of Hebrews, and the Eastern churches continued to challenge James, 2 Peter, 2 and 3 John, and Revelation. Yet, late in the fourth century Augustine of Hippo accepted the canon list of Athanasius and, save for occasional challenges to Hebrews or the minor catholic epistles, or rare attempts to add the *Epistle to the Laodiceans*, the list of Athanasius and Augustine would—in the Western church and a century later in the Eastern churches—stand as the canon of the New Testament until the Protestant Reformation a thousand years later.

Yet through this entire period, the church never adopted a set of criteria by which to determine canonicity. Although unstated, the most significant criterion for inclusion was usage and dissemination. Colossians 4.16, for example, speaks of forwarding letters from church to church. The earliest of the church fathers, the aforementioned Clement of Rome (fl. 90–100), by referring to 1 Corinthians in his letter to the church at Corinth, shows that he has in Rome a copy of a letter that Paul had originally sent to Corinth.

Also important was the criterion of apostolicity, that is, whether the document emanated from an apostle or was connected to an apostolic authority (e.g., Luke and Acts were associated with Paul, Mark with Peter). On the other hand, many of the now noncanonical documents were written in the names of apostles and yet were not cited as scripture by any church father: usage (or lack of it) thus took priority over ascription to an apostle.

A third criterion was conformity to the proper understanding of Christianity (the *regula fidei* or "rule of faith") as the majority church (and certainly the majority of those in power in the church) saw it. The *Gospel of Peter* had failed on this point, possibly because it could be read to support a Gnostic view that the divine aspect of Jesus abandoned him before death (v. 19), and so permission to use it was withdrawn. Such was the fate of numerous other gospels, apocryphal acts, and pseudepigraphic epistles.

Finally, the document had to be sufficiently "catholic," meaning that it had to be understood as applying to the church as a whole. This was most problematic for the so-called catholic epistles (that is, general letters, not sent to specific Christian communities or individuals: the letters of James, 1 and 2 Peter, 1, 2, and 3 John, and Jude) and the epistles of Paul (which had been sent to specific communities or individuals). The former, though not identified with one recipient or community, may have been seen as overly specific; the latter were obviously intended to address specific problems or situations. These documents therefore were reinterpreted so that their message was seen as applying to the entire Christian world.

"Divine inspiration" was not a criterion for acknowledging a document as scripture. The concept itself was developing only during the second century and worked, rather, the other way around. All works of scripture were understood to be divinely inspired, but divine inspiration was never a *limiting* factor in the establishment of the New Testament. Many documents were thought to be inspired without simultaneously being considered scripture. Thus acknowledgement by Clement of Alexandria that the *Shepherd of Hermas* or the *Epistle of Barnabas* were inspired cannot be taken further to demonstrate that he also considered them to be scripture.

Early reformers, particularly Martin Luther (1483–1546), one of those who led what came to be the Protestant Reformation of the sixteenth century, began to challenge those very books that had been questioned in the last decades of the formation of the canon. The issue finally came to a head in 1522 when Luther relegated Hebrews, James, Jude, and Revelation to the end of the New Testament and left them without a sequence number as he had given to the other twenty-three books. He thereby implied that these books ought to have a lower status. Luther's practice was followed by William Tyndale's first English translation in 1525. In response, in 1546 at the Council of Trent, the Roman Catholic Church for the first time formally declared as an article of faith "all of the books the Old and New Testament . . . with an equal sense" to be "canonical" and that anyone who said otherwise was to "be anathema." As far as the New Testament canon was concerned, over the next decades several Protestant churches, including the Church of England and the French and Belgic Confessions, followed suit. The Presbyterians followed nearly a century later in the Westminster Confession. But some Protestants, most notably the Lutherans, have never declared the canon closed, and thus the question of the canon persists to this day.

Protestant theologians have, from time to time, asked whether there is a principle behind the collection that serves to determine what is *truly* canonical, that is, a "canon within the canon." Furthermore, if such a principle exists, not only does Luther's relegation of Hebrews, James, Jude, and Revelation to the back of the New Testament with a somewhat diminished status become understandable from a Protestant perspective, but so too does the current conversation about the possible inclusion of the *Gospel of Thomas*, rejected by the church as early as the third century CE. Since all Roman Catholic churches recognize the authority of the church to determine the principle by which the canon is established, these are not issues for them.

TRANSLATION OF THE BIBLE

Naomi Seidman

The New Testament is bound with the antecedent Jewish Scripture in a finely spun intertextual web: the New Testament models itself after linguistic, literary, and theological patterns in the earlier texts, and direct references are ubiquitous, as when Jesus quotes Deuteronomy 6.5 in exhorting his followers, "You shall love the Lord your God with all your heart" (Mt 22.37) or when Paul quotes God's words (Gen 21.9) to Abraham, "Drive out the slave and her child" (Gal 4.30). The text that lies in the background of the New Testament is often not the Hebrew Bible but rather the Hebrew Bible in Greek—often quoted from memory or modified to suit the new context. (See "The Septuagint," p. 562.)

The use of Greek sources by New Testament writers became a subject of intense Jewish-Christian dispute because of one particularly charged Septuagint (LXX) citation. In linking the birth of Jesus to a prophetic passage in Isaiah, Matthew 1.18–25 quotes not from the Hebrew but rather from the Septuagint version of Isaiah 7.14 (with a slight modification, either deliberate or due to quoting from memory). After the angel urges Joseph to take Mary into his home, "for the child conceived in her is from the Holy Spirit," the narrator continues:

> All this took place to fulfill what had been spoken by the Lord through the prophet: "Look, the virgin [*parthenos*] shall conceive and bear a son, and they shall name him Emmanuel," which means, "God is with us."

The Christian reading of this passage, as it crystallized in the first few centuries, viewed Matthew as saying that Isaiah had prophesied the miraculous birth of Jesus through "the virgin." A Jewish response to this reading can be gleaned from the debate between the Christian writer Justin Martyr (d. ca. 160 CE) and his fictionalized Jewish interlocutor in *Dialogue with Trypho the Jew* (ca. 150 CE). In what would come to be the standard Jewish position, Trypho argued that no virgin appeared in Isaiah's Hebrew text; Isaiah spoke rather of *ha'almah*, the young woman; this prophecy was fulfilled, moreover, in Isaiah's own time since it involved an imminent political and military threat facing Judah and so had nothing to do with Mary. Trypho implied that the Septuagint translation Matthew cites was simply wrong, and that Jews needed no intermediary to understand Isaiah. Nevertheless, the Jewish insistence that the Septuagint was either flawed or had been misunderstood was complicated by the awkward fact that the Septuagint was a translation composed and historically accepted by some Jews, indeed praised as uniquely perfect by such Jewish writers as Philo (see his *Life of Moses*). Some historians surmise that it was precisely this Christian embrace of the Septuagint that led Jewish communities to adopt new Greek translations in the second and third centuries CE, particularly the hyperliteral translation of Aquila, which renders Isaiah's *ha'almah* as *hē neanis*, "the young girl."

Jewish Bible translations since then invariably render Isaiah's *ha'almah* as "the girl," or "the young woman," while translations produced by and for Christians rendered in Isaiah's prophecy, until very recently, *the* virgin, the same virgin that would reappear in Matthew. Thereby, Christian translators avoided opening an uncomfortable gap between Isaiah and Matthew. Not until the Revised Standard Version appeared in 1952 did a mainline Christian Bible translation allow Isaiah to speak of the "young woman" while Matthew cited him as naming the virgin; the translation was burned by Christian fundamentalists for this heresy and perhaps also for the not-unrelated "sin" of including on the translation committee the well-known Jewish Bible scholar and translator, Harry Orlinsky.

The Christian position on the Matthew citation of the Greek Isaiah was complicated by an equally awkward set of circumstances: not only was the Septuagint, as Christian polemicists increasingly discovered, criticized as inaccurate by Jewish interlocutors but also the rarity of Hebrew knowledge in Christian circles often compelled theologians to defer to Jews on questions of what the Hebrew Bible actually said. When Jerome (ca. 347–420), the Christian biblical translator who produced a Latin Bible, departed from the practice of translating the Christian Old Testament portion of the Bible into Latin from the Greek, and announced his turn in his new translation (later called the Vulgate) to the *hebraica veritas*, the "Hebrew truth," he was thus constructing a direct Christian channel to the Hebrew Bible and circumventing what had been an uncomfortable dependence on Jewish expertise. The Vulgate did, however, translate Isaiah 7.14 using the Latin word *virgo*, "virgin," thus perpetuating the Christian practice of reading back from Matthew to Isaiah.

The Vulgate did not resolve these Jewish-Christian tensions; translation has been a major site of Jewish-Christian dispute, and Christian theologians and translators have continued both to seek and to resist Jewish language teachers and Bible interpreters. Nor did Jerome's Vulgate settle matters from the internal Christian viewpoint. Augustine (354–430), the Christian theologian, had argued against Jerome that the established translation, the Septuagint, should be preferred to any new version. Jerome's translation into the "vulgar" tongue carried the day, and eventually it, too, became a canonical translation as the Septuagint had once been, protected by church authority long after Latin had ceased to be a vernacular.

Martin Luther (1483–1546), who began the Protestant Reformation in 1517, produced a German translation of the Bible (NT in 1522, OT/Hebrew Bible in 1534). His was a lively and accessible German translation based directly on the Hebrew of the "Old Testament" and Greek of the New Testament, rather than from the Vulgate. Luther thus repeated the innovative character of Jerome's enterprise even while challenging the supremacy that Jerome's translation had achieved. Luther's translation of Isaiah 7.14 used the German word *Jungfrau*, which has the advantage of a literal meaning—"young woman"—that reflects the underlying Hebrew, but a lexical or usage meaning—"virgin"—that does not. In this it is similar to the English word "maiden," which can mean "virgin"—and metaphorically any entity that is about to have its first trial, as a ship's maiden voyage or a politician's maiden speech—but which also can simply mean "young female," whether sexually experienced or not.

In response to the activities of the Protestant reformers, the Roman Catholic Church convened a council of bishops, which met in the city of Trent (Trento, in northeastern Italy) from 1545 to 1563. The session that met in 1546 awarded the Vulgate canonical status in response to Luther's bold new translation. This meant that both the Latin of the translation, and the contents of the Bible itself (including a larger canon for the Old Testament), were affirmed against the Reformation's call for Bible translations into languages actually spoken at the time and for an Old Testament canon that followed the contents (but not the order) of the Hebrew Bible. The action by the Council of Trent affirming the importance of Latin, therefore, could not obviate the need for new translations. Of course, as time went on, the natural tendency of the Reformation-era translations—for instance, Luther's in Germany and the series of English translations beginning in the sixteenth century and culminating in the early seventeenth century with the King James Version (1611)—was to acquire, with time, their own quasi-canonical status. The history of Bible translation by Christians, from this perspective, moves restlessly between innovation and institutionalization, between the Bible as universal message to be spread in every language and the Bible as untouchable sacred text.

Although such tensions may characterize all traditions with sacred texts, it is particularly acute for Christianity, given its beginnings as a movement that sought to cross ethnic and linguistic lines. The imperative of translation is addressed in the New Testament itself. According to the book of Acts, Jesus' followers have gathered in Jerusalem, and on Shavuot (the Greek term is Pentecost), the first pilgrimage festival after his death, the Holy Spirit (*ruaḥ hakodesh*, in its familiar Hebrew designation) descends upon them in tongues of fire. They begin to speak in languages understood by the multiethnic and multilingual gathering of Jewish pilgrims, "each . . . in our own languages . . . we hear them speaking about God's deeds of power" (Acts 2.8–10). The New Testament can in fact be read as already a translation, presenting in *koinē* Greek, the dominant language of the Roman Empire, experiences that largely took place in other languages, most notably Aramaic, the language of Galilee and Judea; a few passages give tantalizing glimpses of what appear to be Jesus' Aramaic *ipsissima verba*, as in *talitha kumi* (Mk 5.41) and *Eli, Eli, lema sabachthani?* (Mt 27.46; Mk 15.34).

This process of translating Jesus' Jewish-identified Aramaic into the Greek of the empire sometimes extends to an erasing of Jesus' Jewish context. For example, while Jesus is referred to in John 1.38 as Rabbi (followed by a parenthetical explanation, "which translated means Teacher"), nearly everywhere else in the New Testament Jesus is addressed with Greek terms that obscure his Jewish affiliations.

In Matthew 9.20, when the woman with a bloody discharge comes up behind Jesus and touches the "hem of his garment" (KJV) or "the edge of his cloak" (NIV) [in the Greek, *tou kraspedou tou himatiou autou*], she is touching his *tzitzit*, the ritual fringes mandated in Numbers and Deuteronomy, which is similarly (mis)translated in the Septuagint as *kraspedon*, meaning hem, edge, or border. On this point, the NRSV (New Revised Standard Version) correctly reads "the fringe of his cloak." As this example demonstrates, the transformation of the Hebrew Bible into Greek begins not with the New Testament but rather with the Septuagint, which already obscures the Jewish specificity of a number of key biblical terms. Indeed, the Septuagint's translation of "Torah" (the Hebrew is best translated as "instruction") as *nomos*, or "law," underlies the common Christian view that Judaism is legalistic and interested in the "letter of the Law" rather than in faith and grace. More recently, translations have begun to adjust this translation at least as far as the Hebrew Bible is concerned. The NRSV, for example, translates Isaiah 51.4, "*Torah* will go out from me," as "teaching," not "law" as in the RSV and previous translations. (See also "The Law," p. 515.)

Today, missionary New Testament translations for Jews have sometimes attempted to translate the Greek into an English version that "sounds Jewish" and thus quell the sense among potential readers that they are encountering an alien text. David Stern's *Complete Jewish Bible* (CJV), a 1998 Messianic-Jewish translation of both testaments, is in an English sprinkled with Yiddishisms, as if to reinforce the point that the characters of the New Testament are authentic Jews: in Luke 10.4, the apostles are warned: "Don't carry a money-belt or a pack, and don't stop to shmoose with people on the road." Alongside the translational questions surrounding the Jewishness of Jesus and his first followers are those that involve the Jewishness of those who opposed Jesus. The term *hoi Ioudaioi*, generally translated as "the Jews," occurs more than 180 times in the New Testament, 150 of them in John and Acts, usually in describing the adversaries of the Jesus movement. As scholars have pointed out, the term emerges not from the events of Jesus' own day, in which nearly all the major protagonists were Jews, but rather from the enmity and separation arising from the expulsion of the Johannine community from the synagogue (an event "predicted" by Jesus in Jn 16.2). This anachronistic labeling of Jesus' enemies—but not his family or friends—as "the Jews" has contributed to the Christian persecution of Jews. Barclay Newman's 1995 *Holy Bible: Contemporary English Version* was heavily promoted for combating Christian anti-Judaism by translating John's references to *hoi Ioudaioi* as, variously, "the Jewish authorities," "the leaders," or "the crowd." Such attempts have not been universally lauded: The CEV has been attacked, and not only by fundamentalists, on the grounds that it mistranslated the clear words of the New Testament to avoid giving offense to Jews. (See "Ioudaios," p. 524.)

From the first few centuries to our own day, translation has been the stage for some of the most charged and difficult Jewish-Christian arguments. The inclusion of a Jewish Bible scholar on the RSV and NRSV translation committees, the impulse of the CEV to combat Christian anti-Judaism through translation, the production of New Testament translations that seek to transcend religious affiliations, and indeed the publication of the present volume suggest that translation has now also become a productive site of Jewish-Christian dialogue. Nevertheless, controversies and differences continue, as perhaps is inevitable: translation has often served as the ambiguous bridge between the two traditions. Translation, which seeks equivalence, is also a confrontation with difference, in the Jewish-Christian case as elsewhere.

THE SEPTUAGINT

Leonard Greenspoon

Acts 15 narrates a pivotal moment in which disciples of Jesus debated whether "Unless you are circumcised according to the custom of Moses, you cannot be saved" (15.1). During this debate, James cites "the words of the prophets, as it is written" (15.15–18). The first part of this citation "I will rebuild the dwelling of David, which has fallen" is clearly a reference to Amos 9.11 in the traditional Hebrew wording (or Masoretic text [MT]), "I will raise up the booth of David that is fallen." The next line in Acts, "so that all other peoples may seek the Lord," is very different from the MT, "in order that they may possess the remnant of Edom." However, the wording in Acts agrees with the Greek version of the Hebrew Bible known as the Septuagint (LXX). In addition, the vocabulary of the New Testament is clearly reliant on that of the Septuagint: the word "testament" itself is a Latin translation of the Greek word *diathēkē* ("will" or "covenant"): the Greek word was used by the Septuagint translators to render the Hebrew word *berit*, "covenant." Thus, in the account of the Last Supper that Jesus shares with his followers (Mk 14.12–25 and parallels), Jesus states, "This is my blood of the covenant (*haima . . . tēs diathēkēs*)," repeating the Septuagint phrase in Ex 24.8. It is thus clear that anyone seeking to understand the New Testament must take into account its considerable debt to the Septuagint.

The origins of this translation are located at Alexandria, Egypt, in the first third of the third century BCE, during the reign of Ptolemy II Philadelphus (283–246 BCE). The earliest account of how the Septuagint came to be, dating to at least a century after the event, is found in the *Letter of Aristeas*. According to this narrative, the high priest in Jerusalem, at the request of Ptolemy, sent seventy-two elders, skilled in languages and unblemished in morality, to the royal court at Alexandria in order to provide a Greek translation of the Torah (Pentateuch). The number of translators, conventionally given as "seventy" (Gk *septuaginta*) gave the translation its name and its standard abbreviation (LXX). The resultant version was read aloud, to the acclaim of Ptolemy and the Jewish community. The latter went so far as to put a curse on anyone who would make even the slightest change to this Greek text (for a similar curse, see Rev 22.18–19).

Modern scholarship has cast considerable doubt on the value of the *Letter of Aristeas* as a historical source for Septuagint origins. However, as Josephus, among others, demonstrates (*Ant.* Preface), the general contours of the *Letter* were held in high esteem in the first century CE. It is even likely that some embellishments had been introduced by then to support the claim that the Greek translators were in some way inspired. The mid-first century CE Jewish philosopher Philo, himself a resident of Alexandria, spoke of those responsible for the Septuagint as prophets, not just translators (*Life of Moses* 2.7.37). Much later, Christian users of the Septuagint claimed that each translator or pair of translators working in isolation produced identical Greek texts (Augustine, *Doctr. chr.*, 2.15.22). By the first century CE, the term "Septuagint" encompassed the Greek rendering of the entire Hebrew Bible (that is sections of the Bible beyond the Torah). Even some writings originally composed in Greek were included under the rubric Septuagint, such as the Wisdom of Solomon and the books of Maccabees. While evidence for chronology for the production of the Septuagint after the Torah is scarce, the corpus of the Septuagint was completed by the first century CE, but it likely took until the third or fourth century CE before a collection of all of the books of the Septuagint was produced. Such collections are contained in the so-called great manuscripts, written in all capital letters (and therefore called uncial codices): Vaticanus, Alexandrinus, and Sinaiticus. The earliest Greek renderings, which scholars sometimes call the Old Greek to distinguish them from later additions and other changes, were not immune to revision, in spite of the anathema recorded in the *Letter of Aristeas*.

The revisers sought in general to accommodate the Greek text to what they viewed as the Hebrew "original" used in their communities. The Septuagint translators often worked with a Hebrew text that varies from the one later established as the traditional or Masoretic text, and this is one cause of the variances between LXX and MT. Those who were revising the Greek, however, saw such variants, which came from other available Hebrew text traditions, as mistakes, and therefore corrected them.

These other Greek texts include those in a compilation put together by the Christian scholar and theologian Origen (185–254). This compilation consisted of the Hebrew text, a transliteration into Greek letters of the Hebrew, and four Greek translations (the Septuagint and later versions) of the Hebrew. Three revisers are known by name because of their inclusion in Origen's *Hexapla*: Aquila, Symmachus, and Theodotion. For the purposes of New Testament studies, only the last named, Theodotion, is directly relevant. Some of his distinctive readings do appear in the New Testament, making it certain that either he or one of his major sources antedated the first century CE. Thus, we must acknowledge the likelihood that various books of the Greek Scriptures circulated in a variety of forms, differing a little or a lot from each other, in first-century Judea.

In spite of this, much New Testament scholarship prior to the mid-twentieth century (and even some since) spoke of a "Septuagintal" origin for almost all New Testament citations that differed from the received consonantal Hebrew or MT. However, as we have shown, use of the term "Septuagint" or "Septuagintal" is inexact in such contexts, since the Scripture in Greek circulated in so many different forms and revisions.

Taking these and other factors into account suggests a number of questions and raises a number of issues about how New Testament authors might have proceeded. Did the authors know that various books or blocks of Scripture were available in different forms? If so, did they seek out and cite the particular form that best suited their argument? Perhaps the authors compared the Greek text in front of them with the Hebrew text (assuming they could read Hebrew at all). Perhaps some of the authors translated the Hebrew themselves or were able to cite the Greek from memory. In some cases they may have had lists of biblical passages that had already been compiled for preaching or other purposes (e.g., the prophetic and other citations that Matthew uses with his fulfillment formula in 1.22 and other places). At the time of the New Testament writings, few people owned books or scrolls, and biblical passages would have been known and transmitted orally in many instances. What follows are examples of the various phenomena that New Testament specialists wrestle with, and that all readers of the New Testament must at least consider.

Consider again the passage from Amos quoted in Acts. When English readers are faced with clauses as varied as "so that all other peoples may seek the Lord" (Amos, in Acts and LXX) and "in order that they may possess the remnant of Edom" (MT), the connection between their respective wording is tenuous at best. What appears distant in one language may, however, be far closer in another. In unvocalized Hebrew the word for "peoples" (*'-d-m*, *'adam*, "humankind") and "Edom" (*'-d-w-m*, *'Edōm*, "[the land of] Edom") could well have been the same or at the most separated by a single Hebrew letter, *vav*, here represented as "w" because it is a vowel. Although the author/compiler of the Hebrew book of Amos intended "Edom" here, a translator may have seen things differently.

But how did "Edom"/"peoples" move from being the object of the verb to the subject, and how did a Hebrew verb meaning "possess" come to be rendered "seek"? There is no simple route from what is in the Hebrew Bible to what the book of Acts displays for this clause as a whole. The Septuagint translator, on whom Acts depends (given the precise Greek words used), seems to have read and perhaps also misread a consonantal text identical to the MT in a way that made sense to him grammatically and perhaps also theologically. Thus the author of Acts did not create a new version of Amos.

For another example: according to Matthew 21.13, Jesus enters the Temple and exclaims, "It is written, 'My house shall become a house of prayer.'" This saying comes from Isaiah 56.7. Not only is the wording of the MT and the LXX identical but also Matthew uses the same Greek as does the LXX (with one slight exception). Moreover, the Greek wording and sentence structure that the LXX and the New Testament share here are unremarkable. Therefore, although the author of the Gospel may have drawn this citation from the LXX, it is also possible that he independently translated it from the Hebrew (if, in fact, the author of Matthew knew Hebrew).

Galatians 3.6 states "Just as Abraham 'believed God, and it was reckoned to him as righteousness'" likewise shows the possibility (as at Mt 21.13) of fresh translation on the part of the New Testament writer. Both the LXX and Paul add the subject Abraham ("Abraham 'believed God'"), where the Hebrew characteristically relies on the context as well as the verb to give the number and gender of the subject. Moreover, the second verb of the verse is passive in the Greek of the LXX and Paul ("it was reckoned"), while active (again, with implicit subject) in the Hebrew. Given the likely Hebrew consonantal text that the Septuagint translators worked with, which also would have been the one available to Paul if he knew and consulted the Hebrew text, and given also the vocabulary choices made, we cannot state with certainty that Paul arrived at wording identical to the LXX through dependence on the latter.

Prior to the twentieth century, it was regularly asserted that the language of the Septuagint, in following Hebrew language syntax and idiom, displayed numerous features that would have rendered it a mixture of Hebrew and Greek so thorough and unique as to make it difficult or impossible for a reader unfamiliar with the biblical literature to understand. Thus no one outside the Jewish communities where this Hebrew-influenced Greek developed could understand the Septuagint. Subsequent research demonstrated that many of the features that separated the LXX from classical Greek were shared with other early Hellenistic literature. In general, this Greek is now referred to as *koinē*, the "common" Greek of the Hellenistic empire. But Septuagint Greek is not identical to other contemporaneous examples. Much of this distinctiveness is a direct result of the fact that the LXX is at heart a translation of Semitic originals.

Many of these features can be found in vocabulary, through either neologisms (that is, words coined by the LXX translators) or distinctive translations of Hebrew words into already existing Greek words. Thus, throughout the New Testament, as was the case in the LXX, there was a standard way to express "the Lord," *kyrios*, "glory," *doxa*, "angel," *angelos*, "covenant," *diathēkē*, and "Gentiles," *ethnoi*, among other terms. In other instances, the vocabulary of the LXX is adapted by the New Testament writers to reflect their needs, as with the term for "gospel," *euangelion* (used in LXX for "good tidings," as in a positive report from a battle; see, e.g., 2 Sam 18.27) but appropriated in the New Testament to mean specifically the message of Jesus and the preaching about him. The New Testament authors expected their (original) audience to understand key words, especially relating to theology, within a context that had been developed earlier by the LXX.

For readers of the New Testament, whether Jewish or Christian, one final example of the influence of LXX translation on New Testament concepts remains to be explored: that of the citation of Isaiah 7.14 in Matthew 1.23 (see "Translation of the Bible," p. 560). Isaiah's statement to King Ahaz, "The young woman is with child," in its context means a birth that signals the imminent end of a threat to the kingdom of Judah (within two or three years, the point at which a child will be weaned and able to eat solid food). The LXX translates the Hebrew *'almah*, "young woman," with the Greek word *parthenos*, which often means "virgin." In Genesis 34.3, however, the LXX translates *na'arah*, "young woman, girl" the word used for Dinah after she has been raped, as *parthenos*, indicating that its semantic range extends beyond the meaning of "virgin" to that of "young female."

When Matthew quotes the passage from Isaiah, he takes the term *parthenos* literally as meaning that Mary's conception of Jesus occurred without human sexual intercourse and therefore was miraculous. Thus a word choice by the LXX translators led to an assertion of one of Christianity's teachings and a fundamental difference between Christians and Jews. It has also meant that until the twentieth century, with the publication of the Revised Standard Version Old Testament in 1952 (which used "young woman"), the translation of Isaiah 7.14 ("Behold, a virgin shall conceive" in the King James Version) has been influenced not by the meaning of the Hebrew words but by a New Testament quotation of the Septuagint. Thus do translations bring about far-reaching consequences.

MIDRASH AND PARABLES IN THE NEW TESTAMENT

David Stern

No topic touches more directly on the "Jewishness" of the New Testament than the place of midrash—classical Jewish biblical interpretation—in its pages, and few topics are more fraught with complications. These begin with the word "midrash" itself. Midrash refers to the activity of biblical study as pursued specifically by rabbinic sages in the first five centuries CE. It is derived from the root *d-r-sh*, which carries the primary meaning of "inquire, investigate," and by extension came to mean both "explicate" and "study." In more contemporary usage, the word is often used in the sense of an "imaginative interpretation," but readers should know that the rabbis did not have just one way of "studying" scripture, in addition to which they "did" midrash. Midrashic interpretation was part and parcel of biblical study.

By further extension, midrash also refers to the specific interpretations produced by that activity (thus, a "midrash" of a specific verse), and thus to the collections of rabbinic literature in which those originally orally transmitted interpretations were recorded. Those collections—our earliest actual documentation for midrash—first began to be compiled near the end of the third century, that is, two centuries after the Gospels were composed. The earliest collections were the *Mekhilta* (on Exodus), *Sifra* (on Leviticus) and *Sifre* (on Numbers and Deuteronomy). During the fourth through sixth centuries, other collections were compiled, some of which were later included in the sixteenth-century edition of *Midrash Rabbah* (e.g., *Ber. Rab.* and *Lev. Rab.*).

In the development of biblical criticism during the second half of the twentieth century, the term "midrash" came to be used to describe a method of reading the Bible, whether exemplified in the Hebrew Bible, the New Testament writings, or the rabbinic collections. This usage coincided with a wider recognition that biblical interpretation was among the most pervasive activities pursued by all Jews, including the followers of Jesus, throughout the Second Temple period and well into Late Antiquity.

These Jews, as well as most early Gentile Christians, accepted the core of the Hebrew Bible—or its Greek versions—as we know it today (even if the precise text remained in flux); further, they believed that the Bible was a sacred, authoritative text, without inconsistency, contradiction, and superfluity, which could reveal the will of God for their present time through close and intense study of its words and verses. That specific meaning, however, and so the text's true significance, was believed to be by definition *cryptic*, that is, not immediately evident or obvious. The biblical text may have an obvious or plain sense, but its deeper meaning was there to be discovered beneath the surface of its words.

That all biblical readers shared these assumptions by no means meant that their interpretations were identical. All readers *also* read the biblical text through the lens of their times, using their own theological beliefs and ideological tenets, and typically all utilized their own literary forms to convey those interpretations. Nonetheless, there is often a strong resemblance among these interpretations, partly due to the fact that many of these readers also shared a common fund of extra-biblical legends (like the story of Abraham exemplifying his belief in one God by smashing the images in his father's idol shop) that had independently developed in the Hellenistic and Late Antique periods. The New Testament scholars who used the term "midrash" to describe their biblical interpretations correctly recognized this family resemblance even if they did not always account for the profound differences.

Consider, for example, the following New Testament passages and rabbinic midrash that contain a form of interpretation called a "fulfillment narrative," because a verse from scripture, typically a prophecy, is represented as having been "fulfilled," or realized, in a specific occurrence. Thus, Matthew regularly recounts unusual episodes in Jesus' life, which are said to have "fulfilled" scriptural prophecies. For example, after describing how Joseph is told in a dream that Herod will attempt to kill the baby Jesus, and that he should take Mary and the child and flee to Egypt until Herod dies, Mt. 2.15 announces that this happened "to fulfill what had been spoken by the Lord through the prophet, 'Out of Egypt I have called my son.'" The citation is to Hos 11.1. In other words, the reason the family fled to Egypt was not solely out of fear of Herod but so that Hosea's prophecy could be fulfilled (thereby also confirming, in the process, that Jesus was God's son). Similarly, Mt 1.22–23 states that the virginal conception of Jesus by Mary through the Holy Spirit "took place to fulfill what had been spoken by the Lord through the prophet, 'Look, the virgin shall conceive and bear a son, and they shall call him Emmanuel, which means "God is with us."'" (Here, the quotation seems to be based on the Septuagint [LXX] which translates the Hebrew *'almah* ["unmarried young woman"] as Greek *parthenos*, a word meaning either "unmarried young woman" or "virgin.") In both examples, the scripture quoted does double if not triple duty. On the one hand, the verse reads the episode in Jesus' life as a realization of the scriptural prophecy whose meaning is thereby completely exemplified or exhausted. At the same time, those events interpret the verse in an almost literal fashion, thus confirming the validity of the prophecy and showing every detail in Jesus' life to be part of the divine plan.

Rabbinic midrash uses the same literary-exegetical form but for somewhat different purposes. The following passage is from a collection of interpretations of the Scroll of Lamentations compiled in the fourth or fifth century CE, in reference to Lam 2.12, a verse describing the children of Zion as "they cry to their mothers, 'Where is bread and wine?,' as they faint like the wounded in the streets of the city, as their life is poured out on their mothers' bosom":

> It happened to a certain woman who told her husband: This money is not doing me any good. Take it, and go to the marketplace and buy me something to eat so that we won't die. He did this. He took money from her and went to the market and tried to buy something, but he could not find anything to buy, and he fainted and died. They came and said to her elder son: Aren't you going to see what happened to your father? The son went, and he found his father dead in the marketplace. He began to weep over him, and then he too fainted and died. The youngest child wished to be suckled, but he found nothing in his mother's breast, and he too fainted and died.
>
> [All this happened] in order to fulfill what is said, ". . . 'as they faint like the wounded in the streets of the city, as their life is poured out in their mothers' bosom.'" (*Midr. Lam. Rab.*)

Even though Lamentations was compiled in the aftermath of the destruction of the First Temple in 586 BCE, the rabbis viewed the text as a prophecy of the destruction of the Second Temple in 70 CE. As in Matthew, the rabbinic anecdote reads the verse hyperliterally (with part of the novelty of the midrashic reading being to see each separate phrase referring to a different type of death suffered by each member of the hapless family). And, as in Matthew, the biblical prophecy is both fulfilled and exhausted in the historical event, in this case a series of tragic deaths. The verse, far from being read as a mainly rhetorical expression of despair, is shown to have been a lethally precise prophecy.

Yet this example of rabbinic interpretation also points to the exact difference between New Testament fulfillment-narratives and rabbinic midrash. In Matthew the form is used to authorize Jesus as the prophesied Messiah and divine Son. For Matthew's audience, living while the church was still struggling to establish its identity, the fulfillment-narrative served to authorize their theology and their understanding of scripture. In contrast, by the time the midrash was composed, the Temple's destruction was a historical catastrophe of the distant past whose painful memory may still have been alive but whose political charge had long since expired. The function of the midrash is both belated and apologetic: it shows that the catastrophes suffered by the Jews were neither arbitrary nor meaningless but, as prophesied, part of a larger divine plan that continues to govern Israel's destiny.

Of the four Gospels, Matthew is the one most suffused with interpretations that resemble rabbinic midrash (and other modes of early Jewish exegesis). In addition to the fulfillment-narratives, the Gospel's genealogy (Mt 1.1–17) is reminiscent of other "pseudo-genealogies" found in late biblical and early postbiblical documents (for example, Mordecai's ancestry as given in Esth 2.5) seeking to establish their biblical pedigree. The stories of the Magi (2.1–6) and Jesus' infancy (2.7–12) are reminiscent of pseudepigraphic and rabbinic tales about the birth of figures like Noah and Moses, which also contain miraculous and supernatural details. The escape to Egypt (2.13–23) re-enacts in midrashic fashion the descent and exodus of the Israelites from Egypt. Jesus' temptation in the desert (4.1–11) is a virtual exegetical battle, with Jesus' parrying each of Satan's challenges with a scriptural verse, often in its interpreted sense. Comparable exegetical duels between rabbis and heretics are found throughout rabbinic literature.

Of all the New Testament literary forms with rabbinic parallels, none has been more controversial than the narrative parables that Jesus delivers in the Synoptic Gospels. Virtually since the beginnings of modern New Testament scholarship in the nineteenth century, scholars have heatedly debated the relationship between the New Testament parables and the more than a thousand examples of the parable or *mashal* (pl. *meshalim*) found in rabbinic midrash. One reason behind the fervor of the debate is that the Gospel parables have long been considered by New Testament scholars as the parts of the Gospels closest to Jesus' own words, in which he disclosed to his disciples his teachings of salvation and his sense of his divine mission. But part of the debate has also been semantic. "Parable" (Gk *parabolē*, "thrown or placed alongside," and by extension "talking about one thing in terms of another") is the usual translation in the Septuagint of the Hebrew *mashal*. But that word and its verbal root have a wide range of meaning in the Hebrew Bible from "proverb" (as in the plural form *mishlei shlomo*, "proverbs of Solomon") to "byword" (Deut 28.37), allegory (Ezek 24.3), simile (Ps 49.13), and fable (Ezek 17.2). In rabbinic literature, the word continues to carry nearly all these senses, but it also comes to be a generic marker for the narrative parable. Curiously, the one narrative parable in the Bible that actually anticipates the parabolic narratives found in both the Gospels and rabbinic literature, Nathan's parable in 2 Sam 12.1–6, is not called a *mashal*.

What today seems clear to nearly all scholars is that neither Jesus nor the rabbis invented the parable. Both drew upon a widespread genre of oral traditional literature that goes back to the Bible (see, for example, Nathan's parable in 2 Sam 12.1–14 and that of the woman of Tekoa in 2 Sam 14.1–20) and in even earlier Near Eastern literature. Because of their common roots it is not surprising that both New Testament and rabbinic parables share common language-patterns and diction, narrative motifs, character types, and rhetorical strategies, albeit with important differences between them. These differences are especially evident in the way the parabolic narratives are used and interpreted in their respective literary contexts.

No New Testament parable exemplifies these similarities and differences better than that of the wicked tenants (Mk 12.1–12; Mt 21.33; Lk 20.9–19). This parable describes a man who plants a vineyard and then lets it out to tenants; the owner sends his servants and, finally, his own beloved son to collect fruit from the vineyard, but the tenants beat and kill the messengers and the son. "What will the owner of the vineyard do? He will come and destroy the tenants, and give the vineyard to others" (Mk 22.9), which is clearly a reworking of the "Song of the Vineyard" in Isa 5.1–6 and its application in vv. 7–10.

Jesus tells the parable against the "chief priests, the scribes, and the elders" (Mk 11.27), who accost him and ask by what authority he acts as he does. To this question, Jesus responds with his own question: "Did the baptism of John"—who had been executed by Herod Antipas (Mk 6.17–29)—"come from heaven, or was it of human origin?" (Mk 11.30). The authorities refuse to answer—they understand that the question is loaded—and Jesus responds, "Neither will I tell you by what authority I am doing these things" (Mk 11.33). Instead, he tells them the parable.

Within this narrative context, the parable's "meaning" is an attack upon the Jewish leaders—represented in the parable as the wicked tenants—for killing the owner's son. The precise identity of the person whom the son represents is not spelled out explicitly in the Gospel text, but both Matthew and Luke retain Mark's final line (Mk 12.9b), predicting that the owner will destroy the tenants and hand the vineyard over to others. Its next passage quotes Ps 118.22–23:

> Have you not read this scripture, "The stone that the builders rejected has become the cornerstone. This is the Lord's doing; it is amazing in our eyes." (Mk 12.10–11; Mt 21.42; Lk 20.17)

To this Matthew adds the following elaboration:

> Therefore I tell you, the kingdom of God will be taken away from you and given to a people that produces the fruits of the kingdom. The one who falls on this

> stone will be broken to pieces; and it will crush anyone on whom it falls. (21.43–44)

The author of the passage citing Ps 118.22–23 clearly understood Jesus to mean himself, when he described the tenants killing the owner's son, and Matthew's gloss elaborates this understanding by specifying that the Jewish leaders who confront Jesus (the "you" in the passage) are the tenants who will be destroyed for rejecting and killing "the son." In subsequent Christian tradition this text became a primary source for the claim that Jesus' death caused God's rejection of the Jews and the election of the church. New Testament scholars debate whether the Gospels present the parable's original narrative context, whether the original parable contained a reference to a son, and whether Jesus used this parable to explain his own divinely mandated fate. According to the scholars who see its meaning in this way, the parable has a virtually revelatory force as a literary form. Comparison of this parable with a rabbinic *mashal* may prove helpful in understanding the parable's literary strategies, perhaps even offering an alternative path for interpreting it.

Most rabbinic *meshalim* are preserved as parts of biblical exegeses rather than in narrative contexts. The following is recorded in a third-century collection as a midrash on Deut 32.9, "the Lord's own portion was his people, Jacob, his allotted share" (NRSV):

> It is like a king who owned a field and gave it to tenant-farmers. The tenant-farmers began to plunder the field. So he took it away from them, and gave the field to their children, but they were more wicked than their parents. So he took the field away from the children, and gave it to their children, but soon they too proved even more wicked. [Finally,] a son was born to the king. He said to the tenant-farmers: Get off my property. I do not want you on it. Give me back my portion that I may make it known as mine. (*Sifre Deut.* 312)

So goes the first part of the *mashal*, the narrative proper. The resemblances between its stock characters and motifs to those in the New Testament parable are obvious, thereby confirming the view that both parables belonged to the same popular tradition of parable-telling. In most rabbinic *meshalim*, however, the narrative proper is typically followed by an explanatory paragraph, the *nimshal*, which provides the necessary information to apply the narrative to the verse that serves as its exegetical occasion. Here is this *mashal*'s *nimshal*:

> Likewise: when Abraham came into the world, there issued from him inferior progeny—Ishmael and all the children of Keturah. When Isaac came into the world, there issued from him inferior progeny—Esau and all the chiefs of Edom. They were more wicked than their predecessors. But when Jacob came, the progeny that issued forth were not inferior; all his sons were upright persons. As the matter is stated: "Jacob was a perfect man, dwelling in tents" [Gen 25.27]. Now from what point does God make known His portion? From Jacob, as it is said, "For the Lord's portion is His people Jacob, the lot of His inheritance." [Deut 32.9]

The point of this *mashal* is clearly polemical: condemnation of Ishmael and Esau, the rabbinic code names for the Arab and Roman nations, and praise for Jacob's children, the people of Israel, who, according to the *nimshal*'s interpretation of Deut 32.9, alone are God's chosen people, "the lot of His inheritance."

Such a rhetorical function of comparative blame and praise—with some measure of contempt mixed into it—is reminiscent of the message that the Gospels saw in Jesus' parable with its bitter condemnation of the Jewish leaders and implied praise of those whom God chose to replace them. Indeed, the rhetorical resemblance between the two parables increases the historical likelihood that Matthew's interpretation was a plausible one to its early audience. To be sure, we will never know for certain what Jesus originally intended by his parable. But within its narrative context, Jesus' parable may very well have been directed against the Jewish leaders for their presumed *future* responsibility for Jesus' crucifixion. The resemblance between the wicked tenants and the later rabbinic *mashal* may go even farther. Most rabbinic *meshalim* are preserved in an exegetical context that is highlighted in the *nimshal*. The parable of the tenants is the only New Testament one that appends a verse to its narrative (Ps 118.22–23): "The stone that the builders rejected has become the cornerstone. This is the Lord's doing; it is amazing in our eyes." As it is cited, the verse may have been understood in a midrashic sense, with the Hebrew word *rosh pinah*, translated in the NRSV as "cornerstone," meaning the central capstone in an arch (which must be irregularly shaped in order to fit its strategic position)—an interpretation favored by some modern biblical scholars; so, too, the Hebrew for "builders," *ha-bonim*, may have been understood not as deriving from the root *b-n-h* ("to build") but from the root *b-y-n*, "to understand," meaning "those who understand," or think they understand, namely, the Jewish priests and scribes. (Other *midrashim* play on the similarity of these two roots.) In this interpreted sense, then, the verse would have been read as: "The 'stone' that the Jewish leaders rejected as misshapen turned out in the end to be the capstone. How unpredictable is the Lord's doing!" Such messages of unexpected reversal—the last becoming first; the least turning out to be the best—are typical of Jesus' other teachings.

While it would be a mistake to turn Jesus into a third- or fourth-century rabbi, the wicked tenants is the only one of his parables with a *nimshal*, which typifies the rabbinic parable. This text may be, ironically, our earliest example of the literary-exegetical form that becomes so prevalent in rabbinic midrash. Nor does understanding the larger ancient Jewish context for the parable and its resemblance to the later rabbinic tradition change its anti-Jewish message in Christian interpretation. What it does show is that, for all their profound theological differences and mutual conflict, early Christianity and rabbinic Judaism spoke much the same language. Even when they disagreed, they did so in remarkably similar ways.

THE DEAD SEA SCROLLS

Maxine Grossman

The mid-twentieth-century discovery of fragmentary ancient Jewish manuscripts in caves near the Dead Sea proved to be a bonanza for scholars of ancient Judaism. Although the Dead Sea Scrolls (DSS) are important for a variety of reasons to scholars in many fields, from the first the discoveries were framed in terms of the light they might shed on the world of Jesus and the New Testament.

The first seven scrolls came to scholarly attention in Jerusalem in late 1947. These scrolls, from Qumran Cave 1, included two copies of the book of Isaiah (1QIsa[a] and IQIsa[b]); a previously unknown expansion of the book of Genesis in Aramaic, the main language of the period (1QapGen, unrolled last of the seven, because of its advanced deterioration); and four previously unknown sectarian texts. These include a rule for an apparently celibate religious community (1QS); a type of commentary on the book of Habakkuk (1QpHab) and a collection of hymns of thanksgiving (1QH), both reflecting the terminology and worldview found in the rule text; and a highly stylized account of the final battle between the Sons of Light and the Sons of Darkness (1QM). Taken together, these manuscripts offered an evocative look at an ancient Jewish community whose resonance with earliest Christianity included not only shared scriptural interests (Genesis, Isaiah, the Minor Prophets) but also a commitment to celibacy, communitarian ideals, and the expectation of a rapidly impending end-times event.

The interpretive approach known as *pesher* is characteristic of the community's use of scriptural texts, particularly those of the Minor Prophets and the Psalms. The word, which means "interpret" or "discover the meaning of," occurs in Tanakh only in Eccl 8.1 (in Hebrew) and Dan 5.12,16 (in Aramaic); in Daniel it means interpretation of dreams. The scrolls, most clearly 1QpHab, the Habakkuk pesher, exemplify this interpretive strategy: quoting a verse from the biblical text and following it with an interpretation (using a form of the word "pesher") that applies the verse to the current situation as the interpreter sees it. Pesher thus serves to make biblical texts relevant to the community's concerns.

The scrolls reflected a Judaism different from later rabbinic tradition, and scholars were quick to suggest possible contexts for that difference. One of the first scholars to see the scrolls, E. L. Sukenik (1889–1953), suggested as early as 1948 that they might be connected with the Essenes, an ancient Jewish sect that the Roman author Pliny (*Nat.* 5.15 § 73) had located near the shores of the Dead Sea. Accounts of the Essenes from two first-century Jewish writers, Philo (*Good Person* 12.77; *Hypoth.* 10.4; 11.11–12) and Josephus (*Life* 10–12; *J.W.* 2.119, 122, 126; *Ant.* 13.171, 18.11, 20), rounded out the picture of the sect as all male, generally celibate, and highly concerned with a collective life of simplicity and separation from the corrupt society around them. Textual similarities between 1QS and the Damascus Document (CD), a rule text discovered in the late 1890s in the Cairo Geniza by Solomon Schechter (1847–1915), provided further context for the scrolls, by framing 1QS as the rule text for the celibate Essene community at Qumran and CD as a parallel rule for an outside population of "marrying Essenes" mentioned only by Josephus and not by the other sources (*J.W.* 2.160–61). The so-called Essene Hypothesis has framed the order of business in scrolls scholarship up to the present day.

References to a founding Teacher of Righteousness (and to his conflicts with a Wicked Priest, who sought to kill him on account of his teachings) resonated even more intensely with scholars who came to see in the scrolls a possible backdrop for Jesus' ministry. The evidence of the scrolls was brought to bear even more directly in comparison with John the Baptist who, like the scrolls' authors, went out into the wilderness to "prepare a way for the Lord," lived ascetically, and preached baptism for the removal of sins and the preparation for endtimes salvation. The parallels in the scrolls to John's practice of immersion have struck scholars. For instance, the Damascus Document (CD 10.10–13) and the Temple Scroll (11QSTemple 45.7–10) contain rules for this practice. In the Rule of the Community (2.25–3.9), there would seem to be a description of immersion as an initiation into the community. Although some scholars, like Jacob L. Teicher (1904–81), argued for specific correlations between the scrolls and the central figures of early Christianity (Teicher equated the Teacher of Righteousness with Jesus and the Wicked Priest with Paul), the vast majority of scholars saw the scrolls as providing more general religious and cultural contexts for the developments of Christian messianism and eschatological expectations.

There is also the matter of New Testament parallels to imagery in the Qumran materials, especially the emphasis on light versus darkness. This is characteristic of imagery in Tanakh: for instance, light is associated with Torah (Isa 2.5) and darkness with evil (Prov 2.13); God is manifest as light (Ps 104.2). In the Qumran documents, all of humankind is divided into the "sons of light" and the "sons of darkness" (this is further developed in 1QS 1.9–11 and other places). The phrase "children of light" appears in the New Testament at Lk 16.8; Jn 12.36; Eph 5.8; and 1 Thess 5.5, meaning those who are among the righteous. The contrast is also present in many other New Testament passages: e.g., 1 Jn 2.8–11. This imagery is especially prominent in the Gospel of John (1.4–5,7–9; 3.19–21; 8.12; 12.46).

By 1956, excavations at Qumran revealed a habitation site and a cemetery containing some 1,100 graves. Initial arguments dated the founding of the habitation site to the mid-second century BCE, which would fit with early identifications of the Teacher of Righteousness. A recent re-dating of the site by the archaeologist Jodi Magness argues for its founding as a sectarian habitation site around the turn of the first century BCE. Magness' interpretation of the site emphasizes a number of key features: the extensive water installations, which she views as evidence for ritual purity as a chief concern at the site; large quantities of high-quality but simple tableware, which argue for the service of group meals; and the minimal presence of imported fineware and decorative architectural features, which suggest a lack of interest in ostentation. The presence of women at the site remains a point of debate; the evidence from the cemetery reveals few if any ancient female skeletons, and there is little significant evidence in the form of small finds traditionally associated with women (tools for spinning and weaving textiles; hair combs, and decorations). Critiques of the classical Essene Hypothesis suggest variously that the site should be understood as a rustic villa, a pottery-production center, or a commercial entrepôt (warehouse or depot for goods to be exported). None of these theories adequately addresses the material remains of the site and its cemetery, and none adequately refutes the view that the site should be understood in terms of its relationship to the scrolls.

A total of eleven "scroll caves" were discovered near the site of Qumran, and these were found to contain upwards of eight hundred fragmentary manuscripts. A vast proportion of these highly fragmentary manuscripts were found in Cave 4, directly across a wadi or seasonal watercourse from the site of Qumran. Subsequent study identified among these manuscripts evidence for every book of Tanakh except Esther; major fragments of previously known pseudepigrapha such as *1 Enoch* and *Jubilees*; and a wide variety of previously unknown scriptural expansions and scripture-like texts. Finds included additional sectarian rule texts, scriptural commentary, hymns, and prayers as well as an array of calendars and previously unknown legal texts. Notably absent among these texts, which extended until the site's destruction in 68 CE, were books of the New Testament or other early Christian literature. Some Greek fragments from Cave 7 (esp. 7Q5) were speculatively identified as fragments of the Gospel of Mark, but scholars now believe that 7Q5 and related fragments are Greek translations of the book of *1 Enoch*.

Theodor H. Gaster (1906–92) published an early translation of more than a dozen core texts in *The Dead Sea Scriptures* (1956). He saw the scrolls as "the library of an Essene monastery or meeting-house at Qumran" but noted that the texts reflected the larger "religious repertoire of the Essene Brotherhood." He further acknowledged that the scrolls "help us to reconstruct the spiritual climate of early Christianity and throw light especially on the mission of John the Baptist and on the constitution of the primitive Church." Gaster's study reflects the field's early attention to parallels with New Testament texts. He noted such general similarities between the scrolls and the New Testament as the use of covenantal identity markers ("the elect," the "remnant" of God's covenant, those "planted" by God, the true Temple); the term "teacher" as a designation for group leadership; light-language (including "Sons of Light"); and a sense of unique relationship to God and his messengers. Gaster also speculated on parallels in terminology for social relationships, including "council" (*etzah, synhedrion*) or "congregation" (*edah, synagōgē*) along with parallels between Qumran terms for an "overseer" (*mevaker*) and priests and comparable New Testament terms for bishop (*episkopos*, lit., "overseer") and presbyter ("elder"). However, Gaster carefully avoided the impression that the scrolls bore some organic relationship to earliest Christianity.

A less-responsible tendency to search for parallels in the scrolls and the New Testament was a point of significant concern among scholars. Samuel Sandmel (1911–79), in his 1961 presidential address to the Society of Biblical Literature and Exegesis, specifically noted the dangers of what he called "parallelomania" of various sorts, including in scholarship of the New Testament and ancient Jewish literature, as well as the scrolls. He noted in particular the tendency to cherry-pick shared textual references or similar theological claims without attention to their literary contexts or their relationship to larger religious implications: "Two passages may sound the same in splendid isolation from their context, but when seen in context reflect difference rather than similarity." Equally important for understanding such parallels, Sandmel asserted, was the presence of a shared Jewish tradition (or, better, "traditions") within which the writings of Philo, the rabbis, the New Testament authors, and the Qumranites might—variously and partially—be compared but also contrasted with one another. Sandmel also offered a helpful clarification that would come to resonate in later reconsiderations of the Essene Hypothesis: "I would never try to identify the Qumran Community by the Essenes, but I incline to some willingness to identify the Essenes by the Qumran Community."

Geza Vermes (1924–) noted in his introduction to *Jesus the Jew* (1973) that his own approach to the scrolls and other ancient Jewish sources requires using them not "simply as aids in answering queries arising from the New Testament, but as independent spokesmen capable, from time to time at least, of guiding the enquiry, either by suggesting the right angle of approach, or even the right questions to ask." This approach came to the fore most clearly in his treatment of Jesus in light of Jewish messianism; his use of examples from Qumran allowed him to argue for an ancient Jewish messianism that was diverse and capable of including expectations of a Davidic messiah (e.g., in 1QSb 5; 4Q161 8–10; 10–20; 4Q174 1.11; CD 7.20), a priestly messiah (1QS 9.11; CD 6.7; 7.18, 20; 12.23–13.1; 14.19; 1QSa 2.11–14; 19–20; 1QSb 3.1–21; 5.20–29), or a prophetic messianic figure (1QS 9.11; 4Q175 5–20), in any of several possible combinations. From his 1953 dissertation forward, Vermes has argued for linking the scrolls directly to the Essene sect. This argument also underlies his translations of the scrolls, most recently *The Complete Dead Sea Scrolls in English* (1997, 2004; first published as *The Dead Sea Scrolls in English*, 1962, and revised and expanded in four editions through 1995), which continues to serve as a standard general-purpose translation of the scrolls.

In recent years, challenges to the Essene Hypothesis have pushed scholars to rethink their earlier emphases on celibacy, separation, and messianic expectations as hallmarks of the Qumran movement. This shift has necessarily brought with it reconsiderations of the relevance of the scrolls for earliest Christianity.

Chief among the reasons for this shift in focus was the publication of a number of substantial—and substantially different—texts from caves other than Qumran Cave 1. This process began in a 1977 publication by Yigael Yadin (1917–84) of the Temple Scroll (English translation in 1983), which served to highlight the importance for the scrolls and so their authors of Torah, religious praxis, ritual purity, family law, and classical Jewish notions of covenant—concepts that were not emphasized by earlier studies. Yadin also led the archaeological excavation of the Masada fortress in 1963–65, which resulted in textual finds including fragments of Genesis, Leviticus, Deuteronomy, Ezekiel, and Psalms, as well as fragments in Hebrew of Ben Sirach (Ecclesiasticus), apocryphal works based on passages from Genesis and from Joshua, and a collection of Sabbath Songs (this has also been found at Qumran).

The majority of the material from Caves 1–3 and 5–11 had been published in the first decades after their discovery. In contrast, the highly fragmentary (and massive) collection of texts from Cave 4 remained unpublished through the end of the 1980s. Public controversies over the lack of access to these texts peaked in 1991 and ultimately led to a general "freeing" of the scrolls. Although this new material confirmed much of what scholars had gleaned from the scrolls in past decades, it also revealed a much broader theological world than the one framed by the first generation of scrolls research. The themes highlighted by the Temple Scroll, including interpretation of Jewish law and practice, appeared again in multiple copies of the Community Rule (1QS) and the Damascus Document (CD). The Damascus Document also contains collective rules, such as those governing purification rites, which make clear the group's separation from Temple practices of the time. Other sectarian rule texts, legal collections, and calendrical compositions further suggested that the scrolls do not reflect a single sectarian group but rather a movement that developed over time and in sometimes contentious ways.

The most significant text in the context of this latter discussion is 4QMMT (*Miqzat Ma'aseh Ha-Torah,* "A Few Words of Torah"). This text, written in the voice of a communal leader (the Teacher of Righteousness, according to its editors), documents a series of legal disagreements, many related to issues of ritual purity, that distinguish the author and his group from an untrustworthy priestly authority structure from whom they separated. The text is addressed not to the opposition forces but to a third party, who is framed as potentially open to the "words" of the text, and who might yet—in consequence of receiving the text—find a way to bring his people to the side of righteousness before the endtimes. The Teacher of Righteousness (*moreh ha-tzedeq* and variant related phrases) is generally seen as the founding leader of the community. Who this individual was is not known; nor is it known exactly when he would have begun his sectarian efforts. Scholars have focused attention on the second century BCE, between the efforts of the Seleucid ruler Antiochus IV (Epiphanes) to make Jerusalem into a Hellenistic city (ca. 175 BCE) and the Hasmonean rule of Jerusalem after the Maccabean revolt of 167–164 BCE, leading to the Hasmonean choice of Jonathan as high priest (152–143). If this conjecture is correct, then Jonathan is the "wicked priest" who opposes the Teacher, but by the nature of the case all of this is very speculative.

4QMMT emphasizes *halakhah* (legal interpretation) in an eschatological framework, and this combination served as the thematic anchor for Lawrence H. Schiffman (1948–) in his *Reclaiming the Dead Sea Scrolls* (1994). Although the topic of *halakhah* was certainly an element of Qumran studies by the mid-1990s (dating back at least to Schiffman's own monograph, *The Halakhah at Qumran* [1975]), he presented this later publication as a comprehensive effort to "correct a fundamental misreading" of the scrolls, "written to explain their significance in understanding the history of Judaism," instead of concentrating on their relationship to early Christianity.

The Judaism that Schiffman identified in the scrolls was one with priestly connections (as the original Cave 1 scrolls suggested), and one with distinct conflicts with the Jerusalem authority structure (both also suggested by the earlier scrolls). But Schiffman and other scholars also observe that the scrolls assume the presence of marrying sectarians in family structures (the image of isolated men appears only in the Community Rule). Thus celibacy as such appears to have been greatly exaggerated by earlier readings. Messianism, too, came to be seen not as the driving theological focus of the scrolls but rather as one element in the larger ancient Jewish worldview. Schiffman argued for a view of the scrolls sectarians as priestly oriented Jews in conflict with both the Jerusalem priestly authorities and their Pharisaic opponents, and who consequently removed themselves from both camps. The appeal to Zadokite priestly authority in the sectarian scrolls (1QS 5.2, 9; CD 3.21–44) leads Schiffman to speak of their authors as pious (disaffected) Sadducees; their treatment of marriage and sexuality leads him also to note that they might well be equated with the "marrying Essenes" mentioned by Josephus. Although they have not won wholesale approval as such, Schiffman's arguments have contributed a necessary layer of complexity to the scholarly consensus with regard to the Essene Hypothesis.

The scrolls testify to a Jewish religious movement that was at once halakhically oriented, exegetically aware, purity-sensitive, and eschatologically motivated. The scrolls sectarians were not the celibate, monastic Essenes of Pliny's designation, but nor were they "ordinary" Jews of a proto-rabbinic variety. To understand them in their full complexity requires rethinking the Judaism in which they developed, and this, in turn, provides a richer and more nuanced context in which to envision the earliest Christian movements that arose in their wake.

PHILO OF ALEXANDRIA

David Satran

LIFE

Although Philo (ca. 20 BCE–ca. 50 CE) was a contemporary of Jesus, the immediate circle of Jesus' disciples, and the apostle Paul, his writings disclose no direct knowledge of the emergent Christian movement. From the fourth century CE on, however, the church fathers would not hesitate to turn to Philo in their accounts of the origins of Christianity. Following mention of Philo's background and his embassy on behalf of the Jews of Alexandria (*Hist. eccl.* 2.5.1ff.), Eusebius proceeds to cite at length from Philo's work *On the Contemplative Life* as a testimony to the foundations of Christianity in Alexandria (*Hist. eccl.* 2.16–17). Later Christian legend and historiography would claim that Philo was himself involved in the foundation of Alexandrian Christianity, and in Byzantine and early medieval representations he is elevated to the role of a Christian theologian.

We have relatively few secure details of Philo's life, but it is certain that he belonged to a prominent and influential family, deeply involved in the economic, religious, and political life of the Alexandrian Jewish community. His own works (see below) and the testimony of Josephus (*Ant.* 18.8.1) provide ample evidence both of his stature and his involvement in matters of communal welfare. Educated according to the highest standards of Greco-Roman *paideia* (education) and highly proficient in both rhetorical theory and philosophical inquiry, Philo is a strong proponent of the welfare of the Jewish community and its religious observances. His loyalty to the demands of the Hebrew Bible (through the medium of Greek translation) combined with an advocacy of the Greek wisdom traditions foreshadow the medieval religious effort—whether Jewish, Christian, or Islamic—to achieve a harmonious accommodation between scripture and philosophy.

WORKS

Philo was a prolific writer, producing dozens of works of varying length during his writing life. Central in number and significance are varied forms of biblical exegesis (e.g., *On the Creation*; *Allegorical Interpretation of the Laws*; *The Sacrifices of Abel and Cain*; *The Migration of Abraham*; *The Life of Moses*; *The Special Laws*; *Questions and Answers on Genesis*) but notable as well are his apologetic and historical works (e.g., *Every Good Person Is Free*; *On the Contemplative Life*; *The Embassy to Gaius*).

At the very heart of Philo's hermeneutical enterprise lies the unparalleled stature of the Pentateuch: from the account of the opening chapters of Genesis we learn that

> the world [Gk *kosmos*] is in harmony with the Law [Gk *nomos*=Heb *Torah*], and the Law with the world, and that the individual who observes the Law is thus constituted a loyal citizen of the world [*kosmopolitēs*], regulating his actions by the will of Nature [*physis*], according to which the entire world is governed. (*On the Creation* 3)

Philo has linked the Law with the natural order, *kosmos*, and in turn with *physis*, thereby asserting that the moral or spiritual order and the natural order are not in opposition but arise from the same source. This philosophical position creates a complex equation where the Torah, as both legal system and document, is revealed as the blueprint for cosmic and political harmony. God is similarly seen in rabbinic writings as providing the order to the created cosmos, and a famous metaphor in the opening of *Genesis Rabbah* (1.1), often compared with Philo, describes the Torah as a form of "blueprint" for the creation of the world. The Pentateuch is thus established to be a text of universal validity and significance.

THOUGHT

Philo was an important figure in the philosophical tradition that has come to be recognized by scholars of Greco-Roman philosophy as "Middle Platonism." The influence of Plato extended beyond the classical era, through Late Antiquity and into the Middle Ages, and the adaptation of his writings and ideas was an ongoing effort. Historians of philosophy, therefore, distinguish between early Platonism, the philosophical approach that began in the Academy of Plato and extended until the first century BCE; Middle Platonism, from the first century BCE to the early third century CE; and Neoplatonism, associated first and foremost with the philosopher Plotinus, from the third century BCE on. The philosophical schools of the Roman imperial period were characterized by a "syncretistic" approach, assimilating elements from rival outlooks or systems, and Middle Platonism reveals strong influences from and adaptations of the Aristotelian and Stoic traditions. These philosophical movements were deeply significant during the formative period of Christian thought, and Philo himself was a very important figure in this development.

Philo's philosophy, however, is in a sense the underpinnings of his larger agenda. The center of his intellectual project and the overwhelming bulk of his literary output are dedicated to the presentation and explication of the biblical text. Dependent on the Greek version of the Pentateuch (the Septuagint [LXX])—accepted by Alexandrian Judaism as no less accurate or even inspired than the Hebrew text—Philo explicated the characters and themes of scripture in terms that could be grasped not only by Jews with a Hellenistic education but also by non-Jews for whom Judaism was a foreign faith and not well known. Philo also undertook a painstakingly detailed explication of the books of Genesis and Exodus. Philo's labors of interpretation, which anticipate both rabbinic midrash and early Christian commentary, were predicated on the dual assumption of the absolute significance of every aspect of the Greek text of scripture and the unfailing correspondence between biblical precept and philosophical truth. Within his intensive and exhaustive exegesis of the biblical text, we meet a broad range of themes, philosophical and theological, which were to determine Philo's great importance for emergent Christian thought.

A corollary of the supreme status of the Law (Gk *nomos*, Heb *Torah*) in Philo's thought is the unique standing of Moses, who represents a fourfold perfection: philosopher-king, lawgiver, priest, and prophet (*Life of Moses* 2). A wide variety of biblical figures are of great importance for Philo, as they embody and symbolize a wide range of intellectual and moral virtues.

The patriarchs demonstrate varied aspects of the Platonic or Stoic sage, with Abraham, for example, in his departure from his country and kindred, representing the mind leaving behind the senses and bodily inclinations to meditate on that which is imperishable and incorporeal (*Migr.* 7–13). Yet the role and stature of Moses is elevated to a different plane altogether, as he exceeds the patriarchs in his achievement of a superhuman degree of perfection. Philo presents Moses as a supreme example of an ideal in Hellenistic thought, the *theios anēr* or "divine man," the human being who by ascetical practice and concentration on the divine realm becomes a participant in that realm (*Life of Moses* 1.156–59; 2.66–70). By depicting Moses in this way, Philo understands the Pentateuch as "the books of Moses" in the sense that Moses alone embodies the very principles innate in the Law and necessary for its full comprehension (*Life of Moses* 2.10).

This philosophical view, that the "divine man" or exceptional individual can participate to some extent in the divine realm, as well as the broader theme of divine-human interaction, is but one aspect of a central concern of Philo's thought: the relationship between this-worldly physical existence and the realm of a higher spiritual reality. Philo's Platonic outlook assumes that there is a sharp distinction between these two planes, and he explores afresh the anthropological, ethical, and cosmological implications of this earthly-heavenly divide within a scriptural perspective.

At the very core of Philo's religious-philosophical worldview lies his creative and tireless reading of scripture. No aspect or feature of the biblical text, however small or plain, is devoid of an inner meaning, which needs to be recovered through the careful extraction (exegesis) of its added significance. For example, Philo's extended explication of the passage in which Rebekah gives water to Abraham's servant (Gen 24.15–18) presents the inner significance of the scriptural text as the teacher who has accumulated wisdom (as she has drawn water from the well) and is offering it to students according to their capacity to take it in (as she gives the servant water to the extent that he wants or needs it) (*Posterity* 132–41).

Such allegorical interpretation of scripture, in Philo's view, reveals its hidden truth and allows the appreciation of its full philosophical depth and scope. Yet Philo also gives expression to the dangers of this interpretative mode when abused by those who behave

> as though they were living alone by themselves in a wilderness, or as though they had become disembodied souls, and knew neither city nor village nor household nor any company of human beings at all, overlooking all that the mass of men regard, they explore reality in its naked absoluteness. . . . Why, we shall be ignoring the sanctity of the Temple and a thousand other things, if we are going to pay heed to nothing except what is shown us by the inner meaning of things. No, we should look on all these outward observances as resembling the body, and their inner meanings as resembling the soul. It follows that, exactly as we have to take thought for the body, because it is the abode of the soul, so we must pay heed to the letter of the laws. (*Migr.* 90–93)

This search for the spiritual meaning of the Torah combined with a deep concern for its practical observance is the goal toward which Philo aimed in his writings. He was concerned that the spiritual meaning (which for him was the inner philosophical truth) of scripture should be made plain; but at the same time, he strove to show how the moral and legal precepts of scripture were to be obeyed.

INFLUENCE

New Testament scholars (and others whose fields cover that historical period) have brought out parallels between Philo and various New Testament authors and passages. Among the issues that scholars have raised are questions such as these: Could early Christian views of Jesus, particularly those emphasizing his divine status, have drawn on the same Hellenistic currents of thought that underlie Philo's approach to the character of Moses? To what extent does subsequent rabbinic delimitation of the role of Moses reflect a critical sensitivity to this Jewish-Hellenistic model and its influence?

Varied features of Philo's worldview have been compared fruitfully with aspects of a number of New Testament writings, particularly the Gospel of John, the Epistle to the Hebrews, and certain other letters of Paul and his school. Despite numerous, suggestive, and broad similarities, it is doubtful whether any of these authors had firsthand knowledge of Philo and his writings, as the similarities are not specific enough and the ideas found in Philo are known elsewhere as well. In the years following the New Testament era—beginning around the middle of the second century CE—major Christian theologians, including Justin Martyr and Clement of Alexandria, would begin using and citing Philo's works. For example, the concept of the *Logos*, the mediating principle between the divine mind and human reason, as both thought and word, which appears prominently both in Philo's theological system and so dramatically in the prologue to the Gospel of John (1.1–18), is known elsewhere as well (see "John's Prologue as Midrash," p. 546). While it is virtually certain that John's Gospel introduces this term in his presentation of Jesus without any direct reference to or knowledge of Philo, subsequent discussions of the *Logos*, e.g., by Justin Martyr (*1 Apol.*) or Origen (*Cels.*), are heavily indebted to Philo.

Philo's influence, therefore, is not a direct one for the New Testament authors. He is important in showing the prevalence of certain ideas and philosophical approaches that are also present in the New Testament. In addition, Philo's influence on later Christian writers, and particularly on their exegesis of the Jewish scriptures, has established a mode of reading those Jewish writings, which was greatly influential in the development of Christianity. Paul's location of Christ in the Exodus narrative (1 Cor 10.4) set an example that later Christian exegetes, who had absorbed the method that Philo established, would apply to show that the Christian Old Testament foreshadowed the teaching of the New Testament and the ministry of Jesus. Philo's Hellenistic Judaism, therefore, is very much the world in which subsequent generations of the new faith were to find the exegetical and theological tools to forge their new identity.

JOSEPHUS

Shaye J. D. Cohen

Students of the Second Temple period owe enormous gratitude to Joseph son of Matthias, in Hebrew Yosef ben Mattityahu, better known as Flavius Josephus or simply Josephus (37–100 CE). His *Jewish War*, also known as *Judaean War*, completed in the early 80s CE, and *Jewish Antiquities*, also known as *Judaean Antiquities*, completed in 93/94 CE, both written in Greek and in accordance with the conventions of Greek rhetoric and historiography, give a continuous narrative of the history of the Jews of Judea from about 175 BCE to some time after the destruction of the Temple in 70 CE. He also wrote two smaller works in Greek, an autobiography (*The Life*), which focuses on his military career in the Galilee in the spring and summer of 67 CE, and a defense of Judaism (*Against Apion*), which attempts to refute a host of malicious accusations against Jews and Judaism. All of these works were preserved by Christians, not Jews. (A Jewish historical work called *Josippon*, written in Hebrew in Italy in the tenth century, had access to some of Josephus's works in Latin translation.) Without Josephus, even major figures such as John Hyrcanus, Alexander Jannaeus, Herod the Great, and the revolutionaries John of Gischala, Simon bar Giora, and Eleazar ben Yair, would be for us little more than bare names. Similarly, virtually all of what is known about the destruction of the Temple, the fall of Masada, and the history of the Jews of the Diaspora during these centuries, and much of what we know about the Essenes, derives from Josephus.

Josephus was born in 37 CE in Jerusalem to a priestly family of the Hasmonean line. After receiving an education befitting an urban aristocrat, he became involved in politics in 64 CE when he went to Rome in order to secure the release of some priests, "perfect gentlemen," who had been arrested by Judea's Roman governor (*Life* 13). Upon his return to Jerusalem he found the city in turmoil, riven by factional strife and revolutionary fervor. Josephus was caught up in these events, and when the war broke out in the fall of 66 CE he became a general of the revolutionary forces in Galilee. (Josephus gives two inconsistent versions of these events, one in the *Jewish War* and the other in the *Life*.) In Galilee, Josephus spent most of his time escaping various attempts on his life and surviving the maneuvers of his political rivals. The Roman general Vespasian met little resistance when he attacked Galilee in the spring of 67 CE; Josephus was soon captured, and the Romans were on their way toward Judea.

Josephus spent the rest of his life among the Romans. He claims that upon capture by Vespasian, he prophesied that the general would someday become Roman emperor, a prophecy realized in 69 CE. Josephus continues this theme in his *Jewish War*, written under the patronage of Vespasian and his son Titus; its main thesis is that God supported the Romans against the Jews. Titus's destruction of the Temple in the summer of 70 CE proves not divine impotence but divine justice, since the destruction was condign punishment visited upon the sinful Jews. The revolutionaries had rebelled not only against the Romans but also against God, and the Jews should hold themselves to blame for the catastrophe.

The *Jewish Antiquities* is a different kind of work. The first half paraphrases the Bible, beginning with Genesis 1, while the second half gives the postbiblical history of the Jews in both the homeland and the Diaspora, up to the outbreak of the war in 66 CE. Thus Josephus gives two different versions of the reign of Herod the Great and the Roman administration of Judea, one in the opening book and a half of the *Jewish War* and another in the last seven books of the *Jewish Antiquities*. These parallel accounts often disagree.

(For example, the portrait of Herod the Great in *J.W.* is much more favorable than in *Ant.*) The *Antiquities* is a large and complex work that had a wide range of motives, among them to introduce Jews and Judaism to the Greco-Roman world, to correct certain misconceptions about the Jews, and to show that the Jews were a distinguished people with a distinguished past and present. This apologetic motive was taken up further in Josephus's final work, *Against Apion*.

At numerous points the narratives of Josephus intersect directly with the New Testament. For example, Josephus gives a fuller portrait of various political figures mentioned in the Gospels and Acts, including Herod the Great, his sons Archelaus, Herod Antipas, and Philip, his grandson Agrippa I, and his great-grandson Agrippa II; the Roman governors of Judea Pontius Pilate, Antonius Felix, and Porcius Festus; and the first-century high priests Ananus (Annas), Caiaphas, and Ananias son of Nedebaeus.

In *Antiquities* Josephus mentions Jesus, John the Baptist, and James the Just. *Ant.* 18.3.3, the so-called *Testimonium Flavianum*, is Josephus's account of Jesus:

> About this time there lived Jesus, a wise man, if indeed one ought to call him a man. For he was one who performed surprising deeds and was a teacher of such people as accept the truth gladly. He won over many Jews and many of the Greeks. He was the Messiah [Greek: the Christ]. And when, upon the accusation of the principal men among us, Pilate had condemned him to a cross, those who had first come to love him did not cease. He appeared to them spending a third day restored to life, for the prophets of God had foretold these things and a thousand other marvels about him. And the tribe of the Christians, so called after him, has still to this day not disappeared. (trans. W. Whiston)

Most modern scholars believe that Josephus could not have written this text as we have it; specifically, he would not have written "He was the Christ." A shorter text was likely revised by Christian copyists who wanted Josephus to endorse Christianity. Scholars disagree about exactly how to reconstruct the original of the passage.

John the Baptist is mentioned in *Ant.* 18.5.2. Speaking of Herod Antipas, who suffered a military defeat at the hands of the king of the Nabataeans, Josephus says that the conflict arose because Herod Antipas was planning to divorce his wife, daughter of the Nabataean king, in order to marry Herodias, the wife of his half-brother. Josephus continues:

> Now some of the Jews thought that the destruction of Herod's army came from God, and was a very just punishment for what he did against John called the baptist. For Herod had him killed, although he was a good man and had urged the Jews to exert themselves to virtue, both as to justice toward one another and reverence towards God, and having done so join together in baptism. For immersion in water, it was clear to him, could not be used for the forgiveness of sins, but as a sanctification of the body, and only if the soul was already thoroughly purified by right actions. And when others massed about him, for they were very greatly moved by his words, Herod, who feared that such strong influence over the people might lead to a revolt—for they seemed ready to do anything he should advise—much preferred to move now rather than to have him raise a rebellion later and engage him in actions he would regret.
>
> And so John, out of Herod's suspiciousness, was sent in chains to Machaerus, the fort previously mentioned, and there put to death; but it was the opinion of the Jews that out of retribution for John God willed the destruction of the army so as to afflict Herod. (trans. W. Whiston, rev.)

This passage disagrees with the New Testament. In Mark 6.17–28 the femme fatale who sets the story in motion is not Herodias but her daughter, she who does her famous dance. Also, in Mark 1.4 John the Baptist is said to preach a "baptism of repentance for the forgiveness of sins," a position that Josephus's John appears to reject ("For immersion in water, it was clear to him, could not be used for the forgiveness of sins"). In Josephus, John is executed out of fear that he may be a revolutionary, a motif that is absent from the New Testament.

James the Just is mentioned in *Ant.* 20.9.1. The governor Festus has just died, and his successor Albinus has not yet arrived in Judea. During the interregnum the high priest Ananus son of Ananus acts against his enemies:

> Ananus thought he had now a proper opportunity since Festus was now dead, and Albinus was but upon the road; so he assembled a session [Greek: the Sanhedrin] of judges, and brought before them a man named James, the brother of Jesus who was called Christ, and some others. He accused them of being breakers of the law, and delivered them to be stoned. But those who were reputed to be the most equitable of the citizens, and who were strict in observance of the laws—they disliked what was done. They therefore secretly sent to the king [Agrippa II], desiring him to send to Ananus that he should act so no more. (trans. W. Whiston, rev.)

James the Just, brother of Jesus, is mentioned in a number of New Testament passages, but his death is reported only here. What is striking is that Ananus accuses James of transgressing the Torah, but in the New Testament James appears as an advocate of loyalty to the Torah (Gal 2.12; Acts 21.20–24). These three Josephan passages, which parallel and yet differ from what is written in the New Testament, suggest that by the late first century CE, the period when the Gospels were being composed and Josephus was writing his *Antiquities*, a variety of historical traditions were in circulation concerning the founding figures of earliest Christianity.

JEWISH RESPONSES TO BELIEVERS IN JESUS

Claudia Setzer

Contemporary Jews and Christians have a stake in understanding the relations of Jesus and his early followers to other Jews, but we are limited to a few tendentious sources. The majority of sources are Christian: the New Testament; *The Martyrdom of Polycarp* (a late second-century account of the death of Polycarp [ca. 69–155 CE], bishop of Smyrna, at the hands of the Roman authorities); the pseudepigraphical *Gospel of Peter* (second century CE); comments from the mid-second-century apologist Justin Martyr (ca. 100–165 CE) in his *Dialogue with Trypho*. We also have the testimony of the staunch Platonist, the pagan Celsus (as reported in writings of the Christian thinker Origen [ca. 185–254]; his work *Contra Celsum* [*Against Celsus*, mid-third century] quotes extensive portions of Celsus's critique of Christianity, *True Discourse* [*Alēthēs Logos*, ca. 178]); two comments by the Jewish historian Josephus; and a handful of rabbinic references from the third century and later.

Complicating the study is the question of *how* to read each source: Is it stylized rhetoric, symbolic language, or a reflection of lived reality? Were boundaries between groups apparent, or were they erected by later religious thinkers, trying to tame a messy social reality? Christ-followers, both Jew and Gentile, must have had different kinds of relationships with different kinds of Jews in different places, at different times. The dashing of hope for Jewish self-rule after the Bar Kochba revolt (132–35), coupled with the replacement of Jewish church leaders in Jerusalem with Gentile bishops made it very difficult to be both a loyal Jew and a Jesus-follower in Judea. This tells us nothing about the Diaspora, however, and how Jewish and Christian neighbors regarded each other in cities like Antioch and Rome.

VERBAL POLEMIC

The vast majority of references are to Jews *saying* things to or about believers in Jesus. Scattered references in the Gospels and Acts allude to criticism over observance of Jewish law, *orthopraxy*, particularly extra-scriptural laws like particulars of Sabbath observance: not plucking grain, Mt 12.1–8; Mk 2.23–24; not healing (i.e., working) on the Sabbath, Mt 12. 9–14; Mk 3.1–6; hand-washing for religious purposes before eating (Mt 15.1–20; Mk 7.1–4), and some instances of fasting (Mt 9.14–17; Mk 2.18–20). In Acts (e.g., 13.45,50; 14.1–2), Jews opposed to the mission of Paul and Barnabas stir up opposition to it in order to get the missionaries expelled from the area. Although the Gospel references are set in Jesus' time, they more likely represent the period of the redaction of the Gospels from 70s to the 90s; the Acts incidents probably reflect the situation in the early second century.

According to Justin Martyr, writing in Rome ca. 160, Jews slander, ridicule, and even curse Christians in the synagogue (*Dial.* 96). But he also engages in arguments about belief, *orthodoxy* (lit., "right opinion"). He says Jews deny Jesus' resurrection, repeating a charge from the Gospel of Matthew (28.13–15) and the apocryphal *Gospel of Peter* (8.29–31) that Jews claim Jesus' tomb was empty because his disciples stole his body, not because he rose from the dead. Matthew adds: "this story is still told among the Jews to this day" (28.15), placing the debate in his own time. The debate has a long trajectory, and is attested also by the pagan author Celsus (Origen, *Cels.* 2.55), and in Justin's many proofs of the resurrection from scripture in his debate with the Jew Trypho (*Dial.* 32.3–6; 106–108).

Similarly, the nature of Jesus' death by crucifixion led to dispute between Christians and Jews. As early as the 50s Paul notes Christ crucified is "a stumbling block to Jews" (1 Cor 1.23). One hundred years later, Justin (*Dial.* 89,94,96, and other places) attributes to the Jew Trypho the same view: that a Messiah cannot be crucified. Paul suggests (Gal 3.13) that one element of the debate was Deut 21.23, which states (in relation to people executed for a capital crime): "anyone hung on a tree is under God's curse," but the reference is in the context of discussion of Gentile obedience to Torah, not Jewish denial of Jesus' messianic status.

Another tenet of belief for many Christians, the virgin birth, was linked by some Jews to questions of Jesus' legitimacy and pedigree. In John 8.41, when "the Jews" say to Jesus, "we were not born of fornication," they may imply that he was. In Justin's *Dialogue with Trypho* the virgin birth is a full-blown controversy (*Dial.* 66,68,71,77) that depends on whether the word "virgin" appears in Isaiah 7.14 and whether it refers to events at the time of Hezekiah, Isaiah's contemporary, or the time of Jesus' birth. Celsus affirms the proclamation of the virginal conception to be a point of Jewish attack, and he is the earliest source to indicate that some Jews call Jesus "ben Panthera" (Pantera, Pandera, Pantiri), "son of Panthera" (purported name of a Roman legionary), suggesting he was the illegitimate son of a Roman soldier (Origen, *Cels.* 1.28,32,69). Some rabbinic materials, primarily Palestinian, repeat this name (*t. Hul.* 2.22–24; *y. Avodah Zara* 2.2/12; *Eccl. Rab.* 1.8 [3], and others). Tertullian, at the end of the second century, says Jews call Jesus the son of a prostitute (*Spect.* 30.3).

In the Gospel of John, written at the end of the first century, Jesus claims equality with God (5.18; 10.24–25,33,38; 19.7) and applies many "I am" sayings (the meaning of God's name in the Tanakh [see Ex 3.14]) to himself (8.24,28,58; 13.19). To some Jews, these would sound suspiciously like ditheism, claims to be a second God. In fact, later rabbis will reject as an apostate a rabbi who claims there are "two powers in heaven" (*b. Hag.* 15a). Celsus mentions conflict between Jews and Christians over the meaning of scripture and Jesus' identity, calling it bickering over "the shadow of an ass" (Origen, *Cels.* 3.1–4). He adds that Jews resent Christians stirring up the Jewish community and inviting the attention of the Romans.

The broader argument between some Jews and believers in Jesus, Jewish and Gentile, is the question of "Whose book is it?" Who inherits and rightly understands the scriptures of Israel? Such an argument is inevitable, since the Gospels and Paul predicate claims about Jesus on the promises made in the Torah and the Prophets. For all Jews, the Torah was one of the real and symbolic elements left to them after two disastrous revolts and the destruction of the Temple. So the understanding of the Tanakh and the authority to interpret it was fundamental to the development of different groups. The idea that it might belong to Jews *and* Christians, mentioned anonymously in the *Epistle of Barnabas* (4.6; 13.1), did not gain much traction. Justin's *Dialogue with Trypho*, even if a rhetorical composition, shows the urgency of defeating Jewish claims on scripture.

PHYSICAL ACTIONS

Paul relates that he received the thirty-nine lashes five times (2 Cor 11.24), the penalty of flogging imposed by a Jewish court (*m. Makk.* 3.10–11) for a variety of offenses (e.g., prohibited marriages, stealing, consuming what is offered in the Temple while unclean or going into the Temple while unclean [*m. Makk.* 3.1ff.]). This discipline imposed by the synagogue sought to keep a recalcitrant Jew in good standing in the community. That Paul submitted to this punishment indicates that both he and the synagogue regarded him as a Jew. In the same way, Matthew's Gospel, written forty years later, puts in Jesus' mouth the prediction, "they will flog you in their synagogues" (10.17), suggesting the same kind of discipline.

Paul says that before he became a follower of Jesus, he violently persecuted the church (1 Cor 15.9; Phil 3.5–6; Gal 1.13–14,22–23). Acts 7.57–60 depicts the stoning of Stephen, in what—if the story is historically credible—is spontaneous mob violence. He refers (1 Thess 2.14–16) to the disciples in Judea suffering some kind of persecution from the Jews, and Paul says he is in danger from "unbelievers in Judea" (Rom 15.31). These general references suggest a persecution that went beyond verbal polemic.

John 16.2–3 predicts, "an hour is coming when those who kill you [i.e., Jesus' closest followers] will think that by doing so they are offering worship to God. And they will do this because they have not known the Father or me." Justin likewise claims several times (e.g., *Dial.* 123,131) that Jews contribute to the deaths of Christians, but he often includes statements of Jewish powerlessness, such as "you curse Christians in your synagogues, and other nations carry out the curse, putting to death those who simply confess themselves Christians" (*Dial.* 96.2). Justin Martyr further says that Bar Kochba (a second-century CE Jewish military leader, who headed the second revolt against Rome, 132–35) ordered terrible punishments for Christians (*1 Apol.* 31.6). No other reference supports this claim, (an ambiguous mention of "Galileans" in a Bar Kochba letter does not seem to mean "Christians"), but in a situation of siege, a military leader might see anyone loyal to another messiah as a threat. The second revolt finished the work of Roman suppression of Jewish life in Jerusalem that had begun with the first, in 70 CE.

The Roman state was not interested in internal matters, but it did attend to charges of atheism or lack of loyalty to Caesar. Such charges were leveled against the Jews themselves by the Roman historian Tacitus, writing around 110 CE (*Hist.* 5.5). According to John's Gospel, "the Jews" fear Jesus will get them in trouble with the Romans (11.48–50; 18.13–14; 19.12; cf. Acts 5.28). Later sources depict members of the Jewish community as turning the followers of Jesus over to the state. Revelation refers to the "slander of the synagogue of Satan" (2.9), and the mid-second-century *Martyrdom of Polycarp* implicates

Jews as secondary participants in his execution (they gather sticks for the fire) and part of the crowd that called Polycarp an atheist. These sources suggest anxiety that Christ-followers will invite Roman persecution of Jews as a whole. Some references, like the *Martyrdom of Polycarp* may simply be imitating the Gospels. Just as the Jews are there implicated in Jesus' death, so too they play a part in Polycarp's death.

Believers in Jesus were not routinely expelled from synagogues. John's Gospel reports that those who confessed Jesus as Messiah were to be put out of the synagogue (9.22; 12.42–43; 16.2–3). Some scholars have linked this expulsion to a Talmudic statement (*b. Ber.* 28b) that one who falters while reciting the *birchat ha-minim* (a euphemism for curse against the heretics; the prayer is part of the *Shemoneh Esreh*), is to be "removed." Early versions of this prayer, found in the Cairo geniza, in a number of fragments from the early medieval period, targets "Nazoreans [Christians?] and *minim* [sectarians, heretics]." Some scholars have argued that this is a special prayer denouncing Jewish followers of Jesus as heretics, particularly those later called "Nazarenes," who believed in Jesus as the messiah and accepted his divine status. Many questions dog this theory, including the inclusiveness of the term "minim," the earliness of the word "Nazoreans," and the vagueness of the Talmudic reference. (Was one to be removed from the temporary position of praying on behalf of the community, or taken out of the synagogue? Was the removal temporary or permanent?) Recent work has shown that "Nazoreans" seems to be an original and stable tradition, so it is as early or late as the statements in which it appears.

While Justin says (*Dial.* 17.1; 108.2) that Jews send emissaries to warn their communities of the Christian *hairesis* (a Greek term, source of the English word "heresy," [party]; Josephus applies the same term to Pharisees and Sadducees), his examples show these measures are more prescriptive than real, not unlike urging the members of one's group not to associate with the wrong people from another group.

TOLERANCE

People who generally accept one another and tolerate neighbors with differing beliefs and practices usually do not leave much evidence behind. Given the range of people, Jew and Gentile, accommodated in Greco-Roman synagogues, and the variety of attitudes apparent among the rabbis, tolerance might have been *the* most common Jewish response to early Jesus-followers.

Josephus, from the Jewish elite, writing in the 90s under Roman patronage, makes two references to Christians. The famous *Testimonium Flavianum*, about Jesus and his immediate followers, is preserved by the church and contains many Christian interpolations (*Ant.* 18.3.3). The core of the passage is probably authentic, and it suggests that Josephus found Christians a little gullible, but inoffensive. More telling is his information about the execution of James the brother of Jesus at the hands of a Sadducean high priest (*Ant.* 20.197–203), who accused James and perhaps fellow believers "as breakers of the law," and "delivered them to be stoned." (See "Josephus," p. 575.) Josephus speaks approvingly of the "reasonable ones" (perhaps Pharisees), prominent Jews who go to meet the incoming Roman governor, Albinus, to protest the injustice against James, the prominent leader of the first generation of Jesus-followers in Jerusalem after Jesus' death; other Jews brought their protest on James's behalf to King Agrippa II.

In Acts, a variety of Jews defend Jesus' followers or promote a policy of "benign neglect," including Gamaliel (a first-century CE rabbi, sometimes called "the Elder") (5.34–39), Pharisaic scribes (23.6–9), and Roman Jewish leaders (28.21–25). While these scenes are not necessarily historical, Luke assumes his audience could imagine such benevolent Jews who are willing to tolerate the followers of Jesus and who will urge their fellow Jews to treat them with respect. In John's Gospel, not calculated to flatter Jews, "the Jews" comfort Mary and Martha in their grief at their brother's death (Jn 11.19). Even Justin's Trypho emerges as a courtly, fair-minded person, an intellectual Jewish friend to the Gentile Christian Justin, even as Justin complains about Jewish treatment of Christians. If, as seems likely, Trypho is a "type," rather than a specific historical character, that would make this depiction an even stronger witness to perceived Jewish benevolence.

The rabbinic references are relatively few in number, and in materials redacted at the beginning of the third century at the earliest. If anything, they show that from the Jewish perspective, Jews who believed in Jesus did not impinge much on the rabbinic consciousness. Some stories are playful, some cryptic, and some probably fold Christians in with other groups. Rabbinic Jews worried more about other people, like those attracted to Epicureanism, or those who rejected belief in resurrection (*m. Sanh.* 10.1).

Jews who did not believe in Jesus continued to see Jesus-believers as part of their community for some time. If Israel's core identity revolved around God, Torah, and Temple, Christians also made those things central, but with a peculiar (to others) slant. Believers in Jesus may have been a source of anxiety, or in need of group discipline, but they still belonged to the community. Other Jews seemed to hold out hope of their return to the right path, long after Jesus-followers saw themselves as a separate group, with their own practices and identity.

JESUS IN RABBINIC TRADITION

Burton L. Visotzky

Only a very minuscule proportion of rabbinic literature concerns Jesus or Christianity, but even within this small sample attitudes vary depending upon the era and provenance of the tradition's composition.

The earliest rabbinic texts (tannaitic) were composed in Roman Galilee, from the late first century through their editing in the early- to mid-third century. These texts largely ignore Jesus and Christianity, probably because Christianity was seen as but a minor heresy posing no real threat to rabbinic Judaism. One text (*b. Hul.* 2.24) reports Jesus' teaching within the context of Roman persecution of Christianity. While it slurs Jesus' origins, it is somewhat ambivalent about the content of his teaching, even admiring its cleverness. Hence it calls him "Jesus son of the Panther" (a common nickname for a Roman soldier), deriding the Gospels' emphasis on Jesus' divine paternity. But Jesus' teaching on whether money earned from prostitution can be used to benefit the Temple priests (an arcane point of Temple law), is accepted by a prominent rabbi, Eliezer.

One of the few other early rabbinic texts (*t. Shabb.* 14.5) opines that Christian works caught in a fire should not be saved on the Sabbath due to the prohibitions of carrying and extinguishing on that day—although one should save a Torah scroll. Each rabbi who offers an opinion agrees on the impermissibility of saving a Christian text. The Hebrew refers to the *avon gilayon,* which sounds like *euangelion* (the term that comes into English as "Gospel"). The literal meaning of the Hebrew is "the Scroll of Sin." This is a puerile but nevertheless negative assessment of Christian Scripture.

From the time the Roman Empire became Christian (post-312 CE), rabbinic attitudes toward Jesus and Christianity changed. While careful to speak in allegory or thinly veiled code (which makes identification of anti-Christian material notoriously difficult to distinguish from other heterodox views), rabbinic literature in Roman Palestine joins inner-Christian debate, weighing in negatively on questions of virgin birth (e.g., *Lev. Rab.* 14.5) and the resurrection of Jesus (see *Lev. Rab.* 6.6). The Palestinian Talmud (edited in fifth-century Galilee) contains a series of texts refuting the idea of the Trinity and the efficacy of invoking Jesus as a patron for protection (*y. Ber.* 12.9). Yet in their commentaries on Genesis the rabbis share some attitudes with the church fathers as they explicate Adam and Eve's sin as a source of human failings. The rabbis of the land of Israel also employ many of the same methods as the church fathers in their approaches to interpreting Scripture (see "The New Testament between the Hebrew Bible [Tanakh] and Rabbinic Literature," p. 504). These are interpretive methods that both rabbis and church fathers learned from their Hellenistic milieu.

The majority of anti-Christian materials in this latter period (third to sixth centuries CE) are in the Babylonian Talmud. Here, too, these texts are an exceptionally small part of that vast compendium. The Babylonian Talmud recounts stories about the trial and crucifixion of Jesus (*b. Sanh.* 43a), Jesus' repudiation by his disciples (ibid.), Jesus' punishment in hell (*b. Git.* 57a), and the dishonesty of Christian judges (*b. Shabb.* 116a–b; parodying Mt 5.14–17). Peter Schäfer (*Jesus in the Talmud*, Princeton University Press, 2007) has plausibly explained the concentration of these texts in Jewish Babylonia rather than the land of Israel. There, Christianity was known as the oppressive empire to the West, yet it remained a minority religion in the Zoroastrian East. Consequently, the rabbis spoke derisively of Christianity with impunity, something they could not afford to do in the Christian Roman Empire. Midrash *Ecclestiastes Rabbah* (edited sixth to seventh centuries) contains a collection of anti-Christian texts deriding the efficacy and authenticity of Christian conversions of Jews (*Eccl. Rab.* 1. 1.8).

Christianity strengthened its grip on Judaism in Europe, first during the Crusades and then during Inquisition of the High Middle Ages. There were two consequences for rabbinic traditions about Jesus and Christianity. One was the Christian suppression of many rabbinic anti-Christian texts which were removed from manuscripts and printed editions of the Talmud by Christian censors (e.g., *b. Sanh.* 43a and *b. Git.* 57a). Ultimately this practice of suppression led to Christian burning of Talmud texts and other rabbinic books. As a second consequence, this church oppression led Jews to circulate anti-Christian texts, such as a scurrilous "biography" of Jesus, in rabbinic communities of Europe. These texts expressed rabbinic disdain for their Christian rulers.

No rabbinic text, including the earliest, offers any historic evidence regarding Jesus or first-century Christianity. All rabbinic writing reflects the attitudes of the editors toward the Christianity of their own times, at least two centuries after the death of Jesus. By this time, copies of the New Testament and other early Christian writings were circulating in various forms throughout the Roman Empire and the East. Further, rabbinic texts often reflect the interpretations of New Testament that were being offered by the various church fathers in their eras and locales. It is highly unlikely that rabbis read the New Testament per se.

It is important, in looking at these rabbinic texts today, to take account of the various historical contexts in which they were written or edited. By the time the Talmud was coming into final form, Christianity was the dominant religion of the Mediterranean world and beyond. Negative expressions in such writings reflect negative experiences in the time of their creation. Quoting such texts without explaining these contextual influences can grossly distort one's understanding of how Jewish tradition views Jesus.

JESUS IN MEDIEVAL JEWISH TRADITION

Martin Lockshin

The medieval period is not a sharply delineated one. It extends from the centuries after the fall of Rome in 476 CE up to the beginnings of the Renaissance in the fifteenth century. For the purposes of surveying Jewish thought, the medieval period can be said to begin with the conclusion of the formation of the Babylonian Talmud in the sixth century CE.

The earliest medieval Jewish criticism of Jesus originated in the ninth century in the Muslim world. This work, known as the "Polemic of Nestor the Priest," exists in two forms: an Arabic version, the "Disputation," and a Hebrew translation, the "Polemic." The work contends that Christian claims of Jesus' divinity cannot be supported from the New Testament and are also contradicted by the events of Jesus' life: gestation and birth (considered unbecoming for a divine being), Jesus' prayers to God (why, if Jesus were divine, would he pray?), and particularly a shameful death (crucifixion seen as disproving divine status). Within Christendom, only beginning in the thirteenth century did Jewish writers criticize, in ways similar to that of the "Polemic," the character of Jesus or point out the disparity between the Jesus of the Gospels and common Christian dogma. These writers also argued that claims about Jesus as the second person of the Trinity are not philosophically tenable. The most sustained criticism of Jesus is found in the late fourteenth-century satirical work *Be Not Like Your Fathers* (Hebrew title *al tehi ka'avotekha*) by Profiat Duran, a Spanish Jew. It is a satiric letter purportedly commending Christian beliefs while actually undermining them.

In general, Jews in medieval Christian countries did talk about Jesus, but not the Jesus of the Gospels. The most important source of Jewish (mis-)information about Jesus was the scurrilous Hebrew biography *Toledot Yeshu* (*The Chronicle of Yeshu*). "Yeshu" was the preferred form of Jesus' name for most medieval Jews, probably because the more accurate name, Yeshua, is associated with the Hebrew root that means salvation. Other (insulting) terms for Jesus included *ha-talui*, the hanged one (see, e.g., R. Eliezer ben R. Yoel Halevi, *Sefer Raavyah* 1051).

The provenance, date, and even original version of *Toledot Yeshu* are unclear. The book is rarely mentioned explicitly by Jewish writers, for obvious reasons: It would have been dangerous for a Jew to own or perhaps even mention an insulting biography of Jesus. The work survived in part because it was disseminated by Christians who wished to rouse animosity against Jews.

The most common version of the story depicts a Jewish woman named Miriam engaged to a Jewish man named Yoḥanan. A villainous character, Joseph Pandera, disguised himself as Yoḥanan and raped Miriam when she was menstrually impure. The child thus conceived, Yeshu, was intelligent but impertinent. Learning in a deceitful manner how to pronounce God's Name (YHWH, the tetragrammaton), he used this knowledge to perform supernatural deeds, thus seducing people into following him and seeing him as divine. After many twists and turns, the rabbis put Yeshu to death by hanging him on a cabbage plant (!).

A work like *Toledot Yeshu* was meant to make oppressed Jews of medieval Christendom feel better by satirizing their oppressors.

The Jewish idea that Jesus was a sorcerer is found in the Talmud (e.g. *b. Sanh.* 43a and 107b); the New Testament (e.g. Mt 12.24) reports that the charge was leveled against Jesus in his lifetime. But *Toledot Yeshu* greatly expands and develops this theme. Other medieval Jews alluded to Jesus as the paradigmatic false prophet described in biblical texts such as Deut 13.2–6. For example, Joseph Bekhor Shor (late twelfth-century Northern France) states in his Bible commentary: "How much more so if he performs miracles through sorcery, as Yeshu did, bringing [back to the Holy Land] sorcery [that he learned] from Egypt" (see *b. Sanh.* 107b).

The image of Jesus as a false prophet and false messiah appears explicitly in the uncensored versions of Moses Maimonides's *Mishneh Torah*, his code of Jewish law (*Kings* 11). After describing in some detail how the true messiah can be recognized, Maimonides adds:

> So also Jesus of Nazareth who imagined that he was the messiah and was put to death by a Jewish court, was prophesied about by Daniel, who said (11.14) "the lawless sons of your people shall assert themselves to establish the vision; but they shall stumble." Could there be a greater stumbling block than this [episode of Jesus]? All the prophets had said that the messiah would save Israel and redeem them, would gather their exiles and strengthen the commandments [of the Torah]. But he [= Jesus] caused Israel to be put to the sword, caused their remnant to be exiled and degraded, switched their Torah [for another one] and led much of the world to worship someone other than God.

After this scathing attack on Jesus, Maimonides concludes however, with what may be the most liberal Jewish statement about Jesus from the High Middle Ages. He says that despite the many evil outcomes of Jesus' life, it also led to some crucial positive developments:

> All the actions of Jesus . . . . only serve to pave the way for the coming of the [true] messianic king, and to improve our world [by leading all of humanity, eventually] to worship God together, as it is written (Zeph 3.9), "For then I will make the peoples pure of speech so that they all invoke the LORD by name and serve Him with one accord."

Maimonides thus concludes that when the true messiah comes, his mission will have been prepared for by Jesus: even if the preparation has been inadvertent, it will result in good, because great numbers of those outside the Jewish community are now aware of the coming of a messiah. Christian belief thus can be seen, from the Jewish perspective, as producing a benefit for non-Jews. The wider question raised by this approach then becomes: Is Christianity the means by which non-Jews can come to worship the God of Israel?

JESUS IN MODERN JEWISH THOUGHT

Susannah Heschel

The emancipation of Jews from political repression and into secularizing Christian society in the eighteenth century elicited a Jewish interest in Jesus; the principal focus was less an appreciation for Christianity than a justification of Judaism. For example, the noted Jewish German philosopher Moses Mendelssohn (1729–86) sought to win Christian tolerance of Judaism by reminding his audience of Jesus' Jewishness: he wrote in his *Jerusalem: or, On Religious Power and Judaism* (1783) that

> Jesus of Nazareth himself observed not only the law of Moses, but also the ordinances of the rabbis; and whatever seems to contradict this in the speeches and acts ascribed to him appears to do so only at first glance. Closely examined, everything is in complete agreement not only with scripture, but also with the tradition.

Such an emphasis on Jesus' faithfulness to Judaism initially had to proceed with caution. Mendelssohn writes in an unpublished note in 1770,

> It is a disgrace that we should reproach Socrates and Plato because they were pagans! Was this a flaw in their morals? And Jesus a Jew?—And what if, as I believe, he never wanted to give up Judaism? One can only imagine where this remark would lead me.

The answer: into dangerous waters, no doubt, given the generally negative views Christians at the time had toward Judaism. The Jewishness of Jesus was known but not to be publicized.

The next generation saw in Germany the rise of the *Wissenschaft des Judentums*, the historical study of Judaism, which emphasized scholarship on the Second Temple period. Participants in this movement sought not only to elucidate developments in Jewish history, but also to demonstrate how early Christian texts can be clarified with reference to Jewish sources, particularly rabbinic texts. Scholars representing this movement include Abraham Geiger (1810–74), Joseph Salvador (1796–1873), Heinrich Graetz (1817–91), Levi Herzfeld (1810–84), and Joseph Derenbourg (1811–95). In arguing that Jesus can best be understood by studying the Gospel texts in the context of Jewish sources, these scholars were not attempting to build bridges between Synagogue and Church, but to change the prevailing Christian view of Jewish history. Whereas the general Christian view portrayed late Second Temple Judaism as moribund, ossified, heartless, and spiritless, these scholars presented a Judaism of depth and vitality; moreover, they located at the heart of Western civilization not classical Greek or Roman civilization, not Aryan culture, and not the New Testament, but Jewish biblical and rabbinic literature and culture. These Jewish historians argued that even Enlightenment thought, with its claims to secularized, scientific forms of knowing and its insistence on tolerance and diversity, was the product of Judaism, not Christianity. They claimed that while Christianity demanded belief in established dogma, Judaism permitted freedom of belief and required only ethical behavior.

The initial step taken by Jewish historians was to redefine the nature of Judaism during the era when Christianity developed. In 1829, the German-Jewish scholar Issac M. Jost (1793–1860) published the first extensive history of the Jewish people since Josephus wrote his *Antiquities of the Jews* in the first century. Jost simply followed the New Testament narrative that depicts the Pharisees as narrow-minded and hypocritical, responsible for their own destruction and for Jews' turning away to Christianity. By contrast, thirty years later, Abraham Geiger, one of the founders of Reform Judaism, inaugurated a new era of scholarship in 1857 with his magnum opus, the *Urschrift und Übersetzungen der Bibel* (*The Original Text and Versions of the Bible*), one of the nineteenth century's most important works of Jewish scholarship. Geiger defined two tendencies in early Judaism: the liberal Pharisaic and the conservative Sadducean. His Pharisees, far from being the figures of hypocrisy depicted in the New Testament, attempted to liberalize and democratize *halakhah*, Jewish religious law. The Sadducees, whom Geiger associated with the priests of the Jerusalem Temple, represented the aristocratic elite who sought to preserve their privileges by a conservative reading of *halakhah*.

Even though the New Testament is frequently critical of the Pharisees, Geiger suggested that Jesus himself was part of the liberalizing Pharisaic movement of his day. In his *Das Judentum und seine Geschicht* (*Judaism and Its History*) he declared in a passage that became notorious among Protestant theologians that Jesus "was a Jew, a Pharisaic Jew with Galilean coloring–a man who shared the hopes of his time and who believed that these hopes were fulfilled in him. He did not utter a new thought, nor did he break down the barriers of nationality.... He did not abolish any part of Judaism; he was a Pharisee who walked in the way of Hillel." Geiger argued that Christianity was not founded by Jesus, but by Paul, who brought the Jewish monotheism taught by Jesus to the pagan world. There it became corrupted by pagan thought and led to non-Jewish doctrines such as the Trinity. Geiger suggested that Christians find the actual liberal faith of Jesus—Pharisaic Judaism—in Geiger's own Reform Judaism.

The next generation of Jewish scholars, including Leo Baeck (1873–1956), Joseph Eschelbacher (1884–1916), and Felix Perles (1874–1933), extended Geiger's arguments. By the early twentieth century, a cottage industry had developed of Jewish writers who adduced parallels between rabbinic literature and the Gospels. The biblical scholar and Zionist leader Hirsch Perez Chajes wrote in 1919, "You have to be a rabbinical Jew, to know midrash, if you wish to fathom the spirit of Christianity in its earliest years. Above all, you must read the Gospels in the Hebrew translation." Claude Montefiore (1858–1938), one of the founders of liberal Judaism in Great Britain, saw in Jesus the forerunner of his own liberal attitude to Jewish orthopraxy. The Reform theologian Samuel Cohon (1888–1959) argued in a 1928 article published in the prestigious *Journal of Biblical Literature* that Jesus should be seen as a *Hasid* from the *'amei ha-'aretz*, the peoples of the land, rather than as a Pharisee or Essene.

By the twentieth century, most Jewish thinkers followed Geiger in asserting that Jesus said nothing original or unusual. From this there is a short step to Martin Buber's proclamation (from his 1951 *Two Types of Faith*), "From my youth onwards I have found in Jesus my great brother." Such positive comments about Jesus were not always welcomed in the Jewish community. For example, enormous controversy broke out when the American Reform rabbi Stephen Wise declared in his 1929 autobiography, "Jesus was a Jew, Hebrew of Hebrews.... Jesus did not teach or wish to teach a new religion."

Jesus also played an important role in Zionist writings. Christian commentators had long argued that Jesus rejected the nationalist confines of Jewishness as well as the strictures of Jewish law. Joseph Klausner (1874–1958), who taught at the Hebrew University in Jerusalem, published in 1922 the first book on Jesus written in modern Hebrew. There, he presented Jesus as a pious Pharisee, a Galilean poet, and a miracle worker with apocalyptic interests. Klausner's Jesus departed from the boundaries of Jewish nationhood, implying that Jews who reject Zionism end up like Jesus, as Christians. In contrast to Klausner, the liberal theologian and chief rabbi of Stockholm Gottlieb Klein wrote in 1910 that Jesus never abandoned his nationality; in Jesus, "a Jew is speaking, no cult hero, but a Jew with a marked national consciousness." Other Zionist thinkers also claimed Jesus as a member of a self-conscious Jewish nationality, often as a rebel against religious piety.

Among Jews of Eastern Europe, however, the nuances of Jesus' Jewishness are more complex. In Sholem Asch's 1909 Yiddish story, "Jesus climbs down from the cross in St. Peter's Cathedral to become one of the Jewish martyrs persecuted by the Church. The Virgin Mary joins Mother

Rachel in sewing the shrouds." In a 1920 Yiddish poem, "Golgotha," printed in the shape of a cross, the major Yiddish and Hebrew poet Uri Zvi Greenberg writes,

> You've become inanimate, brother Jesus. For two thousand years you've been tranquil on the cross. All around you the world expires. Damn it, you've forgotten everything. Your petrified brain can't grasp: a Star of David at your heart, over the star—hands in a priestly blessing . . . the worship of those millions is a lie . . . Beit Lehem is a Jewish town! Ben-Yosef is a Jewish son!

It is Jesus on the cross who comes to represent the figure of the Jew in Eastern Europe: "*Mir kumen tsu kholem di yidn vos hengen af tslomin* [I dream of the Jews hanging on crosses]," wrote Greenberg in 1923. Jesus becomes the symbol for catastrophe, for the pogroms, and for the Shoah. Marc Chagall frequently painted crucifixion scenes, and his most famous, the 1938 *White Crucifixion*, depicts Jesus wrapped in a tallit (prayer shawl)and nailed to the cross, while around him communist revolutionaries attack, a synagogue burns, Jews flee on foot and by boat, a Torah scroll is in flames, an old Jew weeps, a mother clutches her baby. For Chagall's painting Jesus' death not only fails to end suffering, it is responsible for generating it. Chagall's 1944 *The Crucified* depicts a village with fully clothed Jews hanging from a series of crosses. The Holocaust is the Crucifixion, and the Crucifixion is a mass murder.

Elie Wiesel depicts in his memoir *Night* the heart-wrenching image of three Jews hanging on the gallows at Auschwitz; the middle victim is a child. An anonymous voice asks a question not from Psalm 22 (see Mt 27.46; Mk 15.34), but "Where is God now?" and the narrator responds, "And I heard a voice within me answer him: 'Where is He? Here He is—He is hanging here on this gallows.'" In contrast to Chagall, neither Jesus nor Christianity is the crucifier. In *Night*, the perceived death of God at Auschwitz is expressed in crucifixion imagery.

Other Jews attempted to bring historical precision to studies of Jesus' crucifixion. Solomon Zeitlin (1886–1976), whose 1967 *Rise and Fall of the Judean State* was one of the first modern comprehensive studies of the late Second Temple period, published several articles in the 1940s asking *Who Crucified Jesus?* His answer includes not only Pilate but also the high priests, whom he saw as complicit in Roman rule.

In the 1960s and 1970s, the time of the "new quest" of the historical Jesus, the dominant approach was reconciliatory and optimistic; Jewish writers positively approached Jesus, and they saw in him a Jew who represented much that was good about early Judaism (determined by a selective reading of rabbinic sources). In 1967 Schalom ben Chorin (1913–99) drew upon rabbinic literature, Jewish folk-tradition, and studies of Semitic languages to write *Bruder Jesus—Mensch, Nicht Messias* (*Brother Jesus—Human, not Messiah*). This attempt at building bridges between Jews and Christians presents Jesus as a love-filled proto-rabbi who saw himself as the suffering servant of God (Isa 49–53). Pinchas Lapide (1922–97) argued in his 1970 *Der Jude Jesus: Thesen eines Juden: Antworten eines Christen* (*The Jew Jesus: Theses of a Jew: Answers of a Christian*) and in several other publications both that Jesus was Torah-observant and that the Jews did not reject Jesus. He also claimed that Jesus' resurrection was a physical occurrence, a miracle whose purpose was to bring Gentiles to belief in Israel's God. David Flusser (1917–2000), professor of New Testament and Early Christianity at Hebrew University, took a similarly irenic, fraternal tone. His 1968 *Jesus in Selbstzeugnissen und Bilddokumenten* (*Jesus in Self-Portrayals and Picture-Documents*) depicts Jesus as an observant Jew more concerned with the moral rather than the ritual aspects of the tradition. Instead of associating Jesus with liberal Pharisees, he saw in Jesus Essene connections, including an apocalyptic orientation, a messianic self-identity and a sense of personal call by the Holy Spirit. Samuel Sandmel (1911–79), a Reform rabbi with a PhD in New Testament from Yale, introduced Jesus to Jewish audiences with books such as *We Jews and Jesus* (1965) and *A Jewish Understanding of the New Testament* (1956). Other Jewish scholars of this generation include Hans Joachim Schoeps (1909–80), Yitzhak (Fritz) Baer (1888–1980), Ben-Zion Bokser (1907–84), Haim (Hugo) Mantel (1908–), and Haim Cohen (1911–2002).

The turn to the "Third quest" of the historical Jesus, with its more historical-critical approach to the rabbinic sources and greater attention to other Jewish literature of the late Second Temple period (e.g., the Dead Sea Scrolls, Josephus and Philo, the Pseudepigrapha, archaeological remains) continued the trend of Jewish scholars finding Jesus within, rather than apart from, his Jewish tradition. In several major studies starting with *Jesus the Jew* (1973), Geza Vermes (1924–) locates Jesus in the context of other Jewish-Galilean charismatic miracle workers, such as Ḥoni the Circle Drawer and Ḥanina ben Dosa, and sees Jesus' elevation to messianic status as the invention of the Gentile churches and, especially, of Paul of Tarsus. Asking similar questions, Shmuel Safrai (1919–2003) also located Jesus among the Galilean *Hasidim* but saw him as closer to the Pharisees in his legal opinions. Hyam Maccoby (1924–2004) placed Jesus among apocalyptically inclined Jews who were expecting divine intervention to end Roman occupation; among his more controversial theories are the claim that Judas Iscariot is an invention of the church and that the name "Bar-abbas" originally applied to Jesus of Nazareth.

Jacob Neusner (1932–) has written numerous volumes on Second Temple and rabbinic Judaism, but it was his *A Rabbi Talks with Jesus* (1993) that engaged Pope Benedict XVI's own study of the man from Nazareth. Neusner explains that were he a rabbi listening to Jesus, he would have rejected Jesus' command to leave his family and become a disciple, rejected Jesus' focus on himself as opposed to the community, and concluded that instead of following Jesus, he would follow the Torah.

Paula Fredriksen (1951–), in *From Jesus to Christ* (1988) explains the development of images of Jesus in the church. Her *Jesus of Nazareth: King of the Jews* (1999) calls into historical question the famous Gospel scene in which Jesus "cleanses" the Temple. Combining historical-critical analysis with attention to how popular negative stereotypes of Jews and Judaism infect Christian teaching and preaching, *The Misunderstood Jew: The Church and the Scandal of the Jewish Jesus* (2006) by Amy-Jill Levine (1956–) seeks to both locate Jesus within his diverse Jewish context and show how the historical Jesus has benefits for Jewish-Christian dialogue. *The Historical Jesus in Context* (2006), Levine's collection of studies co-edited with Dale C. Allison Jr. (a Protestant) and John Dominic Crossan (a Roman Catholic) situates Jesus and the Gospel writers in both their Jewish and Roman worlds.

A number of Jewish authors, including Levine, Judith Plaskow, Susannah Heschel, Ross S. Kraemer, Adele Reinhartz, and Pnina Navé Levison, have specifically attended to Jesus' relations with women and to the erroneous Christian stereotype that sees early Judaism as comparable to the Taliban and Jesus as an early feminist. Today, Israeli scholars such as Eyal Regev, Uriel Rappaport, Joshua Efron, and Israel Knohl are making contributions in archaeologically situating Jesus and using increasingly sophisticated methods of textual analysis to see how he fits into a Jewish context.

PAUL IN JEWISH THOUGHT

Daniel R. Langton

Jewish interest in the apostle Paul is essentially a modern phenomenon. Generally speaking, Jews have regarded the apostle to the Gentiles suspiciously as a kind of self-hating Jew and as the "real" founder of the Christian religion. In particular, he has commonly been held responsible for Christianity's traditional antagonism toward the Law.

Rabbinic literature never mentions Paul by name, but there are some tantalizing references. For example: "[He who] profanes the Hallowed Things and despises the set feasts and puts his fellow to shame publicly and makes void the covenant of Abraham our father, and discloses meanings in the Law which are not according to the Halakhah" (*Pirkei Avot* 3.12); "This man . . . estranged himself from circumcision and the commandments of the Torah" (*Ruth Rab. Petikha* 3); a pupil of Gamaliel who "scoffed" at his master's teachings and who exhibited "impudence in matters of learning" (*b. Shabb.* 30b). All of these texts postdate 200 CE and, if they refer to Paul, reflect knowledge of Christian teaching rather than independent knowledge of Paul himself.

Nor does Paul feature in medieval Jewish refutations of Christianity, despite his importance for its theology. This might reflect simple ignorance, a deliberate policy to ignore a dangerous opponent, or, more likely, an awareness of the political danger of engaging with such an authoritative Christian figure. Those few authors that do make brief mention tended to be Karaites (Jews who rejected Rabbinic authority and law), or minor figures living in the relative safety of Muslim lands, or converts (e.g., Al-Mukammis, Kirkisani, Hadassi, Ibn Kammuna, Profiat Duran, and Isaac Troki). One exception is a brief, confused reference in the anonymous *Toledot Yeshu* or *Story of Jesus*, a notorious, popular polemic composed sometime in Late Antiquity on the basis of earlier traditions, some of which may go back to the second century CE. (See "Jesus in Medieval Jewish Tradition," p. 581). Versions of the *Toledot* dating from the thirteenth-century record that the Jewish sages "desired to separate from Israel those who followed Yeshu as the Messiah, and that they called upon a learned man, Simeon Kepha, for help." Simeon Kepha is Simon, called Peter, Jesus' apostle. Claiming to speak on behalf of Yeshu, Simeon Kepha introduced new festivals, and rejected circumcision and the dietary laws. The *Toledot* then confuses Peter and Paul: "All these new ordinances which Simeon Kepha (or Paul, as he was known to the Nazarenes) taught them were really meant to separate these Nazarenes from the people of Israel and to bring the internal strife to an end."

A rough, composite image of the highly fragmentary premodern Jewish conception of Paul finds him portrayed as the innovator of non-Jewish teachings such as the Trinitarian conception of God, the atoning death of Christ, and celibacy, who had modified the calendar, and whose antinomian (anti-*Torah*) misreading of scripture had led him to set aside practices that traditionally separated the Jews from the other nations. But such an image was by no means widespread.

In contrast, early Enlightenment Jewish discussions of Paul were remarkably positive. The Dutch philosopher Baruch Spinoza (1632–77) in his *Theological-Political Treatise* stressed that the apostle spoke from reason rather than revelation and regarded him as the most philosophical of the apostles. Spinoza wrote as a philosopher, not as a theologian; in fact he had been expelled from the Amsterdam Jewish community in 1656. Since he was not a Christian convert, however, it is reasonable to see his views on Paul as reflecting at least one possible Jewish assessment. The German rabbi Jacob Emden (1697–1776) argued in his *Seder olam rabbah vezutai* that Paul had not sought to denigrate Judaism, had "never dreamed of destroying the Torah," and was in fact "well-versed in the laws of the Torah." While Spinoza wrote for a Gentile readership, and Emden wrote to advise the Polish Jewish authorities, both appreciations of this key Christian figure can be seen as strategic in terms of connecting with the wider Gentile world.

In the nineteenth century, German Protestant biblical criticism increasingly viewed Christianity as brought about by Paul's universalistic teaching. As the cliché states, Paul turned the religion *of* Jesus into the religion *about* Jesus. Among the earliest Jewish proponents of this view was the German scholar Heinrich Graetz (1817–91), whose immensely influential *History of the Jews* (1853–76 [English translation 1891–98]) presented Paul as the "inventor" of Christianity, distinguished Paul's superficial Jewish learning from Jesus' high-mindedness and moral purity, and argued that Paul's antinomian theology made him "the destroyer of Judaism."

As German Christian scholarship emphasized Paul's role in injecting pagan elements into the religion of Jesus, it comes as no surprise that the prominent American Reform rabbi, Kaufman Kohler (1843–1926), in his *Jewish Encyclopedia* (1901–16) article on "Saul of Tarsus," found Gnostic influences and Hellenistic mystery religions to account for many of Paul's teachings. Even the German philosopher Martin Buber (1878–1965), whose credentials in interfaith relations were impeccable, contrasted the faith (Heb *'emunah*) of Jesus, a Jewish faith that implied relation with and trust in God, with the faith (Gk *pistis*) of Paul, a Christian faith that was premised upon belief in a proposition.

Insofar as it is legitimate to speak of a popular modern Jewish view of Paul—for he barely registers on the Jewish cultural radar—the apostle is regarded not only as the creator of Christianity but also as a Jewish self-hater. The Chief Rabbi of the United Synagogue in the United Kingdom, Jonathan Sacks (1948–), in his 1993 *One People?: Tradition, Modernity, and Jewish Unity*, even identified a genocidal ring to the apostle's teachings, describing him as "the architect of a Christian theology which deemed that the covenant between God and his people was now broken. . . . Pauline theology demonstrates to the full how remote from and catastrophic to Judaism is the doctrine of a second choice, a new election. *No doctrine has cost more Jewish lives*" [Italics added].

Until recently the majority of Jewish commentators, influenced by the traditional Lutheran teaching that Paul taught freedom from the oppressive yoke of the Law through faith in the Messiah's redemptive sacrifice, denounced Paul's apparent derogation and abrogation of the *Torah* as reflected in statements such as "the power of sin is the law" (1 Cor 15.56) and "For all who rely the works of the law are under a curse" (Gal 3.10). The Rumanian scholar and leader of North American Conservative Judaism, Solomon Schechter (1847–1915), captured perfectly in his *Some Aspects of Rabbinic Theology* (1909) the Jewish puzzlement at Paul's apparent hostility toward the Law: "Either the theology of the Rabbis must be wrong, its conception of God debasing, its leading motives materialistic and coarse, and its teachings lacking in enthusiasm and spirituality, or the Apostle to the Gentiles is quite unintelligible." Jewish scholars understood Paul's antinomian stance as either an opportunistic strategy to convert Gentiles (Graetz and Joseph Klausner), or the result of embittered conflict with contemporary Jews (Kohler), or a mistaken reaction against legalism or "works-righteousness" (Buber and Claude Montefiore), or a consequence of Paul's own frustrated inability to observe its commandments (Hyam Maccoby, Emil Hirsch, Samuel Sandmel).

A few, however, including the German Reform rabbi Leo Baeck (1873–1956), argued that Paul remained authentically Jewish. In his 1952 article "The Faith of Paul" Baeck suggested that like many of his contemporaries, Paul had expected the Law to be transcended (not abrogated) when the messianic age began; the only difference was that this new age had arrived with Jesus. Thus it had not been un-Jewish for him to exclaim, "All things are lawful for me" (1 Cor 6.12) since this closely paralleled the rabbinic teaching that in the "Days of the Messiah . . . there will be no merit or guilt" (*b. Shabb.* 151a). Many noted that Paul's apparent readiness to prioritize a universal dimension at the expense of the more particularistic elements of the *halakhah* (religious law) was somewhat similar to the attitude of nineteenth-century Reform Judaism. While traditionalists were condemnatory (in 1925, the Anglo-Orthodox Chief Rabbi Joseph Hertz denounced the Reform movement as "an echo of Paul, the Christian apostle to the Gentiles"), some Progressives such as Montefiore, Hans Joachim Schoeps, Samson Raphael Hirsch, Joseph Krauskopf, and Isaac Mayer Wise argued that Paul's concern to bring the essential teachings of Judaism to the Gentiles was a profoundly Jewish concern, and, admiring his success, they speculated whether there were lessons to be learned from his methods.

More recently, mainstream New Testament scholarship has questioned the assumed antinomian character of Paul's thought. A number of Jewish scholars are associated with this trend. For example, Mark Nanos (1954–) has gone so far as to claim that Paul was entirely *Torah*-observant and that he expected other Jewish followers of Jesus to be so as well. Nanos interprets the apostle's negative remarks about the Law as expressing the right of Gentiles to follow Jesus without observing the Law, rather than expressive of dissatisfaction with the Law per se. Modern scholars have also been interested in issues relating to gender and Paul's attitude toward women. Against Christian feminists who see the apostle as sexist and placing restrictions on women as a result of his rabbinic training, Amy-Jill Levine (1956–) points out the anachronism of the charge: that Paul belonged to no rabbinic school, and that the rabbinic literature is of a much later date. She further suggests that Paul would have been familiar with women leaders in Diaspora synagogues, and thus recognized women leaders in his churches (e.g., Phoebe the deacon and Junia the apostle [Rom 16]). One might even begin to talk of a sort of Jewish reclamation of the Jewish Paul. Daniel Boyarin (1946–) maintains that despite the fact that Paul had found the Law problematic, his letters ("the spiritual autobiography of a first-century Jew") show him to be a Jew facing many of the same kinds of challenges that Jews face today; furthermore, as a fellow "cultural critic" Paul had asked the right questions (regarding universalist and gender issues in particular) in terms of how Jews should relate to the non-Jewish world.

The classic, negative view of Paul tends to emphasize Paul's Diaspora roots and to locate him within an essentially pagan environment. Kohler and Buber, among others, locate "Paulinism" (i.e., the pessimistic exaggeration of the power of sin and the belief in enslavement of the cosmos) in a heathen world of idolatrous sacrifice, mysteries, and demonic forces. This perspective found its final expression in the eccentric theory of the Ukrainian Zionist writer Micah Berdichevsky (1865–1921), who, determined to expose the essentially non-Jewish origins of the apostle and hence of Christianity itself, argued that Saul and Paul were different people, one a Jew and the other a pagan priest from Damascus. The Anglo-Orthodox scholar Hyam Maccoby (1924–2004) also argued for the Gentile origins of the "inventor of Christianity," maintaining that his poor emulation of rabbinic arguments (e.g., in Rom 7.1–6, where he discusses the limits of the Law) showed that he could not have been a Jew, and certainly not a Pharisee.

Others have had less difficulty placing Paul in an explicitly Jewish context. Among those who regarded him as a Hellenistic Jew, for example, were the founder of Anglo-Liberal Judaism, Claude Montefiore (1858–1938) and the American leading scholar of Jewish-Christian relations, Samuel Sandmel (1911–79). Montefiore suggested that Paul's apparent complaints concerning Judaism and the Law had reflected his experiences of this inferior form of Judaism; thus Paul should *not* be regarded as an enemy of rabbinic Judaism. Others, from Wise in 1883 to the American scholar Alan Segal (1945–2011) in 1990, attending to Paul's vision of paradise in 2 Corinthians 12.2 ("I know a person in Christ who fourteen years ago was caught up to the third heaven—whether in the body or out of the body I do not know"), attribute to Paul an education in Jewish mysticism. Hugh Schonfield even argued in his 1946 *The Jew of Tarsus: An Unorthodox Portrait of Paul*, that Paul's Letter to the Romans parallels parts of the Jewish liturgy.

Broadly speaking, the Jewish relationship with the apostle to the Gentiles has been, and remains, a bitter one. He was largely ignored until the Enlightenment, with Jewish interest gathering real momentum only in the nineteenth century, in tandem with the growth of Protestant biblical scholarship. Thereafter Paul was frequently lambasted as the real founder of Gentile Christianity, under whose influence the lachrymose history of the Jews unfolded. In contrast to the figure of Jesus, who has, in the main, been reclaimed as a good Jew of one sort or another, Paul remains an object of hostility and suspicion. While there have been a number of scholarly exceptions to this rule, one should not expect him, whose likening of the Law to "sin" and "death" still echo down the centuries, to enjoy a more general Jewish reclamation any time soon.

TIMELINE

DATE	PERIOD	GREECE AND ROME
539–333	PERSIAN	Greeks repel Persian invasions Peloponnesian War (431–404)
333–63	HELLENISTIC	Alexander the Great (336–323); Defeats Persians at Issus (332) Occupies the Levant and Egypt Rome gains control over Greece (ca. 188–146); Sack of Carthage and Corinth (146)
63 BCE–135 CE	ROMAN	Julius Caesar named dictator (49); assassinated (44) Octavian (Augustus) defeats Antony at Actium (31); (Emperor 27 BCE–14 CE) Tiberius (14–37 CE) Gaius (Caligula) (37–41) Claudius (41–54) Nero (54–68) Vespasian (69–79) Titus (79–81) Domitian (81–96) Nerva (96–98) Trajan (98–117) Hadrian (117–138)

EASTERN AND MEDITERRANEAN	MESOPOTAMIA
	Cyrus II (the Great) (559–530); Capture of Babylon
Some exiles return from Babylon (538)	Cambyses (530–522); Capture of Egypt (525)
Second Temple built (520–515)	Darius I (522–486)
Prophet Haggai (520); Prophet Zechariah (520–518)	Xerxes I (486–465)
Nehemiah governor of Judah (ca. 445–430)	Artaxerxes I (465–424)
Mission of Ezra the scribe (mid-fifth [or early fourth] century)	Artaxerxes II (405–359)
Seleucus I (312/311–281) controls Syria and Mesopotamia	
Ptolemy I (323–282) controls Egypt, Palestine, Phoenicia	
Antiochus III (223–187) gains control of southern Syria, Phoenicia, and Judea from Ptolemy IV (202–198)	
Ben Sira (Sirach) (early second century)	
Antiochus IV Epiphanes (175–164)	
Revolt of the Maccabees (167–164)	
HASMONEAN RULE OF JUDEA (165–37):	
John Hyrcanus (135–104); Alexander Janneus (103–76);	
Salome Alexandra (76–67)	
Pompey conquers the Levant (66–62); Enters Jerusalem (63)	
Herod the Great king of Judea (37–4); Rebuilds Second Temple	
(Herod) Antipas (4 BCE–39 CE)	
Life of Jesus of Nazareth (ca. 4 BCE– ca. 30 CE)	
Pontius Pilate governor of Judea (26–36)	
(Herod) Agrippa I (39–44)	
Missionary activity of Paul (mid-first century)	
(Herod) Agrippa II (53–93)	
First Jewish Revolt in Judea against Rome (66–73); Jerusalem is captured (70)	
Jewish revolts in Egypt, Libya, Cyprus (115–118)	
Second Jewish Revolt (Bar Kochba Revolt) in Judea against Rome (132–135)	

CHRONOLOGICAL TABLE OF RULERS

DATE	EGYPT	SYRIA
	HELLENISTIC PERIOD	**Alexander** (the Great) (336–323)
300 BCE	Ptolemy I Soter (305–282)	**Seleucus I Nicator** (305–281)
	Ptolemy II Philadelphus (285–246)	Antiochus I Soter (281–261)
		Antiochus II Theos (261–246)
	Ptolemy III Euergetes (246–221)	Seleucus II Callinicus (246–225)
	Ptolemy IV Philopator (221–204)	Seleucus III Soter Ceraunos (225–223)
	Ptolemy V Epiphanes (204–180);	**Antiochus III** (the Great) (223–187)
	Cleopatra I (180–176)	**Seleucus** IV Philopator (187–175)
		Antiochus IV **Epiphanes** (175–164)
	Ptolemy VI **Philometor** (180–145);	**Antiochus** V **Eupator** (164–162)
	Cleopatra II (175–116)	**Demetrius** I Soter (162–150)
	Ptolemy VII Neos Philopator (145)	**Alexander Epiphanes** (Balas) (150–145)
	Ptolemy VIII Euergetes II Physcon (170–116)	**Demetrius** II Nicator (145–141 and 129–125)
		Antiochus VI Epiphanes (145–142)
		Trypho (142–138)
		Antiochus VII Sidetes (138–129)
		Cleopatra Thea (126–121)
		Antiochus VIII Grypus (125–121 and 121–96)
	Cleopatra III (116–101)	Seleucus V (125)
	Ptolemy IX Soter II (116–107 and 88–80)	Antiochus IX Cyzicenus (115–95)
100 BCE	Ptolemy X Alexander I (107–88)	Seleucus VI (95)
		Antiochus X Eusebes (95–83)
		Antiochus XI Philadelphus (95)
	Cleopatra Berenice (101–88)	Demetrius III Eukairos (95–88)
		Philip I Epiphanes Philadelphus (95–84)
	Ptolemy XI Alexander II (80)	Antiochus XII Dionysus Epiphanes (87–84)
		Philip II (67–66)
	Ptolemy XII Auletes (80–59 and 55–51)	Antiochus XIII Asiaticus (69–68 and 65–64)
50 BCE	Cleopatra VII (51–30)	
	Ptolemy XIII (51–47)	
	Ptolemy XIV (47–44)	
		ROMAN EMPIRE
		ROMAN EMPERORS:
		Octavian (**Augustus**) (27 BCE–14 CE)
25 CE		**Tiberius** (14–37)
		Gaius Caligula (37–41)
50 CE		**Claudius** (41–54)
		Nero (54–68)
		Galba (68–69); Otho (69); Vitellius (69)
		Vespasian (69–79)
		Titus (79–81)
100 CE		Domitian (81–96)
		Nerva (96–98)
		Trajan (98–117)
		Hadrian (117–138)

YEHUD/IOUDAIA/JUDEA AND SURROUNDING TERRITORY

HASMONEAN RULERS

[Mattathias d. 166]
Judas Maccabeus, son of Mattathias (165–160)
Jonathan, son of Mattathias (160–142)
Simon, son of Mattathias (142–135)
John Hyrcanus I, son of Simon (135–104)

Judah Aristobulus I , son of John Hyrcanus (104–103)

Alexander Janneus, son of John Hyrcanus (103–76)

Salome Alexandra, wife of Alexander Jannaeus (76–67)
Aristobulus II, son of Alexander Jannaeus and Salome Alexandra (67–63)

Hyrcanus II, son of Alexander Jannaeus and Salome Alexandra (63–40)
Mattathias Antigonus, son of Aristobulus II (40–37)

HERODIAN DYNASTY

Herod the Great, king of the Jews (37–4)
Herod Archelaus, son of Herod the Great, ethnarch of Judea, Samaria, Idumea (4 BCE–6 CE)
Herod Antipas, son of Herod the Great, tetrarch of Galilee and Perea (4 BCE–39 CE)
Herod **Philip**, son of Herod the Great, tetrarch of Batanea, Trachonitis, Auranitis (4 BCE–34 CE)

Herod Agrippa I, grandson of Herod the Great, king of Batanea, Trachonitis, Aurantis (37–44) and of Judea, Galilee, and Perea (41–44)

Herod Agrippa II, son of Herod Agrippa I, king of Chalcis (50–53), king of Batanea, Trachonitis, Auranitis, Galilee, Perea (53–ca. 93)

ROMAN GOVERNORS OF JUDEA

Coponius (6–8 CE)
M. Ambivius (9–12)
Annius Rufus (12–15)
Valerius Gratus (15–26)
Pontius Pilate (26–36)
Marcellus (36–37)
Marullus (37–41)[1]
Cuspius Fadus (44–46)
Tiberius Julius Alexander (46–48)
Ventidius Cumanus (48–52)
M. Antonius **Felix** (52–60?)
Porcius Festus (60?–62)
Clodius Albinus (62–64)
Gessius Florus (64–66)

1. In 41 Judea was made part of the kingdom of Herod Agrippa I, grandson of Herod the Great (see Herodian Dynasty, above). At his death in 44 it became a province again.

SOME TANNAITIC RABBIS

FIRST GENERATION

Gamaliel (sometimes called "the Elder"; late 1st century BCE)
Shimeon ben Gamaliel (1st century CE)
Yoḥanan ben Zakkai (1st century CE)

SECOND GENERATION

Elder

Gamaliel II (of Yavneh; son of R. Shimeon; born ca. 50 CE)
Eliezer ben Hyrcanus (pupil of R. Yoḥanan ben Zakkai; 1st–2nd century)
Yehoshua ben Ḥananiah (pupil of R. Yoḥanan ben Zakkai; 1st–2nd century)

Younger

Akiva ben Yosef (ca. 40–135)
Ishma'el (or Yishma'el) ben Elisha (early 2nd century)
Elishah ben Avuya (late 1st–early 2nd century)

THIRD GENERATION

Students of Akiva

Meir (2nd century)
Shimeon bar Yoḥai (2nd century)
Yose ben Ḥalafta (2nd century)
Yehudah bar Ilai (2nd century)
Shimeon ben Gamaliel II (2nd century)

FOURTH GENERATION

Judah ha-Nasi ("Rabbi"; ca. 135–220)
Eleazar bar Shimeon (2nd century; son of Shimeon bar Yoḥai)

FIFTH GENERATION

Gamaliel III (2nd century).

SOME AMORAIC RABBIS

LAND OF ISRAEL	BABYLONIA
FIRST GENERATION	
Elder	
Ḥiyya (2nd–3rd century)	
Bar Kappara (3rd century)	
Levi bar Sisi (3rd century)	
Ḥaninah bar Ḥama (2nd–3rd century)	
Younger	
Yannai (known as Rabbah, "the Great," or Sabba, "the Elder"; 3rd century)	Rav (Abba Arikha, "the Tall"; died ca. 248)
Yehoshua ben Levi (of Lydda; 3rd century)	Mar Shemuel (died ca. 254)
SECOND GENERATION	
Yoḥanan (ca. 240–279)	Yehudah ben Yeḥezkel (d. 291)
Simeon ben Lakhish (d. ca. 275)	
THIRD GENERATION	
Yosi bar Ḥanina	Rabba bar Naḥmani (d. ca. 321)
Abbahu (ca. 300)	Yosef (d. 333)
Eleazar ben Pedat (3rd century)	
Ammi bar Natan (ca. 279)	
Assi (3rd century)	
Ze'era (3rd century)	
FOURTH GENERATION	
Ḥaggai	Abbayei (ca. 278–338)
Yirmiyahu ben Abba (4th century)	Rava (Abba ben Yosef bar Ḥama; 4th century)
Yonah (4th century)	
Yosa	
Aḥa	
FIFTH GENERATION	
Mana	Papa (d. 376)
Yose bar Abin	
Ḥizkiya	
SIXTH GENERATION	
	Ashi (ca. 335–427)
SEVENTH GENERATION	
	Yemar
	Mar bar R. Ashi

CALENDAR

The Jewish year was composed of twelve lunar months (beginning on the day of the new moon), with an intercalary month added periodically (see perhaps 1 Kings 12.33). In some traditions, and perhaps originally, the year began in the fall, at the autumnal equinox (see Ex 23.16; 34.22). In others, following Babylonian practice, the new year was celebrated in the spring. The fall new year became standard in postbiblical Judaism.

Months in the Bible are usually identified by ordinal numbers, beginning with the spring new year. Some months (in boldface in the following list) are also designated with names derived either from a Canaanite calendar or, in postexilic texts, from a Babylonian one; the names of months not found in the Bible are known from other ancient sources.

	CANAANITE NAME	BABYLONIAN NAME	MODERN EQUIVALENT
First	**'Aviv**	**Nisan**	March–April
Second	**Ziv**	'Iyar	April–May
Third		**Sivan**	May–June
Fourth		Tamuz	June–July
Fifth		Av	July–August
Sixth		**Elul**	August–September
Seventh	**'Etanim**	Tishri	September–October
Eighth	**Bul**	Marḥeshvan	October–November
Ninth		Kislev	November–December
Tenth		**Tevet**	December–January
Eleventh		**Shevat**	January–February
Twelfth		**'Adar**	February–March

The Jewish calendar is based on the lunar month, which is a bit longer than 29½ days, so Jewish lunar months are 29 or 30 days long. Twelve lunar months usually amount to 354 days, 11 days short of a solar year. In order for the festivals to stay in the correct season in relation to the solar year, an extra month is added every few years. Following ancient Babylonian models, the calendar runs on a 19-year cycle: years 3, 6, 8, 11, 14, 17, and 19 of the cycle are intercalated or "leap" years, containing an extra month of Adar, sometimes called *Adar Sheni* (second Adar). Adar was chosen for intercalation because it is the last month of the Babylonian year and of the biblical year beginning in Nisan (an alternate calendar, the one now in use, begins the year in Tishri with Rosh Ha- Shanah). The previous 19-year intercalation cycle began in 5768 (2007–2008 CE).

Observances fall within the calendar as follows:

Rosh Ha-Shanah (the New Year)	1-2 Tishri
Yom Kippur (the Day of Atonement)	10 Tishri
Sukkot (Booths) begins	15 Tishri
Hanukkah begins	25 Kislev
Purim	14 Adar (15 Adar in Jerusalem and other ancient walled cities)
Passover begins	15 Nisan
Shavuot (Weeks) begins	6 Sivan
Tish'ah be' av	9 Av

WEIGHTS AND MEASURES

The modern equivalents for New Testament measures and weights are presented in the following tables.

WEIGHTS IN THE NEW TESTAMENT

GREEK	NRSV	EQUIVALENCE	U.S. AVOIRDUPOIS	METRIC UNITS
talenton	talent	(Hebrew) kikar	75.558 pounds	34.3 kilograms
mna	pound	(Hebrew) maneh	20.148 ounces	571.2 grams
litra	pound	(Latin) libra	0.719 pound	326.4 grams

MEASURES OF LENGTH IN THE NEW TESTAMENT

GREEK	NRSV	U.S. MEASURES	METRIC UNITS
pechus	cubit	about 1.5 feet	.456 meter
orguia	fathom	about 72.44 inches	1.839 meters
stadion	stadia, or the equivalent in miles	about 606 feet	184.7 meters
milion	mile	about 4,854 feet	1.482 kilometers

MEASURES OF CAPACITY IN THE NEW TESTAMENT

GREEK	NRSV	EQUIVALENCE	U.S. MEASURES	METRIC UNITS
batos	measure	(Hebrew) bat	6.073 gallons	23 liters
koros	measure	(Hebrew) kor	60.738 gallons or 6.524 bushels	230 liters
saton	measure	(Hebrew) se'ah	6.959 dry quarts	7.71 liters
metretes	measure		10.3 gallons	39 liters
choinix	quart		0.98 dry quart	1.079 liters
modios	bushel	(Latin) modius	7.68 dry quarts	8.458 liters
xestes	pot	(Latin) sextarius	0.96 dry pint, or 1.12 fluid pints	.53 liter

PARALLEL TEXTS

NEW TESTAMENT

A majority of scholars think that the Gospel of Mark was independently used as a source by Matthew and Luke.

	SYNOPTIC PASSAGES		SUBJECT MATTER
Mk 1.2–8	Mt 3.1–6,11–12	Lk 3.1–6,16	John the Baptist
Mk 1.9–11	Mt 3.13–17	Lk 3.21–22	Baptism of Jesus
Mk 1.12–13	Mt 4.1–2,11	Lk 4.1–2,13	Temptation of Jesus
Mk 1.16–20	Mt 4.18–22	(Lk 5.1–11)	Call of disciples
Mk 1.21–38	(Mt 7.28–29; 8.14–17)	Lk 4.31–43	Teaching and healing by Jesus
Mk 1.40–45	Mt 8.1–4	Lk 5.12–16	Healing of a leper
Mk 2.1–22	Mt 9.1–17	Lk 5.17–39	Events in Jesus' ministry
Mk 2.23–3.30	Mt 12.1–37; 10.1–4	Lk 6.1–19; 11.14–23; 12.10; 6.43–45	Events in Jesus' ministry
Mk 3.31–4.25	Mt 12.46–50; 13.1–13, 18–23	Lk 8.4–21	Sayings of Jesus
Mk 4.30–34	Mt 13.31–32,34–35	Lk 13.18–19	Sayings of Jesus
Mk 4.35–41	Mt 8.23–27	Lk 8.22–35	Stilling the storm
Mk 5.1–43	Mt 8.28–34; 9.18–26	Lk 8.26–56	Healings by Jesus
Mk 6.1–6	Mt 13.51–52		Rejection in Nazareth
Mk 6.7–14	Mt 10.1,9–11; 14.1–2	Lk 9.1–9	Events in Jesus' ministry
Mk 6.17–29	Mt 14.3–12		Death of John the Baptist
Mk 6.30–44	Mt 14.13–21	Lk 9.10–17	Feeding of five thousand
Mk 6.45–8.10	Mt 14.22–15.39		Events in Jesus' ministry
Mk 8.11–21	Mt 16.1–12	(Lk 11.29; 12.1)	Sayings of Jesus
Mk 8.27–9.48	Mt 16.13–17.23; 18.1–9	Lk 9.18–50; 17.1–2	Events in Jesus' ministry
Mk 12.28–31	Mt 22.34–40	Lk 10.25–38	Sayings of Jesus
Mk 10.1–12	Mt 19.1–12		On marriage
Mk 10.13–52	Mt 19.13–30; 20.17–34	Lk 18.15–43; 22.24–27	Sayings of Jesus
Mk 11.1–12.37	Mt 21.1–27,33–46; 22.15-46	Lk 19.28–38,45–48; 20.1–44; (10.25–28)	Jesus in Jerusalem
Mk 12.41–44		Lk 21.1–4	The poor widow
Mk 13.1–32	Mt 24.1–36	Lk 21.5–33	Sayings of Jesus about the end
Mk 14.1–15.47	Mt 26.1–27.2; 27.11–61	Lk 22.1–34,39–71; 23.1–5,18–55	Passion of Jesus
Mk 16.1–8	Mt 28.1–10	Lk 24.1–11	The empty tomb

A majority of scholars think that Matthew and Luke used a source that has not survived (known as "Q").

	SYNOPTIC PASSAGES	SUBJECT MATTER
Mt 3.7–10,12	Lk 3.7–9,17	John the Baptist's preaching
Mt 4.3–10	Lk 3.3–12	Temptation of Jesus
Mt 5.3–12	Lk 6.20–23	Beatitudes
Mt 5.13–16	Lk 14.34–35; 11.33	Sayings of Jesus
Mt 5.21–26	Lk 12.57–59	Sayings of Jesus
Mt 5.38–48	Lk 6.27–36	Sayings of Jesus
Mt 6.9–15	Lk 11.2–4	Lord's Prayer
Mt 6.19–7.27	Lk 12.33–36; 16.13; 12.22–31; 6.37–38, 41–42; 11.9–13; 6.31; 13.23–24; 6.43–49	Sayings of Jesus
Mt 8.5–15	Lk 7.1–10	Healing of a centurion's servant
Mt 8.18–22	Lk 9.57–60	Sayings of Jesus
Mt 10.26–39	Lk 12.2–9,51–53; 14.26–27	Sayings of Jesus
Mt 11.2–19	Lk 7.18–35	On John the Baptist
Mt 11.20–27	Lk 10.13–15,21–22	Sayings of Jesus
Mt 12.38–45	Lk 11.29–32; 11.24–26	Sayings of Jesus
Mt 13.16–17	Lk 10.23–24	Sayings of Jesus
Mt 13.33	Lk 13.20–21	Sayings of Jesus
Mt 18.10–14	Lk 15.3–7	Sayings of Jesus
Mt 22.1–4	Lk 14.16–22	Parable of the marriage feast
Mt 23.37–39	Lk 13.34–35	Lament over Jerusalem
Mt 24.37–51	Lk 17.26–35; 12.39–46	Sayings of Jesus about the end
Mt 25.14–30	Lk 19.12–27	Parable of the talents

CHAPTER/VERSE DIFFERENCES

Chapter/verse differences between standard English numbering and Hebrew text numbering. Books are listed in Hebrew canonical order.

ENGLISH	HEBREW	ENGLISH	HEBREW	ENGLISH	HEBREW
Gen 31.55	Gen 32.1	Mic 5.1	Mic 4.14	Ps 34. title	Ps 34.1
Gen 32.1–32	Gen 32.2–33	Mic 5.2–15	Mic 5.1–14	Ps 34.1–22	Ps 34.2–23
Ex 8.1–4	Ex 7.26–29	Nah 1.15	Nah 2.1	Ps 35. title	Ps 35.1 (1st word)
Ex 8.5–32	Ex 8.1–28	Nah 2.1–13	Nah 2.2–14	Ps 36. title	Ps 36.1
Ex 22.1	Ex 21.37	Zech 1.18–21	Zech 2.1–4	Ps 36.1–12	Ps 36.2–13
Ex 22.2–31	Ex 22.1–30	Zech 2.1–13	Zech 2.5–17	Ps 37. title	Ps 37.1 (1st word)
Lev 6.1–7	Lev 5.20–26	Mal 4.1–6	Mal 3.19–24	Ps 38. title	Ps 38.1
Lev 6.8–30	Lev 6.1–23	Ps 3. title	Ps 3.1	Ps 38.1–22	Ps 38.2–23
Num 16.36–50	Num 17.1–15	Ps 3.1–8	Ps 3.2–9	Ps 39. title	Ps 39.1
Num 17.1–13	Num 17.16–28	Ps 4. title	Ps 4.1	Ps 39.1–13	Ps 39.2–14
Num 26.1a	Num 25.19	Ps 4.1–8	Ps 4.2–9	Ps 40. title	Ps 40.1
Num 29.40	Num 30.1	Ps 5. title	Ps 5.1	Ps 40.1–17	Ps 40.2–18
Num 30.1–6	Num 30.2–17	Ps 5.1–12	Ps 5.2–13	Ps 41. title	Ps 41.1
Deut 12.32	Deut 13.1	Ps 6. title	Ps 6.1	Ps 41.1–13	Ps 41.2–14
Deut 13.1–18	Deut 13.2–19	Ps 6.1–10	Ps 6.2–11	Ps 42. title	Ps 42.1
Deut 22.30	Deut 23.1	Ps 7. title	Ps 7.1	Ps 42.1–11	Ps 42.2–12
Deut 23.1–25	Deut 23.2–26	Ps 7.1–17	Ps 7.2–18	Ps 44. title	Ps 44.1
Deut 29.1	Deut 28.69	Ps 8. title	Ps 8.1	Ps 44.1–26	Ps 44.2–27
Deut 29.2–29	Deut 29.1–28	Ps 8.1–9	Ps 8.2–10	Ps 45. title	Ps 45.1
1 Sam 20.42b	1 Sam 21.1	Ps 9. title	Ps 9.1	Ps 45.1–17	Ps 45.2–18
1 Sam 21.1–15	1 Sam 21.2–16	Ps 9.1–20	Ps 9.2–21	Ps 46. title	Ps 46.1
1 Sam 23.29	1 Sam 24.1	Ps 11. title	Ps 11.1a	Ps 46.1–11	Ps 46.2–12
1 Sam 24.1–22	1 Sam 24.2–23	Ps 12. title	Ps 12.1	Ps 47. title	Ps 47.1
2 Sam 18.33	2 Sam 19.1	Ps 12.1–8	Ps 12.2–9	Ps 47.1–9	Ps 17.2–10
2 Sam 19.1–43	2 Sam 19.2–44	Ps 13. title	Ps 13.1	Ps 48. title	Ps 48.1
1 Kings 4.21–34	1 Kings 5.1–14	Ps 13.1–5	Ps 13.2–6a	Ps 48.1–14	Ps 48.2–15
1 Kings 5.1–18	1 Kings 5.15–32	Ps 13.6	Ps 13.6b	Ps 49. title	Ps 49.1
1 Kings 18.33b	1 Kings 18.34a	Ps 14. title	Ps 14.1a	Ps 49.1–20	Ps 49.2–21
1 Kings 20.2b	1 Kings 20.3a	Ps 15. title	Ps 15.1a	Ps 50. title	Ps 50.1a
1 Kings 22.22a	1 Kings 22.21b	Ps 16. title	Ps 16.1a	Ps 51. title	Ps 51.1–2a
1 Kings 22.43b	1 Kings 22.44	Ps 17. title	Ps 17.1a	Ps 51.1–19	Ps 51.2b–21
1 Kings 22.44–53	1 Kings 22.45–54	Ps 18. title	Ps 18.1–2a	Ps 52. title	Ps 52.1–2a
2 Kings 11.21	2 Kings 12.1	Ps 18.1–50	Ps 18.2–51	Ps 52.1–9	Ps 52.2b–11
2 Kings 12.1–21	2 Kings 12.2–22	Ps 19. title	Ps 19.1	Ps 53. title	Ps 53.1
Isa 9.1	Isa 8.23	Ps 19.1–14	Ps 19.2–15	Ps 53.1–6	Ps 53.2–7
Isa 9.2–21	Isa 9.1–20	Ps 20. title	Ps 20.1	Ps 54. title	Ps 54.1–2
Isa 63.19	Isa 63.19a	Ps 20.1–9	Ps 20.2–10	Ps 54.1–7	Ps 54.3–9
Isa 64.1	Isa 63.19b	Ps 21. title	Ps 21.1	Ps 55. title	Ps 55.1
Isa 64.2–12	Isa 64.1–11	Ps 21.1–13	Ps 21.2–14	Ps 55.1–23	Ps 55.2–24
Jer 9.1	Jer 8.23	Ps 22. title	Ps 22.1	Ps 56. title	Ps 56.1
Jer 9.2–26	Jer 9.1–25	Ps 22.1–31	Ps 22.2–32	Ps 56.1–13	Ps 56.2–14
Ezek 20.45–49	Ezek 21.1–5	Ps 23. title	Ps 23.1a	Ps 57. title	Ps 57.1
Ezek 21.1–32	Ezek 21.6–37	Ps 24. title	Ps 24.1a	Ps 57.1–11	Ps 57.2–12
Hos 1.10–11	Hos 2.1–2	Ps 25. title	Ps 25.1a	Ps 58. title	Ps 58.1
Hos 2.1–23	Hos 2.3–25	Ps 26. title	Ps 26.1a	Ps 58.1–11	Ps 58.2–12
Hos 11.12	Hos 12.1	Ps 27. title	Ps 27.1a	Ps 59. title	Ps 59.1
Hos 12.1–14	Hos 12.2–15	Ps 28. title	Ps 28.1a	Ps 59.1–17	Ps 59.2–18
Hos 13.6	Hos 14.1	Ps 29. title	Ps 29.1a	Ps 60. title	Ps 60.1–2
Hos 14.1–9	Hos 14.2–10	Ps 30. title	Ps 30.1	Ps 60.1–12	Ps 60.3–14
Joel 2.28–32	Joel 3.1–5	Ps 30.1–12	Ps 30.2–13	Ps 61.1–8	Ps 61.2–9
Joel 3.1–21	Joel 4.1–21	Ps 31. title	Ps 31.1	Ps 62.1–12	Ps 62.2–13
Jon 1.17	Jon 2.1	Ps 31.1–24	Ps 31.2–25	Ps 63. title	Ps 63.1
Jon 2.1–10	Jon 2.2–11	Ps 32. title	Ps 32.1a	Ps 63.1–11	Ps 63.2–12

ENGLISH	HEBREW	ENGLISH	HEBREW	ENGLISH	HEBREW
Ps 64. title	Ps 64.1	Ps 87.1	Ps 87.1b	Ps 131. title	Ps 131.1a
Ps 64.1–10	Ps 64.2–11	Ps 88. title	Ps 88.1	Ps 131.1	Ps 131.1b
Ps 65. title	Ps 65.1	Ps 88.1–18	Ps 88.2–19	Ps 132. title	Ps 132.1a
Ps 65.1–13	Ps 65.2–14	Ps 89. title	Ps 89.1	Ps 132.1	Ps 132.1b
Ps 66. title	Ps 66.1a	Ps 89.1–52	Ps 89.2–53	Ps 133. title	Ps 133.1a
Ps 66.1	Ps 66.1b	Ps 90. title	Ps 90.1a	Ps 133.1	Ps 133.1b
Ps 67. title	Ps 67.1	Ps 90.1	Ps 90.1b	Ps 134. title	Ps 134.1a
Ps 67.1–7	Ps 67.2–8	Ps 92. title	Ps 92.1	Ps 134.1	Ps 134.1b
Ps 68. title	Ps 68.1	Ps 92.1–15	Ps 92.2–16	Ps 138. title	Ps 138.1a
Ps 68.1–35	Ps 68.2–36	Ps 98. title	Ps 98.1 (1st word)	Ps 138.1	Ps 138.1b
Ps 69. title	Ps 69.1	Ps 100.1	Ps 100.1b	Ps 139. title	Ps 139.1a
Ps 69.1–36	Ps 69.2–37	Ps 101.1	Ps 101.1b	Ps 139.1	Ps 139.1b
Ps 70. title	Ps 70.1	Ps 102. title	Ps 102.1	Ps 140. title	Ps 140.1
Ps 70.1–5	Ps 70.2–6	Ps 102.1–28	Ps 102.2–29	Ps 140.1–13	Ps 140.2–14
Ps 72. title	Ps 72.1 (1st word)	Ps 103. title	Ps 103.1 (1st word)	Ps 141. title	Ps 141.1a
Ps 73. title	Ps 73.1a	Ps 108. title	Ps 108.1	Ps 141.1	Ps 141.1b
Ps 73.1	Ps 73.1b	Ps 108.1–13	Ps 108.2–14	Ps 142. title	Ps 142.1
Ps 74. title	Ps 74.1a	Ps 109. title	Ps 109.1a	Ps 142.1–7	Ps 142.2–8
Ps 74.1	Ps 74.1b	Ps 109.1	Ps 109.1b	Ps 143. title	Ps 143.1a
Ps 75. title	Ps 75.1	Ps 110. title	Ps 110.1a	Ps 143.1	Ps 143.1b
Ps 75.1–10	Ps 75.2–11	Ps 110.1	Ps 110.1b	Ps 144. title	Ps 144.1 (1st word)
Ps 76. title	Ps 76.1	Ps 120. title	Ps 120.1a	Ps 145. title	Ps 145.1a
Ps 77. title	Ps 77.1	Ps 120.1	Ps 120.1b	Ps 145.1	Ps 145.1b
Ps 77.1–20	Ps 77.2–21	Ps 121. title	Ps 121.1a	Song 6.13	Song 7.1
Ps 78. title	Ps 78.1a	Ps 121.1	Ps 121.1b	Song 7.1–13	Song 7.2–14
Ps 78.1	Ps 78.1b	Ps 122. title	Ps 122.1a	Eccl 5.1	Eccl 4.17
Ps 79. title	Ps 79.1a	Ps 122.1	Ps 122.1b	Eccl 5.2–20	Eccl 5.1–19
Ps 79.1	Ps 79.1b	Ps 123. title	Ps 123.1a	Dan 4.1–3	Dan 3.31–33
Ps 80. title	Ps 80.1	Ps 123.1	Ps 123.1b	Dan 4.4–37	Dan 4.1–34
Ps 80.1–19	Ps 80.2–20	Ps 124. title	Ps 124.1a	Dan 5.31	Dan 6.1
Ps 81. title	Ps 81.1	Ps 124.1	Ps 124.1b	Dan 6.1–28	Dan 6.2–29
Ps 81.1–16	Ps 81.2–17	Ps 125. title	Ps 125.1a	Neh 4.1–6	Neh 3.53–58
Ps 82. title	Ps 82.1a	Ps 125.1	Ps 125.1b	Neh 4.7–23	Neh 4.1–17
Ps 82.1	Ps 82.1b	Ps 126. title	Ps 126.1a	Neh 9.38	Neh 10.1
Ps 83. title	Ps 83.1	Ps 126.1	Ps 126.1b	Neh 10.1–39	Neh 10.2–40
Ps 83.1–18	Ps 83.2–19	Ps 127. title	Ps 127.1a	1 Chr 6.1–15	1 Chr 5.27–41
Ps 84. title	Ps 84.1	Ps 127.1	Ps 127.1b	1 Chr 6.16–81	1 Chr 6.1–66
Ps 84.1–12	Ps 84.2–13	Ps 128. title	Ps 128.1a	1 Chr 12.4	1 Chr 12.4–5
Ps 85. title	Ps 85.1	Ps 128.1	Ps 128.1b	1 Chr 12.5–40	1 Chr 12.6–41
Ps 85.1–13	Ps 85.2–14	Ps 129. title	Ps 129.1a	2 Chr 2.1	2 Chr 1.18
Ps 86. title	Ps 86.1a	Ps 129.1	Ps 129.1b	2 Chr 2.2–18	2 Chr 2.1–17
Ps 86.1	Ps 86.1b	Ps 130. title	Ps 130.1a	2 Chr 14.1	2 Chr 13.23
Ps 87. title	Ps 87.1a	Ps 130.1	Ps 130.1b	2 Chr 14.2–15	2 Chr 14.1–14

CANONS OF THE HEBREW BIBLE/ OLD TESTAMENT WITH ADDITIONS

JEWISH CANON	PROTESTANT CANON	ROMAN CATHOLIC/ORTHODOX CANON
Torah (INSTRUCTION)	PENTATEUCH	PENTATEUCH
Genesis	Genesis	Genesis
Exodus	Exodus	Exodus
Leviticus	Leviticus	Leviticus
Numbers	Numbers	Numbers
Deuteronomy	Deuteronomy	Deuteronomy
Nevi'im (PROPHETS)	HISTORIES	HISTORIES
FORMER PROPHETS	Joshua	Joshua
Joshua	Judges	Judges
Judges	Ruth	Ruth
Samuel (1 & 2)	1 & 2 Samuel	1 & 2 Samuel
Kings (1 & 2)	1 & 2 Kings	1 & 2 Kings
	1 & 2 Chronicles	1 & 2 Chronicles
LATTER PROPHETS	Ezra	Ezra
Isaiah	Nehemiah	Nehemiah
Jeremiah	Esther	Tobit
Ezekiel		Judith
The Twelve	POETICAL/WISDOM BOOKS	Esther
Hosea	Job	1 & 2 Maccabees
Joel	Psalms	
Amos	Proverbs	POETICAL/WISDOM BOOKS
Obadiah	Ecclesiastes	Job
Jonah	Song of Solomon	Psalms
Micah		Proverbs
Nahum	PROPHETS	Ecclesiastes
Habakkuk	Isaiah	Song of Solomon
Zephaniah	Jeremiah	Wisdom of Solomon
Haggai	Lamentations	Sirach
Zechariah	Ezekiel	
Malachi	Daniel	PROPHETS
	Hosea	Isaiah
Ketuvim (WRITINGS)	Joel	Jeremiah
Psalms	Amos	Lamentations
Proverbs	Obadiah	Baruch
Job	Jonah	Ezekiel
(Five Scrolls [order of this section is	Micah	Daniel
variable]):	Nahum	Hosea
Song of Solomon	Habakkuk	Joel
Ruth	Zephaniah	Amos
Lamentations	Haggai	Obadiah
Ecclesiastes	Zechariah	Jonah
Esther	Malachi	Micah
Daniel		Nahum
Ezra-Nehemiah	THE APOCRYPHA	Habakkuk
Chronicles (1 & 2)	1 & 2 Esdras	Zephaniah
	Tobit	Haggai
There is no Apocrypha	Judith	Zechariah
in the Hebrew Bible	Esther (with additions)	Malachi
	Wisdom of Solomon	
	Ecclesiasticus (Sirach)	Orthodox Canons generally include
	Baruch	1 & 2 Esdras
	Letter of Jeremiah (Baruch ch 6)	Prayer of Manasseh
	Prayer of Azariah and Song of Three	Psalm 151
	Daniel and Susanna	3 Maccabees
	Daniel, Bel, & Snake	4 Maccabees (as an Appendix)
	Prayer of Manasseh	
	1 & 2 Maccabees	

TRANSLATIONS OF ANCIENT TEXTS

INTRODUCTORY

Amy-Jill Levine, Dale C. Allison, Jr., and John Dominic Crossan (eds), *The Historical Jesus in Context.* Princeton Readings in Religion. Princeton, NJ: Princeton University Press, 2006; Japanese translation, 2009.

Evans, Craig A. *Ancient Texts for New Testament Studies: A Guide to the Background Literature.* Peabody, Mass. Hendrickson, 2005.

Sparks, Kenton L. *Ancient Texts for the Study of the Hebrew Bible: A Guide to the Background Literature.* Peabody, Mass. Hendrickson, 2005.

EARLY JEWISH

General

Bartlett, John R. *Jews in the Hellenistic World: Josephus, Aristeas, the Sibylline Oracles, Eupolemus.* Cambridge, Eng.: Cambridge University Press, 1985.

Maccoby, Hyam. *Early Rabbinic Writings.* Cambridge, Eng.: Cambridge University Press, 1988.

Dead Sea Scrolls

Abegg, Martin, Jr.; Peter Flint; and Eugene Ulrich, eds. *The Dead Sea Scrolls Bible: The Oldest Known Bible.* San Francisco: HarperSanFrancisco, 1999.

García Martínez, Florentino, ed. *The Dead Sea Scrolls Study Edition.* 2 vols. Grand Rapids, Mich.: Eerdmans, 2000.

Vermes, Geza. *The Complete Dead Sea Scrolls in English.* Rev. ed. New York: Penguin, 2004.

Apocrypha and Pseudepigrapha

Charles, R. H., ed. *The Apocrypha and Pseudepigrapha of the Old Testament.* 2 vols. Oxford: Clarendon, 1913.

Charlesworth, James H., ed. *The Old Testament Pseudepigrapha.* 2 vols. New York: Doubleday, 1983; 1985.

Josephus

Mason, Steve, ed. *Flavius Josephus: Translation and Commentary.* Leiden: E. J. Brill, 2000– .

Whiston, William, trans. *The Works of Josephus Complete and Unabridged.* 1736. New updated edition, Peabody, Mass.: Hendrickson, 1987.

Williamson, G. A., trans. *Josephus: The Jewish War.* New York: Penguin, 1984.

Loeb Classical Library

Philo of Alexandria

Williamson, Ronald. *Jews in the Hellenistic World: Philo.* Cambridge, Eng.: Cambridge University Press, 1989.

Yonge, C. D., trans. *The Works of Philo.* 1854. New updated edition, Peabody, Mass.: Hendrickson, 1993.

Loeb Classical Library

Mishnah

Danby, Herbert. *The Mishnah.* Oxford: Clarendon, 1933.

Neusner, Jacob, trans. *The Mishnah: A New Translation.* New Haven: Yale University Press, 1997.

Talmud

Epstein, I. *The Babylonian Talmud.* 30 vols. London: Soncino, 1935–48.

Neusner, Jacob, trans. *The Babylonian Talmud.* 22 vols. Peabody, MA: Hendrickson, 2011.

Steinsaltz, Adin. *The Talmud.* New York: Random House, 1989–99.

EARLY CHRISTIAN

General

Barrett, C. K. *The New Testament Background: Writings from Ancient Greece and the Roman Empire That Illuminate Christian Origins.* Rev. ed. San Francisco: HarperCollins, 1987.

Cartlidge, David R., and David L. Dungan, eds. *Documents for the Study of the Gospels.* Rev. ed. Minneapolis: Fortress, 1994.

Elliott, J. K. *The Apocryphal New Testament: A Collection of Apocryphal Christian Literature in an English Translation.* Rev ed. Oxford: Oxford University Press, 1999.

Richardson, Cyril D., ed. *Early Christian Fathers.* New York: Macmillan, 1970.

Staniforth, Maxwell, trans. *Early Christian Writings.* New York: Penguin, 1987.

Nag Hammadi

Barnstone, Willis, and Marvin Meyer, eds. *The Gnostic Bible.* Boston: Shambhala, 2003.

Layton, Bentley. *The Gnostic Scriptures: A New Translation.* Garden City, N.Y.: Doubleday, 1987.

Robinson, J. M., ed. *The Nag Hammadi Library in English.* 4th rev. ed. Leiden: E. J. Brill, 1996.

TRANSLATIONS OF ANCIENT TEXTS

ANCIENT TRANSLATIONS OF THE BIBLE

Greek

Brenton, Lancelot C. L. *The Septuagint with Apocrypha: Greek and English*. 1851. Reprint, Peabody, Mass.: Hendrickson, 1986.

Pietersma, Albert, and Benjamin G. Wright, eds. *A New English Translation of the Septuagint and the Other Greek Translations Traditionally included under That Title.* New York: Oxford University Press, 2007.

Aramaic

McNamara, Martin, et al. *The Aramaic Bible: The Targums.* Collegeville, Minn.: Liturgical, 1987– .

CLASSICAL SOURCES

Beard, Mary; John North; and Simon Price. *Religions of Rome.* Vol. 2: *A Sourcebook.* Cambridge, Eng.: Cambridge University Press, 1998.

Translations of the writings of most Greek and Roman authors are available in the Loeb Classical Library.

DIVISIONS AND TRACTATES OF THE MISHNAH, TALMUD, AND TOSEFTA

The following list of all of the divisions and tractates may help to identify citations in this volume for the Mishnah, the Talmud Yerushalmi (Jerusalem Talmud), the Talmud Bavli (Babylonian Talmud), and the Tosefta. The citation begins with *m.* (for Mishnah), *y.* (for Yerushalmi), *b.* (for Bavli), or *t.* (for Tosefta), and is followed by the name or abbreviation of the tractate.

First Division: Zeraim ("Seeds")	
Berakot ("blessings")	*Ber.*
Pe'ah ("gleanings")	
Demai ("produce not certainly tithed")	
Kilaim ("diverse kinds")	*Kil.*
Shebiit ("seventh year")	*Seb.*
Terumot ("heave offerings")	*Ter.*
Ma'aserot ("tithes")	*Ma'as.*
Ma'aser Sheni ("second tithe")	*Ma'as. S.*
Ḥallah ("dough offering")	
Orlah ("the fruit of young trees")	
Bikkurim ("first-fruits")	*Bik.*

Second Division: Mo'ed ("Set Feasts")	
Shabbat ("Sabbath")	*Shabb.*
Eruvin ("Sabbath limits")	*Eruv.*
Pesaḥim ("Passover")	*Pesah.*
Sheqalim ("shekel tax")	*Seqal.*
Yoma ("Day of Atonement")	
Sukkah ("Tabernacles/Booths")	*Sukk.*
Yom Tov or Betzah ("festival days")	
Rosh Ha-Shanah ("New Year")	
Ta'anit ("fasts")	*Ta'an.*
Megillah ("scroll" [of Esther])	*Meg.*
Mo'ed Qatan ("mid-festival days")	*Mo'ed Qat.*
Ḥagigah ("festal offering")	*Hag.*

Third Division: Nashim ("Women")	
Yebamot ("sisters-in-law")	*Yebam.*
Ketubbot ("marriage deeds")	*Ketub.*
Nedarim ("vows")	*Ned.*
Nazir ("Nazirites")	*Naz.*
Sotah ("adulteress")	*Sot.*
Gittin ("bills of divorce")	*Git.*
Qiddushin ("betrothals")	*Qidd.*

Fourth Division: Nezikin ("Damages")	
Bava Kamma ("first gate")	*B. Kamma*
Bava Metzia ("second gate")	*B. Metz.*
Bava Bathra ("last gate")	*B. Bat.*
Sanhedrin ("the Sanhedrin")	*Sanh.*
Makkot ("stripes")	*Makk.*
Shebuot ("oaths")	*Sebu.*
Eduyot ("testimonies")	*Ed.*
Avodah Zara ("idolatry")	
Avot ("fathers")	
Horayot ("instructions")	*Hor.*

Fifth Division: Kodashim ("Hallowed Things")	
Zebahim ("animal offerings")	*Zeb.*
Menahot ("meal offerings")	*Men.*
Hullin ("animals killed for food")	*Hul.*
Bekhorot ("firstlings")	*Bek.*
Arakhin ("vows of valuation")	*Arak.*
Temurah ("substituted offering")	
Kerithot ("extirpation")	*Ker.*
Me'ilah ("sacrilege")	*Me'il.*
Tamid ("daily whole offering")	
Middot ("measurements")	*Midd.*
Kinnim ("bird offerings")	

Sixth Division: Teharot ("Cleannesses")	
Kelim ("vessels")	
Ohalot ("tents")	
Negaim ("signs of leprosy")	
Parah ("the red heifer")	
Teharot ("cleannesses")	*Tehar.*
Mikvaot ("pools of immersion")	
Niddah ("the menstruant")	*Nidd.*
Makshirin ("predisposers")	*Maks.*
Zabim ("sufferers of flux")	
Tebul Yom ("immersed that day")	
Yadaim ("hands")	*Yad.*
Uktzin ("stalks")	

GLOSSARY

A

Aaron According to the Bible, the first high priest, brother of Moses and a Levite (Ex 4.14); he was regarded as the progenitor of all later priests.

Abaddon (Heb "place of destruction") the realm of the dead, a synonym of **Sheol** (Job 26.6; Prov 15.11; Ps 88.10–12; Rev 9.11).

Abba (Aram "father") the word Jesus (Mk 14.36) and, following him, the early church (Rom 8.15; Gal 4.6) used, consistent with Jewish tradition, to address God.

Abraham the first **patriarch** (Gen 17), to whom the covenant of circumcision was given (Gen 17.10–14); the ancestor, with his wife Sarah, of the people Israel. The NT presents him as an archetype of the faithful one (Heb 11.8–12), through whom the Gentiles are blessed (Gal 3.6–9), and the spiritual ancestor of the faithful Israelites and of the followers of Jesus (Rom 9.6–18).

acropolis (Gk "height of the city") fortified upper area of a Greek city.

Acts of Paul and Thecla second-century Christian novel recounting the story of Thecla, a young Greek woman who follows Paul's exhortations to celibacy and who proclaims the gospel. The work describes Paul as small, bald, bowlegged, with a prominent nose and single eyebrow, but noble and full of grace (3), a description that influenced later representations.

Acts of Peter an apocryphal account (probably late second century) of Peter's deeds and martyrdom. It is the source of the well-known story in which Peter encounters Jesus and asks him, "Where are you going?" (Lat *quo vadis?*). Jesus' response, "I am going to Rome to be crucified," prompts Peter to return to Rome and to his death.

AD abbreviation of the Latin *Anno Domini* ["in the year of our Lord"]; see **CE**.

Adar the twelfth and final month (February–March) in the Jewish year. To align the lunar calendar with the solar year, a leap year, in which there are two months of Adar, occurs seven times every nineteen-year cycle.

adelphoi (Gk "brothers"; sing., *adelphos*) a word that can mean either biological brothers or companions. In the former case, the NRSV translates "brothers" (e.g., Mk 3.31); in the latter, "believers" (Acts 1.15), "friends" (Acts 3.17), or "brothers and sisters" (Rom 1.13).

Adonai (Heb "my Lord") a title that in Jewish worship is generally substituted for the **tetragrammaton**, YHWH.

agapē (Gk "love") the term for love used by Jesus' followers (e.g., Jn 13.35) in distinction to *eros* and *philia*.

aggadah (or "haggadah," likely from Heb *huggad*, "things said" or "what is told") non-legal portions of rabbinic writings (see **halakhah**) especially concerned the moral meaning of scripture and with elaborating on the stories in the Bible.

Akedah (Heb "the binding [of Isaac]") See Gen 22. This passage is read during synagogue worship on Rosh Hashanah.

Akiva (ca. 50–135 CE) rabbi and **tanna** martyred in the Hadrianic persecutions connected to the **Bar Kochba** revolt (132–135). He played an instrumental role in assembling the **Oral Torah**.

Alexandrinus (so-called because it was brought to Constantinople from Alexandria) a fifth century **codex** containing most of the Septuagint and the NT.

Aleinu synagogue prayer that begins *aleinu leshabech la'adon ha-kol*, "it is our duty to praise the Lord of all," the conclusion of regular services. It contains the phrase "to You [God] every knee must bend, every tongue vow loyalty" (cf. Phil 2.10–11).

aliyah (Heb "ascent") both pilgrimage or emigration to the land of Israel; or the honor of "ascending" to recite the blessings before and after a Torah reading in synagogue worship.

allegory an extended comparison that directly describes one reality while indirectly describing another (see, e.g., the "Song of the Vineyard" in Isa 5; the parable of the sower in Mt 13.1–8,18–23).

alleluia see **hallelujah**.

amen (Heb "may it be so") word signifying assent; based on biblical precedent (e.g., Deut 27.15; Ps 106.48) it became the standard response to prayers in the synagogue and the church.

Amidah (Heb "standing") the main post-biblical prayer in Jewish worship. Also called the *Shemonah Esrei* (eighteen [blessings]), and *Tefillah* ("prayer"). On regular weekdays (not Shabbat or festivals), it now consists of nineteen blessings.

amora (pl. ***amoraim;*** adj. ***amoraic***) (Aram "speaker") rabbinic teacher of the Talmudic period (third century CE onward).

anathema (Gk "devoted to evil," "accursed") solemn pronouncement condemning a person, thing, or idea as false or evil.

anoint to touch or rub with oil as a sign that the person or thing was dedicated to God. Kings (1 Kings 1.39) and priests (Lev 8.30) were anointed, as were the bodies of those who had died (Lk 26.53).

antichrist originally a term for false teachers and given in the plural (1 Jn 2.18,22; 4.3; 2 Jn 7), the term comes to indicate in the post-NT period an **eschatological** figure who opposes God.

antitheses Designation for the rhetorical form "You have heard that it was said . . . but I say to you" (see Mt 5.21–48).

anti-type something or someone who is prefigured in an earlier event or person. See **typology**.

aphorism short, memorable saying.

apocalypse (Gk *apokalypsis*, "uncovering, revelation") literary genre in which a heavenly being communicates to a human the divine plan for history, the arrangement of the supernatural order, and/or eschatological warnings (see, e.g., Dan 7–12; Mk 13; Revelation).

Apocrypha see **deuterocanonical**.

Apocryphal Acts early post-NT Christian writings, often with novelistic flavor and a stress on celibacy, which narrate activities of various apostles such as Peter, Paul, and Thomas.

apologetics a defense or proof of Christianity.

apologia (Gk "explanation") a defense of one's actions or beliefs, usually in a formal speech or document.

apostle (Gk "one who is sent") a delegate or representative. In the NT, an apostle was one who had known Jesus and could witness to the resurrection (Acts 1.21–22) or a messenger called by God (1 Cor 12.28; Rom 16.7).

Apostles' Creed a statement of belief (second to fourth centuries) still recited by many Christian denominations.

apotheosis the elevation of a person to the rank of a god.

Aramaic a Semitic language used widely in the Near East during the Persian period (sixth to fourth centuries BCE), though it developed earlier. It became the language of Jews in Israel and the eastern **diaspora**, including Jesus and his early followers.

Aramaism the reproduction in another language of phraseology characteristic of Aramaic: "Son of man" (Gk *huios tou anthropou*) may be derived from Daniel's *bar enash* (7.13).

aretology (Gk "words about virtue") a general recounting the deeds of a hero.

Aristeas, Letter of a second century BCE Greek document purporting to describe the translation of the Septuagint for the king of Egypt.

ark (for the Torah) a box or cabinet, typically of wood, in which the Torah scrolls are stored at the front of the synagogue.

Armageddon traditional site of the final battle between good and evil (Rev 16.6), possibly derived from "Megiddo," a battle site in Israel's history (Judg 5.19; 2 Kings 9.27).

ascension (Lat "going up") an account in which a human being goes or is taken into the divine realm. According to Lk 24.51, Jesus ascends soon after his resurrection; Acts 1.1–9 places his ascension forty days later.

asceticism (Gk "training") self-denial or self-punishment for religious purposes.

avodah (Heb "service") the sacred service in the Temple (see e.g., Lev 16.2–34), extended to mean the worship of God through prayer.

Avot (Heb "fathers") a tractate in the **Mishnah** containing sayings of rabbis (also known as **Pirkei Avot** or the *Ethics of the Fathers*).

B

Babylon Mesopotamian empire that destroyed the First Temple in 586. It became a stand-in for any tyrannical empire and is a synonym for Rome in the book of Revelation.

Babylonian exile the forced relocation of some of the population of Judah after the Babylonian conquest in 597–586 BCE. The exile ended with the permitted return to the land under Cyrus of Persia (beginning 538).

Babylonian Talmud also called the **Bavli**. This Talmud, mostly reflecting traditions of the rabbis in Babylon through the fifth century CE, is a commentary on several Mishnaic tractates. In Judaism, it is more authoritative than the **Jerusalem Talmud**. See **Talmud**.

baptism immersion in water, a practice found throughout Mediterranean antiquity for ritual purification. John the Baptist (Mk 1.4) may have been derived his practice from Jewish purification ritual (Lev 15.18). Paul's connection of baptism with the death and resurrection of Christ (Rom 6.1–14) changed its meaning from purification to initiation into a new community and new identity.

Bar Kochba (Aram "son of a star") sobriquet of Shimon Bar Kosiba (d. 135 CE), leader of the unsuccessful second Jewish revolt against Rome; he was proclaimed the messiah by **Akiva**.

bar mitzvah (Aram "son of commandment") a Jewish male who at age 13 takes on adult responsibility for performing the **mitzvoth**. The ritual marking this adult role (also called a Bar Mitzvah) well post-dates the NT.

bat qol (Heb lit. "daughter of [the] voice," "echo") rabbinic term for a heavenly voice and likely the idea behind the voice at Jesus' **baptism** and **transfiguration**.

Bavli see **Babylonian Talmud**.

BCE Before the Common Era, an alternative to BC ("before Christ").

beatitudes (from Lat *beatus*, "blessed") the series of Jesus' pronouncements in Mt 5.3–11 beginning with *makarioi*, "blessed" or "fortunate"; cf. the Heb *ashrei* (e.g., Ps 144.15).

Beelzebul (also Baalzebul, Baalzebub, Beelzebub) ruler of the demons (Mt 12.24–27). The name derives from the Heb *Baalzebul*, "exalted lord," a title of the Phoenician god (2 Kings 1.2–18), transformed into the derogatory Baalzebub, "lord of flies."

beloved disciple follower "whom Jesus loved" (Jn 13.23; 19.26; 21.20) and to whom is attributed (21.24) the Gospel of John.

Bereshit Hebrew title of Genesis (from its first word, "[When] in the beginning").

berit (also *brit* and *bris*; Heb "covenant") the term can specifically refer to circumcision (Heb *brit milah*, lit. the "covenant of circumcision"). See **covenant**.

binyan 'av ("construction of a father") a form of rabbinic argumentation which entails using one Torah passage to reach a conclusion regarding another.

birchat ha-mason (Heb "blessing for nourishment") the Jewish blessing recited after a meal.

birchat ha-minim (Heb "blessing [i.e., 'curse'] on heretics") the twelfth blessing of the ***Amidah***; one ancient version, no longer recited, curses *minim* (heretics) and Nazareans (perhaps Jewish Christians).

birchat ha-motsi (Heb "blessing for bringing out") the Jewish blessing before a meal.

bishop (Old English *bisceop*, from Gk *episkopos*, "overseer") usually the head of the church in a particular area (where there might be more than one congregation). The office seems to have been more definite by the time of the **Pastoral Epistles**; see, e.g., 1 Tim 3.1–7. See **deacon**, **presbyter**.

Booths, Feast (Festival) of see **Sukkoth**.

born again in Jn 3.3,7 Jesus tells Nicodemus, "You must be born *anōthen*": the Greek can be translated "anew," "from above," or "again"; the pun works in Greek, but not in Aramaic or Hebrew. Passages such as Rom 6.3–11 suggest that believers are "reborn" into a new family based on faith rather than biology or marriage.

C

Cairo Genizah the storeroom (a genizah is a storage room for worn, no longer usable copies of Jewish texts) of the synagogue of Fostat in Old Cairo (built 882 CE) where thousands of fragments of texts, including a portion of Ben Sirach (Ecclesiasticus) in Hebrew, rabbinic documents, translations of the Bible, liturgical texts, poetry, letters, and other writings were discovered.

Canaan early designation for the area roughly equivalent to the land of Israel.

canon (Gk "measuring rod") the rule by which something is determined to belong to a category; the official list of the books that comprise the Scriptures. See chart, p. 600.

Catholic Epistles (from Gk *katholikos*, "according to the whole," "universal") designation for the NT letters James, 1 and 2 Peter, 1, 2, and 3 John, and Jude.

CD the Cairo-Damascus Document (earlier called the Zadokite Document), known from discoveries in the **Cairo Genizah**, recapitulates much of the material in the Qumran **Community Rule** (1QS).

CE Common era; an alternative to **AD**.

centurion the commander of a company in the Roman army.

Chaldea, Council of the council (451 CE) that defined the union of divine and human natures in Jesus.

charis NT word for "grace," "kindness."

charisma a gift of spiritual grace, particularly a manifestation of the Holy Spirit such as glossolalia (speaking in tongues) or prophecy.

cherubim composite creatures with body parts from various animals; they often had wings and human heads (see Heb 9.5).

Christ (Gk "anointed") translation of Heb *mashiach*, "messiah." In NT usage, generally a title, "Christ," "the anointed one"; in use today as an alternative name for Jesus.

Christian Hebraists Christian scholars who taught the importance of returning to the Hebrew text of the "Old Testament" as opposed to relying on the **Vulgate** and who studied Hebrew with rabbinic scholars. The beginnings of Christian Hebraism are generally traced to Andrew of St. Victor (d. 1175), and it reached its zenith in the Renaissance.

Christology statements concerning the nature of Christ, or the study of the meaning of Jesus' role, character, and purpose.

church fathers see **patristic writers**.

circumcision removal of the foreskin of the penis (see ***berit***). In Paul's writings, "circumcised" and "uncircumcised" (Gal 2.7) refer to Jews and Gentiles respectively.

Clement of Alexandria Christian theologian (ca. 150–ca. 215) who argued that Christianity fulfilled both the Hebrew Bible and Greek philosophy.

Clement of Rome (fl. 96) the bishop of Rome who wrote the letter known as *1 Clement* to the church at Corinth.

codex (pl. **codices**) a manuscript of separate pages, bound along one edge, like contemporary books.

Christian communities adopted the codex form, while Jews continued to write on scrolls.

colophon (Gk "summit," by extension "finishing touch") a notice, usually written at the end of a book, giving information about authorship (e.g., Sir 50.27).

Community Rule (or "Rule of the Community" or *serech ha-yachad*, 1QS) a **Dead Sea Scroll** that sets out the arrangements under which the community functioned: holding property in common; eating, blessing, and advising one another in unity; preparing for the **eschaton**; training new members.

Coptic Egyptian dialect from approximately the first century CE until it was supplanted by Arabic.

cosmology an account of the nature of the world.

Council of Trent the twenty-ninth ecumenical council of the Roman Catholic Church (1545–1563), held after the Protestant Reformation had begun. Among other decisions, it defined the Catholic **canon**.

covenant (Heb ***berit***) a treaty between God and Israel. In the Septuagint, the word was generally translated by the Greek *diathēkē*, which can mean "testament"; Jeremiah's phrase *berit chadashah* ("new covenant," 31.31) was translated *diathēkē kainē*, (**LXX** Jer 38.31; see Lk 22.20); translated into Latin, *novum testamentum*, it became the name of the collection known as the NT.

D

Day of Atonement Heb **Yom Kippur**, commemorated on the tenth day of the seventh month (Tishri), a day of repentance, fasting and abstinence, as well as performance of special Temple rituals (see Lev 16).

Day of the Lord the time mentioned in many prophetic books (e.g., Am 5.18) where God's justice prevails.

Day of Preparation the day before a Sabbath or festival. Mk 15.42 describes the day of Jesus' crucifixion as "the day of Preparation, that is, the day before the sabbath." In Jn 19.14, Jesus' crucifixion take place on "the day of Preparation for the Passover."

deacon (Gk *diakonos*, "servant") church official; see e.g., 1 Tim 3.8–13.

Dead Sea Scrolls a group of manuscripts found beginning in 1947 in caves near the Dead Sea, at Wadi Qumran. The scrolls were probably the library of a settlement, likely of Essenes, that flourished from the second century BCE until the Romans destroyed it in 68 CE. The library, in Hebrew, Aramaic and Greek, included biblical books older than those previously known, and other scrolls of biblical interpretation (see **pesher**) and of regulations for the life of the community.

Decalogue (Gk "ten words") a name for the list of commandments in Ex 20.1–17, Deut 5.6–21, often called the Ten Commandments.

demon (Gk *daimonion*, originally a minor divinity) an evil spirit to which is ascribed the cause of physical and mental ailments.

demoniac one possessed by demons.

derash (Heb *d-r-sh*, "inquire") interpretation (see **midrash**).

derekh eretz (Heb "way of [the] land") the path of righteousness one should follow.

deuterocanon, deuterocanonical (Gk "second canon") a group of about 20 Jewish works, many included in the Septuagint, which were not accepted into the Jewish canon. These texts (e.g., Judith, 1,2 Maccabees, ben Sirah [Ecclesiasticus]) are extra-canonical for Protestants; some are canonical for Roman Catholics; a few more are canonical for Orthodox Christians (see chart, p. 600). Also known as Old Testament **Apocrypha**.

Deutero-Isaiah scholarly term for Isa 40–55.

Deutero-Pauline designation for letters attributed to Paul but which many modern scholars regard as **pseudonymous**. The list usually includes Ephesians, Colossians, 1 and 2 Timothy, Titus, and sometimes 2 Thessalonians.

deuteronomistic pertaining to the editor(s) of the history comprised in the books of Joshua, Judges, Samuel, and Kings, as prefaced by the book of Deuteronomy.

diaspora (Gk "dispersal") the home of Jews outside the land of Israel (see Jn 7.35); the church adapted the term to refer to its members outside the kingdom of heaven (Jas 1.1; 1 Pet 1.1).

diathēkē (Gk *diatithēmi*, "arrange" or "assign," "dispose of" in making a will) a testament or covenant; see **covenant; testament.**

diatribe a rhetorical argument against another's position.

Didache (Gk "teaching") a late first or early second century Christian writing, also called the *Teaching of the Twelve Apostles*, which contains material similar to the canonical Gospels (esp. Matthew).

disciple a follower, an adherent of a particular teaching.

docetism (from Gk *dokeō*, "seem") early Christian teaching maintaining that Jesus only *seemed* to be a human being.

doxology (Gk "word of glory") a prayer of praise to God (e.g., Rom 16.25–27).

dualism the view that reality consists of two opposing elements, often seen as "good" and "evil."

dynamis (Gk "power," "strength," "might") in the NT often the divinely given ability to do something (Acts 3.12).

E

ecclesia (Gk "assembly," "congregation") a regular convocation of a group; in **LXX** the word usually translates Heb *qahal*, an assembly of Israelites. It comes to designate a Christian congregation, a church.

Eighteen Benedictions see ***Amidah***.

elder see **presbyter**.

elect, election idea that certain persons or groups are chosen for a particular role (2 Pet 1.10). Some NT texts regard the followers of Jesus as assuming Israel's role as God's people (1 Pet 2.4–10; Gal 4.22–5.1).

Elephantine Papyri Aramaic documents, mostly from the fifth century BCE, from a Jewish colony on the island of Elephantine, near modern Aswan in Egypt.

Elohim Heb word usually translated "God," and sometimes "gods."

Enoch, books of writings dating from the third century BCE to the sixth century CE, attributed to Enoch (Gen ch 5). *1 Enoch*, a collection of apocalyptic visions, is quoted in Jude 14–15. *2 Enoch* contains a series of linked visions of ascent through seven heavens.

entolē (Gk "charge," "command" usually for Heb ***mitzvah***) a commandment, especially one from God, e.g., Mt 15.3.

epiphany (Gk "manifestation," "appearance") the appearance of a divine being.

Epicureans Greek philosophical school, founded by Epicurus, who taught that human beings naturally seek pleasure, and that the best way to achieve this pursuit was in moderation.

Epiphanes a title, "[God] made manifest," adopted by Antiochus IV, the **Seleucid**-Greek king who promoted pagan worship in the Jerusalem Temple, thus provoking the Maccabean revolt.

epistle a letter intended for public reading and therefore written according to a particular literary form.

Epistle of Barnabas a late first or early second century anti-Jewish Christian text that claims Jews lost their covenantal status with the incident of the golden calf and that biblical law must be understood allegorically (e.g., prohibition of pork means that people are not to act like swine).

eschaton, eschatological, eschatology (Gk *eschata*, "last things") a concern with the end time or the end of the world.

Essenes Jewish movement, first century BCE to first century CE, which rejected the Jerusalem establishment and kept the law with utmost rigor.

ethnos/ethnē (Gk "nation," "race," "people," or, depending on context, "Gentiles") Heb ***goyyim***.

Eucharist ritual or service of thanksgiving, centering on the sharing of bread and wine, based on Jesus' final meal (see **Last Supper**).

eusebeia Gk "piety," "reverence," "religion."

Eusebius (ca. 263–339) Bishop of Caesarea (from 314). His *Ecclesiastical History* surveys the development of Christianity.

evangelist (from Gk *euangelion*, "good news") the author of a Gospel or, more broadly, one who proclaims the "good news" of Jesus.

exegesis (Gk "lead into") the explanation or interpretation of a text.

F

Festival of Weeks see **Shavuot**.

First Temple the Temple in Jerusalem from Solomon's time (tenth century BCE) until the destruction of Jerusalem by **Babylon** in 586. The First Temple period extends from the tenth to the sixth centuries BCE.

Former Prophets the first part of the biblical section called "the Prophets" **(Nevi'im)**: the books of Joshua, Judges, Samuel, and Kings.

Fourth Ezra chs 3–14 of 2 Esdras, a late-first-century CE Jewish apocalypse, incorporated into a Christian frame, set during the **Babylonian exile** (586–538 BCE) but referring to the destruction of the **Second Temple**.

fulfillment citations quotations from the **Tanakh/LXX** in the Gospel of Matthew and elsewhere that proclaim the events in Jesus' life are "fulfillments" of predictions.

fundamentalist in its narrow meaning, a conservative Protestant who holds to the five fundamentals: the sole authority of Scripture; the Virgin Birth of Jesus; the doctrine of substitutionary atonement; Jesus' bodily resurrection; and his Second Coming to judge the world.

G

Gabriel one of two named angels in **Tanakh** (Dan 8.16; the other is Michael, Dan 12.1). Gabriel serves as a messenger from God (see, e.g., Lk 1.19,26).

Galilee Israel's northernmost geographical area.

Gehenna the place of punishment after death (see Mt 5.22). The name derives from Heb *gei ben hinnom*, "valley of the sons of Hinnom," a place south of Jerusalem thought to be where children were burnt as sacrificial offerings: Josiah (2 Kings 23.10) destroyed the site, but its associations with burning and evil remained, and developed into the image of burning punishment.

Gemara (Aram "completion") commentary that supplements and extends the **Mishnah**. The Mishnah and the Gemara together form the **Talmud**.

gematria (likely from Gk *geometria*) a procedure for interpreting a word or phrase by its numerical value, with each Hebrew letter representing a number (alef=1; bet=2, etc.; see Rev 13.18).

genizah see **Cairo Genizah.**

Gentile a person who is neither a Jew nor a Samaritan.

Gnosticism (from Gk *gnōsis*, "knowledge") a philosophy that regards spirit and matter as opposites and the material world as created by an inferior divine being; in Gnostic teaching, "knowledge" (as opposed to faith or the cross) gains salvation.

Gospel (Old English "god spel," "good news," translating Gk *euangelion*) a written account of Jesus' life or sayings, or more broadly, the "good news" of his life and death.

goyyim (Heb "nations," "peoples") a general term for non-Israelite peoples. See ***ethnē***.

gymnaō (from Gk *gymnos*, "naked") to exercise (in a gymnasion or place of physical training).

H

Hades the abode of the dead in Greek religion; in the NT the general name for the place where souls go after death (e.g., Mt 11.23; Acts 2.27).

haftarah (Heb "conclusion") the reading from a prophetic book that follows the Torah reading in the Sabbath or festival service.

haggadah see **aggadah.**

Haggadah of Pesach ("telling of Passover") the liturgical recitation at the Passover **Seder**; also the book that contains the recitation and instructions of the Seder.

hagioi (Gk "holy ones," "saints") a standard address in NT letters for the members of a congregation; see, e.g., Rom 1.7; 1 Cor 1.2; Eph 1.1.

halakhah (Heb "way," from *halakh* "go"; pl. *halakhot*) the legal portions of the Talmud, or any legal ruling according to Jewish law.

Hallel (Heb "praise") Psalms 113–118, recited on major Jewish festivals.

hallelujah (Gk and Lat "alleluia") Hebrew acclamation, "Praise Yah!"

Ḥaninah ben Dosa first century CE rabbi known for performing miraculous healing.

Hanukkah (Heb "dedication") the commemoration of the rededication of the Temple on 25 Kislev 164 BCE, after the Maccabees defeated the supporters of Antiochus IV.

ha-Shem see **Shem.**

Hasidic, Hasidim (Heb *Hasid*, "pious one") (1) a pietistic Jewish group in the Maccabean period; (2) a Jewish renewal movement that began in eastern Europe under the influence of the Baal Shem Tov ("master of the good Name"), R. Yisrael ben Eliezer (ca. 1700–1760).

Hasmonean the dynasty descended from the Maccabee brothers. It ruled Israel from 135 to 36 BCE, when Herod overthrew it.

Hasmonean Revolt the uprising led by the family of Mattathias Heshmon against Antiochus IV Epiphanes beginning in 167 BCE, which succeeded in liberating Jerusalem and the surrounding territory from Seleucid rule in 164. See **Hannukah.**

ḥaverim [or ***chaverim***] Heb "friends," "those in fellowship."

Hebraism the reproduction in another language of characteristic Hebrew phraseology; see **Son of Man** (Gk *huios tou anthrōpou*), which may be derived from *ben adam*, frequent in Ezekiel.

hekhalot (Heb "palaces") visionary writings in the form of travels through heavenly realms; often connected to ***merkavah*** mysticism.

Hellenism Greek culture, politics, and language spread following the conquests of Alexander the Great (d. 323 BCE).

ḥen Heb "grace," "favor."

Herodian followers and members of the court of Herod the Great and his sons.

ḥesed Heb "lovingkindness," "mercy."

Hexapla the compendium compiled by **Origen** (d. 254 CE) of six Bible versions in columns: 1. Hebrew, 2. Hebrew transliterated into Greek, 3. Greek [Aquila], 4. Greek [Symmachus], 5. Septuagint, 6. Greek [Theodotion]). The original 7,000-page Hexapla is lost, but quotations exist in various writings including a Syriac translation of column 5 (known as the Syro-Hexapla), prepared by a Christian bishop, Paul of Tella (618–19).

high priest leading priest in the Jerusalem Temple. In the first century CE, Roman rulers (or their agent, the ruler of Judea) influenced the choice of the high priest.

hilasterion (Gk "place of propitiation or expiation") the covering of the Ark (Ex 25.17, *kapporet*, **LXX** *hilasterion*), regarded as a place from which to ask mercy or forgiveness; Rom 3.25 applies the term to Jesus' death.

Hillel , Rabbi an important early rabbinic sage of the first century BCE; according to tradition, he migrated from Babylonia to Israel. Tradition also suggests that he set up a "house" or scholarly school. The House of Hillel often differs with the House of **Shammai** in halakhic rulings, and is typically more lenient.

Holy Spirit the Spirit of God regarded as a source of power or love (in **Tanakh** usually "spirit of God" [e.g., Gen 1.2; Num 24.2] or "spirit of the LORD" [e.g., Judg 6.34], but sometimes "holy Spirit" [Ps 51.11; Heb v. 13]). See **Trinity.**

homiletical having the character or function of a sermon.

hosanna a Hebrew phrase *(hosha' na')*, meaning "Save!," used as a cry of acclamation (Ps 118.26; Mt 21.9).

Hoshanah Rabbah (Heb "great Hosanna") the seventh day of **Sukkot** when the worshipers ask for salvation; it marks the end of the days of judgment that began on **Rosh Ha-Shanah**.

household code (German *haustafeln*) prescribed behaviors for the members of an extended family. See, e.g., Eph 5.22–6.9.

hypostatization speaking of an abstract quality as if it were an object or being.

I

idolatry worship of anything other than what the worshiper defines as the true God.

Idumea Greek form of "Edom"; country located south of Judea between the Dead Sea and the Mediterranean.

Ignatius bishop of Antioch (ca. 35–ca. 107). On his way to martyrdom in Rome, Ignatius wrote **epistles** addressed to the Ephesians, Magnesians, Trallians, Romans, Philadelphians, and Smyrnians, as well as to Polycarp, bishop of Smyrna.

incarnation (Lat "enfleshment" from *carne, carnis*, "flesh," translation of Gk *sarx*) the taking on of human flesh (becoming human) by the divine.

inerrancy doctrine that the Bible is without error. In its most expansive form, inerrancy asserts that the Bible's original manuscripts contain no errors—theological, historical, or scientific. A more restrained version claims that the Bible is inerrant in matters of faith, but that it may contain material that cannot be reconciled with science.

inspiration belief that the words uttered by a human being are really the words of a divine being. Christian tradition applies the notion to the Bible (see 2 Tim 3.16, "All scripture is inspired by God and is useful for teaching, for reproof, for correction, and for training in righteousness").

intercalation (1) Adding an extra time unit (day or month) to a calendar to compensate for the inexact fit between the solar year and the lunar cycle. See **Adar**. (2) The sandwiching of one story into another, e.g., the hemorrhaging woman and Jairus's daughter.

interpolation an insertion of material into a previously existent text. Absent textual evidence, e.g., differing manuscript readings, interpolation must be inferred and is often the subject of scholarly disagreement (examples include Jn 8.1–11 and possibly 1 Cor 14.33b–36; 1 Thess 2.14b–16).

intertextuality the interrelationship between one part of a text (or collection of texts) and other parts created by recurrent images (the vineyard in Isa 5.1–10 and 27.2–4), quotation and/or inner biblical interpretation (Jer 25.11–12 is partly quoted in Dan 9.2 before it is reinterpreted; 1 Cor 3.20 quotes Ps 94.11), or allusion (Matthew's Sermon on the Mount [chs 5–7] alludes to the Sinaitic covenant).

Isis the Egyptian mother-goddess.

J

Jerome (ca. 340–420) Christian theologian who produced in 405 a Latin version of the Old Testament, the **Vulgate**, based on the Hebrew.

Jerusalem Talmud also called the Palestinian Talmud. This Talmud, mostly reflecting traditions of the Galilean ***amoraim*** of the third and fourth centuries, is a commentary on several Mishnaic tractates. In Judaism, it is less authoritative than the longer, more comprehensive, and more carefully edited **Babylonian Talmud**. See **Talmud**.

Johannine pertaining to writings traditionally ascribed to John: the Gospel of John and 1, 2, and 3 John, and the book of Revelation.

Joseph and Aseneth a romance (dating ca. second century BCE to first century CE) which recounts the love of the Egyptian Aseneth for Joseph; her conversion to his religion, their marriage; the plot of Pharaoh's son to kill Joseph and abduct Aseneth; and Joseph's appointment as ruler of Egypt.

Josephus Hellenistic Jewish historian ca. 37–100 CE. His extant writings are *The Jewish War*, an account of the rebellion against Rome in 66–70 CE, with background information starting at about 200 BCE; *The Antiquities of the Jews*, a complete history from the creation up to the point where *The Jewish War* begins; *Against Apion*, a defense of Judaism; and an autobiography, *Life*.

***Jubilees*, book of** a book, pseudonymously attributed to Moses, retelling much of Genesis and Exodus and representing itself as a hidden revelation from the Angel of the Presence. It was most likely written in Israel in the third or second century BCE.

Judaizers followers of Jesus who maintained, or were accused of maintaining, Jewish practices such as circumcision and dietary restrictions.

Justin Martyr early Christian author (b. 103) of two *Apologies*, *Dialogue with Trypho*, a (fictional) debate with a Jewish critic, and a fragment of a work on the resurrection. He was executed by Rome in 165.

K

kabbalah "what is received," i.e., matter handed down. In the twelfth century, *kabbalah* came to mean esoteric or mystical teaching.

Kaddish (Aram "holiness," "sanctification") prayer in praise of God that is recited at the conclusion of a principal section of the synagogue service; a special Kaddish is recited in memory of the deceased.

kashrut *see* **kosher**.

kavod Heb "glory," usually as a divine attribute.

Kedushah (Heb "holiness") prayers of sanctification of God, esp. the third blessing of the ***Amidah***, including the words "Holy, holy, holy . . ." (Isa 6.3).

Ketuvim The Writings, the third division of the **Tanakh**.

Kiddush short for *kiddush ha-yom*, "sanctification of the day," both the ceremony and the prayer that proclaims the holiness of the Sabbath (or festival), recited over wine before the Sabbath (or festival) meal.

kiddush ha-Shem (Heb "sanctify the Name") the duty to guard the honor of God and God's name (Lev 22.32) even under threat of martyrdom.

Kimchi, Rabbi David see **Radak**.

kingdom of God/kingdom of heaven in the NT sometimes regarded as aspect of the **eschatological** age (e.g., 1 Cor 15.23–28; Mk 14.25), sometimes as realized in the present (Lk 17.21; Col 1.13).

King James Version (KJV) an English translation of the Bible, published first in 1611.

Kislev third month (November/December) in the Jewish calendar; **Hanukkah** begins on 25 Kislev.

kohen (pl. ***kohanim***) (Heb "priest") a member of the hereditary group traditionally descended from **Aaron**.

koinonia Gk "community," "fellowship."

korban (Heb "offering," "oblation," "sacrifice") a general term for the offering of sacrifice (e.g., Lev 1.2).

kosher (Heb "fit" or "proper") a general term used in post-biblical texts for food permitted under Jewish dietary laws.

kyrios Gk, a title of respect: "lord" or "sir," used in **LXX** in place of the **tetragrammaton**, and applied to Jesus in the NT.

L

L designation for the source of materials unique to Luke's Gospel, such as the parable of the prodigal son (Lk 15.11–32).

Last Supper meal that Jesus and his disciples shared the night before his crucifixion; dated by Matthew (26.17), Mark (14.12), and Luke (22.7–8), but not John (13.1; 19.14,31) to the first night of **Pesach**. See **Eucharist**.

Latter Prophets section of **Nevi'im** comprised of the books of Isaiah, Jeremiah, Ezekiel, and the Book of the Twelve.

law usual English translation of **Torah**. The **Septuagint** uses the word *nomos*, usually meaning "law," to translate *Torah*, and the NT writers follow the Septuagint.

lectionary a list of scriptural readings for Sundays, holy days, and sometimes weekdays (in Christianity). In many churches, readings from the Old Testament, a psalm, a Gospel text, and another NT document, usually a letter.

legalism a pejorative label and stereotype used by Christian writers to indicate that Jews adhere to Torah in a rote manner, unconcerned with mercy or personal spirituality.

legate an official representative.

legion the basic unit of the Roman army, consisting of up to 6,000 men.

Letter of Aristeas see ***Aristeas, Letter of***.

lev, levav Heb "heart," "mind"; the inner person.

levirate marriage (from Lat *levir*, "husband's brother") the provision that if a man died without an heir, his brother would marry the widow and the first son she bore would be regarded as the dead brother's heir (Deut 25.5–10). By rabbinic times *ḥalitzah*, the ceremony that released the levir from this obligation, was preferred.

Levite a member of the tribe of Levi, one set aside for service to God (Deut 18.2); by **Second Temple** times, Levites were Temple functionaries of secondary importance to priests.

lex talionis (Lat "law [of retribution] in kind") punishment fitting the crime, e.g., "an eye for an eye."

litotes a figure of speech negating the opposite of what is meant; emphasizes by understatement.

liturgy the form or rite for communal, public worship.

Logos Gk "word," "reason"; the organizing principle of the cosmos; the rational basis of thought. See Jn 1.1,14; cf. Aram *memre.*

Lord's Prayer prayer given by Jesus as a model for his followers (Mt 6.9–13; Lk 11.2–4).

Lord's Supper see **Eucharist**.

LXX the Roman numeral 70, abbreviation for the **Septuagint**.

lytron Gk "ransom," "payment to secure release from captivity."

M

M designation for the source of materials unique Matthew's Gospel, such as the account of the Magi (2.1–12).

Maccabees see **Hasmonean Revolt**.

maḥloket dispute or argument.

Magnificat (Lat "makes great," "magnifies") the first word in the Latin translation of Mary's hymn (Lk 1.46–55).

Maimonides Rabbi Mosheh ben Maimon (1135–1204), medieval Spanish Jewish scholar, physician, and philosopher also known by the acronym (from his Hebrew name) **Rambam** (Rav Mosheh Ben Maimon). He compiled the *Mishneh Torah*, a codification of rabbinic law and explicated Jewish beliefs as congruent with Aristotelianism in his *Guide to the Perplexed*.

makarisms from *makarioi*, see **beatitudes**.

malkhut shamayim Heb "**kingdom of heaven.**"

martyr (Gk "witness") a person who demonstrates loyalty by remaining faithful even when threatened with death.

Martyrdom of Isaiah a Hellenistic Jewish work that describes how Isaiah died by being sawn in two (see Heb 11.37).

mashiaḥ see **messiah**.

masorah (Heb "tradition") a system of markings (vowel signs, marginal notes, cantillation and accent marks, etc.) added to the consonantal Hebrew text by the **Masoretes**.

Masoretes scholars of the scribal schools that in the early Middle Ages ensured the accurate copying of the Tanakh by a system of markings (**masorah**).

Masoretic text (**MT**) text of the **Tanakh**, established by the **Masoretes**). The text consists of the Hebrew consonants, vowel signs, cantillation and accent markings, and other notes. Texts derived from this effort date from ca. 900 to 1000 CE.

matzah unleavened bread, eaten on Passover.

Megillot Heb "scrolls," specifically the five books of **Ketuvim** that are read on holy days: Song of Songs (**Pesach**), Ruth (**Shavuot**), Lamentations (Ninth of Av, the day commemorating the destruction of the Jerusalem Temple), Ecclesiastes (**Sukkot**), and Esther (**Purim**).

Mekilta (or *Mekhilta*) two halakhic midrashic commentaries on sections of Exodus, one attributed to R. Ishmael and the other to R. Shimeon bar Yoḥai.

Melekh ha-Olam Heb "ruler of the universe," a rabbinic title for God.

merkavah (Heb "chariot") the title for visionary writings that describe the heavenly realms; based on the vision in Ezekiel ch 1. See ***hekhalot***

merit of the fathers (Heb *zekhut avot*) the concept that righteous behavior by the **patriarchs** can redound to the benefit of the people as a whole.

messiah (Heb *mashiaḥ*, "anointed"; see 1 Sam 24.6; Isa 45.1) the term came to designate an eschatological savior and was adopted by Christians to refer to Jesus, called in Gk *christos*, "anointed." In the **Tanakh**, *mashiaḥ* never refers to an eschatological figure.

messianic secret Jesus' practice, particularly in Mark's Gospel, of demanding followers, those he has healed, and demons to remain silent about him and his acts (e.g., Mk 1.34; 1.43–44; 3.12; 5.43; 8.30).

mezuzah (Heb "doorpost") a parchment affixed to the doorpost on which are written the paragraphs of the Shema (Deut 6.4–9; 11.13–21), and on the back *sh-d-y* ("Shaddai," "Almighty"). Many mezuzot (pl. of mezuzah) were found among the Dead Sea Scrolls.

midrash, midrashic (Heb *darash*, "inquire") interpretation to draw out meanings from a text beyond the plain sense (see **peshat**).

Minor Prophets (so-called because compared to the Major Prophets, Isaiah, Jeremiah, and Ezekiel, they are shorter) the books from Hosea through Malachi; in the **Tanakh**, see **Twelve, Book of the**.

miqveh a bath designed for ritual immersion.

Mishnah (Heb "oral instruction," from *shanah*, "repeat") the compilation of oral law, edited ca. 200 CE, that is the basis of the **Talmud**.

mitzvah, mitzvoth (Heb "commandment") a religious obligation; by extension, any good deed.

MT see **Masoretic text**.

mystery in the NT, a divine truth that is kept hidden by God (see Rom 16.25–26); a revelation about God's plan (Eph 1.9–10).

mystery religion any of various religious groups in the Greek and Roman empires which practiced secret initiation rites.

N

Nachmanides see **Ramban**.

Nag Hammadi city in Upper (southern) Egypt where in 1945 were discovered **Coptic codices** of non-canonical Christian writings including the only complete version of the *Gospel of Thomas*.

nativity account of a birth, particularly the accounts of Jesus' birth and infancy in Matthew (1.18–2.23) and Luke (2.1–40).

nazirite one who has taken a vow in accordance with Num 6.1–21: abstention from wine and other intoxicants; refraining from cutting hair; avoiding contact with corpses.

Negev (also **Negeb**) high plateau south of the central hill country of Israel; borders the Sinai Peninsula.

Nevi'im the Prophets, the second division of the **Tanakh**.

NT Apocrypha writings—Gospels, letters, apocalyptic visions, acts—in circulation among early communities of Jesus' followers, but that were not accepted into the Christian **canon**.

Nicene Creed statement of Christian belief, esp. concerning the **Trinity**, set forth at the Council of Nicea (325) and augmented at the Council of Constantinople (381).

Noahide laws seven commandments that according to rabbinic Judaism were established for Noah and therefore for all humanity: they prohibit blasphemy, idolatry, sexual immorality, murder, robbery, and eating blood, and they command justice.

nomos see **law, Torah.**

NRSV New Revised Standard Version Bible translation, published 1989.

O

Odes of Solomon early collection of 42 Christian poems preserved in Greek and Syriac.

olam biblical Hebrew term for unending (time), extended in postbiblical Hebrew to mean all space, i.e., the world or universe.

Old Latin the Latin translation of the Bible based on the **Septuagint**. The Old Latin version was replaced by **Jerome's Vulgate**.

Oral Torah a synonym for the **Mishnah** and **Talmud**. According to rabbinic belief (*b. Shabb.* 31a), the Oral Torah was given to Moses on Sinai along with the Written Torah.

Origen Origen Adamantius (ca. 184–254), Alexandrian Christian, early biblical interpreter, and theologian. Among his accomplishments were his **Hexapla** and commentaries on the Bible, many in the form of homilies. He was among the first Christian scholars to study Hebrew.

P

pagan (originally, Lat *paganus*, a country-dweller) general term for an adherent of traditional polytheistic religions.

Palestine name derived from the Roman designation *Provincia Syria Palaestina*, "Syro-Palestinian Province," which replaced *Provincia Judaea* after the revolt of 135 CE; *Palaestina* was the Roman spelling of "Philistine," and the designation was probably intended as a derogation of Jewish claims to the territory.

Palestinian Talmud the **Jerusalem Talmud** or Talmud Yerushalmi; see **Talmud**.

parable statement or story that uses figurative language to evoke a reality that lies beyond the literal.

Paraclete "Advocate" or "Comforter" (Gk *paraklētos*, "one who stands alongside" [to strengthen or console]) promised by Jesus in John's Gospel to accompany his followers after he ascends. John 14.26 connects the Paraclete to the **Holy Spirit**.

paraenesis moral exhortation.

parallelism characteristic feature of biblical Hebrew poetry in which the second line of a unit in some way echoes the meaning and/or grammatical structure of the first line.

parashah the portion of Torah designated to be read publicly for each week of the year. There are 54 parashiyot, to provide for the maximum possible number of Sabbaths in a year (this maximum can only occur in an intercalated or leap year). In years with fewer Sabbaths, the readings are combined to produce fewer portions. The weekly portion is also sometimes improperly called the *Sidrah*, "arrangement."

parousia (Gk "coming") a secular term for the arrival of a conquering general or emperor, it comes to designate the second coming of Christ at the **eschaton**.

parresia Gk "speaking freely, openly, with confidence and boldness."

paschal pertaining to the Passover.

passim (Lat "here and there") refers to references scattered throughout a source.

Passion narrative (from Lat *passio*, "suffer, undergo") sections of the Gospels narrating Jesus' **Last Supper**, arrest, trial, and death: Mt 26–27, Mk 14–15, Lk 22–23, Jn 18–19.

Passover see **Pesach**.

Passover Haggadah see **Haggadah of Pesach**.

Pastoral Epistles the NT letters of 1 and 2 Timothy and Titus.

patriarchs the founding fathers (*avot*) of Israel: Abraham, Isaac, and Jacob.

patristic writers theologians of the early church, such as **Clement**, Irenaeus, **Origen**, and **Jerome**, from the time of the end of the NT period to about the fifth century.

Pax Romana (Lat "Roman peace") the period from the early first century CE to the end of the second century in the Roman Empire, characterized by absence of major international conflicts and relatively calm internal politics.

peirasmos Gk "trial," "test," "temptation."

Pentateuch (Gk "five scrolls") the first five books of the Bible—Genesis through Deuteronomy—regarded as a unit; the **Torah**.

Pentecost (Gk "fiftieth [day]") Greek name for the Jewish festival of Weeks (**Shavuot**), which occurs fifty days after Passover. On the Pentecost after Jesus' crucifixion, according to Acts 2, the Holy Spirit descended on his followers.

pericope (Gk *perikopē*, "[what is] cut out") a short passage from a longer text that can be read as a complete unit.

Persian era period of Persian dominion over the Near East, beginning ca. 539 BCE when Cyrus the Great defeated **Babylon**, and lasting until ca. 333 BCE, the campaigns of Alexander the Great.

Pesach (probably "protection"; others "pass over") festival commemorating the exodus from Egypt.

peshat (Heb "simple") the "plain sense" or "contextual sense" of a text, often contrasted with ***derash***, the homiletical meaning.

pesher (pl. ***pesharim***) (Heb "interpretation") a type of commentary in the Dead Sea Scrolls in which the biblical text is understood to be actualized or fulfilled in the interpreter's time.

Peshitta Syriac (a dialect of **Aramaic**) word for "simple." It is the name of the Syriac translation of the Bible.

Pesikta Rabbati (Aram *pesikta'*, "section") a collection of midrash that deals with selected biblical passages, dating from the ninth to thirteenth centuries.

Pesikta de Rav Kahana (Aram *pesikta'*, "section") a collection of midrash that deals with selected biblical passages, dating from the fifth to seventh centuries.

Pharisees a movement among Jews that followed **Oral Torah** and extended Jewish practice into all areas of life.

Philo Hellenistic Jewish philosopher and interpreter of Scripture, who lived in Alexandria, Egypt, well known for his allegorical interpretations of the **Septuagint** (ca. 20 BCE–50 CE).

phylacteries (Gk *phylakterion*, "amulet," from *phylax*, "guard") see **tefillin**.

Pirkei Avot ("sayings" or "chapters of the Fathers") a tractate of the Mishnah (called *Avot*) that begins by tracing the transmission of the oral law from Moses to the Rabbis; emphasizes the strong link between Torah study and ethical behavior; and contains nonlegal, moralistic sayings of various Rabbis. ***Avot*** is included in the traditional prayer book and is made part of the liturgical recitation in many communities.

piska a particular note or section in a commentary.

pistis Gk "faith."

Platonism philosophy derived from Plato's teaching that the world of sense experience is essentially an illusion, deriving what reality it has from a correspondence with a true, ultimately real world of Forms.

pleonasm unnecessary word(s), deliberate repetitiveness. "May you be made strong with all strength" (Col 1.11).

pogrom an officially encouraged, organized massacre.

Polycarp, Letter of an early Christian letter of instruction, written by Polycarp (ca. 69–ca. 155), bishop of Smyrna, to the church of Philippi (*To the Philippians*).

poneros Gk "toilsome," "painful," "evil"; *ho poneros* in the Lord's Prayer is lit. "the evil one" (Mt 6.13).

pneumatology study of the role of the Holy Spirit.

Prayer of Nabonidus a Dead Sea Scroll fragment (4Q242), paralleling Dan 4.33–37, but attributing the prayer not to Nebuchadnezzar (as in Daniel) but to Nabonidus and naming the disease as an ulcer, not loss of reason.

prefect Roman administrator, sometimes a civil authority and sometimes (or additionally) a commander of a praetorian guard unit.

presbyter (Gk *presbyteros*, "elder") an office in the early church.

procurator governor of a Roman province who was appointed by the emperor (for larger provinces the appointment was by the Roman Senate). The title could also be used for officials assisting governors of the larger provinces.

prophet (Gk *prophetēs*, "speak out" or "speak forth") the **LXX** translation of *navi* ("one who is called"), the standard Heb term for prophet.

Prophets, the see **Nevi'im**.

Psalms of Solomon eighteen Jewish poems from ca. 63 BCE (Pompey's invasion of Jerusalem) concerned with efforts to live an upright life, and anticipating a messiah who brings justice.

pseudepigrapha (Gk "writings with false attributions of authorship") a diverse group of Jewish or Christian writings, such as ***Jubilees***, that are not included in the **Tanakh**, the **Septuagint**, or the NT. They are typically attributed to ancient figures.

pseudonymous written or published under a false name (e.g., *Testaments of the Twelve Patriarchs*).

Pseudo-Phocylides author of Jewish apocryphal work, *Sentences* (first century BCE to first century CE), written in Greek and containing a series of poetic **aphorisms**.

Purim festival commemorating the delivery of the Jews in Persia from destruction, as recounted in the book of Esther.

Q

Q (abbreviation of German "Quelle," "Source") the posited source of passages, especially Jesus' sayings, common to Matthew and Luke. See **synoptic problem**.

qal vahomer (Heb "light and heavy") a rabbinic exegetical argument that moves from a lesser instance to a greater. It is similar to the philosophical argument *a fortiori* (see e.g., Mt 6.26–30).

Qumran Community settlement near Wadi Qumran at the Dead Sea, most likely composed of Essenes. The library of this group is known as the **Dead Sea Scrolls**.

R

Rabbah comments on scripture, teachings

rabbi (Aram "my great one," "teacher") a Jewish teacher; eventually, one who studied Torah and its commentaries, and offered his own teaching based on that study.

Radak acronym for Rabbi David Kimchi (1160–1235), a prolific biblical commentator and grammarian.

Rambam acronym for **Maimonides**.

Ramban acronym for Rabbi Nachmanides (1194–1270), known for his writings on the **Torah**.

Rapture belief of some Christian groups that, before the trials preceding the **eschaton**, the saved will be taken up into heaven; the belief is based on an interpretation of 1 Thess 5.13–17.

Rashi acronymic name of Rabbi Shlomo Yitzhaki (1040–1105), a medieval French rabbi who compiled important commentaries on the **Talmud** and the **Tanakh**.

Rav a third century Babylonian ***amora*** whose real name was 'Abba ben 'Aivu. "Rav" means "great" and is a tribute to the regard in which he was held by his students at the academy in Sura, which he founded. Rav and Mar Samuel are seen as the main teachers in the tradition that became the Babylonian Talmud. Rav's specialty was issues relating to religious law and interpretation.

realized eschatology the view, primarily associated with the Gospel of John, that salvation and damnation are not future events but are realized in one's response to Jesus.

resident alien a foreigner with legal rights living in Israel.

revelation (Lat "remove the veil," translating Gk *apokalypsis*) insight granted to a human being by a heavenly being.

rhetoric (Gk *rhetor*, "speaker," "orator") the art or study of persuasive speech or writing.

Roman Period the period from 63 BCE onwards, marking the beginning of Roman rule of Judea.

Rosh Chodesh (Heb "new moon") a festival celebrating the beginning of the month.

Rosh Ha-Shanah (Heb "head [i.e., beginning] of the year") the fall New Year in the Jewish calendar, 1(–2) Tishri.

ruaḥ Heb "spirit," "breath," "wind" (Gk *pneuma*; see **pneumatology**).

S

Sabbath see **Shabbat**.

Sadducees Jewish movement that opposed the **Pharisees** in rejecting the **Oral Law** and belief in resurrection; they were based primarily in Jerusalem and in relation to the Temple.

Samaritan Pentateuch text of the Torah used by the **Samaritans**. This text disagrees with the **Masoretic text** at several points.

Samaritans descendants of the population of Samaria after the exile and then repopulation of the Northern Kingdom of Israel by the Assyrians in 722 BCE. The Samaritans worshiped at the Temple on Mount Gerizim; their **canon** consists of the **Pentateuch** only.

Sanhedrin (Gk *synedria,* from *syn-* and *hedra*, "with seat," i.e., "council") court holding authority in Judea under the Roman empire. "Sanhedrin" is also the title of a tractate of the **Mishnah** dealing with law courts.

Satan (Heb "accuser," "opponent," "adversary") title of a heavenly functionary whose task was to test humans (Job 1.6ff.). In later writings, a proper name for a supernatural being opposed to God (e.g., Mk 3.23).

scribe one who could write and interpret documents.

Second Baruch apocalyptic writing (late first or early second century CE) reacting to the destruction of the Temple in 70 CE. *2 Baruch* is included in the canon of the Syriac Orthodox Church, but not in any other Christian or Jewish canon.

Second Temple the Temple constructed ca. 520–516 BCE by the returning exiles; it continued and expanded until its destruction by the Romans in 70 CE.

seder (Heb "order") the ritual **Passover** meal.

Seder Olam ("order of the world") a rabbinic history of the world and the Jewish people up to the second century CE.

Sefer ha-Zikronot a Masoretic concordance labored on for twenty years by Elijah Levita (1468–1549). He was a grammarian, Masorite, and poet. The work is in the Bibliothèque Nationale, Paris.

Seleucids the rulers of Syria and surrounding areas after Alexander the Great's death.

Seliḥot penitential prayers.

semeion Gk "sign"; used especially in John's Gospel (e.g., 2.11) to describe Jesus' acts of power.

Septuagint (abbreviated **LXX**) main ancient Greek translation of the Hebrew Scriptures. The Septuagint was translated over a lengthy period beginning probably in the third century BCE. It contains additional works, grouped in **NRSV** as the Apocryphal/Deuterocanonical Books, most of which were originally written in Greek; some form of it was the Bible of early Christians.

Shabbat (Heb "cessation") the Sabbath day. The church preserved the day of rest but moved it from Saturday to Sunday, both to commemorate the proclamation of Jesus' resurrection and to distinguish its practices from that of the synagogue.

Shammai, Rabbi (50 BCE–30 CE) see **Hillel.**

Shavuot (Heb) the festival of "Weeks" (also "**Pentecost**," Gk for "fiftieth" [day]), the spring harvest, occurring fifty days (seven full weeks) after **Pesach.**

shekhinah a post-biblical term for the "dwelling" or "presence" of God with Israel; by extension, the divine manifestation in the community's life or the sense of divine immanence within the world.

Shem, ha-Shem "name" or "the Name," a circumlocution for the **tetragrammaton** (see Deut 28.58).

Shema (Heb "hear") the first word, used as a title, of the exhortation (Deut 6.4), "Hear, O Israel, the LORD our God is one LORD" (or, "the LORD our God, the LORD is one"); also the name of the best-known prayer in Judaism, comprised of Deut 6.4–9; 11.13–21; Num 15.37–41.

Shemonah Esrei see ***Amidah.***

Sheol the abode of the dead.

Shepherd of Hermas second-century Christian apocalypse.

Shulchan Arukh (Heb "set table") the authoritative compendium of Jewish law, compiled by Yosef Karo and first published in Venice in 1565.

Sibylline Oracles collection of Jewish and Christian texts (dating perhaps from the second century BCE to the first few centuries CE) pseudonymously attributed to the Sybils, Greek prophetesses.

Sicarii (Lat "dagger men") a term for the Jewish movement in Roman Judea which advocated armed rebellion; see **zealot.**

Siddur (Heb "order") the Jewish prayer book.

Sifra (Heb "writing [of]") a rabbinic commentary on Leviticus.

Sifre (Heb "writings [of]") rabbinic commentaries on Numbers and Deuteronomy.

Signs source a posited source used by the author of John's Gospel (Gk *semeia*, sing. ***semeion***).

Sinaiticus (so-called because it was discovered in a Greek Orthodox monastery on Mount Sinai) a fourth century **codex** (containing the entire NT; about half of the Septuagint; the ***Epistle of Barnabas***; and parts of the ***Shepherd of Hermas.***

Son of Man a **Hebraism** (from *ben adam*, e.g., Ps 8.4 [Heb v. 5]; Ezek 2.1) meaning "human being, mortal" or an **Aramaism** (*bar enosh*, e.g., Dan 7.13). It was apparently Jesus' self-designation (e.g., Mk 2.10,28).

soteriology (Gk *sōtēr*, "savior") the study of views of salvation.

source criticism effort to discover the written sources behind a text.

Stoics Greek philosophers who taught that emotions should be controlled by reason.

Sukkot (Heb "booths") autumn harvest pilgrimage festival during which it is customary, following Lev 23.42–43, to dwell in temporary booths.

suffering servant the figure in Isa 52.13–53.11 who bears the disease, punishment, or sins of others. The passage taken by Jesus' followers (e.g., Mt 8.17, in the context of Jesus' healing ministry; Acts 8.27–35, referring to Jesus' death) to be a prophecy of his life; Jewish tradition typically regards the servant as the people Israel.

Symmachus a second to third century translator of the Bible into Greek, see **Hexapla.**

synagogue (Gk "coming together with") an assembly; a congregation; later a building where the community met.

Synoptic Gospels the Gospels of Matthew, Mark, and Luke. "Synoptic" means "view together," and is applied to these writings because they, unlike John, can be readily compared.

synoptic problem The determination of the literary relationship among the Gospels of Matthew, Mark, and Luke. According to the most widely-held theory, Matthew and Luke relied on Mark and on another document, **Q** (now lost), that contained mostly sayings of Jesus. In addition, Matthew and Luke each had their own sources (**M** and **L**).

Syriac eastern form of **Aramaic.**

Syrohexapla see **Hexapla.**

T

tabernacle portable sanctuary used by the Israelites in the wilderness, as described in Exodus, chs 25–30 and chs 35–40.

Taheb in Samaritan teaching, the one who will restore the people to their land and kingdom, analogous to **messiah.**

talion see **lex talionis.**

tallit originally "a garment," also a four-cornered fringed shawl worn during prayer; also called *tallit gadol*, "large tallit," in contrast to *tallit katan*, "small tallit," worn throughout the day beneath the clothing by observant Jewish men (see Num 15.38–39; Deut 22.12).

Talmud (Heb "teaching") the title of the two great collections of rabbinic teaching, the **Jerusalem Talmud** or Yerushalmi and the **Babylonian Talmud** or Bavli. The Talmuds consist of comments on, and extensions of, the **Mishnah** as well as information on a wide range of topics.

Tanakh acronym formed from the beginning letters of the three divisions of the Hebrew Bible: **Torah, Nevi'im, Ketuvim.**

tanna (pl. **tannaim**; adj. **tannaitic**) (Aram/Heb *tanna/shana*, "repeat") rabbis who contributed to and compiled the Mishnah, from ca. 70 to 200 CE.

Tanhuma a rabbi who is often cited in the Midrash Tanhuma. This Midrash compilation was printed by Salomon Buber in 1885.

Targum Aramaic translations of the Bible. There are two main texts on the Torah: *Targum Onkelos* and *Targum Yerushalmi* or the Jerusalem Targum. There is also Targum Jonathan to the prophets, as well as targums to other biblical books such as Ruth and Esther.

Teacher of Righteousness (Heb *moreh ha-tzedek*) presumed founder of the community at **Qumran** (see e.g., CD 1.9–11).

tefillin small black leather boxes containing biblical passages from Ex 13.1–10; 13.11–16; Deut 6.4–9; 11.13–21. Two are worn during weekday morning prayer: one on the head and one on the arm (see e.g., Deut 6.8). Also called "**phylacteries.**" Many copies were found among the **Dead Sea Scrolls**.

Temple the central place of worship for Israelite religion in Jerusalem, referring either to the **First Temple** built by Solomon or the post-exilic **Second Temple** rebuilt and enlarged by Herod the Great.

Temple tax Jewish males annually paid a half-shekel tax for the Jerusalem Temple (Ex 30.11–16; Neh 10.33; cf. *t. Ketub.* 13.3).

Tertullian Quintus Septimius Florens Tertullianus (ca. 160–ca.225), early Christian theologian and exegete. He opposed the views of Marcion, who advocated discarding the "Old Testament" in Christian use.

Testament of Abraham a text dating from the first or second century CE, depicting an encounter between the archangel Michael, a vision of judgment in the context of the death of Abraham, and the ascent of Abraham's soul to heaven.

Testaments of the Twelve Patriarchs the purported last words of the twelve sons of Jacob (separate texts include the Testaments of Benjamin, Judah, Issachar, Levi, and Simeon). Although it may contain material from the second century BCE, as a whole it dates from the second century CE.

Testimonia (1) a Dead Sea Scroll (4Q175), consisting of a series of quotations from Exodus, Numbers, Deuteronomy, and Joshua, all of which may be of messianic interest; (2) any collection of quotations taken as messianic predictions.

tetragrammaton (Gk "four letters") the Hebrew divine name, **YHWH**.

textual criticism the effort to establish, by scholarly assessment of manuscript copies and other sources, an original and accurate version of a text

textus receptus (Lat "received text") the standard text in a tradition. For the Hebrew text the "received text" is the **Masoretic text**, particularly that in the Rabbinic Bible (*Miqraot Gedolot*) in the 1525 edition published in Venice. For the NT (Gk) text, the Stephanus edition of 1550 became known as the received text and was the basis of the King James NT. Most modern NT translations use a critical text based on comparison of numerous manuscripts.

theodicy the effort to justify divine goodness in the face of human suffering.

Theodotion (ca. second century CE) a translator of the Bible into Greek and reviser of the **Septuagint**.

theophany (Gk "appearance of god") a temporary appearance or manifestation of a divine being.

Therapeutae a Jewish community of men and women in Egypt, described by Philo, who practiced temperance, asceticism, and contemplation.

Thomas, Gospel of an early collection of sayings attributed to Jesus. Some sayings resemble those in the canonical Gospels, but other speak of salvation through knowledge of escaping the material world (rather than through the death and resurrection of Jesus).

Torah (Heb "teaching," "instruction") the first division of the **Tanakh** (the **Pentateuch**), and, more broadly, Jewish teaching. See **law**.

Tosefta (Aram "addition") a compilation of oral law, of uncertain provenance and date, that follows the arrangement of the Mishnah.

Transfiguration (Gk *metamorphoō*, "change form") name for the event recounted in Mk 9.2–8; Mt 17.1–8; Lk 9.28–36, in which Jesus' appearance is transformed (see Ex 34.29) and where he speaks with Moses and Elijah.

Tribulation (Gk *thlipsis*, "affliction") the period of earthly oppression before Jesus returns in glory (Rev 7.14, there translated "ordeal").

Trinity Christian doctrine that God, though one in Being, is comprised of three Persons (Father, Son, and Spirit). See **Nicene Creed**.

Twelve, Book of the the **Tanakh**'s designation for the **Minor Prophets** (Hosea through Malachi).

typology (Gk *typos*, the raised design on a seal for imprinting in wax) the understanding of persons or events, especially in the NT, by referring them to earlier biblical "types," such as the exodus (1 Cor 10.1–6); Solomon (Lk 11.31); or narratives like that of Jonah (Lk 11.29–30).

tzedaqah Heb "righteousness" and, by extension, "alms."

tzitzit fringes on the **tallit** or garment (Num 15.37–40) as a reminder of God's commandments (e.g., Mt 9.20).

U

uncircumcised, the Gentiles (Rom 4.9; Gal 2.7).

V

Vaticanus (so called because it is housed in the Vatican library) a **codex** of the Greek Bible (Old and New Testaments) that dates from the fourth century.

vaticinium ex eventu The term applied to a passage in the Prophets or the Gospels which has the form of a prediction but it is in fact written in the knowledge of the event having occurred (e.g., 2 Pet 3.3–4).

vice list a list of sins for the faithful to avoid. See Rom 1.29–31; 1 Cor 5.11; 6.9–10; 1 Tim 1.9–10; 2 Tim 3.2–5; Tob 4.12; *Jub.* 7.20.

Vulgate (Lat "common") Latin translation of the Bible by **Jerome**, completed 405. In the Middle Ages the Vulgate became the standard translation of the Bible for Western Christians. With the Protestant Reformation, its authority was questioned, but was reaffirmed by the Roman Catholic Church at the **Council of Trent** (1546).

W

Weeks, Feast of **Shavuot** or **Pentecost**.

works-righteousness description of a religion that emphasizes the deeds of the faithful as the way of earning God's grace.

Writings see **Ketuvim**.

Y

Yerushalmi see **Talmud**.

YHWH the name of God, which conventionally remains unpronounced and is represented by the Hebrew letters *yod-he-vav-he* (the **tetragrammaton**). In standard English translations, YHWH is represented by the word LORD.

yetzer ha-ra/yetzer ha-tov Heb "inclination to evil/inclination to good."

Yizkor (lit. "remembrance") Philem 4ff. A memorial service recited as part of the prayer service four times during the year.

Yom Kippur (Heb "**day of atonement**") solemn fast observed on 10 Tishri (see Lev 23.26–32). The observance focuses on personal and communal repentance.

Z

Zadokites proponents of re-establishing the priesthood of the Jerusalem Temple as consisting of descendants of Zadok (see 2 Sam 15; 1 Kings 1; 2 Chr 31.10; Neh 11.10–11). The name **Sadducee** may be derived from Zadok.

zealot an advocate of armed resistance in Roman rule.

Zion the name of the fortified hill within Jerusalem and thus, by extension, an alternative name for Jerusalem.

Zohar ("Splendor") kabbalistic writing of the late thirteenth century, partly the work of Moshe de Leon (d. 1305).

INDEX

A

Abraham, 155, 210
as ancestor of Jesus, 3
faithfulness of, 261–63
faith of, 337
family of, 552
as first Jew, 3
Acts of the Apostles, 197–252
ascension of Jesus, 199–200
authorship of, 96, 197
on Jerusalem council, 523
on Last Supper, 522–23
on life of Paul, 554
miracles and signs in, 536
Peter and, 436
on Pharisees, 527
on Sadducees, 527
adultery, 12, 502
divorce and, 503, 517
woman caught in, 174
afterlife, resurrection and, 312–13, 549–51
Agrippa
Paul and, 246–47
Simon dispute, 525
Agrippa I, 198, 510
Agrippa II, 198, 510–11, 538
Alexander the Great, 508
Hellenism and, 507
Ioudaios and, 524
alien, believer in Christ as, 439–41
Amidah prayer, 534
amoraic rabbis, 593
ancient texts, translation of, 601–2
angel, 4; *see also* divine beings
of judgment, 63, 486
Metatron, 465, 544–45
Michael, 460, 531, 545
power of, 13
superiority of Jesus, 407
Angel of the Lord, 544
anger, divine, 502; *see also* wrath
annunciation
by angels, 545
of John the Baptist conception, 98–99
to shepherds, 101–2
Anointed One, 107, 531
anointing, 182
of Jesus, 88
priesthood ordination and, 531
by woman, 48
Antioch, 1, 336
Antiochus IV Epiphanes, 380, 507, 531, 550, 572
apocalypse, 87–88, 463, 467; *see also* Revelation to John
Gog and Magog as, 473
literature of, 3, 535
Markan, 87–88
Apocalypse of Abraham, 544
Apocalypse of Peter, 551
apostasy, 413, 443, 515
apostle, 112, 222; *see also* disciple
council, appear before 208–9
Paul as, 66
Paul meeting with, 335–36
rights of, 301
Apostolic Decree, 522, 523
Aramaic language, 561–62
Genesis in, 569
Aratus, 234
Aristophanes, 304
Aristotle, 155, 187, 352, 399
armor of God, 353
arrest
of Jesus, 91–92, 145, 146
of Peter, 205–6, 510
ascension, of Jesus, 151, 199–200
Augustine, 196, 253, 291, 559, 561, 563
authority
apostolic, 327
of Jesus, 16, 22, 38–39, 161–63
of Peter, 444–45
question on, 84, 141
source of, in interpretation, 274
subordination to higher, 280–81
authorship
of Acts of the Apostles, 96, 197
of Colossians, Letter of Paul to, 362
of Corinthians, Second Letter of Paul to, 315
of Ephesians, Letter of Paul to, 345
of Hebrews, Letter to, 406
of John, First Letter of, 448
of John, Second Letter of, 456
of Jude, Letter of, 460
of Luke, Gospel According to, 96
of Mark, Gospel According to, 55
of Matthew, Gospel According to, 1
of Paul, letters of, 551–52
of Peter, First Letter of, 436

of Philemon, Letter of Paul to, 402
of Philippians, Letter of Paul to, 354
of Romans, Letter of Paul to, 253
of Thessalonians, First Letter of Paul to, 372
of Thessalonians, Second Letter of Paul to, 378

B

Baal, 29, 66, 359
Babylon
 Jewish Diaspora population in, 507
 as whore, in Revelation, 489–92
Babylonian exile, 323, 544
Babylonian Talmud, 580–81
Balaam, prophecy of, 5
baptism
 with Holy Spirit, 58, 81
 of Jesus, 2, 104, 105
 of John the Baptist, 57–58
 new moral life and, 368
 Pharisee rejection of, 110
 as purification ritual, 164–65, 532
 of repentance, 58
Bar Kochba revolt, 506, 537
Bathsheba, 3
beasts, in Revelation, 483–85
beatitudes, 1, 9–10, 96, 113
Beelzebul
 controversy, 125–26
 Satan and, 66–67
beheading, of John the Baptist, 27, 71–72, 147
Behemoth, 483
belief, core of, 449–51
believer in Christ
 as alien, 439–41
 Jewish response to, 577–80
 Justin Martyr on, 577
 Paul as, 242–43
 synagogue expulsion of, 579
 unity of, 349–50
 unmarried, 299
benediction, 389–90
Benedictus, 100–101
Bethsaida, 76, 160
Bible, translation of, 560–62
biblical codex
 Sinaiticus, 153, 559, 563
 Vaticanus, 153, 559, 563
biography, in Hebrew Bible, 505
birth
 angel announcement of, 545
 of Jesus, 4, 101, 578
 of John the Baptist, 100
bishop, qualifications for, 386
blasphemy, 18, 23, 63, 91, 110, 127, 179
blessing, 339, 344, 437
 of children, 35
 in Ephesians, 346–47
blind men, 82
 demoniac and, 19
 healing of, 37, 76, 139, 177–78
blood cry, 2, 501
body
 church and, 365
 metaphor, of Paul, 296–97, 307–8
 names inscribed on, 485
 resurrected, 312–13, 549–51
Booths. *See* Sukkot
bread and wine, at Last Supper, 523
Bread of Life discourse, 155, 169–72
bridegroom, Jesus metaphor of, 18
bureaucracy, of Egypt, 507
burial of Jesus, 93–94, 191–92; *see also* entombment

C

Caesar, taxes to, 40–41, 85, 142
Caiaphas, 38–39, 191, 206
calendar, 594
 rituals, 367
Caligula, 510
 statue in Jerusalem temple, 511, 514
Canaanite woman, Jesus and, 29
canon of the New Testament, 557–60
canons of Hebrew Bible, 600
Capernaum, 9, 16
 healing at, 107, 109
CD. *See* Damascus Document
celibacy, 35, 80
centurion's servant, healing of, 16, 114–15
CEV. *See* Contemporary English Version
Chabad movement, 535
chapter/verse differences, 598–99
charismatic prophet, 536–37
charity, life in community and, 387–88
children
 becoming like, 33
 blessing of, 35
 of darkness, 534
 of God, 158, 338–39, 451–54
 Jesus and, 138
 of light, 570
 love between parents and, 539
 marriage and, 80–81
Christ, 264–65; *see also* believer in Christ; Jesus
 better covenant of, 417–18

hymn to, 365–66
as manifestation of God, 467
return of, 446–47
as sacrifice for sin, 418–19
victory of, 311
Christian, 518
on crucifixion, 577
documents, 557
Gentile, 555–56
grace, 501
Jewish, 554–57
missionary sites, 215
neighbor, concept of, 540–43
suffering as, 441–42
tradition, Peter in, 436
on virgin birth, 578
Christianity
conformity to, 559
rabbinic texts on, 580–81
Chrysostom, John, 554–56
church
body and, 365
discipline, 33–34
expansion, Peter and, 200
in Judea, 374
leaders, 386–87
seven in Revelation, 465–66, 468–72, 470
Cicero, 40, 203, 256, 280, 304, 343, 565
circumcision, 4, 254, 259, 363, 397, 514, 518
faction, Paul on, 523, 552, 555
Gentiles and, 515
of Jesus, 102
of John the Baptist, 100
resistance for, 341–42
Tacitus on, 515
Clement of Alexandria, 152, 558, 574
Colossians, Letter of Paul to, 362–71
authorship of, 362
Ephesians comparison to, 365
commandment, 543; *see also* Ten Commandments
greatest, 41–42, 86, 502
washing of hands and, 73–74
community
charity in, 387–88
controversy in, 399, 400
fellowship, 449
life, early, 203–4
purity, 294
standards, 350–52
Community Rule, 542, 570, 571
Complete Jewish Bible (CJV), 562
conception
of John the Baptist, annunciation of, 98–99
of Moses, 2
condemnation, of Jesus, 22, 147–48, 191–92
confession, 274, 359–60
of Jesus, 77
of Peter, 120
conspiracy, of Jewish leaders, 47–48, 88
Contemporary English Version (CEV), 562
continuing education, on Judaism, 501
controversy story, 62
of healing on the Sabbath, 65–66, 130, 131
of plucking grain on Sabbath, 65, 517
conversion
of Cornelius, 218–20
Ioudaios and, 524–25
Corinth
on dietary law, 522
events in, 234–36
Paul canceled visit to, 317–18
as urban center, 287
Corinthians, First Letter of Paul to, 287–314
plans and farewells in, 314
on sexual morality, 287
on women's role, 287
Corinthians, Second Letter of Paul to, 315–31
appeal to, 323–24
authorship of, 315
on Jewish law, 315
letter of tears in, 318–19
Cornelius
conversion of, 218–20
Holy Spirit and, 523
corporal punishment, Pentateuch on, 516
Council of Trent, 560, 561
covenant
Christ's better, 417–18
inadequacy of first, 416–17
law and, 338
salvation and, 5
creation, 387
social order and, 385
crucifixion, 51–53, 55, 148–49, 156, 193
burial and, 93–94
Christian and Jew on, 577
Psalms on, 505
understanding of, 366–67
curse of law, 337–38
cursing
of fig tree, 83–84
of Jesus, 307

D

Damascus Document (CD), 569–71
 on converts, 528
 on polygamy, 530
Daniel, book of
 date of, 506
 on reward and punishment after death, 550
darkness
 children of, 534
 light and, 323, 449
 power of, 364
David (king), 524
 as eschatological redeemer, 530–31
 Jesus as son of, 2, 19, 86
 Messiah from lineage of, 3
Day of Atonement, 324
Day of Preparation, 94
Day of the Lord, 372, 380–81
Day of Wrath, 369; *see also* wrath
Day of YHWH, 369; *see also* YHWH
Dead Sea, 8, 527
Dead Sea Scrolls (DSS), 55–56, 65, 158, 505, 572
 book of Isaiah and, 569
 Community Rule of, 542, 570, 571
 on divorce, 517, 576
 Genesis in Aramaic, 569
 on Habakkuk, 569
 on high priest, 534
 hymns of thanksgiving, 569
 Judaism and, 569
 on laws, 516
 Qumran Cave and, 569, 570
 on Sadducees, 528
 Teacher of Righteousness and, 508
death
 of Herod Antipas, 222–23
 of Herod the Great, 533
 of Jesus, 2, 578
 of Judas, 200
 Lazarus raising from, 152, 180–82
 reward and punishment after, 549–50
demon, 78–79; *see also* Satan
 casting out of, 17
demoniac
 blind men and, 19
 of Gerasene, 69–70, 117–18
devil. *See* Satan
Diaspora, Hellenistic, 529–30
Diaspora, Jewish, 154, 465, 529, 556
 Babylon population of, 507
 revolt, 512
 synagogue, in pre-70 era, 520
Didache, 556, 558
 on Golden Rule, 543
dietary laws, 363, 515
 concerns of, 300, 303–4
 Jesus on, 522
 observance of, 367
Dio Chrysostom, 237, 256, 296, 304
Diodorus of Sicily, 392
disciple
 call of, 59, 160–61
 commissioning of, 119
 fate of, 20
 instructions to, 127–28
 Jesus appearance to, 150–51, 194
 Jesus' twelve, 19, 66
 mission of, 71, 122–23
 persecution of, 143
 receiving of, 79–80
discipleship, 77–78, 120
 cost of, 132
 demands of, 121–22
discipline, divine, 423–24
disobedience, punishment of, 461
divine anger, 502
divine beings; *see also* angel
 Angel of the Lord, 544
 birth announcement by, 545
 divine council and, 544
 Gabriel angel, 545
 Metatron angel, 465, 544–45
 Michael angel, 460, 531, 545
 Son of Man, 23, 30, 57, 63, 465, 467, 545–46
 Wisdom in Proverbs, 544
 YHWH, 467, 544, 545
divine council, 544
divine discipline, 423–24
divine fidelity, 413–14
divine judgment, 257–58, 411
Divine Liturgy, 523
divine love, 502
divine Wisdom, 289–91
Divine Word, 547
divisions and tractates, Talmudic, 603
divorce, 12, 297–98
 adultery and, 503, 517
 DSS on, 516, 517
 Jesus' protection of women in, 503
 in Jewish family life, in first century CE, 538–39
 marriage and, 34–35, 80–81
 prohibition of, 80
 remarriage after, 135, 502
DSS. *See* Dead Sea Scrolls

E

early Judaism, common errors about, 501–4
on heavenly father, 503
on messiah, 503
on outcasts, 503
on universalism, 504
on women, 502–3
earthquakes, 44, 54
Ecclesiastes, book of, on afterlife, 549–50
Ecclesiastes Rabbah, 580
Ecclesiastical History (Eusebius), 463, 558
education in first century CE, 540
Egypt
bureaucracy of, 507
Diaspora synagogue in, 520
flight to, 5–6
Jesus' family fleeing, 566
elders, 456, 458
qualifications for, 398–99
tradition of, 28–29
Eleazar, 511, 533, 534
exorcism of, 536
Elijah, 53, 78, 107, 160, 164, 531
ascent to heaven, 159
call of, 59
charismatic prophecy of, 536
eschatological act of, 480–81
prophecies about, 79
as prophet, 32
role of, 533
Elisha, 107
charismatic prophecy of, 536
healing by, 79
Emmaus incident, 149–50
end-time signs, 143
endurance, 394–95
exhortation to, 393, 419
Enoch, 63, 77, 164
prophecy of, 462
Enoch, First, on reward and punishment after death, 549–50
entombment, of Jesus, 53–54, 94, 149
Ephesians, Letter of Paul to, 345–53
authorship of, 345
blessing in, 346–47
Colossians comparison to, 365
Paul's speech in, 239–40
Epictetus, 220, 258, 266–67, 279, 296, 398, 404, 525
Epistle of Barnabas, 558, 559
epistles. *See* Pastoral Epistles
Epistle to the Laodiceans, 559
eschatology, 378
David as redeemer and, 530–31
Elijah and, 480–81
Jesus and, 15, 480–81
judgment, 292–93
Matthew elements of, 44
on Messiah timetable, 534
Essene Hypothesis, 569, 570
Essenes, 391, 527
eternal life, sin and, 454–55
ethical law, Paul on, 518
Eucharist, 90, 184–85, 523
Euripides, 248
Eusebius, 1, 152, 463–64, 557, 558
evil, 295
careless speech and, 433–34
of humankind, 255–57
understanding occurrences of, 129
exaltation of Jesus, 408–9
excavations at Qumran, 570
exegesis, 516
exhortation, 366, 375, 395–96, 425–26, 462
to attention, 408
to endurance, 393, 419
on faithfulness in suffering, 392–93
to hope, 445
moral, 368
for patience, 447
for righteousness, 447
salvation and, 400
to virtuous behavior, 444
Exodus, the, 211–13
exorcism, 24, 29, 61, 69, 121, 536
Ezekiel, 464
John of Patmos as new, 473
Ezra, Fourth, on Anointed One, 531

F

faith, 136
of Abraham, 337
children of God through, 338
forgiveness of sin and, 62–64
heroes of, 420–23
importance of, 428
law vs., 336–37
works vs., 337, 431–32
faithfulness
of Abraham, 261–63
of God, 261, 263–64, 282–85
life of, 278–80
in suffering, 392–93
of Thessalonians, 372
faithful obedience, of life in Christ, 264–65

false prophets, 15, 445–46, 453, 581–82
false teachers, 358–59, 384, 389–90, 443
family
  of Abraham, 552
  division within, 129
  of Jesus, 117, 540, 566
  Jewish, in first century CE, 537-40
Farewell discourse, Jesus', 185–87
fasting, 14, 64–65
  of Moses, 7
  of Pharisees, 18
Feast of Tabernacles, 154, 155
Feast of the Dedication, 179
feeding
  of five thousand, 27–28, 72–73, 119, 169–70
  of four thousand, 29–30, 75
Felix, 245–46, 532
festival
  dates, 367
  harvest, of Sukkot, 38
Festival of Tabernacles (Sukkot or Booths), 172–74
Festival of Unleavened Bread, 144
Festus, 246, 532
fidelity, 477
  divine, 413–14
  idolatry vs., 303
  fiduciary. *See* wealth
fig tree
  cursing of, 83–84
  lesson of, 144
  unfruitful, 130
final judgment, 443, 494–95
first century CE, Jewish family life in, 537–40
first Judean revolt, 511–12
  Josephus on, 533
Flavius Josephus. *See* Josephus
food, 1; *see also* feeding; Last Supper; Passover meal; table fellowship
  restrictions within Jesus Movements, 522
  table fellowship and, 521–24
fool's speech, of Paul, 328–30
forgiveness, 34
  redemption and, 364–65
  sin and, 62–64, 135–36
fornication, 369
Fourth Gospel. *See* John, Gospel According to
fulfillment narrative, prophecy and, 566

G

Gabriel, 545
Galatians, Letter of Paul to, 332–44
  locations in, 334
  LXX and, 564
  Paul's rebuke in, 333
  on salvation, 517
Galilee, 6, 8, 59, 106
Gamaliel, 198, 209, 527, 529, 579
Gehenna, 20, 80
gender roles, 304
gender segregation, 539–40
genealogy, of Jesus, 3, 105–6
Genesis, in Aramaic, 569
Gentile Christians, 555–56
Gentiles, 55–56, 378
  circumcision of, 515
  conversion to Judaism, 515, 524–25
  following law by, 518
  in Jerusalem Temple, 503
  Jews' table fellowship with, 523–24
  Jews' union with, 348
  Paul's outreach to, 523, 553
  proselytes and, 273, 574
  redemption of, 107
  Romans, Letter of Paul to, 253–54
Gerasene demoniac, 69–70, 117–18
German Bible, Luther's translation of, 561
Gethsemane, 49–50
  prayer in, 90–91
  women and, 502
God, 58, 259–61, 547–48
  armor of, 353
  children of, 158, 338–39, 451–54
  Christ as manifestation of, 467
  elect of, 397
  faithfulness of, 261, 263–64, 282–85
  Paul deliverance by, 316–17
  promise of rest of, 410–11
  righteous judgment of, 379
Gog, 473
Golden Rule, 448–49, 543
Good Shepherd discourse, 178–80
Gospel of Peter, 559, 577
Gospels
  collection of, 558
  on Pharisees and Sadducees, 527
  parallel texts in, 596-97
grace, of Christian, 501
grain, plucking of, on Sabbath, 65, 517
Great Commandment, 502, 543
  of love, 308–9
Greek sources
  of LXX, 562–63
  in New Testament, 560

H

Habakkuk, 569
Hadrianic persecutions, 506
hand washing, 73–74, 154, 161
Ḥanina ben Dosa, 536–37, 584
Hanukkah, 154, 179, 508, 531
Hasmonean dynasty, 508–9, 531, 572
  High Priest and, 527
  Ioudaios and, 524
  Josephus and, 575
  Pompey and, 509
headcovering, 304, 305
healer, Jesus' authority as, 16
healing, 23, 29, 32, 61, 75, 78–79, 107, 109, 121, 204
  of blind men, 37, 76, 139, 177–78
  of centurion's servant, 16, 114–15
  of Jairus's daughter, 70–71, 118–19
  of lame man, 153, 167–68
  of leprosy, 16, 62, 110, 517
  of paralytic, 17–18, 110–11
  on Sabbath, 65–66, 130, 131
  of woman with a hemorrhage, 70–71, 118–19, 502
heaven
  Elijah's ascent into, 159
  treasures in, 128
  war in, 482
heavenly temple, 487
  cult, 478
Hebrew Bible (Tanakh), 1, 10, 504–7
  biography in, 505
  canons of, 600
  neighbor, concept of, 541
  New Testament comparison to, 505–6
  opinions vary in, 505
  Rabbinic literature and, 506
  YHWH in, 544
Hebrews, Hellenists and, 209–10
Hebrews, Letter to, 406–26
  authorship of, 406
  structure and contents of, 406–7
Hell, 11, 20; *see also* Gehenna; Sheol
Hellenism, 443, 508, 525, 529
  Alexander the Great and, 507
Hellenistic Diaspora, 529
Hellenistic Judaism, of Philo, 575
Hellenists, Hebrews and, 209–10
heresy, 557, 559, 579
Herod Antipas, 8, 66, 76, 104, 576
  death of, 222–23
  Jews and, 509–10
  John the Baptist execution by, 533
  speculations of, 119
  threat of, 131
Herod the Great, 508, 531
  death of, 533
  Idumeans and, 524
  Jesus before, 147
  Josephus on, 575
  Judas and, 533
  temple renovations by, 433, 509, 514
higher authority, subordination to, 280–81
high priest
  DSS on, 534
  Jesus as, 415
  qualifications for, 411–12
  Sadducees and, 527
  Second Temple period and, 534
Hillel (rabbi), 449, 516, 543
holiness, encouragement to, 437–38
Holy Spirit, 4, 373
  baptism with, 58, 81
  Pentecost and, 536
  Peter's teaching and, 201
Homer, 56, 216, 227, 273, 383, 399, 549
Ḥoni, 536–37, 584
hope, exhortation to, 445
Horace, 16, 47, 114
household code, 352–53, 362, 370, 399–400, 403
human responsibility, divine judgment and, 257–58
human wisdom, 289–91
humility, 131–32, 356–57
hymn
  to Christ, 365–66
  of thanksgiving, 569

I

idolatry, 369
  fidelity vs., 303
Idumeans, 509, 524
Ignatius, 1, 54, 239, 402, 405, 555, 557–58
imprisonment
  of John the Baptist, 105
  of Paul, 355–56
Ioudaios, 155–56, 513
  Alexander the Great and, 524
  conversion and, 524–25
  Hasmonean dynasty and, 524
  identity and, 524
  Idumeans as, 524
  proselytes and, 524–25
  translation of, 524–26
Irenaeus, 197, 378, 443, 463, 475, 556, 558
Isaiah
  DSS and, 569

on Mary's conception of Jesus, 560
prophecy, 67
Israel, 36, 66
laws, New Testament and, 505
negative examples of, 302–3
place of, 270–74
restoration of, 275–78
use of scripture of, 439
Israelites
proselytes compared to, 525
Paul's concern for, 273–74

J

Jairus, healing of daughter of, 70–71, 118–19
James, 31, 37, 53, 460
executed by Sadducees, 528
as Judaizer, 556
James, Letter of, 427–35
content and structure of, 427
Jerome, Latin Bible, Vulgate, produced by, 561
Jerusalem, 5, 512
desolation of, 143
Jesus' entry into, 82–83, 121, 182–83
Jesus' lament over, 43, 131
Jesus' second lament over, 140–41
new, 495–97
Paul in, 240–42
Pompey conquest of, 536
Rome destruction of, 2
Jerusalem Council, 227–30, 523
Jerusalem Temple; *see also* Temple, Second; Temple of Solomon
Antiochus IV Epiphanes and, 507
Caligula statue in, 511, 514
destruction of, 1, 2, 64, 406, 520, 537, 575
Gentiles in, 503
incident in, 38
Jesus' authority over, 161–63
Jesus in, 103
Jewish worship in, 513–14
religious life centered on, 528
sacrifice, 11
tax, 32–33, 64, 325
tax collectors in, 503
Zeus's statue in, 44
Jesus, 1, 3, 18, 59, 66, 103, 184, 412, 560; *see also* healing; son of David; Son of God; Son of Man; suffering servant
as Anointed One, 107, 531
arrest of, 91–92, 145, 146
ascension of, 151, 199–200
authority of, 16, 22, 38–39, 161–63
baptism of, 2, 7, 104, 105
birth of, 4, 101, 578
bridegroom, metaphor of, 18
burial of, 93–94, 191–92
children and, 138
circumcision of, 102
condemnation of, 22, 147–48, 191–92
cursing of, 307
death of, 2, 578
on dietary laws, 522
disciples, his appearances to, 150–51, 194
on divorce, 503
entombment of, 53–54, 94, 149
eschatology and, 15, 480–81
exaltation of, 408–9
explains his teachings, 25
as false prophet, 581–82
family of, 117, 540, 566
genealogy of, 3, 105–6
before Herod, 147
as High Priest, 415
Jerusalem entry by, 82–83, 121, 182–83
John the Baptist and, 115–16
Josephus on, 576
as King of the Jews, 51
lamentation over Jerusalem, 43
in medieval Jewish tradition, 581–82
ministry beginning of, 8–9
missionary mandate by, 109
mission of, 62
in modern Jewish thought, 582–85
Moses comparison to, 2, 154, 409–10, 504–5
multiplication of food by, 27–30, 72–73, 75
Nazareth rejection of, 27, 71, 106–7
neighbor, concept of, 543
new covenant of, 506
Peter's denial of, 49, 50, 90, 92, 145, 146
Pharisees questioned him, 42
Pilate and, 51–52, 92–93, 147
prayer of, 189
rabbinic texts on, 580–81
Samaritan woman's encounter with, 152, 155–56, 165–67
as shekhinah, 2, 34, 98
stilling of storm by, 17, 68–69, 117
synagogue expulsion of, 188
synagogue sermon of, 107
teaching in Galilee, 106
on temple domination system, 503
temptation of, 7–8, 106
transfiguration of, 31–32, 78, 120–21, 502
triumphal entry of, 37–38, 140, 181–83

walking on water, 28, 73
Jesus Movements, food restrictions within, 522
Jew, 42, 296, 513, 552
Abraham as first, 3
removal of term from New Testament, 525–26
Jesus' confrontation with, 175–76
on crucifixion, 577
customs of, 514–15
on death of Jesus, 2, 578
Gentiles, table fellowship with, 523–24
Gentiles, union with, 348
Herod and, 509–10
Ioudaios and, 525
as Jesus archenemies, 152
Judea, relocation from, 507
legalism of, 515
Luke on, 96–97
neighbor, concept of, 540–43
Paul, their persecution of, 578
response to believers in Christ, 577–80
Satan association with, 156
in Second Temple period, 158
Jewish Antiquities (Josephus), 513, 514, 575–76, 583
Jewish Christians, 554–57
Jewish family life, in first century CE, 537
demographics of, 538
documents on, 538
domestic arrangements in, 538
education and, 540
gender segregation in, 539–40
Jesus' family and, 117, 540, 560
love between parents and children in, 539
marriage and divorce in, 538–39
polygyny, 538
slaves and, 538
Jewish history (331 BCE-135 CE)
Alexander the Great to Maccabean Revolt, 507–8
Diaspora revolt, 512
first Judean revolt, 511–12, 533
Hasmonean dynasty, 508–9
Roman rule, 509–11
second Judean revolt, 512–13, 534
Jewish law, 62, 315
of circumcision, 514
in New Testament, 515–16
obedience to, 296
Paul on, 516–18
pork abstention, 514, 522
Sabbath, abstention of work, 515
scribes' interpretation of, 63
Jewish movement, of New Testament period, 526
Pharisees vs. Sadducees in, 527–28
rabbis vs. priests in, 527–30
sects in, 529–30
Jewish thought, Paul in, 585–87
Jewish War (Josephus), 575
Jewish worship, 513–15
Job, on afterlife, 549
Johannine community, 152–53, 448
Johannine literature, 156–57, 456
John, 21, 31, 37, 53, 112, 153–54
arrest of, 205–6
John, Gospel According to, 152–96, 546
anonymous author of, 153–54
anti-Judaism and, 155–56
audience of, 154
epilogue of, 195–96
first-century Judaism and, 154–55
geography of, 162
Jewish sources and, 155
on Jews, 578
Johannine community and, 152–53
Johannine narrative in, 156–57
John, First Letter of, 448–55
authorship of, 448
canonical status of, 448
John, Second Letter of, 456–57
authorship of, 456
John, Third Letter of, 458–59
John Hyrcanus, 98, 508, 524, 575
John of Patmos
heavenly call of, 466–68
as new Ezekiel, 473
John the Baptist, 6–7, 18, 55, 64–65, 156, 502, 510, 567
annunciation of conception of, 98–99
baptism of, 57–58
beheading of, 27, 71–72, 147
birth and naming of, 100
imprisonment of, 105
Jesus and, 115–16
Josephus on, 576
in Luke, Gospel According to, 104
as prophetic figure, 532–33
Qumran and, 530
teachings of, 104–5
testimony of, 159–60
Josephus, 2, 502, 508, 537, 577
on afterlife, 549
on Herod Antipas, 510
on Jesus, 576
Jewish Antiquities by, 513, 514, 575–76, 583
on Judaizers, 555
on messianic leaders, 531–33
on neighbor, 542

on royal figures, 533–34
Sicarii denouncement of, 527
on synagogue, 520
Judaean Antiquities. *See Jewish Antiquities*
Judaism, 513–14; *see also* early Judaism
anti-, 155–56
continuing education on, 501
DSS and, 569
first century, John, Gospel According to, and, 154–55
Gentile conversion to, 515, 524–25
historical study of, 582–83
Luke, Gospel According to, on, 96–97
neighbor and, 123
Paul and, 333–34, 551–54
proselytes to, 554
Rabbinic, 505, 516, 518
works-righteousness model on, 502
Judaizers, 554–57
LXX on, 555
Judas Iscariot, 2, 50–51, 144, 460
death of, 200
Pharisees and, 41
Jude, Letter of, 460–62
authorship of, 460
cultural influences in, 460
Judea, 6, 513
church in, 374
Jews relocated from, 507
Judean
Ioudaios and, 525
revolts, 511–13, 533, 534
synagogues, in Second Temple period, 519–20
judgment, 15, 113–14
angel of, 63, 486
divine, 257–58, 411
eschatological, 292–93
final, 443, 494–95
God's righteous, 379
justification, 362
Paul on, 287
Justin Martyr, 558, 560, 574–75, 577

K

Kimchi, David (Radak), 295
kingdom
keys of, 30–31
parable of, 24–25
Kingdom of God, 136, 163
announcement of, 59
parable and, 67–68
riches and, 81
Kingdom of Heaven, 6, 14
King James Version (KJV), 561
King of the Jews, 5, 51, 92

L

Lady Wisdom, in Proverbs, 155
Lamb, opens scroll with seven seals, 474–76
lame man, healing of, 153, 167–68
language
Aramaic, 561–62, 569
of LXX, 564
Last Supper, 28, 48–49, 89–90, 145, 184–85, 305–6
Acts of the Apostles on, 522–23
Late Antiquity
Judaism and Christianity in, 555
synagogue in, 521
law; *see also* Jewish law
covenant and, 338
curse of the, 337–38
DSS on, 516
faith vs., 336–37
freedom from, 296
fulfillment by love, 281
grievances and, 295
Judaism as system of, 513
moral, 518, 541–42
purpose of, 338
ritual, 518
wholeness under, 431
lawyers, 41
challenge of, 124
invectives against, 126–27
Lazarus
raising of, 152, 180–82
rich man and, 135
leper scholar, messiah as, 535
leprosy, healing of, 16, 62, 110, 136, 517
Letter of Aristeas, 522, 563
letter of tears, 318–19
Levitical priests, 414–15
Leviticus, book of, on neighbor, 541–42
life
in community, charity and, 387–88
of faithfulness, 278–80
light
children of, 570
darkness and, 323, 449
literature
of apocalypse, 3, 535
Jewish, of Second Temple period, 584
Johannine, 456
rabbinic, 506, 565, 567, 585–87
visionary, 464

Wisdom, 157, 548, 549
liturgy, of early synagogue, 520–21
Logos, 546–49
Divine Word, 547
Memra comparison to, 547
Lord's Prayer, 1, 13, 34, 96, 125
Lord's Supper. *See* Last Supper
love, 539
commandment of, 449
earning God's, 502
as Greatest Commandment, 308–9
law fulfilled by, 281
mutual, 457
of neighbor, 502, 540–41
Luke, Gospel According to, 96–151
authorship of, 96
geography of, 108
on Jews and Judaism, 96–97
John the Baptist in, 104
on Last Supper, 522
nativity stories in, 96
on Pharisees, 110, 527
on Sadducees, 527
on women, 96
Luther, Martin, 253, 362, 559–61
LXX. *See* Septuagint

M

Maccabean Revolt, 87, 507–8, 517, 550, 572
Maccabees, First (Book of), 563
on Hanukkah, 508
on Hellenism, 507
Maccabees, Second (Book of), 563
on Jews, 513
on martyr, 505
on reward and punishment after death, 550
Maccoby, Hyam, 584, 586, 587
magicians, 391–92
Magnificat, of Mary, 100
Magog, 473
Maimonides (Rambam), 546, 551, 582
Mark, Gospel According to, 1, 55–95
authorship of, 55
on dietary restrictions, 515
on Gentiles, 55–56
geography of, 60
healings in, 61
on Jesus' crucifixion, 505
on Last Supper, 522
letters of Paul comparison, 55
at Qumran cave, 570
scripture fulfillments in, 89
Markan Apocalypse, 87–88
marriage, 266, 376; *see also* wedding at Cana
children and, 80–81
divorce and, 34–35, 80–81
in Jewish family life, first century CE, 538–39
sexuality in, 297
Mary, 2, 53, 125, 560
Magnificat of, 100
Mary Magdalene, 53, 66, 193–94
mashal, 567–68
Masoretic text (MT), 159, 562–63
Mattathias, revolt of, 508
Matthew, Gospel According to, 1–54, 557
authorship of, 1
on crucifixion, 505
eschatological elements in, 44
geography of, 8
on Jesus' conception, 560
on Jewish Christians, 556
on Jewish law, 516
on Last Supper, 522
on neighbor, 542
Peter in, 31
rabbinic midrash in, 567
on tax collecting, 40
medieval Jewish tradition
Babylonian Talmud and, 581
Jesus in, 581–82
Memra, *Logos* comparison to, 547
Messiah, 2, 57, 76, 86, 154, 176, 202–3, 548
from David's lineage, 3
divine, in New Testament, 505
in early Jewish thought, 530–31
early Judaism on, 503
as leper scholar, 535
timetable, 534
messianic leaders, 531–34
priests, 414–15, 527–29, 531, 534
prophetic figures, 531–33
royal figures, 533–34
messianic movements, 530–35
age of Messiah and, 531
apocalyptic literature and, 535
in Jewish history, 535
rabbinic traditions, 534–35, 580–81
Reform Movement, 535
messianic secret, 56-57, 66
Metatron angel, 465, 544–45
Michael angel, 460, 531, 545
midrash, 4, 548
Ecclesiastes Rabbah, 580
in Matthew, Gospel According to, 567

New Testament parables and, 565–69
ministry, 276
of glory, 319
of hardship, 321–22
of Jesus, 183–84
of new covenant, 319–20
of reconciliation, 322–23
miracle, 76, 208
in Gospels and Acts, 536
of conception of Jesus, 4
Mishnah, 502, 551, 557
date of, 506
as law book, 518
on neighbor, 528
on reward and punishment after death, 550
mission, 19, 366
of disciples, 71
of Jesus, 62
of seventy, 122–23
missionary
instructions, 19–20
journeys of Paul, 224, 228, 235
mandate by Jesus, 109
sites, 215
modern Jewish thought, Jesus in, 582–85
Montefiore, Claude, 583, 586, 587
moral exhortation, 368
moral law, 518
on neighbor, 541–42
Moses, 31, 391–92, 513
conception of, 2
eschatological act of, 480–81
exodus and, 211–13
Jesus comparison to, 2, 154, 409–10, 504–5
Philo on, 573–74
radiant face of, 319, 320
Mount of Olives, 44, 49, 82–83, 93, 146, 532
MT. *See* Masoretic text
murder, 11, 127, 502
mustard seed, parable of, 26–27, 130

N

Nachmanides (Ramban), 303, 431
nativity, 4–5, 96
Nazareth, 6
Jesus rejection by, 27, 71, 106–7
neighbor
Golden Rule and, 543
Jesus on, 543
Jewish and Christian concept of, 540–43
Judaism and, 123
Leviticus on, 541–42
love of, 502, 540–41
Mishnah on, 528
neologisms, of LXX, 564–65
Nero, 463, 511
new covenant, 407; *see also* New Testament
of Jesus, 506
ministers of, 319–20
new Jerusalem, in Revelation, 495–97
New Jewish Publication Society (NJPS), 516
New Revised Standard Version (NRSV), 284
translation and Septuagint, 562
translation of "law," 516
New Testament, 504–7
canon of, 557–60
children of light in, 570
divine Messiah in, 505
Greek sources, use in, 560
Hebrew Bible, comparison to, 505–6
Israel's laws and, 505
Jewish law in, 505, 515–16
Josephus narratives and, 576
LXX and, 563, 565
midrash and, 565–69
period, Jewish movements of, 526–30
Philo and, 574–75
as translation, 561
NJPS. *See* New Jewish Publication Society
NRSV. *See* New Revised Standard Version
numerology of Revelation, 475

O

olive tree allegory, 275–76
oral prophecy, 466
Oral Torah, 341, 518
oral tradition, 153
Ovid, 163, 227, 304, 308
Origen, 458, 558, 563, 575, 577

P

pagan, synagogue donated by, 520
Palestinian Talmud, 580
Palestinian Targum, 547–49
Papias, 1, 55, 557
parable, 7, 24, 34, 40, 46–47, 66, 96, 132–35, 139–41
of good Samaritan, 96, 123, 124, 502, 540–43
Kingdom of God and, 67–68
of mustard seed, 26–27, 130
of New Testament, midrash and, 565–69
of Pharisee and tax collector, 137–38
of sower, 25, 116–17
of vineyard, 2, 36, 39, 84–85, 567
of yeast, 26–27, 130

paraenesis (moral exhortation), 368
parallel texts, 598–99
paralytic, Jesus' healing of, 17–18, 110–11
parent, love between child and, 539
parousia, 44, 372, 376
Passion of Jesus
    narrative, 56, 190–91
    prediction of, 32, 36, 76, 77, 79, 81–82, 120, 121, 139
    resurrection and, 47
Passover, 88, 511, 526
    John, Gospel According to, and, 154
    preparations for, 144
Passover meal, 48, 89, 184, 522
Pastoral Epistles, 383, 391, 397–98
patience
    care in speech and, 434
    exhortation for, 447
Paul, 319, 320, 326–27, 384–85, 557
    Agrippa and, 246–47
    apostle, 66
    apostles, meeting with, 335–36
    as believer in Christ, 242–43
    body metaphor of, 297–98, 307–8
    on circumcision faction, 523, 552, 555
    conversion of, 216–18
    defense of, 247–49
    on dietary laws, 522
    doctrine of the Trinity and, 293
    on ethical law, 518
    Felix and, 245–46
    Festus and, 246
    fool's speech of, 328–30
    Gentile outreach by, 523, 553
    God's deliverance of, 316–17
    on God's Spirit, 554
    imprisonment of, 355–56
    in Jerusalem, 240–42
    Jewish Christians and, 555
    on Jewish law, 516–18
    in Jewish thought, 585–87
    journey of, 223, 230–32, 236–39
    Judaism and, 333–34, 551–54
    on justification, 287
    missionary journeys of, 224, 228, 235
    on olive tree allegory, 275–76
    persecuted by the Jews, 578
    persecution of, 552
    as Pharisee, 527, 551
    Philemon, his appeal to, 404–5
    preaching of, 224–27
    on proselytes to Judaism, 554
    Rome, travel to, 249–52, 250
    speech of, in Ephesians, 239–40
    on spiritual gifts, 306, 307, 552
    on table fellowship, 553
Paul, letters of
    authorship of, 551–52
    on dietary law, 522
    interpretation of, 552–54
    non-Jew direction in, 553–54
Pausanias, 233, 276
Pentateuch, 1, 516, 548
    oral traditions of, 518
    Philo on, 573
Pentecost
    Holy Spirit and, 536
    land of, 201
    teaching on, 202
perfection through suffering, 408
persecution
    of disciples, 143
    Hadrianic, 506
    of Paul, 552
    suffering under, 438
Peter, 1, 9, 31, 112, 160, 218, 336, 557
    Agrippa I arrest of, 510
    arrest of, 205–6, 510
    authority of, 444–45
    in Christian tradition, 436
    church expansion and, 200
    on circumcision, 555
    confession of, 77, 120
    denial by, 49, 50, 90, 92, 145, 146
    as Judaizer, 556
    speech of, 202, 204–5, 220–21
    and table fellowship with uncircumcised, 523
    teaching, Holy Spirit and, 201
Peter, First Letter of, 436–42
    authorship of, 436
Peter, Second Letter of, 443–47, 460
Pharisees, 2, 43, 53, 391, 583
    criticize Jesus, 135
    fasting of, 18
    invectives against, 126–27
    Jesus' questioning of, 42
    Jewish movement, 6
    in Luke, Gospel According to, 110, 135, 527
    oral tradition, 153
    parable of tax collector and, 137–38
    Paul as, 527, 551
    reject John's baptism, 110
    on Sabbath laws, 527
    Sadducees vs., 527–28
    sign demanded by, 76

sinners and, 132
tax collectors and, 64, 137–38
water purification rites and, 58
woman who loved Jesus and, 116
yeast of, 30
Philemon, Letter of Paul to, 402–5
authorship of, 402
Paul's appeal to, 404–5
Philippians, Letter of Paul to, 354–61
authorship of, 354
Paul as observant Jew in, 552
Philo of Alexandria, 56, 155, 157, 168, 274, 507, 514, 569
Hellenistic Judaism of, 575
influence of, 574–75
life of, 572–73
on *Logos*, 548
on Moses, 573–74
New Testament and, 574–75
on proselytes, 525
scripture interpretation of, 574
works of, 573
Pilate, 510
Jesus and, 51–52, 92–93, 147
Plato, 206, 233, 270, 304, 312, 414, 539, 573, 582
Pliny, 392, 527, 569
Plutarch, 514, 555
pollution, woman and symbolism of, 489
Polycarp of Smyrna, 448, 558
polygamy, 530, 538
polygyny, 538
Pompey, 380, 509
Jerusalem conquest by, 536
Pontius Pilate. *See* Pilate
pork, abstention of, 515, 522
prayer, 13, 380, 381, 434–35; *see also* Lord's Prayer
Amidah, 534
in Gethsemane, 90–91
of Jesus, 189
persistence in, 125
for spiritual wisdom, 364–65
prediction, of Passion of Jesus, 32, 36, 76, 77, 79, 81–82, 120, 121, 139
priests
anointing of, 531
inherited and chosen roles of, 528–29
Levitical, 414–15
as messianic leaders, 534
rabbis vs., 527–30
prophecy, 39, 78
of Balaam, 5
charismatic, 536–37
of Enoch, 462
fulfillment narratives and, 566
of Isaiah, 67
oral and written, 466
Psalms and, 505
tongues and, 309–10
prophet
charismatic, 536–37
Elijah as, 32
Jesus as false, 581–82
prophetic figures, 531
John the Baptist as, 532–33
proselytes
Gentiles and, 273, 524
Ioudaios and, 524–25
to Judaism, 554
Protestant Reformation, 557, 559, 561
Proverbs
Lady Wisdom in, 155
Wisdom in, 544
Psalms, book of, 1, 569
on Jesus' crucifixion, 505
prophecy and, 505
Ptolemy II Philadelphus, on LXX, 563
purification rites
baptism as, 164–65, 532
hand washing, 73–74, 154, 161
water, 58
purity, 388
community, 294
laws, 123, 363, 502

Q

Q (Quelle), 1, 96
Qumran
cave, 569–70
excavations at, 570
John the Baptist and, 530
on proselytes, 525
sect, 526, 528, 529
Temple Scroll from, 517
Yaḥad, 526–27

R

rabbi, 160, 594
amoraic, 593
inherited and chosen roles of, 528–29
priests vs., 527–28
tannaitic, 592
on radiant face of Moses, 319, 320
rabbinic Judaism, 505, 516
on circumcision, 518
law development by, 518

rabbinic literature, 506
midrash and, 565
parable in, 567
on Paul, 585–87
rabbinic texts, on Christianity and Jesus, 580–81
rabbinic traditions, 534–35, 580–81
Rav, 10, 160, 348, 350, 595
redemption
forgiveness and, 364–65
of Gentiles, 107
Reform Judaism, 583
Reform Movement, 535
remarriage, after divorce, 135, 502
repentance
baptism of, 58
teaching on, 203
rest, promise of God's, 410–11
restoration, of Israel, 275–78
resurrection, 142, 156, 391
afterlife and, 312–13, 549–51
appearances of Jesus, 193–94
centrality of, 311
passion and, 47
questions about, 41
Revelation to John, 463–97, 558
Babylon as whore in, 489–92
beasts in, 483–85
interpretation of, 464
literary history of, 463
numerology of, 475
outline for, 463–64
seven bowls in, 487–88
seven churches in, 465–66, 468–72, 470
seven seals in, 474–76
seven trumpets in, 477–81
Revised Standard Version (RSV), 561
revolt
Bar Kochba, 506, 537
Diaspora, Jewish, 512
first Judean, 511–12, 533
Maccabean, 87, 507–8, 517, 550, 572
Mattathias, 508
second Judean, 512–13, 534
rich
favoring of, 430–31
Lazarus and, 135
poor and, 428
ruler, 138–39
scribe, 86
young man, 35–36
riches; *see also* wealth
emptiness of, 434
Kingdom of God and, 81
righteousness, 4, 7, 273, 421, 447
ritual, 363
calendar, 367
law, 518
purity, 123
ritual practices, 516; *see also* purification rites
hand washing, 73–74, 154, 161
Roman Catholic Church, 31, 253, 560
Roman Empire, tax collectors and, 40
Roman rule, in Jewish history, 509–11
Romans, Letter of Paul to, 253–86
authorship of, 253
commendation in, 285–86
Gentile audience of, 253–54
Paul on gifts in, 306–8, 552
Rome
Jerusalem destruction by, 2
Paul's travel to, 250, 249–52
Rosh Ha-Shanah, 15, 18, 113, 123, 597
royal figures, 533–34
RSV. *See* Revised Standard Version
rulers, chronological table of, 590–91

S

Sabbath, 61, 155
abstention of work on, 515
healing on, 65–66, 130, 131
instructions for, 22–23
John, Gospel According to, and, 154
laws, 1, 527
observance, 363
plucking grain on, 65, 517
practices, 112
sacrifice
atonement of, 450
Christ as, for sin, 418–19
in Temple, 11
Sadducees, 391
dispute with, 85
James's execution by, 528
Luke, Gospel According to, on, 527
oral tradition, 153
Pharisees vs., 527–28
on Sheol, 549
yeast of, 30
salvation, 104, 130–31, 275–78, 362, 376, 517
covenant and, 5
exhortations and, 400
Samaritan, 19–20, 508
parable of good, 96, 123, 124, 502, 540–43
reject the Jews, 121

woman, Jesus' encounter with, 152, 155–56, 165–67
sanctification, 362, 375
Sandmel, Samuel, 571, 584, 586, 587
Sanhedrin council, 206, 243–44
Sanhedrin trial, 50, 91–92, 146–47
Satan, 7, 374, 493–94
Beelzebul and, 66–67
fall of, 482–83
Jews' association with, 156
scribes, 42–43
Jewish law interpretated by, 63
rich, 86
warnings concerning, 142
Scroll of Lamentations, 566
second Judean revolt, 512–13, 534
Second Temple period
on dietary laws, 522
high priest and, 534
Jewish literature of, 584
Jewish miracle workers in, 536–37
Jews in, 158
Judean synagogues in, 519–20
sects, 529–30
Essenes, 391, 526, 527
Pharisees, 2, 6, 18, 30, 42–43, 53, 58, 64, 76, 110, 116, 126–27, 132, 135, 137–38, 153, 391, 526–28, 551, 583
Sadducees, 30, 85, 153, 391, 526–28, 549
Seleucids of Syria-Mesopotamia, 507
Hasmonean dynasty of, 508–9
Mattathias's revolt against, 508
Septuagint (LXX), 504, 560, 562
Acts of Apostles and, 198–99
on Jewish law, 516
on Judaizers, 555
language of, 564
Luke, Gospel According to and, 96
neologisms of, 564–65
New Testament and, 563, 565
origins of, 563
Torah translation by, 561
Word of God in, 546
Sermon on the Mount, 1, 2, 7, 9, 516
servant
centurion's, healing of, 16, 114–15
leadership, 145
unforgiving, parable of, 34
seven bowls, in Revelation, 487–88
seven churches, in Revelation, 465–66, 468–72, 470
seven seals, in Revelation, 474–76
seven trumpets, in Revelation, 477–81
sexual immorality, 294–96
sexual morality, 287, 297, 375–76
Shavuot (Weeks or Pentecost), 88, 526, 561
shekhinah, 2, 34, 98
Sheol, Sadducees on, 549
Shepherd of Hermas, 413, 464, 482, 558–59
Sicarii, 527–29, 532
sign, 125, 126, 157, 161, 169–70, 289, 536; *see also* healing
end-time, 143
from heaven, 30
interpretations of, 129
John, Gospel According to, on, 153
Pharisees demanding of, 76
raising of Lazarus, 152, 180–82
Similitudes of Enoch, 531, 545
Simon, 9
dispute with Agrippa, 525
of Hasmonean dynasty, 508
Simon bar Gioras, 511, 533, 575
sin
Christ as sacrifice for, 418–19
debt and, 34
eternal life and, 454–55
forgiveness and, 62–64, 135–36
freedom from, 266–67
rebirth from, 347–48
Sinaiticus biblical codex, 153, 559, 563
sinners
Jesus' association with, 64, 523
Pharisees and, 132
repentance of, 62
tax collectors and, 18
slaves, 402–3
to all, 301–2
in Jewish family life, 538
social order, 298–99
creation and, 385
social teachings, 79
Passion predictions and, 76
Solomon, 14, 204–5; *see also* Temple of Solomon; Wisdom of Solomon
son of David, 2, 19, 86, 142
Son of God, 58, 152, 154, 159, 160, 176, 406
Son of Man, 23, 30, 57, 63, 465, 467, 545–46
coming of, 44–45, 144
day of, 136–37
final judgment and, 47
suffering of, 77
watchfulness for, 45
sower, parable of, 25, 116–17
Spirit of God, 342–43, 554
Spirit of Life, 267–70
spiritual gifts, 306–8, 552
spiritual wisdom, 364–65

Stephen
arrest, speech and martyrdom of, 210–11
stoning of, 213
storm, stilling of, by Jesus, 17, 68–69, 117
suffering, 268–69
as Christian, 441–42
faithfulness in, 392–93
perfection to, 408
under persecution, 438
of Son of Man, 77
Strabo, 233, 308, 471
Suetonius, 137, 234, 256–57, 287, 314, 484, 510, 533
suffering servant, 56, 63, 505–6, 535, 584
Sukkot (Booths), 38, 88, 172, 526
synagogue, 9, 61, 198, 555
believer in Christ expelled from, 579
Diaspora, in pre-70 era, 520
exclusion from, 152
Jesus' expulsion from, 188
Jesus' sermon in, 107
Jewish worship in, 513–14
Judean, in Second Temple period, 519–20
in late antiquity, 521
leadership of, 519
liturgy of early, 520–21
location of, 519
pagan interest in, 520
participation in, 519
social-communal aspects of, 519
Torah reading ceremony in, 519–21
worship in, 519
Synoptic Gospels, 152, 567

T

Tabernacles. *See* Sukkot
table fellowship
food and, 521–24
between Jews and Gentiles, 523–24
in Luke, Gospel According to, 111
Paul on, 553
Tacitus, 578
on Jewish customs, 514–15
Talmud
Babylonian, 580–81
Jesus as sorcerer in, 581
Tanakh. *See* Hebrew Bible
Tanhuma, 10, 13, 20, 125, 202, 290, 303, 350, 428, 432–33
tannaitic rabbis, 592
tax
for Caesar, 40–41, 85, 142
collecting, 40, 281
Temple, 32–33, 64, 325
tax collectors, 503
Jesus' association with, 64, 96, 523
Pharisees and, 64, 137–38
Roman empire and, 40
sinners and, 18
Teacher of Righteousness, 508, 534, 569–70, 572
teaching
with authority, 61
Holy Spirit and, 201
Jesus' explanation of his, 25
of Jesus in Galilee, 106
of John the Baptist, 104–5
on Pentecost, 202
social, 76, 79
Temple, Second, 515; *see also* Second Temple period
celibacy and, 35
construction of, 93
destruction of, 3, 43–44, 55, 531, 550
Judaism, 582
prophecy and, 39
Temple of Solomon, 198, 503–4; *see also* Jerusalem Temple
construction of, 93
destruction of, 143, 154, 512, 566
Herod the Great renovations of, 433, 509, 514
prediction of destruction of, 87–88
prophetic judgment against, 83–84
Temple Scroll, 570
from Qumran, 517
on temple entry, 528
temptation
good deeds and, 429
of Jesus, 7–8, 106
Ten Commandments, 515, 518
Tertullian, 22, 197, 298, 378, 397, 423, 438, 557–58, 578
Testimonium Flavianum, 536, 576, 579
thanksgiving, 347, 355, 363–64, 373, 381, 402–4, 569
Thessalonians, First Letter of Paul to, 372–77
authorship of, 372
on faithfulness, 372
interpretation of, 372
Thessalonians, Second Letter of Paul to, 378–82
authorship of, 378
Gentiles and, 378
historical context, literary history of, 378–79
Thessalonica, 372
events in, 232–33
third Gospel. *See* Luke, Gospel According to
Thucydides, 240
Timothy, 363, 372
mission to the Thessalonians, 375

travels of, 358
Timothy, First Letter of Paul to, 383–90
Timothy, Second Letter of Paul to, 391–96
Titus, Letter of Paul to, 397–401
Toledot Yeshu
Jesus mis-information in, 581
on Paul, 585
tongues, prophecy and, 309–10
Torah, 1, 516
covenant of, 79
exegetical rules of, 2
LXX translation of, 562
observance, 332, 501
permanence of, 135
purity laws and, 502
reading ceremony, in synagogue, 519–21
on Sabbath, 23
summarization of, 342
views concerning, 10–11
Written and Oral, 516
tractates, Talmudic, 603
Transfiguration, 31–32, 78, 120–21, 502
translation
of ancient texts, 601–2
of Bible, 560–62
of *Ioudaios*, 524–26
trinity, 293, 580
triumphal entry, 37–38, 140, 182–83
"Two Powers in Heaven," 547

U

unclean spirit, 24, 58, 61, 69–70; *see also* demon
unity, 288–89, 356–57
of believers in Christ, 349–50
universal worship, 477
unmarried believers, 299

V

Vaticanus biblical codex, 153, 559, 563
vineyard, parable of, 2, 36, 39, 84–85, 567
virgin birth, of Jesus, 4, 101, 578
visionary literature, 464
vision of heavenly throne, 473–74
Vulgate, Jerome production of, 561

W

warnings, 15–16, 128, 424–25
water
Jesus walking on, 28, 73
purification rites, 58
wealth, 34, 135
Kingdom of Heaven and, 14
warnings against, 128
wedding at Cana, 152, 157
Jesus' first sign of, 161
Weeks of Pentecost. *See* Shavuot
widow
offering of, 143
poor, 86, 115
wilderness, 6
John the Baptist in, 104, 532
Israelites in, 410
messianic movement and, 532
Wisdom
divine vs. human, 289–91
Lady, in Proverbs, 155
in Proverbs, 544
Wisdom literature, 157
on afterlife, 549
on *Logos*, 548
Wisdom of Solomon, 558, 563
Wissenschaft des Judentums, 582–83
woman
adulterous, 174
anointing by, 48
Canaanite, Jesus and, 29
as church leader, 386
divorce and, 503
early Judaism and, 502–3
headcovering of, 304, 305
with hemorrhage, healing of, 70–71, 118–19, 502
home ownership by, 503
Jesus healing of two, 18–19
Luke, Gospel According to, on, 96
pollution symbolism and, 489
role of, 287
Samaritan, Jesus' encounter with, 152, 155–56, 165–67
at tomb, 148
who loved Jesus, 116
Word, Divine, 547
Word of God, in LXX, 546
works
faith vs., 337, 431–32
of Philo of Alexandria, 573
-righteousness model, 502
Sabbath abstention from, 515
worship
places of, 213
in synagogue, 519
universal, 477
wrath, 7
written prophecy, 466
Written Torah, 516

X

Xenophon, 237, 294

Y

Yaḥad, Qumran, 526–27
yeast
  parable of, 26–27, 130
  of Pharisees and Sadducees, 30
YHWH, 467, 544, 545
Yiddishisms, in CJV, 562

Z

Zeus, Jerusalem temple statue of, 44